WHAT'S NEW!

This is our 8th edition of Camps Australia Wide, one of Australia's most comprehensive guides to free, low cost camping and unique out of the way camping sites throughout Australia.

It has been a very busy couple of years. We have driven vast distances all over Australia visiting new and existing sites. Where sites are free we have verified that they are legitimate and approved for camping. Those that have been closed or are no longer suitable for camping/ overnight stays have been removed.

We have also deleted many of the 'day use' listings as your feedback indicated that most of the time preference was for overnight stop information.

To improve and simplify the layout on the maps and make them less crowded and therefore easier to read, we have redesigned the icons used to indicate the sites position and number.

The indexing is now state by state, found at the front of the campsite listings.

As always we are grateful for any feedback about the book, sites or general RV issues, so if you have a comment or suggestion please call or email us.
Phone 07 5474 2542 or philip@campsaustraliawide.com

Safe travels

Philip & Cathryn Fennell

ACKNOWLEDGEMENTS

Camps Australia Wide Pty Ltd
PO Box 1765 Noosaville BC
Queensland Australia 4566
Phone: (07) 5474 2542 Fax: (07) 5474 1715
Email: info@campsaustraliawide.com
Website: www.campsaustraliawide.com

First edition published	October 2001
Second edition published	February 2003
Third edition published	February 2005
Fourth edition published	February 2007
Fifth edition published	February 2009
Sixth edition published	February 2011
Seventh edition published	February 2013
Eighth edition published	February 2015

ISBN: Paperback 978-0-9925732-0-1
A4 Spiral Bound 978-0-9925732-1-8
B4 Spiral Bound 978-0-9925732-2-5

Proprietors of Camps Australia Wide:
Philip & Cathryn Fennell

Compiled, Designed and Published by:
Philip & Cathryn Fennell

Research:
Julie Simpson, Jacqueline Wardle, Philip & Cathryn Fennell

Field Research:
Philip & Cathryn Fennell

Production and Prepress:
Allan & Linda Shearer (Shearer Publishing Systems)
Pauline Gleeson (www.paulinegleesongraphicdesign.com.au)
Gavin James (www.mapuccino.com.au)

Cover Design:
Pauline Gleeson (www.paulinegleesongraphicdesign.com.au)

Photography:
Philip Fennell, Cathryn Fennell

Base Maps:
Hema Maps Pty Ltd

Printed by C&C Offset Printing Co Ltd, China

Further personal acknowledgements to the many people and organisations for their contribution of information over the years, however small, are listed on page 431.

Cover photo: Red Bluff, WA site 348

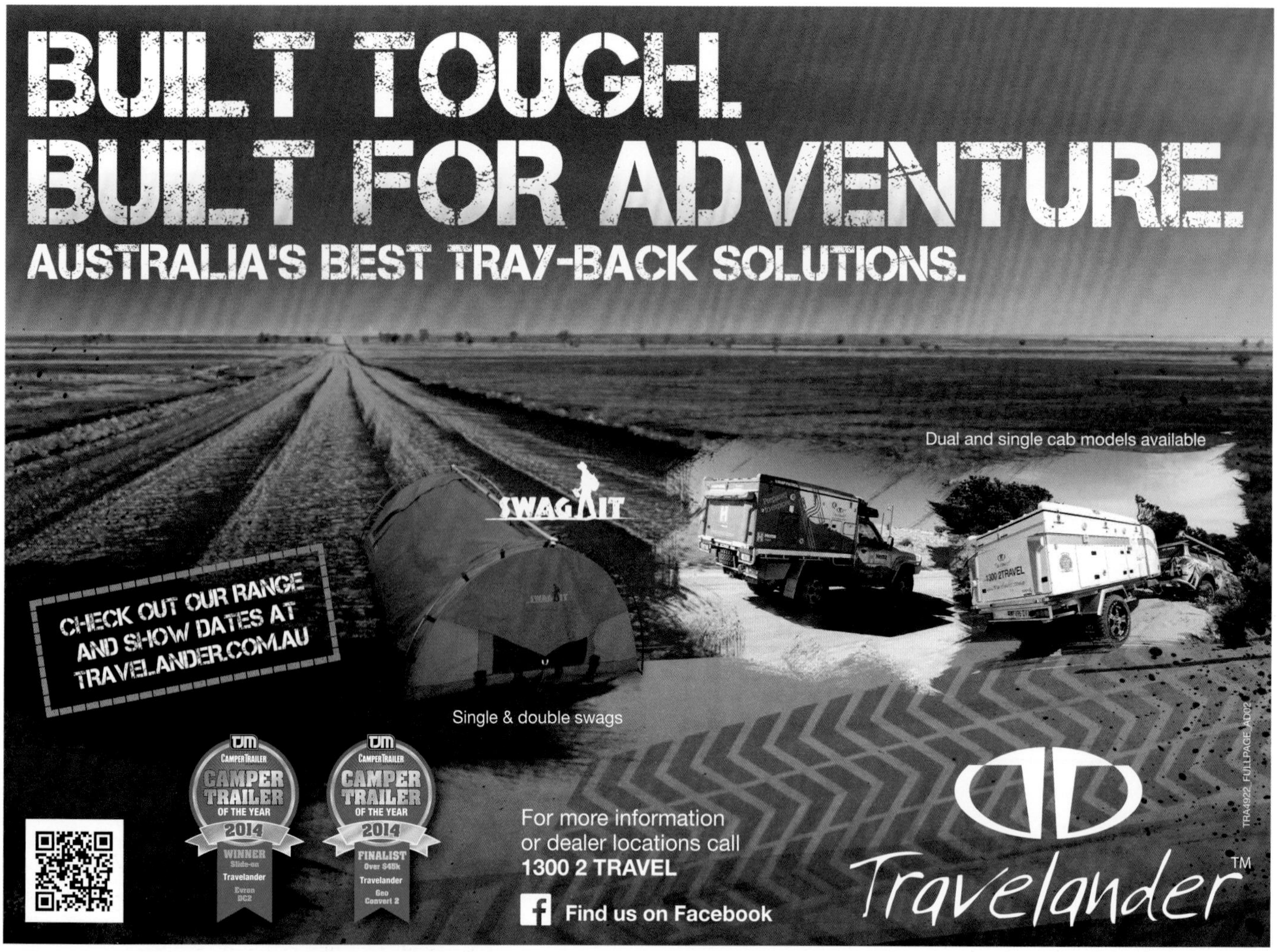
BUILT TOUGH.
BUILT FOR ADVENTURE.
AUSTRALIA'S BEST TRAY-BACK SOLUTIONS.
Dual and single cab models available
SWAG IT
CHECK OUT OUR RANGE AND SHOW DATES AT TRAVELANDER.COM.AU
Single & double swags
CAMPER TRAILER OF THE YEAR 2014 WINNER
CAMPER TRAILER OF THE YEAR 2014 FINALIST
For more information or dealer locations call
1300 2 TRAVEL
Find us on Facebook
Travelander™

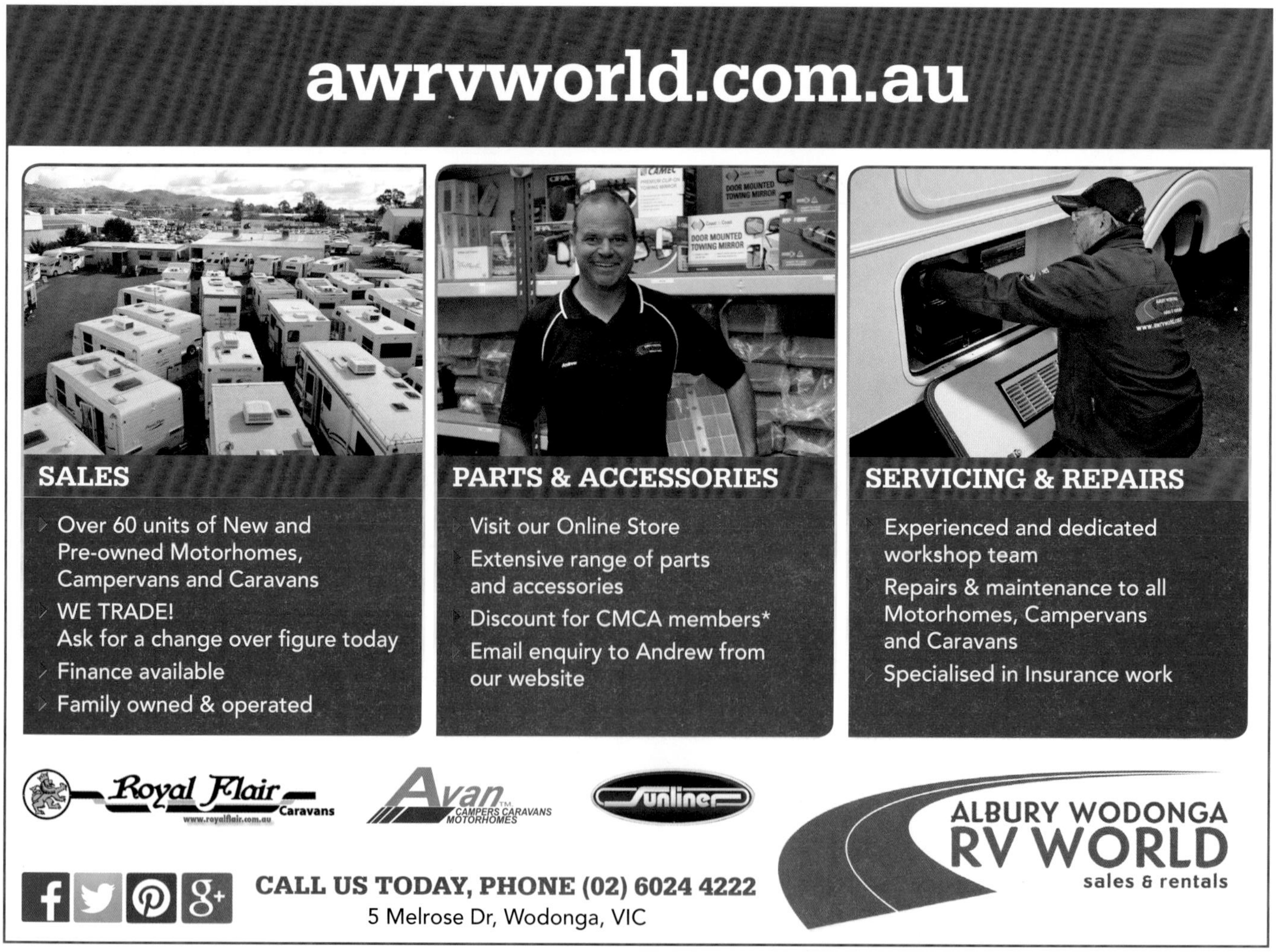
awrvworld.com.au
SALES
Over 60 units of New and Pre-owned Motorhomes, Campervans and Caravans
WE TRADE! Ask for a change over figure today
Finance available
Family owned & operated
PARTS & ACCESSORIES
Visit our Online Store
Extensive range of parts and accessories
Discount for CMCA members*
Email enquiry to Andrew from our website
SERVICING & REPAIRS
Experienced and dedicated workshop team
Repairs & maintenance to all Motorhomes, Campervans and Caravans
Specialised in Insurance work
Royal Flair Caravans
www.royalflair.com.au
Avan CAMPERS CARAVANS MOTORHOMES
Sunliner
ALBURY WODONGA RV WORLD
sales & rentals
CALL US TODAY, PHONE (02) 6024 4222
5 Melrose Dr, Wodonga, VIC

CONTENTS

ABOUT THIS GUIDE

GPS Co-ordinates used in Camps Australia Wide 8

The format used in Camps 8 is d° m' s" (Degrees, Minutes, Seconds).

Most GPS units generally have three GPS format settings. It is important that you select the correct setting in your GPS to match our format. This will ensure you are accurately guided to the site.

Listed below are the three common coordinates formats:

- d.d° (-49.5000°, 123.500°) sometimes called "Degrees".
- d° m.m (49° 30.0, 123° 30.0) sometimes called "Minutes".
- **d° m' s" (49° 30 00 S, 123° 30 00 E) sometimes called "Seconds" (we use this format)**

We now have GPS Point Of Interest (POI) files that have been created by our partner GPSOZ. When these files are loaded into your GPS you can view and select Camps 8 sites from the Custom POI section of your GPS for turn by turn guidance to the selected Camps listing. These files are available as a download for a range of GPS devices and are delivered by email.

Visit our web site www.campsaustraliawide.com for more information about purchasing GPS POI files.

This guide predominantly lists Free and Low Cost Camping, National Parks, State Forests, Rest Areas, Station Stays, Showgrounds.

This guide is NOT a comprehensive Caravan Park Guide, only Caravan Parks where fees are below $25 per night for 2 adults are included, this means the parks are generally in country and remote areas.

Feedback

This type of publication relies on consumer feedback to maintain accuracy and content. Your input would be most appreciated.

You can email us on talktous@campsaustraliawide.com or phone us on (07) 5474 2542.

Any information, no matter how small, can be sent in by mail, fax or email. It won't be ignored.

Dump Point List

Because of the ever-increasing concern for the environment a comprehensive Public Dump Point list has been included. These dump points also have GPS co-ordinates to help you find their positions. Any new addition to our list of Public Dump Points would be most welcome.

Seven Principles of Leave No Trace

- Plan ahead and prepare
- Travel and camp on durable surfaces
- Dispose of waste properly
- Leave what you find
- Minimise campfire impacts
- Respect wildlife
- Be considerate of your hosts and other visitors

For more information visit www.lnt.org.au

This book

This book is intended to be used as a guide only. The representation on the maps of any road or track is not necessarily evidence of public right of way. Third parties who provide information to the publisher and authors concerning roads and other matters do not assert or imply to the publishers that such information is complete, accurate or current. Whilst the author believes the details contained in the book to be correct at the time of publication and all care has been taken to ensure the information is as accurate as possible, inaccuracies may occur. As such, no responsibility is taken for changes, amendments, additions or alterations to any item and no liability will be accepted for any decisions or actions taken based on information contained in the publication. Conditions in Australia are constantly changing, and as such, Federal, State and Local authorities may make changes to conditions relating to sites listed in this guide, which are subject to closure or change without notice. Please obey any signs and do not insist that you are in the right because it says so in the book. The book is not the absolute authority. It's a guide only!

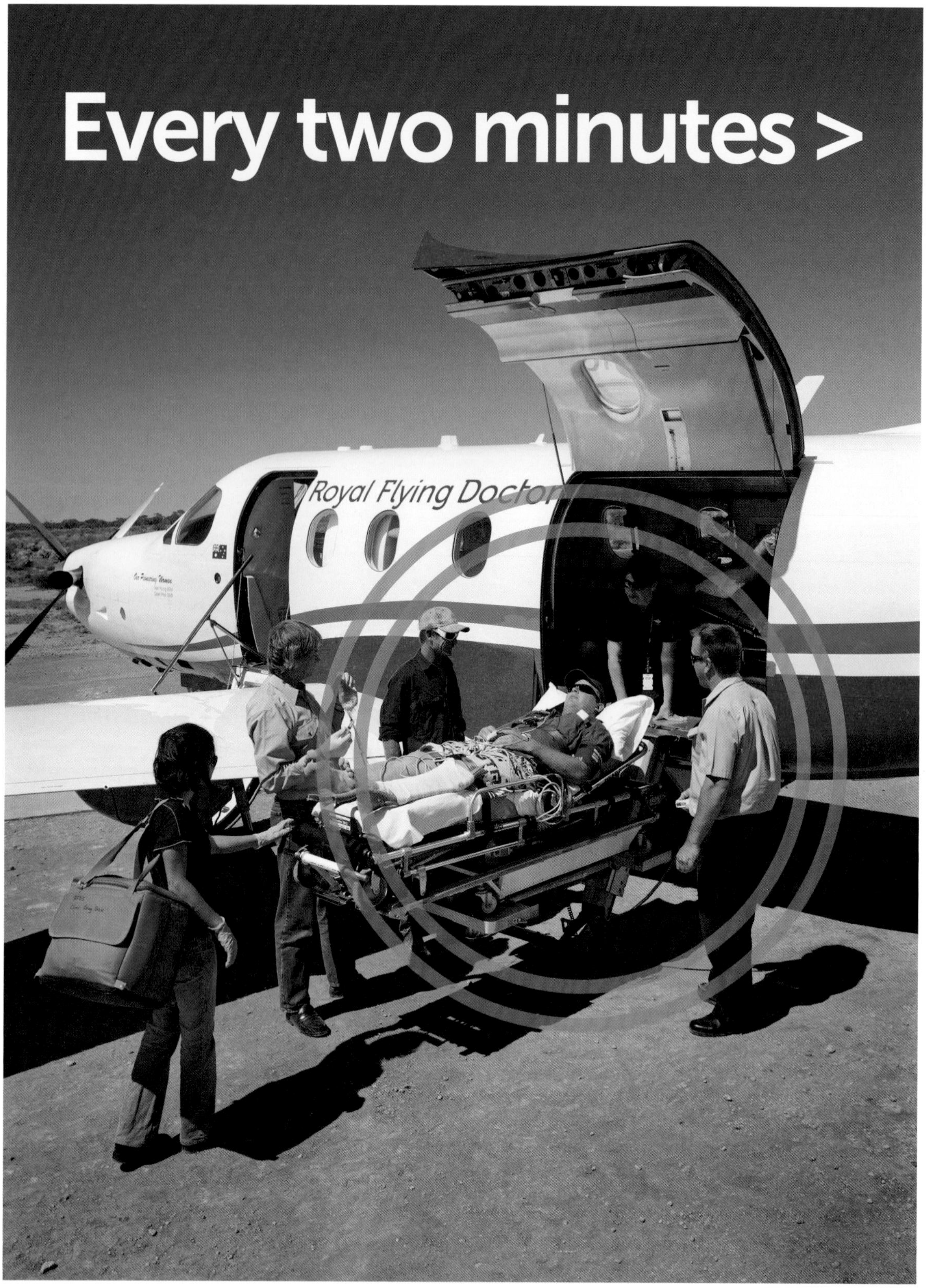
Every two minutes >
Royal Flying Doctor

IMPORTANT: UPDATING THIS BOOK

A free user-friendly searchable update service is provided on our website via the 'Updates' tab. Changes will occur, especially over time after the books release. So it's important to check regularly for updates. Updates for this edition are provided for four years from the date first published.

Step 1

On the Camps Australia Wide website (www.campsaustraliawide.com) select the 'Updates' tab.

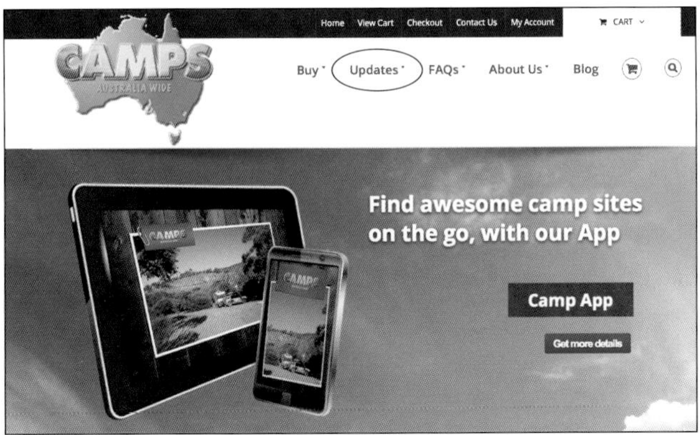

Step 2

Selecting the 'Updates' tab will open the 'Update Service' page which gives you an option to 'Launch Updates Program'. When that is selected, the Updates Program will display in a window floating above the web page.

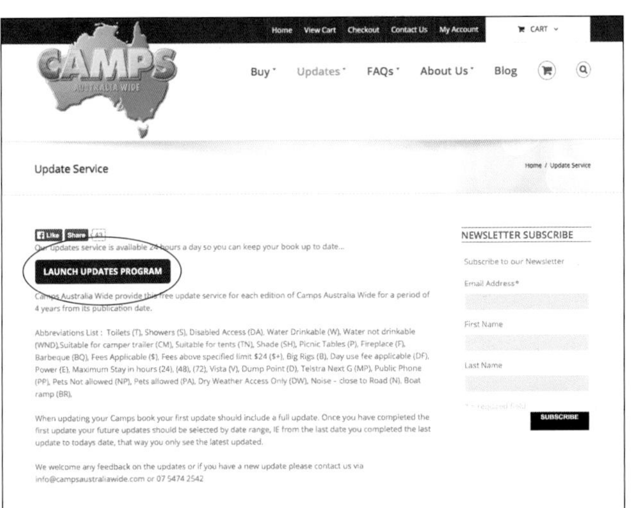

Step 3

The Updates Program window. Here choices are made as to publication, edition, State, and dates.

For the first update leave the date fields blank. For subsequent updates just enter the date range using the pop-up calendar to show new updates only.

Printing. If the Print button is obscured, simply use the scroll bar to reveal it.

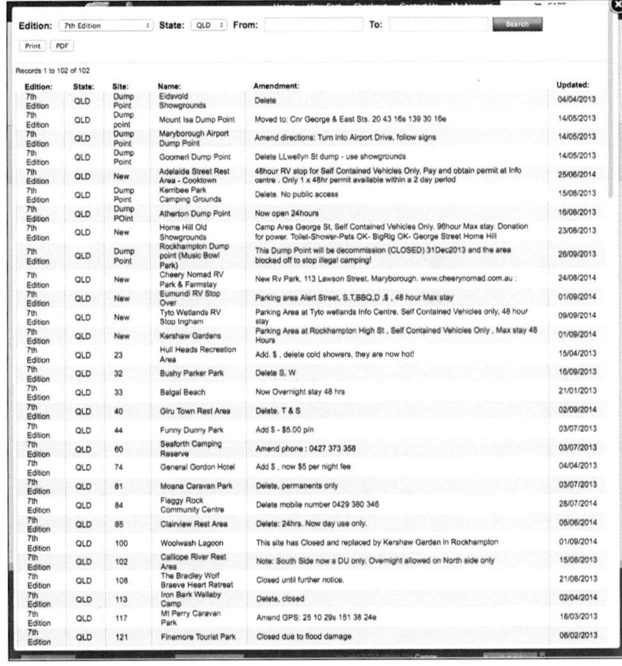

Edition: 7th Edition State: QLD From: To: Search

Print PDF

Records 1 to 102 of 102

Edition:	State:	Site:	Name:	Amendment:	Updated:
7th Edition	QLD	Dump Point	Eidsvold Showgrounds	Delete	04/04/2013
7th Edition	QLD	Dump point	Mount Isa Dump Point	Moved to: Cnr George & East Sts. 20 43 16s 139 30 16e	14/05/2013
7th Edition	QLD	Dump Point	Maryborough Airport Dump Point	Amend directions: Turn into Airport Drive, follow signs	14/05/2013
7th Edition	QLD	Dump Point	Goomeri Dump Point	Delete LLwellyn St dump - use showgrounds	14/05/2013
7th Edition	QLD	New	Adelaide Street Rest Area - Cooktown	48hour RV stop for Self Contained Vehicles Only. Pay and obtain permit at Info centre . Only 1 x 48hr permit available within a 2 day period	25/06/2014
7th Edition	QLD	Dump Point	Kerribee Park Camping Grounds	Delete. No public access	15/08/2013
7th Edition	QLD	Dump POint	Atherton Dump Point	Now open 24hours	16/08/2013
7th Edition	QLD	New	Home Hill Old Showgrounds	Camp Area George St, Self Contained Vehicles Only. 96hour Max stay. Donation for power. Toilet-Shower-Pets OK- BigRig OK- George Street Home Hill	23/08/2013
7th Edition	QLD	Dump Point	Rockhampton Dump point (Music Bowl Park)	This Dump Point will be decommission (CLOSED) 31Dec2013 and the area blocked off to stop illegal camping!	26/09/2013
7th Edition	QLD	New	Cheery Nomad RV Park & Farmstay	New Rv Park, 113 Lawson Street, Maryborough. www.cheerynomad.com.au :	24/08/2014
7th Edition	QLD	New	Eumundi RV Stop Over	Parking area Alert Street, S,T,BBQ,D ,$, 48 hour Max stay	01/09/2014
7th Edition	QLD	New	Tyto Wetlands RV Stop Ingham	Parking Area at Tyto wetlands Info Centre, Self Contained Vehicles only, 48 hour stay	09/09/2014
7th Edition	QLD	New	Kershaw Gardens	Parking Area at Rockhampton High St , Self Contained Vehicles Only , Max stay 48 Hours	01/09/2014
7th Edition	QLD	23	Hull Heads Recreation Area	Add. $, delete cold showers, they are now hot!	15/04/2013
7th Edition	QLD	32	Bushy Parker Park	Delete S, W	16/09/2013
7th Edition	QLD	33	Balgal Beach	Now Overnight stay 48 hrs	21/01/2013
7th Edition	QLD	40	Giru Town Rest Area	Delete. T & S	02/09/2014
7th Edition	QLD	44	Funny Dunny Park	Add $ - $5.00 p/n	03/07/2013
7th Edition	QLD	60	Seaforth Camping Reserve	Amend phone : 0427 373 358	03/07/2013
7th Edition	QLD	74	General Gordon Hotel	Add $, now $5 per night fee	04/04/2013
7th Edition	QLD	81	Moana Caravan Park	Delete, permanents only	03/07/2013
7th Edition	QLD	84	Flaggy Rock Community Centre	Delete mobile number 0429 380 346	28/07/2014
7th Edition	QLD	85	Clairview Rest Area	Delete: 24hrs. Now day use only.	05/06/2014
7th Edition	QLD	100	Woolwash Lagoon	This site has Closed and replaced by Kershaw Garden in Rockhampton	01/09/2014
7th Edition	QLD	102	Calliope River Rest Area	Note: South Side now a DU only. Overnight allowed on North side only	15/08/2013
7th Edition	QLD	108	The Bradley Wolf Braeve Heart Retreat	Closed until further notice.	21/08/2013
7th Edition	QLD	113	Iron Bark Wallaby Camp	Delete, closed	02/04/2014
7th Edition	QLD	117	Mt Perry Caravan Park	Amend GPS: 25 10 29s 151 38 24e	18/03/2013
7th Edition	QLD	121	Finemore Tourist Park	Closed due to flood damage	08/02/2013

Feedback

Our team always welcomes feedback on existing sites and any new site that you think worthwhile sharing with our fellow travellers. Please email us on talktous@campsaustraliawide.com

HOW TO USE THIS GUIDE

Layout of the guide

The book is divided into different coloured sections for each State or Territory for easier navigation.

The listings, in general, are in a linear order along the highways and roads, running from north to south and east to west, where possible.

The list of terms has been amended to better illustrate each site and to avoid the overuse of the word 'camp', which has different connotations to different people.

Abbreviations Some abbreviations have been used to condense the amount of text throughout the book.

They are:

Dr - Drive	Tce - Terrace
Rd - Road	St - Street
Ave - Avenue	cnr - corner
Hwy - highway	jcn - junction
km - kilometre	L - left
R - right	m - metre
N - north	S - south
E - east	W- west
NP - National Park	PO - Post Office

Map References Maps by Hema with sites and site numbers from Camps Australia Wide 8 overlaid.

All the sites are referenced to these maps.

Where the number of sites is quite comprehensive, the more detailed maps should be used for navigation.

Site Classification Symbols and Map Symbols

The following are used in the listings and on the maps:

Explanation	In Listings	On Maps: No Dump Point	On Maps: With Dump Point
Day Use Only	☼	32	30
Overnight Camping and Parking	☾	155	115
Caravan Parks	caravan	121	
Public Dump Point not at a Listed Site		dump point	

Sites' symbols are placed as close as possible to the exact position.

Explanation of terms used in this guide

Rest Area An area usually located close to the highway to enable the traveller to take a break. Some rest areas provide a wide range of facilities, while others are just an area to rest for a while. Overnight camping is permitted at some sites, depending on the relevant authorities regulations. Please take notice of any regulatory signs.

Camp Area An area that has been established for camping overnight or longer, that usually provides at least some basic facilities such as toilets and water, but not necessarily showers or power. A fee is usually charged for most locations.

Camp Spot An area that is not an established camp area, but is adequate for an overnight stay or even longer, usually with limited facilities. A fee may be charged in some instances.

Picnic Area An area that has suitable facilities for a picnic. Overnight stays may be permissible in certain cases.

Parking Area An area with limited or no facilities. Overnight stays may be allowed in certain cases.

Caravan Park An established area for short or long term stays, providing a range of facilities and comforts. A fee is payable depending on the quality and number of facilities offered.

Self Contained Vehicle A vehicle that is fully self contained with respect to shower, toilet, washing, cooking and sleeping facilities and which must have holding tanks for all toilet waste and sullage water sufficient for at least 48 hours' use by the occupants.

Small Vehicle On some site descriptions, we add 'small vehicle only'. This generally indicates the entry into the site is tight and the parking, camping or turning area is restricted, only Toyota HiAce size campers, small camper trailers or caravans are recommended.

How to locate a site

- If you know the name of a site, go to the Site Index at the beginning of each state (alphabetically listed), which gives you the site number and the relevant page number.
- If you want to find sites in any particular area, look at the relevant map for site numbers in that region, then look up those sites in the numerical listing.

There will always be variations in odometer readings and road distance signs, so do allow for those discrepancies when locating sites.

LEGEND – CAMPSITES

The sample below explains how each site is laid out for easy interpretation. Most of the symbols are self-explanatory, but some have been designed to fit certain criteria.

Sample of a Site Listing

Explanation of Symbols

Toilets

Outside of caravan parks these may be longdrops or composting types. As these are not always serviced frequently it is advisable to carry your own supply of toilet tissue.

Disabled facilities

Generally there is at least one dedicated toilet and shower, in some sites this facility is unisex.

Shade

At the time of viewing this site there was shade available for your vehicle.

Fireplace

It is advisable to carry your own supply of firewood for fires and barbeques at some of the more isolated camp spots. Most National Parks do not allow firewood collection within the Park boundaries. Please gather deadwood only, do not destroy trees. Ensure you respect all local fire bans and seasonal restrictions.

Fees applicable

At the time of publication sites with this symbol had a fee below $25 per night for 2 adults. As fees at all site are subject to change without notice it is strongly recommended that you call and verify the fees before you arrive.

Day use fee applicable

Primarily charged at State and National Parks, often in addition to any camping fees.

Fees above specified limit

Sites with this symbol have been included in this edition because of their locations or because they offer something special, even though the cost may be above the upper limit of $24 per night.

BIG RIG **Site suitable for Big Rigs**

We define Big Rigs as large or long vehicles with an overall length of 10 metres or more. There are usually limited sites available for larger vehicles.

Powered sites

These sites may have a concrete pad and/or grassed area with a power point for your vehicle.

Pleasant outlook or vista

The site provides over water, valley, or mountain views.

Mobile phone service

Site has access to Telstra NextG™ Network with a 'Blue Tick Telstra phone'.

Pets

Although pets are allowed at these sites conditions may apply when entering a commercial camping area or caravan park. Some operators now require a fee and/or bond as part of the conditions of entry into the area, and may limit animal size and allow pets only in off-peak periods. It is advisable to call ahead to ensure that your pet is welcome. As a general rule pets must always be on a lead, and must never be left unattended. As always, clean up after your pet!

 **Pets NOT allowed**
Pets are not allowed at this site.

 **Dry weather access only**
Roads used to access the site may become impassable during the wet season or after rain and care is advised. Please check with local authorities for conditions. Usually recommended for 4WD only.

 **Showers**
May be hot or cold and in some isolated areas solar heated only. Some sites have showers available for a gold coin donation.

 **Water**
Even though it is listed as drinkable it is advisable to boil or filter before use. Please use common sense and limit your use, so that others can enjoy the availability as well.

 **Water not drinkable**
While this site has a water supply we recommend that you NOT drink it.

 **Picnic table**
Picnic tables are available and may be shaded at some locations.

BBQ
At camp sites these are usually wood fired. Some caravan parks and National Parks provide a free gas or electric barbeque for guests, others may charge a small fee for the use of the facility. Commonsense and etiquette on use and cleaning after use applies.

 **Camper trailer**
Site is suitable for the setting up of a camper trailer.

 **Tent Site**
Site is suitable for the setting up of a tent. In a commercial camping area tent sites are usually in an open grassed area (subject to local conditions).

 **Maximum stay (hours)**
These may be Main Roads rest areas or sites provided by local authorities. Please use these as intended and honour the time limits as sign posted. Improper use of these sites may be detrimental to travellers' future use of the facility.

✓ **Author's Recommendation**
The authors at the time of their visit found that these sites were appealing, either because of the sites position or vista or because facilities were above average.

 **Dump Point**
This symbol advises that the park or site has a central dump point. These dump points are generally provided for the disposal of cassette toilets. For those vehicles with holding tanks you will need to check with the facility operator to ensure that there is access for the disposal of black or grey water.

 **Public phone**
A public phone is available at this facility or within 100 metres of the site.

 **Site close to road**
These sites may be noisy depending on the amount of passing traffic and time of day.

 **Caravan**
Site is suitable for a caravan.

 **Camper/Motorhome**
Site is suitable for a camper/motorhome (not a Big Rig).

 **Boat ramp**
This site has boat launch facilities nearby. The ramp may be properly built or may be adapted from local conditions. In most cases they are suitable for small 'tinnies'. Check local conditions for tidal flow and other hazards.

Site Symbols

 Day Use Only  Overnight Camping/Parking  Caravan Parks

Public Dump Points

An example of a public dump point listing and the symbols used for dump points are shown on the introductory page of the Public Dump Point section on page 410.

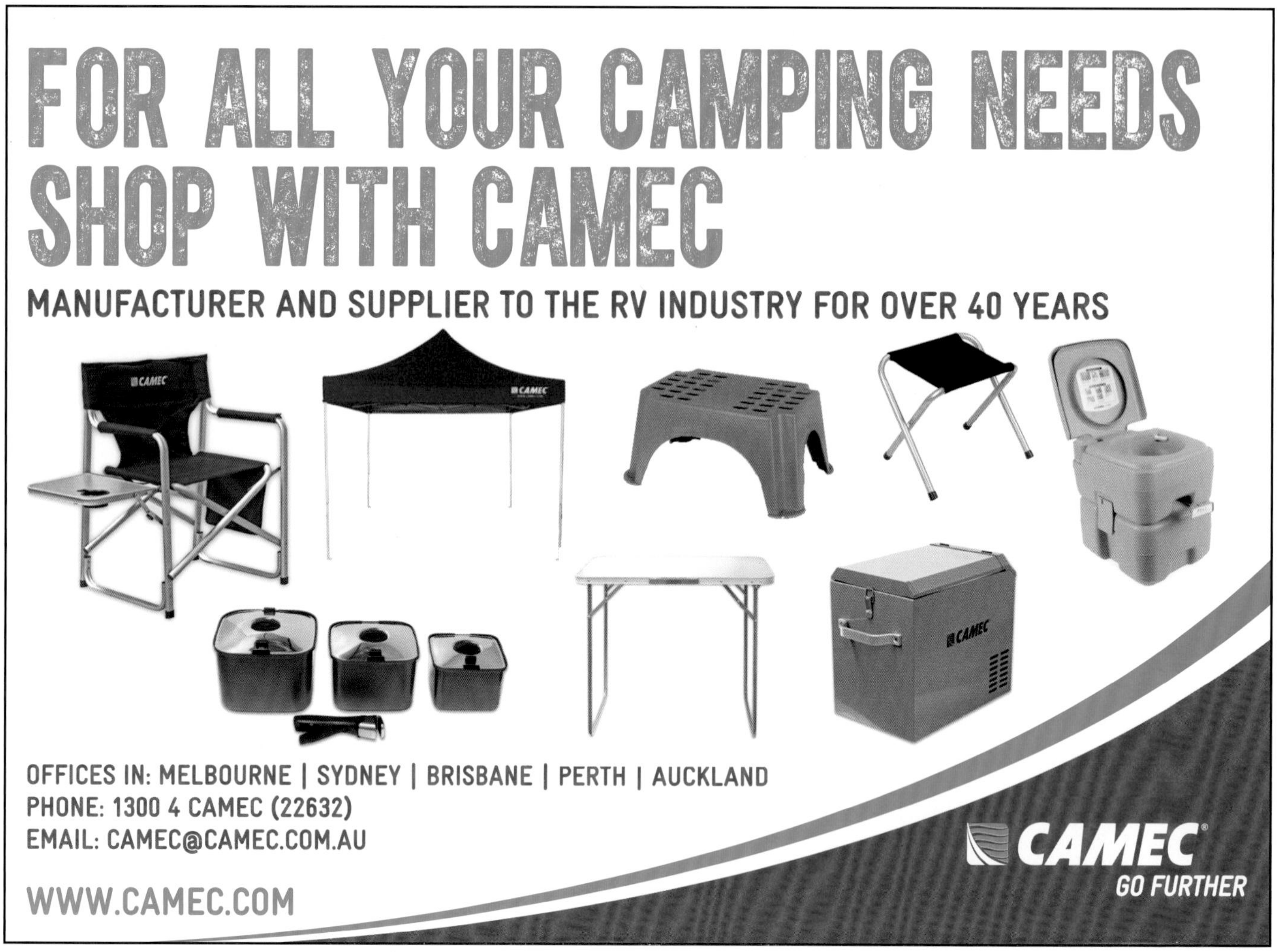
FOR ALL YOUR CAMPING NEEDS
SHOP WITH CAMEC
MANUFACTURER AND SUPPLIER TO THE RV INDUSTRY FOR OVER 40 YEARS
OFFICES IN: MELBOURNE | SYDNEY | BRISBANE | PERTH | AUCKLAND
PHONE: 1300 4 CAMEC (22632)
EMAIL: CAMEC@CAMEC.COM.AU
WWW.CAMEC.COM
CAMEC
GO FURTHER

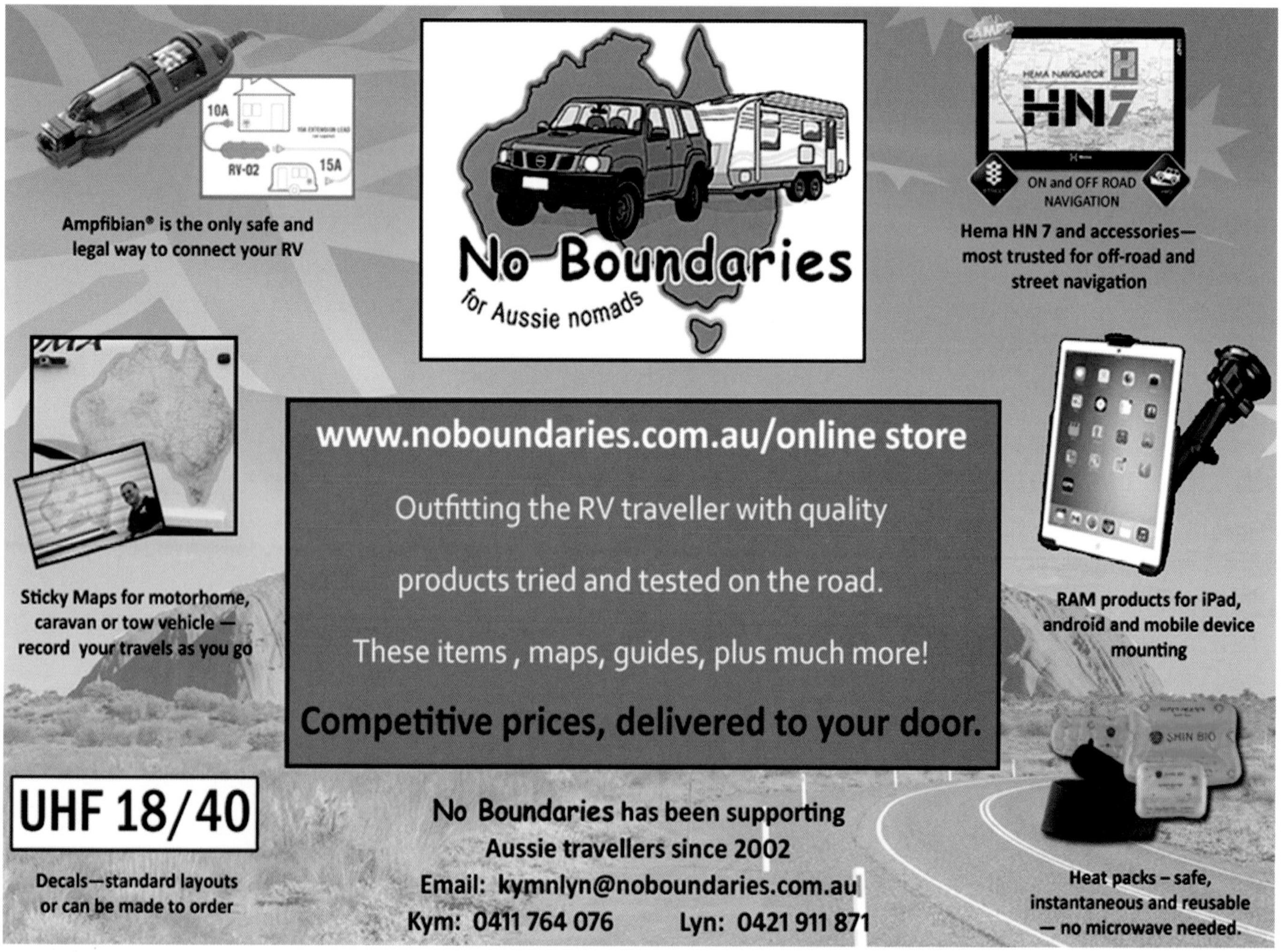
Ampfibian® is the only safe and legal way to connect your RV
No Boundaries
for Aussie nomads
Hema HN 7 and accessories—most trusted for off-road and street navigation
ON and OFF ROAD NAVIGATION
www.noboundaries.com.au/online store
Outfitting the RV traveller with quality
products tried and tested on the road.
These items , maps, guides, plus much more!
Competitive prices, delivered to your door.
Sticky Maps for motorhome, caravan or tow vehicle — record your travels as you go
RAM products for iPad, android and mobile device mounting
UHF 18/40
Decals—standard layouts or can be made to order
No Boundaries has been supporting
Aussie travellers since 2002
Email: kymnlyn@noboundaries.com.au
Kym: 0411 764 076
Lyn: 0421 911 871
Heat packs – safe, instantaneous and reusable — no microwave needed.

Road Conditions

Some of the sites listed are accessed by roads that may be unsuitable for some vehicles and which may also change due to weather conditions. It is recommended that you enquire from local authorities before travelling on roads of uncertain condition.

Pets

Apart from National Parks and some caravan parks, pets are generally accepted, provided they are under control by their owner. Dogs always need to be under control, especially around other dogs or people. Where dogs are accepted in caravan parks, it is usually at the manager's discretion and on condition that they are on a leash at all times. Common sense should prevail. Clean up any mess left behind and respect the area.

Generators

These can be a necessary part of travelling, but do have consideration for your neighbour and run them at respectable hours. Be aware of the noise and fumes put out by these machines and park accordingly. Generators are banned in some National Parks. Consult relevant National Park information for details.

Rubbish

If there are no rubbish bins provided, take your rubbish with you. Leave an area cleaner than you find it and consider cleaning up after someone else. A well-looked-after site will give the authorities a good reason to keep it open for our use.

Toilet Waste

We have provided a comprehensive 'Public Dump Point' listing starting on page 410. For a fee some caravan parks will allow access and use of their Dump Point, enquire at the caravan park. If you have to bury your waste in remote areas, make sure it is buried at least 20 centimetres deep and 200 metres away from any waterway, runoff area or camp site.

Firewood

It is advisable to carry your own supply of firewood for fires and barbeques at some of the more isolated camp spots, rather than destroy any remaining trees. Always observe fire bans and restrictions.

Water

Although the water available at sites should be suitable for drinking, it would be wise to carry sufficient water for drinking as a backup and as an alternative if the water is drinkable but unpleasant.

At all times use common sense with fires, plants, animals and your fellow traveller and protect the environment.

State Regulations

Overnight Camping

There are some differences in the laws relating to overnight camping in rest areas and on private property within each State, and these laws are always changing. Some States and Local Authorities are quite tolerant of overnight camping, while others will enforce the law and move you on, fine you, or both. Observe any regulatory signs, respect people in authority and always use common sense.

IMPORTANT CONTACTS

Police, Ambulance & Fire Brigade 000

International emergency Number 112 (mobile phones only)

National Parks and Wildlife Service

Western Australia
Dept of Parks and Wildlife (DPAW): (08) 9219 900
www.dpaw.wa.gov.au

Queensland
Dept of National Parks, Recreation, Sport & Racing
Ph: 13 74 68 www.nprsr.qld.gov.au or
www.ehp.qld.gov.au

New South Wales
NSW National Parks and Wildlife Service Ph: 1300 361 967
www.nationalparks.nsw.gov.au

South Australia
Dept of Environment, Water and Natural Resources
Ph: (08) 8204 1910
www.environment.sa.gov.au/parks

Tasmania
Parks and Wildlife Service Ph: 1300 827 727
www.parks.tas.gov.au

Northern Territory
Parks and Wildlife Commission Northern Territory
Ph: (08) 8999 5511
www.parksandwildlife.nt.gov.au

Victoria
Parks Victoria Ph: 13 19 63
www.parkweb.vic.gov.au

Australian Capital Territory
Environment and Sustainable Development
Ph: 13 22 81
www.environment.act.gov.au

Aboriginal Land Permits

Western Australia
Dep of Aboriginal Affairs Ph: 1300 651 077
Online Permits: www.dia.wa.gov.au/land/permits

Northern Territory, Central Land Council
Alice Springs
Ngaanyatjarra Shire Council Ph: (08) 8950 1711
www.clc.org.au

Tennant Creek Ph: (08) 8962 2343

South Australia
Yalata Ph: 0407 832 297
Maralinga-Tjarutja Council Ph: (08) 8625 2946

Road Conditions

New South Wales (Outback) Ph: (08) 8082 6660
Queensland Ph: 1300 130 595
South Australia Ph: 1300 361 033
Western Australia Ph: 1800 013 314
Northern Territory Ph: 1800 246 199

Vehicle Assistance

AANT, NRMA, RAA, RAC, RACQ, RACT, RACV
Ph: 13 11 11

Royal Flying Doctor Service

NSW Medical & Emergency Calls (Broken Hill)
Ph: (08) 8088 1188

Qld Medical & Emergency Calls (Charleville)
Ph: (07) 4654 1443

Qld Medical & Emergency Calls (Mt Isa)
Ph: (07) 4743 2802

SA & NT South of Tennant Creek Medical & Emergency Calls Ph: (08) 8648 9555

NT (North of Tennant Creek) After Hours Emergency Calls Ph: 000 (112 for mobile phones)

WA Medical & Emergency Calls Ph: 1800 625 800
(Satphones Ph: (08) 9417 6389)

Weather Information

Bureau of Meterology www.bom.gov.au

Other Useful Contacts

New South Wales Rural Fire Service Ph: 1800 679 737
Queensland Fire & Rescue Service Ph: 13 74 68
Victoria Country Fire Authority – Fire Restrictions Ph: 1800 240 667
Bushfires Council NT Ph: (08) 8922 0844
Tasmanian Fire Service Ph: (03) 6230 8600
Australian National 4WD Radio Network
Ph: (08) 8287 6222, www.vks737.on.net
Birdsville Hotel, Queensland Ph: (07) 4656 3244
Spirit of Tasmania - Information and Reservations
Ph: 1800 634 906, www.spiritoftasmania.com.au
Pink Roadhouse, Oodnadatta, SA Ph: (08) 8670 7822,
www.pinkroadhouse.com.au

Fruit and Quarantine Zones

Western Australian Quarantine & Inspection Service
Kununurra border checkpoint Ph: (08) 9166 4000
South Australia Fruit Fly Exclusion Zone
Ph: 1800 084 881, www.fruitfly.net.au
Queensland DPI & F Coen Quarantine & Inspection Point Ph: 13 25 23, www.daff.qld.gov.au

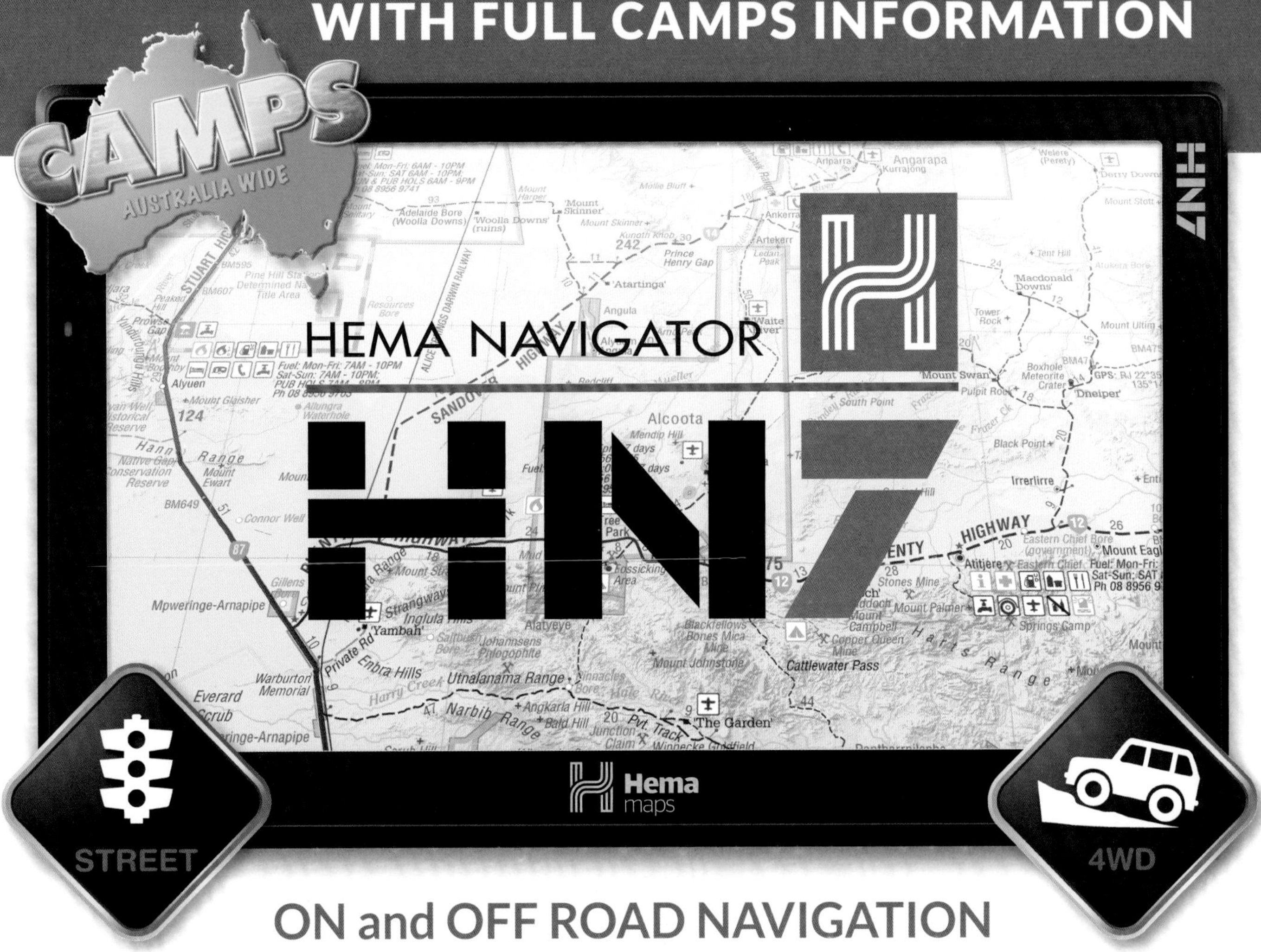

Freeway; Divided Highway
Autobahn
Autoroute; route rapide à chaussées séparées
Autostrada; superstrada
Autosnelweg; hoofdweg met gescheiden rijbanen

Freeway – future
Autobahn – im Bau
Autoroute – en construction
Autostrada – in costruzione
Autosnelweg in aanleg

Major Highway – sealed; unsealed
Durchgangsstraße – befestigt; unbefestigt
Route principale – revêtue; non revêtue
Strada di grande comunicazione – pavimentata; non pavimentata
Hoofdverbindingsweg – verhard; onverhard

Major Road – sealed; unsealed
Hauptstraße – befestigt; unbefestigt
Route de communication – revêtue; non revêtue
Strada principale – pavimentata; non pavimentata
Belangrijke weg – verhard of onverhard

Minor Road – sealed; unsealed
Nebenstraße – befestigt; unbefestigt
Autre route revêtue; non revêtue
Altra strada – pavimentata; non pavimentata
Secundaire weg – verhard of aardeweg

Track, four-wheel drive only
Piste, nur mit 4-Rad-Antrieb befahrbar
Piste, utilisable pour véhicule à 4 roues motrices
Pista, praticabile solo con trazione integrale
Piste, uitsluitend voor 4 x 4

Rough Track, four-wheel drive only
Piste (unwegsam), nur mit 4-Rad-Antrieb befahrbar
Piste rugueux, utilisable pour véhicule à 4 roues motrices
Pista greggio, praticabile solo con trazione integral
Piste moeilijk berijbaar, uitsluitend voor 4 x 4

Walking Track; Gate
Wanderweg; Tor
Sentier; barrière
Sentiero; cancello
Wandelweg; gate

★ 44 ★

Total Kilometres
Entfernung (total) in km
Distance totale en km
Distanza totale in km
Totale afstand in km

20 24

Intermediate Kilometres
Teildistanz in km
Distance partielle en km
Distanza parziale in km
Gedeeltelijke afstand in km

National Route Number/ National Highway Number
Nummer Nationalstraße/ Nummer nationale Durchgangsstraße
Numéro de route nationale/ de route rapide
Numero della strada nazionale/ Numero della strada di grande comunicazione
Wegnummers op nationale/ wegen en expresswegen

B2 B400

State Route Number
Staats-Straßennummer
Numéro de route d'Etat
Numero della strada dello stato
Staatswegnummer

Tourist Route
Touristische Route
Route touristique
Strada turistica
Toeristische route

Railway – in use; disused
Bahnlinie – in Betrieb; stillgelegt
Chemin de fer – en service; abandonné
Ferrovia – in esercizio; interrotto
Spoorweg – in gebruik; buiten gebruik

Ferry Route
Fährverbindung
Route de traversier
Traghetto rotta
Veerdienst

State/ Territory Border
Staats-/ Territoriengrenze
Frontière d'Etat/ territoire
Stato/ territorio di confine
Staats-/ Territorygrens

Pest Free Area
Pest Freie Zone
Zone de ravageur franche
Zona parassiti franca
Pestvrij gebied

Fruit Fly Exclusion Zone
Fruchtfliegen Ausschluss Zone
Zone exclusive de la mouche des fruits
Zona esclusiva de la mosca della frutta
Fruitvliegvrij gebied

National Park
Nationalpark
Parc national
Parco nazionale
Nationaal park

Other Parks & Nature Reserves
Sonstige Parks und Natur Reservate
Autre parks et réserve naturelle
Altri parchi e riserve
Andere parken en natuurreservaten

Resources Reserve
Ressourcen Schutzgebiet
Zone protégée de ressources
Zona protetta da risorse
Ontginnings Reservaat

Scientific Reserve
Naturwissenschaftliches Schutzgebiet
Zone protégée scientifique
Zona protetta scientifica
Wetenschappelijk Reservaat

State Forest & Timber Reserve
Staatsforst & Holz Reservat
Forêt domaniale
Zona protetta da risorse
Staatsbos en bosbouw reservaat

Aboriginal Land
Aborigines-Gebiet
Région d'aborigènes
Regione d'aborigeni
Gebied van de aborigines

World Heritage Area
Weltkulturerbegebiet (UNESCO)
Site du patrimoine mondial
Luogo dell' patrimonio mondiale
Wereld Beschermd Gebied

Marine Park
Meeresschutzgebiet
Parc marin
Parco marino
Zeereservaat

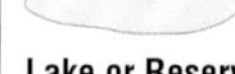

Prohibited Area
Sperrgebiet
Zone interdite
Area vietata
Afgesloten gebied

Lake or Reservoir
See oder Reservoir
Lac ou réservoir
Lago o lago artificiale
Meer of waterreservoir

Intermittent or Salt Lake
Periodischer oder Salzwassersee
Lac périodique ou d'eau salée
Lago periodico o salato
Periodiek of zoutwatermeer

River – perennial; non-perennial
Fluß – dauerhaft; periodisch
Rivière – constant; périodique
Fiume – constante; periodico
Rivier – altijd; periodiek

Saline Coastal Flat
Wattgebiet
Salines côtières
Salino castiero platts
Zeekust vlakte

Swamp
Sumpf
Marais
Palude
Moeras

Subject to Inundation
Überschwemmungsgebiet
Sujet aux inondations
Soggette a inondazioni
Kan onderwater lopen

Sandridges
Sanddüne
Dune de sable
Dune de sabbia
Zandruggen

Mangroves
Mangroven
Mangroves
Mangrovie
Wortelbomen

Built up area
Bebaute Fläche
Zone construite
Costruito nell'area
Bebouwde kom

• **BRISBANE**

Capital City
Hauptstadt
Capitale
Capitale
Hoofdstaad

• **Cairns**

City
Grossstadt
Ville importante
Città grande o importante
Stad of hoofdplaats

• **Gympie**

Large Town
Stadt
Ville
Città
Stad

• **Tully**

Medium Town
Mittelgroße Stadt
Ville moyenne
Città de medie
Middelgrote Stad

• Samford

Small Town
Kleinstadt
Ville petite
Piccola città
Kleine Stad

• Ayton

Locality
Gegend
Localité
Località
Plaats

▪ 'Rostock'

Homestead
Gehöft
Ferme
Masseria
Hofstede

◉ Doomadgee ◉ Urlampe

Aboriginal Community – major; minor
Aborigines Gemeinde – groß; klein
Communauté d'aborigènes
Comunità d'aborigeni
Gebied van aborigines – groot; klein

+ *Mount James*

Mountain/ Hill
Berg/ Hügel
Montagne/ colline
Monte/ colle
Bergen/ heuvel

• *Fruit Bat Falls*

Tourist Point of Interest
Sehenswürdigkeit
Curiosité touristique
Curiosità turistica
Toeristische bezienswaardigheid

• *Lindeman's Hunter Valley*

Winery
Weinkellerei
Établissement vinicole
Cantina
Wijnmakerij

Shipwreck
Schiffswrack
Naufrage
Naufragio
Schipwrak

Lighthouse
Leuchtturm
Phare
Faro
Vuurtoren

Tower
Turm
Tour
Torre
Toren

Hut
Hütte
Hutte
Capanna
Hut

—40—

Distance from GPO (km)
Entfernung zum Hauptpostgebäude (km)
Distance par la route du bureau de poste général (km)
Distanza dalla strada da General Post Office (km)
Afstand uit de algemene postkantoor (km)

Camping Area (with facilities)
Camping (mit Einrichtungen)
Camping (avec équipement)
Campeggio (con equipaggiamento)
Campingplaats (met voorzieningen)

Rest Area (with toilet)
Rastplatz (ohne Einrichtungen)
Aire de repos (sans équipement)
Area di riposo (senza equipaggiamento)
Rustplaats (zonder voorzieningen)

... with overnight camping
Rastplatz (Toilette)
...mit Camping (nur 1 Nacht)
Aire de repos (Toilettes)
...et camping (seulement 1 nuit)
Area di riposo (Gabinetto)
...e campeggio (solo 1 notte)
Rustplaats (toilet)
...en Campingplaats (één overnachting)

...with overnight camping (no toilet)
Rastplatz (ohne Toilette)
Aire de repos (sans Toilettes)
Area di riposo (senza Gabinetto)
Rustplaats (zonder toilet)

Picnic Area/ Rest Area (no facilities)
Picknickplatz (nur in Stadtplänen)
Place pique-nique (Plans de villes)
Picnic (Plante di città)
Piknikplaatsen (allen op stadsplannen)

Accredited Visitor Information Centre
Akkreditiertes Besucher Informationszentrum
Accréditée centre d'information touristique
Accreditato visitatore centro di informazione
Officieel touristenkantoor

Golf Course
Golfplatz
Terrain de golf
Campo da golf
Golfbaan

Caravan Park
Wohnwagen-Park
Terrain pour caravanes
Area per Camper/Roulotte
Het karavaan park

Boat ramp
Bootsrampe
Rampe
Barca rampa
Boothelling

Lookout
Aussichtspunkt
Point de vue
Belvedere
Uitkijk

24 Hour Fuel
Tankstelle 24 Std.
Station-service ouverte 24h
Stazione di servizio aperta 24h
24 uur benzene

Diesel
Diesel erhältlich
Diesel disponible
Diesel disponibile
Diesel beschikbaar

Outback Fuel (Diesel and Unleaded)
(not shown in region pages)
Diesel u. bleifreies Benzin bzw.
Diesel et carburant sans plomb
Diesel e benzina senza piombo
Diesel en loodvrij

Opal (unleaded replacement)
(not shown in region pages)
Opal Bezin erhältlich
Opal disponible
Opale disponible
Opal

Airport; International Airport
Flughafen; Internationaler Flughafen
Aéroport; Aéroport international
Aeroporto; Aeroporto internazionale
Vlieghaven; Vlieghaven internationaal

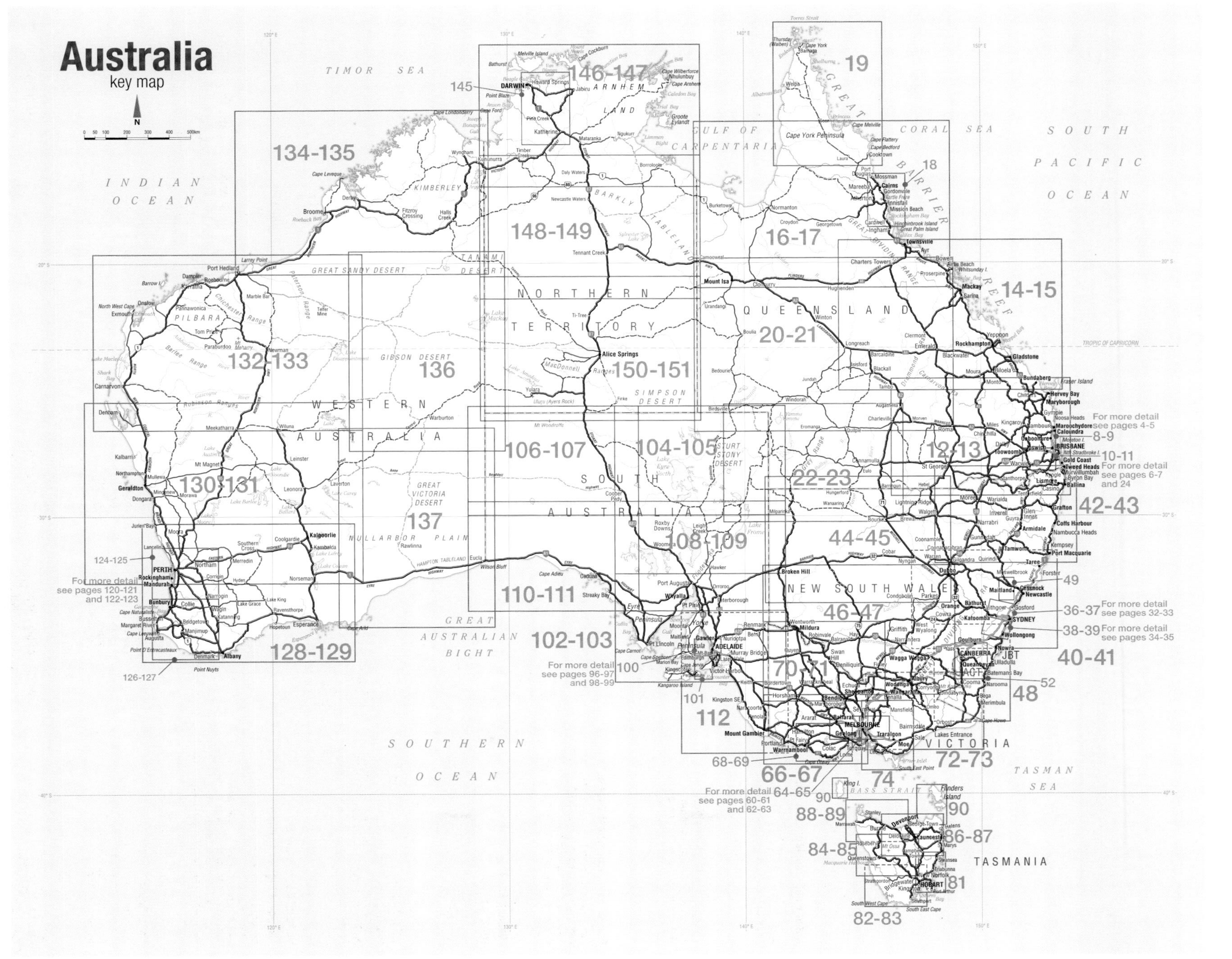
Australia
key map
TIMOR SEA
INDIAN OCEAN
CORAL SEA
SOUTH PACIFIC OCEAN
GULF OF CARPENTARIA
GREAT AUSTRALIAN BIGHT
SOUTHERN OCEAN
TASMAN SEA
WESTERN AUSTRALIA
NORTHERN TERRITORY
QUEENSLAND
SOUTH AUSTRALIA
NEW SOUTH WALES
VICTORIA
TASMANIA
145
146-147
19
18
134-135
148-149
16-17
14-15
132-133
136
20-21
150-151
106-107
104-105
12-13
22-23
130-131
137
42-43
44-45
108-109
124-125
For more detail see pages 120-121 and 122-123
110-111
102-103
46-47
49
36-37
38-39
40-41
128-129
126-127
For more detail see pages 96-97 and 98-99
100
101
112
70-71
48
52
68-69
66-67
74
72-73
For more detail see pages 60-61 and 62-63
64-65
90
88-89
86-87
84-85
81
82-83
For more detail see pages 4-5
8-9
10-11
For more detail see pages 6-7 and 24
For more detail see pages 32-33
For more detail see pages 34-35

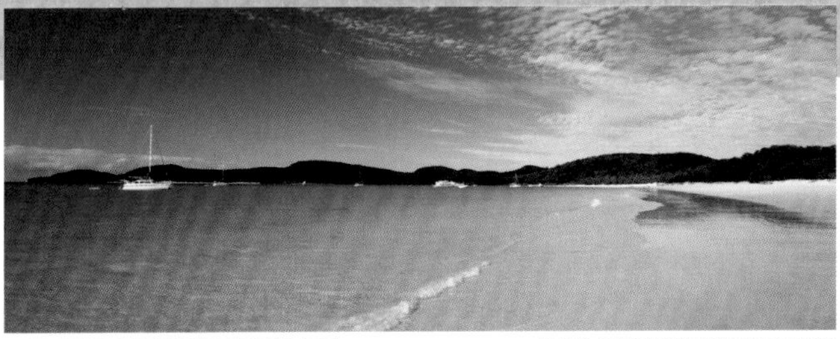

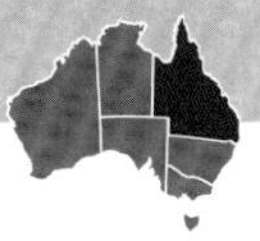

WHITEHAVEN BEACH, WHITSUNDAY ISLAND (15 B8)

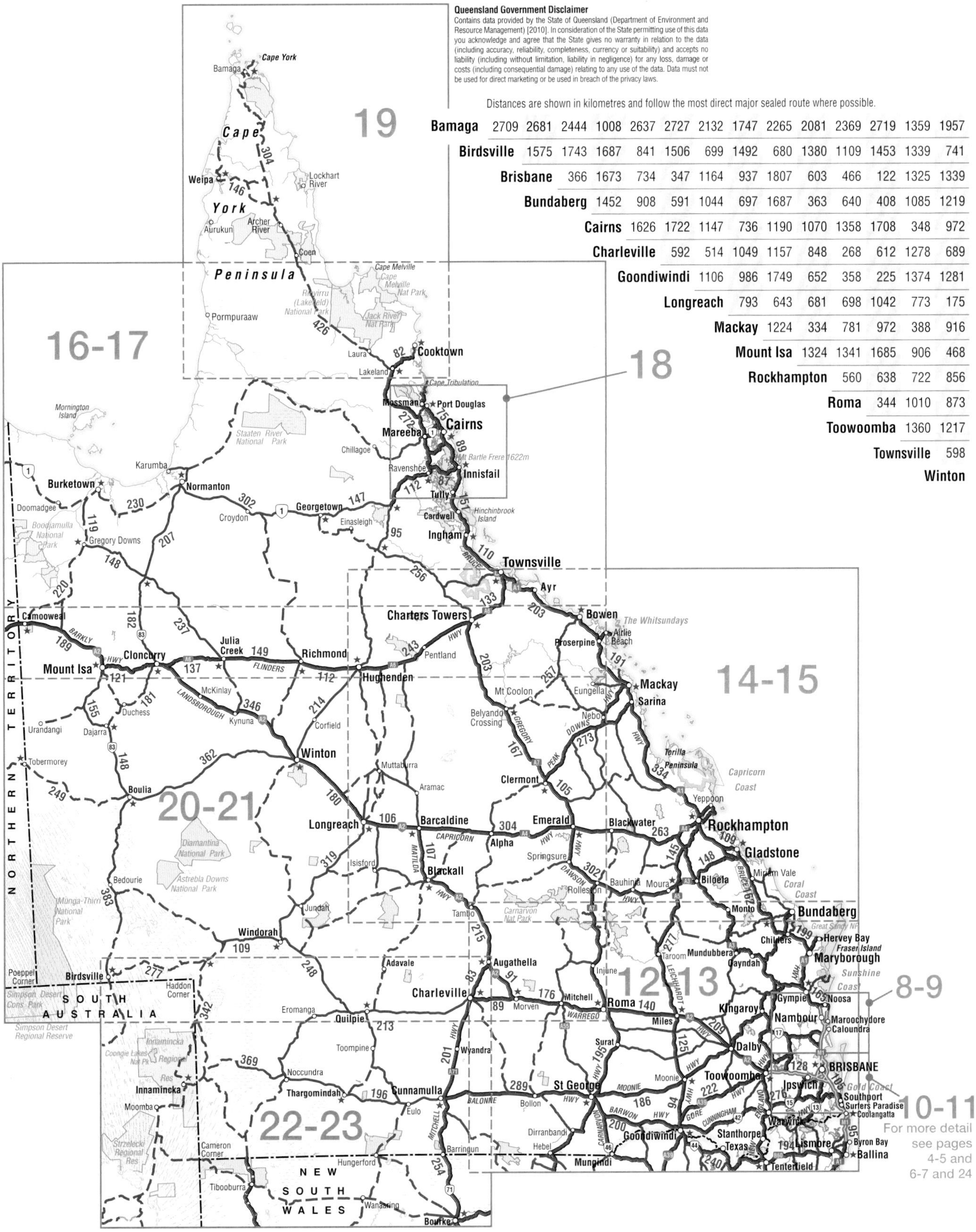

Queensland Government Disclaimer

Contains data provided by the State of Queensland (Department of Environment and Resource Management) [2010]. In consideration of the State permitting use of this data you acknowledge and agree that the State gives no warranty in relation to the data (including accuracy, reliability, completeness, currency or suitability) and accepts no liability (including without limitation, liability in negligence) for any loss, damage or costs (including consequential damage) relating to any use of the data. Data must not be used for direct marketing or be used in breach of the privacy laws.

Distances are shown in kilometres and follow the most direct major sealed route where possible.

	Birdsville	Brisbane	Bundaberg	Cairns	Charleville	Goondiwindi	Longreach	Mackay	Mount Isa	Rockhampton	Roma	Toowoomba	Townsville	Winton
Bamaga	2709	2681	2444	1008	2637	2727	2132	1747	2265	2081	2369	2719	1359	1957
Birdsville		1575	1743	1687	841	1506	699	1492	680	1380	1109	1453	1339	741
Brisbane			366	1673	734	347	1164	937	1807	603	466	122	1325	1339
Bundaberg				1452	908	591	1044	697	1687	363	640	408	1085	1219
Cairns					1626	1722	1147	736	1190	1070	1358	1708	348	972
Charleville						592	514	1049	1157	848	268	612	1278	689
Goondiwindi							1106	986	1749	652	358	225	1374	1281
Longreach								793	643	681	698	1042	773	175
Mackay									1224	334	781	972	388	916
Mount Isa										1324	1341	1685	906	468
Rockhampton											560	638	722	856
Roma												344	1010	873
Toowoomba													1360	1217
Townsville														598
Winton														

19 · 18 · 16-17 · 14-15 · 20-21 · 12-13 · 8-9 · 22-23 · 10-11

For more detail see pages 4-5 and 6-7 and 24

Brisbane CBD

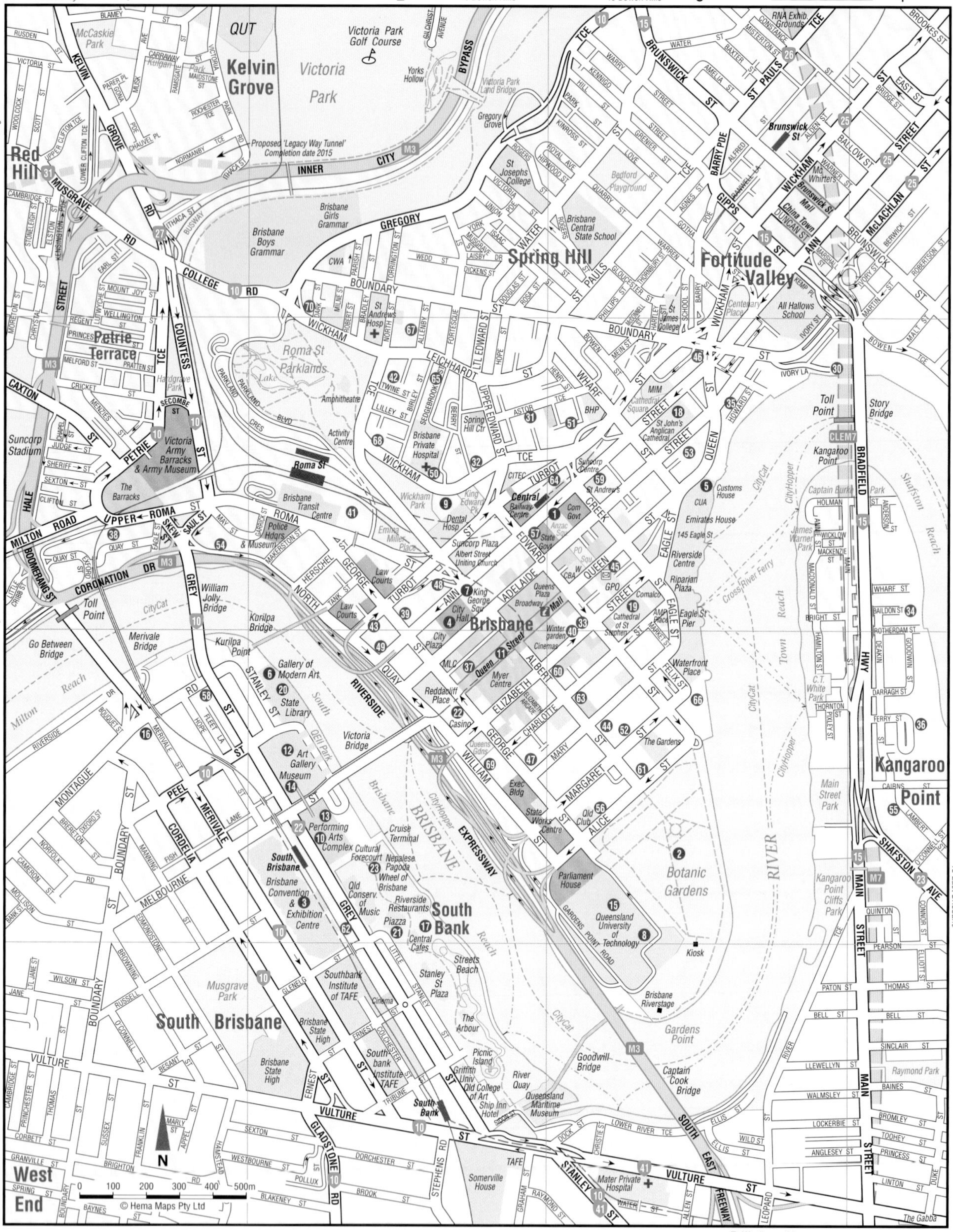

Places of Interest

1. Anzac Memorial B3
2. Botanic Gardens C3
3. Brisbane Convention & Exhib Ctr C2
4. City Hall B2
5. Customs House B3
6. Gallery of Modern Art C2
7. King George Square B2
8. Old Government House C3
9. Old Windmill Observatory B2
10. Performing Arts Complex C2
11. Queen Street Mall C2
12. Queensland Art Gallery C2
13. Queensland Cultural Centre C2
14. Queensland Museum C2
15. Queensland University of Technology C3
16. Queensland Theatre Company C1
17. South Bank C2
18. St John's Cathedral B3
19. St Stephen's Cathedral B3
20. State Library of Queensland C2
21. Suncorp Entertainment Piazza C2
22. Treasury Casino C2
23. Wheel of Brisbane C2

Accommodation

30. Adina Apartment Hotel Brisbane B3
31. Astor Apartments, The B2
32. Astor Metropole Best Western Hotel,The B2
33. Base Brisbane Embassy B3
34. Bridgewater Apartments B4
35. Brisbane Marriott Hotel B3
36. Central Dockside Apartments C4
37. Chifley at Lennons, The C2
38. City Backpackers B1
39. George Williams Hotel B2
40. Hilton Brisbane B3
41. Holiday Inn Hotel Brisbane B2
42. Hotel Grand Chancellor B2
43. Hotel Ibis Brisbane B2
44. iStay River City C3
45. Manor Apartment Hotel, The B3
46. Mantra on Queen B3
47. Marque Hotel, The C2
48. Mercure Brisbane King George Square B2
49. Mercure Hotel Brisbane C2
50. Metro Hotel Tower Mill B2
51. Novotel Brisbane B3
52. Oaks 212 Margaret C3
53. Oaks Aurora B3
54. Park Regis North Quay B1
55. Point Hotel, The C4
56. Quay West Suites Brisbane C3
57. Rendezvous Hotel B2
58. Riverside Hotel C1
59. Rothbury Heritage Apartment Hotel B3
60. Royal Albert Hotel C3
61. Royal on the Park C3
62. Rydges South Bank Hotel C2
63. Sebel Brisbane, The C3
64. Sofitel Brisbane Central B3
65. Spring Hill Centrepoint B2
66. Stamford Plaza Brisbane C3
67. Summit Apartments, The B2
68. Terraces on Wickham B2
69. Treasury Casino & Hotel C2
70. Watermark Hotel Brisbane A2

Freeway, Major Road, Minor Road, Lane / Path, Railway,Station, Busway, CLEM7 Tunnel (Toll), Post Office, Accredited Information, Ferry Route, Major Building, Govt Building, Theatre/Cinema, Shopping, Hospital, Mall

© Hema Maps Pty Ltd

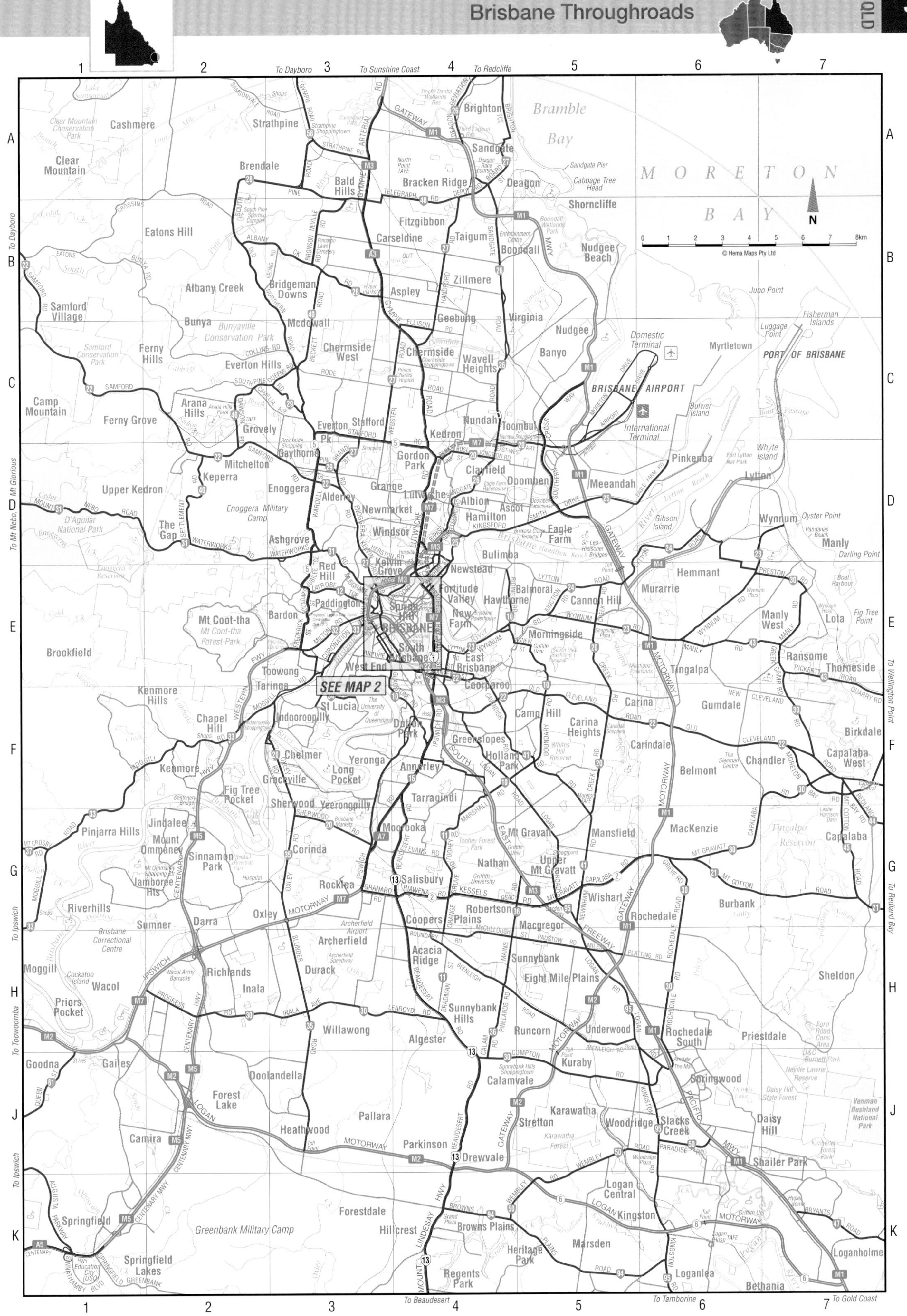
MORETON BAY
Bramble Bay
BRISBANE AIRPORT
PORT OF BRISBANE
SEE MAP 2
BRISBANE
Strathpine
Cashmere
Clear Mountain
Brendale
Bald Hills
Bracken Ridge
Brighton
Sandgate
Deagon
Shorncliffe
Eatons Hill
Fitzgibbon
Carseldine
Taigum
Boondall
Nudgee Beach
Albany Creek
Bridgeman Downs
Aspley
Zillmere
Samford Village
Bunya
Mcdowall
Geebung
Virginia
Nudgee
Ferny Hills
Everton Hills
Chermside West
Chermside
Wavell Heights
Banyo
Camp Mountain
Ferny Grove
Arana Hills
Grovely
Everton Pk
Stafford
Nundah
Toombul
Kedron
Gordon Park
Clayfield
Doomben
Pinkenba
Mitchelton
Keperra
Upper Kedron
Enoggera
Alderley
Grange
Lutwyche
Albion
Ascot
Meeandah
Lytton
Wynnum
Manly
The Gap
Newmarket
Windsor
Hamilton
Eagle Farm
Ashgrove
Kelvin Grove
Newstead
Bulimba
Hemmant
Red Hill
Paddington
Fortitude Valley
Balmoral
Hawthorne
Cannon Hill
Murarrie
Mt Coot-tha
Bardon
Spring Hill
New Farm
Morningside
Manly West
Lota
Brookfield
South Brisbane
West End
East Brisbane
Tingalpa
Ransome
Thorneside
Toowong
Taringa
Coorparoo
Kenmore Hills
St Lucia
Indooroopilly
Dutton Park
Camp Hill
Carina
Carina Heights
Gumdale
Chapel Hill
Birkdale
Greenslopes
Holland Park
Carindale
Kenmore
Chelmer
Yeronga
Long Pocket
Annerley
Belmont
Chandler
Capalaba West
Graceville
Fig Tree Pocket
Sherwood
Yeerongpilly
Tarragindi
Jindalee
Mount Ommaney
Pinjarra Hills
Moorooka
Mt Gravatt
Mansfield
MacKenzie
Capalaba
Corinda
Sinnamon Park
Nathan
Upper Mt Gravatt
Jamboree Hts
Salisbury
Rocklea
Wishart
Riverhills
Oxley
Robertson
Coopers Plains
Rochedale
Burbank
Sumner
Darra
Macgregor
Archerfield
Acacia Ridge
Sunnybank
Moggill
Richlands
Durack
Eight Mile Plains
Sheldon
Wacol
Inala
Priors Pocket
Sunnybank Hills
Runcorn
Underwood
Willawong
Algester
Rochedale South
Priestdale
Goodna
Gailes
Kuraby
Calamvale
Doolandella
Springwood
Forest Lake
Pallara
Karawatha
Daisy Hill
Stretton
Woodridge
Slacks Creek
Heathwood
Camira
Parkinson
Drewvale
Shailer Park
Logan Central
Springfield
Forestdale
Kingston
Hillcrest
Browns Plains
Marsden
Loganholme
Springfield Lakes
Heritage Park
Regents Park
Loganlea
Bethania
Greenbank Military Camp
To Beaudesert
To Tamborine
To Gold Coast
To Dayboro
To Sunshine Coast
To Redcliffe
To Ipswich
To Toowoomba
To Redland Bay
To Wellington Point
To Mt Nebo, Mt Glorious
© Hema Maps Pty Ltd

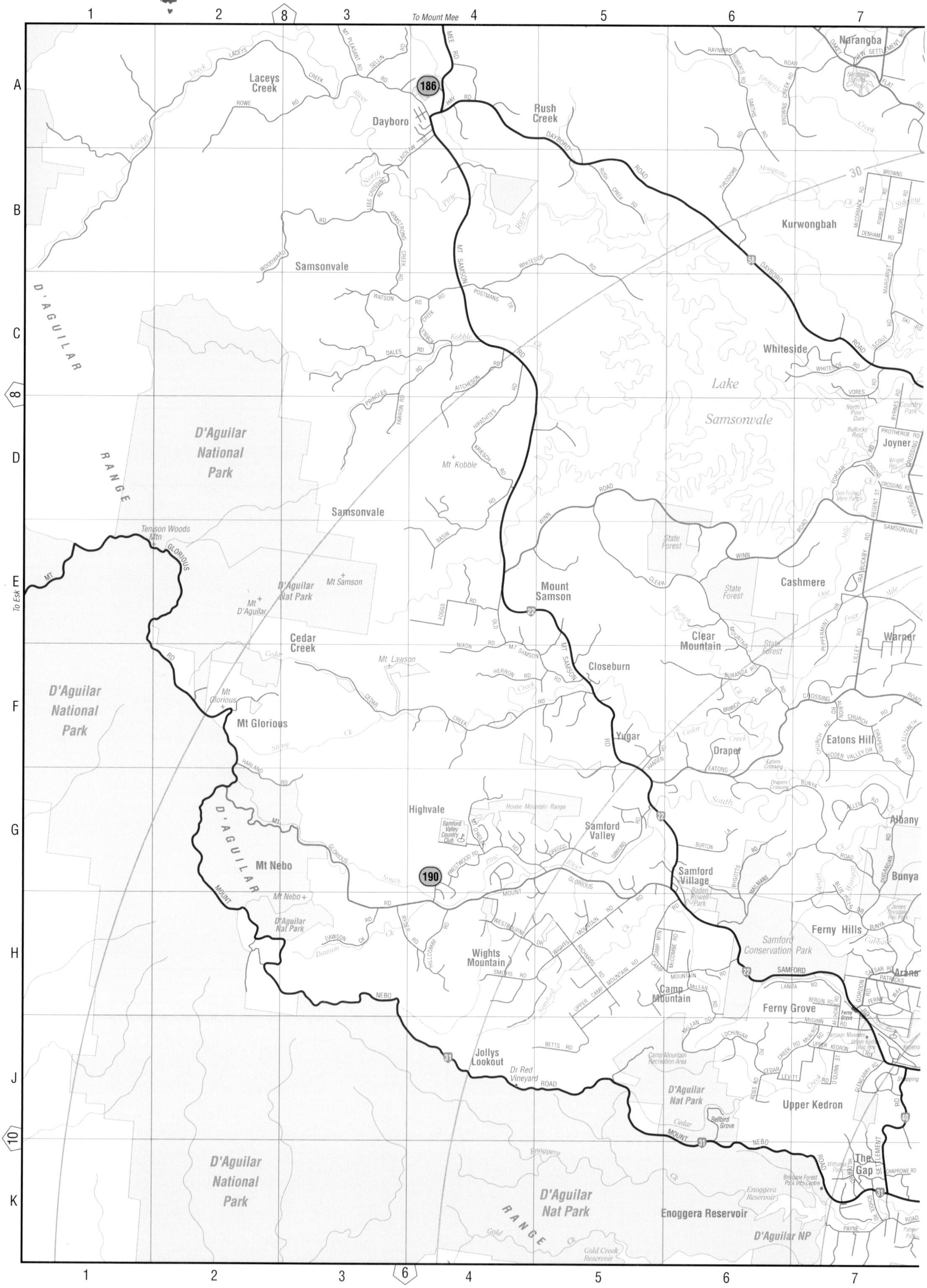

To Mount Mee
Narangba
Laceys Creek
Dayboro
Rush Creek
Kurwongbah
Samsonvale
Whiteside
Lake Samsonvale
D'AGUILAR RANGE
D'Aguilar National Park
Mt Kobble
Joyner
Samsonvale
Tenison Woods Mtn
Cashmere
Mount Samson
Mt Samson
Mt D'Aguilar
D'Aguilar Nat Park
To Esk
Cedar Creek
Mt Lawson
Clear Mountain
Warner
Closeburn
Mt Glorious
Eatons Hill
Yugar
Draper
Highvale
Samford Valley
Albany
Mt Nebo
Samford Village
Bunya
Mt Nebo
Ferny Hills
Samford Conservation Park
Wights Mountain
Arana
Camp Mountain
Ferny Grove
Jollys Lookout
Dr Red Vineyard
Upper Kedron
The Gap
Enoggera Reservoir
D'Aguilar NP
D'Aguilar Nat Park

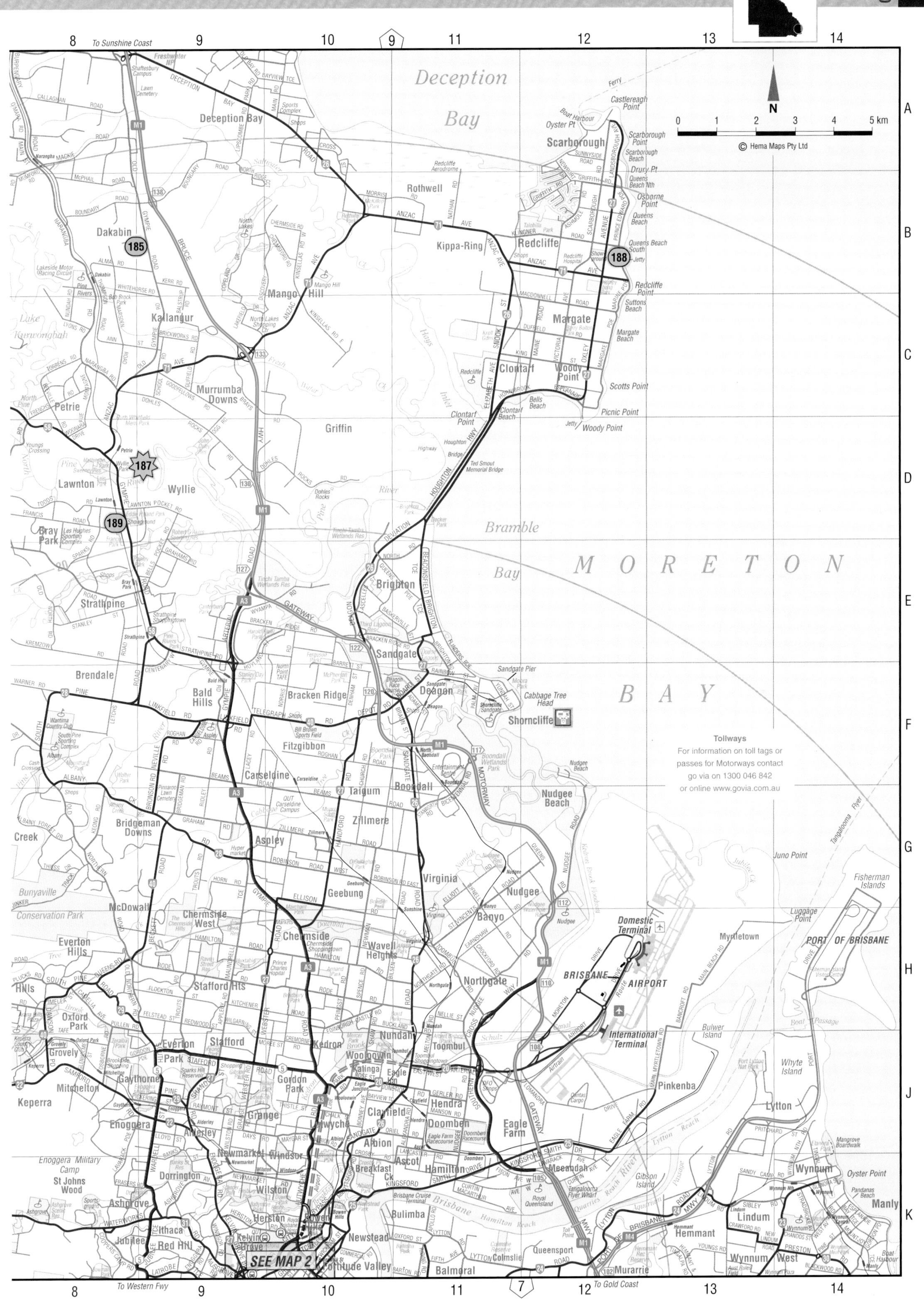
To Sunshine Coast
Deception Bay
Deception Bay
Castlereagh Point
Scarborough
Oyster Pt
Boat Harbour
Redcliffe Aerodrome
Rothwell
Kippa-Ring
Redcliffe
Dakabin
Mango Hill
Kallangur
Margate
Clontarf
Woody Point
Murrumba Downs
Petrie
Griffin
Lawnton
Wyllie
Bray Park
Strathpine
Brighton
Bramble
Bay
MORETON
BAY
Sandgate
Deagon
Shorncliffe
Cabbage Tree Head
Brendale
Bald Hills
Bracken Ridge
Fitzgibbon
Carseldine
Taigum
Boondall
Nudgee Beach
Zillmere
Aspley
Bridgeman Downs
Virginia
Geebung
Nudgee
Banyo
McDowall
Chermside West
Chermside
Wavell Heights
Northgate
Everton Hills
Stafford Hts
Oxford Park
Grovely
Everton Park
Stafford
Kedron
Nundah
Toombul
Mitchelton
Gaythorne
Gordon Park
Wooloowin
Kalinga
Eagle Junction
Hendra
Clayfield
Pinkenba
Lytton
Keperra
Enoggera
Alderley
Grange
Wooloowin
Doomben
Eagle Farm
Newmarket
Windsor
Albion
Ascot
Hamilton
Meeandah
Enoggera Military Camp
St Johns Wood
Dorrington
Wilston
Breakfast Ck
Bulimba
Ashgrove
Herston
Bowen Hills
Newstead
Hemmant
Lindum
Wynnum
Manly
Ithaca
Jubilee
Red Hill
Kelvin Grove
Fortitude Valley
Balmoral
Colmslie
Queensport
Murarrie
Wynnum West
SEE MAP 2
To Western Fwy
To Gold Coast
BRISBANE AIRPORT
Domestic Terminal
International Terminal
PORT OF BRISBANE
Myrtletown
Bulwer Island
Whyte Island
Gibson Island
Fisherman Islands
Juno Point
Luggage Point
Oyster Point
Tollways
For information on toll tags or passes for Motorways contact go via on 1300 046 842 or online www.govia.com.au
© Hema Maps Pty Ltd
0 1 2 3 4 5 km
N
185
187
188
189

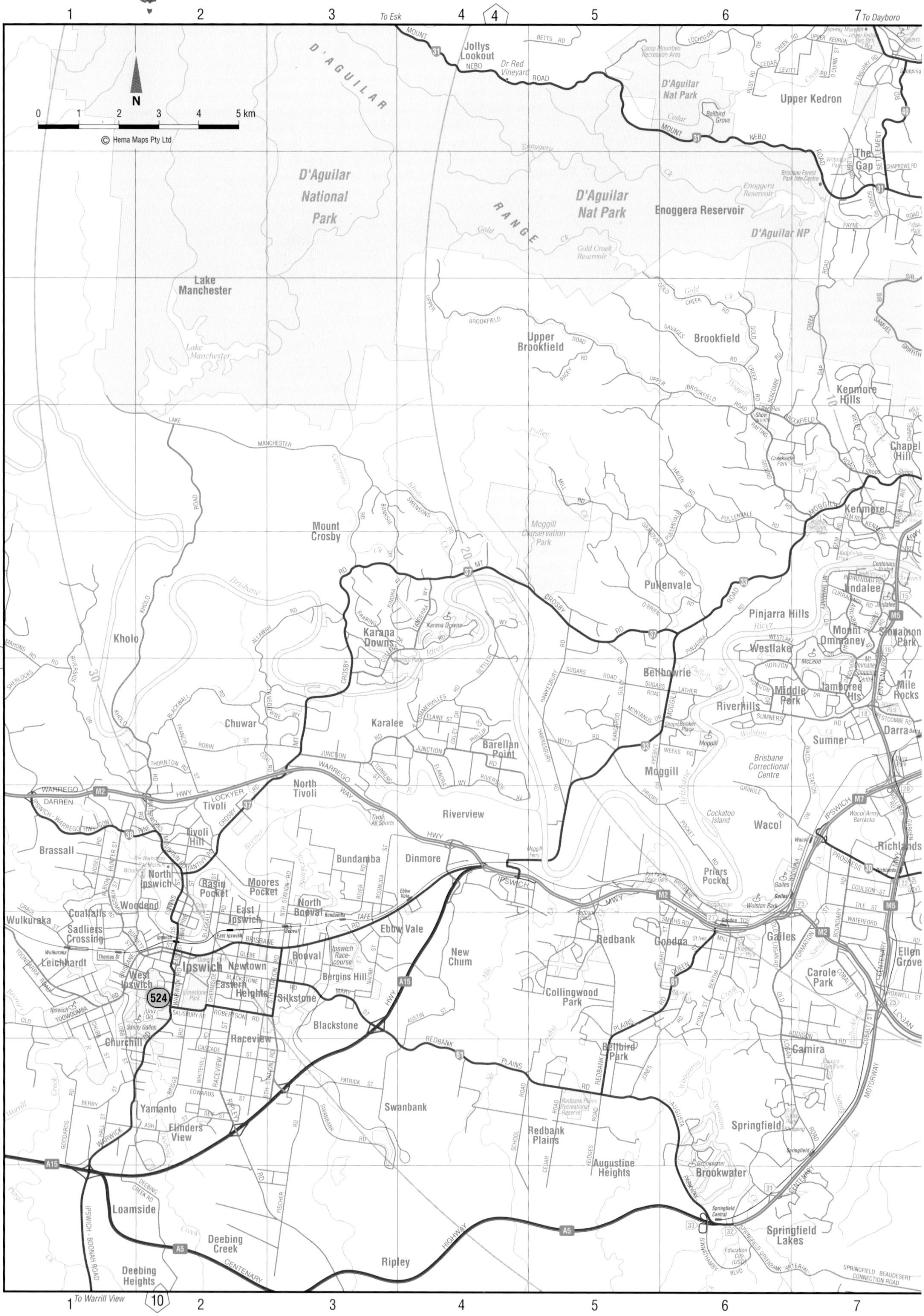

Brisbane Suburbs, Queensland

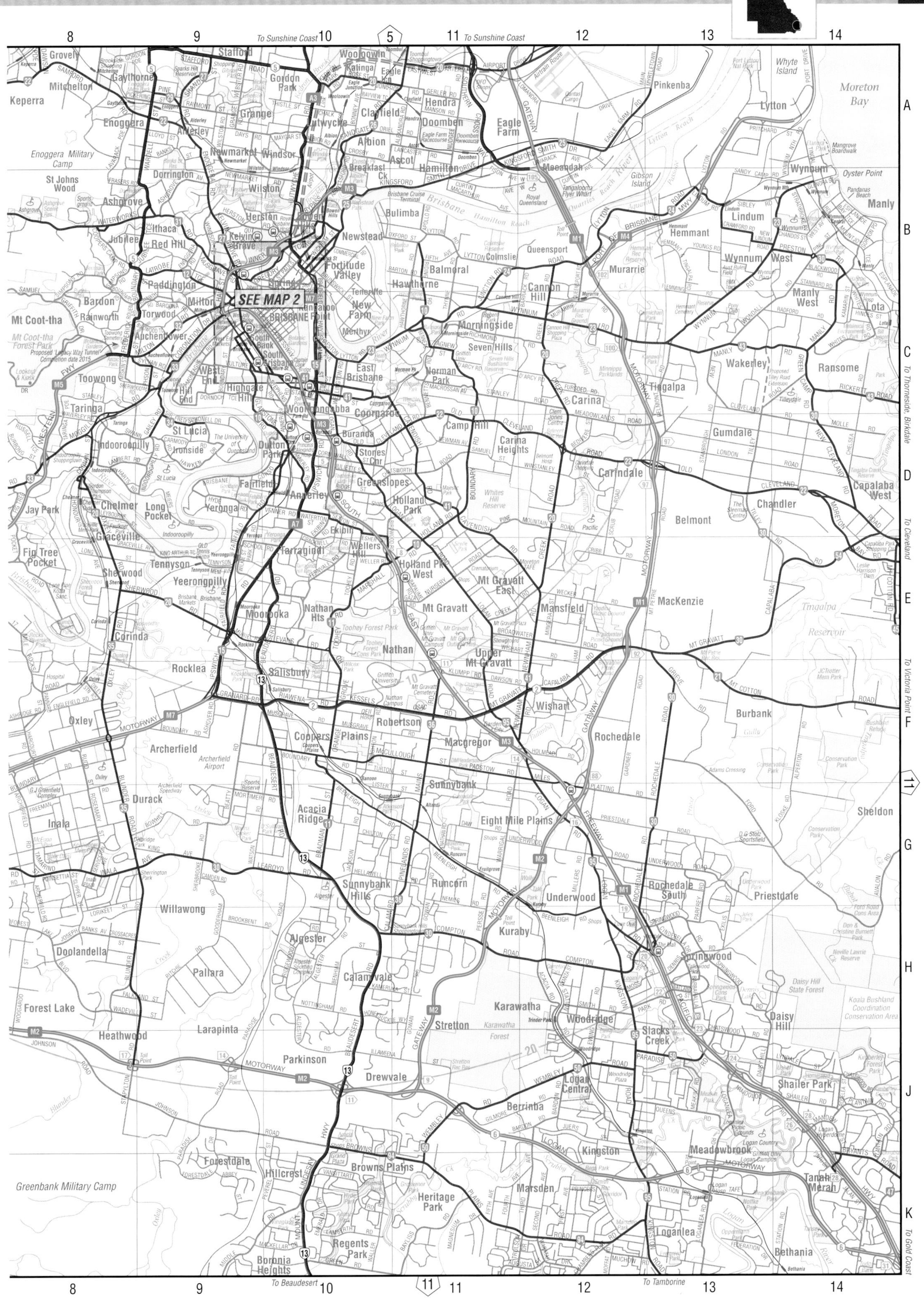
To Sunshine Coast
To Sunshine Coast
SEE MAP 2
Moreton Bay
To Thorneside, Birkdale
To Cleveland
To Victoria Point
To Gold Coast
To Beaudesert
To Tamborine
Grovely
Keperra
Mitchelton
Gaythorne
Stafford
Gordon Park
Wooloowin
Kalinga
Eagle Junction
Hendra
Pinkenba
Whyte Island
Lytton
Enoggera
Alderley
Grange
Clayfield
Lutwyche
Doomben
Eagle Farm
Enoggera Military Camp
Newmarket
Windsor
Albion
Ascot
Hamilton
Meeandah
Gibson Island
Wynnum
Oyster Point
Manly
St Johns Wood
Dorrington
Wilston
Breakfast Ck
Ashgrove
Herston
Bulimba
Kelvin Grove
Ithaca
Jubilee
Red Hill
Newstead
Queensport
Hemmant
Lindum
Murarrie
Wynnum West
Paddington
Fortitude Valley
Balmoral
Colmslie
Cannon Hill
Manly West
Bardon
Milton
Torwood
Rainworth
Mt Coot-tha
Hawthorne
New Farm
Brisbane Point
Morningside
Lota
Auchenflower
Seven Hills
Toowong
West End
Hill End
Highgate Hill
South Brisbane
East Brisbane
Norman Park
Wakerley
Ransome
Tingalpa
Taringa
St Lucia
Woolloongabba
Coorparoo
Camp Hill
Carina
Indooroopilly
Ironside
Dutton Park
Buranda
Stones Cnr
Carina Heights
Gumdale
Carindale
Greenslopes
Fairfield
Annerley
Holland Park
Chandler
Capalaba West
Jay Park
Chelmer
Long Pocket
Yeronga
Belmont
Graceville
Ekibin
Tarragindi
Wellers Hill
Fig Tree Pocket
Sherwood
Tennyson
Holland Pk West
Mt Gravatt East
Yeerongpilly
Moorooka
Nathan Hts
Mt Gravatt
Mansfield
MacKenzie
Corinda
Nathan
Upper Mt Gravatt
Rocklea
Salisbury
Wishart
Burbank
Oxley
Robertson
Coopers Plains
Macgregor
Rochedale
Archerfield
Sunnybank
Sheldon
Durack
Acacia Ridge
Eight Mile Plains
Inala
Runcorn
Sunnybank Hills
Underwood
Rochedale South
Priestdale
Willawong
Kuraby
Algester
Doolandella
Springwood
Pallara
Calamvale
Daisy Hill
Karawatha
Forest Lake
Larapinta
Stretton
Woodridge
Slacks Creek
Heathwood
Parkinson
Drewvale
Logan Central
Shailer Park
Berrinba
Kingston
Meadowbrook
Forestdale
Hillcrest
Browns Plains
Tanah Merah
Greenbank Military Camp
Marsden
Heritage Park
Loganlea
Regents Park
Bethania
Boronia Heights
Tingalpa Reservoir
Archerfield Airport
Karawatha Forest
GATEWAY
MOTORWAY
PACIFIC
LOGAN
BRISBANE
Brisbane River

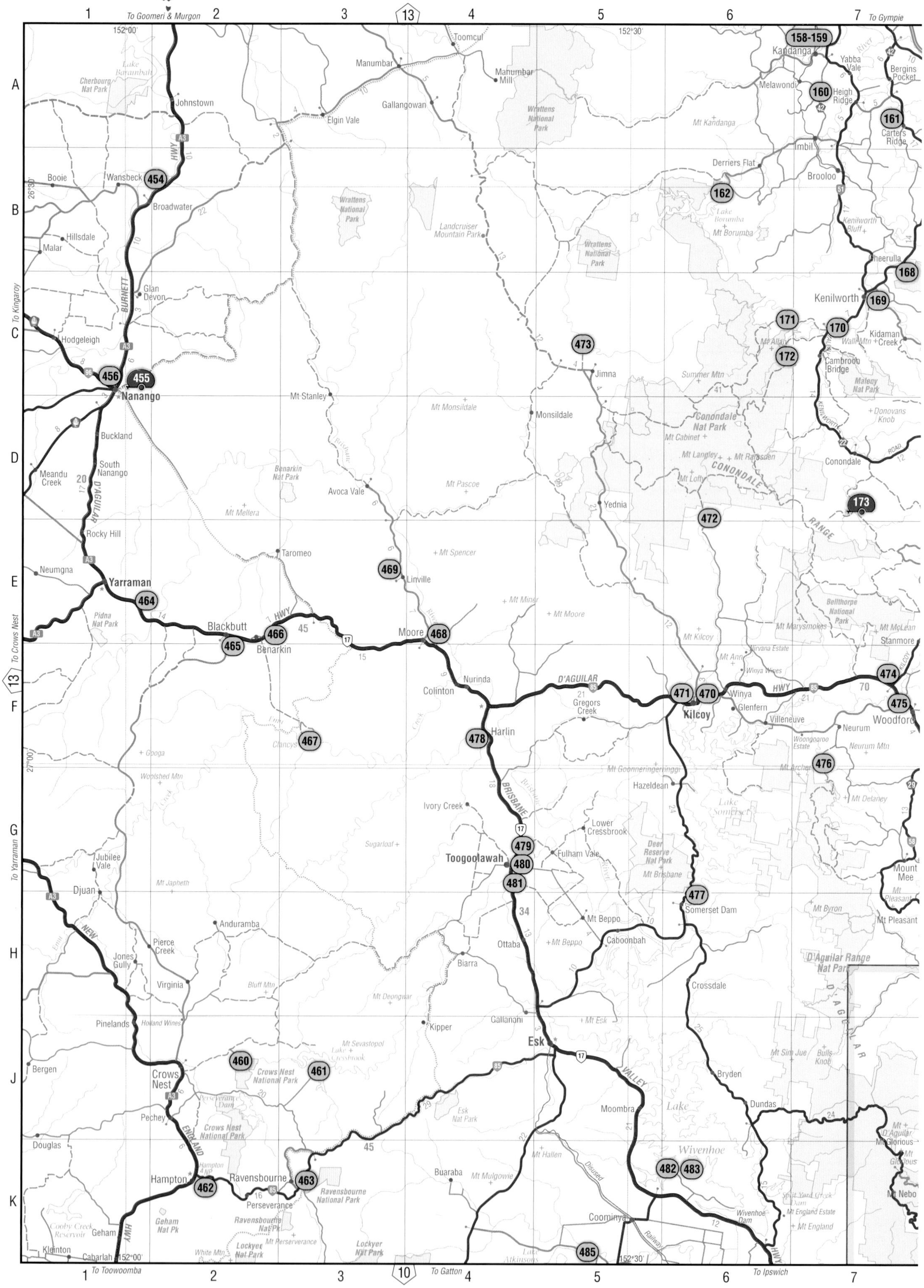

Brisbane Region, Queensland

1 2 3 4 5 6 7

A B C D E F G H J K

To Goomeri & Murgon · To Gympie · To Kingaroy · To Crows Nest · To Yarraman · To Toowoomba · To Gatton · To Ipswich

152°00' · 152°30' · 26°30' · 27°00'

Kandanga · Yabba Vale · Bergins Pocket · Melawondi · Heigh Ridge · Carters Ridge · Imbil · Derriers Flat · Brooloo · Mt Kandanga · Toomcul · Manumbar · Mahumbar Mill · Gallangowan · Elgin Vale · Johnstown · Wrattens National Park · Booie · Wansbeck · Broadwater · Hillsdale · Malar · Lake Boroumba · Mt Borumba · Landcruiser Mountain Park · Kenilworth Bluff · Cheerulla · Kenilworth · Kidaman Creek · Cambroon Bridge · Maleny Nat Park · Donovans Knob · Glan Devon · Hodgeleigh · Nanango · Jimna · Summer Mtn · Mt Allan · Mt Stanley · Mt Monsildale · Monsildale · Conondale Nat Park · Mt Cabinet · Mt Langley · Mt Ramsden · Mt Lofty · Conondale · Conondale Range · Buckland · South Nanango · Meandu Creek · Benarkin Nat Park · Mt Pascoe · Avoca Vale · Yednia · Mt Mellera · Rocky Hill · Taromeo · Mt Spencer · Neumgna · Yarraman · Linville · Mt Miner · Mt Moore · Bellthorpe National Park · Pidna Nat Park · Blackbutt · Benarkin · Moore · Mt Kilcoy · Mt Marysmokes · Mt McLean · Stanmore · Nurinda · Colinton · Mt Ann · Nirvana Estate · Winya Wines · D'Aguilar Hwy · Gregors Creek · Kilcoy · Winya · Glenfern · Villeneuve · Neurum · Woodford · Neurum Mtn · Woongooroo Estate · Harlin · Clancys · Googa · Woolshed Mtn · Mt Goonneringerringgi · Hazeldean · Mt Archer · Mt Delaney · Lake Somerset · Ivory Creek · Brisbane · Lower Cressbrook · Sugarloaf · Fulham Vale · Deer Reserve Nat Park · Mt Brisbane · Toogoolawah · Jubilee Vale · Mount Mee · Mt Pleasant · Djuan · Mt Japheth · Somerset Dam · Mt Byron · Anduramba · Mt Beppo · Caboonbah · Ottaba · Pierce Creek · Jones Gully · Biarra · D'Aguilar Range Nat Park · Virginia · Bluff Mtn · Crossdale · Mt Deongwar · Pinelands · Holland Wines · Kipper · Gallanani · Mt Esk · Esk · Mt Sevastopol · Lake Cressbrook · Bergen · Crows Nest · Crows Nest National Park · Mt Sim Jue · Bulls Knob · Bryden · Valley · Perseverance Dam · Esk Nat Park · Moombra · Lake Wivenhoe · Dundas · Pechey · New England · Mt D'Aguilar · Mt Glorious · Douglas · Mt Hallen · Hampton · Ravensbourne · Buaraba · Mt Mulgowie · Disused Railway · Perseverance · Ravensbourne National Park · Mt Nebo · Split Yard Creek Dam · Mt England Estate · Mt England · Wivenhoe Dam · Geham Nat Pk · Cooby Creek Reservoir · Geham · Ravensbourne Nat Pk · Mt Perseverance · Coominya · Klenton · Cabarlah · White Mtn · Lockyer Nat Park · Lockyer Nat Park · Lake Atkinson

158-159 · 160 · 161 · 162 · 168 · 169 · 170 · 171 · 172 · 173 · 454 · 455 · 456 · 460 · 461 · 462 · 463 · 464 · 465 · 466 · 467 · 468 · 469 · 470 · 471 · 472 · 473 · 474 · 475 · 476 · 477 · 478 · 479 · 480 · 481 · 482 · 483 · 485

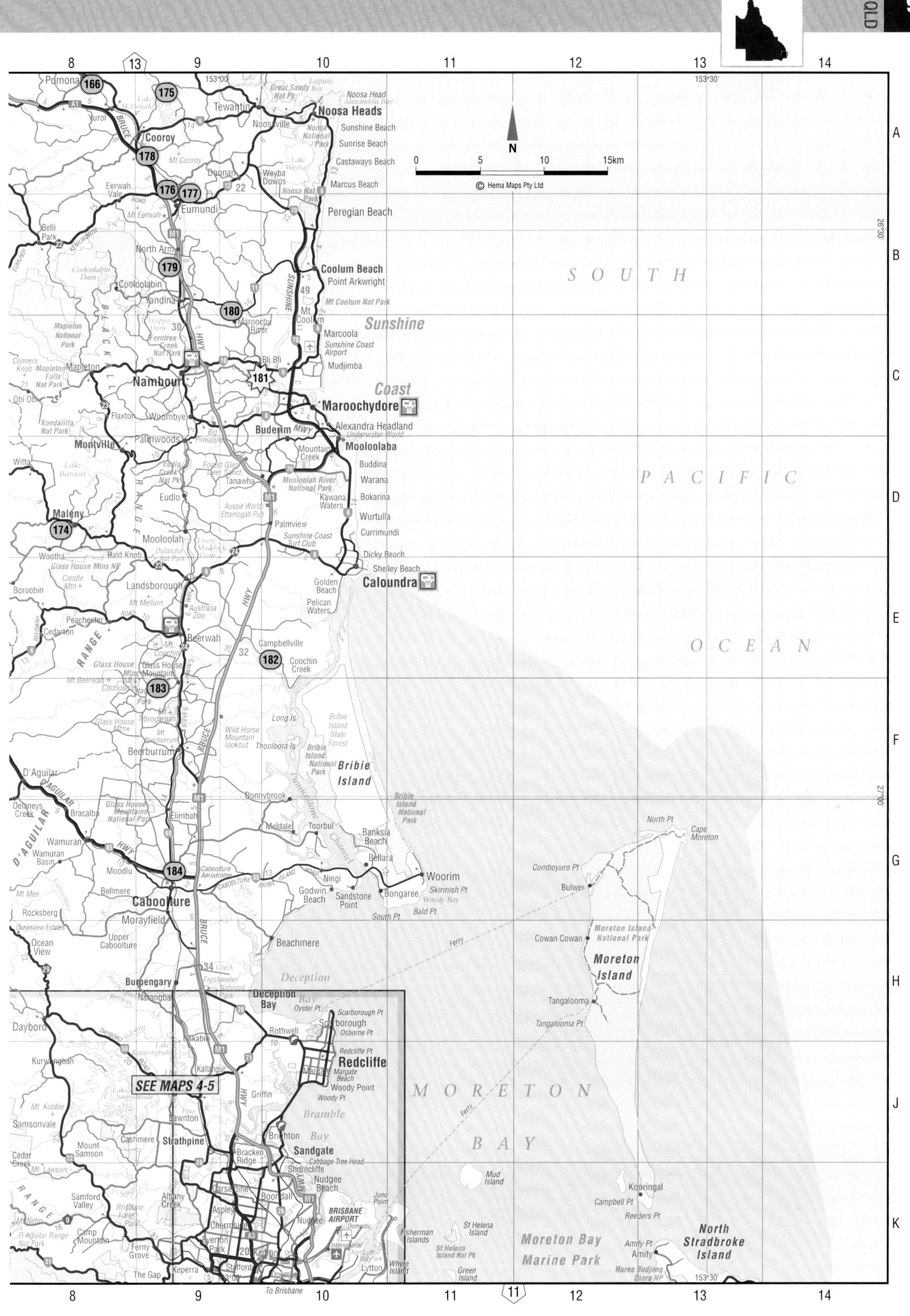
SOUTH PACIFIC OCEAN
Sunshine Coast
Noosa Heads
Maroochydore
Mooloolaba
Caloundra
Nambour
Caboolture
Redcliffe
Bribie Island
Moreton Island
North Stradbroke Island
MORETON BAY
Moreton Bay Marine Park
SEE MAPS 4-5
© Hema Maps Pty Ltd

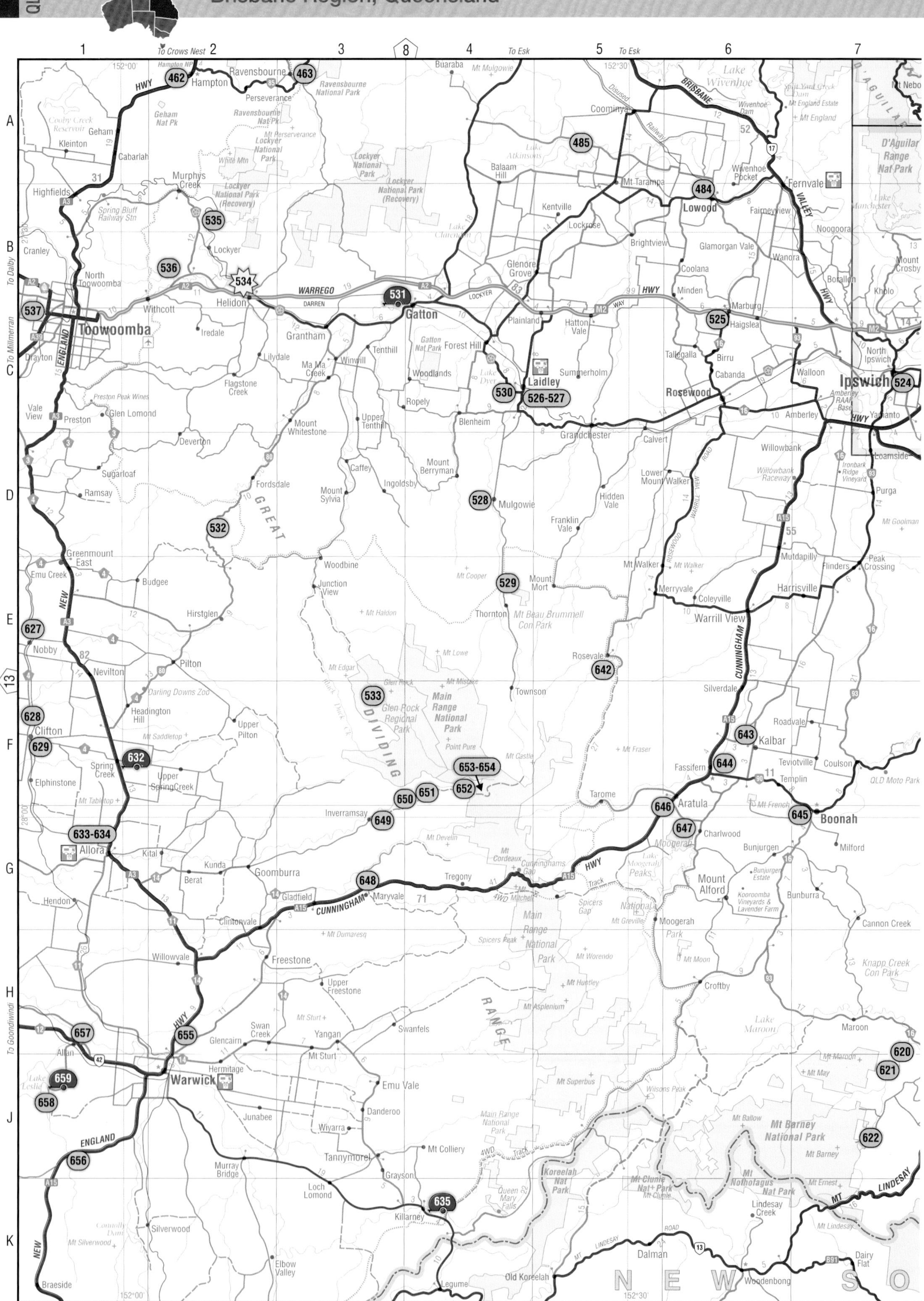

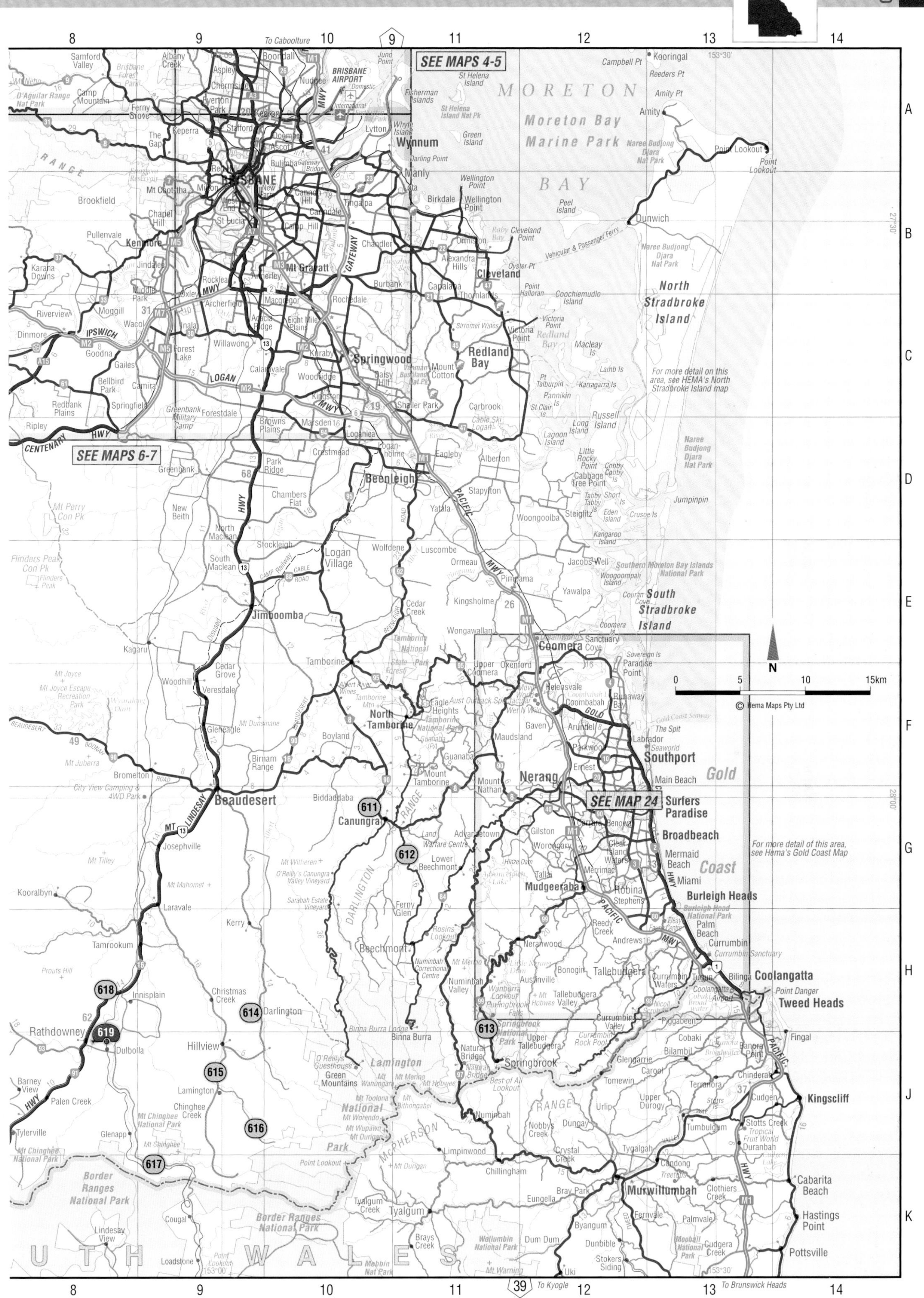
SEE MAPS 4-5
SEE MAPS 6-7
SEE MAP 24
MORETON BAY
Moreton Bay Marine Park
North Stradbroke Island
South Stradbroke Island
For more detail on this area, see HEMA's North Stradbroke Island map
For more detail of this area, see Hema's Gold Coast Map
Gold Coast
BRISBANE
Wynnum
Cleveland
Redland Bay
Springwood
Beenleigh
Logan Village
Jimboomba
Beaudesert
Canungra
Coomera
Nerang
Southport
Surfers Paradise
Broadbeach
Mudgeeraba
Burleigh Heads
Coolangatta
Tweed Heads
Kingscliff
Murwillumbah
Rathdowney
Border Ranges National Park
Lamington National Park
To Caboolture
To Kyogle
To Brunswick Heads
© Hema Maps Pty Ltd
0 5 10 15km

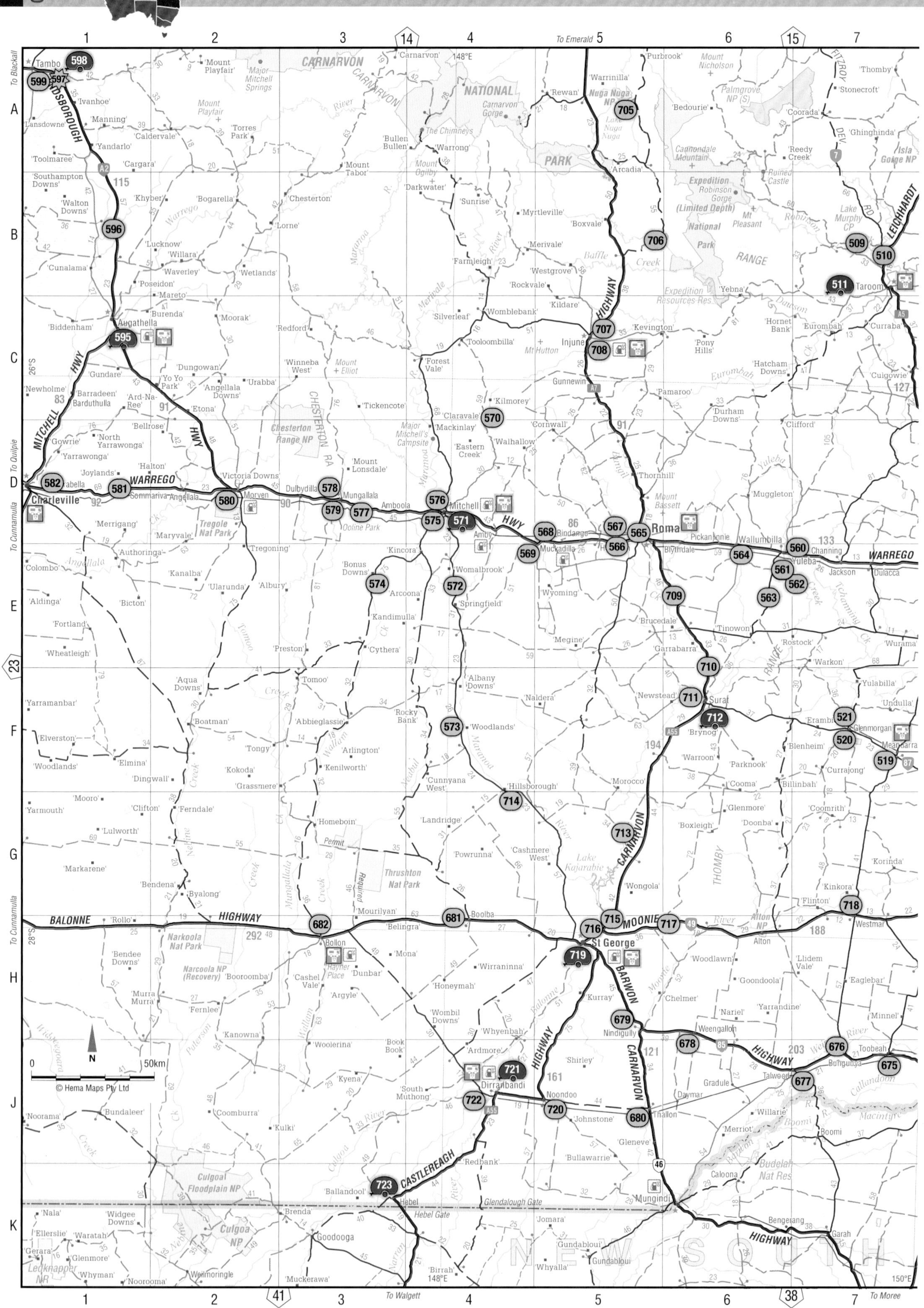

CARNARVON NATIONAL PARK
Tambo
Augathella
Charleville
Morven
Mitchell
Roma
Injune
Taroom
Surat
St George
Dirranbandi
Bollon
Mungindi
Thallon
Hebel
Goodooga
Yuleba
Wallumbilla
Amby
Mungallala
Amboola
Dulbydilla
Muckadilla
Bindango
Nindigully
Talwood
Toobeah
Bungunya
Boomi
Westmar
Alton
Noondoo
Weengallon
Garah
WARREGO HWY
MITCHELL HWY
BALONNE HIGHWAY
MOONIE HIGHWAY
CARNARVON HIGHWAY
CASTLEREAGH HIGHWAY
BARWON HIGHWAY
LEICHHARDT
Chesterton Range NP
Tregole Nat Park
Thrushton Nat Park
Narkoola Nat Park
Culgoa Floodplain NP
Culgoa NP
Nuga Nuga NP
Expedition Robinson Gorge (Limited Depth) National Park
Isla Gorge NP
Alton NP
Budelah Nat Res
Lake Kajarabie
NEW SOUTH
Glendalough Gate
Hebel Gate
To Blackall
To Emerald
To Quilpie
To Cunnamulla
To Walgett
To Moree
26°S
28°S
148°E
150°E
0 50km
© Hema Maps Pty Ltd
N

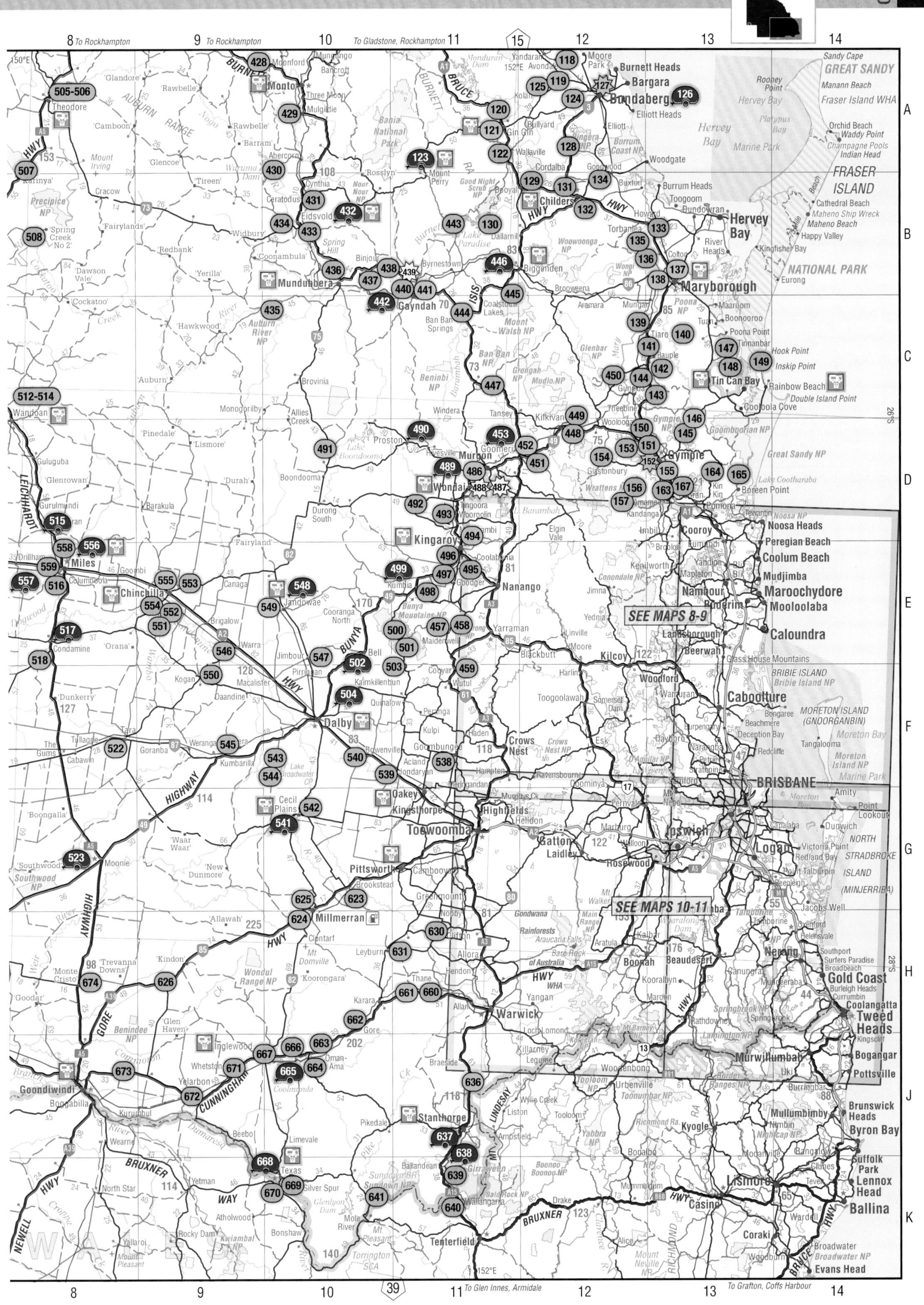

To Rockhampton
To Gladstone, Rockhampton
SEE MAPS 8-9
SEE MAPS 10-11
GREAT SANDY NATIONAL PARK
FRASER ISLAND
Hervey Bay
Bundaberg
Bargara
Burnett Heads
Childers
Maryborough
Gympie
Tin Can Bay
Rainbow Beach
Noosa Heads
Peregian Beach
Coolum Beach
Mudjimba
Maroochydore
Mooloolaba
Caloundra
Caboolture
BRISBANE
Ipswich
Logan
Gold Coast
Coolangatta
Tweed Heads
Murwillumbah
Brunswick Heads
Byron Bay
Suffolk Park
Lennox Head
Ballina
Lismore
Casino
Kyogle
Evans Head
Toowoomba
Dalby
Warwick
Stanthorpe
Tenterfield
Goondiwindi
Texas
Millmerran
Pittsworth
Oakey
Kingaroy
Nanango
Murgon
Wondai
Gayndah
Mundubbera
Eidsvold
Monto
Theodore
Wandoan
Miles
Chinchilla
Condamine
Jandowae
Crows Nest
Gatton
Laidley
Boonah
Beaudesert
Kilcoy
Woodford
Nambour
Cooroy
Biggenden
Moonie
Inglewood
Yelarbon
CUNNINGHAM HWY
BRUXNER HWY
WARREGO HWY
LEICHHARDT HWY
GORE HWY
NEWELL HWY
BRUCE HWY
To Glen Innes, Armidale
To Grafton, Coffs Harbour

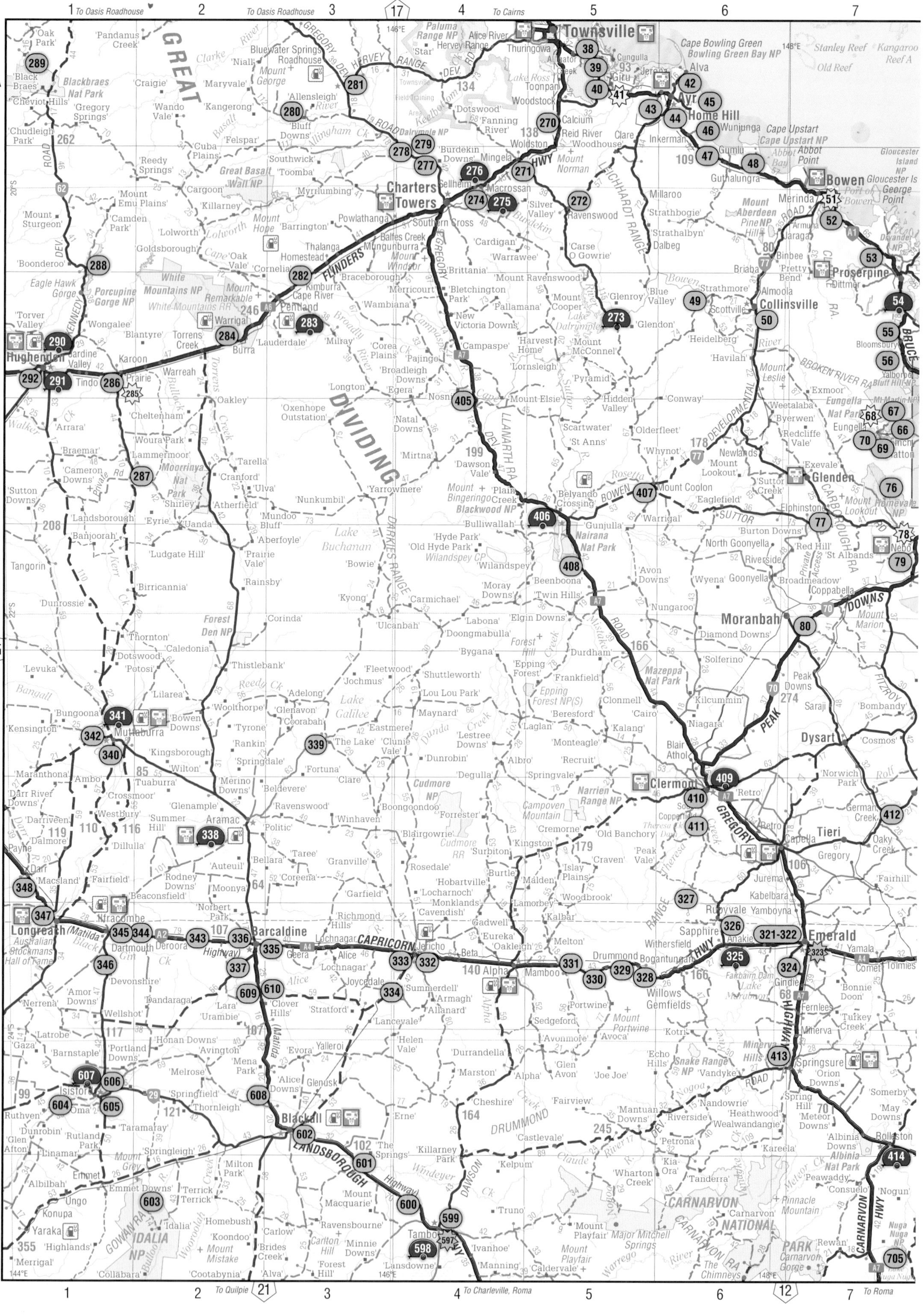

Central-East Queensland

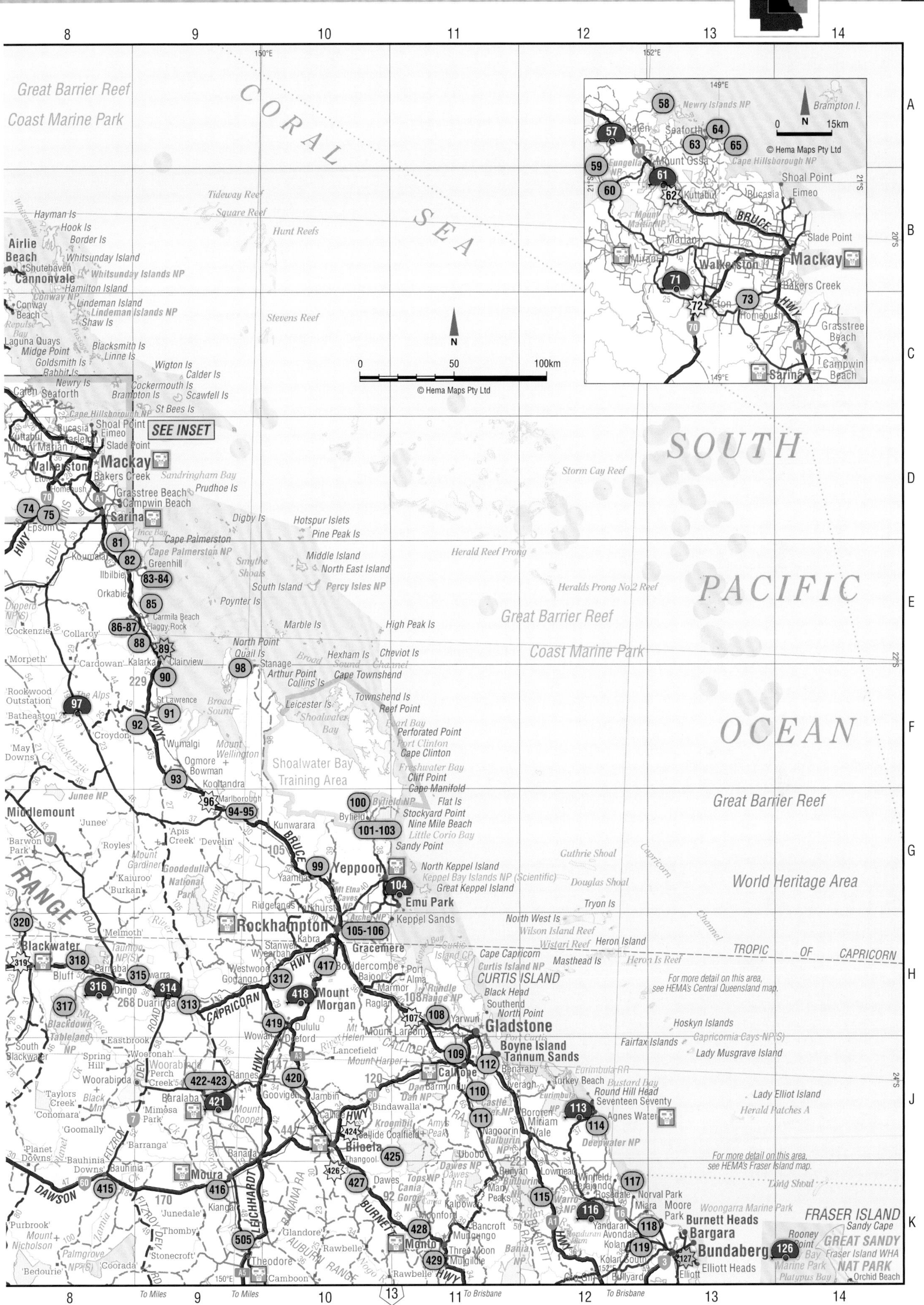

CORAL SEA
SOUTH PACIFIC OCEAN
Great Barrier Reef Coast Marine Park
Great Barrier Reef World Heritage Area
SEE INSET
Mackay
Sarina
Rockhampton
Yeppoon
Emu Park
Gladstone
Boyne Island
Tannum Sands
Biloela
Moura
Monto
Bundaberg
Bargara
Burnett Heads
Blackwater
Mount Morgan
Gracemere
Shoalwater Bay Training Area
CURTIS ISLAND
FRASER ISLAND
TROPIC OF CAPRICORN
For more detail on this area, see HEMA's Central Queensland map.
For more detail on this area, see HEMA's Fraser Island map.
© Hema Maps Pty Ltd
0 50 100km
To Miles
To Brisbane

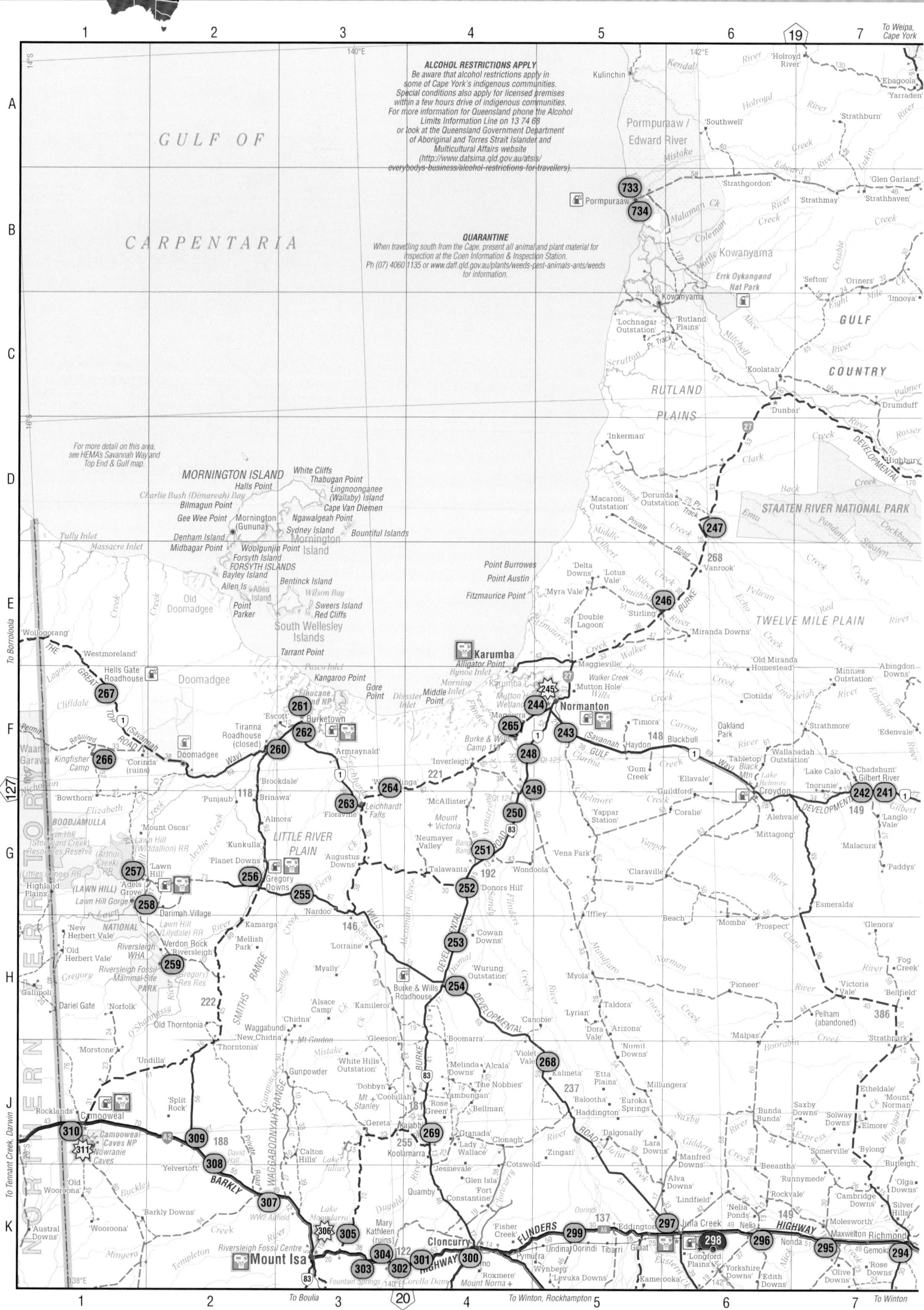
ALCOHOL RESTRICTIONS APPLY
Be aware that alcohol restrictions apply in some of Cape York's indigenous communities. Special conditions also apply for licensed premises within a few hours drive of indigenous communities. For more information for Queensland phone the Alcohol Limits Information Line on 13 74 68 or look at the Queensland Government Department of Aboriginal and Torres Strait Islander and Multicultural Affairs website (http://www.datsima.qld.gov.au/atsis/everybodys-business/alcohol-restrictions-for-travellers).
QUARANTINE
When travelling south from the Cape, present all animal and plant material for inspection at the Coen Information & Inspection Station. Ph (07) 4060 1135 or www.daff.qld.gov.au/plants/weeds-pest-animals-ants/weeds for information.
For more detail on this area, see HEMA's Savannah Way and Top End & Gulf map.
GULF OF CARPENTARIA
MORNINGTON ISLAND
South Wellesley Islands
Pormpuraaw / Edward River
Kowanyama
Karumba
Normanton
Burketown
Croydon
Doomadgee
Camooweal
Mount Isa
Cloncurry
Julia Creek
Richmond
RUTLAND PLAINS
GULF COUNTRY
STAATEN RIVER NATIONAL PARK
TWELVE MILE PLAIN
LITTLE RIVER PLAIN
SMITHS RANGE
WAGGABOONYAH RANGE
Riversleigh Fossil Mammal Site PARK
NORTHERN TERRITORY
To Weipa, Cape York
To Borroloola
To Tennant Creek, Darwin
To Boulia
To Winton, Rockhampton
To Winton

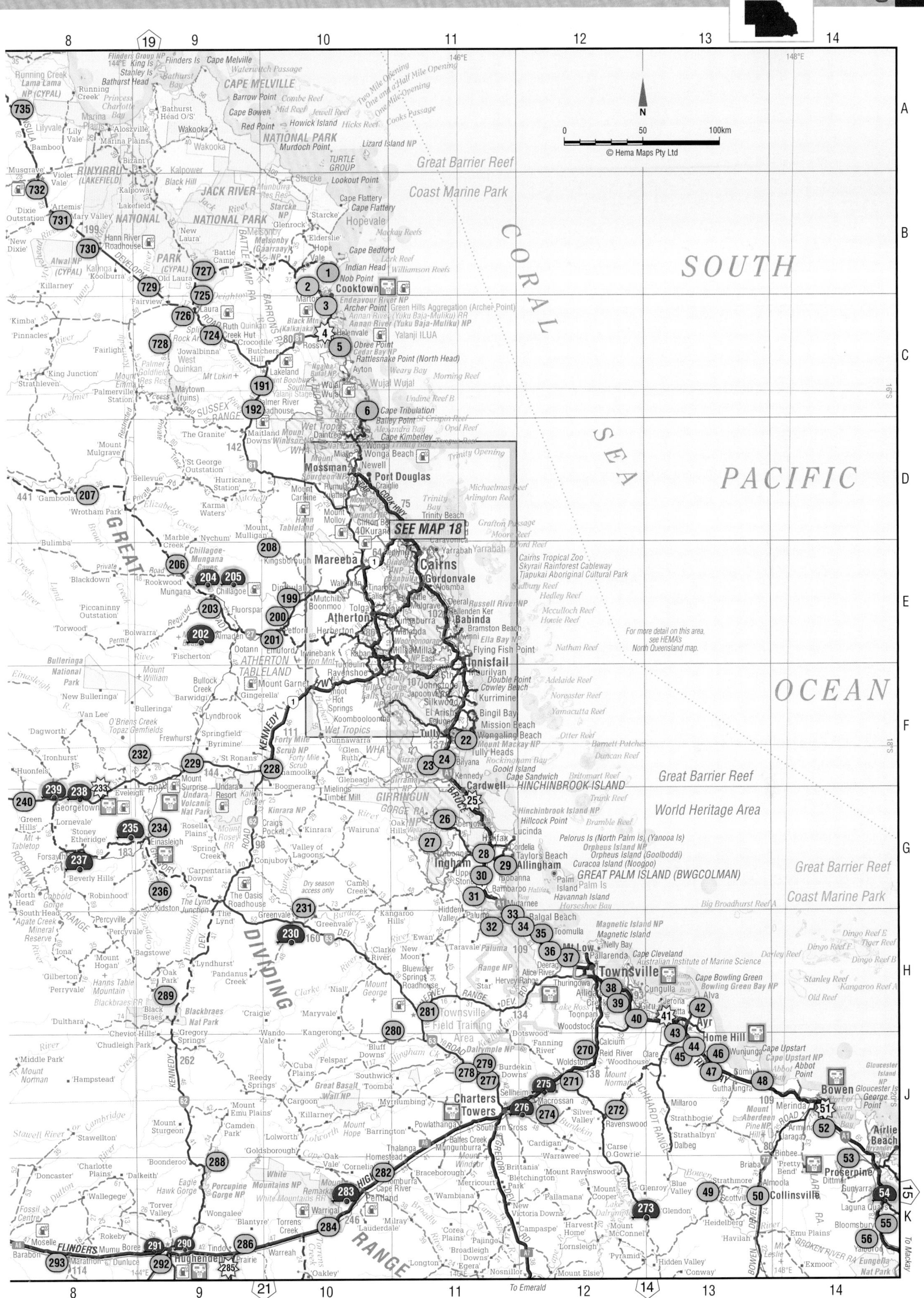

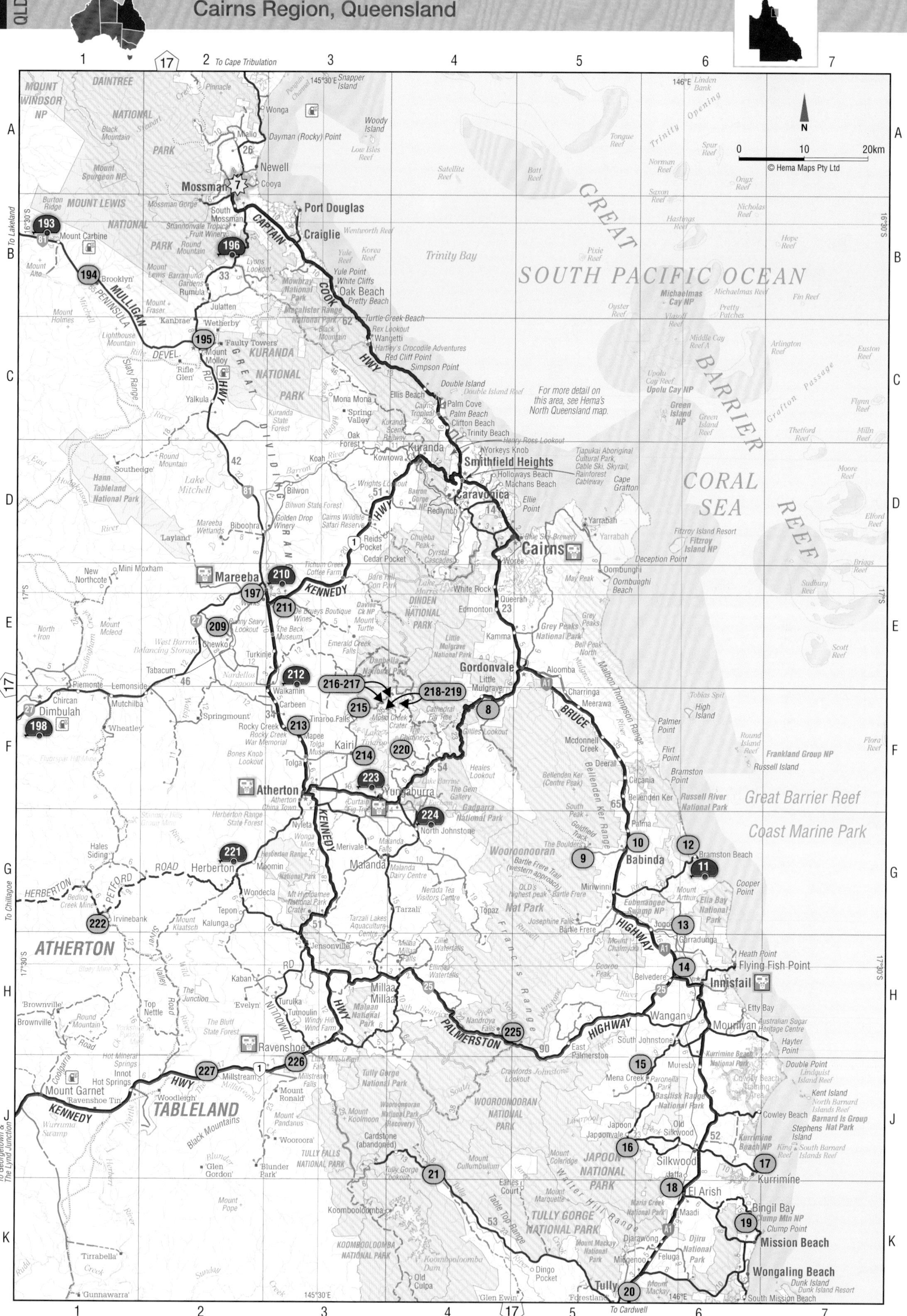
GREAT
SOUTH PACIFIC OCEAN
CORAL SEA
GREAT BARRIER REEF
Great Barrier Reef
Coast Marine Park
Trinity Bay
Mossman
Port Douglas
Craiglie
Newell
Cooya
Mount Carbine
Brooklyn
Julatten
Mount Molloy
Kuranda
Smithfield Heights
Caravonica
Cairns
Mareeba
Atherton
Yungaburra
Malanda
Millaa Millaa
Ravenshoe
Herberton
Dimbulah
Mount Garnet
Gordonvale
Babinda
Innisfail
Flying Fish Point
Wangan
Mourilyan
Silkwood
El Arish
Kurrimine
Bingil Bay
Mission Beach
Wongaling Beach
Tully
ATHERTON
TABLELAND
KENNEDY
HWY
CAPTAIN COOK HWY
MULLIGAN
PENINSULA
BRUCE HIGHWAY
PALMERSTON HIGHWAY
For more detail on this area, see Hema's North Queensland map.
© Hema Maps Pty Ltd
To Lakeland
To Cape Tribulation
To Chillagoe
To Georgetown & The Lynd Junction
To Cardwell

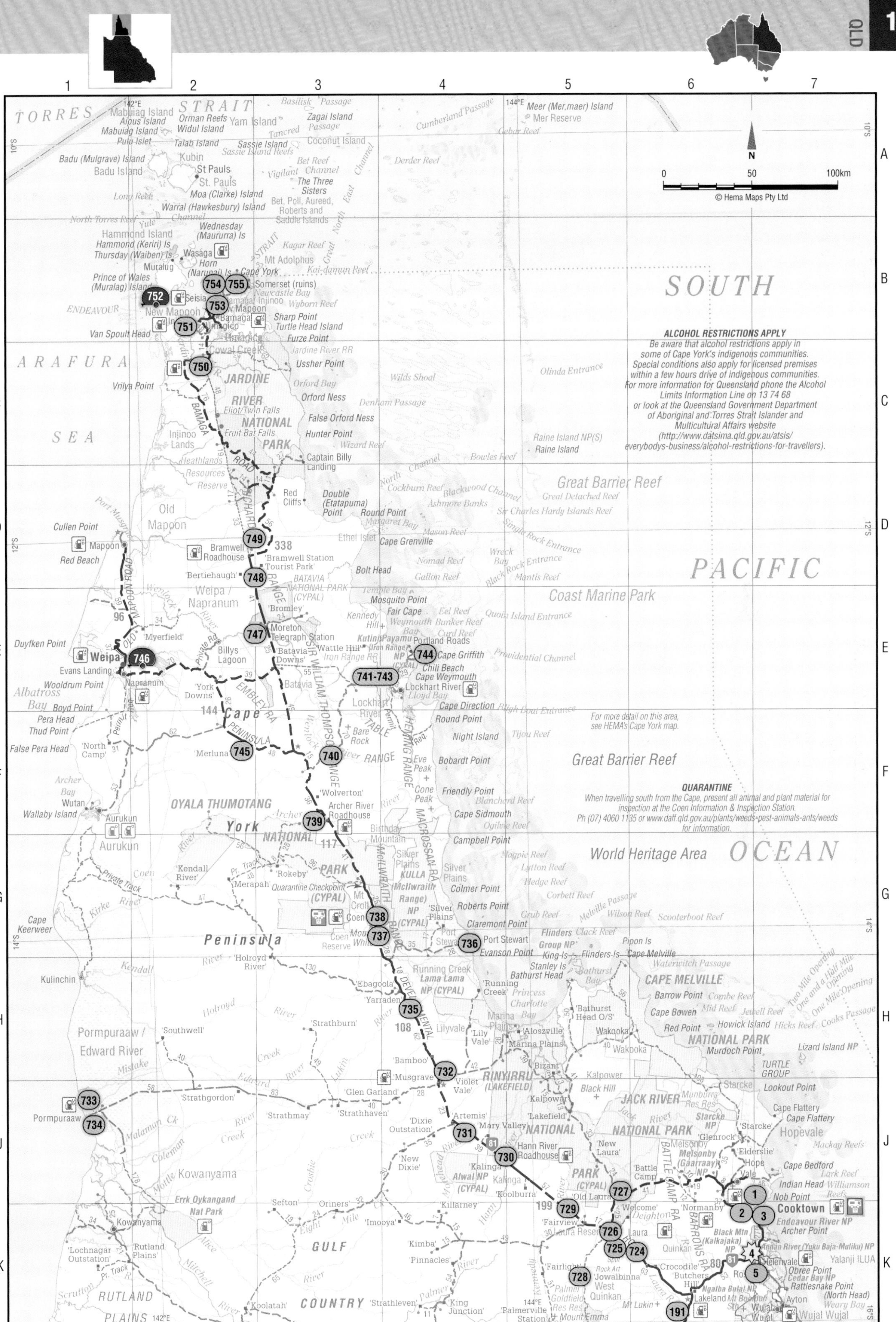
ALCOHOL RESTRICTIONS APPLY
Be aware that alcohol restrictions apply in some of Cape York's indigenous communities. Special conditions also apply for licensed premises within a few hours drive of indigenous communities. For more information for Queensland phone the Alcohol Limits Information Line on 13 74 68 or look at the Queensland Government Department of Aboriginal and Torres Strait Islander and Multicultural Affairs website (http://www.datsima.qld.gov.au/atsis/everybodys-business/alcohol-restrictions-for-travellers).
QUARANTINE
When travelling south from the Cape, present all animal and plant material for inspection at the Coen Information & Inspection Station. Ph (07) 4060 1135 or www.daff.qld.gov.au/plants/weeds-pest-animals-ants/weeds for information.
For more detail on this area, see HEMA's Cape York map.
© Hema Maps Pty Ltd
0 50 100km
TORRES STRAIT
ARAFURA SEA
SOUTH PACIFIC OCEAN
Great Barrier Reef Coast Marine Park
Great Barrier Reef World Heritage Area
JARDINE RIVER NATIONAL PARK
OYALA THUMOTANG
CAPE MELVILLE NATIONAL PARK
JACK RIVER NATIONAL PARK
RINYIRRU (LAKEFIELD) NATIONAL PARK
Peninsula
Cape Peninsula
GULF COUNTRY
RUTLAND PLAINS
Thursday (Waiben) Is
Bamaga
Weipa
Napranum
Mapoon
Aurukun
Coen
Pormpuraaw
Kowanyama
Laura
Cooktown
Hopevale
Lakeland
Wujal Wujal
Archer River Roadhouse
Musgrave
Hann River Roadhouse
Bramwell Roadhouse
Lockhart River
Portland Roads
752 754 755 753 751 750 749 748 747 746 745 744 741-743 740 739 738 737 736 735 734 733 732 731 730 729 728 727 726 725 724 191 1 2 3 4 5
16 17
To Cairns

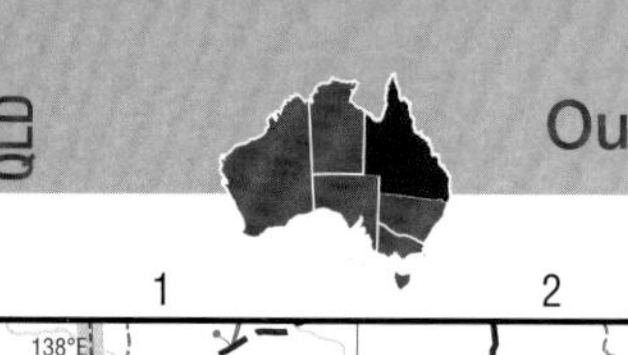

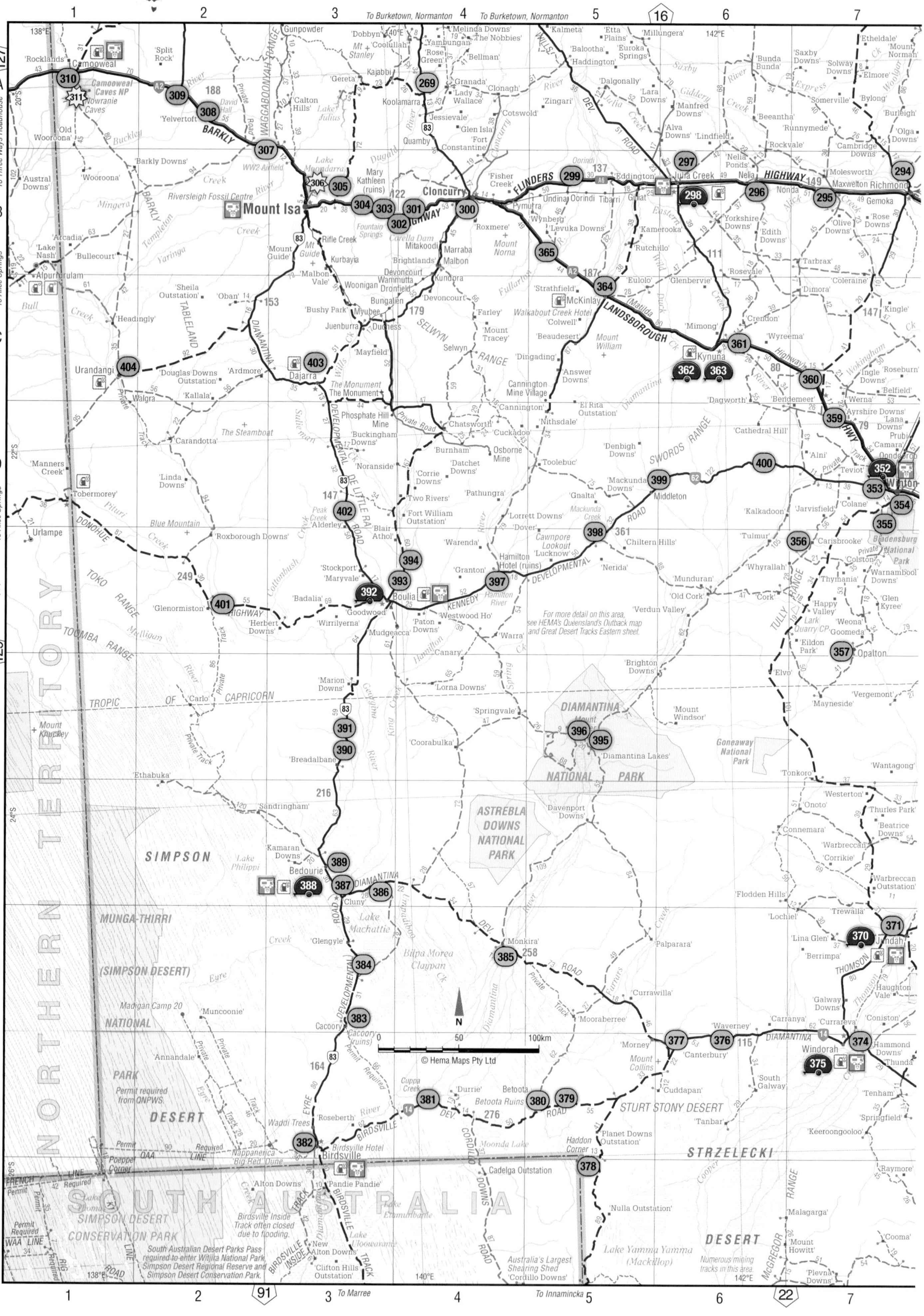

For more detail on this area, see HEMA's Queensland's Outback map and Great Desert Tracks Eastern sheet.

© Hema Maps Pty Ltd

Birdsville Inside Track often closed due to flooding.

South Australian Desert Parks Pass required to enter Witjira National Park, Simpson Desert Regional Reserve and Simpson Desert Conservation Park.

Australia's Largest Shearing Shed 'Cordillo Downs'

Numerous mining tracks in this area.

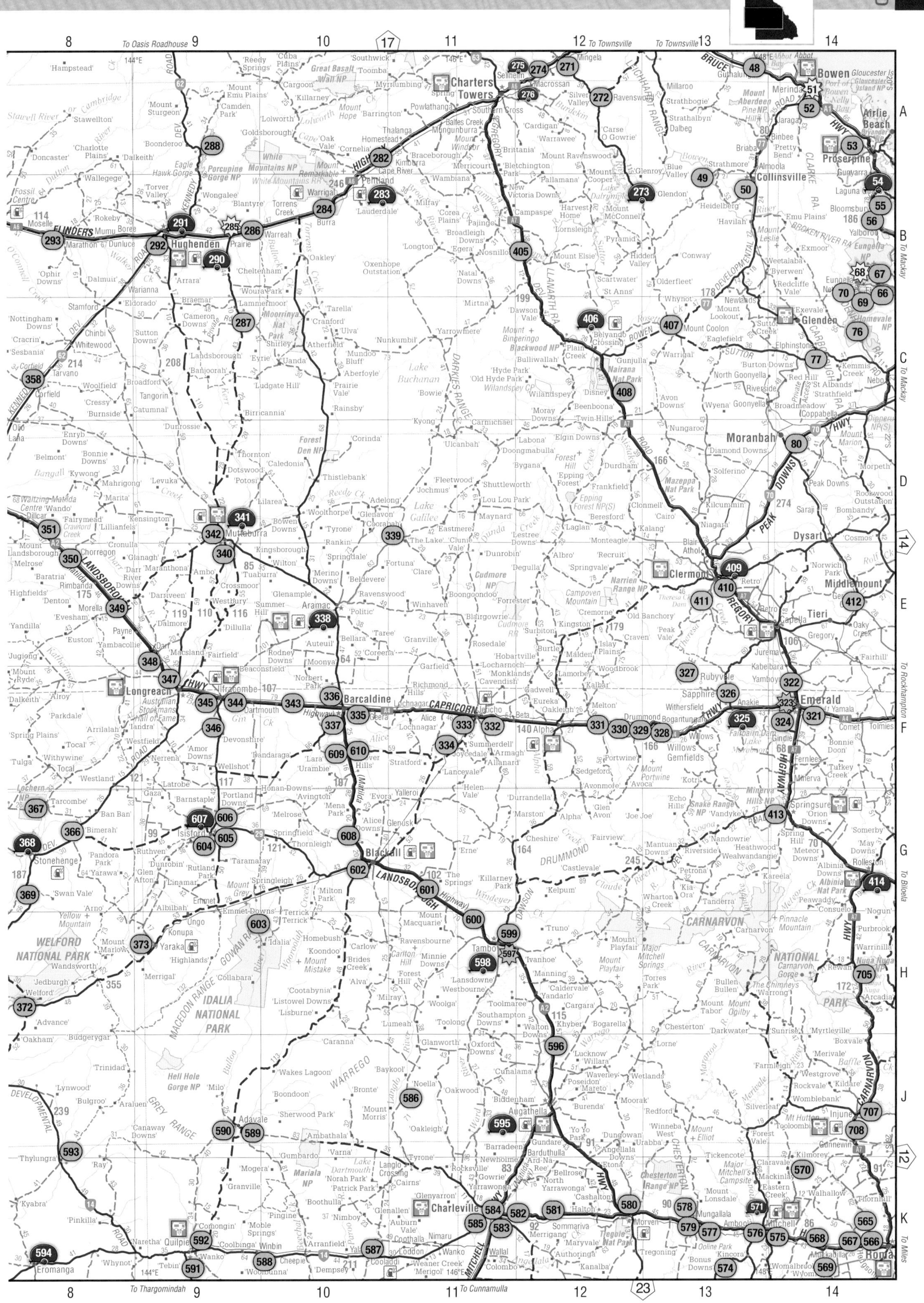
To Oasis Roadhouse
To Townsville
To Townsville
To Mackay
To Rockhampton
To Biloela
To Miles
To Thargomindah
To Cunnamulla
Charters Towers
Pentland
Hughenden
Prairie
Torrens Creek
Muttaburra
Aramac
Barcaldine
Longreach
Ilfracombe
Isisford
Blackall
Tambo
Augathella
Charleville
Morven
Mitchell
Roma
Quilpie
Adavale
Eromanga
Jericho
Alpha
Emerald
Clermont
Moranbah
Collinsville
Bowen
Proserpine
Airlie Beach
Glenden
Dysart
Middlemount
Capella
Tieri
Sapphire
Rubyvale
Anakie
Springsure
Rolleston
Injune
Winton
Stonehenge
Jundah
Yaraka
Welford National Park
Idalia National Park
Carnarvon National Park
White Mountains NP
Porcupine Gorge NP
Moorrinya Nat Park
Forest Den NP
Hell Hole Gorge NP
Mariala NP
Tregole Nat Park
Chesterton Range NP
Snake Range NP
Minerva Hills NP
Narrien Range NP
Epping Forest NP(S)
Blackwood NP
Nairana Nat Park
Mazeppa Nat Park
Homevale NP
Eungella NP
Great Basalt Wall NP
Lake Buchanan
Lake Galilee
Grey Range
Drummond Range
Darkies Range
Carnarvon Range
Flinders Hwy
Landsborough Hwy
Capricorn Hwy
Gregory Hwy
Warrego Hwy
Dawson Hwy
Peak Downs Hwy
Bowen Dev Rd
Bruce Hwy
Kennedy Dev Rd
Developmental Rd
Mitchell Hwy

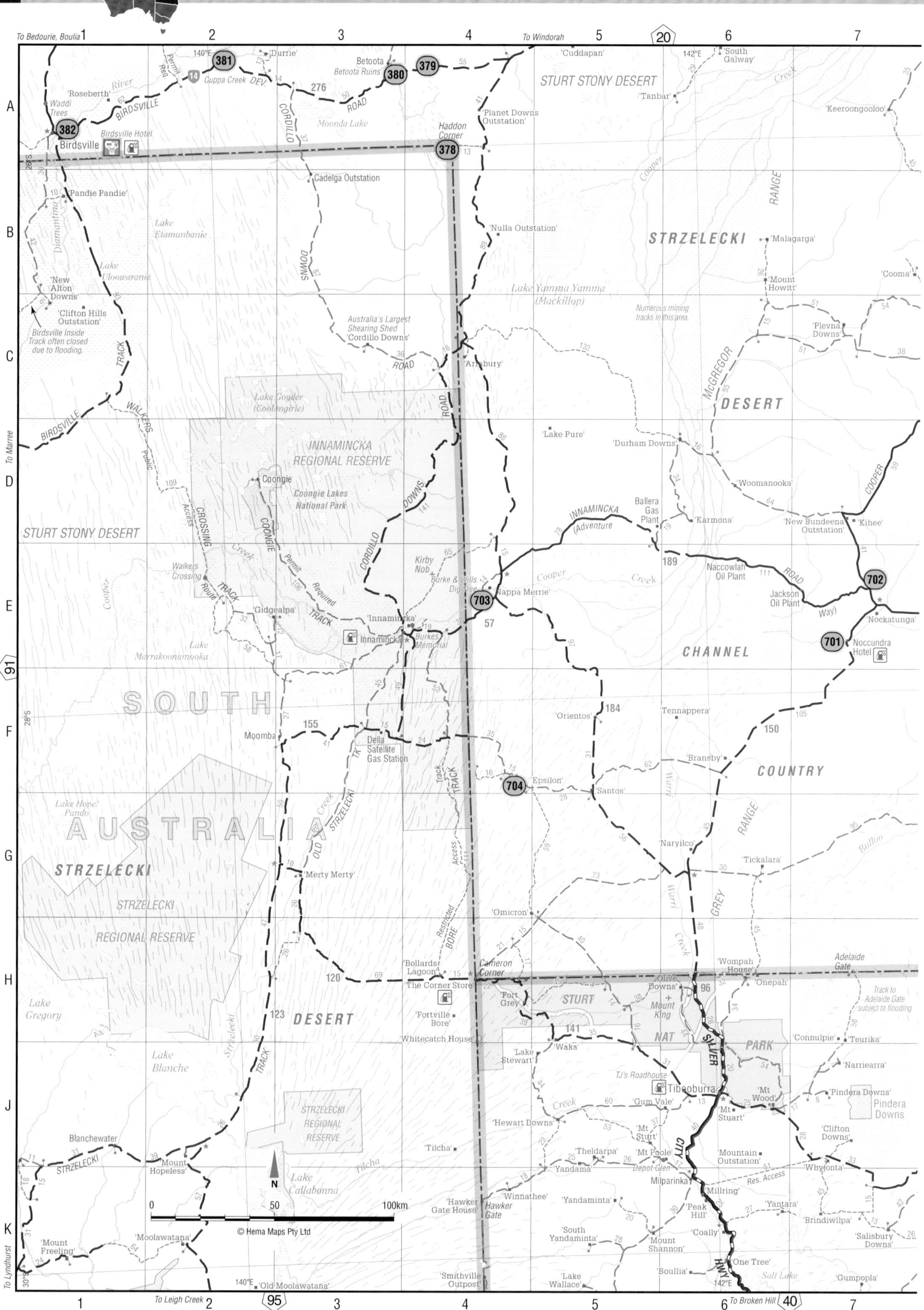
To Bedourie, Boulia
To Windorah
To Marree
To Lyndhurst
To Leigh Creek
To Broken Hill
Birdsville
Birdsville Hotel
'Roseberth'
Waddi Trees
BIRDSVILLE
Cuppa Creek DEV.
'Durrie'
Betoota
Betoota Ruins
CORDILLO
ROAD
Moonda Lake
Haddon Corner
'Cuddapan'
STURT STONY DESERT
'South Galway'
'Tanbar'
'Keeroongooloo'
'Planet Downs Outstation'
Cadelga Outstation
'Pandie Pandie'
Diamantina
Lake Etamunbanie
Lake Uloowaranie
'Nulla Outstation'
STRZELECKI
'Malagarga'
RANGE
Cooper
'New Alton Downs'
'Clifton Hills Outstation'
Birdsville Inside Track often closed due to flooding.
DOWNS
Lake Yamma Yamma (Mackillop)
'Mount Howitt'
'Cooma'
Numerous mining tracks in this area.
'Plevna Downs'
Australia's Largest Shearing Shed 'Cordillo Downs'
'Arrabury'
McGREGOR
DESERT
TRACK
Lake Goyder (Coolongirie)
WALKERS
Public
INNAMINCKA REGIONAL RESERVE
'Lake Pure'
'Durham Downs'
Coongie
Coongie Lakes National Park
'Woomanooka'
COOPER
STURT STONY DESERT
CROSSING
COONGIE
Access
INNAMINCKA (Adventure Way)
Ballera Gas Plant
'Karmona'
'New Bundeena Outstation'
'Kihee'
Walkers Crossing
Route
Permit Required
Kirby Nob
Burke & Wills Dig Tree
Nappa Merrie'
Naccowlah Oil Plant
Jackson Oil Plant
'Nockatunga'
'Gidgealpa'
'Innamincka'
Innamincka
Burkes Memorial
Noccundra Hotel
Lake Marrakoonamooka
CHANNEL
SOUTH
Moomba
Della Satellite Gas Station
'Orientos'
Tennappera'
'Bransby'
COUNTRY
'Epsilon'
'Santos'
Warri
Lake Hope/ Pando
AUSTRALIA
OLD STRZELECKI
Creek
Access
'Naryilco'
'Tickalara'
Bulloo
STRZELECKI
'Merty Merty'
STRZELECKI REGIONAL RESERVE
'Omicron'
Restricted BORE
GREY
'Bollards Lagoon'
Cameron Corner
The Corner Store
'Wompah House'
'Onepah'
Adelaide Gate
Track to Adelaide Gate subject to flooding
Lake Gregory
DESERT
'Fortville Bore'
'Fort Grey'
STURT
'Olive Downs'
Mount King
NAT
PARK
SILVER
'Whitecatch House'
'Waka'
'Connulpie'
'Teurika'
Lake Blanche
Strzelecki
'Lake Stewart'
'Narriearra'
TJ's Roadhouse
Tibooburra
'Pindera Downs'
Pindera Downs
'Gum Vale'
'Mt Wood'
'Mt Stuart'
Blanchewater
STRZELECKI REGIONAL RESERVE
'Hewart Downs'
'Mt Sturt'
'Clifton Downs'
'Tilcha'
Tilcha
CITY
'Theldarpa'
'Mt Poole'
'Mountain Outstation'
Mount Hopeless
Lake Callabonna
'Yandama'
Depot Glen
Milparinka
Res. Access
'Whyjonta'
'Winnathee'
'Millring'
0
50
100km
'Hawker Gate House'
Hawker Gate
'Yandaminta'
'Peak Hill'
'Yantara'
'Brindiwilpa'
© Hema Maps Pty Ltd
'Moolawatana'
'South Yandaminta'
'Mount Shannon'
'Coally'
'Salisbury Downs'
'Mount Freeling'
HWY
'One Tree'
'Smithville Outpost'
'Lake Wallace'
'Boullia'
Salt Lake
'Gumpopla'
'Old Moolawatana'
140°E
142°E
28°S
29°S
30°S
381
380
379
382
378
703
702
701
704
20
91
95
40
14
276
189
57
184
155
150
120
123
141
96

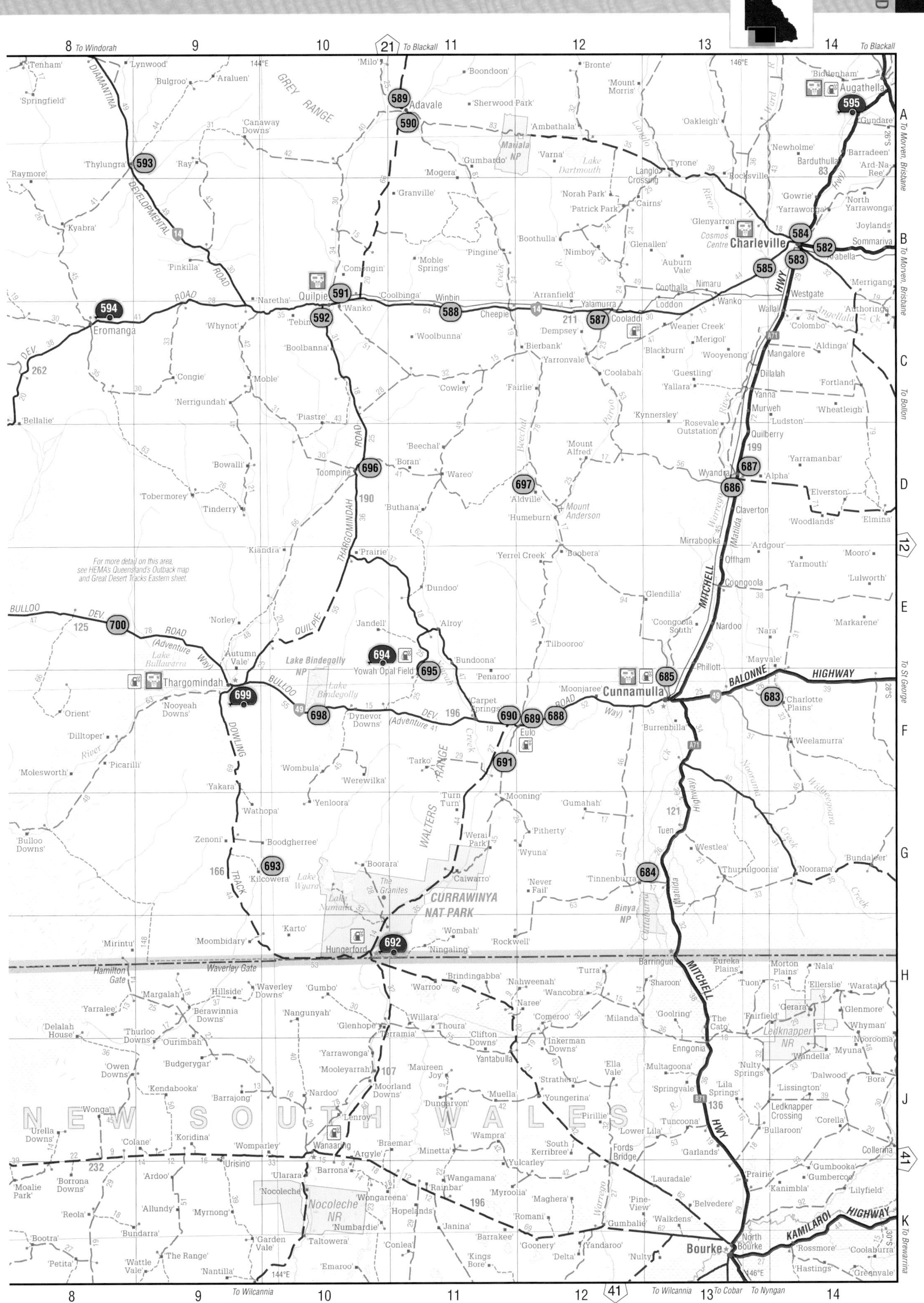
8 To Windorah
9
10
21 To Blackall
11
12
13
14
To Blackall
A
B
C
D
E
F
G
H
J
K
To Morven, Brisbane
To Bollon
To St George
To Brewarrina
To Wilcannia
To Cobar
To Nyngan
'Tenham'
'Lynwood'
'Springfield'
'Bulgroo'
'Araluen'
GREY RANGE
'Milo'
Adavale
'Boondoon'
'Bronte'
'Mount Morris'
'Biddenham'
Augathella
'Sherwood Park'
'Canaway Downs'
'Ambathala'
'Oakleigh'
'Gundare'
Mariala NP
'Varna'
Lake Dartmouth
'Tyrone'
'Newholme'
Barduthulla
'Barradeen'
'Ard-Na-Ree'
'Thylungra'
'Ray'
'Gumbardo'
'Mogera'
Langlo Crossing
'Rocksville'
'Raymore'
DIAMANTINA
DEVELOPMENTAL
ROAD
'Granville'
'Norah Park'
'Gowrie'
'North Yarrawonga'
'Patrick Park'
'Cairns'
'Yarrawonga'
'Joylands'
'Kyabra'
'Glenyarron'
Cosmos Centre
Charleville
Sommariva
'Boothulla'
'Nimboy'
'Glenallen'
'Arabella'
'Pingine'
'Moble Springs'
'Comongin'
'Auburn Vale'
'Pinkilla'
Coothalla
Nimaru
'Merrigang'
'Naretha'
Quilpie
'Coolbinga'
Winbin
'Arranfield'
Yalamurra
Wanko
Westgate
Eromanga
'Wanko'
Cheepie
Cooladdi
Loddon
Wallal
'Authoringa'
'Whynot'
'Tebin'
'Dempsey'
'Weaner Creek'
'Colombo'
Angellala Ck
'Woolbunna'
'Merigol'
'Boolbanna'
'Bierbank'
'Blackburn'
'Wooyenong'
'Mangalore'
'Aldinga'
'Yarronvale'
'Coolabah'
Dillalah
'Congie'
'Moble'
'Cowley'
'Guestling'
'Fortland'
'Fairlie'
'Yallara'
'Nerrigundah'
Yanna
Murweh
'Wheatleigh'
'Bellalie'
'Piastre'
'Kynnersley'
'Ludston'
'Rosevale Outstation'
Quilberry
'Beechal'
'Mount Alfred'
'Bowalli'
Toompine
'Boran'
'Wareo'
'Yarramanbar'
Wyandra
'Alpha'
'Aldville'
'Tobermorey'
'Buthana'
'Mount Anderson'
'Elverston'
'Tinderry'
'Humeburn'
Claverton
'Woodlands'
'Elmina'
THARGOMINDAH
ROAD
Mirrabooka
'Ardgour'
'Kiandra'
'Prairie'
'Yerrel Creek'
'Boobera'
'Mooro'
Offham
'Yarmouth'
For more detail on this area, see HEMA's Queensland's Outback map and Great Desert Tracks Eastern sheet.
'Dundoo'
Coongoola
'Lulworth'
BULLOO DEV. ROAD
'Glendilla'
MITCHELL
'Norley'
'Jandell'
'Alroy'
'Coongoola South'
Nardoo
'Nara'
'Markarene'
(Adventure Way)
Lake Bullawarra
QUILPIE
'Tilbooroo'
Autumn Vale
Lake Bindegolly NP
Yowah Opal Field
'Bundoona'
'Mayvale'
Phillott
BALONNE
HIGHWAY
Thargomindah
'Penaroo'
'Moonjaree'
Cunnamulla
Charlotte Plains'
'Nooyeah Downs'
BULLOO
Lake Bindegolly
Carpet Springs
'Orient'
'Dynevor Downs'
DEV.
(Adventure Way)
'Burrenbilla'
'Dilltoper'
Eulo
'Weelamurra'
River
'Picarilli'
'Tarko'
'Molesworth'
'Wombula'
'Werewilka'
DOWLING
'Yakara'
'Yenloora'
'Mooning'
'Gumahah'
Turn Turn
WALTERS
RANGE
'Wathopa'
'Pitherty'
Tuen
'Bulloo Downs'
'Zenoni'
'Boodgherree'
'Werai Park'
'Wyuna'
'Westlea'
'Boorara'
'Thurulgoonia'
'Noorama'
'Bundaleer'
'Kilcowera'
Lake Wyara
The Granites
'Caiwarro'
'Never Fail'
'Tinnenburra'
TRACK
Lake Numalla
CURRAWINYA NAT PARK
Binya NP
'Karto'
'Wombah'
'Mirintu'
'Moombidary'
Hungerford
'Rockwell'
'Ningaling'
Hamilton Gate
Waverley Gate
Barringun
'Eureka Plains'
'Morton Plains'
'Nala'
'Brindingabba'
'Turra'
'Margalah'
'Hillside'
'Waverley Downs'
'Gumbo'
'Warroo'
'Nahweenah'
'Wancobra'
'Sharoon'
'Tuon'
'Ellerslie'
'Waratah'
'Yarralee'
'Naree'
'Gerara'
'Glenmore'
'Berawinnia Downs'
'Nangunyah'
'Comeroo'
'Milanda'
'Goolring'
'Fairfield'
'Delalah House'
'Glenhope'
'Willara'
'Thoura'
The Cato
Ledknapper NR
'Whyman'
'Thurloo Downs'
'Ourimbah'
'Terramia'
'Clifton Downs'
'Inkerman Downs'
Enngonia
'Nooroomah'
'Owen Downs'
'Yarrawonga'
Yantabulla
'Wandella'
'Myuna'
'Budgerygar'
'Maureen Joy'
'Ella Vale'
'Multagoona'
'Nulty Springs'
'Mooleyarrah'
'Dalwood'
'Bora'
'Strathern'
'Lila Springs'
'Kendabooka'
'Moorland Downs'
'Muella'
'Springvale'
'Lissington'
'Barrajong'
'Nardoo'
'Youngerina'
'Wonga'
'Dungarvon'
Ledknapper Crossing
NEW SOUTH WALES
'Lenroy'
'Pirillie'
'Corella'
'Urella Downs'
'Tuncoona'
'Koridina'
'Wampra'
'Lower Lila'
'Bullaroon'
'Colane'
'Womparley'
Wanaaring
'Braemar'
'South Kerribree'
Fords Bridge
'Argyle'
'Minetta'
'Garlands'
Collerina
Urisino
'Yulcarley'
'Gumbooka'
'Moalie Park'
'Borrona Downs'
'Ardoo'
'Ularara'
'Barrona'
'Wangamana'
'Prairie'
'Gumbercoo'
'Rainbar'
'Lauradale'
'Kanimbla'
'Lilyfield'
'Reola'
'Allundy'
'Myrnong'
'Nocoleche'
'Myroolia'
'Maghera'
'Wongareena'
Nocoleche NR
'Pine View'
'Belvedere'
HIGHWAY
'Hopelands'
'Romani'
'Walkdens'
KAMILAROI
'Bootra'
'Bundarra'
'Numbardie'
'Janina'
Gumbalie
North Bourke
'Garden Vale'
'Barrakee'
'Rossmore'
'Coolaburra'
'Petita'
'The Range'
'Taltowera'
'Conlea'
'Goonery'
'Yandaroo'
Bourke
'Wattle Vale'
'Kings Bore'
'Delta'
'Nulty'
'Hastings'
'Greenvale'
'Nantilla'
'Emaroo'
144°E
146°E
28°S
26°S
30°S
12
41

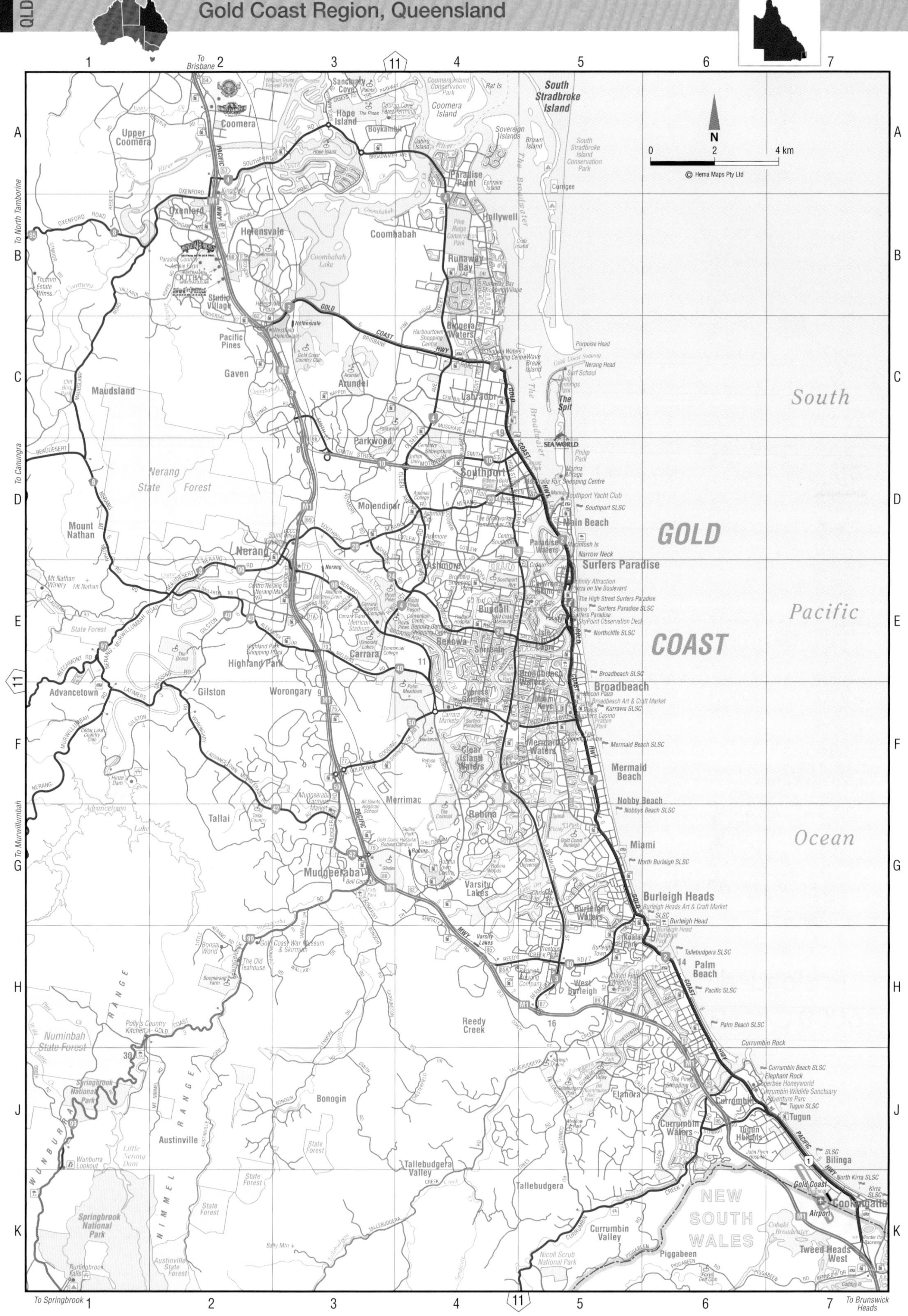
To Brisbane
To North Tamborine
To Canungra
To Murwillumbah
To Springbrook
To Brunswick Heads
N
0 2 4 km
© Hema Maps Pty Ltd
South Pacific Ocean
GOLD COAST
NEW SOUTH WALES
South Stradbroke Island
Coomera Island
Sanctuary Cove
Hope Island
Boykambil
Upper Coomera
Coomera
Oxenford
Helensvale
Coombabah
Paradise Point
Hollywell
Runaway Bay
Biggera Waters
Pacific Pines
Gaven
Maudsland
Arundel
Labrador
The Spit
Parkwood
Southport
Nerang State Forest
Molendinar
Main Beach
Mount Nathan
Nerang
Ashmore
Surfers Paradise
Bundall
Benowa
Sorrento
Carrara
Highland Park
Advancetown
Gilston
Worongary
Broadbeach
Broadbeach Waters
Mermaid Waters
Clear Island Waters
Mermaid Beach
Nobby Beach
Merrimac
Tallai
Robina
Miami
Mudgeeraba
Varsity Lakes
Burleigh Heads
Burleigh Waters
Palm Beach
West Burleigh
Reedy Creek
Numinbah State Forest
Springbrook National Park
Bonogin
Austinville
Elanora
Currumbin
Currumbin Waters
Tugun
Tugun Heights
Bilinga
Tallebudgera Valley
Tallebudgera
Currumbin Valley
Piggabeen
Coolangatta
Tweed Heads West
Gold Coast Airport
Currumbin Rock
SEA WORLD
Southport Yacht Club
Southport SLSC
Surfers Paradise SLSC
Northcliffe SLSC
Broadbeach SLSC
Kurrawa SLSC
Mermaid Beach SLSC
Nobbys Beach SLSC
North Burleigh SLSC
Tallebudgera SLSC
Pacific SLSC
Palm Beach SLSC
Currumbin Beach SLSC
Tugun SLSC
North Kirra SLSC
Kirra SLSC
NUMINBAH
RANGE
NIMMEL RANGE
WUNBURRA RANGE
GOLD COAST HWY
PACIFIC HWY
PACIFIC MWY

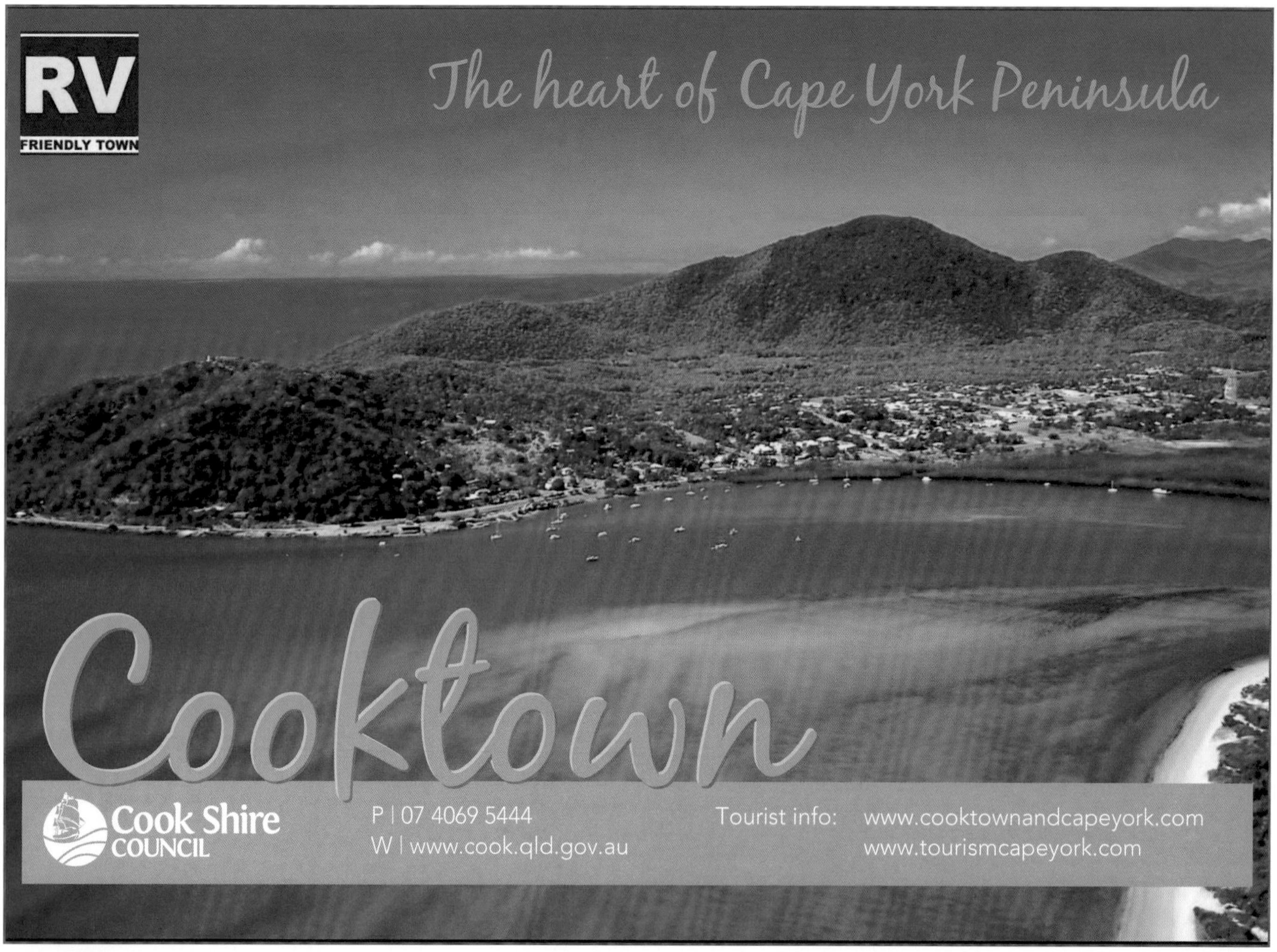

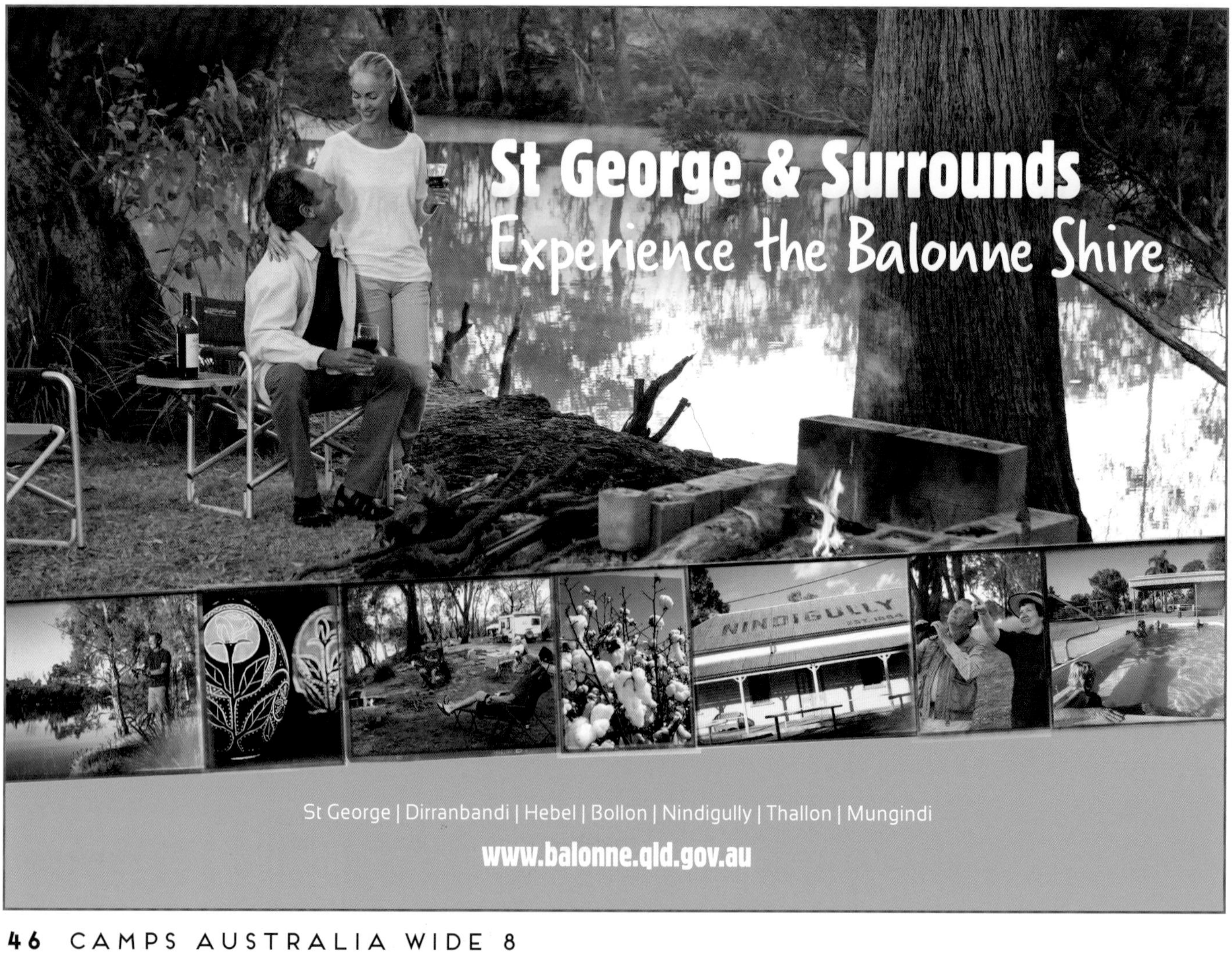

Queensland Highway Index

Queensland Alphabetic Site Index

Symbols

A

B

C

D

E

F

G

H

I

J

K

R

S

T

U

V

W

Y

Z

QUEENSLAND

Mossman to the Gold Coast

Bruce Highway

1 Endeavour River Escape
☎ (07) 4069 5084

Camp Area 17 km N of Cooktown PO. Turn R after Cooktown Airport 5 km along Barretts Creek Rd. Closed during wet season (Dec-Apr)

HEMA 17 B10 15 24 26 S 145 11 24 E

BIG RIG

2 Barradise RV Bush Camp
☎ (07) 4069 5005

Camp Area 14 km WNW of Cooktown. 1133 Endeavour Valley Rd. Self Contained Vehicles only

HEMA 17 B10 15 26 13 S 145 9 53 E

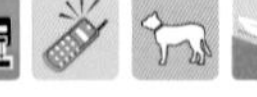

3 Adelaide Street RV Stop
☎ (07) 4069 6004

Parking Area at Cooktown. Cnr Walker & Adelaide St. 1 km S of PO. Register & pay for permit at Visitor Information Centre at Natures Powerhouse in Botanic Gardens off Walker St. Open 7 days 0900 -1700. Self Contained Vehicles only. Only 1 x 48 hour stay within a 90 day period

HEMA 17 C10 15 28 9 S 145 14 51 E

BIG RIG 48

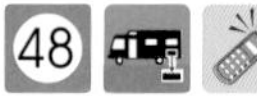

4 Little Annan River Rest Area

Rest Area 28 km SW of Cooktown

HEMA 17 C10 15 40 52 S 145 12 21 E

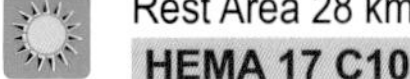

5 Lions Den Hotel Campground
☎ (07) 4060 3911

Camp Area at Helenvale on the Bloomfield Rd

HEMA 17 C10 15 42 21 S 145 13 23 E

BIG RIG

6 Noah Beach Campground
☎ 13 74 68

Daintree National Park

Camp Area 8 km S of Cape Tribulation. Small vehicles only. No Caravans permitted. Bookings required

HEMA 17 D10 16 7 56 S 145 27 8 E

7 Bill Reese Park

44

Rest Area 1 km N of Mossman. N side of Mossman River bridge

HEMA 18 A2 16 27 8 S 145 22 18 E

8 Catch a Barra
☎ (07) 4056 1727

Parking Area at Little Mulgrave 14 km W of Gordonvale. 386 Nielson Rd

HEMA 18 F4 17 7 22 S 145 41 57 E

BIG RIG

9 The Boulders
☎ (07) 4067 1008

Camp Area 6 km W of Babinda. Limited sites

HEMA 18 G5 17 20 27 S 145 52 14 E

48

10 Babinda Rotary Park
☎ (07) 4067 1008

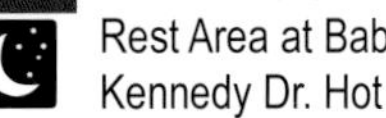

Rest Area at Babinda. Just E of town over railway. S end of Howard Kennedy Dr. Hot showers coin operated

HEMA 18 G6 17 20 54 S 145 55 35 E

BIG RIG 72

11 Bramston Beach Plantation Caravan Park
☎ (07) 4067 4133

Caravan Park at Bramston Beach. Evans Rd

HEMA 18 G6 17 21 32 S 146 1 38 E

BIG RIG

12 Bramston Beach Caravan Park & Campground
☎ (07) 4067 4121

Camp Area at Bramston Beach. N end of Evans Rd

HEMA 18 G6 17 21 8 S 146 1 25 E

BIG RIG

13 Garradunga Hotel
☎ 0428 563 754

Camp Spot at Garradunga. Free stay with a spend at the bar. Fee for hot showers

HEMA 18 G6 17 27 41 S 145 59 43 E

BIG RIG

14 Fred Drew Park

1

Rest Area 4 km N of Innisfail or 25 km S of Babinda. At Palmerston Hwy turnoff

HEMA 18 H6 17 30 55 S 145 59 37 E

BIG RIG 24

15 Mena Creek Hotel
☎ (07) 4065 3201

Camp Area at Mena.19 km SW of Innisfail on the Innisfail Japoon Rd. Free Camping if order a meal at the hotel

HEMA 18 J6 17 39 18 S 145 57 22 E

BIG RIG

16 Upper Liverpool Creek

Rest Area at Japoonvale. 29 km SW of Innisfail or 14 km W of Silkwood. Beside creek

HEMA 18 J5 17 43 25 S 145 56 1 E

24

17 Kurrimine Beach Campground
☎ (07) 4030 2222

Camp Area at Kurrimine. N end of Robert Johnstone Parade. Maximum stay 4 weeks. Caretaker on site

HEMA 18 J6 17 46 31 S 146 6 32 E

18 El Arish Rest Area

1

Rest Area 1 km N of El Arish. Limited space

HEMA 18 K6 17 47 44 S 146 0 39 E

48

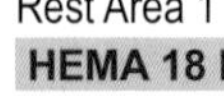

19 Bingil Bay Campground
☎ (07) 4030 2222

Camp Area at Bingil Bay, 3 km N of Mission Beach. Small vehicles only. Beachfront. Maximum stay 4 weeks

HEMA 18 K6 | 17 49 40 S | 146 6 3 E

20 Tully Showground
☎ 07 4068 2288

Camp Area at Tully Showground, Butler Street. Limited sites, Self Contained Vehicles only. Obtain permit from Info Centre.

HEMA 18 K5 | 17 56 2 S | 145 55 47 E

BIG RIG 36

21 Tully Gorge Campground
☎ (07) 4066 8601

Tully Gorge National Park

Camp Area 44 km NW of Tully, via Tully Falls Rd. Cold showers. Must pre-book

HEMA 18 J4 | 17 46 22 S | 145 38 59 E

22 Hull Heads Recreation Area

Camp Area at Hull Heads, 21 km SE of Tully.

HEMA 17 F11 | 17 59 42 S | 146 4 18 E

96

23 Murray Falls Campground
☎ 13 74 68

Murray Falls National Park

Camp Area 36 km SW of Tully or 41 km NW of Cardwell. Turn W 16 km S of Tully at Murrigal or 21 km N of Cardwell at Bilyana. 3 km dirt road. Bookings essential

HEMA 17 F11 | 18 9 11 S | 145 48 57 E

BIG RIG

24 Bilyana Rest Area

Rest Area 22 km S of Tully or 21 km N of Cardwell

1

HEMA 17 F11 | 18 7 7 S | 145 54 43 E

20

25 Five Mile Swimming Hole

Picnic Area 9 km S of Cardwell or 46 km N of Ingham. 700m W of Hwy. Dirt road

HEMA 17 G11 | 18 19 39 S | 146 2 44 E

26 Broadwater Campground
☎ 13 74 68

Abergowrie State Forest

Camp Area 45 km NW of Ingham, via Trebonne along Abergowrie Rd, or turn W off Bruce Hwy 3 km N of Ingham onto Hawkins Creek Rd for 26 km.17 km dirt road. Bookings required

HEMA 17 G11 | 18 24 59 S | 145 56 43 E

Notes...

27 Wallaman Falls Campground
☎ 13 74 68

Girringun National Park

Camp Area 51 km W of Ingham, via Trebonne. 20 km dirt road. Steep, winding road not suitable for caravans. Bookings required

HEMA 17 G11 | 18 35 59 S | 145 48 0 E

28 Tyto Wetlands RV Stop
☎ (07) 4776 4792

Parking Area at Ingham. Tyto Wetlands Info Centre. Cnr Bruce Hwy & Cooper St. Need to get permit from Info Centre. Self Contained Vehicles only

HEMA 17 G11 | 18 39 18 S | 146 9 11 E

48

29 Mungalla Station
☎ (07) 4777 8718

Camp Area at Mungalla Station. 12 km E of Ingham on the Forrest Beach Rd towards Allingham. Signposted at entrance

HEMA 17 G11 | 18 41 49 S | 146 15 52 E

30 Frances Creek

Rest Area 11 km S of Ingham or 98 km N of Townsville

1

HEMA 17 G11 | 18 44 52 S | 146 8 14 E

20

31 Jourama Falls
☎ 13 74 68

Paluma Range National Park

Camp Area 29 km S of Ingham. Turn W off Bruce Hwy 24 km S of Ingham or 85 km N of Townsville for 5 km. 3 km dirt road. Cold showers. Bookings required

HEMA 17 G11 | 18 51 20 S | 146 7 35 E

BIG RIG

32 Big Crystal Creek Camping Area
☎ 13 74 68

Paluma Range National Park

Camp Area 47 km S of Ingham. Turn W off Bruce Hwy 40 km S of Ingham onto Barrett Rd, then R into Spiegelhauer Rd. 5 km to camping area. Not suitable for large motorhomes, caravans. Bookings required

HEMA 17 H11 | 18 58 47 S | 146 15 25 E

33 Bushy Parker Park

Rest Area at Rollingstone. Turn E off Bruce Hwy just N of Rollingstone, across railway line

HEMA 17 H11 | 19 2 46 S | 146 23 37 E

BIG RIG 48

34 Balgal Beach

Rest Area 6 km E of Rollingstone. Turn E off Bruce Hwy 1 km S of Rollingstone. 5 km E of Hwy. N end of town near boat ramp. Limited sites

HEMA 17 H12 | 19 0 37 S | 146 24 18 E

48

35 Toomulla Beach

Rest Area 68 km S of Ingham or 45 km N of Townsville. Turn E off Bruce Hwy 43 km N of Townsville or 66 km S of Ingham. S end of town

HEMA 17 H12 19 5 0 S 146 28 34 E

BIG RIG 48

36 Bluewater Park

Rest Area at Bluewater, 80 km S of Ingham or 29 km N of Townsville. Beside creek. Outside cold shower

1

HEMA 17 H12 19 10 35 S 146 33 5 E

BIG RIG 24

37 Saunders Park

Rest Area at Saunders Beach. Turn E off Bruce Hwy 87 km S of Ingham or 24 km N of Townsville, 1 km N of Yabulu. N side of town. 7 km off Bruce Hwy. No tents

HEMA 17 H12 19 9 14 S 146 36 15 E

48

38 Alligator Creek Roadhouse

Parking Area 22 km SE of Townsville or 66 km NW of Ayr

1

HEMA 14 A5 19 22 59 S 146 55 45 E

BIG RIG 24

39 Alligator Creek Campground ☎ 13 74 68

Bowling Green Bay National Park

Camp Area 25 km SE of Townsville. Turn W off Bruce Hwy 25 km SE of Townsville or 63 km NW of Ayr. Gate locked 1830 - 0630 hrs. Small vehicles only. Online booking

HEMA 14 A5 19 26 2 S 146 56 46 E

$

40 Giru Town Rest Area

Camp Spot at Giru. Cnr Walton St & Brookes St

HEMA 14 A5 19 30 50 S 147 6 27 E

BIG RIG 48

41 Sandy Creek Rest Area

Rest Area 79 km SE of Townsville or 8 km W of Ayr

1

HEMA 14 A5 19 34 16 S 147 20 12 E

BIG RIG

42 Plantation Creek Boat Ramp

Camp Spot 12.5 km NE of Ayr. Take Airdmillan Rd to Old Wharf rd. 5.5 km dirt road

HEMA 14 A6 19 32 5 S 147 30 46 E

BIG RIG 72

43 Red Lilly Rural Stopover ☎ 0428 826 846

Camp Spot at Mt Kelly. 22 km SW of Ayr 450 Barrett Rd Mt Kelly. Self Contained Vehicles only, donation for upkeep of wetlands

HEMA 14 A5 19 38 11 S 147 18 16 E

$ BIG RIG

44 Home Hill Comfort Stop

Rest Area at Home Hill Comfort Stop. Adjacent to old railway station just W of main street. No tents

HEMA 14 A6 19 39 54 S 147 24 50 E

BIG RIG 48

45 Home Hill Old Showgrounds

Camp Area at Home Hill. Sixth Ave, Self Contained Vehicles only. Donation for power

HEMA 14 A6 19 40 11 S 147 24 57 E

$ BIG RIG 96

46 Funny Dunny Park

Camp Area 5 km S of Inkerman. Signposted "Wunjunga". 15 km dirt road. Maximum Stay 4 days in a 2 week period. Donation for use

HEMA 14 A6 19 45 8 S 147 35 45 E

$ BIG RIG 96

47 Wilson Creek Rest Area

Rest Area 28 km S of Home Hill or 12 km N of Gumlu

1

HEMA 14 B6 19 50 5 S 147 35 39 E

BIG RIG 20

48 Guthalungra Rest Area

Rest Area at Guthalungra. Shower at service station for a fee

1

HEMA 14 B6 19 55 24 S 147 50 35 E

BIG RIG 20

49 Bowen River Hotel ☎ (07) 4785 3388

Camp Area 32 km W of Collinsville, via Strathmore

HEMA 14 C6 20 32 1 S 147 33 21 E

$ BIG RIG

50 Collinsville Showgrounds ☎ (07) 4785 5795

Camp Area at Collinsville. Entry from Railway Rd next to Showgrounds. Self Contained Vehicles only

HEMA 14 C6 20 33 24 S 147 50 57 E

BIG RIG 72

51 Bowen Rest Area

Rest Area 4 km S of Bowen turnoff 62 km NW of Proserpine. Opposite "Big Mango" Info Centre

1

HEMA 14 B7 20 2 47 S 148 13 46 E

52 Glen Erin Farm Stay ☎ (07) 4786 4899

Camp Area 20 km S of Bowen. Turn W off Bruce Hwy at Mookara Rd for 4 km. Signposted

HEMA 14 B7 20 7 6 S 148 13 21 E

$+ BIG RIG

53 Camp Kanga
☎ (07) 4947 2600

Camp Area 24 km W of Proserpine, via Crystal Brook Rd. Reservations essential

HEMA 14 B7 20 21 37 S 148 23 53 E

54 O'Connell River Whitsunday Tourist Park
☎ (07) 4947 5148

Caravan Park 22 km S of Proserpine or 18 km N of Bloomsbury. Beside O'Connell River. Bruce Hwy

HEMA 14 C7 20 33 57 S 148 37 0 E

55 Bloomsbury BP
☎ (07) 4947 5739

Parking Area at Bloomsbury. At rear of service station

HEMA 14 C7 20 42 19 S 148 35 45 E

56 Jaxut Camping Area
Cathu State Forest
☎ (07) 4944 7800

Camp Area 30 km NW of Calen. Turn W off Bruce Hwy 13 km S of Bloomsbury or 18 km N of Calen onto Cathu-O'Connell River Rd. 12 km dirt road, steep in places, not suitable for caravans.

HEMA 14 C7 20 47 32 S 148 32 56 E

57 St Helens Gardens Caravan Park
☎ (07) 4958 8152

Caravan Park at Calen. Bruce Hwy. 1 km S of PO

HEMA 15 C8 20 54 15 S 148 46 48 E

58 St Helens Camping Reserve
☎ 1300 622 529

Camp Area 15 km NE of Calen. 1.5 km S of St Helens Beach, via Murrays Rd. Beachfront. Attendant collects fees daily

HEMA 15 C8 20 50 28 S 148 50 38 E

59 Wintermoon Way Camping Oasis
☎ (07) 4958 8390

Camp Area 12 km W of Calen. Via Calen - Mount Charlton Rd

HEMA 15 D8 20 57 47 S 148 41 47 E

60 Boulder Creek

Rest Area 18 km SW of Calen, via Camerons Pocket. 1.5 km dirt road

HEMA 15 D8 21 0 31 S 148 43 10 E

61 Jolimont Caravan Park
☎ (07) 4954 0170

Caravan Park 16 km S of Calen or 6 km N of Kuttabul. Bruce Hwy

HEMA 15 D8 21 0 25 S 148 52 27 E

62 Palm Tree Creek Rest Area

Rest Area 20 km S of Calen or 2 km N of Kuttabul

HEMA 15 D8 21 1 41 S 148 53 35 E

63 Seaforth Camping Reserve
☎ 0427 373 358

Camp Area at Seaforth. On the Esplanade. Maximum stay 6 weeks

HEMA 15 D8 20 53 58 S 148 57 57 E

64 Ball Bay Camping Reserve
☎ 1300 622 529

Camp Area at Ball Bay. 9 km E of Seaforth. Turn N 3 km W of Seaforth onto Cape Hillsborough Rd & Ball Bay Rd. N end of Ward Esplanade. Outside showers

HEMA 15 D8 20 54 11 S 148 59 44 E

65 Smalleys Beach
Cape Hillsborough National Park
☎ 13 74 68

Camp Area 12 km E of Seaforth. Via Cape Hillsborough Rd & Smalleys Beach Rd. Limited sites for larger vehicles. 1.5 km dirt road. Prebook online

HEMA 15 D8 20 54 51 S 149 1 0 E

66 Pioneer Valley Showgrounds
☎ (07) 4958 5666

Camp Area at Finch Hatton. W of Mackay. Closed during show week in early June

HEMA 14 D7 21 8 22 S 148 37 51 E

67 Platypus Bushcamp
☎ (07) 4958 3204

Camp Area at Finch Hatton Gorge. W of Mackay

HEMA 14 D7 21 4 53 S 148 38 16 E

68 Goodes Lookout

Rest Area at Eungella. E end of town, behind tennis courts

HEMA 14 D7 21 7 54 S 148 29 36 E

69 Crediton Hall Campground
Crediton State Forest
☎ 13 74 68

Camp Area 15 km S Eungella. Via Eungella Dam Rd, Crediton Loop Rd, continue 6.7 km to the campground. Steep access road. Not suitable for caravans

HEMA 14 D7 21 12 21 S 148 32 46 E

Notes...

70 Eungella Dam
☎ 13 74 68

Camp Area 28 km SW of Eungella, via Broken River Rd. 20 km dirt road. Cold showers. 28 day maximum stay (Big Rig access from Peak Downs Hwy via Turrawulla Rd, dry weather access only)

HEMA 14 D7 | 21 9 7 S | 148 22 47 E

71 Kinchant Waters Leisure Resort
☎ (07) 4954 1453

Caravan Park 15 km NW of Eton, via North Eton & Kinchant Dam Rd

HEMA 15 D8 | 21 13 14 S | 148 53 34 E

BIG RIG

72 Eton Rest Area

Rest Area at Eton. Beside sports oval

HEMA 15 D8 | 21 15 44 S | 148 58 26 E

BIG RIG

73 General Gordon Hotel
☎ (07) 4959 7324

Camp Area at Homebush, 8 km W of Rosella or 13 km E of Eton

HEMA 15 D8 | 21 15 45 S | 149 4 53 E

74 The Retreat Hotel
☎ (07) 4954 1239

Camp Area 35 km SW of Eton or 28 km NE of Nebo via Peak Downs Hwy

HEMA 15 D8 | 21 28 42 S | 148 48 40 E

BIG RIG

75 The Retreat Hotel Rest Area

Rest Area 35 km SW of Eton or 28 km NE of Nebo. Adjacent to Hotel

70

HEMA 15 D8 | 21 28 48 S | 148 48 40 E

BIG RIG

76 Moonlight Dam
☎ 13 74 68

Homevale National Park

Camp Area 40 km NW of Nebo. Travel 17 km on Suttor Development Rd, turn N into Turrawulla Rd, signposted after passing Homevale-Mount Britton turnoff. 4WD vehicles only. Must Pre book

HEMA 14 D7 | 21 24 34 S | 148 30 13 E

77 Lake Elphinstone
☎ (07) 4944 5888

Camp Spot 136 km SW of Mackay. Turn W off Peak Downs Hwy 86 km SW of Mackay to Elphinstone. 4 km on Suttor Development Rd. Cold shower

HEMA 14 D7 | 21 32 18 S | 148 14 8 E

BIG RIG

78 Nebo Rest Area

Rest Area at Nebo

HEMA 14 E7 | 21 41 20 S | 148 41 15 E

BIG RIG

79 Nebo Showground
☎ 1300 47 22 27

Bowen St. Must register & pay at council office in Reynolds St before camping

HEMA 14 E7 | 21 41 2 S | 148 41 19 E

BIG RIG

80 Isaac River Rest Area

Rest Area 108 km NE of Clermont. 7 km NE of Moranbah turnoff

70

HEMA 14 F7 | 22 2 57 S | 148 7 53 E

BIG RIG

81 Rocky Dam Creek

Camp Spot 10 km NE of Koumala. Turn E into Landings Rd just N of Koumala. 6 km dirt road

HEMA 15 E8 | 21 32 57 S | 149 18 0 E

BIG RIG

82 Ilbilbie Caltex
☎ (07) 4950 3944

Parking Area at Ilbilbie.

HEMA 15 E8 | 21 42 17 S | 149 21 26 E

BIG RIG 20

83 Notch Point Road

Camp Spot 11 km E of Ilbilbie via Greenhill Rd & Notch Point Rd. 1 km dirt road. Limited camp spots alongside Marion Creek

HEMA 15 E9 | 21 43 24 S | 149 26 33 E

24

84 Yarrawonga Park Reserve

Camp Area 14 km E of Ilbilbie. Turn E onto Greenhill Rd, R onto Notch Point Rd, 9 km to gate, then 3 km of narrow rough sandy track. 4WD only

HEMA 15 E9 | 21 44 28 S | 149 28 28 E

85 Carmila Beach

Camp Area 6 km E of Carmila. Camp site off dirt road for 1 km. Last 300m narrow, sandy track

HEMA 15 E9 | 21 54 50 S | 149 27 47 E

86 Flaggy Rock Cafe
☎ 07 4950 2148

Parking Area at Flaggy Rock. Self Contained Vehicles only. Fee waived if cafe is patronised

HEMA 15 E9 | 21 58 13 S | 149 26 9 E

BIG RIG

87 Flaggy Rock Community Centre
☎ 07 4964 5140

Camp Area at Flaggy Rock, 7 km S of Carmila. 85 Flaggy Rock Rd. Self Contained Vehicles only. Entry from Flaggy Rock Rd. Caretaker on site

HEMA 15 E9 | 21 58 6 S | 149 26 43 E

BIG RIG 72

88 Brandy Bottle Camping & Recreation Reserve
☎ 0423 877 288

Camp Area 17 km S of Carmilla or 8 km N of Clairview Northern turnoff. 82943 Bruce Hwy. Limited number of sites, reservations essential. Fee includes golf. Signposted off Hwy

HEMA 15 E9 | 22 2 49 S | 149 29 7 E

90 Kalarka Roadhouse
☎ (07) 4956 0167

Camp Area at Kalarka

HEMA 15 F9 | 22 13 13 S | 149 29 32 E

BIG RIG

91 St Lawrence Recreational Reserve
Camp Spot 1 km W of St Lawrence. 5.5 km off Bruce Hwy
HEMA 15 F9 | 22 21 4 S | 149 31 11 E
BIG RIG

92 Waverley Creek Rest Area
Rest Area 8 km S of St Lawrence turnoff or 64 km N of Marlborough
1
HEMA 15 F9 | 22 26 19 S | 149 28 30 E
BIG RIG 24

93 Tooloombah Creek Roadhouse
☎ (07) 4935 6214
Camp Spot at Roadhouse. 42 km S of St Lawrence turn off or 32 km N of Marlborough. Self Contained Vehicles only. Call in at reception before parking
HEMA 15 F9 | 22 41 18 S | 149 37 41 E

94 Marlborough Hotel
☎ (07) 4935 6103
Camp Area at Marlborough. Head over railway line, turn R into Milman St. Check in with publican on arrival
HEMA 15 G9 | 22 48 48 S | 149 53 18 E
BIG RIG 24

95 Marlborough Caltex
☎ (07) 4935 6135
Camp Spot at Marlborough. Fee for showers. Check in at counter prior to camping. Showers close at 2000 hrs.
HEMA 15 G9 | 22 49 18 S | 149 53 29 E

96 Marlborough Rest Area
Rest Area at Marlborough. Next to swimming pool
HEMA 15 G9 | 22 48 51 S | 149 53 28 E
BIG RIG

97 Lotus Creek Tourist Centre
☎ (07) 4950 7135
Caravan Park Tourist Centre on Alternate Hwy 1. 130 km S of Sarina or 120 km N of Marlborough
HEMA 15 F8 | 22 20 53 S | 149 6 9 E
BIG RIG

98 Stanage Bay
Camp Spot at Stanage Bay. 100 km dirt road. Main camping area at boat ramp. Gold coin donation
HEMA 15 F9 | 22 8 10 S | 150 2 2 E
BIG RIG

99 Yaamba Rest Area
Rest Area at Yaamba
1
HEMA 15 G10 | 23 8 6 S | 150 22 7 E
BIG RIG

Notes...

100 Byfield Campstay
☎ (07) 4935 1002
Camp Area at Byfield. 53 Castle Rock Rd. Travel 2 km N of Byfield, turn L into Castle Rock Rd, then first on the L. Closed Feb-April
HEMA 15 G10 | 22 49 46 S | 150 37 56 E

101 Upper Stony Campground
☎ 13 74 68
Byfield State Forest
Camp Area 37 km N of Yeppoon. Turn W off Byfield Rd 27 km N of Yeppoon for 11 km of dirt road. 6 tonne load limit bridge. Bookings essential. 4WD vehicles only. Book online or at Byfield Store
HEMA 15 G10 | 22 53 31 S | 150 37 5 E

102 Red Rock Campground
☎ 13 74 68
Byfield State Forest
Camp Area 33 km N of Yeppoon. Turn E off Byfield Rd 32 km N of Yeppoon. 1 km dirt road. Maximum stay 14 days. Book online or at Byfield Store
HEMA 15 G10 | 22 52 25 S | 150 41 5 E

103 Water Park Creek Campground
☎ 13 74 68
Byfield State Forest
Camp Area 39 km N of Yeppoon. Turn E off Byfield Rd 36 km N of Yeppoon for 3 km. 1 km dirt road. Small Vehicles only. Bookings essential. Book online or at Byfield store
HEMA 15 G10 | 22 50 8 S | 150 40 20 E

104 Causeway Caravan Park
☎ (07) 4933 6356
Caravan Park 12 km S of Yeppoon. 11 The Esplanade
HEMA 15 G11 | 23 11 54 S | 150 47 16 E

105 Kershaw Gardens
Parking Area at Rockhampton. High Street opposite Bob Janes T-Mart. Self Contained Vehicles only
HEMA 15 H10 | 23 21 27 S | 150 31 9 E
48

106 Woolwash Lagoon
Parking Area 5 km SE of Rockhampton. Turn E off Bruce Hwy at Info Centre onto Port Curtis Rd for 4 km. Long narrow area between road & lake. Self Contained Vehicles only
HEMA 15 H10 | 23 25 59 S | 150 31 46 E
BIG RIG 24

107 Mount Larcom Rest Area
Rest Area at Mount Larcom
1
HEMA 15 H11 | 23 48 40 S | 150 58 50 E

108 Mount Larcom Showgrounds ☎ (07) 4975 1002
Camp Area at Mount Larcom. Entry off The Narrows Rd. No camping during show week (mid June). Caretaker on site
HEMA 15 H11 23 48 37 S 150 59 7 E
BIG RIG

109 Calliope River Camping Grounds
Rest Area 70 km N of Miriam Vale or 27 km S of Mount Larcom. 7 km N of Calliope turnoff. Turn W off Hwy onto Old Bruce Hwy beside Historical Village, follow road to river bank.
HEMA 15 J11 23 57 40 S 151 9 9 E
BIG RIG 48

110 Wallum Reserve
Rest Area at Barmundu, 21 km S of Calliope on the Gladstone-Monto Rd
HEMA 15 J11 24 8 17 S 151 11 45 E
BIG RIG 72

111 Boynedale Bush Camp
Camp Area at Boynedale, 31 km S of Calliope. 2 km E of Gladstone-Monto Rd, beside dam. Maximum stay 7 days. Small dogs only on leash
HEMA 15 J11 24 13 2 S 151 15 0 E
BIG RIG

112 Boyne River Rest Area
Rest Area 49 km SE of Mount Larcom or 49 km N of Miriam Vale. 1 km S of Benaraby. Beside river
HEMA 15 J11 24 0 39 S 151 20 26 E
BIG RIG 20

113 The Reef Caravan Park ☎ (07) 4974 7547
Caravan Park 5 km W of Agnes Water. Rocky Crossing Rd
HEMA 15 J12 24 14 50 S 151 51 39 E

114 Workmans Beach Camping Area ☎ (07) 4902 1515
Camp Area 1 km S of Agnes Water, via Springs Rd. Small vehicles only. Maximum stay 42 days. Cold showers
HEMA 15 J12 24 12 45 S 151 54 51 E

115 Bernie Christensen Rest Area
Rest Area 36 km S of Miriam Vale or 63 km N of Gin Gin
HEMA 15 K12 24 36 44 S 151 40 4 E
BIG RIG 48

116 Rosedale Royal Hotel & Caravan Park ☎ (07) 4156 5322
Caravan Park at Rosedale. 55 km NW of Bundaberg
HEMA 15 K12 24 37 44 S 151 54 59 E
BIG RIG

117 Norval Park Campground ☎ (07) 4153 8888
Camp Area 48 km N of Bundaberg. Via Bundaberg - Lowmead Rd. Entry via Norval Park Rd & Park Rd. Permit required before arrival, booking by phone or online via Bundaberg Tourism web site. Tent & Camper trailers only
HEMA 15 K12 24 36 32 S 152 7 49 E

118 Avondale Homestead Tavern ☎ (07) 4156 1206
Camp Area at Avondale. Large camping area next to the hotel, please check in at the bar
HEMA 15 K12 24 45 48 S 152 9 12 E
BIG RIG

119 Binnowee Bush Camp ☎ (07) 4157 8331
Camp Area 20 km W of Bundaberg. Take the Rosedale Rd for 16 km, turn W into Bucca Rd for 3 km. Signposted
HEMA 13 A12 24 49 42 S 152 11 24 E
BIG RIG

120 Gin Gin Rest Area
Rest Area 2 km N of Gin Gin
HEMA 13 A11 24 58 27 S 151 56 45 E
BIG RIG 20

121 Gin Gin Showgrounds ☎ (07) 4157 3223
Camp Area at Gin Gin. N end of town off King St. Caretaker on site
HEMA 13 A11 24 59 16 S 151 57 7 E
BIG RIG

122 Baffle Bobs Wallaville Hotel
☎ (07) 4157 6110

Camp Area at Wallaville. Turn off E 10 km S of Gin Gin. Seek permission for use of toilet at Hotel

HEMA 13 A11 25 4 32 S 151 59 43 E

BIG RIG

123 Mt Perry Caravan Park
☎ 07 4156 3850

Caravan Park at Mt Perry. 53 km W of Gin Gin

HEMA 13 A11 25 10 29 S 151 38 24 E

124 Sharon Nature Park

Rest Area 36 km E of Gin Gin or 15 km W of Bundaberg. 3 km W of Sharon

HEMA 13 A12 24 53 1 S 152 14 34 E

24

125 Bucca Hotel
☎ (07) 4157 8171

Camp Area 30 km W of Bundaberg. 5 North Bucca Rd

HEMA 13 A12 24 51 33 S 152 5 34 E

BIG RIG 72

126 Oaks Beach Caravan Village & Relocatable Homes Village
☎ (07) 4159 4353

Caravan Park at Bundaberg. Cnr Burnett Heads Rd & Rowlands Rd

HEMA 13 A12 24 46 13 S 152 24 52 E

127 Hinkler Lions Park

3

Rest Area at Bundaberg. 4 km SW of PO. Opposite airport

HEMA 13 A12 24 53 49 S 152 18 51 E

BIG RIG

128 Wallum Reserve

3

Rest Area 28 km SW of Bundaberg or 24 km N of Childers, on Isis Hwy

HEMA 13 A12 25 3 32 S 152 13 50 E

BIG RIG 24

129 Booyal Crossing

1

Camp Spot 30 km N of Childers or 33 km S of Gin Gin. Turn S into Booyal Dallarnil Rd, then W into Causeway Rd

HEMA 13 B12 25 13 45 S 152 0 34 E

BIG RIG 20

130 Paradise Dam
☎ (07) 4127 7278

Camp Area 35 km NE of Biggenden. Turn N off Isis Hwy into Gooroolba Biggenden Rd at Biggenden. Follow signs

HEMA 13 B11 25 21 17 S 151 55 10 E

BIG RIG

Notes...

131 Apple Tree Creek Rest Area

1

Rest Area 7 km N of Childers or 49 km SE of Gin Gin

HEMA 13 B12 25 13 9 S 152 14 18 E

BIG RIG 20

132 Brierley Wines
☎ (07) 4126 1297

Camp Area 7 km SE of Childers. 574 Rainbows Rd. Turn S into Taylors St in town, this then turns into Rainbows Rd. Free overnight camping to customers. Booking required & must be on site by 1500 hrs. Open Tue to Sun

HEMA 13 B12 25 17 15 S 152 17 23 E

24

133 Torbanlea Sports Complex

Camp Area at Torbanlea. Torbanlea - Pialba Rd. Caretaker will find you for payment

HEMA 13 B13 25 20 47 S 152 35 59 E

BIG RIG 72

134 Iron Ridge Park
☎ (07) 4126 8410

Camp Area at Redridge 16 km NW of Childers on the Goodwood Rd. Not suitable for tents

HEMA 13 B12 25 10 6 S 152 22 29 E

BIG RIG

135 Lenthall Dam
☎ (07) 4129 4833

Camp Area 21 km SW of Howard. Turn W off Bruce Hwy 12 km S of Howard or 16 km N of Maryborough, for 2 km, then 7 km NW along rough dirt road. Cold showers. Limited spaces, pre-booking of sites required

HEMA 13 B12 25 24 14 S 152 32 0 E

48

136 Wongi Waterholes Camping Area
☎ 13 74 68

Wongi State Forest Recreation Area

Camp Area 21 km SW of Howard. Turn W off Bruce Hwy 12 km S of Howard or 16 km N of Maryborough, for 9 km of dirt road. Cold showers. No camping at lake. Bookings necessary

HEMA 13 B12 25 26 15 S 152 32 37 E

137 Cheery Nomad RV Park & Farmstay
☎ 0414 754 638

Camp Area 6 km N of Maryborough off Fazio Rd. 113 Lawson Rds

HEMA 13 B13 25 29 34 S 152 42 28 E

BIG RIG

138 Maryborough Showground & Equestrian Park
☎ (07) 4123 5311

Camp Area at Maryborough off the Bruce Hwy. Camping closed during major events

HEMA 13 B13 25 30 22 S 152 39 46 E

BIG RIG 48

QUEENSLAND

139 Petrie Park RV Camp & Rest Area

Rest Area 2 km NW of Tiaro. Turn W over railway line 1 km N of PO, then immediately R for 200m, then L to E bank of Mary River. Self Contained Vehicles only. Limited space

HEMA 13 C13 25 42 52 S 152 34 37 E

20

140 Tiaro Memorial Park

1

Rest Area at Tiaro. Overnight parking in Inman St behind town park. Cold showers. Toilet 100m across park

HEMA 13 C13 25 43 43 S 152 35 2 E

BIG RIG 48

141 Bauple RV Stop

Camp Spot at Bauple Village. 100m from Museum. Self Contained Vehicles only

HEMA 13 C13 25 48 44 S 152 37 8 E

20

142 Rosendale Park RV Stop

1

Rest Area on Bauple Dr. 500m E of Bruce Hwy. Self Contained Vehicles only

HEMA 13 C13 25 50 23 S 152 35 43 E

20

143 Gunalda Rest Area

1

Rest Area 2 km N of Gunalda turnoff

HEMA 13 C13 25 59 10 S 152 34 13 E

BIG RIG 20

144 Prince Alfred Hotel (The Gundy)

☎ (07) 4129 3182

Camp Area at Gundiah. Check in at hotel bar

HEMA 13 C13 25 49 58 S 152 32 31 E

$ BIG RIG

145 Ross Creek Store Rest Area

Rest Area at Goomboorian. 25 km NE of Gympie or 32 km SW of Tin Can Bay

HEMA 13 D13 26 5 26 S 152 46 2 E

24

146 Standown Park

☎ (07) 5486 5144

Camp Area at Goomboorian. 24 km NE of Gympie or 24 km SW of Tin Can Bay. Radtke Rd, opposite Counter Rd. No facilities for children. GPS at entry point

HEMA 13 D13 26 2 8 S 152 47 32 E

$+ BIG RIG

147 Log Dump Campground

☎ (07) 4121 1800

Tuan State Forest

Camp Area 44 km SE of Maryborough. S on Cooloola Coast Rd for 38 km, turn E into Tinnanbar Rd for 6 km. Small vehicles only. Dirt road. Must be pre-booked

HEMA 13 C13 25 48 38 S 152 55 26 E

$

148 Hedleys Campground

☎ (07) 4121 1800

Tuan State Forest

Camp Area 44 km SE of Maryborough. S on Cooloola Coast Rd for 38 km, turn E into Tinnanbar Rd for 9 km. Small vehicles only. Dirt road. Beware that the camp area can only be accessed via private property, access fee applies payable to property owner

HEMA 13 C13 25 47 56 S 152 56 51 E

$ $

149 Inskip Point Campground

☎ 13 74 68

Camp Area 12 km N of Rainbow Beach. Permit required, must be obtained prior to arrival

HEMA 13 C13 25 49 0 S 153 4 15 E

$

150 Curra Country Club

☎ (07) 5483 1686

Parking Area. 7 David Dr, adjacent to Matilda Service Station, 18 km N of Gympie. Donation required at the bar

HEMA 13 D13 26 5 0 S 152 34 49 E

$ BIG RIG 20

151 Chatsworth Park

1

Rest Area 59 km S of Tiaro or 6 km N of Gympie

HEMA 13 D13 26 8 58 S 152 37 37 E

BIG RIG 20

152 Archery Park

1

Parking Area 1 km N of Gympie. Cross St, W side of Hwy. Area not level

HEMA 13 D13 26 11 19 S 152 39 13 E

BIG RIG

153 Glastonbury Creek Campground

☎ 13 74 68

Brooyar State Forest

Camp Area 26 km W of Gympie. Turn N at Glastonbury 16 km W of Gympie for 10 km. 6 km dirt road. Must pre book

HEMA 13 D12 26 9 18 S 152 33 5 E

$ BIG RIG

154 Marg McIntosh Park

Rest Area at Upper Widgee, 26 km W of Gympie. 2 km N of Widgee Primary School

HEMA 13 D12 26 11 30 S 152 25 55 E

BIG RIG 20

155 Six Mile Creek Rest Area

1

Rest Area 6 km S of Gympie or 4 km N of Kybong

HEMA 13 D13 26 13 54 S 152 41 49 E

BIG RIG 20

156 Cedar Grove Campground

☎ 13 74 68

Amamoor State Forest

Camp Area 12 km W of Amamoor, via Amamoor Creek Rd. 5 km dirt road. Must pre-book

HEMA 13 D12 26 21 58 S 152 35 13 E

$ BIG RIG

QUEENSLAND

157 Amamoor Creek Campground
☎ 13 74 68

Amamoor State Forest

Camp Area 16 km W of Amamoor, via Amamoor Creek Rd. 5 km dirt road

HEMA 13 D12 26 21 26 S 152 33 24 E

BIG RIG

158 Kandanga RV Stop
☎ (07) 5488 4605

Parking Area at Kandanga. Self Contained Vehicles only. Toilets across road during opening hours, gold coin donation for upkeep appreciated

HEMA 8 A7 26 23 13 S 152 40 37 E

BIG RIG 72

159 Kandanga Bowls Club
☎ 0438 843 195

Parking Area at Kandanga, Bowls Club Rd, enter off the Kandanga Amamoor Rd

HEMA 8 A7 26 23 11 S 152 40 34 E

BIG RIG

160 Mary Valley Koolewong Par 3 Golf Course
☎ (07) 5484 5999

Camp Spot 5 km N of Imbil. Head N on Kandanga Imbil Rd for 4.5 km, turn E into Barsby Rd, 800m to entrance on L. Self Contained Vehicles only. Limited sites, phone ahead

HEMA 8 A7 26 25 38 S 152 41 12 E

161 Carters Ridge RV Stop

Parking Area at Carters Ridge. Cnr Julile & Poulsen Rd next to RFS shed on grassed area. Store next door. Toilet & BBQ across the road in Mary Fereday Park. Self Contained Vehicles only. Do not park in Mary Fereday Park

HEMA 8 A7 26 27 4 S 152 45 52 E

24

162 Borumba Campground

☎ (07) 5488 6662

Camp Area at Borumba Dam, 12 km W of Imbil, via Yabba Creek Rd

HEMA 8 B6 26 30 6 S 152 35 17 E

BIG RIG

163 Matilda Roadhouse

Parking Area 10 km S of Gympie or 40 km N of Cooroy. Behind roadhouse. Some noise from trucks. Fee for shower payable at roadhouse

HEMA 13 D13 26 18 19 S 152 43 13 E

BIG RIG 24

164 Kin Kin Oval

Camp Area at Kin Kin. Entry at the roundabout Main St. Payment & keys at Pub

HEMA 13 D13 26 15 46 S 152 52 30 E

BIG RIG 48

165 Elanda Point Canoe Company
☎ (07) 5485 3165

Camp Area 6 km N of Boreen Point. 1.5 km dirt road, entry at end of road

HEMA 13 D13 26 15 15 S 152 59 57 E

BIG RIG

166 Pomona Showgrounds
☎ (07) 5485 1477

Camp Area at Pomona. Exhibition St. Maximum stay 6 weeks

HEMA 9 A8 26 21 36 S 152 51 28 E

BIG RIG

167 Cobb & Co Nine Mile Campgrounds
☎ (07) 5483 5065

Camp Area 10 km S of Gympie or 40 km N of Cooroy. Turn E onto Tandur Rd at Matilda Roadhouse, travel 6 km, then turn S onto Old Noosa Rd for 300m. GPS at Gate. Pets on application call ahead to check

HEMA 13 D13 26 17 8 S 152 45 55 E

BIG RIG

168 Gheerulla Campground
☎ 13 74 68

Mapleton Forest Reserve

Camp Area 10 km E of Kenilworth. Turn SE 23 km W of Eumundi or 8 km E of Kenilworth for 2 km. Very small area. Rough dirt road

HEMA 8 C7 26 34 12 S 152 47 29 E

Notes...

169 Kenilworth Show & Recreation Grounds
(07) 5446 0131

Camp Area at Kenilworth. S side of town. Elizabeth Street

HEMA 8 C7 26 35 56 S 152 43 34 E

BIG RIG

170 Little Yabba Picnic Area

Picnic Area 6 km SW of Kenilworth on Kenilworth - Maleny Rd

HEMA 8 C7 26 37 27 S 152 41 25 E

171 Charlie Moreland Campground
13 74 68

Imbil State Forest

Camp Area 12 km SW of Kenilworth. Turn W off Kenilworth-Maleny Rd 7 km S of Kenilworth. 5 km dirt road

HEMA 8 C6 26 36 59 S 152 39 2 E

BIG RIG

172 Booloumba Creek No.4 Campground
13 74 68

Conondale National Park

Camp Area 14 km SW of Kenilworth. Turn W off Kenilworth-Maleny Rd 7 km S of Kenilworth. 7 km dirt road. High clearance 4WD recommended. Alternative 2WD dry-weather access is via Sundy Creek Rd, Funnels Hut Rd & Booloumba Creek Rd. Not suitable for large vehicles

HEMA 8 C6 26 38 46 S 152 38 52 E

173 Crystal Waters Eco Caravan Park
(07) 5494 4590

Caravan Park at Conondale. 65 Kilcoy Lane, via Aherns Rd off Maleny-Kenilworth Rd

HEMA 8 D7 26 46 54 S 152 43 0 E

174 Maleny Showgrounds
(07) 5494 2008

Camp Area at Maleny. Turn S 1 km W of PO onto Myrtle St for 800m. Pay at Secretary's Office next to Pavillion. Contact prior as showground closed to camping during some events

HEMA 9 D8 26 45 45 S 152 50 56 E

BIG RIG 72

175 Camp Cooroora
(07) 5442 5285

Camp Area 10 km NE of Cooroy. Take the Noosa-Cooroy Rd towards Noosa turn L into Sivyers Rd, turn R into Gumboil Rd, following signs to camp. Bookings essential

HEMA 9 A9 26 22 51 S 152 56 14 E

BIG RIG

176 Eumundi Showgrounds
(07) 5442 7224

Camp Area at Eumundi. 1.3 km N of Eumundi on Black Stump Rd. Bookings essential as gates are locked

HEMA 9 B9 26 28 13 S 152 56 34 E

177 Eumundi RV Stop Over
(07) 5442 8762

Parking Area at Eumundi, Cnr Albert St & Napier St. Fees collected. Mobile 0409 280 775

HEMA 9 B9 26 28 34 S 152 57 13 E

BIG RIG 48

178 Cooroy's No Worries Caravan Parking
0427 006 018

Parking Area at Cooroy. 154 Holts Rd. Take Cooroy exit 230B off M1, follow ramp for 200m, Turn R into Mayall St under Hwy & L at Holts Rd. 1.5 km. Entry signposted RH side

HEMA 9 A9 26 26 31 S 152 55 8 E

BIG RIG 96

179 Browns Creek Rest Area

Rest Area 2 km N of Yandina. On Old Bruce Hwy. Limited space

HEMA 9 B9 26 32 19 S 152 57 21 E

48

180 Dunethin Rock Scout Camp
(07) 5446 6246

Camp Area 7 km SE of Yandina or 6 km NW of Bli Bli on the Yandina - Bli Bli Rd. 1 km gravel road from the Yandina entry. Road narrow & steep. Bookings essential

HEMA 9 C9 26 34 42 S 153 0 39 E

72

181 Muller Park

6

Rest Area 1 km E of Bli Bli. David Low Way. E side of Maroochy River

HEMA 9 C9 26 37 21 S 153 2 51 E

182 Coochin Creek Campground
13 74 68

Beerburrum State Forest

Camp Area 30 km NE of Caboolture. Only from the Southbound lane, turn E 11 km S of Caloundra turnoff or 25 km N of Caboolture turnoff onto Roys Rd for 4 km, then S for 500m. Vehicles over 5 tonne access via Bells Creek Rd. Maximum stay 21 days. Must pre book

HEMA 9 E10 26 52 52 S 153 2 46 E

183 Glasshouse Mountains Camping Ground
(07) 5496 9588

Camp Area 4.5 km W of Glasshouse Mountain PO. 2001 Old Gympie Rd, via Coonowrin Rd

HEMA 9 F9 26 54 50 S 152 55 17 E

BIG RIG

184 Caboolture Showgrounds
(07) 5495 2030

Camp Area at Caboolture. Beerburrum Rd. 4 km N of Town Centre

HEMA 9 G9 27 4 4 S 152 56 55 E

BIG RIG

185 Watson Park Convention Centre
Seventh Day Adventist Church
☎(07) 3204 6544
Camp Area at Dakabin. Old Gympie Rd, check in with caretaker. No alcohol, drugs or tobacco permitted
HEMA 5 B8 27 13 13 S 152 59 21 E
BIG RIG

186 Dayboro Showgrounds
☎(07) 3425 1156
Camp Area at Dayboro. Mt Mee Rd
HEMA 4 A4 27 11 25 S 152 49 25 E
BIG RIG

187 Wyllie Park Rest Area
58
Rest Area 1 km S of Petrie. 755 Gympie Rd, beside North Pine River
HEMA 5 D9 27 16 22 S 152 58 49 E
BIG RIG

188 Redcliffe Showgrounds
☎(07) 3205 0555
Camp Area at Redcliffe. Scarborough Rd. Motorhome must be 30ft or over
HEMA 5 B12 27 13 30 S 153 6 22 E
BIG RIG

189 Pine Rivers Showground
☎0459 023 346
Camp Area at Lawnton, Gympie Rd. Check in required with caretaker. Closed to campers in August for Show. Maximum stay 21 days
HEMA 5 D8 27 17 7 S 152 59 13 E
BIG RIG

190 Samford Showground
☎(07) 3289 7057
Camp Spot 7 km W of Samford, off Mt Glorious Rd & Showgrounds Dr. Gates usually locked. Contact caretaker. Closed during July for show
HEMA 4 G4 27 22 14 S 152 49 29 E
BIG RIG

Cairns to Cloncurry
Kennedy Highway, Gulf and Burke Developmental Roads

191 James Earl Lookout
Camp Spot 14.5 km S of Lakeland or 100 km N of Mt Carbine. Limited sites
HEMA 17 C10 15 58 29 S 144 49 44 E

192 Palmer River Roadhouse
☎(07) 4060 2020
Camp Area at Roadhouse. 31 km S of Lakeland or 113 km N of Mount Molloy. Limited generator power
HEMA 17 C9 16 6 25 S 144 46 37 E
BIG RIG

193 Mt Carbine Caravan Park
☎(07) 4094 3160
81
Caravan Park at Mt Carbine. Peninsula Hwy. 300m SE of roadhouse. No cats
HEMA 18 B1 16 31 42 S 145 8 21 E
BIG RIG

194 Bustard Downs
☎(07) 4094 3110
Camp Area 22 km N of Mount Molloy or 10 km S of Mount Carbine. Turn E into East Mary Rd 21 km N of Mount Molloy. Signposted on East Mary Rd
HEMA 18 B1 16 34 31 S 145 11 31 E
BIG RIG

195 Rifle Creek Rest Area
Rest Area 1 km N of Mt Molloy, 33 km S of Mossman or 41 km N of Mareeba. Cold showers. Donation requested
HEMA 18 C2 16 39 58 S 145 19 42 E
BIG RIG 48

196 Tableland Caravan Park
☎(07) 4094 1145
Caravan Park near Julatten. 1045 Rex Hwy. 10.5 km from the Captain Cook Hwy
HEMA 18 B2 16 32 44 S 145 22 59 E

197 Kerribee Park Camping Grounds
☎(07) 4092 1654
Camp Spot 3 km W of Mareeba, 614 Dimbulah Rd.
HEMA 18 E2 16 59 34 S 145 23 43 E
BIG RIG

198 Dimbulah Caravan Park
☎(07) 4093 5242
27
Caravan Park at Dimbulah. Burke Developmental Rd
HEMA 18 F1 17 9 5 S 145 6 20 E
BIG RIG

199 Eureka Creek
Camp Spot 9 km W of Dimbulah. Burke Development Rd
HEMA 17 E10 17 11 12 S 145 2 29 E
BIG RIG 20

200 Emu Creek Outback Holiday Station
☎(07) 4094 8313
Camp Area at Emu Creek Station. 30 km W of Dimbulah on Burke Development Rd. Turn N 23 km W of Dimbulah, cross railway line into driveway. 7 km to Station. Dirt road
HEMA 17 E10 17 17 14 S 144 58 34 E

Notes...

201 Rooky's Retreat
☎ (07) 4093 5465
Camp Area at Petford. Must call ahead to book site. No after hours check in
HEMA 17 E10 17 20 34 S 144 55 47 E

202 Tamarind Gardens Caravan Park
☎ (07) 4094 8201
Caravan Park at Almaden. Schools Rd
HEMA 17 E9 17 20 15 S 144 40 41 E

203 Chillagoe Rodeo Grounds
☎ (07) 4094 7111
Camp Area at Chillagoe. From Queen St turn W onto Frew St, entrance 700m on R. Pay fees at the Hub Information Office in Queen St
HEMA 17 E9 17 9 29 S 144 30 58 E

204 Chillagoe Observatory & Eco Lodge
☎ (07) 4094 7155
Caravan Park at Chillagoe. 1 Hospital Ave
HEMA 17 E9 17 8 55 S 144 31 39 E

205 Chillagoe Tourist Village
☎ (07) 4094 7177
Caravan Park at Chillagoe. 21 - 23 Queen St
HEMA 17 E9 17 9 20 S 144 31 28 E

206 Walsh River
Camp Spot 32 km W of Chillagoe on the Burke Development Rd
HEMA 17 E9 16 59 24 S 144 17 58 E

207 Walsh River West
Camp Spot 120 km W of Chillagoe or 450 km E of Karumba on the Burke Development Rd
HEMA 17 D8 16 32 43 S 143 46 58 E

208 Mount Mulligan Station
☎ (07) 4098 1149
Camp Area at Mount Mulligan Station. Enquires at Homestead. 55 km N of Dimbulah. Dirt road not suitable for caravans
HEMA 17 E10 16 51 21 S 144 52 28 E

209 Granite Gorge Nature Park
☎ (07) 4093 2259
Camp Area 14 km SW of Mareeba via Rankin St & Chewko Rd. Riverside camping. Fee includes entry to 3 gorge walks
HEMA 18 E2 17 2 31 S 145 21 6 E

210 Riverside Caravan Park
☎ (07) 4092 2309
Caravan Park at Mareeba. 13 Egan St. E side of town
HEMA 18 E3 17 0 4 S 145 25 39 E

211 Ringers Rest
☎ 0447 136 865
Camp Area 7 km from PO SE of Mareeba, take Kennedy Hwy E turn S into Tinaroo Creek Rd then turn S into Fichera Rd. Alt phone number 0421 253 259
HEMA 18 E3 17 1 55 S 145 27 15 E

212 Walkamin Central Van Park
☎ (07) 4093 3990
1
Caravan Park at Walkamin. 15 km S of Mareeba or 18 km N of Atherton. S side of town
HEMA 18 E3 17 7 56 S 145 25 41 E

213 Rocky Creek Memorial Park & Camping Reserve
1
Rest Area 23 km S of Mareeba or 12 km N of Atherton. Donation box at toilet block
HEMA 18 F3 17 10 54 S 145 27 19 E

214 Kairi Lions Park
Parking Area at Kairi. Irvine St, opposite hotel
HEMA 18 F3 17 12 57 S 145 32 34 E

215 Platypus Campground
☎ 13 74 68
Danbulla State Forest
Camp Area 6 km NE of Tinaroo off Danbulla Forest Dr. 3 km dirt road. Small sites not suitable for caravans. Must be prebooked. Lakefront
HEMA 18 F3 17 9 38 S 145 33 34 E

216 Downfall Creek Campground
☎ 13 74 68
Danbulla State Forest
Camp Area 8 km NE of Tinaroo off Danbulla Forest Dr. 5 km dirt road. Must be prebooked. Lakefront
HEMA 18 F4 17 8 52 S 145 35 18 E

217 Kauri Creek Campground
☎ 13 74 68
Danbulla State Forest
Camp Area 10 km NE of Tinaroo off Danbulla Forest Dr. 7 km dirt road. Must be prebooked. Lakefront
HEMA 18 F4 17 8 18 S 145 35 53 E

218 School Point Campground
☎ 13 74 68

Danbulla State Forest

Camp Area 18 km NE of Tinaroo off Danbulla Forest Dr. 13 km dirt road. Lakefront. Small sites not suitable for caravans. Must be prebooked

HEMA 18 F4 | 17 8 54 S | 145 36 39 E

219 Fong-On Bay Campground
☎ 13 74 68

Danbulla State Forest

Camp Area 22 km E of Tinaroo off Danbulla Forest Dr. 19 km dirt road. Lakefront. Must be prebooked

HEMA 18 F4 | 17 9 13 S | 145 35 55 E

220 Genazzano Retreat Motorhome & Caravan Park
☎ (07) 4095 3232

Camp Area 16 km W of Yungaburra. Take Gillies Hwy W for 9 km, turn N into Powley Rd for 7 km

HEMA 18 F4 | 17 12 8 S | 145 37 1 E

BIG RIG

221 Wild River Caravan Park
☎ (07) 4096 2121

Caravan Park at Herberton. Holdcroft Dr. E end of town

HEMA 18 G2 | 17 22 3 S | 145 23 20 E

BIG RIG

222 Irvinebank Town Common
☎ (07) 4096 4176

Camp Spot at Irvinebank. 28 km W of Herberton (12 km dirt road) or 45 km E of Petford. Open grassed area opposite tavern

HEMA 18 G1 | 17 25 41 S | 145 12 13 E

BIG RIG

223 Lakeside Motor Inn & Caravan Park
☎ (07) 4095 3563

Caravan Park at Yungaburra. Tinaburra Dr, follow signs to public boat ramp

HEMA 18 F3 | 17 15 5 S | 145 35 0 E

BIG RIG

224 Lake Eacham Caravan Park
☎ (07) 4095 3730

Caravan Park 6 km SE of Yungaburra. 198 Lakes Dr

HEMA 18 G4 | 17 17 44 S | 145 38 7 E

BIG RIG

225 Henrietta Creek
☎ 13 74 68

25

Wooroonooran National Park

Camp Area 22 km SE of Millaa Millaa or 33 km W of Bruce Hwy/ Palmerston Hwy intersection. Must be prebooked

HEMA 18 H5 | 17 35 56 S | 145 45 31 E

226 Ravenshoe Heritage Steam Railway & Travellers Rest
☎ 07 4097 7402

Camp Area at Ravenshoe. Just S of town centre, enter from Kuridilla St. Maximum stay 7 Days

HEMA 18 J3 | 17 36 30 S | 145 28 59 E

BIG RIG

227 Archer Creek Rest Area

1

Rest Area 16 km W of Ravenshoe or 28 km E of Mount Garnet. Large area beside creek

HEMA 18 J2 | 17 38 48 S | 145 20 51 E

BIG RIG 48

228 Junction Parking Area

1

Parking area 67 km W of Mount Garnet 51 km E of Mount Surprise

HEMA 17 F10 | 18 8 19 S | 144 48 43 E

BIG RIG 20

229 Planet Earth Adventures
☎ (07) 4062 3127

Camp Area at Mount Surprise

HEMA 17 F9 | 18 8 49 S | 144 19 7 E

BIG RIG

230 Greenvale Caravan Park & Cabins
☎ (07) 4788 4155

A7

Caravan Park at Greenvale. 3 Kylee Crt

HEMA 17 H10 | 19 0 4 S | 144 59 0 E

BIG RIG

231 Greenvale RV Stop

Parking Area on Redbank Dr, N of the Three Rivers Hotel. Self Contained Vehicles only

HEMA 17 H10 | 18 59 55 S | 144 58 56 E

BIG RIG 24

232 Elizabeth (O'Briens) Creek Campgound
☎ (07) 4062 3001

Camp Area 30 km NW of Mount Surprise township. Turn onto O'Briens Creek Rd opposite Police Station. Dirt road

HEMA 17 F9 | 18 2 43 S | 144 3 42 E

BIG RIG

233 Routh Creek

1

Parking Area 65 km W of Mount Surprise or 20 km E of Georgetown

HEMA 17 G8 | 18 18 43 S | 143 46 35 E

BIG RIG

Notes...

234 The Einasleigh Hotel
(07) 4062 5222

Camp Spot at Einasleigh. Check in with publican, fee for showers & power. Maximum stay 7 days

HEMA 17 G9 18 30 45 S 144 5 40 E

BIG RIG

235 Copperfield Lodge Camping & Caravan Park
(07) 4062 5102

Caravan Park at Einasleigh. Baroota St. Open between Easter & Labour day weekend in October. No children allowed

HEMA 17 G9 18 30 35 S 144 5 37 E

236 Oaks Rush Outback Resort
(07) 4062 4100

Camp Area 40 km S of Einasleigh via Georgetown-Mt Garnet Rd, turn S onto Kidston Rd for 19 km. Signposted

HEMA 17 G9 18 49 41 S 144 10 5 E

237 Forsayth Tourist Park & Store
(07) 4062 5548

Caravan Park at Forsayth. First St

HEMA 17 G8 18 35 16 S 143 36 6 E

BIG RIG

238 Goldfields Caravan Park
(07) 4062 1269

Caravan Park at Georgetown. St George St

HEMA 17 G8 18 17 14 S 143 32 58 E

BIG RIG

239 Midway Caravan Park
(07) 4062 1219

Caravan Park at Georgetown. North St (Main Hwy). 500m W of PO

HEMA 17 G8 18 17 22 S 143 32 48 E

BIG RIG

240 Cumberland Mine Historic Site

Picnic Area 20 km W of Georgetown or 128 km E of Croydon. Beside chimney & billabong

HEMA 17 G8 18 17 59 S 143 21 4 E

BIG RIG 20

241 Gilbert River East

Parking Area 72 km W of Georgetown or 75 km E of Croydon

HEMA 16 F7 18 11 36 S 142 53 49 E

BIG RIG

242 Gilbert River

Rest Area 75 km W of Georgetown or 73 km E of Croydon. W side of River

1

HEMA 16 F7 18 12 2 S 142 52 25 E

BIG RIG 48

243 Leichhardt Lagoon Camping Park
(07) 4745 1330

Camp Area 128 km W of Croydon or 24 km SE of Normanton. 800m off Hwy through gate. Closed during wet season. AH 0487 675 173

HEMA 16 F5 17 51 2 S 141 7 47 E

BIG RIG

244 Norman River Reserve
(07) 4745 1065

Parking Area 2 km NE of Normanton. 150m N of Norman River. Self Contained Vehicles only. Permit required from Info Centre. Do not confuse this site with the "day use" rest area on the SW side of the Norman River

HEMA 16 F5 17 39 48 S 141 5 26 E

48

245 Normanton North Rest Area

Rest Area 2 km N of Normanton, 100m S of Norman River

HEMA 16 F5 17 39 52 S 141 5 13 E

246 Gilbert River North

Camp Spot 112 km NE of Karumba on Burke Development Rd. Tracks on S side of river

HEMA 16 E5 17 10 17 S 141 45 59 E

247 Pebbles Drop

Camp Spot 175 NE of Karumba on Burke Development Rd at Wyaaba Creek. Various tracks off road

HEMA 16 D6 16 41 34 S 141 57 1 E

248 QT125

Rest Area 39 km S of Normanton or 161 km N of Burke & Wills Roadhouse

83

HEMA 16 F4 17 57 40 S 140 54 13 E

BIG RIG 20

249 Flinders River

Camp Spot 62 km S of Normanton or 138 km N of Burke & Wills Roadhouse. Sites both sides of the river

HEMA 16 G4 18 9 27 S 140 51 35 E

250 QT124

Rest Area 78 km S of Normanton or 114 km N of Burke & Wills Roadhouse

83

HEMA 16 G4 18 17 17 S 140 48 35 E

BIG RIG 20

251 Bang Bang Rest Area

Rest Area 112 km S of Normanton or 90 km N of Burke & Wills Roadhouse

83

HEMA 16 G4 18 31 36 S 140 39 11 E

BIG RIG 20

252 Donors Hill Rest Area

Rest Area 135 km S of Normanton or 63 km N of Burke & Wills Roadhouse

83

HEMA 16 G4 18 41 54 S 140 30 43 E

BIG RIG 20

253 Cowan Downs
☎ (07) 4745 2200

Parking Area 169 km S of Normanton or 28 km N of Burke & Wills Roadhouse

83

HEMA 16 H4 | 18 59 12 S | 140 26 5 E

BIG RIG

254 Burke & Wills Roadhouse
☎ (07) 4742 5909

Camp Area 207 km S of Normanton or 183 km N of Cloncurry

HEMA 16 H4 | 19 13 37 S | 140 20 49 E

BIG RIG

255 Firey Creek

Camp Spot 118 km W of Burke & Wills Roadhouse or 31 km E of Gregory Downs. Various tracks off road

HEMA 16 G3 | 18 41 45 S | 139 31 21 E

BIG RIG

256 Gregory Downs

Camp Spot at Gregory Downs. On vacant land NW cnr of Lawn Hill Rd & Wills Development Rd. Facilities opposite Hotel. No camping on river bank per Council

84

HEMA 16 G2 | 18 38 51 S | 139 15 13 E

BIG RIG

257 Adels Grove Camping Park
☎ (07) 4748 5502

Camp Area 88 km W of Gregory Downs. Bookings essential in high season. Dirt road

HEMA 16 G1 | 18 41 24 S | 138 31 54 E

BIG RIG

258 Boodjamulla (Lawn Hill) National Park
☎ 13 74 68

Boodjamulla National Park

Camp Area 10 km W of Adels Grove. Bookings essential in high season. Dirt road

HEMA 16 G1 | 18 42 5 S | 138 29 16 E

259 Miyumba Bush Camp
☎ 13 74 68

Boodjamulla National Park

Camp Area 185 km N of Camooweal via "Riversleigh", 48 km S of Adels Grove. 4.2 km S of Riversleigh Fossil site. Open March - Oct. Reservations essential. Dry weather access only

HEMA 16 H2 | 19 1 6 S | 138 43 21 E

260 Beames Brook

Camp Spot 93 km N of Gregory Downs or 27 km S of Burketown, 3 km S of Savannah Way jcn. Tracks off road, small vehicles only

HEMA 16 F2 | 17 52 37 S | 139 20 35 E

261 Burketown North River

Camp Spot along river N of Burketown. 6.5 km N of town on Beames St & Truganini Rd

HEMA 16 F3 | 17 43 58 S | 139 35 32 E

262 Albert River

Parking Area 3 km SE of Burketown. NE side of river, tracks to sites

HEMA 16 F3 | 17 45 55 S | 139 33 42 E

263 Leichhardt River Falls

Camp Spot 72 km E of Burketown or 154 km W of Normanton

HEMA 16 G3 | 18 13 15 S | 139 52 35 E

BIG RIG

264 Tower Layby

Camp Spot 100 km E of Burketown or 126 km W of Normanton

HEMA 16 G3 | 18 9 9 S | 140 5 48 E

BIG RIG

265 Little Bynoe River

Camp Spot 189 km E of Burketown or 37 km W of Normanton. Tracks on SW side of river, limited space

HEMA 16 F4 | 17 52 0 S | 140 49 28 E

266 Kingfisher Camp
☎ (07) 4745 8212

Camp Area 170 km SW of Burketown or 366 km SE of Borroloola. Signposted

HEMA 16 F1 | 17 52 7 S | 138 17 5 E

BIG RIG

267 Hells Gate Roadhouse
☎ (07) 4745 8258

Camp Area at Hells Gate Roadhouse

HEMA 16 F1 | 17 27 18 S | 138 21 22 E

268 Jack and Lil's Parking Area

Parking Area 89 km SE of Burke & Wills Roadhouse or 156 km NW of Julia Creek. Small area

HEMA 16 J5 | 19 40 7 S | 140 56 33 E

269 Terry Smith Lookout

Rest Area 103 km S of Burke & Wills Roadhouse or 78 km N of Cloncurry

83

HEMA 16 J4 | 20 4 49 S | 140 13 39 E

BIG RIG 20

Townsville to Camooweal

Flinders and Barkly Highways

270 Reid River

Rest Area 58 km S of Townsville or 75 km NE of Charters Towers

A6

HEMA 14 A5 | 19 45 24 S | 146 50 2 E

BIG RIG 20

Notes...

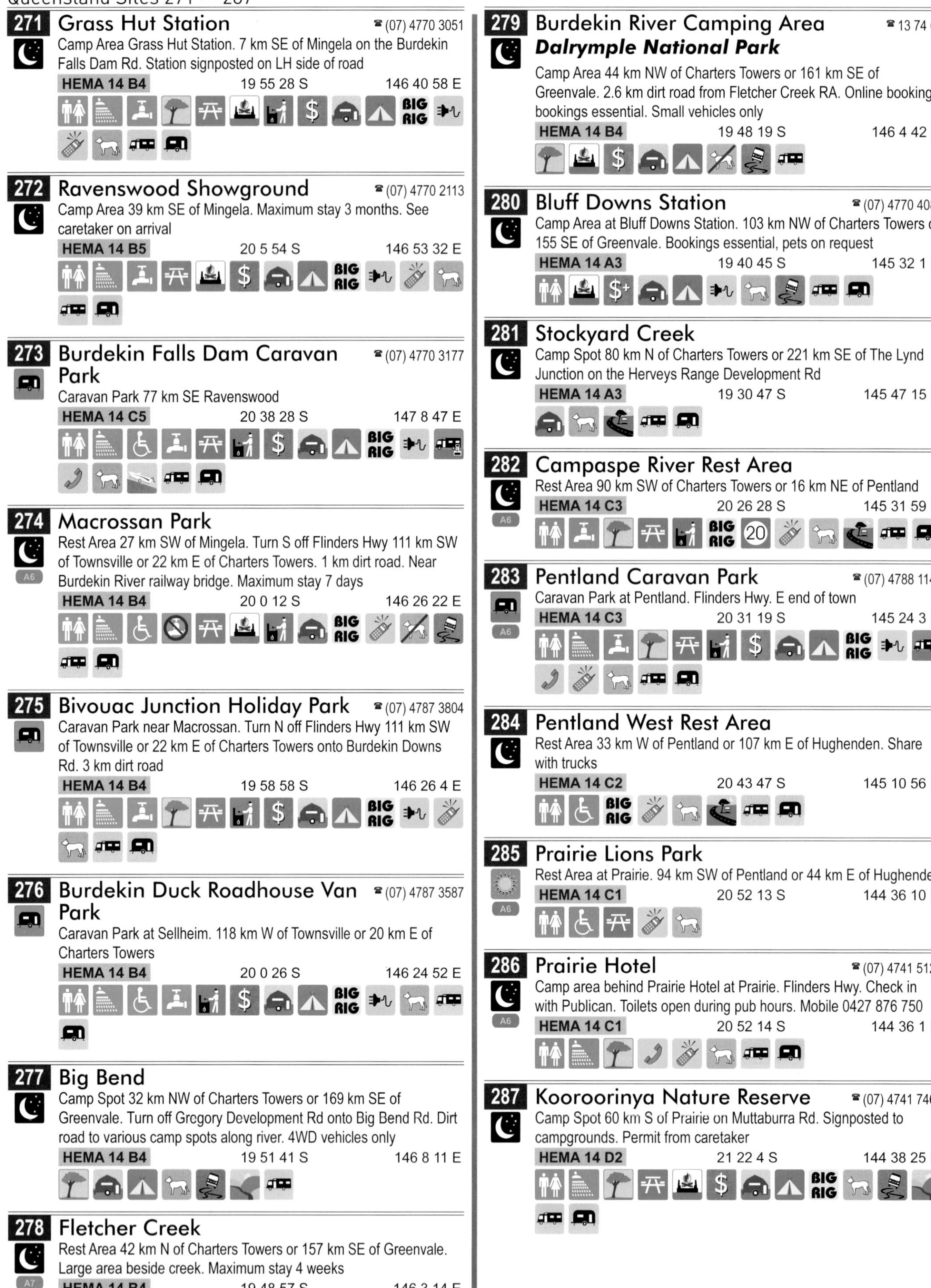

271 Grass Hut Station
☎ (07) 4770 3051
Camp Area Grass Hut Station. 7 km SE of Mingela on the Burdekin Falls Dam Rd. Station signposted on LH side of road
HEMA 14 B4 19 55 28 S 146 40 58 E

272 Ravenswood Showground
☎ (07) 4770 2113
Camp Area 39 km SE of Mingela. Maximum stay 3 months. See caretaker on arrival
HEMA 14 B5 20 5 54 S 146 53 32 E

273 Burdekin Falls Dam Caravan Park
☎ (07) 4770 3177
Caravan Park 77 km SE Ravenswood
HEMA 14 C5 20 38 28 S 147 8 47 E

274 Macrossan Park
A6
Rest Area 27 km SW of Mingela. Turn S off Flinders Hwy 111 km SW of Townsville or 22 km E of Charters Towers. 1 km dirt road. Near Burdekin River railway bridge. Maximum stay 7 days
HEMA 14 B4 20 0 12 S 146 26 22 E

275 Bivouac Junction Holiday Park
☎ (07) 4787 3804
Caravan Park near Macrossan. Turn N off Flinders Hwy 111 km SW of Townsville or 22 km E of Charters Towers onto Burdekin Downs Rd. 3 km dirt road
HEMA 14 B4 19 58 58 S 146 26 4 E

276 Burdekin Duck Roadhouse Van Park
☎ (07) 4787 3587
Caravan Park at Sellheim. 118 km W of Townsville or 20 km E of Charters Towers
HEMA 14 B4 20 0 26 S 146 24 52 E

277 Big Bend
Camp Spot 32 km NW of Charters Towers or 169 km SE of Greenvale. Turn off Gregory Development Rd onto Big Bend Rd. Dirt road to various camp spots along river. 4WD vehicles only
HEMA 14 B4 19 51 41 S 146 8 11 E

278 Fletcher Creek
A7
Rest Area 42 km N of Charters Towers or 157 km SE of Greenvale. Large area beside creek. Maximum stay 4 weeks
HEMA 14 B4 19 48 57 S 146 3 14 E

279 Burdekin River Camping Area
☎ 13 74 68
Dalrymple National Park
Camp Area 44 km NW of Charters Towers or 161 km SE of Greenvale. 2.6 km dirt road from Fletcher Creek RA. Online booking, bookings essential. Small vehicles only
HEMA 14 B4 19 48 19 S 146 4 42 E

280 Bluff Downs Station
☎ (07) 4770 4084
Camp Area at Bluff Downs Station. 103 km NW of Charters Towers or 155 SE of Greenvale. Bookings essential, pets on request
HEMA 14 A3 19 40 45 S 145 32 1 E

281 Stockyard Creek
Camp Spot 80 km N of Charters Towers or 221 km SE of The Lynd Junction on the Herveys Range Development Rd
HEMA 14 A3 19 30 47 S 145 47 15 E

282 Campaspe River Rest Area
A6
Rest Area 90 km SW of Charters Towers or 16 km NE of Pentland
HEMA 14 C3 20 26 28 S 145 31 59 E

283 Pentland Caravan Park
☎ (07) 4788 1148
A6
Caravan Park at Pentland. Flinders Hwy. E end of town
HEMA 14 C3 20 31 19 S 145 24 3 E

284 Pentland West Rest Area
Rest Area 33 km W of Pentland or 107 km E of Hughenden. Share with trucks
HEMA 14 C2 20 43 47 S 145 10 56 E

285 Prairie Lions Park
A6
Rest Area at Prairie. 94 km SW of Pentland or 44 km E of Hughenden
HEMA 14 C1 20 52 13 S 144 36 10 E

286 Prairie Hotel
☎ (07) 4741 5121
A6
Camp area behind Prairie Hotel at Prairie. Flinders Hwy. Check in with Publican. Toilets open during pub hours. Mobile 0427 876 750
HEMA 14 C1 20 52 14 S 144 36 1 E

287 Kooroorinya Nature Reserve
☎ (07) 4741 7460
Camp Spot 60 km S of Prairie on Muttaburra Rd. Signposted to campgrounds. Permit from caretaker
HEMA 14 D2 21 22 4 S 144 38 25 E

288 Pyramid Campground
☎ 13 74 68

Porcupine Gorge National Park

Camp Area 73 km N of Hughenden, via Kennedy Developmental Rd & Emu Plains Rd. 1 km dirt road. Advanced booking essential in the holidays, ebooking online or at Info Centre Hughenden

HEMA 14 B1 20 20 44 S 144 27 39 E

289 Emu Swamp Campground
☎ 13 74 68

Blackbraes Resources Reserve

Camp Area 170 km N of Hughenden. 20.5 km from park entrance. 4WD only, suitable for high clearance caravans & camper trailers only. Permit required, closed during wet season

HEMA 14 A1 19 25 3 S 144 9 47 E

290 Hughenden Allan Terry Caravan Park
☎ (07) 4741 1190

Caravan Park at Hughenden. 2 Resolution St. 2 km SW of PO

HEMA 14 C1 20 50 57 S 144 11 46 E

BIG RIG

291 Rest Easi Motel & Caravan Park
☎ (07) 4741 1633

Caravan Park at Hughenden. Flinders Hwy

HEMA 14 C1 20 50 55 S 144 11 59 E

292 Hughenden RV Parking Area
☎ (07) 4741 1021

Parking Area at Hughenden. E end of Stansfield St on N side of road. Self Contained Vehicles only. Permit required from Info Centre, Grey St adjacent to showgrounds

HEMA 14 C1 20 50 41 S 144 12 20 E

BIG RIG 48

293 Marathon Rest Area
A6

Rest Area 65 km W of Hughenden or 47 km E of Richmond. Share with trucks

HEMA 17 K8 20 51 31 S 143 34 7 E

BIG RIG 20

294 Richmond RV Parking Area
A6

Parking Area at Richmond. 300m off main rd, via Harris St & Hillier St. Self Contained Vehicles only. Register at Kronosaurus Korner

HEMA 16 K7 20 43 44 S 143 8 36 E

BIG RIG 72

295 Maxwelton Rest Area
A6

Rest Area 50 km W of Richmond or 99 km E of Julia Creek

HEMA 16 K7 20 43 23 S 142 40 42 E

BIG RIG 20

296 Corella Creek Country Stay N Store
☎ (07) 4746 7555

A5

Camp Area at Nelia. 1 Main St. 2 km off Flinders Hwy

HEMA 16 K6 20 39 17 S 142 12 49 E

BIG RIG

297 Julia Creek
☎ (07) 4746 7690

Camp Spot 1.3 km E of Julia Creek. 200m off main road. Camping either side of bridge. Permit required from Info Centre. Self Contained Vehicles only

HEMA 16 K6 20 39 21 S 141 45 22 E

96

298 Julia Creek Caravan Park
☎ (07) 4746 7108

Caravan Park at Julia Creek. Old Normanton Rd. 500m N of PO

HEMA 16 K6 20 39 9 S 141 44 41 E

299 Oorindi Rest Area
A6

Rest Area 69 km W of Julia Creek or 68 km E of Cloncurry

HEMA 16 K5 20 38 32 S 141 6 15 E

BIG RIG 20

300 Wal's Camp
☎ (07) 4742 1606

Camp Area 1 km S of Cloncurry. Turn S at bowls club onto Sheaffe & Philips Sts. Follow signs. Mobile 0408 700 302

HEMA 16 K4 20 42 58 S 140 29 47 E

BIG RIG

301 Burke & Wills Memorial Rest Area (Corella River)
A2

Rest Area 44 km W of Cloncurry or 77 km E of Mt Isa

HEMA 16 K4 20 46 56 S 140 6 45 E

20

302 Clem Walton Park & Corella Dam
A2

Camp Spot at Corella Dam. 65 km E of Mt Isa or 53 km W of Cloncurry. Turn S off Hwy, through gate, its only locked if the water is high so check lock. Veer L at first Y jcn. At 2nd Y veer L to Clem Walton Park (1.7 km). Veer R to camp spots by dam. Toilets at Clem Walton

HEMA 16 K3 20 49 36 S 140 2 56 E

303 Fountain Springs Rest Area
A2

Rest Area 60 km W of Cloncurry or 61 km E of Mt Isa

HEMA 16 K3 20 48 1 S 139 59 48 E

BIG RIG 20

304 Mary Kathleen Old Mine Township

Parking Area 63 km W of Cloncurry or 56 km E of Mt Isa. This is private land please respect notices for no litter & no fires

HEMA 16 K3 20 46 50 S 139 58 24 E

BIG RIG

Notes...

305 West Leichhardt Station
☎ (070 4743 8947

Camp Area at West Leichardt Station. 30 km NW of Mt Isa via Lake Julius Rd. Bookings are essential, pets on request

HEMA 16 K3 20 37 12 S 139 42 0 E

BIG RIG

306 Lake Moondarra Picnic Area

Picnic Area at Lake Moondarra

HEMA 16 K3 20 35 17 S 139 34 37 E

BIG RIG

307 WW2 Airfield

A2

Rest Area 50 km NW of Mt Isa or 139 km E of Camooweal. Near monument on Barkly Hwy

HEMA 16 K2 20 22 23 S 139 15 50 E

BIG RIG 48

308 David Hall Rest Area

A2

Rest Area 90 km NW of Mt Isa or 99 km E of Camooweal

HEMA 16 K2 20 11 23 S 138 53 52 E

BIG RIG 48

309 Inca Creek Rest Area

A2

Rest Area 119 km NW of Mt Isa or 70 km E of Camooweal

HEMA 16 J2 20 3 58 S 138 45 34 E

BIG RIG 48

310 Camooweal Billabong

A2

Camp Spot at Camooweal. Head W across Georgina River Bridge turn S immediately W of bridge onto dirt road. Follow gravel road for 2 km, tracks for various camping spots next to river

HEMA 16 J1 19 55 37 S 138 6 54 E

BIG RIG 72

311 Nowranie Waterhole
☎ 13 74 68

Camooweal Caves National Park

Picnic Area 21 km S of Camooweal signposted off the Camooweal Urandangi Rd. 19 km dirt road

HEMA 16 J1 20 2 37 S 138 10 19 E

Rockhampton to Cloncurry

Capricorn and Landsborough Highways

312 Westwood Rest Area

A4

Rest Area at Westwood, behind the hall

HEMA 15 H10 23 37 18 S 150 9 23 E

313 Duaringa Rest Area

A4

Rest Area at Duaringa. E end of town

HEMA 15 H9 23 43 18 S 149 40 20 E

BIG RIG 48

314 Duaringa Motel & Caravan Park
☎ (07) 4935 7202

Caravan Park Edward St off Hwy

HEMA 15 H9 23 43 14 S 149 40 9 E

BIG RIG

315 Bridgewater Creek Rest Area

A4

Rest Area 26 km W of Duaringa or 10 km E of Dingo

HEMA 15 H8 23 39 50 S 149 25 41 E

BIG RIG 20

316 Dingo Caravan Park
☎ (07) 4935 9121

Caravan Park at Dingo. Cairns St, off Fitzroy Developmental Rd. N end of town

HEMA 15 H8 23 38 33 S 149 19 48 E

BIG RIG

317 Munall Campground

Blackdown Tableland National Park

Camp Area in Blackdown Tableland National Park. Turn off is 11 km W of Dingo then campsite is 8 km from Park entrance. Steep winding road suitable for small vehicles only, not suitable for caravans. Bookings essential, E Permit required

HEMA 15 H8 23 47 41 S 149 4 12 E

318 Bluff Hotel
☎ (07) 4982 9158

Parking Area at Bluff. Parking at hotel, free camping if a meal or beverage is purchased from the bar

HEMA 15 H8 23 34 56 S 149 4 13 E

319 Blackwater Rest Area

A4

Rest Area at Blackwater. Mackenzie St. Next to water tower

HEMA 15 H9 23 35 6 S 148 52 48 E

320 Bedford Weir

Camp Area 27 km N of Blackwater. Turn N 2 km W of Blackwater. S side of weir upper banks only, near Ski Club. Maximum stay 7 days. Donation please for upkeep

HEMA 15 H8 23 22 21 S 148 50 20 E

BIG RIG

321 Emerald Botanical Gardens

A4

Rest Area at Emerald. E end of town beside Nogoa River bridge. Facilities in gardens, but no camping inside

HEMA 14 H7 23 31 49 S 148 9 59 E

20

322 Emerald Showgrounds
☎ 0400 258 714

Camp Area at Emerald. Capricorn Hwy. Call caretaker before arrival to access key & payment

HEMA 14 H7 23 31 23 S 148 9 7 E

BIG RIG

323 Emerald Rest Area
Rest Area at Emerald. W end of town, near Tourist Information Centre
HEMA 14 H7 23 31 18 S 148 9 20 E
A4

324 Higher Ground Homestay
(07) 4987 4562
Camp area 16 km SW Emerald. 1467 Selma Rd. Some camping on river. Self Contained Vehicles only
HEMA 14 H7 23 37 28 S 148 4 8 E

325 Anakie Gemfields Caravan Park
(07) 4985 4142
Caravan Park at Anakie. Richardson Street
HEMA 14 H6 23 33 8 S 147 44 41 E

326 Sapphire Reserve
Picnic Area at Sapphire. Rifle Range Rd, opposite general store
HEMA 14 H6 23 27 57 S 147 43 13 E
BIG RIG 48

327 Tomahawk Creek Fossicking Area
Camp Spot 42 km NW of Rubyvale. Take the Rubyvale Clermont Rd, turn W into Recklaw Rd for 6.5 km, then R into Recklaw Park Track for 10.5 km. Well signposted. Permit required for fossicking & camping
HEMA 14 H6 23 21 6 S 147 27 35 E

328 Bogantungan Rest Area
Rest Area at Bogantungan. 98 km W of Emerald or 70 km E of Alpha. 400m S of Hwy. Toilets at Railway Station 1 km from rest area
A4
HEMA 14 H5 23 38 53 S 147 17 22 E
BIG RIG 24

329 Drummond Range Lookout
Rest Area 108 km W of Emerald or 60 km E of Alpha. 300m N of Hwy. Small vehicles only. Unlevel area steep approach
A4
HEMA 14 H5 23 38 38 S 147 12 16 E

330 Drummond West Rest Area
Rest Area 120 km W of Emerald or 48 km E of Alpha
HEMA 14 H5 23 40 14 S 147 5 27 E
BIG RIG

331 Belyando River Rest Area
Rest Area 137 km W of Emerald or 31 km E of Alpha. Area subject to flooding
A4
HEMA 14 H5 23 39 38 S 146 55 51 E
BIG RIG

332 Jericho Showground
Camp Area 1 km NE of Jericho. At E end of town, turn N just E of railway crossing.
A4
HEMA 21 F11 23 35 42 S 146 7 54 E
BIG RIG

333 Redbank Park
Camp Area on river bank in Jericho. Turn S off Hwy into Darwin St & R into Lyon St to park. Donation appreciated
A4
HEMA 21 F11 23 36 21 S 146 7 47 E
BIG RIG 48

334 Outback Pioneer Centre & Bush Camping
(07) 4651 0420
Slygo Station
Camp Area 27 km SW of Jericho or 94 km NE of Blackall on the Jericho-Blackall Rd
HEMA 21 F11 23 46 36 S 145 59 27 E

335 Barcaldine East Rest Area
Rest Area 2 km E of Barcaldine
A4
HEMA 21 F10 23 33 9 S 145 18 26 E
BIG RIG 20

336 Barcaldine Showgrounds
(07) 4651 1211
Camp Area at Barcaldine. E end of town. Fees payable at Council Office or see Caretaker. Maximum stay 72 hours
HEMA 21 F10 23 33 2 S 145 17 37 E
BIG RIG 72

337 Lloyd Jones Weir
Camp Area 15 km SW of Barcaldine. Turn W off Landsborough Hwy 5 km S of Barcaldine for 9 km. 1 km dirt road. Donation appreciated
HEMA 21 F10 23 39 0 S 145 12 57 E
BIG RIG

338 Aramac Shire Caravan Park
(07) 4652 9999
Caravan Park at Aramac. 67 km N of Barcaldine. Booker St. Pay fee at Council Office or after hours book return at Aramac Library, Gordon St
HEMA 21 E10 22 58 2 S 145 14 20 E
BIG RIG

339 Lake Dunn
Camp Area 63 km NE of Aramac. Off Eastmere Rd. Owners collect fees daily
HEMA 21 D11 22 36 16 S 145 40 24 E
BIG RIG

Notes...

340 The Broadwater
Camp Spot 6 km S of Muttaburra via Muttaburra Westside Rd & Broadwater Rd. Bush campsites along Thomson River
HEMA 21 E9 22 39 39 S 144 34 6 E

341 Muttaburra Caravan Park
☎ (07) 4658 7191
Caravan Park at Muttaburra. Cnr Mary & Bridge Sts
HEMA 21 D9 22 35 36 S 144 33 7 E
BIG RIG

342 Pump Hole
Camp Spot 4.5 km W of Muttaburra. Turn N off the Muttaburra-Aramac Rd 3 km W of Muttaburra. 1.2 km dirt road to camp spots
HEMA 21 D9 22 34 59 S 144 33 57 E

343 Packsaddle Creek Rest Area
A2
Rest Area 30 km W of Barcaldine or 76 km E of Longreach. Share with trucks
HEMA 21 F10 23 32 7 S 144 59 46 E
BIG RIG

344 Dartmouth Rest Area
A2
Rest Area 63 km W of Barcaldine or 43 km E of Longreach. Shared with trucks
HEMA 21 F9 23 30 44 S 144 40 13 E
BIG RIG

345 Newstead Creek Rest Area
A2
Rest Area 74 km W of Barcaldine or 32 km E of Longreach
HEMA 21 F9 23 30 8 S 144 33 6 E
BIG RIG

346 12 Mile Hotel Site Rest Area
Rest Area 20 km S of Ilfracombe or 70 km N of Isisford
HEMA 21 F9 23 39 25 S 144 30 27 E
BIG RIG

347 Apex Riverside Park
A2
Rest Area 4 km NW of Longreach. 1 km E of Hwy, via River Farms Rd. Maximum stay 4 days
HEMA 21 F9 23 24 37 S 144 13 47 E
BIG RIG

348 Macsland Rest Area
A2
Rest Area 24 km NW of Longreach or 156 km SE of Winton
HEMA 21 E9 23 16 34 S 144 7 39 E
BIG RIG 20

349 Morella Rest Area
A2
Rest Area 68 km NW of Longreach or 112 km SE of Winton
HEMA 21 E8 22 58 31 S 143 51 36 E
BIG RIG 20

350 Chorregon Rest Area
A2
Rest Area 112 km NW of Longreach or 68 km SE of Winton
HEMA 21 E8 22 41 28 S 143 34 24 E
BIG RIG

351 Crawford Creek
A2
Rest Area 132 km NW of Longreach or 46 km SE of Winton
HEMA 21 D8 22 33 29 S 143 25 30 E
BIG RIG 20

352 Pelican Caravan Park
☎ (07) 4657 1478
A2
Caravan Park at Winton. 92 Elderslie St
HEMA 20 D7 22 23 25 S 143 2 5 E
BIG RIG

353 North Gregory Hotel
☎ (07) 4657 0647
Parking Area at Winton. Area behind Hotel entry off Oondooroo St. Register at hotel
HEMA 20 D7 22 23 21 S 143 2 21 E
BIG RIG

354 Long Waterhole
Camp Spot 4 km S of Winton. Turn E off the Winton-Jundah Rd 2 km S of Winton for 2 km of dirt road. Signposted
HEMA 20 D7 22 24 46 S 143 3 33 E
BIG RIG

355 Bough Shed Hole Campground
☎ 13 74 68
Bladensburg National Park
Camp Area 28 km S of Winton. Turn E off the Winton-Jundah Rd 14 km S of Winton onto Opalton Rd for 12 km, then N along River Gums Route for 2 km. Beside creek. 14 km dirt road. Permits required must be pre booked
HEMA 20 D7 22 33 37 S 142 57 39 E

356 Carisbrooke Station
☎ (07) 4657 0084
Camp Area at Carisbrooke Station. 85 km SW of Winton. Via Cork Mail Rd. Pets by arrangement
HEMA 20 E7 22 39 36 S 142 31 17 E

357 Opalton Bush Camp
Camp Area at Opalton. 124 km S of Winton
HEMA 20 E7 23 14 45 S 142 45 46 E

358 Corfield Rest Area
62
Rest Area at Corfield. 86 km NE of Winton or 128 km SW of Hughenden. Donation for RFDS to stay
HEMA 21 C8 21 42 51 S 143 22 27 E
48

359 Ayshire Hills
Parking Area 65 km NW of Winton or 99 kn SE of Kynuna
HEMA 20 D7 21 58 17 S 142 39 40 E
BIG RIG

360 Wanora Downs Rest Area
A2
Rest Area 90 km NW of Winton or 74 km SE of Kynuna
HEMA 20 C7 21 45 20 S 142 31 7 E
BIG RIG

361 Kynuna East Rest Area
Rest Area 18 km E of Kynuna or 146 km W of Winton
HEMA 20 C6 21 32 25 S 142 4 37 E
BIG RIG

362 Blue Heeler Caravan Park
(07) 4746 8650
Caravan Park at Kynuna. At Blue Heeler Hotel
A2
HEMA 20 C6 21 34 43 S 141 55 23 E
BIG RIG

363 Kynuna Roadhouse Caravan Park
(07) 4746 8683
Caravan Park at Kynuna. No bookings
A2
HEMA 20 C6 21 34 44 S 141 55 13 E
BIG RIG

364 Walkabout Hotel
(07) 4746 8424
Camp Area at McKinlay. Cnr Middleton St & Landsborough Hwy
A2
HEMA 20 C5 21 16 19 S 141 17 23 E
BIG RIG

365 Fullarton River North Rest Area
Rest Area 46 km NW of McKinlay or 60 km SE of Cloncurry. 2 km W of Fullarton River. Share with trucks
A2
HEMA 20 B5 21 1 16 S 140 56 24 E
BIG RIG

Longreach - Birdsville - Mt Isa

366 Isisford Road Rest Area
Rest Area 121 km S of Longreach or 96 km N of Jundah
HEMA 21 G8 24 14 1 S 143 33 27 E
BIG RIG

367 Broadwater Waterhole Camping Area
13 74 68
Lochern National Park
Camp Area in Lochern National Park. Turn W 100 km S Longreach or 45 km N of Stonehenge onto access Rd. Follow for 45 km to waterhole t/off. Signposted. Dirt road 4WD recommended
HEMA 21 G8 24 6 19 S 143 21 13 E

368 Stonehenge Caravan Park
(07) 4658 5857
Caravan Park at Stonehenge. Stratford St
HEMA 21 G8 24 21 16 S 143 17 11 E
BIG RIG

Notes...

369 Swan Vale Rest Area
Rest Area 179 km SW of Longreach or 39 km N of Jundah, on Thompson Developmental Rd
HEMA 21 G8 24 35 9 S 143 16 8 E
BIG RIG

370 Jundah Caravan Park
(07) 4658 6225
Caravan Park at Jundah. Miles St
HEMA 20 H7 24 49 51 S 143 3 37 E
BIG RIG

371 Thomson River
Camp Spot 1 km W of Jundah or 95 km N of Windorah
HEMA 20 H7 24 49 48 S 143 3 4 E
BIG RIG

372 Little Boomerang Waterhole Camping Area
13 74 68
Welford National Park
Camp Area 60 km SE of Jundah on the Barcoo River. Turn W off the Jundah-Quilpie Rd. Campground is approx 10 km from turn off. Signposted. 4WD recommended. Dirt road. Small vehicles only. Must be pre-booked.
HEMA 21 H8 25 10 33 S 143 8 23 E

373 Yaraka Town Park
(07) 4657 5526
Camp Area at Yaraka. Behind the town hall next to swimming pool
HEMA 21 H9 24 52 59 S 144 4 43 E
BIG RIG

374 Cooper Creek
Camp Spot 10 km E of Windorah or 238 km NW of Quilpie. Various sites along riverbank
HEMA 20 J7 25 22 14 S 142 44 46 E
BIG RIG

375 Windorah Caravan Park
(07) 4656 3063
Caravan Park at Windorah. 1 Albert St
HEMA 20 J7 25 25 13 S 142 39 9 E
BIG RIG

376 JC Hotel Ruins
Camp Spot 75 km W of Windorah or 34 km E of Birdsville Developmental Rd Jcn
HEMA 20 J6 25 22 38 S 141 53 55 E
BIG RIG

377 Morney Rest Area
Rest Area 108 km W of Windorah or 95 km E of Betoota on the Diamantina Developmental Rd
HEMA 20 J6 25 22 50 S 141 37 24 E
BIG RIG

378 Haddon Corner
Camp Spot 55 km SW of Diamantina Developmental Rd & Birdsville Developmental Rd. Sandy road, caution
HEMA 22 A4 25 59 46 S 140 59 58 E
BIG RIG

379 Deons Lookout
Rest Area 200 km W of Windorah or 20 km E of Betoota, on the Birdsville Developmental Rd
HEMA 22 A4 25 43 4 S 140 53 40 E
BIG RIG

380 Betoota Rest Area
Rest Area at Betoota
HEMA 22 A3 25 41 36 S 140 44 52 E
BIG RIG

381 Cuppa Rest Area
Rest Area 81 km W of Betoota or 85 km E of Birdsville, on the Birdsville Developmental Rd
HEMA 22 A2 25 40 0 S 140 4 1 E
BIG RIG

382 Birdsville Windmill
Parking Area 2 km E of Birdsville, on riverbank near windmill
HEMA 22 A1 25 54 22 S 139 22 24 E
BIG RIG

383 Cacoory Ruins
Rest Area 81 km N Birdsville or 107 km S of Bedourie. Alternate sites on N side of creek
HEMA 20 H3 25 14 34 S 139 33 30 E
BIG RIG

384 Cuttaburra Crossing Rest Area
Rest Area 121 km N of Birdsville or 68 km S of Bedourie
HEMA 20 H3 24 54 49 S 139 38 58 E
BIG RIG

385 Monkira Rest Area
Rest Area on Diamantina Development Rd, 121 km E of Eyre Dev. Rd Jcn or 138 km W of Birdsville Dev. Rd Jcn
HEMA 20 H4 24 49 11 S 140 32 28 E
BIG RIG

386 No 3 Bore Rest Area
Rest Area on Diamantina Development Rd. 28 km E of Eyre Development Rd jcn
HEMA 20 G3 24 28 31 S 139 48 33 E
BIG RIG

387 King Creek
Rest Area 22 km S of Bedourie or 2 km N of the Diamantina Development Rd Jcn
HEMA 20 G3 24 31 4 S 139 33 28 E

388 Simpson Desert Oasis Caravan Park
☎ (07) 4746 1291
Caravan Park at Bedourie. Herbert St, opposite Roadhouse
HEMA 20 G3 24 21 23 S 139 28 16 E
$ BIG RIG

389 Bedourie Campground
Camp Area at Bedourie. Nappa St next to Aquatic Spa, S end of town. Fees payable at Info Centre
HEMA 20 G3 24 21 45 S 139 28 12 E
$ BIG RIG

390 Vaughan Johnson Lookout
Rest Area on Diamantina Development Rd, 88 km N of Bedourie or 107 km S of Boulia. Access via 3 km of steep dirt Rd. Small vehicles only
HEMA 20 F3 23 41 21 S 139 38 7 E
20

391 Amaroo Picnic Area
Picnic Area on Diamantina Development Rd, 89 km N of Bedourie or 106 km S of Boulia
HEMA 20 F3 23 40 44 S 139 38 9 E

392 Boulia Caravan Park
☎ (07) 4746 3320
83
Caravan Park at Boulia. Winton Rd
HEMA 20 E3 22 54 36 S 139 55 4 E
$ BIG RIG

393 Burke River
Camp Spot 5 km NE of Boulia. Turn N onto Chatsworth-Boulia Rd (known as Cloncurry Rd), then onto Racecourse Rd. Veer L at signs follow track behind racecourse to river
HEMA 20 E3 22 53 24 S 139 56 19 E

394 Old Police Barracks Waterhole
Picnic Area 25 km N of Boulia via Selwyn Rd. 1.5 km E of road, signposted. Dirt road
HEMA 20 E4 22 43 12 S 140 1 52 E
BIG RIG

395 Hunters Gorge Camping Area
☎ 13 74 68
Diamantina National Park
Camp Area 183 km SE of Boulia via Springvale Rd. Signposted, follow track 4 km to Mundawerra Waterhole. 4WD only. Must be pre booked
HEMA 20 F5 23 40 55 S 141 6 8 E
$

396 Gum Hole Camping Area
☎ 13 74 68
Diamantina National Park
Camp Area 180 km SE of Boulia via Springvale Rd. Signposted, follow track 4 km to Gumhole. 4WD only. Small vehicles only, limited space
HEMA 20 F5 23 40 21 S 140 59 13 E
$

397 Hamilton Hotel Historic Site
Rest Area 76 km E of Boulia or 286 km W of Winton
83
HEMA 20 E4 22 46 23 S 140 34 54 E
BIG RIG 20

398 Lilley Vale
Rest Area 146 km E of Boulia or 216 km W of Winton
83
HEMA 20 E5 22 36 14 S 141 12 54 E
BIG RIG 20

399 Hotel Hilton
Parking Area at Middleton. Opposite the hotel
HEMA 20 D5 22 21 11 S 141 32 59 E
BIG RIG

400 Poddy Creek Rest Area
Rest Area 90 km W of Winton or 271 km E of Boulia
HEMA 20 D6 22 12 46 S 142 13 49 E
BIG RIG 20

401 Georgina River
Camp Spot 122 km W of Boulia or 124 km E of Tobermorey Station. Dirt road. Both sides of bridge. 4WD recommended
HEMA 20 E2 22 54 44 S 138 52 19 E
BIG RIG

402 Peak Creek
Rest Area 64 km N of Boulia or 84 km S of Dajarra
83
HEMA 20 D3 22 24 40 S 139 39 47 E
BIG RIG

403 Dajarra Campground
Camp Area at Dajarra. Fee for power
83
HEMA 20 C3 21 41 46 S 139 30 49 E
BIG RIG

404 Dangi Bush Resort ☎ (07) 4748 4988
Camp Area at Urandangie. Free camping if you spend a gold coin in the pub
HEMA 20 C1 21 36 33 S 138 19 0 E
BIG RIG

Charters Towers to Banana

Gregory and Dawson Highways

405 Cape River
Parking Area 112 km S of Charters Towers or 91 km N of Belyando Crossing
A7
HEMA 14 C4 20 59 16 S 146 25 13 E
BIG RIG

406 Belyando Crossing Service Station Caravan Park ☎ (07) 4983 5269
Caravan Park at Belyando Crossing. Gregory Developmental Rd. $2 deposit for toilet key
A7
HEMA 14 D5 21 31 56 S 146 51 31 E

407 Mount Coolon Hotel ☎ (07) 4983 5530
Camp Area at Mount Coolon
HEMA 14 D5 21 23 6 S 147 20 33 E
BIG RIG

408 Belyando South
Parking Area 31 km S of Belyando Crossing
HEMA 14 E5 21 46 20 S 146 58 18 E
BIG RIG

409 Clermont Caravan Park ☎ (07) 4983 1927
Caravan Park at Clermont. Haig St. 500m SE of PO
HEMA 14 G6 22 49 39 S 147 38 46 E
BIG RIG

410 BP Roadhouse
Parking Area at Clermont. Patronise shop for free showers & parking
HEMA 14 G6 22 48 7 S 147 38 46 E
BIG RIG 24

411 Theresa Creek Dam ☎ (07) 4983 2327
Camp Area 22 km SW of Clermont. See caretaker
HEMA 14 G6 22 58 16 S 147 33 13 E

412 Bundoora Dam
Camp Area 69 km NE of Capella or 26 km SW of Middlemount. Turn W 200m N of German Creek or 2.8 km S of German Creek Mine entrance. Go over railway line 400m to dam. Rough road
HEMA 14 G7 22 57 13 S 148 32 15 E
BIG RIG

413 Virgin Rock Rest Area
Rest Area 1.5 km N of Springsure or 63.5 km S of Emerald. W side of road
A7
HEMA 14 J7 24 5 37 S 148 5 48 E
BIG RIG 20

414 Rolleston Caravan Park ☎ (07) 4984 3145
Caravan Park at Rolleston. Comet St
A7
HEMA 14 J7 24 27 54 S 148 37 21 E
BIG RIG

415 Bauhinia Store ☎ (07) 4996 4146
Camp Area at Bauhinia
HEMA 15 K8 24 34 13 S 149 17 31 E
BIG RIG

416 Moura Apex River Park
Rest Area 66 km E of Bauhinia or 7 km W of Moura. Beside river. Donation appreciated to upkeep facility
60
HEMA 15 K9 24 35 58 S 149 54 36 E
BIG RIG

Notes...

Rockhampton to Toowoomba

Burnett Highway

417 Royal Hotel
☎ (07) 4934 0120

Camp Area at Bouldercombe. Cnr Burnett Hwy & Mount Usher Rd. Toilets in park across the road

HEMA 15 H10 | 23 34 17 S | 150 28 7 E

BIG RIG 48

418 Mount Morgan Motel & Van Park
☎ (07) 4938 1952

17

Caravan Park at Mount Morgan. Cnr Burnett Hwy & Showgrounds Rd

HEMA 15 H10 | 23 39 37 S | 150 23 13 E

$+ BIG RIG

419 Dululu Rest Area

17

Rest Area at Dululu, 70 km SW of Rockhampton or 75 km N of Biloela. Bryant St, S end of town, near tennis courts. Fee for showers & power. Keys from Hotel. No generators allowed

HEMA 15 H10 | 23 50 54 S | 150 15 40 E

$ BIG RIG 48

420 Goovigen Showground

Camp Area at Goovigen, Stone Cres. Pay fee at Goovigen Hotel

HEMA 15 J10 | 24 8 44 S | 150 17 8 E

$ BIG RIG 48

421 Country Caravan Park
☎ (07) 4998 1103

Caravan Park at Baralaba. 16 Wooroonah Rd. 500m SW of PO. Limited Sites

HEMA 15 J9 | 24 11 8 S | 149 48 56 E

$+

422 Baralaba Showgrounds

Camp Area at Baralaba. Entry off Wooroonah Rd

HEMA 15 J9 | 24 11 6 S | 149 48 54 E

$ BIG RIG

423 Neville Hewitt Weir
☎ (07) 4998 1142

Camp Spot at Baralaba. S end of Stopford St. Beside weir. Cold shower

HEMA 15 J9 | 24 11 7 S | 149 48 26 E

BIG RIG

424 Callide Dam

Picnic Area 15 km NE of Biloela. Turn S off Dawson Hwy 5 km NE of Biloela. Beside lake

HEMA 15 J10 | 24 22 26 S | 150 36 46 E

BIG RIG

425 Lochenbar Station - Kroombit Farmstay
☎ (07) 4992 2186

Camp Area at Lochenbar Station. 35 km E of Biloela, via Valentine Plains Rd. 12 km dirt road

HEMA 15 J10 | 24 27 8 S | 150 47 54 E

$+ BIG RIG

426 Mt Scoria Conservation Park

Picnic Area 7 km SW of Thangool. Turn W off Hwy at Thangool

HEMA 15 K10 | 24 31 50 S | 150 36 4 E

BIG RIG

427 Lawgi Hall Rest Area

17

Rest Area 27 km SE of Biloela or 66 km NW of Monto

HEMA 15 K10 | 24 34 5 S | 150 39 40 E

BIG RIG

428 Coominglah Range Rest Area

17

Rest Area 75 km SE of Biloela or 22 km NW of Monto. 100m W of Hwy

HEMA 13 A9 | 24 47 58 S | 150 59 4 E

BIG RIG

429 Mulgildie Hotel
☎ (07) 4167 2107

17

Camp Spot at Mulgildie, 5 km S of Monto. Monal St. Rear of hotel. Contact manager. Fee for showers (business hours only)

HEMA 13 A10 | 24 57 50 S | 151 7 56 E

$ BIG RIG 24

430 Wuruma Dam
☎ (07) 4165 7200

Camp Area 48 km NW of Eidsvold, via Abercorn. Turn W 19 km N of Eidsvold. 1 km dirt road. Beside lake

HEMA 13 B10 | 25 10 52 S | 150 59 14 E

BIG RIG

431 Ceratodus Rest Area

17

Rest Area 65 km S of Monto or 11 km N of Eidsvold. Beside Burnett River

HEMA 13 B10 | 25 16 53 S | 151 8 20 E

BIG RIG 20

432 Eidsvold Caravan Park
☎ (07) 4165 1168

17

Caravan Park at Eidsvold. Esplanade St

HEMA 13 B10 | 25 22 6 S | 151 7 23 E

$

433 RM Williams Australian Bush Centre
☎ (07) 4165 7272

Parking Area at Eidsvold. Gayndah Monto Rd. Parking in Car Park for Self Contained Vehicles only. Payment & Permit from the Centre office

HEMA 13 B10 | 25 22 17 S | 151 7 42 E

$ 24

434 Tolderodden Campground
☎ 13 74 68

Tolderodden Conservation Park

73

Camp Area 4.5 km W of Eidsvold or 82 km E of Cracow. Beside Burnett River. Bookings required

HEMA 13 B10 | 25 22 36 S | 151 5 14 E

$ BIG RIG

435 Auburn River Campground
☎ 13 74 68

Auburn River National Park

Camp Area 42 km SW of Mundubbera. Turn W off Mundubbera-Durong Rd 15 km S of Mundubbera or 91 km N of Durong South onto Hawkwood Rd for 20 km, then S for 7 km of dirt road. Bookings required

HEMA 13 C10 25 42 41 S 151 3 10 E

436 Jaycees Park

Rest Area 3 km N of Mundubbera, 35 km SE of Eidsvold or 44 km W of Gayndah. 500m E of Mundubbera turnoff

17 **HEMA 13 B10** 25 34 24 S 151 18 40 E

437 Glenden Organic Farm & Working Bullock Team
☎ 0429 137 224

Camp Area 23 km NW of Gayndah or 23 km SW of Mundubbera off Slab Creek Rd

HEMA 13 B10 25 34 11 S 151 27 2 E

BIG RIG

438 Binjour Range Rest Area

Rest Area 28 km E of Mundubbera or 17 km NW of Gayndah

17 **HEMA 13 B10** 25 32 0 S 151 29 59 E

BIG RIG 20

439 Claude Wharton Weir

Rest Area 3 km N of Gayndah. 600m W of Hwy. Beside lake

17 **HEMA 13 B11** 25 36 48 S 151 35 35 E

440 Gayndah Showgrounds

Camp Area at Gayndah. Entry off Spencer St. Call number listed at the gate to pay & get keys for toilet & showers. Closed Easter for show week

HEMA 13 B11 25 37 35 S 151 35 55 E

BIG RIG 24

441 Zonhoven Park

Rest Area at Gayndah. E end of town

17 **HEMA 13 B11** 25 37 44 S 151 37 33 E

BIG RIG 24

442 Riverview Caravan Park
☎ (07) 4161 1280

Caravan Park at Gayndah. 3 Barrow St. 1 km N of PO

HEMA 13 C11 25 37 17 S 151 36 10 E

Notes...

443 Mingo Crossing Recreation Area
☎ 07 4161 6200

Camp Area at Mingo Crossing. 30 km S of Mt Perry or 40 km N of Gayndah

HEMA 13 B11 25 23 38 S 151 46 38 E

BIG RIG

444 Ban Ban Springs

Rest Area 28 km SE of Gayndah or 74 km N of Goomeri

17 **HEMA 13 C11** 25 40 54 S 151 48 57 E

BIG RIG 20

445 Glengariff (Rocky Creek) Bush Camping
☎ (07) 4127 1377

Camp Area 36 km E of Ban Ban Springs or 12 km W of Biggenden. Turn S onto Lords Rd 31 km E of Ban Ban Springs or 7 km W of Biggenden. Follow signs for 6 km to campground. Caravans OK to Campground not beyond

HEMA 13 B11 25 35 11 S 152 0 30 E

446 Mountain View Caravan Park
☎ (07) 4127 1399

Caravan Park at Biggenden. Walsh St. 1 km W of PO

52 **HEMA 13 B12** 25 30 49 S 152 2 25 E

BIG RIG

447 Lawless Park (Booubyjan)

Rest Area 40 km S of Ban Ban Springs or 34 km N of Goomeri

17 **HEMA 13 C11** 25 56 40 S 151 57 11 E

BIG RIG 48

448 Kilkivan Bush Camping Park
☎ (07) 5484 1340

Camp Area 8 km E of Kilkivan. Turn S 2 km E of Kilkivan onto Rossmore Rd

HEMA 13 D12 26 7 1 S 152 17 25 E

BIG RIG

449 Fat Hen Creek

Rest Area 6 km E of Kilkivan or 32 km W of Bruce Hwy jcn

HEMA 13 D12 26 5 24 S 152 17 18 E

BIG RIG 20

450 Munna Creek Hall
☎ 0429 912 154

Parking Area at Munna Creek. 23 km E of Woolooga

HEMA 13 C12 25 53 48 S 152 28 34 E

BIG RIG 48

451 Kinbombi Falls

Picnic Area 11 km E of Goomeri or 24 km W of Kilkivan. Turn S off Wide Bay Hwy 6 km E of Goomeri or 19 km W of Kilkivan. 5 km to area

HEMA 13 D12 26 13 19 S 152 9 3 E

452 Goomeri Showgrounds
☎ 0431 520 316

Camp Area at Goomeri. Cnr Burnett Hwy & Laird St. S end of town

HEMA 13 D12 26 11 6 S 152 4 8 E

BIG RIG

453 Goomeri Roadhouse Caravan Park
☎ (07) 4168 4203

Caravan Park at Goomeri. Moore St (Burnett Hwy)

HEMA 13 D11 26 11 10 S 152 4 13 E

454 Broadwater Recreational Reserve

Camp Spot 22 km N of Nanango, on Broadwater Access Rd

HEMA 8 B1 26 30 4 S 152 2 12 E

455 Nango Caravan Park
☎ (07) 4163 1376

17

Caravan Park at Nanango. Cnr of Scott & Arthur Sts. 1 km S of PO

HEMA 8 C1 26 40 49 S 151 59 54 E

BIG RIG

456 Tipperary Flat Park

17

Rest Area at Nanango. 1.5 km S of PO

HEMA 8 C1 26 40 48 S 151 59 47 E

BIG RIG 20

457 Maidenwell Rest Area

Rest Area at Maidenwell. 27 km SW of Nanango or 19 km N of Cooyar. Opposite hall on Coomba Falls Rd. Donation for showers

HEMA 13 E11 26 50 48 S 151 48 0 E

48

458 Maidenwell Hotel
☎ (07) 4164 6133

Camp Spot at Maidenwell. 27 km SW of Nanango or 19 km N of Cooyar. Gold coin donation for showers

HEMA 13 E11 26 50 49 S 151 47 56 E

48

459 Swinging Bridge Park

61

Rest Area at Cooyar. Behind Cooyar Hotel. Fee for power. Key from pub. Toilets opposite hotel in Memorial Park

HEMA 13 F11 26 58 54 S 151 49 57 E

BIG RIG 48

460 Crows Nest Camping Area
☎ 13 74 68

Crows Nest National Park

Camp Area 7 km E of Crows Nest, via Three Mile Rd. Prebook on ParksQ website

HEMA 8 J2 27 15 15 S 152 6 25 E

461 Cressbrook Dam
☎ (07) 4688 6540

Camp Area 17 km E of Crows Nest. Prebook on ParksQ website. GPS at entry

HEMA 8 J3 27 17 20 S 152 9 49 E

462 Chapman Park

61

Rest Area at Hampton. Visitor Information Centre

HEMA 8 K2 27 21 30 S 152 4 9 E

20

463 Ravensbourne Rest Area

Rest Area 14 km E of Hampton or 32 km SW of Esk

HEMA 8 K3 27 21 36 S 152 10 35 E

BIG RIG 24

Yarraman to Ipswich

D'Aguilar and Burnett Highways

464 Harland Park

Camp Spot 8.6 km W of Blackbutt or 6 km E of Yarraman

HEMA 8 E1 26 52 7 S 152 1 26 E

BIG RIG

465 Blackbutt Showgrounds
☎ (07) 4163 0633

Camp Area at Blackbutt Showgrounds. Bowmans Rd

HEMA 8 E2 26 52 50 S 152 6 7 E

BIG RIG

466 First Settlers Park

85

Rest Area at Benarkin. 4 km E of Blackbutt or 42 km NW of Toogoolawah. Donation welcomed

HEMA 8 E2 26 53 18 S 152 8 10 E

20

467 Clancys Campground
☎ 1300 130 372

Benarkin State Forest

Camp Area 15 km SE of Blackbutt, via Benarkin Forest Dr. Turn S 4 km E of Blackbutt. 12 km dirt road. Maximum stay 14 days. Small area, 4WD recommended

HEMA 8 F3 26 58 36 S 152 10 19 E

468 Moore Rest Area

85

Rest Area at Moore. Opposite local store

HEMA 8 E4 26 53 37 S 152 17 25 E

24

469 Linville Village

Camp Spot at Linville. Turn through white gates opposite Linville Hotel. Donation welcomed

HEMA 8 E3 26 50 36 S 152 16 33 E

BIG RIG 48

470 Kilcoy Camping Area (Anzac Memorial park)
☎ (07) 5422 4900

85

Camp Area at Kilcoy. E end of town at cnr of Seib & William Sts

HEMA 8 F6 26 56 32 S 152 34 2 E

BIG RIG 72

471 Kilcoy Showgrounds
☎ (07) 5422 4900

Camp Area at Showgrounds. Turn NE 2 km W of Kilcoy off the D'Aguilar Hwy. Caretaker will collect fee

HEMA 8 F6 26 56 37 S 152 32 45 E

BIG RIG

472 Yandilla Farm
☎ (07) 5498 1220

Camp Area 22 km NE of Kilcoy. 1785 Mt Kilcoy Rd. Travel N from Kilcoy on the Kilcoy Murgon Rd, turn E at Mt Kilcoy Rd. Small dogs may be permitted on enquiry. Bookings Essential

HEMA 8 D6 26 47 15 S 152 34 26 E

BIG RIG

473 Peach Trees Camping Area
☎ 13 1304

Jimna State Forest

Camp Area 4 km N of Jimna, 44 km N of Kilcoy. Permit required. Four Tonne Load Limit in park

HEMA 8 C5 26 38 15 S 152 26 59 E

474 Cruice Park

Rest Area 4 km NW of Woodford or 29 km W of Beerwah at jcn of Kilcoy-Beerwah Rd & D'Aguilar Hwy

53

HEMA 8 F7 26 55 40 S 152 45 33 E

BIG RIG 20

475 Woodford Showgrounds
☎ (07) 5422 9681

Camp Area at Woodford . Neurem Rd. Register with onsite caretaker on arrival

HEMA 8 F7 26 56 51 S 152 46 12 E

BIG RIG

476 Neurum Creek Bush Retreat
☎ (07) 5496 3692

Camp Area 14 km W of Woodford. 268 Rasmussen Rd, Neurum. Bookings essential, a $7 site fee applies to all bookings for the first night only

HEMA 8 F7 26 59 56 S 152 41 13 E

477 Somerset Dam Campground
☎ (07) 5426 4729

Camp Area at Somerset Dam. 27 km S of Kilcoy or 24 km NE of Esk. Showers $1 coin operated

HEMA 8 H6 27 7 25 S 152 33 3 E

BIG RIG

478 Sim Lord Park

Rest Area at Harlin. Small area

17

HEMA 8 F4 26 58 33 S 152 21 34 E

Notes...

479 Toogoolawah Drop Zone
☎ (07) 5423 1159

Camp Area 3 km N of Toogoolawah or 12 S of Harlin

17

HEMA 8 G4 27 4 11 S 152 23 21 E

BIG RIG 48

480 Toogoolawah Showgrounds
☎ (07) 5423 1336

Camp Area at Toogoolawah Showgrounds. Ivory Creek Rd

17

HEMA 8 G4 27 4 41 S 152 22 31 E

BIG RIG

481 Poll Crandell (B.E.M.) Park

Rest Area 1 km S of Toogoolawah

17

HEMA 8 G4 27 5 50 S 152 22 50 E

BIG RIG

482 Captain Logan Camp
☎ (07) 5426 4729

Wivenhoe Dam

Camp Area at Lake Wivenhoe. Logan Inlet Rd

HEMA 8 K6 27 21 6 S 152 33 5 E

483 Lumley Hill Campground
☎ (07) 5426 4729

Wivenhoe Dam

Camp Area at Lake Wivenhoe. Logan Inlet Rd

HEMA 8 K6 27 20 50 S 152 33 8 E

484 Lowood Showgrounds & Caravan Park
☎ 0455 187201

Camp Area at Lowood. Station St

HEMA 10 B6 27 27 45 S 152 35 1 E

BIG RIG

485 Atkinson Dam Cabin Village & Shoreline Camping
☎ (07) 5426 4211

Camp Area at Atkinsons Dam. 381 Atkinsons Dam Rd. 18 km W of Lowood

HEMA 10 A5 27 25 12 S 152 27 11 E

BIG RIG

Goomeri to Dalby

Bunya Highway

486 Murgon RV Stop
☎ (07) 4189 9387

Camp Area at Murgon. 3 Krebs St. 1 km NE of PO

49

HEMA 13 D11 26 14 32 S 151 56 17 E

BIG RIG 48

487 George Bernard Roberts Place

Picnic Area at Bjelke Petersen Dam. 14 km SE of Murgon

HEMA 13 D11 26 18 14 S 151 59 9 E

BIG RIG

488 Dingo Creek Bicentennial Park

49

Rest Area at Wondai. N end of town

HEMA 13 D11 26 18 49 S 151 52 13 E

BIG RIG

489 Wondai Caravan Park

☎ (07) 4169 2555

49

Caravan Park at Wondai. McKenzie St. Centre of town, next to swimming pool & railway line. $10 deposit for shower & toilet key. Payment & key available from Council Chambers or Wondai Diggers Club

HEMA 13 D11 26 19 10 S 151 52 18 E

490 Proston Caravan Park

☎ (07) 4168 9272

Caravan Park at Proston. Next to Showgrounds Proston Boondooma Rd. Check in & pay fee at Golden Spurs Hotel, 2 Blake St

HEMA 13 D11 26 9 39 S 151 35 55 E

BIG RIG

491 Boondooma Homestead

☎ (07) 4168 0159

Camp Area 81 km S of Mundubbera or 112 km SW of Chinchilla. Off the Mundubbera Durong Rd. Pay fees to caretaker

HEMA 13 D10 26 12 10 S 151 17 35 E

BIG RIG

492 Stuart River Rest Area

82

Rest Area 19 km W of Tingoora or 44 km E of Durong South

HEMA 13 D11 26 22 22 S 151 38 52 E

BIG RIG 20

493 Wooroolin Rest Area

49

Rest Area at Wooroolin. Opposite PO. Gold coin for Showers

HEMA 13 D11 26 24 38 S 151 48 58 E

BIG RIG 48

494 Kingaroy Showgrounds Caravan Park

☎ (07) 4162 5037

Camp Area at Kingaroy. 1.5 km from PO. 31 Youngman St. S side of town

HEMA 13 E11 26 32 49 S 151 49 56 E

BIG RIG

495 Coolabunia Rest Area

Rest Area 7 km SE of Kingaroy or 17 km NW of Nanango. Small area

HEMA 13 E11 26 34 49 S 151 52 41 E

20

496 Soren Hansen Bridge

Rest Area 7 km SW of Kingaroy. Turn W 4 km S of Kingaroy at S end of golf course onto Burrandowan Rd for 3 km. Large area beside river

HEMA 13 E11 26 35 12 S 151 47 24 E

BIG RIG 20

497 Alwyn Francis Bridge

49

Rest Area 10 km SW of Kingaroy or 17 km NE of Kumbia. Large area beside river

HEMA 13 E11 26 36 41 S 151 47 0 E

BIG RIG 20

498 Kumbia Apex Park

49

Rest Area at Kumbia. Opposite Police Station. Honesty box for power

HEMA 13 E11 26 41 32 S 151 39 10 E

48

499 Kumbia Caravan Park

☎ (07) 4164 4375

Caravan Park at Kumbia. Bell St

HEMA 13 E11 26 41 23 S 151 39 18 E

500 Dandabah Campground

☎ 13 74 68

Bunya Mountains National Park

Camp Area 62 km SW of Kingaroy. Permit required must pre book

HEMA 13 E11 26 52 45 S 151 35 52 E

501 Bushland Park Cabins & Camping

☎ 0407 113 514

Camp Area 52 km N of Dalby or 62 km S of Kingaroy on Bunya Mountain Rd

HEMA 13 E11 26 54 48 S 151 37 52 E

502 Bells & Whistle Caravan Park

☎ (07) 4663 1265

49

Caravan Park at Bell. Bunya Hwy. 200m S of PO

HEMA 13 E10 26 55 57 S 151 26 49 E

BIG RIG

503 Yamsion Rest Area

Rest Area 44 km S of Kumbia or 42 km NE of Dalby on Bunya Mountains Rd

HEMA 13 F11 26 59 5 S 151 34 42 E

48

504 Glasbys Caravan Park

☎ (07) 4663 4228

Caravan Park at Kaimkillenbun. Mofatt St

HEMA 13 F10 27 3 39 S 151 26 3 E

Rockhampton to Goondiwindi

Leichhardt Highway

505 Junction Park

☎ (07) 4993 1900

Rest Area at Theodore. S end of The Boulevard. Donations requested

HEMA 13 A8 24 57 14 S 150 4 29 E

BIG RIG 48

506 Theodore Recreation Reserve

☎ 0427 367 069

Camp Area at Theodore. The Boulevard E side of town

HEMA 13 A8 24 56 22 S 150 4 34 E

BIG RIG

507 Isla Gorge Campground
☎ 13 74 68

Isla Gorge National Park

A5

Camp Area 38 km S of Theodore. Turn W 37 km S of Theodore or 57 km N of Taroom. 1 km dirt road. GPS at entry point

HEMA 13 A8 25 12 5 S 149 58 34 E

BIG RIG

508 Glebe Weir
☎ 07 4628 6113

Camp Area 93 km S of Theodore. Turn E 66 km S of Theodore or 28 km NE of Taroom. Honesty box for payment. Maximum stay 4 weeks

HEMA 13 B8 25 27 49 S 150 2 2 E

BIG RIG

509 Lake Murphy Conservation Park
☎ 13 74 68

Camp Area 39 km NW of Taroom. Turn NW 76 km S of Theodore or 18 km N of Taroom onto Fitzroy Developmental Rd, then W after 1 km onto Glenhaughton Rd for 11 km dirt road

HEMA 12 B7 25 29 8 S 149 39 36 E

510 Chain Lagoons

A5

Parking Area 80 km S of Theodore or 16 km N of Taroom. 1 km E of Hwy. GPS at entry point

HEMA 12 B7 25 31 38 S 149 46 26 E

BIG RIG

511 Taroom Village Resort

A5

Caravan Park at Taroom. Short St. 1 km NW of PO

HEMA 12 B7 25 38 18 S 149 47 25 E

BIG RIG

512 Waterloo Plain Environmental Park

Camp Spot in Wandoan. 100m from PO. Toilets located in football ground next door

HEMA 13 D8 26 7 7 S 149 57 42 E

BIG RIG 48

513 Wandoan Showgrounds

Camp Area at Wandoan. 92 Roche Creek Rd. 3 km NE of PO

HEMA 13 D8 26 6 55 S 149 58 55 E

BIG RIG

514 Juandah Heritage Site
☎ 0417 760 883

Camp Area at Wandoan. 92 Windeyer Rd, limited power. Donation to the Juandah Heritage Society for upkeep

HEMA 13 D8 26 7 40 S 149 58 23 E

BIG RIG

Notes...

515 Possum Park Caravan & Camping Park
☎ (07) 4627 1651

A5

Caravan Park 20 km N of Miles or 46 km S of Wandoan. Leichhardt Hwy

HEMA 13 D8 26 30 49 S 150 6 0 E

BIG RIG

516 Gil Weir

Camp Area 6 km S of Miles or 29 km N of Condamine. Turn W off Leichhardt Hwy

HEMA 13 E8 26 42 33 S 150 10 46 E

BIG RIG 48

517 Condamine River Caravan Park
☎ (07) 4627 7179

A5

Caravan Park at Condamine. Wambo St

HEMA 13 E8 26 55 36 S 150 7 59 E

BIG RIG

518 Caliguel Lagoon

Picnic Area 7 km SW of Condamine, via Condamine-Meandarra Rd

HEMA 13 E8 26 59 1 S 150 6 40 E

BIG RIG

519 Brigalow Creek

Camp Spot at Meandarra. Bush camping along creek. Toilets, dump point & BBQ at Leo Gordon Apex Park, Condamine Meandarra Rd & Dillon St. Max stay 14 days

HEMA 12 F7 27 19 41 S 149 52 40 E

BIG RIG

520 Glenmorgan

Camp Spot at Glenmorgan. 64 km E of Surat at Old Railway Station. Donation welcome

HEMA 12 F7 27 14 56 S 149 40 34 E

BIG RIG

521 Myall Park Botanic Garden
☎ (07) 4665 6705

Camp Area 5 km N of Glenmorgan, Riverglen Rd. Fee includes admission to the Gardens

HEMA 12 F7 27 12 17 S 149 39 25 E

522 Tara Lagoon

Camp Area at Tara. Showground Rd

HEMA 13 F8 27 16 21 S 150 27 36 E

BIG RIG 72

523 Moonie Motel Caravan Park
☎ (07) 4665 0200

A5

Caravan Park at Moonie. Cnr Moonie & Leichhardt Hwys

HEMA 13 G8 27 43 3 S 150 22 11 E

BIG RIG

Brisbane to Barcaldine

Warrego and Landsborough Highways

524 Ipswich Showgrounds
☎ (07) 3281 1577

Camp Area at showgrounds. Cnr Warwick & Salisbury Rds. Pay at office Mon to Fri, 0830 - 1630 hrs. Maximum stay 7 days

HEMA 6 H2 27 37 38 S 152 45 33 E

525 Marburg Showground
☎ (07) 5464 4457

Camp Spot at Marburg. 1 km S of Warrego Hwy, via Queen Street. Fee in honour box

HEMA 10 C6 27 34 17 S 152 35 50 E

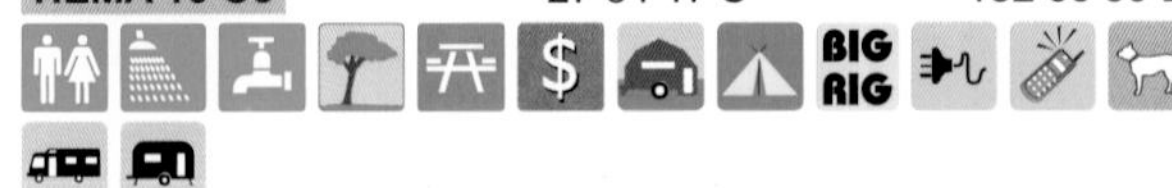

526 Narda Lagoon

Parking Area at Laidley. S end of town Cnr Drayton & Pioneer St

HEMA 10 C4 27 39 1 S 152 23 27 E

527 Laidley Showground
☎ (07) 5465 1284

Camp Area at Laidley. Use McGregor St entrance

HEMA 10 C4 27 38 16 S 152 23 22 E

528 Mulgowie Community Hall
☎ (07) 5465 9127

Camp Spot at Mulgowie 12 km S of Laidley. Beckman Rd. Advance booking required, fee payable at the Mulgowie Hotel

HEMA 10 D4 27 43 48 S 152 21 48 E

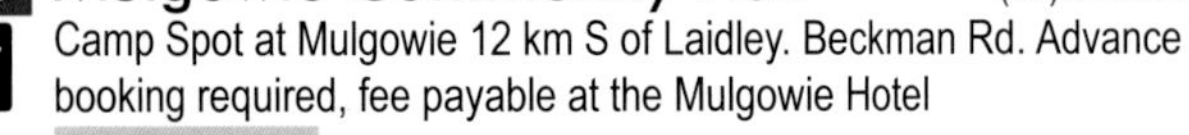

529 Thornton Centenary Park Camping Ground
☎ (07) 5465 3698

Camp Area at Thornton. 24 km S of Laidley. Maximum stay 7 nights. Key for access to power via Lake Dyer Camping ground office

HEMA 10 E4 27 47 54 S 152 22 27 E

530 Lake Dyer Caravan & Camping Ground
☎ (07) 5465 3698

Camp Area 1.5 km NW of Laidley off Gatton-Laidey Rd.

HEMA 10 C4 27 37 57 S 152 22 40 E

531 Gatton Caravan Park
☎ (07) 5462 1198

Caravan Park at Gatton. 291 Eastern Dr

HEMA 10 B4 27 33 19 S 152 17 19 E

532 Heifer Creek

Rest Area 41 km SW of Gatton or 25 km NE of New England Hwy. On Clifton-Gatton Rd. Beside creek

HEMA 10 D2 27 44 56 S 152 5 23 E

533 Casuarina Camping Area
☎ 13 74 68

Glen Rock Park

Camp Area 42 km SW of Gatton. From Gatton take Mt Sylvia Rd via Tenthill to Junction View. Turn E onto East Haldon Rd. Signposted to Park. Permit required. Maximum stay 30 days

HEMA 10 F3 27 53 18 S 152 14 50 E

534 James Hedges Park

A2

Rest Area at Helidon beside Warrego Hwy

HEMA 10 B2 27 33 4 S 152 7 9 E

535 Murphy's Creek Escape Camping Park
☎ 07 4630 5353

Camp Area at Upper Lockyer. 356 Thomas Rd. 14 km N of Helidon or 17 km SE of Cabarlah

HEMA 10 B2 27 28 53 S 152 5 35 E

536 Six Mile Country Retreat
☎ 0417 780 194

Camp Area NW of Postmans Ridge. Follow Murphy's Creek Rd, after 0.5 km turn L into Six Mile Creek Rd, follow for 2.9 km, cross creek & camp area is on your R

HEMA 10 B2 27 31 27 S 152 2 16 E

537 Toowoomba Showground
☎ (07) 4634 7400

Camp Area at Towoomba. Glenvale Rd. Available to Motorhomes over 30 ft & travellers with pets. Must register at office. Closed during events

HEMA 10 C1 27 33 36 S 151 53 4 E

538 Goombungee Haden Showgounds
☎ 0457 183 406

Camp Area at Goombungee. Lau St. NE side of town off Pechey Maclagan Rd

HEMA 13 F11 27 18 19 S 151 51 27 E

539 Jondaryan Woolshed
☎ (07) 4692 2229

Camp Area 3 km S of Jondaryan

HEMA 13 F11 27 23 32 S 151 34 30 E

540 Bowenville Reserve

Rest Area 5 km S of Bowenville on Bowenville-Norwin Rd

HEMA 13 F10 27 19 40 S 151 27 17 E

BIG RIG

541 Cecil Plains Rural Retreat Caravan Park

☎ 0428 913 779

Caravan Park at Cecil Plains. Taylor St

HEMA 13 G10 27 31 59 S 151 11 45 E

BIG RIG

542 Cecil Plains Apex Park

☎ (07) 4695 1399

Picnic Area at Cecil Plains. 1 km E of PO on the Toowoomba-Cecil Plains Rd, beside the Condamine River. Self Contained Vehicles only

HEMA 13 G10 27 31 56 S 151 12 16 E

BIG RIG 72

543 Wilga Campground

☎ 13 74 68

Lake Broadwater Conservation Park

Camp Area 28 km SW of Dalby. Turn S off Moonie Hwy 20 km SW of Dalby or 92 km NE of Moonie along Lake Broadwater. Register on arrival, no prebooking available

HEMA 13 F10 27 19 55 S 151 5 46 E

BIG RIG

544 The Lake Campground

☎ 13 74 98

Lake Broadwater Conservation Park

Camp Area 30 km SW of Dalby. Turn S off Moonie Hwy 20 km SW of Dalby or 92 km NE of Moonie along Lake Broadwater Rd. Register on arrival. No prebooking available.

HEMA 13 F10 27 21 13 S 151 5 34 E

BIG RIG

545 Kumbarilla Rest Area

Rest Area 46 km SW of Dalby or 66 km NE of Moonie

49

HEMA 13 F9 27 19 28 S 150 52 39 E

BIG RIG

546 Warra Rest Area

Rest Area 46 km NW of Dalby or 35 km SE of Chinchilla

A2

HEMA 13 E9 26 55 43 S 150 55 10 E

48

547 Jimbour Rest Area

Rest Area at Jimbour. Next to War Memorial Hall

HEMA 13 E10 26 57 50 S 151 12 59 E

BIG RIG 20

Notes...

548 Jandowae Accommodation Park

☎ (07) 4668 5071

Caravan Park at Jandowae. High St

HEMA 13 E10 26 47 12 S 151 6 46 E

BIG RIG

549 Jandowae Showgrounds

☎ (07) 4668 5268

Camp Area at Showgrounds. Warra St. Caretaker collects fees. Mob 0458 595 796

HEMA 13 E10 26 47 13 S 151 6 38 E

BIG RIG

550 Kogan Memorial Hall

☎ (07) 4668 1762

Camp Area at Kogan. W side of Memorial Hall. Phone to pay & get the key

HEMA 13 F9 27 2 24 S 150 45 40 E

551 Archers Crossing (South side)

☎ (07) 4668 9564

Camp Area 24 km S of Chinchilla. Turn S 26 km NW of Warra or 9 km SE of Chinchilla, onto Hopelands Rd for 9 km to school. Turn R for 2 km to Archers Crossing Rd, then 4 km of dirt road to river

HEMA 13 E9 26 47 57 S 150 40 46 E

48

552 Archers Crossing (North side)

☎ (07) 4668 9564

Camp Area 11 km SE of Chinchilla. Turn S 28 km NW of Warra or 7 km SE of Chinchilla onto No Through Rd for 4 km of dirt road. GPS at entry point

HEMA 13 E9 26 47 44 S 150 40 40 E

48

553 Round Water Hole Rest Area

Rest Area 5.5 km NE of Chinchilla on the Chinchilla - Wondai Rd

HEMA 13 E9 26 43 18 S 150 40 3 E

BIG RIG 24

554 Chinchilla Weir

☎ (07) 4668 9564

Rest Area 9 km SW of Chinchilla on Chinchilla -Tara Rd. Power available.

HEMA 13 E9 26 48 2 S 150 34 52 E

BIG RIG 48

555 Chinchilla Showgrounds

☎ (07) 4662 7194

Camp Area at Chinchilla. Entrance at Cnr Zeller St & Gaske Ln

HEMA 13 E9 26 45 2 S 150 37 5 E

BIG RIG

556 Columboola Country Caravan Park

☎ (07) 4665 8293

Caravan Park at Columboola. Ryalls Rd

HEMA 13 E8 26 32 46 S 150 19 52 E

BIG RIG

QUEENSLAND

557 Miles Crossroads Caravan Park ☎(07) 4627 2165
Caravan Park at Miles. 132 Murilla St
HEMA 13 E8 26 39 36 S 150 11 42 E
A2 BIG RIG

558 Miles Showgrounds ☎0419 028 905
Camp Area at Miles. Entry off Hawkins St, contact caretaker on arrival
HEMA 13 E8 26 39 41 S 150 10 56 E
BIG RIG

559 Moraby Park
Rest Area 1 km W of Miles. Both sides of the road
HEMA 13 E8 26 39 20 S 150 10 46 E
A2

560 Yuleba East Rest Area
Rest Area 17 km W of Jackson or 7.5 km E of Yuleba
HEMA 12 E7 26 37 16 S 149 27 25 E
A2

561 Judds Lagoon ☎(07) 4623 5155
Camp Spot 3 km SE of Yuleba, turn W onto Forestry Rd just before the town Cemetery then onto Moongool Rd. Signposted
HEMA 12 E6 26 38 12 S 149 23 46 E
BIG RIG

562 Old Yuleba ☎1300 007 662
Camp Spot 13 E of Yuleba. Via Forestry Rd & Moongool Rd
HEMA 12 E7 26 41 50 S 149 25 59 E

563 The Maryanne
Camp Spot 16 km S of Yuleba on the Yuleba Surat Rd. (The Cobb & Co Way) past the windmill follow track to lagoon & open area
HEMA 12 E6 26 46 45 S 149 19 33 E

564 Wallumbilla Showgrounds
Camp Area at Wallumbilla. W end of town
HEMA 12 E6 26 35 14 S 149 11 1 E
A2 BIG RIG 72

565 Roma Showgrounds ☎0408 988 002
Camp Area at Roma Showgrounds (Bassett Park) Carnarvon Hwy. Only available when all caravan parks in town are full or for large club groups
HEMA 12 D5 26 33 13 S 148 47 6 E
BIG RIG

566 Meadowbank 'Museum' Farm Stay ☎(07) 4622 3836
Camp Area at Meadowbank Station. 60 Bindango Rd Warrego Hwy. 12 km W of Roma, turn N for 2 km. Signposted
HEMA 12 D5 26 34 46 S 148 40 48 E
A2 BIG RIG

567 Bungeworgorai Creek
Camp Spot 10 km W of Roma or 31 km E of Muckadilla. Tracks on S of Rd, E of bridge
HEMA 12 D5 26 35 32 S 148 41 39 E
A2 BIG RIG

568 Muckadilla Community Park
Rest Area at Muckadilla. Donation box E side of Community Hall for showers & upkeep of facility
HEMA 12 D5 26 35 7 S 148 23 17 E
A2 BIG RIG 24

569 Muckadilla Hotel ☎(07) 4626 8318
Camp Area at Muckadilla. Fee for Power
HEMA 12 D5 26 35 6 S 148 23 6 E
A2

570 Natural Wilderness Experience 'Claravale' ☎(07) 4623 2721
Camp Area 52 km NE of Mitchell. 500m E of Mitchell on the Warrego Hwy turn N onto Warroonga-Tooloombilla Rd. 25 km of dirt road
HEMA 12 C4 26 8 43 S 148 7 51 E
BIG RIG

571 Caltex Bridge Service Station & Caravan Park ☎(07) 4623 1125
Caravan Park at Mitchell. 3 Cambridge St. Limited sites
HEMA 12 D4 26 29 8 S 147 58 45 E
A2

572 Womallilla Creek
Camp Spot 37 km S of Mitchell or 176 km NW of St George. Near bridge at jcn of Maranoa River & Womalilla Creek
HEMA 12 E4 26 46 20 S 148 1 51 E
BIG RIG 48

573 Woodlands Rest Area
Rest Area 91 km S of Mitchell or 114 km N of St George
HEMA 12 F4 27 15 59 S 148 3 16 E
BIG RIG

574 Bonus Downs Station ☎(07) 4623 1573
Camp Area at Bonus Downs Station. 46 km SW of Mitchell on the Mitchell Bollon Rd. Bookings essential
HEMA 12 E3 26 42 41 S 147 41 1 E

575 Neil Turner Weir
Rest Area 3.2 km W of Mitchell. Turn N off Warrego Hwy 2 km W of Mitchell. Cnr Alexandra & River St
HEMA 12 D4 26 28 28 S 147 57 21 E
BIG RIG

576 Fisherman's Rest
Camp Spot 5.5 km W of Mitchell. Turn N off Warrego Hwy 5 km W of Mitchell
HEMA 12 D4 26 28 30 S 147 55 42 E
48

577 Ooline Park
Rest Area 36 km W of Mitchell or 9.6 km E of Mungallala. Turn S off Hwy, follow track for 1 km. Limited space, small vehicles only
HEMA 12 D3 26 27 53 S 147 37 49 E

578 Mungallala RV Stop
Camp Spot at Mungallala. 45 km W of Mitchell or 44 km E of Morven. Donation required for use
A2
HEMA 12 D3 26 26 44 S 147 32 29 E

579 Mungallala Hotel
☎ (07) 4623 6192
Camp Area at Mungallala Hotel. Main St
A2
HEMA 12 D3 26 26 46 S 147 32 36 E

580 Morven Recreation Ground
☎ (07) 4654 8281
Camp Area at Morven. S side of town via Victoria St. $5 Donation per night appreciated for upkeep of facilities. Maximum stay 7 days
HEMA 12 D2 26 25 6 S 147 6 58 E

581 Sommariva Rest Area
Rest Area 49 km W of Morven or 39 km E of Charleville
HEMA 12 D1 26 24 51 S 146 37 30 E

582 Charleville Rockpool
Camp Spot 11 km W of Charleville on Warrego Hwy
HEMA 23 B14 26 25 6 S 146 21 5 E

583 The Red Lizard Camping Ground
☎ (07) 4654 7047
Camp Area 7 km S of Charleville on the Mitchell Hwy
A71
HEMA 23 B14 26 27 45 S 146 14 2 E

584 Charleville Bush Camp
☎ 0428 545 200
Caravan Park (Bush) 1.5 km NW of Charleville on Adavale Rd. Total Non Smoking park. No Power. Separate generator area. Self Contained Vehicles only
HEMA 23 B14 26 23 20 S 146 13 47 E

585 Ward River
Camp Spot 18 km W of Charleville. Turn NW off Diamantina Hwy 17 km W of Charleville onto old Hwy, follow for 500m. Tracks along river. Signposted "Ward River Fishing"
HEMA 23 B13 26 29 39 S 146 6 1 E

586 Nungil Station
☎ (07) 4654 0151
Camp Area At Nungill Station 117 km NW of Charlieville. Via Charlieville Adavale & Langlo Rds. Bookings are essential
HEMA 21 J11 25 44 45 S 145 39 3 E

587 Cooladdi Foxtrap Roadhouse
☎ (07) 4654 0347
Camp Spot at Cooladdi. 88 km W of Charleville or 122 km E of Quilpie. Camp sites available near pub & river
HEMA 23 C12 26 38 53 S 145 28 4 E

588 Winbin East Rest Area
Rest Area 159 km W of Charleville or 53 km E of Quilpie
HEMA 23 C11 26 38 15 S 144 47 48 E

589 Adavale Town Camping Area
☎ (07) 4656 4656
Camp Area at Adavale. Beside Community Hall, Blackall Adavale Rd call into Pub for more info. Donation required
HEMA 23 A11 25 54 29 S 144 35 59 E

590 Adavale Bush Camping
☎ (07) 4656 4656
Camp Area 1 km W of Adavale off the Charleville Adavale Rd. Collect Map from the pub for other bush camping & fishing spots in the area
HEMA 23 A11 25 54 30 S 144 37 0 E

591 Wanco Station
Lake Houdraman

Camp Spot 7 km NE of Quilpie at Lake Houdraman. Turn N 2 km E of Quilpie, follow rd for 2 km then turn E at grid. 4.5 km dirt road
HEMA 23 B10 26 35 7 S 144 18 22 E

592 Quilpie River
Camp Spot at Quilpie. Turn S 1 km E of Quilpie, just W of John Waugh Bridge (Bulloo River). Follow track to camp spots along river near old crossing
HEMA 23 C10 26 36 55 S 144 17 3 E

593 Kyabra Creek Rest Area
Rest Area 116 km NW of Quilpie or 130 km SE of Windorah on Diamantina Development Rd
HEMA 23 A9 26 5 50 S 143 26 38 E

594 Eromanga Motel & Caravan Park
☎ (07) 4656 4885
Caravan Part at Eromanga. Webber St
HEMA 23 C8 26 40 7 S 143 16 21 E

Notes...

QUEENSLAND

595 Augathella Motel & Caravan Park
☎ (07) 4654 5255

Caravan Park at Augathella. Matilda Hwy

A2

HEMA 21 J12 | 25 47 36 S | 146 35 35 E

BIG RIG

596 Augathella North Rest Area
Rest Area 42 km N of Augathella or 72 km S of Tambo

A2

HEMA 21 J12 | 25 28 15 S | 146 35 42 E

BIG RIG 20

597 Tambo Lake
Rest Area at Tambo. At S entrance to town.

A2

HEMA 21 H11 | 24 52 55 S | 146 15 35 E

BIG RIG

598 Tambo Caravan Park
☎ (07) 4654 6463

Caravan Park at Tambo. Next to Football Grounds

A2

HEMA 21 H11 | 24 53 6 S | 146 14 52 E

599 Stubby Bend
Camp Spot 2 km NE of Tambo. First turn right after bridge on Alpha-Springsure Rd. Signposted

HEMA 21 H11 | 24 52 34 S | 146 15 46 E

BIG RIG 72

600 Tambo North Rest Area
Rest Area 25 km NW of Tambo or 75 km SE of Blackall

A2

HEMA 21 H11 | 24 45 3 S | 146 6 20 E

BIG RIG 24

601 Barcoo River Rest Area
Rest Area 59 km N of Tambo or 41 km S of Blackall. Self Contained Vehicles only

A2

HEMA 21 G11 | 24 34 53 S | 145 48 45 E

BIG RIG

602 Barcoo River Camp (Blackall)
☎ (07) 4657 4637

Camp Spot at Blackall. 500m W of PO. Self Contained Vehicles only. Toilets & showers across road

A2

HEMA 21 G10 | 24 25 29 S | 145 27 41 E

BIG RIG 72

603 Monks Tank Camping Area
☎ 13 74 68

Idalia National Park

Camp Area in Idalia National Park. Turn S off Yaraka Rd at Benlidi Siding, then 54 km to camp area. Signposted. Dirt road, 4WD access only

HEMA 21 H9 | 24 47 37 S | 144 42 16 E

604 Oma Waterhole
Camp Area 17 km SW of Isisford, next to Oma Station. Take St Helens Rd out of Isisford then join Yaraka River Rd

HEMA 21 G9 | 24 17 11 S | 144 18 32 E

605 Yaranigh's Pond
Camp Spot 7 km S of Isisford on the Isisford Emmet Rd

HEMA 21 G9 | 24 17 59 S | 144 28 44 E

606 Barcoo River Nature Park
☎ (07) 4658 8900

Camp Area at Isisford. E of town beside river. Showers in town park. Fee payable at Council Office

HEMA 21 G9 | 24 15 28 S | 144 26 36 E

607 Golden West Hotel Caravan Park
☎ (07) 4658 8222

Caravan Park at Isisford

HEMA 21 G9 | 24 15 30 S | 144 26 29 E

BIG RIG

608 Douglas Ponds Creek
Rest Area 23 km N of Blackall or 84 km S of Barcaldine. Self Contained Vehicles only

A2

HEMA 21 G10 | 24 16 34 S | 145 20 29 E

BIG RIG

609 Lara Wetland Camping Grounds
☎ 0457 661 243

Camp Area at Lara Station. Turn W at signpost 79 km N of Blackall or 28 km S of Barcaldine onto access road. 13 km dirt road. GPS at the gate

HEMA 21 F10 | 23 47 51 S | 145 18 31 E

BIG RIG

610 Barcaldine South Rest Area
Rest Area 79 km N of Blackall or 28 km S of Barcaldine

A2

HEMA 21 F10 | 23 48 1 S | 145 18 34 E

BIG RIG

Brisbane to Rathdowney

Mt Lindesay Highway

611 Canungra Recreation Ground
☎ (07) 5543 5904

Camp Area at Canungra. On RHS past hotel along Lamington National Park Rd. Follow signs to rec grounds

HEMA 11 G10 | 28 1 18 S | 153 9 36 E

BIG RIG

612 Sharp Park
☎ 0409 550 745

Camp Area 4 km SE of Canungra. On Beechmont Rd, on either side of Coomera River. Bookings essential during peak season. Max stay 3 weeks

HEMA 11 G11 | 28 2 59 S | 153 11 18 E

BIG RIG

613 The Settlement Camping Area ☎ 13 74 68
Springbrook National Park
Camping area on Carricks Rd. Suitable for small vehicles only, not suitable for caravans. Booking required
HEMA 11 J11 28 11 36 S 153 16 19 E

614 Darlington Park ☎ (07) 5544 8120
Camp Area 24 km S of Beaudesert, via Kerry Rd. Beside Albert River
HEMA 11 H9 28 11 4 S 153 2 26 E
BIG RIG

615 Burgess Park ☎ (07) 5544 8120
Camp Area 19 km SE of Laravale on Christmas Creek Rd. 3 km S of Hillview
HEMA 11 J9 28 14 20 S 152 59 45 E
BIG RIG

616 Stinson Memorial Park ☎ (07) 5544 8008
Camp Area 27 km SE of Laravale on Christmas Creek Rd. 11 km S of Hillview. Bookings preferred
HEMA 11 J9 28 17 16 S 153 2 13 E

617 Andrew Drynan Park ☎ (07) 5544 1281
Camp Area 18 km SE of Rathdowney. Turn E 4 km N of Rathdowney onto Running Creek Rd (Lions Tourist Rd). 3.5m clearance, 5 tonne limit, steep grades & sharp curves into NSW via Lions Tourist Rd, access only from the N due to damaged road S of the camp area.
HEMA 11 K9 28 19 8 S 152 55 59 E

618 Langdon Reserve
13
Rest Area 25 km S of Beaudesert or 6 km N of Rathdowney
HEMA 11 H8 28 10 9 S 152 53 28 E
BIG RIG 20

619 Rathdowney Caravan Park
Caravan Park at Rathdowney. Running Creek Rd, just E of PO
HEMA 11 J8 28 12 42 S 152 51 55 E
BIG RIG

620 Bigriggen Park Reserve ☎ (07) 5463 6190
Camp Area 9 km W of Rathdowney. Turn W off Mt Lindesay Hwy 1 km S of Rathdowney onto Rathdowney-Boonah Rd for 7 km, S onto Upper Logan Rd for 500m, then R onto Bigriggen Rd. Dirt road. Bookings required
HEMA 11 J8 28 11 53 S 152 46 46 E
BIG RIG

Notes...

621 Flanagans Reserve ☎ (07) 5544 3128
Camp Area 14 km W of Rathdowney. Turn S off Rathdowney-Boonah Rd onto Upper Logan Rd (4 km), then Flanagans Reserve Rd. Dirt road
HEMA 10 J7 28 12 50 S 152 45 55 E
BIG RIG

622 Mt Barney Lodge Country Retreat ☎ (07) 5544 3233
Camp Area 19 km W of Rathdowney, 1093 Upper Logan Rd. Dirt road. Bookings essential
HEMA 10 J7 28 16 32 S 152 44 19 E

Toowoomba to Goondiwindi
Gore Highway

623 Yarramalong Weir ☎ (07) 4695 1399
Camp Spot 25 km SW of Pittsworth. From Gore Hwy, turn E 11 km N of Millmerran or 33 km S of Pittsworth onto Leyburn Rd for 11 km, then N onto Yarramalong Rd. 3 km to weir. Signposted
HEMA 13 G10 27 50 7 S 151 27 2 E
BIG RIG 72

624 Walpole Park
Rest Area at Millmerran. In Charles St between Walpole & Charlotte Sts. 400m E of PO. Dump point opposite park. Self Contained Vehicles only
HEMA 13 G10 27 52 20 S 151 16 27 E
72

625 Millmerran Showgrounds ☎ (07) 4695 1241
Camp Area at Millmerran Showgrounds. N end of town on Millmerran-Cecil Plains Rd. Entry just past Aerodrome. Call 0427 957 176 to gain access
HEMA 13 G10 27 51 37 S 151 16 40 E
BIG RIG

626 Wyaga Creek Rest Area
A39
Rest Area 74 km SW of Millmerran or 64 km NE of Goondiwindi. At Yelarbon turnoff
HEMA 13 H9 28 9 32 S 150 39 23 E
BIG RIG

Toowoomba to Stanthorpe
New England Highway

627 Nobby Town Park
Rest Area at Nobby. Opposite Rudds Hotel. Limited power available for a fee. Pay at hotel
HEMA 10 E1 27 51 8 S 151 54 13 E
BIG RIG 72

628 Clifton Recreation Grounds
☎ (07) 4697 4222

Camp Area at Clifton. N side of town in Morton St, via Clark & Devonport Sts. Caretaker on site for payment or Shire Offices. Maximum stay 7 days

HEMA 10 F1 27 55 34 S 151 54 45 E

BIG RIG

629 O'Shanley's Pub
☎ (07) 4697 3288

Camp Area at Clifton. Check in with publican. Clarke Street

HEMA 10 F1 27 55 54 S 151 54 24 E

BIG RIG

630 Clifton Golf Club
☎ 0427 933 638

Camp Spot 12 km W of Clifton on the Clifton-Leyburn Rd

HEMA 13 H11 27 56 41 S 151 47 35 E

631 Leyburn Rest Area

Rest Area 66 km SW of Toowoomba or 24 km N of Karara. Across bridge near General Store

HEMA 13 H10 28 0 27 S 151 34 58 E

BIG RIG

632 Spring Creek Caravan Park
☎ (07) 4697 3397

42

Caravan Park 8 km E of Clifton or 9 km N of Allora. New England Hwy

HEMA 10 F1 27 57 0 S 151 59 28 E

BIG RIG

633 Allora Showgrounds
☎ 0402 717 836

Camp Area at Allora. Darling St. Maximum stay 7 nights. Alt mobile 0427 100 210

HEMA 10 G1 28 2 19 S 151 59 24 E

BIG RIG

634 Allora Rest Area

42

Rest Area at Allora. N side of town. Access from Herbert St off Allora Dr. Beside Dalrymple Creek

HEMA 10 G1 28 1 45 S 151 58 58 E

BIG RIG 24

635 Killarney Sundown Motel Tourist Park
☎ (07) 4664 1318

Caravan Park at Killarney. 2-4 Pine St

HEMA 10 K4 28 20 29 S 152 17 46 E

BIG RIG

636 Jim Mitchell Park

15

Rest Area at Dalveen. 40 km S of Warwick or 18 km N of Stanthorpe. Mountain Park Rd

HEMA 13 J11 28 29 20 S 151 58 14 E

12

637 Blue Topaz Caravan Park & Camping Ground
☎ (07) 4683 5279

Caravan Park 6 km S of Stanthorpe on the New England Hwy

HEMA 13 J11 28 41 50 S 151 54 21 E

638 Country Style Tourist Accommodation Park
☎ (07) 4683 4358

15

Caravan Park 1 km N of Glen Aplin or 9 km S of Stanthorpe. New England Hwy. Beside river

HEMA 13 J11 28 43 24 S 151 53 19 E

BIG RIG

639 Bald Rock & Castle Rock Campgrounds
☎ 13 74 68

Girraween National Park

Camp Area 35 km S of Stanthorpe. Turn E off New England Hwy 7 km S of Ballandean or 11 km N of Wallangarra onto Pyramids Rd for 9 km

HEMA 13 K11 28 49 58 S 151 56 16 E

640 Wallangarra Lions Park

Rest Area at Wallangarra

HEMA 13 K11 28 55 18 S 151 55 41 E

BIG RIG

641 Broadwater Campground
☎ 13 74 68

Sundown National Park

Camp Area 79 km SW of Stanthorpe or 70 km W of Tenterfield, via Bruxner Hwy & Glenlyon Dam Rd. 5 km E of Glenlyon Dam Rd along Permanents Rd. Small vehicles only. 4 km of gravel road

HEMA 13 K10 28 55 9 S 151 34 36 E

Brisbane to Goondiwindi

Cunningham Highway

642 Rosevale Retreat Hotel
☎ (07) 5464 9258

Camp Spot at Rosevale, 16 km SW of Warrill View. Free camping for hotel customers. Fee for showers pay at bar

HEMA 10 E5 27 51 43 S 152 28 35 E

BIG RIG

643 Kalbar Showground
☎ 0409 973 608

Camp Area at Kalbar. N end of town

HEMA 10 F6 27 56 15 S 152 37 32 E

BIG RIG

644 Fassifern Memorial Reserve

15

Rest Area 5 km NE of Aratula or 16 km S of Warrill View

HEMA 10 F6 27 57 30 S 152 34 46 E

BIG RIG 20

645 Boonah Showgrounds
☎ (07) 5463 4080

Camp Area at Showgrounds. Entry via Melbourne St

HEMA 10 G7 | 27 59 51 S | 152 41 6 E

BIG RIG

646 Aratula Hotel Motel
☎ (07) 5463 8100

Parking Area at Aratula. Check in with manager on arrival. Self Contained Vehicles only

HEMA 10 F6 | 27 58 57 S | 152 32 51 E

BIG RIG 24

647 The Gorge Campground
☎ (07) 5526 0683

Camp Area 3 km S of Aratula, via Charlwood Rd & Gorge Rd. Dirt road

HEMA 10 G6 | 28 0 37 S | 152 33 16 E

648 Maryvale Crown Hotel
☎ (07) 4666 1148

Camp Spot at Maryvale. 47 Taylor St. Self Contained Vehicles only

HEMA 10 G3 | 28 4 18 S | 152 14 22 E

BIG RIG 48

649 Janowen Hills Camping and 4WD Park
☎ (07) 4666 6207

Camp Area 15 km E of Goomburra on Inverramsay Rd

HEMA 10 G3 | 27 59 44 S | 152 15 18 E

BIG RIG

650 Goomburra Valley Campground
☎ (07) 4666 6006

Camp Area 20 km E of Goomburra. 2013 Inverramsay Rd . Dogs- Vaccination Certificate must be sighted upon arrival. Dog bond payable

HEMA 10 F3 | 27 58 49 S | 152 17 37 E

BIG RIG

651 Gordon Country
☎ (07) 4666 6179

Camp Area 20 km E of Goomburra. Take Inverramsay Rd out of Goomburra

HEMA 10 F4 | 27 58 39 S | 152 17 52 E

BIG RIG

652 Goomburra Forest Retreat
☎ (07) 4666 6058

Camp Area 25 km NW of Goomburra on Forestry Reserve Rd

HEMA 10 F4 | 27 58 44 S | 152 20 16 E

Notes...

653 Poplar Flat Camping Area
☎ 13 74 68

Main Range National Park

Camp Area 25 km E of Goomburra on Inverramsay Rd into Forest Reserve Rd

HEMA 10 F4 | 27 58 44 S | 152 20 32 E

654 Manna Gum Camp Site
☎ 13 74 68

Main Range National Park

Camp Area 26 km E of Goomburra. E on Inverramsay Rd, into Forest Reserve Rd

HEMA 10 F4 | 27 58 51 S | 152 20 49 E

655 Caltex Truck Stop Roadhouse

Parking Area 6 km N of Warwick

15

HEMA 10 H2 | 28 11 5 S | 152 3 15 E

BIG RIG 12

656 The Glen

Rest Area 14.5 km S of Warwick or 47 km N of Stanthorpe. Share with trucks

HEMA 10 J1 | 28 17 14 S | 151 56 57 E

BIG RIG

657 Darling Downs Hotel
☎ (07) 4661 3413

Camp Spot 10 km W of Warwick. Turn N off Cunningham Hwy 7 km W of Warwick or 41 km E of Karara onto Sandy Creek Rd for 3 km. Fee for shower

HEMA 10 H1 | 28 11 1 S | 151 56 49 E

BIG RIG

658 Washpool Camping Reserve
☎ (07) 4661 7844

Leslie Dam

Camp Area 18 km W of Warwick. Turn S off Cunningham Hwy 9 km W of Warwick or 39 km E of Karara. Beside lake

HEMA 10 J1 | 28 14 25 S | 151 54 59 E

BIG RIG

659 Lake Leslie Tourist Park
☎ (07) 4661 9166

Caravan Park 12 km W of Warwick. 113 Saddledam Rd

HEMA 10 J1 | 28 13 37 S | 151 55 29 E

BIG RIG

660 Cunningham Rest Area

Rest Area 33 km W of Warwick or 17 km E of Karara

HEMA 13 H11 | 28 10 10 S | 151 43 52 E

BIG RIG 20

661 Glendon Camping Grounds
☎ (07) 4667 4756

Camp Area 38 km W of Warwick or 10 km E of Karara. 222 Glendon Rd, Thane

HEMA 13 H11 | 28 10 30 S | 151 41 48 E

BIG RIG

662 Gore Rest Area
Rest Area at Gore, next to store. 63 km W of Warwick or 47 km E of Inglewood
HEMA 13 H10 28 17 42 S 151 29 19 E
BIG RIG 20

663 Omanama Rest Area
Rest Area at Omanama. 88 km W of Warwick or 22 km E of Inglewood. E side of Servo
HEMA 13 J10 28 23 50 S 151 17 42 E
BIG RIG 12

664 Lake Coolmunda Camping Area
(07) 4652 4171
Camp Area at Lake Coolmunda, 16 km E of Inglewood, via Coolmunda Dam Access Rd. Register & pay at Caravan Park
HEMA 13 J10 28 25 18 S 151 12 49 E
BIG RIG

665 Lake Coolmunda Caravan Park
(07) 4652 4171
Caravan Park 16 km E of Inglewood. Turn S 7 km W of Oman-ama store or 13 km E of Inglewood
HEMA 13 J10 28 24 34 S 151 12 45 E
BIG RIG

666 Lake Roadhouse
(07) 4652 4274
Parking Area 13 km E of Inglewood on the Cunningham Hwy. Showers available during operating hours (day only)
HEMA 13 J10 28 24 28 S 151 12 13 E
BIG RIG 24

667 Inglewood RV Stop
Parking Area at Inglewood. N end of town, grassed area just S of McIntyre Brook bridge. Opposite the park. Self Contained Vehicles only
HEMA 13 J10 28 24 42 S 151 5 9 E
BIG RIG 72

668 Texas 3 Rivers Caravan Park
(07) 4653 1194
Caravan Park at Texas. Avon St
HEMA 13 K10 28 50 56 S 151 10 8 E
BIG RIG

669 Dumaresq River
Picnic Area 1 km S of Texas. Opposite stock inspection station. Maximum stay 14 days. Self Contained Vehicles only
HEMA 13 K10 28 52 3 S 151 9 51 E
BIG RIG

670 Goat Rock Camping Ground & Tourist Park
(07) 4653 0999
Camp Area 16 km S of Texas. 1040 Goat Rock Rd off Bruxner Way
HEMA 13 K10 28 57 43 S 151 6 2 E
BIG RIG

671 Carisbrooke Camping & Fishing Reserve
Camp Spot 14.5 km SW of Inglewood on Cunningham Hwy. 300m N of McDougalls Rd, beside river. N side of road
HEMA 13 J9 28 27 58 S 150 57 32 E

672 Yelarbon Recreation Ground
(07) 4675 1224
Camp Area at Yelarbon, 41 km SW of Inglewood. Wyemo St. AH contact 0438 024 158
42
HEMA 13 J9 28 34 34 S 150 45 24 E
BIG RIG

673 Mundi Rest Area
Rest Area 69 km W of Inglewood or 21 km E of Goondiwindi
42
HEMA 13 J8 28 29 19 S 150 29 10 E
BIG RIG 20

674 Monte Cristo Rest Area
Rest Area 41 km N of Goondiwindi or 52 km S of Moonie on Leichhardt Hwy
A5
HEMA 13 H8 28 10 49 S 150 16 49 E
BIG RIG 24

Goondiwindi to Thargomindah
Barwon and Balonne Highways

675 Toobeah Coronation Hotel
(07) 4677 5280
Camp spot at Toobeah. Behind hotel, please check in at the bar before parking. Free to patrons
HEMA 12 J7 28 25 1 S 149 52 14 E
BIG RIG

676 Bungunya Rest Area
Rest Area at Bungunya, 69 km W of Goondiwindi or 87 km E of Nindigully
HEMA 12 J7 28 25 23 S 149 39 28 E
BIG RIG 48

677 Talwood Sports Ground
Camp Spot at Talwood, 91 km W of Goondiwindi or 65 km E of Nindigully. Donation appreciated for upkeep of grounds. Limited power
HEMA 12 J7 28 29 12 S 149 28 8 E
BIG RIG 72

678 Weengallon Rest Area
Rest Area at Weengallon. 40 km W of Talwood or 26 km E of Nindigully S side of Hwy
HEMA 12 H6 28 21 29 S 149 3 17 E
BIG RIG 20

679 Nindigully Hotel

Camp Spot at Nindigully, 1 km S of Barwon Hwy jcn. Camping beside Moonie River. In front of the hotel. Donation for upkeep of facilities

46

HEMA 12 H5 | 28 21 17 S | 148 49 15 E

BIG RIG

680 Thallon Recreation Ground

☎ 0427 259 095

Camp Spot at Thallon. Call mobile for access key or see PO during business hours

46

HEMA 12 J5 | 28 37 58 S | 148 51 59 E

BIG RIG

681 Boolba Rest Area

Rest Area 56 km W of St George or 56 km E of Bollon

49

HEMA 12 H4 | 27 58 10 S | 148 2 36 E

BIG RIG

682 Yumbai Creek

Camp Spot at Bollon. Willliam St. 500m N of Fire Station beside river. Donation for upkeep

HEMA 12 H3 | 28 1 40 S | 147 28 41 E

BIG RIG 24

683 Charlotte Plains

☎ (07) 4655 4923

Camp Area Turn S 135 km W of Bollon or 46 km E of Cunnamulla, then 15 km dirt road to homestead. Signposted. Advance bookings preferred

HEMA 23 F14 | 28 4 55 S | 146 10 32 E

684 Warrego River

Camp Spot 95.7 km S of Cunnamulla or 38.7 km N of Barringum. Turn W 89 km S of Cunnamulla into Tinnenburra Rd for 6.7 km to bush camping area by river

HEMA 23 G13 | 28 44 4 S | 145 36 38 E

685 Bowra Sanctuary

☎ (07) 4655 1238

Camp Area 10 km N of Cunnamulla via the Humeburn Rd. Turn W at Signposted gate, then 6 kms to house. Bookings essential limited sites & power. Closed to public summer period Dec to Feb

HEMA 23 F13 | 27 59 32 S | 145 40 22 E

686 Wyandra Camping Ground

☎ (07) 4655 2481

Camp Area at Wyandra, N end of town, behind school. Donations requested

A71

HEMA 23 D13 | 27 14 37 S | 145 58 36 E

BIG RIG

687 Wyandra Post & General Store

☎ (07) 4654 9212

Camp Area at Wyandra, N end of town, behind PO & General Store

A71

HEMA 23 D13 | 27 14 46 S | 145 58 48 E

BIG RIG

688 Paddabilla Bore

Camp Spot 50 km W of Cunnamulla or 16 km E of Eulo. 300m behind bore

HEMA 23 F12 | 28 7 2 S | 145 11 40 E

BIG RIG

689 Eulo Queen Hotel

☎ (07) 4655 4867

Camp Area at Hotel in Eulo. Leo St

HEMA 23 F12 | 28 9 37 S | 145 2 49 E

BIG RIG

690 Paroo River

Camp Spot 1.5 km W of Eulo or 128 km E of Thargomindah. Both sides of bridge

HEMA 23 F11 | 28 9 38 S | 145 2 12 E

BIG RIG

691 Wandilla Station

☎ (07) 4655 4065

Camp Area at Wandilla Station. 15 km S of Eulo. From Eulo, head S on Pitherty Rd, turn W at the Big Yellow Sponge Bob letterbox

HEMA 23 F11 | 28 17 4 S | 144 59 9 E

BIG RIG

692 Southern Cross Caravan Park

☎ (07) 4655 4105

Caravan Park at Hungerford. Honesty box provided for outside hours

HEMA 23 H11 | 28 59 51 S | 144 24 35 E

693 Kilcowera Station

☎ (07) 4655 4960

Camp Area at Kilcowera Station. 95 km S Tharomindah or 90 km N of Hungerford. Bookings essential. High clearance 4WD. Open 1st March to 31st October

HEMA 23 G9 | 28 40 52 S | 143 56 14 E

BIG RIG

694 Artesian Waters Caravan Park

☎ (07) 4655 4953

Caravan Park at Yowah Opal Field. 87 km NW of Eulo. Bluff Rd

HEMA 23 E10 | 27 58 15 S | 144 38 17 E

BIG RIG

695 Yowah Rest Area

Rest Area at Yowah. First turn L after school. Donation requested

HEMA 23 F11 | 27 58 1 S | 144 37 59 E

696 Toompine Hotel

☎ (07) 4656 4863

Camp Area at Toompine Hotel, 76 km S of Quilpie or 120 km N of Thargomindah. Donation

HEMA 23 D10 | 27 13 30 S | 144 22 5 E

BIG RIG

Notes...

697 Aldville Station
☎ 07 4655 4814

Camp Area at Aldville Station. 120 km NW of Cunnamulla or 110 kms W of Wyandra. Advance booking appreciated

HEMA 23 D12 27 17 45 S 145 9 12 E

698 Lake Bindegolly Bush Camping

Camp Spot 34 km E of Thargomindah or 90 km W of Eulo. Turn S 100m W of National Park Rest Area entrance, follow track. Signposted. Do not camp in rest area

HEMA 23 F10 28 5 35 S 144 12 12 E

699 Thargomindah Explorers Caravan Park
☎ (07) 4655 3307

Caravan Park at Thargomindah. Dowling St. 500m W of PO

HEMA 23 F9 27 59 51 S 143 49 11 E

BIG RIG

700 Bulloo Development Rd

Parking Area 75 km W of Thargomindah or 63 E of Noccundra turn off

HEMA 23 E8 27 46 24 S 143 21 22 E

BIG RIG

701 Wilson River Camp
☎ (07) 4655 3055

Camp Spot at Noccundra. Opposite hotel, beside river. Facilities at hall

HEMA 22 E7 27 49 16 S 142 35 26 E

BIG RIG

702 Jackson Oil Field Rest Area

Rest Area at the cnr of Cooper Development Rd & Adventure Way

HEMA 22 E7 27 37 59 S 142 41 1 E

BIG RIG

703 Burke & Wills Dig Tree
☎ (07) 4655 4323

Nappa Merrie Station

Camp Area 46 km E of Innamincka or 225 km W of Noccundra on the Adventure Way. Signposted

HEMA 22 E4 27 37 19 S 141 4 24 E

704 Epsilon Station
☎)07) 4655 4324

Camp Area at Epsilon Station. 116 km SE of Innamincka. Bookings essential, pets on request

HEMA 22 F4 28 17 58 S 141 12 7 E

BIG RIG

Rolleston to Hebel (NSW border)

Carnarvon and Castlereagh Highways

705 Lake Nuga Nuga
☎ 13 74 68

Nuga Nuga National Park

Camp Area 85 km SE of Rolleston. Access via Arcadia Valley Access Rd, 28 km SE of Rolleston on Dawson Hwy. 58 km gravel road, then W onto Lake Nuga Nuga Access Rd. Dirt road

HEMA 12 A5 24 59 32 S 148 41 4 E

706 Lonesome Bush Camping Area
☎ 13 74 68

Expedition National Park

Camp Area 55 km NE of Injune. Travel N for 26 km on Carnarvon Hwy, turn E onto Arcadia Valley Rd, 18 km to campsite. 4 km dirt road

HEMA 12 B5 25 29 28 S 148 49 51 E

BIG RIG

707 Injune Rodeo Ground
☎ (07) 4626 0503

Camp Spot at Injune. 1.6 km S of town

HEMA 12 C5 25 51 14 S 148 33 28 E

BIG RIG 48

708 Possum Park
☎ (07) 4626 0503

Camp Area at Injune. Racecourse Rd, off the Carnarvon Hwy. Pay at Info Centre, caretaker will visit

HEMA 12 C5 25 50 49 S 148 33 25 E

BIG RIG 72

709 Croydon Rest Area

55

Parking Area 31 km S of Roma or 47 km N of Surat

HEMA 12 E6 26 46 47 S 148 56 3 E

BIG RIG

710 Toalki Rest Area

55

Rest Area 65 km S of Roma or 13 km N of Surat

HEMA 12 E6 27 2 4 S 149 4 58 E

BIG RIG

711 Surat Fishing & Restocking Club Park
☎ (07) 4626 5058

55

Camp Area 1 km N of Surat. Just over Balonne River. Gold Coin donation

HEMA 12 F6 27 8 57 S 149 4 23 E

BIG RIG 72

712 Surat Caravan Park
☎ (07) 4626 5218

Caravan Park at Surat. Marcus St. Key & payment at Hotel opposite

HEMA 12 F6 27 9 5 S 149 3 59 E

BIG RIG

713 Warroo Bridge

Camp Spot 60 km N of St George. Turn W at Wycombe School, 66 km S of Surat or 51 km N of St George for 9 km of dirt road

HEMA 12 G5 27 38 34 S 148 44 28 E

48

714 Begonia Farm Stay
☎ (07) 4625 7415

Camp Area at Begonia Farm Stay. 74 km N of St George or 135 km S of Mitchell. Advance bookings essential, pets on request

HEMA 12 G4 27 30 11 S 148 18 52 E

BIG RIG

715 Beardmore

Camp Spot 15 km N of St George. Turn W off Carnarvon Hwy 103 km S of Surat or 14 km N of St George onto Beardmore Dam Rd for 1 km. Left at 1st grid. Camp beside river

HEMA 12 H5 27 57 25 S 148 40 59 E

QUEENSLAND

716 Kapunda Tourist & Fishing Park
☎ (07) 4625 5546

55

Camp Area at St George. 9 km N of PO on Carnarvon Hwy. GPS at gate

HEMA 12 H5 27 59 14 S 148 39 33 E

BIG RIG

717 Toorumbee Rest Area

49

Rest Area 38 km E of St George or 148 km W of Moonie

HEMA 12 H6 27 58 8 S 148 56 17 E

BIG RIG

718 Westmar Rest Area

49

Rest Area at Westmar. Adjacent to Pub

HEMA 12 H7 27 55 8 S 149 43 5 E

BIG RIG

719 Kamarooka Tourist Park
☎ (07) 4625 3120

55

Caravan Park at St George. 56 Victoria St

HEMA 12 H5 28 2 1 S 148 35 12 E

BIG RIG

720 Noondoo Rest Area

Rest Area 19.5 km E of Dirranbandi or 76 km S of St George. Share with trucks

HEMA 12 J5 28 36 36 S 148 25 23 E

BIG RIG

721 Dirranbandi Caravan Park
☎ (07) 4625 8707

Caravan Park at Dirranbandi. 45 Kirby St

HEMA 12 J4 28 34 53 S 148 13 44 E

BIG RIG

722 Balonne Minor Bridge

Rest Area 3 km W of Dirranbandi, on Dirranbandi-Bollon Rd

HEMA 12 J4 28 35 56 S 148 12 34 E

723 Hebel Caravan Park
☎ (07) 4625 0920

Caravan Park at Hebel. William St, behind general store

HEMA 12 K3 28 58 18 S 147 47 44 E

Cairns to Cape York

This road is seasonal and more suitable to 4WD vehicles, camper trailers and off road caravans. Road conditions phone Main Roads 131 940, Cooktown Shire 07 4069 5444 or RACQ 1300 130 595

724 Ang-Ganrra Aboriginal Community
☎ (07) 4060 3214

Camp Spot 61 km NW of Lakeland or 1 km SE of Laura. Signposted

HEMA 19 K5 15 39 1 S 144 32 2 E

725 Quinkan Hotel & Camp Ground
☎ (07) 4060 3393

Camp Area at Laura, 62 km NW of Lakeland or 76 km SE of Hann River Roadhouse. At hotel. Limited power available

HEMA 19 K5 15 33 59 S 144 27 1 E

BIG RIG

726 Quinkan Remote Community Campground
☎ (07) 4060 3419

Camp Spot at Laura, 62 km NW of Lakeland or 76 km SE of Hann River Roadhouse. Pay at Laura Roadhouse

HEMA 19 K5 15 33 57 S 144 26 57 E

BIG RIG

727 Rinyirru (Lakefield) National Park
☎ 13 74 68

Lakefield National Park

Various camp spots in Lakefield National Park. Permit required. Maximum stay 21 days, GPS taken at Old Laura Homestead, S entrance to the park. Must purchase an epermit before arriving

HEMA 19 J5 15 20 43 S 144 27 17 E

728 Jowalbinna Rock Art Safari Camp
☎ (07) 4060 3236

Camp Area 36 km SW of Laura. Turn SW 1 km N of Laura. Signposted. Open May-Nov, reservations preferred

HEMA 19 K5 15 45 39 S 144 15 25 E

729 Kennedy River Rest Area

Rest Area 33 km N of Laura or 43 km S of Hann River Roadhouse

HEMA 19 K5 15 25 13 S 144 11 12 E

730 Hann River Roadhouse
☎ (07) 4060 3242

Camp Area at Hann River. 74 km NW of Laura or 62 km S of Musgrave

HEMA 19 J5 15 11 20 S 143 52 22 E

731 Morehead River Rest Area

Rest Area 27 km N of Hann River Roadhouse or 63 km S of Musgrave Roadhouse

HEMA 19 J4 15 1 22 S 143 39 50 E

732 Musgrave Roadhouse
☎ (07) 4060 3229

Camp Area at Musgrave. 62 km N of Hann River Roadhouse or 107 km S of Coen

HEMA 19 J4 14 46 51 S 143 30 14 E

Notes...

733 Mungkan River Camping Area
☎ (07) 4060 4155

Camp Area at Pormpuraaw. 210 km W of Musgrave. 7.5 km N of township. Permit required from Ranger

HEMA 19 J1 14 51 31 S 141 36 13 E

734 Chapman River
☎ (07) 4060 4155

Camp Area at Pormpuraaw. 210 km W of Musgrave. 2.5 km S of township. Permit required from Ranger

HEMA 19 J1 14 55 0 S 141 37 18 E

735 Lukin River Rest Area

Rest Area 55 km S of Coen or 53 km N of Musgrave Roadhouse. Small area

HEMA 19 H4 14 23 43 S 143 21 42 E

736 Port Stewart Campground

Camp Area at Port Stewart. 19 km E of Peninsula Development Rd. Register at community offices

HEMA 19 G4 14 4 10 S 143 40 58 E

737 Charlies Mine

Camp Area 2 km SE of Coen

HEMA 19 G3 13 57 39 S 143 12 45 E

738 The Bend

Camp Spot on Peninsula Development Rd. 3 km N of Coen. Bush camping

HEMA 19 G3 13 55 27 S 143 11 38 E

739 Archer River Roadhouse
☎ (07) 4060 3266

Camp Area at Archer River Crossing. 64 km N of Coen or 123 km S of Moreton Telegraph Station

HEMA 19 F3 13 26 16 S 142 56 27 E

740 Chuulangun Aboriginal Corporation Campgrounds
☎ (07) 4060 3240

Camp Area 16 km E of the Peninsula Development Rd, 7 km off the Portland Roads Rd. Permit required

HEMA 19 F3 13 6 27 S 142 57 52 E

741 Rainforest Campground
☎ 13 74 68

Kutini-Payamu (Iron Range) National Park

Camp Area 130 km NE of Archer River Roadhouse. Camp site near the Portland & Lockhart River Rd jcn. Permit required. 2 small sites. Must be prebooked

HEMA 19 E3 12 42 49 S 143 17 13 E

742 Cooks Hut Campground
☎ 13 74 68

Kutini-Payamu (Iron Range) National Park

Camp Area 130 km NE of Archer River Roadhouse. Camp site near the Portland & Lockhart River Rd jcn. Permit required

HEMA 19 E4 12 42 35 S 143 17 33 E

743 Gordon Creek Campground Sth
☎ 13 74 68

Kutini-Payamu (Iron Range) National Park

Camp Area 135 km NE of Archer River Roadhouse. Camp site near the Portland & Lockhart River Rd jcn. Permit required must be pre booked

HEMA 19 E3 12 42 48 S 143 17 53 E

744 Chilli Beach Campground
☎ 13 74 68

Kutini-Payamu (Iron Range) National Park

Camp Area 170 km NE of Archer River Rd Roadhouse. Permit required must be pre booked

HEMA 19 E4 12 37 52 S 143 25 36 E

745 Merluna Station Stay & Tourist Park
☎ (07) 4060 3209

Camp Area 150 km NW of Coen or 150 km SE of Weipa on the Peninsula Development Rd. Signposted.

HEMA 19 F2 13 3 54 S 142 27 1 E

BIG RIG

746 Weipa Caravan Park & Camping Ground
☎ (07) 4069 7871

Caravan Park at Weipa. Newbold Dr. Bookings essential in high season (June-Sep)

HEMA 19 E1 12 38 20 S 141 51 38 E

BIG RIG

747 Moreton Telegraph Station Camping Ground
☎ (07) 4060 3360

Camp Area at Morton Telegraph Station. 123 km N of Archer River Roadhouse. Limited power

HEMA 19 E3 12 27 13 S 142 38 19 E

BIG RIG

748 Bramwell Station
☎ (07) 4060 3300

Camp Area at Bramwell Station. 37 km NE of Moreton Telegraph Station or 8 km SE of Bramwell Junction

HEMA 19 D3 12 8 26 S 142 37 19 E

BIG RIG

749 Bramwell Roadhouse
☎ (07) 4060 3230

Camp Area at Bramwell Junction

HEMA 19 D2 12 5 33 S 142 33 37 E

BIG RIG

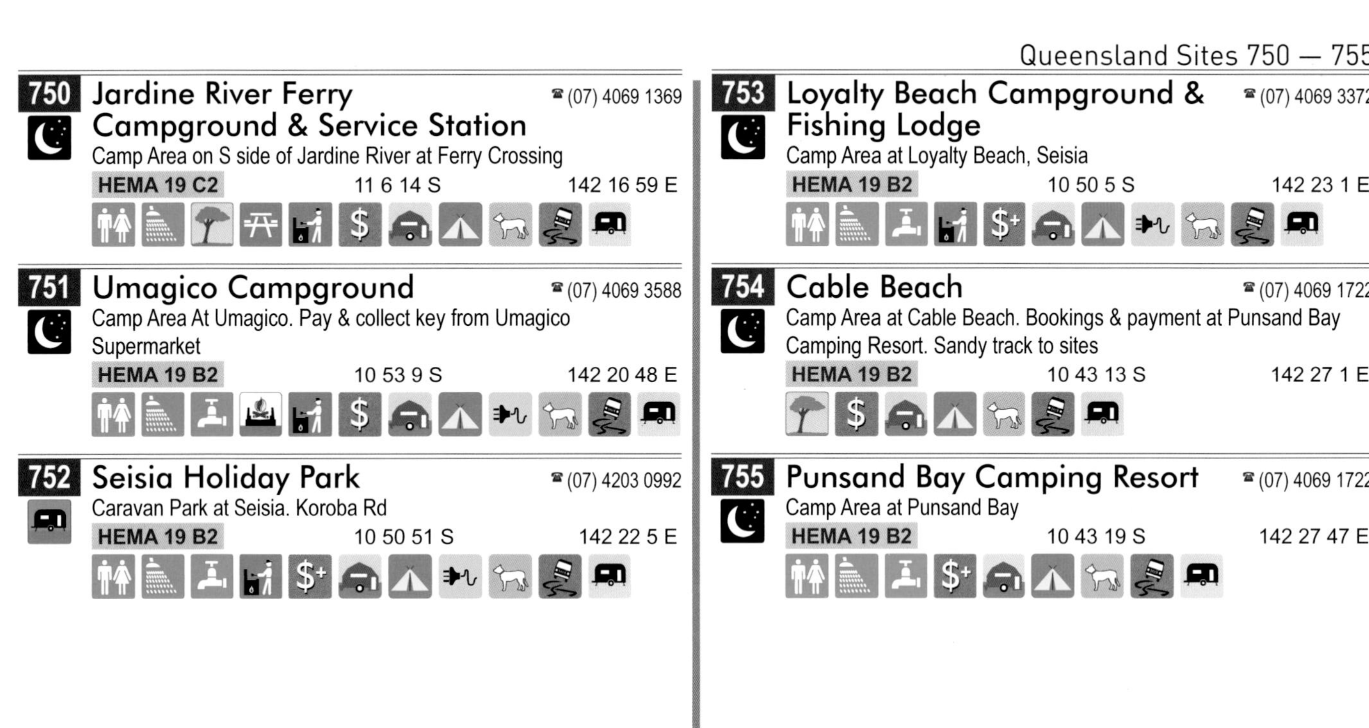

750 Jardine River Ferry Campground & Service Station

☎ (07) 4069 1369

Camp Area on S side of Jardine River at Ferry Crossing

HEMA 19 C2 11 6 14 S 142 16 59 E

751 Umagico Campground

☎ (07) 4069 3588

Camp Area At Umagico. Pay & collect key from Umagico Supermarket

HEMA 19 B2 10 53 9 S 142 20 48 E

752 Seisia Holiday Park

☎ (07) 4203 0992

Caravan Park at Seisia. Koroba Rd

HEMA 19 B2 10 50 51 S 142 22 5 E

753 Loyalty Beach Campground & Fishing Lodge

☎ (07) 4069 3372

Camp Area at Loyalty Beach, Seisia

HEMA 19 B2 10 50 5 S 142 23 1 E

754 Cable Beach

☎ (07) 4069 1722

Camp Area at Cable Beach. Bookings & payment at Punsand Bay Camping Resort. Sandy track to sites

HEMA 19 B2 10 43 13 S 142 27 1 E

755 Punsand Bay Camping Resort

☎ (07) 4069 1722

Camp Area at Punsand Bay

HEMA 19 B2 10 43 19 S 142 27 47 E

Notes...

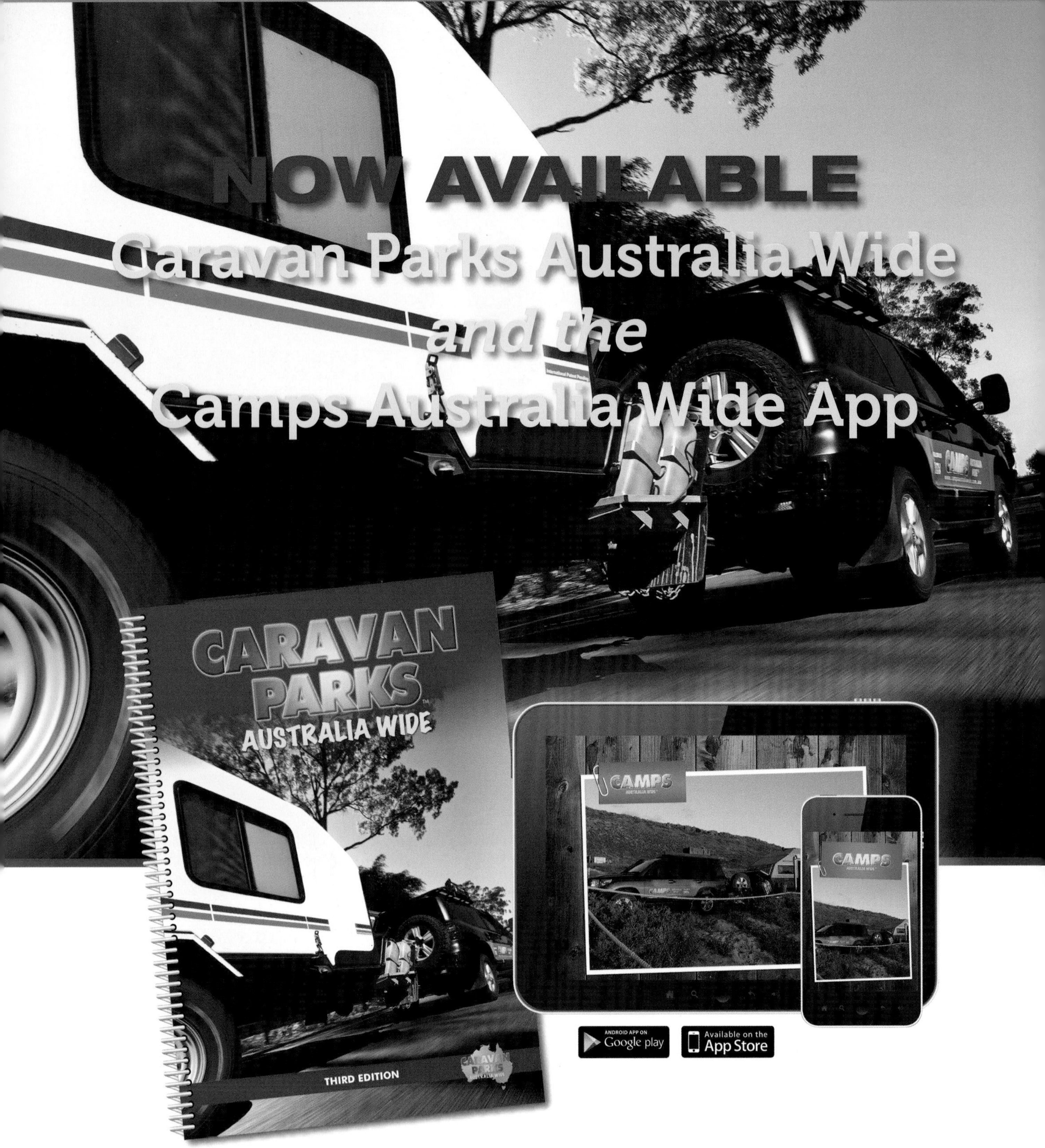

NOW AVAILABLE
Caravan Parks Australia Wide
and the
Camps Australia Wide App
CARAVAN PARKS
AUSTRALIA WIDE
THIRD EDITION
CAMPS
AUSTRALIA WIDE
ANDROID APP ON Google play
Available on the App Store

NEW SOUTH WALES

key map

THE THREE SISTER, BLUE MOUNTAINS (34 E4) PHOTO: © ISTOCK.COM/TOMOGRAF

	Wagga Wagga	Tamworth	Sydney	Port Macquarie	Newcastle	Mildura	Lismore	Grafton	Goulburn	Dubbo	Canberra	Broken Hill	Bathurst	Armidale	Albury
Armidale															993
Bathurst														547	446
Broken Hill													981	1119	832
Canberra												1133	263	810	340
Dubbo											475	775	206	446	537
Goulburn										410	89	1155	174	721	362
Grafton									809	641	899	1314	742	195	1188
Lismore								134	943	775	1048	1448	876	329	1322
Mildura							1576	1442	859	801	807	296	810	1247	617
Newcastle						1188	628	479	358	428	448	1094	355	398	721
Port Macquarie					251	1411	397	248	600	603	671	1276	578	235	944
Sydney				382	159	1029	759	610	205	403	289	1177	196	529	562
Tamworth			414	272	283	1132	444	310	619	331	703	1004	432	115	878
Wagga Wagga		752	465	847	624	564	1224	1075	265	411	243	890	320	857	126
Wollongong	400	492	78	460	237	964	837	688	134	481	224	1255	274	607	526

Distances are shown in kilometres and follow the most direct major sealed route where possible.

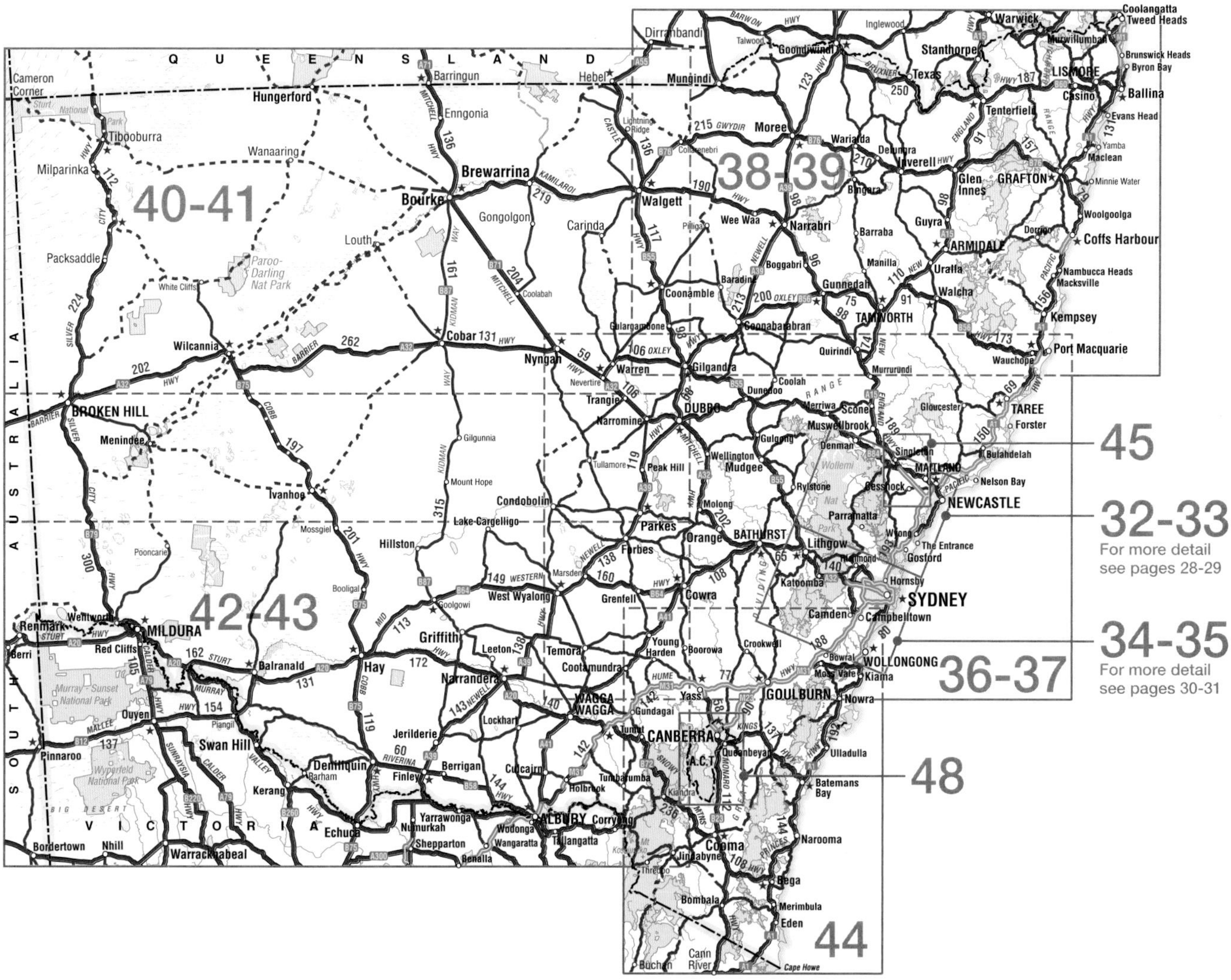

40-41

38-39

42-43

36-37

45

32-33
For more detail see pages 28-29

34-35
For more detail see pages 30-31

48

44

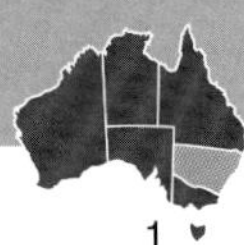

Sydney CBD

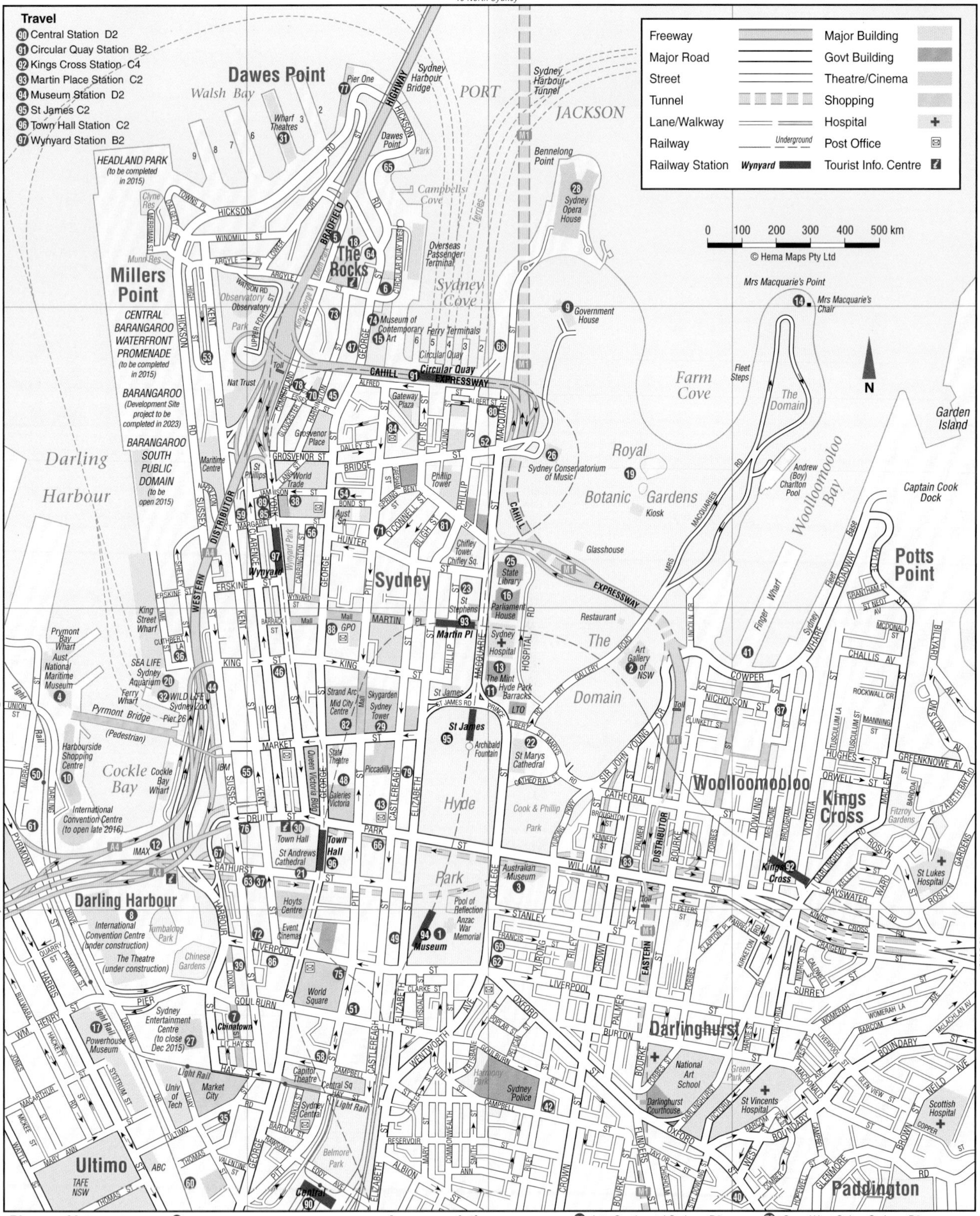

Travel
- 90 Central Station D2
- 91 Circular Quay Station B2
- 92 Kings Cross Station C4
- 93 Martin Place Station C2
- 94 Museum Station D2
- 95 St James C2
- 96 Town Hall Station C2
- 97 Wynyard Station B2

Freeway		Major Building	
Major Road		Govt Building	
Street		Theatre/Cinema	
Tunnel		Shopping	
Lane/Walkway		Hospital	
Railway	Underground	Post Office	
Railway Station	Wynyard	Tourist Info. Centre	

0 100 200 300 400 500 km

© Hema Maps Pty Ltd

Places of Interest

1. Anzac War Memorial D2
2. Art Gallery of NSW C3
3. Australian Museum C3
4. Australian Nat. Maritime Museum C1
5. Bridge Climb Sydney A2
6. Cadmans Cottage A2
7. Chinatown D1
8. Darling Harbour D1
9. Government House B3
10. Harbourside Shopping Centre C1
11. Hyde Park Barracks C3
12. LG IMAX Theatre Sydney C1
13. Mint, The C3
14. Mrs Macquarie's Chair A4
15. Museum of Contemporary Art B2
16. Parliament House B3
17. Powerhouse Museum D1
18. Rocks, The A2
19. Royal Botanic Gardens B3
20. SEA LIFE Sydney Aquarium C1
21. St Andrews Cathedral C2
22. St Marys Cathedral C3
23. St Stephens Church B2
24. Star, The C1
25. State Library of NSW B3
26. Sydney Conservatorium of Music B3
27. Sydney Entertainment Centre D1
28. Sydney Opera House A3
29. Sydney Tower Eye & SKYWALK C2
30. Sydney Town Hall C2
31. Wharf Theatres A2
32. WILD LIFE Sydney Zoo C1

Accommodation

35. Aarons Hotel Sydney D1
36. Adina Apartment Hotel Harbourside C1
37. Adina Apartment Hotel Sydney C2
38. Amora Hotel Jamison Sydney B2
39. APX Apartments Darling Hbr D1
40. Arts Hotel D4
41. Blue Sydney C4
42. Cambridge Hotel Sydney D3
43. Castlereagh Boutique Hotel C2
44. Four Points by Sheraton Sydney C1
45. Four Seasons Hotel Sydney B2
46. Grace Hotel Sydney (The) C2
47. Harbour Rocks Hotel (The) B2
48. Hilton Sydney C2
49. Hyde Park Inn D2
50. Ibis Sydney Darling Harbour C1
51. Ibis Sydney World Square D2
52. InterContinental Sydney B2
53. Langham Sydney (The) B1
54. Mantra 2 Bond Street B2
55. Mantra on Kent C1
56. Menzies Sydney (The) B2
57. Mercure Sydney D1
58. Metro Hotel Sydney Central D2
59. Napoleon on Kent B1
60. Novotel Sydney Central D1
61. Novotel Sydney on Darling Harbour C1
62. Oaks Hyde Park Plaza D3
63. Oaks Maestri Towers C1
64. Old Sydney Holiday Inn A2
65. Park Hyatt Hotel Sydney A2
66. Park Regis City Centre C2
67. Parkroyal Darling Harbour C1
68. Pullman Quay Grand Sydney Harbour B3
69. Pullman Sydney Hyde Park Hotel D3
70. Quay West Suites Sydney B2
71. Radisson Blue Plaza Hotel Sydney B2
72. Radisson Sydney D2
73. Rendezvous Hotel Sydney The Rocks B2
74. Russell Hotel B2
75. Rydges World Square Sydney D2
76. Seasons Harbour Plaza Sydney C1
77. Sebel Pier One Sydney (The) A2
78. Shangri-La Hotel Sydney B2
79. Sheraton on the Park C2
80. Sir Stamford at Circular Quay B2
81. Sofitel Sydney Wentworth B2
82. Swissotel Sydney C2
83. Sydney Boulevard Hotel (The) C3
84. Sydney Harbour Marriott Hotel B2
85. Travelodge Wynyard B2
86. Waldorf Apartment Hotel (The) D2
87. Waldorf Woolloomooloo Waters C4
88. Westin Sydney (The) C2
89. York by Swiss - Belhotel (The) B2

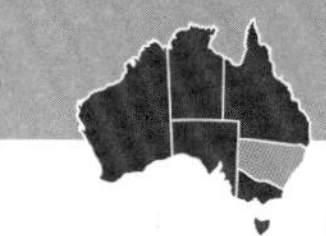

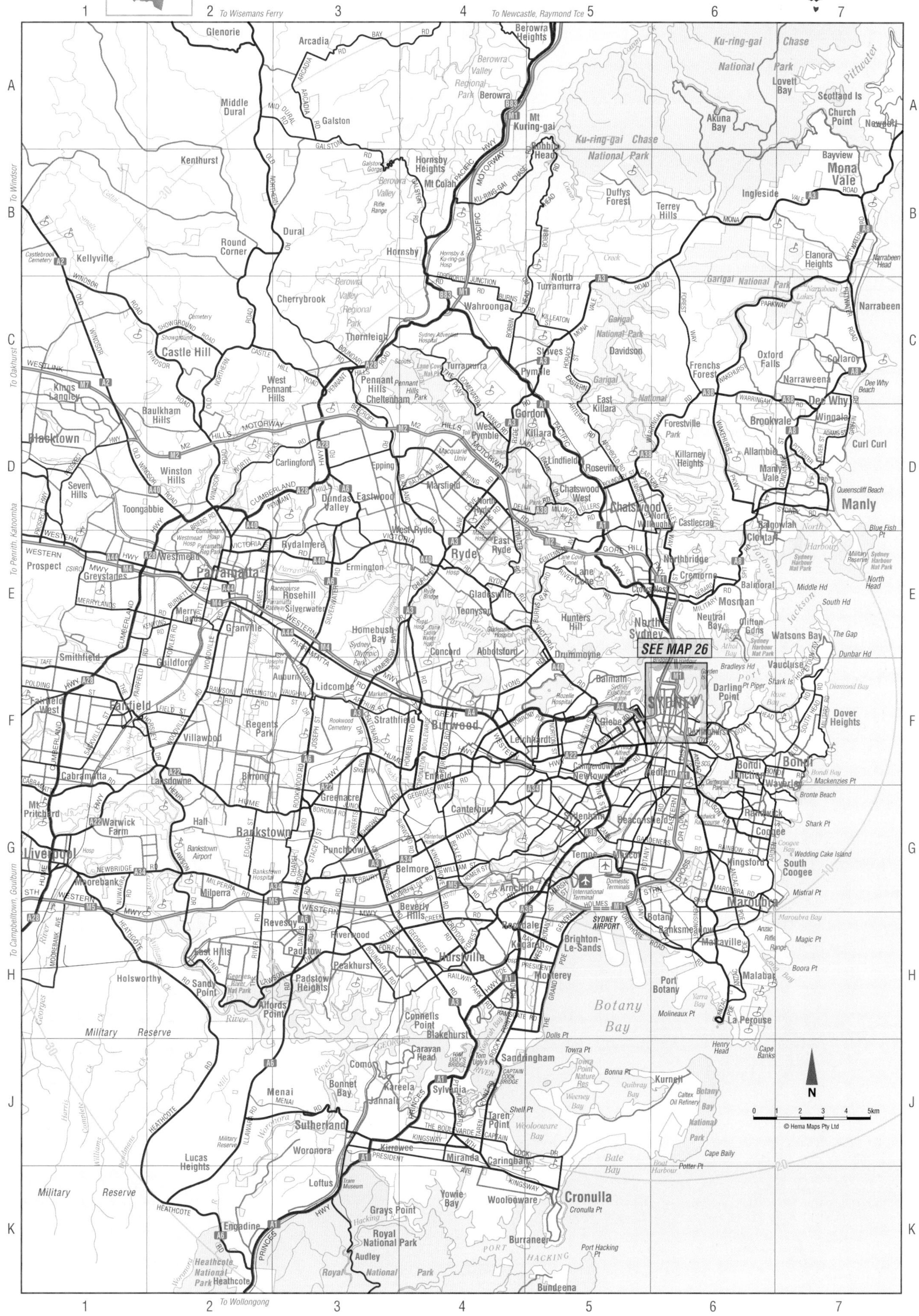

To Wisemans Ferry
Glenorie
Arcadia
Berowra Heights
Berowra Valley Regional Park
Berowra
Ku-ring-gai Chase National Park
Pittwater
Lovett Bay
Scotland Is
Church Point
Newport
Akuna Bay
Middle Dural
Galston
Mt Kuring-gai
Cobbitty Head
Kenthurst
Hornsby Heights
Mt Colah
Duffys Forest
Terrey Hills
Bayview
Mona Vale
Ingleside
Dural
Round Corner
Kellyville
Hornsby
North Turramurra
Elanora Heights
Narrabeen
Garigal National Park
Cherrybrook
Wahroonga
Castle Hill
Thornleigh
Davidson
Oxford Falls
Collaroy
Frenchs Forest
Narraweena
Dee Why
Kings Langley
West Pennant Hills
Pennant Hills
Cheltenham
Turramurra
St Ives
Pymble
East Killara
Brookvale
Curl Curl
Baulkham Hills
Blacktown
Gordon
West Pymble
Killara
Forestville
Killarney Heights
Allambie
Manly Vale
Winston Hills
Carlingford
Epping
Lindfield
Roseville
Seven Hills
Toongabbie
Dundas Valley
Eastwood
Marsfield
North Ryde
Chatswood West
Chatswood
Castlecrag
Manly
Balgowlah
Clontarf
Rydalmere
West Ryde
Ryde
East Ryde
Westmead
Parramatta
Prospect
Greystanes
Ermington
Lane Cove
Northbridge
Cremorne
Balmoral
North Head
Rosehill
Silverwater
Merrylands
Gladesville
Tennyson
Hunters Hill
Mosman
Neutral Bay
Clifton Gdns
Middle Hd
Granville
Homebush Bay
North Sydney
Watsons Bay
Smithfield
Guildford
Concord
Abbotsford
Drummoyne
SEE MAP 26
Vaucluse
Auburn
Lidcombe
Balmain
Darling Point
Fairfield West
Fairfield
Villawood
Regents Park
Strathfield
Burwood
Leichhardt
Glebe
SYDNEY
Darlinghurst
Dover Heights
Bondi
Bondi Junction
Waverley
Cabramatta
Lansdowne
Birrong
Enfield
Camperdown
Newtown
Redfern
Centennial Park
Bronte Beach
Mt Pritchard
Warwick Farm
Hall
Bankstown
Greenacre
Canterbury
Sydenham
Beaconsfield
Randwick
Coogee
Liverpool
Moorebank
Milperra
Punchbowl
Belmore
Tempe
Mascot
Kingsford
South Coogee
Revesby
Beverly Hills
Arncliffe
Maroubra
Riverwood
Rockdale
Botany
Banksmeadow
Matraville
East Hills
Padstow
Peakhurst
Hurstville
Kogarah
Brighton-Le-Sands
SYDNEY AIRPORT
Holsworthy
Sandy Point
Padstow Heights
Alfords Point
Monterey
Malabar
Port Botany
Botany Bay
La Perouse
Military Reserve
Connells Point
Blakehurst
Caravan Head
Sandringham
Como
Bonnet Bay
Kareela
Jannali
Sylvania
Kurnell
Menai
Taren Point
Woolooware Bay
Sutherland
Woronora
Kirrawee
Miranda
Caringbah
Lucas Heights
Loftus
Yowie Bay
Woolooware
Cronulla
Engadine
Grays Point
Royal National Park
Audley
Burraneer
Port Hacking
Heathcote National Park
Heathcote
Bundeena
© Hema Maps Pty Ltd

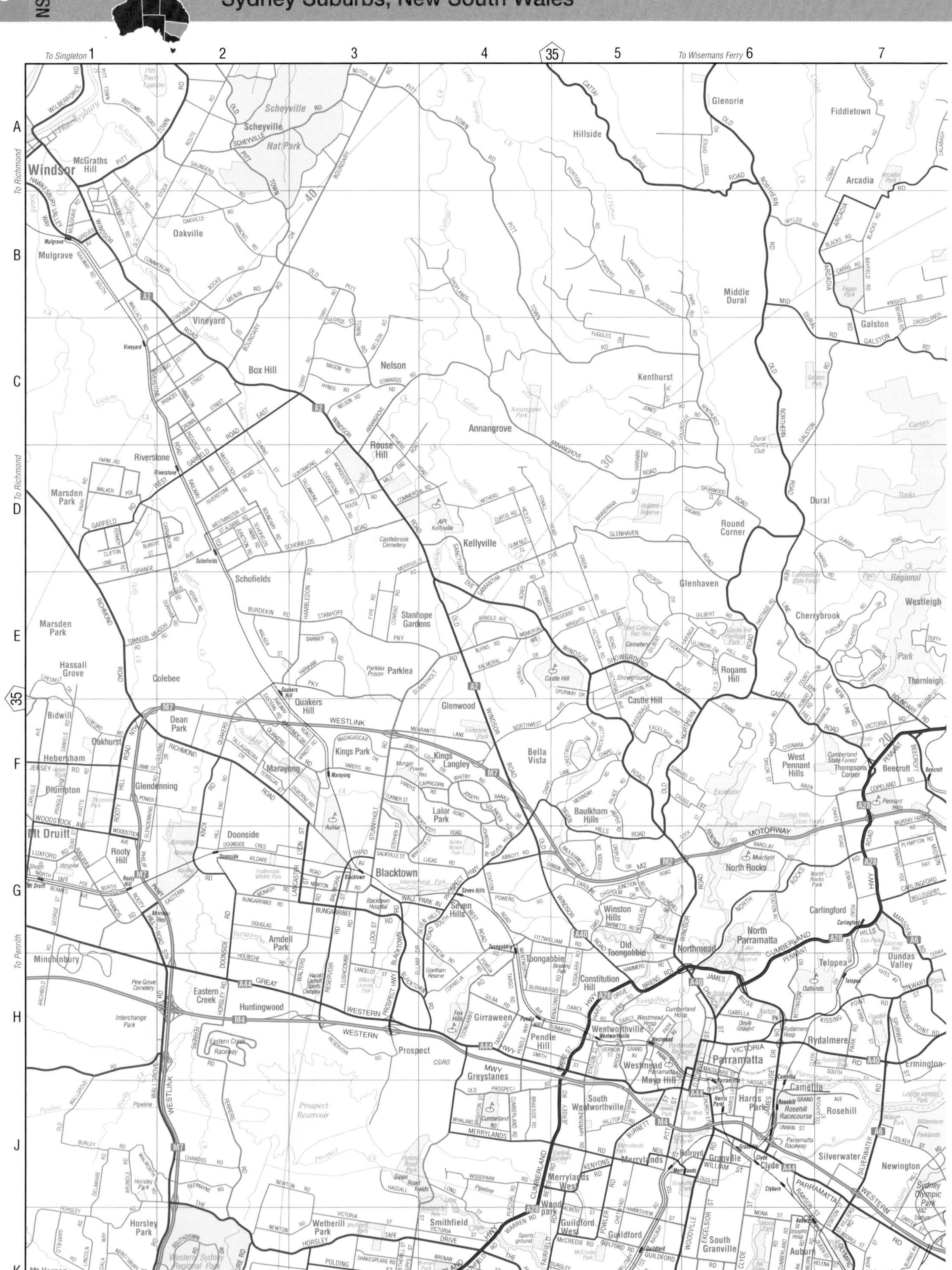
To Singleton
To Wisemans Ferry
To Richmond
To Penrith
To Campbelltown
To Liverpool
To Bankstown
Windsor
McGraths Hill
Mulgrave
Scheyville Nat Park
Oakville
Vineyard
Box Hill
Nelson
Glenorie
Fiddletown
Hillside
Arcadia
Middle Dural
Galston
Kenthurst
Annangrove
Rouse Hill
Riverstone
Marsden Park
Schofields
Kellyville
Dural
Round Corner
Glenhaven
Stanhope Gardens
Parklea
Colebee
Hassall Grove
Cherrybrook
Westleigh
Rogans Hill
Thornleigh
Castle Hill
Bidwill
Dean Park
Quakers Hill
Glenwood
Bella Vista
Oakhurst
Hebersham
Kings Park
Kings Langley
West Pennant Hills
Thompsons Corner
Beecroft
Plumpton
Marayong
Glendenning
Lalor Park
Baulkham Hills
Mt Druitt
Doonside
Rooty Hill
Blacktown
North Rocks
Seven Hills
Winston Hills
Carlingford
Arndell Park
Minchinbury
Toongabbie
Old Toongabbie
Northmead
North Parramatta
Telopea
Dundas Valley
Constitution Hill
Eastern Creek
Huntingwood
Girraween
Wentworthville
Pendle Hill
Prospect
Parramatta
Rydalmere
Ermington
Greystanes
Westmead
Mays Hill
Camellia
South Wentworthville
Harris Park
Rosehill
Prospect Reservoir
Merrylands
Holroyd
Granville
Clyde
Silverwater
Newington
Merrylands West
Smithfield
Guildford
Guildford West
Horsley Park
Wetherill Park
South Granville
Auburn
Lidcombe
Mt Vernon
Abbotsbury
Bossley Park
Prairiewood
Fairfield West
Fairfield
Fairfield Heights
Yennora
Old Guildford
Fairfield East
Rookwood
Cecil Park
Western Sydney Regional Park
Sydney Olympic Park

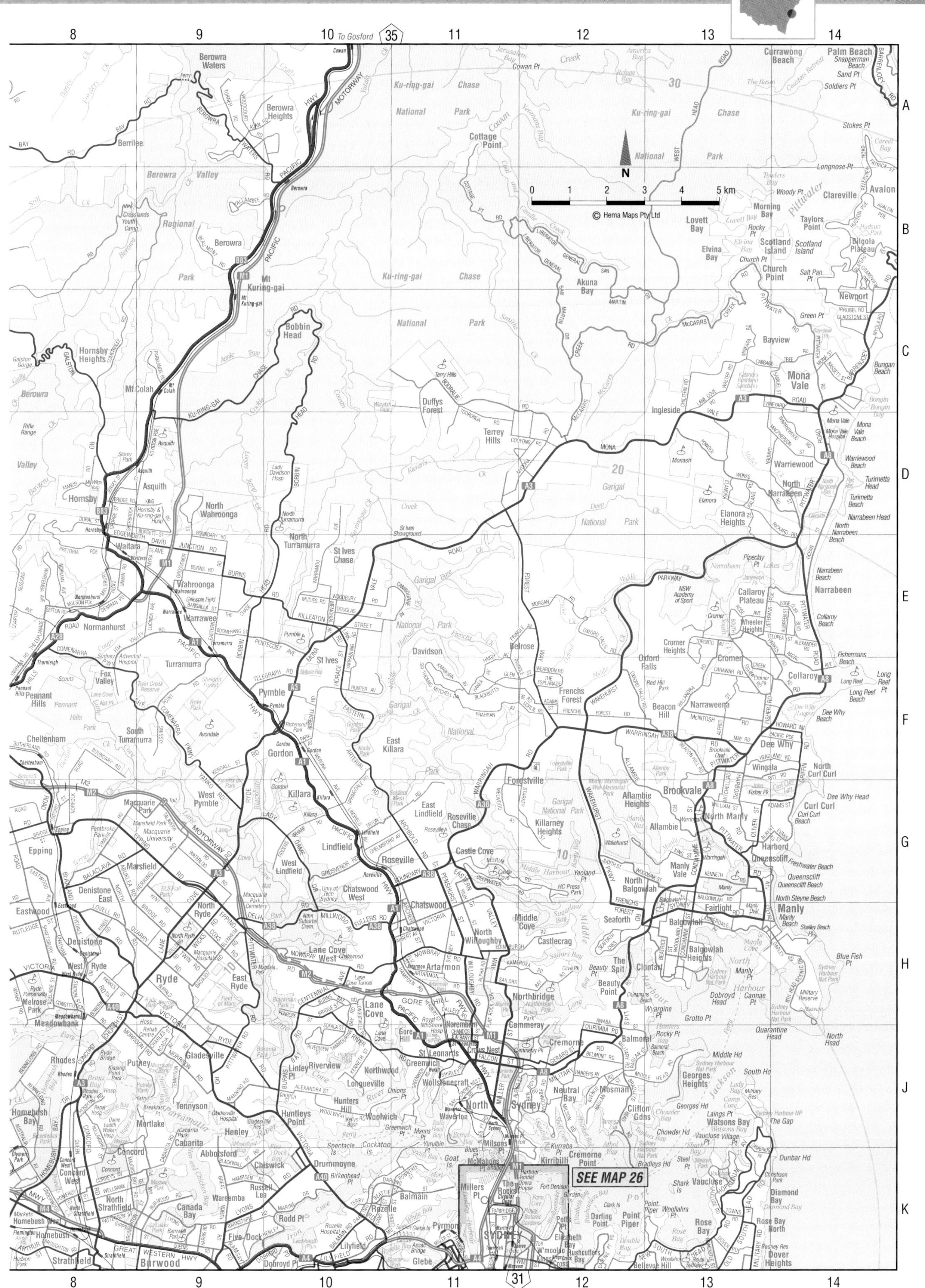

8
9
10 To Gosford
35
11
12
13
14
A
B
C
D
E
F
G
H
J
K
31
0 1 2 3 4 5 km
N
© Hema Maps Pty Ltd
Berowra Waters
Berowra Heights
Berrilee
Berowra Valley Regional Park
Berowra
Mt Kuring-gai
Ku-ring-gai Chase National Park
Cottage Point
Cowan Pt
Jerusalem Bay
Currawong Beach
Palm Beach
Snapperman Beach
Sand Pt
Soldiers Pt
Stokes Pt
Longnose Pt
Clareville
Avalon
Morning Bay
Lovett Bay
Taylors Point
Bilgola Plateau
Elvina Bay
Scotland Island
Church Point
Newport
Akuna Bay
Bobbin Head
Hornsby Heights
Mt Colah
Terrey Hills
Duffys Forest
Ingleside
Bayview
Mona Vale
Mona Vale Beach
Warriewood
Warriewood Beach
North Narrabeen
Elanora Heights
Garigal National Park
Asquith
Hornsby
North Wahroonga
Waitara
Wahroonga
Normanhurst
Warrawee
Turramurra
North Turramurra
St Ives Chase
St Ives
Pymble
Gordon
Killara
Lindfield
East Killara
Davidson
Belrose
Frenchs Forest
Oxford Falls
Cromer Heights
Cromer
Collaroy
Collaroy Plateau
Narrabeen
Narrabeen Head
Narraweena
Beacon Hill
Dee Why
Dee Why Head
Wingala
North Curl Curl
Curl Curl
Brookvale
Allambie Heights
Allambie
Forestville
Killarney Heights
Roseville Chase
Roseville
East Lindfield
West Lindfield
West Pymble
South Turramurra
Fox Valley
Pennant Hills
Cheltenham
Macquarie Park
Epping
Marsfield
Denistone East
Denistone
Eastwood
North Ryde
West Ryde
Ryde
East Ryde
Melrose Park
Meadowbank
Chatswood
Chatswood West
Lane Cove West
Lane Cove
Artarmon
North Willoughby
Middle Cove
Castle Cove
Castlecrag
Northbridge
Cammeray
Cremorne
Neutral Bay
Mosman
Balmoral
Clontarf
Beauty Point
The Spit
Seaforth
Balgowlah
Balgowlah Heights
Fairlight
Manly
Manly Vale
North Balgowlah
North Manly
Harbord
Queenscliff
North Head
Quarantine Head
Middle Head
Georges Heights
Clifton Gdns
Chowder Hd
Watsons Bay
South Hd
Vaucluse
Rose Bay
Rose Bay North
Dover Heights
Diamond Bay
Point Piper
Darling Point
Double Bay
Rushcutters Bay
Elizabeth Bay
Potts Pt
Kings Cross
W'mooloo
Kirribilli
Milsons Pt
McMahons Pt
Waverton
Wollstonecraft
North Sydney
Crows Nest
St Leonards
Greenwich
Naremburn
Riverview
Northwood
Longueville
Linley Pt
Hunters Hill
Woolwich
Huntleys Point
Gladesville
Putney
Tennyson
Henley
Rhodes
Mortlake
Cabarita
Abbotsford
Chiswick
Russell Lea
Drummoyne
Birkenhead Pt
Rodd Pt
Five Dock
Wareemba
Canada Bay
Concord
Concord West
North Strathfield
Homebush Bay
Homebush West
Homebush
Strathfield
Burwood
Dobroyd Pt
Lilyfield
Rozelle
Balmain
Glebe
Pyrmont
Millers Pt
The Rocks
SEE MAP 26
Sydney
Bellevue Hill
Cockatoo Is
Spectacle Is
Goat Is
Shark Is
CAMPS AUSTRALIA WIDE 8

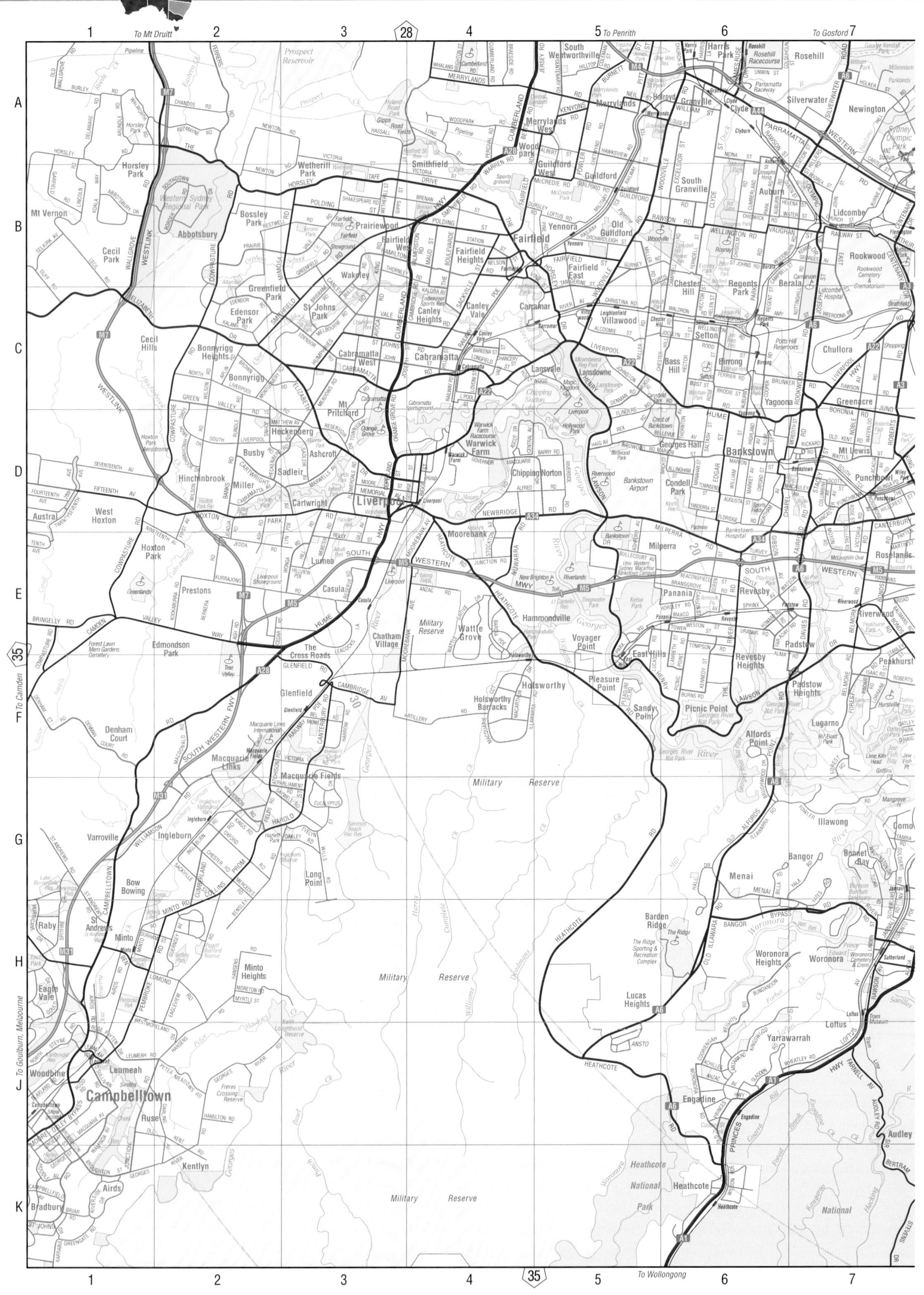

To Mt Druitt
To Penrith
To Gosford
To Camden
To Goulburn, Melbourne
To Wollongong
Prospect Reservoir
Horsley Park
Mt Vernon
Cecil Park
Abbotsbury
Bossley Park
Wetherill Park
Smithfield
Prairiewood
Fairfield West
Fairfield
Fairfield Heights
Wakeley
Greenfield Park
Edensor Park
St Johns Park
Canley Heights
Canley Vale
Cecil Hills
Bonnyrigg Heights
Bonnyrigg
Cabramatta West
Cabramatta
Mt Pritchard
Heckenberg
Busby
Ashcroft
Sadleir
Hinchinbrook
Miller
Cartwright
Liverpool
West Hoxton
Austral
Hoxton Park
Prestons
Lurnea
Casula
Moorebank
Chatham Village
Wattle Grove
Warwick Farm
Chipping Norton
Hammondville
Voyager Point
Holsworthy
Holsworthy Barracks
Edmondson Park
The Cross Roads
Glenfield
Denham Court
Macquarie Links
Macquarie Fields
Varroville
Ingleburn
Bow Bowing
Minto
Minto Heights
Raby
St Andrews
Eagle Vale
Leumeah
Campbelltown
Woodbine
Ruse
Kentlyn
Airds
Bradbury
Military Reserve
South Wentworthville
Merrylands
Merrylands West
Woodpark
Guildford West
Guildford
Holroyd
Granville
Clyde
Harris Park
Rosehill
Silverwater
Newington
South Granville
Auburn
Lidcombe
Yennora
Old Guildford
Villawood
Carramar
Lansvale
Lansdowne
Chester Hill
Regents Park
Berala
Rookwood
Sefton
Bass Hill
Birrong
Yagoona
Chullora
Greenacre
Georges Hall
Bankstown
Bankstown Airport
Condell Park
Mt Lewis
Punchbowl
Milperra
Panania
Revesby
Padstow
Picnic Point
East Hills
Revesby Heights
Padstow Heights
Pleasure Point
Sandy Point
Alfords Point
Riverwood
Roselands
Peakhurst
Lugarno
Illawong
Menai
Bangor
Bonnet Bay
Barden Ridge
Lucas Heights
Woronora Heights
Woronora
Loftus
Yarrawarrah
Engadine
Heathcote
Heathcote National Park
Audley
Como

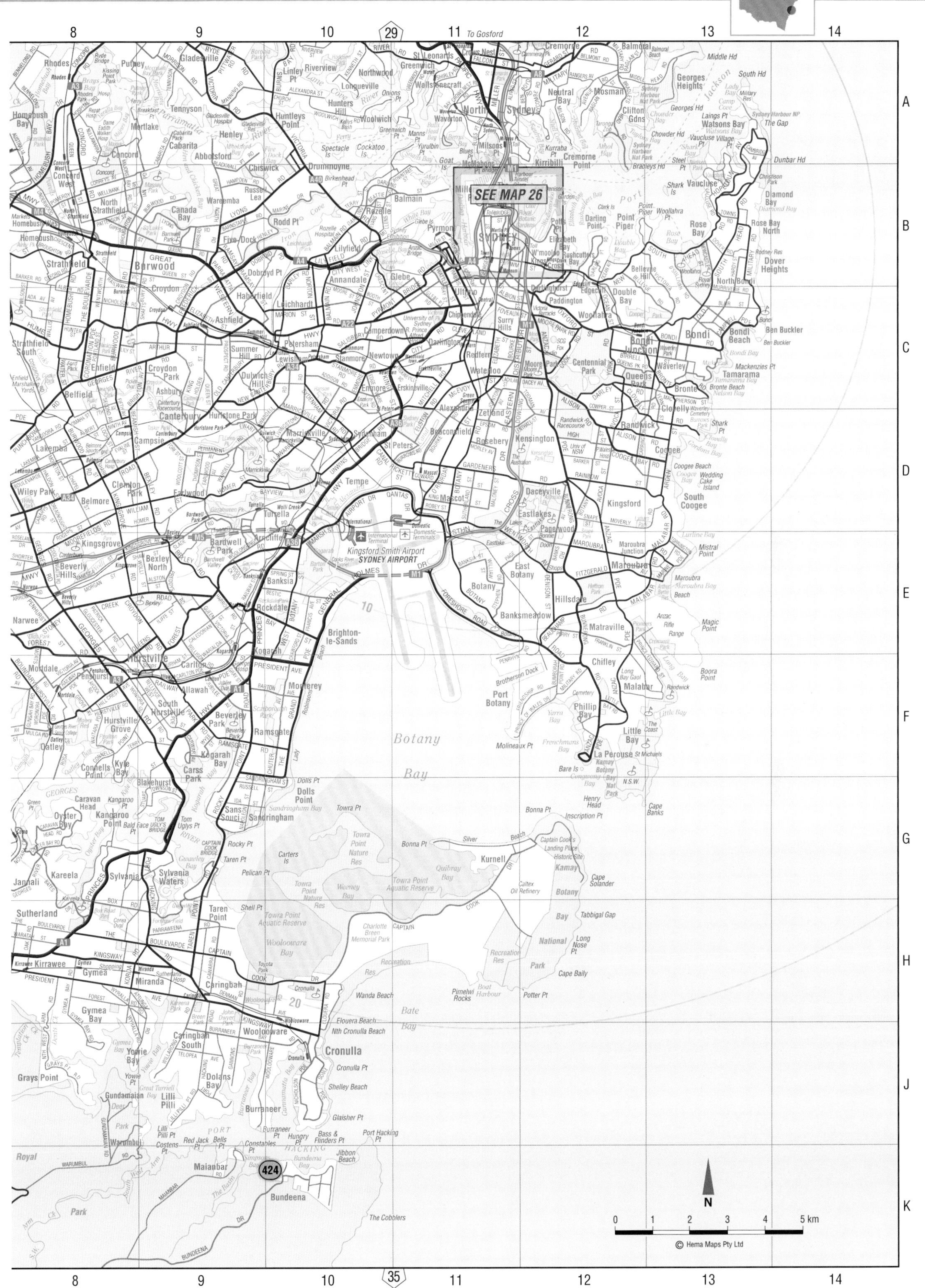

SEE MAP 26
To Gosford
Rhodes
Putney
Gladesville
Ryde
Riverview
Linley Pt
Northwood
Greenwich
St Leonards
Crows Nest
Cremorne
Balmoral
Middle Hd
South Hd
Georges Heights
Mosman
Neutral Bay
North Sydney
Wollstonecraft
Waverton
Longueville
Hunters Hill
Woolwich
Tennyson
Homebush Bay
Mortlake
Huntleys Point
Henley
Cabarita
Concord
Abbotsford
Chiswick
Drummoyne
Concord West
Milsons Pt
Kirribilli
Cremorne Point
Watsons Bay
The Gap
Vaucluse
Dunbar Hd
Diamond Bay
Rose Bay
Rose Bay North
Dover Heights
North Bondi
Bondi
Bondi Beach
Bondi Junction
Ben Buckler
Tamarama
Bronte
Waverley
Queens Park
Clovelly
Randwick
Coogee
South Coogee
Kingsford
Maroubra
Maroubra Junction
Matraville
Chifley
Malabar
Little Bay
La Perouse
Phillip Bay
Hillsdale
Banksmeadow
Eastlakes
Daceyville
Pagewood
Kensington
Mascot
Rosebery
Zetland
Waterloo
Alexandria
Redfern
Surry Hills
Darlinghurst
Paddington
Woollahra
Edgecliff
Double Bay
Point Piper
Darling Point
Centennial Park
Moore Park
Sydney
Ultimo
Chippendale
Glebe
Annandale
Pyrmont
Balmain
Rozelle
Lilyfield
Leichhardt
Haberfield
Five Dock
Rodd Pt
Russell Lea
Wareemba
Canada Bay
North Strathfield
Strathfield
Strathfield South
Burwood
Croydon
Ashfield
Summer Hill
Dobroyd Pt
Petersham
Lewisham
Stanmore
Camperdown
Newtown
Darlington
Enmore
Erskineville
Marrickville
Sydenham
St Peters
Tempe
Dulwich Hill
Hurlstone Park
Canterbury
Campsie
Ashbury
Croydon Park
Enfield
Belfield
Lakemba
Wiley Park
Clemton Park
Belmore
Earlwood
Turrella
Arncliffe
Bardwell Park
Kingsgrove
Bexley North
Beverly Hills
Narwee
Bexley
Rockdale
Banksia
Kogarah
Hurstville
Carlton
Allawah
Penshurst
Mortdale
South Hurstville
Beverley Park
Ramsgate
Monterey
Brighton-le-Sands
Kyle Bay
Connells Point
Hurstville Grove
Oatley
Blakehurst
Kogarah Bay
Carss Park
Sans Souci
Sandringham
Dolls Point
Kingsford Smith Airport
SYDNEY AIRPORT
Botany Bay
Botany
East Botany
Port Botany
Kurnell
Cape Solander
Kamay Botany Bay National Park
Cape Baily
Potter Pt
Bate Bay
Wanda Beach
Elouera Beach
Cronulla
Woolooware
Caringbah
Caringbah South
Miranda
Gymea
Gymea Bay
Kirrawee
Sutherland
Jannali
Kareela
Sylvania
Sylvania Waters
Taren Point
Oyster Bay
Kangaroo Point
Caravan Head
Como
Yowie Bay
Dolans Bay
Grays Point
Gundamaian
Lilli Pilli
Burraneer
Port Hacking
Maianbar
Bundeena
Royal National Park
The Cobblers
Jibbon Beach
N
0 1 2 3 4 5 km
© Hema Maps Pty Ltd

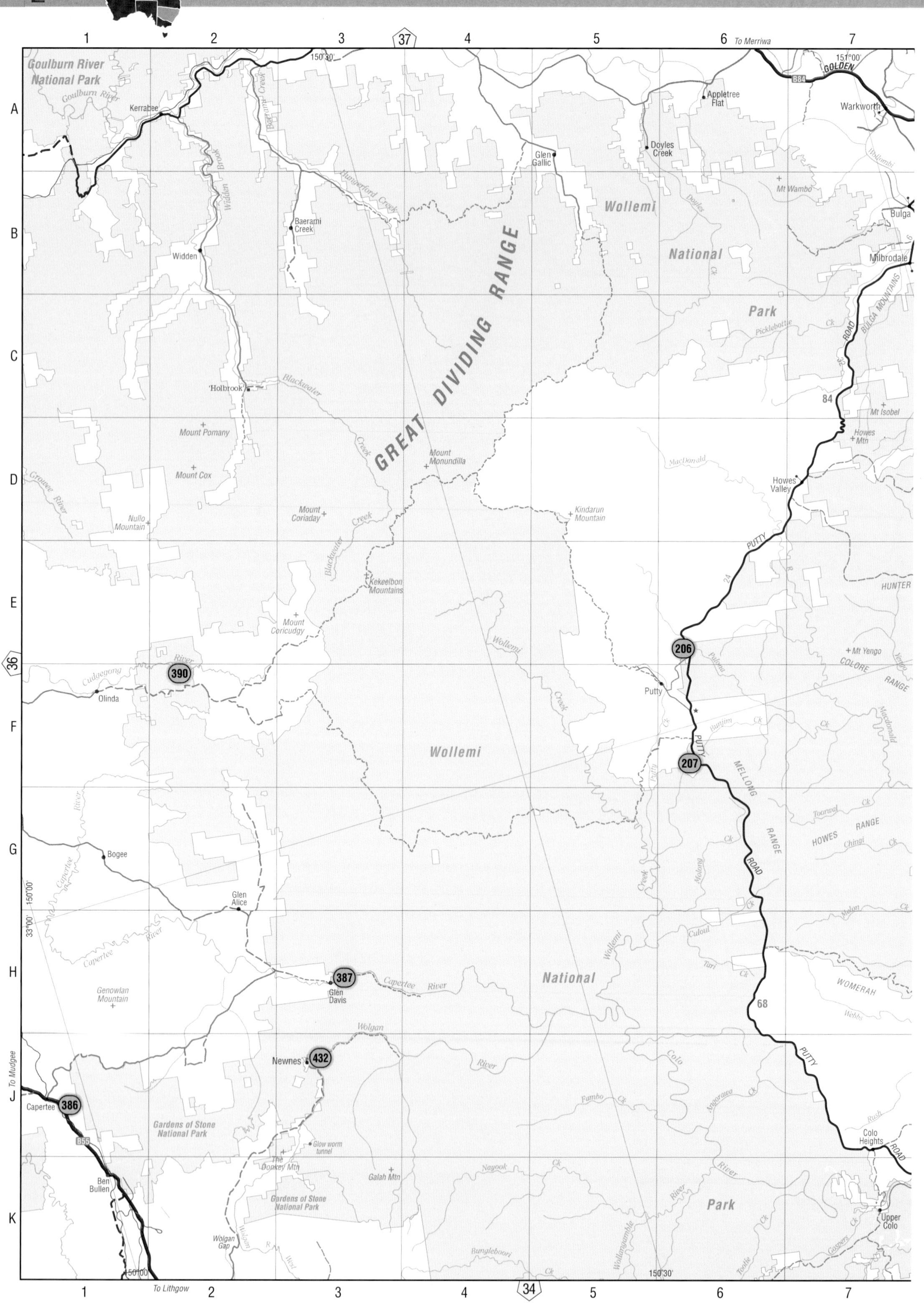
Goulburn River National Park
Kerrabee
Widden
Baerami Creek
'Holbrook'
Mount Pomany
Mount Cox
Nullo Mountain
GREAT DIVIDING RANGE
Mount Monundilla
Mount Coriaday
Kekeelbon Mountains
Mount Coricudgy
Glen Gallic
Appletree Flat
Doyles Creek
Wollemi National Park
Mt Wambo
Warkworth
Bulga
Milbrodale
BULGA MOUNTAINS
Mt Isobel
Howes Mtn
Howes Valley
Kindarun Mountain
PUTTY ROAD
HUNTER
Mt Yengo
COLORE RANGE
Putty
206
207
390
Olinda
Wollemi
MELLONG RANGE
HOWES RANGE
Bogee
Glen Alice
Genowlan Mountain
387
Glen Davis
Capertee River
National
WOMERAH
Newnes
432
Capertee
386
Gardens of Stone National Park
Glow worm tunnel
The Donkey Mtn
Galah Mtn
Ben Bullen
Wolgan Gap
Park
Colo Heights
Upper Colo
To Merriwa
To Mudgee
To Lithgow
GOLDEN
B84
B55
84
68
24
37
36
34
150°30'
151°00'
150°00'
33°00'

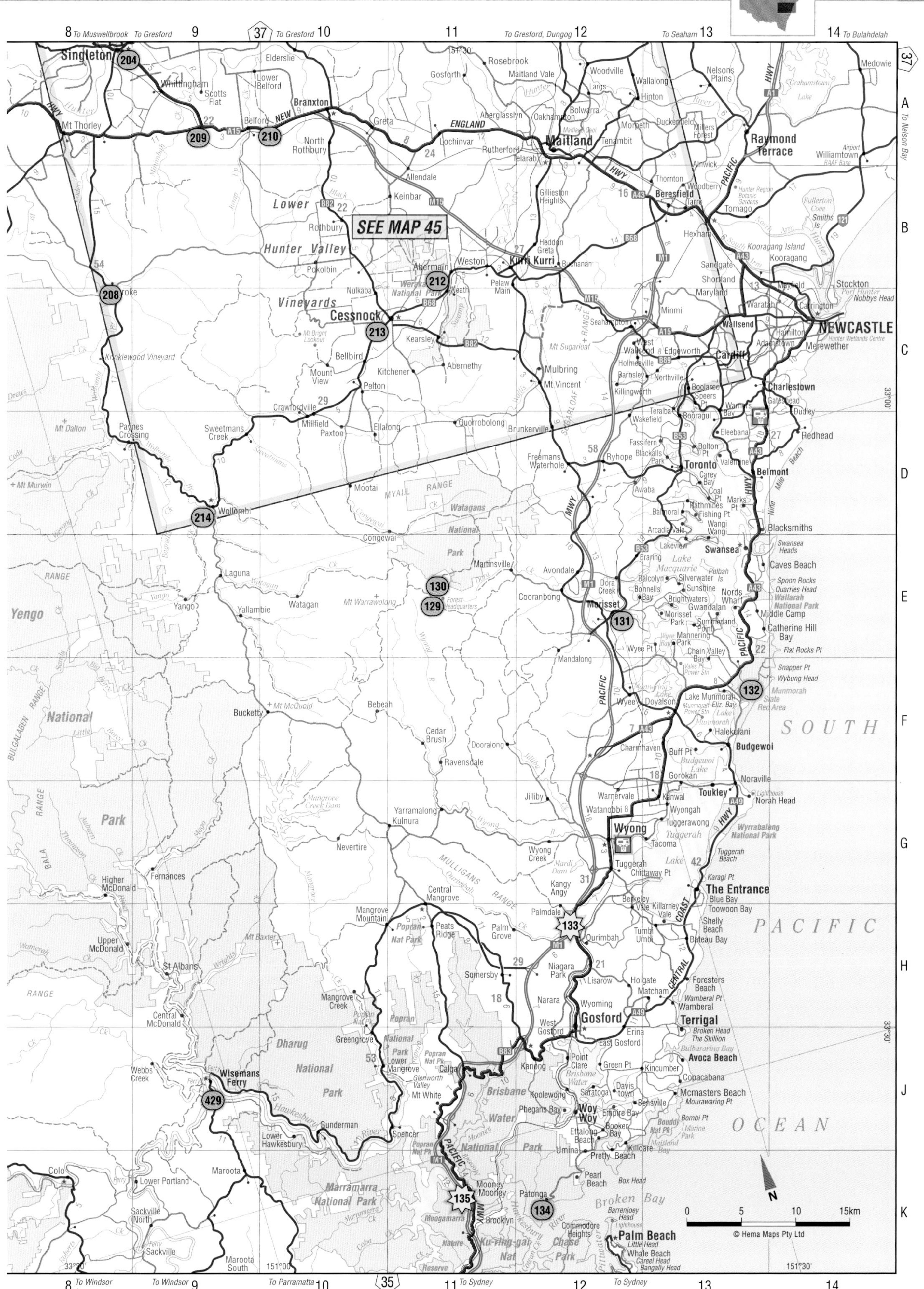

To Muswellbrook
To Gresford
To Gresford
To Gresford, Dungog
To Seaham
To Bulahdelah
To Nelson Bay
Singleton
Whittingham
Scotts Flat
Elderslie
Lower Belford
Branxton
Belford
NEW ENGLAND HWY
Mt Thorley
North Rothbury
Greta
Gosforth
Rosebrook
Maitland Vale
Woodville
Largs
Bolwarra
Wallalong
Hinton
Nelsons Plains
Medowie
Grahamstown Lake
Aberglasslyn
Oakhampton
Lochinvar
Rutherford
Maitland
Telarah
Tenambit
Morpeth
Duckenfield
Millers Forest
Raymond Terrace
Airport
Williamtown
Allendale
Keinbar
Lower Hunter Valley Vineyards
Rothbury
SEE MAP 45
Gillieston Heights
Thornton
Beresfield
Woodberry
Tarro
Tomago
Hunter Region Botanic Gardens
Fullerton Cove
Smiths Is
Heddon Greta
Kurri Kurri
Buchanan
Weston
Abermain
Pokolbin
Nulkaba
Werakata National Park
Neath
Pelaw Main
Hexham
Kooragang Island
Kooragang
Sandgate
Shortland
Maryland
Mayfield
Stockton
Port Hunter
Nobbys Head
Carrington
Waratah
Wallsend
Hamilton
NEWCASTLE
Adamstown
Merewether
Hunter Wetlands Centre
Minmi
Seahampton
Cessnock
Mt Bright Lookout
Kearsley
Bellbird
Mount View
Kitchener
Abernethy
Mt Sugarloaf
West Wallsend
Edgeworth
Cardiff
Holmesville
Barnsley
Northville
Killingworth
Charlestown
Gateshead
Dudley
Redhead
Mulbring
Mt Vincent
Boolaroo
Speers Pt
Teralba
Booragul
Warners Bay
Wakefield
Eleebana
Kirkwood Vineyard
Pelton
Crawfordville
Millfield
Paxton
Ellalong
Quorrobolong
Brunkerville
Mt Dalton
Paynes Crossing
Sweetmans Creek
Fassifern
Blackalls Park
Bolton Pt
Toronto
Valentine
Belmont
Nine Mile Beach
Freemans Waterhole
Ryhope
Carey Bay
Coal Pt
Awaba
Marks Pt
Mt Murwin
Mootai
MYALL RANGE
Watagans National Park
Wollombi
Balmoral
Rathmines
Fishing Pt
Wangi Wangi
Arcadia Vale
Lakeview
Swansea
Swansea Heads
Blacksmiths
Congewai
Eraring
Lake Macquarie
Caves Beach
Martinsville
Avondale
Dora Creek
Balcolyn
Silverwater
Pulbah Is
Spoon Rocks
Quarries Head
Laguna
Watagan
Cooranbong
Sunshine
Bonnells Bay
Brightwaters
Nords Wharf
Wallarah National Park
Yengo
Yango
Yallambie
Mt Warrawolong
Forest Headquarters
Morisset
Gwandalan
Middle Camp
Morisset Park
Summerland Point
Catherine Hill Bay
Wyee Pt
Wyee Bay
Mannering Park
Chain Valley Bay
Vales Pt Power Stn
Flat Rocks Pt
Mandalong
Snapper Pt
Wybung Head
Munmorah State Rec Area
National Park
Bucketty
Mt McQuoid
Bebeah
Wyee
Doyalson
Lake Munmorah
Munmorah Power Stn
Elizabeth Bay
Lake Munmorah
SOUTH
Cedar Brush
Dooralong
Ravensdale
Halekulani
Budgewoi
Charmhaven
Buff Pt
Budgewoi Lake
Gorokan
Noraville
Jilliby
Warnervale
Kanwal
Toukley
Lighthouse
Norah Head
Mangrove Creek Dam
Yarramalong
Kulnura
Watanobbi
Wyong
Wyongah
Tuggerawong
Tuggerah
Wyrrabalong National Park
BULGALABEN RANGE
BALA RANGE
Park
Nevertire
Tacoma
Tuggerah Beach
Wyong Creek
Mardi Dam
Tuggerah
Chittaway Pt
Lake
Karagi Pt
The Entrance
Blue Bay
Toowoon Bay
MULLIGANS RANGE
Higher McDonald
Fernances
Central Mangrove
Kangy Angy
Berkeley Vale
Killarney Vale
Shelly Beach
Bateau Bay
PACIFIC
Mangrove Mountain
Popran Nat Park
Peats Ridge
Palm Grove
Palmdale
Ourimbah
Tumbi Umbi
Upper McDonald
Mt Baxter
St Albans
Somersby
Niagara Park
Lisarow
Holgate
Matcham
Foresters Beach
Wamberal Pt
Wamberal
Terrigal
Broken Head
The Skillion
RANGE
Central McDonald
Mangrove Creek
Popran
Narara
Wyoming
Gosford
West Gosford
Erina
East Gosford
Dharug National Park
Greengrove
Popran National Park
Popran Nat Pk
Lower Mangrove
Calga
Kariong
Point Clare
Green Pt
Kincumber
Bulbararing Bay
Avoca Beach
Copacabana
Webbs Creek
Wisemans Ferry
Glenworth Valley
Mt White
Brisbane Water National Park
Koolewong
Saratoga
Davistown
Empire Bay
Bensville
Mcmasters Beach
Mourawaring Pt
Bombi Pt
Bouddi Nat Pk
Marine Park
OCEAN
Gunderman
Hawkesbury River
Lower Hawkesbury
Spencer
Phegans Bay
Woy Woy
Booker Bay
Ettalong Beach
Umina
Killcare
Pretty Beach
Maitland Bay
Colo
Lower Portland
Maroota
Marramarra National Park
Mooney Mooney
Patonga
Pearl Beach
Box Head
Broken Bay
Barrenjoey Head
Lighthouse
Sackville North
Sackville
Muogamarra Nature Reserve
Brooklyn
Ku-ring-gai Chase Nat Park
Commodore Heights
Palm Beach
Little Head
Whale Beach
Careel Head
Bangally Head
Maroota South
0 5 10 15km
© Hema Maps Pty Ltd
N
To Windsor
To Windsor
To Parramatta
To Sydney
To Sydney

Sydney Region South, New South Wales

To Wisemans Ferry
To Gosford
Broken Bay
Palm Beach
Marramarra National Park
Ku-ring-gai Chase National Park
SEE MAPS 28-29
SEE MAPS 30-31
Windsor
Hornsby
Castle Hill
Blacktown
Parramatta
Ryde
Chatswood
Manly
Dee Why
Mona Vale
Avalon
SYDNEY
Bondi
Coogee
Maroubra
Strathfield
Burwood
Bankstown
Hurstville
Liverpool
Fairfield
Cronulla
Sutherland
Campbelltown
Camden
Picton
Appin
Royal National Park
Heathcote National Park
Stanwell Park
WOLLONGONG
Port Kembla
SOUTH PACIFIC OCEAN
TASMAN SEA
MILITARY RESERVE
To Kiama, Moss Vale
0 5 10 15km
© Hema Maps Pty Ltd

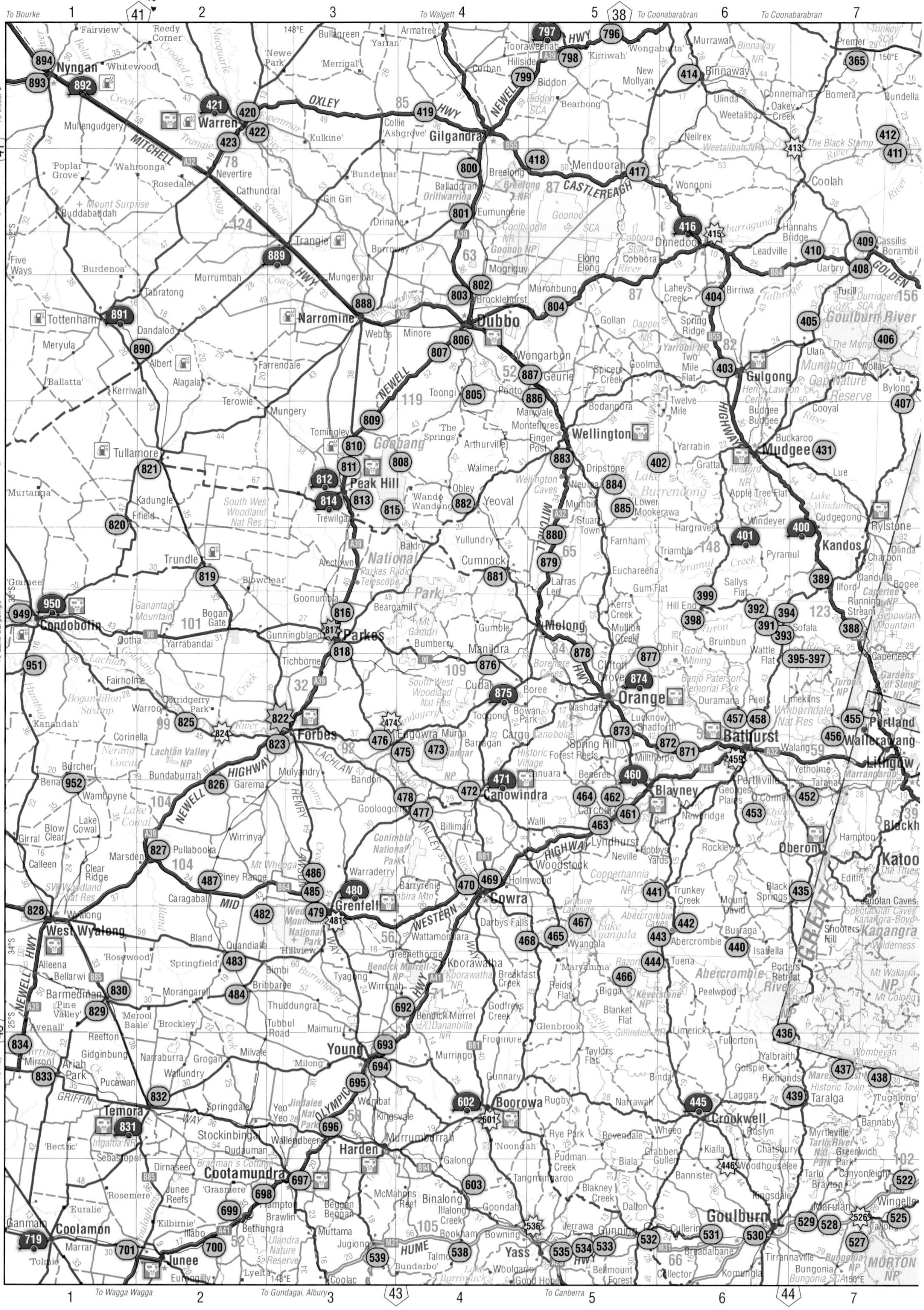

Central-East New South Wales

To Bourke 1 41 2 3 To Walgett 4 5 38 To Coonabarabran 6 To Coonabarabran 7

A B C D E F G H J K

To Cobar 41 · To Lake Cargelligo · To Hay 43

1 To Wagga Wagga 2 To Gundagai, Albury 3 43 4 To Canberra 5 6 44 7

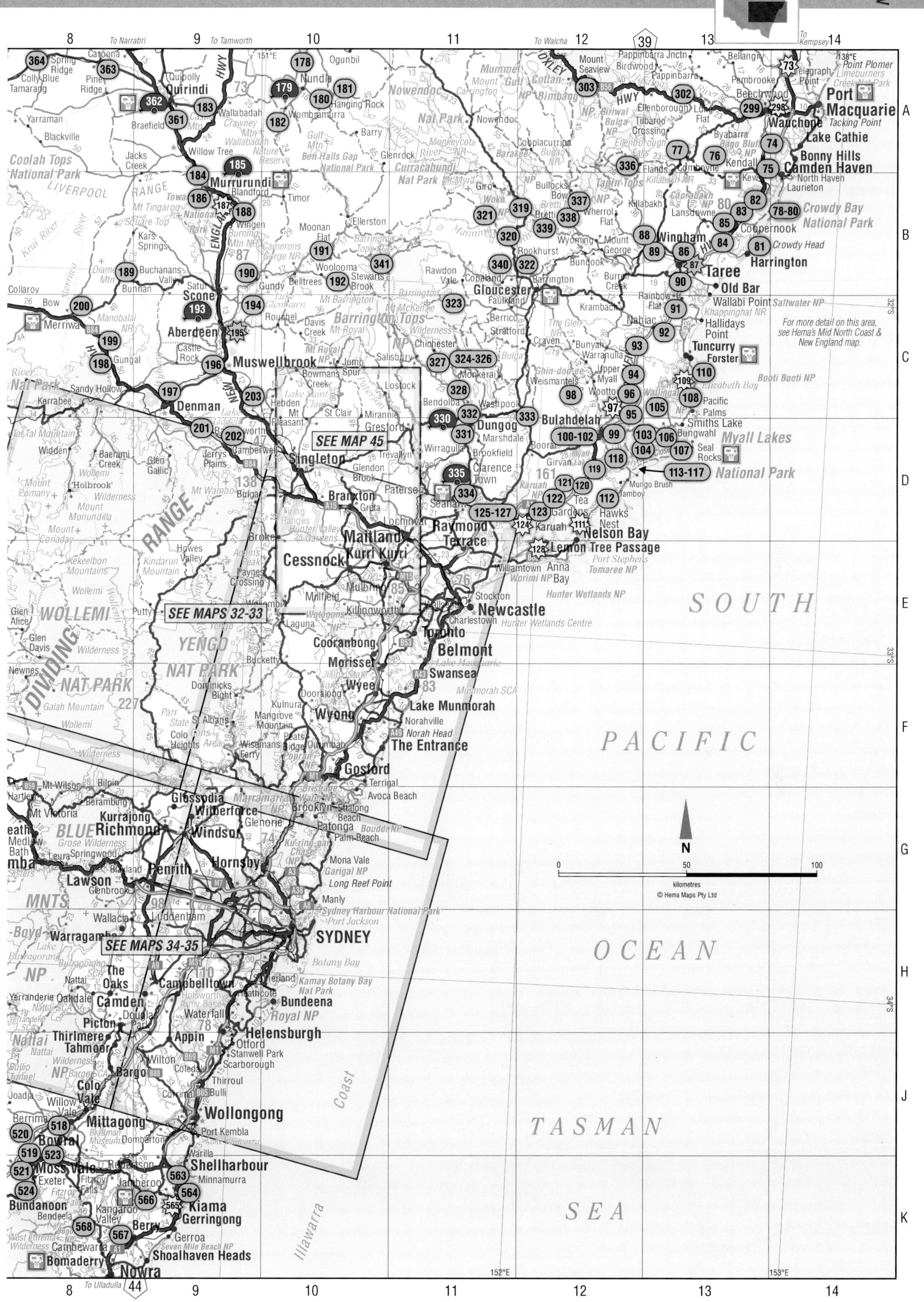

SEE MAP 45
SEE MAPS 32-33
SEE MAPS 34-35
SOUTH
PACIFIC
OCEAN
TASMAN
SEA
For more detail on this area, see Hema's Mid North Coast & New England map.
kilometres
© Hema Maps Pty Ltd
Port Macquarie
Newcastle
SYDNEY
Wollongong
Taree
Maitland
Cessnock
Gosford
Nowra

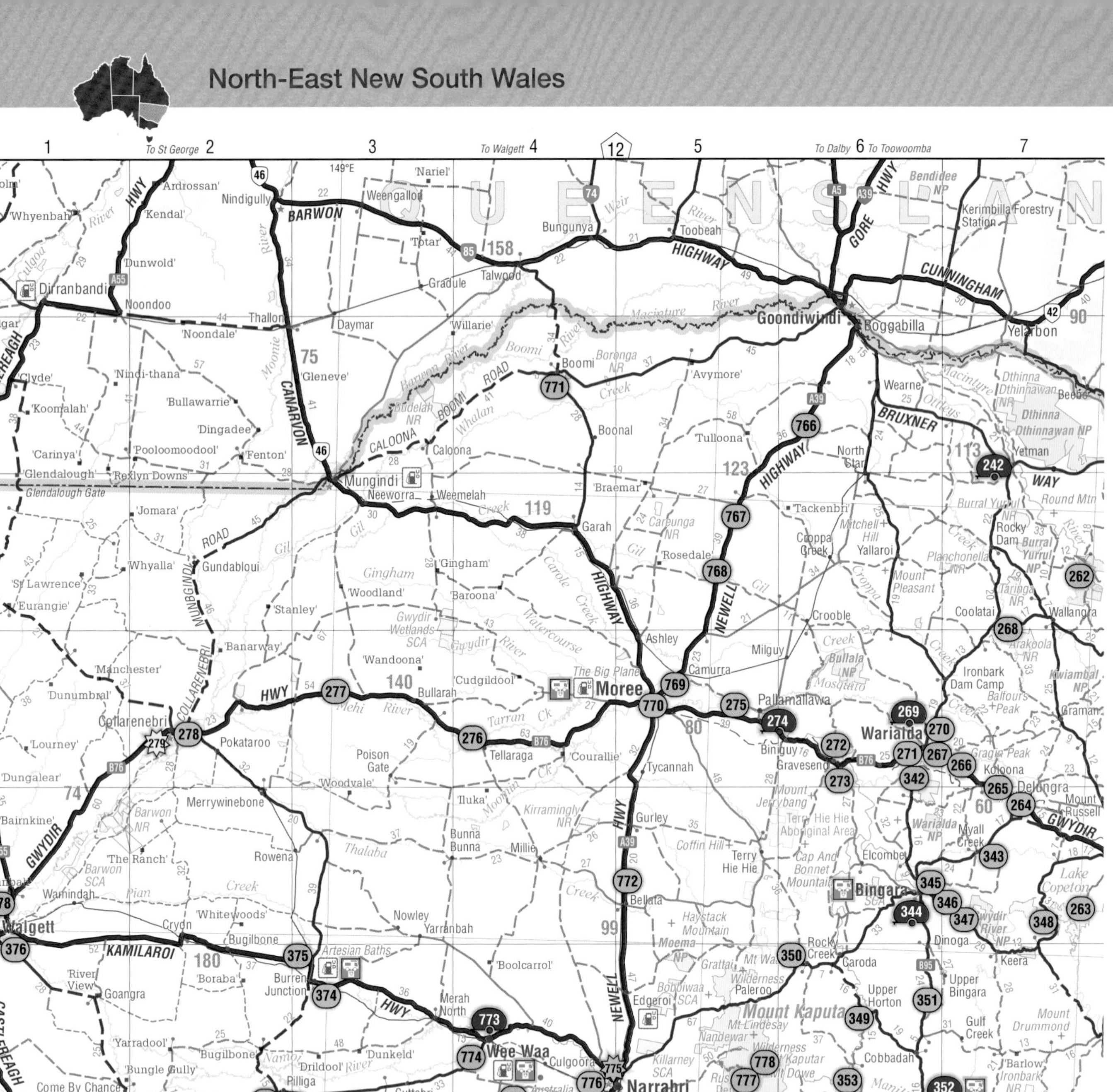

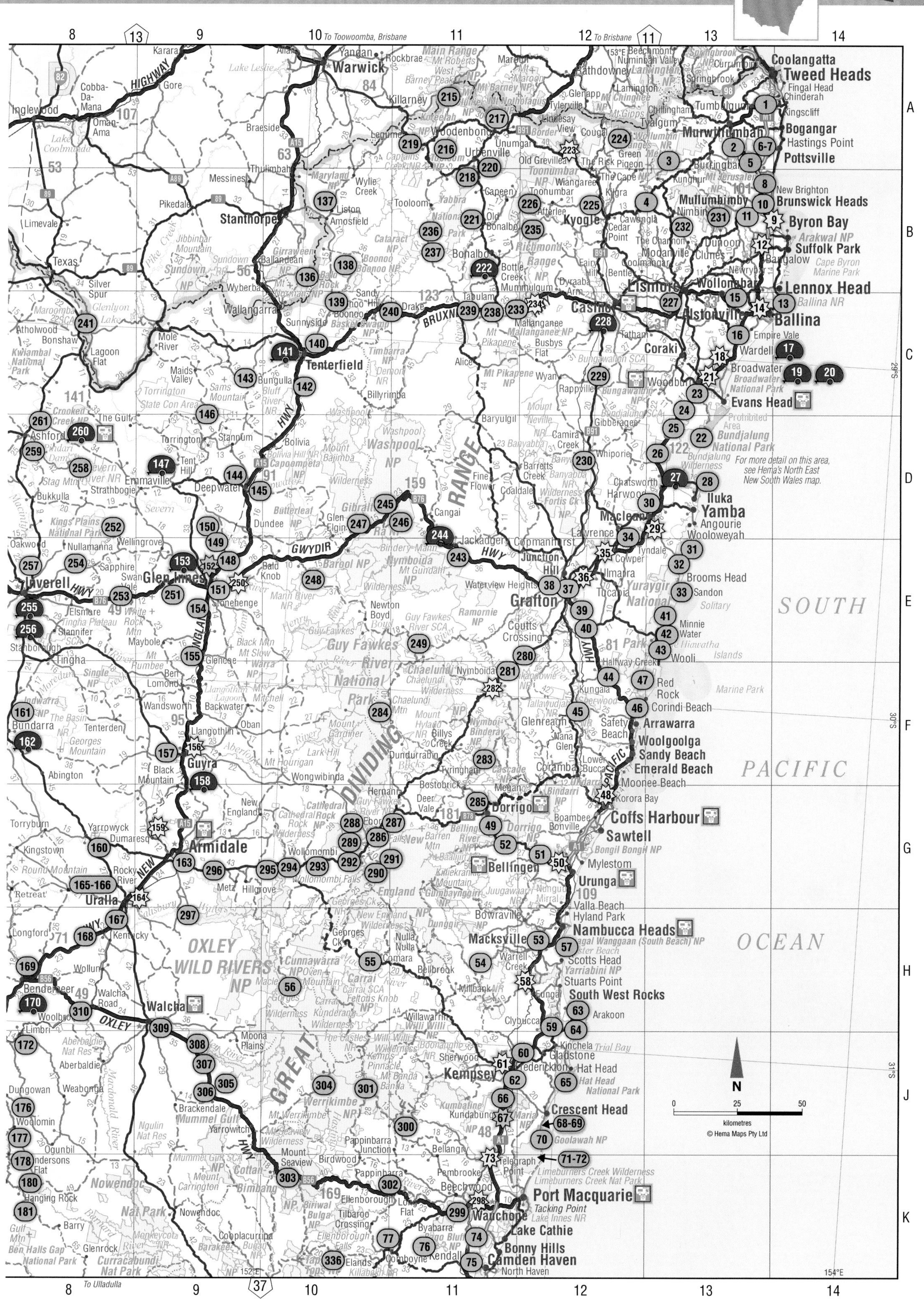
To Toowoomba, Brisbane
To Brisbane
Coolangatta
Tweed Heads
Fingal Head
Chinderah
Kingscliff
Bogangar
Hastings Point
Pottsville
Murwillumbah
Tumbulgum
New Brighton
Brunswick Heads
Mullumbimby
Byron Bay
Arakwal NP
Suffolk Park
Bangalow
Cape Byron Marine Park
Lennox Head
Ballina NR
Ballina
Alstonville
Wollongbar
Lismore
Casino
Kyogle
Empire Vale
Wardell
Broadwater
Broadwater National Park
Evans Head
Coraki
Woodburn
Bundjalung National Park
For more detail on this area, see Hema's North East New South Wales map.
Iluka
Yamba
Angourie
Wooloweyah
Maclean
Harwood
Chatsworth
Brooms Head
Sandon
Minnie Water
Wooli
Yuraygir National Park
Grafton
Coutts Crossing
Ulmarra
Red Rock
Corindi Beach
Arrawarra
Woolgoolga
Sandy Beach
Emerald Beach
Moonee Beach
Korora Bay
Coffs Harbour
Sawtell
Bongil Bongil NP
Mylestom
Urunga
Valla Beach
Hyland Park
Nambucca Heads
Macksville
Scotts Head
Stuarts Point
South West Rocks
Arakoon
Kempsey
Frederickton
Gladstone
Hat Head
Hat Head National Park
Crescent Head
Goolawah NP
Limeburners Creek Wilderness
Limeburners Creek Nat Park
Port Macquarie
Tacking Point
Lake Innes NR
Wauchope
Lake Cathie
Bonny Hills
Camden Haven
North Haven
Kendall
SOUTH
PACIFIC
OCEAN
Solitary Islands Marine Park
Warwick
Killarney
Stanthorpe
Wallangarra
Tenterfield
Texas
Inglewood
Goondiwindi
Glen Innes
Inverell
Emmaville
Deepwater
Guyra
Armidale
Uralla
Walcha
Bendemeer
Tingha
Bundarra
Dorrigo
Bellingen
Ebor
Wollomombi
OXLEY WILD RIVERS NP
GREAT DIVIDING RANGE
Guy Fawkes River National Park
Washpool NP
GWYDIR HWY
BRUXNER HWY
NEW ENGLAND HWY
OXLEY HWY
PACIFIC HWY
N
0 25 50
kilometres
© Hema Maps Pty Ltd
To Ulladulla

North-West New South Wales

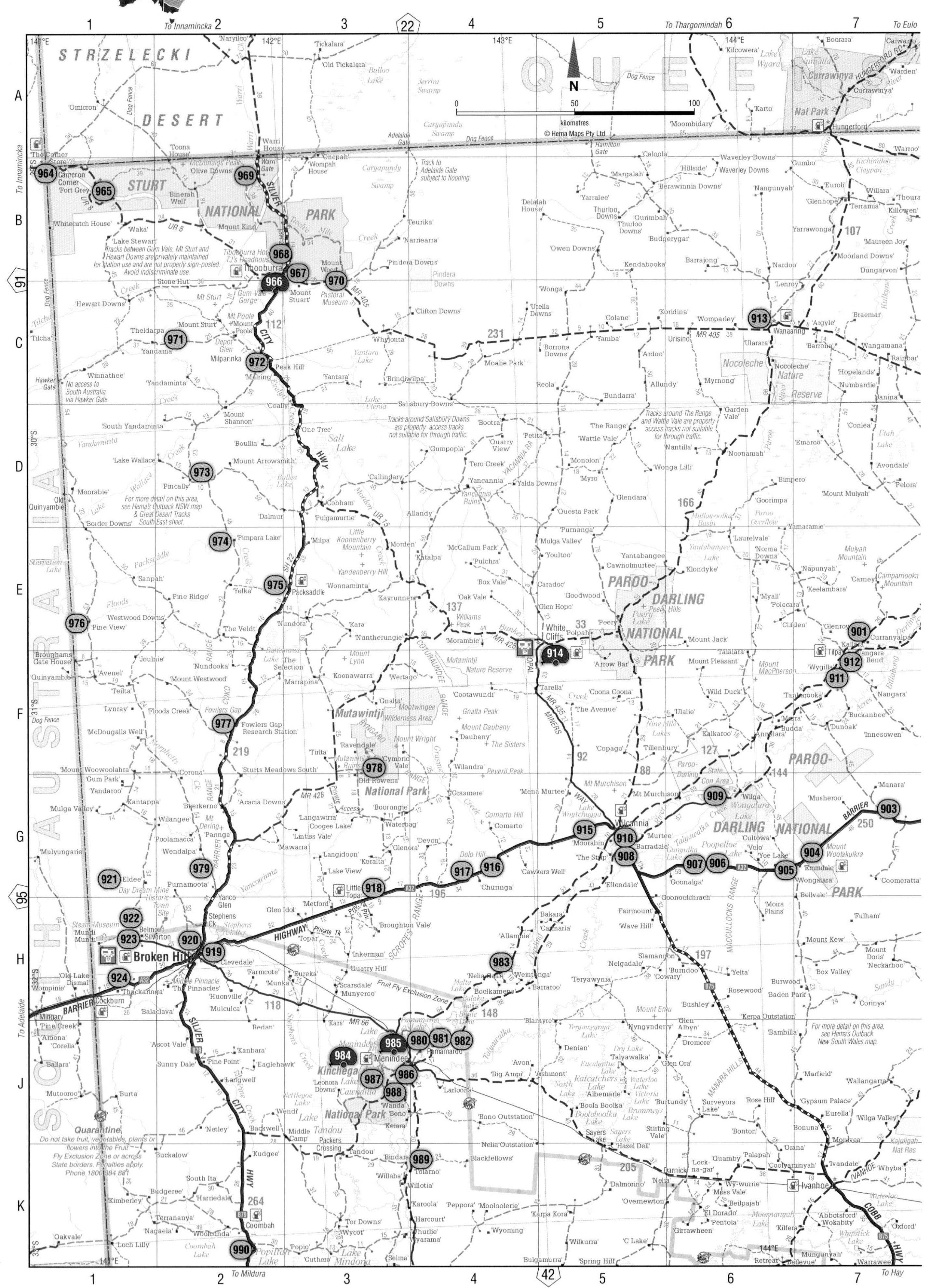

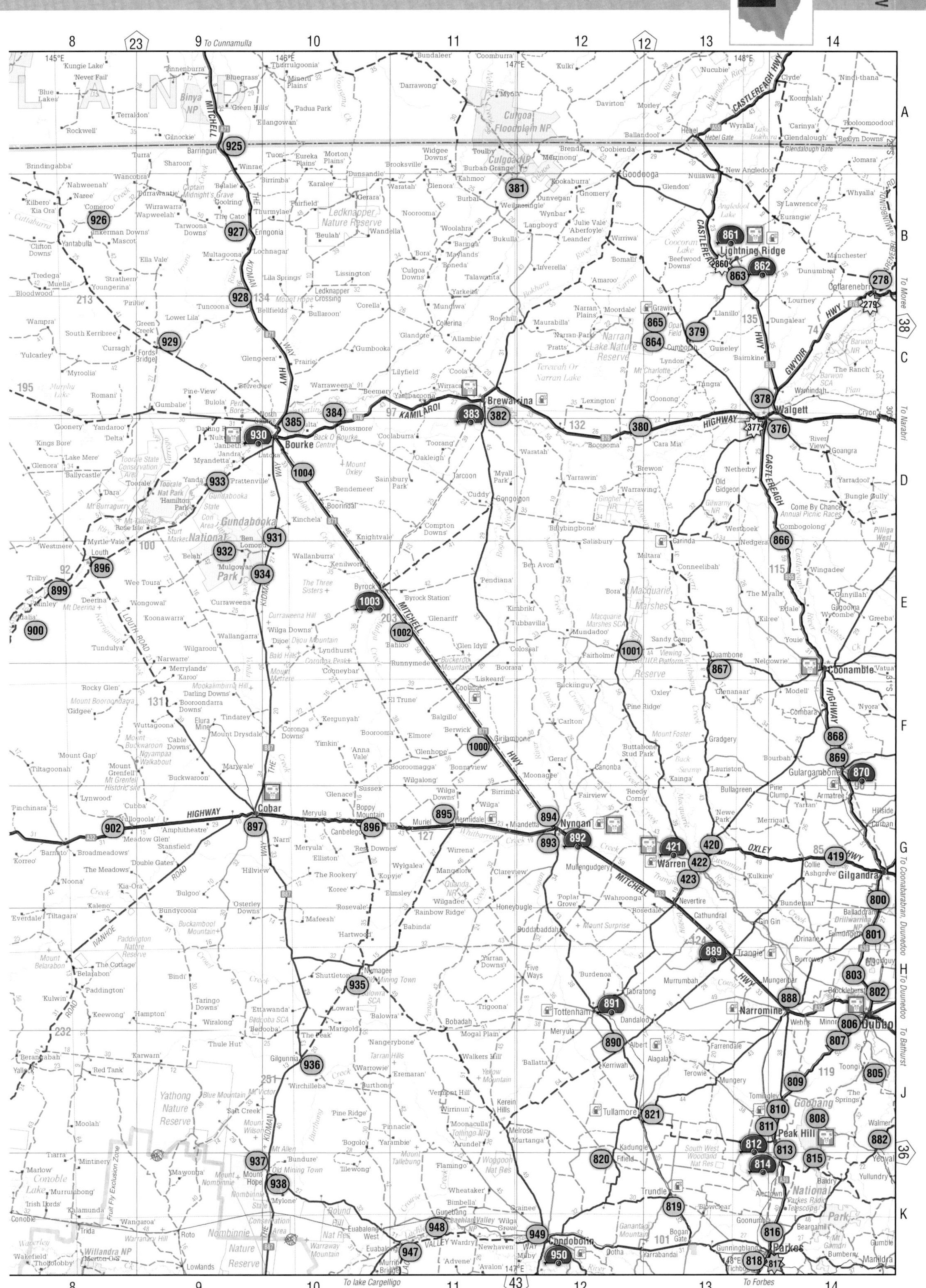

To Cunnamulla
Binya NP
Culgoa Floodplain NP
Culgoa NP
Hebel
Goodooga
Lightning Ridge
Collarenebri
To Moree
Barringun
Bourke
Brewarrina
Walgett
KAMILAROI HIGHWAY
CASTLEREAGH HWY
MITCHELL HWY
THE KIDMAN WAY
GWYDIR HWY
Ledknapper Nature Reserve
Narran Lake Nature Reserve
Toorale State Conservation Area
Toorale Nat Park
Gundabooka State Con Area
Gundabooka National Park
Louth
Byrock
Macquarie Marshes
Macquarie Marshes SCA
Coonamble
Gulargambone
Cobar
Nyngan
Warren
Gilgandra
To Narrabri
To Coonabarabran, Dunedoo
To Dunedoo
To Bathurst
Girilambone
Hermidale
Trangie
Narromine
Dubbo
Tottenham
Albert
Peak Hill
Tullamore
Trundle
Yathong Nature Reserve
Nombinnie Nature Reserve
Willandra NP
Condobolin
Parkes
Goobang National Park
To lake Cargelligo
To Forbes
OXLEY HWY
Mount Hope
Nymagee
Gilgunnia
Euabalong
Lachlan Valley Way

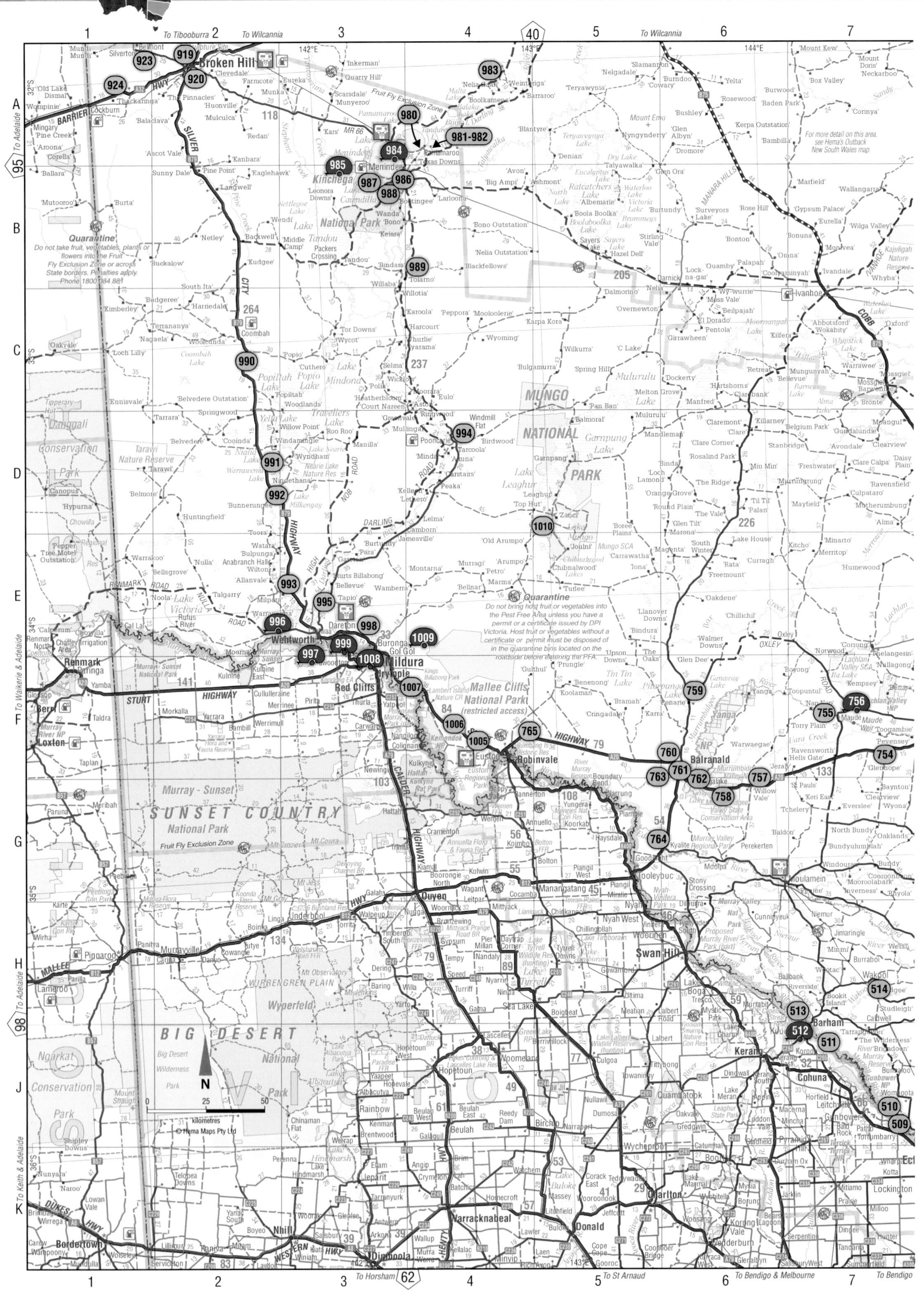
Broken Hill
Menindee
Kinchega National Park
Mungo National Park
Wentworth
Mildura
Red Cliffs
Robinvale
Balranald
Ivanhoe
Mallee Cliffs National Park (restricted access)
Murray - Sunset
Sunset Country National Park
Big Desert
Wyperfeld
Ouyen
Swan Hill
Kerang
Barham
Cohuna
Charlton
Donald
Warracknabeal
Hopetoun
Nhill
Dimboola
Bordertown
Renmark
Loxton
Pinnaroo
Quarantine
Do not take fruit, vegetables, plants or flowers into the Fruit Fly Exclusion Zone or across State borders. Penalties apply. Phone 1800 084 881
Quarantine
Do not bring host fruit or vegetables into the Pest Free Area unless you have a permit or a certificate issued by DPI Victoria. Host fruit or vegetables without a certificate or permit must be disposed of in the quarantine bins located on the roadside before entering the PFA.
For more detail on this area, see Hema's Outback New South Wales map.
Fruit Fly Exclusion Zone
To Tibooburra
To Wilcannia
To Adelaide
To Walkerie & Adelaide
To Keith & Adelaide
To Horsham
To St Arnaud
To Bendigo & Melbourne
To Bendigo
kilometres
© Hema Maps Pty Ltd

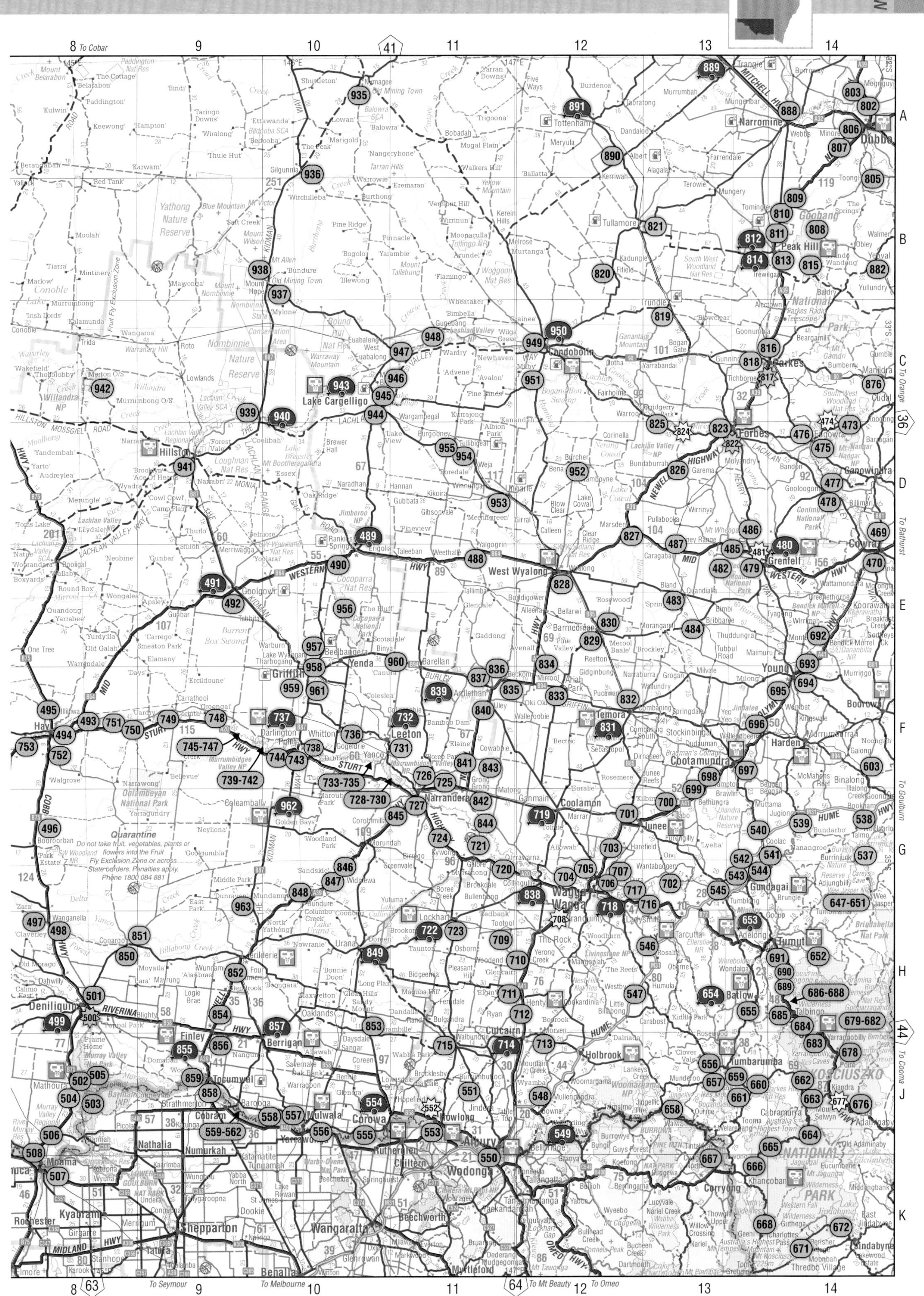
To Cobar
To Orange
To Bathurst
To Goulburn
To Cooma
To Seymour
To Melbourne
To Mt Beauty
To Omeo
Narromine
Dubbo
Tottenham
Tullamore
Peak Hill
Trundle
Condobolin
Parkes
Forbes
Eugowra
Canowindra
Cowra
Grenfell
West Wyalong
Lake Cargelligo
Hillston
Goolgowi
Griffith
Yenda
Leeton
Narrandera
Hay
Darlington Point
Temora
Young
Cootamundra
Harden
Junee
Coolamon
Wagga Wagga
Gundagai
Tumut
Batlow
Tumbarumba
Holbrook
Culcairn
Henty
Lockhart
Urana
Jerilderie
Berrigan
Finley
Deniliquin
Tocumwal
Mathoura
Moama
Cobram
Barooga
Mulwala
Corowa
Howlong
Albury
Wodonga
Rutherglen
Chiltern
Wangaratta
Beechworth
Myrtleford
Benalla
Shepparton
Kyabram
Numurkah
Nathalia
Rochester
Tatura
Corryong
Khancoban
Jindabyne
Thredbo Village
Adelong
Tarcutta
Ardlethan
Barellan
Yanco
Whitton
Griffith
Stockinbingal
Grong Grong
Gilgunnia
Mount Hope
Nombinnie Nature Reserve
Yathong Nature Reserve
Cocoparra Nat Res
Oolambeyan National Park
Kosciuszko National Park
Quarantine
Do not take fruit, vegetables, plants or flowers into the Fruit Fly Exclusion Zone or across State borders. Penalties apply. Phone 1800 084 881
Fruit Fly Exclusion Zone
MITCHELL HWY
NEWELL HIGHWAY
MID WESTERN HWY
STURT HWY
RIVERINA HWY
HUME HWY
OLYMPIC HWY
COBB HWY
KIDMAN WAY
MIDLAND HWY
OMEO HWY
LACHLAN VALLEY WAY
HILLSTON MOSSGIEL ROAD
41
36
44
63
64

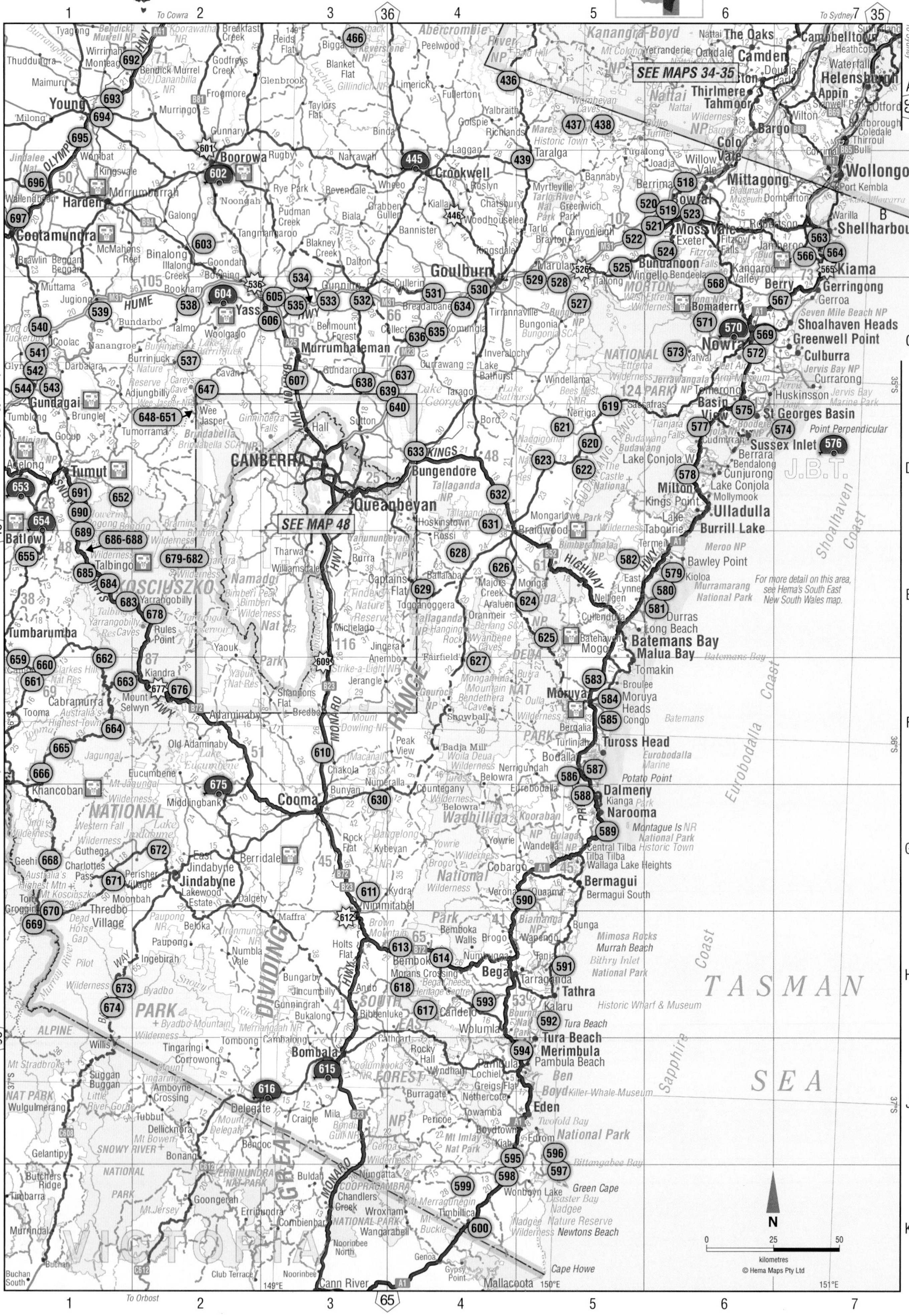

South-East New South Wales

SEE MAPS 34-35

SEE MAP 48

For more detail on this area, see Hema's South East New South Wales map.

TASMAN SEA

kilometres 0 25 50

© Hema Maps Pty Ltd

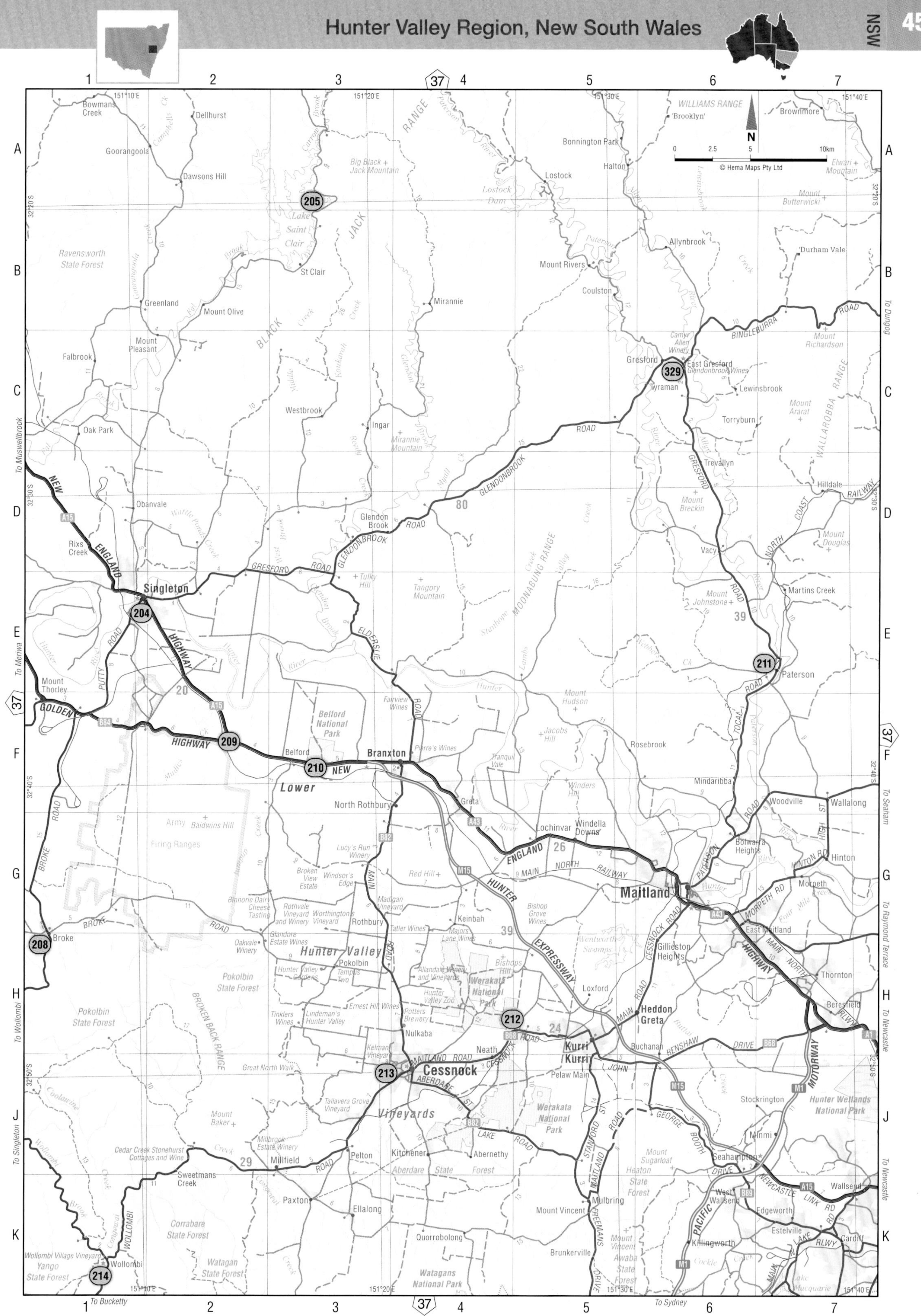
Singleton
Maitland
Cessnock
Kurri Kurri
Branxton
Paterson
Broke
Wollombi
Gresford
Lower Hunter Valley Vineyards
Werakata National Park
Belford National Park
Hunter Wetlands National Park
Watagans National Park
Heddon Greta
East Maitland
Thornton
Beresfield
Morpeth
Greta
Lochinvar
Rothbury
North Rothbury
Pokolbin
Nulkaba
Kearsley
Abermain
Kitchener
Ellalong
Paxton
Millfield
Pelton
Sweetmans Creek
Quorrobolong
Mulbring
Mount Vincent
Kilingworth
Edgeworth
Cardiff
Wallsend
Seahampton
Minmi
Stockrington
Buchanan
Loxford
Gillieston Heights
Bolwarra Heights
Hinton
Woodville
Wallalong
Mindaribba
Rosebrook
Martins Creek
Vacy
Trevallyn
Torryburn
Lewinsbrook
East Gresford
Allynbrook
Mount Rivers
Coulston
Lostock
Halton
Bonnington Park
St Clair
Lake Saint Clair
Mirannie
Westbrook
Ingar
Glendon Brook
Mount Olive
Greenland
Mount Pleasant
Falbrook
Oak Park
Obanvale
Rixs Creek
Mount Thorley
Dellhurst
Goorangoola
Dawsons Hill
Bowmans Creek
Ravensworth State Forest
Pokolbin State Forest
Corrabare State Forest
Watagan State Forest
Yango State Forest
Aberdare State Forest
Heaton State Forest
Awaba State Forest
To Muswellbrook
To Merriwa
To Wollombi
To Singleton
To Bucketty
To Sydney
To Newcastle
To Raymond Terrace
To Seaham
To Dungog
© Hema Maps Pty Ltd
NEW ENGLAND HIGHWAY
GOLDEN HIGHWAY
HUNTER EXPRESSWAY
PACIFIC MOTORWAY
GLENDONBROOK ROAD
GRESFORD ROAD
BROKE ROAD
PUTTY ROAD
MAIN NORTH RAILWAY
204
205
208
209
210
211
212
213
214
329

Major Building
Govt Building
Accommodation
Shopping
Post Office
Embassy
National Highway
Tourist Route
Cycleway
Picnic Area

0 100 200 300 400 500m
© Hema Maps Pty Ltd

Places of Interest

1 ACT Legislative Assembly A3
2 Acton Ferry Terminal B2
3 Acton Park B2
4 Albert Hall C2
5 Aust. and New Zealand Memorial B4
6 Australian Army National Memorial A4
7 Australian Hellenic Memorial A4
8 Australian National Botanic Gardens A1
9 Aust. National Korean War Memorial B4
10 Australian National University A2
11 Aust. Service Nurses National Mem B4
12 Aust. Vietnam Forces National Mem B4
13 Australian War Memorial A4
14 Black Mountain Tower A1
15 Blundell's Cottage B4
16 Canberra Centre A3
17 Canberra Institute of Technology B3
18 Canberra Museum & Gallery A3
19 Canberra Olympic Pool B3
20 Canberra Sthn Cross Yacht Club C2
21 Canberra Theatre Centre A3
22 Capital Hill D2
23 Captain Cook Memorial Water Jet B3
24 Casino Canberra A3
25 Civic Square A3
26 Commonwealth Park B3
27 Commonwealth Place C3
28 CSIRO Discovery Centre A1
29 Dendy Cinemas A3
30 Glebe Park A3
31 Gorman House Arts Centre A3
32 High Court of Australia C3
33 Jolimont Tourist Centre A3
34 Kings Park C4
35 Museum of Australian Democracy C3
36 National Archives of Australia C3
37 National Capital Exhibition B3
38 National Carillon C4
39 National Convention Centre B3
40 National Film & Sound Archive A2
41 National Gallery of Australia C3
42 National Library of Australia C3
43 National Museum of Australia B2
44 National Portrait Gallery C3
45 National Rose Garden C3
46 Old Parliament House C3
47 Palace Electric Cinema B2
48 Parliament House D2
49 Prime Minister's Lodge D2
50 Questacon-Nat. Science & Tech. Ctr C3
51 RAAF Memorial B4
52 RAN Memorial B4
53 Rats of Tobruk Memorial B4
54 Regatta Point Jetty B3
55 School of Art A2
56 School of Music A2
57 St John's Schoolhouse Museum B4
58 Stage 88 Music Bowl B3
59 Stirling Park C1
60 Telopea Park D3

Accommodation

61 Bentley Suites Canberra D3
62 BreakFree Capital Tower B2
63 Canberra City YHA A3
64 Comfort Inn Downtown A3
65 Crowne Plaza Canberra A3
66 Forrest Hotel & Apartments D3
67 Hotel Kurrajong Canberra D3
68 Hyatt Hotel Canberra C2
69 Kingston Court Serviced Apartments D4
70 Medina Executive James Crt Canberra A3
71 Novotel Canberra A3
72 Olims Canberra Hotel A4
73 QT Canberra A2
74 Quest Canberra A3
75 Rydges Capital Hill D3
76 Telopea Inn on the Park D3
77 The Brassey of Canberra D3
78 The York Canberra D4
79 University House at ANU A2
80 Waldorf Apartment Hotel Canberra A3

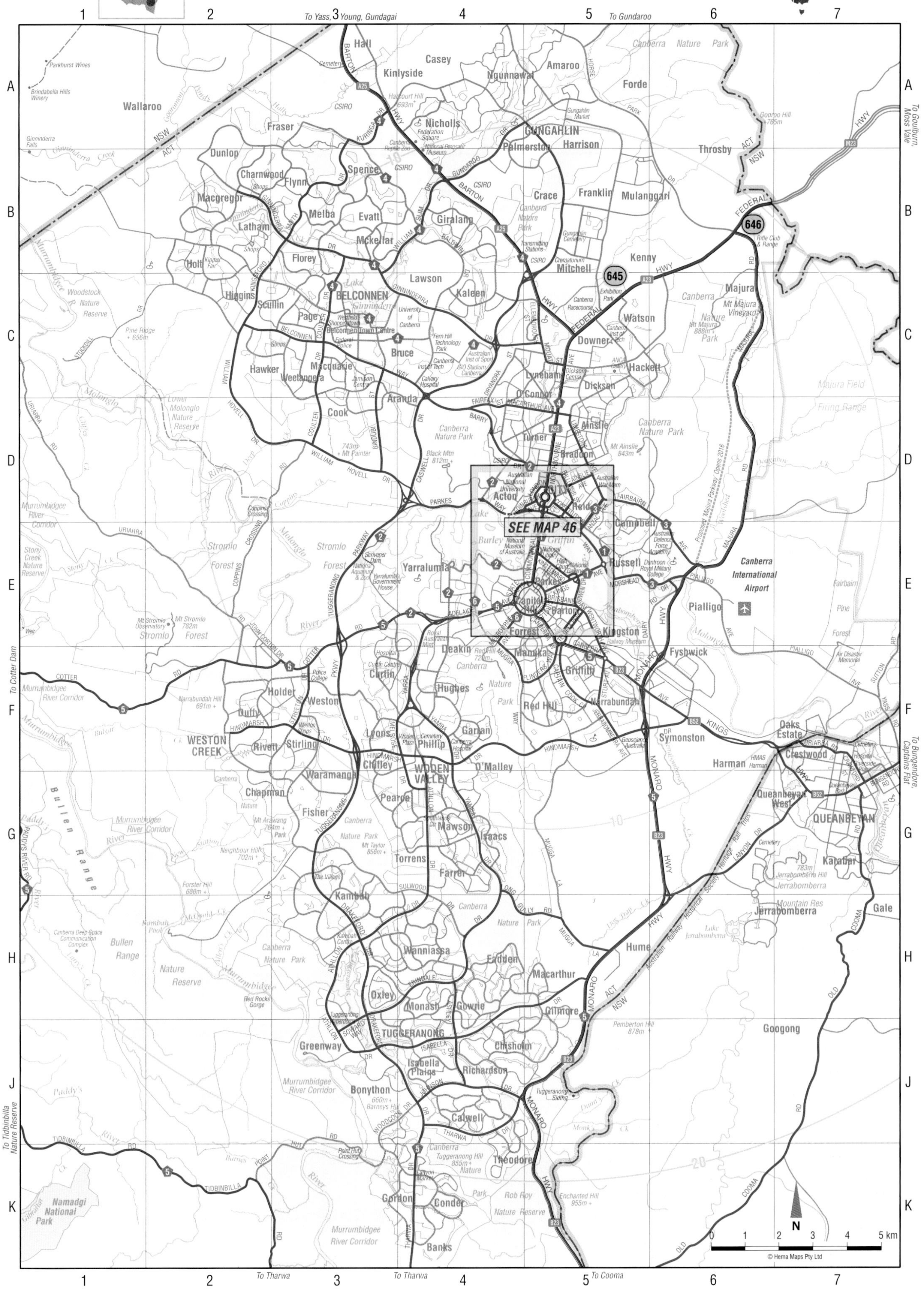
To Yass, Young, Gundagai
To Gundaroo
To Goulburn, Moss Vale
To Bungendore, Captains Flat
To Cotter Dam
To Tidbinbilla Nature Reserve
To Tharwa
To Tharwa
To Cooma
SEE MAP 46
Hall
Casey
Kinlyside
Ngunnawal
Amaroo
Forde
Canberra Nature Park
Wallaroo
Fraser
Nicholls
GUNGAHLIN
Palmerston
Harrison
Throsby
Dunlop
Spence
Charnwood
Flynn
Macgregor
Melba
Evatt
Giralang
Crace
Franklin
Mulanggari
Latham
McKellar
Holt
Florey
Lawson
Kaleen
Mitchell
Kenny
Higgins
Scullin
BELCONNEN
Page
Bruce
Watson
Majura
Downer
Hawker
Weetangera
Macquarie
Aranda
Lyneham
Hackett
O'Connor
Dickson
Cook
Turner
Ainslie
Braddon
Acton
Reid
Campbell
Yarralumla
Russell
Parkes
Canberra International Airport
Pialligo
Capital Hill
Barton
Forrest
Kingston
Deakin
Manuka
Griffith
Fyshwick
Curtin
Hughes
Red Hill
Narrabundah
Holder
Weston
Duffy
WESTON CREEK
Rivett
Stirling
Lyons
Phillip
Garran
Symonston
Oaks Estate
Crestwood
Harman
Chifley
WODEN VALLEY
O'Malley
Waramanga
Chapman
Fisher
Pearce
Queanbeyan West
QUEANBEYAN
Mawson
Isaacs
Torrens
Farrer
Karabar
Kambah
Jerrabomberra
Gale
Bullen Range
Wanniassa
Fadden
Hume
Macarthur
Oxley
Monash
Gowrie
Gilmore
TUGGERANONG
Greenway
Chisholm
Isabella Plains
Richardson
Googong
Bonython
Calwell
Theodore
Gordon
Conder
Banks
Namadgi National Park
Rob Roy Nature Reserve
Murrumbidgee River Corridor
Stromlo Forest
Mt Stromlo 782m
Black Mtn 812m
Mt Ainslie 843m
Mt Majura 888m
0 1 2 3 4 5 km
© Hema Maps Pty Ltd

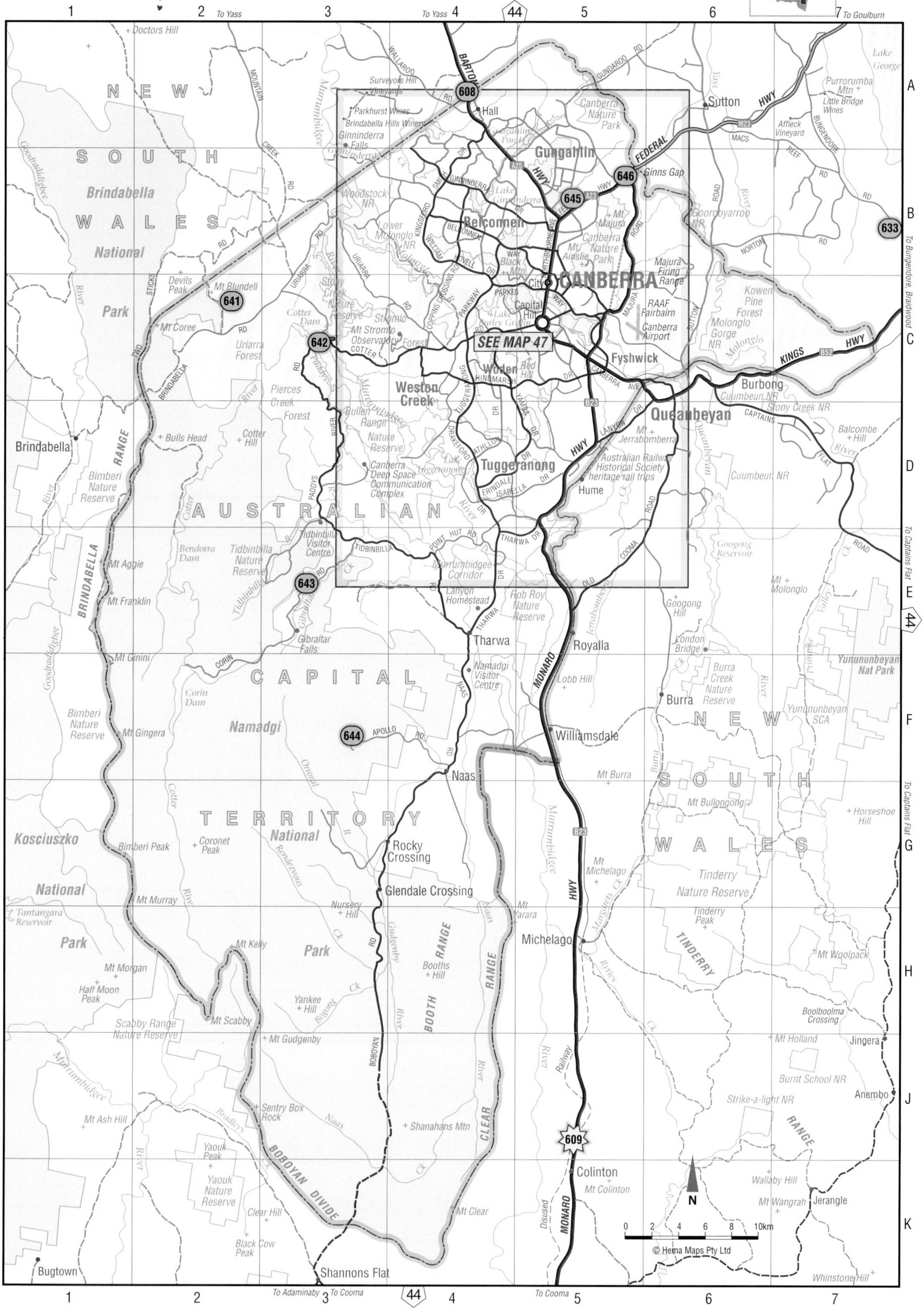

1 2 To Yass 3 To Yass 4 44 5 6 7 To Goulburn

A B C D E F G H J K

Doctors Hill
NEW SOUTH WALES
Brindabella National Park
Goodradigbee
MOUNTAIN CREEK RD
Murrumbidgee
WALLAROO RD
Surveyors Hill Vineyards
608
BARTON HWY
Hall
Parkhurst Wines
Brindabella Hills Winery
Ginninderra Falls
Gungahlin
GUNDAROO RD
Canberra Nature Park
Sutton
FEDERAL HWY
M23
Purrorumba Mtn
Little Bridge Wines
Affleck Vineyard
Lake George
MACS REEF RD
BUNGENDORE RD
646
Ginns Gap
645
Belconnen
Lake Ginninderra
Woodstock NR
Lower Molonglo NR
Mt Majura
Canberra Nature Park
Mt Ainslie
Gooroobyarroo NR
633
NORTON RD
Black Mtn
City
CANBERRA
Majura Firing Range
Devils Peak
Mt Blundell
641
STICKS RD
TWO STICKS RD
Mt Coree
Uriarra Forest
URIARRA RD
Cotter Dam
Stony Creek Nature Reserve
Stromlo
Mt Stromlo Observatory
Forest
642
COTTER RD
Capital Hill
PARKES WAY
Lake Burley Griffin
RAAF Fairbairn
Canberra Airport
Kowen Pine Forest
Molonglo Gorge NR
SEE MAP 47
Fyshwick
KINGS HWY
B52
Burbong
Cuumbeun NR
Stony Creek NR
To Bungendore, Braidwood
Pierces Creek Forest
Weston Creek
Woden
Red Hill
Queanbeyan
CAPTAINS FLAT RD
Bullen Range Nature Reserve
Mt Jerrabomberra
Balcombe Hill
Brindabella
RANGE
Bulls Head
Cotter Hill
Bimberi Nature Reserve
Canberra Deep Space Communication Complex
Tuggeranong
Australian Railway Historical Society heritage rail trips
Hume
Cuumbeun NR
AUSTRALIAN
PADDYS RIVER
Tidbinbilla Visitor Centre
TIDBINBILLA RD
POINT HUT RD
THARWA DR
COOMA RD
To Captains Flat
Bendorra Dam
Tidbinbilla Nature Reserve
Mt Aggie
BRINDABELLA RANGE
Googong Reservoir
643
Murrumbidgee Corridor
Lanyon Homestead
Rob Roy Nature Reserve
OLD COOMA RD
Mt Molonglo
Mt Franklin
Googong Hill
44
Gibraltar Falls
Tharwa
Royalla
London Bridge
Mt Ginini
CORIN RD
CAPITAL
Namadgi Visitor Centre
Lobb Hill
MONARO HWY
Burra Creek Nature Reserve
Yurununbeyan Nat Park
Corin Dam
Burra
Yurununbeyan SCA
Bimberi Nature Reserve
Mt Gingera
Namadgi
644
APOLLO RD
NAAS RD
Williamsdale
NEW SOUTH WALES
Naas
Mt Burra
Mt Bullongong
Horseshoe Hill
TERRITORY
Kosciuszko
Bimberi Peak
Coronet Peak
National
Rocky Crossing
B23
Mt Michelago
Tinderry Nature Reserve
National
Mt Murray
Glendale Crossing
Tantangara Reservoir
Park
Nursery Hill
Mt Yarara
Tinderry Peak
Mt Kelly
Park
BOOTH RANGE
Michelago
TINDERRY
Mt Woolpack
Mt Morgan
Half Moon Peak
Booths Hill
Yankee Hill
Scabby Range Nature Reserve
Mt Scabby
Boolboolma Crossing
Mt Gudgenby
BOBOYAN RD
Mt Holland
Jingera
Burnt School NR
Murrumbidgee
Sentry Box Rock
Naas
Strike-a-light NR
Anembo
Mt Ash Hill
Shanahans Mtn
CLEAR RANGE
609
RANGE
Yaouk Peak
Yaouk Nature Reserve
BOBOYAN DIVIDE
Colinton
Mt Colinton
Wallaby Hill
N
Mt Wangrah
Jerangle
Clear Hill
Mt Clear
Disused Railway
MONARO HWY
0 2 4 6 8 10km
© Hema Maps Pty Ltd
Black Cow Peak
Bugtown
Shannons Flat
Whinstone Hill

1 2 To Adaminaby 3 To Cooma 44 4 To Cooma 5 6 7

New South Wales Highway Index

New South Wales Alphabetic Site Index

Symbols

A

B

New South Wales Alphabetic Site Index

N

O

P

Q

R

S

T

U

V

W

X

Y

Gold Coast to Sydney

Pacific Highway

1 Stotts Creek Rest Area

Rest Area 14 km NE of Murwillumbah or 4 km SW of Chinderah, on Tweed Valley Way

HEMA 39 A13 28 16 27 S 153 30 17 E

2 Hosanna Farmstay

☎ (02) 6677 9023

Camp Area at Stokes Landing. 11 km S of Murwillumbah on the Tweed Valley Way

HEMA 39 A13 28 24 2 S 153 24 33 E

3 Cutters Campground

☎ (02) 6670 8600

Mebbin National Park

Camp Area 13 km S of Tyalgum, via Byrrill Creek Rd. 11 km dirt road. Alternative access from Kyogle Rd & Cadell Rd. Small vehicles only

HEMA 39 A13 28 26 40 S 153 11 41 E

4 Wadeville Woolies

☎ (02) 6689 7285

Camp Area at Wadeville. 20 km N of Kyogle or 48 km S of Murwillumbah. Turn N onto Link Rd

HEMA 39 B12 28 33 59 S 153 7 40 E

5 Burringbar Park

Camp Spot at Burringbar. Entrance opposite PO

HEMA 39 A13 28 26 3 S 153 28 14 E

6 Sleepy Hollow Rest Area Southbound

Rest Area 22 km S of Chinderah or 63 km N of Ballina. Southbound only

1

HEMA 39 A13 28 24 50 S 153 31 31 E

7 Sleepy Hollow Rest Area Northbound

Rest Area 24 km S of Chinderah or 61 km N of Ballina. Northbound only

1

HEMA 39 A13 28 25 25 S 153 31 14 E

8 Yelgun Rest Area

Rest Area 32 km S of Chinderah or 50 km N of Ballina

1

HEMA 39 B13 28 29 31 S 153 31 22 E

Notes...

9 Tyagarah Rest Area

Rest Area at Tyagarah. 8 km S of Brunswick Heads or 40 km N of Ballina

1

HEMA 39 B13 28 35 54 S 153 32 41 E

10 Mullumbimby Leagues Club

☎ 0405 198 866

Camp Area at Mullumbimby. Manns Rd. Camping at riverbank, next to Leagues Club. 2 km NE of PO

HEMA 39 B13 28 33 11 S 153 30 59 E

11 Mullumbimby Showground

☎ 0474 100 189

Camp Area at Mullumbimby. Main Arm Rd. 2 km W of PO

HEMA 39 B13 28 32 48 S 153 29 20 E

12 Bangalow North Rest Area

Rest Area 19 km S of Brunswick Heads or 1 km N of Bangalow. Southbound lane

1

HEMA 39 B13 28 39 58 S 153 31 35 E

13 Flat Rock Tent Park

☎ (02) 6686 4848

Camp Area at East Ballina. 38 Flat Rock Rd. Tents & camper trailers only

HEMA 39 C14 28 50 37 S 153 36 10 E

14 Bicentennial Gardens

Rest Area 3 km N of Ballina

1

HEMA 39 C13 28 50 52 S 153 32 59 E

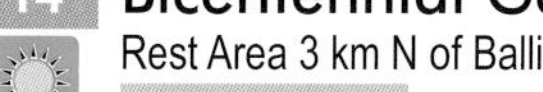

15 Alstonville Showground

☎ (02) 6628 0358

Camp Area at Alstonville. Entry is South St cnr Commercial Rd. Contact caretaker

HEMA 39 C13 28 50 23 S 153 26 26 E

16 Wardell Rest Area

Rest Area 14 km S of Ballina or 3 km N of Wardell, South & Northbound

1

HEMA 39 C13 28 56 7 S 153 28 19 E

17 Sandalwood Van & Leisure Park

☎ (02) 6683 4221

Caravan Park at Wardell, 12 km S of Ballina S turnoff or 21 km NE of Woodburn. 978 Pimlico Rd

HEMA 39 C13 28 56 29 S 153 28 21 E

NEW SOUTH WALES

18 Broadwater West Rest Area
Rest Area 4 km W of Broadwater or 10 km NW of Woodburn, on Broadwater - Coraki Rd. W side of Richmond River
HEMA 39 C13 28 59 56 S 153 23 54 E

19 Broadwater Stopover Tourist Park
(02) 6682 8254
Caravan Park at Broadwater. 1 - 5 Pacific Hwy
HEMA 39 C13 29 1 12 S 153 25 26 E
BIG RIG

20 Sunrise Caravan Park
(02) 6682 8388
Caravan Park at Broadwater. 74 - 92 Pacific Hwy. 1 km N of PO
HEMA 39 C13 29 0 54 S 153 25 49 E
BIG RIG

21 Riverside Park
Rest Area at Woodburn, beside Richmond River
1
HEMA 39 C13 29 4 16 S 153 20 40 E
BIG RIG

22 Black Rocks Campground
(02) 6627 0200
Bundjalung National Park
Camp Area 24 km SE of Woodburn. Turn E off Pacific Hwy 3.6 km from Woodburn onto Gap Rd. 15 km dirt road
HEMA 39 D13 29 15 2 S 153 21 59 E

23 Woodburn Park Rest Area
Rest Area 3 km S of Woodburn or 9 km N of New Italy. Southbound only
1
HEMA 39 C13 29 6 14 S 153 20 24 E
BIG RIG

24 New Italy Rest Area
Rest Area at New Italy. 12 km S of Woodburn or 38 km N of Maclean. Near museum
1
HEMA 39 C13 29 9 13 S 153 17 55 E
12

25 Tabbimoble Rest Area
Rest Area 5 km S of New Italy or 35 km N of MacLean
HEMA 39 D13 29 11 37 S 153 16 25 E
BIG RIG

26 Beekeepers Rest Area
Rest Area 17 km S of New Italy or 23 km N of Maclean
HEMA 39 D13 29 16 56 S 153 12 56 E
BIG RIG

27 Woombah Woods Caravan Park
(02) 6646 4544
Caravan Park 36 km S of Woodburn or 8 km N of Harwood, cnr Pacific Hwy & Iluka Rd
1
HEMA 39 D13 29 21 12 S 153 15 13 E
BIG RIG

28 Woody Head Campground
(02) 6641 1500
Bundjalung National Park
Camp Area 4 km N of Iluka. Turn E off Pacific Hwy 9 km N of Harwood Bridge or 36 km S of Woodburn onto Iluka Rd. 13 km E of Hwy
HEMA 39 D13 29 21 59 S 153 22 16 E
BIG RIG

29 Ferry Park
Rest Area at Maclean. Near Southern Hwy exit
1
HEMA 39 D13 29 28 20 S 153 12 17 E

30 Maclean Showground
Camp Area at Maclean. Entry off Cameron St. Honesty box for payment
HEMA 39 D13 29 27 50 S 153 11 58 E
BIG RIG

31 Red Cliff Campground
(02) 6641 1500
Yuraygir National Park
Camp Area 5 km N of Brooms Head or 19 km SE of Maclean. Turn E off Brooms Head Rd 18 km SE of Maclean. 1 km dirt road
HEMA 39 E13 29 34 35 S 153 20 6 E
BIG RIG

32 Lake Arragan
(02) 6641 1500
Yuraygir National Park
Camp Area 6 km N of Brooms Head or 20 km SE of Maclean. Turn E off Brooms Head Rd 18 km SE of Maclean. 2 km dirt road
HEMA 39 E13 29 34 0 S 153 20 10 E
BIG RIG

33 Sandon River Campground
(02) 6641 1500
Yuraygir National Park
Camp Area 10 km S of Brooms Head. Turn W off Brooms Head Rd 21 km SE of Maclean onto Sandon River Rd. 9 km dirt road
HEMA 39 E13 29 40 27 S 153 19 37 E

34 Lawrence Park
Rest Area at Lawrence. Cnr Richmond & Grafton St, next to river. Parking permitted E side of toilet block near General Store
HEMA 39 D12 29 30 1 S 153 6 4 E
BIG RIG 20

35 Brushgrove Recreation Triangle
Rest Area at Brushgrove 19 km NE of Grafton or 26 km SW of MacLean. Woodford St
HEMA 39 E12 29 33 59 S 153 4 42 E
BIG RIG

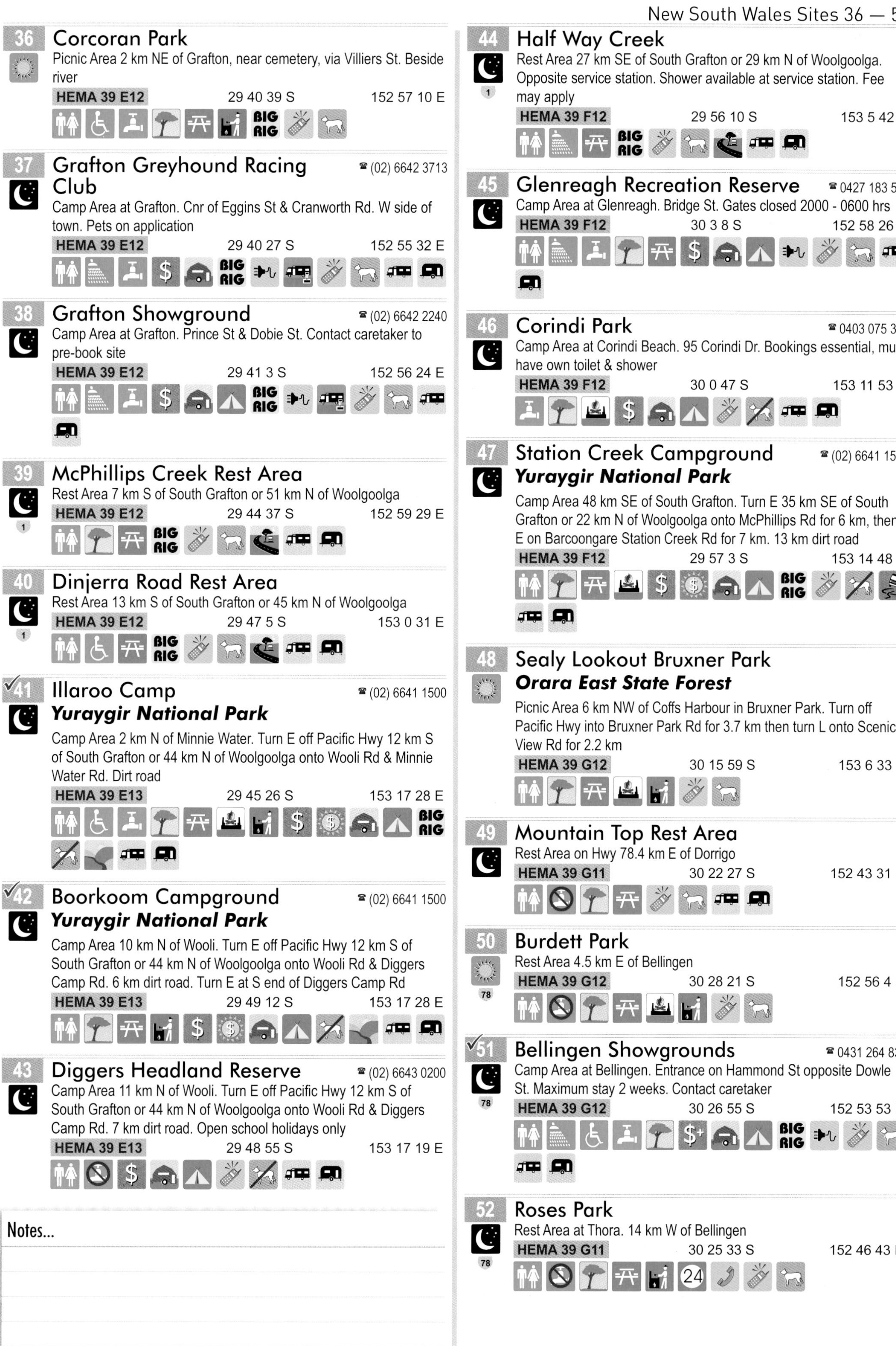

36 Corcoran Park
Picnic Area 2 km NE of Grafton, near cemetery, via Villiers St. Beside river
HEMA 39 E12 29 40 39 S 152 57 10 E
BIG RIG

37 Grafton Greyhound Racing Club
☎ (02) 6642 3713
Camp Area at Grafton. Cnr of Eggins St & Cranworth Rd. W side of town. Pets on application
HEMA 39 E12 29 40 27 S 152 55 32 E
BIG RIG

38 Grafton Showground
☎ (02) 6642 2240
Camp Area at Grafton. Prince St & Dobie St. Contact caretaker to pre-book site
HEMA 39 E12 29 41 3 S 152 56 24 E
BIG RIG

39 McPhillips Creek Rest Area
Rest Area 7 km S of South Grafton or 51 km N of Woolgoolga
1
HEMA 39 E12 29 44 37 S 152 59 29 E
BIG RIG

40 Dinjerra Road Rest Area
Rest Area 13 km S of South Grafton or 45 km N of Woolgoolga
1
HEMA 39 E12 29 47 5 S 153 0 31 E
BIG RIG

41 Illaroo Camp
☎ (02) 6641 1500
Yuraygir National Park
Camp Area 2 km N of Minnie Water. Turn E off Pacific Hwy 12 km S of South Grafton or 44 km N of Woolgoolga onto Wooli Rd & Minnie Water Rd. Dirt road
HEMA 39 E13 29 45 26 S 153 17 28 E
BIG RIG

42 Boorkoom Campground
☎ (02) 6641 1500
Yuraygir National Park
Camp Area 10 km N of Wooli. Turn E off Pacific Hwy 12 km S of South Grafton or 44 km N of Woolgoolga onto Wooli Rd & Diggers Camp Rd. 6 km dirt road. Turn E at S end of Diggers Camp Rd
HEMA 39 E13 29 49 12 S 153 17 28 E

43 Diggers Headland Reserve
☎ (02) 6643 0200
Camp Area 11 km N of Wooli. Turn E off Pacific Hwy 12 km S of South Grafton or 44 km N of Woolgoolga onto Wooli Rd & Diggers Camp Rd. 7 km dirt road. Open school holidays only
HEMA 39 E13 29 48 55 S 153 17 19 E

Notes...

44 Half Way Creek
Rest Area 27 km SE of South Grafton or 29 km N of Woolgoolga. Opposite service station. Shower available at service station. Fee may apply
1
HEMA 39 F12 29 56 10 S 153 5 42 E
BIG RIG

45 Glenreagh Recreation Reserve
☎ 0427 183 553
Camp Area at Glenreagh. Bridge St. Gates closed 2000 - 0600 hrs
HEMA 39 F12 30 3 8 S 152 58 26 E

46 Corindi Park
☎ 0403 075 335
Camp Area at Corindi Beach. 95 Corindi Dr. Bookings essential, must have own toilet & shower
HEMA 39 F12 30 0 47 S 153 11 53 E

47 Station Creek Campground
☎ (02) 6641 1500
Yuraygir National Park
Camp Area 48 km SE of South Grafton. Turn E 35 km SE of South Grafton or 22 km N of Woolgoolga onto McPhillips Rd for 6 km, then E on Barcoongare Station Creek Rd for 7 km. 13 km dirt road
HEMA 39 F12 29 57 3 S 153 14 48 E
BIG RIG

48 Sealy Lookout Bruxner Park
Orara East State Forest
Picnic Area 6 km NW of Coffs Harbour in Bruxner Park. Turn off Pacific Hwy into Bruxner Park Rd for 3.7 km then turn L onto Scenic View Rd for 2.2 km
HEMA 39 G12 30 15 59 S 153 6 33 E

49 Mountain Top Rest Area
Rest Area on Hwy 78.4 km E of Dorrigo
HEMA 39 G11 30 22 27 S 152 43 31 E

50 Burdett Park
Rest Area 4.5 km E of Bellingen
78
HEMA 39 G12 30 28 21 S 152 56 4 E

51 Bellingen Showgrounds
☎ 0431 264 836
Camp Area at Bellingen. Entrance on Hammond St opposite Dowle St. Maximum stay 2 weeks. Contact caretaker
78
HEMA 39 G12 30 26 55 S 152 53 53 E
BIG RIG

52 Roses Park
Rest Area at Thora. 14 km W of Bellingen
78
HEMA 39 G11 30 25 33 S 152 46 43 E
24

53 Macksville Lions Park
Picnic Area at Macksville. N side of river, beside bridge. Self Contained Vehicles only

1

HEMA 39 H12 30 42 14 S 152 55 15 E

24

54 Taylors Arm Reserve
Parking Area 27 km W of Macksville. "Pub with No Beer". Toilets & showers at hotel. Gold coin donation

HEMA 39 H11 30 46 4 S 152 42 58 E

20

55 Blackbird Flat Reserve
☎ (02) 6563 1555

Picnic Area 69 km NW of Kempsey or 68 km SE of Wollomombi near Comara. 16 km dirt road. Not suitable for caravans

HEMA 39 H10 30 46 20 S 152 22 6 E

56 West Kunderang Wilderness Retreat
☎ (02) 6778 1264

Camp Area 50 km E of Armidale. Off Raspberry Rd. Bookings essential. Dirt road. Suitable for off-road caravans & camper trailers only

HEMA 39 H10 30 50 38 S 152 4 36 E

57 Gumma Crossing Reserve
☎ (02) 6568 2555

Camp Area 7.5 km E of Macksville. Turn E off Pacific Hwy 200m S of bridge at Macksville onto Partridge St then onto Gumma Rd for 5 km. L at Boltons Crossing Rd. 2 km dirt road. Fairly large area beside Warrell Creek, but narrow access. Check re dogs at peak times

HEMA 39 H12 30 42 24 S 152 59 0 E

58 Paddy's Rest
Rest Area 5 km S of Warrell Creek or 17 km N of Clybucca

1

HEMA 39 H12 30 48 47 S 152 52 15 E

BIG RIG

59 Clybucca BP Roadhouse
Parking Area at Clybucca. Self Contained Vehicles only

1

HEMA 39 H12 30 56 17 S 152 56 33 E

BIG RIG 24

60 Frederickton Golf Club
☎ 02 6566 8261

Parking Area at Frederickton Golf Club. Please check in with bar manager. Toilets only open during Club House hours. Self Contained Vehicles only

HEMA 39 J12 31 1 50 S 152 52 41 E

BIG RIG 20

61 Riverside Park Rest Area
Rest Area at Kempsey. Turn S at N end of bridge

HEMA 39 J11 31 4 56 S 152 50 29 E

BIG RIG

62 Kempsey Showgrounds
☎ (02) 6562 5231

Camp Area at Kempsey. 19 Sea St

1

HEMA 39 J11 31 4 24 S 152 49 45 E

BIG RIG

63 Trial Bay Goal Campground
☎ (02) 6566 6168

Arakoon National Park
Camp Area 4 km E of South West Rocks. Near Trial Bay Gaol. Very expensive in peak season

HEMA 39 H12 30 52 41 S 153 4 16 E

64 Smoky Cape Campground
☎ (02) 6566 6168

Hat Head National Park
Camp Area 9 km SE of South West Rocks, via Arakoon Rd & Lighthouse Rd. Bush camping in confined area. Near beach. Maximum stay 6 weeks

HEMA 39 H12 30 55 45 S 153 4 37 E

65 Hungry Gate Campground
☎ (02) 6566 6168

Hat Head National Park
Camp Area 3.5 km S of Hat Head via Gap Rd, turn R into Hungry Rd. 3 km dirt road. Not suitable for caravans.

HEMA 39 J12 31 4 47 S 153 2 31 E

66 Bloodwood Ridge Rest Area
Rest Area 6 km S of Kempsey. Northbound only. Combined truck bay

1

HEMA 39 J11 31 9 50 S 152 49 10 E

BIG RIG

67 Kundabung Rest Area
Rest Area 15 km S of Kempsey. Southbound only. Combined truck bay

1

HEMA 39 J11 31 12 14 S 152 49 25 E

BIG RIG

68 Racecourse Headland Campground
☎ (02) 6566 6168

Goolawah National Park
Camp Area 8 km S of Crescent Head via Point Plomer Rd. 7 km dirt road. Beside beach. Outside cold showers. Maximum stay 6 weeks. Small vehicles only

HEMA 39 J12 31 14 57 S 152 57 37 E

69 Delicate Campground
☎ (02) 6566 6168

Goolawah National Park
Camp Area 10 km S of Crescent Head via Point Plomer Rd. 9 km dirt road. Beside beach. Outside cold showers. Maximum stay 6 weeks. Small vehicles only

HEMA 39 J12 31 15 37 S 152 58 6 E

70 Delicate Nobby Camping Ground
☎ (02) 6566 0144

Camp Area 11 km S of Cresent Head. 954 Point Plomer Rd

HEMA 39 J12 31 15 43 S 152 58 2 E

71 Melaleuca Campground
☎ (02) 6566 6168

Limeburners Creek National Park

Camp Area 12 km S of Crescent Head via Point Plomer Rd. 11 km dirt road. Beside creek. Maximum stay 6 weeks

HEMA 39 K12 31 16 49 S 152 57 45 E

72 Point Plomer Campground
☎ (02) 6566 6168

Limeburners Creek National Park

Camp Area 17 km S of Crescent Head via Point Plomer Rd. 16 km dirt road. Beside beach. Maximum stay 6 weeks

HEMA 39 K12 31 18 48 S 152 58 12 E

73 Log Wharf Reserve

Rest Area 1 km S of Telegraph Point or 14 km N of Pacific Hwy/Oxley Hwy jcn. Access via Hacks Ferry Rd, just S of bridge

1

HEMA 39 K11 31 19 36 S 152 47 46 E

BIG RIG

74 Burrawan Rest Area

Rest Area 10 km N of Kew. Northbound only

1

HEMA 39 K11 31 33 6 S 152 45 17 E

BIG RIG

75 Kendall Showgrounds
☎ (02) 6559 4463

Camp Area at Kendall. 23 Batar Creek Rd

HEMA 37 A13 31 38 12 S 152 42 7 E

BIG RIG

76 Swans Creek Crossing
☎ 1300 655 687

Kerewong State Forest

Camp Area 16 km NW of Kendall. Turn N 4 km W of Kendall off Kendall-Lorne Rd onto Upsalls Creek Rd for 12 km. 10 km dirt road

HEMA 37 A13 31 36 29 S 152 34 55 E

BIG RIG

77 Comboyne Showgrounds
☎ (02) 6550 4305

Camp Area at Comboyne. Showgrounds Rd off Main St. Call into general store or cafe for details & access information. Sealed road from Wauchope

HEMA 37 A13 31 36 28 S 152 27 58 E

BIG RIG

78 Diamond Head Campground
☎ (02) 6588 5555

Crowdy Bay National Park

Camp Area 9 km S of Laurieton, via Diamond Head Rd. 5 km dirt road. Cold showers. Beside beach

HEMA 37 B14 31 43 5 S 152 47 39 E

BIG RIG

Notes...

79 Indian Head Campground
☎ (02) 6588 5555

Crowdy Bay National Park

Camp Area 11 km S of Laurieton. 7 km dirt road. Cold showers

HEMA 37 B14 31 43 49 S 152 47 39 E

BIG RIG

80 Kylies Beach Campground
☎ (02) 6588 5555

Crowdy Bay National Park

Camp Area 13 km S of Laurieton. 9 km dirt road. Cold showers. Near beach

HEMA 37 B14 31 44 6 S 152 47 29 E

BIG RIG

81 Crowdy Gap Cultural Camp
☎ (02) 6552 4097

Crowdy Bay National Park

Camp Area 4 km N of Crowdy Head on Crowdy Bay Rd. Narrow access not suitable for large vehicles. Dirt road

HEMA 37 B13 31 49 59 S 152 43 48 E

82 Blacksmiths Inn Tavern & Cafe
☎ (02) 6556 5001

Camp Spot at Johns River. 400m E of Hwy. Spend a gold coin

HEMA 37 B13 31 43 53 S 152 41 40 E

BIG RIG 20

83 Tom Cat Creek Rest Area

Rest Area 20 km S of Kew or 2 km N of Moorland

1

HEMA 37 B13 31 45 53 S 152 40 15 E

BIG RIG 20

84 Coopernook Hotel
☎ (02) 6556 3150

Camp Spot at Coopernook. S end of Coopernook on George Gibson Dr. Parking at the rear of the hotel for Self Contained Vehicles, check in with publican on arrival. Toilet available during hotel opening hours

HEMA 37 B13 31 49 57 S 152 36 23 E

BIG RIG 48

85 Coopernook Forest Park
☎ (02) 6585 3744

Camp Area 4 km NW of Coopernook. Turn N onto West St, N onto Lansdowne Rd, N onto Forest Rd. 4 km dirt road

HEMA 37 B13 31 47 19 S 152 36 29 E

BIG RIG

86 Taree Showgrounds
☎ (02) 6552 4056

Camp Area at Taree. Mudford St, off Muldoon St. Gates close at 1800 hrs

HEMA 37 B13 31 54 4 S 152 27 36 E

BIG RIG

87 Taree Rotary Park

Rest Area at Taree, via Victoria St. 4 km NE of PO, just W of Info Centre

HEMA 37 B13 31 53 57 S 152 29 27 E

NEW SOUTH WALES

NEW SOUTH WALES

88 Wingham Showground
☎ (02) 6553 4083
Camp Area at Wingham. Gloucester Rd. Check in with caretaker
HEMA 37 B13 31 52 25 S 152 21 43 E
BIG RIG

89 Wingham Riverside Reserve
Picnic Area at Wingham. E of Central Park on Farquhar St. Toilets closed 1900 - 0600 hrs. Self Contained Vehicles only
HEMA 37 B13 31 52 17 S 152 22 51 E
BIG RIG 24

90 Four Mile Hill Rest Area
Rest Area 6 km S of Taree or 21 km N of Nabiac. Combined truck bay. Northbound only
1
HEMA 37 B13 31 57 49 S 152 27 53 E
BIG RIG 20

91 Talawahl Creek Rest Area
Rest Area 18 km S of Taree or 9 km N of Nabiac. Southbound only
1
HEMA 37 C13 32 2 57 S 152 26 49 E
BIG RIG 20

92 The National Motorcycle Museum
☎ (02) 6554 1333
Camp Area at Nabiac. 33 Clarkson St. For power arrive prior to 1530 hrs. Self Contained Vehicles only
HEMA 37 C13 32 5 44 S 152 23 0 E
BIG RIG

93 Wang Wauk Rest Area
Rest Area 8 km S of Nabiac or 8 km N of Coolongolook
1
HEMA 37 C12 32 9 16 S 152 19 19 E
BIG RIG 20

94 Kennedys Gap Road Rest Area
Rest Area 3 km S of Coolongolook or 26 km NE of Bulahdelah. Southbound only
1
HEMA 37 C12 32 15 2 S 152 19 24 E
BIG RIG 20

95 Newmans Road Rest Area
Rest Area 16 km S of Coolongolook or 13 km NE of Bulahdelah
1
HEMA 37 C12 32 21 9 S 152 18 51 E
BIG RIG 20

96 Wootton Rest Area
Rest Area at Wootton. On Wootton Way
HEMA 37 C12 32 17 38 S 152 18 14 E
BIG RIG

97 O'Sullivans Gap Picnic Area
Myall Lakes National Park
Picnic Area 9 km SW of Wootton or 10 km NE of Bulahdelah. On Wootton Way
HEMA 37 C12 32 20 37 S 152 15 36 E

98 Strike a Light Campground
☎ (02) 4997 4981
Camp Area 24 km NW of Bulahdelah, via Cabbage Tree Creek & Strike a Light Rds. 4WD high clearance vehicles only
HEMA 37 C12 32 17 42 S 152 5 29 E

99 Bulahdelah Showgrounds
☎ (02) 4997 4981
Camp Area at showgrounds. Cnr Stuart St & Prince St. Pay fee at Info Centre
HEMA 37 D12 32 24 18 S 152 12 16 E
BIG RIG 72

100 Bulahdelah Lions Park
Camp Spot at Bulahdelah. 1 km S of PO, entry 600m before bridge on old Pacific Hwy Rd. Entry only from N bound lane. Self Contained Vehicles only
HEMA 37 D12 32 24 50 S 152 12 21 E
BIG RIG 20

101 Bulahdelah Golf Club
Parking Area at Bulahdelah. Golf Rd. Self Contained Vehicles only
HEMA 37 D12 32 23 34 S 152 13 16 E
BIG RIG 24

102 Bulahdelah Bowling Club
☎ (02) 4997 4365
Parking Area at Bulahdelah. 50 Jackson St, check in with the bar, toilets & showers available during opening hours, a small fee applies
HEMA 37 D12 32 24 25 S 152 12 14 E
BIG RIG 72

103 Bungaree Bay Camping Area
☎ (02) 6591 0300
Myall Lakes National Park
Camp Area 18 km E of Bulahdelah. Turn S off The Lakes Way onto Violet Hill Rd, 10 km E of Bulahdelah near Boolambayte. 8 km dirt road. Small area beside lake
HEMA 37 D12 32 27 34 S 152 19 9 E

104 Violet Hill Campground
☎ (02) 6591 0300
Myall Lakes National Park
Camp Area 20 km E of Bulahdelah. Turn S off The Lakes Way onto Violet Hill Rd, 10 km E of Bulahdelah near Boolambayte. 10 km dirt road. Beside lake
HEMA 37 D12 32 28 16 S 152 19 37 E

105 Wallingat River Forest Park
☎ (02) 4984 8200
Wallingat National Park
Camp Area 15 km N of Bungwahl. Turn N off Lakes Way 2 km E of Bungwahl or 10 km SW of Pacific Palms onto Sugar Creek Rd, then River Rd. 13 km dirt road, not suitable for caravans. Beside river
HEMA 37 C13 32 19 39 S 152 24 10 E

106 Neranie Head Campground
☎ (02) 6591 0300
Myall Lakes National Park
Camp Area 5 km S of Bungwahl. Turn W off Seal Rocks Rd after 4 km at Fishermans Co-Op Neranie Rd. 1 km dirt road. Beside lake
HEMA 37 D13 32 24 33 S 152 27 8 E

107 Yagon Campground
☎ (02) 6591 0300

Myall Lakes National Park

Camp Area 4 km SW of Seal Rocks, via Thomas Rd

HEMA 37 D13 | 32 27 11 S | 152 29 41 E

108 The Ruins Campground
☎ (02) 6591 0300

Booti Booti National Park

6

Camp Area 16 km S of Forster or 5 km N of Pacific Palms

HEMA 37 C13 | 32 18 36 S | 152 31 10 E

BIG RIG

109 Sailing Club Picnic Area

Booti Booti National Park

6

Picnic Area 12 km S of Forster or 9 km N of Pacific Palms. 200m W of Hwy. Beside lake

HEMA 37 C13 | 32 16 24 S | 152 31 30 E

110 Camp Elim
☎ (02) 6554 0277

Camp Area 11.5 km S of Foster or 9.5 km N of Pacific Palms. Bookings essential as limited sites

HEMA 37 C13 | 32 16 8 S | 152 31 42 E

111 Tea Gardens Rest Area

Rest Area 1 km W of Tea Gardens. Turn S 30 km S of Bulahdelah or 14 km NE of Karuah

HEMA 37 D12 | 32 38 23 S | 152 8 39 E

112 Myall River Camp
☎ 0409 836 828

Camp Area 4 km N of Hawks Nest. Mungo Brush Rd

4

HEMA 37 D12 | 32 38 23 S | 152 10 44 E

BIG RIG

113 Banksia Green Campground
☎ (02) 6591 0300

Myall Lakes National Park

Camp Area 19.5 km NE of Hawks Nest, via Mungo Brush Rd. Access also via Bombah Pt ferry from Bulahdelah (Crawford St, Ann St, Lakes Rd). Small vehicles only

HEMA 37 D12 | 32 32 58 S | 152 18 26 E

114 Mungo Brush Campground
☎ (02) 6591 0300

Myall Lakes National Park

4

Camp Area 19 km NE of Hawks Nest, via Mungo Brush Rd. Access also via Bombah Pt ferry from Bulahdelah (Crawford St, Ann St, Lakes Rd)

HEMA 37 D12 | 32 32 37 S | 152 18 37 E

BIG RIG

115 Dees Corner Campground
☎ (02) 6591 0300

Myall Lakes National Park

4

Camp Area 20 km NE of Hawks Nest, via Mungo Brush Rd. Access also via Bombah Pt ferry from Bulahdelah (Crawford St, Ann St, Lakes Rd)

HEMA 37 D12 | 32 32 19 S | 152 18 59 E

116 White Tree Bay Campground
☎ (02) 6591 0300

Myall Lakes National Park

4

Camp Area 22 km NE of Hawks Nest, via Mungo Brush Rd. Access also via Bombah Pt ferry from Bulahdelah (Crawford St, Ann St, Lakes Rd)

HEMA 37 D12 | 32 31 41 S | 152 19 21 E

117 The Wells Camp Ground
☎ (02) 6591 0300

Myall Lakes National Park

4

Camp Area 23 km NE of Hawks Nest, via Mungo Brush Rd. Access also via Bombah Pt ferry from Bulahdelah (Crawford St, Ann St, Lakes Rd)

HEMA 37 D12 | 32 31 29 S | 152 19 22 E

118 Korsmans Landing Campground
☎ (02) 6591 0300

Myall Lakes National Park

4

Camp Area in Myall Lakes National Park. From Pacific Hwy turn S onto Lakes Rd at Bulahdelah, for 12 km then L to Korsmanns Landing

HEMA 37 D12 | 32 28 36 S | 152 17 8 E

119 Nerong Waterholes Rest Area

Rest Area 19 km S of Bulahdelah or 10 km N of Tea Gardens turnoff. Northbound

1

HEMA 37 D12 | 32 32 53 S | 152 9 15 E

BIG RIG 20

120 Browns Flat Rest Area

Rest Area 20 km S of Bulahdelah or 9 km N of Tea Gardens turnoff. Southbound only

1

HEMA 37 D12 | 32 33 15 S | 152 9 1 E

BIG RIG 20

121 Station Creek Rest Area

Rest Area 30 km S of Bulahdelah or 500m N of Tea Gardens turnoff. Northbound only

1

HEMA 37 D12 | 32 36 33 S | 152 5 43 E

BIG RIG 20

122 Ayers Rock Roadhouse

Parking Area 14 km E of Karuah or 1 km W of Tea Gardens turnoff. 100m off Hwy

1

HEMA 37 D12 | 32 36 52 S | 152 4 47 E

BIG RIG 20

Notes...

NEW SOUTH WALES

NEW SOUTH WALES

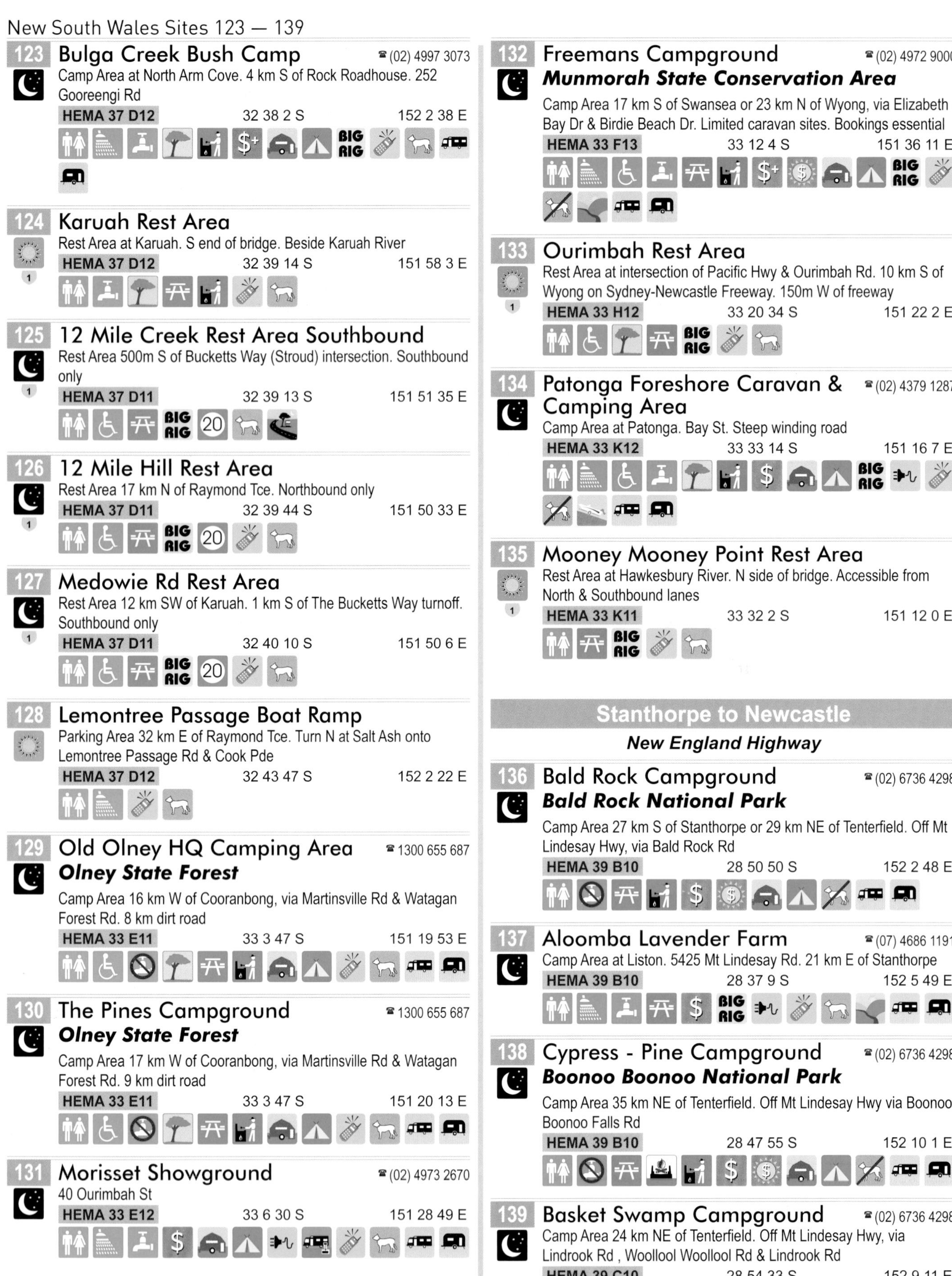

123 Bulga Creek Bush Camp
☎ (02) 4997 3073

Camp Area at North Arm Cove. 4 km S of Rock Roadhouse. 252 Gooreengi Rd

HEMA 37 D12 | 32 38 2 S | 152 2 38 E

BIG RIG

124 Karuah Rest Area

Rest Area at Karuah. S end of bridge. Beside Karuah River

HEMA 37 D12 | 32 39 14 S | 151 58 3 E

125 12 Mile Creek Rest Area Southbound

Rest Area 500m S of Bucketts Way (Stroud) intersection. Southbound only

HEMA 37 D11 | 32 39 13 S | 151 51 35 E

BIG RIG 20

126 12 Mile Hill Rest Area

Rest Area 17 km N of Raymond Tce. Northbound only

HEMA 37 D11 | 32 39 44 S | 151 50 33 E

BIG RIG 20

127 Medowie Rd Rest Area

Rest Area 12 km SW of Karuah. 1 km S of The Bucketts Way turnoff. Southbound only

HEMA 37 D11 | 32 40 10 S | 151 50 6 E

BIG RIG 20

128 Lemontree Passage Boat Ramp

Parking Area 32 km E of Raymond Tce. Turn N at Salt Ash onto Lemontree Passage Rd & Cook Pde

HEMA 37 D12 | 32 43 47 S | 152 2 22 E

129 Old Olney HQ Camping Area
☎ 1300 655 687

Olney State Forest

Camp Area 16 km W of Cooranbong, via Martinsville Rd & Watagan Forest Rd. 8 km dirt road

HEMA 33 E11 | 33 3 47 S | 151 19 53 E

130 The Pines Campground
☎ 1300 655 687

Olney State Forest

Camp Area 17 km W of Cooranbong, via Martinsville Rd & Watagan Forest Rd. 9 km dirt road

HEMA 33 E11 | 33 3 47 S | 151 20 13 E

131 Morisset Showground
☎ (02) 4973 2670

40 Ourimbah St

HEMA 33 E12 | 33 6 30 S | 151 28 49 E

132 Freemans Campground
☎ (02) 4972 9000

Munmorah State Conservation Area

Camp Area 17 km S of Swansea or 23 km N of Wyong, via Elizabeth Bay Dr & Birdie Beach Dr. Limited caravan sites. Bookings essential

HEMA 33 F13 | 33 12 4 S | 151 36 11 E

BIG RIG

133 Ourimbah Rest Area

Rest Area at intersection of Pacific Hwy & Ourimbah Rd. 10 km S of Wyong on Sydney-Newcastle Freeway. 150m W of freeway

HEMA 33 H12 | 33 20 34 S | 151 22 2 E

BIG RIG

134 Patonga Foreshore Caravan & Camping Area
☎ (02) 4379 1287

Camp Area at Patonga. Bay St. Steep winding road

HEMA 33 K12 | 33 33 14 S | 151 16 7 E

BIG RIG

135 Mooney Mooney Point Rest Area

Rest Area at Hawkesbury River. N side of bridge. Accessible from North & Southbound lanes

HEMA 33 K11 | 33 32 2 S | 151 12 0 E

BIG RIG

Stanthorpe to Newcastle

New England Highway

136 Bald Rock Campground
☎ (02) 6736 4298

Bald Rock National Park

Camp Area 27 km S of Stanthorpe or 29 km NE of Tenterfield. Off Mt Lindesay Hwy, via Bald Rock Rd

HEMA 39 B10 | 28 50 50 S | 152 2 48 E

137 Aloomba Lavender Farm
☎ (07) 4686 1191

Camp Area at Liston. 5425 Mt Lindesay Rd. 21 km E of Stanthorpe

HEMA 39 B10 | 28 37 9 S | 152 5 49 E

BIG RIG

138 Cypress - Pine Campground
☎ (02) 6736 4298

Boonoo Boonoo National Park

Camp Area 35 km NE of Tenterfield. Off Mt Lindesay Hwy via Boonoo Boonoo Falls Rd

HEMA 39 B10 | 28 47 55 S | 152 10 1 E

139 Basket Swamp Campground
☎ (02) 6736 4298

Camp Area 24 km NE of Tenterfield. Off Mt Lindesay Hwy, via Lindrook Rd , Woollool Woollool Rd & Lindrook Rd

HEMA 39 C10 | 28 54 33 S | 152 9 11 E

140 Tenterfield Showground
☎ (02) 6736 3666

Camp Area located at Tenterfield. Miles St. Turn W opposite Info Centre

HEMA 39 C10 | 29 3 25 S | 152 0 55 E

141 Craigs Caravan Park
☎ (02) 6736 1585

Caravan Park at Tenterfield. 102 Rouse St. 800m S of PO

HEMA 39 C10 | 29 3 40 S | 152 0 59 E

142 Bluff Rock Rest Area

Rest Area 11 km S of Tenterfield or 41 km N of Deepwater

HEMA 39 C10 | 29 9 15 S | 152 0 7 E

143 Eagle Creek Bush Camp
☎ 0419 631 301

Camp Spot 33 km SW of Tenterfield via Bruxner Hwy & Woodside Rd. Self Contained Vehicles only

HEMA 39 C10 | 29 8 40 S | 151 51 17 E

144 Deepwater
☎ (02) 6734 5111

Camp Spot at Deepwater behind the Old Deepwater Inn. Turn E off Hwy into Cadell St, entry 100m. Please register at bar

HEMA 39 D9 | 29 26 12 S | 151 50 53 E

145 Gunyah - Deepwater River Camping
☎ 0429 462 642

Camp Area at Gunyah. 1 km E of Deepwater. Access via Simpson St off New England Hwy. Follow signs across stock route to property

HEMA 39 D9 | 29 26 42 S | 151 51 1 E

146 Blatherarm Creek Campground
☎ (02) 6736 4298

Camp Area 11 km N of Torrington, via Blatherarm Rd off Silent Grove Rd

HEMA 39 C9 | 29 14 25 S | 151 41 58 E

147 Emmaville Caravan Park
☎ 0429 347 249

Caravan Park at Emmaville. Park Rd

HEMA 39 D9 | 29 26 51 S | 151 36 8 E

148 Beardy Creek (Heritage Park)

Rest Area 31 km S of Deepwater or 9 km N of Glen Innes

HEMA 39 E9 | 29 39 50 S | 151 46 37 E

Notes...

149 Three Waters High Country Holidays
☎ (02) 6732 4863

Camp Area 15 km NW of Glen Innes. Turn W off New England Hwy onto Gwydir Hwy travel 1.4 km. Turn N off Gwydir Hwy onto Emmaville Rd. Travel 4 km into Bullock Mountain Rd, 9 km to Homestead

HEMA 39 E9 | 29 37 12 S | 151 43 46 E

150 Bullock Mountain Homestead

Camp Area 17 km N of Glen Innes. Turn N off the Gwydir Hwy 5.5 km (towards Inverell) into Bullock Mountain Rd, travel 10 km to blue signs at grid, the homestead is another 2 km

HEMA 39 D9 | 29 36 11 S | 151 43 42 E

151 Glen Innes Showgrounds
☎ (02) 6732 3186

Camp Area at Glen Innes. Torrington Street. Caretaker will collect fees. Showgrounds closes Feb for Show Days

HEMA 39 E9 | 29 44 30 S | 151 44 31 E

152 Glen Innes Anzac Park

Rest Area at Glen Innes. 2 blocks W of main street on East Ave

HEMA 39 E9 | 29 44 3 S | 151 44 4 E

153 Poplar Caravan Park
☎ (02) 6732 1514

Caravan Park at Glen Innes. 15 Church St. 1 km S of PO

HEMA 39 E9 | 29 45 5 S | 151 44 9 E

154 Balancing Rock Rest Area

Rest Area 5 km S of Glen Innes or 16 km N of Glencoe

HEMA 39 E9 | 29 47 15 S | 151 43 55 E

155 Red Lion Tavern
☎ (02) 6733 3271

Camp Area at Glencoe. Fee for use of hot shower & toilet

HEMA 39 E9 | 29 55 34 S | 151 43 24 E

156 Guyra Rotary Park

Rest Area at Guyra. Toilets closed 1900 - 0700 hrs

HEMA 39 F9 | 30 13 7 S | 151 40 21 E

157 Mother of Ducks Lagoon

Rest Area at Guyra. White St. S end of town, turn W off Hwy into McKie Parkway

HEMA 39 F9 | 30 13 21 S | 151 40 10 E

158 Guyra Summit Caravan Park
☎(02) 6779 1241
Caravan Park at Gurya. 245 New England Hwy. 1.8 km S of Info Centre
HEMA 39 F9 30 14 4 S 151 40 17 E
BIG RIG

159 Dumaresq Dam Recreation Area
☎(02) 6772 4655
Picnic Area 14 km NW of Armidale. Turn N off Boorolong Rd onto Dumaresq Dam Rd, 9 km NW of Armidale, via Donnelly St (past UNE).
HEMA 39 G9 30 25 46 S 151 35 46 E
BIG RIG

160 Boorrolong Creek
Parking Area 26 km W of Armidale or 54 km SE of Bundarra on Thunderbolts Way
HEMA 39 G8 30 28 46 S 151 25 41 E

161 Bundarra Lions Park
Rest Area 3 km S of Bundarra or 73 km NW of Uralla. On Thunderbolts Way, beside river. Donations welcome
HEMA 39 F8 30 11 36 S 151 4 42 E
BIG RIG

162 Bundarra Caravan Park
☎(02) 6723 7162
Caravan Park at Bundarra. Court St. Pay at hotel
HEMA 39 F8 30 10 14 S 151 4 35 E
BIG RIG

163 Armidale Showgrounds
☎0400 966 650
Camp Area at Armidale. Dumaresq St
HEMA 39 G9 30 30 54 S 151 40 47 E
BIG RIG

164 Alma Park
Rest Area at Uralla. Cnr of Hill St & Queen St. Opposite bowling club
HEMA 39 G8 30 38 20 S 151 30 1 E
BIG RIG

165 Rocky River Fossicking Area
☎(02) 6778 4496
Camp Area 6 km W of Uralla, via Kingstown & Devoncourt Rds. Turn W off New England Hwy 800m S of Tourist Information Centre. Beside river
HEMA 39 G8 30 37 44 S 151 28 20 E

166 Wooldridge Recreation & Fossicking Reserve
Camp Area 6 km W of Uralla. Take Kingstown Rd for 4.5 km, turn N onto Devoncourt Rd, follow to end. Cattle grid at reserve entrance
HEMA 39 G8 30 37 53 S 151 28 0 E

167 Thunderbolts Rock
15
Rest Area 7 km SW of Uralla or 41 km NE of Bendemeer
HEMA 39 H8 30 41 52 S 151 28 7 E
BIG RIG 20

168 Uralla South Rest Area
15
Rest Area 18 km SW of Uralla or 32 km NE of Bendemeer
HEMA 39 H8 30 45 11 S 151 23 2 E

169 Bendemeer Camping Area
Camp Area at Bendemeer. Access via 800m dirt road, parallel to Hwy, between Hwy & service station. Behind rodeo grounds. Beside river
HEMA 39 H8 30 53 14 S 151 9 25 E
BIG RIG 24

170 Bendemeer Tourist Park
☎(02) 6769 6604
Caravan Park at Bendemeer. Havannah St. Single fee rate for solo travellers
HEMA 39 H8 30 52 50 S 151 9 29 E
BIG RIG

171 Moonbi Park & Lookout
15
Rest area 6 km N of Moonbi or 11 km S of Bendemeer on Moonbi Lookout Rd
HEMA 38 H7 30 58 34 S 151 5 57 E
BIG RIG

172 Cockburn River
☎(02) 6764 5100
Camp Area 11 km E of Kootingal or 2 km W of Limbri, via Kootingal-Limbri Rd. Beside Cockburn River
HEMA 39 J8 31 3 7 S 151 8 38 E
BIG RIG

173 Tamworth Rest Area
15
☎(02) 6755 4555
Rest Area at Tamworth. 2 km E of PO. Tight area to access
HEMA 38 J7 31 6 30 S 150 57 16 E

174 Tamworth Airport Rest Area
34
Rest Area 8 km W of Tamworth or 67 km E of Gunnedah. On Hwy opposite airport
HEMA 38 J7 31 4 40 S 150 51 2 E
BIG RIG 20

175 The Laura Byrne Park
25
Rest Area at Currabubula. Near Currabubula Creek. Toilets at sports oval
HEMA 38 J7 31 15 41 S 150 44 21 E
20

✓176 Woolomin Reserve
☎(02) 6764 2243
Camp Area at Woolomin. Beside Peel River. Fee for power payable at store. Maximum stay 30 days
HEMA 39 J8 31 18 12 S 151 8 51 E
BIG RIG

177 Bowling Alley Point Rec Reserve
Chaffey Dam

23

Camp Area 7 km S of Woolomin or 15 km N of Nundle. Maximum stay 7 days

HEMA 39 J8 | 31 21 38 S | 151 8 0 E

BIG RIG

178 Swamp Creek
☎ (02) 6764 5100

Camp Area 4 km N of Nundle. Beside Peel River on Bowling Alley Point Rd. 2 km dirt road

HEMA 37 A10 | 31 26 7 S | 151 8 33 E

BIG RIG

179 Fossickers Tourist Park
☎ (02) 6769 3355

Caravan Park at Nundle. Jenkins St

HEMA 37 A10 | 31 27 28 S | 151 7 41 E

180 Sheba Dams Reserve
☎ (02) 6764 5100

Camp Area 11 km E of Nundle, via Hanging Rock Rd. 1 km SE of Hanging Rock. Steep climb

HEMA 37 A10 | 31 29 56 S | 151 11 46 E

BIG RIG

181 Ponderosa Park Campground
☎ 1300 655 687

Hanging Rock State Forest

Camp Area 17 km E of Nundle. Turn N off Hanging Rock Rd after 8 km onto Forest Way. 8 km dirt road

HEMA 37 A10 | 31 27 49 S | 151 15 25 E

BIG RIG

182 Teamsters Rest Campground
☎ (02) 6764 5100

Camp Area 14 km S of Nundle, via Crawney Rd. Beside Wombramurra Creek. 5 km dirt road

HEMA 37 A10 | 31 33 24 S | 151 3 22 E

183 Wallabadah Rest Area

15

Rest Area at Wallabadah, behind First Fleet Gardens, beside Quirindi Creek. Gold coin donation to gardens

HEMA 37 A9 | 31 32 17 S | 150 49 52 E

BIG RIG 24

184 Nowlands Gap Rest Area

15

Rest Area 16 km SE of Willow Tree or 4 km NW of Murrurundi. Southbound only

HEMA 37 B9 | 31 44 25 S | 150 47 52 E

BIG RIG

185 Murrurundi Caravan Park
☎ (02) 6546 6288

Caravan Park at Murrurundi. 11 Bernard St. 1 km N of PO

HEMA 37 B9 | 31 45 30 S | 150 49 21 E

BIG RIG

186 Murrundi Self Contained Vehicle Park
☎ (02) 6546 6288

Camp Area attached to caravan park. Self Contained Vehicles only

HEMA 37 B9 | 31 45 30 S | 150 49 21 E

BIG RIG

187 Blandford Rest Area

15

Rest Area at Blandford. N end of town

HEMA 37 B9 | 31 46 39 S | 150 53 32 E

188 Burning Mountain Reserve
☎ (02) 6540 2300

15

Rest Area 10 km S of Blandford or 23 km N of Scone. 5 km N of Wingen. 200m in from Hwy on sloping parking area

HEMA 37 B9 | 31 51 21 S | 150 53 58 E

BIG RIG 20

189 Bunnan Rest Area

Rest Area at Bunnan. High St, N end of town

HEMA 37 B9 | 32 2 4 S | 150 35 8 E

BIG RIG 24

190 Gundy Showgrounds
☎ (02) 6545 8045

Camp Area at Gundy. 23 km E of Scone or 27 km W of Moonan Flat. Keys from general store. Site not available on show-event days

HEMA 37 B9 | 32 0 46 S | 150 59 43 E

BIG RIG

191 Belmadar Campground
☎ (02) 6546 3130

29

Camp Area 51 km E of Scone. At Moonan Flat, via Gundy Ellerston St. Amenity key available from PO. Caretaker collects fees

HEMA 37 B10 | 31 55 26 S | 151 14 13 E

192 Stewarts Brook Recreation Reserve
☎ (02) 6546 1237

Camp Area at Stewarts Brook. From Gundy take Hunter Rd, then turn SE onto Stewarts Brook Rd, follow to reserve, signposted. Maximum 6 weeks, fees payable to caretaker. 10 km dirt road

HEMA 37 B10 | 32 0 12 S | 151 18 29 E

BIG RIG

193 Scone Caravan Park
☎ (02) 6545 2024

Caravan Park at Scone. New England Hwy. 1 km N of PO

HEMA 37 B9 | 32 2 33 S | 150 51 56 E

BIG RIG

194 Lake Glenbawn Holiday Park
☎ (02) 6543 7193

Camp Area 13 km SE of Scone or 13 km NE of Aberdeen

HEMA 37 C9 | 32 6 28 S | 150 59 25 E

BIG RIG

Notes...

NEW SOUTH WALES

195 Taylor Park
Rest Area at Aberdeen. N end of town
15
HEMA 37 C9 | 32 9 39 S | 150 53 17 E
BIG RIG

196 Muswellbrook Showgrounds ☎ 0428 493 731
Camp Area at Muswellbrook. Entry off Rutherford Rd. Call ahead to confirm with caretaker
HEMA 37 C9 | 32 16 51 S | 150 53 48 E
BIG RIG

197 Cawsey Rotary Park
Rest Area 2 km NE of Denman or 24 km SW of Muswellbrook. Beside Hunter River. Small vehicles only
HEMA 37 C9 | 32 23 0 S | 150 41 59 E

198 Gungal Rest Area
Rest Area at Gungal. 11 km NW of Sandy Hollow or 24 km SE of Merriwa
84
HEMA 37 C8 | 32 16 24 S | 150 30 6 E
BIG RIG

199 Battery Rock Rest Area
Rest Area 20 km NW of Sandy Hollow or 15 km SE of Merriwa
84
HEMA 37 C8 | 32 12 51 S | 150 27 33 E

200 Merriwa Sports Club ☎ (02) 6548 2028
Camp Spot at Merriwa. King George Ave, entry at Golf Course sign. Check in at bar in club for parking directions. Self Contained Vehicles only
HEMA 37 C8 | 32 8 24 S | 150 21 47 E
BIG RIG

201 Bowmans Crossing
Camp Spot 7.5 km NW of Jerrys Plain or 22.5 km SE of Denman. Next to Hunter River
84
HEMA 37 D9 | 32 27 17 S | 150 51 8 E
BIG RIG 24

202 Jerrys Plains Recreation Ground
Camp Spot at Jerrys Plains. S end of town
HEMA 37 D9 | 32 29 54 S | 150 54 34 E
BIG RIG

203 Lake Liddell Recreation Area ☎ (02) 6541 2010
Camp Area 16 km S of Muswellbrook or 39 km NW of Singleton. Turn E off Hwy 15, 12 km S of Muswellbrook or 35 km NW of Singleton onto Hebden Rd for 4 km
HEMA 37 C9 | 32 21 3 S | 150 59 48 E
BIG RIG

204 Singleton Showground ☎ 0488 722 424
Camp Area at Singleton. Access gates in Church St, directly opposite Dight Ave. Max stay 5 days. Closed for show late September
HEMA 45 E1 | 32 34 5 S | 151 10 19 E
BIG RIG

205 Lake St Clair Campground ☎ (02) 6577 3370
Camp Area 35 km N of Singleton, via Bridgeman Rd. Beside lake
HEMA 45 A3 | 32 20 4 S | 151 17 30 E

206 Boggy Swamp Creek
Rest Area 56 km SW of Bulga or 61 km N of Colo Heights. 5 km N of Putty turnoff
HEMA 32 E6 | 32 56 27 S | 150 42 6 E
48

207 Grey Gum Cafe ☎ (02) 6579 7015
Camp Area 86 kms S of Singleton or 87 kms N of Windsor on the Putty Rd. Pay for showers
69
HEMA 32 F6 | 33 1 49 S | 150 40 25 E
BIG RIG

208 McNamara Park
Camp Spot at Broke. Beside river
HEMA 45 H1 | 32 44 52 S | 151 6 1 E
BIG RIG 72

209 Singleton East Rest Area
Rest Area 11 km W of Branxton or 11 km SE of Singleton, at jcn of New England Hwy & Golden Hwy
15
HEMA 45 F2 | 32 38 33 S | 151 13 56 E
BIG RIG

210 Pothana Lane Rest Area
Rest Area 5 km W of Branxton or 17 km SE of Singleton
15
HEMA 45 F3 | 32 39 30 S | 151 17 32 E
BIG RIG

211 Paterson Sports Ground ☎ (02) 4938 5029
Camp Area at Paterson. Entry from Webbers Creek Rd
HEMA 45 E7 | 32 36 12 S | 151 36 40 E
BIG RIG 72

212 Abermain Bowling & Recreation Club ☎ (02) 4930 4285
Camp Spot at Abermain. Goulburn St
HEMA 45 H5 | 32 48 26 S | 151 25 36 E
72

213 Cessnock Showground ☎ 0412 235 447
Camp Area at Cessnock. Access gates beside indoor sports centre Mount View Rd. Closed Feb & early Mar for show
HEMA 45 J4 | 32 49 51 S | 151 20 26 E
BIG RIG

214 The Wollombi Tavern ☎ (02) 4998 3261
Camp Spot at Wollombi. Parking at hotel, check in with publican for directions
HEMA 45 K1 | 32 56 19 S | 151 8 25 E
48

Woodenbong to Grafton

Summerland Way

215 Koreelah Creek Campground ☎ (02) 6632 0000

Koreelah National Park

Camp Area 35 km NW of Woodenbong. Turn N off the Mt Lindesay Rd 23 km W of Woodenbong or 22 km E of Legume at Old Koreelah onto White Swamp Rd for 12 km. 3 km dirt road. Beside creek. Maximum stay 2 weeks

HEMA 39 A11 28 18 30 S 152 27 58 E

216 Levuka ☎ (02) 6634 1338

Camp Area 16 km SW of Woodenborg. 6 km W of Woodenborg turn S into Beaury Creek Rd then turn W into Plantation Rd to Levuka. Bookings essential

HEMA 39 A11 28 25 20 S 152 30 33 E

217 Woodenbong Campground ☎ (02) 6635 1300

Camp Area at Woodenbong. W end of town next to swimming pool. Payable at Mobil or Ampol Service Station. Fee for showers

HEMA 39 A11 28 23 20 S 152 36 21 E

BIG RIG

218 Tooloom Falls Campground

Camp Area 6 km S of Urbenville. Turn S off Urbenville-Warwick Rd 3 km SW of Urbenville onto Tooloom Falls Rd. 3 km dirt road

HEMA 39 A11 28 30 46 S 152 31 36 E

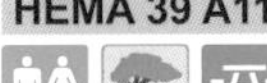     

BIG RIG

219 Legume

Camp Spot at Legume. Behind Community Hall, Killarney St. Donation welcomed, committe member will collect

HEMA 39 A11 28 24 23 S 152 18 25 E

BIG RIG 48

220 Urbenville Forest Park ☎ (02) 6634 1254

Camp Area at Urbenville. N end of town. Keys at Urbenville News

HEMA 39 A11 28 28 6 S 152 32 56 E

BIG RIG

221 Old Bonalbo Pioneers Park

Rest Area 23 km S of Urbenville or 1 km N of Old Bonalbo

HEMA 39 B11 28 38 35 S 152 35 49 E

BIG RIG 24

222 Bonalbo Caravan Park ☎ (02) 6632 1204

Caravan Park at Bonalbo. See onsite caretaker

HEMA 39 B11 28 44 19 S 152 37 43 E

BIG RIG

223 Moore Park Nature Reserve

Picnic Area 1.2 km N of Old Grevillia. 32 km SE of Woodenbong or 13 km NW of Wiangaree. Via Findon Creek Rd. Beside Richmond River

HEMA 39 A12 28 26 11 S 152 52 42 E

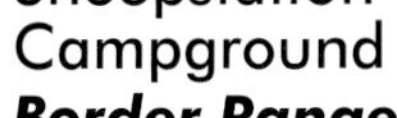

224 Sheepstation Creek Campground ☎ (02) 6632 0000

Border Ranges National Park

Camp Area 17 km NE of Wiangaree, via Lynchs Creek Rd & Tweed Range Scenic Dr. 11 km dirt road. Maximum stay 2 weeks

HEMA 39 A12 28 24 47 S 153 1 23 E

225 Kyogle Showground ☎ 0459 537 601

91

Camp Area at Kyogle. N end of town

HEMA 39 B12 28 36 57 S 153 0 0 E

BIG RIG

226 Bells Bay ☎ (02) 6633 9140

Toonumbar Dam

Camp Area 29 km W of Kyogle, via Afterlee Rd & Dam Access Rd. Some dirt road

HEMA 39 B12 28 37 0 S 152 47 39 E

227 Lismore Showgrounds ☎ (02) 6621 5916

Camp Area at Lismore. Alexandra Parade, North Lismore. Not available during events, call ahead to check availability. Maximum stay 14 days

HEMA 39 B13 28 47 50 S 153 16 25 E

BIG RIG

228 Casino Village ☎ (02) 6662 1069

Caravan Park at Casino. Light St. S side of town

HEMA 39 C12 28 52 31 S 153 3 0 E

BIG RIG

229 Breamer Park

91

Rest Area 28 km S of Casino or 22 km N of Whiporie

HEMA 39 C12 29 5 16 S 153 0 7 E

BIG RIG

230 Whiporie General Store ☎ (02) 6661 9100

91

Camp Spot at Whiporie. Beside store. Ask owner's permission

HEMA 39 D12 29 16 56 S 152 59 22 E

BIG RIG 24

Notes...

Ballina to Goondiwindi

Bruxner Highway

231 Rummery Park ☎ (02) 6627 0200

Whian Whian State Conservation Area

Camp Area 32 km NE of Lismore. Turn N off Dunoon Rd 7 km NE of Dunoon onto Minyon Falls Rd (Nightcap Range Rd) & Peates Mountain Rd for 8 km. 7 km narrow, winding, dirt road

HEMA 39 B13 28 35 55 S 153 22 41 E

232 Nimbin Showgrounds ☎ 0458 872228

Camp Area at Nimbin. Cecil St. Maximum stay 7 days

HEMA 39 B13 28 35 56 S 153 13 36 E

233 Mallanganee Oval

Camp Spot at Mallanganee. Access via Pine St, behind Bush Fire Brigade Building. Self Contained Vehicles only. Ask at Info Centre, do not take water, town is on tank water

HEMA 39 C11 28 54 29 S 152 43 17 E

234 Mallanganee Lookout

Rest Area cnr Bruxner Hwy & Bulmer Rd

HEMA 39 C12 28 53 56 S 152 44 25 E

235 Peacock Creek Camping Area ☎ (02) 6632 0000

Richmond Range National Park

Camp Area 18 km NE of Bonalbo. Turn N off Clarence Way 3 km E of Bonalbo onto Peacock Creek Rd. 13.5 km to campsite. Dirt road. 4WD only when wet

HEMA 39 B11 28 39 36 S 152 42 56 E

236 Clarence River Wilderness Lodge ☎ (02) 6665 1337

Camp Area 45 km NW of Tabulam. Turn N 3 km S of Tabulam off the Bruxner Hwy onto Paddy's Flat Rd, travel 38 km to entrance. 7 km to camp area, 38 km of gravel road. GPS at entrance

HEMA 39 B11 28 41 8 S 152 24 53 E

237 Lanikai Campground & Wildlife Refuge ☎ (02) 6666 1272

Camp Area 28 km NW of Tabulam. Turn N 3 km S of Tabulam off Bruxner Hwy onto Paddy's Flat Rd. 28 km gravel road. Book in at farmhouse for payment & directions

HEMA 39 B11 28 44 41 S 152 25 36 E

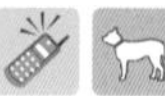

238 West of The Range Rest Area

44

Rest Area 10 km E of Tabulam or 9 km W of Mallanganee, at jcn of Bruxner Hwy & Bonalbo Rd

HEMA 39 C11 28 54 2 S 152 39 15 E

239 Tabulam Racecourse ☎ (02) 6666 1535

Camp Area 2 km S of Tabulam. On Racecourse Rd & Creek St. Keys & payment at the service station or co-op in town. Campdraft has the site during the June long weekend for private use

HEMA 39 C11 28 54 22 S 152 33 16 E

240 Crooked Creek Picnic Area

44

Picnic Area 9 km W of Drake or 40 km E of Tenterfield. Steep descent for last 200m. Inspect first

HEMA 39 C11 28 55 37 S 152 18 44 E

241 Bonshaw Weir ☎ (02) 6728 8161

44

Camp Area 8 km N of Bonshaw or 21 km SE of Texas

HEMA 39 C8 28 59 8 S 151 16 31 E

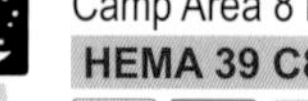

242 Yetman Caravan Park ☎ (07) 4675 3231

44

Caravan Park at Yetman. MacIntyre St. Opposite picnic area, behind tennis courts. Pay caretaker at house next door

HEMA 38 B7 28 54 6 S 150 46 42 E

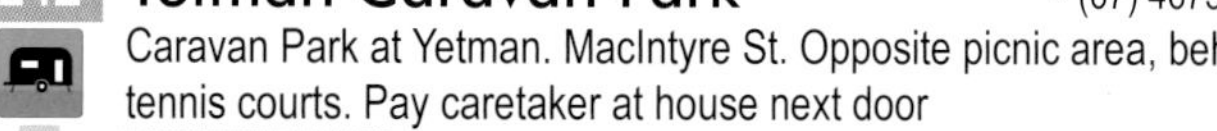

Grafton to Walgett

Gwydir Highway

243 Lollback Rest Area

38

Rest Area at Jackadgery, 43 km W of South Grafton or 111 km E of Glen Innes. Beside Mann River Bridge

HEMA 39 E11 29 34 39 S 152 33 25 E

244 Mann River Caravan Park ☎ (02) 6647 4662

38

Caravan Park at Jackadgery, 44 km W of South Grafton or 110 km E of Glen Innes. Gwydir Hwy

HEMA 39 E11 29 34 36 S 152 33 3 E

245 Bellbird Campground ☎ (02) 6739 0700

Washpool National Park

Camp Area 85 km W of South Grafton or 75 km E of Glen Innes. Turn N off Gwydir Hwy 82 km W of South Grafton or 72 km E of Glen Innes, onto Coachwood Rd. 3 km dirt road. Small vehicles only

HEMA 39 D10 29 28 27 S 152 18 58 E

246 Mulligans Hut Campground ☎ (02) 6739 0700

Gibraltar Range National Park

Camp Area 94 km W of South Grafton or 78 km E of Glen Innes. Turn S at Info Centre 85 km W of South Grafton or 69 km E of Glen Innes, onto Mulligans Dr. 9 km dirt road. Cold showers

HEMA 39 D11 29 30 57 S 152 21 34 E

247 Boundary Creek Falls
☎ (02) 6739 0700

Gibraltar Range National Park

Camp Area 95 km W of South Grafton or 63 km E of Glen Innes. Turn N off Gwydir Hwy 93 km W of South Grafton or 61 km E of Glen Innes. 1.5 km dirt road

HEMA 39 D10 | 29 32 2 S | 152 14 56 E

248 Mann River Nature Reserve
☎ (02) 6739 0700

Camp Area 131 km W of South Grafton or 47 km E of Glen Innes. Turn S off Gwydir Hwy 119 km W of South Grafton or 35 km E of Glen Innes onto Old Glen Innes - Grafton Rd. 12 km to campsites, open grassy area beside Mann River. Narrow winding road steep in places, some dirt road

HEMA 39 E10 | 29 41 15 S | 152 5 55 E

249 Dalmorton Campground
☎ (02) 6657 2309

Guy Fawkes River National Park

Camp Area 65 km W of Grafton via Old Grafton - Glen Innes Rd. Turn onto Chaelundi Rd 58 km along Grafton Rd, 1 km to campground

HEMA 39 E11 | 29 51 56 S | 152 26 52 E

250 Beardy Waters Woodland Park

Rest Area 148 km W of South Grafton or 6 km E of Glen Innes

38

HEMA 39 E9 | 29 43 33 S | 151 47 20 E

BIG RIG

251 Sinclair Lookout

Rest Area 15 km W of Glen Innes or 52 km E of Inverell

HEMA 39 E9 | 29 43 35 S | 151 35 56 E

BIG RIG

252 Kings Plains Creek Campground
☎ (02) 6739 0700

Kings Plains National Park

Camp Area 48 km NW of Glen Innes or 2.5 km SW of Jindalee. Via Jindalee Rd after Kings Plains Rd. Turn W, site off Iron Bark Rd. Dirt road from Wellingrove

HEMA 39 D8 | 29 35 25 S | 151 23 25 E

253 Swan Brook Rest Area

Rest Area 32 km W of Glen Innes or 35 km E of Inverell

38

HEMA 39 E8 | 29 46 18 S | 151 26 7 E

BIG RIG

254 7 Oaks Sapphire Fossicking & Camping
☎ (02) 6725 1582

Camp Area 23 km NE of Inverell. Turn E into Swanbrook Rd just N of town, turn R into Rickeys Ln

HEMA 39 E8 | 29 41 14 S | 151 16 48 E

Notes...

255 Fossickers Rest Caravan Park
☎ (02) 6722 2261

Caravan Park at Inverell. Lake Inverell Dr, 3 km E of PO. 300m off Gwydir Hwy

HEMA 39 E8 | 29 47 10 S | 151 8 15 E

BIG RIG

256 Sapphire City Caravan Park
☎ (02) 6722 1830

Caravan Park at Inverell. 93-103 Moore St

HEMA 39 E8 | 29 46 32 S | 151 7 52 E

BIG RIG

257 Inverell Showground
☎ (02) 6722 3435

Camp Area at Inverell. 1 km E of town, enter off Tingha Rd, in between Sporting Complex & Pioneer Village. Limited sites

HEMA 39 E8 | 29 46 57 S | 151 7 14 E

BIG RIG

258 Pindari Dam

Camp Area 80 km N of Inverell or 22 km SE of Ashford. Small vehicles only

HEMA 39 D8 | 29 23 46 S | 151 15 36 E

259 Wells Crossing

Camp Area 7 km E of Ashford on the Pindari Dam Rd, beside Severn River

HEMA 39 D8 | 29 21 44 S | 151 8 36 E

BIG RIG

260 Ashford Caravan Park
☎ (02) 6725 4014

Caravan Park at Ashford. 57 km N of Inverell. Bukkulla St. Payment in honesty box

HEMA 39 D8 | 29 19 24 S | 151 5 52 E

BIG RIG

261 Severn River

Rest Area 4 km N of Ashford

HEMA 39 D8 | 29 17 52 S | 151 7 5 E

BIG RIG

262 Lemon Tree Flat Campground
☎ (02) 6736 4298

Kwiambal National Park

Camp Area 38 km NW of Ashford. 17 km on sealed Wallangra Rd, then R for 21 km of unsealed road. Limited caravan sites (6)

HEMA 38 C7 | 29 8 50 S | 150 59 24 E

263 Copeton Dam (Northern Foreshore)
☎ (02) 6723 0250

Camp Area 17 km SW of Inverell, via Auburn Vale Rd. 4 km dirt road. Check ahead for dogs permitted

HEMA 38 E7 | 29 53 37 S | 150 59 50 E

NEW SOUTH WALES

264 Delungra Recreation Ground
☎ (02) 6724 8275

Camp Spot at Delungra. W end of town

38

HEMA 38 E7 29 39 4 S 150 49 33 E

265 Dumboy Creek Rest Area
Rest Area 4 km NW of Delungra or 25 km SE of Warialda

38

HEMA 38 E7 29 38 24 S 150 47 51 E

BIG RIG

266 Cranky Rock Recreation Reserve
☎ (02) 6729 1402

Camp Area 26 km NW of Delungra or 8 km E of Warialda. Turn N off Gwydir Hwy 23 km NW of Delungra or 5 km E of Warialda for 3 km dirt road. Pay at kiosk

HEMA 38 D7 29 33 39 S 150 38 46 E

BIG RIG

267 Warialda Rotary Park
Rest Area 27 km NW of Delungra or 2 km E of Warialda. S side of Hwy

38

HEMA 38 D6 29 32 59 S 150 35 27 E

BIG RIG

268 The Coolatai Hall
Camp Spot at Coolatai at the Community Hall. Donation box at hall for upkeep & hot showers

HEMA 38 C7 29 15 0 S 150 44 59 E

269 Warialda Caravan Park
☎ 0427 291 008

Caravan Park at Warialda. Cnr Holden St & Gwydir Hwy. W end of town. Caretaker in attendance

38

HEMA 38 D6 29 32 32 S 150 34 11 E

270 Warialda Rest Area
Rest Area in Warialda, Gwydir Hwy

HEMA 38 D6 29 32 43 S 150 34 52 E

BIG RIG 20

271 Warialda Creek Rest Area
Rest Area 2 km W of Warialda or 78 km E of Moree. N side of Hwy

38

HEMA 38 D6 29 32 46 S 150 33 14 E

BIG RIG

272 Gravesend Recreation Reserve
☎ (02) 6729 7012

Camp Area at Gravesend, Gwydir St. Phone for key to facilities & payment

HEMA 38 D6 29 35 6 S 150 20 2 E

BIG RIG

273 Gravesend Hotel
Camp Spot at Gravesend at rear of hotel. Check in with publican. Fee for power

HEMA 38 D6 29 34 59 S 150 20 15 E

274 The Golden Grain Motel & Caravan Park
☎ (02) 6754 9236

Caravan Park at Pallamallawa

HEMA 38 D5 29 28 28 S 150 8 7 E

BIG RIG

275 Gum Flat Public Reserve
Camp Spot 58 km W of Warialda or 28 km E of Moree. Turn N 55 km W of Warialda or 25 km E of Moree. 3 km dirt road N of Hwy. Signposted

HEMA 38 D5 29 27 54 S 150 4 54 E

276 Telleraga Rest Area
Rest Area 50 km W of Moree or 92 km E of Collarenebri

HEMA 38 D4 29 33 45 S 149 23 42 E

BIG RIG

277 Mehi River Rest Area
Rest Area 91 km W of Moree or 48 km E of Collarenebri

HEMA 38 D3 29 27 10 S 149 0 20 E

BIG RIG

278 Collarenebri Primitive Campground
Camp Area at Collarenebri. Gwydir Hwy, E end of town. Next to football grounds

HEMA 38 D2 29 32 56 S 148 34 55 E

279 Lions Park
Rest Area at Collarenebri

HEMA 38 D2 29 32 45 S 148 34 37 E

BIG RIG

Grafton / Dorrigo to Armidale

280 Blaxlands Creek Riverside Reserve
Camp Spot 33 km SW of Grafton or 86 km NE of Ebor. Just N of bridge

HEMA 39 E12 29 54 28 S 152 47 12 E

281 Nymboida Canoe Centre
☎ (02) 6649 4155

Camp Area at Nymboida. 37 km SW of Grafton or 81 km NE of Ebor. Cash only

HEMA 39 F11 29 55 33 S 152 44 52 E

BIG RIG

282 James Cartmill Memorial Park
Picnic Area 45 km SW of Grafton or 77 km NE of Ebor. Just W of Nymboida, beside Nymboida River

HEMA 39 F11 29 58 42 S 152 43 33 E

283 Platypus Flat Campground
☎ (02) 6657 2309

Nymboi-Binderay National Park

Camp Area 29 km N of Dorrigo, via Bostobrick or Cascade. Turn N 1 km W of Bostobrick via Moonpar Forest Dr

HEMA 39 F11 30 11 9 S 152 41 29 E

284 Chaelundi Campground
☎ (02) 6657 2309

Guy Fawkes River National Park

Camp Area 38 km NW of Ebor. Turn W 78 km SW of Grafton or 14 km N of Ebor at Hernani. 24 km dirt road. No caravans or motorhomes

HEMA 39 F11 30 4 7 S 152 19 59 E

285 Dangar Falls Lodge & Camping
☎ (02) 6657 2131

Camp Area 2 km N of Dorrigo, 180 Coramba Rd. Entrance is 100m N of Dangar Falls car park. Entry through gate

HEMA 39 G11 30 19 18 S 152 42 51 E

286 Ebor Rest Area

78

Rest Area at Ebor. 600m W of town, next to sportsground. Opposite Ebor Falls turnoff

HEMA 39 G10 30 24 29 S 152 20 45 E

287 Ebor Falls Hotel Motel
☎ (02) 6775 9155

78

Camp Area at Ebor. Behind Ebor Hotel

HEMA 39 G10 30 24 11 S 152 20 51 E

BIG RIG

288 Native Dog Creek Campground
☎ (02) 6657 2309

Cathedral Rock National Park

17

Camp Area 12 km NW of Ebor or 67 km SE of Guyra, via Ebor - Guyra Rd. 200m W of Hwy. Small vehicles only

HEMA 39 G10 30 23 15 S 152 16 6 E

289 Barokee Campground
☎ (02) 6657 2309

Cathedral Rock National Park

Camp Area 14 km SW of Ebor or 38 km E of Wollomombi. Turn W off Waterfall Way 6 km SW of Ebor or 32 km E of Wollomombi, onto Round Mountain Rd. 8 km dirt road. Small vehicles only. Not suitable for caravans

HEMA 39 G10 30 26 38 S 152 15 2 E

290 Little Styx River Campground

Camp Area 21 km S of Ebor or 37 km E of Wollomombi. Turn E off Waterfall Way 11 km SW of Ebor or 27 km E of Wollomombi, onto Point Lookout Rd.10 km dirt road. At entrance to New England National Park

HEMA 39 G10 30 30 28 S 152 21 59 E

BIG RIG

Notes...

291 Thungutti Camping Ground
☎ (02) 6657 2309

New England National Park

Camp Area 23 km S of Ebor or 35 km E of Wollomombi. Turn E off Waterfall Way onto Point Lookout Rd. 11 km dirt road. Tent camping only. Small vehicles only

HEMA 39 G11 30 30 2 S 152 23 15 E

292 Oaky Creek Rest Area

78

Rest Area 16 km SW of Ebor or 22 km E of Wollomombi

HEMA 39 G10 30 30 0 S 152 15 14 E

293 Dingo Fence Rest Area

78

Rest Area 28 km SW of Ebor or 10 km E of Wollomombi

HEMA 39 G10 30 30 8 S 152 8 43 E

294 Wollomombi Rest Area

Rest Area at Wollomombi. 1 km NW off Waterfall Way. Toilets at Memorial Hall

HEMA 39 G10 30 30 42 S 152 2 40 E

BIG RIG 24

295 Green Gully Campground
☎ (02) 6738 9100

Oxley Wild Rivers National Park

Camp Area 4 km W of Wollomombi. Turn S off Waterfall Way 2 km W of Wollomombi or 38 km E of Armidale. Near Wollomombi Gorge. Narrow entrance way

HEMA 39 G10 30 31 54 S 152 1 40 E

296 Gara River Rest Area

78

Rest Area 27 km W of Wollomombi or 13 km E of Armidale

HEMA 39 G9 30 32 38 S 151 47 39 E

BIG RIG

297 Dangars Gorge Campground
☎ (02) 6738 9100

Oxley Wild Rivers National Park

Camp Area 22 km SE of Armidale via Dangarsleigh, Dangars Falls Rd. 10 km dirt road

HEMA 39 H9 30 40 20 S 151 43 32 E

Port Macquarie-Tamworth-Coonabarabran

Oxley Highway

298 Rocks Ferry Reserve

Rest Area at Wauchope N end of town. River Ferry Rd

HEMA 39 K11 31 27 7 S 152 44 46 E

BIG RIG

299 Wauchope Showgrounds
☎ (02) 6585 3485

Camp Area at Wauchope, enter via High St

HEMA 39 K11 31 27 28 S 152 43 27 E

BIG RIG 96

300 **Wild Bull Camping Area** ☎ 1300 655 687
Mount Boss State Forest
Camp Area 40 km NW of Wauchope, via Beechwood, Bellangry, Hastings Forest Way & Cobrabald Rd. 17 km dirt road
HEMA 39 J11 31 14 45 S 152 30 47 E

301 **Brushy Mountain Campground** ☎ (02) 6588 5555
Werrikimbe National Park
Camp Area 61 km NW of Wauchope, via Beechwood, Bellangry & Hastings Forest Way. 38 km dirt road. Small vehicles only
HEMA 39 J10 31 8 52 S 152 21 42 E

302 **Ellenborough Reserve**
Camp Area at Ellenborough. 500m N of Hwy on E side of bridge, beside river. Maximum stay 14 days
HEMA 39 K11 31 26 25 S 152 27 40 E
BIG RIG

303 **Stockyard Creek Rest Area**
Rest Area 82 km W of Wauchope or 83 km SE of Walcha. Just E of Gingers Creek store
34
HEMA 39 K10 31 24 10 S 152 7 26 E
BIG RIG

304 **Mooraback Campground** ☎ (02) 6777 4700
Werrikimbe National Park
Camp Area 84 km E of Walcha. Turn N off the Oxley Hwy 111 km W of Wauchope or 54 km SE of Walcha onto Kangaroo Flat Rd, Mooraback Rd. 30 km dirt road. Small vehicles only
HEMA 39 J10 31 8 51 S 152 12 54 E

305 **Tia Falls Campground** ☎ (02) 6777 4700
Oxley Wild Rivers National Park
Camp Area 42 km SE of Walcha. Turn N off Oxley Hwy 128 km NW of Wauchope or 37 km SE of Walcha. 5 km dirt road
HEMA 39 J9 31 9 37 S 151 51 16 E

306 **Tia River Rest Area**
Rest Area 129 km NW of Wauchope or 36 km SE of Walcha
34
HEMA 39 J9 31 11 17 S 151 49 51 E
BIG RIG

307 **Stoney Creek Rest Area**
Rest Area 143 km NW of Wauchope or 22 km SE of Walcha
34
HEMA 39 J9 31 4 35 S 151 46 39 E
BIG RIG

308 **Apsley Gorge Campground** ☎ (02) 6777 4700
Oxley Wild Rivers National Park
Camp Area 20 km SE of Walcha. Turn N off Oxley Hwy 146 km NW of Wauchope or 19 km SE of Walcha for 1 km
HEMA 39 J9 31 3 16 S 151 45 45 E

309 **Walcha East Rest Area**
Rest Area 161 km NW of Wauchope or 4 km E of Walcha
34
HEMA 39 H9 31 0 13 S 151 37 48 E
BIG RIG

310 **Woolbrook Rest Area**
Rest Area at Woolbrook. 26 km W of Walcha or 26 km E of Bendemeer. 1 km S of Hwy beside river
HEMA 39 H8 30 57 55 S 151 20 50 E
BIG RIG

311 **Somerton Hotel - Cathys Tavern** ☎ (02) 6769 7683
Camp Area at Somerton. Check in at the bar for directions for parking
HEMA 38 H6 30 56 26 S 150 38 26 E
BIG RIG

312 **Eastern Foreshore Campground** ☎ (02) 6769 7605
Lake Keepit State Park
Camp Area 56 km NW of Tamworth. Turn N off Oxley Hwy 46 km W of Tamworth or 29 km E of Gunnedah. 3 km dirt road. Pets only permitted in bush camping area, not caravan park area
HEMA 38 H6 30 53 20 S 150 31 6 E
BIG RIG

313 **Lake Keepit Holiday Park** ☎ (02) 6769 7605
Lake Keepit State Park
Caravan Park 56 km NW of Tamworth. Turn N off Oxley Hwy 46 km W of Tamworth or 29 km E of Gunnedah
HEMA 38 H6 30 53 45 S 150 30 21 E
BIG RIG

314 **Red Bank Rest Area**
Rest Area 7 km W of Carroll or 12 km E of Gunnedah
34
HEMA 38 H6 30 59 39 S 150 22 40 E
BIG RIG

315 **South St RV Park** ☎ (02) 6742 1589
Camp Area at Gunnedah South St, next to showgrounds. Caretaker collects fees
34
HEMA 38 H6 30 58 44 S 150 14 42 E
BIG RIG 72

316 **150 Meridian Rest Area**
Rest Area 27 km W of Gunnedah or 10 km E of Mullaley
34
HEMA 38 H5 31 3 46 S 149 59 55 E
BIG RIG

317 **Mullaley Hotel** ☎ (02) 6743 7820
Camp Area at Mullaley. Oxley Hwy. W end of town
34
HEMA 38 J5 31 6 1 S 149 54 15 E
BIG RIG

318 **Oxleys Crossing Rest Area**
Rest Area 37 km W of Mullaley or 31 km E of Coonabarabran
34
HEMA 38 J4 31 7 56 S 149 32 38 E

Walcha to Raymond Terrace

Thunderbolts Way, Bucketts Way

319 Bretti Reserve
☎ (02) 6558 1408

Camp Area 44 km S of Nowendoc or 34 km N of Gloucester. On Thunderbolts Way beside Manning River. Maximum stay 1 month

HEMA 37 B12 31 47 29 S 151 54 56 E

BIG RIG

320 Gloryvale Reserve
☎ (02) 6558 1408

Camp Area 55 km S of Nowendoc or 23 km N of Gloucester. On Thunderbolts Way, beside Manning River. Maximum stay 1 month

HEMA 37 B11 31 51 25 S 151 52 42 E

321 Woko Campground
☎ (02) 6538 5300

Woko National Park

Camp Area 33 km NW of Gloucester. Turn W off Thunderbolts Way 59 km S of Nowendoc or 19 km N of Gloucester onto Curricarbark Rd & Flood Detour Rd for 14 km. 10 km dirt road. Beside river

HEMA 37 B11 31 48 5 S 151 47 42 E

322 Barrington Reserve
☎ (02) 6558 4249

Camp Area 1.5 km W of Barrington. W side of bridge, beside Barrington River. Steep dip at entrance. Pay fee at Barrington Store

HEMA 37 B11 31 58 17 S 151 53 59 E

BIG RIG

323 Gloucester River Campground
☎ (02) 6538 5300

Barrington Tops National Park

Camp Area 38 km W of Gloucester. Turn W off Bucketts Way 9 km S of Gloucester onto Gloucester Tops Rd. 15 km dirt road

HEMA 37 C11 32 3 33 S 151 40 44 E

324 Telegherry Forest Park
☎ 1300 655 687

Chichester State Forest

Camp Area 26 km N of Dungog. From Dungog take Chichester Dam Rd, turn N into Wangat Rd, E into Middle Rd. Dirt road

HEMA 37 C11 32 13 21 S 151 44 40 E

325 Coachwood Camping Area
☎ 1300 655 687

Chichester State Forest

Camp Area 29 km N of Dungog, take Chichester Dam Rd N into Wangat Rd turn E into Middle Rd E into Frying Pan Rd. Dirt road

HEMA 37 C11 32 12 58 S 151 45 39 E

326 Frying Pan Creek Camping Area
☎ 1300 655 687

Chichester State Forest

Camp Area 29.5 km N of Dungog, take Chichester Dam Rd N into Wangat Rd turn E into Middle Rd E into Frying Pan Rd. Dirt road

HEMA 37 C11 32 13 9 S 151 45 42 E

327 Ferndale Camping Area
☎ (02) 4995 9239

Camp Area 25 km N of Dungog on Chichester Dam Rd. Signposted

HEMA 37 C11 32 14 45 S 151 41 21 E

BIG RIG

328 Bandon Grove Reserve

Camp Spot 13 km N of Dungog on the Chichester Dam Rd

HEMA 37 C11 32 18 6 S 151 43 1 E

BIG RIG 48

329 East Gresford Showground

Camp Area at East Gresford on the Gresford-Paterson Rd

HEMA 45 C6 32 25 56 S 151 33 27 E

BIG RIG

330 Dungog Caravan Park
☎ (02) 4992 2212

Caravan Park 1 km NE of Dungog on the Dungog - Stroud Rd. Key for facilities from the Info Centre

HEMA 37 D11 32 23 49 S 151 45 46 E

331 Dungog Showground
☎ (02) 4992 1810

Camp Area at Dungog Showground. Main entrance from Chapman St. Caretaker will collect fees

HEMA 37 D11 32 24 19 S 151 45 3 E

BIG RIG

332 Dungog Memorial Bowls, Sport & Recreation CLub
☎ (02) 4992 1635

Camp Area at Dungog. 5 powered sites, check in at reception

HEMA 37 D11 32 24 8 S 151 45 10 E

BIG RIG 24

333 Stroud Showground
☎ (02) 4994 5204

Camp Area at Stroud. 47 km S of Gloucester or 47 km N of Raymond Tce

HEMA 37 D12 32 23 59 S 151 57 51 E

334 Wharf Reserve
☎ (02) 4996 4231

Camp Spot at Clarence Town. Rifle St

HEMA 37 D11 32 35 27 S 151 46 40 E

335 Williams River Holiday Park
☎ (02) 4996 4231

Caravan Park at Clarence Town. Durham St

HEMA 37 D11 32 34 56 S 151 46 55 E

BIG RIG

Notes...

Kew to Scone

336 Little Plains Sportsground

Camp Area at Elands. 39 km N of Wingham or 24 km W of Comboyne. Ask at shop for directions

HEMA 37 A12 31 37 56 S 152 17 44 E

BIG RIG

337 Rocks Crossing Reserve ☎ (02) 6552 1900

Camp Area 43 km NW of Wingham. Access along Nowendoc Rd, via Killawarra & Mount George

HEMA 37 B12 31 46 7 S 152 4 30 E

338 Knorrit Flat Riverside Retreat & Camping Ground ☎ (02) 6550 7541

Camp Area 35 km NW of Wingham, via Nowendoc Rd

HEMA 37 B12 31 47 49 S 152 3 36 E

BIG RIG

339 Cundle Flat Farm ☎ (02) 6550 7565

Camp Area 22 km NW of Bundook via Gloucester or 60 km W of Taree via Wingham. Dirt road. Bookings required

HEMA 37 B12 31 48 45 S 151 59 2 E

340 Copeland Reserve ☎ (02) 6558 1408

29

Camp Area 12 km W of Gloucester on Scone Rd. Maximum stay 1 month

HEMA 37 B11 31 58 21 S 151 51 32 E

BIG RIG

341 Polblue Campground ☎ (02) 6540 2300

Barrington Tops National Park

29

Camp Area 64 km W of Gloucester, via Barrington, Copeland & Barrington Tops Rd. Dirt road

HEMA 37 B10 31 57 19 S 151 25 28 E

Warialda-Tamworth

Fossickers Way

342 Ti Tree Creek Rest Area

95

Rest Area 11 km S of Warialda or 31 km N of Bingara

HEMA 38 D6 29 36 50 S 150 32 36 E

BIG RIG

343 Myall Creek Rest Area

Rest Area 18 km SW of Delungra or 24 km NE of Bingara

HEMA 38 E7 29 46 30 S 150 43 1 E

BIG RIG

344 Bingara Riverside Caravan Park ☎ 0427 241 300

Caravan Park at Bingara. Keera St

HEMA 38 E6 29 51 49 S 150 34 38 E

BIG RIG

345 Bingara Riverside Camping

Camp Spot at Bingara, 3 areas of riverside camping. Information & map for camp areas on board at entrance to S side camp area, Copeton Dam Rd. Maximum stay 7 nights. Self Contained Vehicles only. GPS at entry gate

HEMA 38 E6 29 51 45 S 150 34 45 E

346 Gwydir River Camps ☎ (02) 6724 0066

Camp Spots 8 km E of Bingara, via Keera Rd. Various sites along riverbank

HEMA 38 E7 29 53 26 S 150 37 17 E

347 Allawah 4WD & Camping ☎ (02) 6724 1240

Camp Area 10 km E of Bingara on the Bundarra - Bingara Rd. Bush camping

HEMA 38 E7 29 54 40 S 150 38 46 E

348 Copeton Waters Holiday Park ☎ (02) 6723 6269

Camp Area 52 km E of Bingara or 44 km SW of Inverell. Fees higher in peak season. Bush camping also available

HEMA 38 E7 29 55 12 S 150 56 18 E

BIG RIG

349 Upper Horton Caravan and Camping Area

Camp Area at Upper Horton. Cobbadah St, next to tennis courts

HEMA 38 F6 30 8 24 S 150 26 36 E

BIG RIG

350 Rocky Creek Glacial Area

Camp Spot 36 km SW of Bingara or 66 km NE of Narrabri. Some dirt road

HEMA 38 F6 30 2 4 S 150 19 1 E

351 The Ponds Camp

95

Rest Area 29 km S of Bingara or 32 km N of Barraba

HEMA 38 F6 30 6 39 S 150 35 51 E

BIG RIG

352 Barraba Caravan Park ☎ (02) 6782 1818

95

Caravan Park at Barraba. Bridge St. N end of town

HEMA 38 G6 30 22 23 S 150 36 36 E

BIG RIG

353 Little Creek Reserve ☎ (02) 6782 1255

Picnic Area 21 km W of Barraba, via Trevallyn Rd. Beside creek

HEMA 38 F6 30 18 38 S 150 26 4 E

BIG RIG

354 Barraba Lions Park

95

Rest Area 5 km S of Barraba or 40 km N of Manilla

HEMA 38 G6 30 25 15 S 150 36 59 E

BIG RIG 24

355 **Glen Riddle Recreation Reserve** ☎ (02) 6782 1255
Camp Area 17 km S of Barraba. Turn E 9 km S of Barraba or 36 km N of Manilla onto Crow Mountain Rd for 8 km
HEMA 38 G7 30 27 1 S 150 41 34 E
BIG RIG

356 **Split Rock Dam** ☎ (02) 6767 5555
Camp Area 39 km S of Barraba. Turn E 30 km S of Barraba or 15 km N of Manilla for 7 km, then N onto Recreation Area Rd. Payment at council office in Manilla
HEMA 38 G7 30 33 50 S 150 40 35 E
BIG RIG

357 **Warrabah National Park** ☎ (02) 6739 0700
Camp Area 35 km NE of Manilla, via Namoi Rd. 22 km dirt road. Not suitable for caravans, small vehicles only
HEMA 38 G7 30 34 7 S 150 54 55 E

358 **Manilla Rivergums Caravan Park** ☎ (02) 6785 1166
95
Caravan Park at Manilla. 2 km E of PO
HEMA 38 H7 30 44 40 S 150 43 52 E
BIG RIG

359 **Lions Park**
Rest Area 7.5 km S of Manilla or 37.5 km N of Tamworth on the Fossickers Way
HEMA 38 H7 30 48 14 S 150 45 12 E
BIG RIG 24

360 **Attunga Creek**
95
Rest Area 24 km S of Manilla or 21 km N of Tamworth
HEMA 38 H7 30 55 45 S 150 50 48 E
BIG RIG

Quirindi to Bourke

Kamilaroi Highway

361 **Braefield Rest Area**
Rest Area 9 km N of Willow Tree or 7 km S of Quirindi. Next to railway line
HEMA 38 K7 31 33 54 S 150 41 53 E
BIG RIG

362 **Quirindi Caravan Park** ☎ (02) 6746 2407
Caravan Park at Quirindi. 15 Rose St
HEMA 38 K6 31 30 37 S 150 40 59 E
BIG RIG

Notes...

363 **Caroona Hall** ☎ (02) 6747 4749
Parking Area at Caroona. Next to hall
HEMA 38 J6 31 24 23 S 150 25 29 E
BIG RIG 48

364 **Spring Ridge Showground**
Camp Area at Spring Ridge. Entry from Tungenbone Rd. Donation box on site
HEMA 38 J6 31 23 45 S 150 14 42 E
BIG RIG 48

365 **Premer Lions Park**
Camp Area, midway between Quirindi & Coonabarabran. Donation to Lions Club payable at honesty box
HEMA 38 K5 31 27 9 S 149 54 3 E
BIG RIG

366 **Werris Creek League Club** ☎ (02) 6768 7108
Camp Area at Werris Creek, entry off Parks St. Pay fee at service station
HEMA 38 J6 31 20 28 S 150 38 56 E
BIG RIG

367 **Square Bush Rest Area**
37
Rest Area 34 km NW of Quirindi or 7 km S of Breeza
HEMA 38 J6 31 17 55 S 150 29 43 E
BIG RIG

368 **Gunnedah South Rest Area**
37
Rest Area 11 km N of Curlewis or 7 km S of Gunnedah
HEMA 38 H6 31 1 32 S 150 16 28 E
BIG RIG

369 **Gunnedah North No 2 Rest Area**
37
Rest Area 8 km N of Gunnedah or 31 km S of Boggabri
HEMA 38 H5 30 55 22 S 150 11 15 E
BIG RIG

370 **Boggabri South Rest Area**
37
Rest Area 33 km N of Gunnedah or 6 km S of Boggabri
HEMA 38 H5 30 44 41 S 150 4 35 E
BIG RIG

371 **Gins Leap**
37
Rest Area 6 km N of Boggabri or 51 km SE of Narrabri
HEMA 38 G5 30 39 21 S 150 2 29 E

372 **Pilliga Pub** ☎ (02) 6796 4320
Camp Area at the Pilliga Pub. 55 km SW of Wee Waa or 38 km S of Burren Junction
HEMA 38 F2 30 21 7 S 148 53 4 E
BIG RIG

373 **Pilliga Bore Baths** ☎ (02) 6799 6760
Camp Spot 1.6 km E of Pilliga on the Wee Waa Pilliga Rd at the Hot Mineral Bore
HEMA 38 F2 30 21 19 S 148 54 25 E
BIG RIG

NEW SOUTH WALES

374 Burren Junction Baths Reserve
☎ (02) 6828 1399

Camp Spot 51 km W of Wee Waa or 3 km E of Burren Junction. Self Contained Vehicles only

HEMA 38 F3 30 6 52 S 148 59 44 E

BIG RIG

375 Junction City Hotel
☎ (02) 6796 1440

Camp Area at Burren Junction

HEMA 38 F3 30 6 19 S 148 58 12 E

BIG RIG

376 Alex Trevallion Park

Camp Spot 2 km S of Walgett. E side of Hwy

55

HEMA 38 E1 30 2 4 S 148 6 55 E

BIG RIG 48

377 Gray Park

Rest Area at Walgett

HEMA 38 E1 30 1 25 S 148 7 4 E

BIG RIG

378 Pagan Creek Bridge

Camp Spot 6 km N of Walgett. 1.5 km N of the Castlereagh Hwy & Kamilaroi Hwy jcn

HEMA 38 E1 29 59 15 S 148 9 16 E

379 Cumborah Park Reserve
☎ 0418 317 002

Camp Area at Cumborah. Entry to the park is at the S end of the main road

HEMA 41 C13 29 44 45 S 147 46 17 E

BIG RIG

380 Boorooma Creek

Parking Area 75.5 km E of Brewarrina or 56.5 km W of Walgett. N side of the road, entry W of The Big Warrambool Bridge

HEMA 41 D12 30 4 39 S 147 33 36 E

BIG RIG

381 Culgoa River Campground
☎ (02) 6871 2744

Culgoa National Park

Camp Area 25 km N of Weilmoringle or 60 km W of Goodooga. Turn N 6 km W of Weilmoringle for 17 km, (or turn W 24 km NW of Goodooga for 34 km), then S for 9 km. Rough dirt road

HEMA 41 A12 29 10 11 S 146 59 51 E

382 Four Mile Campground
☎ (02) 6830 5152

Camp Area 6 km E of Brewarrina. Via Coolabah - Brewarrina Rd & Billybingbone Brae for 5 km. Follow blue signs. Cold showers

HEMA 41 C11 29 59 6 S 146 55 2 E

383 Brewarrina Caravan & Camping Park
☎ 0467 064 316

Caravan Park at Brewarrina. Church St

HEMA 41 C11 29 58 0 S 146 51 40 E

BIG RIG

384 Food & Huts by Mt Oxley
☎ 0428 723 275

Rossmore Station

Camp Spot 28 km E of Bourke or 70 km W of Brewarrina. Check in at homestead for directions to camp area. Self Contained Vehicles only. Bush camping

HEMA 41 D10 30 2 51 S 146 12 55 E

BIG RIG

385 May's Bend

Camp Spot 13 km NE of Bourke on Mitchell Hwy. Turn E 10 km from Bourke onto dirt road, take R fork at Y jcn. Check with Bourke Info Centre for road conditions (02 6872 1321)

HEMA 41 D10 30 2 20 S 146 1 23 E

BIG RIG

Bathurst-Mudgee-Gilgandra-Nevertire

386 Capertee

Parking Area at Capertee. Railway St

86

HEMA 32 J1 33 8 48 S 149 59 5 E

BIG RIG

387 Glen Davis Campground
☎ (02) 6353 1859

Camp Area 35 km E of Capertee or 52 km SE of Rylestone. Signposted off Castlereagh Hwy at Capertee, 26 km dirt road. 10 km dirt road from Rylestone

HEMA 32 H3 33 7 31 S 150 16 55 E

388 McDonalds Hole Road Rest Area

Rest Area 15 km S of Ilford or 11 km N of Capertee

86

HEMA 36 E7 33 3 57 S 149 56 8 E

BIG RIG

389 Ilford Rest Area

Rest Area at Ilford. Ilford Hall Rd, 400m E of Hwy beside hall

HEMA 36 E7 32 57 47 S 149 51 41 E

BIG RIG

390 Dunns Swamp - Ganguddy Campground
☎ (02) 6370 9000

Wollemi National Park

Camp Area 27 km E of Rylstone, via Narrango Rd. Beside lake. 8 km dirt road

HEMA 32 F2 32 50 9 S 150 12 26 E

391 Wallaby Rocks Crossing

Camp Spot 4.6 km W of Sofala on Hill End Rd. E side of Turon River Bridge, camp spots along river. Small vehicles only

HEMA 36 E6 33 4 29 S 149 38 59 E

392 **Coles Bridge Camping Area**
Camp Area 13 km W of Sofala on Turondale Rd, via Hill End Rd. Turn R over bridge then 200m rough access track
HEMA 36 E6 33 3 33 S 149 37 15 E

393 **Ration Point**
Camp Spot 3 km E of Sofala, via Upper Turon Rd. Beside river. Small vehicles only
HEMA 36 E6 33 5 30 S 149 42 56 E

394 **Greens Point**
Camp Spot 6 km E of Sofala via Upper Turon Rd. Beside river
HEMA 36 E6 33 5 44 S 149 43 55 E

395 **Wattle Flat Racecourse**
Camp Area 3 km E of Wattle Flat on Limekilns Rd
HEMA 36 F6 33 10 33 S 149 42 35 E

396 **Wattle Flat Heritage Land (North)**
Camp Area 800m W of Wattle Flat. Turn W onto Thompson St. Signposted at entrance. GPS at gate
HEMA 36 F6 33 8 19 S 149 41 8 E

397 **Wattle Flat Heritage Land (South)**
Camp Spot at Wattle Flat. 1 km SW of Wattle Flat on Peel Rd
HEMA 36 F6 33 8 55 S 149 41 23 E

398 **Village Campground** ☎(02) 6337 8206
Hill End Historic Site
Camp Area at Hill End, 38 km W of Sofala, via Clarke St & Warrys Rd. Coin operated hot showers. Camp closes for a period in winter, please phone ahead
HEMA 36 E6 33 2 1 S 149 24 51 E

399 **Glendora Campground** ☎(02) 6337 8206
Hill End Historic Site
Camp Area at Hill End, 38 km W of Sofala. 1 km NE of town, via Beyers Ave & Lees Lane. Coin operated hot showers. Camp closes for a period in winter, please phone ahead
HEMA 36 E6 33 1 39 S 149 24 34 E

400 **Cudgegong Waters Caravan Park** ☎(02) 6358 8462
Caravan Park 22 km N of Ilford or 35 km SE of Mudgee. 1 km E of Hwy beside Lake Windamere
HEMA 36 D7 32 48 44 S 149 49 24 E

401 **Bushlands Tourist Park** ☎(02) 6373 8252
Caravan Park at Windeyer. 1879 Windeyer Rd. Turn W off Hwy 86, 3 km N of Mudgee onto Windeyer Rd. 40 km to Windeyer
HEMA 36 D6 32 47 44 S 149 33 25 E

402 **Cudgegong River Park** ☎(02) 6373 0378
Camp Area 36 K W of Mudgee, off Yarrabin Rd
HEMA 36 D5 32 37 37 S 149 15 28 E

403 **Gulgong Showground** ☎(02) 6374 1255
Camp Area at Gulgong Showgrounds. 1 km S of Gulgong off Mudgee Rd. Entrance on cnr of Grevillia Rd & Guntawang Rd
HEMA 36 C6 32 22 15 S 149 31 41 E

404 **Tallawang Rest Area**
Rest Area 28 km N of Gulgong or 22 km S of Dunedoo
86
HEMA 36 C6 32 8 51 S 149 26 38 E

405 **Goulburn River Reserve The Drip** ☎(02) 6370 9000
Camp Spot 10 km N of Ulan or 14 km S of Turill. Small vehicles only, limited space
HEMA 36 C7 32 12 56 S 149 47 16 E

406 **Spring Gully Camp Ground** ☎(02) 6370 9000
Goulburn River National Park
Camp Area 15 km NE of Wollar, via Mogo Rd. Dry weather only. Not suitable for caravans. Small vehicles only
HEMA 36 C7 32 14 35 S 150 2 43 E

407 **Bylong Public Hall**
Camp Area at Bylong. Bylong Valley Way, opposite shop. Coin operated shower
HEMA 36 C7 32 24 58 S 150 6 52 E

408 **Cassilis Park Rest Area**
Rest Area 9 km NE of Turill or 7 km SW of Cassilis
HEMA 36 B7 32 3 16 S 149 56 0 E

Notes...

409 Cassilis War Memorial Park
☎ (02) 6376 1002

Camp Area at Cassilis. Mudgee Rd, adjacent to Bowling Club. Pay at Bowling Club. Limited power

HEMA 36 B7 32 0 41 S 149 58 46 E

BIG RIG

410 Uarbry Hall

Camp Spot at Village of Uarbry. 39 km E of Dunedoo or 22 km W of Cassilis. Church Rd, next to hall

HEMA 36 B7 32 2 43 S 149 45 53 E

BIG RIG

411 The Barracks Campground
☎ (02) 6370 9000

Coolah Tops National Park

Camp Area 35 km NE of Coolah, via Pinnacle Rd. 15 km dirt road

HEMA 36 A7 31 43 51 S 150 0 54 E

412 The Pines Campground
☎ (02) 6947 7025

Coolah Tops National Park

Camp Area 37 km NE of Coolah, via Hildegarde Rd. Approx 16 km rough unsealed road

HEMA 36 B7 31 44 35 S 150 1 46 E

BIG RIG

413 The Black Stump Rest Area

Rest Area 11 km N of Coolah or 42 km SE of Binnaway

HEMA 36 A7 31 44 44 S 149 42 22 E

BIG RIG

414 Pumphouse Caravan & Camp Area

Camp Area at Binnaway. Cnr Warrumbungle Way & Castlereagh Ave. Fee for showers & power. Limited powered sites

HEMA 36 A6 31 32 48 S 149 22 44 E

BIG RIG 72

415 Dunedoo Rest Area

86

Rest Area at Dunedoo. Opposite PO

HEMA 36 B6 32 0 57 S 149 23 44 E

BIG RIG

416 Dunedoo Caravan Park
☎ (02) 6375 1455

86

Caravan Park at Dunedoo. Bolaro St. 600m W of PO

HEMA 36 B6 32 0 56 S 149 23 22 E

BIG RIG

417 Mendooran Rest Area

86

Rest Area at Mendooran, beside river. Cold showers

HEMA 36 B5 31 49 28 S 149 6 53 E

BIG RIG 48

418 Breelong Rest Area

86

Rest Area at Breelong. 17 km E of Gilgandra or 39 km W of Mendooran

HEMA 36 B4 31 48 40 S 148 47 43 E

BIG RIG 20

419 Marthaguy West Rest Area

34

Rest Area 23 km W of Gilgandra or 14 km E of Collie

HEMA 36 A4 31 39 28 S 148 26 51 E

BIG RIG

420 Warren North Rest Area

34

Rest Area 44 km W of Collie or 6 km NE of Warren

HEMA 36 A2 31 40 2 S 147 51 30 E

421 Macquarie Caravan Park
☎ (02) 6847 4706

Caravan Park at Warren. 2 Hospital Rd

HEMA 36 A2 31 41 43 S 147 50 23 E

BIG RIG

422 Bob Christensen Reserve
☎ (02) 6847 6665

Parking Area at Warren. Via Burton St, Dubbo St onto Industrial Access Rd. Self Contained Vehicles only

HEMA 36 A2 31 41 8 S 147 50 1 E

BIG RIG 96

423 Sandy Creek

34

Rest Area 8 km SW of Warren or 12 km N of Nevertire

HEMA 36 A2 31 44 56 S 147 47 0 E

BIG RIG

Greater Sydney Area

424 Bonnie Vale Campground
☎ (02) 9542 0648

Royal National Park

Camp Area 25 km NE of waterfall. Near Bundeena. Pre-booking essential

HEMA 31 K9 34 4 58 S 151 8 8 E

425 Bents Basin Campground
☎ (02) 4774 6800

Bents Basin State Conservation Area

Camp Area 25 km S of Penrith, via Northern, Greendale Rd & Wolstenholme Rd. Bookings essential

HEMA 34 F7 33 55 58 S 150 38 14 E

426 Cattai Campground
☎ (02) 4572 3100

Cattai National Park

Camp Area at Cattai. 800m N of Cattai on the Wiseman Ferry Rd turn W into road leading to the camping ground. Signposted. No caravans, small vehicles only

HEMA 35 B8 33 33 33 S 150 53 24 E

427 Wanderest Travellers Park
☎ (02) 4578 1144

Camp Area at Richmond. 71 Francis St. Fee for power. Self Contained Vehicles only

HEMA 34 B7 33 35 48 S 150 45 18 E

BIG RIG 72

428 Robert Martin Family Camp
☎ (02) 4777 4494

Camp Area at Londonderry. 66 Kenmare Rd

HEMA 34 C7 33 38 56 S 150 44 15 E

429 NSW Ski Gardens
☎ (02) 4566 4212

Camp Area Sydney Side of Hawkesbury River. 1.2 km from Wisemans Ferry Township

HEMA 33 J9 33 23 45 S 150 58 57 E

BIG RIG

430 Bilpin Reserve

40

Rest Area 30 km NW of Richmond or 35 km E of Bell. Next to recreation area

HEMA 34 B5 33 29 49 S 150 31 1 E

48

431 Old Barra
☎ 02 6373 6555

Camp Area 28 km E of Mudgee on Bara Rd via Lue Rd & Hayes Gap Rd

HEMA 36 D6 32 34 39 S 149 48 22 E

432 Newnes Campground
☎ (02) 4787 8877

Wollemi National Park

Camp Area 35 km NE of Lithgow. Turn NE at Lidsdale, 11 km N of Lithgow, onto Wolgan Rd. 9 km dirt road. Small vehicles only

HEMA 32 J3 33 10 21 S 150 14 19 E

433 Millionth Acre Picnic Area
☎ (02) 6331 2044

Hampton State Forest

Picnic Area 4 km S of Hampton. Intersection of Jenolan Caves Rd & Oberon Rd

HEMA 34 E2 33 40 37 S 150 3 0 E

BIG RIG

434 Boyd River Campground
☎ (02) 4787 8877

Kanangra-Boyd National Park

Camp Area 30 km S of Jenolan Caves, via Kanangra Walls Rd. 27 km dirt road

HEMA 34 H3 33 58 16 S 150 3 21 E

435 Black Springs Campground
☎ (02) 6331 2044

Vulcan State Forest

Camp Spot at Black Springs. 24 km SW of Oberon or 26 NE of Burraga. Opposite General Store

HEMA 36 G6 33 50 51 S 149 44 38 E

BIG RIG

436 Bummaroo Ford
☎ (02) 6336 1972

Abercrombie River National Park

Camp Area 25 km N of Taralga. On Abercrombie Rd at Abercrombie River crossing

HEMA 36 H6 34 11 40 S 149 44 10 E

437 Wombeyan Caves Campground
☎ (02) 4843 5976

Wombeyan Karst Conservation Reserve

Camp Area 33 km NE of Taralga. Near Visitors Centre. 13 km dirt road. Small vehicles only

HEMA 36 J7 34 18 36 S 149 57 58 E

438 Wollondilly River Station
☎ (02) 4888 9207

Camp Area Wollondilly River Station. 50 km W Bowral on Wombeyan Caves Rd. 15 km W of Wombeyan Caves. Dirt road. Small vehicles only

HEMA 36 J7 34 18 28 S 150 4 0 E

439 Taralga Showgrounds

Camp Area at Taralga. Bannaby Rd. Pay at Taralga General Store or Taralga Gifts & Goodies. AH 0425 270 763

HEMA 36 J7 34 24 16 S 149 49 26 E

BIG RIG 24

440 Burraga Dam
☎ (02) 6337 0255

Camp Area 3 km NE of Burraga. Turn N off Arkstone Rd 1.7 km E of Burraga, opposite Jeremy Station. 1.3 km dirt road

HEMA 36 H6 33 56 9 S 149 33 8 E

441 Trunkey Creek Showground
☎ (02) 6368 8604

Camp Spot at Trunkey Creek. Church St. Information at hotel

HEMA 36 G6 33 49 3 S 149 19 23 E

BIG RIG

442 Abercrombie Caves Campground
☎ (02) 6368 8603

Camp Area 14 km S of Trunkey Creek. 2 km narrow, winding road

HEMA 36 H6 33 54 50 S 149 21 30 E

443 Abercrombie River Camp

Camp Spot 19 km S of Trunkey Creek. S of bridge turn W. Some spots next to river

HEMA 36 H6 33 57 23 S 149 19 13 E

444 Tuena Camping & Picnic Ground
☎ (02) 4834 5235

Camp Area at Tuena. Bathurst Rd. Fee for power please pay at the General Store

HEMA 36 H6 34 0 59 S 149 19 40 E

BIG RIG

Notes...

NEW SOUTH WALES

445 Crookwell Caravan Park
☎ 0408 250 652

Caravan Park at Crookwell. Laggan Rd. Register at Visitor Information Centre or Council office

HEMA 36 J6 | 34 27 17 S | 149 28 3 E

446 Pejar Dam Rest Area

Rest Area at Pejar Dam. S of dam wall. 22 km S of Crookwell or 24 km NW of Goulburn

HEMA 36 K6 | 34 35 14 S | 149 34 47 E

Sydney to Echuca

Great Western, Mid Western, Sturt Highways

447 Bulls Camp Reserve

Rest Area 17 km W of Blaxland or 2 km E of Woodford

HEMA 34 D5 | 33 43 32 S | 150 29 26 E

32

BIG RIG

448 Sutton Park Rest Area

Rest Area at Blackheath. 1.5 km S of PO or 10 km N of Katoomba. Alternative for pets at Whitley Park, 500m towards town

HEMA 34 D4 | 33 38 48 S | 150 17 3 E

32

BIG RIG

449 Blackheath Glen Reserve

Camp Spot 6.5 km S of Blackheath via Megalong Valley Rd

HEMA 34 D4 | 33 40 30 S | 150 16 8 E

450 Old Ford Reserve

Camp Area 15.3 km S of Blackheath. Via Shipley Rd & Megalong Valley Rd

HEMA 34 E3 | 33 43 54 S | 150 14 6 E

48

451 Lake Lyell Campground
☎ (02) 6355 6347

Camp Area 13 km SW of Lithgow. Magpie Hollow Rd. Fee for showers

HEMA 34 C2 | 33 31 30 S | 150 4 38 E

452 Flat Rock

Camp Spot 13 km W of Tarana or 7 km E of O'Connell. At Rainville Creek, Mutton Falls Rd, beside Fish River

HEMA 36 G7 | 33 32 54 S | 149 47 31 E

BIG RIG

453 Chifley Dam Primitive Camping Area
☎ (02) 6632 1444

Camp Area at Chifley Dam. 20 km S of Bathurst, travel 6 km S of Bathurst along Vale Rd, turn E into Lagoon Rd then Chifley Dam Rd 14 km. Only 4 sites, no pre-booking. Access gates locked after dark

HEMA 36 G6 | 33 33 43 S | 149 38 0 E

BIG RIG 72

454 Lake Wallace

Camp Spot at Wallerawang. Barton Ave, beside lake. Turn N off Great Western Hwy 8 km W of Lithgow or 57 km E of Bathurst

HEMA 34 B1 | 33 24 56 S | 150 4 24 E

BIG RIG 72

455 Kremer Park

Camp Spot at Portland. Kiln St

HEMA 36 F7 | 33 21 11 S | 149 58 28 E

BIG RIG 72

456 Sunny Corner Recreation Reserve

Camp Spot 7 km N of Meadow Flat. Turn N off Great Western Hwy 26 km W of Lithgow or 33 km E of Bathurst. S end of village, E side of road

HEMA 36 F7 | 33 23 16 S | 149 53 34 E

BIG RIG

457 Bathurst Showground
☎ (02) 6331 1349

Camp Area at Bathurst, Kendell Ave. Mobile 0418 637 682

HEMA 36 F6 | 33 25 5 S | 149 35 22 E

BIG RIG

458 Lions Club Berry Park

Parking Area at Bathurst, Lions Club Dr, E side of city. Self Contained Vehicles only

HEMA 36 F6 | 33 25 1 S | 149 35 38 E

72

459 McPhillamy Park

Rest Area 5 km SW of Bathurst. On top of Mt Panorama

HEMA 36 F6 | 33 27 23 S | 149 32 55 E

BIG RIG

460 Blayney Tourist Park
☎ (02) 6368 4455

Caravan Park at Blayney. 18 Quamby Place

HEMA 36 G5 | 33 32 15 S | 149 14 36 E

BIG RIG

461 Carcoar Dam
☎ (02) 6367 3103

Camp Spot 12 km SW of Blayney or 16 km NE of Mandurama. Turn S 9 km SW of Blayney or 13 km NE of Mandurama

HEMA 36 G5 | 33 36 39 S | 149 10 47 E

BIG RIG

462 Carcoar Rest Area

Rest Area 11 km SW of Blayney or 11 km NE of Mandurama

HEMA 36 G5 | 33 35 54 S | 149 9 53 E

24

BIG RIG

463 Mandurama East Rest Area

Rest Area 3 km E of Mandurama or 19 km SW of Blayney

HEMA 36 G5 | 33 38 24 S | 149 6 6 E

24

464 Bakers Shaft Reserve
Camp Area 15 km N of Mandurama. Turn W off Mandurama - Burnt Yards Rd after 10 km onto Bakers Rd, then onto Junction Park Rd. 5 km dirt road. Beside Belubula River
HEMA 36 G5 | 33 36 34 S | 149 0 43 E

465 Wyangala Waters Holiday Parks ☎ (02) 6345 0877
Camp Area 37 km SE of Cowra, via Darbys Falls. Bookings required for powered sites
HEMA 36 H5 | 33 57 46 S | 148 57 17 E
BIG RIG

466 Bigga Recreation Centre
Camp Area at Bigga 81 km SE of Cowra or 56 km NW of Crookwell. Bistro at golf club Friday night, General Store & pub in town centre
HEMA 36 H5 | 34 4 59 S | 149 9 6 E
72

467 Grabine Lakeside Park ☎ (02) 4835 2345
Camp Area 97 km SE of Cowra or 71 km NW of Crookwell, via Bigga Rd & Grabine Rd. NE side of Lake Wyangala. Some dirt road
HEMA 36 H5 | 33 57 3 S | 149 1 44 E

468 Darbys Falls River Reserve
Rest Area 26 km SE of Cowra or 17 km NW of Wyangala. Beside Lachlan River. 2 km S of township
HEMA 36 H5 | 33 56 53 S | 148 51 45 E
24

469 Cowra Overnight Rest Area
81
Rest Area at Cowra, Lachlan Valley Way, 100m S Mid Western Hwy intersection. Self Contained Vehicles only. Dump Point 100m S
HEMA 36 G4 | 33 50 8 S | 148 40 55 E
24

470 Cowra Showground ☎ 0428 405 245
Camp Area at Cowra Showground. Entrance off Grenfell Rd. Must register with caretaker
HEMA 36 G4 | 33 50 4 S | 148 40 29 E
BIG RIG

471 Canowindra Caravan Park ☎ 0428 233 769
Caravan Park at Canowindra. Tilga St. Next to swimming pool. 300m S of PO
HEMA 36 G4 | 33 34 8 S | 148 39 50 E

472 Canowindra Rest Area
Rest Area 2 km W of Canowindra, beside river
HEMA 36 G4 | 33 33 35 S | 148 39 5 E

473 Terarra Creek Camping & Picnic Area ☎ (02) 6851 4429
Nangar National Park
Camp Area 18 km E of Eugowra or 76 km W of Orange on Escort Way. Turn S 11 km E of Eugowra onto Dripping Rock Rd. Camp sites are 7 km from this point
HEMA 36 F4 | 33 25 8 S | 148 29 54 E

474 Escort Rock Rest Area
Rest Area 5 km NE of Eugowra or 36 km SW of Cudal
HEMA 36 F4 | 33 24 4 S | 148 24 35 E

475 Eugowra Showground ☎ 0427 639 701
Camp Spot at Eugowra. 1 km E of PO. Noble St
HEMA 36 F3 | 33 26 1 S | 148 23 0 E
BIG RIG 72

476 Byrne's Park
Parking Area at Eugowra. Myall St, adjacent to bridge
HEMA 36 F3 | 33 25 40 S | 148 22 11 E
BIG RIG 48

477 Gooloogong Camping Ground
Camping Ground at Gooloogong. Power available. Gold coin donation
HEMA 36 G4 | 33 36 49 S | 148 26 3 E
BIG RIG 72

478 Gooloogong West Campspot
Camp Spot 2 km NW of Gooloogong or 49 km SE of Forbes. Turn N into Grey St 1 km W of Gooloogong. Near old Anglican church site. Beside river
HEMA 36 G4 | 33 36 31 S | 148 25 12 E
72

479 John Channon Park
24
Rest Area 1 km W of Grenfell
HEMA 36 H3 | 33 53 25 S | 148 8 43 E

480 Grenfell Caravan Park ☎ (02) 6343 1194
24
Caravan Park at Grenfell. Mid Western Hwy. 2 km W of PO
HEMA 36 H3 | 33 53 30 S | 148 9 6 E
BIG RIG

481 Companys Dam
Picnic Area 2 km W of Grenfell, via Bradley St. 700m dirt road
HEMA 36 G3 | 33 53 1 S | 148 9 10 E

Notes...

482 Ben Halls Campground
(02) 6851 4429

Weddin Mountains National Park

Camp Area 20 km W of Grenfell. Turn W off Mid Western Hwy 5.5 km NW Grenfell onto Back Piney Range Rd, then Weddin View Rd, Nowlans Rd. Turn E onto signposted track to campground. Dirt road

HEMA 36 H3 | 33 54 23 S | 147 55 11 E

483 Quandialla Showgrounds
(02) 6347 1221

Camp Area at Quandialla, bookings essential

HEMA 36 H2 | 34 0 28 S | 147 47 24 E

BIG RIG

484 Bribbaree Showgrounds
(02) 6347 1221

Camp Area at Bribbaree, Bookings essential

HEMA 36 H2 | 34 7 16 S | 147 51 44 E

BIG RIG

485 Bogolong Creek Rest Area

24

Rest Area 9 km NW of Grenfell or 35 km E of Caragabal

HEMA 36 G3 | 33 50 58 S | 148 5 27 E

BIG RIG

486 Ooma Creek Rest Area

Rest Area 14 km N of Grenfell or 50 km S of Forbes. Henry Lawson Way

HEMA 36 G3 | 33 48 33 S | 148 4 34 E

BIG RIG

487 Caragabal Rest Area

24

Rest Area at Caragabal

HEMA 36 G2 | 33 50 38 S | 147 44 23 E

BIG RIG

488 Yalgogrin Rest Area

24

Rest Area 36 km W of West Wyalong or 57 km E of Rankins Springs

HEMA 43 E11 | 33 50 41 S | 146 49 44 E

489 Rankins Springs Caravan Park
(02) 6966 1346

Caravan Park at Rankins Springs. Mid Western Hwy

HEMA 43 E10 | 33 50 29 S | 146 15 44 E

BIG RIG

490 John Oxley Rest Area

24

Rest Area 12 km W of Rankins Springs or 44 km E of Goolgowi

HEMA 43 E10 | 33 52 22 S | 146 11 3 E

BIG RIG

491 Goolgowi Caravan Park
(02) 6965 1900

Caravan Park at Goolgowi. Combo St. 1 km NE of PO. Pay fees & key collection at Council office. After hours at Royal Mail Hotel

HEMA 43 E9 | 33 58 47 S | 145 42 22 E

BIG RIG

492 Goolgowi Rest Area

24

Rest Area 1 km W of Goolgowi

HEMA 43 E9 | 33 59 22 S | 145 41 42 E

BIG RIG

493 Meriola Reserve

Camp Spot 19 km E of Hay. Turn S off Mid Western Hwy onto Murrumbidgee River Rd 16 km E of Hay or 241 km W of West Wyalong for 3.1 km. Turn S at River sign, through gate, veer L follow track for 1 km to river. Various sites. GPS at gate

HEMA 43 F8 | 34 28 1 S | 145 0 56 E

BIG RIG

494 Hay Showground
(02) 6993 1087

Camp Spot at Hay. Showground Rd. 1.5 km N of PO. Dump point 200m W

HEMA 43 F8 | 34 29 51 S | 144 50 17 E

BIG RIG

495 Sandy Point Reserve

Parking Area at Hay. Turn W off Cobb Hwy just N of bridge onto Brunker St, then S for 1 km to N bank of Murrumbidgee River. Use entry from Water St, near Hatty St for large vehicles

HEMA 43 F8 | 34 30 55 S | 144 50 8 E

496 Royal Mail Hotel
(02) 6993 0694

75

Camp Area at Booroorban. 6 acres of camping grounds. Limited power available

HEMA 43 G8 | 34 55 54 S | 144 45 44 E

BIG RIG

497 Wanganella Weir

Camp Spot at Wanganella. Turn SW on N side of bridge (opposite store) follow track for 1 km. Camp spots along river

HEMA 43 H8 | 35 13 3 S | 144 48 26 E

498 Wanganella Creek Camp Park
(03) 5882 3509

Camp Area at Wanganella. Murray St, behind Pepin Ram Memorial. Call ahead to arrange key from store

HEMA 43 H8 | 35 12 57 S | 144 48 59 E

BIG RIG

499 Deni Car O Tel & Caravan Park
(03) 5881 1732

Caravan Park at Deniliquin. 700m E of PO opposite RSL Club

HEMA 43 H8 | 35 32 8 S | 144 58 7 E

500 Deniliquin Rest Area

75

Rest Area at Deniliquin. Davidson St. Recreation reserve N side of town

HEMA 43 H8 | 35 31 31 S | 144 58 41 E

501 **Willoughby's Beach Campground** ☎(03) 5483 9100
Murray Valley National Park
Camp Area at Deniliquin. Take Memorial Dr past showgrounds to Regional Park entrance. Campground 200m inside gate, various sites
HEMA 43 H8 | 35 31 53 S | 144 58 36 E

502 **Gulpa Island State Forest** ☎(03) 5483 9100
Camp Spot 3 km E of Mathoura, via Picnic Point Rd & Gulpa Creek Rd. Signposted Gulpa Island Forest Dr, veer R at fork. 1.1 km track to bush camping beside creek
HEMA 43 J8 | 35 48 41 S | 144 54 36 E

503 **Porters Creek Camp Ground** ☎(03) 5483 9100
Murray Valley National Parks
Camp Area 13 km SE of Mathoura. Turn E 5 km S of Mathoura or 35 km N of Moama. Access via Coolamon Rd, Poverty Creek Rd & Porters Creek Rd. 8 km of dirt road. Bush camping beside creek
HEMA 43 J8 | 35 53 45 S | 144 57 51 E

504 **Mathoura Bowling Club** ☎(03) 5880 3200
Camp Spot at Mathoura. Cobb Hwy. Behind Bowling Club, entry from Steven St. Contact manager on arrival
HEMA 43 J8 | 35 48 34 S | 144 53 59 E
48

505 **Edward River Bridge Campground** ☎(03) 5483 9100
Murray Valley Regional Park
Camp Area 8.5 km E of Mathoura. Off Mathoura-Tocumwal Rd. Bush camping beside Edward River
HEMA 43 J8 | 35 48 38 S | 144 57 45 E

506 **Moama North Rest Area**
Rest Area 30 km S of Mathoura or 10 km N of Moama
HEMA 43 J8 | 36 2 8 S | 144 46 42 E

507 **Rich River Golf Club Resort** ☎(03) 5481 333
Parking Area at Moama. Twenty Four Lane, via Perricoota Rd. Self Contained Vehicles only. Register at reception, must join as a social member to stay
HEMA 43 K8 | 36 4 35 S | 144 43 35 E
BIG RIG 48

508 **Moama (5 Mile) Campground** ☎(03) 5483 9100
Murray Valley National Park
Camp Area 8 km W of Moama, via Perricoota Rd
HEMA 43 J8 | 36 4 3 S | 144 41 30 E

Notes...

509 **Benarca Campground** ☎(03) 5483 9100
Murray Valley National Park
Camp Area 18 km NW of Moama. Take Perricoota Rd (Moama - Barnham Rd) for 15 km, turn S onto Benarca Forest Rd, follow signs to campground
HEMA 42 J7 | 36 3 15 S | 144 37 25 E

510 **Perricoota State Forest** ☎(02) 6841 4288
Camp Spot 33 km NW of Moama, via Perricoota Rd, Nineteen Mile Rd, then signposted Perricoota Forest Rd & River Rd. Various tracks to campspots. GPS at gate
HEMA 42 J7 | 35 56 14 S | 144 29 32 E
BIG RIG

511 **Koondrook State Forest** ☎1300 655 687
Murray River Reserve
Camp Area 12 km SE of Barham, via East Barham Rd, River Rd. Bush camping sites beside river
HEMA 42 J7 | 35 41 30 S | 144 12 58 E

512 **Barham Lakes Caravan Park** ☎(03) 5453 2009
Caravan Park at Barham. East Barham Rd. 1 km E of PO
HEMA 42 J7 | 35 38 23 S | 144 8 19 E
BIG RIG

513 **Campbells Island State Forest** ☎1300 655 687
Camp Area 5 km NW of Barham, via Cobwell St & North Barham Rd, Little Murray Rd. Signposted Campbells Island. Bush camping sites along river
HEMA 42 H7 | 35 35 25 S | 144 6 22 E

514 **Wakool River**
Camp Spot 11 km E of Wakool or 53 km W of Deniliquin. Turn E just S of Wakool River bridge, follow tracks to camp spots on river
HEMA 42 H7 | 35 29 58 S | 144 27 30 E
BIG RIG

Sydney-Albury-Tocumwal
Hume and Riverina Highways

515 **Partridge VC Rest Area**
31
Rest Area 42 km S of Campbelltown or 10 km N of Picton Rd. Southbound only
HEMA 35 H8 | 34 9 22 S | 150 44 18 E
BIG RIG

516 **Coledale Camping Reserve** ☎(02) 4267 4302
Camp Area at Coledale. Lawrence Hargrave Dr. Advance bookings are essential. Minimum stay applies on a seasonal basis, please confirm with the booking office
HEMA 35 J10 | 34 17 13 S | 150 56 54 E

517 Pheasants Nest Service Centre
Rest Area 6 km S of Picton Rd or 8 km N of Yanderra on South Western Fwy
31
HEMA 35 J8 34 17 0 S 150 38 11 E
BIG RIG

518 Berrima Reserve
☎ 1300 125 944
Camp Area at Berrima. Just NW of town, past White Horse Inn. W onto Oxley St, L at fork. No discharge of grey water permitted, no generators & only 4 sites. Permit required
1
HEMA 44 B6 34 29 9 S 150 19 57 E
48

519 Gordon VC Rest Area
Rest Area 17 km SW of Mittagong or 33 km NE of Marulan. 7 km N of Illawarra Hwy jcn near Belanglo State Forest turnoff. Northbound only
31
HEMA 44 B6 34 32 11 S 150 16 49 E

520 Dalys Clearing Campground
☎ 1300 655 687
Belanglo State Forest
Camp Area 10 km W of Moss Vale. Turn W off Hume Hwy 6 km N of Illawarra Hwy jcn onto Bunnigalore Rd & Dalys Rd at Gordon VC Rest Area. Follow Belanglo Rd for 4 km R onto Dalys Rd for 0.9 km
HEMA 44 B6 34 31 38 S 150 14 30 E

521 MacKay VC Rest Area
Rest Area 26 km SW of Mittagong or 27 km NE of Marulan. 2 km N of Illawarra Hwy jcn. 100m off Hwy. Southbound only
31
HEMA 44 B6 34 34 45 S 150 15 10 E
BIG RIG

522 Kingsbury VC Rest Area
Rest Area 28 km SW of Mittagong or 25 NE of Marulan. 6 km S of Illawarra Hwy jcn. Southbound only. 100m off Hwy
31
HEMA 44 B5 34 37 8 S 150 12 46 E
BIG RIG

523 Moss Vale Showgrounds
☎ 0427 737 495
Camp Area at Moss Vale. Entry via Robertson Rd, call to gain entry into grounds. Closed during show week
HEMA 44 B6 34 32 52 S 150 22 53 E
BIG RIG 72

524 Gambells Rest Campground
☎ (02) 4887 7270
Morton National Park
Camp Area 2 km S of Bundanoon, via Church St & Gullies Rd. Dirt road. Bookings essential
HEMA 44 B6 34 40 7 S 150 17 48 E

525 HQ Camp
☎ 1300 655 687
Wingello State Forest
Camp Area 4 km SE of Wingello, via Forest Rd. Dirt road
HEMA 44 B5 34 42 57 S 150 11 20 E
BIG RIG

526 Marulan Service Centre
Rest Area 29 km SW of Illawarra Hwy jcn or 42 km NE of Federal Hwy jcn
31
HEMA 44 B5 34 43 13 S 149 59 42 E
BIG RIG

527 Bungonia Campground
☎ (02) 4844 4277
Bungonia National Park
Camp Area 15 km NE of Bungonia, via Lookdown Rd
HEMA 44 C5 34 48 26 S 150 0 11 E

528 Chowne VC Rest Area
Rest Area 39 km E of Federal Hwy jcn. Eastbound only
31
HEMA 44 C5 34 44 37 S 149 53 14 E
BIG RIG

529 Derrick VC Rest Area
Rest Area 21 km W of Marulan. 100m off Hwy. Westbound only
31
HEMA 44 C5 34 44 11 S 149 49 48 E
BIG RIG

530 French VC Rest Area
Rest Area 4 km E of Federal Hwy jcn. Eastbound only. 100m off Hwy
31
HEMA 44 C4 34 47 13 S 149 38 24 E
BIG RIG

531 Breadalbane Rest Area
Rest Area 10 km W of Federal Hwy jcn or 1 km E of Breadalbane
HEMA 44 C4 34 48 12 S 149 29 40 E

532 Barbour Park Gunning
Parking Area at Gunning. N end of public pool car park. Limited sites
HEMA 44 C3 34 46 48 S 149 16 5 E
BIG RIG 48

533 Mundoonen Rest Area Westbound
Rest Area 14 km E of Barton or 16 km W of Gunning. Westbound only
31
HEMA 44 C3 34 48 56 S 149 6 34 E
BIG RIG

534 Mundoonen Rest Area Eastbound
Rest Area 17 km W of Gunning or 13 km E of Barton Hwy jcn
31
HEMA 44 C3 34 49 33 S 149 4 37 E
BIG RIG

535 Yass Valley Way Rest Area
Rest Area at jcn of Yass Valley Way & Hume Hwy
31
HEMA 44 C3 34 50 16 S 149 0 50 E
BIG RIG

536 Derringullen Creek Service Centre
Rest Area 9 km W of Barton Hwy jcn or 24 km E of Bookham
31
HEMA 44 C2 34 47 40 S 148 52 6 E
BIG RIG

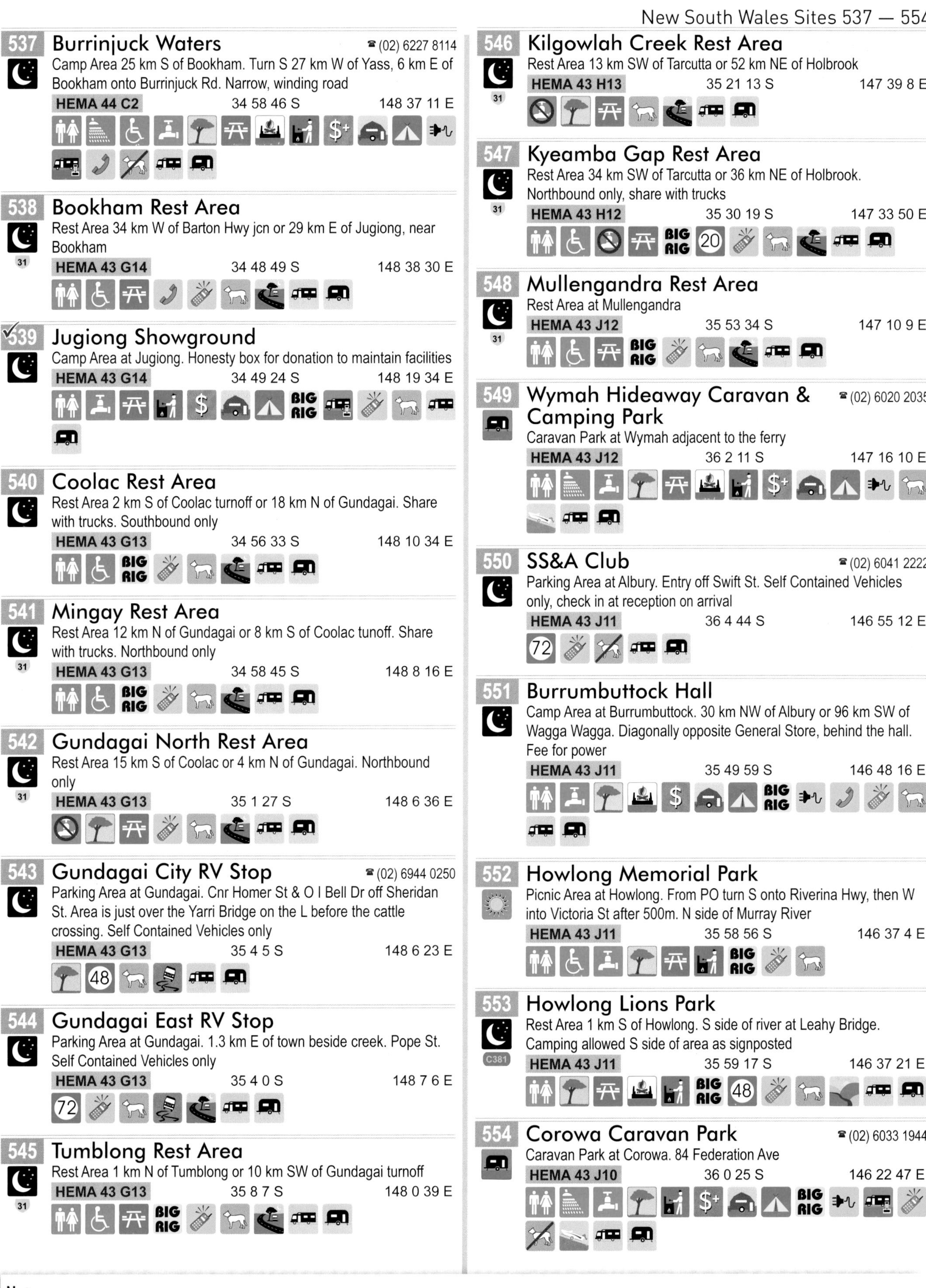

537 Burrinjuck Waters
☎ (02) 6227 8114

Camp Area 25 km S of Bookham. Turn S 27 km W of Yass, 6 km E of Bookham onto Burrinjuck Rd. Narrow, winding road

HEMA 44 C2 | 34 58 46 S | 148 37 11 E

538 Bookham Rest Area
31

Rest Area 34 km W of Barton Hwy jcn or 29 km E of Jugiong, near Bookham

HEMA 43 G14 | 34 48 49 S | 148 38 30 E

BIG RIG

539 Jugiong Showground

Camp Area at Jugiong. Honesty box for donation to maintain facilities

HEMA 43 G14 | 34 49 24 S | 148 19 34 E

BIG RIG

540 Coolac Rest Area

Rest Area 2 km S of Coolac turnoff or 18 km N of Gundagai. Share with trucks. Southbound only

HEMA 43 G13 | 34 56 33 S | 148 10 34 E

BIG RIG

541 Mingay Rest Area
31

Rest Area 12 km N of Gundagai or 8 km S of Coolac tunoff. Share with trucks. Northbound only

HEMA 43 G13 | 34 58 45 S | 148 8 16 E

BIG RIG

542 Gundagai North Rest Area
31

Rest Area 15 km S of Coolac or 4 km N of Gundagai. Northbound only

HEMA 43 G13 | 35 1 27 S | 148 6 36 E

543 Gundagai City RV Stop
☎ (02) 6944 0250

Parking Area at Gundagai. Cnr Homer St & O I Bell Dr off Sheridan St. Area is just over the Yarri Bridge on the L before the cattle crossing. Self Contained Vehicles only

HEMA 43 G13 | 35 4 5 S | 148 6 23 E

48

544 Gundagai East RV Stop

Parking Area at Gundagai. 1.3 km E of town beside creek. Pope St. Self Contained Vehicles only

HEMA 43 G13 | 35 4 0 S | 148 7 6 E

72

545 Tumblong Rest Area
31

Rest Area 1 km N of Tumblong or 10 km SW of Gundagai turnoff

HEMA 43 G13 | 35 8 7 S | 148 0 39 E

BIG RIG

546 Kilgowlah Creek Rest Area
31

Rest Area 13 km SW of Tarcutta or 52 km NE of Holbrook

HEMA 43 H13 | 35 21 13 S | 147 39 8 E

547 Kyeamba Gap Rest Area
31

Rest Area 34 km SW of Tarcutta or 36 km NE of Holbrook. Northbound only, share with trucks

HEMA 43 H12 | 35 30 19 S | 147 33 50 E

BIG RIG 20

548 Mullengandra Rest Area
31

Rest Area at Mullengandra

HEMA 43 J12 | 35 53 34 S | 147 10 9 E

BIG RIG

549 Wymah Hideaway Caravan & Camping Park
☎ (02) 6020 2035

Caravan Park at Wymah adjacent to the ferry

HEMA 43 J12 | 36 2 11 S | 147 16 10 E

550 SS&A Club
☎ (02) 6041 2222

Parking Area at Albury. Entry off Swift St. Self Contained Vehicles only, check in at reception on arrival

HEMA 43 J11 | 36 4 44 S | 146 55 12 E

72

551 Burrumbuttock Hall

Camp Area at Burrumbuttock. 30 km NW of Albury or 96 km SW of Wagga Wagga. Diagonally opposite General Store, behind the hall. Fee for power

HEMA 43 J11 | 35 49 59 S | 146 48 16 E

BIG RIG

552 Howlong Memorial Park

Picnic Area at Howlong. From PO turn S onto Riverina Hwy, then W into Victoria St after 500m. N side of Murray River

HEMA 43 J11 | 35 58 56 S | 146 37 4 E

BIG RIG

553 Howlong Lions Park
C381

Rest Area 1 km S of Howlong. S side of river at Leahy Bridge. Camping allowed S side of area as signposted

HEMA 43 J11 | 35 59 17 S | 146 37 21 E

BIG RIG 48

554 Corowa Caravan Park
☎ (02) 6033 1944

Caravan Park at Corowa. 84 Federation Ave

HEMA 43 J10 | 36 0 25 S | 146 22 47 E

BIG RIG

Notes...

NEW SOUTH WALES

555 Collendina State Forest
☎ (03) 5483 9100

Murray Valley Regional Park

Camp Spots 8.5 km W of Corowa or 31 km E of Mulwala. Turn S off Mulwala Corowa Rd onto signposted access track. Bush camping at river. GPS at gate

HEMA 43 J10 36 1 2 S 146 17 57 E

BIG RIG

556 Kyffins Reserve

Camp Spot 32 km W of Corowa or 7 km E of Mulwala. Spring Rd. Visitors are required to use portable toilets & dispose in the appropriate manner offsite. Camping in marked areas only

HEMA 43 J10 35 58 34 S 146 3 50 E

BIG RIG

557 Mulwala Regional Park
☎ (02) 6841 4288

Camp Spots 8 km W of Mulwala. Bush camping via Mulwala - Barooga Rd. Signposted. Hinches Beach 4 km from entrance. GPS at gate

HEMA 43 J10 35 57 12 S 145 57 40 E

558 Boomanoomana State Forest
☎ (02) 6841 4288

Camp Spot 15 km W of Mulwala or 21 km E of Barooga. Bush camping via Mulwala - Barooga Rd. Signposted. Sandy Beach 4.5 km, Little Pebble Beach 4 km from entrance. GPS at gate

HEMA 43 J10 35 55 55 S 145 53 26 E

559 Quicks Beach
☎ (03) 5483 9100

Murray Valley National Park

Camp Area 4 km SE of Barooga. Turn S off Mulwala - Barooga Rd 34 km W of Mulwala or 2 km E of Barooga onto Quicks Rd

HEMA 43 J9 35 55 37 S 145 42 1 E

BIG RIG

560 Paradise Beach
☎ (03) 5483 9100

Murray Valley Regional Park

Camp Area 2.5 km W of Barooga. Turn S off Cobram - Barooga Rd for 1.8 km. Signposted. Dirt road

HEMA 43 J9 35 55 46 S 145 41 7 E

561 Wattle Tree Beach
☎ (03) 5483 9100

Murray Valley Regional Park

Camp Area 2 km W of Barooga. Turn S off Cobram - Barooga Rd for 1.1 km then turn R for 0.5 km. Signposted. Dirt road

HEMA 43 J9 35 55 27 S 145 40 27 E

BIG RIG

562 Ski Beach
☎ (03) 5483 9100

Murray Valley National Park

Camp Area 2 km S of Barooga. Turn E off Cobram - Barooga Rd just N of bridge. Self Contained Vehicles only

HEMA 43 J9 35 55 4 S 145 40 17 E

BIG RIG 48

Sydney to Victorian Border via Eden

Princes Highway

563 Killalea Campground
☎ (02) 4237 8589

Killalea State Park

Camp Area 6 km S of Shellharbour or 9 km N of Kiama, off Shellharbour Rd. Gates closed between 1930 - 0430 hrs

HEMA 44 B7 34 36 41 S 150 51 12 E

$+

564 Kiama North Rest Area

1

Rest Area 5 km N of Kiama. Northbound traffic only

HEMA 44 B7 34 38 5 S 150 49 56 E

BIG RIG

565 Kiama South Rest Area

1

Rest Area 5 km N of Kiama. Southbound traffic only

HEMA 44 B7 34 37 50 S 150 50 7 E

BIG RIG

566 Jamberoo Valley Motorhome Grounds
☎ 0431 759 015

Camp Area at Jamberoo. Kevin Walsh Oval, Churchill St

HEMA 44 B7 34 38 50 S 150 46 28 E

BIG RIG 72

567 Berry Showground
☎ 0427 605 200

Camp Area at Berry. 500m S of PO. Alexandra St

HEMA 44 C7 34 46 46 S 150 41 46 E

$ BIG RIG

568 Bendeela Reserve

Camp Area 7 km W of Kangaroo Valley. Turn W N of Hampden Bridge onto Bendeela Rd. Short steep access into camp area

HEMA 44 C6 34 44 21 S 150 28 15 E

569 Shoalhaven Zoo
☎ (02) 4421 3949

Camp Area at Nowra. Turn W just N of Nowra Bridge onto Illaroo Rd, McMahons Rd & Rockhill Rd. Riverfront

HEMA 44 C6 34 52 17 S 150 33 59 E

$ BIG RIG

570 Shoalhaven Ski Park
☎ (02) 4423 2488

Caravan Park, 70 Rockhill Rd. 4 km W of Nowra on river. Pets welcome on weekdays

HEMA 44 C6 34 52 18 S 150 34 12 E

$+ BIG RIG

571 Coolendel Bush Camp
☎ (02) 4421 4586

Camp Area 30 km W of Nowra, via Yalwal Rd & Grassy Gully Rd (Burrier Rd). 10 km dirt road. Beside Shoalhaven River

HEMA 44 C6 34 50 38 S 150 25 18 E

$

572 Nowra Showground
☎ 1300 662 808

Camp Area at Nowra. West St. Bookings required

HEMA 44 C6 34 52 30 S 150 35 31 E

BIG RIG

573 Yalwal Campground
☎ 1300 662 808

Camp Area at Yalwal, 24 km W of Nowra, via Burrier Rd & Yalwal Rd. Overlooking Danjera Dam. 17 km dirt road, not suitable for caravans. Bookings required

HEMA 44 C6 34 55 23 S 150 23 3 E

574 Green Patch Campground
☎ (02) 4443 0977

Booderee National Park

Camp Area 25 km SE of Falls Creek. Access via Iluka Rd off Jervis Bay Rd. Bookings essential

HEMA 44 D7 35 8 17 S 150 43 17 E

575 Bewong Rest Area

Rest Area 27 km S of Nowra or 38 km N of Ulladulla. Share with trucks

HEMA 44 D6 35 5 6 S 150 31 59 E

BIG RIG

576 Alamein Caravan Park
☎ (02) 4441 2031

Caravan Park at Sussex Inlet. Alamein Rd, S side of town. More expensive in school holidays

HEMA 44 D6 35 10 24 S 150 35 21 E

577 Jerrawangala Rest Area

Rest Area 38 km S of Nowra or 23 km N of Ulladulla. Small vehicles only

1

HEMA 44 D6 35 8 43 S 150 27 39 E

578 Milton Showground
☎ 0429 934 067

Camp Area at Milton Showgrounds. Croobyar Rd. Please camp in signposted designated camping areas only

1

HEMA 44 D6 35 19 9 S 150 25 48 E

BIG RIG

579 Pretty Beach
☎ 1300 072 757

Murramarang National Park

Camp Area 2 km S of Kioloa. Turn E off Hwy at Termeil onto Bawley Point Rd

HEMA 44 E6 35 34 6 S 150 22 1 E

BIG RIG

Notes...

580 Pebbly Beach
☎ (02) 4478 6582

Murramarang National Park

Camp Area 8 km E of East Lynne, via Mount Agony Rd 5 km S of East Lynne. No caravans

HEMA 44 E6 35 36 26 S 150 19 33 E

581 Depot Beach Campground
☎ 1300 072 757

Murramarang National Park

Camp Area 9 km E of East Lynne. Via Mt Agony Rd & North Durras Rd

HEMA 44 E6 35 37 45 S 150 19 20 E

582 Shallow Crossing Camp Ground
☎ (02) 4478 1183

Camp Area 21 km N of Nelligan via The River Rd

HEMA 44 E5 35 31 55 S 150 11 55 E

583 Waldrons Swamp Rest Area

Rest Area 20 km S of Batemans Bay or 7 km N of Moruya. Shared with trucks

1

HEMA 44 F5 35 51 54 S 150 7 9 E

BIG RIG

584 North Head Primitive Campground
☎ 0428 633 447

Camp Area 7 km E of Moruya. From Moruya turn E along North Head Dr just N of bridge, then into Bruce Cameron Dr beside airport. Cold showers. Fees higher in peak season

HEMA 44 F5 35 54 11 S 150 8 55 E

BIG RIG

585 Congo Point Campground
☎ (02) 4476 0800

Eurobodalla National Park

Camp Area at Congo. 10 km SE of Moruya, via South Head Dr & Congo Rd. Beachside. Cold showers

HEMA 44 F5 35 57 17 S 150 9 31 E

BIG RIG

586 Brou Lake Campground
☎ (02) 4476 0800

Eurobodalla National Park

Camp Area 14 km S of Bodalla. Turn E 9 km S of Bodalla onto Brou Lake Rd, veer R at fork. 5 km dirt road to camp area. Bush camping, small vehicles only

HEMA 44 F5 36 8 52 S 150 7 9 E

587 Bodalla Park Forest Rest Area
☎ (02) 4472 6211

Rest Area 9 km S of Bodalla or 9 km N of Narooma

1

HEMA 44 F5 36 9 3 S 150 5 46 E

24

588 Dalmeny Camp Ground
☎ 0428 635 641

Camp Area at Dalmeny. Turn E off Princes Hwy onto Mort Ave 38 km S of Moruya or 5 km N of Narooma

HEMA 44 G5 | 36 9 46 S | 150 7 38 E

BIG RIG

589 Mystery Bay Primitive Campground
☎ 0428 622 357

Camp Area 12 km S of Narooma. Turn SE 10 km S of Narooma or 27 km NE of Cobargo onto Mystery Bay Rd. Big rigs on grass near road. Cold showers. Fees higher in peak season

HEMA 44 G5 | 36 17 54 S | 150 8 0 E

BIG RIG

590 Dry River Rest Area

1

Rest Area 12 km S of Cobargo or 30 km N of Bega

HEMA 44 G5 | 36 28 7 S | 149 51 58 E

591 Gillards Beach
☎ (02) 4476 0800

Mimosa Rocks National Park

Camp Area 13 km N of Tathra, via Tathra - Bermagui Rd & Gillards Rd. 4 km single lane dirt road care needed. Maximum stay 1 month

HEMA 44 H5 | 36 39 35 S | 150 0 5 E

592 Hobart Beach
☎ (02) 6495 5000

Bournda National Park

Camp Area 13 km S of Tathra or 18 km N of Merimbula. Turn E off Sapphire Coast Dr 10 km S of Tathra or 15 km N of Merimbula. 3 km dirt road

HEMA 44 H5 | 36 47 49 S | 149 56 21 E

593 Candelo Rest Area

Rest Area at Candelo. Opposite General Store Williams St

HEMA 44 H4 | 36 46 0 S | 149 41 42 E

594 Merimbula Caravan & Motor Home Park
☎ 0428 260 734

1

Camp Area 6 km W of Merimbula or 4 km N of Pambula Village on Princes Hwy. 2529 Princes Hwy. Self Contained Vehicles only

HEMA 44 J5 | 36 53 14 S | 149 52 13 E

BIG RIG

595 East Ben Boyd Forest Rest Area

1

Rest Area 18 km S of Eden or 41 km N of Genoa. Both sides of the road

HEMA 34 J4 | 37 12 9 S | 149 50 43 E

BIG RIG 12

596 Saltwater Creek
☎ (02) 6495 5000

Ben Boyd National Park

Camp Area 41 km SE of Eden or 29 km NE of Narrabarba. Turn E 19 km S of Eden or 7 km N of Narrabarba, onto Edrom Rd, Greencape Rd, Saltwater Rd. 16 km winding dirt road. Limited space for trailers & caravans, small vehicles only. Bookings required Christmas, Easter

HEMA 44 J5 | 37 10 8 S | 149 59 58 E

597 Bittangabee Bay
☎ (02) 6495 5000

Ben Boyd National Park

Camp Area 43 km SE of Eden. Turn E 19 km S of Eden or 7 km N of Narrabarba, onto Edrom Rd & Green Cape Rd. 18 km winding dirt road. Small vehicles only. Bookings required Christmas, Easter

HEMA 44 K5 | 37 13 4 S | 150 0 58 E

598 Scrubby Creek Forest Picnic Area

1

Picnic Area 20 km S of Eden or 39 km N of Genoa. 700m W of Hwy. GPS at entrance

HEMA 44 K4 | 37 13 39 S | 149 49 51 E

599 Newtons Crossing Picnic Area
☎ (02) 9871 3377

Yambulla State Forest

Camp Area 56 km SW of Eden. Turn W into Imlay Rd 25 km S of Eden or 36 km N of Genoa. Follow for 12 km, turn S into Allan Brook Rd, 6 km dirt road to campsite. Last 100m rough track. Small vehicles only

HEMA 44 K4 | 37 16 3 S | 149 40 30 E

600 Wallagaraugh River Rest Area

1

Rest Area 40 km S of Eden or 19 km N of Genoa. Small vehicles only

HEMA 44 K4 | 37 22 10 S | 149 43 0 E

Cowra to Cann River

Lachlan Valley Way, Barton and Monaro Highways

601 Boorowa Rest Area

81

Rest Area at Boorowa. Pudman St

HEMA 44 B2 | 34 26 13 S | 148 43 11 E

602 Boorowa Caravan Park
☎ (02) 6385 3658

81

Caravan Park at Boorowa. Brial St. 1 km N of PO

HEMA 44 B2 | 34 26 4 S | 148 43 10 E

BIG RIG

603 Binalong Rest Area

94

Rest Area at Binalong

HEMA 44 C2 | 34 40 33 S | 148 38 1 E

24

604 **Yass Caravan Park** ☎ (02) 6226 1173
Caravan Park at Yass. Cnr Old Hume Hwy & Grampian St. 1 km SW of PO
HEMA 44 C2 — 34 50 2 S — 148 54 30 E

605 **Yass Showgrounds** ☎ (02) 6226 1615
Camp Area at Yass. Entry off Grand Junction Rd. Closed during show week mid-March. Honesty box
HEMA 44 C2 — 34 50 27 S — 148 55 18 E

606 **Joe O'Connor Park**
Parking Area at Yass off Laidlaw St, W side of town. Self Contained Vehicles only
HEMA 44 C2 — 34 50 10 S — 148 54 21 E

607 **Jeir Creek**
Rest Area 10 km S of Murrumbateman or 28 km N of Canberra
HEMA 44 C3 — 35 2 27 S — 149 1 23 E

608 **ACT Border Rest Area**
Rest Area 23 km S of Murrumbateman or 15 km N of Canberra
HEMA 48 A4 — 35 9 29 S — 149 3 39 E

609 **Colinton Rest Area**
Rest Area 15 km S of Michelago or 13 km N of Bredbo
HEMA 48 J5 — 35 50 16 S — 149 9 44 E

610 **Numeralla River Rest Area**
Rest Area 14 km S of Bredbo or 20 km N of Cooma. Beside river
HEMA 44 F3 — 36 4 36 S — 149 9 33 E

611 **Nimmitabel Campground** ☎ 0427 406 668
Camp Area at Nimmitabel. N end of town. Call caretaker to use amenties block. Fees collected
HEMA 44 G3 — 36 30 31 S — 149 17 4 E

612 **Lake Williams**
Rest Area at Nimmitabel. S end of town
HEMA 44 H3 — 36 30 53 S — 149 16 56 E

613 **Brown Mountain**
Parking Area 22 km SE of Nimmitabel or 17 km W of Bemboka. Behind truck parking area
HEMA 44 H4 — 36 36 31 S — 149 25 58 E

614 **Bemboka Sports Ground** ☎ 0408 020 636
Camp Spot 1 km E of Bemboka. Turnoff at Colombo Creek Bridge. Fee for power & shower, phone for key & payment
HEMA 44 H4 — 36 38 8 S — 149 34 41 E

615 **Bombala Caravan Park** ☎ (02) 6458 3817
Caravan Park at Bombala. Monaro Hwy
HEMA 44 J3 — 36 54 30 S — 149 14 20 E

616 **Delegate Caravan Park** ☎ (02) 6458 8167
Caravan Park at Delegate. Bill Jeffery's Park, Topping St
HEMA 44 J3 — 37 2 24 S — 148 56 48 E

617 **Six Mile Creek** ☎ (02) 6458 4080
South East Forest National Park
Camp Area 20 km NE of Cathcart or 12 km W of Candelo on the Tantawangalo Mountain Rd. Dirt road. Small vehicles only
HEMA 44 H4 — 36 47 11 S — 149 32 18 E

618 **Nunnock Campground** ☎ (02) 6458 4080
South East Forests National Park
Camp Area in SE Forests National Park. Turn N off Mount Darragh Rd onto Tantawangalo Mountain Rd. N onto New Line Rd, then E into Packers Swamp Rd, then onto Cattlemans Link Trail, follow to campsite. Small vehicles only. 15 km dirt road
HEMA 44 H4 — 36 42 12 S — 149 26 49 E

Tomerong to Braidwood

Trunk Road 92

619 **Endrick River Crossing**
Camp Spot 55 km W of Tomerong or 5 km NE of Nerriga on Turpentine Rd. 100m N of bridge on N side of the road. Dirt road
HEMA 44 D5 — 35 5 22 S — 150 7 15 E

620 **Corang River**
Camp Spot 12 km S of Nerriga or 41 km NE of Braidwood. On the Braidwood - Nerriga Rd. Dirt road. N side of bridge beside river
HEMA 44 D5 — 35 12 21 S — 150 3 6 E

621 **Oallen Ford**
Camp Spot 18 km W of Nerriga or 37 E of Tarago, via Oallen Rd (dirt road). Access 200m E of bridge. Overlooking river. 5 tonne load limit if entering from Tarago
HEMA 44 D5 — 35 9 6 S — 149 57 19 E

Notes...

NEW SOUTH WALES

622 Wog Wog Campground
(02) 4423 2170

Morton National Park

Camp Area 22 km S of Nerriga or 41 km NE of Braidwood. Turn S off Braidwood - Nerriga Rd 17 km S of Nerriga or 36 km NE of Braidwood onto Mongarlowe Rd. Dirt road

HEMA 44 D5 35 16 6 S 150 2 8 E

623 Charleyong Crossing

Camp Spot 31 km SW of Nerriga or 26 km NE of Braidwood. Turn W off Braidwood - Nerriga Rd 29 km SW of Nerriga or 24 km NE of Braidwood onto Mayfield - Tarago Rd for 2.5 km. Dirt road

HEMA 44 D5 35 14 43 S 149 53 29 E

Batemans Bay to Canberra

Kings Highway

624 Araluen Creek

Deua National Park

Camp Area 24 km S of Braidwood or 3 km N of Araluen Hotel. 200m along Majors Creek Mountain Rd

HEMA 44 E4 35 37 27 S 149 47 37 E

BIG RIG

625 Deua River Campground

Deua National Park

Camp Area 48 km S of Braidwood on Araluen Rd. Small vehicles only. No caravans

HEMA 44 E5 35 44 52 S 149 55 0 E

626 Majors Creek Recreation Reserve

Camp Spot at Majors Creek, 16 km S of Braidwood. Araluen St. Big rig access via King St

HEMA 44 E4 35 34 8 S 149 44 31 E

BIG RIG 24

627 Wyanbene Caves
(02) 4476 0800

Deua National Park

Camp Area 47 km S of Braidwood, via the Braidwood - Cooma Rd. 7 km dirt road

HEMA 44 E4 35 47 41 S 149 40 59 E

628 Lowden Forest Park
1300 655 687

Tallaganda State Forest

Camp Area 38 km SW of Braidwood. Via the Krawarree Rd to Ballalaba, then Harolds Cross Rd (Parlour Creek), Coxes Creek Rd, into Lowden Forest Rd. Dirt road

HEMA 44 E4 35 30 34 S 149 36 16 E

629 Wilkins Memorial Park

Camp Area at Captains Flat. Foxlow St, S end of town. Small vehicles only. Donation welcome

HEMA 44 E4 35 35 26 S 149 26 46 E

24

630 Badja Recreation Reserve
(02) 6450 1777

Camp Spot at Numeralla, 22 km E of Cooma. Numeralla Peak View Rd. Beside river

HEMA 44 G3 36 10 25 S 149 21 1 E

631 Bombay Reserve

Camp Spot 9 km W of Braidwood via Cooma Rd & Bombay Rd. 200m past bridge on R. 100m off road, beside Shoalhaven River

HEMA 44 D4 35 25 37 S 149 42 48 E

632 Warri Camping Reserve

52

Camp Area 14 km N of Braidwood or 35 km SE of Bungendore. Beside Shoalhaven River

HEMA 44 D4 35 20 39 S 149 44 15 E

BIG RIG

633 Bungendore Showground
0457 528 344

52

Camp Spot 4 km NW of Bungendore on Bungendore - Sutton Rd. Caretaker on site. Maximum stay 7 days. Check ahead for availability

HEMA 44 D4 35 14 30 S 149 24 37 E

BIG RIG

Goulburn to Canberra

Federal Highway

634 Kibby VC Rest Area

23

Rest Area 2 km S of Hume Hwy/Federal Hwy jcn. Southbound only

HEMA 44 C4 34 48 55 S 149 36 14 E

BIG RIG

635 Edmondson VC Rest Area

23

Rest Area 15 km SW of Hume Hwy/Federal Hwy jcn or 62 km NE of Barton/Federal Hwy jcn. Beside Rowes Lagoon, 300m off Hwy

HEMA 44 C4 34 53 46 S 149 30 37 E

BIG RIG

636 Gurney VC Rest Area

23

Rest Area 33 km SW of Hume Hwy/Federal Hwy jcn or 44 km NE of Barton/Federal Hwy jcn

HEMA 44 C4 34 54 42 S 149 26 35 E

BIG RIG

637 Badcoe VC Rest Area

23

Rest Area 37 km SW of Hume Hwy/Federal Hwy jcn or 40 km NE of Barton/Federal Hwy jcn

HEMA 44 C4 35 2 5 S 149 22 40 E

BIG RIG

638 Gundaroo Sport & Recreation Ground

Camp Area at Gundaroo. Cork St. Donation please for upkeep at General Store/PO

HEMA 44 C3 35 1 25 S 149 15 57 E

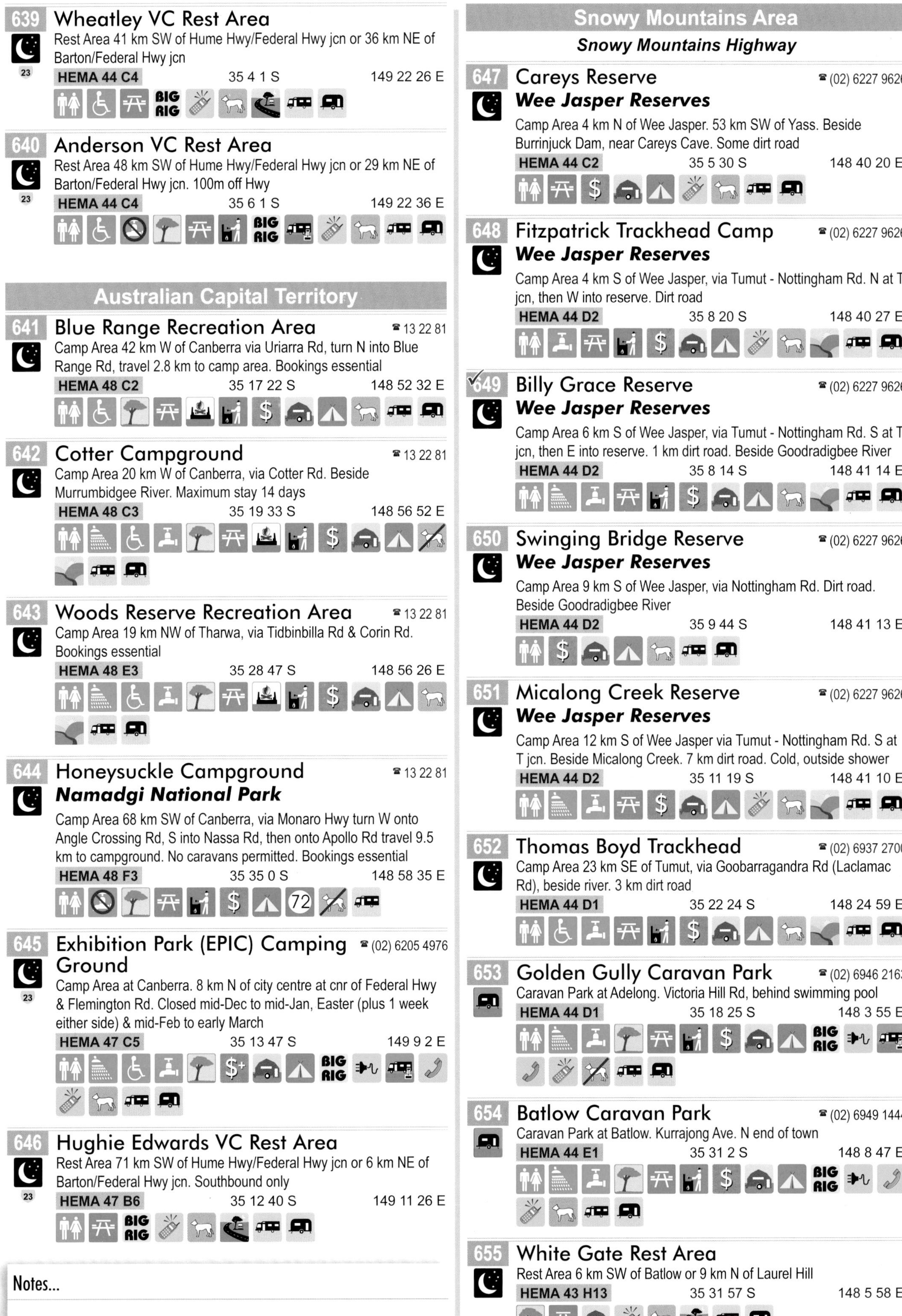

639 **Wheatley VC Rest Area**
Rest Area 41 km SW of Hume Hwy/Federal Hwy jcn or 36 km NE of Barton/Federal Hwy jcn
23
HEMA 44 C4 35 4 1 S 149 22 26 E
BIG RIG

640 **Anderson VC Rest Area**
Rest Area 48 km SW of Hume Hwy/Federal Hwy jcn or 29 km NE of Barton/Federal Hwy jcn. 100m off Hwy
23
HEMA 44 C4 35 6 1 S 149 22 36 E
BIG RIG

Australian Capital Territory

641 **Blue Range Recreation Area** ☎ 13 22 81
Camp Area 42 km W of Canberra via Uriarra Rd, turn N into Blue Range Rd, travel 2.8 km to camp area. Bookings essential
HEMA 48 C2 35 17 22 S 148 52 32 E

642 **Cotter Campground** ☎ 13 22 81
Camp Area 20 km W of Canberra, via Cotter Rd. Beside Murrumbidgee River. Maximum stay 14 days
HEMA 48 C3 35 19 33 S 148 56 52 E

643 **Woods Reserve Recreation Area** ☎ 13 22 81
Camp Area 19 km NW of Tharwa, via Tidbinbilla Rd & Corin Rd. Bookings essential
HEMA 48 E3 35 28 47 S 148 56 26 E

644 **Honeysuckle Campground** ☎ 13 22 81
Namadgi National Park
Camp Area 68 km SW of Canberra, via Monaro Hwy turn W onto Angle Crossing Rd, S into Nassa Rd, then onto Apollo Rd travel 9.5 km to campground. No caravans permitted. Bookings essential
HEMA 48 F3 35 35 0 S 148 58 35 E
72

645 **Exhibition Park (EPIC) Camping Ground** ☎ (02) 6205 4976
Camp Area at Canberra. 8 km N of city centre at cnr of Federal Hwy & Flemington Rd. Closed mid-Dec to mid-Jan, Easter (plus 1 week either side) & mid-Feb to early March
23
HEMA 47 C5 35 13 47 S 149 9 2 E
BIG RIG

646 **Hughie Edwards VC Rest Area**
Rest Area 71 km SW of Hume Hwy/Federal Hwy jcn or 6 km NE of Barton/Federal Hwy jcn. Southbound only
23
HEMA 47 B6 35 12 40 S 149 11 26 E
BIG RIG

Notes...

Snowy Mountains Area

Snowy Mountains Highway

647 **Careys Reserve** ☎ (02) 6227 9626
Wee Jasper Reserves
Camp Area 4 km N of Wee Jasper. 53 km SW of Yass. Beside Burrinjuck Dam, near Careys Cave. Some dirt road
HEMA 44 C2 35 5 30 S 148 40 20 E

648 **Fitzpatrick Trackhead Camp** ☎ (02) 6227 9626
Wee Jasper Reserves
Camp Area 4 km S of Wee Jasper, via Tumut - Nottingham Rd. N at T jcn, then W into reserve. Dirt road
HEMA 44 D2 35 8 20 S 148 40 27 E

649 **Billy Grace Reserve** ☎ (02) 6227 9626
Wee Jasper Reserves
Camp Area 6 km S of Wee Jasper, via Tumut - Nottingham Rd. S at T jcn, then E into reserve. 1 km dirt road. Beside Goodradigbee River
HEMA 44 D2 35 8 14 S 148 41 14 E

650 **Swinging Bridge Reserve** ☎ (02) 6227 9626
Wee Jasper Reserves
Camp Area 9 km S of Wee Jasper, via Nottingham Rd. Dirt road. Beside Goodradigbee River
HEMA 44 D2 35 9 44 S 148 41 13 E

651 **Micalong Creek Reserve** ☎ (02) 6227 9626
Wee Jasper Reserves
Camp Area 12 km S of Wee Jasper via Tumut - Nottingham Rd. S at T jcn. Beside Micalong Creek. 7 km dirt road. Cold, outside shower
HEMA 44 D2 35 11 19 S 148 41 10 E

652 **Thomas Boyd Trackhead** ☎ (02) 6937 2700
Camp Area 23 km SE of Tumut, via Goobarragandra Rd (Laclamac Rd), beside river. 3 km dirt road
HEMA 44 D1 35 22 24 S 148 24 59 E

653 **Golden Gully Caravan Park** ☎ (02) 6946 2163
Caravan Park at Adelong. Victoria Hill Rd, behind swimming pool
HEMA 44 D1 35 18 25 S 148 3 55 E
BIG RIG

654 **Batlow Caravan Park** ☎ (02) 6949 1444
Caravan Park at Batlow. Kurrajong Ave. N end of town
HEMA 44 E1 35 31 2 S 148 8 47 E
BIG RIG

655 **White Gate Rest Area**
Rest Area 6 km SW of Batlow or 9 km N of Laurel Hill
HEMA 43 H13 35 31 57 S 148 5 58 E

NEW SOUTH WALES

656 Mannus Campsite
☎ (02) 6948 3444

Camp Area 7 km W of Tumbarumba, via Jingellic Rd. Beside Mannus Creek

HEMA 43 J13 35 46 46 S 147 56 44 E

657 Lake Mannus Boat Ramp

Camp Spot 12 km W of Tumbarumba. Turn S at Mannus Campsite on Lake Rd, follow dirt road for 5 km to boat ramp

HEMA 43 J13 35 48 40 S 147 58 39 E

658 Jingellic Reserve
☎ (02) 6037 1290

Camp Area at Jingellic. Beside Murray River & hotel. Toilets & showers at hotel for a fee. Dogs must be on lead. Maximum stay 4 weeks.

HEMA 43 J13 35 55 44 S 147 42 14 E

659 Henry Angel Flat
☎ (02) 6948 3444

Camp Area 8 km SE of Tumbarumba or 26 km N of Tooma. Beside river. Maximum stay 4 weeks

HEMA 43 J13 35 49 41 S 148 3 38 E

BIG RIG

660 Paddys River Falls
☎ (02) 6948 9100

Camp Area 16 km SE of Tumbarumba or 22 km N of Tooma. Turn S 14 km SE of Tumbarumba or 20 km N of Tooma. Maximum stay 4 weeks

HEMA 43 J13 35 51 32 S 148 6 56 E

661 Paddys River Flats
☎ (02) 6948 9100

Camp Area 18 km SE of Tumbarumba or 16 km N of Tooma. Beside river. Maximum stay 4 weeks

HEMA 43 J13 35 51 6 S 148 8 23 E

BIG RIG

662 O'Hares Campground
☎ (02) 6947 7025

Kosciuszko National Park

Camp Area 22 km N of Cabramurra or 48 km SE of Tumbarumba on Elliot Way. Steep & winding road

HEMA 43 J14 35 49 20 S 148 21 55 E

663 Three Mile Dam Campground
☎ (02) 6947 7025

Kosciuszko National Park

T1

Camp Area 6 km W of Kiandra or 12 km NE of Cabramurra. 300m N of road

HEMA 43 J14 35 53 18 S 148 26 56 E

664 Bradley's Hutt
☎ (02) 6076 9373

Kosciuszko National Park

Camp Area 47 km NE of Khancoban or 17 km SE of Cabramurra. E side of road. Steep & winding road

HEMA 43 J14 36 0 57 S 148 22 46 E

665 Clover Flat Campground
☎ (02) 6076 9373

Kosciuszko National Park

Camp Area 25 km NE of Khancoban or 35 km SW of Cabramurra. Steep & winding road, limited space, small vehicles only

HEMA 43 J14 36 4 21 S 148 13 2 E

666 Bradneys Gap Campground
☎ (02) 6076 9373

Kosciuszko National Park

Camp Area 10 km NE of Khancoban or 50 km SW of Cabramurra

HEMA 43 K13 36 9 56 S 148 9 24 E

667 Towong Reserve
☎ (02) 6948 9100

Camp Area 25 km S of Tooma or 1 km E of Towong. Beside Murray River bridge

HEMA 43 J13 36 7 25 S 147 59 49 E

BIG RIG

668 Geehi Flats Campground
☎ (02) 6076 9373

Kosciuszko National Park

T1

Camp Area 30 km S of Khancoban or 81 km W of Jindabyne. Steep & winding road. Small vehicles only

HEMA 44 G1 36 23 5 S 148 10 51 E

669 Tom Groggin Campground
☎ (02) 6076 9373

Kosciuszko National Park

T1

Camp Area 53 km S of Khancoban or 58 km W of Jindabyne. Steep & winding road. Small vehicles only

HEMA 44 H1 36 32 22 S 148 8 6 E

670 Leatherbarrel Creek Campground
☎ (02) 6076 9373

Kosciuszko National Park

T1

Camp Area 61 km S of Khancoban or 50 km W of Jindabyne. Steep & winding road. Small vehicles only

HEMA 44 H1 36 31 33 S 148 11 35 E

671 Thredbo Diggings Campground
☎ (02) 6450 5600

Kosciuszko National Park

T1

Camp Area 92 km SE of Khancoban or 19 km W of Jindabyne, beside Thredbo River. Steep & winding road. Small vehicles only

HEMA 44 G1 36 26 49 S 148 25 31 E

672 **Kosciuszko Mountain Retreat** ☎ (02) 6456 2224
Kosciuszko National Park
T1
Camp Area 13 km N of Jindabyne, at Sawpit Creek
HEMA 44 G2 36 21 6 S 148 33 53 E

673 **Jacob River Campground** ☎ (02) 6450 5600
Kosciuszko National Park
Camp Area 51 km S of Jindabyne or 37 km N of Suggan Buggan on Barry Way
HEMA 44 H1 36 44 58 S 148 26 38 E

674 **Pinch River Campground** ☎ (02) 6450 5600
Kosciuszko National Park
Camp Area 58 km S of Jindabyne or 31 km N of Suggan Buggan on Barry Way
HEMA 44 H1 36 47 32 S 148 24 27 E

675 **Buckenderra Holiday Village** ☎ (02) 6453 7242
Caravan Park on the shore of Lake Eucumbene. From Cooma, turn R onto Snowy Mountain Hwy, travel 2.5 km turn L onto Slacks Creek Rd. 26 km to boomgate/office
HEMA 44 F2 36 10 55 S 148 45 52 E
BIG RIG

676 **Rocky Plain Campground** ☎ (02) 6947 7025
Kosciuszko National Park
18
Camp Area 28 km NW of Adaminaby or 10 km S of Kiandra. Turn NE 300m S of The Rest House. 500m dirt access track. Not suitable for caravans
HEMA 44 F2 35 53 30 S 148 32 30 E

677 **The Rest House** ☎ (02) 6947 7025
Kosciuszko National Park
18
Rest Area 29 km NW of Adaminaby or 9 km S of Kiandra
HEMA 44 F2 35 53 45 S 148 32 24 E
BIG RIG

678 **Long Plain Hut Campground** ☎ (02) 6450 5600
Kosciuszko National Park
Camp Area 15 km SE of Yarrangobilly. 10.5 km S of Yarrangobilly turn E into Long Plain Rd for 3.5 km, turn L at signpost, 1 km to camping area near hut. 4WD recommended
HEMA 44 E2 35 41 49 S 148 32 23 E

679 **Cooinbil Hut Campground** ☎ (02) 6947 7025
Kosciuszko National Park
Camp Area 25 km SE of Yarrangobilly. 10.5 km S of Yarrangobilly turn E into Long Plain Rd for 10.5 km, turn R at signpost, 1 km to camping area near hut. 4WD recommended
HEMA 44 E2 35 37 53 S 148 35 49 E

680 **Cooleman Mountain Campground** ☎ (02) 6450 5600
Kosciuszko National Park
Camp Area 30 km SE of Yarrangobilly. 10.5 km S of Yarrangobilly turn E into Long Plains Rd for 17 km, turn R into Blue Waterhole Trail for 2.6 km. 4WD recommended
HEMA 44 E2 35 35 51 S 148 38 23 E

681 **Magpie Flat Campground** ☎ (02) 6450 5600
Kosciuszko National Park
Camp Area 35 km SE of Yarrangobilly. 10.5 km S of Yarrangobilly turn E into Long Plain Rd for 16.5 km, turn R into Blue Waterholes Trail for 8 km. 4WD recommended
HEMA 44 E2 35 37 16 S 148 40 49 E

682 **Blue Waterholes Campground** ☎ (02) 6947 7025
Kosciuszko National Park
Camp Area 35.5 km SE of Yarrangobilly. 10.5 km S of Yarrangobilly turn E into Long Plain Rd for 16.5 km, turn R into Blue Waterholes Trail for 8.5 km. 4WD recommended
HEMA 44 E2 35 37 36 S 148 41 3 E

683 **Yarrangobilly Village Campground** ☎ (02) 6947 7025
Kosciuszko National Park
18
Rest Area 29 km N of Kiandra or 24 km S of Talbingo turnoff. Beside river
HEMA 44 E2 35 39 7 S 148 27 44 E
BIG RIG

684 **Black Perry Rest Area** ☎ (02) 6947 7025
Kosciuszko National Park
18
Rest Area 45 km N of Kiandra or 10 km S of Talbingo turnoff
HEMA 44 E1 35 36 4 S 148 22 23 E

685 **Jounama Creek Campground** ☎ (02) 6947 7025
Kosciuszko National Park
18
Camp Area opposite Talbingo turnoff. 500m E of Hwy. Beside creek
HEMA 44 E1 35 33 56 S 148 19 55 E

686 **Yolde Campground** ☎ (02) 6947 7025
Kosciuszko National Park
18
Camp Area 5 km N of Talbingo turnoff or 35 km S of Tumut. Small vehicles only
HEMA 44 E1 35 32 18 S 148 17 43 E

Notes...

687 Yachting Point Campground
(02) 6947 7025

Kosciuszko National Park

18

Camp Area 10 km N of Talbingo turnoff or 30 km S of Tumut

HEMA 44 E1 35 30 39 S 148 16 3 E

BIG RIG

688 Humes Crossing Campground
(02) 6947 7025

Kosciuszko National Park

18

Camp Area 15 km N of Talbingo turnoff or 25 km S of Tumut

HEMA 44 E1 35 28 25 S 148 16 34 E

BIG RIG

689 The Pines Campground
(02) 6947 7025

Kosciuszko National Park

18

Camp Area 18 km N of Talbingo turnoff or 22 km S of Tumut

HEMA 44 D1 35 26 51 S 148 17 6 E

BIG RIG

690 Log Bridge Creek Campground
(02) 6947 7025

Kosciuszko National Park

18

Camp Area 22 km N of Talbingo turnoff or 18 km S of Tumut. Turn SE off Hwy, follow road back across Hwy for 1.5 km to main camp area

HEMA 44 D1 35 25 7 S 148 16 23 E

691 Tumut River Rest Area

Rest Area 9 km S of Tumut. Turn S off Snowy Mountains Hwy onto Blowering Dam Access Rd. 1.5 km to rest area next to river. Self Contained Vehicles only

HEMA 44 D1 35 22 23 S 148 15 27 E

BIG RIG 48

Cowra to Albury

Olympic Highway

692 Bendick Murrell Rest Area

Rest Area 44 km SW of Cowra or 26 km NE of Young

41

HEMA 36 H4 34 10 2 S 148 27 33 E

BIG RIG

693 Lions Lookout Rest Area

Rest Area 62 km SW of Cowra or 8 km NE of Young

41

HEMA 36 J3 34 17 14 S 148 21 16 E

BIG RIG

694 Young Showground
(02) 6382 2079

Camp Area at Young. Entry from Whitman Ave. Self Contained Vehicles only. Entry from Whitman Ave. Bookings essential 0455 141 801

HEMA 36 J3 34 18 58 S 148 18 50 E

$ BIG RIG 48

695 Big Spring Creek

Rest Area 8 km S of Young or 23 km NE of Wallendbeen

41

HEMA 36 J3 34 22 28 S 148 15 35 E

BIG RIG

696 Mackay Park

Rest Area at Wallendbeen

41

HEMA 36 J3 34 31 45 S 148 9 46 E

BIG RIG 20

697 Cootamundra Showgrounds
0428 555 241

Camp Area at Cootamundra off Pinkerton Rd

HEMA 36 K3 34 38 24 S 148 2 27 E

$+ BIG RIG

698 Cunjigong Creek Rest Area

Rest Area 12 km SW of Cootamundra or 12 km NE of Bethungra. Rotary Park

41

HEMA 36 K2 34 42 9 S 147 56 30 E

699 Bethungra Dam & Reserve

Camp Area 5 km E of Bethungra. 100m N of Bethungra Village turn E onto dirt road under viaduct, onto Bethungra Waterworks Rd, follow to Dam

HEMA 36 K2 34 45 50 S 147 54 27 E

BIG RIG

700 Illabo Rest Area

Rest Area at Illabo. Opposite hotel

41

HEMA 36 K2 34 48 57 S 147 44 21 E

BIG RIG

701 Old Junee Rest Area

Rest Area at Old Junee. N side of town

85

HEMA 43 G12 34 50 13 S 147 31 16 E

BIG RIG

702 Sandy Beach Reserve

Camp Area 3 km SE of Wantabadgery on River Rd

HEMA 43 G13 35 4 3 S 147 44 21 E

BIG RIG

703 Wallacetown Rest Area

Rest Area 20 km S of Junee or 21 km N of Wagga Wagga. Opposite service station

41

HEMA 43 G12 34 57 34 S 147 26 54 E

BIG RIG 24

704 Wagga Wagga Showgrounds

Camp Area at Wagga Wagga. Entry via Urana St. Self Contained Vehicles only

HEMA 43 G12 35 7 31 S 147 21 15 E

$ BIG RIG 24

705 Wilks Park

Rest Area at Wagga Wagga. Turn E off Olympic Hwy at Travers St, cross bridge to Hampden Ave. N side of town, E side of Murrumbidgee River. Self Contained Vehicles only

HEMA 43 G12 35 5 59 S 147 22 17 E

BIG RIG 72

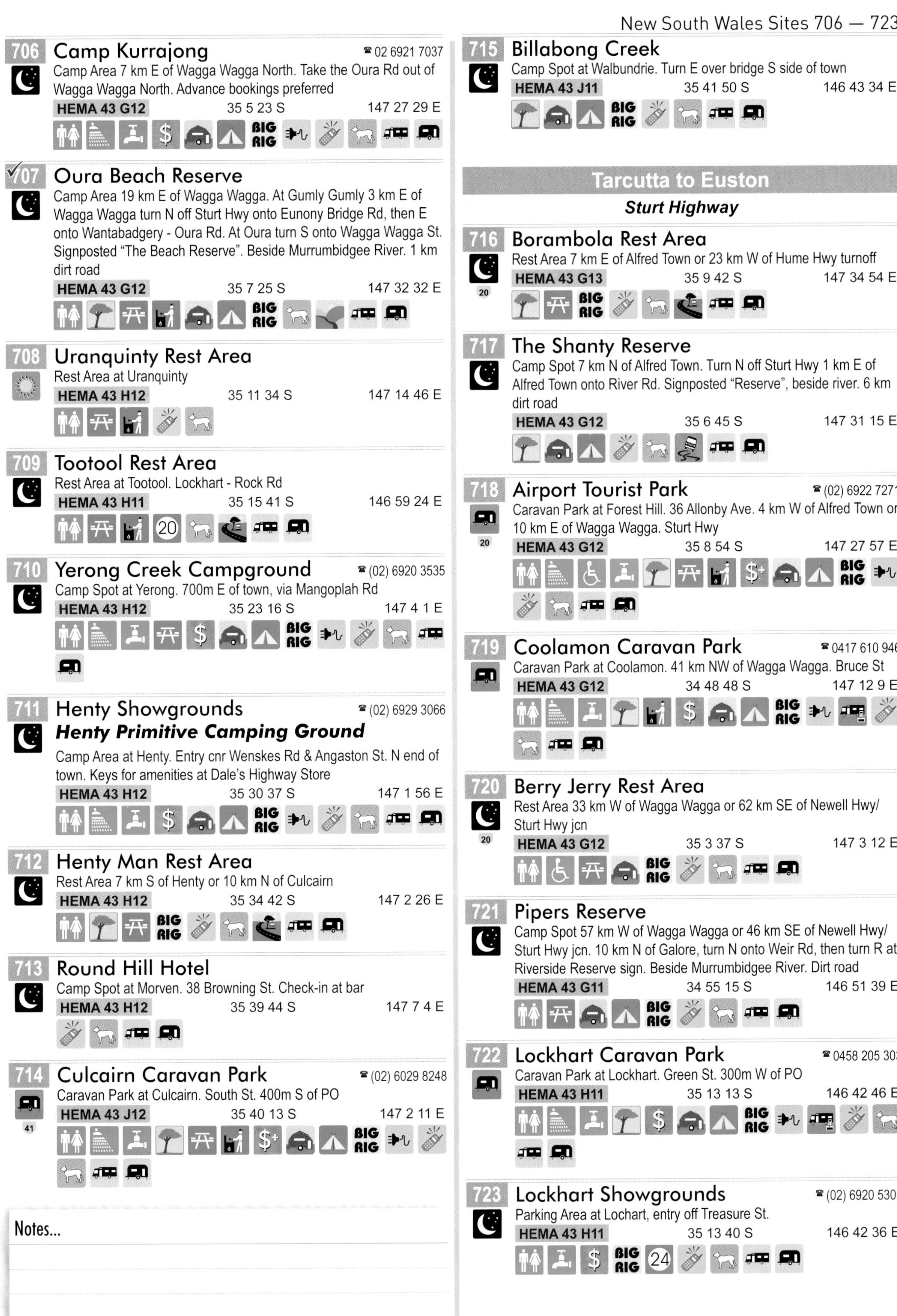

706 **Camp Kurrajong** ☎ 02 6921 7037
Camp Area 7 km E of Wagga Wagga North. Take the Oura Rd out of Wagga Wagga North. Advance bookings preferred
HEMA 43 G12 35 5 23 S 147 27 29 E

707 **Oura Beach Reserve**
Camp Area 19 km E of Wagga Wagga. At Gumly Gumly 3 km E of Wagga Wagga turn N off Sturt Hwy onto Eunony Bridge Rd, then E onto Wantabadgery - Oura Rd. At Oura turn S onto Wagga Wagga St. Signposted "The Beach Reserve". Beside Murrumbidgee River. 1 km dirt road
HEMA 43 G12 35 7 25 S 147 32 32 E

708 **Uranquinty Rest Area**
Rest Area at Uranquinty
HEMA 43 H12 35 11 34 S 147 14 46 E

709 **Tootool Rest Area**
Rest Area at Tootool. Lockhart - Rock Rd
HEMA 43 H11 35 15 41 S 146 59 24 E

710 **Yerong Creek Campground** ☎ (02) 6920 3535
Camp Spot at Yerong. 700m E of town, via Mangoplah Rd
HEMA 43 H12 35 23 16 S 147 4 1 E

711 **Henty Showgrounds** ☎ (02) 6929 3066
Henty Primitive Camping Ground
Camp Area at Henty. Entry cnr Wenskes Rd & Angaston St. N end of town. Keys for amenities at Dale's Highway Store
HEMA 43 H12 35 30 37 S 147 1 56 E

712 **Henty Man Rest Area**
Rest Area 7 km S of Henty or 10 km N of Culcairn
HEMA 43 H12 35 34 42 S 147 2 26 E

713 **Round Hill Hotel**
Camp Spot at Morven. 38 Browning St. Check-in at bar
HEMA 43 H12 35 39 44 S 147 7 4 E

714 **Culcairn Caravan Park** ☎ (02) 6029 8248
Caravan Park at Culcairn. South St. 400m S of PO
HEMA 43 J12 35 40 13 S 147 2 11 E

Notes...

715 **Billabong Creek**
Camp Spot at Walbundrie. Turn E over bridge S side of town
HEMA 43 J11 35 41 50 S 146 43 34 E

Tarcutta to Euston
Sturt Highway

716 **Borambola Rest Area**
Rest Area 7 km E of Alfred Town or 23 km W of Hume Hwy turnoff
HEMA 43 G13 35 9 42 S 147 34 54 E

717 **The Shanty Reserve**
Camp Spot 7 km N of Alfred Town. Turn N off Sturt Hwy 1 km E of Alfred Town onto River Rd. Signposted "Reserve", beside river. 6 km dirt road
HEMA 43 G12 35 6 45 S 147 31 15 E

718 **Airport Tourist Park** ☎ (02) 6922 7271
Caravan Park at Forest Hill. 36 Allonby Ave. 4 km W of Alfred Town or 10 km E of Wagga Wagga. Sturt Hwy
HEMA 43 G12 35 8 54 S 147 27 57 E

719 **Coolamon Caravan Park** ☎ 0417 610 946
Caravan Park at Coolamon. 41 km NW of Wagga Wagga. Bruce St
HEMA 43 G12 34 48 48 S 147 12 9 E

720 **Berry Jerry Rest Area**
Rest Area 33 km W of Wagga Wagga or 62 km SE of Newell Hwy/Sturt Hwy jcn
HEMA 43 G12 35 3 37 S 147 3 12 E

721 **Pipers Reserve**
Camp Spot 57 km W of Wagga Wagga or 46 km SE of Newell Hwy/Sturt Hwy jcn. 10 km N of Galore, turn N onto Weir Rd, then turn R at Riverside Reserve sign. Beside Murrumbidgee River. Dirt road
HEMA 43 G11 34 55 15 S 146 51 39 E

722 **Lockhart Caravan Park** ☎ 0458 205 303
Caravan Park at Lockhart. Green St. 300m W of PO
HEMA 43 H11 35 13 13 S 146 42 46 E

723 **Lockhart Showgrounds** ☎ (02) 6920 5305
Parking Area at Lochart, entry off Treasure St.
HEMA 43 H11 35 13 40 S 146 42 36 E

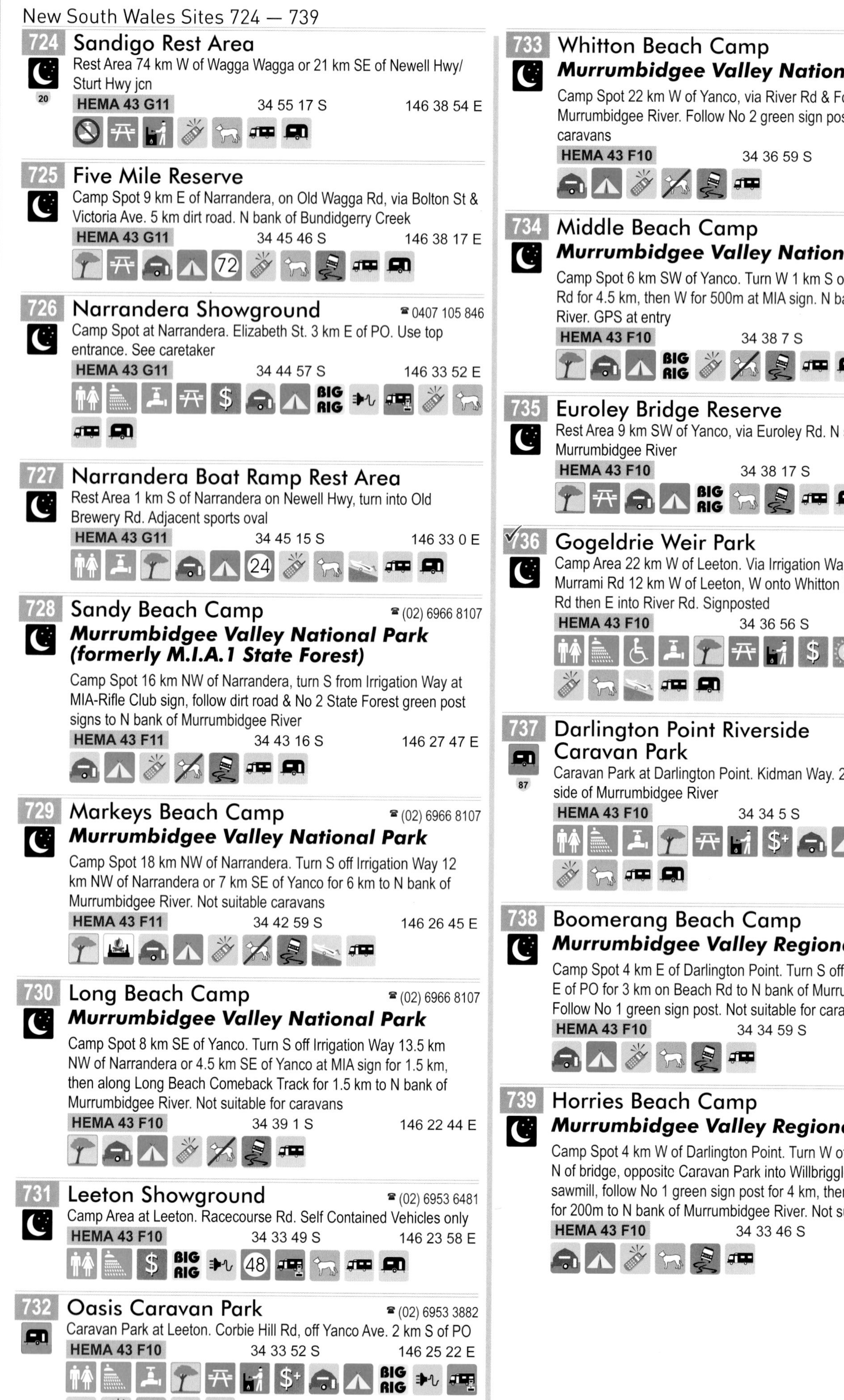

724 Sandigo Rest Area
Rest Area 74 km W of Wagga Wagga or 21 km SE of Newell Hwy/ Sturt Hwy jcn
20
HEMA 43 G11 | 34 55 17 S | 146 38 54 E

725 Five Mile Reserve
Camp Spot 9 km E of Narrandera, on Old Wagga Rd, via Bolton St & Victoria Ave. 5 km dirt road. N bank of Bundidgerry Creek
HEMA 43 G11 | 34 45 46 S | 146 38 17 E
72

726 Narrandera Showground
☎ 0407 105 846
Camp Spot at Narrandera. Elizabeth St. 3 km E of PO. Use top entrance. See caretaker
HEMA 43 G11 | 34 44 57 S | 146 33 52 E
BIG RIG

727 Narrandera Boat Ramp Rest Area
Rest Area 1 km S of Narrandera on Newell Hwy, turn into Old Brewery Rd. Adjacent sports oval
HEMA 43 G11 | 34 45 15 S | 146 33 0 E
24

728 Sandy Beach Camp
☎ (02) 6966 8107
Murrumbidgee Valley National Park (formerly M.I.A.1 State Forest)
Camp Spot 16 km NW of Narrandera, turn S from Irrigation Way at MIA-Rifle Club sign, follow dirt road & No 2 State Forest green post signs to N bank of Murrumbidgee River
HEMA 43 F11 | 34 43 16 S | 146 27 47 E

729 Markeys Beach Camp
☎ (02) 6966 8107
Murrumbidgee Valley National Park
Camp Spot 18 km NW of Narrandera. Turn S off Irrigation Way 12 km NW of Narrandera or 7 km SE of Yanco for 6 km to N bank of Murrumbidgee River. Not suitable caravans
HEMA 43 F11 | 34 42 59 S | 146 26 45 E

730 Long Beach Camp
☎ (02) 6966 8107
Murrumbidgee Valley National Park
Camp Spot 8 km SE of Yanco. Turn S off Irrigation Way 13.5 km NW of Narrandera or 4.5 km SE of Yanco at MIA sign for 1.5 km, then along Long Beach Comeback Track for 1.5 km to N bank of Murrumbidgee River. Not suitable for caravans
HEMA 43 F10 | 34 39 1 S | 146 22 44 E

731 Leeton Showground
☎ (02) 6953 6481
Camp Area at Leeton. Racecourse Rd. Self Contained Vehicles only
HEMA 43 F10 | 34 33 49 S | 146 23 58 E
BIG RIG
48

732 Oasis Caravan Park
☎ (02) 6953 3882
Caravan Park at Leeton. Corbie Hill Rd, off Yanco Ave. 2 km S of PO
HEMA 43 F10 | 34 33 52 S | 146 25 22 E
BIG RIG

733 Whitton Beach Camp
☎ (02) 6966 8107
Murrumbidgee Valley National Park
Camp Spot 22 km W of Yanco, via River Rd & Forest Dr. N bank of Murrumbidgee River. Follow No 2 green sign post. Not suitable for caravans
HEMA 43 F10 | 34 36 59 S | 146 11 1 E

734 Middle Beach Camp
☎ (02) 6966 8107
Murrumbidgee Valley National Park
Camp Spot 6 km SW of Yanco. Turn W 1 km S of Yanco onto Euroley Rd for 4.5 km, then W for 500m at MIA sign. N bank of Murrumbidgee River. GPS at entry
HEMA 43 F10 | 34 38 7 S | 146 22 32 E
BIG RIG

735 Euroley Bridge Reserve
☎ (02) 6841 4288
Rest Area 9 km SW of Yanco, via Euroley Rd. N side of Murrumbidgee River
HEMA 43 F10 | 34 38 17 S | 146 22 32 E
BIG RIG

736 Gogeldrie Weir Park
☎ (02) 6955 9267
Camp Area 22 km W of Leeton. Via Irrigation Way. Turn S onto Murrami Rd 12 km W of Leeton, W onto Whitton Rd, S onto Gogeldrie Rd then E into River Rd. Signposted
HEMA 43 F10 | 34 36 56 S | 146 15 29 E
BIG RIG

737 Darlington Point Riverside Caravan Park
☎ (02) 6968 4237
87
Caravan Park at Darlington Point. Kidman Way. 200m E of PO on N side of Murrumbidgee River
HEMA 43 F10 | 34 34 5 S | 146 0 15 E
BIG RIG

738 Boomerang Beach Camp
☎ (02) 6966 8107
Murrumbidgee Valley Regional Park
Camp Spot 4 km E of Darlington Point. Turn S off Whitton Rd 1.2 km E of PO for 3 km on Beach Rd to N bank of Murrumbidgee River. Follow No 1 green sign post. Not suitable for caravans
HEMA 43 F10 | 34 34 59 S | 146 1 13 E

739 Horries Beach Camp
☎ (02) 6966 8107
Murrumbidgee Valley Regional Park
Camp Spot 4 km W of Darlington Point. Turn W off Kidman Way just N of bridge, opposite Caravan Park into Willbriggle State Forest, pass sawmill, follow No 1 green sign post for 4 km, then S at sign "Beach" for 200m to N bank of Murrumbidgee River. Not suitable for caravans
HEMA 43 F10 | 34 33 46 S | 145 58 38 E

740 Swaggys Beach Camp
☎ (02) 6966 8107

Camp Spot 7 km W of Darlington Point. Turn W off Kidman Way just N of bridge, opposite caravan park into Willbriggle State Forest, past sawmill, follow No1 green sign post 7 km, then S to N bank of Murrumbidgee River. Not suitable for caravans

HEMA 43 F10 34 33 33 S 145 57 30 E

741 Cookoothama Reserve

Camp Spot 8 km W of Darlington Point. Turn W 3 km N of Darlington Point onto Murrumbidgee River Rd. N bank of Murrumbidgee River

HEMA 43 F10 34 32 47 S 145 56 49 E

742 Nobles Beach Camp
☎ (02) 6966 8107

Murrumbidgee Valley National Park

Camp Spot 15 km W of Darlington Point. Turn W 3 km N of Darlington Point onto Murrumbidgee River Rd. N bank of Murrumbidgee River

HEMA 43 F9 34 33 20 S 145 54 12 E

743 Common Beach

Camp Spot at Darlington Point. From W end of King St, cross grid, then immediate R to S bank of Murrumbidgee River. GPS at entry

HEMA 43 F10 34 33 57 S 145 59 32 E

744 Bunyip Hole Reserve

Camp Spot at Darlington Point. From W end of King St, cross grid, then 2nd track to R, then L at T jcn, then R to S bank of Murrumbidgee River. GPS at Entry

HEMA 43 F10 34 33 57 S 145 59 32 E

745 Birdcage Reserve Rest Area West

20

Rest Area 86 km W of Newell Hwy/Sturt Hwy jcn or 86 km E of Hay. Westbound

HEMA 43 F9 34 31 27 S 145 42 8 E

BIG RIG

746 Birdcage Reserve Rest Area East

20

Rest Area 86 km W of Newell Hwy/Sturt Hwy jcn or 86 km E of Hay. Eastbound

HEMA 43 F9 34 31 27 S 145 42 8 E

BIG RIG

747 Birdcage Reserve

Camp Spot 86 km W of Newell Hwy/Sturt Hwy jcn or 86 km E of Hay. Turn N at sign "Birdcage Reserve" for 400m to S bank of Murrumbidgee River. Dirt road

HEMA 43 F9 34 31 12 S 145 41 56 E

BIG RIG

748 Tonganmain Reserve

Camp Spot 90 km W of Newell Hwy/Sturt Hwy jcn or 82 km E of South Hay. Turn N at sign "Tonganmain Reserve" 87 km W of Newell Hwy/Sturt Hwy jcn or 79 km of Hay for 3 km of dirt road to S bank of Murrumbidgee River

HEMA 43 F9 34 28 17 S 145 38 19 E

BIG RIG

749 Campbells Reserve

Camp Spot 114 km W of Newell Hwy/Sturt Hwy jcn or 58 km E of Hay. Turn N at sign "Campbells Reserve" for 1 km of dirt road to S bank of Murrumbidgee River

HEMA 43 F9 34 28 0 S 145 23 19 E

BIG RIG

750 Mulberrygong Reserve

Camp Spot 134 km W of Newell Hwy/Sturt Hwy jcn or 38 km E of South Hay. Turn N at signs "River" & "Mulberrygong Reserve" for 1 km of dirt road to S bank of Murrumbidgee River. GPS at gate

HEMA 43 F8 34 30 43 S 145 13 59 E

BIG RIG

751 Burrabogie Reserve

Camp Spot 141 km W of Newell Hwy/Sturt Hwy jcn or 31 km E of Hay. Turn N at signs "Burrabogie Reserve" for 600m of dirt road to S bank of Murrumbidgee River. GPS at entry

HEMA 43 F8 34 30 5 S 145 9 32 E

BIG RIG

752 Brandons Bend Reserve

Camp Spot 169 km W of Newell Hwy/Sturt Hwy jcn or 3 km E of Hay. Turn N at sign "Brandons Bend Reserve" for 150m dirt road to S bank of Murrumbidgee River. GPS at entry

HEMA 43 F8 34 31 14 S 144 51 52 E

753 Nine Mile Reserve

20

Camp Spot 14 km W of Hay or 117 km E of Balranald. Turn N onto signposted track. Beside river. Limited flat ground

HEMA 43 F8 34 32 56 S 144 42 37 E

754 Pevensey Rest Area

20

Rest Area 27 km W of Hay or 104 km E of Balranald. Shared with trucks

HEMA 42 F7 34 36 14 S 144 34 2 E

BIG RIG

755 Yang Yang (Maude)

Camp Spot at Maude. Turn W off Moulamein Rd along Nap Nap Rd for 300m. S side of Murrumbidgee River

HEMA 42 F7 34 28 40 S 144 17 49 E

BIG RIG

756 Maude Caravan Park
☎ (02) 6993 6112

Caravan Park at Maude. Part of Post Office Hotel

HEMA 42 F7 34 28 25 S 144 18 7 E

757 Willowvale Rest Area

Rest Area 91 km W of Hay or 40 km E of Balranald. Share with trucks

HEMA 42 G6 34 43 23 S 143 55 41 E

BIG RIG

Notes...

NEW SOUTH WALES

758 The Willows Campground
(03) 5020 1764

Murrumbidgee Valley National Park

Camp Area in Murrumbidgee Valley National Park. Turn S off Sturt Hwy 100 km W of Hay or 24 km E of Balranald onto Impimi Rd. Travel 1 km to park entrance, follow track 1.5 km to camping area. GPS at entrance. No fires

HEMA 42 G6 | 34 44 46 S | 143 45 5 E

759 Homebush Hotel Campground
(03) 5020 6803

Camp Area at Penarie 28 km N of Balranald or 201 km S of Ivanhoe

HEMA 42 F6 | 34 24 27 S | 143 36 47 E

BIG RIG

760 Swimming Pool Car Park

Parking Area in Balranald. Church St, next to blue towers. Self Contained Vehicles only

HEMA 42 F6 | 34 38 7 S | 143 33 43 E

BIG RIG 24

761 Balranald RV Stop
(03) 5020 1599

Parking Area in Balranald. River St, behind Info Centre. Self Contained Vehicles only

HEMA 42 F6 | 34 38 25 S | 143 33 53 E

BIG RIG 24

762 Yanga Rest Area

20

Rest Area 121 km W of Hay or 10 km E of Balranald

HEMA 42 G6 | 34 42 1 S | 143 35 41 E

BIG RIG

763 Mamanga Campground
(03) 5020 1764

Murrumbidgee Valley National Park

Camp Area 9 km SW Balranald. Via Sturt Hwy & Windomal Rd. Signposted. GPS at entrance

HEMA 42 G6 | 34 40 40 S | 143 31 13 E

764 Wakool River

Camp Spot 17 km NE of Tooleybuc or 36 km SW of Balranald, turn SE on the S side of Wakool River bridge, dirt road to tracks by river

HEMA 42 G6 | 34 56 47 S | 143 28 41 E

BIG RIG

765 Lake Benanee

20

Rest Area 65 km W of Balranald or 15 km E of Euston. Lakefront. Cold shower

HEMA 42 F4 | 34 31 13 S | 142 52 39 E

BIG RIG 96

Goondiwindi to Tocumwal

Newell Highway

766 North Star Road Rest Area

39

Rest Area 40 km S of Goondiwindi or 84 km N of Moree

HEMA 38 B6 | 28 50 26 S | 150 13 34 E

BIG RIG

767 Kiga Bore Rest Area

39

Rest Area 69 km S of Goondiwindi or 55 km N of Moree. Combined truck stop. Both sides of road

HEMA 38 C5 | 29 2 18 S | 150 3 11 E

BIG RIG

768 Gil Gil Creek North Rest Area

39

Rest Area 83 km S of Goondiwindi or 41 km N of Moree. 2 km N of Gil Gil Creek

HEMA 38 C5 | 29 9 50 S | 150 0 48 E

BIG RIG

769 Boolooroo Rest Area

39

Rest Area 116 km S of Goondiwindi or 8 km N of Moree. Combined truck stop

HEMA 38 D5 | 29 25 12 S | 149 54 15 E

BIG RIG

770 Moree Showgrounds
0428 205 098

Camp Area at showgrounds. Entrance off River St, via Alice St & Warialda St. Caretaker on site. Closed show weeks April

HEMA 38 D5 | 29 28 7 S | 149 50 53 E

BIG RIG

771 Boomi Community Co-Op Campground
(02) 6753 5336

Camp Area at Boomi. Opposite Police Station, adjacent to artesian pools

HEMA 38 B4 | 28 43 32 S | 149 34 45 E

772 Tookey Creek Rest Area

39

Rest Area 47 km S of Moree or 51 km N of Narrabri

HEMA 38 E5 | 29 52 28 S | 149 47 19 E

BIG RIG

773 Mainway Caravan Park
(02) 6795 4268

Caravan Park at Wee Waa. 210 Rose St. 1 km NE of PO

HEMA 38 F4 | 30 13 16 S | 149 27 12 E

774 Wee Waa Showgrounds

Camp Area at Wee Waa. Entry off Maitland St

HEMA 38 F4 | 30 13 8 S | 149 26 57 E

BIG RIG

775 Cameron Park

39

Rest Area at Narrabri. 700m S of Info Centre. S bank of Narrabri Creek. Beside bridge

HEMA 38 F5 | 30 19 37 S | 149 46 43 E

BIG RIG

776 Narrabri Showground
(02) 6792 3913

Camp Area at Narrabri. Turn off Cooma (Newell Hwy) Rd onto Belar St at Eathers Creek Bridge. S of town

HEMA 38 F5 | 30 20 19 S | 149 45 48 E

BIG RIG

777 **Bark Hut** ☎ (02) 6792 7300
Mt Kaputar National Park
Camp Area 50 km E of Narrabri. Access steep & narrow in parts. Some sections of dirt road, but all steep sections are sealed. No caravans allowed in the park, motorhomes up to size of coaster allowed
HEMA 38 F5 30 17 25 S 150 8 35 E

778 **Dawsons Spring** ☎ (02) 6792 7300
Mt Kaputar National Park
Camp Area 56 km E of Narrabri. Some sections of unsealed road, but all steep sections are sealed. Access steep & narrow in parts. No caravans allowed in the park, motorhomes up to size of coaster & camper trailers allowed
HEMA 38 F5 30 16 51 S 150 9 47 E

779 **Yarrie Lake** ☎ 0427 666 105
2
Camp Area 27 km W of Narrabri. Turn W off Newell Hwy 3 km S of Narrabri onto Yarrie Lake Rd, towards Australia Telescope for 19 km then S for 7 km, turn R on Lake Circuit. 1 km dirt road
HEMA 38 G4 30 22 7 S 149 31 5 E
BIG RIG

780 **Bohena Creek Rest Area**
Rest Area 16 km S of Narrabri or 103 km N of Coonabarabran. Share with trucks
HEMA 38 G4 30 26 12 S 149 40 42 E
BIG RIG 12

781 **Pilliga No 2 Rest Area**
39
Rest Area 25 km S of Narrabri or 95 km N of Coonabarabran
HEMA 38 G4 30 29 41 S 149 38 9 E
BIG RIG

782 **Schwagers Bore Picnic Area** ☎ (02) 6843 1607
Picnic Area 61 km SW of Narrabri or 50 km NE of Baradine, turn SW onto Pilliga Forest Way 27 km SW of Narrabri. Dirt road
HEMA 38 G3 30 36 13 S 149 18 57 E

783 **Salt Caves Picnic Area** ☎ (02) 6825 4364
Pilliga National Park
Picnic Area 68 km SW of Narrabri or 37 km NE of Baradine, turn SW onto Pilliga Forest Way 27 km SW of Narrabri, then S onto County Line Rd. Dirt road
HEMA 38 H3 30 44 46 S 149 17 28 E

784 **The Aloes Picnic Area** ☎ (02) 6843 1607
Picnic Area 88 km SW of Narrabri or 23 km N of Baradine, via Pilliga Forest Way. Dirt road. Beside Etoo Creek
HEMA 38 H3 30 44 57 S 149 6 38 E

785 **Anzac Park Primitive Campground** ☎ (02) 6799 6760
Camp Spot at Gwabegar, Anzac Parade
HEMA 38 G3 30 36 30 S 148 58 15 E
BIG RIG 24

786 **Camp Cypress** ☎ (02) 6843 1035
Camp Area at Baradine. 1 km W of PO at showground. Lachlan St
HEMA 38 H3 30 56 49 S 149 3 21 E
BIG RIG

787 **Yarraman Rest Area**
Rest Area 49 km S of Narrabri or 71 km N of Coonabarabran. Northbound only, share with trucks
HEMA 38 G4 30 41 43 S 149 32 13 E
BIG RIG

788 **Pilliga Rest Area**
39
Rest Area 52 km S of Narrabri or 68 km N of Coonabarabran
HEMA 38 G4 30 43 22 S 149 31 28 E
BIG RIG

789 **Yamminba Rest Area**
39
Rest Area 68 km S of Narrabri or 52 km N of Coonabarabran
HEMA 38 H4 30 51 14 S 149 27 26 E
BIG RIG

790 **Sculptures in the Scrub Camping & Picnic Area** ☎ (02) 6843 4011
Timallallie National Park
Camp Area 33 km E of Baradine. From Baradine, N on Indian Lane for 9.5 km, E into No 1 Break Rd for 11 km, S into Top Crossing Rd for 11 km, E at "Sculptures in the Scrub" sign for 1.5 km. 27 km dirt road
HEMA 38 H3 30 59 46 S 149 14 3 E
BIG RIG

791 **Barkala Farmstay** ☎ (02) 6842 2239
Camp Area 34 km NW of Coonabarabran or 105 km SW of Narrabri via Newwell Hwy. Turn W 23 km N of Coonabarabran into Borambitty, travel for approx 11 km. Signposted
HEMA 38 J3 31 2 42 S 149 19 4 E

792 **Gowan North Rest Area**
39
Rest Area 111 km S of Narrabri or 9 km N of Coonabarabran. 2 km N of Gowan Truck parking bay
HEMA 38 J3 31 13 5 S 149 19 34 E
BIG RIG

793 **Neilson Park**
39
Rest Area at Coonabarabran. Essex St beside river
HEMA 38 J3 31 16 16 S 149 16 46 E
BIG RIG

Notes...

NEW SOUTH WALES

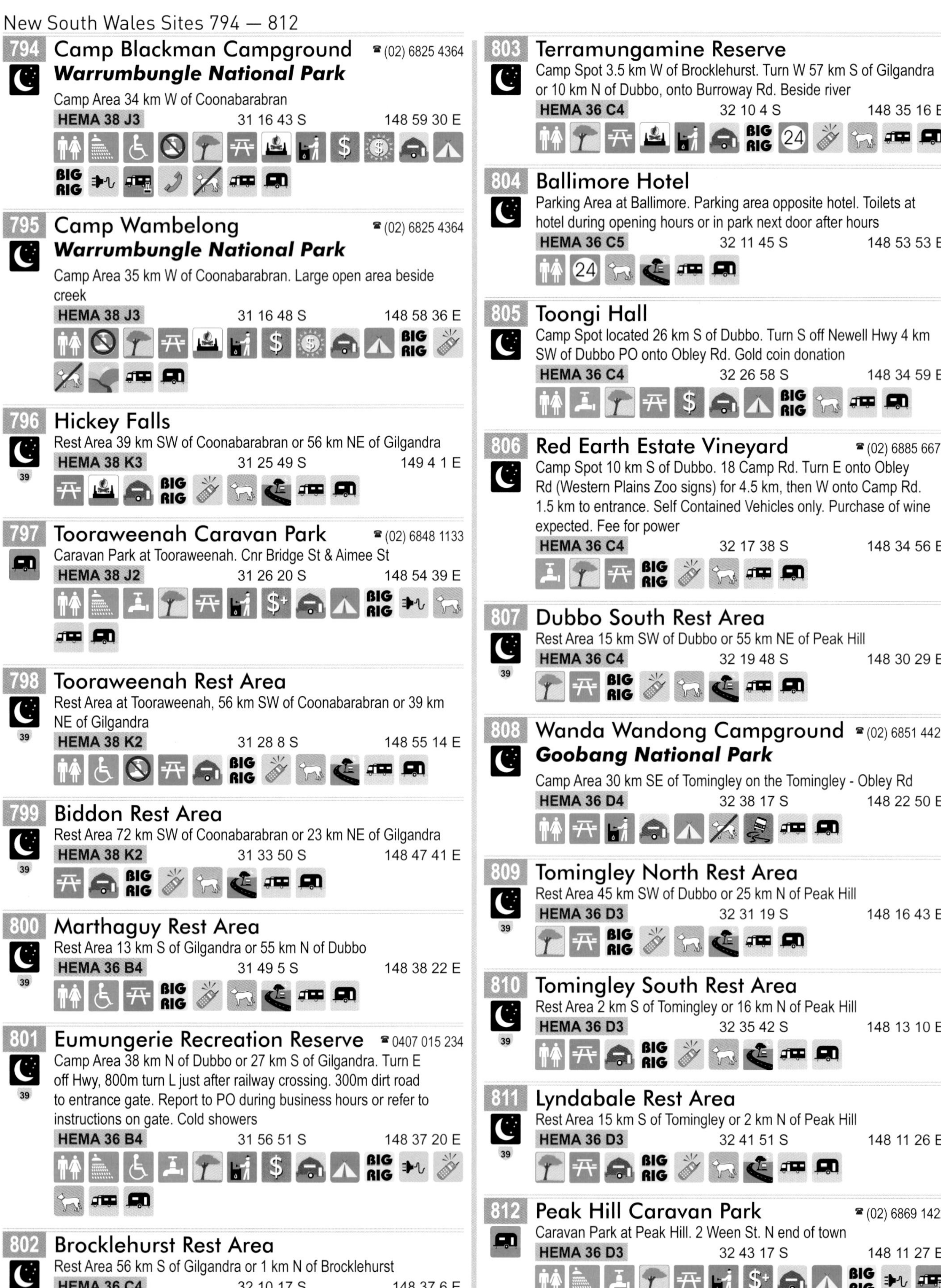

794 Camp Blackman Campground ☎ (02) 6825 4364
Warrumbungle National Park

Camp Area 34 km W of Coonabarabran

HEMA 38 J3 31 16 43 S 148 59 30 E

BIG RIG

795 Camp Wambelong ☎ (02) 6825 4364
Warrumbungle National Park

Camp Area 35 km W of Coonabarabran. Large open area beside creek

HEMA 38 J3 31 16 48 S 148 58 36 E

BIG RIG

796 Hickey Falls
39

Rest Area 39 km SW of Coonabarabran or 56 km NE of Gilgandra

HEMA 38 K3 31 25 49 S 149 4 1 E

BIG RIG

797 Tooraweenah Caravan Park ☎ (02) 6848 1133
Caravan Park at Tooraweenah. Cnr Bridge St & Aimee St

HEMA 38 J2 31 26 20 S 148 54 39 E

BIG RIG

798 Tooraweenah Rest Area
39

Rest Area at Tooraweenah, 56 km SW of Coonabarabran or 39 km NE of Gilgandra

HEMA 38 K2 31 28 8 S 148 55 14 E

BIG RIG

799 Biddon Rest Area
39

Rest Area 72 km SW of Coonabarabran or 23 km NE of Gilgandra

HEMA 38 K2 31 33 50 S 148 47 41 E

BIG RIG

800 Marthaguy Rest Area
39

Rest Area 13 km S of Gilgandra or 55 km N of Dubbo

HEMA 36 B4 31 49 5 S 148 38 22 E

BIG RIG

801 Eumungerie Recreation Reserve ☎ 0407 015 234
39

Camp Area 38 km N of Dubbo or 27 km S of Gilgandra. Turn E off Hwy, 800m turn L just after railway crossing. 300m dirt road to entrance gate. Report to PO during business hours or refer to instructions on gate. Cold showers

HEMA 36 B4 31 56 51 S 148 37 20 E

BIG RIG

802 Brocklehurst Rest Area
39

Rest Area 56 km S of Gilgandra or 1 km N of Brocklehurst

HEMA 36 C4 32 10 17 S 148 37 6 E

BIG RIG

803 Terramungamine Reserve
Camp Spot 3.5 km W of Brocklehurst. Turn W 57 km S of Gilgandra or 10 km N of Dubbo, onto Burroway Rd. Beside river

HEMA 36 C4 32 10 4 S 148 35 16 E

BIG RIG 24

804 Ballimore Hotel
Parking Area at Ballimore. Parking area opposite hotel. Toilets at hotel during opening hours or in park next door after hours

HEMA 36 C5 32 11 45 S 148 53 53 E

24

805 Toongi Hall
Camp Spot located 26 km S of Dubbo. Turn S off Newell Hwy 4 km SW of Dubbo PO onto Obley Rd. Gold coin donation

HEMA 36 C4 32 26 58 S 148 34 59 E

BIG RIG

806 Red Earth Estate Vineyard ☎ (02) 6885 6676
Camp Spot 10 km S of Dubbo. 18 Camp Rd. Turn E onto Obley Rd (Western Plains Zoo signs) for 4.5 km, then W onto Camp Rd. 1.5 km to entrance. Self Contained Vehicles only. Purchase of wine expected. Fee for power

HEMA 36 C4 32 17 38 S 148 34 56 E

BIG RIG

807 Dubbo South Rest Area
39

Rest Area 15 km SW of Dubbo or 55 km NE of Peak Hill

HEMA 36 C4 32 19 48 S 148 30 29 E

BIG RIG

808 Wanda Wandong Campground ☎ (02) 6851 4429
Goobang National Park

Camp Area 30 km SE of Tomingley on the Tomingley - Obley Rd

HEMA 36 D4 32 38 17 S 148 22 50 E

809 Tomingley North Rest Area
39

Rest Area 45 km SW of Dubbo or 25 km N of Peak Hill

HEMA 36 D3 32 31 19 S 148 16 43 E

BIG RIG

810 Tomingley South Rest Area
39

Rest Area 2 km S of Tomingley or 16 km N of Peak Hill

HEMA 36 D3 32 35 42 S 148 13 10 E

BIG RIG

811 Lyndabale Rest Area
39

Rest Area 15 km S of Tomingley or 2 km N of Peak Hill

HEMA 36 D3 32 41 51 S 148 11 26 E

BIG RIG

812 Peak Hill Caravan Park ☎ (02) 6869 1422
Caravan Park at Peak Hill. 2 Ween St. N end of town

HEMA 36 D3 32 43 17 S 148 11 27 E

BIG RIG

813 Peak Hill Showgrounds
Camp Area at Peak Hill, Coradgery Rd
HEMA 36 D3 32 43 42 S 148 10 33 E
BIG RIG 48

814 Double D Caravan Park
☎ (02) 6869 1797
Caravan Park at Peak Hill. Bogan St. 1 km SW of PO. 5 tonne limit no access for 5th wheelers
HEMA 36 D3 32 43 46 S 148 11 10 E

815 Greenbah Creek Campground
☎ (02) 6851 4429
Goobang National Park
Camp Area 24 km E of Trewilga on the Trewilga - Balbry Rd. 16 km along Trewilga - Balbry Rd turn N into gravel road. Signposted
HEMA 36 D3 32 46 18 S 148 21 11 E

816 Currajong Rest Area
Rest Area 116 km SW of Dubbo or 3 km N of Parkes. Combined truck stop
HEMA 36 E3 33 6 45 S 148 10 30 E
BIG RIG

817 Kelly Reserve
39
Rest Area at Parkes. N end of town. Beside lake
HEMA 36 E3 33 7 28 S 148 10 23 E
BIG RIG

818 Parkes Showground
☎ (02) 6862 2580
Camp Area at Parkes. Victoria St. Not available during show August or Elvis Festival 1-14 Jan
HEMA 36 E3 33 7 52 S 148 9 47 E
BIG RIG

819 Trundle Showgrounds
☎ (02) 6892 1025
Camp Area at Trundle Showgrounds, Austral St. Must collect key & pay fee at Lucky Seven store. AH phone number (02) 6892 1183
HEMA 36 E2 32 55 33 S 147 42 6 E
BIG RIG

820 Fifield Hotel
☎ (02) 6892 7276
Camp Spot at Fifield, behind hotel. See publican for parking area, limited space. Fee for showers & power
HEMA 36 D1 32 48 25 S 147 27 28 E
48

821 Tullamore Showground
☎ (02) 6892 5194
Camp Area at Tullamore. Cornet St, camping at end of road. Keys & registration at Tullamore Hotel
HEMA 36 D2 32 37 39 S 147 34 11 E
BIG RIG

Notes...

822 Forbes Lions Park
Rest Area at Forbes. Cnr of Lachlan St & Junction St. 500m S of PO, beside lake
HEMA 36 F3 33 23 22 S 148 0 14 E
BIG RIG

823 Wheogo Park
Rest Area at Forbes. Cnr Junction St & Show St. Self Contained Vehicles only
HEMA 36 F3 33 23 16 S 148 0 5 E
BIG RIG 48

824 Jemalong Weir
Picnic Area 24 km W of Forbes or 76 km E of Condobolin. On Lachlan Valley Way. Facilities inside reserve
HEMA 36 F2 33 24 2 S 147 46 40 E

825 Straneys Bridge
Camp Spot 37 km W of Forbes or 63 km E of Condobolin. On Lachlan Valley Way, beside river
HEMA 36 F2 33 22 19 S 147 39 13 E
BIG RIG

826 Bundaburrah Rest Area
39
Rest Area 31 km SW of Forbes or 71 km NE of Wyalong
HEMA 36 G2 33 31 20 S 147 44 0 E
BIG RIG

827 Marsden Rest Area
39
Rest Area 67 km SW of Forbes or 35 km NE of Wyalong. 1 km S of Hwy 24 jcn, near Bland Creek
HEMA 36 G2 33 45 46 S 147 31 14 E
BIG RIG

828 West Wyalong Showground
☎ 0428 518 329
24
Camp Area at West Wyalong. Entry by Duffs Rd only off the West Wyalong Bypass Rd
HEMA 43 F12 33 56 18 S 147 12 50 E
BIG RIG

829 Barmedman Mineral Pool
85
Parking Area at Barmedman, opposite mineral pool. Cnr Nobbys Rd & Goldfield Way. Donation welcome
HEMA 43 F12 34 8 21 S 147 23 7 E
BIG RIG 24

830 Barmedman Recreation Ground
Camp Area at Barmedman, Cnr DeBoors St & Star St. Check notice board for fee payment & contact number
HEMA 43 F12 34 8 34 S 147 23 16 E

831 Temora Caravan Park
☎ 0418 780 251
Caravan Park at Temora. Junee Rd
HEMA 43 F12 34 27 22 S 147 32 5 E
BIG RIG

NEW SOUTH WALES

832 Temora Showground
☎ (02) 6977 1801

Camp Area at Temora. Entry via Mimosa St. Caretaker collects fees

HEMA 43 F12 | 34 26 23 S | 147 31 17 E

BIG RIG

833 Ariah Park Camping Area
☎ 0458 184 033

Camp Area at Ariah Park. 33 km E of Ardlethan or 39 km W of Temora. 1 km N of Hwy. Maximum stay 14 days

HEMA 43 F12 | 34 21 8 S | 147 13 9 E

BIG RIG

834 Royal Hotel

39

Camp Area at Mirrool at hotel. Limited opening hours. 300m W of Hwy

HEMA 43 F12 | 34 18 26 S | 147 5 19 E

BIG RIG

835 Beckom Rest Area

Rest Area 5 km E of Beckom, 52 km S of West Wyalong or 16 km E of Ardlethan

HEMA 43 F11 | 34 20 9 S | 147 0 53 E

BIG RIG

836 BP Roadhouse Beckom
☎ (02) 6978 2329

Camp Area at BP Roadhouse. Newell Hwy. 500m W of Beckom turnoff. Fee for powered sites

HEMA 43 F11 | 34 19 53 S | 146 57 31 E

BIG RIG

837 Ardlethan Community Park

Rest Area at Ardlethan. On main street, next to bowling club. Power available for a fee. Self Contained Vehicles only

HEMA 43 F11 | 34 21 28 S | 146 54 9 E

BIG RIG 72

838 X Roads Van Park
☎ 02 6920 0166

Caravan Park at Collingullie next to hotel

HEMA 43 G12 | 35 5 16 S | 147 7 30 E

BIG RIG

839 'The Kelpie' Caravan Park
☎ (02) 6978 2396

Caravan Park at Ardlethan. Stewart St. 1 km NW of PO. Payment & keys from IGA

HEMA 43 F11 | 34 21 10 S | 146 53 59 E

BIG RIG

840 Ardlethan Rest Area

39

Rest Area 14 km S of Ardlethan or 55 km NE of Narrandera

HEMA 43 F11 | 34 26 50 S | 146 50 20 E

BIG RIG

841 Firetail Rest Area

Rest Area 42 km S of Ardlethan or 5 km N of Grong Grong. Share with trucks

HEMA 43 F11 | 34 41 36 S | 146 47 12 E

BIG RIG 24

842 Grong Grong Park
☎ (02) 6956 2101

Picnic Area 47 km S of Ardlethan or 23 km E of Narrandera. Parking adjacent. Ask at store, donation welcomed for upkeep

HEMA 43 F11 | 34 44 19 S | 146 46 59 E

BIG RIG 24

843 Grong Grong Royal Hotel
☎ (02) 6956 2117

Camp Spot at Grong Grong, rear of hotel. Check with publican for parking. Gold coin donation for shower

HEMA 43 F11 | 34 44 24 S | 146 46 58 E

BIG RIG

844 Berembed Weir

Camp Spot 19 km S of Grong Grong, signposted track, 12 km dirt road. Follow road across weir to campspots. Toilets at picnic area. Beside Murrumbidgee River

HEMA 43 G11 | 34 52 47 S | 146 50 8 E

845 Gillenbah Rest Area

39

Rest Area 12 km SW of Narrandera or 98 km NE of Jerilderie. Share with trucks

HEMA 43 G11 | 34 48 54 S | 146 28 42 E

BIG RIG

846 Widgiewa Rest Area

39

Rest Area 51 km SW of Narrandera or 59 km NE of Jerilderie

HEMA 43 G10 | 35 3 21 S | 146 10 45 E

BIG RIG

847 Sandside Rest Area

39

Rest Area 53 km SW of Narrandera or 57 km NE of Jerilderie. Share with trucks

HEMA 43 G10 | 35 3 39 S | 146 9 47 E

BIG RIG

848 Bundure Rest Area

39

Rest Area 71 km SW of Narrandera or 39 km NE of Jerilderie. Share with trucks

HEMA 43 G10 | 35 9 1 S | 146 0 36 E

BIG RIG

849 Urana Caravan Park & Aquatic Centre
☎ (02) 6920 8192

Caravan Park at Urana. Corowa Rd. 1 km S of PO. Beside lake

HEMA 43 H10 | 35 20 18 S | 146 16 23 E

BIG RIG

850 Conargo

Parking Area at Conargo. Parking bays adjacent tennis courts

HEMA 43 H8 | 35 18 18 S | 145 10 53 E

BIG RIG

851 Bills Park
☎ (03) 5880 1200

Rest Area at Conargo. W end of town, near school

HEMA 43 H8 | 35 18 24 S | 145 10 38 E

852 Jerilderie South Rest Area
39

Rest Area 8 km S of Jerilderie or 28 km N of Finley

HEMA 43 H9 | 35 25 1 S | 145 41 28 E

853 Daysdale Recreation Reserve

Camp Area at Daysdale. 1 km N of Daysdale Hotel on Federation Way. Gold coin for use of shower

HEMA 43 H10 | 35 38 7 S | 146 18 17 E

854 Tongabo Rest Area
39

Rest Area 27 km S of Jerilderie or 9 km N of Finley

HEMA 43 H9 | 35 34 24 S | 145 36 56 E

855 Finley Lakeside Caravan Park
39

☎ (03) 5883 1170

Caravan Park at Finley. Newell Hwy. 2 km N of PO

HEMA 43 H9 | 35 38 3 S | 145 34 49 E

856 Finley Showgrounds
☎ 0417 495 245

Camp Area at Finley. Enter via Tongs St. See caretaker for keys & payment

HEMA 43 J9 | 35 39 0 S | 145 34 9 E

857 Berrigan Lions Caravan Park
58

☎ 0400 563 979

Caravan Park at Berrigan. Jerilderie St. 1 km S of PO

HEMA 43 J9 | 35 39 37 S | 145 48 49 E

858 Town Beach
39

☎ (03) 5874 2517

Camp Area at Tocumwal. From Tocumwal - Corawa Rd turn W onto Hennessy St then S on Town Beach Rd. 700m dirt road. Cold showers. Caretaker on site. Maximum stay 6 weeks. Beside river

HEMA 43 J9 | 35 49 6 S | 145 33 43 E

859 Sonnermans Travelling Stock Reserve
☎ 03 5874 2517

Camp Area 3 km W of Tocumal. Entrance off Tuppal Rd. Premit required from Tocumal Info Centre

HEMA 43 J9 | 35 48 9 S | 145 32 20 E

Notes...

Hebel to Gilgandra

Castlereagh Highway

860 Bore Baths - Lightning Ridge

Rest Area at Lightning Ridge. Cnr Opal St & Pandora St. Hot bore baths

HEMA 41 B13 | 29 25 22 S | 147 59 52 E

861 Crocodile Caravan Park
☎ (02) 6829 0437

Caravan Park at Lightning Ridge. Morilla St. 500m W of PO

HEMA 41 B13 | 29 25 45 S | 147 58 30 E

862 Lightning Ridge Tourist Park
☎ (02) 6829 0532

Caravan Park at Lightning Ridge. Harlequin St. 200m SE of PO

HEMA 41 B13 | 29 25 42 S | 147 58 54 E

863 Lorne Holiday Station
☎ (02) 6829 0253

Camp Area at Lorne Station. 5 km S of Lightning Ridge. Turn off 3 km S on Opal St - Lorne Rd. Mobile 0418 211 024

HEMA 41 B13 | 29 27 44 S | 147 58 33 E

864 The Sheepyard Inn
☎ (02) 6829 3932

Camp Area at Grawin. Approx 73 km W of Lightning Ridge via Cumborah & Walgett Goodooga Rd. Self Contained Vehicles only

HEMA 41 C13 | 29 41 20 S | 147 37 41 E

865 Glengarry Hilton
☎ (02) 6829 3983

Camp Area 75 km W of Lighting Ridge Via Cumborah & Walgett Goodooga Rd

HEMA 41 C13 | 29 40 11 S | 147 36 56 E

866 Wingadee Rest Area
55

Rest Area 53 km S of Walgett or 62 km N of Coonamble. 4 km S of Combogolong

HEMA 41 E14 | 30 28 5 S | 148 11 40 E

867 Quambone Primitive Camp Site
☎ (02) 6827 1923

Camp Area at Quambone. Mungie St near swimming pool & tennis courts. Keys for pool & courts at Quambone General Store, hours 0800 - 1900 hrs

HEMA 41 E13 | 30 56 1 S | 147 52 16 E

868 John Oxley Rest Area

Rest Area 32 km S of Coonamble or 13 km N of Gulargambone

HEMA 41 F14 | 31 13 36 S | 148 27 25 E

869 Gulargambone Rest Area

Rest Area 42 km S of Coonamble or 3 km N of Gulargambone

HEMA 41 F14 31 18 20 S 148 28 8 E

BIG RIG

870 Gulargambone Caravan Park

☎ (02) 6825 1666

Caravan Park at Gulargambone. Skulthorpe St

55

HEMA 38 J1 31 19 51 S 148 28 12 E

$ BIG RIG

Bathurst to Broken Hill

Mitchell and Barrier Highways

871 The Rocks Rest Area

Rest Area 20 km W of Bathurst or 34 SE of Orange

32

HEMA 36 F6 33 25 56 S 149 22 48 E

872 Macquarie Woods

☎ (02) 6331 2044

Vittoria State Forest

Camp Area 28 km W of Bathurst or 26 km SE of Orange. 2 km N of Hwy on Cashens Lane, dirt road

HEMA 36 F6 33 24 34 S 149 18 44 E

BIG RIG

873 Shadforth Reserve

Rest Area 40 km NW of Bathurst or 4 km SE of Lucknow. Cnr of Mitchell Hwy & Millthorpe Rd

32

HEMA 36 F5 33 22 31 S 149 11 18 E

874 Colour City Caravan Park

☎ (02) 6362 7254

Caravan Park at Orange. 203 Margaret St. Beside showground

HEMA 36 F5 33 16 19 S 149 6 33 E

$+ BIG RIG

875 Cudal Caravan Park

☎ (02) 6390 7100

Caravan Park at Cudal. Main St. 400m E of PO

HEMA 36 F4 33 17 3 S 148 44 39 E

$

876 Manildra Showground

☎ 0428 697 685

Camp Area at Manildra. Entry off Orange St. Fees collected

HEMA 36 F4 33 10 38 S 148 41 16 E

$ BIG RIG 96

877 Ophir Reserve

☎ 1800 069 466

Camp Area 26 km NE of Orange. At Ophir goldfields. Steep sections. Best entry from the S. Obtain permit from Orange Visitor Centre

HEMA 36 F5 33 10 10 S 149 14 21 E

$

878 Gamboola Rest Area

Rest Area 17 km NW of Orange or 17 km SE of Molong

32

HEMA 36 F5 33 9 44 S 149 0 36 E

BIG RIG

879 Bell River Rest Area

Rest Area 22 km N of Molong or 41 km S of Wellington. E side of Hwy

32

HEMA 36 E5 32 54 42 S 148 53 27 E

BIG RIG

880 Two Mile Creek Rest Area

Rest Area 31 km N of Molong or 32 km S of Wellington. W side of Hwy

32

HEMA 36 E5 32 50 3 S 148 54 27 E

BIG RIG

881 Cumnock Showgrounds

☎ 0403 054 754

Camp Area at Cumnock, 21 km NW of Molong or 90 km SE of Dubbo. Key at General Store or hotel after hours

HEMA 36 E4 32 55 43 S 148 44 46 E

$ BIG RIG

882 Yeoval Showground

☎ (02) 6846 4190

Camp Spot at Yeoval. 45 km NW of Molong or 40 km SW of Wellington. Warne St

HEMA 36 D4 32 44 37 S 148 38 42 E

$ BIG RIG

883 Caves Turnoff Rest Area

Rest Area 56 km N of Molong or 9 km S of Wellington. Near Wellington Caves turnoff

32

HEMA 36 D5 32 37 23 S 148 56 51 E

884 Lake Burrendong Holiday Park

☎ (02) 6846 7435

Camp Area 7 km NE of Mumbil or 27 km SE of Wellington, via Burrendong Dam Rd

HEMA 36 D5 32 41 24 S 149 6 29 E

$+ BIG RIG

885 Mookerawa Waters Holiday Park

☎ (02) 6846 8426

Camp Area 11 km E of Stuart Town or 39 km SE of Wellington

5

HEMA 36 D5 32 45 58 S 149 9 27 E

$+ BIG RIG

886 Ponto Falls

Camp Area 19 km NW of Wellington. Turn W off Mitchell Hwy 10 km NW of Wellington or 11 km S of Geurie. 5 km dirt road. Beside river. Maximum stay 14 days

HEMA 36 C5 32 27 57 S 148 49 12 E

BIG RIG

887 Geurie North Rest Area

Rest Area 2 km N of Geurie or 26 km SE of Dubbo

32

HEMA 36 C5 32 23 17 S 148 48 57 E

BIG RIG

888 Macks Reserve

Camp Spot 4 km N of Narromine. Turn N off Mitchell Hwy onto Warren Rd for 3.5 km, then turn E at signpost, follow track to river, various campspots beside Macquarie River

HEMA 36 C3 32 11 45 S 148 14 46 E

889 Tandara Caravan Park
☎(02) 6888 7330

Caravan Park at Trangie. 55 John St. 2 km S of PO

HEMA 36 B3 32 2 11 S 147 58 46 E

BIG RIG

890 Rabbit Trap Hotel
☎(02) 6892 8201

Camp Area at Albert. 55 km SW of Trangie or 67 km N of Trundle. Cabins also available. Donation for use of showers, limited power available for a fee

HEMA 36 C2 32 21 25 S 147 30 29 E

891 The State Centre Caravan Park
☎(02) 6892 4126

Caravan Park at Tottenham. Tullamore Rd

HEMA 36 C1 32 14 44 S 147 21 50 E

BIG RIG

892 Nyngan Leisure & Van Park
☎(02) 6832 2366

Caravan Park at Nyngan. S end of town, via Hospital Rd, Old Warren Rd

HEMA 41 G12 31 34 0 S 147 12 29 E

BIG RIG

893 Mid-State Shearing Shed Car Park

Parking Area in Nyngan. Nymagee St. Not suitable for tents or camper trailers

HEMA 41 G12 31 33 44 S 147 11 49 E

BIG RIG 24

894 Teamsters Rest Area

Rest Area at Nyngan. Self Contained Vehicles only. Limited space

HEMA 41 G12 31 33 43 S 147 11 40 E

24

895 Hermidale West Rest Area

Rest Area 1.5 km W of Hermidale

HEMA 41 G11 31 32 53 S 146 42 28 E

BIG RIG

896 Florida Rest Area

32

Rest Area 82 km W of Nyngan or 50 km E of Cobar

HEMA 41 G10 31 31 56 S 146 21 5 E

BIG RIG

897 Cornish (Cobar) Rest Area

32

Rest Area at Cobar. 500m S of Info Centre. Share with trucks, park on grass area behind toilet to keep away from truck parking area. Self Contained Vehicles only

HEMA 41 G9 31 29 57 S 145 50 41 E

BIG RIG 24

Notes...

898 Louth Camp Spot

Camp Spot at Louth beside Darling River. Turn W go over bridge, camping on S side of river. Showers at park opposite hotel for gold coin donation

HEMA 41 E8 30 32 7 S 145 6 45 E

899 Trilby Station
☎(02) 6874 7420

Camp Area Trilby Station. 160 km NW of Cobar via Louth or 141 km SW of Bourke via Louth. W bank of the Bourke to Wilcannia Rd

HEMA 41 E8 30 38 20 S 144 56 34 E

BIG RIG

900 Idalia Outback River Stay
☎(02) 6874 7401

Camp Area 43 km SW of Louth or 47 km NE of Tilpa on W bank section of Bourke to Wilcannia Rd. 600m from turnoff to Homestead Office. Pets by prior arrangement

HEMA 41 E8 30 43 51 S 144 46 37 E

901 Kallara Station
☎(02) 6837 3963

Camp Area at Kallara Station. 208 km NW of Cobar via Louth or 202 km SW of Bourke via Louth. Signed turn off 80 km SW of Louth or 10 km NE of Tilps on the W bank section of Burke to Wilcannia Rd. 2 km from turn off to Homestead Office

HEMA 40 E7 30 53 27 S 144 30 55 E

BIG RIG

902 Meadow Glen Rest Area

32

Rest Area 63 km W of Cobar or 196 km E of Wilcannia. Site off tracks

HEMA 41 G8 31 33 33 S 145 11 16 E

BIG RIG

903 Bulla Park Rest Area

32

Rest Area 119 km W of Cobar or 140 km E of Wilcannia

HEMA 40 G7 31 33 30 S 144 37 35 E

BIG RIG

904 Emmdale Roadhouse
☎(02) 6837 3979

32

Parking Area 159 km W of Cobar or 100 km E of Wilcannia. Limited power available

HEMA 40 G7 31 39 11 S 144 16 6 E

BIG RIG

905 Baden Park Rest Area

32

Rest Area 172 km W of Cobar or 89 km E of Wilcannia

HEMA 40 G6 31 42 50 S 144 8 34 E

BIG RIG

906 MacCullochs Range Rest Area

32

Rest Area 204 km W of Cobar or 55 km E of Wilcannia

HEMA 40 G6 31 41 42 S 143 48 53 E

BIG RIG

907 Caltigeena Rest Area
Rest Area 212 km W of Cobar or 48 km E of Wilcannia
HEMA 40 G6 31 41 43 S 143 44 23 E
32
BIG RIG

908 Wilcannia South Rest Area
Rest Area 250 km W of Cobar or 9 km SE of Wilcannia
HEMA 40 G5 31 37 21 S 143 24 43 E
32
BIG RIG

909 Coach & Horses Campground
☎ (08) 8083 7900
Paroo - Darling National Park
Camp Area 52 km NE of Wilcannia or 282 km SW of Bourke on the Bourke - Wilcannia Rd. E side of Darling River
HEMA 40 G6 31 27 23 S 143 49 37 E
$ BIG RIG

910 Warrawong on the Darling
☎ 1300 688 225
Camp Area 3 km S of Wilcannia. Barrier Hwy
HEMA 40 G5 31 34 3 S 143 23 39 E
$ BIG RIG

911 Old Buckanbe Station
☎ (02) 6837 3940
Camp Area at Old Buckanbe Station. 7 km SW of Tilpa. 140 km NE of Wilcannia or 199 km SW of Bourke. E side of Darling River
HEMA 40 F7 30 59 12 S 144 22 54 E
$ BIG RIG

912 Tilpa Weir
☎ (02) 6837 3928
Camp Spot 6 km NE of Tilpa on E side of Darling River. 139 km NE of Wilcannia or 186 km SW of Bourke
HEMA 40 F7 30 55 10 S 144 27 29 E
BIG RIG

913 Wanaaring Store & Caravan Park
☎ (02) 6874 7720
Camp Area at Wanaaring 192 km W Bourke or 234 km E Tibooburra
HEMA 40 C6 29 42 9 S 144 8 57 E
$ BIG RIG

914 Opal Pioneer Caravan & Camping Tourist Park
☎ (08) 8091 6688
Caravan Park at White Cliffs. Johnston St. 200m N of PO
HEMA 40 E5 30 50 58 S 143 5 23 E
$

915 Netallie Rest Area
Rest Area 18 km W of Wilcannia or 176 km E of Broken Hill
HEMA 40 G5 31 34 7 S 143 13 0 E
32
BIG RIG

916 Dolo Rest Area
Rest Area 60 km W of Wilcannia or 136 km E of Broken Hill
HEMA 40 G4 31 40 23 S 142 48 47 E
32
BIG RIG

917 Spring Hill Rest Area
Rest Area 74 km W of Wilcannia or 122 km E of Broken Hill
HEMA 40 G4 31 43 23 S 142 41 9 E
32
BIG RIG

918 Little Topar Roadhouse
Rest Area 128 km W of Wilcannia or 76 km E of Broken Hill
HEMA 40 H3 31 46 47 S 142 13 39 E
32
BIG RIG

919 Round Hill Rest Area
Rest Area 190 km W of Wilcannia or 6 km E of Broken Hill. Combined truck stop
HEMA 40 H2 31 56 15 S 141 31 6 E
32
BIG RIG

920 Broken Hill Racecourse
☎ 0437 250 286
Camp Area 5 km NE of Broken Hill, Racecourse Rd, off Tibooburra Rd. See caretaker before parking. Self Contained Vehicles only
HEMA 40 H2 31 54 48 S 141 28 51 E
32
$+ BIG RIG

921 Eldee Station
Camp Area at Eldee Station. 52 km NW of Broken Hill
HEMA 40 G1 31 40 10 S 141 15 33 E
$+ BIG RIG

922 Umberumberka Reservoir
Parking Area 36 km WNW of Broken Hill via Silverton
HEMA 40 H1 31 48 53 S 141 12 33 E

923 Penrose Park
☎ (08) 8088 5307
Camp Area at Silverton, 24 km NW of Broken Hill
HEMA 40 H1 31 52 57 S 141 13 55 E
$ BIG RIG

924 Thackaringa Rest Area
Rest Area 36 km W of Broken Hill or 14 km E of Cockburn
HEMA 40 H1 32 2 44 S 141 7 39 E
32
BIG RIG

Barringun to Jerilderie
Kidman Way

925 Bush Tucker Inn
☎ (02) 6874 7584
Camp Area at Barringun. Check in at office. Mitchell Hwy
HEMA 41 A9 29 0 36 S 145 42 44 E
71
$ BIG RIG

926 Comeroo Camel Station
☎ (02) 6874 7735
Camp Area at Comeroo Station. 150 km NW of Bourke. 20 km off Bourke - Hungerford Rd or 80 km W of Enngonia. Dirt road
HEMA 41 B8 29 14 36 S 145 8 23 E

927 Oasis Hotel Enngonia
☎ (02) 6874 7577
71
Camp Area at Enngonia. Register & pay at the bar for access to secure parking
HEMA 41 B9 29 19 14 S 145 50 46 E

928 Enngonia South Rest Area
71
Rest Area 70 km S of Barringun or 66 km N of Bourke
HEMA 41 C9 29 35 10 S 145 50 32 E

929 Warrego Pub
☎ (02) 6874 7877
Camp Area at Fords Bridge 70 km NW of Burke or 145 km SE of Hungerford on Bourke - Hungerford Rd
HEMA 41 C9 29 45 9 S 145 25 30 E

930 Mitchell Caravan Park
☎ (02) 6872 2791
Caravan Park at Bourke. Mitchell St. 2 Becker St, 1 km E of Tourist Centre
HEMA 41 D10 30 5 25 S 145 56 59 E

931 Kinchela Rest Area
87
Rest Area 41 km S of Bourke or 120 km N of Cobar
HEMA 41 D10 30 27 27 S 145 56 7 E

932 Dry Tank Campground
☎ (02) 6830 0200
Gundabooka National Park
87
Camp Area 49 km S of Bourke or 111 km N of Cobar. Turn W for 18 km to campsites. Dirt road. Bookings essential
HEMA 41 E9 30 31 4 S 145 42 53 E

933 Yanda Campground
☎ (02) 6830 0200
Gundabooka National Park
Camp Area 46 km S of Bourke or 114 km N of Cobar. Turn W off Louth Rd opposite Telstra tower, follow signs to campground. GPS at turn off
HEMA 41 E9 30 19 28 S 145 36 21 E

Notes...

934 Curraweena Rest Area
87
Rest Area 61 km S of Bourke or 100 km N of Cobar
HEMA 41 E9 30 38 16 S 145 52 20 E

935 Four Corners Farm Stay
☎ 0438 683 626
Camp Area 8 km S of Nymagee township on Burthong Rd. Cabins also available
HEMA 41 H10 32 9 2 S 146 18 7 E

936 Gilgunnia Rest Area
87
Rest Area at Gilgunnia
HEMA 41 J10 32 25 4 S 146 2 5 E

937 Royal Hotel
☎ (02) 6897 7988
Camp Spot at Mt Hope. 161 km S of Cobar or 94 km N of Hillston. Camp area S of hotel or shared with trucks opposite
HEMA 43 B10 32 50 24 S 145 52 47 E

938 Mt Hope Community Hall
Parking Area at Mt Hope. 161 km S of Cobar or 94 km N of Hilston. Fees & power arranged at Mt Hope Hotel
HEMA 43 B10 32 50 19 S 145 52 44 E

939 Lachlan River Rest Area
Rest Area 219 km S of Cobar or 36 km N of Hillston. Beside old bridge
HEMA 43 C9 33 20 29 S 145 50 10 E

940 Billabourie Riverside Tourist Park
☎ 0427 674 131
Caravan Park 48 km NE of Hillston. Turn E 38 km N of Hillston at Coopers Bridge into Mt Grace Rd (Wallanthery Rd). Entry 10 km along road. Signposted
HEMA 43 C10 33 22 32 S 145 55 38 E

941 Hillston Rest Area
Rest Area 1.5 km S of Hillston. Shared with trucks
HEMA 43 D9 33 30 15 S 145 31 56 E

942 Group Campground
☎ (02) 6966 8100
Willandra National Park
Camp Area 62 km NW of Hillston, via Hillston-Mossgeil Rd. Dirt road
HEMA 43 C8 33 11 36 S 145 7 5 E

943 Lake View Caravan Park
☎ (02) 6898 1077
Caravan Park at Lake Cargelligo. Cnr of Naradhan St & Wonboyn St. 1 km SE of PO
HEMA 43 C10 33 18 8 S 146 22 39 E

944 Frog Hollow
☎ (02) 6898 1501

Camp Spot at Lake Cargelligo. 1.5 km SE of PO, via Canada St & Narrandera St. Turn R at foreshore, beside lake

HEMA 43 C10 33 18 16 S 146 22 57 E

BIG RIG

945 Dead Mans Point
☎ (02) 6898 1501

Parking Area 3.5 km NE of Lake Cargelligo, via Canada St & Uabba St. Beside lake

HEMA 43 C10 33 16 46 S 146 23 44 E

946 Cargelligo Weir
☎ (02) 6898 1009

Camp Area 22 km NE of Lake Cargelligo. Sites along river. Turn N off Condobolin Rd 7 km E of PO onto Weir Rd. 9 km dirt road. Over grids, various sites along river

HEMA 43 C11 33 12 3 S 146 27 13 E

947 Euabalong Campground
☎ (02) 6836 5888

Camp Area at Euabalong. 28 km N of Lake Cargelligo. Signposted "Caravan Park". Fee payable at hotel for key to access toilet/shower

HEMA 43 C11 33 6 42 S 146 28 20 E

BIG RIG

948 Booberoi Weir
☎ (02) 6836 5888

Camp Spot 20 km NE of Euabalong or 56 km W of Condobolin. Access from Euabalong via Euabalong West Rd & Booberoi Rd (15 km dirt) or from Condobolin via Kiacatoo Rd & Euabalong West Rd. Turn S opposite radio tower for 1 km to river

HEMA 43 C11 33 2 13 S 146 38 36 E

949 Gum Bend Lake
☎ (02) 6895 4444

Camp Area 4 km W of Condobolin, via Bathurst St. Dogs in signed area only

HEMA 43 C12 33 4 41 S 147 6 0 E

BIG RIG

950 River View Caravan Park
☎ (02) 6895 2611

Caravan Park at Condobolin. Diggers Ave. S end of town

HEMA 43 C12 33 5 40 S 147 8 50 E

BIG RIG

951 Wallaroi Creek Rest Area

Rest Area 15 km S of Condobolin or 90 km N of West Wyalong. Beside creek

HEMA 43 C12 33 12 34 S 147 6 10 E

BIG RIG

952 Burcher Camping Ground
☎ (02) 6972 5244

Camp Area at Burcher. Kurrajong St

HEMA 43 D12 33 31 0 S 147 15 7 E

BIG RIG

953 Ungarie Showground

Camp Area at Ungarie. Crown Camp Rd, entrance beyond school. Collect key from Ampol Service Station, Main St. Gold coin donation

HEMA 43 D11 33 38 7 S 146 58 43 E

BIG RIG

954 Tullibigeal Sportsground
☎ (02) 6972 9176

Camp Spot at Tullibigeal. 44 km SE of Lake Cargelligo or 82 km NW of West Wyalong. Call ahead during office hours to arrange keys. Fee for showers

HEMA 43 D11 33 25 0 S 146 43 28 E

BIG RIG

955 Tullibigeal Pioneer Park
☎ (02) 6972 9176

Rest Area at Tullibigeal, 44 km SE of Lake Cargelligo or 82 km NW of West Wyalong

HEMA 43 D11 33 25 16 S 146 43 40 E

BIG RIG

956 Woolshed Flat
☎ (02) 6966 8100

Cocoparra National Park

Camp Area 25 km NE of Griffith. Access via Mackay Ave, Yenda Rd, N along Myall Park Rd (Whitton Stock Route) then E onto Mt Bingar Rd. Signposted. Some dirt road

HEMA 43 E10 34 4 45 S 146 13 26 E

957 Lake Wyangan
☎ (02) 6962 4145

Camp Area 8 km NW of Griffith. From Main St via roundabout onto Ulong St, L onto Binya St then onto Wyangan Ave. Cold showers only

HEMA 43 E10 34 12 46 S 146 1 2 E

BIG RIG 72

958 Griffith Showgrounds Caravan Park
☎ 0403 655 123

Caravan Park at Griffith. Cnr Merrigal St & Walla Ave. See notice board for caretaker details & payment

HEMA 43 F10 34 17 25 S 146 1 46 E

BIG RIG

959 Willow Park
☎ (02) 6962 4145

87

Rest Area at Griffith. Walla Ave off Kookora St. 1.5 km W of PO, near TAFE college

HEMA 43 F10 34 17 16 S 146 1 55 E

BIG RIG 24

960 Garoolgan Rest Area

94

Rest Area at Garoolgan. 40 km E of Griffith or 45 km W of Ardlethan

HEMA 43 E11 34 15 10 S 146 26 56 E

BIG RIG

961 Nugan Bend

87

Rest Area 10 km S of Griffith or 24 km N of Darlington Point

HEMA 43 F10 34 22 8 S 146 2 3 E

BIG RIG

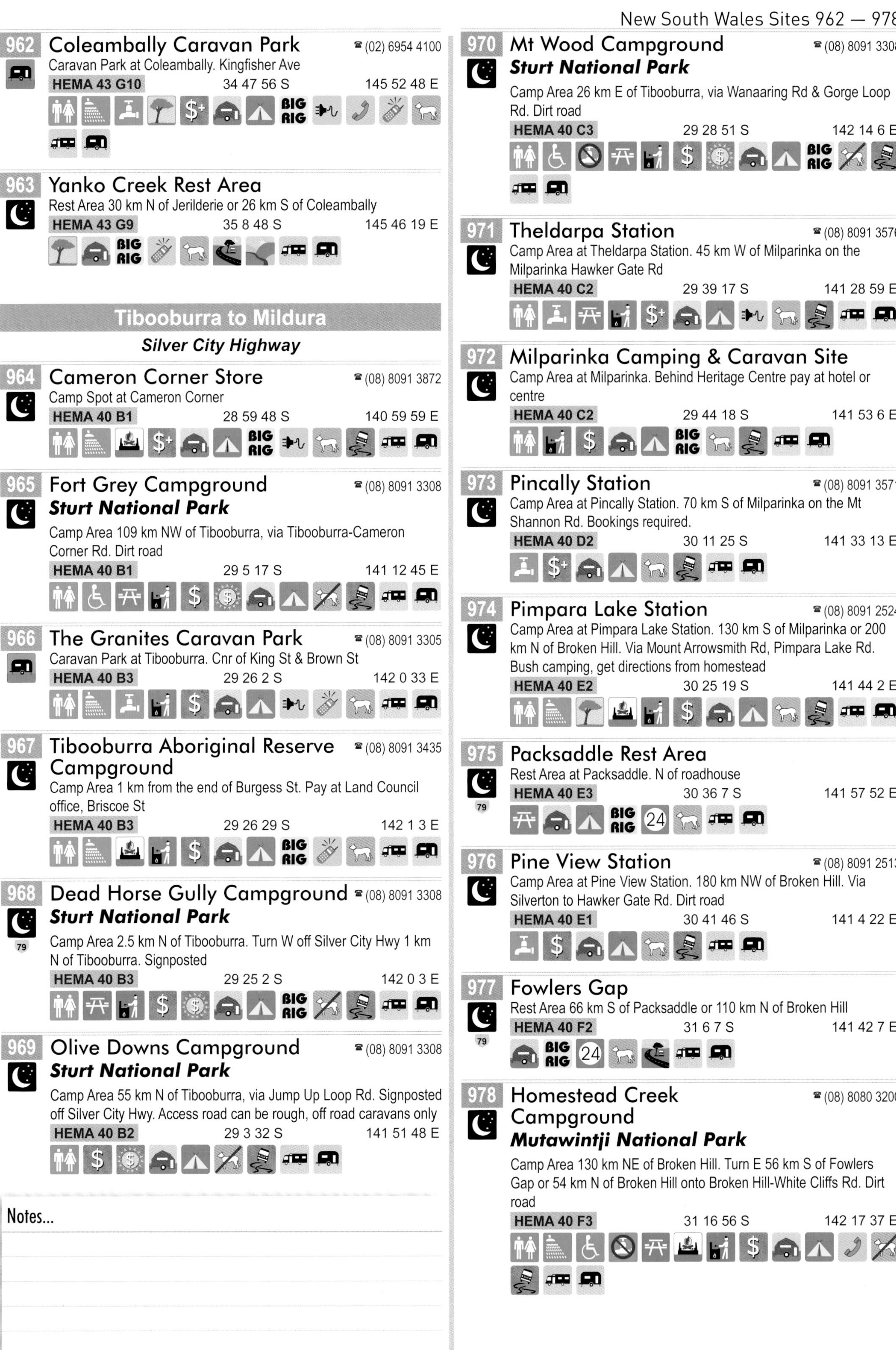

962 **Coleambally Caravan Park** ☎ (02) 6954 4100
Caravan Park at Coleambally. Kingfisher Ave
HEMA 43 G10 34 47 56 S 145 52 48 E

963 **Yanko Creek Rest Area**
Rest Area 30 km N of Jerilderie or 26 km S of Coleambally
HEMA 43 G9 35 8 48 S 145 46 19 E

Tibooburra to Mildura

Silver City Highway

964 **Cameron Corner Store** ☎ (08) 8091 3872
Camp Spot at Cameron Corner
HEMA 40 B1 28 59 48 S 140 59 59 E

965 **Fort Grey Campground** ☎ (08) 8091 3308
Sturt National Park
Camp Area 109 km NW of Tibooburra, via Tibooburra-Cameron Corner Rd. Dirt road
HEMA 40 B1 29 5 17 S 141 12 45 E

966 **The Granites Caravan Park** ☎ (08) 8091 3305
Caravan Park at Tibooburra. Cnr of King St & Brown St
HEMA 40 B3 29 26 2 S 142 0 33 E

967 **Tibooburra Aboriginal Reserve Campground** ☎ (08) 8091 3435
Camp Area 1 km from the end of Burgess St. Pay at Land Council office, Briscoe St
HEMA 40 B3 29 26 29 S 142 1 3 E

968 **Dead Horse Gully Campground** ☎ (08) 8091 3308
Sturt National Park
79
Camp Area 2.5 km N of Tibooburra. Turn W off Silver City Hwy 1 km N of Tibooburra. Signposted
HEMA 40 B3 29 25 2 S 142 0 3 E

969 **Olive Downs Campground** ☎ (08) 8091 3308
Sturt National Park
Camp Area 55 km N of Tibooburra, via Jump Up Loop Rd. Signposted off Silver City Hwy. Access road can be rough, off road caravans only
HEMA 40 B2 29 3 32 S 141 51 48 E

Notes...

970 **Mt Wood Campground** ☎ (08) 8091 3308
Sturt National Park
Camp Area 26 km E of Tibooburra, via Wanaaring Rd & Gorge Loop Rd. Dirt road
HEMA 40 C3 29 28 51 S 142 14 6 E

971 **Theldarpa Station** ☎ (08) 8091 3576
Camp Area at Theldarpa Station. 45 km W of Milparinka on the Milparinka Hawker Gate Rd
HEMA 40 C2 29 39 17 S 141 28 59 E

972 **Milparinka Camping & Caravan Site**
Camp Area at Milparinka. Behind Heritage Centre pay at hotel or centre
HEMA 40 C2 29 44 18 S 141 53 6 E

973 **Pincally Station** ☎ (08) 8091 3571
Camp Area at Pincally Station. 70 km S of Milparinka on the Mt Shannon Rd. Bookings required.
HEMA 40 D2 30 11 25 S 141 33 13 E

974 **Pimpara Lake Station** ☎ (08) 8091 2524
Camp Area at Pimpara Lake Station. 130 km S of Milparinka or 200 km N of Broken Hill. Via Mount Arrowsmith Rd, Pimpara Lake Rd. Bush camping, get directions from homestead
HEMA 40 E2 30 25 19 S 141 44 2 E

975 **Packsaddle Rest Area**
79
Rest Area at Packsaddle. N of roadhouse
HEMA 40 E3 30 36 7 S 141 57 52 E

976 **Pine View Station** ☎ (08) 8091 2513
Camp Area at Pine View Station. 180 km NW of Broken Hill. Via Silverton to Hawker Gate Rd. Dirt road
HEMA 40 E1 30 41 46 S 141 4 22 E

977 **Fowlers Gap**
79
Rest Area 66 km S of Packsaddle or 110 km N of Broken Hill
HEMA 40 F2 31 6 7 S 141 42 7 E

978 **Homestead Creek Campground** ☎ (08) 8080 3200
Mutawintji National Park
Camp Area 130 km NE of Broken Hill. Turn E 56 km S of Fowlers Gap or 54 km N of Broken Hill onto Broken Hill-White Cliffs Rd. Dirt road
HEMA 40 F3 31 16 56 S 142 17 37 E

NEW SOUTH WALES

979 Mount Gipps Station
☎ (08) 8091 3537

Camp Area at Mount Gipps Station. 40 km N of Broken Hill. Via Corona Rd. Dirt road. Bookings preferred. Permission required for pets

HEMA 40 G2 | 31 37 47 S | 141 33 25 E

980 Lake Pamamaroo Campsites
☎ (08) 8091 4274

Camp Spots along Lake Pamamaroo. 16 km NE of Menindee. Turn E off Menindee-Broken Hill Rd 8 km N of Menindee onto Main Weir Rd. Various spots along lake

HEMA 42 A4 | 32 18 59 S | 142 27 58 E

BIG RIG

981 Burke and Wills Campground
☎ (08) 8091 4274

Camp Area 18 km NE of Menindee. Turn E off Menindee-Broken Hill Rd 8 km N of Menindee onto Main Weir Rd. Beside Darling River

HEMA 42 A4 | 32 18 18 S | 142 29 55 E

982 Main Weir Campground
☎ (08) 8091 4274

Camp Area 19 km NE of Menindee. Turn E off Menindee-Broken Hill Rd 8 km N of Menindee onto Main Weir Rd. Beside Darling River

HEMA 42 A4 | 32 18 49 S | 142 30 26 E

BIG RIG

983 Nelia Gaari Station
☎ (08) 8091 6496

Camp Area at Nelia Gaari Station. 80 km E of Menindee or 90 km W of Wilcannia

HEMA 42 A4 | 32 6 8 S | 142 51 4 E

BIG RIG

984 Menindee Lakes Caravan Park
☎ (08) 8091 4315

Caravan Park 5 km NW of Menindee. Menindee Lakes Shore Dr

HEMA 42 B3 | 32 21 15 S | 142 24 12 E

BIG RIG

985 Menindee Bridge Caravan Park
☎ (08) 8091 4282

Caravan Park at Menindee. Pooncarie Rd

HEMA 42 B3 | 32 23 59 S | 142 24 48 E

BIG RIG

986 River Drive Campgrounds
☎ (08) 8080 3200

Kinchega National Park

Camp Area 4.5 km SW of Menindee. 34 sites beside Darling River via River Dr, first site starts at park entry point. Showers & bore water available at the Shearer's Quarters at the historic woolshed, gold coin for use

HEMA 42 B3 | 32 23 52 S | 142 22 24 E

987 Lake Cawndilla Campground
☎ (08) 8080 3200

Kinchega National Park

Camp Area 21 km SW of Menindee. Turn off Menindee-Pooncarie Rd onto Lake Dr, signposted. Showers & bore water available at the Shearer's Quarters at the historic woolshed, gold coin for use

HEMA 42 B3 | 32 26 5 S | 142 15 7 E

988 Emu Lake Campground
☎ (08) 8080 3200

Kinchega National Park

Camp Area 24 km S of Menindee. Turn off Menindee-Pooncarie Rd onto Emu Lake Dr, signposted. Showers & bore water available at the Shearer's Quarters at the historic woolshed, gold coin for use

HEMA 42 B3 | 32 28 12 S | 142 20 46 E

989 Bindara on the Darling
☎ (08) 8091 7412

Camp Area 92 km N of Pooncarie. Cross the Darling at Pooncarie, after about 3 km turn R at T intersection (Polia Rd). Continue for approx 20 km to the next T intersection & turn R onto Polia/RooRoo Rd. Follow this road approx 68 km to Bindara

HEMA 42 B3 | 32 45 30 S | 142 22 22 E

990 Popiltah Rest Area

79

Rest Area 137 km S of Broken Hill or 129 km N of Wentworth

HEMA 42 C2 | 33 4 2 S | 141 38 37 E

BIG RIG

991 Seven Tree Rest Area

Rest Area 183 km S of Broken Hill or 82 km N of Wentworth. W side of Hwy

HEMA 42 D2 | 33 27 49 S | 141 42 37 E

BIG RIG

992 Bunnerungee Bridge

79

Rest Area 198 km S of Broken Hill or 68 km N of Wentworth. S side of bridge

HEMA 42 D2 | 33 34 50 S | 141 45 21 E

BIG RIG

993 Milpara Rest Area

79

Rest Area 240 km S of Broken Hill or 26 km N of Wentworth. Small vehicles only

HEMA 42 E3 | 33 55 34 S | 141 47 45 E

994 Padda Park
☎ (03) 5029 5205

Camp Area at Pooncarie, 117 km NE of Wentworth. Tarcoola St, beside Darling River. Pay at Telegraph Hotel. Refundable deposit power key

HEMA 42 D4 | 33 22 44 S | 142 33 59 E

BIG RIG

995 Darling Campsites
☎ 0427 816 136

Camp Area 16 km N of Wentworth. Please call ahead to book & arrange access, gate locked. GPS at gate

HEMA 42 E3 | 33 58 40 S | 141 56 51 E

BIG RIG

996 Fort Courage Angling & Caravan Park
☎ (03) 5027 3097

Caravan Park 20 km W of Wentworth on Old Renmark Rd. Beside Murray River

HEMA 42 E2 | 34 5 3 S | 141 43 53 E

997 Willow Bend Caravan Park
☎ (03) 5027 3213

Caravan Park at Wentworth. Darling St. 400m from PO

HEMA 42 E3 | 34 6 36 S | 141 55 12 E

BIG RIG

998 Ramond Deed Veterans Retreat
☎ (03) 5027 4447

Camp Area at Dareton. Scout Rd off Tallawalla Rd. Limited sites bookings essential, this facility is available for ex & current defence personnel only

HEMA 42 E3 | 34 5 58 S | 142 3 43 E

BIG RIG

999 Curlwaa Caravan Park
☎ (03) 5027 6210

79

Caravan Park at Curlwaa. 5 km E of Wentworth

HEMA 42 E3 | 34 6 45 S | 141 59 21 E

BIG RIG

Nyngan to Bourke

Mitchell Highway

1000 Memorial Park

Rest Area at Girilambone. Turn E of Hwy. See signage for access. Overflow parking at hotel, see publican

HEMA 41F11 | 31 14 52 S | 146 54 24 E

BIG RIG

1001 Willie Retreat Macquarie Marshes
☎ (02) 6824 4361

Camp Area 110 km N of Warren or 76 km S of Carinda on the Carinda - Nyngan Rd, turn E into Gibson Way, entrance 1.5 km on the S side of road. Bush camping also available. Pets by prior arrangement

HEMA 41 E12 | 30 53 47 S | 147 29 8 E

BIG RIG

1002 Glenariff Rest Area

71

Rest Area 26 km NW of Coolabah or 25 km SE of Byrock

HEMA 41 E11 | 30 49 51 S | 146 32 46 E

BIG RIG

1003 Mulga Creek Hotel Caravan Park
☎ (02) 6874 7311

71

Caravan Park at Byrock. Behind hotel

HEMA 41 E10 | 30 39 47 S | 146 24 10 E

BIG RIG

1004 Maroona Rest Area

71

Rest Area 56 km NW of Byrock or 22 km SE of Bourke

HEMA 41 D10 | 30 14 44 S | 146 3 30 E

BIG RIG

Euston to Mildura

1005 Tapalin Rest Area

Rest Area 10 km NE of Euston or 61 km SE of Gol Gol. North & Southbound

HEMA 42 F4 | 34 32 21 S | 142 39 7 E

BIG RIG

1006 Mail Route Rest Area

20

Rest Area 24 km NW of Euston or 47 km SE of Gol Gol. Combined truck stop

HEMA 42 F4 | 34 27 53 S | 142 32 26 E

BIG RIG

1007 Bottle Bend Conservation Reserve
☎ (03) 5051 6205

Picnic Area 57 km NW of Euston or 18 km SE of Gol Gol. Turn S 56 km NW of Euston or 15 km SE of Gol Gol at signpost. 2 km dirt road. Beside river. Self Contained Vehicles only

HEMA 42 F4 | 34 18 12 S | 142 17 55 E

BIG RIG 24

1008 Trentham Cliffs Caravan Village
☎ (03) 5024 8545

Caravan Park 7 km SE of Gol Gol or 11 km SE of Mildura. Sturt Hwy

HEMA 42 F3 | 34 13 29 S | 142 14 50 E

BIG RIG

1009 Buronga Riverside Tourist Park
☎ (03) 5023 3040

Caravan Park 5 km N of Mildura. From Mildura cross George Chaffey Bridge, then W off Sturt Hwy onto West Rd

HEMA 42 E3 | 34 10 54 S | 142 10 9 E

BIG RIG

1010 Main Campground
☎ (03) 5021 8900

Mungo National Park

Camp Area 150 km NW of Balranald or 110 km NE of Mildura. Signposted. Dirt road

HEMA 42 D5 | 33 44 5 S | 143 0 55 E

Notes...

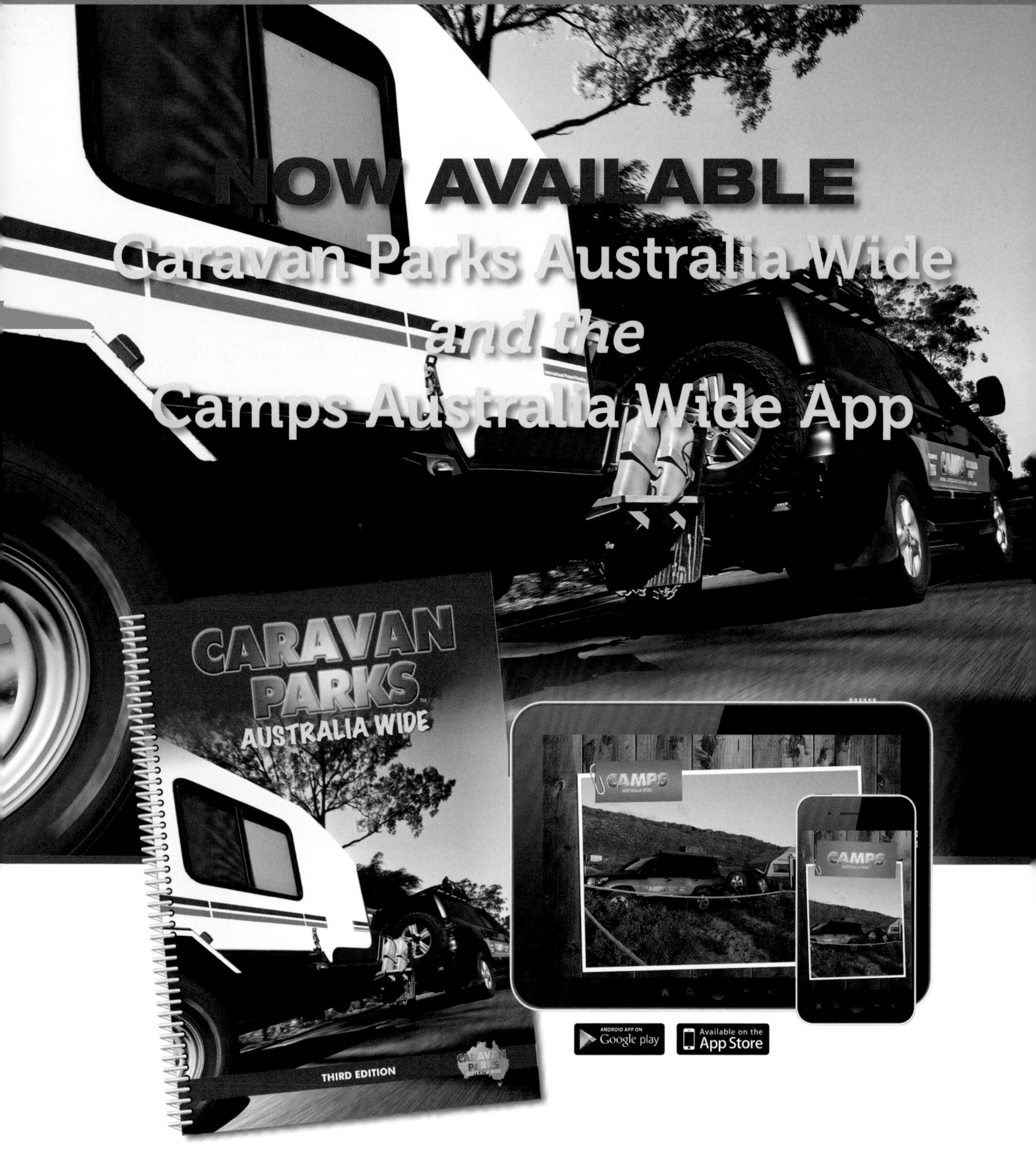
NOW AVAILABLE
Caravan Parks Australia Wide
and the
Camps Australia Wide App
CARAVAN PARKS AUSTRALIA WIDE
THIRD EDITION
CAMPS AUSTRALIA WIDE
ANDROID APP ON Google play
Available on the App Store

key map

TWELVE APOSTLES, GREAT OCEAN RD (60 H6) PHOTO: © ISTOCK.COM

Distances are shown in kilometres and follow the most direct major sealed route where possible.

	Ballarat	Bairnsdale	Bendigo	Echuca	Eden (NSW)	Geelong	Hamilton	Horsham	Melbourne	Mildura	Shepparton	Swan Hill	Traralgon	Wangaratta	Warrnambool
Albury	428	333	310	245	542	372	608	524	305	624	178	403	456	77	601
Ballarat		410	118	201	693	88	180	188	116	449	240	307	287	359	173
Bairnsdale			447	578	283	366	590	598	294	859	511	636	123	410	552
Bendigo				92	730	206	298	214	153	426	122	189	324	230	291
Echuca					787	298	390	306	204	379	68	157	405	176	383
Eden (NSW)						649	873	881	577	1127	794	919	386	619	835
Geelong							233	276	72	537	260	395	273	308	186
Hamilton								128	296	436	420	487	497	532	111
Horsham									304	308	336	403	505	444	239
Melbourne										579	188	342	201	236	258
Mildura											447	220	780	555	547
Shepparton												225	389	108	413
Swan Hill													543	333	480
Traralgon														437	459
Wangaratta															532
Warrnambool															

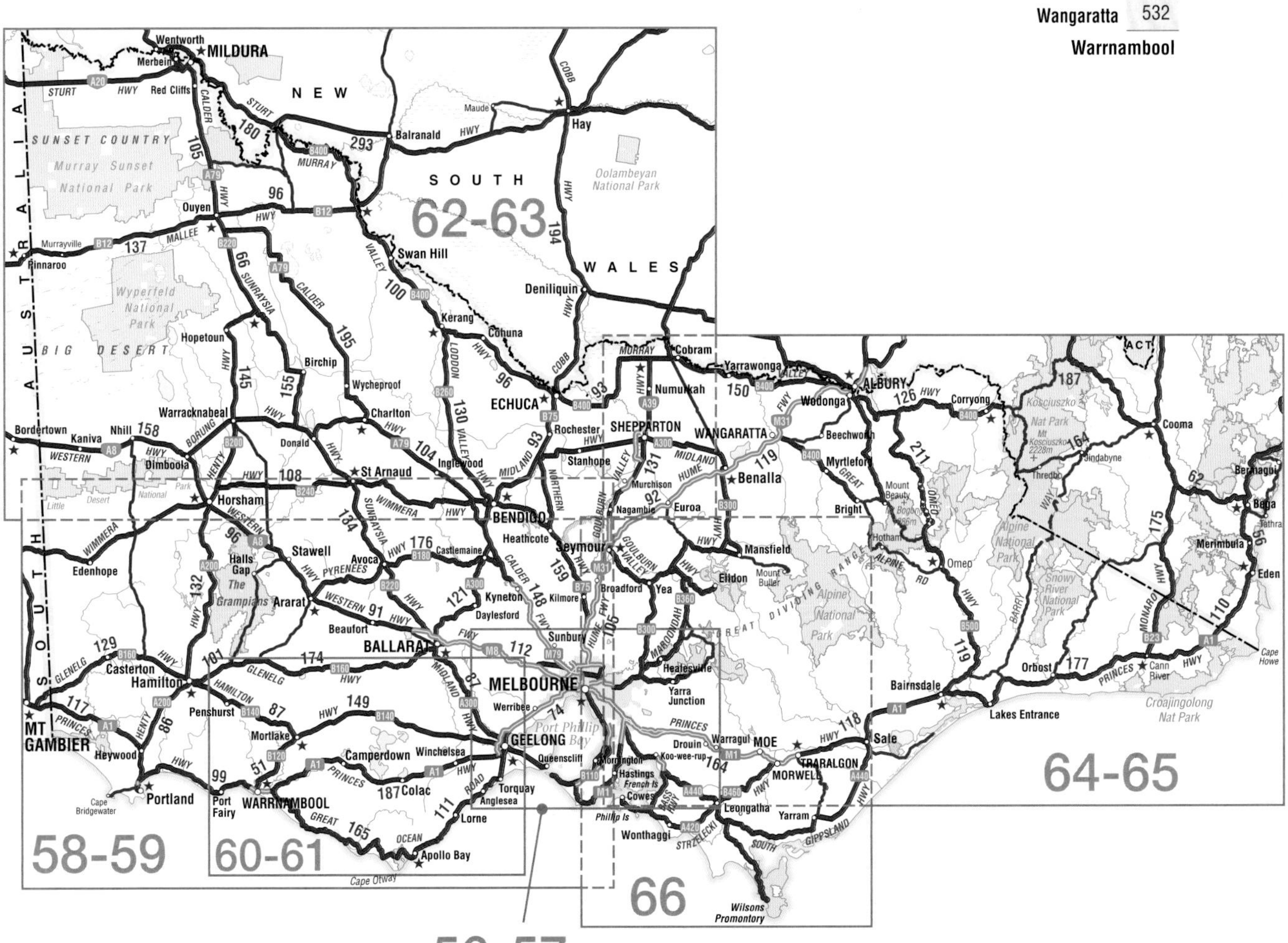

62-63

58-59

60-61

66

64-65

56-57

For more detail see pages 52-53 and 54-55

Melbourne CBD

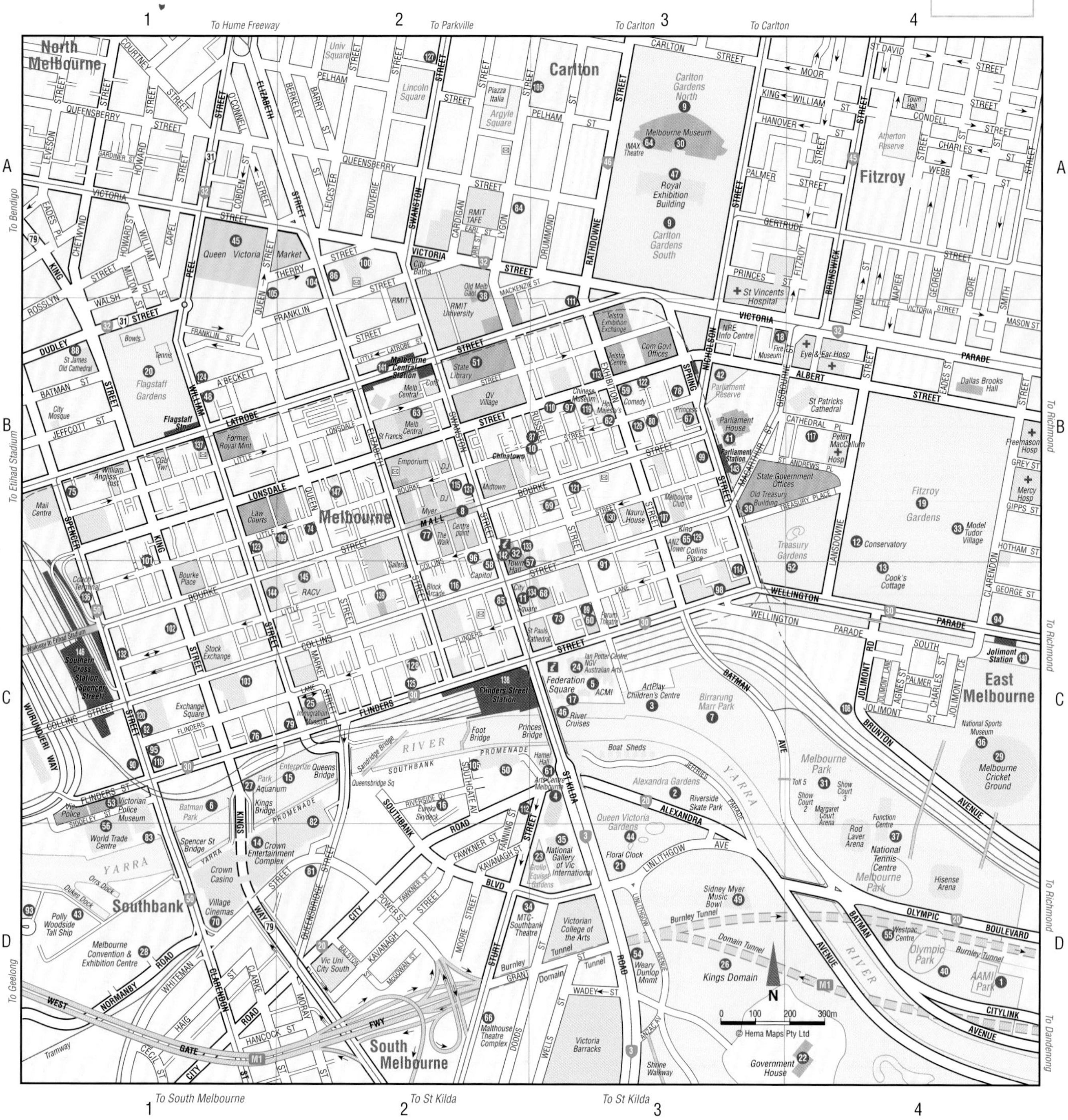

Legend	
Freeway/Tunnel	FREEWAY
Main Road	
Secondary Road	ROAD
Minor Road	STREET
Lane/Footbridge	
National Route	M1 79
Metropolitan Route	22
One Way Street	→
Railway	Underground
Tram	
Park/Garden	
Railway Station	
Major Building	
Government Building	
Theatre/Cinema	
Shopping	
Hospital	+
Post Office	
Accredited Information	

Places of Interest

1 AAMI Park D4
2 Alexandra Gardens C3
3 Artplay Children's Centre C3
4 Arts Centre Melbourne, The C3
5 Aust Ctr for the Moving Image (ACMI) C3
6 Batman Park C1
7 Birrarung Marr Park C3
8 Bourke Street Mall B2
9 Carlton Gardens A3
10 Chinatown B2
11 City Square C2
12 Conservatory B4
13 Cook's Cottage C4
14 Crown Entertainment Complex D1
15 Enterprize Park C2
16 Eureka Skydeck C2
17 Federation Square C3
18 Fire Services Museum B3
19 Fitzroy Gardens B4
20 Flagstaff Gardens B1
21 Floral Clock D3
22 Government House D4
23 Grollo Equiset Gardens D3
24 Ian Potter Centre NGV Australia C3
25 Immigration Museum C2
26 Kings Domain D3
27 Melbourne Aquarium C1
28 Melbourne Convention & Exhibition Cnt (MCEC) D1
29 Melbourne Cricket Ground C4
30 Melbourne Museum A3
31 Melbourne Park C4
32 Melbourne Town Hall B2
33 Model Tudor Village B4
34 MTC - Southbank Theatre D2
35 National Gallery of Victoria International D3
36 National Sports Museum C4
37 National Tennis Centre D4
38 Old Melbourne Gaol A2
39 Old Treasury Building B3
40 Olympic Park D4
41 Parliament House B3
42 Parliament Reserve B3
43 Polly Woodside D1
44 Queen Victoria Gardens D3
45 Queen Victoria Market A1
46 River Cruises C3
47 Royal Exhibition Building A3
48 Royal Historical Society B1
49 Sidney Myer Music Bowl D3
50 Southgate Arts & Leisure Pct C2
51 State Library of Victoria B2
52 Treasury Gardens C4
53 Victorian Police Museum C1
54 Weary Dunlop Monument D3
55 Westpac Centre D4
56 World Trade Centre D1

Theatres

57 Athenaeum Theatre C2
58 Capitol Theatre C2
59 Comedy Theatre B3
60 Forum Theatre C3
61 Hamer Hall C3
62 Her Majesty's Theatre B3
63 Hoyts Melbourne Central B2
64 IMAX Cinema A3
65 Kino Dendy Cinemas B3
66 Malthouse Theatre Complex D2
67 Princess Theatre B3
68 Regent Theatre C3
69 Russell Street Cinemas B3
70 Village Cinemas D1

Accommodation

73 Adelphi Hotel C3
74 Adina Apartment Hotel Melbourne B2
75 Atlantis Hotel B1
76 Best Western Riverside Apts C1
77 Causeway Inn on the Mall B2
78 City Limits Hotel B3
79 Clarion Suites Gateway C2
80 Crossley Hotel, The B3
81 Crown Promenade Hotel D2
82 Crown Towers D2
83 Crowne Plaza Melbourne D1
84 Downtowner on Lygon A2
85 Econo Ledge City Square Motel C2
86 Elizabeth Hostel A2
87 Exford Hotel, The B3
88 Flagstaff City Inn B1
89 Flinders Landing Apartment C3
90 Grand Hotel Melbourne C1
91 Grand Hyatt Melbourne C3
92 Great Southern Hotel, The C1
93 Hilton Melbourne South Wharf D1
94 Hilton on the Park Melbourne C4
95 Holiday Inn Melbourne on Flinders C1
96 Hotel Causeway B2
97 Hotel Grand Chancellor Melbourne B3
98 Hotel Lindrum C3
99 Hotel Windsor, The B3
100 Ibis Hotel A2
101 Ibis Melbourne Little Bourke Street Hotel B1
102 Ibis Styles Kingsgate Hotel C1
103 InterContinental Melbourne The Rialto C1
104 Jasper Hotel A2
105 Langham Melbourne, The C2
106 Lygon Lodge A3
107 Mantra 100 Exhibition B3
108 Mantra on Jolimont C4
109 Mantra on Little Bourke B2
110 Mantra on Russell B3
111 Mantra on the Park B3
112 Mantra Southbank Melbourne C2
113 Melbourne Marriott Hotel B3
114 Mercure Melbourne Treasury Gardens C3
115 Mercure Welcome Melbourne B2
116 Novotel Melbourne on Collins C2
117 Park Hyatt Melbourne B4
118 Pensione Hotel Melbourne C1
119 Punthill Little Bourke Apartments B3
120 Quality Hotel Batman's Hill on Collins C1
121 Quest on Bourke B3
122 Quest on Lonsdale B3
123 Quest on William B1
124 Radisson on Flagstaff Gardens B1
125 Rendezvous Grand Hotel C2
126 Rydges Melbourne B3
127 Rydges on Swanston Melbourne A2
128 Sebel Melbourne Flinders Lane, The C2
129 Sofitel Melbourne on Collins B3
130 Stamford Plaza Melbourne B3
131 Swanston Hotel Melbourne Grand Mercure, The B2
132 Vibe Savoy Hotel Melbourne C1
133 Victoria Hotel, The B2
134 Westin Melbourne, The C3

Travel Information

136 Coach & Bus Terminals C1
137 Flagstaff Station B1
138 Flinders Street Station C2
139 Information Victoria C2
140 Jolimont Station C4
141 Melbourne Central Station B2
142 Met Shop C2
143 Parliament Station B3
144 Qantas Terminal C1
145 RACV Travel C2
146 Southern Cross Station C1
147 YHA Office B2

© Hema Maps Pty Ltd

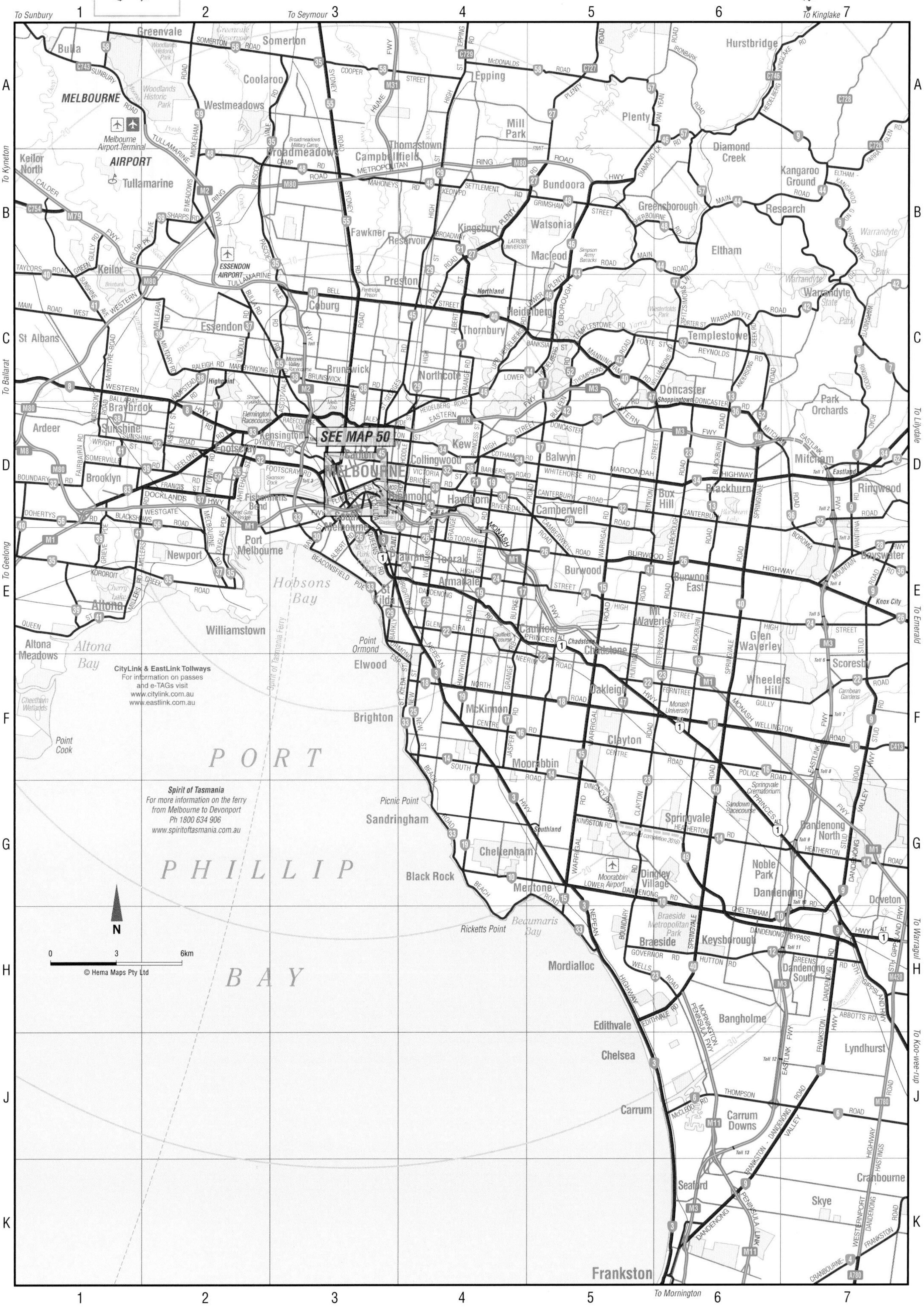

CityLink & EastLink Tollways
For information on passes
and e-TAGs visit
www.citylink.com.au
www.eastlink.com.au

Spirit of Tasmania
For more information on the ferry
from Melbourne to Devonport
Ph 1800 634 906
www.spiritoftasmania.com.au

SEE MAP 50

PORT PHILLIP BAY

0 3 6km

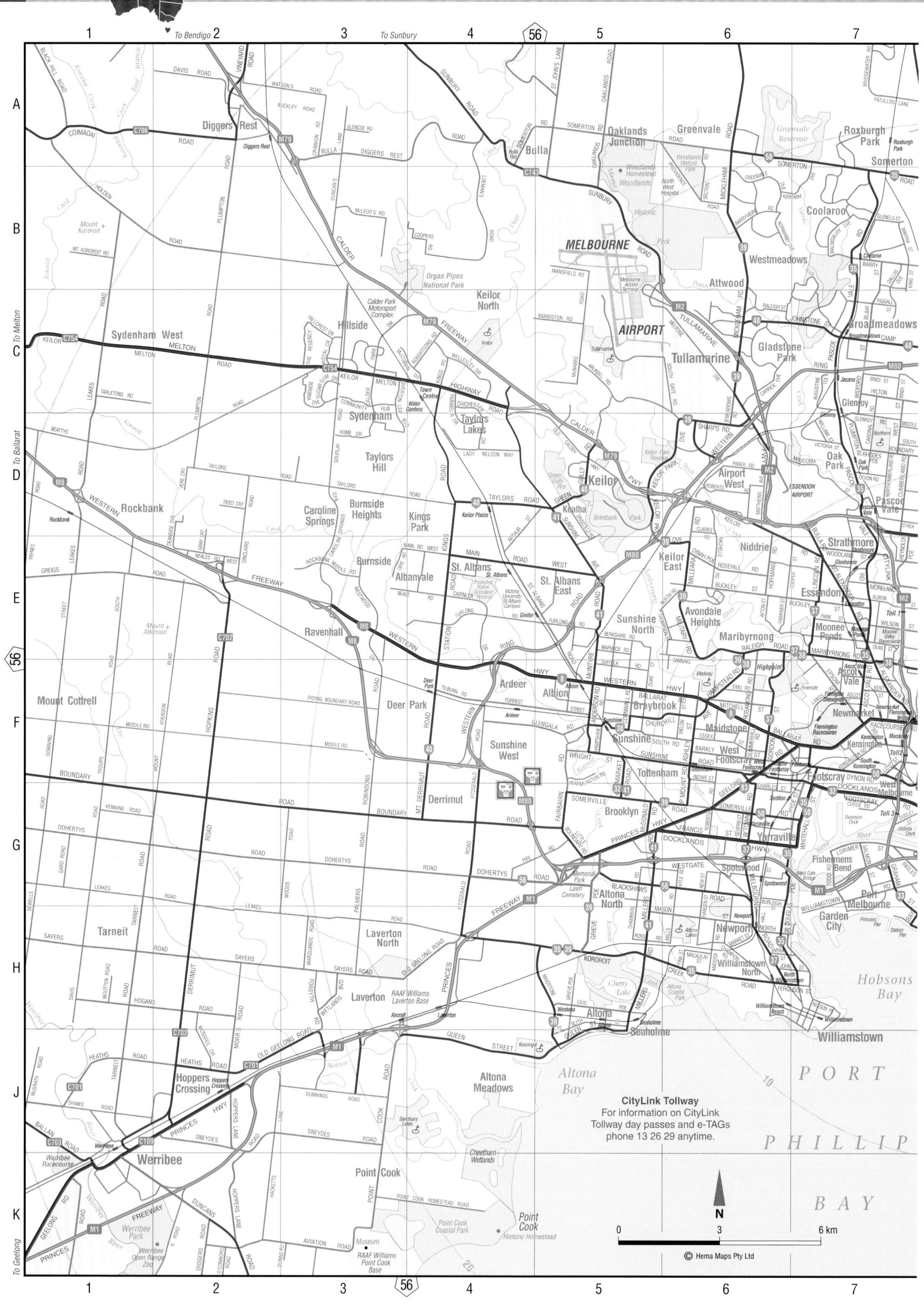
To Bendigo
To Sunbury
To Melton
To Ballarat
To Geelong
Diggers Rest
Bulla
Oaklands Junction
Greenvale
Roxburgh Park
Somerton
Coolaroo
MELBOURNE AIRPORT
Westmeadows
Attwood
Broadmeadows
Gladstone Park
Tullamarine
Organ Pipes National Park
Keilor North
Calder Park Motorsport Complex
Hillside
Sydenham West
Sydenham
Taylors Lakes
Taylors Hill
Keilor
Airport West
Glenroy
Oak Park
Pascoe Vale
Rockbank
Caroline Springs
Burnside Heights
Kings Park
Kealba
Niddrie
Strathmore
Burnside
Albanvale
St. Albans
St. Albans East
Keilor East
Essendon
Sunshine North
Avondale Heights
Maribyrnong
Moonee Ponds
Ravenhall
Ascot Vale
Mount Cottrell
Deer Park
Ardeer
Albion
Braybrook
Flemington
Newmarket
Sunshine
Maidstone
Kensington
Sunshine West
West Footscray
Tottenham
Footscray
West Melbourne
Derrimut
Brooklyn
Yarraville
Fishermens Bend
Spotswood
Altona North
Port Melbourne
Garden City
Tarneit
Laverton North
Newport
Williamstown North
Laverton
Altona
Seaholme
Williamstown
Hobsons Bay
Hoppers Crossing
Altona Meadows
Altona Bay
PORT PHILLIP BAY
Werribee
Point Cook
Cheetham Wetlands
Werribee Park
Point Cook Coastal Park
Point Cook Historic Homestead
RAAF Williams Point Cook Base
CityLink Tollway
For information on CityLink
Tollway day passes and e-TAGs
phone 13 26 29 anytime.
N
0
3
6 km
© Hema Maps Pty Ltd

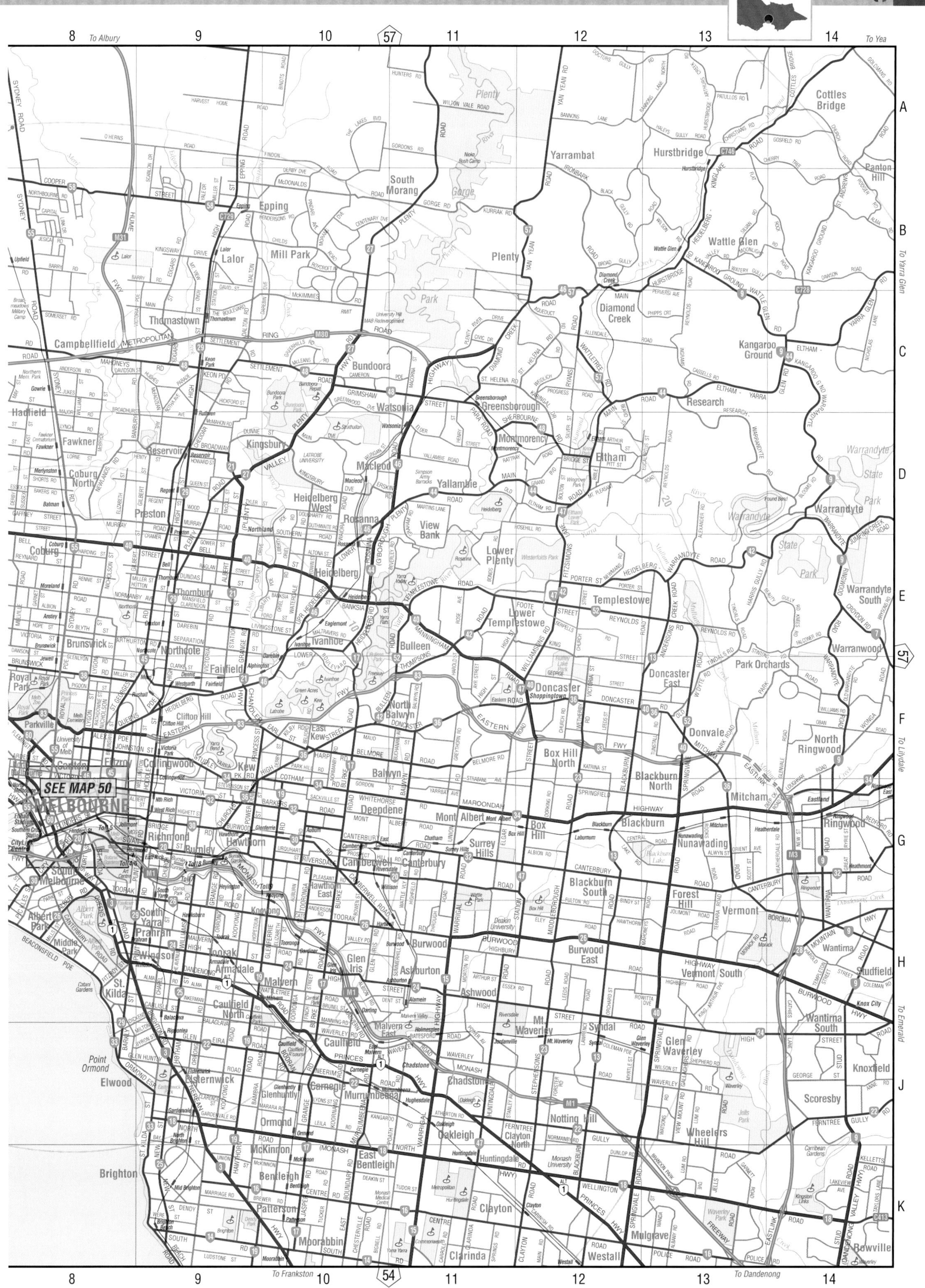

To Albury
To Yea
To Yarra Glen
To Lilydale
To Emerald
To Frankston
To Dandenong
SEE MAP 50
MELBOURNE
Epping
South Morang
Mill Park
Lalor
Thomastown
Campbellfield
Plenty
Yarrambat
Hurstbridge
Cottles Bridge
Panton Hill
Wattle Glen
Diamond Creek
Kangaroo Ground
Research
Eltham
Bundoora
Watsonia
Greensborough
Montmorency
Fawkner
Hadfield
Reservoir
Kingsbury
Macleod
Yallambie
Coburg North
Preston
Heidelberg West
Rosanna
View Bank
Lower Plenty
Warrandyte
Warrandyte South
Warranwood
Coburg
Heidelberg
Thornbury
Templestowe
Lower Templestowe
Brunswick
Northcote
Ivanhoe
Bulleen
Doncaster
Doncaster East
Park Orchards
Donvale
North Ringwood
Fairfield
Clifton Hill
Parkville
North Balwyn
East Kew
Kew
Collingwood
Fitzroy
Carlton
Box Hill North
Blackburn North
Mitcham
Ringwood
Balwyn
Deepdene
Mont Albert
Box Hill
Blackburn
Nunawading
Richmond
Hawthorn
Burnley
Surrey Hills
Canterbury
Camberwell
Blackburn South
Forest Hill
Vermont
South Melbourne
South Yarra
Prahran
Albert Park
Middle Park
Hawthorn East
Kooyong
Toorak
Burwood
Burwood East
Wantirna
Windsor
Armadale
Glen Iris
Ashburton
Vermont South
Heathmont
St. Kilda
Malvern
Caulfield North
Malvern East
Ashwood
Mt. Waverley
Syndal
Glen Waverley
Wantirna South
Knoxfield
Point Ormond
Elwood
Elsternwick
Caulfield
Carnegie
Murrumbeena
Chadstone
Scoresby
Glenhuntly
Ormond
Oakleigh
Notting Hill
Clayton North
Wheelers Hill
McKinnon
East Bentleigh
Huntingdale
Brighton
Bentleigh
Patterson
Clayton
Moorabbin
Clarinda
Mulgrave
Westall
Bowville
Studfield

To Melbourne
To Rosebud
To Hastings
CityLink Tollway
For information on CityLink Tollway day passes and e-TAGs phone 13 26 29 anytime.
© Hema Maps Pty Ltd
PORT PHILLIP BAY
Brighton
Hampton
Picnic Point
Sandringham
Black Rock
Ricketts Point
Beaumaris Bay
Beaumaris
Mentone
Parkdale
Mordialloc
Aspendale
Edithvale
Chelsea
Chelsea Heights
Bonbeach
Carrum
Patterson Lakes
Carrum Downs
Seaford
Frankston
Frankston North
Daveys Bay
Half Moon Bay
Mount Eliza
Moondah Beach
Schnapper Point
Mornington
Langwarrin
Baxter
Skye
Bangholme
Dandenong
Dandenong North
Dandenong South
Keysborough
Braeside
Dingley Village
Noble Park
South Springvale
Springvale
Mulgrave
Wheelers Hill
Notting Hill
Clayton
Clayton North
Clayton South
Westall
Clarinda
Oakleigh
Huntingdale
Carnegie
Murrumbeena
Glenhuntly
Ormond
McKinnon
Bentleigh
East Bentleigh
Patterson
Moorabbin
Highett
Heatherton
Cheltenham
Cheltenham North
Monash University
Braeside Metropolitan Park
Edithvale Seaford Wetland Education Centre
Springvale Crematorium
Sandown Racecourse
Langwarrin Flora & Fauna Reserve
Frankston Reservoir

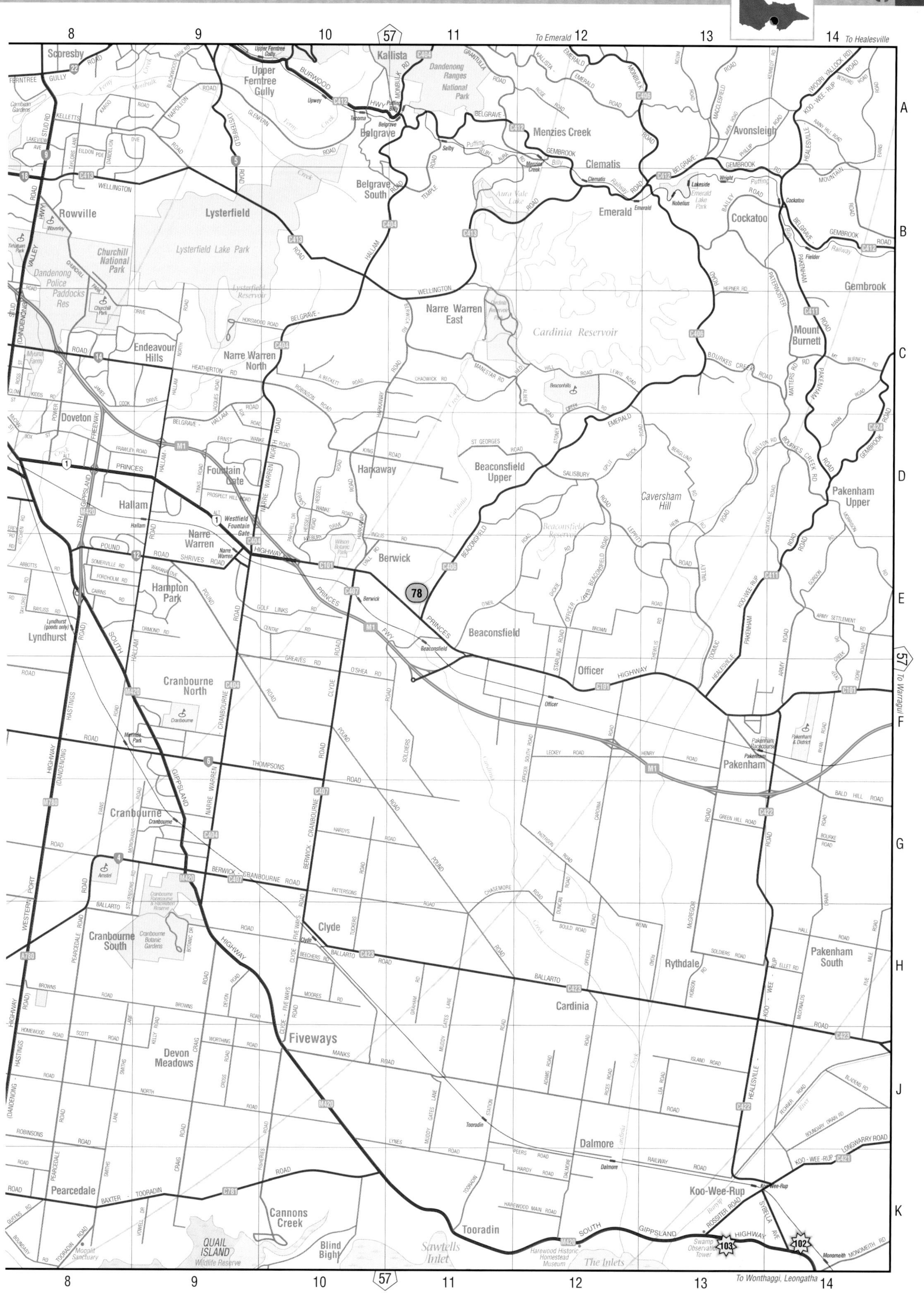

To Emerald
To Healesville
To Warragul
To Wonthaggi, Leongatha
Scoresby
Upper Ferntree Gully
Kallista
Dandenong Ranges National Park
Belgrave
Menzies Creek
Clematis
Avonsleigh
Emerald
Cockatoo
Gembrook
Belgrave South
Rowville
Lysterfield
Lysterfield Lake Park
Churchill National Park
Dandenong Police Paddocks Res
Narre Warren East
Cardinia Reservoir
Mount Burnett
Endeavour Hills
Narre Warren North
Doveton
Harkaway
Beaconsfield Upper
Caversham Hill
Pakenham Upper
Hallam
Fountain Gate
Narre Warren
Berwick
Hampton Park
Beaconsfield
Lyndhurst
Officer
Cranbourne North
Pakenham
Cranbourne
Clyde
Cranbourne South
Rythdale
Pakenham South
Cardinia
Fiveways
Devon Meadows
Dalmore
Pearcedale
Koo-Wee-Rup
Cannons Creek
Tooradin
Blind Bight
Quail Island Wildlife Reserve
Sawtells Inlet
The Inlets
78
102
103

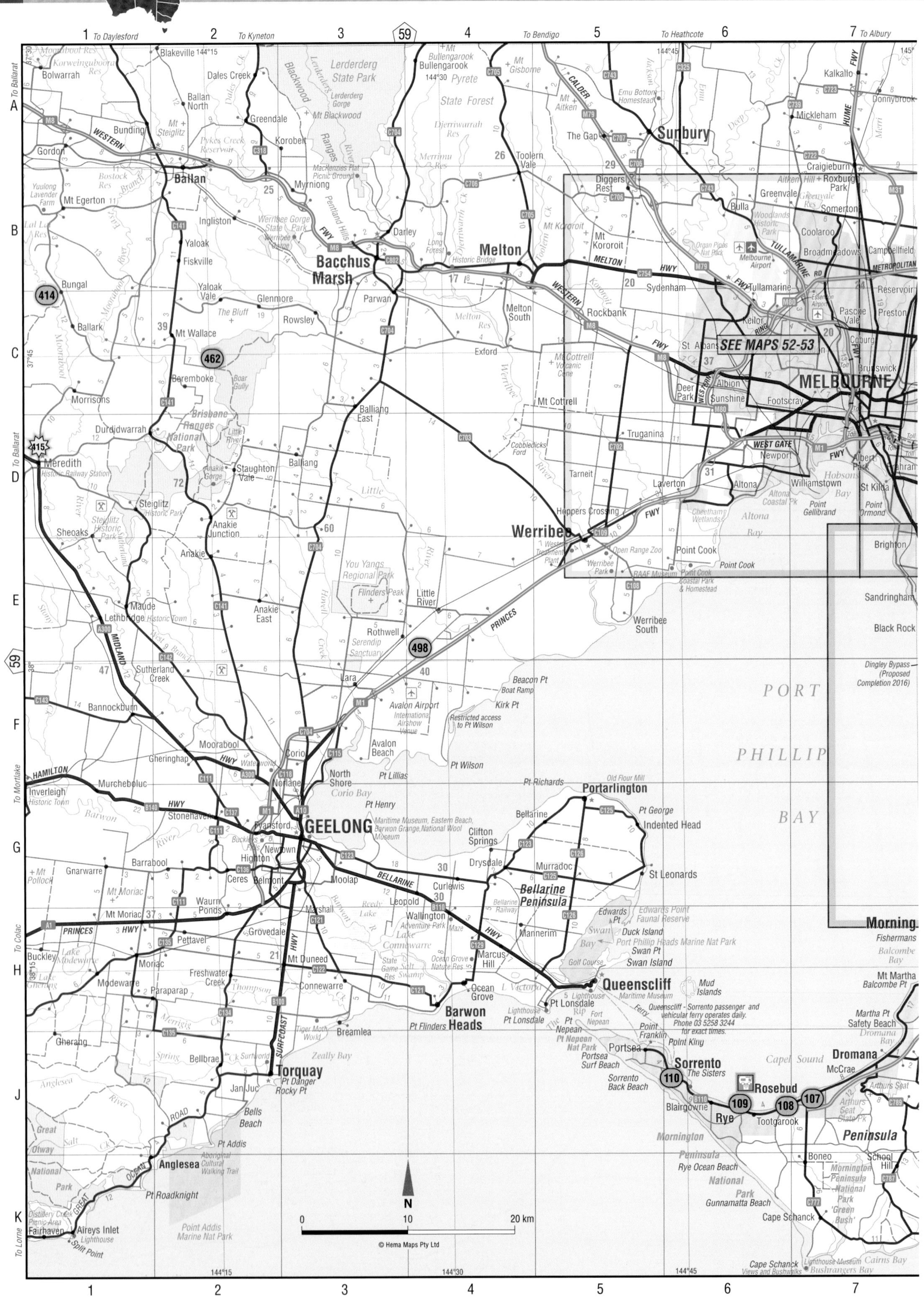
To Daylesford
To Kyneton
To Bendigo
To Heathcote
To Albury
To Ballarat
To Mortlake
To Colac
To Lorne
Bolwarrah
Blakeville
Dales Creek
Ballan North
Greendale
Lerderderg State Park
Blackwood
Bullengarook
Pyrete State Forest
Mt Gisborne
Mt Aitken
Emu Bottom Homestead
Kalkallo
Donnybrook
Mickleham
Bunding
Gordon
Mt Egerton
Korobeit
Ballan
Myrniong
Toolern Vale
The Gap
Sunbury
Diggers Rest
Craigieburn
Roxburgh Park
Greenvale
Somerton
Bulla
Coolaroo
Campbellfield
Broadmeadows
Ingliston
Yaloak
Fiskville
Darley
Bacchus Marsh
Melton
Mt Kororoit
Melbourne Airport
Tullamarine
Sydenham
Reservoir
Preston
Pascoe Vale
Coburg
Brunswick
Bungal
Ballark
Yaloak Vale
Glenmore
Rowsley
Parwan
Melton South
Exford
Rockbank
St Albans
SEE MAPS 52-53
MELBOURNE
Mt Wallace
Greenvale
Keilor
Deer Park
Albion
Sunshine
Footscray
Morrisons
Beremboke
Balliang East
Mt Cottrell
Truganina
Williamstown
Newport
Altona
Laverton
Tarneit
Durdidwarrah
Brisbane Ranges National Park
Meredith
Staughton Vale
Balliang
Hoppers Crossing
Werribee
Point Cook
St Kilda
Brighton
Steiglitz
Sheoaks
Anakie Junction
Anakie
You Yangs Regional Park
Flinders Peak
Little River
Maude
Lethbridge
Anakie East
Rothwell
Werribee South
Sandringham
Black Rock
Sutherland Creek
Lara
Avalon Airport
Beacon Pt
Kirk Pt
Dingley Bypass (Proposed Completion 2016)
Bannockburn
Moorabool
Avalon Beach
Pt Wilson
PORT PHILLIP BAY
Gheringhap
Corio
North Shore
Corio Bay
Pt Lillias
Inverleigh
Murgheboluc
Norlane
Pt Henry
Pt Richards
Portarlington
Stonehaven
GEELONG
Bellarine
Pt George
Indented Head
Fyansford
Clifton Springs
Barrabool
Highton
Newtown
Drysdale
Gnarwarre
Ceres
Belmont
Moolap
Murradoc
St Leonards
Waurn Ponds
Curlewis
Bellarine Peninsula
Mt Moriac
Marshall
Leopold
Wallington
Edwards Pt
Grovedale
Mannerim
Duck Island
Swan Pt
Swan Island
Morning...
Fishermans
Balcombe Bay
Pettavel
Buckley
Moriac
Mt Duneed
Marcus Hill
Queenscliff
Mt Martha
Balcombe Pt
Modewarre
Paraparap
Freshwater Creek
Connewarre
Ocean Grove
Mud Islands
Pt Lonsdale
Barwon Heads
Pt Flinders
Queenscliff - Sorrento passenger and vehicular ferry operates daily. Phone 03 5258 3244 for exact times.
Martha Pt
Safety Beach
Gherang
Bellbrae
Bream Lea
Point Franklin
Point King
Portsea
Sorrento
The Sisters
Dromana
McCrae
Torquay
Pt Danger
Rocky Pt
Zeally Bay
Portsea Surf Beach
Sorrento Back Beach
Rosebud
Arthurs Seat
Jan Juc
Bells Beach
Blairgowrie
Rye
Tootgarook
Mornington Peninsula
Great Otway National Park
Pt Addis
Anglesea
Rye Ocean Beach
Boneo
School Hill
Mornington Peninsula National Park
Pt Roadknight
Gunnamatta Beach
Cape Schanck
Aireys Inlet
Fairhaven
Split Point
Point Addis Marine Nat Park
Cape Schanck Lighthouse Museum
Bushrangers Bay
Cairns Bay
N
0 10 20 km
© Hema Maps Pty Ltd
WESTERN FWY
MELTON HWY
CALDER FWY
HUME FWY
TULLAMARINE FWY
WEST GATE FWY
PRINCES FWY
MIDLAND HWY
HAMILTON HWY
PRINCES HWY
BELLARINE HWY
SURF COAST HWY
GREAT OCEAN ROAD

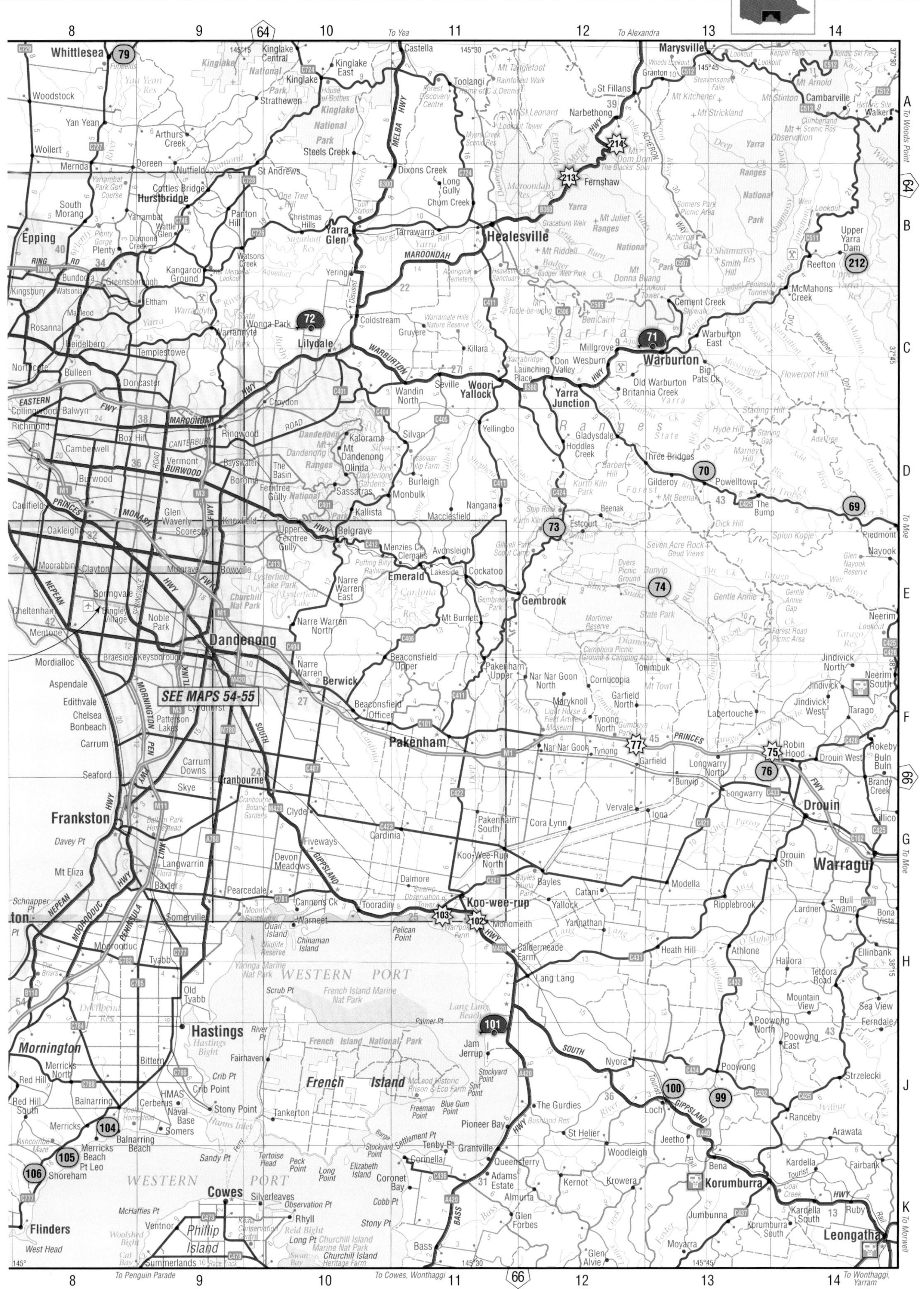

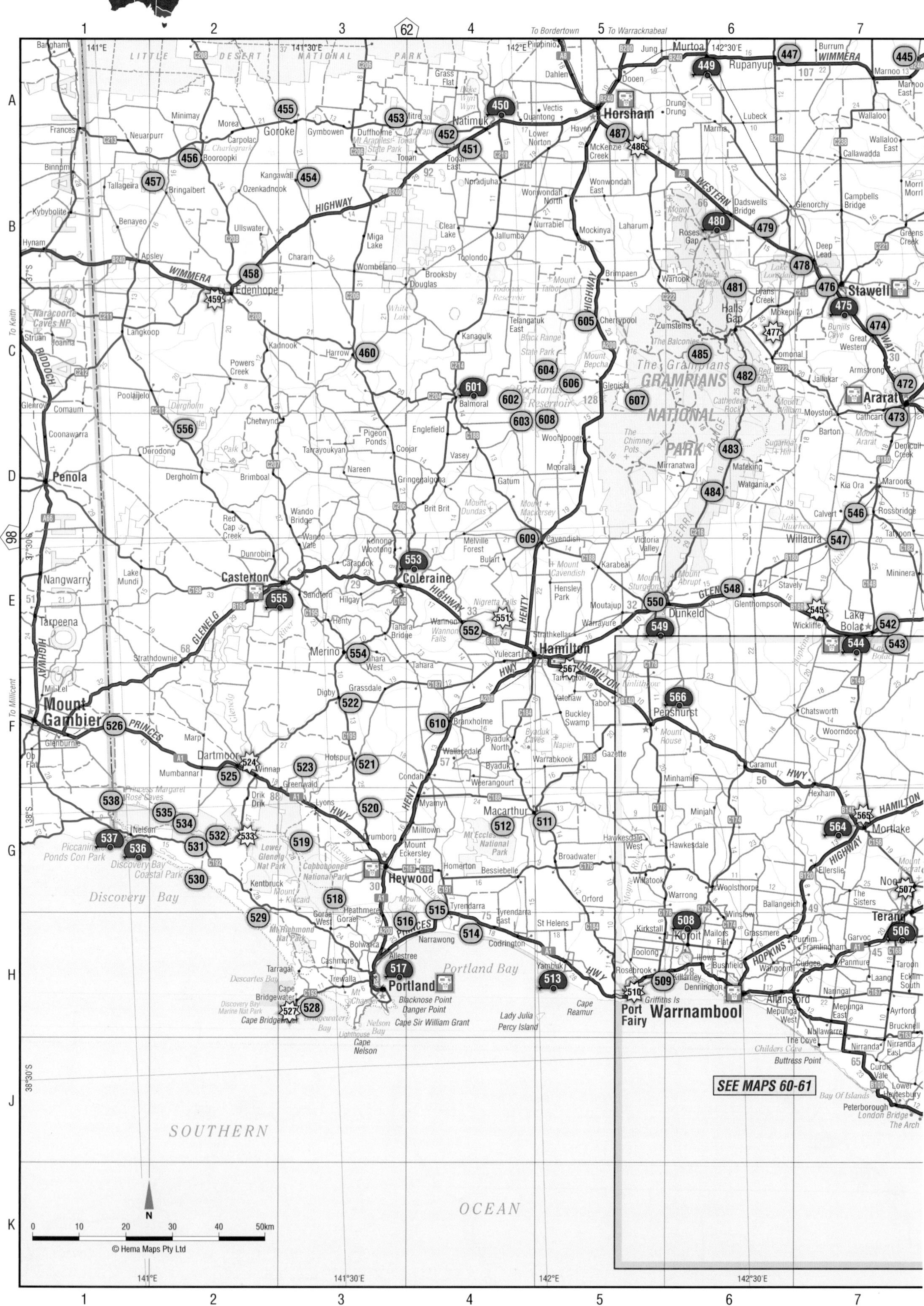
To Bordertown
To Warracknabeal
LITTLE DESERT NATIONAL PARK
Horsham
Murtoa
Rupanyup
Natimuk
Goroke
Edenhope
WIMMERA
HIGHWAY
WESTERN
Stawell
Halls Gap
Ararat
THE GRAMPIANS
GRAMPIANS NATIONAL PARK
Dunkeld
Penola
Casterton
Coleraine
Hamilton
Merino
Mount Gambier
PRINCES
Dartmoor
Heywood
Portland
Portland Bay
Discovery Bay
Port Fairy
Warrnambool
Mortlake
Terang
Penshurst
Macarthur
Balmoral
Harrow
Naracoorte Caves NP
To Keith
To Millicent
Cape Bridgewater
Cape Nelson
Lady Julia Percy Island
SEE MAPS 60-61
SOUTHERN
OCEAN
© Hema Maps Pty Ltd

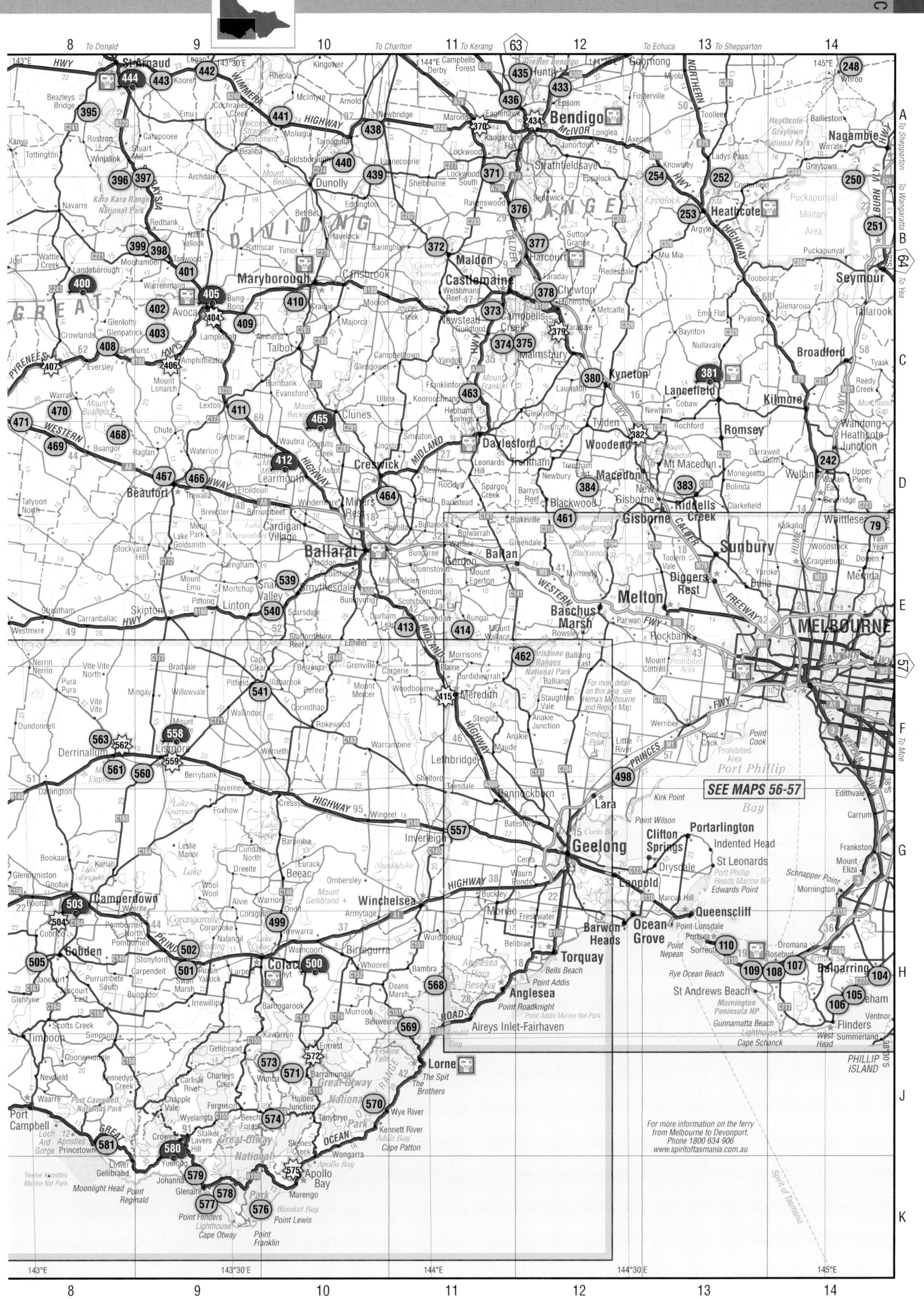
To Donald
To Charlton
To Kerang
To Echuca
To Shepparton
St Arnaud
Bendigo
Heathcote
Nagambie
Seymour
Maryborough
Castlemaine
Maldon
Kyneton
Lancefield
Broadford
Kilmore
Daylesford
Creswick
Clunes
Ballarat
Beaufort
Avoca
Talbot
Woodend
Macedon
Gisborne
Sunbury
Melton
Bacchus Marsh
MELBOURNE
Skipton
Linton
Meredith
Geelong
Lara
Camperdown
Cobden
Colac
Winchelsea
Torquay
Anglesea
Lorne
Apollo Bay
Queenscliff
Portarlington
Ocean Grove
Barwon Heads
Sorrento
Flinders
Port Campbell
Timboon
Lismore
Derrinallum
Inverleigh
SEE MAPS 56-57
Port Phillip Bay
For more detail on this area, see Hema's Melbourne and Region Map.
For more information on the ferry from Melbourne to Devonport, Phone 1800 634 906 www.spiritoftasmania.com.au
PHILLIP ISLAND
Spirit of Tasmania

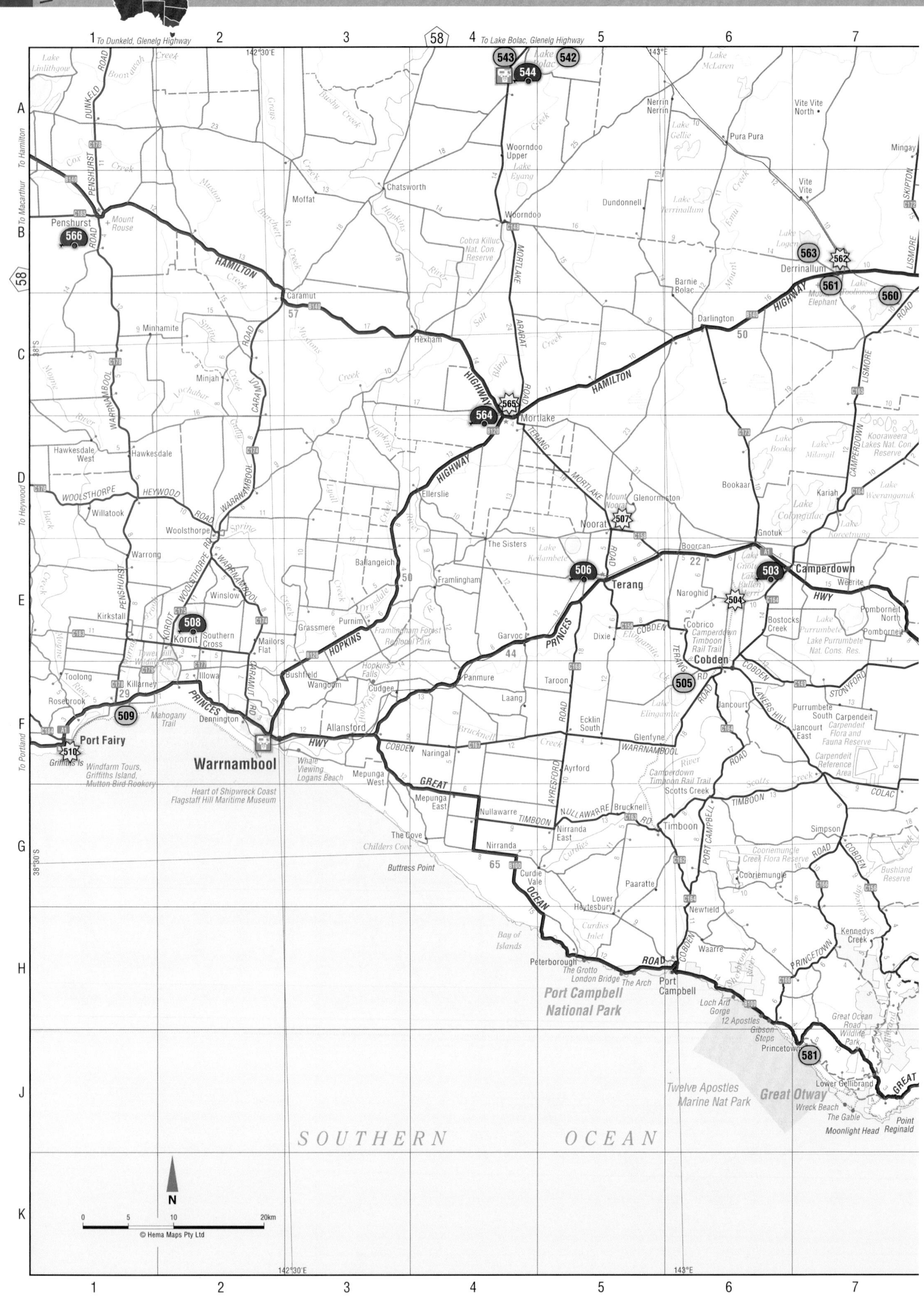
To Dunkeld, Glenelg Highway
To Lake Bolac, Glenelg Highway
Penshurst
Warrnambool
Port Fairy
Mortlake
Terang
Camperdown
Cobden
Timboon
Port Campbell
Port Campbell National Park
Twelve Apostles Marine Nat Park
Great Otway
SOUTHERN OCEAN
© Hema Maps Pty Ltd

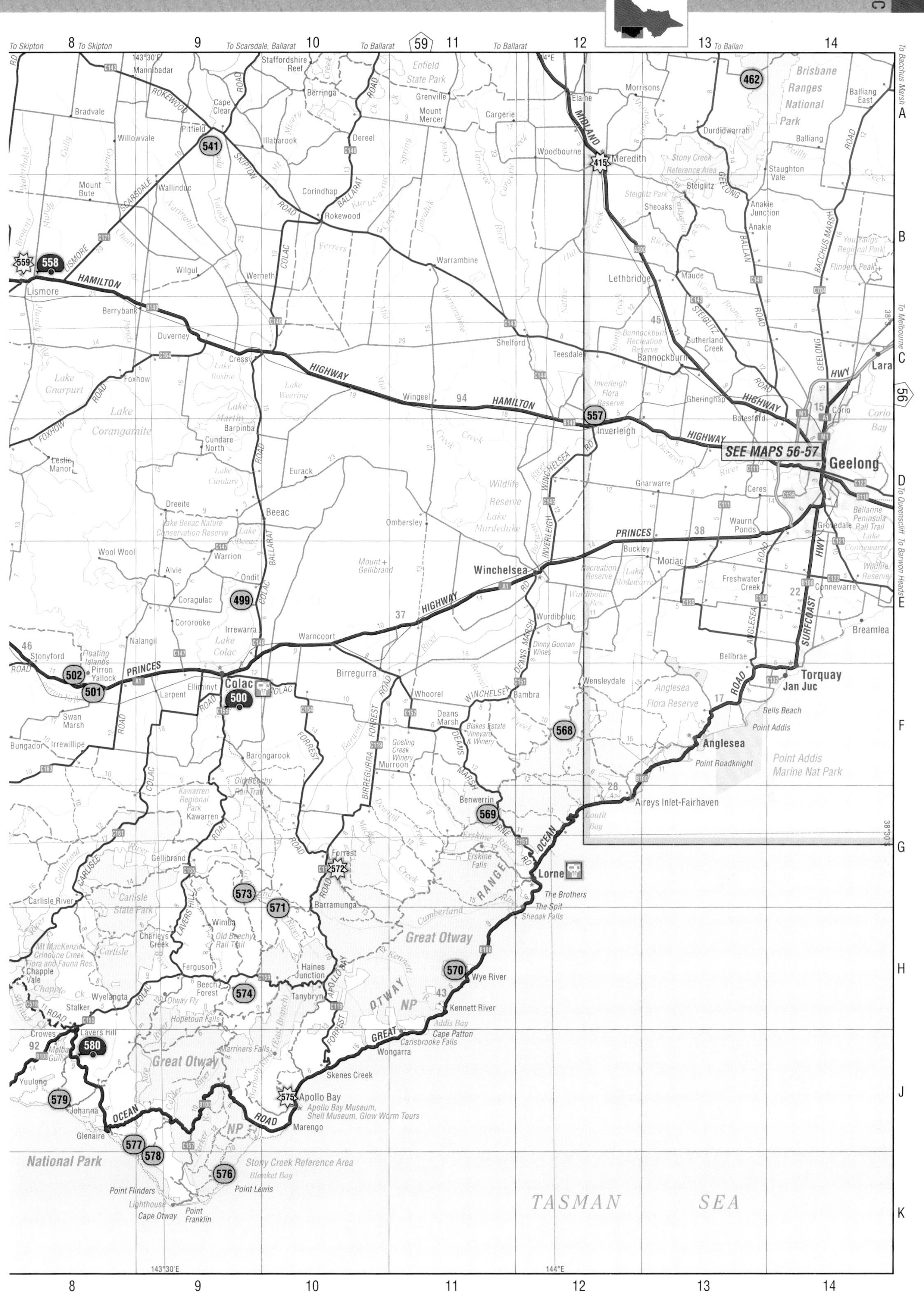
Lismore
Colac
Winchelsea
Geelong
Torquay
Jan Juc
Anglesea
Lorne
Apollo Bay
Meredith
Inverleigh
Bannockburn
Lara
Beeac
Birregurra
Forrest
Great Otway
Otway NP
Tasman Sea
SEE MAPS 56-57
Hamilton Highway
Princes Highway
Great Ocean Road
Surfcoast Hwy

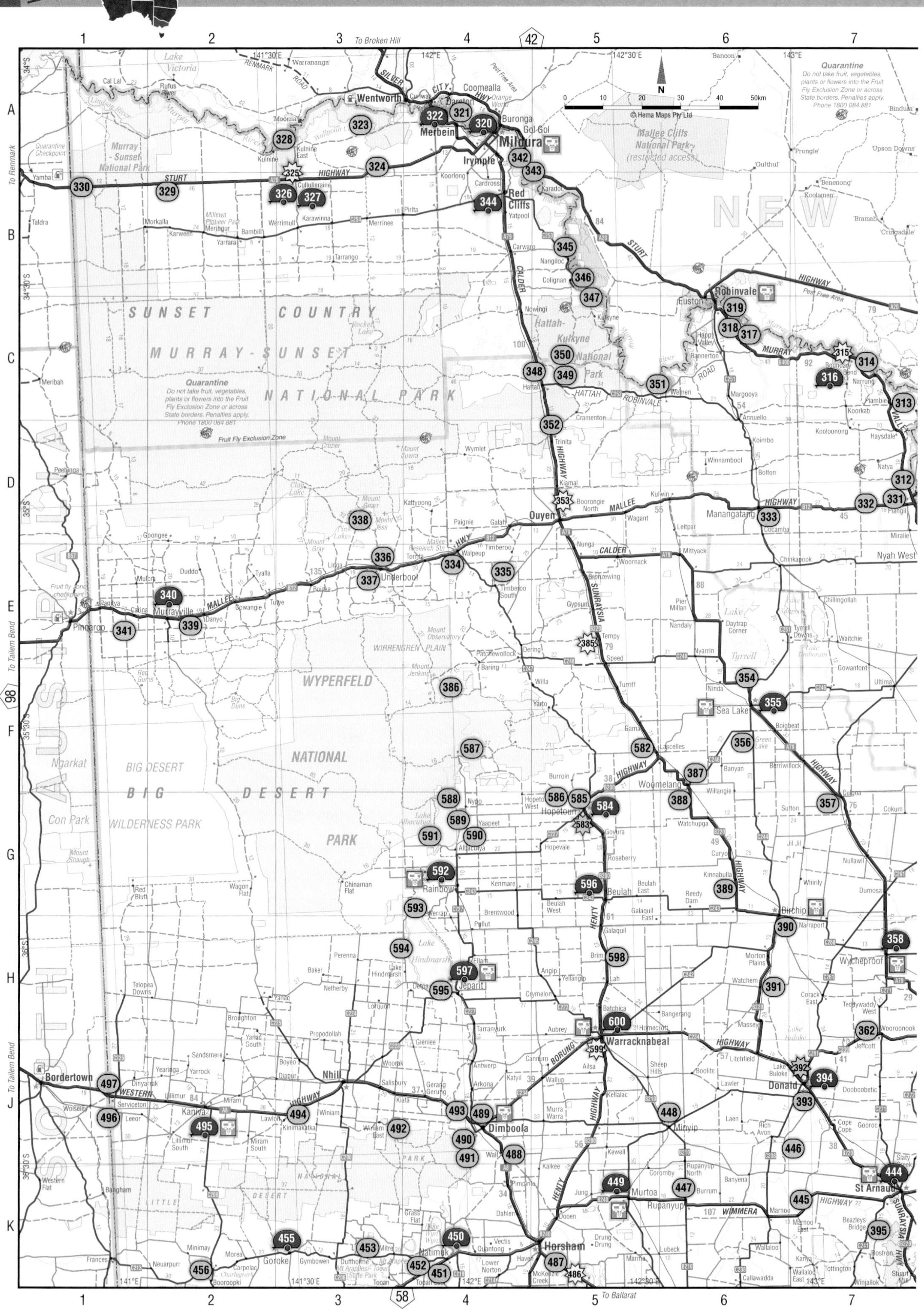
To Broken Hill
Wentworth
Merbein
Mildura
Irymple
Red Cliffs
Buronga
Gol Gol
Coomealla
Dareton
Mallee Cliffs National Park (restricted access)
© Hema Maps Pty Ltd
Quarantine
Do not take fruit, vegetables, plants or flowers into the Fruit Fly Exclusion Zone or across State borders. Penalties apply. Phone 1800 084 881
Fruit Fly Exclusion Zone
Murray - Sunset National Park
SUNSET COUNTRY
MURRAY-SUNSET NATIONAL PARK
STURT HIGHWAY
CALDER HIGHWAY
MALLEE HIGHWAY
SUNRAYSIA HIGHWAY
HENTY HIGHWAY
BORUNG HIGHWAY
WESTERN HIGHWAY
WIMMERA HIGHWAY
Hattah-Kulkyne National Park
Robinvale
Euston
Ouyen
Underbool
Murrayville
Pinnaroo
Sea Lake
Hopetoun
Rainbow
Jeparit
Beulah
Birchip
Wycheproof
Warracknabeal
Donald
St Arnaud
Dimboola
Nhill
Kaniva
Bordertown
Minyip
Murtoa
Rupanyup
Horsham
Natimuk
Goroke
WYPERFELD NATIONAL PARK
BIG DESERT
BIG DESERT WILDERNESS PARK
LITTLE DESERT NATIONAL PARK
Ngarkat Con Park
SOUTH AUSTRALIA
NEW SOUTH WALES
To Renmark
To Tailem Bend
To Ballarat
34°S
34°30'S
35°S
35°30'S
36°S
36°30'S
141°E
141°30'E
142°E
142°30'E
143°E

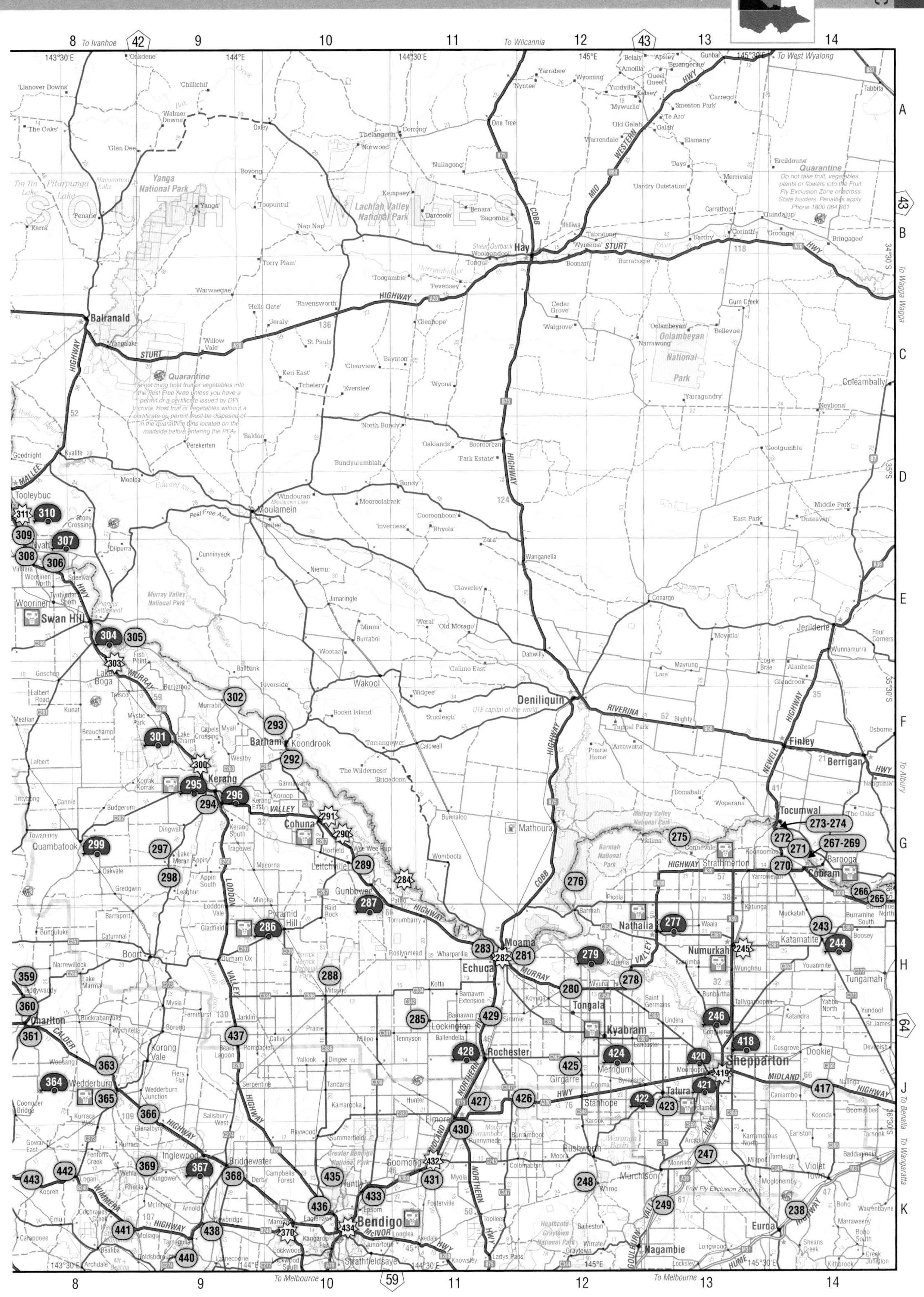
Balranald
Hay
Moulamein
Deniliquin
Swan Hill
Kerang
Barham
Koondrook
Cohuna
Echuca
Moama
Shepparton
Tocumwal
Finley
Jerilderie
Cobram
Numurkah
Nathalia
Kyabram
Tongala
Rochester
Tatura
Bendigo
Wedderburn
Charlton
Nagambie
Euroa
Yanga National Park
Lachlan Valley National Park
Oolambeyan National Park
Murray Valley National Park
Barmah National Park
Quarantine
Do not take fruit, vegetables, plants or flowers into the Fruit Fly Exclusion Zone or across State borders. Penalties apply. Phone 1800 084 881
To Wagga Wagga
To Albury
To Benalla
To Wangaratta
To Melbourne
To Ivanhoe
To Wilcannia
To West Wyalong

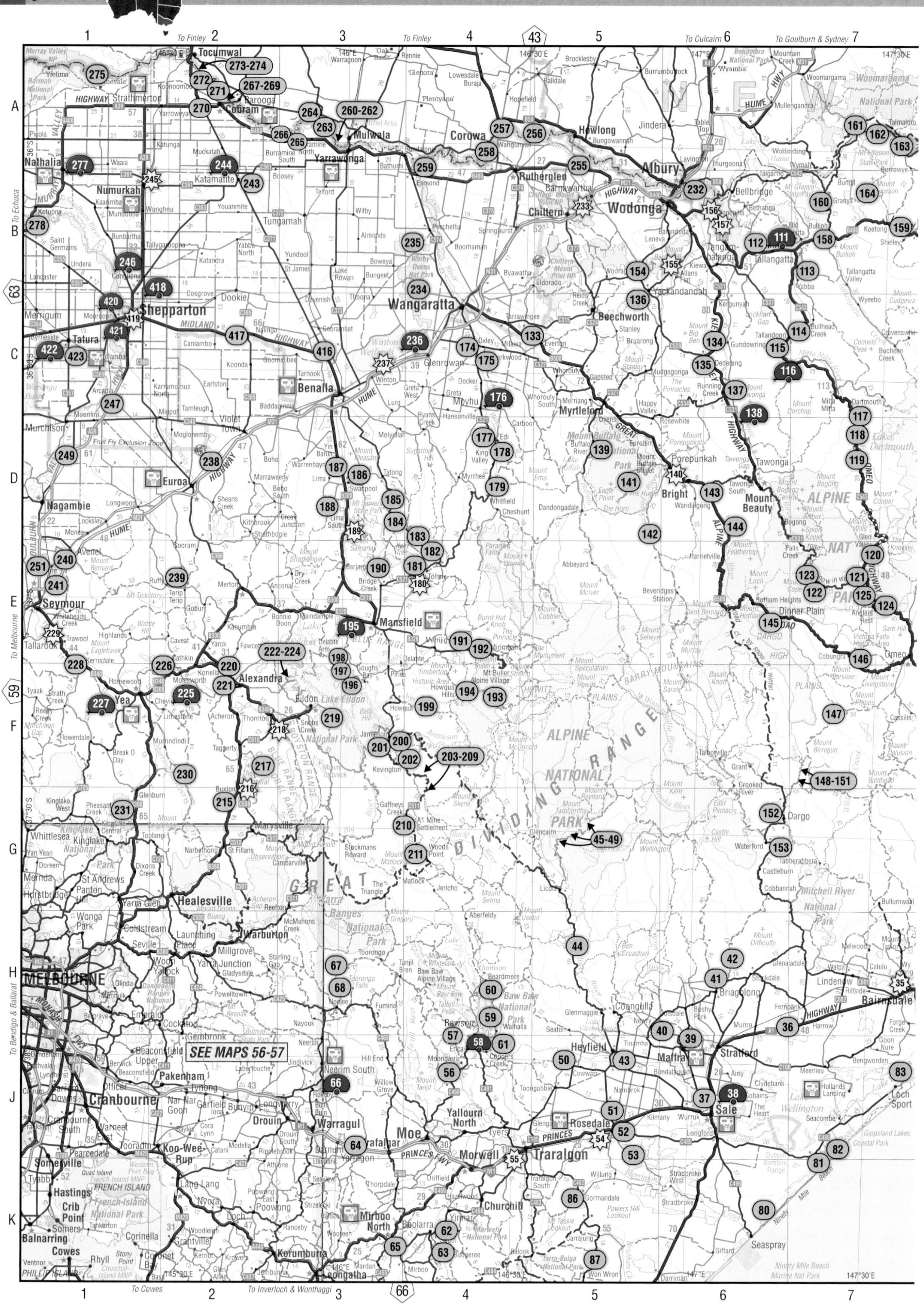

To Finley
To Culcairn
To Goulburn & Sydney
To Echuca
To Melbourne
To Bendigo & Ballarat
To Cowes
To Inverloch & Wonthaggi
SEE MAPS 56-57
Tocumwal
Strathmerton
Cobram
Barooga
Mulwala
Yarrawonga
Corowa
Rutherglen
Howlong
Albury
Wodonga
Chiltern
Nathalia
Numurkah
Katamatite
Tungamah
Shepparton
Tatura
Dookie
Benalla
Wangaratta
Glenrowan
Beechworth
Yackandandah
Tallangatta
Bellbridge
Myrtleford
Bright
Mount Beauty
Porepunkah
Dinner Plain
Omeo
Euroa
Nagambie
Seymour
Avenel
Mansfield
Alexandria
Yea
Eildon
Jamieson
Marysville
Whittlesea
Kinglake
Healesville
Warburton
Yarra Junction
MELBOURNE
Cranbourne
Pakenham
Warragul
Drouin
Moe
Morwell
Traralgon
Churchill
Rosedale
Sale
Maffra
Heyfield
Stratford
Bairnsdale
Mirboo North
Korumburra
Leongatha
Hastings
Cowes
Balnarring
Dargo
Licola
ALPINE NATIONAL PARK
GREAT DIVIDING RANGE
HUME HIGHWAY
MIDLAND HIGHWAY
PRINCES HIGHWAY
GREAT ALPINE ROAD

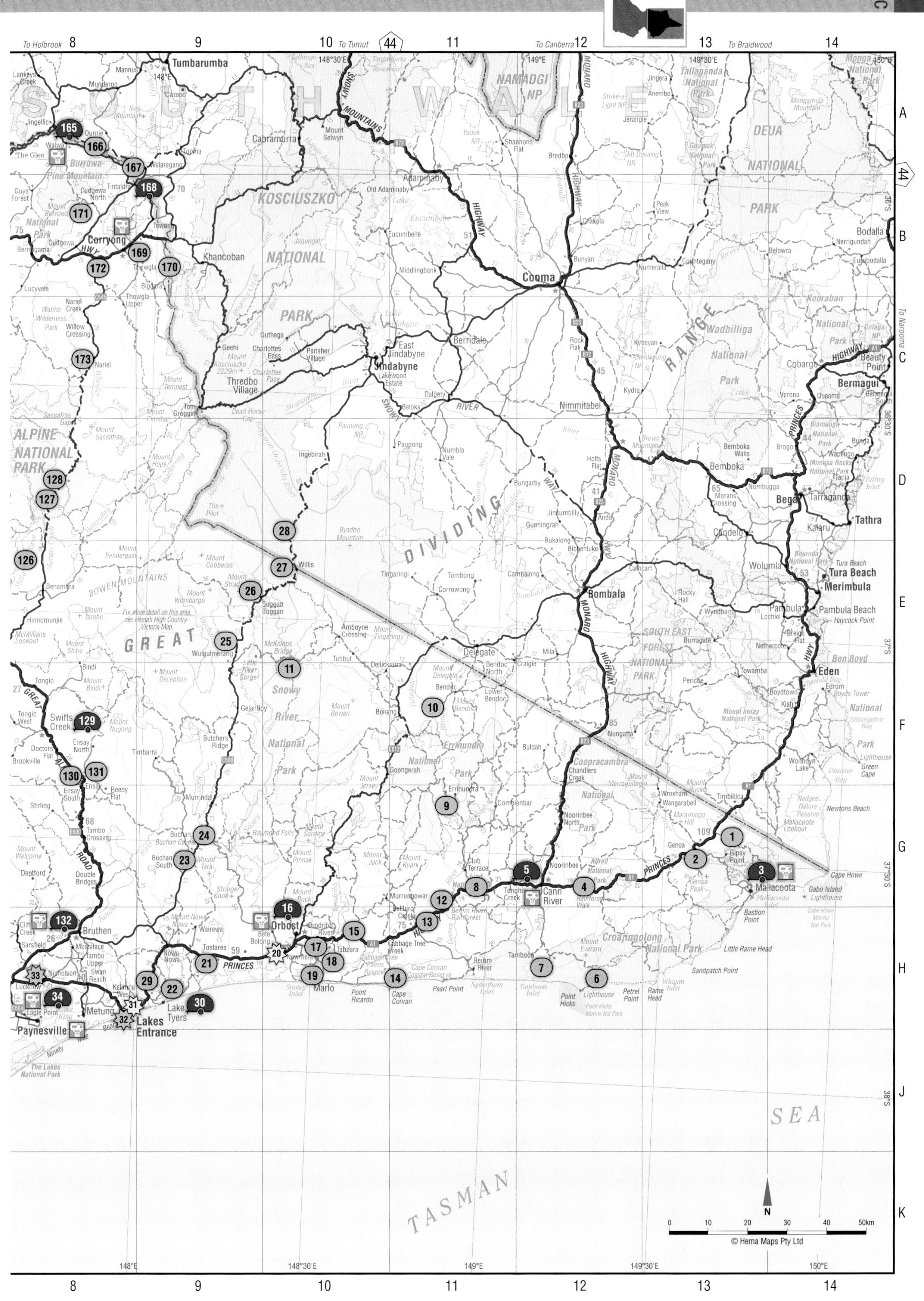

Gippsland Region, Victoria

SEE MAPS 56-57

Victoria Highway Index

Victoria Alphabetic Site Index

Symbols

A

B

C

D

E

F

Y

NSW Border to Melbourne

Princes Highway

1 Wallagaraugh River Retreat
☎ (03) 5158 8211

Camp Area 17 km S of Timbillica. 80 Piesley Rd. Turn E just N of bridge 9 km S of Timbillica or 9 km N of Genoa. 8 km dirt road. Generator power

HEMA 65 G13 37 27 14 S 149 41 25 E

2 Genoa Rest Area

A1

Rest Area 1 km N of Genoa before bridge. Donation welcome

HEMA 65 G13 37 28 21 S 149 35 27 E

3 Mallacoota Foreshore Holiday Park
☎ (03) 5158 0300

Caravan Park at Mallacoota, Allan Dr

HEMA 65 G13 37 33 26 S 149 45 32 E

4 Thurra River Rest Area (Drummond Creek)

A1

Rest Area 36 km W of Genoa or 11 km E of Cann River. 200m off Hwy

HEMA 65 G12 37 34 10 S 149 16 15 E

5 Cann River Rainforest Caravan Park
☎ (03) 5158 6369

Caravan Park at Cann River. 7536 Princes Hwy

HEMA 65 G12 37 33 59 S 149 8 46 E

6 Thurra River Campground
☎ (03) 5158 4268

Croajingolong National Park

Camp Area 42 km S of Cann River. At the mouth of the Thurra River near Point Hicks. Dirt road. Not suitable caravans

HEMA 65 H12 37 46 38 S 149 19 25 E

7 Peach Tree Creek Camping Area
☎ 131 963

Croajingolong National Park

Camp Area 27 km S of Cann River. Turn S onto Tamboon Rd for 21 km, then veer R onto Fishermans Track. 6 km to campground. Dirt road. Small vehicles only

HEMA 65 H12 37 44 33 S 149 8 12 E

8 Brightlight Saddle Rest Area

A1

Rest Area 19 km W of Cann River or 57 km E of Orbost

HEMA 65 G11 37 35 20 S 148 57 26 E

9 Ada River Campground

C616

Camp Area 22 km N of Club Tce. Turn NW off the Club Tce-Combienbar Rd 11 km N of Club Tce onto Errinundra Valley Rd. 12 km dirt road. Beside Little Ada River

HEMA 65 G11 37 24 15 S 148 53 33 E

10 Delegate River Campground
☎ (02) 6458 1456

C616

Camp Area 9 km SW of Bendoc. Beside Delegate River, via Gap Rd. Some dirt road

HEMA 65 F11 37 11 48 S 148 49 41 E

11 McKillop Bridge Campground
☎ 131 963

Snowy River National Park

Camp Area 30 km E of Wulgulmerang or 53 km W of Bonang. Tight winding road not suitable for caravans

HEMA 65 E10 37 5 25 S 148 24 42 E

12 Bemm River Rest Area

A1

Rest Area 30 km W of Cann River or 46 km E of Orbost. Toilets 300m off Hwy

HEMA 65 H11 37 37 37 S 148 53 20 E

13 Bellbird Hotel

A1

Rest Area 38 km W of Cann River or 38 km E of Orbost. Toilets at hotel with permission

HEMA 65 H11 37 39 8 S 148 49 4 E

14 Banksia Bluff Campground
☎ (03) 5154 8438

Cape Conran Coastal Park

Camp Area 19 km E of Marlo, via Marlo Rd & Yeerung River Rd. 1.5 km dirt road. Cold showers

HEMA 65 H11 37 47 44 S 148 44 56 E

15 Murrungower Picnic Area

A1

Rest Area 18 km W of Bellbird or 20 km E of Orbost

HEMA 65 H10 37 41 22 S 148 37 6 E

16 Orbost Caravan Park
☎ (03) 5154 1097

A1

Caravan Park at Orbost. 2-6 Lochiel St

HEMA 65 H10 37 42 38 S 148 27 14 E

17 Snowy River Rest Area 1

C107

Rest Area 8 km S of Orbost or 8 km N of Marlo. Beside river. Self Contained Vehicles only

HEMA 65 H10 37 44 24 S 148 30 26 E

18 Snowy River Rest Area 2

C107

Rest Area 12 km S of Orbost or 4 km N of Marlo. Beside river. Self Contained Vehicles only

HEMA 65 H10 37 46 2 S 148 32 13 E

19 Corringle Slips Campground
☎ (03) 5161 1222
Corringle Foreshore Reserve
Camp Area 18 km S of Newmerella, via Corringle Rd. Dirt road
HEMA 65 H10 37 48 0 S 148 31 21 E

20 Newmerella Rest Area
A1
Rest Area 6 km W of Orbost or 31 km E of Nowa Nowa
HEMA 65 H10 37 44 24 S 148 25 18 E
BIG RIG

21 Tostaree Tavern
☎ (03) 5155 7254
Parking Area at Tostaree. Jonsons Rd. Check in with Tavern before parking
HEMA 65 H9 37 44 51 S 148 11 3 E

22 The Glasshouse Camping Area
☎ 131 963
Lake Tyers Forest Reserve
Camp Area 22 km SE of Nowa Nowa or 48 km W Orbost. Turn S 6 km E of Nowa Nowa or 32 km W of Orbost onto Lake Tyers Rd, follow to end. 16 km dirt road
HEMA 65 H9 37 50 47 S 148 6 33 E

23 Stonehenge Caravan and Camping Park
☎ (03) 5155 9312
Camp Area at Buchan South. 9 km N of Nowa Nowa turn N onto Buchan Caves Rd, 15 km to Buchan South Rd, then onto Buchan South Gillingall Rd. Signposted. GPS at gate
HEMA 65 G9 37 31 51 S 148 8 8 E

24 Buchan Caves Camping Reserve
☎ 131 963
Camp Area at Buchan Caves. Buchan Caves Rd. Bookings necessary
HEMA 65 G9 37 29 43 S 148 9 50 E

25 Wulgulmerang Recreation Reserve
☎ (03) 5155 0244
C608
Camp Area at Wulgulmerang. 133 km NE of Bairnsdale or 112 km SW of Jindabyne
HEMA 65 E9 37 4 6 S 148 15 37 E
BIG RIG

Notes...

26 Suggan Buggan Campground
☎ 131 963
Camp Area 80 km N of Buchan or 87 km S of Jindabyne. Tight winding road in places, not suitable for caravans
HEMA 65 E9 36 57 9 S 148 19 27 E

27 Willis Campground
☎ 131 963
Camp Area 99 km N of Buchan or 68 km S of Jindabyne. Tight winding road in places, not suitable for caravans
HEMA 65 E10 36 53 41 S 148 25 22 E

28 Running Waters Creek Campground
Camp Area 102 km N of Buchan or 65 km S of Jindabyne. Tight winding road in places, not suitable for caravans
HEMA 65 D10 36 48 47 S 148 24 16 E

29 Burned Bridge Reserve
A1
Rest Area 12 km E of Lakes Entrance or 10 km W of Nowa Nowa
HEMA 65 H9 37 48 56 S 148 1 50 E

30 Lake Tyers Camp & Caravan Park
☎ (03) 5156 5530
Caravan Park at Lake Tyers Beach. 558 Lake Tyers Beach Rd
HEMA 65 H9 37 51 30 S 148 4 59 E

31 Lakes Entrance Apex Park
A1
Rest Area at Lakes Entrance. Opposite Tourist Information Centre
HEMA 65 H8 37 52 55 S 147 58 22 E
BIG RIG

32 Lakes Entrance-Gippsland Lakes Fishing Club
A1
Picnic Area at Lakes Entrance. Turn SW from roundabout opposite Info Centre, 50m turn R into car park of fishing club. Dump point next to jetty
HEMA 65 H8 37 52 58 S 147 58 18 E
BIG RIG

33 Nicholson River Reserve
A1
Rest Area at Nicholson. W side of bridge beside river
HEMA 65 H8 37 49 2 S 147 44 24 E
BIG RIG

34 Eagle Point Caravan Park
☎ (03) 5156 1183
Caravan Park at Eagle Point. 40 School Rd
HEMA 65 H8 37 53 32 S 147 40 53 E

35 Howitt Park
A1
Rest Area 1 km E of Bairnsdale. N side of bridge beside river
HEMA 64 H7 37 49 27 S 147 38 28 E
BIG RIG

36 Providence Ponds
Rest Area 34 km W of Bairnsdale or 18 km E of Stratford
HEMA 64 H6 37 55 14 S 147 16 25 E
A1
BIG RIG

37 Sale Showground Caravan & Motorhome Park
☎ (03) 5144 6432
Camp Area at Sale. Maffra-Sale Rd. N end of town
HEMA 64 J6 38 5 31 S 147 3 58 E
BIG RIG

38 Sale Motor Village
☎ (03) 5144 1366
Princes Hwy. 1 km W of PO. Power is pay per usage
HEMA 64 J6 38 6 45 S 147 3 24 E

39 Maffra Golf Club
☎ (03) 5147 1884
Camp Area at Maffra Golf Club. Via Stratford Rd, Fulton Rd. Behind Clubrooms
HEMA 64 J6 37 57 4 S 147 0 1 E
BIG RIG

40 Newry Recreation Reserve
Camp Area at Newry Recreation Reserve. 2 km N of Newry via Newry - Boisdale & Three Chain Rd. Adjacent to golf course. Donation welcomed
HEMA 64 H5 37 54 20 S 146 54 28 E
BIG RIG 72

41 The Quarries Campground
☎ 136 186
Camp Area 4 km N of Briagolong, via Freestone Creek Rd. Beside river. Pay at Briagolong Store
HEMA 64 H6 37 48 50 S 147 5 19 E
BIG RIG

42 Blue Pools Campground
☎ 136 186
Camp Area 10 km N of Briagolong. 6 km N of The Quarries Campground. Small vehicles only
HEMA 64 H6 37 46 50 S 147 6 46 E

43 Heyfield RV Rest Stop
☎ 0418 108 691
Camp Area 700m SE of Heyfield PO, cnr MacFarlane & Clark Sts. Camping in S area of reserve. Please take away own rubbish
HEMA 64 J5 37 59 6 S 146 47 15 E
BIG RIG 48

44 Cheynes Bridge
☎ 136 186
Camp Area 20.5 km S of Licola or 32 km N of Heyfield
HEMA 66 D6 37 45 50 S 146 40 7 E
C486
BIG RIG

45 Currawong Camp
☎ 131 963
Alpine National Park
Camp Area 11 km N of Licola on Tamboritha Rd. Beside Wellington River
HEMA 66 D6 37 33 7 S 146 36 44 E
BIG RIG

46 Manna Gums Camp
☎ 131 963
Alpine National Park
Camp Area 16 km N of Licola on Tamboritha Rd. Beside Wellington River
HEMA 66 C6 37 31 58 S 146 36 30 E
BIG RIG

47 Muttonwood Camp
☎ 131 963
Alpine National Park
Camp Area 16.5 km N of Licola on Tamboritha Rd. Beside Wellington River
HEMA 66 C6 37 31 49 S 146 36 52 E
BIG RIG

48 Red Box Camp
☎ 131 963
Alpine National Park
Camp Area 19.6 km N of Licola on Tamboritha Rd. Beside Wellington River
HEMA 66 C6 37 31 7 S 146 37 22 E
BIG RIG

49 Platypus Camp
☎ 131 963
Alpine National Park
Camp Area 22.3 km N of Licola on Tamboritha Rd. Beside Wellington River
HEMA 66 C6 37 30 43 S 146 38 40 E
BIG RIG

50 Cowwarr Weir
☎ (03) 5139 3100
Camp Spot 5 km W of Cowwarr at Cowwarr Weir. From Toongabbie - Cowwarr Rd turn N onto Weir Rd, follow signs to weir. At weir follow signs around to camping area. Self Contained Vehicles only. Narrow bridge crossing 10 tonne gross
HEMA 66 F6 37 59 49 S 146 39 34 E

51 Willow Park
Rest Area 1 km N of Rosedale. Beside La Trobe River. Gold coin donation
A1
HEMA 66 F7 38 8 31 S 146 47 28 E
BIG RIG 48

52 The Aussie Pub Rosedale
☎ (03) 5199 2504
Camp Spot at Rosedale Hotel. Check in with publican
HEMA 66 F6 38 9 7 S 146 47 24 E

53 Harriers Swamp Campground
☎ 131 963
Holey Plains State Park
Camp Area 10 km SE of Rosedale. Turn E 3.5 km S of Rosedale off Willung Rd onto Rosedale-Stradbroke Rd for 6.6 km, then S for 1.8 km of dirt road
HEMA 66 F7 38 12 31 S 146 50 45 E

54 Blind Joes Creek Rest Area
Rest Area 2 km W of Rosedale or 21 km E of Traralgon
A1
HEMA 66 F6 38 9 18 S 146 45 54 E
BIG RIG

55 Traralgon West Rest Area
A1
Rest Area 5 km W of Traralgon or 8 km E of Morwell
HEMA 66 F6 38 12 40 S 146 29 11 E
BIG RIG

56 Seninis Campground
☎ 131 963
Moondarra State Park
Camp Area 26 km NE of Moe. Turn W off C466 25 km NE of Moe or 6 km S of Erica onto Seninis Track. 1.3 km dirt road
HEMA 66 F5 38 1 24 S 146 20 24 E

57 Caringal Scout Camp
☎ (03) 5165 3210
Camp Area 9 km W of Erica. Turn W off C466 29 km NE of Moe or 2 km S of Erica onto Telbit Rd. 7 km dirt road. Beside Tyers River. Limited power
HEMA 66 E5 37 57 36 S 146 20 2 E

58 Erica Caravan Park
☎ (03) 5165 3315
C466
Caravan Park at Erica. 14 Station St
HEMA 66 E5 37 58 45 S 146 22 24 E

59 North Gardens Campground
☎ 131 963
C461
Camp Area at Walhalla. 1 km N of PO. Other campsites & big rigs at S entrance to town
HEMA 66 E5 37 55 57 S 146 26 55 E
BIG RIG

60 Aberfeldy River Camping Area
☎ 131 963
Baw Baw National Park
Camp Area 17 km N of Walhalla. Signposted off Walhalla - Aberfeldy Rd. Not suitable for caravans
HEMA 66 E5 37 51 13 S 146 25 52 E

61 Coopers Creek Campground
☎ 131 963
Camp Area 9 km SE of Rawson or 9 km SW of Walhalla. Turn E off C481 22.5 km N of Tyers or 5.5 km S of Rawson onto Coopers Creek Rd. 3 km narrow dirt road. 500m NE of Copper Mine Hotel. Alternatively, turn S off C461, 6.5 km from Walhalla
HEMA 66 E5 37 58 52 S 146 25 29 E

62 Boolarra Club Hotel
☎ (03) 5169 6420
C456
Camp Spot at Boolarra Hotel. Monash Way. Check in with Publican
HEMA 66 G5 38 22 48 S 146 16 36 E

Notes...

63 Boolarra Apex Park
Camp Area 8 km SE of Boolarra, via Morwell River Rd. Turn W at Boolarra South sign, then after 30m S into Morwell River Rd
HEMA 66 G5 38 25 45 S 146 18 32 E
BIG RIG

64 Gippsland Food & Wine
Parking Area at Yarragon. Princess Hwy, in rear car park, register with shop. Self Contained Vehicles only. Toilet only open during shop hours
HEMA 66 F4 38 12 14 S 146 3 44 E
20

65 Cafe Escargot
☎ (03) 5668 1589
Parking Area at Mirboo North. 10 Old Nichols Rd. SE of town via Grand Ridge East Rd, free overnight parking with a purchase. Self Contained Vehicles only
HEMA 66 G5 38 25 5 S 146 10 17 E
24

66 Neerim South Caravan Park
☎ (03) 5628 1248
Caravan Park 4 km E of Neerim South. Neerim East Rd
HEMA 66 E4 38 0 46 S 145 59 25 E
BIG RIG

67 Loch Valley Campground
Camp Area 9 km N of Noojee, via Loch Valley Rd & Loch Valley Ext Rd. 5 km dirt road. Beside river. Steep access
HEMA 66 E4 37 49 8 S 145 59 38 E

68 Toorongo Falls Campground
☎ 136 186
Camp Area 9 km NE of Noojee. Turn N off Mt Baw Baw Rd 4 km E of Noojee onto Toorongo Valley Rd. 4 km dirt road. Unlevel area beside river
HEMA 66 E4 37 51 19 S 146 2 28 E

69 Latrobe River Camping Area
☎ 136 186
Camp Area 15 km W of Noojee. Turn N off C425, 11 km W of C425/ C426 jcn or 14 km E of Powelltown. 400m off Hwy on Ada River Rd. Small vehicles only
HEMA 57 D14 37 52 54 S 145 53 35 E

70 Powelltown Rest Area
C425
Rest Area at Powelltown. W end of town
HEMA 57 D13 37 51 38 S 145 44 41 E
BIG RIG

71 Warburton Caravan & Camping Park
☎ (03) 5966 2277
Caravan Park at Warburton. 30 Woods Point Rd 1.5 km E of PO
HEMA 57 C13 37 45 11 S 145 42 19 E

72 Chirnside Park Resort
☎ 0404 044 098
Caravan Park at Chirnside Park
HEMA 57 C10 37 44 4 S 145 18 10 E
BIG RIG

VICTORIA

73 Kurth Kiln
☎ 131 963

Kurth Kiln Regional Park

Camp Area 8 km N of Gembrook or 23 km S of Launching Place, turn W into Soldiers Rd then 1.8 km of dirt road to Kurth Kiln. Small vehicles only. 4WD recommended

HEMA 57 D12 37 53 59 S 145 34 31 E

74 Nash Creek Campground
☎ 131 963

Bunyip State Park

Camp Area in Bunyip State Park 65 km E of Melbourne. From Gembrook via Beenak East Rd & Black Snake Creek Rd. 1.4 km E of Dyers Picnic Area. Small vehicles only

HEMA 57 E12 37 56 48 S 145 41 15 E

75 Picnic Point

Rest Area 14 km W of Warragul or 32 km E of Pakenham. 2 km W of Robin Hood Inn on the old Princes Hwy. Beside river

HEMA 57 F13 38 5 1 S 145 48 47 E

BIG RIG

76 Longwarry North Rest Area

M1

Rest Area on Princes Hwy 2 km W of Robin Hood turn off. Westbound traffic only

HEMA 57 F13 38 5 26 S 145 48 25 E

BIG RIG 20

77 Brew Road Rest Area

M1

Rest Area 27 km W of Warragul or 19 km E of Pakenham

HEMA 57 F12 38 4 18 S 145 39 48 E

78 Akoonah Park
☎ 0427 057 768

Camp Area at Berwick. Park is 2.5 km SE of Berwick along the Princes Hwy, entry into park via Cardinia St "Gate 5" . Bookings advised during peak period. Closed in February each year. Max stay 21 days

HEMA 55 E11 38 2 20 S 145 21 51 E

BIG RIG

79 Whittlesea Showgrounds

Camp Area at Whittlesea, McPhees Rd entry off Beech St. Not available during first week of Nov

HEMA 57 A8 37 30 38 S 145 7 30 E

BIG RIG 48

Sale - Leongatha - Dandenong

South Gippsland Highway

80 Gippsland Lakes Coastal Park
☎ 131 963

C496

Camp Areas between Seaspray & Golden Beach. 20 numbered Camp Areas, facilities & sizes vary. Dogs permitted in sites 1-6 only. Showers at Golden Beach

HEMA 64 K6 38 20 26 S 147 14 15 E

81 Golden Beach RV Rest Stop Area

Camp Area at Golden Beach. Self Contained Vehicles only. Donations appreciated

HEMA 64 K7 38 12 40 S 147 23 56 E

BIG RIG 48

82 Paradise Beach Campground
☎ 131 963

Camp Area 2.5 km N of Golden Beach, via Shoreline Dr

HEMA 64 J7 38 11 39 S 147 25 20 E

BIG RIG

83 Emu Bight Campground
☎ 131 963

The Lakes National Park

Camp Area 5 km E of Lochsport, via Lake Victoria Track. Bookings required

HEMA 64 J7 37 59 44 S 147 39 10 E

84 Reeves Beach Coastal Reserve
☎ 131 963

C459

Camp Area 10 km S of Woodside. Via Woodside Beach Rd, Balloong Rd & Reeves Beach Rd

HEMA 66 H7 38 34 24 S 146 57 8 E

85 White Womans Waterhole
☎ (03) 5183 9100

Won Wron State Forest

Picnic Area 5 km E of Won Wron, via Napier Rd. 5 km dirt road

HEMA 66 H6 38 28 55 S 146 46 19 E

86 Gormandale Recreation Reserve
☎ (03) 5197 7200

C482

Camp Spot at Gormandale, 20 km SE of Traralgon. Hyland Hwy

HEMA 66 G6 38 17 32 S 146 42 3 E

BIG RIG

87 Won Wron North Rest Area

C482

Rest Area 2 km N of Won Wron or 25 km S of Gormandale

HEMA 66 G6 38 27 32 S 146 43 47 E

88 Tarra River Rest Area

B440

Rest Area 1 km NE of Yarram. 10 tonne bridge limit

HEMA 66 H6 38 33 2 S 146 40 59 E

89 Port Albert Parking Area

Parking Area at Port Albert. 6 overnight bays available. Self Contained Vehicles only

HEMA 66 H6 38 40 22 S 146 41 38 E

BIG RIG 24

90 John Crew Memorial Picnic Area

B440

Picnic Area 2 km S of Alberton or 22 km E of Welshpool

HEMA 66 H6 38 37 25 S 146 39 30 E

BIG RIG

91 Agnes River Rest Area

B440

Rest Area 5 km W of Welshpool or 6 km E of Toora

HEMA 66 H5 38 40 18 S 146 23 11 E

BIG RIG

VICTORIA

92 Franklin River Reserve Rest Area
B440
Rest Area 2 km W of Toora or 10 km E of Foster. Beside river
HEMA 66 H5 38 39 6 S 146 18 0 E
BIG RIG

93 Yanakie Rest Area
C444
Rest Area at Yanakie. Near hall
HEMA 66 J5 38 48 41 S 146 12 16 E

94 Shallow Inlet Campground
☎ (03) 5687 1365
Shallow Inlet Coastal Reserve
Camp Area 8 km W of Yanakie. Turn W off C444 19 km S of Foster or 4 km N of Yanakie onto Lester Rd. Past caravan park. 4 km dirt road. Bush camping adjacent to beach. Open Nov to April inclusive
HEMA 66 J4 38 49 16 S 146 10 18 E

95 Tidal River
☎ 131 963
Wilsons Promontory National Park
C444
Camp Area 63 km S of Foster
HEMA 66 K5 39 1 48 S 146 19 16 E
BIG RIG

96 Bear Gully Reserve
☎ 131 963
Cape Liptrap Coastal Park
Camp Area 35 km SW of Fish Creek, via Walkerville-Fish Creek Rd. Turn SE at Cape Liptrap turnoff onto Walkerville South Rd for 3 km, then S along Bear Gully Rd for 5 km to beach. Dirt road. Small vehicles only
HEMA 66 J4 38 53 18 S 145 59 14 E

97 Foster Station Park
Camp Area at Foster. At old railway station site, via Station Rd & Lower Franklin Rd. Self Contained Vehicles only
HEMA 66 H5 38 39 42 S 146 12 42 E
BIG RIG 96

98 Foster North Scenic Lookout
A440
Rest Area 16 km E of Meeniyan or 6 km W of Foster
HEMA 66 H4 38 37 20 S 146 10 32 E

99 Bass Valley Camping Ground
Camp Area 8 km N of Bena or 1 km S of Poowong on Bass Valley Rd. Beside Bass River. Toilets only open 1Oct to 30April
HEMA 57 J13 38 21 38 S 145 45 52 E
BIG RIG

100 Loch Recreation Reserve
☎ (03) 5659 4360
A440
Camp Spot 1 km NE of Loch. N of Hwy off Loch-Poowong Rd. Big rigs at second entrance
HEMA 57 J13 38 22 3 S 145 42 44 E
BIG RIG

101 Lang Lang Foreshore Caravan Park
☎ (03) 5997 5220
Caravan Park at Lang Lang. Jetty Lane
HEMA 57 H11 38 18 25 S 145 31 16 E
BIG RIG

102 Yallock Creek Rest Area
M420
Rest Area 8 km W of Lang Lang or 2 km E of Koo-wee-rup. Eastbound only
HEMA 57 H11 38 12 57 S 145 30 10 E
BIG RIG

103 Swamp Tower Reserve
M420
Rest Area 3 km W of Koo-wee-rup or 21 km W of Cranbourne
HEMA 57 H11 38 12 47 S 145 27 32 E
BIG RIG

104 Balnarring Beach Camping Reserve
☎ (03) 5983 5582
Camp Areas at Balnarring Beach. Three camping areas. Signposted from Rangers Office. 154 Balnarring Rd. Open Sept-June. Bookings essential
HEMA 57 J8 38 23 24 S 145 7 29 E

105 Point Leo Foreshore Camping Reserve
☎ (03) 5989 8333
Camp Area at Point Leo. Point Leo Rd. Bookings essential for peak periods
HEMA 57 K8 38 25 19 S 145 4 19 E

106 Shoreham Foreshore Reserve
☎ (03) 5989 8325
Camp Area at Shoreham. 57 Prout Webb Rd. Bookings essential for peak periods
HEMA 57 K8 38 25 44 S 145 3 3 E

107 Rosebud Foreshore Reserve
☎ (03) 5950 1011
Camp Area at Rosebud. Bookings essential for peak periods. Open November to April
HEMA 56 J7 38 21 41 S 144 53 1 E

108 Capel Sound Foreshore Reserves - Rosebud West & Tootgarook
☎ (03) 5986 4382
Camp Areas at Rosebud West & Tootgarook. Bookings essential for peak periods. Tootgarook only open November to April
HEMA 56 J6 38 21 46 S 144 52 49 E
BIG RIG

Notes...

VICTORIA

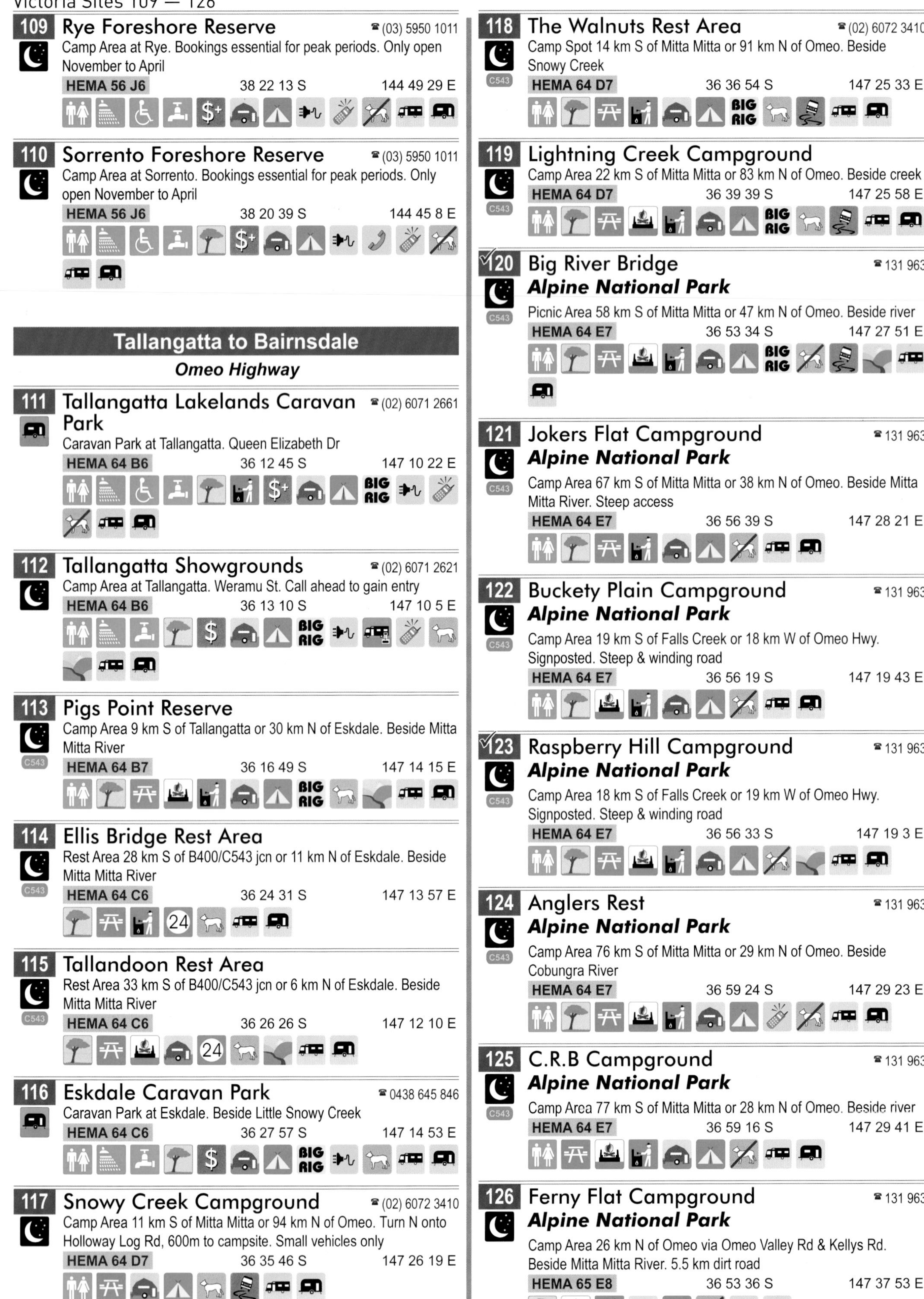

109 Rye Foreshore Reserve
☎ (03) 5950 1011

Camp Area at Rye. Bookings essential for peak periods. Only open November to April

HEMA 56 J6 38 22 13 S 144 49 29 E

110 Sorrento Foreshore Reserve
☎ (03) 5950 1011

Camp Area at Sorrento. Bookings essential for peak periods. Only open November to April

HEMA 56 J6 38 20 39 S 144 45 8 E

Tallangatta to Bairnsdale
Omeo Highway

111 Tallangatta Lakelands Caravan Park
☎ (02) 6071 2661

Caravan Park at Tallangatta. Queen Elizabeth Dr

HEMA 64 B6 36 12 45 S 147 10 22 E

112 Tallangatta Showgrounds
☎ (02) 6071 2621

Camp Area at Tallangatta. Weramu St. Call ahead to gain entry

HEMA 64 B6 36 13 10 S 147 10 5 E

113 Pigs Point Reserve
C543

Camp Area 9 km S of Tallangatta or 30 km N of Eskdale. Beside Mitta Mitta River

HEMA 64 B7 36 16 49 S 147 14 15 E

114 Ellis Bridge Rest Area
C543

Rest Area 28 km S of B400/C543 jcn or 11 km N of Eskdale. Beside Mitta Mitta River

HEMA 64 C6 36 24 31 S 147 13 57 E

24

115 Tallandoon Rest Area
C543

Rest Area 33 km S of B400/C543 jcn or 6 km N of Eskdale. Beside Mitta Mitta River

HEMA 64 C6 36 26 26 S 147 12 10 E

24

116 Eskdale Caravan Park
☎ 0438 645 846

Caravan Park at Eskdale. Beside Little Snowy Creek

HEMA 64 C6 36 27 57 S 147 14 53 E

117 Snowy Creek Campground
☎ (02) 6072 3410

Camp Area 11 km S of Mitta Mitta or 94 km N of Omeo. Turn N onto Holloway Log Rd, 600m to campsite. Small vehicles only

HEMA 64 D7 36 35 46 S 147 26 19 E

118 The Walnuts Rest Area
☎ (02) 6072 3410

C543

Camp Spot 14 km S of Mitta Mitta or 91 km N of Omeo. Beside Snowy Creek

HEMA 64 D7 36 36 54 S 147 25 33 E

119 Lightning Creek Campground
C543

Camp Area 22 km S of Mitta Mitta or 83 km N of Omeo. Beside creek

HEMA 64 D7 36 39 39 S 147 25 58 E

120 Big River Bridge
☎ 131 963

Alpine National Park

C543

Picnic Area 58 km S of Mitta Mitta or 47 km N of Omeo. Beside river

HEMA 64 E7 36 53 34 S 147 27 51 E

121 Jokers Flat Campground
☎ 131 963

Alpine National Park

C543

Camp Area 67 km S of Mitta Mitta or 38 km N of Omeo. Beside Mitta Mitta River. Steep access

HEMA 64 E7 36 56 39 S 147 28 21 E

122 Buckety Plain Campground
☎ 131 963

Alpine National Park

C543

Camp Area 19 km S of Falls Creek or 18 km W of Omeo Hwy. Signposted. Steep & winding road

HEMA 64 E7 36 56 19 S 147 19 43 E

123 Raspberry Hill Campground
☎ 131 963

Alpine National Park

C543

Camp Area 18 km S of Falls Creek or 19 km W of Omeo Hwy. Signposted. Steep & winding road

HEMA 64 E7 36 56 33 S 147 19 3 E

124 Anglers Rest
☎ 131 963

Alpine National Park

C543

Camp Area 76 km S of Mitta Mitta or 29 km N of Omeo. Beside Cobungra River

HEMA 64 E7 36 59 24 S 147 29 23 E

125 C.R.B Campground
☎ 131 963

Alpine National Park

C543

Camp Area 77 km S of Mitta Mitta or 28 km N of Omeo. Beside river

HEMA 64 E7 36 59 16 S 147 29 41 E

126 Ferny Flat Campground
☎ 131 963

Alpine National Park

Camp Area 26 km N of Omeo via Omeo Valley Rd & Kellys Rd. Beside Mitta Mitta River. 5.5 km dirt road

HEMA 65 E8 36 53 36 S 147 37 53 E

127 Gibbo River Bush Camping
☎ 131 963

C545

Camp Spot 26.5 km N of Benambra or 97.5 km S of Corryong. From Benambra 15 km winding dirt road. Not suitable for caravan access from Corryong. Steep creek crossing at entrance. Large open area beside river

HEMA 65 D8 | 36 45 25 S | 147 42 15 E

128 Ah Sye's Camping Area
☎ 13 19 63

C545

Camp Area 31 km N of Benambra or 93 km S of Corryong. From Benambra 20 km winding dirt road. Not suitable for caravan access from Corryong

HEMA 65 D8 | 36 43 52 S | 147 44 2 E

129 Swifts Creek Caravan & Tourist Park
☎ (03) 5159 4205

B500

Caravan Park at Swifts Creek. McMillan Ave, 500m E of PO. Adjacent to the Tambo River

HEMA 65 F8 | 37 15 47 S | 147 43 24 E

BIG RIG

130 Ensay Recreation Ground
☎ (03) 5157 3227

B500

Camp Area at Ensay. Doctors Flat Rd. Pay & pick up key call land line or mobile 0419 249 535

HEMA 65 F8 | 37 22 53 S | 147 49 25 E

131 The Little River Inn
☎ (03) 5157 3311

Camp Area at Ensay. Large open grassed area behind hotel, check in & pay at the bar

HEMA 65 F8 | 37 21 46 S | 147 50 7 E

BIG RIG

132 Bruthen Caravan Park
☎ (03) 5157 5753

B500

Caravan Park at Bruthen. Tambo Upper Rd. 600m E of PO

HEMA 65 H8 | 37 42 43 S | 147 50 8 E

BIG RIG

Wangaratta to Omeo

Great Alpine Road

133 Pioneer Bridges

Rest Area 2 km SW of Everton or 3 km NE of Markwood. Turn S 700m W of Everton onto Markwood Everton Rd. Beside Ovens River

HEMA 64 C5 | 36 26 32 S | 146 31 30 E

BIG RIG

134 Dederang North Rest Area

C531

Rest Area 5 km N of Dederang or 13 km S of Kergunyah

HEMA 64 C6 | 36 26 40 S | 147 1 1 E

BIG RIG

Notes...

135 Dederang Hotel
☎ (02) 6028 9325

Camp Spot at Dederang, Kiewa Valley Hwy. Check in with publican, camp area is behind the hotel. Toilets at hotel during opening hours

HEMA 64 C6 | 36 27 58 S | 147 0 46 E

72

136 Yackandandah Creek
☎ 136 186

Yackandandah State Forest

Camp Area 4.5 km SW of Yackandandah. Take Bell's Flat Rd to Yack Gate Rd. There are a number of sites along Yack Gate Rd & Number One Rd

HEMA 64 C5 | 36 20 18 S | 146 48 24 E

137 Running Creek Rest Area

C534

Rest Area 37 km E of Myrtleford or 1 km W of C531/C534 jcn

HEMA 64 C6 | 36 32 40 S | 147 2 47 E

BIG RIG

138 Mongans Bridge Caravan Park
☎ (03) 5754 5226

Caravan Park 13 km N of Tawonga or 18 km S of Dederang. Turn E 12 km N of Tawonga or 7 km S of C531/C534 jcn onto Bay Creek Lane

HEMA 64 C6 | 36 35 5 S | 147 5 37 E

139 Nug Nug Reserve
☎ 0418 336 272

Camp Area 15 km S of Myrtleford. Turn E off C526, 13 km S of Myrtleford before McGuffies Bridge onto Nug Nug Rd. Turn L after 1 km, then next R. Cold showers

HEMA 64 D5 | 36 39 42 S | 146 42 20 E

140 Porepunkah East Rest Area

B500

Rest Area 2 km SE of Porepunkah or 4 km NW of Bright

HEMA 64 D6 | 36 42 32 S | 146 55 35 E

BIG RIG

141 Lake Catani Campground
☎ 131 963

Mt Buffalo National Park

C535

Camp Area 28 km W of Porepunkah. Closed May to October. Bookings essential

HEMA 64 D5 | 36 44 7 S | 146 48 43 E

142 AH Youngs Camping Area
☎ 136 186

Camp Area 18 km S of Porepunkah. From Porepunkah roundabout turn S onto Buckland Valley Rd, follow for 18 km to campsites along river. 5.6 km dirt road

HEMA 64 D5 | 36 50 30 S | 146 51 4 E

143 Freeburgh Bridge

Rest Area 7 km S of Bright or 16 km N of Harrietville. Turn E off B500 onto Old Harrietville Rd. Camp spots on W side of bridge, entry track 5m from intersection. No camping on E side of bridge in picnic area

HEMA 64 D6 | 36 45 22 S | 147 1 24 E

144 Smoko Camping Area
☎ 136 186

B500

Camp Area 16 km S of Bright or 11.5 km N of Harrietville. Turn E off Great Alpine Rd (opposite house) follow track for 700m veering R to campsite. Beside river

HEMA 64 D6 | 36 49 39 S | 147 4 36 E

145 Scrubbers End Overnight Parking
☎ 1300 734 365

B500

Parking Area at Dinner Plain Alpine Village. Enter via Big Muster Dr & Scrubbers End Ln, E side of village. Permit required in winter

HEMA 64 E6 | 37 1 28 S | 147 14 36 E

BIG RIG 48

146 Victoria Falls Historic Area
☎ 131 963

Alpine National Park

Camp Area 25 km W of Omeo or 90 km SE of Bright. Near Cobungra Station

HEMA 64 E7 | 37 5 37 S | 147 25 30 E

Omeo-Dargo-Bairnsdale

147 Dogs Grave Campground
☎ 136 186

C601

Camp Area 22 km SW of Omeo or 44 km NE of Dargo. Turn S off B500, 3 km W of Omeo onto Swifts Ck-Omeo Rd for 7 km, then SW onto Upper Livingstone Rd for 6 km, then W onto Birregun Rd for 6 km. Winding dirt road

HEMA 64 F7 | 37 14 1 S | 147 22 51 E

148 Ollies Jumpup Campground
☎ 136 186

C601

Camp Area 61 km SW of Omeo or 12 km N of Dargo. 5.5 km N of Dargo turn NE onto Upper Dargo Rd. Winding dirt road. Signposted

HEMA 64 F7 | 37 23 9 S | 147 16 39 E

149 Jimmy Iversons Campground
☎ 136 186

C601

Camp Area 63 km SW of Omeo or 10 km N of Dargo. 5.5 km N of Dargo turn NE onto Upper Dargo Rd. Winding dirt road. Beside river. Signposted

HEMA 64 F7 | 37 23 54 S | 147 16 21 E

150 Italian Flat Campground
☎ 136 186

C601

Camp Area 65 km SW of Omeo or 8 km N of Dargo. 5.5 km N of Dargo turn NE onto Upper Dargo Rd. Winding dirt road. Beside river. Signposted

HEMA 64 G7 | 37 24 25 S | 147 16 3 E

151 Two Mile Creek
☎ 136 186

C601

Camp Area 66 km SW of Omeo or 7 km N of Dargo. 5.5 km N of Dargo turn NE onto Upper Dargo Rd. Winding dirt road. Beside Two Mile Creek. Signposted

HEMA 64 G6 | 37 24 31 S | 147 15 28 E

152 Dargo River Inn
☎ (03) 5140 1330

Camp Spot at Dargo River Inn, Lower Dargo Rd. Open Fri - Sun, for midweek bookings call ahead.

HEMA 64 G6 | 37 28 16 S | 147 15 17 E

$ BIG RIG

153 Meyers Flat Campsite
☎ 136 186

C601

Camp Area 12.5 km S of Dargo. Signposted access, next to Dargo Bairnsdale Rd beside river

HEMA 64 G6 | 37 30 59 S | 147 13 53 E

Far North East Victoria

154 Yackandandah North Rest Area

C315

Rest Area 22 km SW of Wodonga or 5 km NW of Yackandandah. Jcn of C532 & C315

HEMA 64 B5 | 36 16 33 S | 146 48 15 E

BIG RIG

155 Allans Flat Reserve

T6

Picnic Area 8 km NE of Yackandandah. Turn E off C527 7 km NE of Yackandandah or 13 km SW of Baranduda for 700m. Beside lake

HEMA 64 B6 | 36 16 27 S | 146 54 34 E

156 Ebden Reserve

B400

Rest Area 2 km SE of Bonegilla or 25 km NW of Tallangatta. Beside Lake Hume

HEMA 64 B6 | 36 9 6 S | 147 1 33 E

BIG RIG

157 Ludlows Reserve

B400

Rest Area 5 km SE of Bonegilla or 22 km NW of Tallangatta. Beside Lake Hume

HEMA 64 B6 | 36 10 16 S | 147 2 9 E

BIG RIG

158 Tallangatta Creek Rest Area

B400

Rest Area 13 km E of Tallangatta or 2 km W of B400/C546 jcn

HEMA 64 B7 | 36 11 46 S | 147 19 5 E

159 Tom Mitchell Reserve Rest Area

B400

Rest Area 6.5 km E of Koetong or 24 km W of Cudgewa- Tintaldra Rd intersection. Cnr of Murray Valley Hwy & Avondale Rd

HEMA 64 B7 | 36 10 43 S | 147 32 59 E

160 Cottontree Creek Campground
☎ 131 963

Mt Granya State Park

Camp Area 2 km W of Granya. Dirt road

HEMA 64 B7 | 36 6 53 S | 147 18 18 E

BIG RIG

161 The Kurrajongs Campground
☎ 131 963

Mount Lawson State Park

Camp Area 40 km W of Walwa or 16 km NE of Bungil Junction. Via Murray River Rd. Small vehicles only

HEMA 64 A7 | 35 57 22 S | 147 25 11 E

162 Burrowye West Rest Area

Rest Area 37 km W of Walwa or 23 km NE of C542/C546 jcn. Beside Murray River

C546

HEMA 64 A7 35 57 33 S 147 26 37 E

BIG RIG

163 Burrowye Reserve ☎ 131 963

Camp Area 25 km W of Walwa or 35 km NE of C542/C546 jcn. Beside Murray River

C546

HEMA 64 A7 35 59 15 S 147 31 39 E

BIG RIG

164 Koetong Creek Campsites ☎ 131 963

Mount Lawson State Park

Camp Area 7 km NW of Koetong . Off Mount Lawson Rd & Koetong Creek Track. Small vehicles only

HEMA 64 B7 36 5 54 S 147 26 49 E

165 Walwa Riverside Caravan Park ☎ (02) 6037 1388

Caravan Park at Walwa. River Rd. 1 km N of PO

HEMA 65 A8 35 57 16 S 147 44 14 E

BIG RIG

166 Neils Reserve ☎ 131 963

Camp Spot 7 km E of Walwa or 17 km NW of Tintaldra. 300m dirt road off Hwy. Beside Murray River

C546

HEMA 65 A8 35 58 22 S 147 48 46 E

167 Clarke Lagoon Reserve ☎ (02) 6076 2277

Camp Area 19 km SE of Walwa or 5 km NW of Tintaldra. 300m dirt road off Hwy. Beside Murray River

C546

HEMA 65 A8 36 1 20 S 147 54 39 E

BIG RIG

168 Clear Water by the Upper Murray Caravan & Tourist Park ☎ (02) 6077 9207

Caravan Park at Tintaldra. 17 Tintaldra Back Rd

HEMA 65 B9 36 2 46 S 147 55 46 E

169 Corryong Recreation Reserve ☎ (02) 6076 2277

Camp Area at Corryong. Showgrounds Rd via Strezlecki Way. Self Contained Vehicles only. Closed first 2 weeks in April

HEMA 65 B8 36 11 34 S 147 54 6 E

20

170 Indi Bridge Reserve ☎ (02) 6076 2277

Camp Area 4 km S of Towong Upper, 16 km S of Towong. Upper Murray Rd

HEMA 65 B9 36 14 3 S 148 2 0 E

171 Bluff Creek Campground ☎ 131 963

Burrowa - Pine Mountain National Park

Camp Area 21 km SW of Tintaldra. Take the Cudgewa - Tintaldra Rd, turn N into Cudgewa N Rd & S into Bluff Falls Rd. Dirt road. Small caravans only

HEMA 65 B8 36 7 19 S 147 46 40 E

172 Nariel Creek Recreation Reserve ☎ (02) 6076 2277

Camp Area 9 km S of Corryong or 24 km N of Nariel Creek. Via Corryong-Benambra Rd

C545

HEMA 65 B8 36 14 31 S 147 49 51 E

48

173 Staceys Bridge ☎ (02) 6076 2277

Camp Area 44 km S of Corryong. Via Corryong-Benambra Rd

C545

HEMA 65 C8 36 26 37 S 147 49 45 E

Wangaratta-Mansfield-Healesville

North East Victoria

174 Stan Allen Reserve

Rest Area at Oxley. 300m W of town over bridge. Toilets 100m towards town

C522

HEMA 64 C4 36 26 35 S 146 22 44 E

BIG RIG 20

175 Oxley Recreation Reserve

Rest Area 3 km S of Oxley, via Oxley Meadowcreek Rd. Donation for upkeep of facility

HEMA 64 C4 36 28 14 S 146 23 6 E

BIG RIG

176 Moyhu Caravan Park ☎ (03) 5727 9217

Caravan Park at Moyhu. Byrne St

HEMA 64 C4 36 34 37 S 146 22 43 E

BIG RIG

177 Edi Turnoff Rest Area

Rest Area 9 km S of Moyhu or 15 km N of Whitfield. Beside King River. Camp in permitted ares only, no generators permitted

C521

HEMA 64 D4 36 38 51 S 146 25 19 E

BIG RIG

178 Edi Cutting

Camp Area 10 km S of Moyhu or 14 km N of Whitfield. 1 km S of Edi turnoff. Dirt track to camps along King River. N area more suited to 2WD & large vehicle access

C521

HEMA 64 D4 36 39 48 S 146 25 11 E

Notes...

179 Gentle Annie Caravan & Camping Reserve
☎ (03) 5729 8205

Camp Area 24 km S of Moyhu or 2 km N of Whitfield. Turn E 23 km S of Moyhu or 1 km N of Whitfield onto Gentle Annie Lane for 1 km. Beside King River

HEMA 64 D4 36 45 12 S 146 25 26 E

BIG RIG

180 Tolmie Rest Area

C521

Rest Area at Tolmie, opposite hotel. Small area

HEMA 64 E4 36 55 4 S 146 15 55 E

181 Tolmie Recreation Reserve
☎ (03) 5776 2113

C521

Camp Area at Tolmie. 20 km NE Mansfield or 20 km SW of Whitfield. Donation for upkeep of facilities

HEMA 64 E4 36 56 5 S 146 14 14 E

182 Toombullup School Site
☎ 136 186

Toombullup State Forest

C517

Camp Area 6 km NW of Tolmie or 33 km SE of Tatong, along Tolmie-Tatong Rd. Dirt road. Small area 100m off road

HEMA 64 E4 36 53 16 S 146 14 6 E

183 Kelly Tree & Stringybark Creek Campground
☎ 136 186

Toombullup State Forest

C517

Camp Area 11 km NW of Tolmie or 28 km SE of Tatong, via Tolmie-Tatong Rd. Dirt road. Large area 400m off road

HEMA 64 D4 36 52 22 S 146 12 6 E

BIG RIG

184 Jones Campground
☎ 136 186

Toombullup State Forest

Camp Area 23 km NW of Tolmie or 16 km SE of Tatong, via Tolmie-Tatong Rd & Jones Rd. Turn W 21 km NW of Tolmie or 16 km SE of Tatong. 3 km dirt road from Tatong

HEMA 64 D3 36 50 22 S 146 8 37 E

185 Dodds Bridge Rest Area

C517

Rest Area 28 km NW of Tolmie or 11 km S of Tatong

HEMA 64 D3 36 47 39 S 146 8 6 E

186 Swanpool Reserve

Parking Area at Swanpool, S end of town. Self Contained Vehicles only

HEMA 64 D3 36 44 59 S 146 0 3 E

BIG RIG 24

187 Lima East Creek Rest Area

B300

Rest Area 18 km S of B300/M31 jcn or 2 km N of Swanpool

HEMA 64 D3 36 43 26 S 145 59 30 E

BIG RIG

188 James Camping Reserve
☎ 136 186

Strathbogie Ranges State Forest

Camp Area 13 km SW of Swanpool. From Swanpool turn W onto Swanpool - Lima Rd, then turn S along Lima East Rd for 11 km. 5.5 km dirt road. Beside Black Charlies Creek

HEMA 64 D3 36 50 11 S 145 56 49 E

189 Lake Nillahcootie

B300

Picnic Area 13 km S of Swanpool or 26 km N of Mansfield

HEMA 64 D3 36 51 27 S 146 0 16 E

BIG RIG

190 Blue Range Creek Campground
☎ 136 186

Camp Area 14 km N of Mansfield. Turn N 18 km W of Tolmie or 10 km N of Mansfield onto Blue Range Rd. 4 km dirt road

HEMA 64 E3 36 56 7 S 146 5 42 E

191 Carters Road Campground
☎ 136 186

C320

Camp Area 10 km E of Merrijig or 3 km W of Mirimbah. Turn N along Carters Rd for 400m. Unlevel area

HEMA 66 B5 37 6 11 S 146 22 2 E

192 Mirimbah West Rest Area

C320

Rest Area 12 km E of Merrijig or 1 km W of Mirimbah. Small vehicles only

HEMA 66 B5 37 6 31 S 146 23 10 E

193 8 Mile Campground
☎ 131 963

Alpine National Park

Camp Area 29 km SE of Merrijig. Turn S off C320 2 km E of Merrijig into Howqua Hills Rd. 27 km dirt road, steep in places. Small vehicles only. 4WD recommended

HEMA 66 B5 37 11 54 S 146 25 44 E

194 Sheepyard Flat
☎ 131 963

Camp Area 19 km SE of Merrijig. Turn S off C320 2 km E of Merrijig onto Howqua Hills Rd. 17 km dirt road. Beside river

HEMA 66 B5 37 11 33 S 146 20 46 E

195 Mansfield Lakeside Ski Village
☎ (03) 5775 2735

Caravan Park 7 km SW of Mansfield. 540 Howes Creek Rd

HEMA 66 A4 37 4 14 S 146 0 25 E

196 Blue Gum Flat
☎ 131 963

Delatite Arm Reserve

Camp Area 8 km N of Goughs Bay, via Howes Creek Rd (500m before Goughs Bay). Mostly dirt road

HEMA 66 B4 37 10 29 S 145 59 54 E

VICTORIA

197 Picnic Point ☎ 131 963
Delatite Arm Reserve
Camp Area 10 km N of Goughs Bay, via Howes Creek Rd (500m before Goughs Bay). Mostly dirt road
HEMA 66 B4 37 9 43 S 145 59 36 E

198 Delatite Arm Campgrounds ☎ 131 963
Delatite Arm Reserve
Camp Areas N of Goughs Bay, via Howes Creek Rd (500m before Goughs Bay). Mostly dirt road. 24 campgrounds of various sizes
HEMA 66 B4 37 8 18 S 145 58 38 E

199 Running Creek Campground ☎ 136 186
Camp area 7 km E of Howqua. From Howqua turn E onto Howqua River Rd. Dirt road, steep in places, numerous sites beside river. Water is from the river
HEMA 66 B5 37 14 11 S 146 13 54 E

200 Doctors Creek Reserve ☎ 136 186
C511
Camp Area 5 km S of Jamieson or 51 km N of Woods Point. Camping beside river
HEMA 66 C4 37 19 55 S 146 7 50 E

201 Skipworth Reserve ☎ 136 186
C511
Camp Area 7.5 km S of Jamieson or 48.5 km N of Woods Point. Beside river
HEMA 66 C4 37 20 46 S 146 8 34 E
BIG RIG

202 Kevington Hotel ☎ (03) 5777 0543
C511
Camp Spot next to Kevington Hotel. Pay at hotel. Fee for showers
HEMA 66 C5 37 21 30 S 146 9 41 E

203 Flour Bag Creek Reserve ☎ 131 963
C511
Camp Area 19 km S of Jamieson or 37 km N of Woods Point
HEMA 66 C5 37 22 59 S 146 13 31 E
BIG RIG

204 Tunnel Bend Reserve ☎ 131 963
C511
Camp Area 20.5 km S of Jamieson or 35.5 km N of Woods Point
HEMA 66 C5 37 23 1 S 146 12 44 E
BIG RIG

205 Twelve Mile Reserve ☎ 131 963
C511
Camp Area 21 km S of Jamieson or 35 km N of Woods Point
HEMA 66 C5 37 23 5 S 146 13 43 E
BIG RIG

Notes...

206 Blue Hole Reserve ☎ 131 963
C511
Camp Area 23.5 km S of Jamieson or 32.5 km N of Woods Point
HEMA 66 C5 37 23 26 S 146 14 56 E
BIG RIG

207 Picnic Point Reserve ☎ 131 963
C511
Camp Area 26.5 km S of Jamieson or 29.5 km N of Woods Point
HEMA 66 C5 37 24 31 S 146 14 41 E
BIG RIG

208 Snakes Reserve ☎ 131 963
C511
Camp Area 28 km S of Jamieson or 28 km N of Woods Point. Dirt road
HEMA 66 C5 37 25 0 S 146 14 24 E
BIG RIG

209 Knockwood Reserve ☎ 131 963
C511
Camp Area 31 km S of Jamieson or 25 km N of Woods Point. Dirt road
HEMA 66 C5 37 26 4 S 146 13 46 E
BIG RIG

210 Gaffneys Creek Campground ☎ 131 963
Camp Area 37 km S of Jamieson or 19 km N of Woods Point
HEMA 66 C5 37 28 40 S 146 11 33 E

211 Scotts Reserve ☎ 131 963
C511
Camp Area 53 km S of Jamieson or 3 km NW of Woods Point. Dirt road
HEMA 66 D5 37 33 34 S 146 14 21 E

212 Upper Yarra Reservoir Park ☎ 131 963
Camp Area 24 km NE of Warburton. Turn E 21 km NE of Warburton onto Woods Point Rd. Bookings required - gates close at 1700 hrs
HEMA 57 B14 37 40 10 S 145 53 25 E

213 Fernshaw Picnic Ground ☎ 131 963
Yarra Ranges National Park
B360
Picnic Area 11 km NE of Healesville or 11 km S of Narbethong
HEMA 57 B12 37 36 54 S 145 36 14 E

214 Dom Dom Saddle Picnic Ground ☎ 131 963
Yarra Ranges National Park
B360
Rest Area 16 km NE of Healesville or 6 km S of Narbethong
HEMA 57 A12 37 35 30 S 145 38 32 E
BIG RIG

215 Buxton Silver Gum Nature Conservation Reserve ☎ 131 963
B360
Rest Area 12 km N of Narbethong or 3 km S of Buxton
HEMA 66 C3 37 26 59 S 145 41 39 E
BIG RIG

216 Buxton Nature Reserve

Picnic Area at Buxton

B360

HEMA 66 C3 37 25 34 S 145 42 26 E

217 Cooks Mill Campground

☎ 131 963

Cathedral Range State Park

Camp Area 10 km SE of Taggerty. Turn E off B360 9 km N of Buxton or 2 km S of Taggerty onto Cathedral Lane & Little River Rd. 6 km dirt road

HEMA 66 C3 37 22 46 S 145 45 38 E

218 Rubicon River Rest Area

Rest Area 9.5 km NE of Taggerty or 2.5 km S of Thornton. Beside river

C515

HEMA 66 B3 37 16 46 S 145 47 58 E

BIG RIG

219 Jerusalem Creek Campground

☎ 131 963

Lake Eildon National Park

Camp Area 10 km SE of Eildon. Access via Jerusalem Creek Rd. At Jerusalem Inlet. Bush camping for small vehicles only

HEMA 66 B4 37 15 51 S 145 58 8 E

220 Koriella Rest Area

Rest Area 6 km NW of Alexandra or 11 km E of Molesworth

B340

HEMA 66 B3 37 9 28 S 145 39 42 E

BIG RIG

221 Brookes River Reserve

☎ 136 186

Camp Area 5 km W of Alexandra. Turn W off Maroonda Hwy 1 km N of Alexandra onto Binns McCraes Rd, Brookes Cutting Rd. 3.2 km to Camp Area. Signposted. Beside river

HEMA 66 B3 37 11 25 S 145 40 16 E

222 Lakeside Campground

☎ 131 963

Lake Eildon National Park

Camp Area 19 km NE of Alexandra or 18 km NW of Eildon. Access via U.T. Creek Rd from Alexandra or Skyline Rd from Eildon

HEMA 66 B4 37 10 37 S 145 51 44 E

223 Candlebark Campground

☎ 131 963

Lake Eildon National Park

Camp Area 17 km NE of Alexandra or 16 km NW of Eildon. Access via U.T. Creek Rd from Alexandra or Skyline Rd from Eildon

HEMA 66 B4 37 10 36 S 145 50 26 E

224 Devils Cove Campground

☎ 131 963

Lake Eildon National Park

Camp Area 18 km NE of Alexandra or 17 km NW of Eildon. Access via U.T. Creek Rd from Alexandra or Skyline Rd from Eildon. In Fraser Camping Area

HEMA 66 B4 37 10 25 S 145 50 21 E

225 Molesworth Caravan Park

☎ (03) 5797 6278

Caravan Park at Molesworth. Entrance opposite Hall. 300m off Hwy. Limited powered sites

B300

HEMA 66 B2 37 9 49 S 145 32 23 E

226 Sheepwash Lagoon Rest Area

Rest Area 2 km W of Molesworth or 11 km E of Yea

B300

HEMA 66 B2 37 9 48 S 145 31 23 E

227 Yea Family Caravan Park

☎ (03) 5797 2972

Caravan Park at Yea. 1 Court St. 800m E of PO

HEMA 66 B2 37 12 45 S 145 25 57 E

228 King Parrot Creek Rest Area

Rest Area 18 km NW of Yea or 20 km SE of Seymour

B340

HEMA 66 B2 37 8 46 S 145 16 1 E

BIG RIG

229 Trawool Rest Area

Rest Area 28 km NW of Yea or 10 km SE of Seymour. Just N of B340/ C383 jcn

B340

HEMA 66 B1 37 5 26 S 145 12 6 E

230 Murrindindi Scenic Reserve

☎ 13 61 86

Camp Areas 18 to 27 km NE of Toolangi. Turn E off B300 at Devlins Bridge onto Murrindindi Rd & Wilhelmina Falls Rd. Several campgrounds. Alternative access from Toolangi via Myers Creek Rd & Murrindindi Rd. Dirt road

HEMA 66 C3 37 23 26 S 145 33 14 E

231 The Gums Campground

☎ 131 963

Kinglake National Park

Camp Area 10 km N of Kinglake. Access via Eucalyptus Rd (Glenburn Rd)

C724

HEMA 66 C2 37 28 8 S 145 23 40 E

Wodonga to Melbourne

Hume Highway

232 Wodonga Showgrounds

☎ (02) 6024 1872

Camp Area at Wodonga. Entry off Victoria Cross Parade

HEMA 64 B6 36 8 16 S 146 53 37 E

BIG RIG 96

233 Chiltern Iron Bark Rest Area

Rest Area 5 km SW of Barnawartha or 4 km NE of Chiltern

M31

HEMA 64 B5 36 8 16 S 146 38 51 E

BIG RIG

234 Wenhams Camp
☎ 131 963

Warby-Ovens National Park

Camp Area 15 km W of Wangaratta, via Wangandry Rd, Gerret & Booth Rds. Small vehicles only

HEMA 64 B4 — 36 20 21 S — 146 12 14 E

235 The Forest Camp
☎ 131 963

Warby-Ovens National Park

Camp Area 21 km NW of Wangaratta or 17 km SW of Peechelba. Turn W 13 km N of Wangaratta or 9 km S of Peechelba along Boweya Rd, then N along Camp Rd after 6 km

HEMA 64 B4 — 36 13 19 S — 146 10 43 E

236 Glenrowan Caravan & Tourist Park
☎ (03) 5766 2288

Caravan Park at Glenrowan. 2 km N of PO

HEMA 64 C4 — 36 27 6 S — 146 14 13 E

BIG RIG

237 Mokoan Rest Area

M31

Rest Area 30 km SW of B500/M31 jcn or 17 km NE of B300/M31 jcn. Both sides of road

HEMA 64 C3 — 36 29 54 S — 146 6 25 E

BIG RIG

238 Balmattum Rest Area

M31

Rest Area 7 km NE of Euroa. Northbound only

HEMA 64 D2 — 36 42 49 S — 145 38 7 E

BIG RIG

239 Ruffy Recreation Reserve (Maygar Park)

Parking Area at Ruffy, 1.5 km N of Ruffy Noye Ln via Buntings Hill Rd

HEMA 64 E2 — 36 58 5 S — 145 30 56 E

48

240 Coach Road Rest Area

M31

Rest Area 33 km SW of Euroa or 6 km NE of A39/M31 jcn. Southbound only

HEMA 64 E1 — 36 56 31 S — 145 12 43 E

BIG RIG

241 Grass Tree Rest Area

M31

Rest Area 36 km SW of Euroa or 3 km NE of A39/M31 jcn. Northbound only

HEMA 64 E1 — 36 57 47 S — 145 10 50 E

BIG RIG

242 Great Divide Rest Area

M31

Rest Area 44 km S of C384/M31 jcn or 6 km N of B75/M31 jcn

HEMA 59 D14 — 37 24 12 S — 145 0 56 E

BIG RIG

Notes...

Tocumwal to Seymour

Goulburn Valley Highway

243 Katamatite Lions Memorial Park

Rest Area at Katamatite. 550m S of PO. Beside creek. Toilets near PO

HEMA 64 B2 — 36 4 50 S — 145 41 26 E

BIG RIG

244 Katy Caravan Park
☎ (03) 5865 1322

Caravan Park at Katamatite, Beek St

HEMA 64 B2 — 36 4 40 S — 145 41 19 E

245 Numurkah Lions Community Park

Picnic Area 1.5 km S of Numurkah. Nathalia-Katamatite Rd. Next to fitness centre, beside creek

HEMA 64 B1 — 36 5 52 S — 145 26 22 E

BIG RIG

246 Four Corners Motel & Caravan Park
☎ (03) 5829 9404

Caravan Park at Congupua. Goulburn Valley Hwy

HEMA 63 J13 — 36 18 13 S — 145 25 55 E

247 Calder-Woodburn Rest Area

A39

Rest Area 25 km S of Shepparton or 33 km N of Nagambie. Northbound

HEMA 64 C1 — 36 34 24 S — 145 20 29 E

BIG RIG

248 Greens Campground
☎ 13 19 63

Whroo Historic Reserve

Camp Area 8 km S of Rushworth, via Rushworth-Nagambie Rd & Reedy Creek Rd. 1 km dirt road. Beyond Balaclava Hill Info Centre

HEMA 63 K12 — 36 38 45 S — 145 1 41 E

249 Nagambie North Rest Area

A39

Rest Area 41 km S of Shepparton or 12 km N of Nagambie. Southbound only. Share with trucks

HEMA 64 D1 — 36 41 43 S — 145 12 51 E

BIG RIG

250 Major Creek Reserve
☎ 131 963

Camp Spot 14 km SW of Nagambie. Turn W off Goulburn Valley Hwy 6 km S of Nagambie onto Mitchellstown Rd for 8 km

HEMA 59 A14 — 36 51 19 S — 145 4 1 E

251 Taungurung Country Rest Area

M39

Rest Area 20 km S of Nagambie or 7 km N of Seymour. Southbound

HEMA 59 B14 — 36 56 54 S — 145 8 41 E

BIG RIG

252 Dargile Reserve
☎ 136 186

Camp Spot 15 km NE of Heathcote. Access via Plantation Rd off Heathcote-Costerfield Rd. Some dirt road

HEMA 59 A13 — 36 51 4 S — 144 44 34 E

253 Heathcote Rest Area

Rest Area at Heathcote. Ambers Dr. Self Contained Vehicles only

HEMA 59 B13 36 55 34 S 144 42 50 E

24

254 Knowsley Rest Area

B280

Rest Area 12 km SE of Axedale or 14 km NW of Heathcote

HEMA 59 A13 36 50 22 S 144 36 7 E

BIG RIG

Wodonga to Mildura

Murray Valley Highway

255 Rutherglen East Rest Area

B400

Rest Area 26 km W of Wodonga or 18 km E of Rutherglen

HEMA 64 A5 36 2 50 S 146 38 4 E

BIG RIG

256 Police Paddocks

☎ 131 963

Gooramadda State Forest

Camp Area 12 km NE of Rutherglen, via Gooramadda Rd (1.7 km E of Rutherglen) & Police Paddocks Rd. Beside Murray River. 1 km dirt road

HEMA 64 A5 35 58 45 S 146 30 34 E

BIG RIG

257 Granthams Bend

☎ 131 963

Camp Area 6 km N of Wahgunyah or 1 km S of Riverina Hwy. Turn E off Federation Way just S of John Foord Bridge, follow track. Signposted

HEMA 64 A4 35 59 8 S 146 24 45 E

258 'Willows' Camping & Recreation Reserve

Camp Area at Wahgunyah. End of Short St . Donation per day for Park Projects

HEMA 43 A4 36 0 28 S 146 23 26 E

$

259 Parolas Bend

☎ 131 963

Lower Ovens Regional Park

Camp Area 24 km W of Rutherglen or 7 km SE of Bundalong. Turn N off B400 just E of Ovens River, opposite Riverside Caravan Park, along Parolas Track. Big rigs just inside park entrance. Camping beside Ovens River. GPS at enterance

HEMA 64 A4 36 4 3 S 146 12 10 E

BIG RIG

260 Green Bank

☎ 131 963

Murray River Reserve

Camp Area 5 km W of Yarrawonga. Turn N off B400, 3 km W of Yarrawonga or 34 km SE of Cobram onto Cullens Rd. Left fork at info board. Camping beside river

HEMA 64 A3 36 0 35 S 145 58 38 E

BIG RIG

261 Chinamans Bend

☎ 131 963

Murray River Reserve

Camp Area 6.6 km W of Yarrawonga. Turn N off B400, 4 km W of Yarrawonga or 33 km SE of Cobram onto Brears Rd. L at gate onto Chinamans Track. Camping beside river

HEMA 64 A3 36 0 20 S 145 58 15 E

BIG RIG

262 Forges Beach No2

☎ 131 963

Murray River Reserve

Camp Area 10.6 km NW of Yarrawonga. Turn N off B400, 8 km W of Yarrawonga or 29 km SE of Cobram onto Forges Pump Rd. Signposted along Forges Bend Track. Camping beside river

HEMA 64 A3 35 59 35 S 145 57 21 E

BIG RIG

263 Bruces Beach No2

☎ 131 963

Murray River Reserve

Camp Area 13.2 km NW of Yarrawonga. Turn N off B400, 9 km W of Yarrawonga or 28 km SE of Cobram onto Bruces Rd. L at fork onto Bruces Track. Camping beside river

HEMA 64 A3 35 57 58 S 145 54 52 E

264 Nevins Beach East

☎ 131 963

Murray River Reserve

Camp Area 20.2 km NW of Yarrawonga. Turn N off B400, 14 km W of Yarrawonga or 23 km SE of Cobram onto Thoms Rd. R at info board along Collins Ln & Nevins Track. Camping beside river

HEMA 64 A3 35 57 20 S 145 53 31 E

265 Bourkes Bridge Rest Area

B400

Rest Area 19 km W of Yarrawonga or 18 km SE of Cobram

HEMA 64 A3 35 59 53 S 145 49 34 E

BIG RIG

266 Bourkes Bend No 3

☎ 131 963

Murray River Reserve

Camp Area 22.5 km W of Yarrawonga. Turn N off B400, 19 km W of Yarrawonga or 18 km SE of Cobram onto Burkes Bend Track. Camping beside river

HEMA 64 A3 35 58 44 S 145 49 33 E

267 Horseshoe Bend

☎ 131 963

Cobram Regional Park

Camp Area 6.8 km E of Cobram. Turn S off Barooga Rd onto River Rd for 4.8 km, then N onto Horseshoe Track. Camping beside river

HEMA 64 A2 35 55 41 S 145 41 45 E

268 Little Toms Beach

Cobram Regional Park

Camp Area 2.4 km N of Cobram. Turn N onto Wondah St from C370 (Cobram Barooga Rd). Cross over levy at end of road, take middle track for .6 km. Signposted

HEMA 64 A2 35 54 3 S 145 39 24 E

269 Big Toms Beach

☎ 131 963

Cobram Regional Park

Camp Area 3 km N of Cobram. Turn N onto Wondah St from C370 (Cobram Baroonga Rd). At end of street take track over the levee. After grid take middle dirt track for 2 km. Camp areas along river. Toilet block 1 km away

HEMA 64 A2 35 53 37 S 145 38 52 E

BIG RIG

270 The Big Strawberry

☎ (03) 5871 1300

Parking Area at Koonoomoo. Check in with the cafe. Power available for a fee

HEMA 64 A2 35 53 19 S 145 34 28 E

BIG RIG 24

271 Dead River Beach

☎ 131 963

Murray River Reserve

Camp Area 5.5 km NW of Cobram. Turn N off Cobram-Koonoomo Rd 1.7 km W of Cobram onto Racecourse Rd. Travel to end of road through gate/grid. After 200m take middle track for 500m, then R into Dead River Track. Camping beside river

HEMA 64 A2 35 52 49 S 145 37 45 E

BIG RIG

272 Weiss Beach

Cobram Regional Park

Camp Area 13.5 km N of Cobram or 17.5 km S of Tocumwal. Turn E off Cobram Koonoomoo Rd (C357) onto Fresian Rd, then L into Levings Rd, cross levy at end of road & take Cobram Track for 3.5 km. Signposted

HEMA 64 A2 35 51 41 S 145 35 45 E

273 Finley Beach

☎ 131 963

Tocumwal Regional Park

Camp Area 2.5 km S of Tocumwal. Turn E off A39, 2 km S of Tocumwal along Finley Track. Camping beside river

HEMA 64 A2 35 49 22 S 145 33 34 E

274 Apex Beach

☎ 131 963

Tocumwal Regional Park

Camp Area 2.5 km SW of Tocumwal. Turn W off A39, 200m S of bridge, signposted "Time-Out Resort", then L over railway line onto Pumps Bend Track for 1 km. Camping beside river

HEMA 64 A2 35 48 47 S 145 32 54 E

275 Barmah National Park

☎ 131 963

Camp Area 20 km W of Tocumwal. Various sites along Murray River

HEMA 64 A1 35 51 39 S 145 17 44 E

Notes...

276 Barmah Lakes Campground

☎ 131 963

Barmah National Park

Camp Area 7 km N of Barmah. Turn N at Hotel onto Moira Lake Rd, follow to park entrance

HEMA 63 G12 35 57 17 S 144 57 32 E

BIG RIG

277 Riverbank Caravan Park

☎ (03) 5866 2821

Caravan Park at Nathalia. 1-5 Park St. 1 km E of PO

HEMA 63 H12 36 3 15 S 145 12 35 E

$ BIG RIG

278 McCoys Bridge

B400

Rest Area 18 km S of Nathalia or 8 km E of Wyuna, beside Goulburn River

HEMA 63 H12 36 10 41 S 145 6 58 E

BIG RIG

279 Wakiti Creek Resort

☎ (03) 5867 3237

Caravan Park 34 km E of Echuca. Turn N off Murray Valley Hwy 22 km E of Echuca onto Curr Rd for 7 km, then E along Yambuna Bridge Rd for 5 km

HEMA 63 H12 36 8 13 S 145 1 46 E

$ BIG RIG

280 Tongala Turnoff Rest Area

B400

Rest Area 10 km W of Wyuna or 21 km E of Echuca

HEMA 63 H12 36 11 57 S 144 57 5 E

BIG RIG

281 Christies Beach Campground

☎ 131 963

Echuca Regional Park

Camp Area 8.5 km E of Echuca. Turn N off Echuca-Bangerang Rd 6 km E of Echuca onto Simmie Rd, 2 km to various camping areas. 2.5 km dirt road. Camping beside river. GPS at entry

HEMA 63 H12 36 7 21 S 144 48 49 E

282 Echuca Lions Park

B75

Rest Area at Echuca. S end of town, 1 km E of roundabout at jcn of B75/B400. W bank of Campaspe River

HEMA 63 H11 36 8 23 S 144 44 24 E

BIG RIG

283 Wharparilla Flora Reserve Rest Area

B400

Rest Area 4 km NW of Echuca or 38 km SE of Gunbower

HEMA 63 H11 36 7 20 S 144 43 9 E

BIG RIG

284 Torrumbarry Weir

Murray River Reserve

Picnic Area 38 km NW of Echuca or 18 km E of Gunbower. Turn E 31 km NW of Echuca or 11 km SE of Gunbower

HEMA 63 G11 35 56 41 S 144 27 54 E

VICTORIA

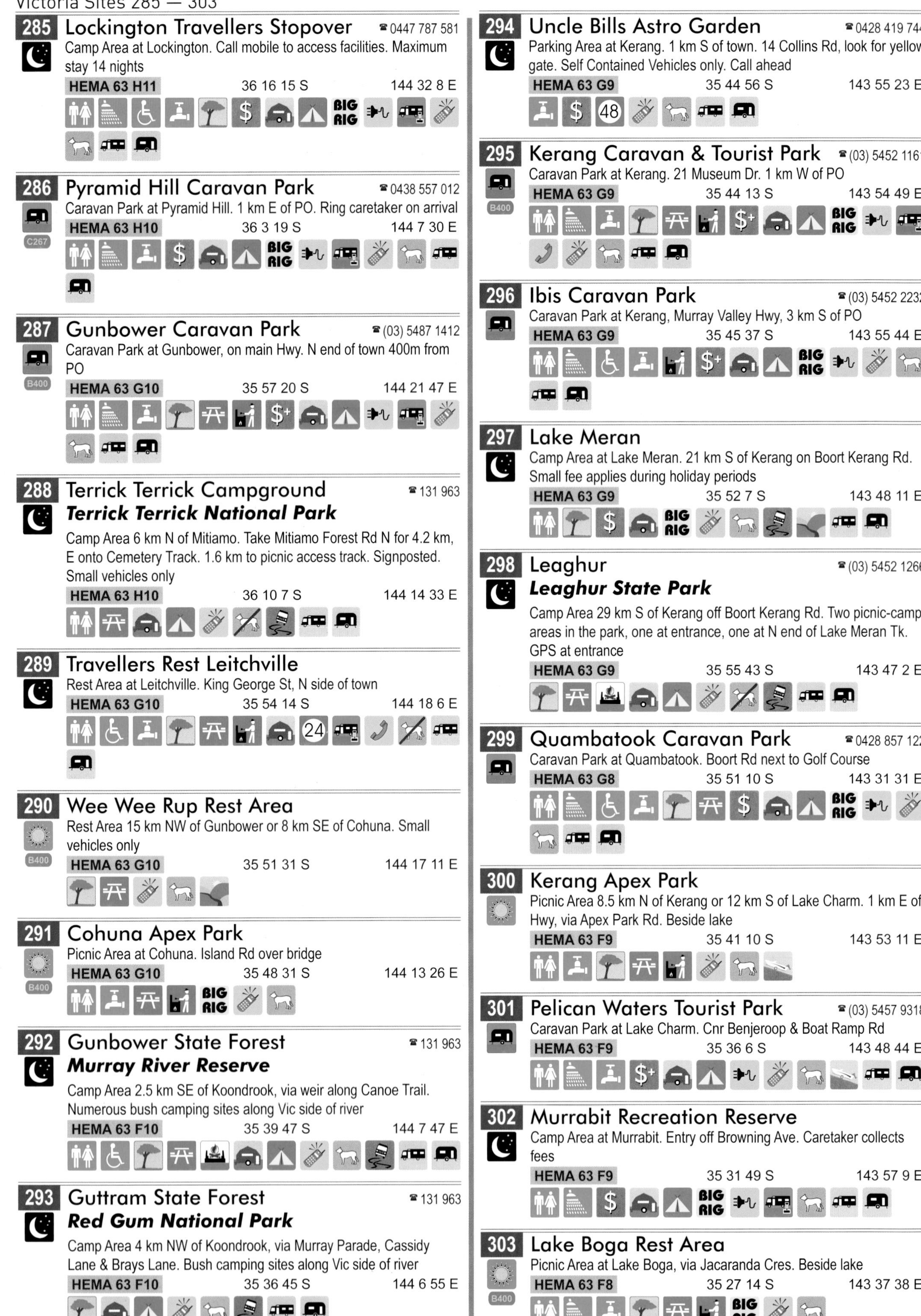

285 Lockington Travellers Stopover
☎ 0447 787 581

Camp Area at Lockington. Call mobile to access facilities. Maximum stay 14 nights

HEMA 63 H11 | 36 16 15 S | 144 32 8 E

286 Pyramid Hill Caravan Park
☎ 0438 557 012

C267

Caravan Park at Pyramid Hill. 1 km E of PO. Ring caretaker on arrival

HEMA 63 H10 | 36 3 19 S | 144 7 30 E

287 Gunbower Caravan Park
☎ (03) 5487 1412

B400

Caravan Park at Gunbower, on main Hwy. N end of town 400m from PO

HEMA 63 G10 | 35 57 20 S | 144 21 47 E

288 Terrick Terrick Campground
☎ 131 963

Terrick Terrick National Park

Camp Area 6 km N of Mitiamo. Take Mitiamo Forest Rd N for 4.2 km, E onto Cemetery Track. 1.6 km to picnic access track. Signposted. Small vehicles only

HEMA 63 H10 | 36 10 7 S | 144 14 33 E

289 Travellers Rest Leitchville

Rest Area at Leitchville. King George St, N side of town

HEMA 63 G10 | 35 54 14 S | 144 18 6 E

24

290 Wee Wee Rup Rest Area

B400

Rest Area 15 km NW of Gunbower or 8 km SE of Cohuna. Small vehicles only

HEMA 63 G10 | 35 51 31 S | 144 17 11 E

291 Cohuna Apex Park

B400

Picnic Area at Cohuna. Island Rd over bridge

HEMA 63 G10 | 35 48 31 S | 144 13 26 E

292 Gunbower State Forest
☎ 131 963

Murray River Reserve

Camp Area 2.5 km SE of Koondrook, via weir along Canoe Trail. Numerous bush camping sites along Vic side of river

HEMA 63 F10 | 35 39 47 S | 144 7 47 E

293 Guttram State Forest
☎ 131 963

Red Gum National Park

Camp Area 4 km NW of Koondrook, via Murray Parade, Cassidy Lane & Brays Lane. Bush camping sites along Vic side of river

HEMA 63 F10 | 35 36 45 S | 144 6 55 E

294 Uncle Bills Astro Garden
☎ 0428 419 744

Parking Area at Kerang. 1 km S of town. 14 Collins Rd, look for yellow gate. Self Contained Vehicles only. Call ahead

HEMA 63 G9 | 35 44 56 S | 143 55 23 E

48

295 Kerang Caravan & Tourist Park
☎ (03) 5452 1161

B400

Caravan Park at Kerang. 21 Museum Dr. 1 km W of PO

HEMA 63 G9 | 35 44 13 S | 143 54 49 E

296 Ibis Caravan Park
☎ (03) 5452 2232

Caravan Park at Kerang, Murray Valley Hwy, 3 km S of PO

HEMA 63 G9 | 35 45 37 S | 143 55 44 E

297 Lake Meran

Camp Area at Lake Meran. 21 km S of Kerang on Boort Kerang Rd. Small fee applies during holiday periods

HEMA 63 G9 | 35 52 7 S | 143 48 11 E

298 Leaghur
☎ (03) 5452 1266

Leaghur State Park

Camp Area 29 km S of Kerang off Boort Kerang Rd. Two picnic-camp areas in the park, one at entrance, one at N end of Lake Meran Tk. GPS at entrance

HEMA 63 G9 | 35 55 43 S | 143 47 2 E

299 Quambatook Caravan Park
☎ 0428 857 122

Caravan Park at Quambatook. Boort Rd next to Golf Course

HEMA 63 G8 | 35 51 10 S | 143 31 31 E

300 Kerang Apex Park

Picnic Area 8.5 km N of Kerang or 12 km S of Lake Charm. 1 km E of Hwy, via Apex Park Rd. Beside lake

HEMA 63 F9 | 35 41 10 S | 143 53 11 E

301 Pelican Waters Tourist Park
☎ (03) 5457 9318

Caravan Park at Lake Charm. Cnr Benjeroop & Boat Ramp Rd

HEMA 63 F9 | 35 36 6 S | 143 48 44 E

302 Murrabit Recreation Reserve

Camp Area at Murrabit. Entry off Browning Ave. Caretaker collects fees

HEMA 63 F9 | 35 31 49 S | 143 57 9 E

303 Lake Boga Rest Area

B400

Picnic Area at Lake Boga, via Jacaranda Cres. Beside lake

HEMA 63 F8 | 35 27 14 S | 143 37 38 E

304 Pental Island Holiday Park
(03) 5032 2071

Caravan Park 6 km S of Swan Hill. Pental Island Rd

HEMA 63 E8 35 22 38 S 143 36 43 E

BIG RIG

305 Loddon Floodway

Camp Spot 19 km SE of Swan Hill. Turn E 2 km S of Swan Hill onto Pental Island Rd for 14 km, then N into Caelli Lane. 3 km dirt road. Small vehicles only

HEMA 63 E8 35 22 40 S 143 41 22 E

306 Vinifera State Forest
131 963

Murray River Reserve

Camp Area 10.5 km NW of Beverford or 4.5 km SE of Vinifera. Turn N 7.5 km NW of Beverford or 1 km S of Vinifera via Forest Rd. 3 km dirt road. Various sites along riverbank

HEMA 63 E8 35 11 42 S 143 25 2 E

BIG RIG

307 Nyah Village Caravan Park
(03) 5030 2284

B400

Caravan Park at Nyah. Murray Valley Hwy. 1 km S of PO

HEMA 63 E8 35 10 56 S 143 22 38 E

BIG RIG

308 Nyah Recreation Reserve

B400

Camp Spot at Nyah. On riverbank behind Harness Club. Maximum stay 7 days. Honesty box for donations

HEMA 63 E8 35 10 18 S 143 22 53 E

BIG RIG

309 Nyah State Forest
131 963

Murray River Reserve

Camp Area between Nyah & Wood Wood. Various camping sites along W bank of river

HEMA 63 E8 35 9 19 S 143 22 56 E

BIG RIG

310 Wood Wood Caravan Park
(03) 5030 5444

B400

Caravan Park at Wood Wood. Murray Valley Hwy. Close to river

HEMA 63 D8 35 6 17 S 143 20 44 E

BIG RIG

311 Wood Wood Rest Area

B400

Rest Area at Wood Wood. Beside river, opposite Riverhaven Caravan Park

HEMA 63 D8 35 6 15 S 143 20 46 E

BIG RIG

312 Piangil North Rest Area

B400

Rest Area 2 km N of B12/B400 jcn or 45 km S of Boundary Bend. Beside river

HEMA 62 D7 35 2 34 S 143 19 29 E

BIG RIG

313 Wakool Junction
131 963

Murray River Reserve

Camp Area 7 km E of Piambie. Turn E off B400 27 km N of B400/ B12 jcn or 20 km SE of Boundary Bend onto Coghill Rd. Dirt road. Camping beside river. Small vehicles only

HEMA 62 C7 34 51 28 S 143 20 35 E

314 Passage Camp
131 963

Murray River Reserve

Camp Area 5 km SE of Boundary Bend. Turn E onto Mills Lane. Veer N at end of lane onto Passage Camp Track. Signposted to Passage Camp. 2 km to river. Small vehicles only

HEMA 62 C7 34 43 1 S 143 11 58 E

315 Boundary Bend Rest Area

B400

Rest Area 1 km E of Boundary Bend

HEMA 62 C7 34 43 8 S 143 9 58 E

316 Boundary Bend General Store & Caravan Park
(03) 5026 8201

Caravan Park at Boundary Bend. 27 Murray Valley Hwy. 300m W of PO

HEMA 62 C7 34 42 55 S 143 8 51 E

BIG RIG

317 Beggs Bend State Forest
131 963

Camp Spot approx 15 km SE of Robinvale. Take Murray Valley Hwy, turn NE 5 km E of Robinvale onto Tol Tol Rd for approx 5 km to signposted entry. Follow tracks to river. GPS at entrance

HEMA 62 C6 34 38 19 S 142 51 3 E

BIG RIG

318 Walshs Bend Camp

Camp Spot 5 km E of Robinvale. Turn N into Tol Tol Rd for 600m. Turn N onto track, signposted Walshs Bend. Follow dirt track for 2 km to camping areas along river. Beware low branches. GPS at entrance

HEMA 62 C6 34 37 16 S 142 48 45 E

319 Pump Road Camp

Camp Spot 2 km E of Robinvale. Turn N onto Pump Rd (E of Cemetery) for 500m. Bridge has a 2T weight limit. Turn E over water pipes, follow dirt tracks to various spots along river

HEMA 62 C6 34 36 25 S 142 48 10 E

BIG RIG

Notes...

Mildura to Yamba

Sturt Highway

320 River Road Caravan Park
☎ (03) 5025 2772

Caravan Park 7 km W of Mildura. 199 Ranfurly Way. Dogs by prior arrangement

HEMA 62 A4 | 34 10 40 S | 142 6 12 E

321 Horseshoe Bend
☎ 131 963

Camp Spot at Merbein Common. E end of town via River Ave & Old Wentworth Rd. Camping beside river

HEMA 62 A4 | 34 9 21 S | 142 4 27 E

BIG RIG

322 Merbein Caravan Park
☎ (03) 5025 2198

Caravan Park at Merbein. Box St. 1 km NW of PO

HEMA 62 A4 | 34 9 58 S | 142 3 3 E

323 Wallpolla Island

Camp Spot 26 km W of Merbein, via Channel Rd & Old Mail Rd. Dirt road. Camping beside river

HEMA 62 A3 | 34 9 13 S | 141 46 45 E

324 Merrinee North Rest Area

A20

Rest Area 35 km W of Mildura or 22 km E of Cullulleraine

HEMA 62 B3 | 34 15 37 S | 141 49 27 E

BIG RIG

325 Johansen Memorial Reserve

A20

Picnic Area at Cullulleraine. Beside lake

HEMA 62 B3 | 34 16 34 S | 141 36 0 E

BIG RIG

326 Bushmans Rest Caravan Park
☎ (03) 5028 2252

A20

Caravan Park at Cullulleraine. 70 Sturt Hwy, beside lake

HEMA 62 B3 | 34 16 23 S | 141 35 13 E

BIG RIG

327 Lake Cullulleraine Holiday Park
☎ (03) 5028 2226

Caravan Park at Cullulleraine. Off Sturt Hwy beside lake

HEMA 62 B3 | 34 16 40 S | 141 36 0 E

BIG RIG

328 Lock 9

Camp Spot 10 km N of Cullulleraine. Turn N 1 km W of Cullulleraine. 9 km dirt road. Turn W at boat ramp sign, follow track. Camp spots near boat ramp. No camping at Lock car park

HEMA 62 A2 | 34 11 30 S | 141 35 39 E

329 Cullulleraine West Rest Area

A20

Rest Area 32 km W of Cullulleraine or 35 km E of Yamba

HEMA 62 B2 | 34 16 30 S | 141 13 55 E

330 VIC/SA Border Rest Area

A20

Rest Area 113 km W of Mildura or 25 km E of Renmark

HEMA 62 B1 | 34 16 26 S | 140 57 52 E

BIG RIG

Tooleybuc to Pinnaroo

Mallee Highway

331 Piangil Rest Area

Rest Area at Piangil. Hall St. Self Contained Vehicles only

HEMA 62 D7 | 35 3 19 S | 143 18 43 E

BIG RIG 24

332 Piangil West Rest Area

B12

Rest Area 9 km W of Piangil or 31 km E of Manangatang

HEMA 62 D7 | 35 3 25 S | 143 13 1 E

BIG RIG

333 Manangatang Travellers Rest

B12

Rest Area at Manangatang. Wattle St. Opposite Hotel, donation welcome for upkeep

HEMA 62 D6 | 35 3 10 S | 142 53 0 E

BIG RIG 24

334 Walpeup Wayside Stop

B12

Camp Area at Walpeup. Centre of town. Place camp fees in box at toilet block

HEMA 62 E4 | 35 8 10 S | 142 1 30 E

BIG RIG

335 Lake Walpeup Reserve

Camp Spot 14 km SE of Walpeup. Take Walpeup-Patchewollock Rd, turn N into Walpeup Lake Rd then E into Mclivena Rd. 6 km dirt road

HEMA 62 E4 | 35 11 53 S | 142 8 18 E

336 Underbool Rest Area

B12

Rest Area at Underbool. Cotter St .Honesty box for power

HEMA 62 E3 | 35 10 11 S | 141 48 35 E

BIG RIG

337 Underbool Recreation Reserve

B12

Camp Area at Underbool Gnarr Rd, N of railway line. Power box & water on W side of grounds, access around oval. Honesty box at toilet block

HEMA 62 E3 | 35 10 8 S | 141 48 47 E

338 Lake Crosbie Campground
☎ 131 963

Murray Sunset National Park

Camp Area 13.5 km N of Linga. Turn N 60 km W of Ouyen or 76 km E of Pinnaroo. 13 km dirt road. Signposted

HEMA 62 D3 | 35 3 19 S | 141 43 53 E

BIG RIG

339 Murrayville East Rest Area
B12
Rest Area 12 km W of Cowangie or 7 km E of Murrayville
HEMA 62 E2 35 15 43 S 141 15 3 E
BIG RIG

340 Murrayville Caravan Park
☎ (03) 5095 2126
Caravan Park at Murrayville. Reed St. Honesty box. Mobile 0439 952 126
HEMA 62 E2 35 15 57 S 141 10 54 E
$ BIG RIG

341 Ngallo Park
Camp Area 21 km SW of Murrayville. Turn S off Mallee Hwy onto Ngallo South Rd. E side of road. 3 km dirt road
HEMA 62 E1 35 16 23 S 141 4 9 E
BIG RIG

Mildura to Melbourne

Calder Highway

342 Kings Billabong Reserve
☎ 131 963
Camp Spot 8 km SE of Mildura, via Eleventh St. Right into Cureton Ave, then L at sign to Kings Billabong Reserve. Camping beside billabong. Maximum stay 7 days
HEMA 62 A4 34 14 42 S 142 13 7 E
BIG RIG

343 Psyche Bends
☎ 131 963
Camp Spot 12 km SE of Mildura, via Eleventh St. Right into Cureton Ave, then L at sign to Psyche Bends. 4 km dirt road. Camping beside river
HEMA 62 A4 34 15 16 S 142 13 55 E
BIG RIG

344 Red Cliffs Caravan Park
☎ (03) 5024 2261
Caravan Park at Red Cliffs. 8760 Calder Hwy
HEMA 62 B4 34 17 56 S 142 11 12 E
$+

345 Spences Bend
☎ 131 963
Camp Spot 1 km N of Nangiloc. Camping beside river
HEMA 62 B5 34 27 47 S 142 21 14 E
BIG RIG

346 Watts Bend
☎ 131 963
Camp Spot 2 km S of Colignan. Camping beside river
HEMA 62 B5 34 32 7 S 142 22 16 E

Notes...

347 Emmerts Bend
☎ 131 963
Murray Kulkyne Park
Camp Spot 7 km S of Colignan. Veer L at Info board. Camping beside river
HEMA 62 C5 34 34 10 S 142 24 36 E

348 Hattah North Rest Area
A79
Rest Area 51 km S of Red Cliffs or 3 km N of Hattah
HEMA 62 C5 34 44 31 S 142 16 18 E
BIG RIG

349 Lake Hattah Campground
☎ 131 963
Hattah-Kulkyne National Park
Camp Area 6 km E of Hattah. Turn N 5 km E of Hattah for 1 km. Dirt road. Narrow for last 100m. Must pre book
HEMA 62 C5 34 45 8 S 142 20 32 E
$+ BIG RIG

350 Lake Mournpall Campground
☎ 131 963
Hattah-Kulkyne National Park
Camp Area 15 km NE of Hattah. Turn N 5 km E of Hattah for 10 km. 9 km sandy road. Must pre book
HEMA 62 C5 34 42 18 S 142 20 8 E
$+ BIG RIG

351 Wemen Rest Area
C252
Rest Area at Wemen, beside river. Small vehicles only
HEMA 62 C6 34 46 56 S 142 38 13 E

352 Hattah South Rest Area
A79
Rest Area 12 km S of Hattah or 22 km N of Ouyen
HEMA 62 D5 34 51 49 S 142 17 58 E
BIG RIG

353 Blackburn Park
A79
Rest Area at Ouyen. Calder Hwy. 1 km SE of PO
HEMA 62 D5 35 4 24 S 142 19 14 E
BIG RIG

354 Lake Tyrrell Rest Area
A79
Rest Area 20 km S of Daytrap Corner or 7 km N of Sea Lake
HEMA 62 F6 35 27 12 S 142 49 44 E
BIG RIG

355 Sea Lake Recreation Reserve Caravan Park
☎ 0427 701 261
A79
Caravan Park at Sea Lake. 71-91 Calder Hwy. Honesty box for payment
HEMA 62 F6 35 30 12 S 142 50 56 E
$ BIG RIG

356 Green Lake Camping & Caravan Park
☎ (03) 5070 1058
Camp Area 10 km S of Sea Lake on Birchip Rd
HEMA 62 F6 35 35 48 S 142 50 54 E
$ BIG RIG

VICTORIA

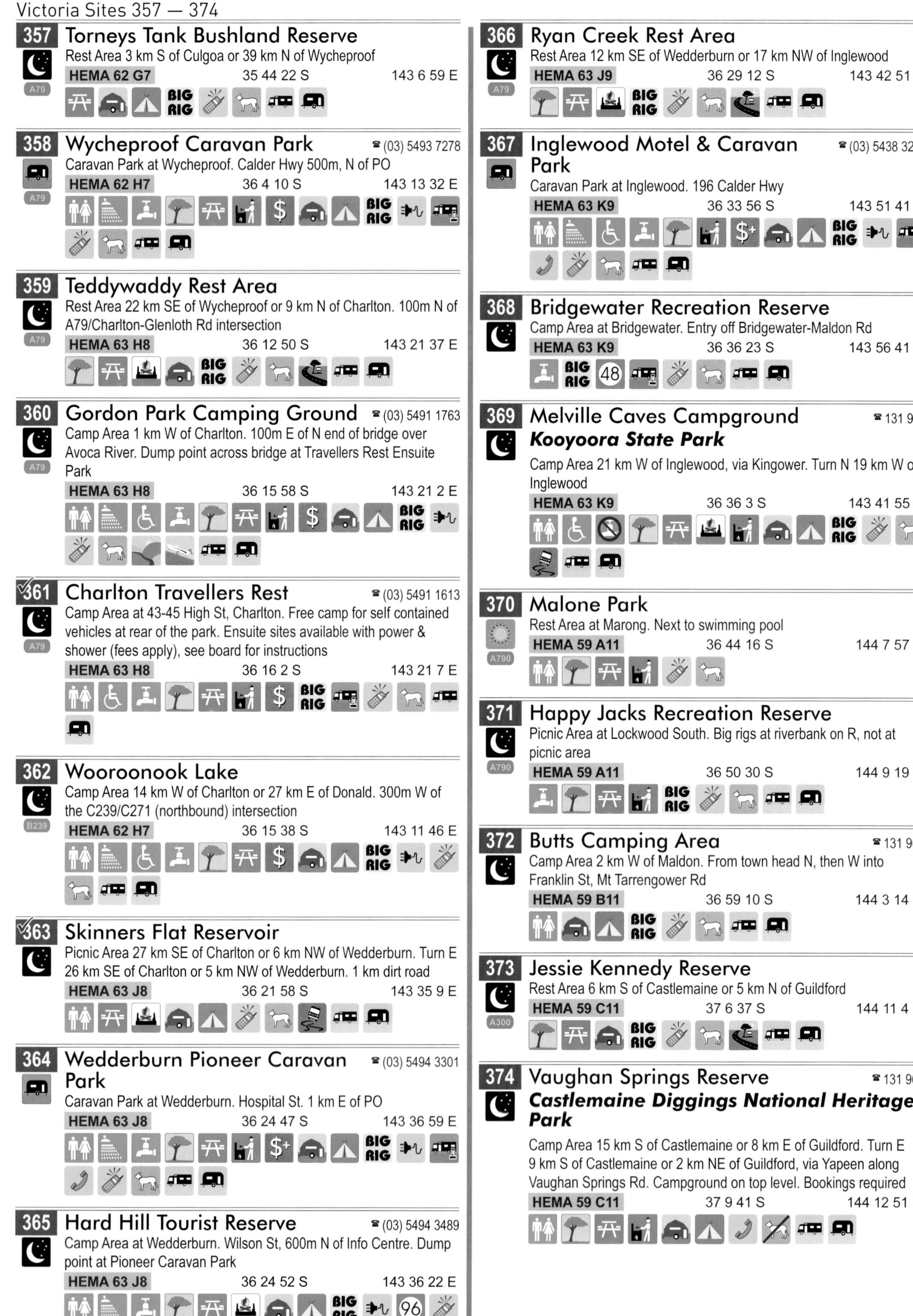

357 Torneys Tank Bushland Reserve
A79
Rest Area 3 km S of Culgoa or 39 km N of Wycheproof
HEMA 62 G7 35 44 22 S 143 6 59 E
BIG RIG

358 Wycheproof Caravan Park
☎ (03) 5493 7278
A79
Caravan Park at Wycheproof. Calder Hwy 500m, N of PO
HEMA 62 H7 36 4 10 S 143 13 32 E
BIG RIG

359 Teddywaddy Rest Area
A79
Rest Area 22 km SE of Wycheproof or 9 km N of Charlton. 100m N of A79/Charlton-Glenloth Rd intersection
HEMA 63 H8 36 12 50 S 143 21 37 E
BIG RIG

360 Gordon Park Camping Ground
☎ (03) 5491 1763
A79
Camp Area 1 km W of Charlton. 100m E of N end of bridge over Avoca River. Dump point across bridge at Travellers Rest Ensuite Park
HEMA 63 H8 36 15 58 S 143 21 2 E
BIG RIG

361 Charlton Travellers Rest
☎ (03) 5491 1613
A79
Camp Area at 43-45 High St, Charlton. Free camp for self contained vehicles at rear of the park. Ensuite sites available with power & shower (fees apply), see board for instructions
HEMA 63 H8 36 16 2 S 143 21 7 E
BIG RIG

362 Wooroonook Lake
B239
Camp Area 14 km W of Charlton or 27 km E of Donald. 300m W of the C239/C271 (northbound) intersection
HEMA 62 H7 36 15 38 S 143 11 46 E
BIG RIG

363 Skinners Flat Reservoir
Picnic Area 27 km SE of Charlton or 6 km NW of Wedderburn. Turn E 26 km SE of Charlton or 5 km NW of Wedderburn. 1 km dirt road
HEMA 63 J8 36 21 58 S 143 35 9 E

364 Wedderburn Pioneer Caravan Park
☎ (03) 5494 3301
Caravan Park at Wedderburn. Hospital St. 1 km E of PO
HEMA 63 J8 36 24 47 S 143 36 59 E
BIG RIG

365 Hard Hill Tourist Reserve
☎ (03) 5494 3489
Camp Area at Wedderburn. Wilson St, 600m N of Info Centre. Dump point at Pioneer Caravan Park
HEMA 63 J8 36 24 52 S 143 36 22 E
BIG RIG 96

366 Ryan Creek Rest Area
A79
Rest Area 12 km SE of Wedderburn or 17 km NW of Inglewood
HEMA 63 J9 36 29 12 S 143 42 51 E
BIG RIG

367 Inglewood Motel & Caravan Park
☎ (03) 5438 3232
Caravan Park at Inglewood. 196 Calder Hwy
HEMA 63 K9 36 33 56 S 143 51 41 E
BIG RIG

368 Bridgewater Recreation Reserve
Camp Area at Bridgewater. Entry off Bridgewater-Maldon Rd
HEMA 63 K9 36 36 23 S 143 56 41 E
BIG RIG 48

369 Melville Caves Campground
☎ 131 963
Kooyoora State Park
Camp Area 21 km W of Inglewood, via Kingower. Turn N 19 km W of Inglewood
HEMA 63 K9 36 36 3 S 143 41 55 E
BIG RIG

370 Malone Park
A790
Rest Area at Marong. Next to swimming pool
HEMA 59 A11 36 44 16 S 144 7 57 E

371 Happy Jacks Recreation Reserve
A790
Picnic Area at Lockwood South. Big rigs at riverbank on R, not at picnic area
HEMA 59 A11 36 50 30 S 144 9 19 E
BIG RIG

372 Butts Camping Area
☎ 131 963
Camp Area 2 km W of Maldon. From town head N, then W into Franklin St, Mt Tarrengower Rd
HEMA 59 B11 36 59 10 S 144 3 14 E
BIG RIG

373 Jessie Kennedy Reserve
A300
Rest Area 6 km S of Castlemaine or 5 km N of Guildford
HEMA 59 C11 37 6 37 S 144 11 4 E
BIG RIG

374 Vaughan Springs Reserve
☎ 131 963
Castlemaine Diggings National Heritage Park
Camp Area 15 km S of Castlemaine or 8 km E of Guildford. Turn E 9 km S of Castlemaine or 2 km NE of Guildford, via Yapeen along Vaughan Springs Rd. Campground on top level. Bookings required
HEMA 59 C11 37 9 41 S 144 12 51 E

375 Warburton Bridge Reserve
☎ 131 963

Castlemaine Diggings National Heritage Park

Camp Area 18 km S of Castlemaine or 11 km E of Guildford. Turn E 9 km S of Castlemaine or 2 km NE of Guildford, via Yapeen along Vaughan Springs Rd & Vaughan-Drummond Rd. At Loddon River bridge

HEMA 59 C11 37 10 11 S 144 14 16 E

BIG RIG

376 Ravenswood Rest Area

A300

Rest Area on Calder Hwy. 19 km N of Castlemaine. Northbound only

HEMA 59 B11 36 54 36 S 144 13 10 E

BIG RIG

377 Picnic Gully
☎ 131 963

Mt Alexander Regional Park

Picnic Area 3 km E of Harcourt. E end of Market St from BP servo. Follow sign post to "Picnic Gully" along dirt road. L at "Xmas Tree" sign, then R at "Oak Plantation" sign. Small vehicles only. Low trees

HEMA 59 B12 36 59 54 S 144 17 26 E

378 Elphinstone North Rest Area

A79

Rest Area 10 km S of Harcourt or 8 km N of Taradale

HEMA 59 B12 37 4 14 S 144 18 23 E

BIG RIG

379 Taradale Mineral Springs Reserve

A79

Picnic Area at Taradale, next to fire station

HEMA 59 C12 37 8 19 S 144 20 59 E

380 Kyneton Mineral Springs Reserve

Parking Area 3.5 km W of Kyneton on Burton Ave

HEMA 59 C12 37 14 9 S 144 25 10 E

BIG RIG 48

381 Lancefield Caravan Park
☎ (03) 5429 1434

C325

Caravan Park at Lancefield. 30 Chauncey St

HEMA 59 C13 37 16 44 S 144 43 48 E

BIG RIG

382 Woodend Town Park

A79

Rest Area at Woodend

HEMA 59 D12 37 21 14 S 144 31 46 E

383 Treetops Scout Camp
☎ (03) 5428 6756

Camp Area at Riddells Creek. 140 Royal Parade off Melvins Rd

HEMA 59 D13 37 26 47 S 144 39 49 E

BIG RIG

Notes...

384 Firth Park Campground
☎ 136 186

Wombat State Forest

Camp Area 24 km W of Gisborne. Take Woodend exit off Calder Hwy. Turn W into Ashbourne Rd, 11k turn S into Chanters Ln, turn W into Pearson Rd, turn S into Beatties Rd into Firth Rd. 5 km dirt road

HEMA 59 D12 37 26 7 S 144 24 35 E

Ouyen-Ballarat-Geelong

Sunraysia and Midland Highways

385 BJ Robertson Memorial Park

B220

Rest Area at Tempy

HEMA 62 E5 35 20 43 S 142 25 28 E

386 Casuarina Campground
☎ 131 963

Wyperfeld National Park

Camp Area 23 km W of Patchewollock, via Pine Plains Rd & Meridian Rd from Baring. 15 km dirt road. Signposted. Must pre book

HEMA 62 F4 35 26 43 S 141 59 43 E

387 Woomelang RV Stop

Camp Area at Woomelang. Cnr Gloucester Ave & Proctor St, donation, please pay at PO / Store

HEMA 62 F6 35 40 54 S 142 39 52 E

BIG RIG 96

388 Cronomby Tanks

Parking Area at Woomelang. Entry off Cronomby Tanks Rd. Self Contained Vehicles only

HEMA 62 F6 35 41 10 S 142 39 48 E

BIG RIG 24

389 Kinnabulla Rest Area

B220

Rest Area at Kinnabulla, 24 km NW of Birchip

HEMA 62 G6 35 54 6 S 142 47 49 E

390 Tchum Lake Camping
☎ (03) 5492 2767

Camp Area 8 km E of Birchip

HEMA 62 H7 35 59 44 S 143 0 14 E

BIG RIG

391 Lake Watchem

Camp Area 1 km W of Watchem. Fees payable at community store

HEMA 62 H6 36 8 54 S 142 50 51 E

BIG RIG

392 Donald Apex Park

B220

Rest Area at Donald. N end of town

HEMA 62 J7 36 22 3 S 142 58 39 E

393 Byrne St Rest Area

Rest Area at Donald. Byrne St W side of town. Self Contained Vehicles only

HEMA 62 J7 36 22 21 S 142 58 56 E

20

394 Donald Lakeside Caravan Park
(03) 5497 1764
Caravan Park at Donald. 2 Corack Rd. 1 km N of PO
HEMA 62 J7 | 36 21 52 S | 142 59 16 E
C261
BIG RIG

395 Beazleys Bridge Rest Area
Rest Area 24 km N of Navarre or 14 km SW of St Arnaud
HEMA 62 K7 | 36 42 7 S | 143 9 45 E
C241
BIG RIG

396 Teddington Reservoir
131 963
Kara Kara National Park
Camp Spot 6 km SW of Stuart Mill. Turn W at Stuart Mill onto Teddington Rd. Some dirt road
HEMA 59 A8 | 36 50 36 S | 143 15 46 E
BIG RIG

397 Stuart Mill South Rest Area
Rest Area 5 km S of Stuart Mill or 34 km N of Avoca
HEMA 59 A8 | 36 50 23 S | 143 19 10 E
B220
BIG RIG

398 Moonambel Recreation Reserve
(03) 5467 2225
Camp Area at Moonambel. Entry to reserve is as you approch from the E. Payment & key at store
HEMA 59 B9 | 36 59 24 S | 143 20 12 E
BIG RIG

399 Mountain Creek Picnic Area
Picnic Area 400m N of Moonambel, via Greens Lane
HEMA 59 B9 | 36 59 7 S | 143 19 9 E

400 Landsborough Caravan Park
(03) 5356 9110
Caravan Park at Landsborough. Call into general store to pick up key & pay fees
HEMA 59 B8 | 37 0 30 S | 143 8 11 E
BIG RIG

401 Tanwood South Rest Area
Rest Area 29 km S of Stuart Mill or 10 km N of Avoca
HEMA 59 B9 | 37 1 3 S | 143 24 23 E
B220
BIG RIG

402 Waterfalls Campground
(03) 5465 1000
Camp Area 12.5 km W of Avoca. Turn W 200m N of PO onto Duke St, then R at T jcn onto Vinoca Rd. 5 km dirt road
HEMA 59 C9 | 37 5 55 S | 143 22 1 E

403 Glenpatrick Reserve
(03) 5354 8290
Camp Area at Glenpatrick. 9 km NE of Elmhurst on Elmhurst Glenpatrick Rd. Gold coin donation
HEMA 59 C9 | 37 8 15 S | 143 19 38 E
BIG RIG

404 Avoca Lions Park
Rest Area at Avoca. Bridport St. Beside Avoca River
HEMA 59 C9 | 37 5 25 S | 143 28 22 E
B180
BIG RIG

405 Avoca Caravan Park
(03) 5465 3073
Caravan Park at Avoca. Liebig St. 1.2 km W of PO
HEMA 59 C9 | 37 5 36 S | 143 28 7 E

406 Amphitheatre Rest Area
Rest Area at Amphitheatre. 13 km SW of Avoca or 50 km NE of Ararat
HEMA 59 C9 | 37 10 55 S | 143 23 59 E
BIG RIG

407 Dunneworth Rest Area
Rest Area 46 km SW of Avoca or 17 km NE of Ararat
HEMA 59 C8 | 37 11 50 S | 143 5 7 E
BIG RIG

408 Elmhurst Recreation Reserve
Camp Area at Elmhurst. Off Green St. Pay at Hotel
HEMA 59 C8 | 37 10 56 S | 143 14 34 E
BIG RIG 72

409 Bung Bong Rest Area
Rest Area 8 km E of Avoca or 18 km W of Maryborough. Next to historical church
HEMA 59 C9 | 37 5 53 S | 143 34 9 E
B180
BIG RIG

410 Paddys Ranges State Park
131 963
Camp Spot 8 km SW of Maryborough or 25 km E of Avoca, via Karri Track (dirt road) from Old Avoca Rd
HEMA 59 B10 | 37 4 58 S | 143 41 27 E

411 Lexton South Rest Area
Rest Area 4 km SE of Lexton or 21 km NW of Learmonth
HEMA 59 C9 | 37 17 20 S | 143 32 53 E
B220
BIG RIG

412 Lake Learmonth Caravan Park
(03) 5343 2406
Caravan Park at Learmonth. Laidlaw St, Alexander Park
HEMA 59 D10 | 37 25 22 S | 143 42 39 E

413 Clarendon Rest Area
Rest Area 2 km S of Clarendon or 8 km N of Elaine
HEMA 59 E11 | 37 42 33 S | 143 58 56 E
A300
BIG RIG

414 Hunts Bridge Camping Area
131 963
Lal Lal State Forest
Camp Area 13 km NE of Elaine. From N side of town take Settlement Rd for 5.6 km, R at T jcn onto Doran-Egerton Rd for 5.3 km, L at T jcn for 400m, L at jcn for 1.7 km. Beside river. 6 km dirt road
HEMA 59 E11 | 37 42 37 S | 144 5 41 E

415 Meredith Pioneer Park

Rest Area at Meredith. Wilson St. S end of town

HEMA 59 F11 37 50 49 S 144 4 23 E

Benalla to Naracoorte

Midland and Wimmera Highways

416 Casey Weir Rest Area

Rest Area 10 km NW of Benalla or 52 km E of Shepparton. Beside river

A300

HEMA 64 C3 36 28 29 S 145 56 41 E

BIG RIG

417 Nalinga West Rest Area

Rest Area 33 km NW of Benalla or 29 km E of Shepparton

A300

HEMA 64 C2 36 25 47 S 145 41 47 E

BIG RIG

418 Riverside Cabin Park

☎ (03) 5823 1561

Caravan Park at Shepparton. Melbourne Rd 2.5 km S of PO

HEMA 63 J13 36 24 24 S 145 23 36 E

419 W B Ferrari Park

Rest Area at Mooroopna. W end of town

A300

HEMA 63 J13 36 23 43 S 145 21 10 E

BIG RIG

420 Acacia Gardens Caravan Park

☎ (03) 5825 2793

Caravan Park at Mooroopna. 3 km W of PO 6705 Midland Hwy

HEMA 63 J13 36 23 59 S 145 19 10 E

421 Aspen Lodge Caravan Park

☎ (03) 5825 2245

Caravan Park at Mooroopna. 1 Lawson St

HEMA 63 J13 36 23 52 S 145 21 40 E

422 Country Gardens Caravan Park

☎ (03) 5824 2652

Caravan Park 2 km W of Tatura. 270 Winter Rd

HEMA 63 J13 36 26 29 S 145 12 16 E

423 Hilltop Golf & Country Club

☎ (03) 5824 1689

Camp Area at Tatura. 71 Gowrie St. Bookings are essential, limited sites

HEMA 63 J13 36 25 57 S 145 14 13 E

Notes...

424 Merrigum Caravan Park

☎ (03) 5855 2727

Caravan Park at Merrigum. 84 Waverley Ave

HEMA 63 J12 36 22 26 S 145 7 52 E

425 Girgarre Town Park

Camp Area at Girgarre. On outer grounds of Town Park, cnr Winter & Station Sts, either side of Hall. No camping within fenced play area. Key for showers at PO, deposit required. Not available 2nd Sunday of the month due to markets

HEMA 63 J12 36 23 53 S 144 58 48 E

BIG RIG

426 Green Lake Recreation Reserve

Camp Area 16 km W of Stanhope or 24 km E of Elmore. Turn N off Midland Hwy 14 km W of Stanhope or 22 km E of Elmore. 1 km dirt road. Donation please for upkeep for facilities

HEMA 63 J12 36 26 16 S 144 49 42 E

BIG RIG

427 Aysons Reserve (Campaspe River)

Camp Area 8 km NE of Elmore. Turn N off Midland Hwy 32 km W of Stanhope or 5 km NE of Elmore along Burnewang Rd for 3 km. Old Elmore Field Day site, beside river. Permit required, see signage

HEMA 63 J11 36 27 34 S 144 40 8 E

BIG RIG

428 Rochester Caravan & Camping Park

☎ (03) 5484 1622

Caravan Park at Rochester. 1 Church St. 400m E of PO

HEMA 63 J11 36 21 36 S 144 42 16 E

429 Rochester North Rest Area

Rest Area 11 km N of Rochester or 18 km S of Echuca, beside Campaspe River

B75

HEMA 63 H11 36 16 31 S 144 42 5 E

BIG RIG

430 Runnymede Highway Park

Rest Area 47 km N of Heathcote or 5 km SE of Elmore. Beside river

B75

HEMA 63 J11 36 31 25 S 144 37 39 E

BIG RIG

431 English's Bridge

☎ 136 186

Camp Spot 3 km E of Goornong. Turn E off A300 15 km S of Elmore or 36 km NE of Bendigo onto English's Rd for 3 km, then N for 400m at signpost "English's Bridge". Beside Campaspe River

HEMA 63 K11 36 37 23 S 144 33 42 E

432 Goornong Village Green

Rest Area at Goornong

A300

HEMA 63 K11 36 36 56 S 144 30 13 E

433 Huntly Lions Park
Rest Area at Huntly. S end of town. Small area
HEMA 63 K10 36 40 11 S 144 19 34 E
A300

434 Lake Weeroona
Rest Area at Bendigo. 2 km NE of PO. Big rigs on roadside
HEMA 63 K10 36 44 54 S 144 17 30 E
A300

435 Notleys Picnic Area
☎ 131 963
Greater Bendigo National Park
Camp Area 21 km N of Eaglehawk. Turn E off Bendigo-Pyramid Rd (C336) 12 km N of Eaglehawk onto Evans Rd for 4 km, then S at T jcn along Neilborough-Eaglehawk Rd for 5 km
HEMA 63 K10 36 38 59 S 144 15 47 E

436 Myers Flat Rest Area
Rest Area 3 km NW of Eaglehawk or 1 km E of Myers Flat
HEMA 63 K10 36 42 41 S 144 13 28 E
B260

437 Bears Lagoon Fruit Fly Rest Area
Rest Area 2 km N of Bears Lagoon or 21 km S of Durham Ox
HEMA 63 J9 36 18 47 S 143 58 28 E
B260

438 Newbridge Recreation Reserve
☎ 0487 703 434
Camp Area at Newbridge. E side of Loddon River. Token for shower at general store - hotel
HEMA 59 A10 36 44 18 S 143 54 10 E
B240

439 Laanecoorie River Reserve
Camp Spot at Laanecoorie. Beside Loddon River
HEMA 59 A10 36 49 32 S 143 53 55 E
C277

440 Waanyarra Recreation
☎ 136 186
Camp Area 10 km NE of Dunolly or 33 km S of Bridgewater. Turn E onto Waanyarra Cemetery Rd. 2 km dirt road
HEMA 59 A10 36 49 0 S 143 48 2 E

441 Moliagul Rest Area
Rest Area 14 km N of Dunolly or 21 km S of Logan
HEMA 59 A10 36 45 6 S 143 39 50 E
C240

442 Logan Pub
☎ (03) 5496 2220
Camp Spot at Logan. 23 km E of St Arnaud or 35 km NW of Dunolly. Behind hotel. Ask landlord's permission. Fee for power.
HEMA 59 A9 36 37 18 S 143 29 27 E
B240

443 Kooreh Hall
Parking Area at Kooreh. 36 km SW of Wedderburn or 12 km E of St Arnaud
HEMA 59 A9 36 38 26 S 143 23 8 E
B240

444 St Arnaud Caravan Park
☎ (03) 5495 1447
Caravan Park at St Arnaud. Cnr Dundas St & Alma St
HEMA 59 A8 36 36 43 S 143 15 32 E

445 Avon River
Rest Area 27 km W of St Arnaud or 50 km E of Murtoa
HEMA 62 K7 36 38 24 S 142 58 43 E
B240

446 Lake Batyo Catyo Campground
Camp Area 22 km NE of Marnoo or 28 km S of Donald, via Donald-Stawell Rd. Then on St Arnoud-Banyena Rd. Last 7 km dirt road
HEMA 62 J7 36 30 58 S 142 56 45 E

447 Jack Emmett Billabong
Rupanyup Memorial Park
Camp Spot at Rupanyup, 63 km W of St Arnaud or 14 km E of Murtoa. Cnr of Wimmera Hwy & Minyip-Rupanyup Rds
HEMA 62 K6 36 37 35 S 142 37 45 E
B240

448 Minyip Wetlands Travellers Rest
☎ 0499 010 463
Camp Area at Minyip. Cnr Petering St & Stawell-Warracknabeal Rd. Limited power. See notice board for payment details
HEMA 62 J6 36 27 23 S 142 35 12 E

449 Murtoa Caravan Park
☎ (03) 5385 2407
Caravan Park at Murtoa. Beside Lake Marma
HEMA 58 A6 36 37 18 S 142 27 58 E

450 Natimuk Lake Caravan Park
☎ 0407 800 753
Caravan Park 4 km N of Natimuk. Beside lake
HEMA 58 A4 36 42 56 S 141 56 30 E

451 Philip of Sherewoods
Rest Area 9 km W of Natimuk or 61 km NE of Edenhope
HEMA 58 A4 36 46 29 S 141 51 56 E

VICTORIA

452 Centenary Park Campground
131 963

Mount Arapiles-Tooan State Park

Camp Area 12 km W of Natimuk or 60 km NE of Edenhope. 2 km N of Wimmera Hwy along Centenary Park Rd

HEMA 58 A4 36 45 33 S 141 51 3 E

453 Jane Duff Highway Park

Picnic Area 21 km W of Natimuk or 24 km E of Goroke

HEMA 58 A3 36 43 59 S 141 43 21 E

BIG RIG

454 Lake Ratzcastle Camp Area

Camp Area 10 km S of Goroke, 2 km off Goroke-Harrow Rd

HEMA 58 B3 36 48 38 S 141 27 58 E

BIG RIG

455 Goroke Camping Accommodation
(03) 5386 1187

Camp Area Goroke. 108 Main St next to swimming pool. See noticeboard for fees

HEMA 58 A3 36 43 13 S 141 28 1 E

BIG RIG

456 Lake Charlegrark Campground
(03) 5386 6281

C208

Camp Area 33 km N of Edenhope or 23 km W of Goroke. 2 km S off C213 on Natimuk Frances Rd

HEMA 58 A2 36 46 6 S 141 14 4 E

BIG RIG

457 Lake Bringalbert

Camp Area 5 km N of Bringalbert. Donation welcomed

HEMA 58 B2 36 50 5 S 141 9 22 E

BIG RIG

458 Parsons (Collins) Lake Lake Reserve

Picnic Area. 63 km SW of Natimuk or 7 km NE of Edenhope

HEMA 58 B2 37 0 5 S 141 21 5 E

459 Edenhope Lake Wallace Recreation Ground

C240

Rest Area at Edenhope, next to caravan park

HEMA 58 B2 37 2 4 S 141 17 46 E

Notes...

460 Johnny Mullagh Park

C206

Camp Area at Harrow. Blair St. S side of Harrow, beside Glenelg River. Pay at Harrows Cafe

HEMA 58 C3 37 10 12 S 141 35 21 E

BIG RIG

Melbourne to Bordertown

Western Highway

461 O'Briens Crossing
131 963

Lerderderg State Park

Camp Area 13 km NE of Greendale or 10 km SE of Blackwood. Turn E off C318, 7 km N of Greendale or 4 km S of Blackwood onto O'Briens Rd. 6 km dirt road. Not suitable for caravans. Small vehicles only

HEMA 59 D12 37 29 46 S 144 21 39 E

462 Boar Gully Campground
131 963

Brisbane Ranges National Park

Camp Area 6 km E of Mount Wallace. Turn E off C141, 18 km S of Ballan onto Brisbane Ranges Rd. Permit required

HEMA 59 E12 37 46 0 S 144 15 47 E

463 Mount Franklin Reserve Campground
131 963

Hepburn Regional Park

Camp Area 11 km N of Daylesford. Turn E 9 km N of Daylesford

HEMA 59 C11 37 15 47 S 144 8 57 E

464 Slaty Creek Campground
131 963

Creswick Regional Park

Camp Area 5 km SE of Creswick. Turn W off C291, 2 km SE of Creswick onto Slaty Creek Rd. 3 km dirt road. There are 2 other camp areas within 400m with no facilities

HEMA 59 D10 37 27 46 S 143 54 15 E

465 Clunes Caravan Park
(03) 5345 3278

C287

Caravan Park at Clunes. Purcell St

HEMA 59 C10 37 17 35 S 143 47 15 E

466 Trawalla State Forest Rest Area

A8

Rest Area 4 km W of Trawalla or 4 km E of Beaufort

HEMA 59 D9 37 26 7 S 143 25 21 E

BIG RIG

467 Red Kangaroo Roadhouse
(03) 5349 3180

A8

Camp Area 3 km W of Beaufort or 17 km E of Buangor. Fee for shower

HEMA 59 D9 37 25 28 S 143 21 14 E

BIG RIG 72

VICTORIA

468 Middle Creek Campground ☎131 963
Mt Buangor State Park
Camp Area 20 km NW of Beaufort or 16 km NE of Buangor. Turn N off Western Hwy 12 km NW of Beaufort or 8 km SE of Buangor onto Ferntree Gully Rd. 8 km dirt road
HEMA 59 D8 37 19 57 S 143 14 47 E

469 Langi Ghiran Rest Area
Rest Area 14 km E of Ararat. Eastbound only
A8
HEMA 59 D8 37 20 15 S 143 6 7 E

470 Langi Ghiran Campground ☎131 963
Langi Ghiran State Park
Camp Area 15 km NW of Buangor or 17 km SE of Ararat. Turn N off Western Hwy 10 km NW of Buangor or 12 km SE of Ararat onto Langi Ghiran Picnic Ground Rd. 5 km dirt road
HEMA 59 C8 37 17 23 S 143 5 30 E
BIG RIG

471 Green Hill Lake Reserve
Camp Area 19 km W of Buangor or 3 km E of Ararat. 500m N of Hwy. Turn at offical sign to the lake & cross railway line to track. Donation requested
A8
HEMA 59 C8 37 17 47 S 142 58 53 E
BIG RIG

472 Ararat
Parking Area at Ararat. Queen St entry. Self Contained Vehicles only
HEMA 58 C7 37 16 50 S 142 55 59 E
20

473 Cathcart Rest Area
Rest Area 6 km W of Ararat, on Ararat-Pomonal Rd
C222
HEMA 58 C7 37 17 43 S 142 52 42 E
BIG RIG

474 Great Western Rest Area
Rest Area 1 km N of Great Western or 13 km SE of Stawell
A8
HEMA 58 C7 37 8 41 S 142 50 32 E
BIG RIG

475 Stawell Park Caravan Park ☎(03) 5358 2709
Caravan Park 9 km N of Great Western or 5 km S of Stawell. Western Hwy, opposite "Sisters Rocks"
HEMA 58 B7 37 5 48 S 142 47 34 E
BIG RIG

476 Federation Park
Rest Area at Stawell. Cnr Western Hwy & Grampians Rd. Self Contained Vehicles only. Small area
HEMA 58 B7 37 3 39 S 142 45 27 E
24

477 Kellers Beach
Picnic Area 17 km SW of Stawell. Turn N off Lake Fyans Rd 14 km SW of Stawell or 7 km NE of Pomonal. W shore of Lake Fyans
HEMA 58 C6 37 8 36 S 142 36 45 E

478 Canadian Gully Bushland Reserve ☎131 963
Rest Area 8 km NW of Stawell turnoff or 21 km SE of Dadswells Bridge
A8
HEMA 58 B7 37 0 20 S 142 42 31 E
BIG RIG

479 Dadswells Bridge South Rest Area
Rest Area 22 km NW of Stawell turnoff or 7 km SE of Dadswells Bridge
A8
HEMA 58 B6 36 57 15 S 142 34 45 E
BIG RIG

480 The Grampians Edge Caravan Park ☎(03) 5359 5241
Caravan Park at Dadswells Bridge. Caravan Park Rd
HEMA 58 B6 36 55 0 S 142 30 29 E

481 Plantation Campground ☎(03) 5361 4000
North Grampians
Camp Area 10 km N of Halls Gap Info Centre. Turn N off C216 before bridge onto Mt Zero Rd for 8.8 km. Dirt road for 8.4 km. Permit required
HEMA 58 B6 37 3 34 S 142 30 53 E
BIG RIG

482 Borough Huts Campground ☎(03) 5361 4000
Central Grampians
Camp Area 11 km S of Halls Gap. Access via Grampians Rd near Fyans Creek. Permit required
C216
HEMA 58 C6 37 13 27 S 142 32 25 E

483 Jimmy Creek Campground ☎(03) 5361 4000
South East Grampians
Camp Area 29 km S of Halls Gap, via Grampians Rd. Permit required
C216
HEMA 58 D6 37 22 19 S 142 30 11 E

484 Wannon Crossing Campground ☎131 963
Central Grampians
Camp Area 35 km S of Halls Gap, access via Grampians Rd at Knight Bridge on Wannon River. Small vehicles only. Permit required
HEMA 58 D6 37 26 0 S 142 28 33 E

485 Boreang Campground ☎(03) 5361 4000
Central Grampians
Camp Area 18 km SW of Halls Gap. Access via Mount Victory Rd & Glenelg River Rd. Dirt road. Not suitable for caravans
HEMA 58 C6 37 10 27 S 142 25 7 E

486 Green Lake
Rest Area 24 km NW of Dadswells Bridge or 13 km SE of Horsham. Big rigs at roadside lay-by
A8
HEMA 58 A5 36 47 13 S 142 17 52 E
BIG RIG

487 Burnt Creek
Rest Area 32 km NW of Dadswells Bridge or 5 km SE of Horsham
A8
HEMA 58 A5 36 45 39 S 142 15 1 E
BIG RIG

488 Wail Picnic Area
Parking Area 12 km S of Dimboola or 24 km N of Horsham
A8
HEMA 62 J4 36 30 35 S 142 6 11 E
BIG RIG 20

489 Dimboola Recreation Reserve
Parking Area at Dimboola, Lloyd St. Self Contained Vehicles only
HEMA 62 J4 36 27 30 S 142 1 43 E
BIG RIG 24

490 Ackle Bend
☎ 131 963
Little Desert National Park
Camp Area 6 km S of Dimboola. Access via Riverside Rd & Horseshoe Bend Rd. 3 km dirt road
HEMA 62 J4 36 30 10 S 142 1 11 E
BIG RIG

491 Horseshoe Bend
☎ 131 963
Little Desert National Park
Camp Area 7 km S of Dimboola. Access via Riverside Rd & Horseshoe Bend Rd. 4 km dirt road
HEMA 62 J4 36 29 51 S 142 1 5 E

492 Kiata Campground
☎ 131 963
Little Desert National Park
Camp Area 12 km S of Kiata, via Kiata South Rd. Signposted. 4 km dirt road
HEMA 62 J3 36 26 51 S 141 47 53 E
BIG RIG

493 Lochiel Rest Area
Rest Area 6 km W of Dimboola or 32 km E of Nhill
A8
HEMA 62 J4 36 25 6 S 141 58 52 E
BIG RIG

494 Camerons Reserve
Rest Area 14 km W of Nhill or 27 km E of Kaniva
A8
HEMA 62 J3 36 23 23 S 141 30 31 E
BIG RIG

Notes...

495 Kaniva Caravan Park
☎ 0458 687 054
Caravan Park at Kaniva. Baker St
HEMA 62 J2 36 22 54 S 141 14 25 E
BIG RIG

496 Serviceton Recreational Reserve
☎ 0419 032 418
Camp Spot at Serviceton, S of township on Baldocks-Grossers Rd. Call for key to facilities & payment
HEMA 62 J1 36 23 16 S 140 58 56 E
BIG RIG

497 Tolmer Reserve
Rest Area 25 km W of Kaniva or 18 km E of Bordertown at Vic/SA border
A8
HEMA 62 J1 36 20 40 S 140 57 58 E
BIG RIG

Melbourne to Mt Gambier
Princes Highway

498 Avalon Rest Area
Rest Area 51 km SW of Melbourne or 23 km NE of Geelong. Both sides of Hwy
M1
HEMA 56 E4 38 0 7 S 144 29 31 E
BIG RIG

499 Meredith Park
Camp Area 12 km N of Colac or 11 km S of Beeac. Turn W off C146 10 km N of Colac or 9 km S of Beeac. Beside Lake Colac
HEMA 61 E9 38 16 7 S 143 36 38 E
BIG RIG

500 Central Caravan Park
☎ (03) 5231 3586
Caravan Park at Colac. Bruce St. At showground. Not available show weekend in November
HEMA 61 F9 38 20 9 S 143 36 12 E
BIG RIG

501 Pirron Yallock West Rest Area
Rest Area 2 km W of Pirron Yallock or 7 km E of Stoneyford. Both sides of road
A1
HEMA 61 F8 38 20 49 S 143 24 45 E
BIG RIG

502 Floating Islands Lagoon Nature Reserve
Rest Area 3 km W of Pirron Yallock or 6 km E of Stoneyford
A1
HEMA 61 F8 38 20 56 S 143 23 57 E

503 Lakes & Craters Holiday Park
☎ (03) 5593 1253
Caravan Park 5 km SW of Camperdown. Access via Park Rd, off Princes Hwy
HEMA 60 E6 38 14 8 S 143 7 0 E
BIG RIG

504 Lake Bullen Merri Reserve

Rest Area 4 km SW of Camperdown. Turn W on to Naroghid Rd, N on to Bullen-Merri Rd

HEMA 60 E6 38 15 45 S 143 5 41 E

BIG RIG

505 Lake Elingamite

Camp Spot 7 km SW of Cobden. Turn W off Cobden-Warrnambool Rd 5 km SW of Cobden onto Oates Rd. 2 km dirt road

HEMA 60 F6 38 20 56 S 143 0 56 E

BIG RIG

506 Terang Apex Caravan Park

☎ (03) 5592 1687

A1

Caravan Park at Terang. Princes Hwy. 1 km W of PO

HEMA 60 E5 38 14 31 S 142 54 34 E

507 Noorat Rest Area

Rest Area at Noorat

HEMA 60 D5 38 11 29 S 142 55 38 E

BIG RIG

508 Koroit-Tower Hill Caravan Park

☎ (03) 5565 7926

Caravan Park at Koroit. High St. 500m SE of PO, adjacent to Botanical Gardens

HEMA 60 E2 38 17 49 S 142 22 10 E

BIG RIG

509 Killarney Beach Caravan Park

☎ 0428 314 823

Camp Area at Killarney. Mahoneys Rd. 2 km S of Hwy

HEMA 60 F1 38 21 19 S 142 18 28 E

BIG RIG

510 Martins Point

Picnic Area at Port Fairy. S end of Gipps St

HEMA 60 F1 38 23 24 S 142 14 39 E

BIG RIG

511 Macarthur Recreation Reserve

☎ (03) 5576 1113

C184

Camp Spot at Macarthur. 700m S of town off Port Fairy-Hamilton Rd, entry to reserve just S of river crossing. Self Contained Vehicles only

HEMA 58 G4 38 2 15 S 142 0 27 E

BIG RIG 48

512 Lake Surprise Campground

☎ 131 963

Mt Eccles National Park

Camp Area 10 km SW of Macarthur

HEMA 58 G4 38 3 30 S 141 55 22 E

513 Yambuk Caravan Park

☎ 0419 006 201

Caravan Park 4 km S of Yambuk

HEMA 58 H5 38 20 22 S 142 3 16 E

BIG RIG

514 Fitzroy River Reserve

Camp Area 26 km NW of Yambuk or 11 km SE of Tyrendarra. Turn S off A1, 22 km NW of Yambuk or 7 km SE of Tyrendarra onto Thompsons Rd, signposted "River Outlet". At river mouth

HEMA 58 H4 38 15 29 S 141 50 51 E

515 Fitzroy River

A1

Parking Area 1 km W of Tyrendarra or 25 km NE of Portland. Quieter sites 400m off Hwy

HEMA 58 H4 38 13 25 S 141 45 45 E

BIG RIG

516 Sawpit Picnic Area

☎ 136 186

Mt Clay State Forest

Picnic Area 4 km NW of Narrawong. Turn N 1 km W of Narrawong onto Boyers Rd for 3 km

HEMA 58 H4 38 14 7 S 141 41 17 E

517 Dutton Way Caravan Park

☎ (03) 5523 1904

Caravan Park at Portland 6 km NE of PO. 215 Dutton Way.

HEMA 58 H3 38 18 20 S 141 36 34 E

518 Surry Ridge Picnic Area

☎ 136 186

Cobboboonee National Park

Picnic Area 18 km W of Heywood. Turn W off A1, 6 km S of Heywood or 21 km N of Portland onto Coffeys Lane. Left at Jackys Swamp Rd, then R at Cut Out Dam Rd. 9 km dirt road

HEMA 58 G3 38 11 2 S 141 30 15 E

519 Jackass Fern Gully Picnic and Campground

☎ 136 186

Cobboboonee National Park

Camp Area 24 km NW of Heywood. Turn W off A1, 7 km NW of Heywood onto Sinclair Settlement Rd, Mt Deception Rd & T&W Rd. Alternative route via T&W Rd off A1, 5 km SE of Greenwald. 9 km dirt road

HEMA 58 G3 38 4 29 S 141 25 32 E

520 Annya Road Picnic Area

☎ 136 186

Annya State Forest

Picnic Area 15 km NW of Heywood or 25 km S of Digby. Turn E off C195, 7.5 km NW of A1/C195 jcn or 24.5 km S of Digby onto Annya Rd. 500m off Hwy. Dirt road

HEMA 58 G3 38 1 7 S 141 34 58 E

521 Hotspur Bridge (Crawford River)

C195

Camp Spot 20 km NW of A1/C195 jcn or 13 km S of Digby

HEMA 58 F3 37 55 33 S 141 33 40 E

BIG RIG

522 Digby Hotel
☎ (03) 5579 3281

C195

Camp Spot at Digby Hotel. Portland Casterton Rd. Check in with publican

HEMA 58 F3 37 48 17 S 141 31 51 E

24

523 Hiscocks Crossing
☎ 131 963

Crawford River Regional Park

Picnic Area 16 km W of Hotspur. Turn W off C195, 600m N of Hotspur Bridge onto Mill Rd & The Boulevard. Dirt road. Bush camping beside river. Alternative route from Greenwald not suitable for caravans. 9 km dirt road

HEMA 58 F3 37 56 19 S 141 26 47 E

524 Glenelg River

A1

Rest Area 1 km E of Dartmoor or 4 km W of Winnap

HEMA 58 F2 37 55 40 S 141 16 37 E

525 Fort O'Hare Campground

Camp Area at Dartmoor. 500m E of PO, beside river

HEMA 58 F2 37 55 33 S 141 17 6 E

BIG RIG

526 Pinaster Picnic Area

A1

Rest Area 33 km W of Dartmoor or 17 km E of Mt Gambier, near VIC/SA border

HEMA 58 F1 37 50 29 S 140 58 42 E

Portland to Mt Gambier

via Nelson

527 Cape Bridgewater

C193

Rest Area 24 km W of Portland. Beachside car park at Surf Club

HEMA 58 H3 38 22 8 S 141 24 23 E

BIG RIG

528 Cape Bridgewater Coastal Camp
☎ (03) 5526 7247

Camp Area at Cape Bridgewater. 300m from the beach heading up Bridgewater Rd S side of town

HEMA 58 H3 38 22 15 S 141 24 5 E

BIG RIG

529 Swan Lake Campground
☎ (08) 8738 4051

Discovery Bay Coastal Park

Camp Area 36 km W of Portland or 45 km E of Nelson. Turn S onto Swan Lake Rd 30 km W of Portland or 38 km E of Nelson. 6 km to campsite. Dirt road, steep in places. Bookings & prepayment required. Not recommended for caravans

HEMA 58 H2 38 12 50 S 141 18 44 E

Notes...

530 Lake Monibeong Campground
☎ (08) 8738 4051

Discovery Bay Coastal Park

Camp Area 72 km W of Portland or 23 km E of Nelson. Turn S onto Lake Monibeong Rd 65 km W of Portland or 16 km E of Nelson. 7 km to campsite. Bookings & prepayment required.

HEMA 58 G2 38 8 2 S 141 11 8 E

531 Dartmoor Turnoff Rest Area

C192

Rest Area 54 km NW of Portland or 15 km E of Nelson

HEMA 58 G2 38 4 31 S 141 9 54 E

532 Pritchards Campground - Southern Shore
☎ (08) 8738 4051

Lower Glenelg National Park

Camp Area 18 km NW of Kentbruck, 21 km E of Nelson or 21 km S of Winnap. Turn N off C192, 12 km W of Kentbruck or 15 km E of Nelson. Access via Winnap-Nelson Rd. 1.5 km dirt road. Permit required

HEMA 58 G2 38 3 23 S 141 13 5 E

533 Moleside Creek Picnic Area
☎ 131 963

Lower Glenelg National Park

Picnic Area 23 km NW of Kentbruck, 26 km E of Nelson or 14 km S of Winnap. Turn N 12 km W of Kentbruck or 15 km E of Nelson. Access via Winnap-Nelson Rd

HEMA 58 G2 38 3 16 S 141 16 17 E

534 Forest Camp
☎ 131 963

Lower Glenelg National Park

Camp Area 26 km E of Nelson off Winnap-Nelson Rd. 8 km dirt road. Permit required

HEMA 58 G2 38 1 52 S 141 8 18 E

535 Wilson Hall Camping Area - Northern Shore
☎ (08) 8738 4171

Lower Glenelg National Park

Camp Area on North Shore. Signposted access off Wanwin Rd turn S onto Wilson Hall Track. Dirt road. Small to medium vehicles. Some low trees. Permit required

HEMA 58 G2 38 1 9 S 141 6 25 E

536 Kywong Caravan Park
☎ (08) 8738 4174

Caravan Park at Nelson. North Nelson Rd. 1 km N of Hwy

HEMA 58 G1 38 2 20 S 141 0 31 E

BIG RIG

537 River Vu Park
☎ (08) 8738 4123

Caravan Park at Nelson. Kellett St

HEMA 58 G1 38 2 57 S 141 0 27 E

538 Princess Margaret Rose Caves - Northern Shore ☎ (08) 8738 4171
Lower Glenelg National Park
Camp Area 16 km N of Nelson or 28 km SE of Mt Gambier. Turn N 4 km W of Nelson or S 10 km E of Mt Gambier off the A1. Permit required
HEMA 58 G1 | 37 59 12 S | 140 59 31 E

Ballarat to Mt Gambier
Glenelg Highway

539 Smythesdale Gardens Rest Area
Camp Area at Smythesdale. Garden St. Donation for upkeep of facilities appreciated
HEMA 59 E10 | 37 38 21 S | 143 41 9 E
BIG RIG 48

540 Woady Yaloak Creek Rest Area
B160
Rest Area 2 km W of Scarsdale or 7 km E of Linton
HEMA 59 E10 | 37 40 41 S | 143 38 19 E
BIG RIG

541 J C Stretch Memorial Park
C143
Rest Area at Pitfield. Near jcn of C143 & C171
HEMA 59 F9 | 37 48 28 S | 143 35 7 E

542 East Beach Reserve
Camp Area 4 km SE of Lake Bolac. Turn S off B160, 3 km E of Lake Bolac. Lakefront
HEMA 58 E7 | 37 43 17 S | 142 52 43 E
BIG RIG

543 Lake Bolac Foreshore ☎ 136 186
Camp Area 2 km S of Lake Bolac, via Sago Rd & Frontage Rd. Various sites around lake
HEMA 58 E7 | 37 43 16 S | 142 51 22 E
BIG RIG

544 Lake Bolac Caravan Park ☎ (03) 5350 2329
Caravan Park 2 km S of Lake Bolac. Frontage Rd. Lakeside
HEMA 58 E7 | 37 43 15 S | 142 50 26 E
BIG RIG

545 Wickliffe Rest Area
Rest Area at Wickliffe. 12 km W of Bolac or 34 km E of Dunkel
HEMA 58 E7 | 37 41 26 S | 142 43 21 E
BIG RIG

546 Lake Buninjon
B180
Rest Area 7 km SW of Maroona or 8 km NE of Willaura
HEMA 58 D7 | 37 29 5 S | 142 47 38 E
BIG RIG

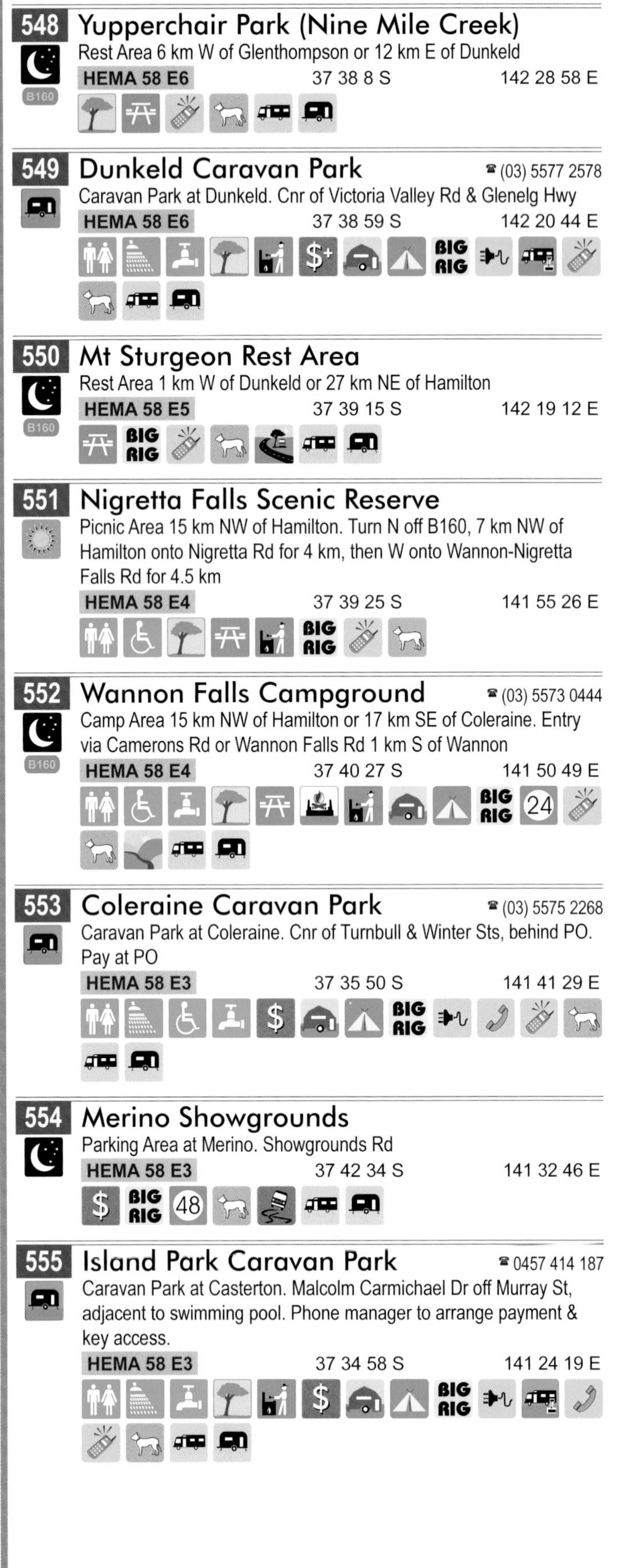

547 Willaura Recreation Grounds ☎ 0429 953 150
Camp Area at Willaura, Delacome Way. Limited powered sites, call caretaker on arrival
HEMA 58 E7 | 37 32 41 S | 142 44 36 E
BIG RIG

548 Yupperchair Park (Nine Mile Creek)
B160
Rest Area 6 km W of Glenthompson or 12 km E of Dunkeld
HEMA 58 E6 | 37 38 8 S | 142 28 58 E

549 Dunkeld Caravan Park ☎ (03) 5577 2578
Caravan Park at Dunkeld. Cnr of Victoria Valley Rd & Glenelg Hwy
HEMA 58 E6 | 37 38 59 S | 142 20 44 E
BIG RIG

550 Mt Sturgeon Rest Area
B160
Rest Area 1 km W of Dunkeld or 27 km NE of Hamilton
HEMA 58 E5 | 37 39 15 S | 142 19 12 E
BIG RIG

551 Nigretta Falls Scenic Reserve
Picnic Area 15 km NW of Hamilton. Turn N off B160, 7 km NW of Hamilton onto Nigretta Rd for 4 km, then W onto Wannon-Nigretta Falls Rd for 4.5 km
HEMA 58 E4 | 37 39 25 S | 141 55 26 E
BIG RIG

552 Wannon Falls Campground ☎ (03) 5573 0444
B160
Camp Area 15 km NW of Hamilton or 17 km SE of Coleraine. Entry via Camerons Rd or Wannon Falls Rd 1 km S of Wannon
HEMA 58 E4 | 37 40 27 S | 141 50 49 E
BIG RIG 24

553 Coleraine Caravan Park ☎ (03) 5575 2268
Caravan Park at Coleraine. Cnr of Turnbull & Winter Sts, behind PO. Pay at PO
HEMA 58 E3 | 37 35 50 S | 141 41 29 E
BIG RIG

554 Merino Showgrounds
Parking Area at Merino. Showgrounds Rd
HEMA 58 E3 | 37 42 34 S | 141 32 46 E
BIG RIG 48

555 Island Park Caravan Park ☎ 0457 414 187
Caravan Park at Casterton. Malcolm Carmichael Dr off Murray St, adjacent to swimming pool. Phone manager to arrange payment & key access.
HEMA 58 E3 | 37 34 58 S | 141 24 19 E
BIG RIG

556 Baileys Rocks Campground ☎ 131 963
Dergholm State Park
Camp Area 45 km NW of Casterton or 27 km SE of Langkoop. Turn E 9 km N of Dergholm or 25 km SE of Langkoop onto Baileys Rocks Rd. 3 km dirt road
HEMA 58 D2 | 37 17 17 S | 141 10 38 E
BIG RIG

Geelong to Hamilton
Hamilton Highway

557 Leigh River
B140
Rest Area 28 km W of Geelong or 1 km E of Inverleigh. Big Rig parking E of river
HEMA 61 D12 | 38 5 59 S | 144 3 40 E
BIG RIG

558 Browns Waterhole Caravan Park ☎ 0439 983 679
Caravan Park at Lismore. High St. Contact caretaker for key, atlernative number 0439 036 265
HEMA 61 B8 | 37 57 16 S | 143 20 48 E

559 Lismore Town Park
B140
Rest Area at Lismore
HEMA 61 B8 | 37 57 14 S | 143 20 38 E
BIG RIG

560 Lake Tooliorook ☎ 0487 337 946
Camp Area 6 km S of Lismore. Turn W off C165, 5 km S of Lismore. 1 km dirt road. Good idea to check availability with caretaker
HEMA 60 C7 | 37 58 38 S | 143 17 5 E

561 Derrinallum Recreation Reserve
B140
Camp Spot at Derrinallum. E end of town
HEMA 60 B7 | 37 56 56 S | 143 13 39 E
BIG RIG 24

562 Derrinallum Town Park
B140
Rest Area at Derrinallum
HEMA 60 B7 | 37 56 53 S | 143 13 26 E
BIG RIG

563 Deep Lake Recreation Reserve ☎ 0407 201 735
Camp Area 5 km NW of Derrinallum via Chatsworth Rd at W end of town. Pay fees at cafe
HEMA 60 B7 | 37 55 53 S | 143 10 37 E

Notes...

564 Mortlake Caravan Park ☎ 0409 428 870
Caravan Park at Mortlake. Jamieson Ave. 1 km E of PO
HEMA 60 D4 | 38 5 1 S | 142 48 32 E
BIG RIG

565 Tea Tree Lake
Rest Area at Mortlake. Terang Mortlake Rd
HEMA 60 D4 | 38 4 54 S | 142 48 33 E

566 Penshurst Caravan Park ☎ (03) 5576 5220
Caravan Park at Penshurst. Cox St, 100m from PO. Pay at PO
HEMA 60 B1 | 37 52 26 S | 142 17 26 E
BIG RIG

567 Tarrington Town Park
B140
Rest Area at Tarrington
HEMA 58 F5 | 37 45 59 S | 142 5 54 E

Geelong to Warrnambool
Great Ocean Road

568 Hammond Road Campground ☎ 131 963
Great Otway National Park
Camp Area 8 km NW of Aireys Inlet. Access from Aireys Inlet, via Bambra Rd & Hammonds Rd. Dirt road
HEMA 61 F12 | 38 23 55 S | 144 1 23 E

569 Big Hill Campground ☎ 131 963
Great Otway National Park
Camp Area 12 km NW of Lorne or 13 km SE of Deans Marsh Lorne Rd on Big Hill track. Signposted. Only open November to April
HEMA 61 G11 | 38 28 29 S | 143 55 57 E

570 Wye River Foreshore Reserve ☎ (03) 5289 0412
Camp Area at Wye River. Bookings essential for peak periods. Only open December to April
HEMA 61 H11 | 38 38 2 S | 143 53 32 E

571 Stevenson Falls Scenic Reserve ☎ 131 963
Great Otway State Park
Camp Area 5 km W of Barramunga. Turn W off C119, 26 km N of Apollo Bay or 8 km S of C119/C154 jcn onto Upper Gellibrand Rd. Narrow winding dirt road
HEMA 61 G10 | 38 33 49 S | 143 39 23 E

572 West Barwon Reservoir
Picnic Area 1 km S of Forrest or 5 km N of Barramunga. 700m off Hwy
HEMA 61 G10 | 38 31 52 S | 143 43 15 E
BIG RIG

573 Dando's Campground ☎ 131 963
Great Otway National Park
Camp Area 13 km SE of Gellibrand. Turn E off C155, 1 km S of Gellibrand onto Gellibrand East Rd, Lardners Track & Sayers Track. Dirt road. Camping beside river

HEMA 61 G9 38 33 16 S 143 37 5 E

574 Beauchamp Falls Reserve ☎ 131 963
Great Otway National Park
Camp Area 4 km SE of Beech Forest. Turn S off C159, 1 km E of Beech Forest onto Aire Valley Rd & Beauchamp Falls Rd. Dirt road

HEMA 61 H9 38 39 5 S 143 36 24 E

575 Apollo Bay Foreshore
B100

Rest Area at Apollo Bay. N of Info Centre

HEMA 61 J10 38 45 9 S 143 40 9 E

576 Blanket Bay Campground ☎ 131 963
Great Otway National Park
Camp Area 36 km W of Apollo Bay. Turn S onto Cape Otway Lighthouse Rd, then Blanket Bay Rd. Must prebook

HEMA 61 K9 38 49 41 S 143 34 58 E

577 Aire River (East) Campground ☎ 131 963
Great Otway National Park
Camp Area 29 km W of Apollo Bay or 29 km SE of Lavers Hill. Turn S off B100, 24 km W of Apollo Bay or 24 km SE of Lavers Hill onto Hordern Vale Rd. 4.5 km to campsites. 2 km dirt road. First camp on R, larger camp area over bridge. Must prebook

HEMA 61 K9 38 48 2 S 143 28 55 E

578 Aire River (West) Campground ☎ 131 963
Great Otway National Park
Camp Area 38 km W of Apollo Bay or 20 km S of Lavers Hill. Turn S off B100, 33 km W of Apollo Bay or 15 km S of Lavers Hill onto Sand Rd. 5 km narrow dirt track. Beside river. Small vehicles only. Must prebook

HEMA 61 J8 38 48 6 S 143 28 40 E

579 Johanna Beach Campground ☎ 131 963
Great Otway National Park
Camp Area 15 km S of Lavers Hill. Turn W off B100, 38 km W of Apollo Bay or 10 km S of Lavers Hill, onto Red Johanna Rd. Must prebook

HEMA 61 J8 38 45 44 S 143 22 44 E

580 Lavers Hill Roadhouse ☎ (03) 5237 3251
B100

Caravan Park at Lavers Hill. Great Ocean Rd. Limited powered sites

HEMA 61 J8 38 40 58 S 143 23 6 E

581 Princetown Recreation Reserve ☎ 0429 985 176
Camp Area 1 km S of Princetown. Old Coach Rd, beside Gellibrand River. 15 tonne limit on bridge. Some dirt road

HEMA 60 J7 38 41 56 S 143 9 31 E

BIG RIG

Lascelles to Portland
Henty Highway

582 Lascelles Camping Ground ☎ (03) 5081 6242
B220

Camp Area at Lascelles. Call into Minapre Hotel for payment

HEMA 62 F6 35 36 26 S 142 34 47 E

BIG RIG

583 Hopetoun Rest Area
B200

Rest Area 1 km NE of Hopetoun

HEMA 62 G5 35 43 21 S 142 21 53 E

BIG RIG

584 Hopetoun Caravan Park ☎ 0417 237 587
Caravan Park at Hopetoun. Austin St

HEMA 62 G5 35 43 34 S 142 22 1 E

BIG RIG

585 Lake Lascelles
Rest Area at Hopetoun. E end of Austin St. Turn N at the end of Austin St, follow track around lake to Eastern Foreshore. 1.5 km dirt road

HEMA 62 G5 35 43 31 S 142 22 29 E

BIG RIG 24

586 Mallee Bush Retreat ☎ (03) 5083 3236
Camp Area at Hopetoun. Austin St

HEMA 62 G5 35 43 39 S 142 22 15 E

BIG RIG

587 Wonga Campground ☎ 131 963
Wyperfeld National Park
Camp Area 28 km N of Yaapeet. Turn W 3 km N of Yaapeet, then N after 3 km onto Park Rd

HEMA 62 F4 35 35 12 S 142 3 2 E

BIG RIG

588 OTIT Campground ☎ 131 963
Lake Albacutya Regional Park
Camp Area 8 km NW of Yaapeet. W end of Yaapeet-Hopetoun Rd. 2 km dirt road past "OTIT Well" sign. Lake can be dry

HEMA 62 G4 35 43 40 S 141 59 30 E

589 Yaapeet Beach Campground
☎ 131 963

Lake Albacutya Regional Park

Camp Area 4 km W of Yaapeet. Beside lake. Dirt road. Lake can be dry. No bookings

HEMA 62 G4 — 35 46 1 S — 142 0 23 E

590 Yaapeet Camp Ground
☎ (03) 5395 7243

Camp Area at Yaapeet. Sites are at rear of hall, honesty box or pay at school. Entry off Yaapeet-Kenmare Rd

HEMA 62 G4 — 35 46 1 S — 142 3 7 E

591 Western Beach Campground
☎ 131 963

Lake Albacutya Regional Park

Camp Area 17 km NW of Rainbow. Access via Western Beach Rd off Albacutya Rd. Lake can be dry. No bookings

HEMA 62 G4 — 35 46 50 S — 141 56 8 E

592 Rainbow Caravan Park
☎ (03) 5395 1062

C227

Caravan Park at Rainbow. Railway St. 1 km SW of PO

HEMA 62 G4 — 35 54 17 S — 141 59 35 E

593 The Wattles

Lake Hindmarsh Lake Reserve

Camp Area 16 km SW of Rainbow on Rainbow-Nhill Rd. Beside lake, sandy track

HEMA 62 G4 — 35 56 41 S — 141 52 27 E

594 Schulzes Beach

Lake Hindmarsh Lake Reserve

Camp Area 22 km SW of Rainbow on Rainbow-Nhill Rd. Beside lake, sandy track

HEMA 62 H4 — 36 2 46 S — 141 51 25 E

595 Four Mile Beach Camping Ground
☎ 0458 565 889

Lake Hindmarsh Lake Reserve

Camp Area 7 km W of Jeparit on Nhil Jeparit Rd. Beside lake. Caretaker on duty, see notice board

HEMA 62 H4 — 36 8 1 S — 141 55 41 E

596 Beulah Caravan Park
☎ (03) 5390 2430

Caravan Park at Beulah. Higgbotham St, in sportsground. Payment & keys from Cafe 67 Phillip St

HEMA 62 G5 — 35 56 32 S — 142 25 4 E

597 Jeparit Caravan Park
☎ (03) 5397 2193

Caravan Park at Jeparit. Peterson Ave. 500m SW of PO. See noticeboard for caretaker details

HEMA 62 H4 — 36 8 41 S — 141 59 3 E

598 Brim Redda's Park
☎ (03) 5390 4212

Camp Area 1 km W of Brim, via Swann St. Fee for power, payable Dixon Garage

HEMA 62 H5 — 36 4 32 S — 142 24 26 E

599 Yarriambiak Creek Picnic Area

Rest Area 1 km N of Warracknabeal, via Warracknabeal-Jeparit Rd. Turn S after single-lane bridge for 100m. Beside creek

HEMA 62 H5 — 36 14 29 S — 142 23 25 E

600 Warracknabeal Caravan Park
☎ 0400 915 125

Caravan Park at Warracknabeal. Lyle St (Dimboola Rd). 1 km SW of PO

HEMA 62 H5 — 36 15 11 S — 142 23 15 E

601 Balmoral Caravan Park
☎ (03) 5570 1400

Caravan Park at Balmoral. 5 Glendinning St. 100m N of PO

HEMA 58 C4 — 37 14 49 S — 141 50 26 E

602 Brodies Campground
☎ 136 186

Rocklands Reservoir

Camp Area 20 km E of Balmoral off Rocklands-Cherrypool Rd. Dirt road

HEMA 58 C4 — 37 15 0 S — 141 59 37 E

603 Glendinning Campground

Rocklands Reservoir

Camp Area 20 km SE of Balmoral, via Yarramyljup or Glendinning Rds

HEMA 58 D4 — 37 17 51 S — 141 59 52 E

604 Mountain Dam Campground
☎ 13 61 86

Rocklands Reservoir

Camp Area 23 km SW of Cherrypool. Turn W off A200, 49 km S of Horsham or 55 km N of Cavendish, then L at HGH Cnr after 7 km. Dirt road

HEMA 58 C5 — 37 13 39 S — 142 5 16 E

Notes...

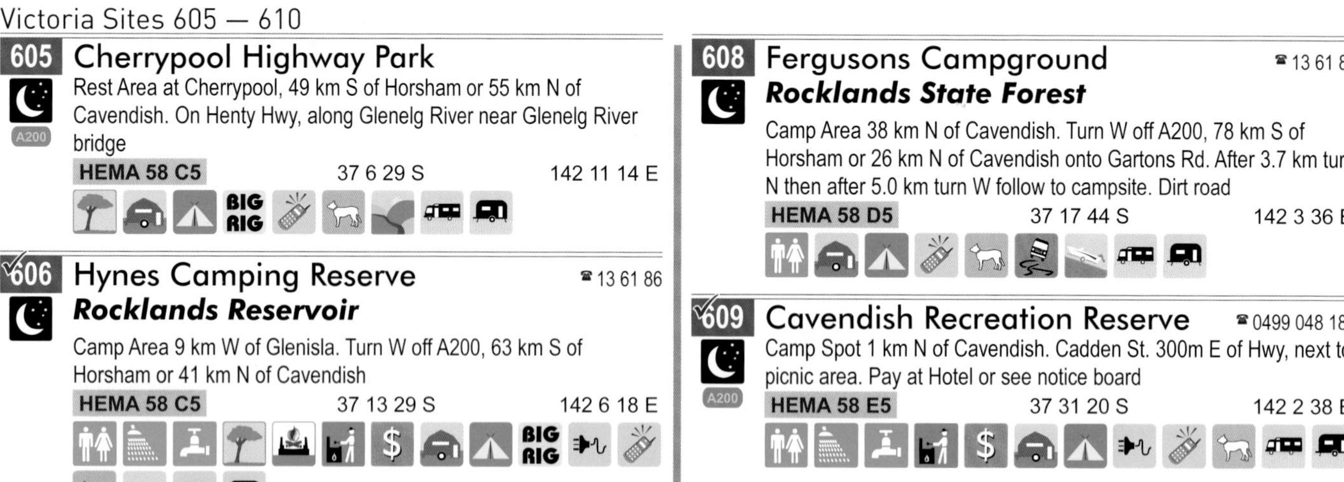

605 Cherrypool Highway Park

A200

Rest Area at Cherrypool, 49 km S of Horsham or 55 km N of Cavendish. On Henty Hwy, along Glenelg River near Glenelg River bridge

HEMA 58 C5 37 6 29 S 142 11 14 E

BIG RIG

606 Hynes Camping Reserve ☎ 13 61 86

Rocklands Reservoir

Camp Area 9 km W of Glenisla. Turn W off A200, 63 km S of Horsham or 41 km N of Cavendish

HEMA 58 C5 37 13 29 S 142 6 18 E

BIG RIG

607 Buandik Campground ☎ 131 963

Grampians National Park

Camp Area 10 km E of Glenisla. Turn E off A200, 66 km S of Horsham or 38 km N of Cavendish onto Billiwing Rd, Harrop Trk & Goat Trk. 9 km dirt road

HEMA 58 C5 37 15 9 S 142 16 43 E

608 Fergusons Campground ☎ 13 61 86

Rocklands State Forest

Camp Area 38 km N of Cavendish. Turn W off A200, 78 km S of Horsham or 26 km N of Cavendish onto Gartons Rd. After 3.7 km turn N then after 5.0 km turn W follow to campsite. Dirt road

HEMA 58 D5 37 17 44 S 142 3 36 E

609 Cavendish Recreation Reserve ☎ 0499 048 184

A200

Camp Spot 1 km N of Cavendish. Cadden St. 300m E of Hwy, next to picnic area. Pay at Hotel or see notice board

HEMA 58 E5 37 31 20 S 142 2 38 E

610 Branxholme Rest Area

A200

Rest Area at Branxholme. Next to Recreation Reserve

HEMA 58 F4 37 51 29 S 141 48 9 E

Notes...

WINEGLASS BAY, FREYCINET NATIONAL PARK (69 B7) PHOTO: ROB BOEGHEIM

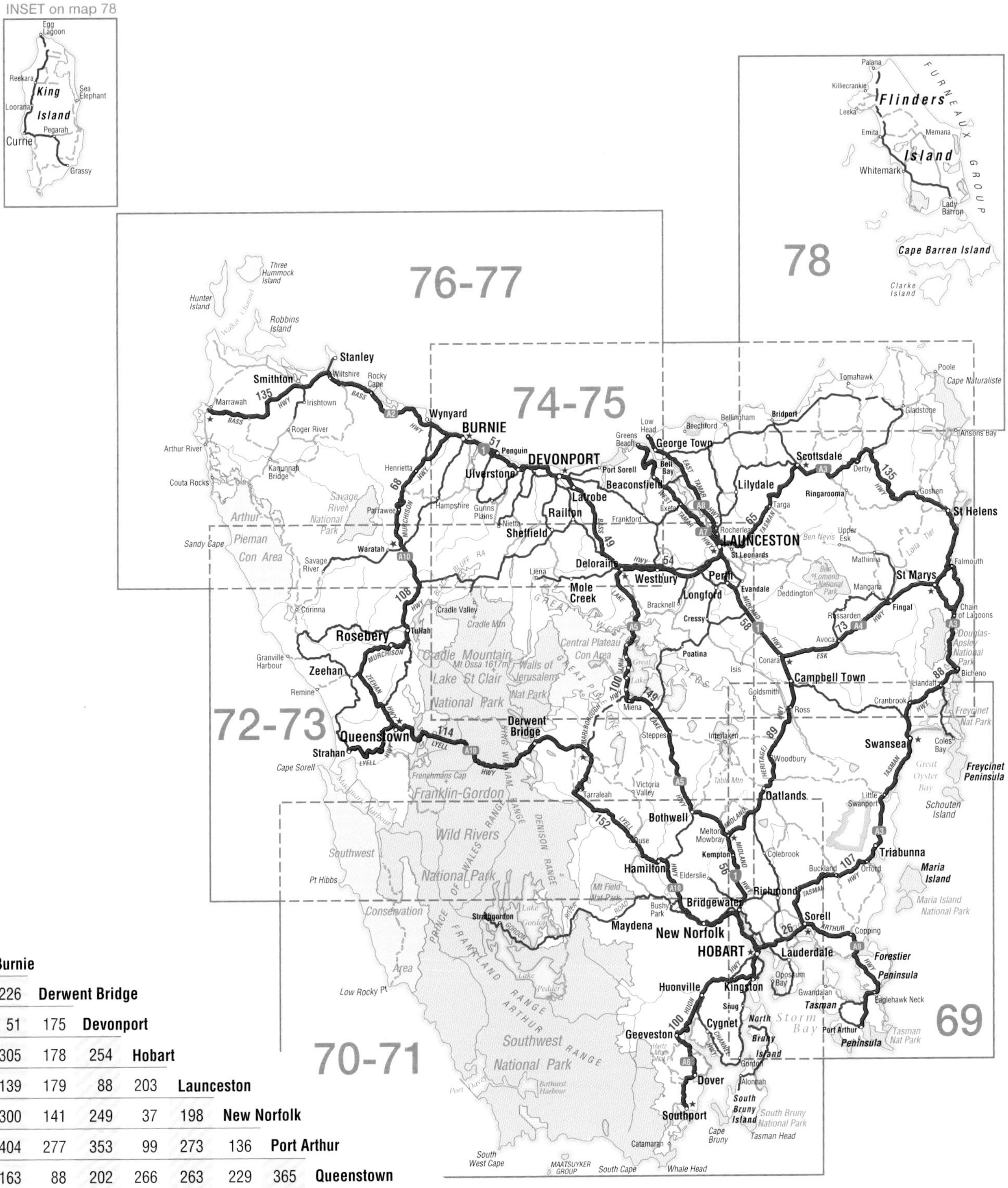

key map

INSET on map 78

Egg Lagoon, Reekara, King Island, Sea Elephant, Loorana, Pegarah, Currie, Grassy

78

Palana, Killiecrankie, Flinders Island, Furneaux Group, Leeka, Emita, Memana, Whitemark, Lady Barron, Cape Barren Island, Clarke Island

76-77

Three Hummock Island, Hunter Island, Robbins Island, Stanley, Smithton, Marrawah, Wiltshire, Rocky Cape, Irishtown, Wynyard, BURNIE, Roger River, Arthur River, Kanunnah Bridge, Couta Rocks, Henrietta, Penguin, Ulverstone, DEVONPORT, Savage River National Park, Sandy Cape, Waratah

74-75

Low Head, Greens Beach, George Town, Beechford, Bellingham, Bridport, Tomahawk, Poole, Cape Naturaliste, Gladstone, Ansons Bay, Scottsdale, Derby, Port Sorell, Beaconsfield, Lilydale, Ringarooma, Latrobe, Railton, Sheffield, Frankford, Targa, LAUNCESTON, St Helens, Deloraine, Westbury, Perth, Mole Creek, Longford, Cressy, Evandale, St Marys, Fingal, Mathinna, Falmouth, Chain of Lagoons, Avoca, Poatina, Campbell Town

72-73

Pieman Con Area, Savage River, Corinna, Cradle Valley, Rosebery, Tullah, Granville Harbour, Zeehan, Remine, Cradle Mountain Lake St Clair National Park, Mt Ossa 1617m, Walls of Jerusalem Nat Park, Central Plateau Con Area, Queenstown, Strahan, Cape Sorell, Derwent Bridge, Miena, Franklin-Gordon Wild Rivers National Park, Tarraleah, Bothwell, Oatlands, Ross, Swansea, Coles Bay, Freycinet Peninsula, Schouten Island, Bicheno

70-71

Southwest National Park, Strathgordon, Maydena, New Norfolk, HOBART, Hamilton, Bridgewater, Richmond, Sorell, Lauderdale, Kingston, Huonville, Cygnet, Geeveston, Dover, Southport, Bruny Island, South West Cape, South Cape, Whale Head, Low Rocky Pt

69

Triabunna, Maria Island, Orford, Buckland, Copping, Forestier Peninsula, Tasman Peninsula, Eaglehawk Neck, Port Arthur, Storm Bay

	Burnie	Derwent Bridge	Devonport	Hobart	Launceston	New Norfolk	Port Arthur	Queenstown	Rosebery	Sorell	Southport	St Helens	Stanley	Swansea
Burnie														
Derwent Bridge	226													
Devonport	51	175												
Hobart	305	178	254											
Launceston	139	179	88	203										
New Norfolk	300	141	249	37	198									
Port Arthur	404	277	353	99	273	136								
Queenstown	163	88	202	266	263	229	365							
Rosebery	109	142	148	320	209	283	419	54						
Sorell	331	204	280	26	200	63	73	292	346					
Southport	405	278	354	100	303	137	199	366	420	126				
St Helens	302	288	251	253	163	250	300	376	375	227	353			
Stanley	79	323	130	384	218	379	483	235	181	410	484	381		
Swansea	275	249	224	133	141	170	180	349	327	107	233	120	354	

Distances are shown in kilometres and follow the most direct major sealed route where possible.

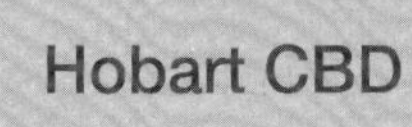

Hobart CBD

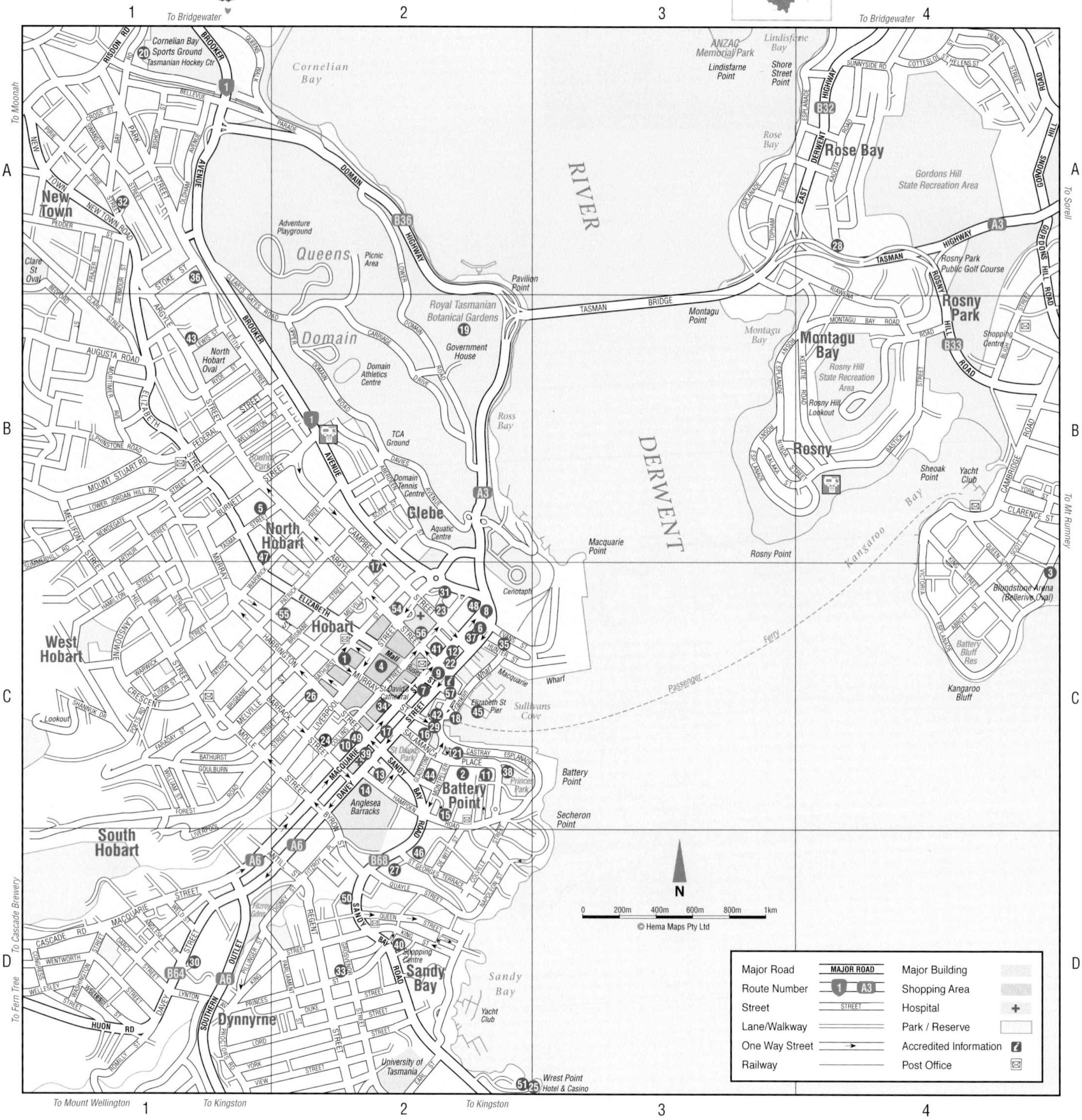

Places of Interest

1. Allport Library & Museum of Fine Arts C2
2. Battery Point Area C2
3. Blundstone Arena C4
4. Cat & Fiddle Arcade C2
5. Designed Objects Tasmania B1
6. Federation Concert Hall C2
7. Franklin Square C2
8. Gasworks Cellar Door C2
9. Hobart Town Hall C2
10. International Wall of Friendship C2
11. Kelly Steps C2
12. Maritime Museum of Tasmania C2
13. Markree House Museum & Gardens C2
14. Military Museum of Tasmania C2
15. Narryna Heritage Museum C2
16. Parliament House C2
17. Penitentiary Chapel Historic Site C2
18. Peppermint Bay Cruises C2
19. Royal Tasmanian Botanical Gardens B2
20. Runnymede A1
21. Salamanca Market (Saturday) C2
22. Tasmanian Museum & Art Gallery C2
23. Theatre Royal C2
24. Village Cinemas C2
25. Wrest Point Casino D2

Accommodation

26. Best Western Hobart C2
27. Blue Hills Motel D2
28. City View Motel A4
29. Customs House Waterfront Hotel C2
30. Davey Place Holiday Town Houses D1
31. Fountainside Hotel C2
32. Graham Court Apartments A1
33. Grosvenor Court Apartments D2
34. Hadleys Hotel C2
35. Henry Jones Art Hotel C2
36. Hobart Tower Motel A1
37. Hotel Grand Chancellor C2
38. Lenna of Hobart C2
39. Macquarie Manor C2
40. Mayfair Plaza Motel D2
41. Montgomery's Hotel Hobart C2
42. Quest Waterfront C2
43. Rydges Hobart B1
44. Salamanca Inn C2
45. Somerset on the Pier C2
46. St Ives Motel Apartments D2
47. The Lodge on Elizabeth B1
48. The Old Woolstore C2
49. Travelodge Hobart C2
50. Woolmers Inn D2
51. Wrest Point Hotel Casino D2

Services

54. Police Headquarters C2
- Post Office C2,D2
55. RACT C2
56. Royal Hobart Hospital C2
57. Tasmanian Visitor Information Centre C2

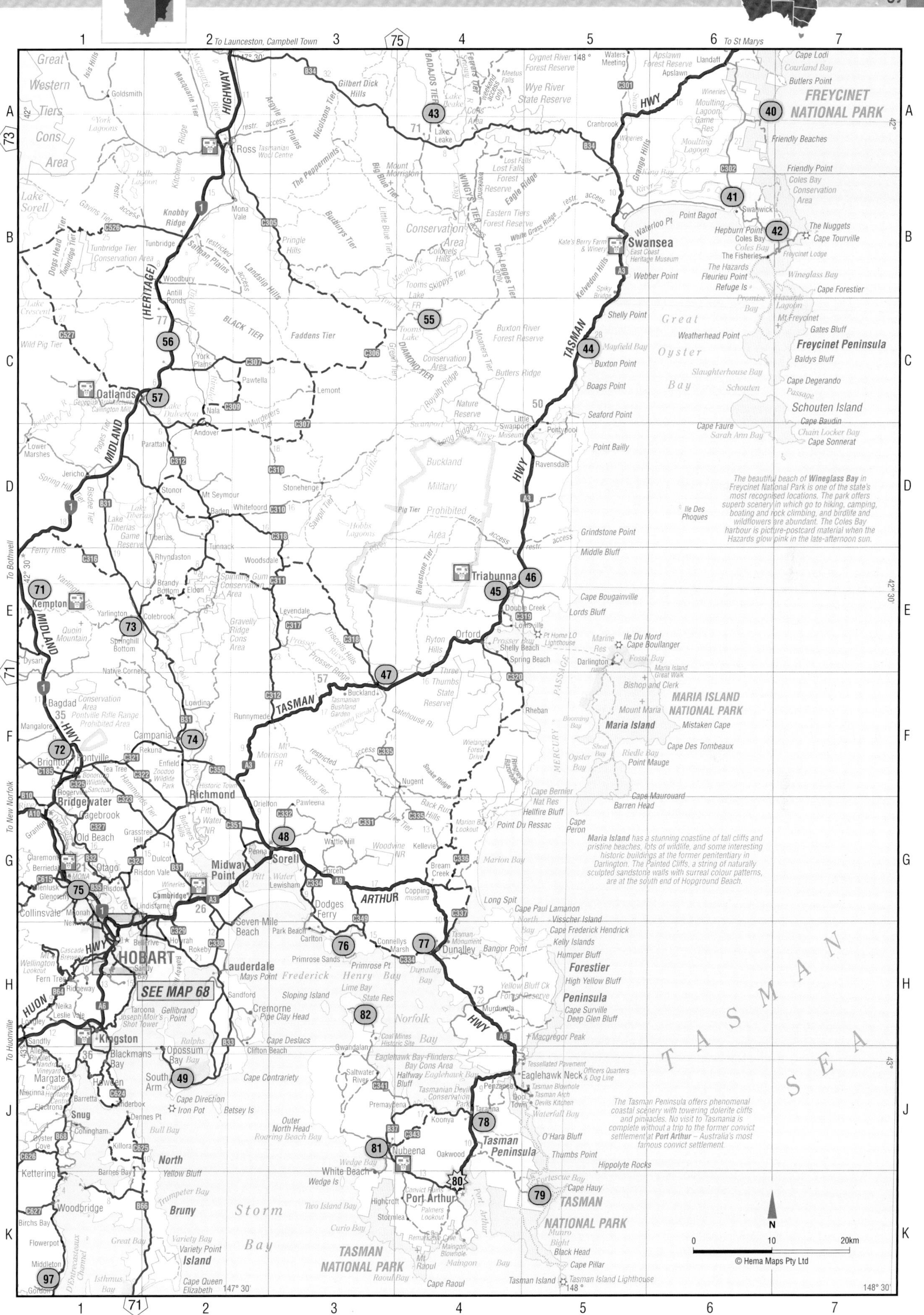
To Launceston, Campbell Town
To St Marys
FREYCINET NATIONAL PARK
Cape Lodi
Courland Bay
Butlers Point
Friendly Beaches
Friendly Point
Coles Bay Conservation Area
Swanwick
The Nuggets
Cape Tourville
Coles Bay
The Fisheries
The Hazards
Fleurieu Point
Refuge Is
Wineglass Bay
Cape Forestier
Promise Bay
Hazards Lagoon
Mt Freycinet
Gates Bluff
Freycinet Peninsula
Baldys Bluff
Cape Degerando
Passage
Schouten Island
Cape Baudin
Chain Locker Bay
Cape Sonnerat
Great Oyster Bay
Slaughterhouse Bay
Schouten
Weatherhead Point
Cape Faure
Sarah Ann Bay
The beautiful beach of Wineglass Bay in Freycinet National Park is one of the state's most recognised locations. The park offers superb scenery in which go to hiking, camping, boating and rock climbing, and birdlife and wildflowers are abundant. The Coles Bay harbour is picture-postcard material when the Hazards glow pink in the late-afternoon sun.
Swansea
East Coast Heritage Museum
Kate's Berry Farm & Winery
Waterloo Pt
Point Bagot
Hepburn Point
Webber Point
Shelly Point
Mayfield Bay
Buxton Point
Boags Point
Seaford Point
Point Bailly
Grindstone Point
Middle Bluff
Ile Des Phoques
Cape Bougainville
Lords Bluff
Ile Du Nord
Cape Boullanger
Marine Res
Darlington
Fossil Bay
Maria Island Great Walk
Bishop and Clerk
MARIA ISLAND NATIONAL PARK
Mount Maria
Maria Island
Mistaken Cape
Cape Des Tombeaux
Riedle Bay
Point Mauge
Oyster Bay
Shoal Bay
Booming Bay
MERCURY PASSAGE
Cape Maurouard
Barren Head
Cape Bernier
Nat Res
Hellfire Bluff
Cape Peron
Point Du Ressac
Marion Bay
Maria Island has a stunning coastline of tall cliffs and pristine beaches, lots of wildlife, and some interesting historic buildings at the former penitentiary in Darlington. The Painted Cliffs, a string of naturally sculpted sandstone walls with surreal colour patterns, are at the south end of Hopground Beach.
Long Spit
Cape Paul Lamanon
North Bay
Visscher Island
Cape Frederick Hendrick
Kelly Islands
Humper Bluff
Forestier Peninsula
High Yellow Bluff
Cape Surville
Deep Glen Bluff
Macgregor Peak
Tessellated Pavement
Officers Quarters & Dog Line
Eaglehawk Neck
Tasman Blowhole
Tasman Arch
Devils Kitchen
Doo Town
Waterfall Bay
O'Hara Bluff
Thumbs Point
Hippolyte Rocks
The Tasman Peninsula offers phenomenal coastal scenery with towering dolerite cliffs and pinnacles. No visit to Tasmania is complete without a trip to the former convict settlement at Port Arthur – Australia's most famous convict settlement.
TASMAN SEA
Fortescue Bay
Cape Hauy
TASMAN NATIONAL PARK
Munro Bight
Black Head
Cape Pillar
Tasman Island
Tasman Island Lighthouse
Cape Raoul
Raoul Bay
Mt Raoul
Maingon Blowhole
Maingon Bay
Remarkable Cave
Palmers Lookout
Port Arthur
Stormlea
Highcroft
Curio Bay
Two Island Bay
Wedge Is
White Beach
Wedge Bay
Nubeena
Oakwood
Tasman Peninsula
Taranna
Koonya
Premaydena
Tasmanian Devil Conservation Park
Saltwater River
Coal Mines Historic Site
Eaglehawk Bay-Flinders Bay Cons Area
Halfway Bluff
Gwandalan
Norfolk Bay
Lime Bay State Res
Primrose Pt
Frederick Henry Bay
Dunalley
Dunalley Bay
Tasman Monument
Bangor Point
Connellys Marsh
Copping
Storm Bay
Outer North Head
Roaring Beach Bay
Betsey Is
Cape Contrariety
Cape Deslacs
Clifton Beach
Cremorne
Pipe Clay Head
Sloping Island
Primrose Sands
Carlton
Park Beach
Dodges Ferry
Lewisham
Sorell
Midway Point
Pitt Water
Penna
Lauderdale
Mays Point
Sandford
Gellibrand Point
Ralphs Bay
Opossum Bay
South Arm
Cape Direction
Iron Pot
Bull Bay
North Bruny
Yellow Bluff
Trumpeter Bay
Variety Bay
Variety Point Island
Cape Queen Elizabeth
Great Bay
Isthmus Bay
D'Entrecasteaux Channel
Gordon
Middleton
Flowerpot
Birchs Bay
Woodbridge
Kettering
Barnes Bay
Killora
Oyster Cove
Coningham
Snug
Dennes Pt
Tinderbox
Barretta
Electrona
Margate
Howden
Blackmans Bay
Kingston
Taroona
Sandfly
Longley
Neika
Leslie Vale
Ridgeway
Fern Tree
Wellington Lookout
HOBART
SEE MAP 68
Bellerive
Howrah
Rokeby
Seven Mile Beach
Cambridge
Lindisfarne
Risdon Vale
Dulcot
Grasstree Hill
Otago
Risdon
Old Beach
Gagebrook
Bridgewater
Granton
Brighton
Pontville
Tea Tree
Rekuna
Enfield
Campania
Richmond
Historic Town
Orielton
Pawleena
Wattle Hill
Woodvine NR
Kellevie
Bream Creek
Nugent
Back Run Hills
Rheban
Buckland
Three Thumbs State Reserve
Runnymede
TASMAN HWY
ARTHUR HWY
Levendale
Ryton Hills
Orford
Triabunna
Spring Beach
Shelly Beach
Louisville
Double Creek
Buckland Military Prohibited Area
Little Swanport
Pontypool
Ravensdale
Nature Reserve
Butlers Ridge
Buxton River Forest Reserve
Conservation Area
Tooms Lake
Lemont
Woodsdale
Tunnack
Rhyndaston
Stonehenge
Whitefoord
Baden
Mt Seymour
Stonor
Parattah
Andover
Oatlands
Lake Dulverton
Jericho
Lake Tiberias
Tiberias
Brandy Bottom
Eldon
Colebrook
Yarlington
Springhill Bottom
Kempton
Quoin Mountain
Dysart
Bagdad
Mangalore
Native Corners
Pontville Rifle Range Prohibited Area
Lowdina
MIDLAND HWY
HERITAGE HIGHWAY
Ross
Tasmanian Wool Centre
Mona Vale
Tunbridge
Woodbury
Antill Ponds
York Plains
Pawtella
Nala
Knobby Ridge
Great Western Tiers
Cons Area
Lake Sorell
Lake Crescent
Wild Pig Tier
Lower Marshes
Goldsmith
Gilbert Dick Hills
Lake Leake
Wye River State Reserve
Cygnet River Forest Reserve
Apslawn Forest Reserve
Apslawn
Llandaff
Waters Meeting
Cranbrook
Moulting Lagoon Game Res
Mount Morriston
Eastern Tiers Forest Reserve
Pringle Hills
Colonels Hills
Hema Maps Pty Ltd

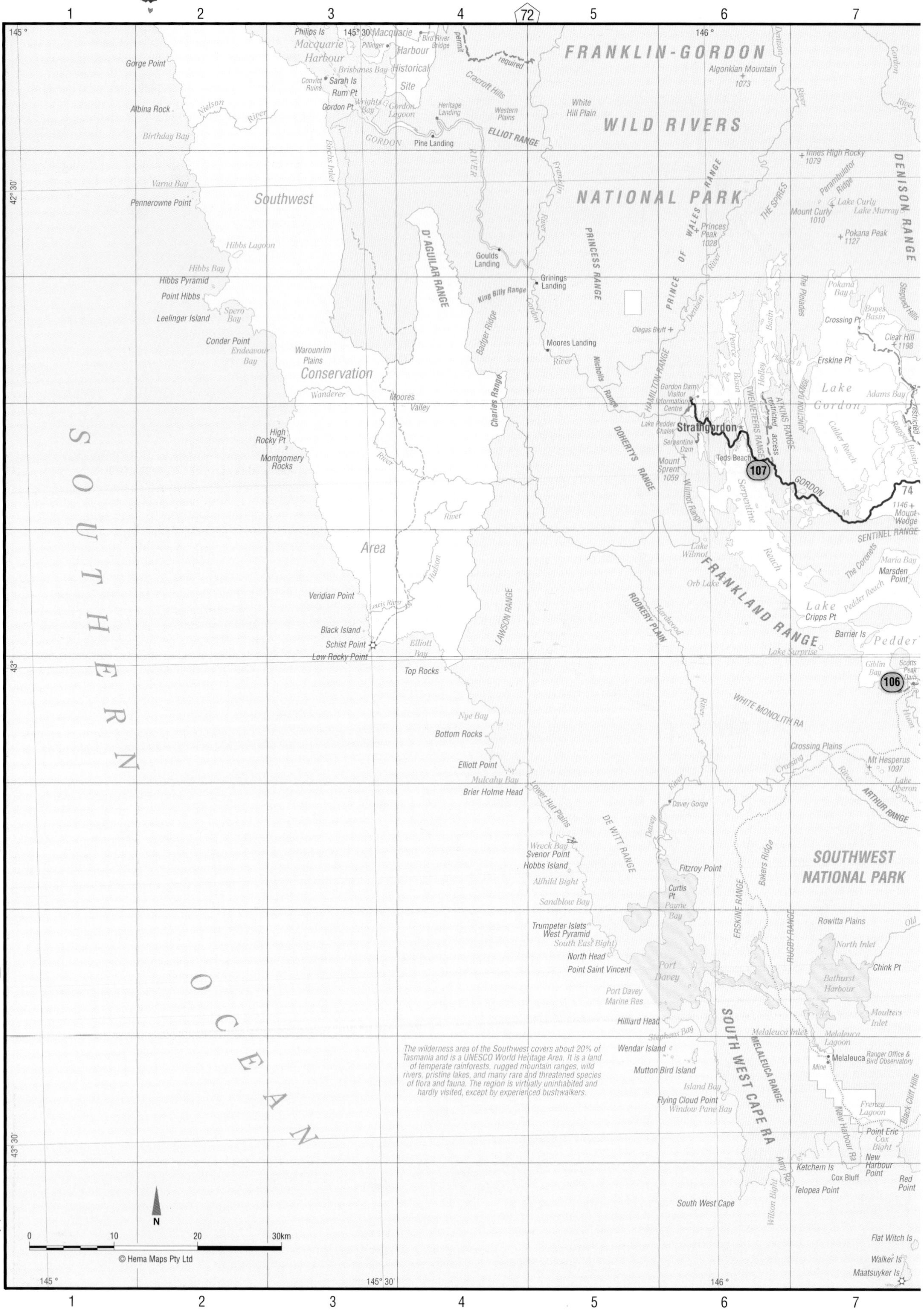
FRANKLIN-GORDON
WILD RIVERS
NATIONAL PARK
Macquarie Harbour
Macquarie Harbour Historical Site
Philips Is
Bird River Bridge
Pillinger
Brisbanes Bay
Convict Ruins
Sarah Is
Rum Pt
Gordon Pt
Wrights Bay
Gordon Lagoon
Heritage Landing
Pine Landing
Gorge Point
Albina Rock
Nielson River
Birthday Bay
Varna Bay
Pennerowne Point
Southwest Conservation Area
Hibbs Lagoon
Hibbs Bay
Hibbs Pyramid
Point Hibbs
Spero Bay
Leelinger Island
Conder Point
Endeavour Bay
Birchs Inlet
D'AGUILAR RANGE
Cracroft Hills
Western Plains
ELLIOT RANGE
Goulds Landing
King Billy Range
Grinings Landing
Badger Ridge
Moores Landing
Charles Range
Warounrim Plains
Wanderer River
Moores Valley
High Rocky Pt
Montgomery Rocks
Veridian Point
Lewis River
Black Island
Schist Point
Low Rocky Point
Elliott Bay
Top Rocks
Nye Bay
Bottom Rocks
Elliott Point
Mulcahy Bay
Brier Holme Head
Lower Hut Plains
Hudson
LAWSON RANGE
ROOKERY PLAIN
DE WITT RANGE
Wreck Bay
Svenor Point
Hobbs Island
Allhild Bight
Sandblow Bay
Trumpeter Islets
West Pyramid
South East Bight
North Head
Point Saint Vincent
Port Davey
Port Davey Marine Res
Hilliard Head
Stephens Bay
Wendar Island
Mutton Bird Island
Island Bay
Flying Cloud Point
Window Pane Bay
South West Cape
Wilson Bight
Amy Ra
SOUTH WEST CAPE RA
MELALEUCA RANGE
Davey Gorge
Davey
Fitzroy Point
Curtis Pt
Payne Bay
ERSKINE RANGE
Bakers Ridge
RUGBY RANGE
SOUTHWEST NATIONAL PARK
Rowitta Plains
North Inlet
Bathurst Harbour
Chink Pt
Moulters Inlet
Melaleuca Inlet
Melaleuca Lagoon
Melaleuca
Ranger Office & Bird Observatory
Mine
Freney Lagoon
Black Cliff Hills
New Harbour Ra
Point Eric
Cox Bight
New Harbour Point
Ketchem Is
Cox Bluff
Red Point
Telopea Point
Flat Witch Is
Walker Is
Maatsuyker Is
White Hill Plain
Algonkian Mountain 1073
Denison River
Innes High Rocky 1079
Perambulator Ridge
Lake Curly
Lake Murray
Mount Curly 1010
DENISON RANGE
THE SPIRES
PRINCE OF WALES RANGE
Princes Peak 1028
PRINCESS RANGE
Pokana Peak 1127
Pokana Bay
Boyes Basin
Stepped Hills
The Pleiades
Crossing Pt
Clear Hill 1198
Olegas Bluff
Erskine Pt
Lake Gordon
Adams Bay
HAMILTON RANGE
Gordon Dam Visitor Information Centre
Lake Pedder Chalet
Strathgordon
Serpentine Dam
Teds Beach
Nicholls Range
DOHERTYS RANGE
Mount Sprent 1059
Wilmot Range
TWELVETREES RANGE
ATKINS RANGE
JUNCTION RANGE
restricted access
Calder Reach
Gordon
107
74
1146 Mount Wedge
SENTINEL RANGE
The Coronets
Maria Bay
Marsden Point
Lake Wilmot
Orb Lake
FRANKLAND RANGE
Serpentine Reach
Lake Pedder
Pedder Reach
Cripps Pt
Barrier Is
Lake Surprise
Giblin Bay
Scotts Peak Dam
106
Huon
WHITE MONOLITH RA
Crossing Plains
Crossing River
Mt Hesperus 1097
Lake Oberon
ARTHUR RANGE
SOUTHERN OCEAN
The wilderness area of the Southwest covers about 20% of Tasmania and is a UNESCO World Heritage Area. It is a land of temperate rainforests, rugged mountain ranges, wild rivers, pristine lakes, and many rare and threatened species of flora and fauna. The region is virtually uninhabited and hardly visited, except by experienced bushwalkers.
N
0 10 20 30km
© Hema Maps Pty Ltd
145°
145° 30'
146°
42° 30'
43°
43° 30'
72
1 2 3 4 5 6 7
A B C D E F G H J K

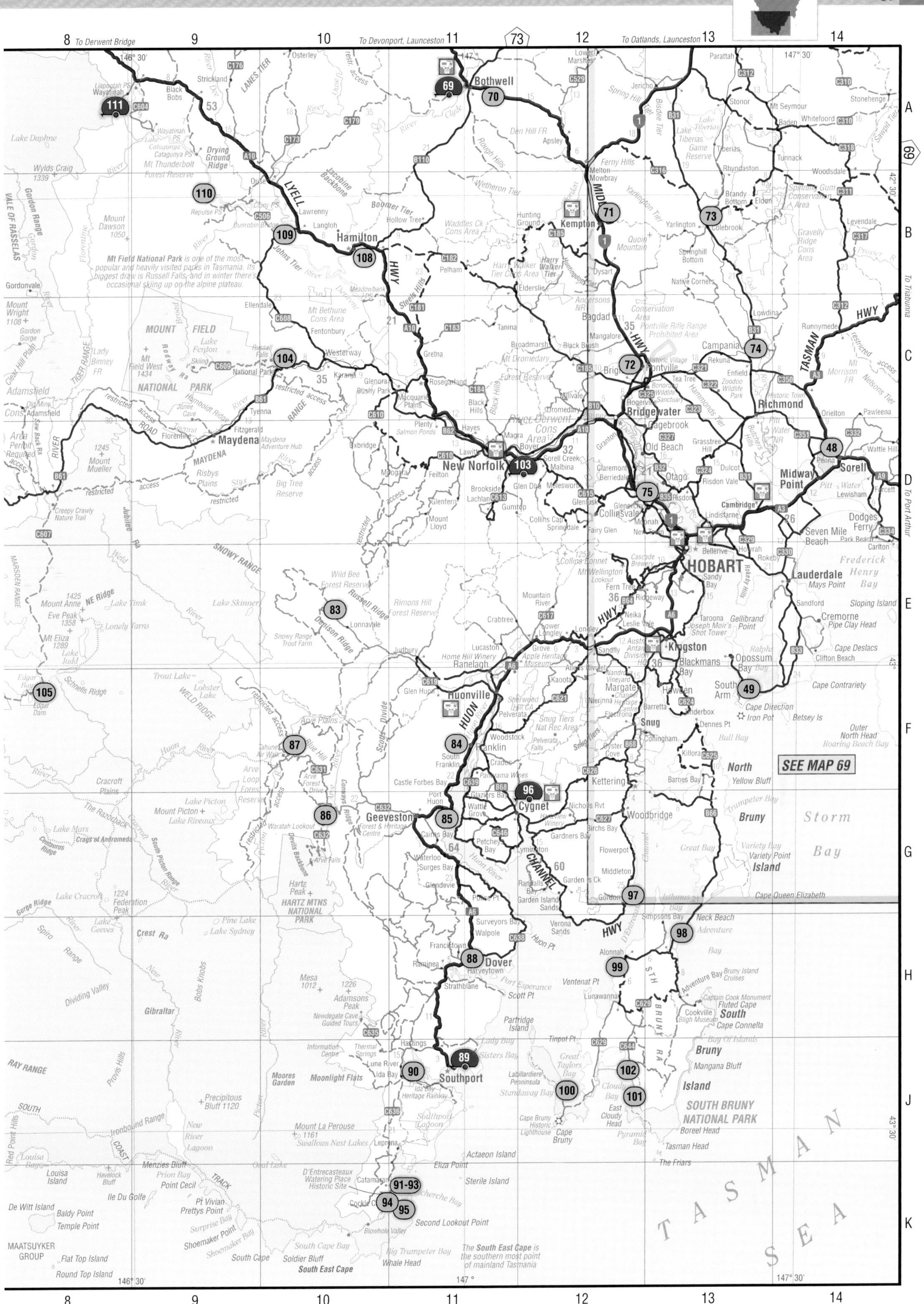
To Derwent Bridge
To Devonport, Launceston
To Oatlands, Launceston
Bothwell
Hamilton
Mt Field National Park is one of the most popular and heavily visited parks in Tasmania. Its biggest draw is Russell Falls, and in winter there's occasional skiing up on the alpine plateau.
MOUNT FIELD NATIONAL PARK
Maydena
New Norfolk
Kempton
Bagdad
Brighton
Pontville
Bridgewater
Richmond
Campania
Sorell
Midway Point
HOBART
Lauderdale
Kingston
Huonville
Cygnet
Geeveston
Dover
Southport
Snug
Kettering
Woodbridge
North Bruny
South Bruny
Bruny Island
SOUTH BRUNY NATIONAL PARK
HARTZ MTNS NATIONAL PARK
SEE MAP 69
Storm Bay
TASMAN SEA
The South East Cape is the southern most point of mainland Tasmania
South East Cape
To Triabunna
To Port Arthur

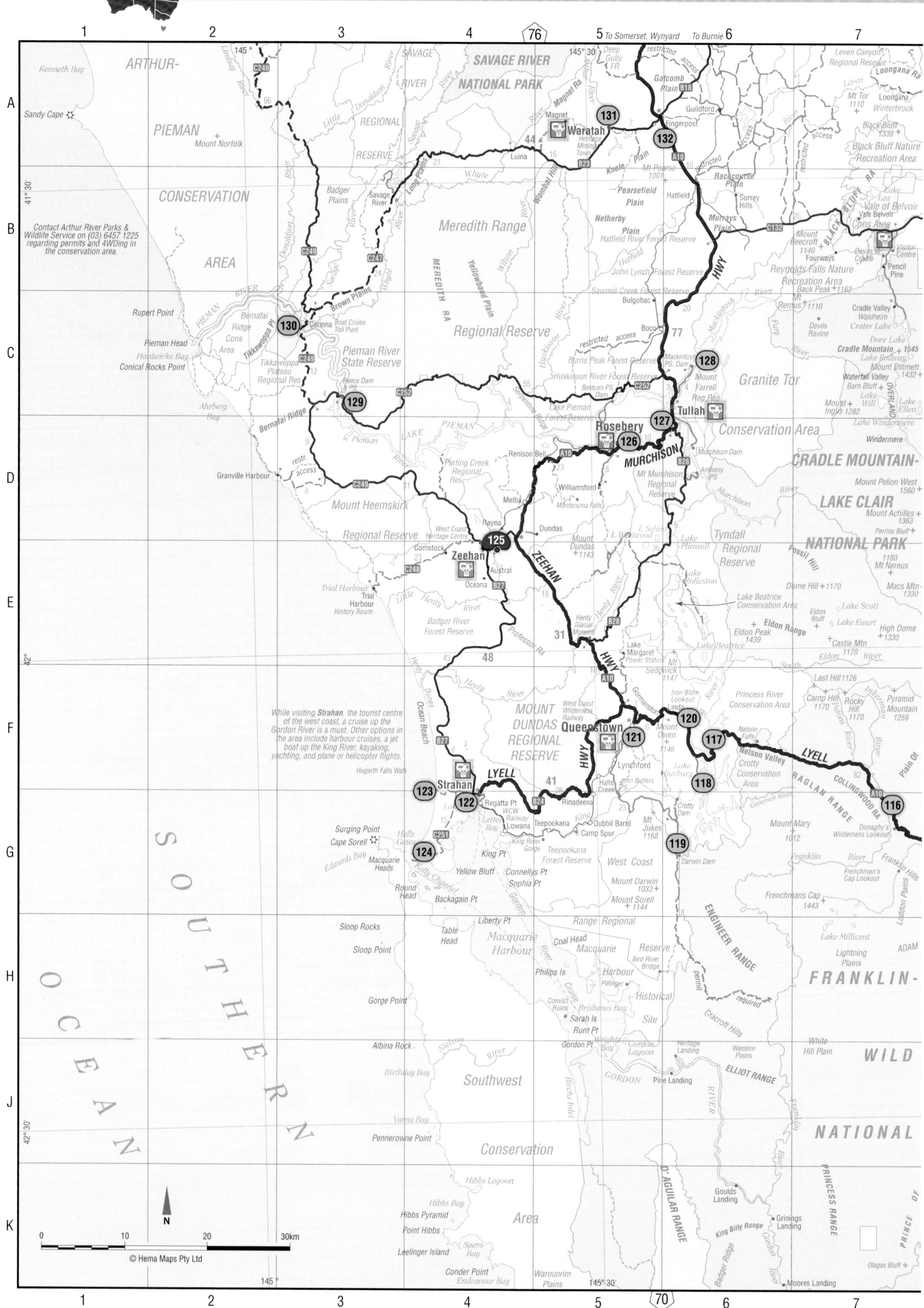

To Somerset, Wynyard
To Burnie
ARTHUR-PIEMAN CONSERVATION AREA
SAVAGE RIVER NATIONAL PARK
SAVAGE RIVER REGIONAL RESERVE
Sandy Cape
Mount Norfolk
Contact Arthur River Parks & Wildlife Service on (03) 6457 1225 regarding permits and 4WDing in the conservation area.
Waratah
Luina
Magnet
Guildford
Fingerpost
Hatfield
Meredith Range
Meredith Range Regional Reserve
Badger Plains
Savage River
Mount Beecroft
Vale of Belvoir
Black Bluff Nature Recreation Area
Reynolds Falls Nature Recreation Area
Cradle Valley
Cradle Mountain
Rupert Point
Pieman Head
Conical Rocks Point
Corinna
Pieman River State Reserve
Reece Dam
Bulgobac
Boco
Granite Tor Conservation Area
Tullah
Rosebery
Renison Bell
Williamsford
CRADLE MOUNTAIN-LAKE CLAIR NATIONAL PARK
Granville Harbour
Mount Heemskirk Regional Reserve
Zeehan
Dundas
Rayna
Comstock
Austral
Oceana
Trial Harbour
Tyndall Regional Reserve
Lake Beatrice Conservation Area
Eldon Range
Badger River Forest Reserve
Professor Ra
MOUNT DUNDAS REGIONAL RESERVE
Queenstown
Gormanston
Linda
Princess River Conservation Area
Nelson Valley
Crotty Conservation Area
RAGLAN RANGE
COLLINGWOOD RA
While visiting Strahan, the tourist centre of the west coast, a cruise up the Gordon River is a must. Other options in the area include harbour cruises, a jet boat up the King River, kayaking, yachting, and plane or helicopter flights.
Ocean Beach
Strahan
Regatta Pt
Lowana
Teepookana
Rinadeena
Lynchford
Mount Jukes
Darwin Dam
Surging Point
Cape Sorell
Hells Gates
Macquarie Heads
Round Head
Yellow Bluff
Backagain Pt
Sophia Pt
Connellys Pt
King Pt
West Coast Range Regional Reserve
Mount Darwin
Mount Sorell
Sloop Rocks
Sloop Point
Table Head
Macquarie Harbour
Macquarie Harbour Historical Site
Coal Head
Philips Is
ENGINEER RANGE
Frenchmans Cap
FRANKLIN-GORDON WILD RIVERS NATIONAL PARK
Gorge Point
Albina Rock
Birthday Bay
Sarah Is
Gordon Pt
Heritage Landing
Pine Landing
ELLIOT RANGE
Southwest Conservation Area
Varna Bay
Pennerowne Point
Hibbs Lagoon
Hibbs Bay
Hibbs Pyramid
Point Hibbs
Leelinger Island
Spero Bay
Conder Point
Endeavour Bay
Warounrin Plains
D'AGUILAR RANGE
Goulds Landing
Grinings Landing
King Billy Range
PRINCESS RANGE
Moores Landing
SOUTHERN OCEAN
0 10 20 30km
© Hema Maps Pty Ltd

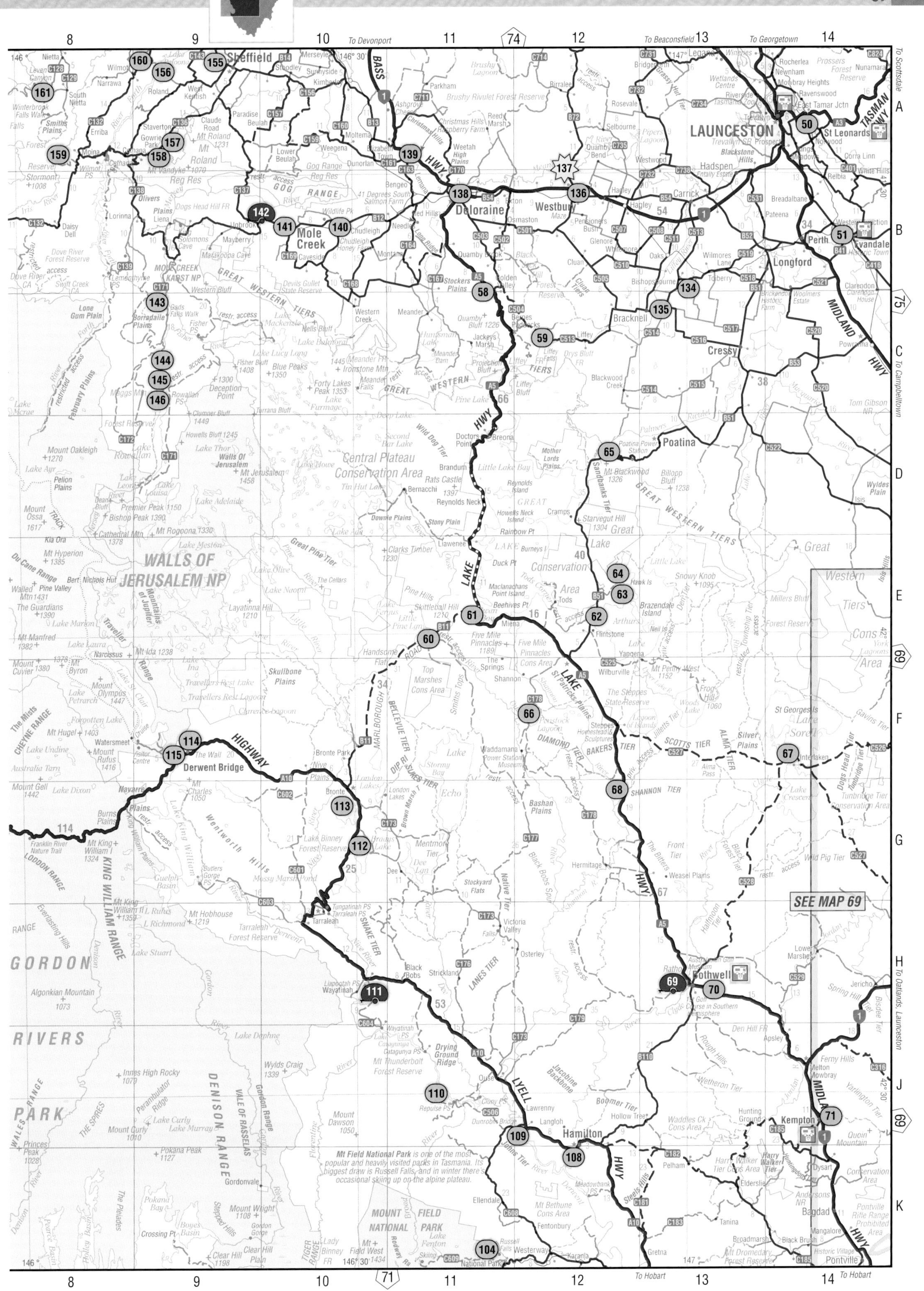
Sheffield
To Devonport
To Beaconsfield
To Georgetown
To Scottsdale
LAUNCESTON
St Leonards
Evandale
Perth
Longford
Cressy
Bracknell
Carrick
Hadspen
Westbury
Deloraine
Mole Creek
Poatina
Railton
Elizabeth Town
BASS HWY
MIDLAND HWY
TASMAN HWY
GREAT WESTERN TIERS
Central Plateau Conservation Area
WALLS OF JERUSALEM NP
MOLE CREEK KARST NP
GOG RANGE
Great Lake
Miena
Liawenee
LAKE HWY
Bothwell
Hamilton
LYELL HWY
Derwent Bridge
Tarraleah
Wayatinah
Ouse
Bronte Park
HIGHWAY
GORDON
RIVERS
PARK
KING WILLIAM RANGE
DENISON RANGE
MOUNT FIELD NATIONAL PARK
Westerway
National Park
Kempton
Pontville
SEE MAP 69
To Campbelltown
To Oatlands, Launceston
To Hobart
Mt Field National Park is one of the most popular and heavily visited parks in Tasmania. Its biggest draw is Russell Falls, and in winter there's occasional skiing up on the alpine plateau.

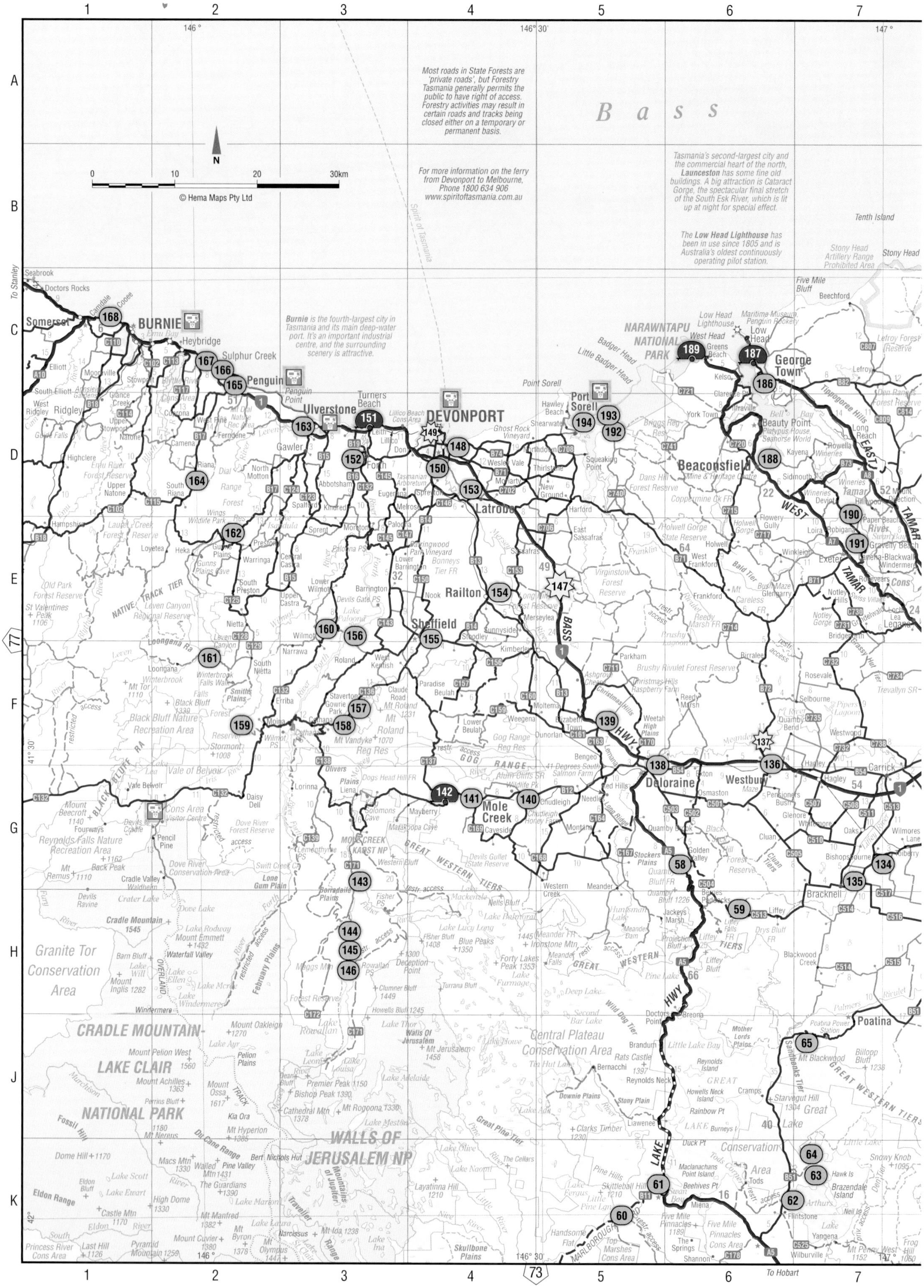

North-East Tasmania

Most roads in State Forests are 'private roads', but Forestry Tasmania generally permits the public to have right of access. Forestry activities may result in certain roads and tracks being closed either on a temporary or permanent basis.

For more information on the ferry from Devonport to Melbourne, Phone 1800 634 906 www.spiritoftasmania.com.au

Tasmania's second-largest city and the commercial heart of the north, **Launceston** has some fine old buildings. A big attraction is Cataract Gorge, the spectacular final stretch of the South Esk River, which is lit up at night for special effect.

The **Low Head Lighthouse** has been in use since 1805 and is Australia's oldest continuously operating pilot station.

Burnie is the fourth-largest city in Tasmania and its main deep-water port. It's an important industrial centre, and the surrounding scenery is attractive.

© Hema Maps Pty Ltd

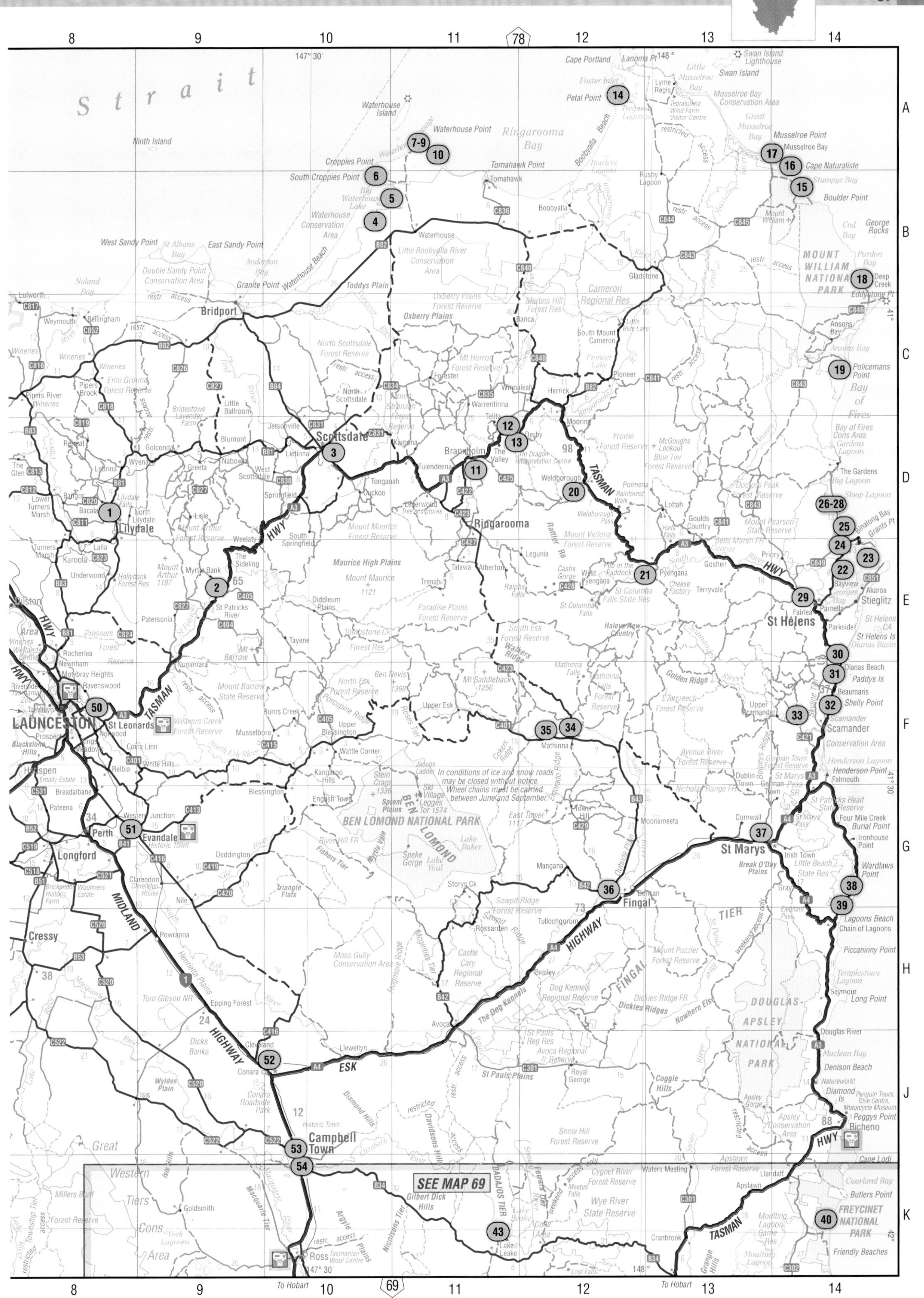
Strait
Ninth Island
Waterhouse Island
Waterhouse Point
Ringarooma Bay
Tomahawk Point
Tomahawk
Croppies Point
South Croppies Point
Waterhouse Conservation Area
West Sandy Point
East Sandy Point
Double Sandy Point Conservation Area
Granite Point
Waterhouse Beach
Toddys Plain
Noland Bay
Lulworth
Weymouth
Bellingham
Bridport
Little Boobyalla River Conservation Area
Oxberry Plains Forest Reserve
Oxberry Plains
Cape Portland
Lanoma Pt
Foster Inlet
Petal Point
Boobyalla Beach
Boobyalla
Lyme Regis
Little Musselroe Bay
Swan Island Lighthouse
Swan Island
Musselroe Bay Conservation Area
Great Musselroe Bay
Musselroe Point
Musselroe Bay
Cape Naturaliste
Stumpys Bay
Boulder Point
Rushy Lagoon
Mount William
Cod Bay
George Rocks
Purdon Bay
MOUNT WILLIAM NATIONAL PARK
Deep Creek
Eddystone Pt
Gladstone
Cameron Regional Res
South Mount Cameron
Little Blue Lake
Pioneer
Ansons Bay
Policemans Point
Bay of Fires
Bay of Fires Cons Area
Gardens Lagoon
The Gardens
Big Lagoon
Sloop Lagoon
Binalong Bay
Grants Pt
Herrick
Moorina
Frome Forest Reserve
McGoughs Lookout
Blue Tier Forest Reserve
Poimena Rainforest Walk
Lottah
Goulds Country
Goshen
Priory
Pyengana
St Columba Falls State Res
St Columba Falls
Cheese Factory
Terryvale
Bayview
Akaroa
Stieglitz
Parnella
Fairlea
St Helens
Parkside
St Helens CA
St Helens Is
Dianas Basin
Dianas Beach
Paddys Is
Beaumaris
Shelly Point
Scamander
Upper Scamander
Scamander Conservation Area
Henderson Lagoon
Henderson Point
Falmouth
German Town
Dublin Town
Nicholas Range FR
Four Mile Creek
Burial Point
Ironhouse Point
Wardlaws Point
Irish Town
Little Beach State Res
St Marys
Cornwall
Break O'Day Plains
Gray
Lagoons Beach
Chain of Lagoons
Piccaninny Point
Templestowe Lagoon
Seymour
Long Point
DOUGLAS-APSLEY NATIONAL PARK
Douglas River
Maclean Bay
Denison Beach
Diamond Is
Peggys Point
Bicheno
Apsley Conservation Area
Cape Lodi
Courland Bay
Butlers Point
FREYCINET NATIONAL PARK
Friendly Beaches
Apslawn
Llandaff
Cranbrook
Waters Meeting
Wye River State Reserve
Cygnet River Forest Reserve
Lake Leake
Snow Hill Forest Reserve
Royal George
Coggle Hills
St Pauls Plains
Avoca
Fingal
Mangana
Tullochgorum
Rossarden
Castle Cary Regional Reserve
Mount Puzzler Forest Reserve
Dog Kennels Regional Reserve
Dickies Ridges
Mathinna
Mathinna Falls
Golden Ridge
Evercreech Forest Reserve
Halls Falls
Legunia
Weldborough
Weldborough Pass
Derby
The Valley
Branxholm
Warrentinna
Winnaleah
Telita
Ringarooma
Talawa
Alberton
Tulendeena
Legerwood
Forester
Scottsdale
North Scottsdale
Jetsonville
Lietinna
Kamona
Tonganah
Cuckoo
Springfield
South Springfield
West Scottsdale
Nabowla
Blumont
Little Ballroom
Golconda
Wyena
Lebrina
Greta
Lisle
Lilydale
North Lilydale
Bacala
Bangor
Lower Turners Marsh
Turners Marsh
Karoola
Lalla
Underwood
Pipers River
Pipers Brook
Weelaty
The Sideling
Myrtle Bank
St Patricks River
Patersonia
Mount Arthur
Mount Maurice
Maurice High Plains
Diddleum Plains
Trenah
Tayene
Nunamara
Ben Nevis
Mt Saddleback
Upper Esk
Burns Creek
Musselboro
Upper Blessington
Wattle Corner
Blessington
Ben Lomond
BEN LOMOND NATIONAL PARK
Legges Tor 1574
In conditions of ice and snow roads may be closed without notice. Wheel chains must be carried between June and September.
Moonameeta
Mt Barrow
Rocherlea
Newnham
Mowbray Heights
Ravenswood
LAUNCESTON
St Leonards
Prospect
Norwood
Corra Linn
White Hills
Relbia
Hadspen
Breadalbane
Pateena
Perth
Evandale
Western Junction
Longford
Deddington
Nile
Clarendon
Cressy
Powranna
Epping Forest
Cleveland
Conara
Campbell Town
Ross
Tom Gibson NR
Dicks Banks
Isis
Wyldes Plain
Llewellyn
Goldsmith
Great Western Tiers
SEE MAP 69
Gilbert Dick Hills
Midland Highway
Tasman Hwy
Esk Highway
To Hobart

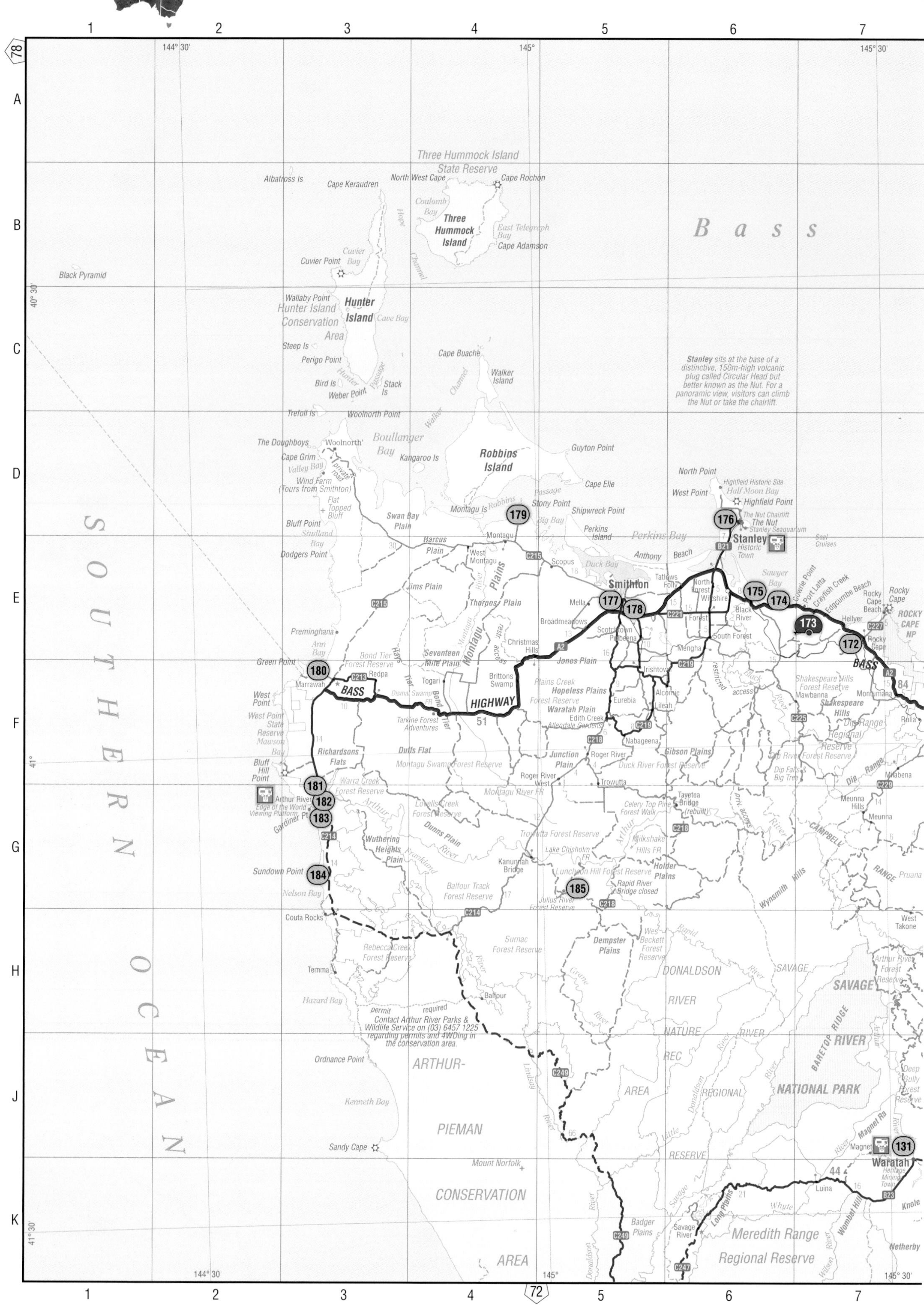
Three Hummock Island State Reserve
Albatross Is
Cape Keraudren
North West Cape
Cape Rochon
Three Hummock Island
East Telegraph Bay
Cape Adamson
Coulomb Bay
Hope Channel
Cuvier Point
Cuvier Bay
Black Pyramid
Wallaby Point
Hunter Island Conservation Area
Hunter Island
Cave Bay
Steep Is
Perigo Point
Bird Is
Weber Point
Stack Is
Hunter Passage
Cape Buache
Walker Island
Walker Channel
Trefoil Is
Woolnorth Point
B a s s
Stanley sits at the base of a distinctive, 150m-high volcanic plug called Circular Head but better known as the Nut. For a panoramic view, visitors can climb the Nut or take the chairlift.
The Doughboys
Woolnorth
Cape Grim
Valley Bay
Wind Farm (Tours from Smithton)
Boullanger Bay
Kangaroo Is
Robbins Island
Guyton Point
Cape Elie
Passage
Stony Point
Shipwreck Point
Montagu Is
Big Bay
Perkins Island
Perkins Bay
North Point
West Point
Highfield Historic Site
Half Moon Bay
Highfield Point
The Nut Chairlift
The Nut
Stanley Seaquarium
Stanley
Historic Town
Seal Cruises
Flat Topped Bluff
Bluff Point
Studland Bay
Dodgers Point
Swan Bay Plain
Harcus Plain
Montagu
West Montagu
Scopus
Duck Bay
Anthony
Beach
Sawyer Bay
Smithton
Tatlows
North Forest
Wiltshire
Black River
Forest
South Forest
Godfrey Point
Port Latta
Crayfish Creek
Edgcumbe Beach
Rocky Cape
Rocky Cape Beach
Hellyer
ROCKY CAPE NP
S O U T H E R N   O C E A N
Jims Plain
Thorpes Plain
Montagu Plains
Mella
Broadmeadows
Scotchtown
Christmas Hills
Mengha
Irishtown
Preminghana
Arm Bay
Green Point
Bond Tier Forest Reserve
Seventeen Mile Plain
Redpa
Marrawah
BASS
HIGHWAY
Togari
Brittons Swamp
Jones Plain
Pines Creek
Hopeless Plains
Forest Reserve
Waratah Plain
Edith Creek
Allendale Gardens
Eurebia
Alcomie
Lileah
Nabageena
West Point
West Point State Reserve
Mawson Bay
Tarkine Forest Adventures
Richardsons Flats
Duffs Flat
Montagu Swamp Forest Reserve
Junction Plain
Roger River
Gibson Plains
Duck River Forest Reserve
Bluff Hill Point
Roger River West
Trowutta
Montagu River FR
Warra Creek Forest Reserve
Arthur River
Edge of the World Viewing Platform
Gardiner Pt
Lowells Creek Forest Reserve
Dunns Plain
Celery Top Pine Forest Walk
Tayetea Bridge (rebuilt)
Shakespeare Hills Forest Reserve
Mawbanna
Shakespeare Hills
Dip Range Regional Reserve
Dip River Forest Reserve
Dip Falls & Big Tree
Dip Range
Meunna Hills
Meunna
Mooreville
Takone
Wuthering Heights Plain
Trowutta Forest Reserve
Milkshake Hills FR
Lake Chisholm FR
Kanunnah Bridge
Luncheon Hill Forest Reserve
Holder Plains
Rapid River Bridge closed
Sundown Point
Nelson Bay
Balfour Track Forest Reserve
Julius River Forest Reserve
Wynsmith Hills
CAMPBELL RANGE
Pruana
West Takone
Couta Rocks
Sumac Forest Reserve
Dempster Plains
West Beckett Forest Reserve
Rebecca Creek Forest Reserve
Temma
DONALDSON RIVER NATURE REC AREA
SAVAGE RIVER REGIONAL RESERVE
SAVAGE RIVER NATIONAL PARK
BARETOP RIDGE
Arthur River Forest Reserve
Hazard Bay
Balfour
permit required
Contact Arthur River Parks & Wildlife Service on (03) 6457 1225 regarding permits and 4WDing in the conservation area.
Ordnance Point
ARTHUR-PIEMAN CONSERVATION AREA
Kenneth Bay
Deep Gully Forest Reserve
Sandy Cape
Mount Norfolk
Magnet
Waratah
Heritage Mining Town
Luina
Long Plains
Whyte
Meredith Range Regional Reserve
Badger Plains
Savage River
Knole
Netherby
144° 30'
145°
145° 30'
40° 30'
41°
41° 30'

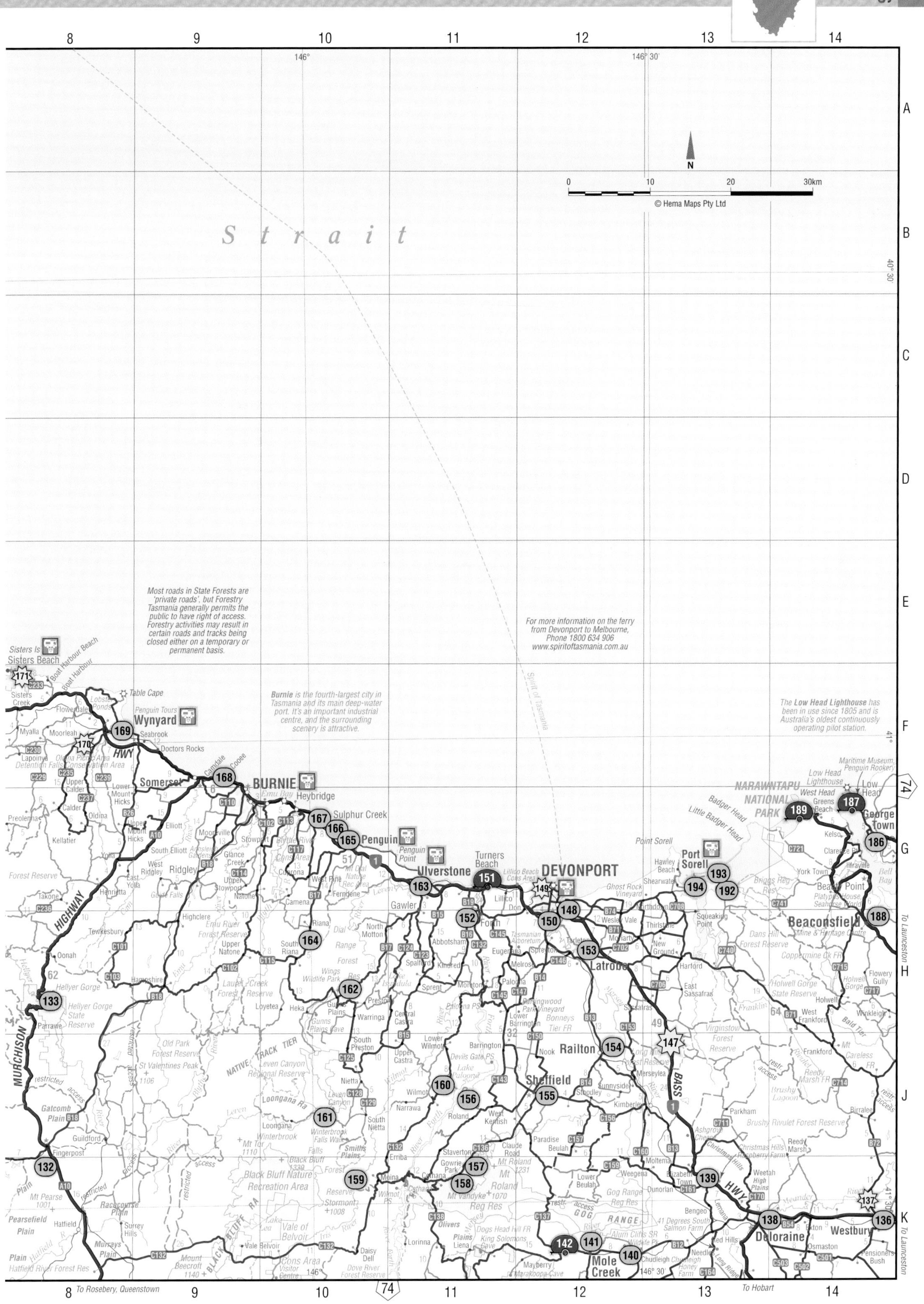

Strait
© Hema Maps Pty Ltd
0 10 20 30km
Most roads in State Forests are 'private roads', but Forestry Tasmania generally permits the public to have right of access. Forestry activities may result in certain roads and tracks being closed either on a temporary or permanent basis.
For more information on the ferry from Devonport to Melbourne, Phone 1800 634 906 www.spiritoftasmania.com.au
Burnie is the fourth-largest city in Tasmania and its main deep-water port. It's an important industrial centre, and the surrounding scenery is attractive.
The Low Head Lighthouse has been in use since 1805 and is Australia's oldest continuously operating pilot station.
Spirit of Tasmania
Sisters Beach
Table Cape
Wynyard
Penguin Tours
Doctors Rocks
Somerset
BURNIE
Heybridge
Sulphur Creek
Penguin
Ulverstone
Turners Beach
DEVONPORT
Port Sorell
NARAWNTAPU NATIONAL PARK
Badger Head
Little Badger Head
Low Head Lighthouse
Maritime Museum, Penguin Rookery
Low Head
George Town
Beaconsfield
Latrobe
Railton
Sheffield
Deloraine
Westbury
Mole Creek
Hellyer Gorge State Reserve
MURCHISON HIGHWAY
BASS HWY
NATIVE TRACK TIER
Black Bluff Nature Recreation Area
Mt Roland
To Rosebery, Queenstown
To Hobart
To Launceston

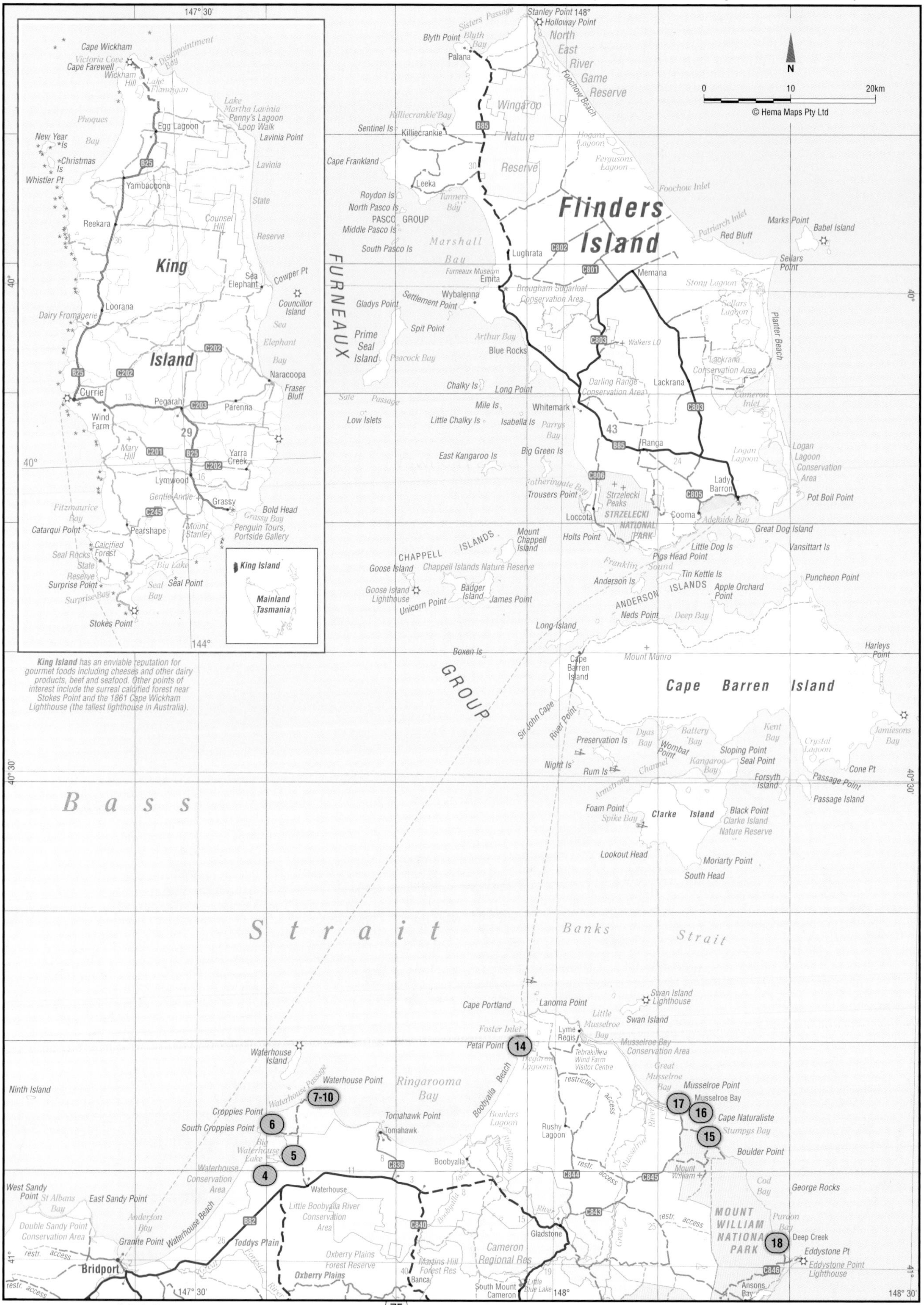

Flinders & King Islands, Tasmania

King Island has an enviable reputation for gourmet foods including cheeses and other dairy products, beef and seafood. Other points of interest include the surreal calcified forest near Stokes Point and the 1861 Cape Wickham Lighthouse (the tallest lighthouse in Australia).

© Hema Maps Pty Ltd

Tasmania Highway Index

Tasmania Alphabetic Site Index

Launceston - St Helens - Hobart

Tasman Highway

1 Lilydale Falls

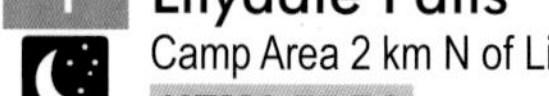

Camp Area 2 km N of Lilydale

B81

HEMA 75 D8 41 13 47 S 147 12 34 E

24

2 Myrtle Park Recreation Ground ☎(03) 6399 3368

Camp Area 32 km NE of Launceston or 31 km SW of Scottsdale, beside St Patricks River. Maximum stay 7 days

A3

HEMA 75 E9 41 18 31 S 147 21 55 E

BIG RIG

3 Northeast Park

Camp Area at Scottsdale. Ringarooma Rd, 1 km E of PO. Maximum stay 7 days. Donation & hot showers gold coin

A3

HEMA 75 D10 41 9 54 S 147 31 24 E

BIG RIG

4 Blackmans Lagoon Camping Area ☎(03) 6356 1173

Waterhouse Conservation Area

Camp Area 26.5 km NE of Bridport. Turn N off the B82, 24 km NE of Bridport. 2.5 km dirt road. Camping beside pine forest. Small vehicles only. Maximum stay 1 month

HEMA 75 B10 40 54 46 S 147 35 44 E

5 Big Waterhouse Lake Camping Area ☎(03) 6356 1173

Waterhouse Conservation Area

Camp Area 34 km NE of Bridport. Turn N off the B82, 27 km NE of Bridport onto Homestead Rd, then L after 4.3 km for 2.5 km. 7 km dirt road. Maximum stay 1 month

HEMA 75 B10 40 53 32 S 147 36 57 E

6 South Croppies Point Camping Area ☎(03) 6356 1173

Waterhouse Conservation Area

Camp Area 37 km NE of Bridport. Turn N off the B82, 27 km NE of Bridport onto Homestead Rd, then L after 6.3 km for 4 km. 10 km dirt road. Camping beside road just after fork. Maximum stay 1 month

HEMA 75 B10 40 51 56 S 147 35 37 E

✓7 Waterhouse Point Camping Area ☎(03) 6356 1173

Waterhouse Conservation Area

Camp Area 40 km NE of Bridport. Turn N off the B82, 27 km NE of Bridport onto Homestead Rd, then L after 12.4 km for 800m. 13 km dirt road. Small vehicles only. Beachfront. Maximum stay 1 month

HEMA 75 A11 40 49 39 S 147 40 8 E

8 Village Green Camping Area ☎(03) 6356 1173

Waterhouse Conservation Area

Camp Area 41 km NE of Bridport. Turn N off the B82, 27 km NE of Bridport onto Homestead Rd, then L after 12.4 km for 1.6 km. 14 km dirt road. Maximum stay 1 month

HEMA 75 A11 40 49 35 S 147 39 39 E

9 Mathers Camping Area

Waterhouse Conservation Area

Camp Area 40 km NE of Bridport. Turn N off the B82, 27 km NE of Bridport onto Homestead Rd, follow signs. 13 km dirt road. Beachfront. Maximum stay 1 month

HEMA 75 A11 40 49 40 S 147 40 9 E

10 Ransons Beach Camping Area ☎(03) 6356 1173

Waterhouse Conservation Area

Camp Area 41.4 km NE of Bridport. Turn N off the B82, 27 km NE of Bridport onto Homestead Rd for 14.4 km of dirt road. Beachfront. Maximum stay 1 month

HEMA 75 A11 40 50 24 S 147 41 14 E

11 Branxholm Camping Ground ☎(03) 6354 6168

Camp Area at Branxholm, beside swimming pool. Bookings & payment at the IGA supermarket

A3

HEMA 75 D11 41 10 6 S 147 44 15 E

BIG RIG

✓12 Derby Park

Camp Spot at Derby. W end of town, beside tennis courts & river

A3

HEMA 75 D11 41 8 31 S 147 47 52 E

BIG RIG

13 Derby Works Depot

Parking Area at Derby. E end of town, beside council depot

A3

HEMA 75 D11 41 9 0 S 147 48 16 E

BIG RIG

14 Petal Point Campground

Camp Area 21 km N of Gladstone, via Cape Portland Rd. Dirt road

C844

HEMA 75 A12 40 46 38 S 147 57 2 E

BIG RIG

15 Stumpys Bay Campground ☎(03) 6356 1173

Mt William National Park

Camp Area 26 km NE of Gladstone, via C843, C845 & Forester Kangaroo Dr. Mostly dirt road. Turn E 6 km N of park entrance. Small vehicles only. 4 camp areas

HEMA 75 B14 40 52 16 S 148 13 19 E

16 Top Camp Campground ☎(03) 6356 1173

Mt William National Park

Camp Area 27 km NE of Gladstone, via C843, C845 & Forester Kangaroo Dr. Turn E 300m N of Musselroe Bay township for 2.5 km. Mostly dirt road. Narrow access track. Oceanfront

HEMA 75 A14 40 50 34 S 148 12 12 E

TASMANIA

17 Musselroe Bay ☎(03) 6356 1173
Musselroe Bay Conservation Area
C845

Camp Area 24 km NE of Gladstone, via C843, C845 & Forester Kangaroo Dr. 800m N of Musselroe Bay fire station. Mostly dirt road. Oceanfront

HEMA 75 A14 40 50 7 S 148 10 39 E

18 Deep Creek Campground ☎(03) 6356 1173
Mt William National Park

Camp Area 37 km E of Gladstone. Turn N off C846, 34 km E of Gladstone at Eddystone Point Rd jcn for 3 km. Mostly dirt road. Small vehicles only

HEMA 75 B14 40 58 11 S 148 18 44 E

19 Policemans Point Campground ☎(03) 6376 1550
Bay of Fires Conservation Area

Camp Area 40 km E of Gladstone. Turn S off C843, 35 km E of Gladstone at South Ansons Bay Rd for 5 km. Mostly dirt road. Maximum stay 1 month

HEMA 75 C14 41 3 44 S 148 17 27 E

20 Weldborough Hotel & Campground ☎(03) 6354 2223
A3

Camp Spot at Weldborough, 21 km E of Derby or 44 km NW of St Helens. Behind Hotel

HEMA 75 D12 41 11 38 S 147 54 16 E

BIG RIG

21 Pub in the Paddock ☎(03) 6373 6121

Camp Spot at Pyengana. 750m W of the Pyengana Dairy Company. Self Contained Vehicles only

HEMA 75 D12 41 17 32 S 147 59 49 E

BIG RIG

22 Moulting Bay Camping Area ☎(03) 6376 1550
Humbug Point Nature Recreation Area

Camp Area 8 km NE of St Helens, via Binalong Bay Rd (C850). Turn E off C850 after 7 km. 1 km dirt road. Beside bay. Maximum stay 1 month

HEMA 75 E14 41 16 48 S 148 16 57 E

BIG RIG

23 Dora Point Camping Area ☎(03) 6376 1550
Humbug Point Nature Recreation Area

Camp Area 13 km NE of St Helens, via Binalong Bay Rd (C850). Turn E off C850 after 8.2 km. 4.7 km dirt road to various sites behind sand dunes. Beside bay. Cold showers. Maximum stay 1 month

HEMA 75 E14 41 16 37 S 148 19 36 E

24 Grants Lagoon ☎(03) 6376 1550
Bay of Fires Conservation Area
C848

Camp Area 10 km NE of St Helens, via Binalong Bay Rd (C850) & The Gardens Rd (C848). Turn E off C848, 9.5 km NE of St Helens, then R after 300m. Near lagoon. Maximum stay 1 month

HEMA 75 D14 41 15 17 S 148 17 25 E

BIG RIG

25 Jeanneret Beach Campground ☎(03) 6376 1550
Bay of Fires Conservation Area
C848

Camp Area 12 km NE of St Helens, via Binalong Bay Rd (C850) & The Gardens Rd (C848). Turn E off C848, 11.4 km NE of St Helens. Beachfront. Maximum stay 1 month

HEMA 75 D14 41 14 13 S 148 17 27 E

26 Swimcart Beach Campground ☎(03) 6376 1550
Bay of Fires Conservation Area
C848

Camp Area 13 km NE of St Helens, via Binalong Bay Rd (C850) & The Gardens Rd (C848). Turn E off C848, 12.3 km NE of St Helens. 1 km dirt road. Beachfront. Maximum stay 1 month

HEMA 75 D14 41 13 46 S 148 17 4 E

27 Cosy Corner South Camp Ground ☎(03) 6376 1550
Bay of Fires Conservation Area
C848

Camp Area 14 km NE of St Helens, via Binalong Bay Rd (C850) & The Gardens Rd (C848). Turn E off C848, 13.6 km NE of St Helens. 500m dirt road. Beachfront. Maximum stay 1 month

HEMA 75 D14 41 13 23 S 148 16 59 E

28 Cosy Corner North Camp Ground ☎(03) 6376 1550
Bay of Fires Conservation Area
C848

Camp Area 15 km NE of St Helens, via Binalong Bay Rd (C850) & The Gardens Rd (C848). Turn E off C848, 13.9 km NE of St Helens. 500m dirt road. Beachfront. Maximum stay 1 month

HEMA 75 D14 41 13 16 S 148 16 55 E

BIG RIG

29 St Helens Sporting Complex

Camp Area at St Helens. Tully St. Self contained motorhomes & campervans only

HEMA 75 E14 41 19 0 S 148 14 8 E

BIG RIG 24

30 Diana's Basin ☎(03) 6376 1550
St Helens Point State Rec Area

Camp Area 9 km S of St Helens or 4 km N of Beaumaris. Turn E 8 km S of St Helens or 3 km N of Beaumaris for 900m. Turn L after 500m. Waterfront. Maximum stay 1 month

HEMA 75 E14 41 22 34 S 148 17 16 E

BIG RIG

31 Paddys Island Campground ☎(03) 6376 1550
Scamander Conservation Area

Camp Area 10.5 km S of St Helens or 2.5 km NW of Beaumaris. Small area, limited sites. Beachfront

HEMA 75 F14 41 23 43 S 148 17 21 E

Notes...

TASMANIA

32 Shelly Point
(03) 6376 1550

Camp Area 2 km S of Beaumaris or 3 km N of Scamander Bridge. 400m off Hwy. No camping on oceanfront

HEMA 75 F14 41 26 5 S 148 16 36 E

33 Scamander Forest Reserve (Trout Creek)
(03) 6374 2102

Camp Area 11 km W of Beaumaris, via Upper Scamander Rd, Eastern Creek Rd & Trout Rd. Dirt road. Beside river

HEMA 75 F14 41 26 8 S 148 13 30 E

34 South Esk River Picnic Area

Camp Spot 3 km N of Mathinna. Turn N at Mathinna, then W onto Griffin Rd after bridge. Camp Spot at jcn

HEMA 75 F12 41 27 49 S 147 53 21 E

BIG RIG

35 Griffin Camping Area
(03) 6352 6520

Camp Area 5.5 km N of Mathinna. Turn N at Mathinna, then W onto Griffin Rd for 2.5 km. Signposted access tracks to various campsites. Beside river

HEMA 75 F12 41 27 57 S 147 51 10 E

36 Fingal Park

Parking Area at Fingal. Talbot St, located behind toilet block at the Info Board. Fee for shower

HEMA 75 G12 41 38 17 S 147 58 6 E

24

37 St Marys Sportsground & Golf Course

Camp Area at St Marys. 22 Harefield Rd. Fee for hot shower

HEMA 75 G13 41 35 5 S 148 11 2 E

BIG RIG 72

38 Little Beach Campground
(03) 6256 7000

Little Beach Conservation Area

A3

Camp Area 17 km S of A3/A4 jcn or 5.5 km N of Chain of Lagoons. 200m off Hwy. Beachfront. Maximum stay 1 month

HEMA 75 G14 41 37 35 S 148 18 44 E

39 Lagoons Beach
(03) 6256 7000

Lagoons Beach Conservation Area

A3

Camp Area 20 km S of A3/A4 jcn or 2.5 km N of Chain of Lagoons. 300m off Hwy. Beachfront. Maximum stay 1 month

HEMA 75 G14 41 38 48 S 148 17 52 E

BIG RIG

40 Friendly Beaches Campground
(03) 6256 7000

Freycinet National Park

Camp Area 13 km S of A3/C302 jcn. Turn E off C302, 9 km S of jcn. 3 km dirt road. Beachfront

HEMA 69 A6 41 59 27 S 148 17 15 E

41 River and Rocks Campground
(03) 6256 7000

Camp Area 19 km S of A3/C302 jcn or 8 km N of Coles Bay, via River & Rocks Rd. 1 km dirt road W of Hwy

HEMA 69 B6 42 5 12 S 148 14 3 E

42 Richardsons Beach Campground
(03) 6256 7000

Freycinet National Park

Camp Area at Coles Bay. Adjacent to National Parks Visitors Centre. Beachfront. Bookings essential. Small vehicles only. Maximum stay 10 days

HEMA 69 B6 42 7 27 S 148 17 46 E

43 Lake Leake Campground
(03) 6381 1319

Camp Area 39 km NW of Swansea or 32 km E of Campbell Town, via Lake Leake Rd. 4 km dirt road. Limited space

HEMA 69 A4 42 0 44 S 147 48 2 E

44 Mayfield Bay Campground
(03) 6256 7000

Mayfield Bay Conservation Area

A3

Camp Area 16 km S of Swansea or 34 km N of Triabunna. Beachfront. Gold coin donation

HEMA 69 C5 42 14 21 S 148 0 45 E

45 Triabunna Spring Bay Hotel
(03) 6257 3115

A3

Parking Area at Triabunna. Gold coin donation to the RFD at Bar. Self Contained Vehicles only

HEMA 69 E4 42 30 33 S 147 54 51 E

BIG RIG 48

46 Triabunna RV Stop

Parking Area at Triabunna. Cnr Esplanade W & Charles St, opposite Visitor Information Centre. Self Contained Vehicles only. Toilets near Info Centre

HEMA 69 E4 42 30 31 S 147 54 53 E

BIG RIG 48

47 Ye Old Buckland Inn
(03) 6257 5114

Camp Spot at Buckland. Parking at rear of pub. Self Contained Vehicles only. Check in with publican. Gold coin donation to Fire Brigade at the bar

HEMA 69 F3 42 36 24 S 147 43 12 E

BIG RIG 48

48 Sorell RV Stop
(03) 6269 0000

Camp Spot at Sorell. Montagu St. Self Contained Vehicles only. Permit available from Council office, 12 Somerville St, or honesty box on site. Maximum stay 5 days

HEMA 69 G3 42 47 2 S 147 33 24 E

BIG RIG

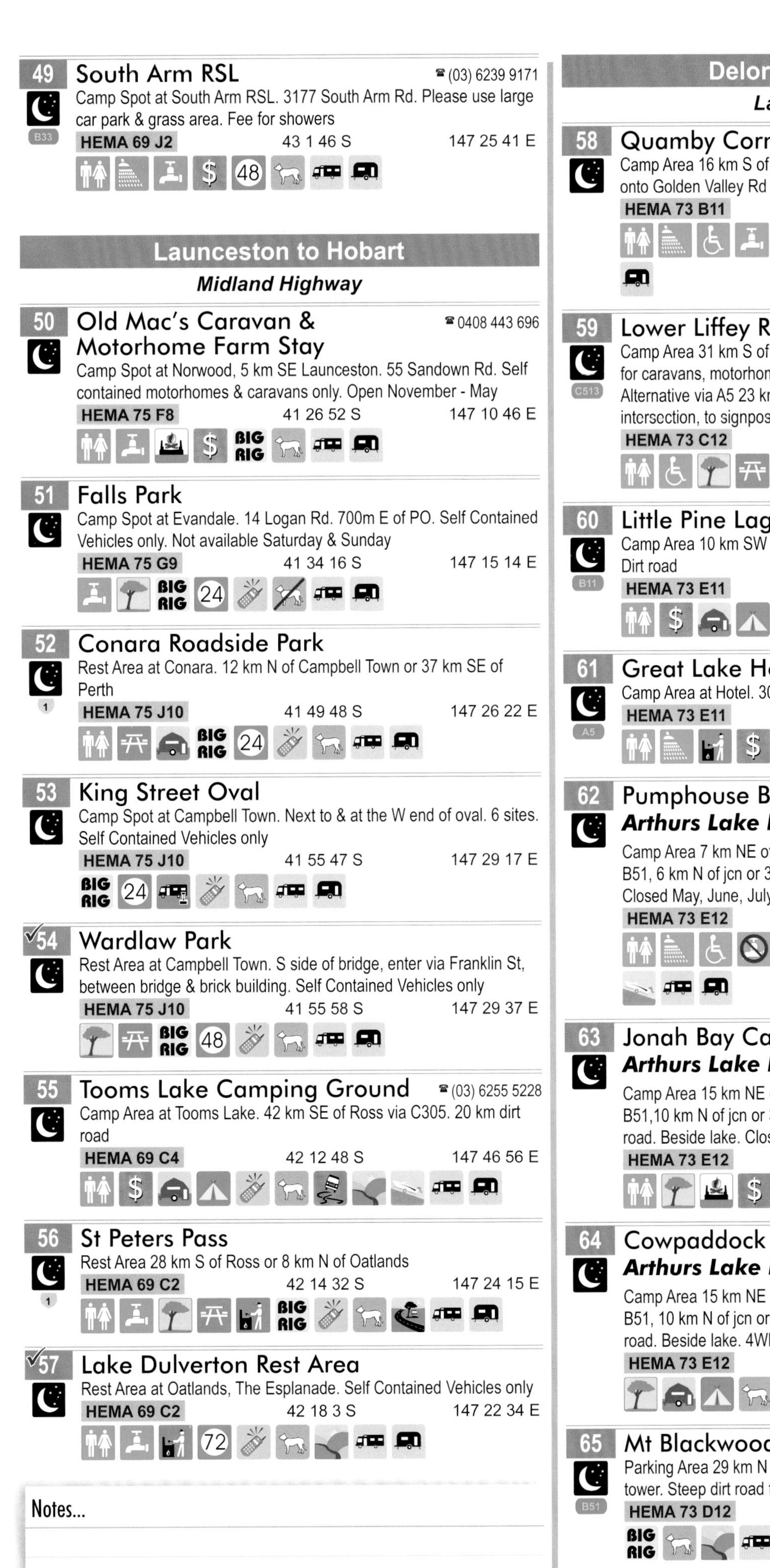

49 South Arm RSL
☎ (03) 6239 9171

Camp Spot at South Arm RSL. 3177 South Arm Rd. Please use large car park & grass area. Fee for showers

B33

HEMA 69 J2 43 1 46 S 147 25 41 E

48

Launceston to Hobart

Midland Highway

50 Old Mac's Caravan & Motorhome Farm Stay
☎ 0408 443 696

Camp Spot at Norwood, 5 km SE Launceston. 55 Sandown Rd. Self contained motorhomes & caravans only. Open November - May

HEMA 75 F8 41 26 52 S 147 10 46 E

BIG RIG

51 Falls Park

Camp Spot at Evandale. 14 Logan Rd. 700m E of PO. Self Contained Vehicles only. Not available Saturday & Sunday

HEMA 75 G9 41 34 16 S 147 15 14 E

BIG RIG 24

52 Conara Roadside Park

Rest Area at Conara. 12 km N of Campbell Town or 37 km SE of Perth

1

HEMA 75 J10 41 49 48 S 147 26 22 E

BIG RIG 24

53 King Street Oval

Camp Spot at Campbell Town. Next to & at the W end of oval. 6 sites. Self Contained Vehicles only

HEMA 75 J10 41 55 47 S 147 29 17 E

BIG RIG 24

54 Wardlaw Park

Rest Area at Campbell Town. S side of bridge, enter via Franklin St, between bridge & brick building. Self Contained Vehicles only

HEMA 75 J10 41 55 58 S 147 29 37 E

BIG RIG 48

55 Tooms Lake Camping Ground
☎ (03) 6255 5228

Camp Area at Tooms Lake. 42 km SE of Ross via C305. 20 km dirt road

HEMA 69 C4 42 12 48 S 147 46 56 E

56 St Peters Pass

Rest Area 28 km S of Ross or 8 km N of Oatlands

1

HEMA 69 C2 42 14 32 S 147 24 15 E

BIG RIG

57 Lake Dulverton Rest Area

Rest Area at Oatlands, The Esplanade. Self Contained Vehicles only

HEMA 69 C2 42 18 3 S 147 22 34 E

72

Notes...

Deloraine to Hobart

Lake Highway

58 Quamby Corner
☎ (03) 6369 5156

Camp Area 16 km S of Deloraine. 13436 Highland Lakes Rd. Turn E onto Golden Valley Rd (C502). 150m to entrance

HEMA 73 B11 41 37 35 S 146 42 39 E

BIG RIG

59 Lower Liffey Reserve

Camp Area 31 km S of Deloraine or 7 km W of Liffey. Best access for caravans, motorhomes signposted from Liffey off C513. Alternative via A5 23 km S Deloraine. Turn L at Jcn after 2 km, R at T intersection, to signposted access Rd

C513

HEMA 73 C12 41 40 58 S 146 46 54 E

60 Little Pine Lagoon
☎ (03) 6261 8050

Camp Area 10 km SW of Miena or 24 km NE of Bronte Park, via B11. Dirt road

B11

HEMA 73 E11 41 59 57 S 146 36 44 E

61 Great Lake Hotel
☎ (03) 6259 8163

Camp Area at Hotel. 3096 Marlborough Hwy, Miena

A5

HEMA 73 E11 41 58 49 S 146 40 36 E

BIG RIG

62 Pumphouse Bay Campground
☎ (03) 6259 4049

Arthurs Lake Recreation Area

Camp Area 7 km NE of A5/B51 jcn or 35 km S of Poatina. Turn E off B51, 6 km N of jcn or 34 km S of Poatina. 1 km dirt road. Beside lake. Closed May, June, July

HEMA 73 E12 41 59 5 S 146 51 41 E

BIG RIG

63 Jonah Bay Campground
☎ (03) 6259 4049

Arthurs Lake Recreation Area

Camp Area 15 km NE of A5/B51 jcn or 40 km S of Poatina. Turn E off B51,10 km N of jcn or 30 km S of Poatina, then R at Y jcn. 5 km dirt road. Beside lake. Closed May, June, July

HEMA 73 E12 41 57 31 S 146 54 10 E

64 Cowpaddock Bay Campground
☎ (03) 6261 8050

Arthurs Lake Recreation Area

Camp Area 15 km NE of A5/B51 jcn or 40 km S of Poatina. Turn E off B51, 10 km N of jcn or 30 km S of Poatina, then L at Y jcn. 5 km dirt road. Beside lake. 4WD recommended

HEMA 73 E12 41 56 10 S 146 53 46 E

65 Mt Blackwood Lookout

Parking Area 29 km N of A5/B51 jcn or 11 km SW of Poatina. Past tower. Steep dirt road for 750m

B51

HEMA 73 D12 41 49 3 S 146 53 21 E

BIG RIG

66 Penstock Lagoon

C178

Camp Spot at Penstock Lagoon. Turn W off A5 10 km S of Miena or 47 km N of Bothwell onto Waddamana Rd. 9 km to camp spot on W shore. Dirt road

HEMA 73 F12 42 4 58 S 146 46 5 E

67 Dago Point Campground

☎ (03) 6259 4049

Camp Area 26 km E of Steppes or 1.4 km W of Interlaken. Turn N 600m W of Interlaken. Dirt road. Lakeside. Big rigs at boat ramp. Closed May, June, July

HEMA 73 F14 42 7 57 S 147 10 7 E

BIG RIG

68 Blackburn Creek

A5

Parking Area 9 km S of Steppes or 25 km N of Bothwell. Beside creek

HEMA 73 G12 42 10 21 S 146 54 17 E

BIG RIG

69 Bothwell Caravan Park

☎ (03) 6259 5503

Caravan Park at Bothwell. Market Place, behind Info Centre

HEMA 73 H13 42 22 58 S 147 0 29 E

70 Pub With No Beer

A5

Parking Area 3 km E of Bothwell or 17 km NW of Melton Mowbray

HEMA 73 H13 42 23 18 S 147 2 36 E

BIG RIG

71 The "Blue Place"

Rest Area at Kempton, beside the "Blue Place". Self Contained Vehicles only. Fee for use of showers, toilets & power

HEMA 73 J14 42 31 55 S 147 12 8 E

BIG RIG 48

72 Pontville Park RV Stop

☎ (03) 6268 7000

Parking Area at Pontville. Entry off Glen Lea Rd. Self Contained Vehicles only

HEMA 69 F1 42 41 12 S 147 15 37 E

BIG RIG 48

73 Colebrook Tavern

☎ (03) 6259 7164

Camp Spot at Colebrook. 1 km N of PO. Self Contained Vehicles only. Meals available Fri & Sat

HEMA 69 E1 42 31 34 S 147 21 32 E

BIG RIG 48

74 Campania Flour Mill Park

Rest Area at Campania, Colebrook Main Rd. Self Contained Vehicles only

HEMA 69 F2 42 39 59 S 147 25 15 E

24

75 Hobart Showgrounds

☎ (03) 6272 6812

Camp Area. 2 Howard Rd Glenorchy. Maximum stay 14 days. Report to Administration building, if closed use self registration forms. Self Contained Vehicles only. Closed during October for show

HEMA 69 G1 42 50 2 S 147 17 6 E

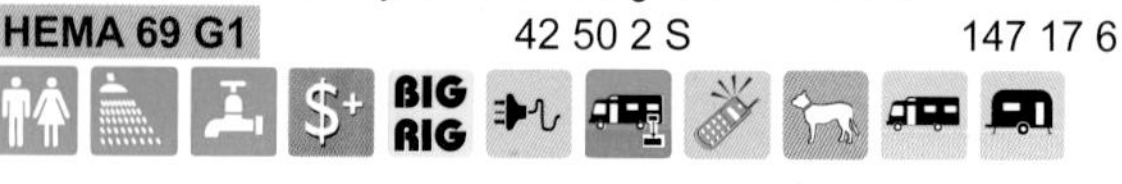

Sorell to Port Arthur

Arthur Highway

76 Primrose Sands RSLA Club

☎ (03) 6265 5655

Parking Area at Primrose Sands, 22 km SE of Sorell. Self Contained Vehicles only. Toilets available during Club opening hours

HEMA 69 H3 42 53 9 S 147 40 9 E

BIG RIG

77 Dunalley Hotel

☎ (03) 6253 5101

Camp Spot at Dunalley, Arthur Hwy

HEMA 69 H4 42 53 36 S 147 48 18 E

BIG RIG

78 Taranna Cottages & Self Contained Campers Park

☎ (03) 6250 3436

Camp Spot at Taranna. 19 Nubeena Rd, near Cnr of Arthur Hwy. Self Contained Vehicles only

HEMA 69 J4 43 3 45 S 147 51 43 E

BIG RIG

79 Fortescue Bay Campground

Tasman National Park

☎ (03) 6250 2433

C344

Camp Area 17 km E of Port Arthur. Turn E off the A9, 6 km S of Taranna or 5 km N of Port Arthur. 12 km dirt road. Bookings necessary

HEMA 69 K5 43 8 32 S 147 58 2 E

80 Stewarts Bay State Reserve

Picnic Area 1 km N of Port Arthur, via Stewarts Bay Rd

HEMA 69 K4 43 8 14 S 147 51 13 E

81 Tasman RSL Club Nubeena

☎ (03) 6250 2135

Camp Spot at Nubeena. Cnr Main & Alfred St. Next to RSL Club. Self Contained Vehicles only. Fee for use of showers

HEMA 69 J3 43 6 28 S 147 44 45 E

BIG RIG 48

82 Lime Bay Campground

☎ (03) 6250 3497

C341

Camp Area 16 km N of Premaydena. 6 km dirt road. Waterfront

HEMA 69 H3 42 57 27 S 147 42 16 E

Hobart to Cockle Creek

Huon Highway

83 Rivers Edge Camping

☎ 0439 760 007

Camp Area 28 km W of Huonville. 1322 Lonnavale Rd. Turn W, S of Houn bridge into Glen Houn Rd (C619) travel 14 km, turn W into Lonnavalle Rd for 14 km to campground. Open weekends only in June/July & August

HEMA 71 E10 42 56 50 S 146 48 1 E

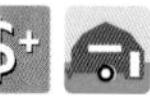

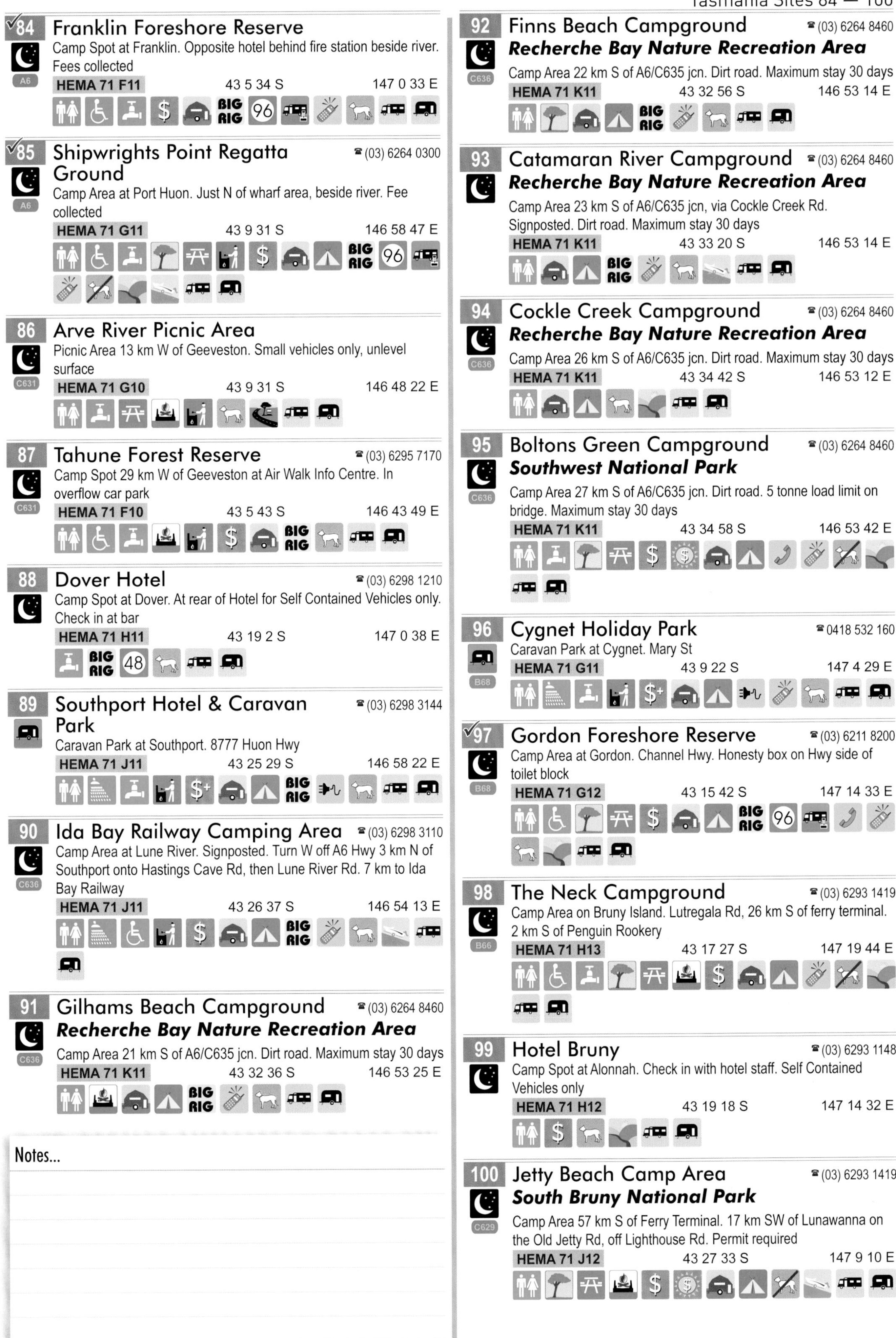

84 Franklin Foreshore Reserve
Camp Spot at Franklin. Opposite hotel behind fire station beside river. Fees collected
A6
HEMA 71 F11 43 5 34 S 147 0 33 E
BIG RIG 96

85 Shipwrights Point Regatta Ground
☎ (03) 6264 0300
Camp Area at Port Huon. Just N of wharf area, beside river. Fee collected
A6
HEMA 71 G11 43 9 31 S 146 58 47 E
BIG RIG 96

86 Arve River Picnic Area
Picnic Area 13 km W of Geeveston. Small vehicles only, unlevel surface
C631
HEMA 71 G10 43 9 31 S 146 48 22 E

87 Tahune Forest Reserve
☎ (03) 6295 7170
Camp Spot 29 km W of Geeveston at Air Walk Info Centre. In overflow car park
C631
HEMA 71 F10 43 5 43 S 146 43 49 E
BIG RIG

88 Dover Hotel
☎ (03) 6298 1210
Camp Spot at Dover. At rear of Hotel for Self Contained Vehicles only. Check in at bar
HEMA 71 H11 43 19 2 S 147 0 38 E
BIG RIG 48

89 Southport Hotel & Caravan Park
☎ (03) 6298 3144
Caravan Park at Southport. 8777 Huon Hwy
HEMA 71 J11 43 25 29 S 146 58 22 E
BIG RIG

90 Ida Bay Railway Camping Area
☎ (03) 6298 3110
Camp Area at Lune River. Signposted. Turn W off A6 Hwy 3 km N of Southport onto Hastings Cave Rd, then Lune River Rd. 7 km to Ida Bay Railway
C636
HEMA 71 J11 43 26 37 S 146 54 13 E
BIG RIG

91 Gilhams Beach Campground
☎ (03) 6264 8460
Recherche Bay Nature Recreation Area
Camp Area 21 km S of A6/C635 jcn. Dirt road. Maximum stay 30 days
C636
HEMA 71 K11 43 32 36 S 146 53 25 E
BIG RIG

Notes...

92 Finns Beach Campground
☎ (03) 6264 8460
Recherche Bay Nature Recreation Area
Camp Area 22 km S of A6/C635 jcn. Dirt road. Maximum stay 30 days
C636
HEMA 71 K11 43 32 56 S 146 53 14 E
BIG RIG

93 Catamaran River Campground
☎ (03) 6264 8460
Recherche Bay Nature Recreation Area
Camp Area 23 km S of A6/C635 jcn, via Cockle Creek Rd. Signposted. Dirt road. Maximum stay 30 days
HEMA 71 K11 43 33 20 S 146 53 14 E
BIG RIG

94 Cockle Creek Campground
☎ (03) 6264 8460
Recherche Bay Nature Recreation Area
Camp Area 26 km S of A6/C635 jcn. Dirt road. Maximum stay 30 days
C636
HEMA 71 K11 43 34 42 S 146 53 12 E

95 Boltons Green Campground
☎ (03) 6264 8460
Southwest National Park
Camp Area 27 km S of A6/C635 jcn. Dirt road. 5 tonne load limit on bridge. Maximum stay 30 days
C636
HEMA 71 K11 43 34 58 S 146 53 42 E

96 Cygnet Holiday Park
☎ 0418 532 160
Caravan Park at Cygnet. Mary St
B68
HEMA 71 G11 43 9 22 S 147 4 29 E

97 Gordon Foreshore Reserve
☎ (03) 6211 8200
Camp Area at Gordon. Channel Hwy. Honesty box on Hwy side of toilet block
B68
HEMA 71 G12 43 15 42 S 147 14 33 E
BIG RIG 96

98 The Neck Campground
☎ (03) 6293 1419
Camp Area on Bruny Island. Lutregala Rd, 26 km S of ferry terminal. 2 km S of Penguin Rookery
B66
HEMA 71 H13 43 17 27 S 147 19 44 E

99 Hotel Bruny
☎ (03) 6293 1148
Camp Spot at Alonnah. Check in with hotel staff. Self Contained Vehicles only
HEMA 71 H12 43 19 18 S 147 14 32 E

100 Jetty Beach Camp Area
☎ (03) 6293 1419
South Bruny National Park
Camp Area 57 km S of Ferry Terminal. 17 km SW of Lunawanna on the Old Jetty Rd, off Lighthouse Rd. Permit required
C629
HEMA 71 J12 43 27 33 S 147 9 10 E

101 Cloudy Bay Corner Camp Area ☎ (03) 6293 1419

South Bruny National Park

C644

Camp Area 49 km S of Ferry Terminal. 9 km S of Lunawanna on Cloudy Bay Rd. Beach access only, approximately 3 km, check tides for access. Permit required. 4WD only recommended

HEMA 71 J12 43 27 55 S 147 15 9 E

102 The Pines Camp Area ☎ (03) 6293 1419

South Bruny National Park

C644

Camp Area 49 km S of Ferry Terminal. 8 km S of Lunawanna on Cloudy Bay Rd. Permit required

HEMA 71 J12 43 26 15 S 147 14 48 E

New Norfolk to Strathgordon

Gordon River Road

103 New Norfolk Caravan Park ☎ (03) 6261 1268

Caravan Park at New Norfolk. The Esplanade. 1.5 km N of PO. Waterfront

HEMA 71 D11 42 46 33 S 147 3 58 E

BIG RIG

104 Mount Field Campground ☎ (03) 6288 1149

Mt Field National Park

C609

Camp Area at Mount Field National Park, via Lake Dobson Rd. 66 Lake Dobson Rd. Limited sites

HEMA 71 C10 42 40 56 S 146 43 6 E

BIG RIG

105 Edgar Campground ☎ 1300 360 441

Camp Area off Scotts Peak Dam Rd, S end of Lake Pedder. 30 km dirt road. Signposted off B61, 42 km E of Strathgordon or 51 km W of Westerway

HEMA 71 F8 43 1 52 S 146 20 35 E

106 Huon Campground ☎ (03) 6288 1149

Camp Area 7 km W of Edgar Campground. Turn L off Scotts Peak Rd opposite dam. 1 km to camping area. Small vehicles only

HEMA 70 F7 43 2 18 S 146 17 57 E

107 Teds Beach Campground ☎ (03) 6288 1149

B61

Camp Area 4 km E of Strathgordon

HEMA 70 D6 42 47 13 S 146 3 39 E

Hobart-Queenstown-Burnie

Lyell, Zeehan and Murchison Highways

108 Hamilton Camping Ground ☎ (03) 6286 3202

A10

Camp Area at Hamilton. W end of town, beside river

HEMA 73 J12 42 33 33 S 146 49 50 E

BIG RIG 72

109 Bethune Park ☎ 1300 360 441

Camp Area 10 km W of Hamilton. Turn S off A10 onto C608 8 km W of Hamilton or 7 km SE of Ouse. On W side of Lake Meadowbank. Maximum stay 7 days

HEMA 73 J12 42 32 11 S 146 43 49 E

110 Lake Repulse Bush Camping ☎ (03) 6233 7449

Camp Area 20 km SW of Ouse. Turn W onto Ellendale Rd 7 km S of Ouse, then onto Dawson Rd for 11 km to forest & track on R to lakefront. Various tracks to sites. 4WD recommended. Not suitable for caravans

HEMA 73 J11 42 29 59 S 146 37 10 E

111 Wayatinah Lakeside Caravan Park ☎ (03) 6289 3317

Caravan Park 24 km NW of Ouse or 16 km S of Tarraleah. Turn S 23 km W of Ouse or 15 km S of Tarraleah. 1.2 km sealed road from Lyell Hwy

HEMA 73 H10 42 23 9 S 146 30 19 E

BIG RIG

112 Bradys Lake ☎ 1300 360 441

Camp Spot 17 km N of Tarraleah or 8 km S of A10/B11 jcn. 800m dirt road E of Hwy. Beside lake. Maximum stay 7 days

HEMA 73 G10 42 13 57 S 146 29 46 E

113 Bronte Lagoon Camping Area ☎ 1300 360 441

A10

Camp Area 26 km N of Tarraleah. Turn S 250m S of A10/B11 jcn. 2 km to campsites. Signposted. Limited space, small vehicles only. Maximum stay 7 days

HEMA 73 G10 42 11 12 S 146 28 49 E

114 Derwent Bridge Hotel ☎ (03) 6289 1144

Parking Area at Derwent Bridge. Self Contained Vehicles only in hotel car park. Must check in with publican

HEMA 73 F9 42 8 11 S 146 13 48 E

BIG RIG 20

115 Lake King William

A10

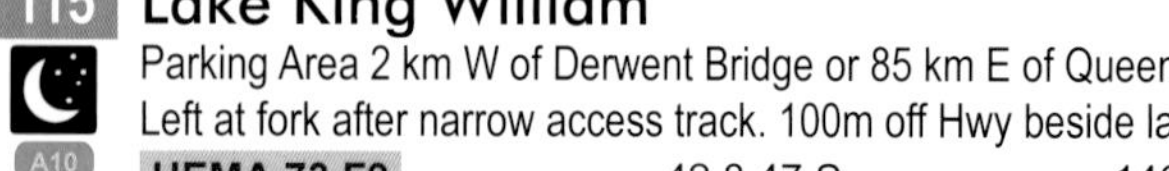

Parking Area 2 km W of Derwent Bridge or 85 km E of Queenstown. Left at fork after narrow access track. 100m off Hwy beside lake

HEMA 73 F9 42 8 47 S 146 13 7 E

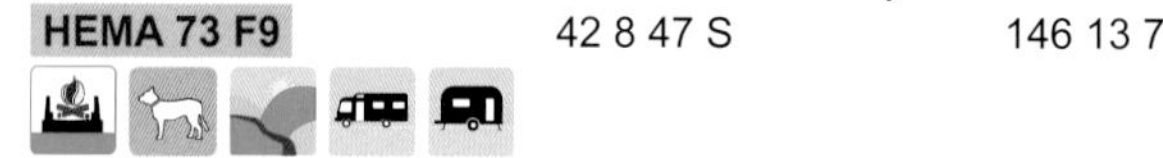

116 Collingwood River Reserve
(03) 6471 7122

Franklin Gordon Wild Rivers National Park

A10

Camp Area 43 km E of Queenstown or 45 km W of Derwent Bridge. Lyell Hwy, entry 100m W of Collingwood River bridge

HEMA 72 G7 42 9 44 S 145 55 37 E

117 Lake Burbury Campground
(03) 6471 2762

Camp Area 23 km E of Queenstown. Turn N 86 km W of Derwent Bridge or 22 km E of Queenstown. 800m off Hwy

HEMA 72 F6 42 5 47 S 145 40 27 E

BIG RIG

118 Thureau Hills Camping Area
(03) 6471 5880

Camp Area 76 km W of Derwent Bridge or 20 km E of Queenstown. Turn S 72 km W of Derwent Bridge or 16 km E of Queenstown. 3.5 km to lakeside camping

HEMA 72 F6 42 8 37 S 145 39 3 E

119 Lake Burbury South Boat Ramp

Picnic Area 23 km SW of Queenstown. On Mt Jukes Rd

HEMA 72 G6 42 12 24 S 145 37 8 E

120 Lake Burbury Foreshore

Parking Area 12 km E of Queenstown. Turn N 77 km W of Derwent Bridge or 11 km E of Queenstown. W side of lake, 800m N of Hwy along old bitumen road

HEMA 72 F6 42 4 25 S 145 38 17 E

121 Gravel Oval

Camp Spot at Queenstown. Wilsdon St, off Batchelor St. Self Contained Vehicles only

HEMA 72 F5 42 4 30 S 145 33 32 E

BIG RIG 24

122 Strahan Golf Course
(03) 6471 7242

Camp Spot at Strahan. Access via Meredith St only. Permit required, register in Clubhouse. 400m W of Clubhouse via gravel road. Self Contained Vehicles only

HEMA 72 G4 42 8 46 S 145 18 59 E

BIG RIG 96

123 Ocean Beach Coastal Reserve

C250

Picnic Area 7 km W of Strahan. 3 km dirt road

HEMA 72 G4 42 8 41 S 145 15 53 E

24

Notes...

124 Macquarie Heads Campground
(03) 6471 7382

C251

Camp Area 15 km S of Strahan, via Ocean Beach Rd. 12 km dirt road

HEMA 72 G4 42 13 16 S 145 13 44 E

125 Zeehan Treasure Island Caravan Park
(03) 6471 6633

Hurst St, enter off Dodd St. 1 km NE of PO

HEMA 72 E4 41 52 40 S 145 19 59 E

BIG RIG

126 Stitt Park

Parking Area at Rosebery. Murchison Hwy. S end of town. Self Contained Vehicles only

HEMA 72 D5 41 46 57 S 145 32 25 E

BIG RIG 20

127 Lake Rosebery Foreshore

A10

Parking Area 12 km E of Rosebery or 3 km S of Tullah. Turn W 50m N of Murchison Bridge or 200m S of Murchison Dam Rd intersection. Sharp turn from S. 200m off Hwy. Limited space

HEMA 72 D6 41 45 39 S 145 37 8 E

128 Lake Mackintosh Camping

Camp Spot 2 km N of Mackintosh Dam. Signposted from Tullah, via Mackintosh Dam Rd. Access over Mackintosh Dam wall. No access when dam spilling. Maximum stay 7 days

HEMA 72 C6 41 41 7 S 145 39 23 E

BIG RIG

129 Reece Dam

C252

Parking Area 44 km NW of Zeehan or 58 km W of Tullah. At boatramp, off Pieman Rd

HEMA 72 C3 41 43 51 S 145 8 5 E

BIG RIG 24

130 Corinna Campground
(03) 6446 1170

C249

Camp Area 49 km NW of Zeehan or 26 km SW of Savage River. Dirt road from Savage River. Limited small campsites, reservations essential. Access from S by barge. Barge maximum length 9m is from mid front hub to mid rear hub

HEMA 72 C3 41 39 3 S 145 4 39 E

131 Waratah Camping Ground
(03) 6439 7100

B23

Camp Area at Waratah, Smith St behind council offices. Key required for access to facilities

HEMA 72 A5 41 26 44 S 145 31 58 E

BIG RIG

132 Fossey River Rest Area

A10

Rest Area 38 km N of Tullah or 2 km S of A10/B23 jcn

HEMA 72 A6 41 27 4 S 145 37 16 E

BIG RIG

133 Hellyer Gorge Rest Area

A10

Rest Area 25 km N of A10/B23 jcn or 24 km S of Yolla

HEMA 77 H8 41 16 25 S 145 36 54 E

BIG RIG

Launceston to Stanley

Bass Highway

134 Bishopsbourne RV Stop

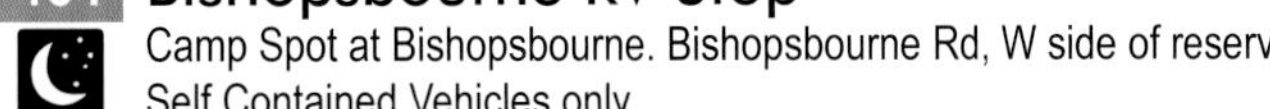

Camp Spot at Bishopsbourne. Bishopsbourne Rd, W side of reserve. Self Contained Vehicles only

C513

HEMA 74 G7 41 36 59 S 146 59 41 E

BIG RIG 20

135 Riverside Park

Parking Area at Bracknell. 700m E of general store, via Louisa St & Esplanade

HEMA 74 G7 41 39 0 S 146 57 1 E

20

136 Andys Bakery Café

☎ (03) 6393 1846

Camp Spot at Westbury. Meander Valley Rd, E end of town. Self Contained Vehicles only

B54

HEMA 74 G6 41 31 32 S 146 50 42 E

BIG RIG 72

137 Egmont Reserve

Picnic Area 4 km N of Westbury, beside river

B54

HEMA 74 F6 41 29 43 S 146 49 1 E

BIG RIG

138 Deloraine East Overnight Park

☎ (03) 6393 5300

Camp Spot at Deloraine. 700m E of PO. Turn N off A5 at Police Station, E side of river. Travel 200m over railway line, then turn R. Self Contained Vehicles only

HEMA 74 G5 41 31 19 S 146 39 43 E

48

139 Christmas Hills Raspberry Farm

☎ (03) 6362 2186

Parking Area at Elizabeth Town. 3 km S on Bass Hwy, Christmas Hills Rd. Limited parking in cafe car park for 5 customer vehicles. Self Contained Vehicles only. Register with the Cafe during opening hours

HEMA 74 F5 41 28 58 S 146 35 49 E

24

140 Chudleigh Showground

Camp Area at Chudleigh. Burnett & Sorrel St. Self Contained Vehicles only. Payment at Chudleigh General store

B12

HEMA 74 G4 41 33 25 S 146 28 58 E

BIG RIG 72

   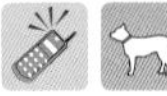  

141 Mole Creek Hotel

☎ (03) 6363 1102

Parking Area at Mole Creek. Pioneer Dr at W end of town. Fee for power, check in at bar

HEMA 74 G4 41 33 21 S 146 24 2 E

BIG RIG 72

142 Mole Creek Caravan Park

☎ (03) 6363 1150

Caravan Park 4 km W of Mole Creek. Beside creek

B12

HEMA 74 G4 41 33 4 S 146 21 37 E

143 Lake Parangana Recreation Area

Camp Spot 29 km SW of Mole Creek. 1 km S of dam wall, via picnic area. Beside lake

C171

HEMA 74 G3 41 38 43 S 146 13 35 E

144 Mersey White Water Forest Reserve

Picnic Area 36 km SW of Mole Creek. 9 km S of dam wall. 1 km dirt road

C171

HEMA 74 H3 41 41 59 S 146 13 4 E

145 Lake Rowallan Bridge

Parking Area 39 km SW of Mole Creek. 1 km N of dam wall, beside river. Small vehicles only. 4 km dirt road

C171

HEMA 74 H3 41 43 23 S 146 13 9 E

146 Lake Rowallan Boat Ramp

Parking Area 41 km SW of Mole Creek. 600m S of dam wall at second boat ramp. E side of lake. 6 km dirt road

C171

HEMA 74 H3 41 44 12 S 146 13 12 E

147 Parramatta Creek Roadside Park

Parking Area 15 km S of Latrobe or 17 km N of Elizabeth Town

1

HEMA 77 J13 41 19 47 S 146 31 49 E

148 East Devonport Recreation Centre (Girdlestone Park)

☎ (03) 6424 4466

Camp Spot at East Devonport, John St. Self Contained Vehicles only. Pay for permit at the Devonport Info Centre, 92 Formby Rd

HEMA 77 G12 41 11 10 S 146 22 45 E

BIG RIG 48

149 Coles Beach Rest Area

☎ (03) 6424 4466

Rest Area at Devonport

HEMA 77 G12 41 9 45 S 146 20 24 E

BIG RIG

150 Horsehead Creek

☎ (03) 6424 4466

Camp Spot at Devonport. Off Devonport Rd N side of Mersey River Bridge. Self Contained Vehicles only. Permit required from Visitor Information Centre

HEMA 77 G12 41 12 4 S 146 21 30 E

BIG RIG 72

151 OC Ling Memorial Caravan Park

☎ (03) 6428 2582

Caravan Park at Turners Beach. The Esplanade

HEMA 77 G11 41 9 29 S 146 14 35 E

152 Forth Recreation Ground

Camp Spot at Forth. Self Contained Vehicles only, limited space

HEMA 77 H11 41 11 19 S 146 15 0 E

48

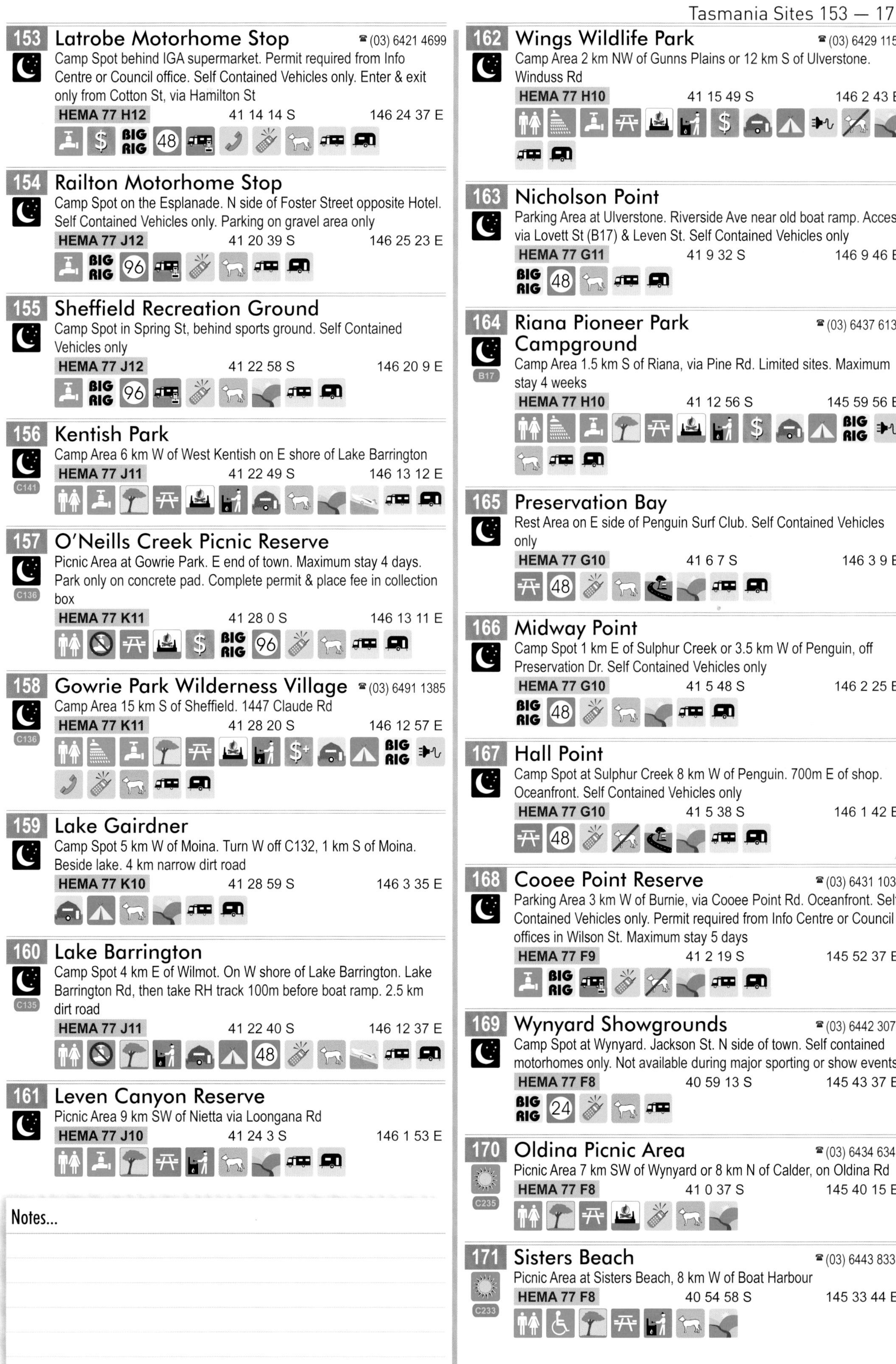

153 Latrobe Motorhome Stop ☎ (03) 6421 4699
Camp Spot behind IGA supermarket. Permit required from Info Centre or Council office. Self Contained Vehicles only. Enter & exit only from Cotton St, via Hamilton St
HEMA 77 H12 | 41 14 14 S | 146 24 37 E
BIG RIG 48

154 Railton Motorhome Stop
Camp Spot on the Esplanade. N side of Foster Street opposite Hotel. Self Contained Vehicles only. Parking on gravel area only
HEMA 77 J12 | 41 20 39 S | 146 25 23 E
BIG RIG 96

155 Sheffield Recreation Ground
Camp Spot in Spring St, behind sports ground. Self Contained Vehicles only
HEMA 77 J12 | 41 22 58 S | 146 20 9 E
BIG RIG 96

156 Kentish Park
C141
Camp Area 6 km W of West Kentish on E shore of Lake Barrington
HEMA 77 J11 | 41 22 49 S | 146 13 12 E

157 O'Neills Creek Picnic Reserve
C136
Picnic Area at Gowrie Park. E end of town. Maximum stay 4 days. Park only on concrete pad. Complete permit & place fee in collection box
HEMA 77 K11 | 41 28 0 S | 146 13 11 E
BIG RIG 96

158 Gowrie Park Wilderness Village ☎ (03) 6491 1385
C136
Camp Area 15 km S of Sheffield. 1447 Claude Rd
HEMA 77 K11 | 41 28 20 S | 146 12 57 E
BIG RIG

159 Lake Gairdner
Camp Spot 5 km W of Moina. Turn W off C132, 1 km S of Moina. Beside lake. 4 km narrow dirt road
HEMA 77 K10 | 41 28 59 S | 146 3 35 E

160 Lake Barrington
C135
Camp Spot 4 km E of Wilmot. On W shore of Lake Barrington. Lake Barrington Rd, then take RH track 100m before boat ramp. 2.5 km dirt road
HEMA 77 J11 | 41 22 40 S | 146 12 37 E
48

161 Leven Canyon Reserve
Picnic Area 9 km SW of Nietta via Loongana Rd
HEMA 77 J10 | 41 24 3 S | 146 1 53 E

Notes...

162 Wings Wildlife Park ☎ (03) 6429 1151
Camp Area 2 km NW of Gunns Plains or 12 km S of Ulverstone. Winduss Rd
HEMA 77 H10 | 41 15 49 S | 146 2 43 E

163 Nicholson Point
Parking Area at Ulverstone. Riverside Ave near old boat ramp. Access via Lovett St (B17) & Leven St. Self Contained Vehicles only
HEMA 77 G11 | 41 9 32 S | 146 9 46 E
BIG RIG 48

164 Riana Pioneer Park Campground ☎ (03) 6437 6137
B17
Camp Area 1.5 km S of Riana, via Pine Rd. Limited sites. Maximum stay 4 weeks
HEMA 77 H10 | 41 12 56 S | 145 59 56 E
BIG RIG

165 Preservation Bay
Rest Area on E side of Penguin Surf Club. Self Contained Vehicles only
HEMA 77 G10 | 41 6 7 S | 146 3 9 E
48

166 Midway Point
Camp Spot 1 km E of Sulphur Creek or 3.5 km W of Penguin, off Preservation Dr. Self Contained Vehicles only
HEMA 77 G10 | 41 5 48 S | 146 2 25 E
BIG RIG 48

167 Hall Point
Camp Spot at Sulphur Creek 8 km W of Penguin. 700m E of shop. Oceanfront. Self Contained Vehicles only
HEMA 77 G10 | 41 5 38 S | 146 1 42 E
48

168 Cooee Point Reserve ☎ (03) 6431 1033
Parking Area 3 km W of Burnie, via Cooee Point Rd. Oceanfront. Self Contained Vehicles only. Permit required from Info Centre or Council offices in Wilson St. Maximum stay 5 days
HEMA 77 F9 | 41 2 19 S | 145 52 37 E
BIG RIG

169 Wynyard Showgrounds ☎ (03) 6442 3079
Camp Spot at Wynyard. Jackson St. N side of town. Self contained motorhomes only. Not available during major sporting or show events
HEMA 77 F8 | 40 59 13 S | 145 43 37 E
BIG RIG 24

170 Oldina Picnic Area ☎ (03) 6434 6345
C235
Picnic Area 7 km SW of Wynyard or 8 km N of Calder, on Oldina Rd
HEMA 77 F8 | 41 0 37 S | 145 40 15 E

171 Sisters Beach ☎ (03) 6443 8333
C233
Picnic Area at Sisters Beach, 8 km W of Boat Harbour
HEMA 77 F8 | 40 54 58 S | 145 33 44 E

172 Rocky Cape Tavern
☎ (03) 6443 4110

Camp Area at Rocky Cape Tavern. 19375 Bass Hwy. Fees apply for use of power & shower/toilet facilities. Check in at Tavern Bar

HEMA 76 E7 | 40 53 7 S | 145 27 56 E

173 Crayfish Creek Van & Cabin Park
☎ (03) 6443 4228

A2

Caravan Park at Crayfish Creek. Coin operated showers

HEMA 76 E7 | 40 51 29 S | 145 23 56 E

174 Peggs Beach Campground
☎ (03) 6458 1480

A2

Camp Area 2.3 km W of Port Latta or 11.5 km E of A2/B21 jcn. Closed 01 May - 31 October

HEMA 76 E6 | 40 51 4 S | 145 21 10 E

175 Black River Campground
☎ (03) 6458 1480

Camp Area 4.8 km W of Port Latta or 9 km E of A2/B21 jcn. 1 km of dirt road N of Hwy. Maximum stay 30 days

HEMA 76 E6 | 40 50 36 S | 145 19 0 E

176 Stanley Recreation Ground
☎ (03) 6458 1266

Parking Area at Stanley, Marine Esplanade, beach side of the road adjacent to Golf Club. Self Contained Vehicles only. Fees collected by site manager. Maximum stay 7 nights

HEMA 76 E6 | 40 45 51 S | 145 17 22 E

177 Smithton Esplanade

Parking Area. W Esplanade. Self Contained Vehicles only

HEMA 76 E5 | 40 50 20 S | 145 7 12 E

178 Tall Timbers Hotel
☎ (03) 6452 9000

Parking Area at hotel. 5/15 Scotchtown Rd. Self Contained Vehicles only. Maximum stay 72 hours in any 14 day period. Available October 1 - 31 May

HEMA 76 E5 | 40 51 24 S | 145 7 10 E

179 Montagu Camping Ground
☎ (03) 6452 4800

Camp Area 20 km NW of Smithton. Turn N off C215, 16 km NW of Smithton, onto Old Port Rd. 4 km dirt road. Open from 01 Nov- 30 April, caretaker collects fees

HEMA 76 D4 | 40 44 40 S | 144 58 44 E

180 Marrawah Green Point Beach Camping Area

Camp Area 3 km W of Marrawah, via Green Point Rd & Beach Rd. Outside cold shower. Oceanfront

HEMA 76 F3 | 40 54 35 S | 144 40 45 E

181 Manuka Campground
☎ (03) 6457 1225

Arthur-Pieman Conservation Area

C214

Camp Area 15 km S of Marrawah or 1 km N of Arthur River

HEMA 76 G3 | 41 2 41 S | 144 40 4 E

182 Peppermint Campground
☎ (03) 6457 1225

Arthur-Pieman Conservation Area

C214

Camp Area at Arthur River. Next to Ranger Station. Not suitable for caravans or motorhomes

HEMA 76 G3 | 41 2 53 S | 144 40 3 E

183 Prickly Wattles Campground
☎ (03) 6457 1225

Arthur-Pieman Conservation Area

C214

Camp Area 2 km S of Arthur River. 4 entry points, 2 & 3 easiest access for caravans

HEMA 76 G3 | 41 3 36 S | 144 40 45 E

184 Nelson Bay
☎ (03) 6457 1225

Arthur-Pieman Conservation Area

Camp Spot at Nelson Bay. 15 km S of Arthur River. Turn R at beach, past fishing boats. Camp on beach side of road

HEMA 76 G3 | 41 7 39 S | 144 40 19 E

185 Julius River Forest Reserve
☎ (03) 6452 4900

C218

Camp Spot 10 km E of Kanunnah Bridge. 600m E of Picnic Area. 7 km gravel road. Toilets at picnic area

HEMA 76 G5 | 41 9 8 S | 145 2 2 E

George Town to Beaconsfield

East/West Tamar Highways

186 George Town Rest Area

A8

Rest Area at George Town. Main Rd, behind Info Centre. Self Contained Vehicles only

HEMA 74 C6 | 41 6 33 S | 146 50 18 E

187 Low Head Tourist Park
☎ (03) 6382 1573

Caravan Park at Low Head. 136 Low Head Rd. Low rates at the Old Caravan Park area only

HEMA 74 C6 | 41 5 2 S | 146 48 42 E

188 Beaconsfield Recreation Ground
☎ (03) 6383 6350

A7

Camp Spot at Beaconsfield. E end of Grubb St. 1700 - 0900 hrs. Self Contained Vehicles only

HEMA 74 D6 | 41 11 57 S | 146 49 19 E

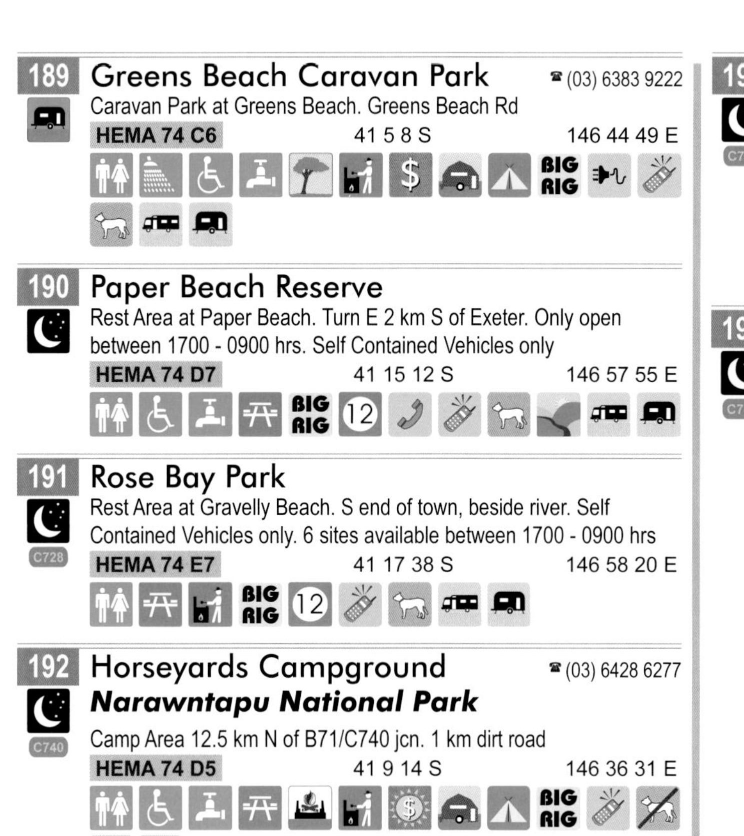

189 Greens Beach Caravan Park
☎ (03) 6383 9222

Caravan Park at Greens Beach. Greens Beach Rd

HEMA 74 C6 41 5 8 S 146 44 49 E

190 Paper Beach Reserve

Rest Area at Paper Beach. Turn E 2 km S of Exeter. Only open between 1700 - 0900 hrs. Self Contained Vehicles only

HEMA 74 D7 41 15 12 S 146 57 55 E

191 Rose Bay Park

C728

Rest Area at Gravelly Beach. S end of town, beside river. Self Contained Vehicles only. 6 sites available between 1700 - 0900 hrs

HEMA 74 E7 41 17 38 S 146 58 20 E

192 Horseyards Campground
☎ (03) 6428 6277

Narawntapu National Park

C740

Camp Area 12.5 km N of B71/C740 jcn. 1 km dirt road

HEMA 74 D5 41 9 14 S 146 36 31 E

193 Springlawn Campground
☎ (03) 6428 6277

Narawntapu National Park

C740

Camp Area 13.5 km N of B71/C740 jcn. 2 km dirt road

HEMA 74 D5 41 8 52 S 146 36 9 E

194 Bakers Point Campground (3)
☎ (03) 6428 6277

Narawntapu National Park

C740

Camp Area 18 km N of B71/C740 jcn. 6 km dirt road

HEMA 74 D5 41 9 44 S 146 34 5 E

Notes...

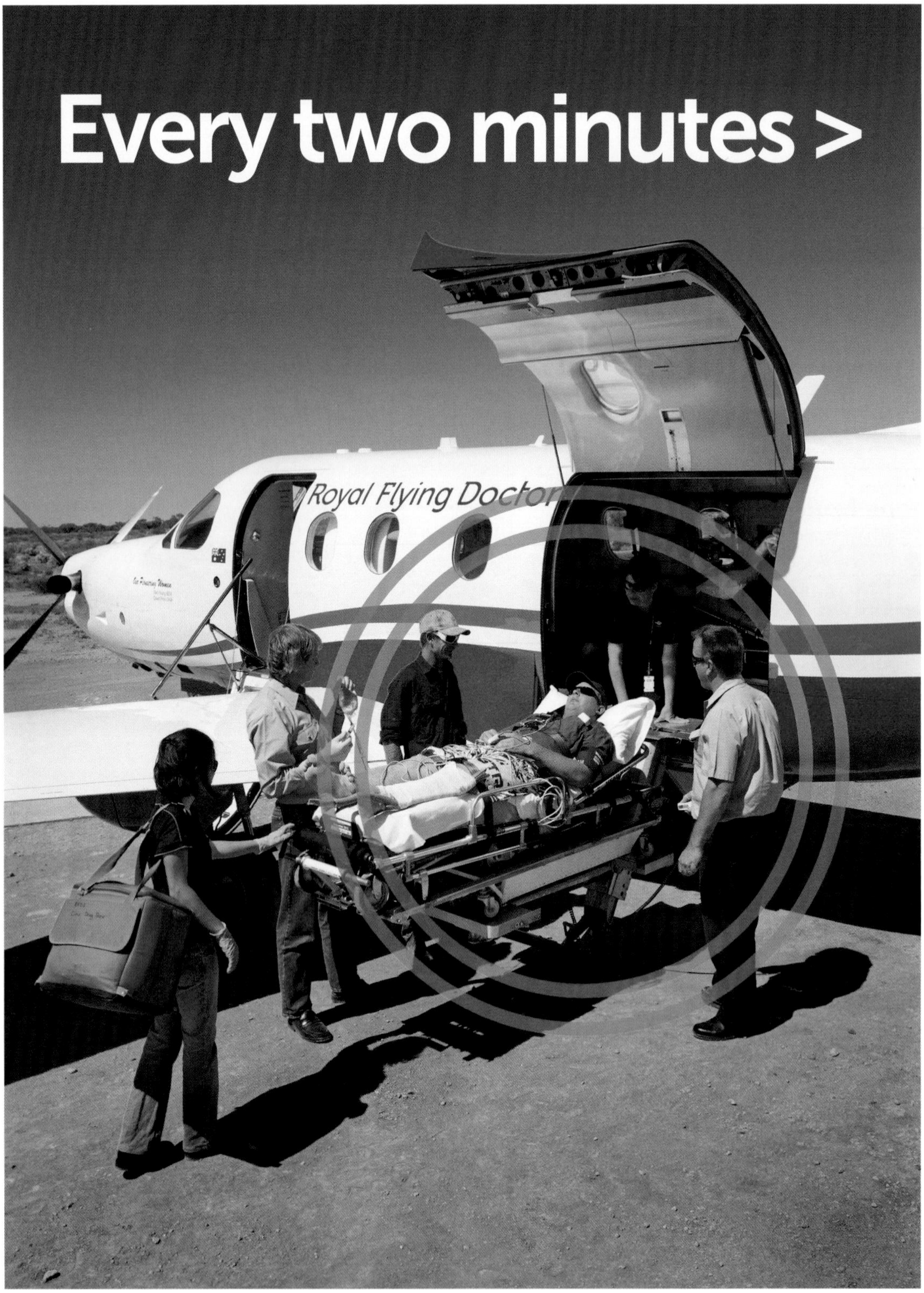
Every two minutes >
Royal Flying Doctor

key map

REMARKABLE ROCKS, KANGAROO ISLAND (88 J5) PHOTO: © ISTOCK.COM/YEKORZH

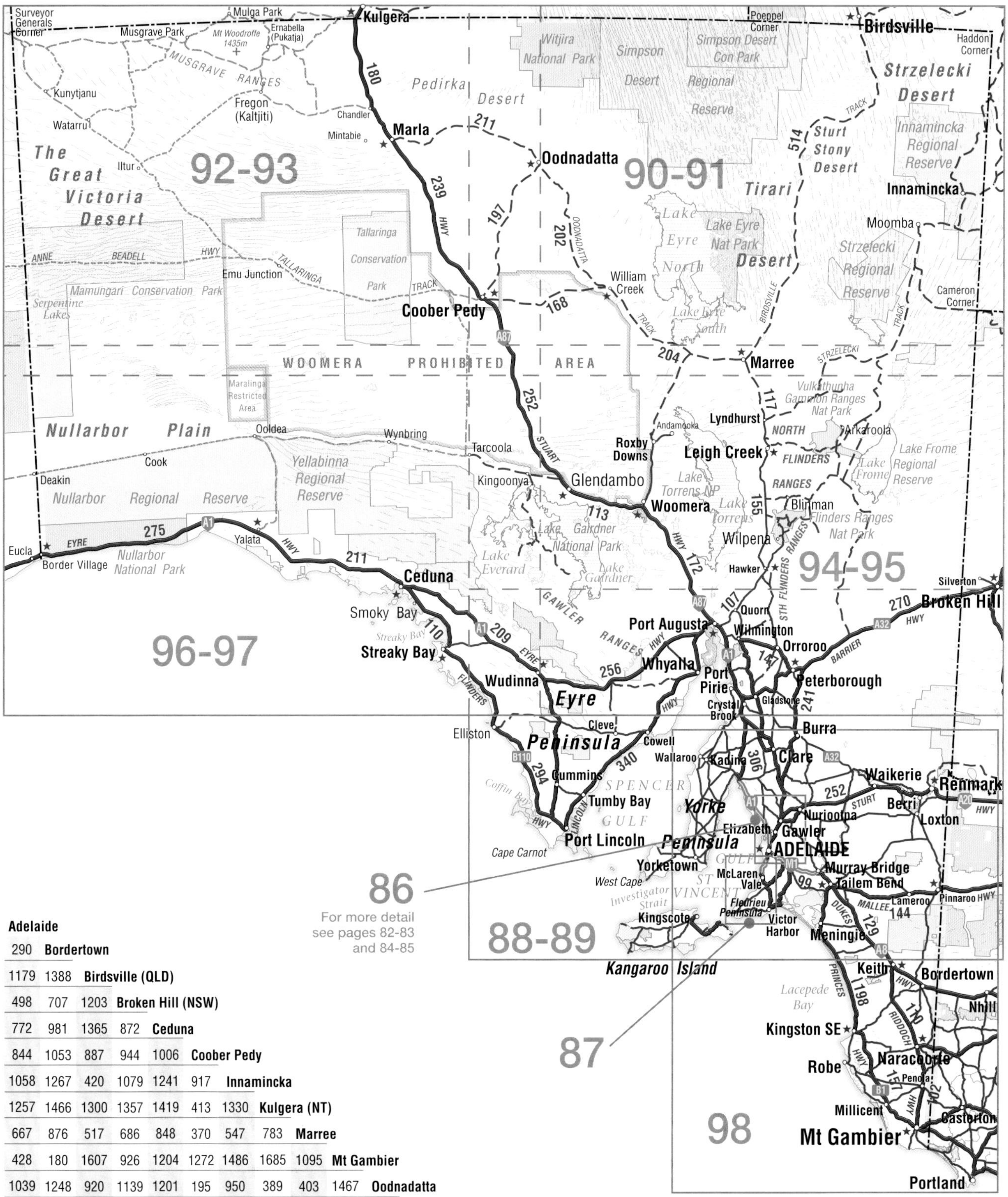

92-93

90-91

94-95

96-97

86

For more detail see pages 82-83 and 84-85

88-89

87

98

	Adelaide	Bordertown	Birdsville (QLD)	Broken Hill (NSW)	Ceduna	Coober Pedy	Innamincka	Kulgera (NT)	Marree	Mt Gambier	Oodnadatta	Pinnaroo	Port Augusta	Port Lincoln	Renmark
Bordertown	290														
Birdsville (QLD)	1179	1388													
Broken Hill (NSW)	498	707	1203												
Ceduna	772	981	1365	872											
Coober Pedy	844	1053	887	944	1006										
Innamincka	1058	1267	420	1079	1241	917									
Kulgera (NT)	1257	1466	1300	1357	1419	413	1330								
Marree	667	876	517	686	848	370	547	783							
Mt Gambier	428	180	1607	926	1204	1272	1486	1685	1095						
Oodnadatta	1039	1248	920	1139	1201	195	950	389	403	1467					
Pinnaroo	240	132	1419	738	1012	1084	1298	1497	907	312	1279				
Port Augusta	305	514	898	405	467	539	774	952	381	690	734	545			
Port Lincoln	648	857	1241	748	401	882	1117	1295	724	1033	1077	888	343		
Renmark	253	288	1234	549	903	975	1110	1388	717	468	1170	156	436	779	
WA-SA Border Village	1252	1461	1845	1352	480	1486	1721	1899	1328	1680	1681	1492	947	881	1383

Distances are shown in kilometres and follow the most direct major sealed route where possible.

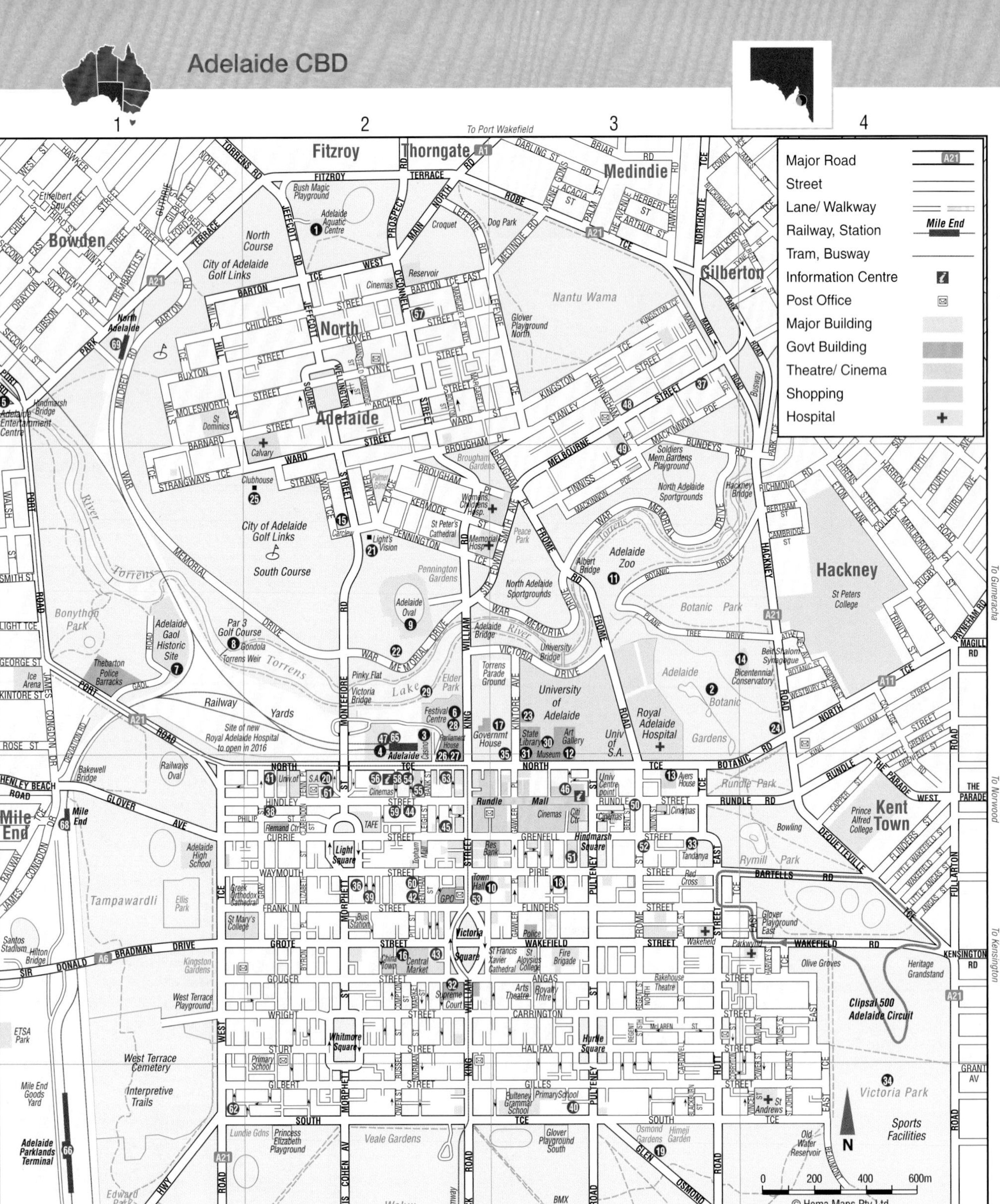

Places of Interest

1. Adelaide Aquatic Centre A2
2. Adelaide Botanic Gardens B3
3. Adelaide Casino B2
4. Adelaide Convention/Exhibition Ctr B2
5. Adelaide Entertainment Centre A1
6. Adelaide Festival Centre B2
7. Adelaide Gaol Historic Site B1
8. Adelaide Gondola B1
9. Adelaide Oval B2
10. Adelaide Town Hall C2
11. Adelaide Zoo B3
12. Art Gallery of South Australia B3
13. Ayers House C3
14. Bicentennial Conservatory B4
15. Carclew Youth Arts Centre B2
16. Central Market/China Town C2
17. Government House B3
18. Hill Smith Gallery C3
19. Himeji Japanese Garden D3
20. Jam Factory Craft & Design Centre C2
21. Light's Vision B2
22. Memorial Drive Tennis Courts B2
23. Migration Museum B3
24. National Wine Centre of Australia B4
25. North Adelaide Golf Links B2
26. Old Parliament House – Museum B2
27. Parliament House B2
28. Performing Arts Collection of SA B2
29. Popeye Motor Launches B2
30. South Australian Museum B3
31. State Library of SA B3
32. Supreme Court Building C2
33. Tandanya National Aboriginal Cultural Inst C3
34. Victoria Park Raceway D4
35. War Memorial B3

Accommodation

36. Adelaide Central YHA C2
37. Adelaide Meridien A3
38. Breakfree Adelaide C2
39. Cannon Street Backpackers C2
40. Chifley on South Terrace, The D3
41. Comfort Hotel Adelaide Riviera C2
42. Franklin Central Apartments C2
43. Hilton Adelaide C2
44. Holiday Inn Adelaide C2
45. Hotel Grand Chancellor Adelaide C2
46. Hotel Richmond C3
47. InterContinental Adelaide B2
48. Majestic Minima Hotel A3
49. Majestic Old Lion Apartments B3
50. Majestic Roof Garden Hotel C3
51. Mantra Hindmarsh Square C3
52. Mantra on Frome C3
53. Medina Grand Adelaide Treasury C2
54. Mercure Grosvenor Hotel Adelaide C2
55. Motel Adjacent Casino C2
56. Oaks Embassy, The C2
57. Old Adelaide Inn A2
58. Playford Adelaide, The C2
59. Plaza Hotel C2
60. Rendezvous Allegra Hotel C2
61. Rockford Hotel C2
62. Rydges South Park Adelaide D1
63. Stamford Plaza Adelaide C2

Railway Stations

65. Adelaide B2
66. Adelaide Parklands Terminal D1
67. Adelaide Showground D1
68. Mile End C1
69. North Adelaide A1

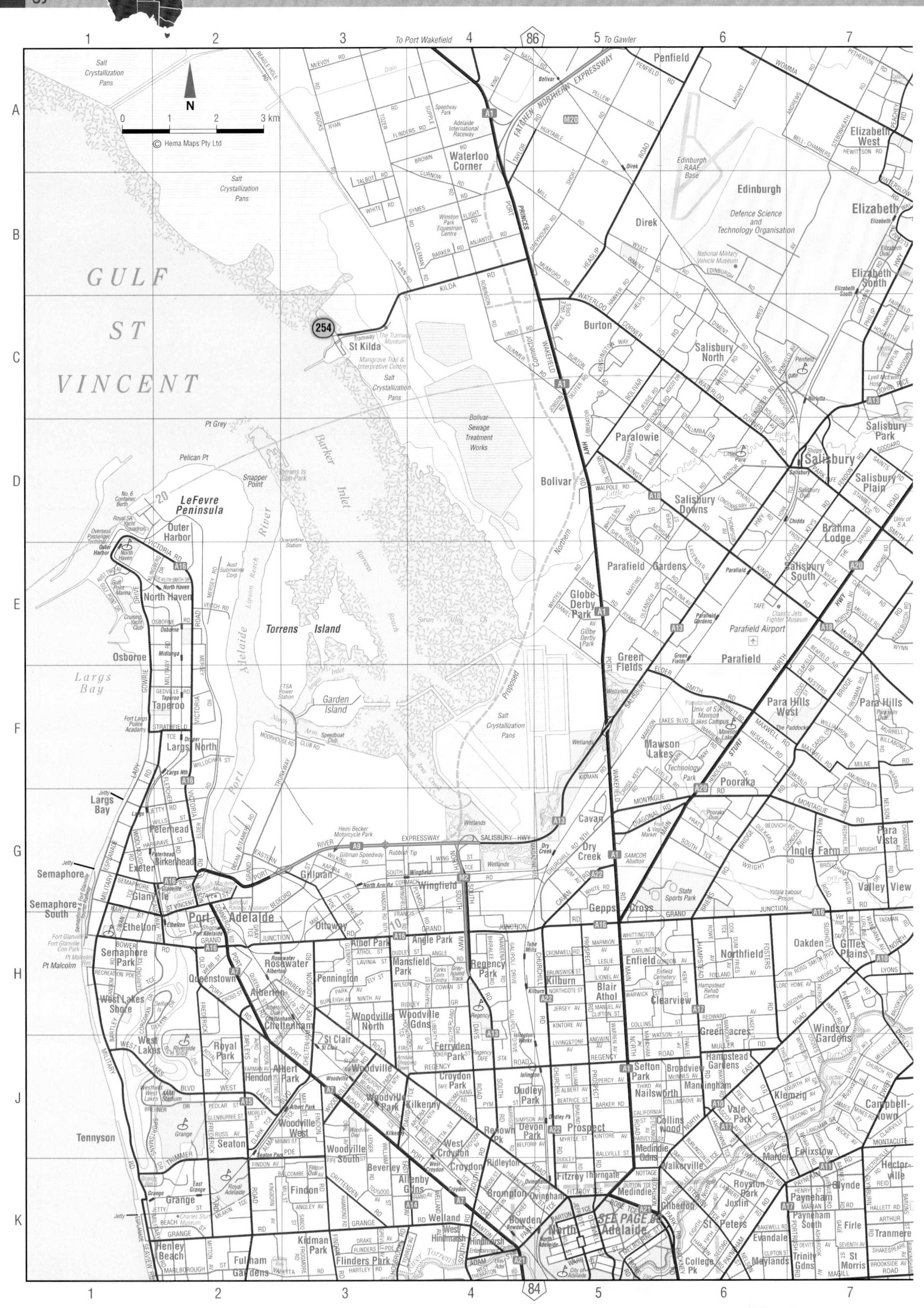
GULF
ST
VINCENT
Torrens Island
LeFevre Peninsula
Port Adelaide
St Kilda
Salisbury
Elizabeth
Edinburgh
Parafield Airport
Bolivar
© Hema Maps Pty Ltd
SEE PAGE 86 Adelaide

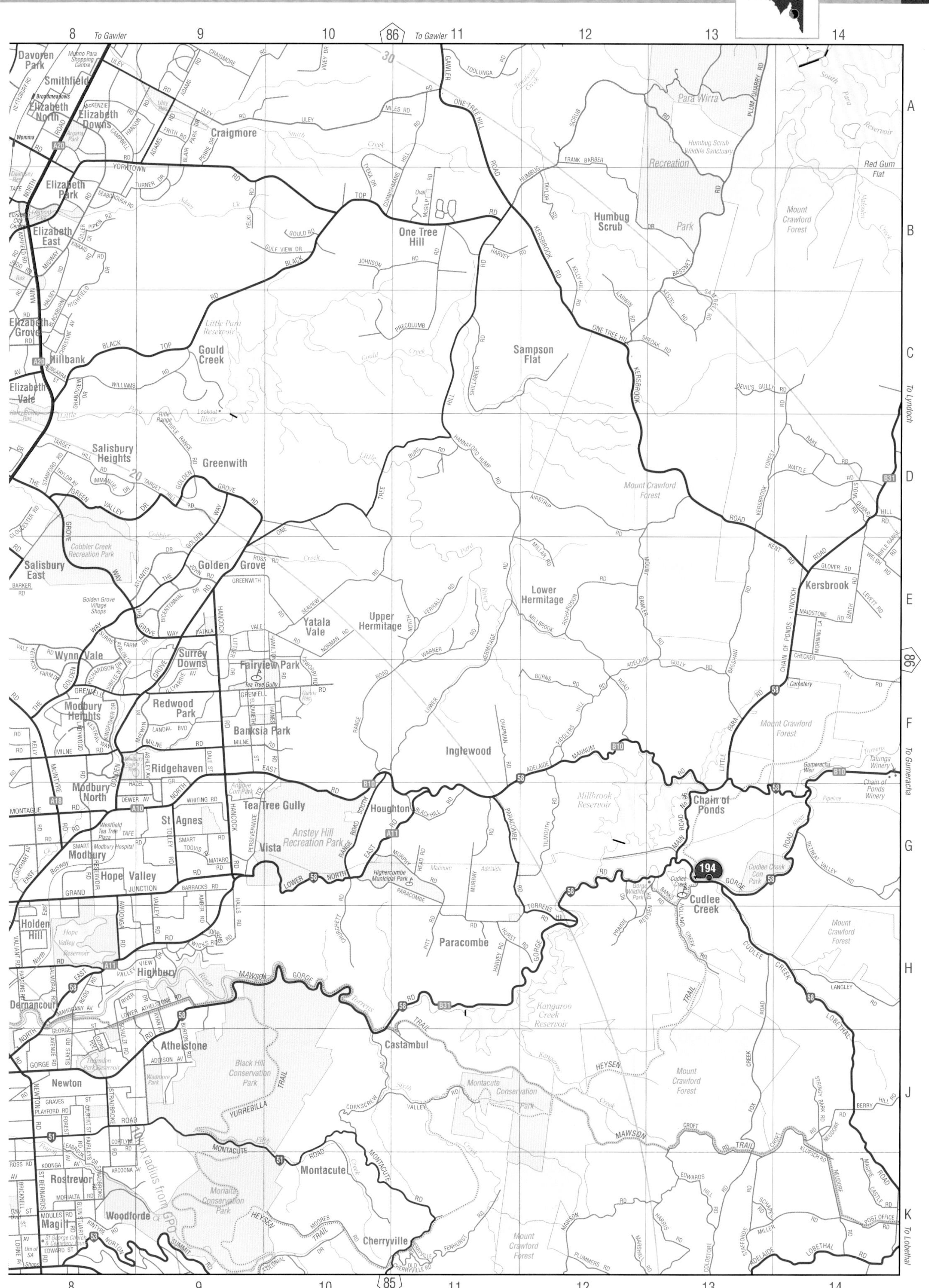
To Gawler
To Gawler
Davoren Park
Smithfield
Elizabeth North
Elizabeth Downs
Craigmore
Elizabeth Park
Elizabeth East
Elizabeth Grove
Hillbank
Elizabeth Vale
One Tree Hill
Humbug Scrub
Para Wirra Recreation Park
Humbug Scrub Wildlife Sanctuary
Mount Crawford Forest
Red Gum Flat
Sampson Flat
Gould Creek
Little Para Reservoir
Salisbury Heights
Greenwith
Cobbler Creek Recreation Park
Salisbury East
Golden Grove
Golden Grove Village Shops
Wynn Vale
Surrey Downs
Fairview Park
Yatala Vale
Upper Hermitage
Lower Hermitage
Kersbrook
To Lyndoch
Modbury Heights
Redwood Park
Banksia Park
Ridgehaven
Inglewood
Modbury North
Tea Tree Gully
St Agnes
Houghton
Chain of Ponds
Millbrook Reservoir
Modbury
Hope Valley
Vista
Anstey Hill Recreation Park
Highercombe Municipal Park
194
Cudlee Creek
Cudlee Creek Con Park
Holden Hill
Hope Valley Reservoir
Paracombe
Highbury
Dernancourt
Athelstone
Castambul
Kangaroo Creek Reservoir
Black Hill Conservation Park
Newton
Montacute Conservation Park
Rostrevor
Montacute
Morialta Conservation Park
Woodforde
Magill
Cherryville
Chain of Ponds Winery
Talunga Winery
To Gumeracha
To Lobethal
HEYSEN TRAIL
10 km radius from GPO

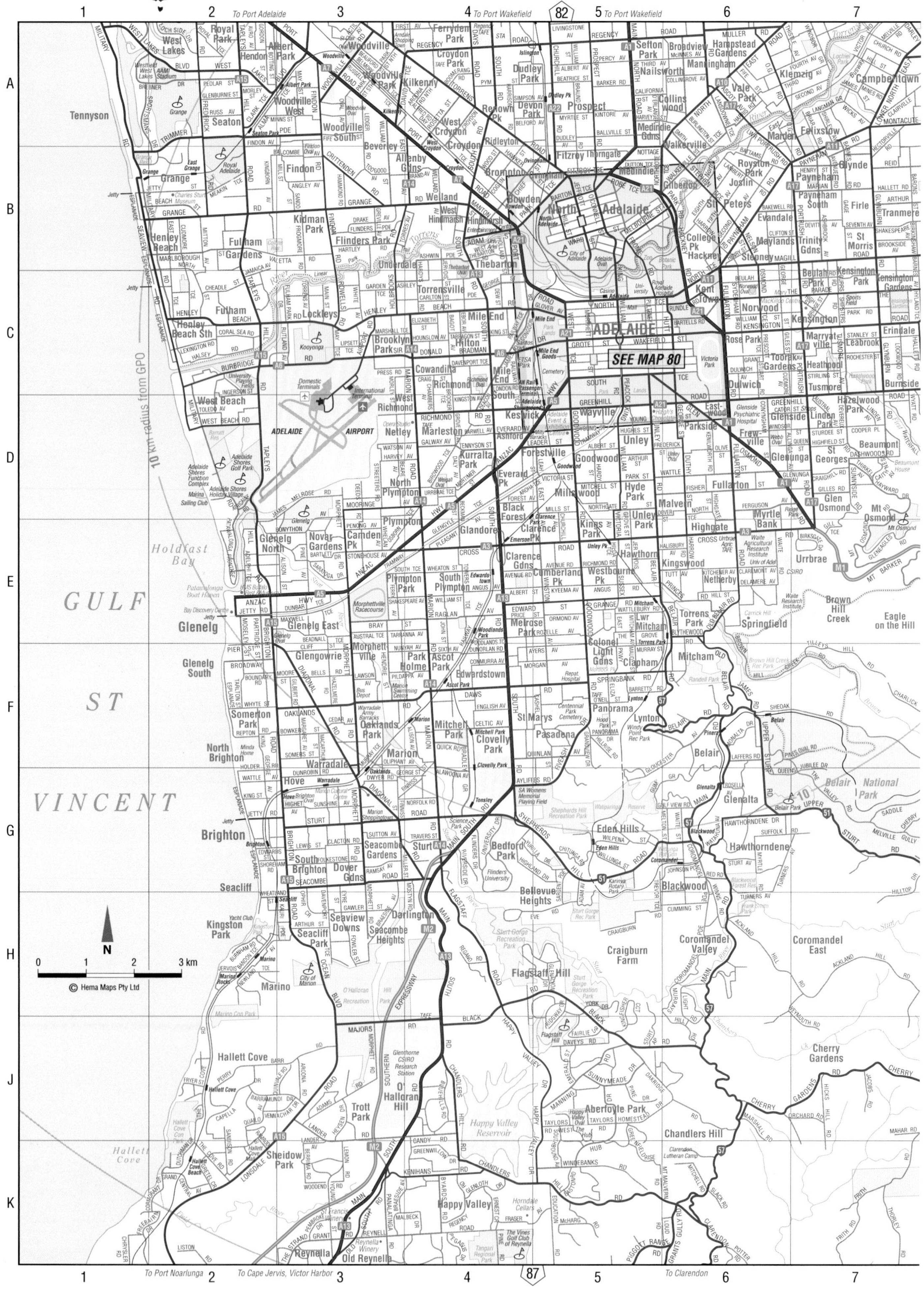

Adelaide Suburbs, South Australia

To Port Adelaide
To Port Wakefield
82
To Port Wakefield

Tennyson
West Lakes
Royal Park
Albert Park
Hendon
Woodville
Ferryden Park
Croydon Park
Dudley Park
Prospect
Sefton Park
Broadview
Nailsworth
Hampstead Gardens
Manningham
Vale Park
Klemzig
Campbelltown
Seaton
Woodville West
Woodville South
Woodville Park
Kilkenny
West Croydon
Renown Pk
Devon Park
Collinswood
Medindie Gdns
Walkerville
Felixstow
Payneham
Grange
Findon
Beverley
Allenby Gdns
Croydon
Ridleyton
Brompton
Fitzroy
Thorngate
Medindie
Gilberton
Royston Park
Joslin
St Peters
Glynde
Payneham South
Firle
Tranmere
Henley Beach
Fulham Gardens
Kidman Park
Flinders Park
Welland
West Hindmarsh
Hindmarsh
Bowden
North Adelaide
College Pk
Hackney
Evandale
Maylands
Stepney
Trinity Gdns
St Morris
Underdale
Torrensville
Thebarton
Kent Town
Norwood
Beulah Park
Kensington Park
Kensington Gardens
Henley Beach Sth
Fulham
Lockleys
Brooklyn Park
Hilton
Mile End
ADELAIDE
Rose Park
Kensington
Marryatville
Leabrook
Erindale
SEE MAP 80
Cowandilla
Richmond
Mile End South
Toorak Gardens
Heathpool
Tusmore
Burnside
West Beach
ADELAIDE AIRPORT
West Richmond
Keswick
Wayville
Parkside
Eastwood
Dulwich
Glenside
Linden Park
Hazelwood Park
Netley
Marleston
Ashford
Forestville
Unley
Frewville
Glenunga
Beaumont
St Georges
Kurralta Park
North Plympton
Everard Pk
Goodwood
Millswood
Hyde Park
Malvern
Fullarton
Glen Osmond
Mt Osmond
Plympton
Black Forest
Clarence Pk
Kings Park
Unley Park
Highgate
Myrtle Bank
Glenelg North
Novar Gardens
Camden Pk
Glandore
Clarence Gdns
Cumberland Pk
Westbourne Pk
Hawthorn
Kingswood
Netherby
Urrbrae
Holdfast Bay
Plympton Park
South Plympton
Brown Hill Creek
Eagle on the Hill
GULF
Glenelg
Glenelg East
Melrose Park
Lwr Mitcham
Torrens Park
Springfield
Glengowrie
Morphettville
Park Holme
Ascot Park
Colonel Light Gdns
Clapham
Mitcham
Glenelg South
Edwardstown
ST
Somerton Park
Oaklands Park
Mitchell Park
Clovelly Park
St Marys
Pasadena
Panorama
Lynton
North Brighton
Marion
Warradale
Belair
Hove
VINCENT
Glenalta
Belair National Park
Brighton
Seacombe Gardens
Sturt
Bedford Park
Eden Hills
Hawthorndene
South Brighton
Dover Gdns
Seacliff
Bellevue Heights
Blackwood
Kingston Park
Seaview Downs
Darlington
Seacombe Heights
Seacliff Park
Craigburn Farm
Coromandel Valley
Coromandel East
Flagstaff Hill
Marino
Hallett Cove
Cherry Gardens
O'Halloran Hill
Trott Park
Happy Valley Reservoir
Aberfoyle Park
Chandlers Hill
Sheidow Park
Hallett Cove
Happy Valley
Reynella
Old Reynella

10 km radius from GPO

N
0 1 2 3 km
© Hema Maps Pty Ltd

To Port Noarlunga
To Cape Jervis, Victor Harbor
87
To Clarendon

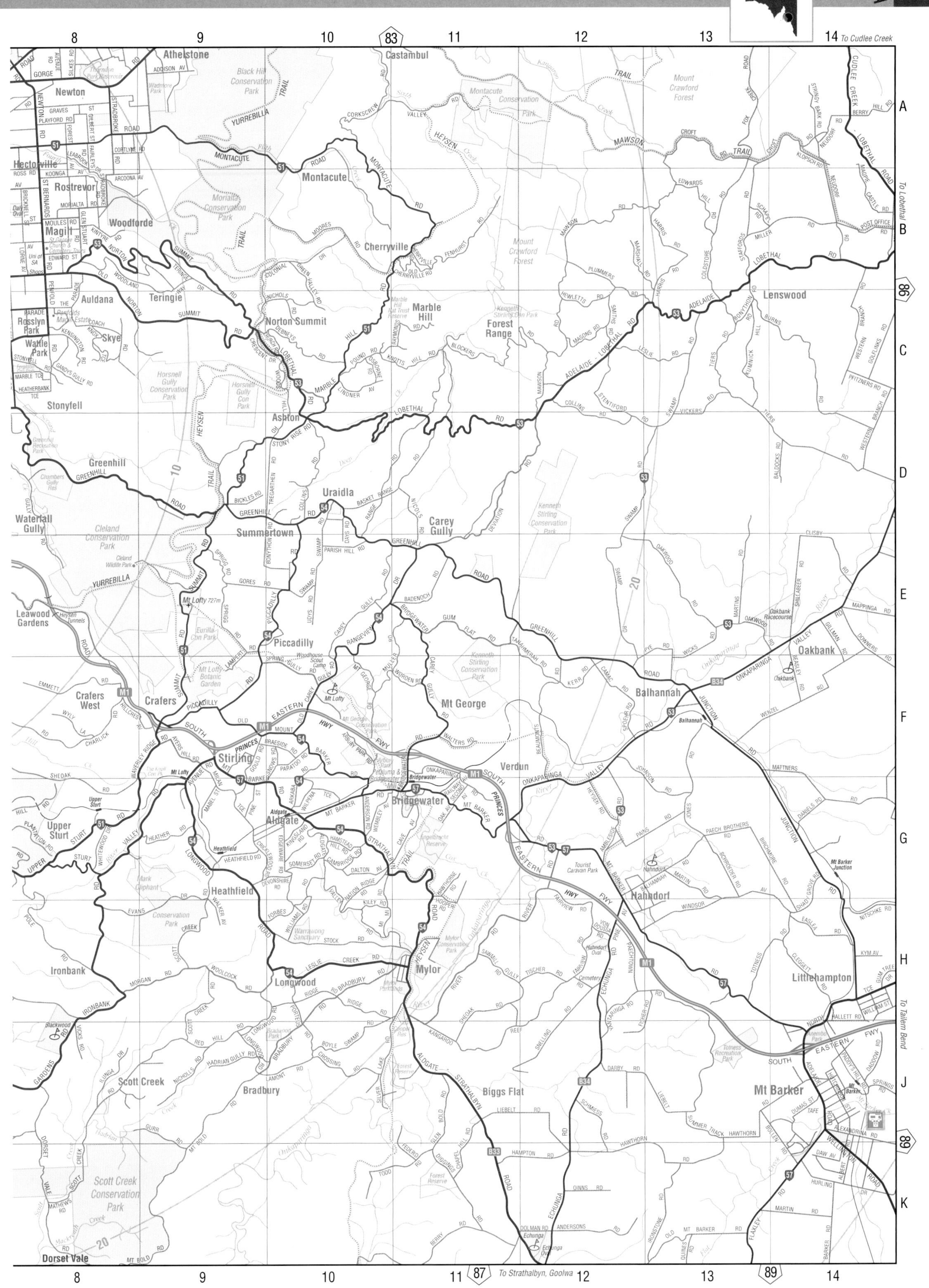
To Cudlee Creek
Athelstone
Castambul
Newton
Black Hill Conservation Park
Montacute Conservation Park
Mount Crawford Forest
YURREBILLA TRAIL
HEYSEN TRAIL
MAWSON TRAIL
Hectorville
Montacute
Rostrevor
Morialta Conservation Park
Magill
Woodforde
Cherryville
Mount Crawford Forest
To Lobethal
Auldana
Teringie
Lenswood
Rosslyn Park
Skye
Norton Summit
Marble Hill
Forest Range
Wattle Park
Horsnell Gully Conservation Park
Stonyfell
Ashton
Greenhill
Uraidla
Carey Gully
Waterfall Gully
Cleland Conservation Park
Summertown
Kenneth Stirling Conservation Park
Mt Lofty 727m
Leawood Gardens
Piccadilly
Oakbank
Crafers West
Crafers
Mt George
Balhannah
Stirling
Verdun
Bridgewater
Upper Sturt
Aldgate
Heathfield
Hahndorf
Ironbank
Longwood
Mylor
Littlehampton
To Tailem Bend
Scott Creek
Bradbury
Biggs Flat
Mt Barker
Scott Creek Conservation Park
Dorset Vale
Echunga
To Strathalbyn, Goolwa
ADELAIDE - LOBETHAL RD
ONKAPARINGA VALLEY RD
SOUTH EASTERN FWY
STRATHALBYN RD
ECHUNGA RD

Adelaide to Barossa Region, South Australia

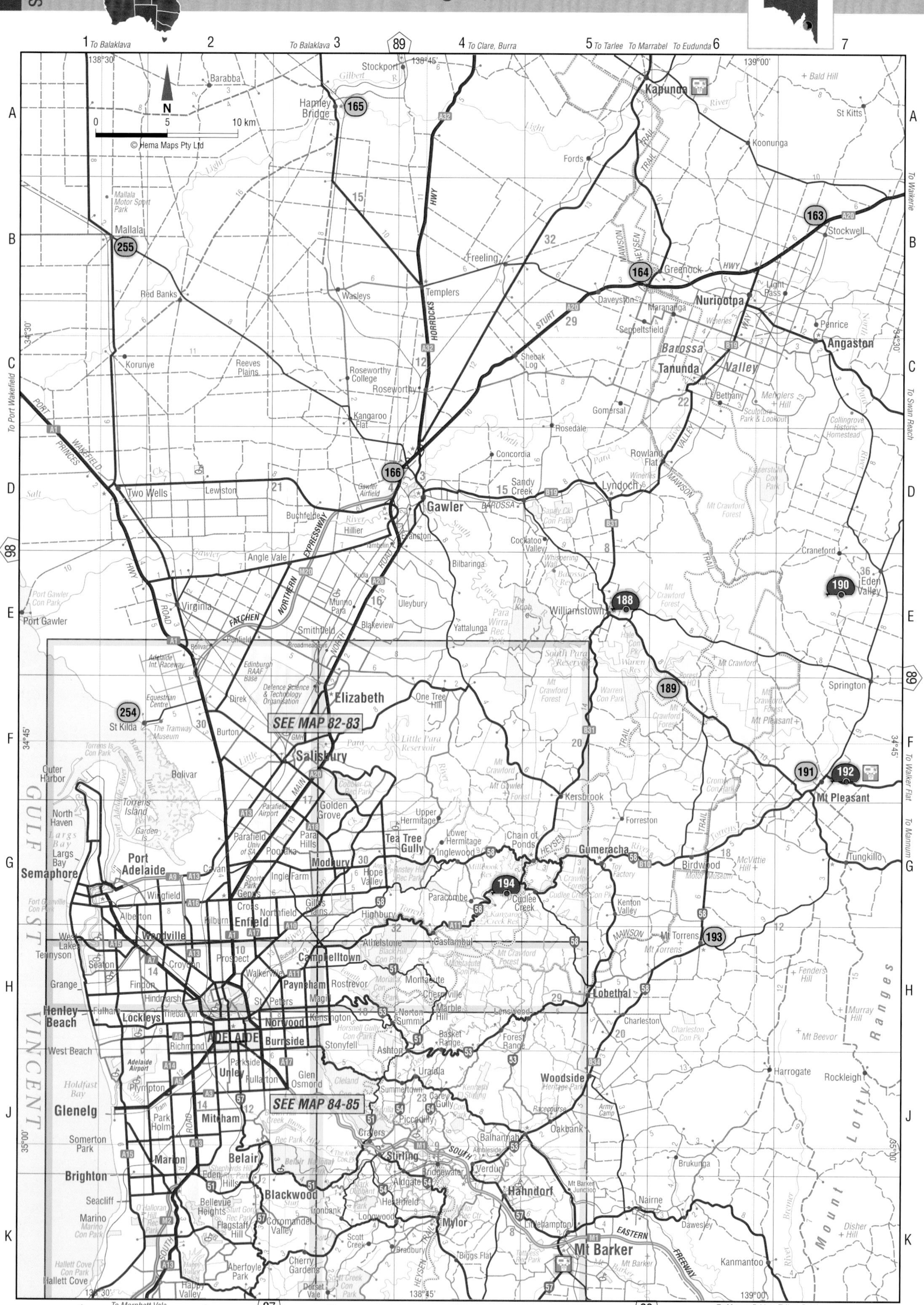

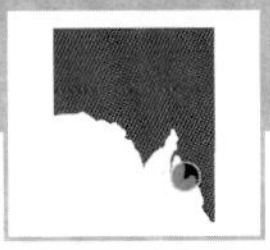

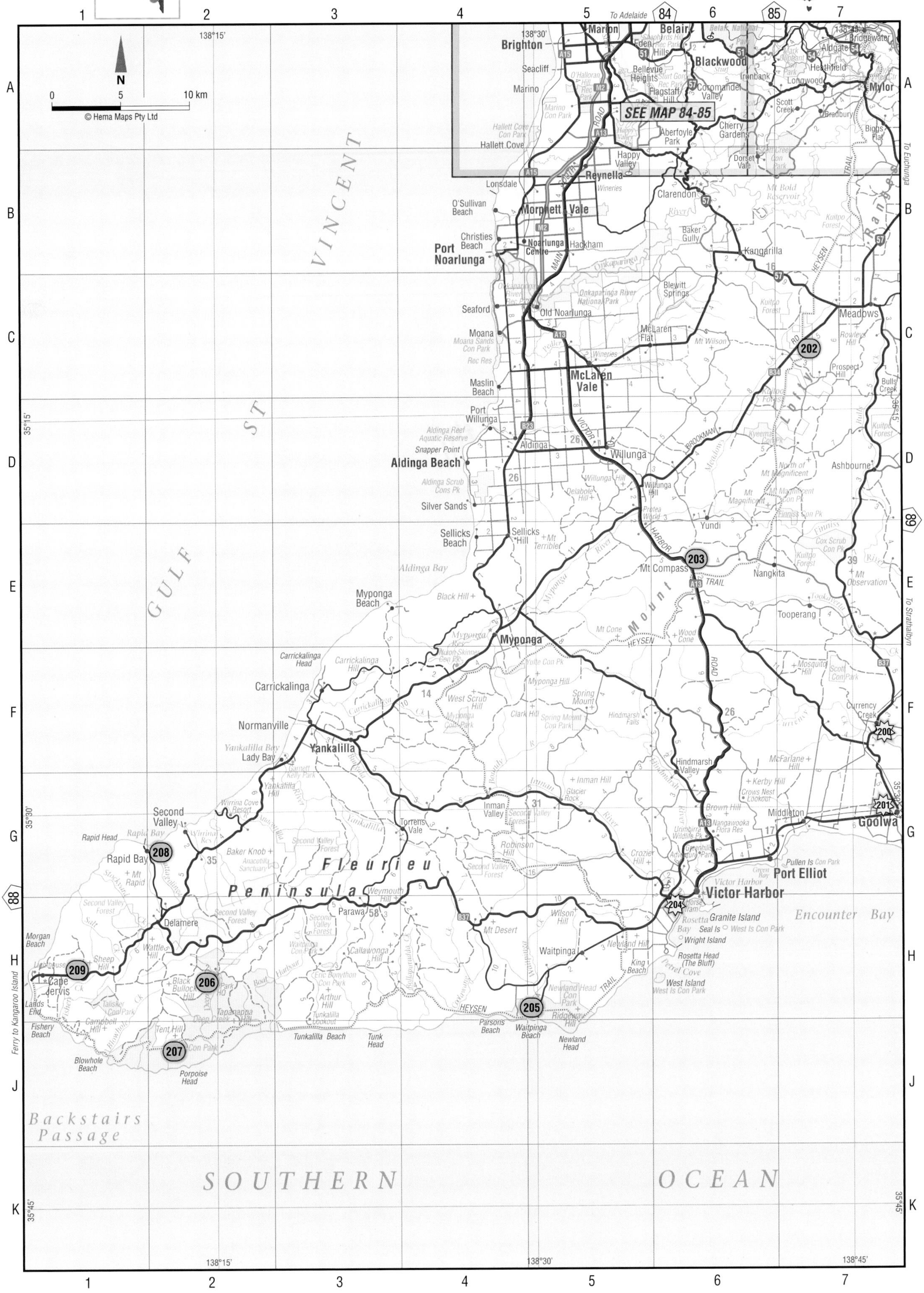

© Hema Maps Pty Ltd
0
5
10 km
N
To Adelaide
SEE MAP 84-85
Marion
Brighton
Belair
Blackwood
Aldgate
Bridgewater
Seacliff
Marino
Heathfield
Mylor
Bellevue Heights
Flagstaff Hill
Coromandel Valley
Ironbank
Longwood
Scott Creek
Bradbury
Hallett Cove
Aberfoyle Park
Cherry Gardens
Biggs Flat
Happy Valley
Reynella
Dorset Vale
To Echunga
Lonsdale
Clarendon
O'Sullivan Beach
Morphett Vale
Mt Bold Reservoir
Christies Beach
Noarlunga Centre
Hackham
Baker Gully
Port Noarlunga
Kangarilla
Onkaparinga River National Park
Blewitt Springs
Seaford
Old Noarlunga
Meadows
Moana
McLaren Flat
Mt Wilson
Rowley Hill
Prospect Hill
McLaren Vale
Maslin Beach
Bulls Creek
Port Willunga
Aldinga Reef Aquatic Reserve
Snapper Point
Aldinga
Willunga
Aldinga Beach
Ashbourne
North of Mt Magnificent
Willunga Hill
Mt Magnificent
Silver Sands
Yundi
Sellicks Beach
Sellicks Hill
Mt Terrible
Aldinga Bay
Mt Compass
Nangkita
Mt Observation
Myponga Beach
Black Hill
Tooperang
To Strathalbyn
Mt Cone
Wood Cone
Myponga
HEYSEN
Carrickalinga Head
Carrickalinga Hill
Carrickalinga
West Scrub Hill
Spring Mount
Clark Hill
Hindmarsh Falls
Currency Creek
Normanville
Yankalilla
Yankalilla Bay
Lady Bay
McFarlane Hill
Yankalilla Hill
Hindmarsh Valley
Wirrina Cove Resort
Inman Hill
Glacier Rock
Kerby Hill
Crows Nest Lookout
Second Valley
Inman Valley
Brown Hill
Middleton
Goolwa
Rapid Head
Rapid Bay
Torrens Vale
Baker Knob
Robinson Hill
Crozier Hill
Pullen Is Con Park
Port Elliot
Mt Rapid
Fleurieu Peninsula
Victor Harbor
Encounter Bay
Weymouth Hill
Parawa
Granite Island
Delamere
Mt Desert
Wilson Hill
Rosetta Bay
Seal Is
West Is Con Park
Wright Island
Morgan Beach
Wattle Hill
Callawonga Hill
Waitpinga
Newland Hill
King Beach
Rosetta Head (The Bluff)
Petrel Cove
Sheep Hill
Cape Jervis
Black Bullock Hill
West Island
Arthur Hill
Newland Head Con Park
Lands End
Tapanappa Hill
Deep Creek
Ridgeway Hill
Campbell Hill
Fishery Beach
Tent Hill
Tunkalilla Beach
Tunk Head
Parsons Beach
Waitpinga Beach
Newland Head
Blowhole Beach
Porpoise Head
Ferry to Kangaroo Island
Backstairs Passage
GULF ST VINCENT
SOUTHERN OCEAN
200
201
202
203
204
205
206
207
208
209

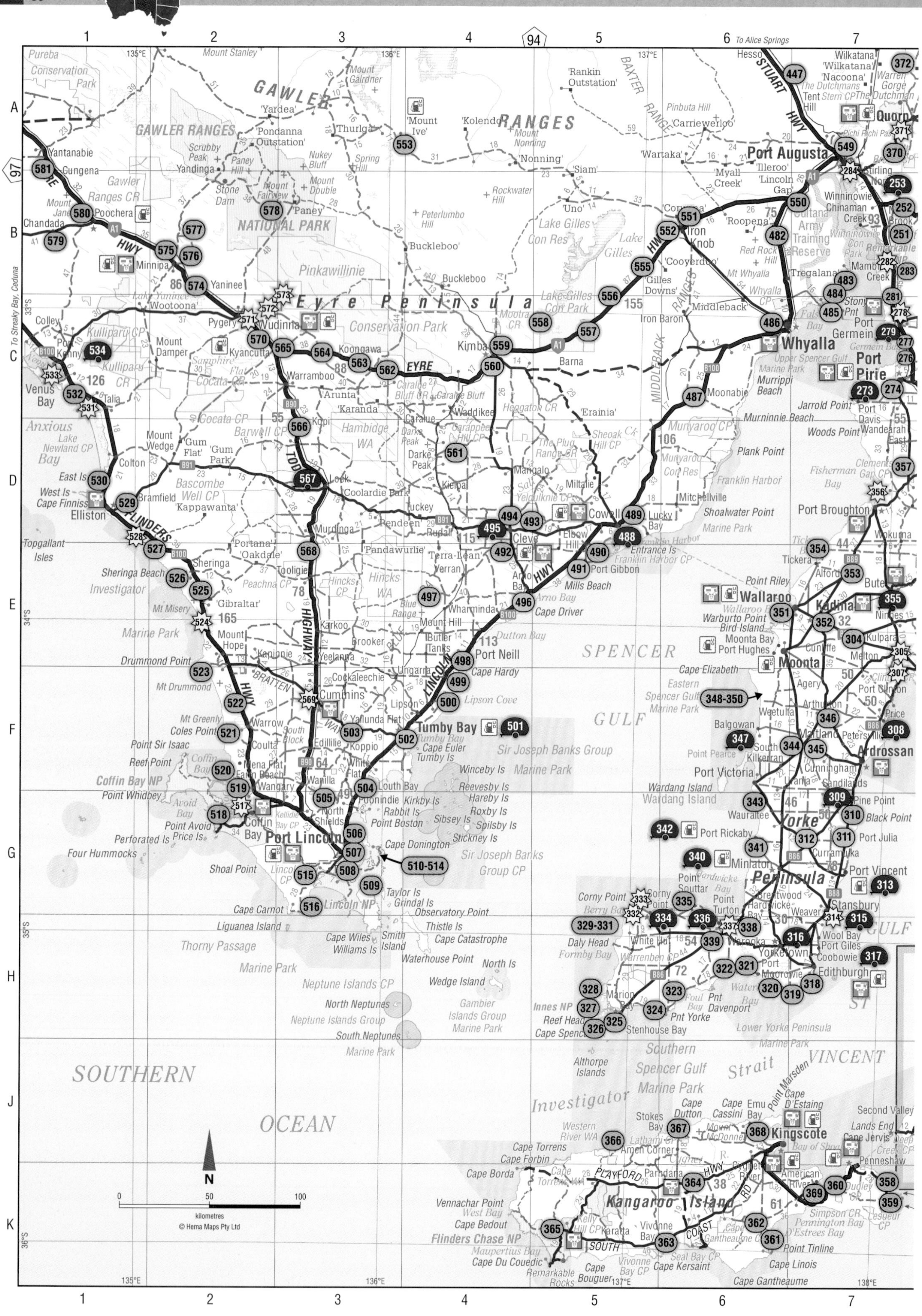

GAWLER RANGES
NATIONAL PARK
Eyre Peninsula
Port Augusta
Whyalla
Port Pirie
Wallaroo
Moonta
Kadina
Ardrossan
Yorketown
Edithburgh
Minlaton
Port Victoria
Yorke Peninsula
Kimba
Cleve
Cowell
Wudinna
Minnipa
Poochera
Elliston
Venus Bay
Port Lincoln
Tumby Bay
Cummins
Coffin Bay
Lincoln NP
SPENCER GULF
SOUTHERN OCEAN
Investigator Strait
Kangaroo Island
Kingscote
Penneshaw
Flinders Chase NP
Sir Joseph Banks Group
Neptune Islands CP
To Alice Springs
To Streaky Bay, Ceduna
N
0 50 100
kilometres
© Hema Maps Pty Ltd

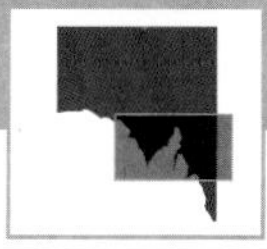

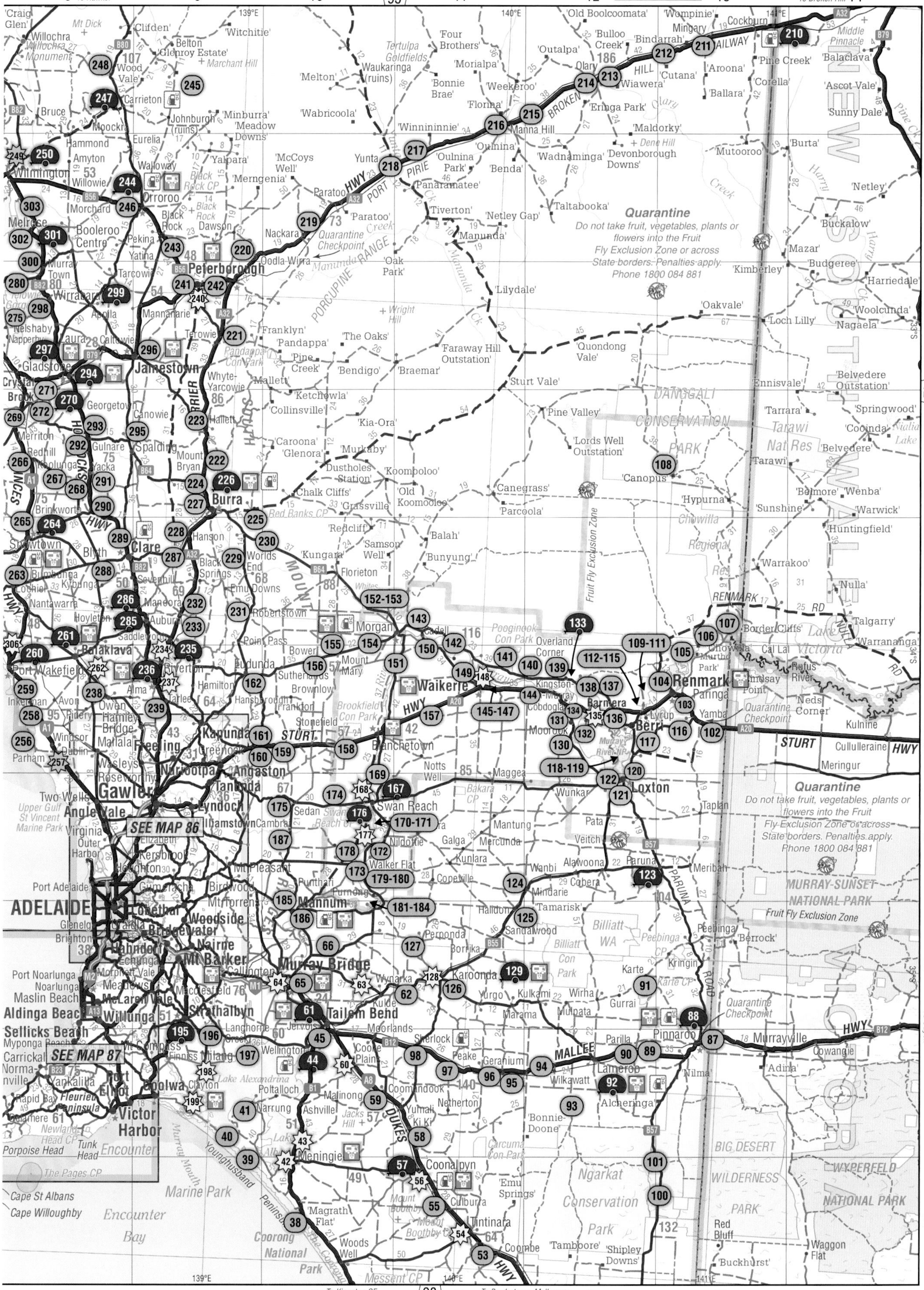

To Hawker
To Broken Hill
To Wentworth
To Mildura
To Ouyen
To Kingston SE
To Bordertown, Melbourne

Quarantine
Do not take fruit, vegetables, plants or flowers into the Fruit Fly Exclusion Zone or across State borders. Penalties apply.
Phone 1800 084 881

Quarantine
Do not take fruit, vegetables, plants or flowers into the Fruit Fly Exclusion Zone or across State borders. Penalties apply.
Phone 1800 084 881

Fruit Fly Exclusion Zone
Quarantine Checkpoint
SEE MAP 86
SEE MAP 87

BARRIER HWY
BROKEN HILL HWY
PORT PIRIE HWY
STURT HWY
MALLEE HWY
DUKES HWY
RENMARK RD
PARUNA RD

NEW SOUTH WALES
VICTORIA

ADELAIDE
Gawler
Peterborough
Jamestown
Burra
Clare
Kapunda
Nuriootpa
Angaston
Waikerie
Renmark
Berri
Barmera
Loxton
Morgan
Mannum
Murray Bridge
Tailem Bend
Pinnaroo
Murrayville
Karoonda
Lameroo
Meningie
Coonalpyn
Tintinara
Victor Harbor
Goolwa
Strathalbyn
Mt Barker
Willunga
McLaren Vale
Orroroo
Wilmington
Melrose
Laura
Gladstone
Crystal Brook
Snowtown
Balaklava
Port Wakefield
Eudunda
Blanchetown
Swan Reach
Paringa
Cockburn
Olary
Yunta
Manna Hill
Paratoo

Danggali Conservation Park
Chowilla Regional Reserve
Murray-Sunset National Park
Ngarkat Conservation Park
Big Desert Wilderness Park
Wyperfeld National Park
Coorong National Park
Encounter Marine Park
Upper Gulf St Vincent Marine Park

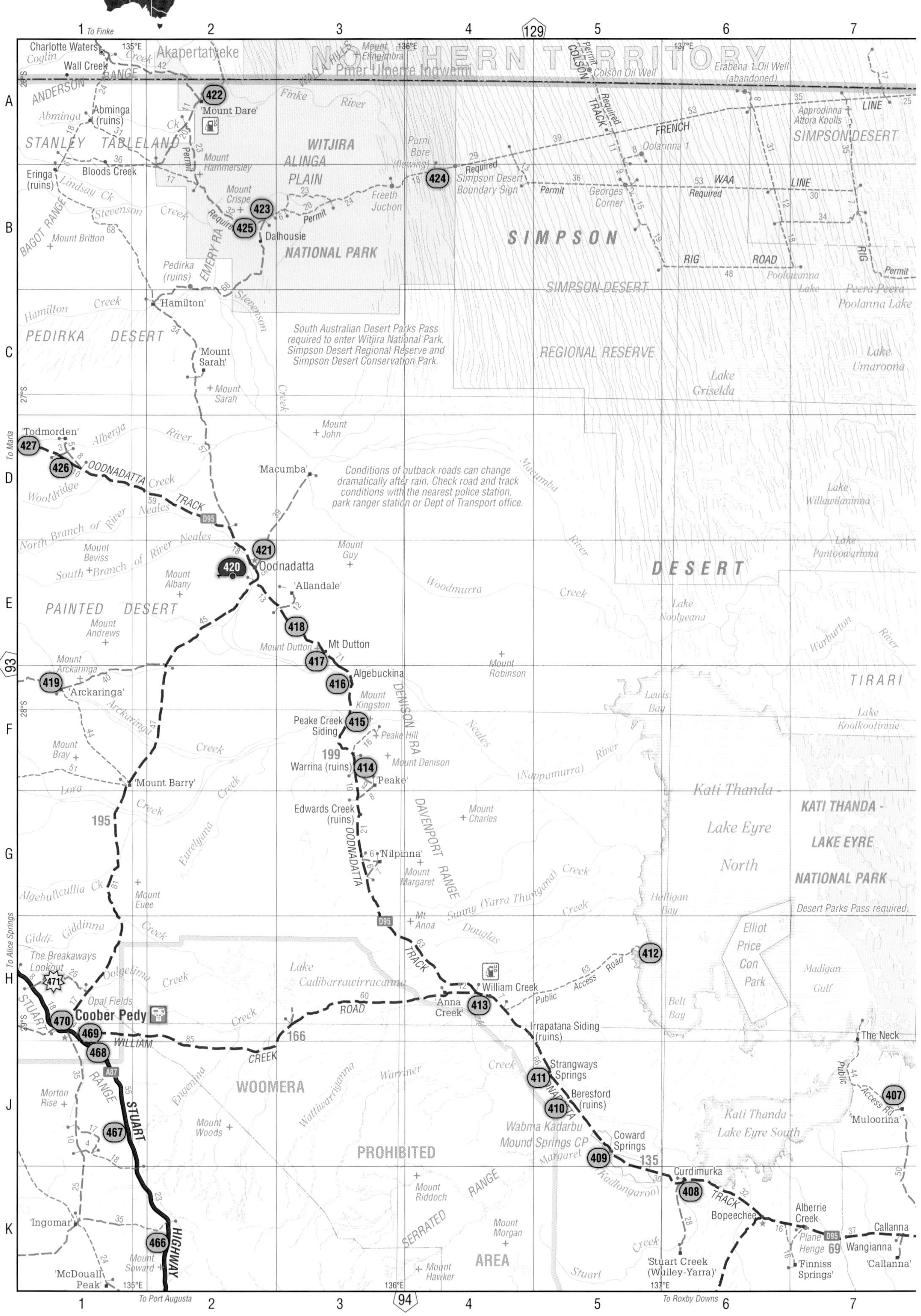
South Australian Desert Parks Pass required to enter Witjira National Park, Simpson Desert Regional Reserve and Simpson Desert Conservation Park.
Conditions of outback roads can change dramatically after rain. Check road and track conditions with the nearest police station, park ranger station or Dept of Transport office.
WITJIRA ALINGA PLAIN NATIONAL PARK
SIMPSON DESERT REGIONAL RESERVE
KATI THANDA - LAKE EYRE NATIONAL PARK
Desert Parks Pass required.
Oodnadatta
Coober Pedy
William Creek
Dalhousie
'Mount Dare'
Marree
WOOMERA PROHIBITED AREA
To Finke
To Marla
To Alice Springs
To Port Augusta
To Roxby Downs

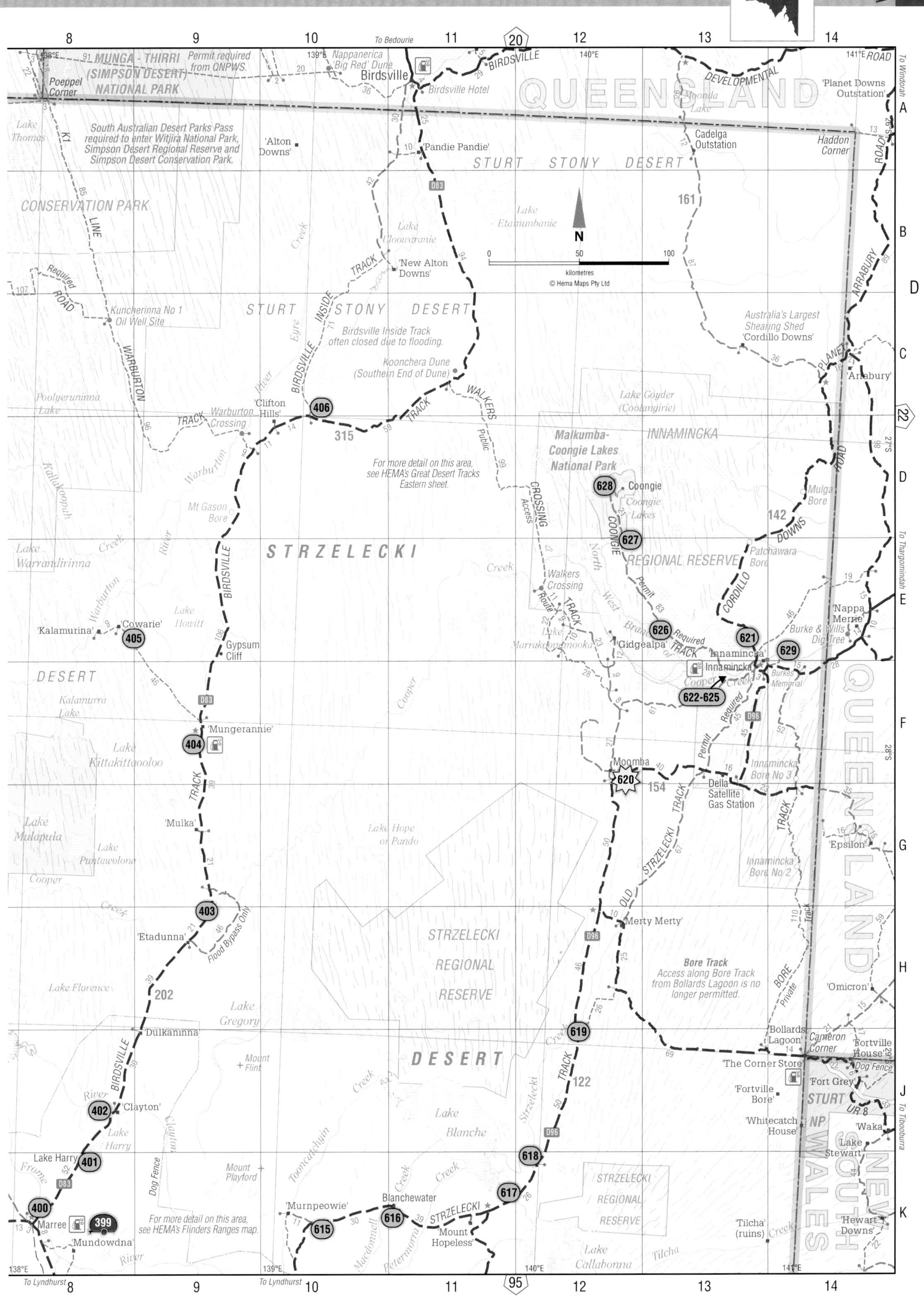
MUNGA - THIRRI (SIMPSON DESERT) NATIONAL PARK
Permit required from QNPWS.
Poeppel Corner
Nappanerica 'Big Red' Dune
Birdsville
Birdsville Hotel
BIRDSVILLE
DEVELOPMENTAL ROAD
QUEENSLAND
'Planet Downs Outstation'
South Australian Desert Parks Pass required to enter Witjira National Park, Simpson Desert Regional Reserve and Simpson Desert Conservation Park.
'Alton Downs'
'Pandie Pandie'
Cadelga Outstation
Haddon Corner
STURT STONY DESERT
CONSERVATION PARK
Lake Etamunbanie
New Alton Downs'
Kuncherinna No 1 Oil Well Site
Birdsville Inside Track often closed due to flooding.
Koonchera Dune (Southern End of Dune)
Australia's Largest Shearing Shed 'Cordillo Downs'
'Arrabury'
Lake Goyder (Coolangirie)
'Clifton Hills'
Warburton Crossing
WALKERS CROSSING
For more detail on this area, see HEMA's Great Desert Tracks Eastern sheet.
Malkumba-Coongie Lakes National Park
INNAMINCKA REGIONAL RESERVE
Coongie
Mt Gason Bore
STRZELECKI
Walkers Crossing
Mulga Bore
Patchawara Bore
'Nappa Merrie'
Burke & Wills Dig Tree
'Kalamurina'
'Cowarie'
Gypsum Cliff
'Gidgealpa'
Innamincka
Burkes Memorial
DESERT
'Mungerannie'
Moomba
Della Satellite Gas Station
Innamincka Bore No 3
'Mulka'
Lake Hope or Pando
'Epsilon'
Innamincka Bore No 2
'Merty Merty'
'Etadunna'
Flood Bypass Only
STRZELECKI REGIONAL RESERVE
Bore Track
Access along Bore Track from Bollards Lagoon is no longer permitted.
'Omicron'
Lake Florence
Lake Gregory
'Dulkaninna'
'Bollards Lagoon'
Cameron Corner
'Fortville House'
'The Corner Store'
'Fort Grey'
Mount Flint
'Clayton'
DESERT
'Fortville Bore'
STURT NP
'Whitecatch House'
'Waka'
Lake Blanche
Lake Harry
Lake Stewart
Mount Playford
NEW SOUTH WALES
'Murnpeowie'
Blanchewater
For more detail on this area, see HEMA's Flinders Ranges map.
Marree
'Mundowdna'
Mount Hopeless'
'Tilcha' (ruins)
Lake Callabonna
'Hewart Downs'
To Lyndhurst
kilometres
© Hema Maps Pty Ltd

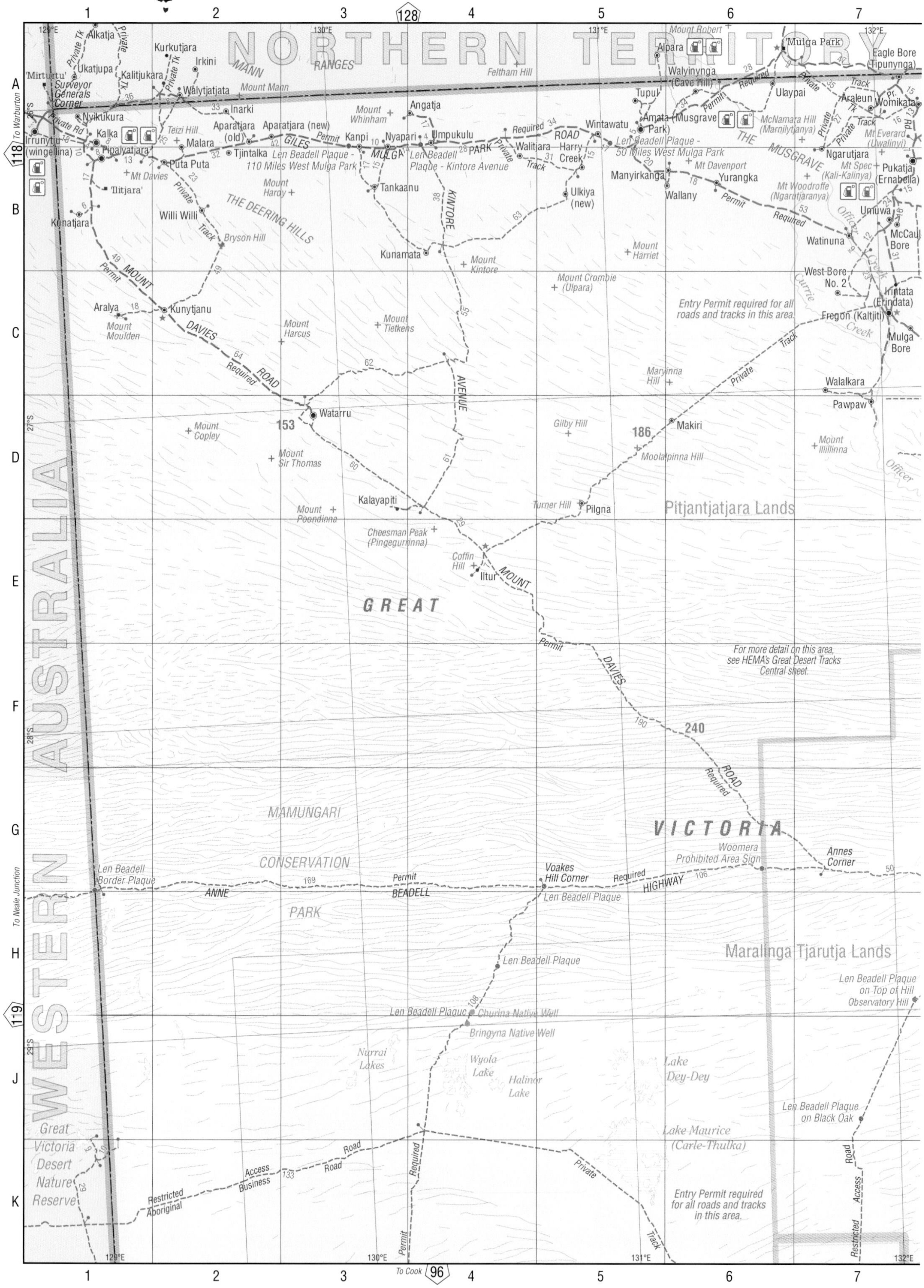
NORTHERN TERRITORY
WESTERN AUSTRALIA
Alkatja
Kurkutjara
Irkini
Ukatjupa
Kalitjukara
'Mirturtu'
Surveyor Generals Corner
Walytjatjata
Mount Mann
MANN RANGES
Feltham Hill
Mount Robert
Alpara
'Mulga Park'
Eagle Bore (Tipunynga)
Walyinynga (Cave Hill)
Ulaypai
Tupul
Araleun
Womikata
Nyikukura
Inarki
Angatja
Mount Whinham
Amata (Musgrave Park)
McNamara Hill (Marnilytjanya)
Irrunytju (wingellina)
Kalka
Pipalyatjara
Teizi Hill
Malara
Aparatjara (old)
Aparatjara (new)
GILES
Kanpi
Nyapari
Umpukulu
MULGA PARK ROAD
Wintawatu
Len Beadell Plaque - 50 Miles West Mulga Park
Mt Everard (Uwalinyi)
Ngarutjara
Pukatja (Ernabella)
Tjintalka
Len Beadell Plaque - 110 Miles West Mulga Park
Len Beadell Plaque - Kintore Avenue
Walitjara
Harry Creek
Manyirkanga
Mt Davenport
Yurangka
THE MUSGRAVE
Mt Spec (Kali-Kalinya)
Puta Puta
Mt Davies
'Ilitjara'
Tankaanu
Mount Hardy
Wallany
Mt Woodroffe (Ngarutjaranya)
Ulkiya (new)
Umuwa
Kunatjara
Willi Willi
THE DEERING HILLS
Bryson Hill
KINTORE AVENUE
McCaul Bore
Watinuna
Kunamata
Mount Kintore
Mount Harriet
MOUNT DAVIES ROAD
West Bore No. 2
Mount Crombie (Ulpara)
Iritata (Erindata)
Aralya
Kunytjanu
Mount Moulden
Entry Permit required for all roads and tracks in this area.
Fregon (Kaltjiti)
Currie Creek
Mulga Bore
Mount Harcus
Mount Tietkens
Maryinna Hill
Walalkara
Pawpaw
Watarru
Mount Copley
Gilby Hill
Makiri
Mount Illillinna
Mount Sir Thomas
Moolalpinna Hill
Officer
Kalayapiti
Mount Poondinna
Turner Hill
Pilgna
Pitjantjatjara Lands
Cheesman Peak (Pingegurrinna)
Coffin Hill
Iltur
GREAT
For more detail on this area, see HEMA's Great Desert Tracks Central sheet.
DAVIES ROAD
MAMUNGARI CONSERVATION PARK
VICTORIA
Woomera Prohibited Area Sign
Annes Corner
Len Beadell Border Plaque
Voakes Hill Corner
ANNE BEADELL HIGHWAY
Len Beadell Plaque
To Neale Junction
To Warburton
Maralinga Tjarutja Lands
Len Beadell Plaque on Top of Hill Observatory Hill
Churina Native Well
Bringyna Native Well
Narrai Lakes
Wyola Lake
Halinor Lake
Lake Dey-Dey
Len Beadell Plaque on Black Oak
Lake Maurice (Carle-Thulka)
Great Victoria Desert Nature Reserve
Restricted Aboriginal Business Access Road
Entry Permit required for all roads and tracks in this area.
Restricted Access Road
Private Track
Permit Required
To Cook
129°E
130°E
131°E
132°E
27°S
28°S
29°S
118
119
128
96
153
186
240

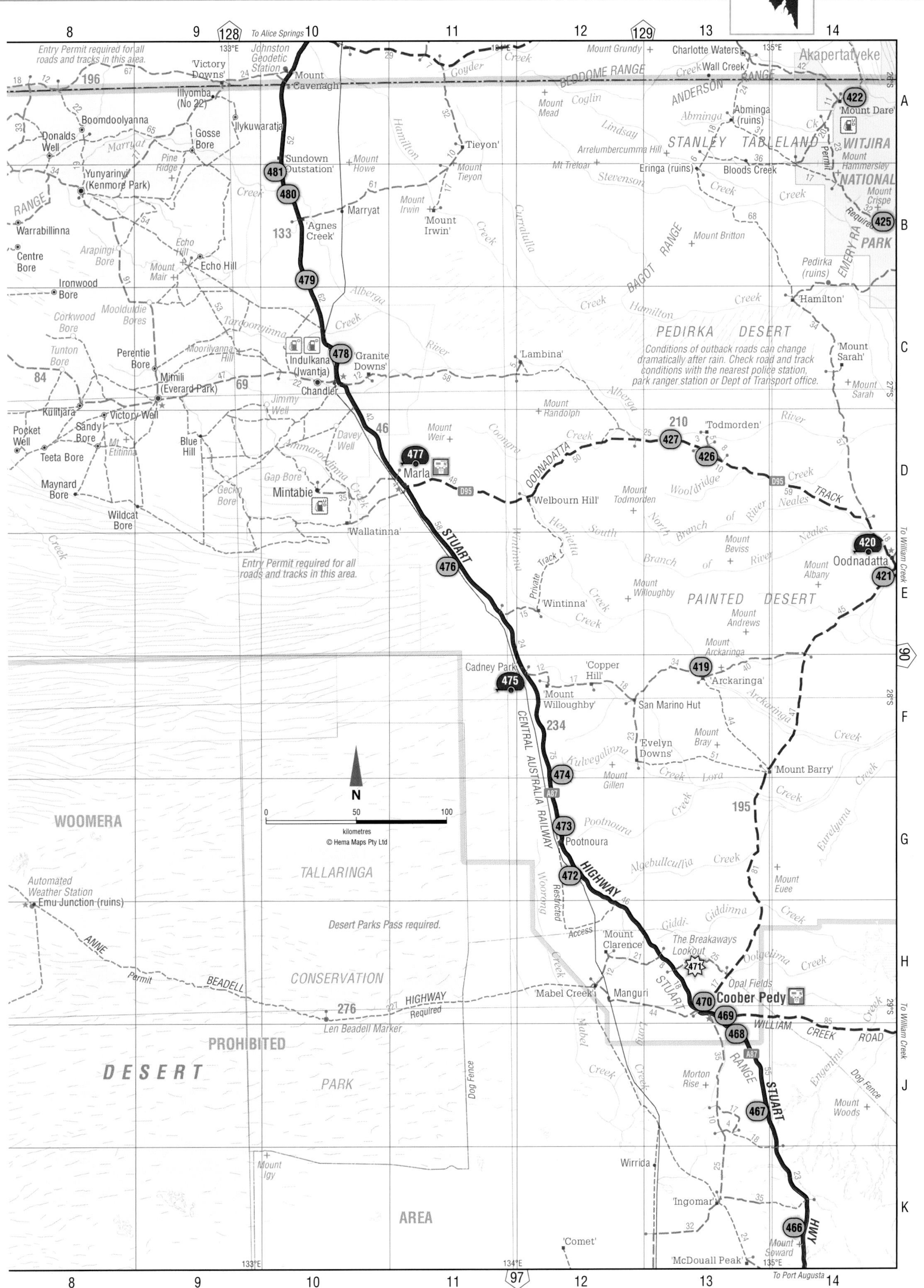
Entry Permit required for all roads and tracks in this area.
To Alice Springs
Johnston Geodetic Station
Mount Cavenagh
'Victory Downs'
Illyomba (No 22)
Boomdoolyanna
Donalds Well
Gosse Bore
Ilykuwaratja
Yunyarinyi (Kenmore Park)
Warrabillinna
Centre Bore
Ironwood Bore
Echo Hill
'Sundown Outstation'
Marryat
'Agnes Creek'
'Tieyon'
Mount Irwin
'Mount Irwin'
Mount Howe
Mount Tieyon
Mount Grundy
Charlotte Waters
Wall Creek
BEDDOME RANGE
Coglin
Mount Mead
ANDERSON RANGE
Abminga (ruins)
STANLEY TABLELAND
Arrelumbercumma Hill
Mt Treloar
Eringa (ruins)
Bloods Creek
Akapertatyeke
'Mount Dare'
WITJIRA NATIONAL PARK
Mount Hammersley
Mount Crispe
Mount Britton
BAGOT RANGE
PEDIRKA DESERT
Pedirka (ruins)
'Hamilton'
Conditions of outback roads can change dramatically after rain. Check road and track conditions with the nearest police station, park ranger station or Dept of Transport office.
'Mount Sarah'
Mount Sarah
Corkwood Bore
Mooldudie Bores
Tunton Bore
Perentie Bore
Moorilyanna Hill
Mimili (Everard Park)
Indulkana (Iwantja)
Chandler
'Granite Downs'
'Lambina'
Mount Randolph
Kuiltjara
Victory Well
Pocket Well
Sandy Bore
Teeta Bore
Blue Hill
Jimmy Well
Davey Well
Mount Weir
Marla
Maynard Bore
Gap Bore
Mintabie
Gecko Bore
Wildcat Bore
'Wallatinna'
OODNADATTA TRACK
'Welbourn Hill'
Mount Todmorden
'Todmorden'
Wooldridge
Neales
Oodnadatta
Mount Albany
Mount Beviss
Entry Permit required for all roads and tracks in this area.
STUART
Private Track
'Wintinna'
Mount Willoughby
PAINTED DESERT
Mount Andrews
Mount Arckaringa
'Arckaringa'
Cadney Park
'Copper Hill'
'Mount Willoughby'
San Marino Hut
CENTRAL AUSTRALIA RAILWAY
'Evelyn Downs'
Mount Bray
'Mount Barry'
Mount Gillen
WOOMERA
N
0 50 100
kilometres
© Hema Maps Pty Ltd
Pootnoura
TALLARINGA
HIGHWAY
Mount Eyee
Automated Weather Station
Emu Junction (ruins)
Desert Parks Pass required.
ANNE BEADELL HIGHWAY
Permit Required
'Mount Clarence'
The Breakaways Lookout
Opal Fields
CONSERVATION
'Mabel Creek'
Manguri
Coober Pedy
Len Beadell Marker
PROHIBITED
WILLIAM CREEK ROAD
DESERT
PARK
Dog Fence
Morton Rise
RANGE
STUART
Mount Woods
Mount Igy
Wirrida
'Ingomar'
AREA
'Comet'
'McDoulall Peak'
Mount Seward
HWY
To William Creek
To Port Augusta
8 9 10 11 12 13 14
A B C D E F G H J K

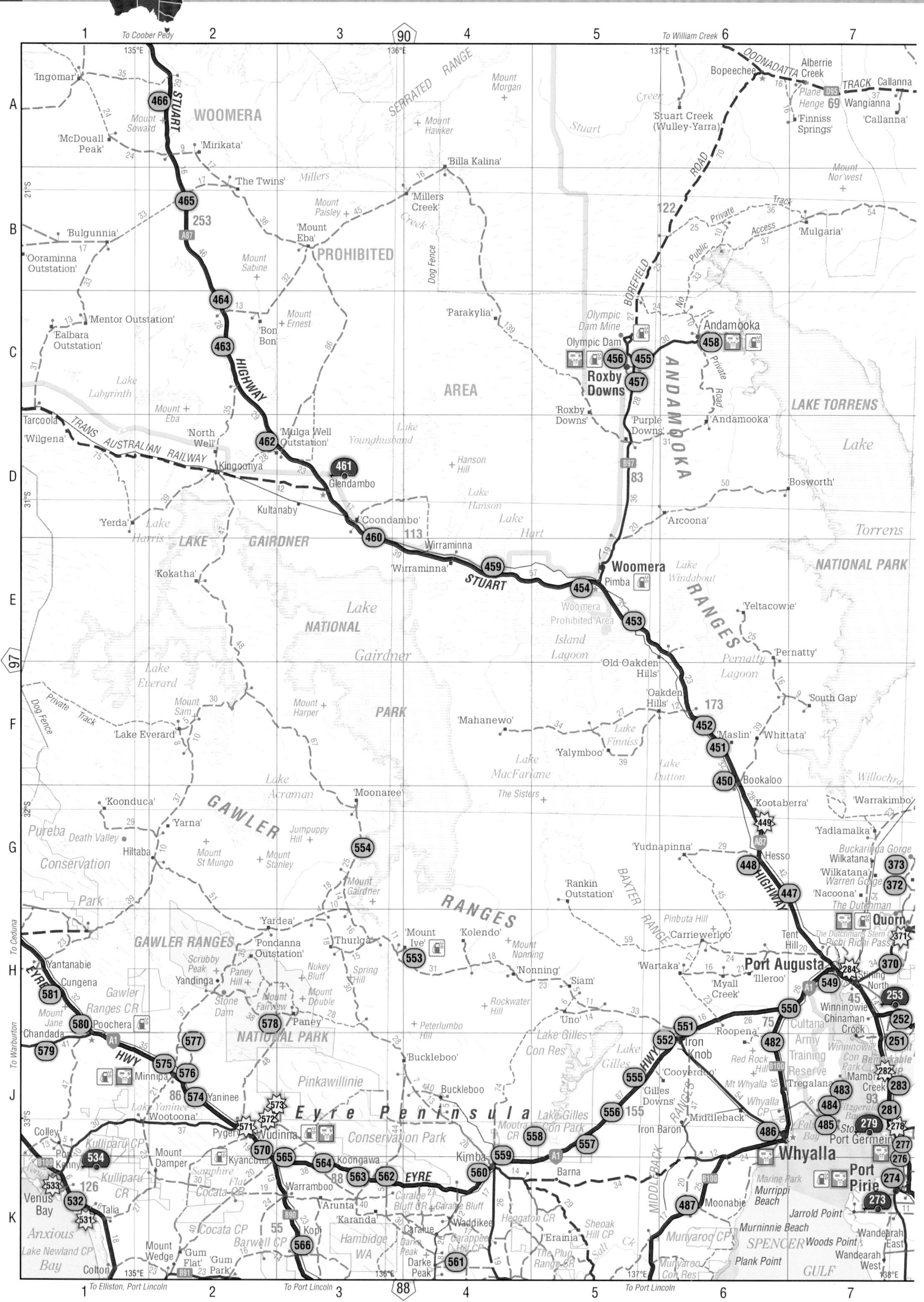

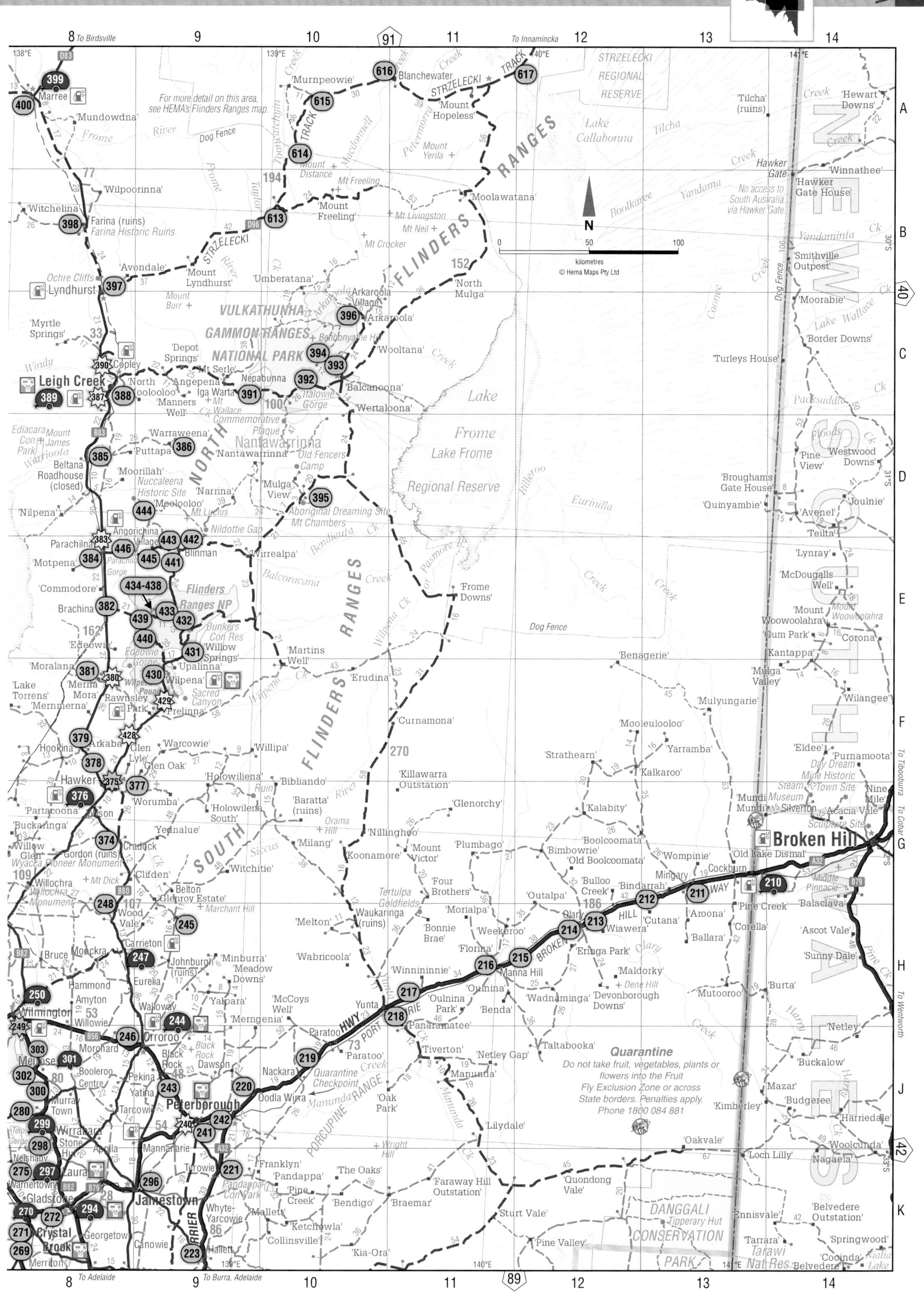
To Birdsville
To Innamincka
For more detail on this area, see HEMA's Flinders Ranges map.
Marree
'Mundowdna'
Dog Fence
'Murnpeowie'
Blanchewater
STRZELECKI TRACK
STRZELECKI REGIONAL RESERVE
'Mount Hopeless'
Mount Yerila
Lake Callabonna
Tilcha
'Tilcha' (ruins)
'Hewart Downs'
'Wilpoorinna'
Mount Distance
Mt Freeling
'Mount Freeling'
Mt Livingston
Mt Neil
Mt Crocker
'Moolawatana'
No access to South Australia via Hawker Gate
Hawker Gate
'Hawker Gate House'
'Winnathee'
'Witchelina'
Farina (ruins)
Farina Historic Ruins
'Avondale'
'Mount Lyndhurst'
'Umberatana'
Ochre Cliffs
Lyndhurst
Mount Burr
VULKATHUNHA-GAMMON RANGES NATIONAL PARK
Arkaroola Village
'Arkaroola'
'North Mulga'
'Smithville Outpost'
'Moorabie'
'Myrtle Springs'
'Depot Springs'
Copley
Leigh Creek
Mt Serle
'Angepena'
'North Moolooloo'
Nepabunna
Iga Warta
'Manners Well'
Mt Wallace
Italowie Gorge
'Balcanoona'
'Wertaloona'
'Wooltana'
Lake Frome
Lake Frome Regional Reserve
'Border Downs'
'Turleys House'
Packsaddle
kilometres
© Hema Maps Pty Ltd
Ediacara Conservation Park
Mount James
Warraweena
'Puttapa'
Nantawarrinna
'Nantawarrinna'
Old Fencers Camp
Beltana Roadhouse (closed)
'Moorillah'
Nuccaleena Historic Site
'Narrina'
'Mulga View'
'Meolooloo'
Mt Lurius
Aboriginal Dreaming Site
Mt Chambers
Nildottie Gap
'Nilpena'
Parachilna
Angorichina Village
Blinman
'Wirrealpa'
'Motpena'
'Commodore'
Brachina
Flinders Ranges NP
Bunkers Con Res
Willow Springs
'Upalinna'
Wilpena
Sacred Canyon
'Edeowie'
'Moralana'
'Merna Mora'
Rawnsley Park
'Lake Torrens'
'Mernmerna'
Prelinna
'Martins Well'
'Erudina'
'Frome Downs'
Dog Fence
'Benagerie'
'Mulyungarie'
'Broughams Gate House'
'Quinyambie'
'Pine View'
'Westwood Downs'
'Avenel'
'Joulnie'
'Teilta'
'Lynray'
'McDougalls Well'
'Mount Woowoolahra'
Woowoolahra
'Gum Park'
'Corona'
Kantappa
'Mulga Valley'
'Wilangee'
FLINDERS RANGES
NORTH FLINDERS RANGES
SOUTH FLINDERS RANGES
'Curnamona'
'Mooleulooloo'
'Yarramba'
'Strathearn'
'Kalkaroo'
'Eldee'
'Purnamoota'
Day Dream Mine Historic
Steam Town Site
Hookina
Arkaba
Glen Lyle
'Warcowie'
'Willipa'
Glen Oak
'Holowiliena'
'Bibliando'
'Killawarra Outstation'
Hawker
'Worumba'
'Holowiliena South'
'Baratta' (ruins)
'Glenorchy'
'Kalabity'
Mundi Mundi
Museum
Silverton
Nine Mile
'Acacia Vale'
Sculpture Site
To Tibooburra
To Cobar
'Partacoona'
'Buckaringa'
'Yednalue'
Orama Hill
'Nillinghoo'
'Plumbago'
'Boolcoomata'
'Bimbowrie'
'Old Boolcoomata'
'Wompinie'
Broken Hill
Willow Glen
Gordon (ruins)
Cradock
'Milang'
'Koonamore'
'Mount Victor'
Wyacca Pioneer Monument
'Witchitie'
Willochra
Mt Dick
Clifden
Willochra Monument
Belton
Glenroy Estate
Marchant Hill
'Four Brothers'
Tertulpa Goldfields
'Bulloo Creek'
'Outalpa'
'Bindarrah'
Mingary
Cockburn
'Old Lake Dismal'
Middle Pinnacle
'Balaclava'
'Pine Creek'
'Melton'
Waukaringa (ruins)
'Morialpa'
'Weekeroo'
Olary
BARRIER HWY
'Wiawera'
'Cutana'
'Aroona'
'Corella'
'Ascot Vale'
Wood Vale
Carrieton
'Bonnie Brae'
'Florina'
'Ballara'
'Sunny Dale'
Bruce
Moockra
'Wabricoola'
'Erinlga Park'
Johnburgh (ruins)
'Minburra'
'Meadow Downs'
'Winnininnie'
Manna Hill
'Maldorky'
Dene Hill
'Burta'
Hammond
Eurelia
Amyton
'Oulnina'
'Wadnaminga'
'Devonborough Downs'
'Mutooroo'
To Wentworth
Wilmington
Walloway
'Yalpara'
'McCoys Well'
'Oulnina Park'
'Benda'
Willowie
Orroroo
'Merngenia'
Yunta
Paratoo
'Panaramatee'
'Netley'
Morchard
Black Rock
Melrose
Booleroo Centre
Dawson
PORT PIRIE HWY
'Paratoo'
'Tiverton'
'Netley Gap'
'Taltabooka'
Quarantine
Do not take fruit, vegetables, plants or flowers into the Fruit Fly Exclusion Zone or across State borders. Penalties apply. Phone 1800 084 881
'Buckalow'
Pekina
Nackara
Quarantine Checkpoint
'Manunda'
Mazar
Yatina
Murray Town
Tarcowie
Peterborough
Oodla Wirra
'Oak Park'
PORCUPINE RANGE
'Kimberley'
'Budgeree'
'Harriedale'
Wirrabara
Stone Hut
Appila
Mannanarie
'Lilydale'
Wright Hill
'Oakvale'
'Loch Lilly'
'Woolcunda'
'Nagaela'
Terowie
'Franklyn'
'Pandappa'
Pandappa Con Park
'The Oaks'
'Faraway Hill Outstation'
'Quondong Vale'
Laura
Warnertown
Gladstone
Jamestown
'Pine Creek'
'Bendigo'
'Braemar'
DANGGALI CONSERVATION PARK
Tipperary Hut
'Ennisvale'
'Belvedere Outstation'
Whyte-Yarcowie
'Mallett'
'Ketchowla'
'Sturt Vale'
Crystal Brook
Georgetown
Canowie
Hallett
'Collinsville'
'Kia-Ora'
'Pine Valley'
'Tarrara'
Tarawi Nat Res
'Springwood'
'Cooinda'
Kalia Lake
'Belvedere'
Merriton
To Adelaide
To Burra, Adelaide
NEW SOUTH WALES

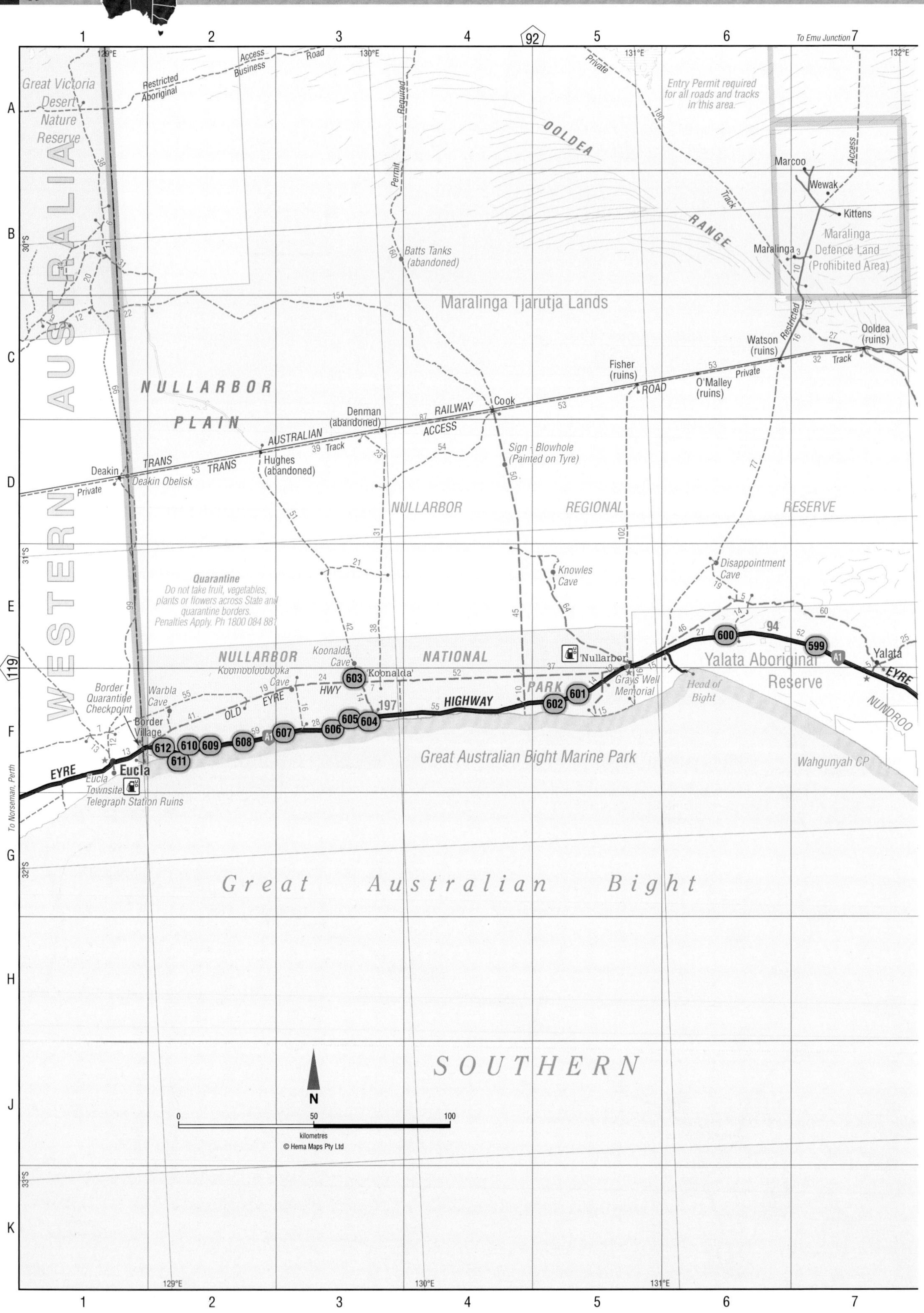
Great Victoria Desert Nature Reserve
WESTERN AUSTRALIA
Restricted Aboriginal
Access Business Road
Permit Required
OOLDEA RANGE
Private Track
Entry Permit required for all roads and tracks in this area.
Marcoo
Wewak
Kittens
Maralinga
Maralinga Defence Land (Prohibited Area)
Batts Tanks (abandoned)
Maralinga Tjarutja Lands
Watson (ruins)
Restricted
Ooldea (ruins)
Fisher (ruins)
O'Malley (ruins)
Private Track
NULLARBOR PLAIN
Denman (abandoned)
TRANS AUSTRALIAN RAILWAY ACCESS ROAD
Cook
Track
Deakin
Deakin Obelisk
Private
Hughes (abandoned)
Sign - Blowhole (Painted on Tyre)
NULLARBOR REGIONAL RESERVE
Knowles Cave
Disappointment Cave
Quarantine
Do not take fruit, vegetables, plants or flowers across State and quarantine borders. Penalties Apply. Ph 1800 084 881
NULLARBOR NATIONAL PARK
Koonalda Cave
'Koonalda'
Koomoolooboka Cave
'Nullarbor'
Grays Well Memorial
Yalata Aboriginal Reserve
Yalata
Head of Bight
Border Quarantine Checkpoint
Warbla Cave
Border Village
OLD EYRE HWY
EYRE HIGHWAY
NUNDROO
Eucla
Eucla Townsite
Telegraph Station Ruins
Great Australian Bight Marine Park
Wahgunyah CP
To Norseman, Perth
To Emu Junction
Great Australian Bight
SOUTHERN
N
kilometres
© Hema Maps Pty Ltd

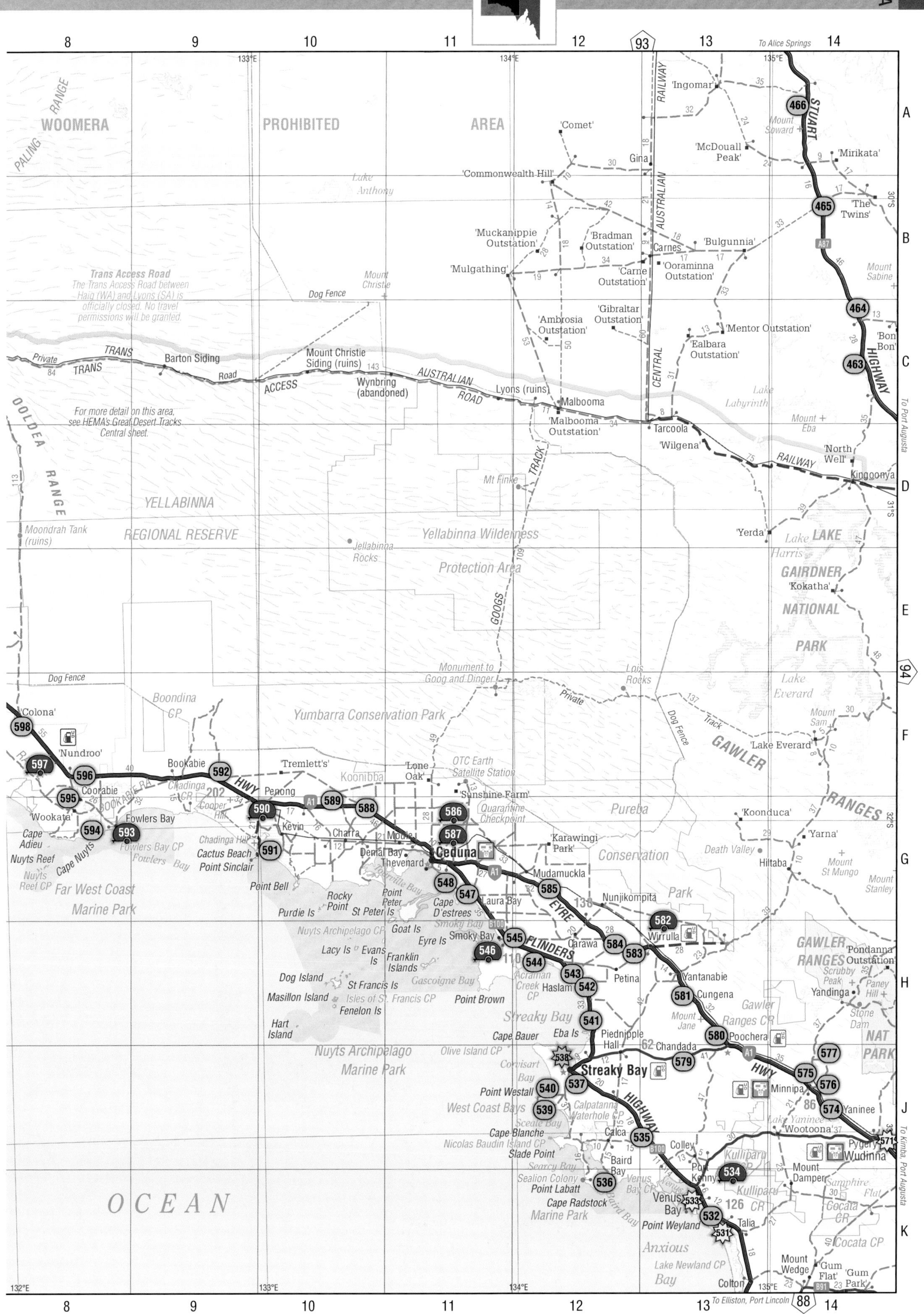
WOOMERA
PROHIBITED
AREA
Ceduna
Streaky Bay
Wudinna
Tarcoola
Kingoonya
Yellabinna Wilderness
Protection Area
Yumbarra Conservation Park
Nuyts Archipelago Marine Park
LAKE GAIRDNER NATIONAL PARK
GAWLER RANGES
OCEAN
EYRE HWY
FLINDERS HIGHWAY
STUART HIGHWAY
TRANS AUSTRALIAN RAILWAY

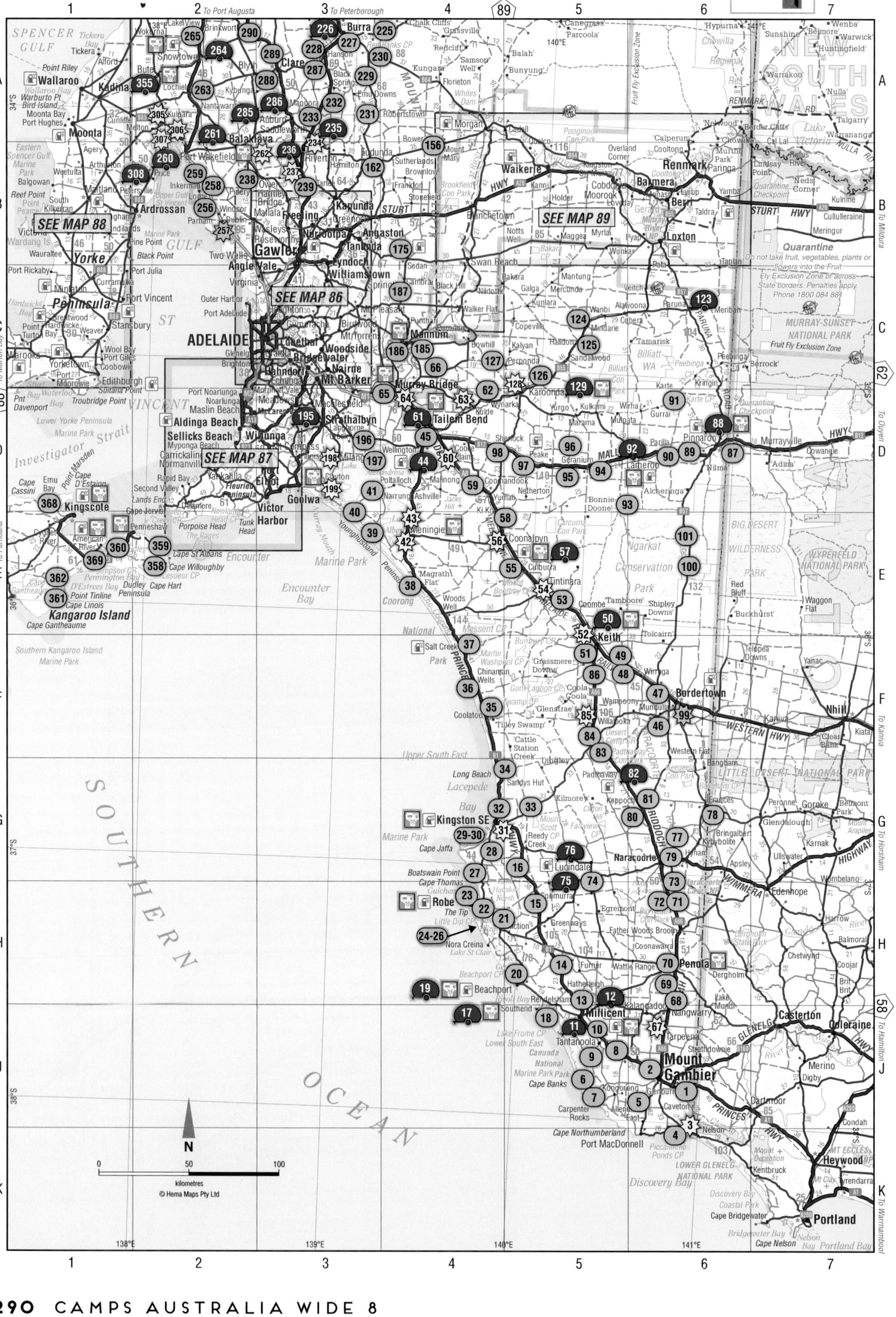

SEE MAP 88
SEE MAP 89
SEE MAP 86
SEE MAP 87

Quarantine
Do not take fruit, vegetables, plants or flowers into the Fruit Fly Exclusion Zone or across State borders. Penalties apply.
Phone 1800 084 881

kilometres
© Hema Maps Pty Ltd

South Australia Highway Index

South Australia Alphabetic Site Index

Y

SOUTH AUSTRALIA

Mt Gambier to Tailem Bend

Princes Highway

1 Kromelite Rd Rest Area
A1

Rest Area 23 km W of Mumbannar or 17 km E of Mt Gambier. 1 km W of SA/VIC border

HEMA 98 J6 37 50 46 S 140 55 14 E

2 Mt Gambier Showgrounds ☎0408 492 182

Camp Area at Mt Gambier, Pick Ave. Caretaker on site. Maximum stay 28 days

HEMA 98 J6 37 50 16 S 140 47 51 E

3 Donovans Landing

Picnic Area 31 km SE of Mt Gambier or 7 km W of Nelson. Turn E 27 km SE of Mt Gambier or turn N 4 km NW of Nelson onto Glenelg River Rd

HEMA 98 J6 38 0 40 S 140 57 36 E

4 Piccaninnie Ponds Conservation Park ☎(08) 8735 1177

Camp Area 32 km SE of Mt Gambier or 10 km W of Nelson. Turn S 29 km SE of Mount Gambier or 7 km W of Nelson for 2 km dirt road. Small vehicles only. Permit required

HEMA 98 K6 38 3 8 S 140 56 42 E

5 Little Blue Lake

Parking Area 17 km S of Mt Gambier or 17 km N of Port MacDonnell. Turn W 14 km S of Mt Gambier or 14 km N of Port MacDonnell along Mt Salts Rd for 3 km

HEMA 98 J6 37 55 40 S 140 40 49 E

6 Cape Banks Lighthouse ☎(08) 8735 1177
Canunda National Park

Camp Area 4 km N of Carpenter Rocks, via Cape Banks Rd

HEMA 98 J5 37 53 51 S 140 22 37 E

7 Carpenter Rocks Community Assoc Camp

Camp Area Carpenter Rocks. Next to community hall & tennis courts. Pay at Store or at payment box at the store

HEMA 98 J5 37 54 49 S 140 23 55 E

8 Tantanoola East
B1

Parking Area 31 km NW of Mt Gambier or 19 km SE of Millicent. Opposite SAFF Service Station

HEMA 98 J5 37 42 21 S 140 29 54 E

9 Tantanoola Rest Area

Rest Area at Tantanoola, opposite hotel

HEMA 98 J5 37 41 46 S 140 27 20 E

10 Millicent South
B1

Parking Area 45 km NW of Mt Gambier or 5 km S of Millicent

HEMA 98 J5 37 38 1 S 140 23 29 E

11 Hillview Caravan Park ☎(08) 8733 2806
B1

Caravan Park. 2.6 km S of Millicent. Dalton St

HEMA 98 J5 37 36 42 S 140 22 19 E

12 Millicent Lakeside Caravan Park ☎(08) 8733 1188

Caravan Park at Millicent. 12 Park Tce. 1 km S of PO

HEMA 98 J5 37 35 28 S 140 20 22 E

13 Millicent North
B1

Parking Area 4 km N of Millicent or 103 km S of Kingston SE

HEMA 98 H5 37 33 50 S 140 21 16 E

14 Drain M
B1

Parking Area 23 km N of Millicent or 84 km S of Kingston SE

HEMA 98 H5 37 23 37 S 140 14 17 E

15 Greenways West
B1

Parking Area 65 km N of Millicent or 42 km S of Kingston SE

HEMA 98 H5 37 6 55 S 140 6 13 E

16 Reedy Creek South
B1

Parking Area 77 km N of Millicent or 30 km S of Kingston SE

HEMA 98 G5 37 0 49 S 140 0 34 E

17 Southend Sands Caravan Park (Lynnies) ☎(08) 8735 6200

Caravan Park at Southend. Cnr of Leake & Eliza Sts

HEMA 98 J5 37 34 7 S 140 7 38 E

18 Kotgee Camping Area ☎(08) 8735 1177
Canunda National Park

Camp Area at Southend. Entry off Boozy Gully Rd, 2 km sandy dirt road. Permit required. Self registration available, small vehicles only

HEMA 98 J5 37 34 50 S 140 8 14 E

19 Beachport Caravan Park ☎(08) 8735 8128

Caravan Park at Beachport. Beach Rd

HEMA 98 H5 37 28 44 S 140 0 55 E

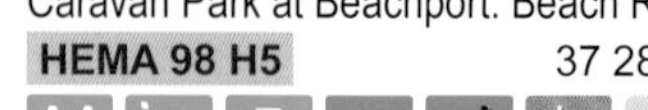

SOUTH AUSTRALIA

20 Three Mile Bend Campground ☎ (08) 8735 1177
Beachport Conservation Park
Camp Area 5 km N of Beachport, via Five Mile Rd. Small vehicles only. 2 km dirt road. Permit required
HEMA 98 H5 37 27 9 S 139 59 31 E

21 Springs Road
Parking Area 36 km N of Beachport or 14 km S of Robe. 400m N of The Springs Rd turnoff
B101
HEMA 98 H4 37 12 49 S 139 53 15 E

22 Jumbo's Jetty
Parking Area 5 km SE of Robe, via Southern Ports Hwy & Wildfield Rd. Beside Lake Battye. Small vehicles only
HEMA 98 H4 37 10 36 S 139 47 42 E
24

23 The Obelisk
Parking Area at Robe. W end of Obelisk Rd
HEMA 98 H4 37 9 21 S 139 44 40 E
24

24 Old Man Lake ☎ (08) 8735 1177
Little Dip Conservation Park
Camp Area 10 km N of Nora Creina or 13 km S of Robe, via Nora Creina Dr. Some dirt road. Small vehicles only. Low trees. Permit required
HEMA 98 H4 37 15 38 S 139 49 18 E

25 Long Gully Campground ☎ (08) 8735 1177
Little Dip Conservation Park
Camp Area 12 km N of Nora Creina or 14 km S of Robe, via Nora Creina Dr. 6 km dirt road. Permit required
HEMA 98 H4 37 15 17 S 139 48 3 E
BIG RIG

26 The Gums Campground ☎ (08) 8735 1177
Little Dip Conservation Park
Camp Area 3 km S of Robe, via Robe St. Small vehicles only not suitable for caravans. Some dirt road. Permit required
HEMA 98 H4 37 11 14 S 139 46 2 E

27 Wrights Bay Bush Camping ☎ 0428 340 717
Camp Spot at Wrights Bay. Turn W into Wrights Bay Rd 19 km N of Robe or 25 km S of Kingston. See Caretaker
HEMA 98 G4 37 2 31 S 139 44 33 E
BIG RIG

28 Kingston South
Parking Area 32 km N of Robe or 12 km S of Kingston SE
B101
HEMA 98 G4 36 55 30 S 139 49 16 E

29 Pinks Beach
Parking Area 6 km S of Kingston SE on PInks Beach Rd (Cnr Marine Pde). Self Contained Vehicles only
HEMA 98 G4 36 52 23 S 139 48 52 E
BIG RIG 24

30 Wyomi Beach
Parking Area 2 km N of Pinks Beach or 4 km S of Kingston SE. Opposite store. Self Contained Vehicles only. Max 5 Day stay
HEMA 98 G4 36 51 36 S 139 49 30 E
BIG RIG

31 Apex Park
Rest Area at Kingston. Cnr East Tce & Princes Hwy
HEMA 98 G4 36 49 34 S 139 51 39 E

32 Kingston SE Jetty Parking Area
Parking Area at Kingston SE Jetty. Cold shower. Self Contained Vehicles only
HEMA 98 G4 36 49 37 S 139 51 1 E
BIG RIG 24

33 Mt Scott Conservation Park
Camp Area 24 km NE of Kingston SE. Turn SE off Desert Camp-Kingston Rd (Rowney Rd) 19 km NE of Kingston SE. 5 km dirt road
HEMA 98 G5 36 46 49 S 140 3 19 E
BIG RIG

34 Coorong Rest Area
Rest Area 25 km N of Kingston SE or 59 km S of Salt Creek
B1
HEMA 98 G4 36 37 15 S 139 52 36 E
BIG RIG

35 Old Coorong Road Campgrounds ☎ (08) 8575 1200
Coorong National Park
Camp Area 39 km N of Kingston SE or 45 km S of Salt Creek. Many campsites beside Old Coorong Rd (dirt road). Permit required
HEMA 98 F4 36 23 20 S 139 45 51 E

36 42 Mile Crossing Campground ☎ (08) 8575 1200
Coorong National Park
Camp Area 69 km N of Kingston SE or 21 km S of Salt Creek. Turn W 66 km N of Kingston SE or 18 km S of Salt Creek. 3 km dirt road. Permit required
HEMA 98 F4 36 17 15 S 139 42 42 E
BIG RIG

37 Adventures Rest Camp Ground ☎ (08) 8575 7021
Camp Area at Salt Creek. Next to roadhouse
B1
HEMA 98 F4 36 7 38 S 139 38 55 E

Notes...

SOUTH AUSTRALIA

38 Parnka Point
(08) 8575 1200

Coorong National Park

Camp Area 42 km N of Salt Creek or 28 km S of Meningie. Turn W 38 km N of Salt Creek or 24 km S of Meningie. 3 km dirt road. Permit required. 2 camp areas

HEMA 89 K10 35 53 49 S 139 24 5 E

39 Long Point
(08) 8575 1200

Coorong National Park

Camp Area 23 km W of Meningie. Permit required

HEMA 89 K9 35 41 40 S 139 9 49 E

BIG RIG

40 Mark Point
(08) 8575 1200

Coorong National Park

Camp Area 34 km W of Meningie. 11 km unsealed road, tracks to camp sites on sandy track. 4WD recommended

HEMA 89 J9 35 37 30 S 139 4 37 E

41 Narrung Jetty Reserve

Rest Area at Narrung, beside ferry terminal. W side

HEMA 89 J9 35 30 49 S 139 11 4 E

BIG RIG 72

42 Meningie Lions Jubilee Park

B1

Rest Area at Meningie

HEMA 89 K10 35 41 7 S 139 20 21 E

BIG RIG

43 Lake Albert Foreshore

B1

Picnic Area 3 km N of Meningie, beside lake

HEMA 89 J10 35 40 19 S 139 20 37 E

BIG RIG

44 Wellington Caravan Park
(08) 8572 7302

Caravan Park at Wellington. Main Rd

HEMA 89 J10 35 19 50 S 139 22 55 E

BIG RIG

45 Tailem Bend South Rest Area

B1

Rest Area 45 km N of Meningie or 7 km S of Tailem Bend

HEMA 89 J10 35 18 16 S 139 25 51 E

BIG RIG

Bordertown to Adelaide

Dukes Highway

46 Mundulla Showground
(08) 8752 0700

Camp Area at Mundulla. Cnr North Tce & Mile Ln. Honesty box

HEMA 98 F6 36 21 30 S 140 41 25 E

BIG RIG 48

47 Poocher Swamp Rest Area

Rest Area 8 km W of Bordertown, via Crocker St from Shell Station & Cannawigara Rd

HEMA 98 F6 36 17 55 S 140 40 56 E

48 Brimbago Rest Area

A8

Rest Area 29 km NW of Bordertown or 16 km SE of Keith

HEMA 98 F5 36 10 19 S 140 28 52 E

49 Pendleton Farmstay
(08) 8756 7042

Camp Area 14 km S of Keith or 34 km N of Bordertown. Eckerts Rd. Signposted

HEMA 98 F5 36 9 21 S 140 28 44 E

BIG RIG

50 Keith Caravan Park
(08) 8755 1957

Caravan Park at Keith. Naracoorte Rd

HEMA 98 F5 36 6 4 S 140 21 4 E

51 Keith Showgrounds
0407 392 231

Camp Area at Keith. Enter via Showgrounds Rd. No camping during Show Week October

HEMA 98 F5 36 5 44 S 140 21 30 E

BIG RIG 72

52 Keith Town Park

A8

Rest Area at Keith. Heritage St. N end of town. No camping, go to Showground for over night camping, fee applies

HEMA 98 F5 36 5 45 S 140 21 8 E

BIG RIG

53 Tintinara South Rest Area

A8

Rest Area 29 km NW of Keith or 8 km S of Tintinara

HEMA 89 K11 35 56 17 S 140 7 27 E

BIG RIG

54 Tintinara Lions Park

A8

Rest Area at Tintinara

HEMA 89 K11 35 53 6 S 140 3 26 E

BIG RIG

55 Culburra North Rest Area

A8

Rest Area 3 km NW of Culburra, 14 km NW of Tintinara or 13 km SE of Coonalpyn

HEMA 89 K11 35 47 49 S 139 56 37 E

BIG RIG

56 Coonalpyn Rest Area

A8

Rest Area at Coonalpyn. Opposite hotel

HEMA 89 K11 35 41 47 S 139 51 25 E

BIG RIG

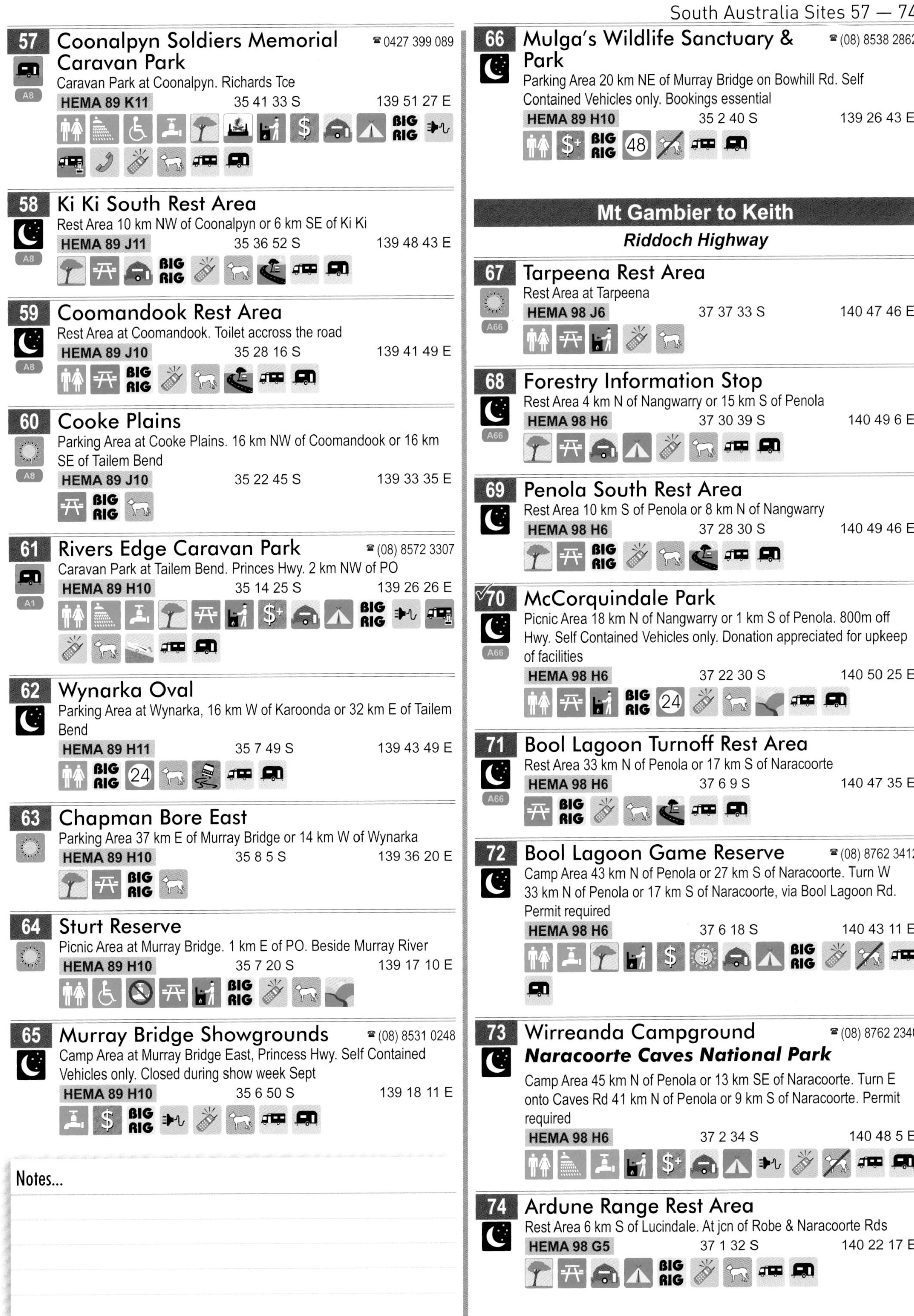

57 Coonalpyn Soldiers Memorial Caravan Park
☎ 0427 399 089

A8

Caravan Park at Coonalpyn. Richards Tce

HEMA 89 K11 35 41 33 S 139 51 27 E

BIG RIG

58 Ki Ki South Rest Area

A8

Rest Area 10 km NW of Coonalpyn or 6 km SE of Ki Ki

HEMA 89 J11 35 36 52 S 139 48 43 E

BIG RIG

59 Coomandook Rest Area

A8

Rest Area at Coomandook. Toilet accross the road

HEMA 89 J10 35 28 16 S 139 41 49 E

BIG RIG

60 Cooke Plains

A8

Parking Area at Cooke Plains. 16 km NW of Coomandook or 16 km SE of Tailem Bend

HEMA 89 J10 35 22 45 S 139 33 35 E

BIG RIG

61 Rivers Edge Caravan Park
☎ (08) 8572 3307

A1

Caravan Park at Tailem Bend. Princes Hwy. 2 km NW of PO

HEMA 89 H10 35 14 25 S 139 26 26 E

BIG RIG

62 Wynarka Oval

Parking Area at Wynarka, 16 km W of Karoonda or 32 km E of Tailem Bend

HEMA 89 H11 35 7 49 S 139 43 49 E

BIG RIG 24

63 Chapman Bore East

Parking Area 37 km E of Murray Bridge or 14 km W of Wynarka

HEMA 89 H10 35 8 5 S 139 36 20 E

BIG RIG

64 Sturt Reserve

Picnic Area at Murray Bridge. 1 km E of PO. Beside Murray River

HEMA 89 H10 35 7 20 S 139 17 10 E

BIG RIG

65 Murray Bridge Showgrounds
☎ (08) 8531 0248

Camp Area at Murray Bridge East, Princess Hwy. Self Contained Vehicles only. Closed during show week Sept

HEMA 89 H10 35 6 50 S 139 18 11 E

BIG RIG

Notes...

66 Mulga's Wildlife Sanctuary & Park
☎ (08) 8538 2862

Parking Area 20 km NE of Murray Bridge on Bowhill Rd. Self Contained Vehicles only. Bookings essential

HEMA 89 H10 35 2 40 S 139 26 43 E

BIG RIG 48

Mt Gambier to Keith

Riddoch Highway

67 Tarpeena Rest Area

A66

Rest Area at Tarpeena

HEMA 98 J6 37 37 33 S 140 47 46 E

68 Forestry Information Stop

A66

Rest Area 4 km N of Nangwarry or 15 km S of Penola

HEMA 98 H6 37 30 39 S 140 49 6 E

69 Penola South Rest Area

Rest Area 10 km S of Penola or 8 km N of Nangwarry

HEMA 98 H6 37 28 30 S 140 49 46 E

BIG RIG

70 McCorquindale Park

A66

Picnic Area 18 km N of Nangwarry or 1 km S of Penola. 800m off Hwy. Self Contained Vehicles only. Donation appreciated for upkeep of facilities

HEMA 98 H6 37 22 30 S 140 50 25 E

BIG RIG 24

71 Bool Lagoon Turnoff Rest Area

A66

Rest Area 33 km N of Penola or 17 km S of Naracoorte

HEMA 98 H6 37 6 9 S 140 47 35 E

BIG RIG

72 Bool Lagoon Game Reserve
☎ (08) 8762 3412

Camp Area 43 km N of Penola or 27 km S of Naracoorte. Turn W 33 km N of Penola or 17 km S of Naracoorte, via Bool Lagoon Rd. Permit required

HEMA 98 H6 37 6 18 S 140 43 11 E

BIG RIG

73 Wirreanda Campground
☎ (08) 8762 2340

Naracoorte Caves National Park

Camp Area 45 km N of Penola or 13 km SE of Naracoorte. Turn E onto Caves Rd 41 km N of Penola or 9 km S of Naracoorte. Permit required

HEMA 98 H6 37 2 34 S 140 48 5 E

74 Ardune Range Rest Area

Rest Area 6 km S of Lucindale. At jcn of Robe & Naracoorte Rds

HEMA 98 G5 37 1 32 S 140 22 17 E

BIG RIG

SOUTH AUSTRALIA

75 Lucindale Country Club Caravan Park
☎ (08) 8766 7028

Caravan Park at Lucindale at Golf Course. E of the town, limited sites

HEMA 98 G5 36 58 17 S 140 24 49 E

76 Lucindale Caravan Park
☎ (08) 8766 2038

Caravan Park at Lucindale. Oak Ave

HEMA 98 G5 36 58 8 S 140 21 59 E

BIG RIG

77 Black Cockatoo Bush Camp
☎ (08) 8762 1612

Camp Area 14 km NE of Naracoorte. Travel NE from Naracoorte along Cadgee Rd for 11 km, then E along Chapples Rd for 3 km

HEMA 98 G6 36 52 0 S 140 49 33 E

BIG RIG

78 The Frances Recreation Ground

Camp Area at Frances. Natimuk-Frances Rd

HEMA 98 G6 36 42 45 S 140 57 30 E

BIG RIG 24

79 Naracoorte Showgrounds
☎ 0428 621 127

A66

Camp Area at Naracoorte. Smith St, enter beside bowls club. Check for events. 7 day maximum stay. Alt mobile 0408 838 668 for bookings

HEMA 98 G6 36 57 16 S 140 44 48 E

BIG RIG

80 Cockatoo Lake Reserve

Camp Spot 105 km S of Keith or 30 km N of Naracoorte. Turn W 93 km S of Keith or 18 km N of Naracoorte. 12 km unsealed road

HEMA 98 G6 36 44 55 S 140 34 54 E

BIG RIG

81 Morambro Creek

A66

Rest Area 26 km N of Naracoorte or 21 km S of Padthaway

HEMA 98 G6 36 44 52 S 140 37 45 E

BIG RIG

82 Padthaway Caravan Park
☎ (08) 8765 5212

Caravan Park at Padthaway. Beeamma Rd, 600m off Riddoch Hwy

HEMA 98 G5 36 35 59 S 140 30 14 E

BIG RIG

83 Padthaway North Rest Area

A66

Rest Area 14 km N of Padthaway or 48 km S of Keith

HEMA 98 F5 36 30 24 S 140 23 36 E

BIG RIG

84 Desert Camp Conservation Reserve

Parking Area 20 km N of Padthaway or 42 km S of Keith

HEMA 98 F5 36 28 0 S 140 21 54 E

BIG RIG

85 Willalooka Roadhouse Rest Area

A66

Rest Area at Willalooka. 34 km S of Keith. Opposite roadhouse

HEMA 98 F5 36 23 34 S 140 21 2 E

BIG RIG

86 Keith South Rest Area

A66

Rest Area 50 km N of Padthaway or 12 km S of Keith

HEMA 98 F5 36 11 39 S 140 20 29 E

BIG RIG

Pinnaroo to Tailem Bend

Mallee Highway

87 Border Rest Area

B12

Rest Area 6 km E of Pinnaroo or 21 km W of Murrayville

HEMA 89 J13 35 14 23 S 140 57 40 E

BIG RIG

88 Pinnaroo Caravan Park
☎ 0430 465 304

B12

Caravan Park at Pinnaroo. Mallee Hwy

HEMA 89 J13 35 15 46 S 140 54 35 E

89 Tailem Bend Rest Area

Rest Area 20 km W of Pinnaroo or 6 km E of Parilla. Both sides of road, share with trucks

HEMA 89 J13 35 17 45 S 140 43 51 E

BIG RIG

90 Parilla Rest Area

B12

Rest Area at Parilla. Opposite Store/PO

HEMA 89 J12 35 17 47 S 140 40 0 E

BIG RIG

91 Karte Conservation Park
☎ (08) 8576 3690

Camp Area 31 km NW of Pinnaroo, via Parilla Well Rd. Bush camping

HEMA 89 H12 35 5 25 S 140 44 12 E

92 Lameroo Caravan Park
☎ (08) 8576 3006

Caravan Park at Lameroo. Bookings, payment & keys at the Lameroo Hotel

HEMA 89 J12 35 19 41 S 140 31 17 E

BIG RIG

93 Baan Hill Soak

Picnic Area 25 km SW of Lameroo. Turn S 8 km W of Lameroo onto Bews South Rd. 19 km dirt road

HEMA 89 J12 35 30 0 S 140 26 19 E

BIG RIG

94 Parrakie East Rest Area

B12

Rest Area 20 km W of Lameroo or 6 km E of Parrakie

HEMA 89 J12 35 21 42 S 140 18 37 E

BIG RIG

95 Geranium Rest Area
Rest Area at Geranium, opposite Geranium turnoff
HEMA 89 J11 35 22 40 S 140 9 42 E
B12

96 Geranium Oval
(08) 8577 2257
Camp Spot at Geranium. Entry off Geranium North Rd. Fee for power
HEMA 89 J11 35 22 45 S 140 9 35 E

97 Peake Rest Area
Rest Area at Peake. Toilets at Hall
HEMA 89 J11 35 21 58 S 139 57 5 E
B12

98 Sherlock Rest Area
Rest Area at Sherlock, opposite hall
HEMA 89 J11 35 19 6 S 139 48 7 E
B12

Bordertown to Pinnaroo

99 Bordertown Recreation Lake
Rest Area at Bordertown, off Golf Course Rd
HEMA 98 F6 36 18 21 S 140 46 31 E

100 Comet Bore Campground
(08) 8576 3690
Ngarkat Conservation Park
Camp Area 61 km S of Pinnaroo or 72 km N of Bordertown
HEMA 98 E6 35 44 38 S 140 48 1 E
B57

101 Pertendi Hut Campground
(08) 8576 3690
Ngarkat Conservation Park
Camp Area 48 km S of Pinnaroo or 84 km N of Bordertown
HEMA 98 E6 35 38 23 S 140 46 35 E
B57

Renmark to Adelaide
Sturt Highway

102 Yamba East Rest Area
Rest Area 119 km W of Mildura or 23 km E of Renmark. 5 km W of VIC/SA border. S area quieter
HEMA 89 F13 34 16 7 S 140 54 13 E
A20

Notes...

103 T Dix Memorial Park
Picnic Area 1 km W of Paringa. SE side of bridge, beside river. Self contained motorhomes only, no caravans, campertrailers or tents
HEMA 89 F13 34 10 59 S 140 46 37 E
A20
12

104 Renmark Swimming Pool Car Park
Parking Area at Renmark. Cnr Cowra & Fifteenth St. In swimming pool car park. Self Contained Motorhomes only
HEMA 89 F13 34 10 8 S 140 44 41 E
24

105 Murtho Forest Landing
(08) 8586 6704
Camp Area 17 km NE of Paringa, via Paringa-Murtho Rd & Headings Rd. 4 km dirt road. Beside river
HEMA 89 F13 34 3 56 S 140 46 49 E

106 Little Gums Campground
(08) 8595 2111
Chowilla Game Reserve
Camp Area 32 km NE of Renmark, via Old Wentworth Rd. Turn S onto signposted road to park entrance (6.5 km). Dirt road. 4WD only. Permit required
HEMA 89 E13 34 0 28 S 140 51 22 E

107 Border Cliffs Campground
(08) 8595 2111
Chowilla Game Reserve
Camp Area 30 km NE of Paringa. Take road E of river, Murtho Rd to campsite. Permit available at general store
HEMA 89 E13 33 58 24 S 140 57 28 E

108 Black Oak Campground
(08) 8595 2111
Danggali Conservation Park
Camp Area 62 km N of Renmark, near Canopus Homestead. Dirt road. Permit required
HEMA 89 D13 33 29 52 S 140 42 20 E

109 Plushs Bend
(08) 8586 6704
Camp Area 6 km S of Renmark. Turn S 2 km SW of Renmark for 4 km along Twenty -Third St. 1 km dirt road. Beside river. Maximum stay 7 days
HEMA 89 F13 34 12 31 S 140 45 15 E

110 T M Price Rotary Park
Rest Area 6 km W of Renmark or 12 km E of Berri. Self Contained Motorhomes only
HEMA 89 F13 34 12 23 S 140 42 10 E
A20
24

111 Black Box Campground
(08) 8595 2111
Murray River National Park
Camp Area 2.5 km NE of Lyrup. Turn S 8 km SW of Renmark or 8 km E of Berri. 3 km dirt road. Bush camping beside river. Low trees. Permit required
HEMA 89 F13 34 14 39 S 140 39 44 E

SOUTH AUSTRALIA

SOUTH AUSTRALIA

112 Tea Tree Campground
(08) 8595 2111
Murray River National Park
Camp Area 1.5 km N of Lyrup. Turn S 9 km SW of Renmark or 6 km E of Berri. Entrance next to ferry crossing. 500m dirt road. Bush camping beside river. Permit required
HEMA 89 F12 | 34 14 57 S | 140 39 7 E

113 S.S. Ellen Park
Rest Area at Lyrup. S side of river. W of ferry crossing. Self Contained Motorhomes Only
HEMA 89 F12 | 34 15 14 S | 140 38 52 E
BIG RIG 72

114 Lyrup Turnoff
A20
Parking Area 12 km W of Renmark or 6 km E of Berri
HEMA 89 F12 | 34 14 14 S | 140 38 33 E
BIG RIG

115 Colligans Campground
(08) 8595 2111
Murray River National Park
Camp Area 17 km W of Renmark. Turn S 12 km W of Renmark (just past Renmark Country Club). Bush camping next to river. 5 km dirt road. Permit required
HEMA 89 F12 | 34 15 14 S | 140 41 49 E
BIG RIG

116 Berri Club
(08) 8582 1697
Parking Area at Berri. Old Stuart Hwy. W side of town. Self Contained Vehicles only. Please register at reception
HEMA 89 F12 | 34 16 56 S | 140 35 22 E
BIG RIG 96

117 Martins Bend Campground
(08) 8582 2423
Camp Area 3 km E of Berri, via Riverview Rd. Beside river. Maximum stay 30 days. Obtain permit from caretaker before set-up
HEMA 89 F12 | 34 17 24 S | 140 37 49 E
BIG RIG

118 Lock 4 Section Katarapko
(08) 8595 2111
Murray River National Park
Camp Area 5 km SW Berri. Via Draper Rd, under Murray River Bridge, 4.5 km dirt road to park entrance. Designated sites. Permit required
HEMA 89 F12 | 34 19 6 S | 140 34 16 E

119 Eckerts Creek Campground
(08) 8595 2111
Murray River National Park
Camp Area 13 km SW of Berri. From Old Sturt Hwy turn S onto Lower Winkie Rd (3.5 km) & E onto Migga Rd taking the R fork to park entry (1 km). Bush camping beside river. Permit required
HEMA 89 F12 | 34 20 9 S | 140 32 47 E

120 Thiele's Sandbar
Camp Area 3.5 km NE of Loxton via Bookpurnong Rd. Turn W at water tower (Tower Dr). At T jcn turn R, 1.5 km dirt track to river. GPS at entry
HEMA 89 F12 | 34 26 29 S | 140 35 1 E
BIG RIG

121 Loxton Motorhome Reserve
(08) 8584 8071
Camp Area at Loxton. Coral St, opposite Loxton Sporting Club. Self Contained Vehicles only. Permit available from Visitor Information Centre. Donation for water
HEMA 89 G12 | 34 27 6 S | 140 34 42 E
BIG RIG 72

122 Rilli Reserve
Camp Spot at Loxton, Briers Rd, bush camping in the reserve
HEMA 89 G12 | 34 23 37 S | 140 34 57 E

123 Paruna Comfort Stop
Caravan Park at Paruna. Railway Tce. Honesty box for fees
HEMA 89 G13 | 34 43 11 S | 140 43 44 E
BIG RIG

124 Mindarie
B55
Parking Area at Mindarie. 500m W of town
HEMA 89 G12 | 34 48 59 S | 140 12 50 E

125 Halidon Rest Area
B55
Rest Area 1 km W of Halidon
HEMA 89 H11 | 34 53 2 S | 140 9 50 E

126 Karoonda East
B55
Parking Area 15 km SW of Borrika or 1 km E of Karoonda
HEMA 89 H11 | 35 5 14 S | 139 54 34 E

127 Perponda Oval
Parking Area at Perponda. 16 km N of Karoonda
HEMA 89 H11 | 34 59 6 S | 139 48 55 E
BIG RIG 24

128 Karoonda Lions Park
B55
Picnic Area at Karoonda
HEMA 89 H11 | 35 5 42 S | 139 53 46 E
BIG RIG

129 Karoonda Apex Caravan Park
(08) 8578 1071
B55
Caravan Park at Karoonda, next to oval
HEMA 89 H11 | 35 5 47 S | 139 53 23 E
BIG RIG

130 Moorook Riverfront Camping Reserve
(08) 8584 7221

Camp Area at Moorook. Loxton Rd, beside Murray River. Honesty box for fees

HEMA 89 F12 | 34 17 17 S | 140 22 6 E

BIG RIG

131 Moorook Game Reserve
(08) 8595 2111

Camp Area 4 km N of Moorook. 1 km dirt road. Bush campsites by river. Permit required

HEMA 89 F12 | 34 15 59 S | 140 22 10 E

132 Kaiser Strip Campground
(08) 8595 2111

Loch Luna Game Reserve

Camp Spot 2 km W of Cobdogla, via Shueard Dr. Various sites either side of Hwy along river. Permit required

HEMA 89 F12 | 34 14 0 S | 140 23 16 E

BIG RIG

133 Kingston-on-Murray Caravan Park
(08) 8583 0209

Caravan Park at Kingston-on-Murray. 461 Holmes Rd

HEMA 89 F12 | 34 13 22 S | 140 21 6 E

BIG RIG

134 Cobdogla Pump Station

Camp Spot 2 km S of Cobdogla. From Shueard Rd turn S onto Park Tce, Schell Rd for 2 km. Turn W across causeway to Pump Station. Camping N & S of station

HEMA 89 F12 | 34 15 45 S | 140 24 2 E

BIG RIG

135 Barmera Lakefront Reserve

Picnic Area at Barmera

HEMA 89 F12 | 34 14 59 S | 140 27 33 E

BIG RIG

136 Bruce Oval

Camp Spot at Barmera. Sims St. Pay at Visitor Information Centre. Self Contained Vehicles only

HEMA 89 F12 | 34 15 13 S | 140 28 3 E

BIG RIG 96

137 Lake Bonney Reserve
(08) 8582 1922

Camp Area 11 km NW of Barmera, via Morgan Rd, Nappers Bridge & Queen Elizabeth Dr. 200m E of Nappers Bridge, beside lake. Sandy area, walk in first to check

HEMA 89 F12 | 34 11 43 S | 140 25 37 E

138 Campground 10
(08) 8595 2111

Loch Luna Game Reserve

Camp Area 18 km NW of Barmera, via Morgan Rd. 7 km W of Nappers Bridge. Dirt road. Bush camping by Chambers Ck. Other sites available, signposted

HEMA 89 F12 | 34 13 20 S | 140 23 39 E

139 Heron Bend

Overland Corner Conservation Reserve

Camp Spot at Overland Corner. 1.2 km W of Overland Corner Hotel. Bush camping by river

HEMA 89 F12 | 34 9 18 S | 140 20 10 E

140 Morgan East Rest Area 1

B64

Rest Area 12 km W of Overland Corner or 57 km E of Morgan

HEMA 89 F12 | 34 9 1 S | 140 13 0 E

BIG RIG

141 Pooginook Conservation Park
(08) 8595 2111

Camp Area 45 km E of Morgan or 43 km W of B64/ Sturt Hwy jcn. Sign posted, 1.9 km N to campsite. GPS at entrance

HEMA 89 F11 | 34 8 21 S | 140 7 17 E

142 Morgan East Rest Area 2

B64

Rest Area 44 km W of Overland Corner or 25 km E of Morgan. Both sides of Hwy

HEMA 89 E11 | 34 3 29 S | 139 53 52 E

143 Cadell Recreation Ground
0497 799 284

Camp Area at Cadell, via Heinrich, Dalzell Roads. Caretaker on site. Fee for showers

HEMA 89 E11 | 34 2 16 S | 139 45 26 E

144 Police Heritage Monument Rest Area

A20

Rest Area 20 km W of Barmera or 29 km E of Waikerie

HEMA 89 F11 | 34 11 39 S | 140 17 15 E

BIG RIG

145 Lowbank Landing

A20

Camp Spot 10 km E of Waikerie. Turn N off Sturt Hwy into Lowbank Rd (dirt). Follow to riverbank

HEMA 89 F11 | 34 11 1 S | 140 4 8 E

BIG RIG

146 Maize Island Lagoon Conservation Park
(08) 8595 2111

Camp Area 7 km E of Waikerie. Turn N 3 km E of Waikerie onto Holder Top Rd for 4 km. Turn R at T intersection, then take R fork dirt road. Bush camping along river bank

HEMA 89 F11 | 34 9 58 S | 140 0 42 E

147 Holder Bend Reserve & Boat Ramp

Camp Spot 5 km E of Waikerie. Turn N 3 km E of Waikerie onto Holder Top Rd (300m), NW onto Holder Bottom Rd (1 km), then W into Reserve via dirt road. Camping along river bank

HEMA 89 F11 | 34 11 4 S | 140 0 48 E

BIG RIG

Notes...

148 Lions Riverfront Park

Picnic Area at Waikerie. Leonard Norman Dr

HEMA 89 F11 34 10 30 S 139 59 7 E

BIG RIG

149 Ricciuto Creek

Camp Spot 4 km NW Waikerie. Turn N onto Ricciuto Rd for 400m then NW onto track to river

HEMA 89 F11 34 9 49 S 139 57 2 E

150 Hogwash Bend

☎ (08) 8541 2332

Picnic Area 25 km NW of Waikerie or 22 km E of Morgan, via Morgan-Waikerie Rd. Turn N 23 km NW of Waikerie or 20 km E of Morgan. 2 km dirt road. Bush camping by river

HEMA 89 F11 34 3 55 S 139 51 12 E

151 Cordola Camping Area - Pelican Point

Camp Area 11 km SW of Morgan. Turn S off B81 onto Blanchetown Rd for 8.5 km then turn E onto Pelican Point Rd for 2 km. S into property gate (500m). Follow River Rd to camp spots along river. Honesty box

HEMA 89 F10 34 7 47 S 139 39 54 E

BIG RIG

152 Morgan Conservation Park

☎ (08) 8595 2111

Northern Section

Camp Area 1 km E of Morgan, via Old Cadell Rd. 600m N of ferry crossing, E side of river. Dirt road. Permit required

HEMA 89 E11 34 2 3 S 139 40 40 E

$

153 Morgan Conservation Park

☎ (08) 8595 2111

Southern Section

Camp Area 1.6 km E of Morgan. 1.2 km S of ferry crossing, E side of river. Dirt road. Small area only. Permit required

HEMA 89 E11 34 2 43 S 139 41 4 E

$

154 Morgan West

B81

Parking Area 7 km W of Morgan or 26 km E of Bower

HEMA 89 F10 34 3 52 S 139 35 9 E

155 Mount Mary Hotel

☎ (08) 8581 0581

B81

Camp Area at Mount Mary Hotel. 22 km W of Morgan or 11 km E of Bower. Limited powered sites

HEMA 89 F10 34 6 16 S 139 26 22 E

$

156 Bower Reserve

B81

Camp Area at Bower. Next to tennis court. Fee for power. Honesty box near BBQ

HEMA 89 F10 34 7 23 S 139 21 11 E

$ BIG RIG

157 Stockyard Plain Rest Area

A20

Rest Area 20 km SW of Waikerie or 22 km NE of Blanchetown

HEMA 89 F11 34 15 55 S 139 48 21 E

BIG RIG

158 Eight Mile Corner

A20

Parking Area 16 km W of Blanchetown or 31 km E of Truro

HEMA 89 F10 34 23 22 S 139 27 41 E

BIG RIG

159 Truro East Rest Area

A20

Rest Area 8 km E of Truro or 38 km W of Blanchetown

HEMA 89 F10 34 24 9 S 139 12 47 E

BIG RIG

160 Truro Rest Area

A20

Rest Area 1 km E of Truro

HEMA 89 F10 34 24 30 S 139 8 9 E

BIG RIG

161 Truro Hotel

☎ (08) 8564 0218

Camp Spot at Hotel. Check in with publican

HEMA 89 F9 34 24 29 S 139 7 28 E

162 Eudunda

B81

Parking Area W side of Eudunda. Kupunda Rd

HEMA 89 F9 34 10 41 S 139 4 53 E

20

163 Stockwell Rest Area

A20

Rest Area 6 km E of Nuriootpa or 9 km W of Truro

HEMA 86 B7 34 25 31 S 139 3 27 E

164 Greenock Oval

Camp Aea at Greenock. Entry off Martin Lane, small fee

HEMA 86 B6 34 27 32 S 138 55 43 E

$ 24

165 Hamley Bridge Community & Sports Centre

Parking Area at Hamley Bridge, entry off Stockport Rd

HEMA 86 A3 34 21 14 S 138 40 53 E

BIG RIG 48

166 Adelaide Soaring Club

☎ (08) 8522 1877

Camp Area at Gawler. Ward Belt Rd beside Gawler Bypass Rd

HEMA 86 D3 34 35 31 S 138 43 47 E

$+ BIG RIG

Blanchetown to Murray Bridge

167 Swan Reach Caravan Park

☎ (08) 8570 2010

Caravan Park at Swan Reach. Victoria St

HEMA 89 G10 34 34 5 S 139 35 46 E

$+ BIG RIG

168 Len White Reserve

Picnic Area at Swan Reach. Just W of town over 12 tonne limit bridge

HEMA 89 G10 34 33 59 S 139 35 42 E

BIG RIG

169 Tenbury - Hunter Reserve
☎ (08) 8569 0100

Camp Spot at Swan Reach, take ferry N across to W side of river. Bush camping on river bank. 500m E of ferry crossing

HEMA 89 G10 | 34 33 43 S | 139 36 1 E

BIG RIG 96

170 Big Bend River

Camp Spot 6 km S of Swan Reach or 17 km N of Nildottie, turn W onto Old Loxton Rd, dirt road for 4 km, bush camping beside Murry River

HEMA 89 G10 | 34 38 12 S | 139 36 50 E

BIG RIG 48

171 Big Bend Lookout

Rest Area 10 km S of Swan Reach or 5 km N of Nildottie. E side of river

HEMA 89 G10 | 34 37 56 S | 139 39 56 E

BIG RIG

172 Len Kroehn Lookout

Parking Area 8 km S of Nildottie or 6 km N of Walker Flat turnoff. E side of river

HEMA 89 G10 | 34 42 13 S | 139 35 16 E

BIG RIG

173 Forster Lookout

Parking Area 1 km E of Walker Flat (ferry crossing). E side of river. Walkers Flat Rd

HEMA 89 G10 | 34 45 19 S | 139 34 18 E

BIG RIG 20

174 Swan Reach Conservation Park
☎ (08) 8576 3690

Camp Spot 14 km W of Swan Reach or 16 km E of Sedan. 2 km of dirt road S of Hwy

HEMA 89 G10 | 34 34 29 S | 139 28 44 E

175 Sedan Hotel
☎ (08) 8565 2252

Parking Area at Sedan. Area at rear of hotel, check in with the publican. Self Contained Vehicles only. Fee for power

HEMA 89 G10 | 34 34 23 S | 139 17 41 E

176 Punyelroo Caravan Park
☎ (08) 8570 2021

Caravan Park 10 km S of Swan Reach. W side of river. 7 km dirt road

HEMA 89 G10 | 34 36 13 S | 139 36 8 E

BIG RIG

177 Wongulla Boat Ramp

Picnic Area 10 km N of Walker Flat ferry crossing, via Mt Pleasant Rd & Mongulla Rd. W side of river. 8 km dirt road

HEMA 89 G10 | 34 42 29 S | 139 34 19 E

178 John S Christian Reserve
☎ (08) 8569 0100

Camp Spot 19 km NW of Walker Flat, via Walker Flat- Mt Pleasant Rd (10 km), Mannum-Swan Reach Rd (5 km N) & Black Hill Rd (4 km W). 9 km dirt road

HEMA 89 G10 | 34 41 56 S | 139 29 12 E

179 Walker Flat Boat Ramp Reserve
☎ (08) 8569 0100

Camp Spot at Walker Flat. 1 km N of ferry crossing on W side of river. Dirt road

HEMA 89 G10 | 34 45 8 S | 139 33 43 E

BIG RIG

180 Hettner Landing
☎ (08) 8569 0100

Camp Spot at Walker Flat. Bush camping 50m N of General Store. Access track opposite Walkers Flat Rd

HEMA 89 G10 | 34 45 1 S | 139 33 16 E

181 Caurnamont Reserve
☎ (08) 8569 0100

Parking Area at Caurnamont. 100m N of Purnong ferry crossing on W side of river

HEMA 89 G10 | 34 51 17 S | 139 36 55 E

182 Caurnamont North

Camp Spot 3.5 km N of Purnong Ferry on W side of river

HEMA 89 G10 | 34 50 32 S | 139 35 11 E

BIG RIG

183 Lakeside Camping Ground
☎ (08) 8570 4309

Camp Area 5.5 km SE of Caurnamont Ferry. From ferry follow road through Caurnamont for 3.5 km. Turn SE into Craignook Rd. 2 km dirt road

HEMA 89 G10 | 34 51 25 S | 139 36 28 E

184 Purnong Reserve
☎ (08) 8569 0100

Parking Area at Purnong. E side of river, beside ferry crossing

HEMA 89 G10 | 34 51 15 S | 139 37 1 E

BIG RIG

185 Haythorpe Reserve
☎ (08) 8569 0100

Parking Area 1 km NE of Mannum, on Bowhill Rd. E side of river. N of ferry crossing.

HEMA 89 H10 | 34 54 33 S | 139 19 24 E

186 Bolto Reserve
☎ (08) 8569 0100

Parking Area 1 km SE of Mannum, via Khartoum Rd. E side of river. S of ferry crossing. Maximum stay 5 nights

HEMA 89 H10 | 34 54 54 S | 139 18 58 E

BIG RIG

187 Marne River Reserve

Picnic Area 1.7 km S of Cambrai or 34 km N of Mannum

HEMA 89 G10 | 34 39 59 S | 139 16 56 E

BIG RIG

Notes...

SOUTH AUSTRALIA

Adelaide Greater Area

188 Williamstown Queen Victoria Jubilee Park
☎ (08) 8524 6363

Caravan Park at Williamstown. Springton Rd. 1 km E of PO

HEMA 86 E5 | 34 40 26 S | 138 54 15 E

BIG RIG

189 Rocky Paddock Campground
☎ (08) 8521 1700

Mount Crawford Forest

Camp Area 8 km SE of Williamstown, via Warren Rd. 1 km S of Forest Info Centre, via Tower Rd. Permit required. Closed 01 December - 31 March, fire season

HEMA 86 F6 | 34 43 1 S | 138 56 26 E

190 Murray Recreation Park

Caravan Park at Eden Valley. On the Eden Valley-Springton Rd. 1.2 km S of PO

HEMA 86 E7 | 34 39 15 S | 139 6 7 E

BIG RIG

191 Totness Inn Hotel
☎ (08) 8568 2346

Parking Area at Mount Pleasant. 143 Melrose St in the middle of town. Check in with manager at bar, toilet only open during hotel hours. Self Contained Vehicles only

HEMA 86 F7 | 34 46 18 S | 139 3 7 E

20

192 Talunga Park Caravan Park (Showgrounds)
☎ (08) 8568 1934

Caravan Park at Mount Pleasant. Melrose St. At showground

HEMA 86 F7 | 34 46 34 S | 139 2 34 E

BIG RIG

193 Mount Torrens Hotel
☎ (08) 8389 4252

Parking Area at Mount Torrens. Check in with publican, limited parking for Self Contained Vehicles only. Toilet access only during pub hours

HEMA 86 H6 | 34 52 32 S | 138 57 31 E

24

194 Cudlee Creek Tavern Caravan Park
☎ (08) 8389 2270

Caravan Park at Cudlee Creek, 30 km E of Adelaide. Gorge Rd

HEMA 83 G13 | 34 50 23 S | 138 48 58 E

195 Strathalbyn Caravan Park
☎ (08) 8536 3681

Caravan Park at Strathalbyn. Ashbourne Rd

B45

HEMA 89 H9 | 35 15 33 S | 138 53 9 E

BIG RIG

196 Frank Potts Reserve

Rest Area 1 km E of Langhorne Creek

HEMA 89 J9 | 35 17 56 S | 139 2 33 E

BIG RIG

197 Tolderol Game Reserve
☎ (08) 8575 1200

Camp Area 14 km SE of Langhorne Creek, via Langhorne Creek-Wellington Rd & Dog Lake Rd. Turn S 5 km E of Langhorne Creek. Dirt road. Permit required

HEMA 89 J9 | 35 22 31 S | 139 8 55 E

198 Milang Foreshore

Picnic Area at Milang. Coin-operated showers

HEMA 89 J9 | 35 24 26 S | 138 58 29 E

199 Clayton Bay Beach Rest Area

Picnic Area at Clayton

HEMA 89 J9 | 35 29 48 S | 138 55 25 E

BIG RIG

200 Currency Creek Lions Park

Picnic Area at Currency Creek

HEMA 87 F7 | 35 27 16 S | 138 45 31 E

201 Briston-Smith Park

Picnic Area at Goolwa South

HEMA 87 G7 | 35 30 51 S | 138 47 4 E

BIG RIG

202 Chookarloo Campground
☎ (08) 8391 8800

Kuitpo Forest Reserve

Camp Area 5 km SW of Meadows. Permit available from Kuitpo Forest Info Centre. Closed December to March

HEMA 87 C7 | 35 12 15 S | 138 42 55 E

BIG RIG

203 Mount Compass

Parking Area at Mount Compass, cnr Victor Harbour & Nangkita Rds

HEMA 87 E6 | 35 20 50 S | 138 37 17 E

BIG RIG 20

204 Kent Reserve

Picnic Area 2 km S of Victor Harbor, via Bay Rd & Harbour View Tce

HEMA 87 H6 | 35 33 50 S | 138 36 44 E

BIG RIG

205 Waitpinga Campground
☎ (08) 8552 3677

Newland Head Conservation Park

Camp Area 17 km SE of Victor Harbour. Access via Waitpinga Rd. Small vehicles only, not suitable for caravans

HEMA 87 H5 | 35 37 41 S | 138 29 59 E

206 Stringybark Campground ☎ (08) 8598 0263
Deep Creek Conservation Park
Camp Area 9 km SE of Delamere, via Tapanappa Rd. Dirt road. Permit required
HEMA 87 H2 35 36 24 S 138 14 20 E

207 Trig Campground ☎ (08) 8598 0263
Deep Creek Conservation Park
Camp Area 12 km S of Delamere, via Tent Rock Rd. Dirt road. Permit required
HEMA 87 J2 35 38 59 S 138 12 54 E

208 Rapid Bay Camping Area ☎ (08) 8598 3003
Camp Area at Rapid Bay. Outside cold shower
HEMA 87 G2 35 31 29 S 138 11 30 E
BIG RIG

209 Cape Jervis Station Caravan & Camping ☎ (08) 8598 0288
Camp Area at Cape Jervis Station. Main South Rd
HEMA 87 H1 35 36 19 S 138 7 41 E

Broken Hill to Adelaide

Barrier Highway

210 Cockburn Village ☎ (08) 8091 1999
Caravan Park in Cockburn. Elder Tce
HEMA 95 G13 32 4 41 S 140 59 48 E
BIG RIG

211 Mingary Siding
A32
Rest Area 25 km SW of Cockburn or 42 km NE of Olary
HEMA 95 G13 32 7 43 S 140 44 27 E
BIG RIG

212 Cutana Rest Area
A32
Rest Area 32 km SW of Cockburn or 35 km NE of Olary. Both sides of the road
HEMA 95 G13 32 11 10 S 140 34 56 E
BIG RIG

213 Olary Creek
A32
Rest Area 2 km E of Olary. 65 km SW of Cockburn or 39 km NE of Mannahill
HEMA 95 H12 32 16 8 S 140 20 46 E

Notes...

214 Olary Rest Area
A32
Rest Area at Olary
HEMA 95 H12 32 16 53 S 140 19 39 E
BIG RIG 20

215 Wawirra Creek
A32
Parking Area 26 km SW of Olary or 11 km NE of Mannahill
HEMA 95 H12 32 23 52 S 140 5 38 E
BIG RIG

216 Mannahill Rest Area
A32
Rest Area at Mannahill. 38 km SW of Olary or 44 km NE of Yunta. Donation welcomed
HEMA 95 H11 32 25 51 S 139 59 12 E
BIG RIG

217 Winnininnie Creek
A32
Rest Area 36 km SW of Mannahill or 9 km NE of Yunta
HEMA 95 H11 32 32 38 S 139 39 21 E
BIG RIG

218 Yunta Centennial Park ☎ (08) 8650 5009
A32
Rest Area at Yunta. Next to Telecentre on Hwy
HEMA 95 H10 32 34 54 S 139 33 46 E
20

219 Nackara East
A32
Parking Area 35 km SW of Yunta or 25 km NE of Oodla Wirra. W side of road
HEMA 95 J10 32 46 3 S 139 17 13 E
BIG RIG

220 Oodla Wirra Rest Area
A32
Rest Area 4 km SW of Oodla Wirra or 7 km NE of Hwy 56 jcn
HEMA 95 J9 32 53 58 S 139 2 40 E
BIG RIG

221 Terowie Railway Yard
Camp Spot at Terowie at the old railway siding. Railway Tce. Toilets in Main St
HEMA 89 C9 33 9 1 S 138 55 17 E
BIG RIG

222 Mount Bryan Rest Area
A32
Rest Area 16 km N of Burra or 16 km S of Hallett. Opposite Mount Bryan Hotel
HEMA 89 D9 33 33 1 S 138 53 32 E
BIG RIG

223 Hallett Recreation Area ☎ (08) 8894 2078
Parking Area at Hallett. Entry off West Tce. Pay fee & collect key from Mini Mart. AH pay & get key from Hotel
HEMA 89 D9 33 24 34 S 138 53 28 E
BIG RIG 96

224 Spalding Junction Rest Area
A32
Rest Area 9 km N of Burra or 7 km S of Mount Bryan
HEMA 89 D9 33 36 49 S 138 53 41 E
BIG RIG

SOUTH AUSTRALIA

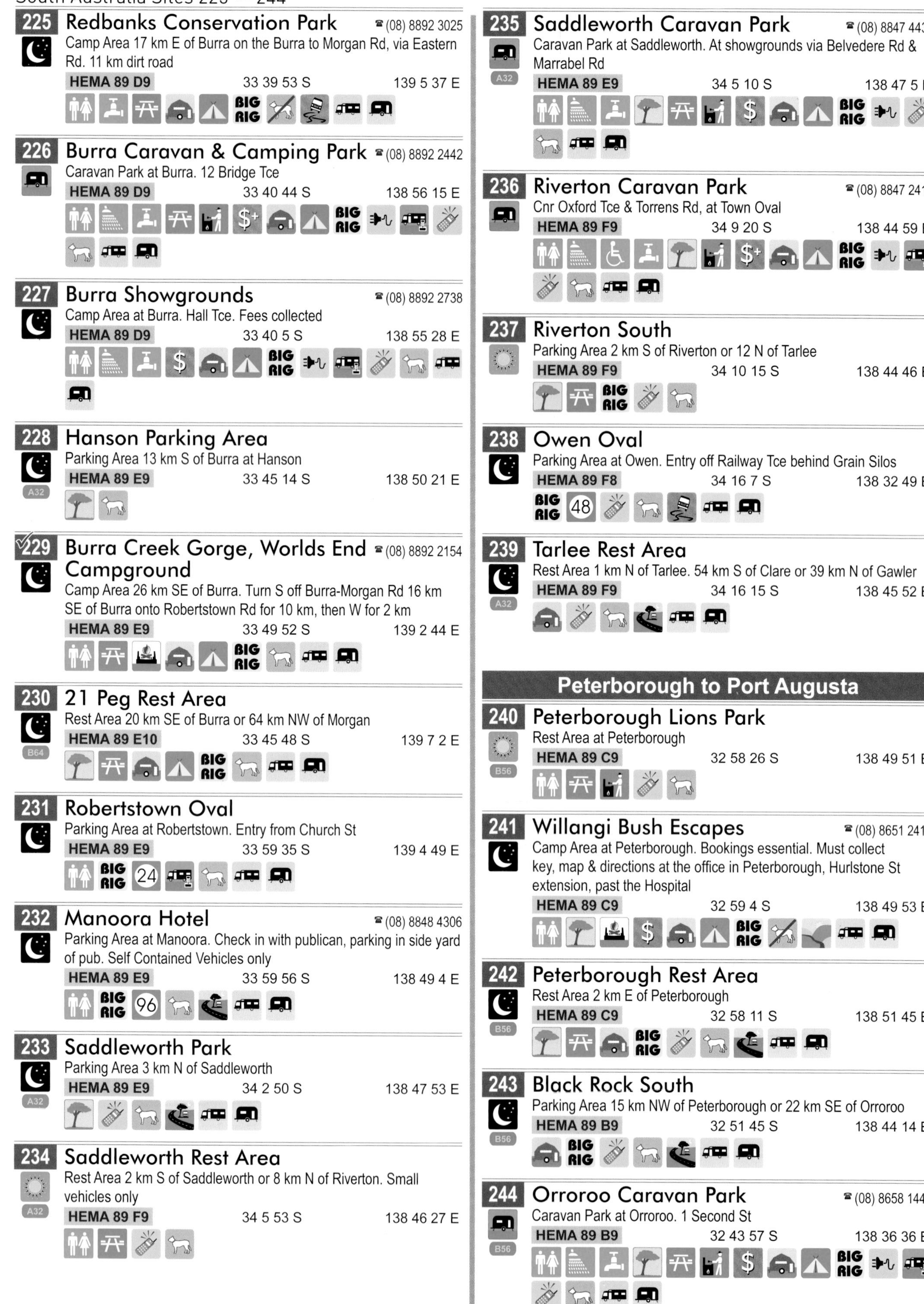

225 Redbanks Conservation Park
(08) 8892 3025
Camp Area 17 km E of Burra on the Burra to Morgan Rd, via Eastern Rd. 11 km dirt road
HEMA 89 D9 33 39 53 S 139 5 37 E
BIG RIG

226 Burra Caravan & Camping Park
(08) 8892 2442
Caravan Park at Burra. 12 Bridge Tce
HEMA 89 D9 33 40 44 S 138 56 15 E
BIG RIG

227 Burra Showgrounds
(08) 8892 2738
Camp Area at Burra. Hall Tce. Fees collected
HEMA 89 D9 33 40 5 S 138 55 28 E
BIG RIG

228 Hanson Parking Area
A32
Parking Area 13 km S of Burra at Hanson
HEMA 89 E9 33 45 14 S 138 50 21 E

229 Burra Creek Gorge, Worlds End Campground
(08) 8892 2154
Camp Area 26 km SE of Burra. Turn S off Burra-Morgan Rd 16 km SE of Burra onto Robertstown Rd for 10 km, then W for 2 km
HEMA 89 E9 33 49 52 S 139 2 44 E
BIG RIG

230 21 Peg Rest Area
B64
Rest Area 20 km SE of Burra or 64 km NW of Morgan
HEMA 89 E10 33 45 48 S 139 7 2 E
BIG RIG

231 Robertstown Oval
Parking Area at Robertstown. Entry from Church St
HEMA 89 E9 33 59 35 S 139 4 49 E
BIG RIG 24

232 Manoora Hotel
(08) 8848 4306
Parking Area at Manoora. Check in with publican, parking in side yard of pub. Self Contained Vehicles only
HEMA 89 E9 33 59 56 S 138 49 4 E
BIG RIG 96

233 Saddleworth Park
A32
Parking Area 3 km N of Saddleworth
HEMA 89 E9 34 2 50 S 138 47 53 E

234 Saddleworth Rest Area
A32
Rest Area 2 km S of Saddleworth or 8 km N of Riverton. Small vehicles only
HEMA 89 F9 34 5 53 S 138 46 27 E

235 Saddleworth Caravan Park
(08) 8847 4439
A32
Caravan Park at Saddleworth. At showgrounds via Belvedere Rd & Marrabel Rd
HEMA 89 E9 34 5 10 S 138 47 5 E
BIG RIG

236 Riverton Caravan Park
(08) 8847 2419
Cnr Oxford Tce & Torrens Rd, at Town Oval
HEMA 89 F9 34 9 20 S 138 44 59 E
BIG RIG

237 Riverton South
Parking Area 2 km S of Riverton or 12 N of Tarlee
HEMA 89 F9 34 10 15 S 138 44 46 E
BIG RIG

238 Owen Oval
Parking Area at Owen. Entry off Railway Tce behind Grain Silos
HEMA 89 F8 34 16 7 S 138 32 49 E
BIG RIG 48

239 Tarlee Rest Area
A32
Rest Area 1 km N of Tarlee. 54 km S of Clare or 39 km N of Gawler
HEMA 89 F9 34 16 15 S 138 45 52 E

Peterborough to Port Augusta

240 Peterborough Lions Park
B56
Rest Area at Peterborough
HEMA 89 C9 32 58 26 S 138 49 51 E

241 Willangi Bush Escapes
(08) 8651 2410
Camp Area at Peterborough. Bookings essential. Must collect key, map & directions at the office in Peterborough, Hurlstone St extension, past the Hospital
HEMA 89 C9 32 59 4 S 138 49 53 E
BIG RIG

242 Peterborough Rest Area
B56
Rest Area 2 km E of Peterborough
HEMA 89 C9 32 58 11 S 138 51 45 E
BIG RIG

243 Black Rock South
B56
Parking Area 15 km NW of Peterborough or 22 km SE of Orroroo
HEMA 89 B9 32 51 45 S 138 44 14 E
BIG RIG

244 Orroroo Caravan Park
(08) 8658 1444
B56
Caravan Park at Orroroo. 1 Second St
HEMA 89 B9 32 43 57 S 138 36 36 E
BIG RIG

245 Bendleby Ranges Bush Camping & Accommodation
☎ (08) 8658 9064

Camp Area 50 km N of Orroroo. Take Jonburgh Rd for 42 km, turn E onto Crotta Rd. 8 km to Station. Bookings required

HEMA 89 A9 | 32 21 15 S | 138 47 33 E

246 Orroroo Rest Area

B56

Rest Area 8 km W of Orroroo or 5 km E of Morchard

HEMA 89 B8 | 32 44 2 S | 138 32 13 E

BIG RIG

247 Horseshoe View Caravan Park
☎ (08) 8658 9090

B80

Caravan Park at Carrieton. Fourth St

HEMA 89 A8 | 32 25 29 S | 138 31 55 E

BIG RIG

248 Almerta Station
☎ (08) 8658 9076

Camp Area at Almerta Station. 18 km N of Carrieton or 65 km S of Hawker on the RM Williams Way. Turn W 12 km N of Carrieton onto Carrieton Quorn Rd, 6 km dirt road. Signposted.

HEMA 89 A8 | 32 17 2 S | 138 27 24 E

249 Wilmington Centenary Park

B56

Rest Area at Wilmington. E end of town

HEMA 89 B8 | 32 39 13 S | 138 6 6 E

250 Stony Creek Bush Camp Caravan Park
☎ 0488 156 850

Caravan Park 4 km E of Wilmington, via Second St & Stony Creek Rd. 1 km dirt road

HEMA 89 B8 | 32 38 54 S | 138 8 6 E

BIG RIG

251 Hancocks Lookout

Camp Spot 13 km W of Wilmington. Turn S off Horrocks Pass Rd 3 km W of Wilmington or 40 km SE of Port Augusta. 7 km dirt road

HEMA 88 B7 | 32 42 21 S | 138 1 37 E

BIG RIG

252 Horrocks Pass

B56

Parking Area 7 km NW of Wilmington or 36 km SE of Port Augusta

HEMA 88 B7 | 32 38 29 S | 138 2 15 E

BIG RIG

Notes...

253 Spear Creek Caravan Park
☎ 0428 822 644

Caravan Park 25 km SE of Port Augusta. On Old Wilmington Rd

HEMA 88 B7 | 32 34 10 S | 137 59 23 E

BIG RIG

Adelaide to Port Augusta

254 St Kilda Adventure Park

Parking Area at St Kilda, Cockle St, check in at Tackle & Tucker Store for permit. Self Contained Vehicles only

HEMA 82 C3 | 34 44 31 S | 138 32 0 E

BIG RIG 24

255 Mallala Sports Ground

A1

Camp Area at Mallala. Wasleys Rd. 200m E of PO. Fee for showers

HEMA 86 B1 | 34 26 18 S | 138 30 49 E

BIG RIG

256 Port Parham Foreshore

Camp Spot at Port Parham, on the Esplanade. Limit 5 Tonne

HEMA 89 F8 | 34 25 34 S | 138 15 20 E

257 Dublin Lions Park

Rest Area at Dublin. Old Port Wakefield Rd

HEMA 89 F8 | 34 27 7 S | 138 21 5 E

BIG RIG

258 Dublin North Rest Area

A1

Rest Area 21 km N of Dublin or 14 km S of Port Wakefield. Northbound only

HEMA 89 F8 | 34 17 29 S | 138 14 30 E

BIG RIG

259 Port Wakefield South Rest Area

A1

Rest Area 25 km N of Dublin or 10 km S of Port Wakefield. Southbound only

HEMA 89 F8 | 34 15 19 S | 138 13 22 E

260 Port Wakefield Caravan Park
☎ (08) 8867 1151

Caravan Park at Port Wakefield. Wakefield St

HEMA 89 F8 | 34 11 10 S | 138 8 44 E

BIG RIG

261 Balaklava Caravan Park
☎ 0400 264 075

Caravan Park at Balaklava. Short Tce. Next to swimming pool

HEMA 89 F8 | 34 8 57 S | 138 25 8 E

BIG RIG

262 Rocks Reserve

Picnic Area 12 km E of Balaklava or 15 km N of Owen. Turn NE 8 km SE of Balaklava or 11 km NW of Owen at Hoskin Corner. 4 km dirt road

HEMA 89 F8 | 34 10 4 S | 138 31 8 E

263 Lochiel Memorial Hall
Parking Area at Lochiel. Princes Hwy next to Hotel N end of town. Self Contained Vehicles only
HEMA 89 E8 33 55 37 S 138 9 40 E
BIG RIG 48

264 Snowtown Centenary Park Caravan Park
(08) 8865 2252
Caravan Park at Snowtown. North Tce. See notice board for payment details & keys
HEMA 89 E8 33 46 42 S 138 12 59 E

265 Snowtown (North) Rest Area
A1
Rest Area 3 km N of Snowtown or 13 km S of Lake View
HEMA 89 E8 33 44 45 S 138 12 36 E

266 Redhill RV Area
(08) 8636 7020
A1
Camp Area at Redhill. On Ellis St between railway line & Mundoora Tce. Gold coin donation appreciated drop at Redhill Corner Store. Self Contained Vehicles only. Toilets 100m from site
HEMA 89 D8 33 32 16 S 138 13 10 E
BIG RIG 48

267 Bunyip Park
Camp Area at Koolunga. 45 km NE of Clare or 11 km SW of Red Hill. Park at S end of town. Limited power sites. Key from garage or hotel
HEMA 89 D8 33 35 20 S 138 20 1 E
$ 24

268 White Cliffs Reserve
Camp Spot 5 km E of Koolunga, via Koolunga-Yacka Rd. Dirt road
HEMA 89 D8 33 35 29 S 138 23 38 E

269 Merriton Rest Area
A1
Rest Area 2 km N of Merriton or 8 km SW of Crystal Brook
HEMA 89 D8 33 24 59 S 138 9 36 E
BIG RIG

270 Crystal Brook Caravan Park
(08) 8636 2640
Caravan Park at Crystal Brook. Eyre Rd. 1 km N of PO
HEMA 89 D8 33 20 48 S 138 12 13 E

271 Jubilee Park
Rest Area at Crystal Brook. Railway Tce. Self Contained Vehicles only
HEMA 89 D8 33 21 13 S 138 12 23 E
BIG RIG 24

272 Bowman Park
Parking Area 5 km NE of Crystalbrook, via Huddlestone Rd & Bowman Park Dr. Self Contained Vehicles only
HEMA 89 D8 33 19 54 S 138 14 24 E
48

273 Rangeview Caravan & Cabin Park
(08) 8634 4221
A1
Caravan Park at Port Pirie. Hwy A1
HEMA 88 C7 33 10 6 S 138 4 6 E
BIG RIG

274 Port Pirie Overnight Parking Area
(08) 8633 9777
Parking Area at Port Pirie. Warnertown Rd, E of Globe Oval, in service lane. Self Contained Vehicles only. Limited spaces
HEMA 88 C7 33 11 14 S 138 1 43 E
BIG RIG 24

275 Lawrie Park
Camp Spot 10 km NE of Port Pirie. Turn E off Port Augusta Hwy onto Nelshaby Rd for 5 km then E onto Flinders View Dr. Signposted. Self Contained Vehicles only
HEMA 95 K8 33 7 43 S 138 6 37 E
BIG RIG 48

276 Port Germein South Rest Area 2
A1
Rest Area 21 km N of Port Pirie turnoff or 4 km S of Port Germein turnoff. Northbound only
HEMA 88 C7 33 2 46 S 138 1 51 E
BIG RIG

277 Port Germein South Rest Area 1
A1
Rest Area 22 km N of Port Pirie turnoff or 3 km S of Port Germein turnoff. Southbound only
HEMA 88 C7 33 2 31 S 138 1 48 E
BIG RIG

278 Port Germein Foreshore
Picnic Area at Port Germein. N side of jetty
HEMA 88 C7 33 1 21 S 137 59 55 E
BIG RIG

279 Port Germein Caravan Park
(08) 8634 5266
Caravan Park at Port Germein. Cnr High St & The Esplanade
HEMA 88 C7 33 1 21 S 138 0 0 E
BIG RIG

280 Germein Gorge
Parking Area 9 km E of Port Germein turnoff, 20 km W of Murray Town or 17 km W of B82 Hwy jcn. 200m S along Telowie Gorge Rd
HEMA 89 C8 32 59 7 S 138 4 52 E

281 Barootta Rodeo Ground & Camping Area
0427 878 017
Camp Area near Baroota, 6 km N of Port Germein turnoff or 14 km S of Mambray Creek Roadhouse. 1 km W of Hwy. Dirt road. Call the number if the gate locked to gain access
HEMA 88 C7 32 57 39 S 137 58 33 E
$ BIG RIG

282 Mambray Creek Rest Area

Rest Area at Mambray Creek. 46 km S of Port Augusta or 21 km N of Port Germein. E side of road

A1

HEMA 88 B7 32 50 47 S 137 58 55 E

BIG RIG

283 Mambray Creek Campground ☎ (08) 8634 7068

Mount Remarkable National Park

Camp Area 26 km NE of Port Germein. Turn E 46 km S of Port Augusta or 21 km N Port Germein. Signposted

HEMA 88 B7 32 50 26 S 138 2 14 E

284 Bird Lake

Picnic Area 4 km SE of Port Augusta. Power Station Rd

A1

HEMA 88 A7 32 30 31 S 137 47 17 E

BIG RIG

Gawler to Wilmington

Main North Road

285 Auburn Caravan Park ☎ 0417 550 781

Caravan Park at Auburn. Turn E into Ford St. Signposted

B82

HEMA 89 E9 34 1 42 S 138 41 30 E

BIG RIG

286 Leasingham Village Cabins & Caravan Park ☎ (08) 8843 0136

Caravan Park at Leasingham. 6 km N of Auburn or 14 km S of Clare. Main North Rd

B82

HEMA 89 E9 33 58 56 S 138 39 1 E

287 Farrell Flat Oval

Parking Area at Farrell Flat. Entry off Cameron Tce. Self Contained Vehicles only

HEMA 89 E9 33 49 40 S 138 47 36 E

BIG RIG 24

288 Blyth Oval

Parking Area at Blyth. Entry off South Tce

HEMA 89 E8 33 50 53 S 138 29 24 E

48

Notes...

289 Clare Valley Racecourse ☎ (08) 8842 1033

Camp Area at Clare. Main North Rd heading N, entrance off Stradbroke Rd. Must make an advance booking to stay. Limited 10amp power outlet

HEMA 89 E8 33 47 13 S 138 35 16 E

BIG RIG 48

290 Brinkworth Travellers Overnight Stay ☎ (08) 8846 2152

Camp Area at Brinkworth. Turn E onto Edgar St. Entry off East Tce (next to entrance to the bowling club). Payment & key at the Junction Hotel

HEMA 89 D8 33 41 33 S 138 24 18 E

BIG RIG 72

291 Yackamoorundie Park ☎ (08) 8846 4077

Camp Spot at Yacka. N side of town on banks of Broughton River. Cnr of Main N Rd & North Tce. Key required, see info on gate

B82

HEMA 89 D8 33 34 6 S 138 26 43 E

BIG RIG

292 Gulnare Hotel ☎ (08) 8662 6202

Camp Spot at Gulnare. 18 Railway Tce

HEMA 89 D8 33 28 4 S 138 26 35 E

293 James Ainsworth Horrock Monument Rest Area

Rest Area 5 km N of turnoff to Gulnare. 1.5 km S of Crystal Brook turnoff

B82

HEMA 89 D8 33 27 34 S 138 25 58 E

BIG RIG

294 Gladstone Caravan Park ☎ (08) 8662 2522

Caravan Park at Gladstone. West Tce. S side of town

B82

HEMA 89 C8 33 16 8 S 138 21 5 E

BIG RIG

295 Barbed Wire Pub ☎ (08) 8845 2006

Parking Area at Spalding. Area behind Pub, check in with publican on arrival during opening hours. Self Contained Vehicles only

HEMA 89 D8 33 29 49 S 138 36 29 E

BIG RIG

296 Robinson Park ☎ (08) 8664 0070

Camp Spot at Jamestown. Vohr St (RM Williams Way) Self Contained Vehicles only. Permit required from Foodland in Ayr St

HEMA 89 C9 33 12 6 S 138 36 12 E

BIG RIG 96

297 Laura Caravan Park ☎ (08) 8663 2296

Caravan Park at Laura. Mill St. N side of town

B82

HEMA 89 C8 33 10 54 S 138 18 2 E

BIG RIG

298 Ippinitchie Campground ☎ (08) 8668 5000
Camp Area 8 km SW of Wirrabara, via Wirrabara-Forest Rd. Dirt road. Permit required
HEMA 89 C8 33 4 1 S 138 13 58 E

299 Wirrabara Oval Caravan Park ☎ (08) 8668 4250
B82
Caravan Park at Wirrabara. Via Crew Rd. 400m dirt road. N end of town. Key at Wirrabara Craft House
HEMA 89 C8 33 1 51 S 138 15 53 E
BIG RIG

300 Murray Town Park ☎ (08) 8666 4253
Camp Area at Murray Town. Main North Rd. Honesty box
HEMA 89 C8 32 56 10 S 138 14 26 E
BIG RIG

301 Melrose Caravan Park ☎ (08) 8666 2060
B82
Caravan Park at Melrose. Joes Rd
HEMA 89 B8 32 49 30 S 138 11 11 E
BIG RIG

302 Melrose Showground ☎ 0428 662 140
B82
Camp Area 2 km N of Melrose or 23 km S of Wilmington
HEMA 89 B8 32 48 36 S 138 11 46 E
BIG RIG

303 Goyder's Line Memorial
B82
Parking Area 3 km N of Melrose or 22 km S of Wilmington
HEMA 89 B8 32 48 6 S 138 12 31 E
BIG RIG

Yorke Peninsula

304 Paskeville Oval
Camp Spot at Paskeville. Railway Tce South at oval. Fees collected. Self Contained Vehicles only. Maximum stay 14 days
HEMA 88 E7 34 2 22 S 137 54 15 E
BIG RIG

305 Kulpara Plantation
B85
Parking Area at Kulpara. Bute Rd. 100m N of Hwy
HEMA 88 E7 34 3 27 S 138 2 9 E
BIG RIG

306 Yorke Peninsula Information Bay
B86
Parking Area 9 km N of Port Wakefield or 11 km SE of Kulpara at jcn of B86 & B85
HEMA 89 E9 34 7 1 S 138 7 31 E
BIG RIG

307 Port Arthur Rest Area
B86
Rest Area 17 km W of Port Wakefield or 10 km N of Clinton
HEMA 88 F7 34 8 55 S 138 3 49 E
BIG RIG

308 Price Caravan Park ☎ (08) 8837 6311
Caravan Park at Price. Fowler Tce
HEMA 88 F7 34 17 14 S 137 59 48 E
BIG RIG

309 Pine Point Caravan Park ☎ (08) 8838 2239
Caravan Park at Pine Point. Main Coast Rd
HEMA 88 G7 34 34 28 S 137 52 40 E
BIG RIG

310 Black Point Camping Area (Harvey Campground) ☎ (08) 8838 2239
Camp Area 4 km S of Pine Point. Next to boat ramp. Caretaker collects fees
HEMA 88 G7 34 36 26 S 137 52 55 E
BIG RIG

311 Port Julia Oval (Reichenbach Memorial Park) ☎ (08) 8853 8115
B98
Camp Spot at Port Julia, via Osprey St. Caretaker collects fees in the afternoon
HEMA 88 G7 34 39 46 S 137 52 38 E
BIG RIG

312 Curramulka Sports Complex
Parking Area at Curramulka. Mount Rat Rd, next to the bowling club & tennis courts. Self Contained Vehicles only
HEMA 88 G7 34 41 52 S 137 42 24 E
BIG RIG 48

313 Port Vincent Seaside Caravan Park & Seaside Cabins ☎ (089) 8853 7011
Caravan Park at Port Vincent. 17 Minlacowie Rd. Beachfront
HEMA 88 G7 34 46 53 S 137 51 38 E

314 Stansbury Boat Ramp
B98
Parking Area at Stansbury
HEMA 88 G7 34 54 14 S 137 47 48 E
BIG RIG

315 Oyster Point Drive Caravan Park ☎ (08) 8852 4171
Caravan Park at Stansbury. Oyster Point Dr. 2 km S of PO
HEMA 88 G7 34 55 0 S 137 47 46 E
BIG RIG

316 Yorketown Community Caravan Park ☎ 0499 213 605
Caravan Park at Yorketown. Memorial Dr
HEMA 88 H6 35 1 13 S 137 36 37 E
BIG RIG

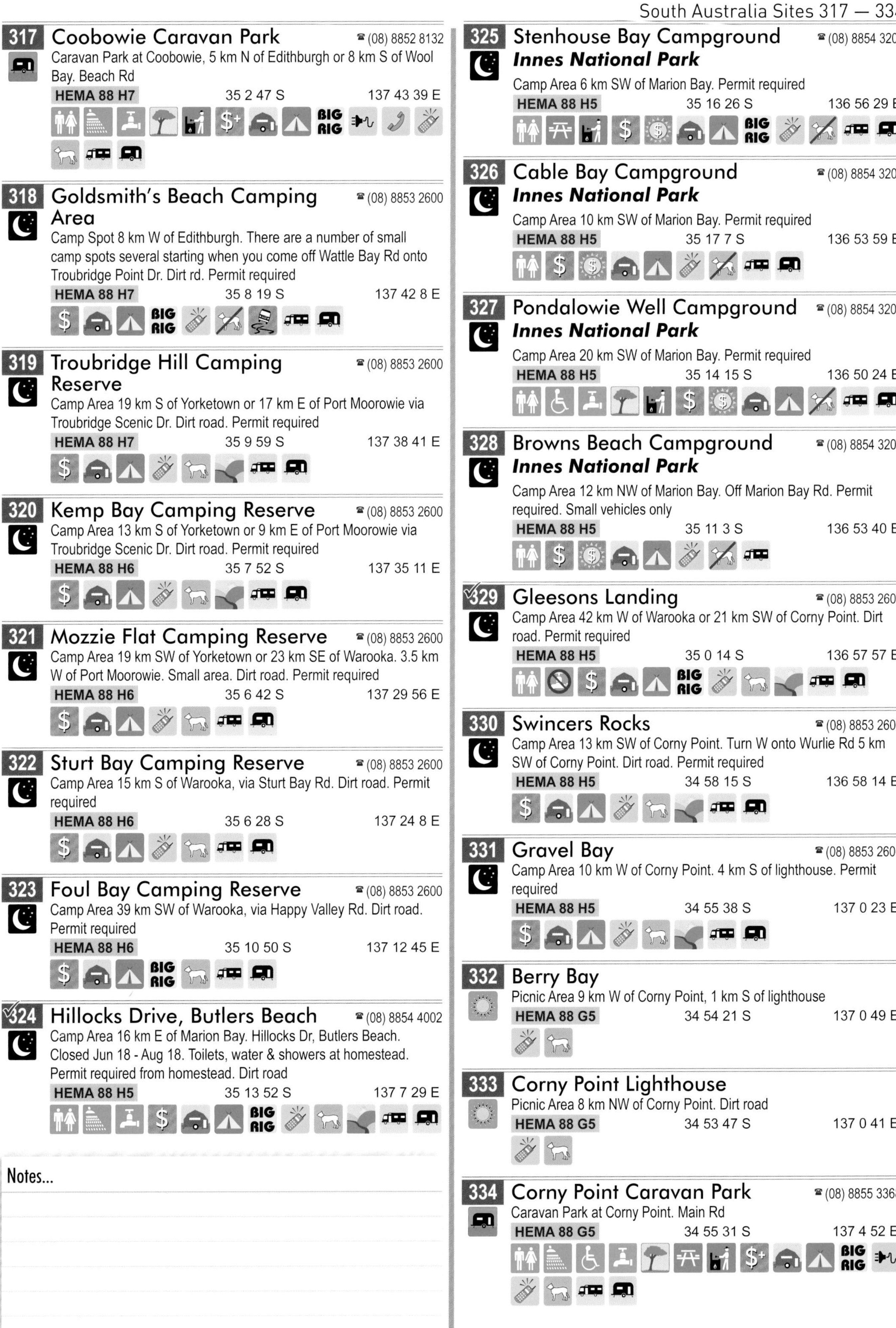

317 Coobowie Caravan Park
☎ (08) 8852 8132

Caravan Park at Coobowie, 5 km N of Edithburgh or 8 km S of Wool Bay. Beach Rd

HEMA 88 H7 | 35 2 47 S | 137 43 39 E

BIG RIG

318 Goldsmith's Beach Camping Area
☎ (08) 8853 2600

Camp Spot 8 km W of Edithburgh. There are a number of small camp spots several starting when you come off Wattle Bay Rd onto Troubridge Point Dr. Dirt rd. Permit required

HEMA 88 H7 | 35 8 19 S | 137 42 8 E

BIG RIG

319 Troubridge Hill Camping Reserve
☎ (08) 8853 2600

Camp Area 19 km S of Yorketown or 17 km E of Port Moorowie via Troubridge Scenic Dr. Dirt road. Permit required

HEMA 88 H7 | 35 9 59 S | 137 38 41 E

320 Kemp Bay Camping Reserve
☎ (08) 8853 2600

Camp Area 13 km S of Yorketown or 9 km E of Port Moorowie via Troubridge Scenic Dr. Dirt road. Permit required

HEMA 88 H6 | 35 7 52 S | 137 35 11 E

321 Mozzie Flat Camping Reserve
☎ (08) 8853 2600

Camp Area 19 km SW of Yorketown or 23 km SE of Warooka. 3.5 km W of Port Moorowie. Small area. Dirt road. Permit required

HEMA 88 H6 | 35 6 42 S | 137 29 56 E

322 Sturt Bay Camping Reserve
☎ (08) 8853 2600

Camp Area 15 km S of Warooka, via Sturt Bay Rd. Dirt road. Permit required

HEMA 88 H6 | 35 6 28 S | 137 24 8 E

323 Foul Bay Camping Reserve
☎ (08) 8853 2600

Camp Area 39 km SW of Warooka, via Happy Valley Rd. Dirt road. Permit required

HEMA 88 H6 | 35 10 50 S | 137 12 45 E

BIG RIG

324 Hillocks Drive, Butlers Beach
☎ (08) 8854 4002

Camp Area 16 km E of Marion Bay. Hillocks Dr, Butlers Beach. Closed Jun 18 - Aug 18. Toilets, water & showers at homestead. Permit required from homestead. Dirt road

HEMA 88 H5 | 35 13 52 S | 137 7 29 E

BIG RIG

Notes...

325 Stenhouse Bay Campground
☎ (08) 8854 3200

Innes National Park

Camp Area 6 km SW of Marion Bay. Permit required

HEMA 88 H5 | 35 16 26 S | 136 56 29 E

BIG RIG

326 Cable Bay Campground
☎ (08) 8854 3200

Innes National Park

Camp Area 10 km SW of Marion Bay. Permit required

HEMA 88 H5 | 35 17 7 S | 136 53 59 E

327 Pondalowie Well Campground
☎ (08) 8854 3200

Innes National Park

Camp Area 20 km SW of Marion Bay. Permit required

HEMA 88 H5 | 35 14 15 S | 136 50 24 E

328 Browns Beach Campground
☎ (08) 8854 3200

Innes National Park

Camp Area 12 km NW of Marion Bay. Off Marion Bay Rd. Permit required. Small vehicles only

HEMA 88 H5 | 35 11 3 S | 136 53 40 E

329 Gleesons Landing
☎ (08) 8853 2600

Camp Area 42 km W of Warooka or 21 km SW of Corny Point. Dirt road. Permit required

HEMA 88 H5 | 35 0 14 S | 136 57 57 E

BIG RIG

330 Swincers Rocks
☎ (08) 8853 2600

Camp Area 13 km SW of Corny Point. Turn W onto Wurlie Rd 5 km SW of Corny Point. Dirt road. Permit required

HEMA 88 H5 | 34 58 15 S | 136 58 14 E

331 Gravel Bay
☎ (08) 8853 2600

Camp Area 10 km W of Corny Point. 4 km S of lighthouse. Permit required

HEMA 88 H5 | 34 55 38 S | 137 0 23 E

332 Berry Bay

Picnic Area 9 km W of Corny Point, 1 km S of lighthouse

HEMA 88 G5 | 34 54 21 S | 137 0 49 E

333 Corny Point Lighthouse

Picnic Area 8 km NW of Corny Point. Dirt road

HEMA 88 G5 | 34 53 47 S | 137 0 41 E

334 Corny Point Caravan Park
☎ (08) 8855 3368

Caravan Park at Corny Point. Main Rd

HEMA 88 G5 | 34 55 31 S | 137 4 52 E

BIG RIG

SOUTH AUSTRALIA

335 Burners Beach
☎ (08) 8853 2600
Camp Area 24 km NW of Warooka. Turn N 14 km W of Warooka onto Souttar Rd. Campsite 1 km W along beachfront. 1 km dirt road. Permit required
HEMA 88 G6 34 54 0 S 137 14 38 E

336 Point Turton Caravan Park
☎ (08) 8854 5222
Caravan Park at Point Turton, overlooking jetty
HEMA 88 H6 34 56 3 S 137 21 4 E
BIG RIG

337 Warooka Rest Area
B96
Rest Area at Warooka. Opposite Warooka Hotel Motel
HEMA 88 H6 34 59 29 S 137 24 4 E
BIG RIG

338 Warooka Caravan & Camping Ground
☎ (08) 8854 5055
B96
Camp Area at Warooka. At Warooka Oval via Oval St. Donation to Progress Assocation. Pay at Rays Takeaway Main Street
HEMA 88 H6 34 59 32 S 137 23 53 E
BIG RIG 24

339 Inland Sea Restaurant
☎ (08) 8854 5499
B86
Camp Spot 4 km W of Warooka on White Hut Rd. Self Contained Vehicles only. Patronage of seafood or restaurant required
HEMA 88 H6 34 59 6 S 137 21 33 E
BIG RIG

340 Minlaton Caravan Park
☎ (08) 8853 2435
B97
Caravan Park at Minlaton. Cnr of Bluff & Maitland Rds
HEMA 88 G6 34 45 58 S 137 35 47 E
BIG RIG

341 Barkers Rocks
☎ (08) 8853 2600
Camp Area 13 km NW of Minlaton. Turn W 10 km NW of Minlaton. 3 km dirt road. Small vehicles only. Permit required
HEMA 88 G6 34 42 52 S 137 29 14 E

342 Port Rickaby Caravan Park
☎ (08) 8853 1177
Caravan Park at Port Rickaby. Main St
HEMA 88 G6 34 40 21 S 137 29 44 E

343 Wauraltee Beach
☎ (08) 8853 2600
Camp Area 4 km W of Wauraltee. Turn W at Wauraltee, 17 km S of Port Victoria. 4 km dirt road. Permit required
HEMA 88 G6 34 35 16 S 137 30 28 E

344 Maitland Rest Area
☎ (08) 8832 0000
B97
Rest Area at Maitland. Roberts St N end of town opposite hospital. Small vehicles only
HEMA 88 F7 34 22 14 S 137 40 29 E
24

345 Maitland Showground
☎ (08) 8832 2171
B97
Camp Spot at Maitland. Rogers Tce. Caretaker collects fees
HEMA 88 F7 34 22 18 S 137 40 39 E
BIG RIG

346 Arthurton Rest Area
Rest Area at Arthurton. 15 km NE of Maitland or 35 km SW of Kulpara. Behind St Agatha's Church in Third St
HEMA 88 F7 34 15 27 S 137 45 25 E
BIG RIG 24

347 Balgowan Caravan & Camping Area
All enquiries & collection of keys go to the Kiosk at 11 Main Street
HEMA 88 F6 34 19 26 S 137 29 38 E
BIG RIG

348 Tiparra Rocks
☎ (08) 8853 2600
Camp Area 4.4 km N of Balgowan. Take Tiparra West Rd, then L fork after 1 km. Dirt road. Permit required
HEMA 88 F6 34 17 10 S 137 29 56 E

349 The Bamboos Campground
☎ (08) 8853 2600
Camp Area 8.5 km N of Balgowan. Take Tiparra West Rd, then L fork after 1 km. Dirt road. Permit required
HEMA 88 F6 34 15 10 S 137 30 5 E

350 The Gap Campground
☎ (08) 8853 2600
Camp Area 15 km N of Balgowan. Take Tiparra West Rd, then L fork after 1 km. Alternate route from Moonta, head S 24 km to Weetulta turn W on Gap Rd, campsite 15 km on dirt road. Permit required
HEMA 88 F6 34 14 3 S 137 30 6 E

351 Wallaroo Parking Area
Parking Area at Wallaroo. Cnr of Cornish Tce & Wildman St. W end of town. Self Contained Vehicles only
HEMA 88 E7 33 56 4 S 137 37 18 E
BIG RIG 20

352 Kadina Showgrounds
☎ (08) 8821 2333
Camp Area at Kadina. Entry off Agery St. Self Contained Vehicles only. Pay fee & collect access key from Copper Coast Info Centre Mines Rd
HEMA 88 E7 33 58 3 S 137 42 57 E
BIG RIG 48

353 Alford Community Park
Camp Area at Alford opposite tennis courts in main road. Donation please
HEMA 88 E7 33 49 1 S 137 49 18 E
BIG RIG 72

354 Tickera North
Parking Area 4.5 km N of Tickera on the Coast Rd. Turn W to beach
HEMA 88 E7 33 45 37 S 137 43 49 E

355 **Bute Caravan Park** ☎ (08) 7007 6589
Caravan Park at Bute. Railway Tce
HEMA 88 E7 33 51 57 S 138 0 22 E

356 **Fisherman Bay**
Parking Area 5 km N of Port Broughton. On Whiting Rd, at boat ramp car park
HEMA 88 D7 33 33 15 S 137 56 35 E
BIG RIG

357 **Clement Gap Old School**
Camp Spot 19.5 km NE of Port Broughton or 10.5 km SW of Merriton. Camp site in old school grounds, close to Clements Gap Conservation Park
HEMA 88 D7 33 29 45 S 138 5 4 E
48

Kangaroo Island

358 **Antechamber Bay West Campground** ☎ (08) 8553 2381
Lashmar Conservation Park
Camp Area 17.5 km NE of Penneshaw. 5 sites. Permit required. Self registration
HEMA 88 K7 35 47 2 S 138 4 1 E

359 **Antechamber Bay East Campground** ☎ (08) 8553 2381
Lashmar Conservation Park
Camp Area 20 km NE of Penneshaw. 5 sites. Permit required. Self registration
HEMA 88 K7 35 47 11 S 138 3 59 E

360 **Browns Beach Campground** ☎ (08) 8553 4500
Camp Area at Browns Bay. Permit required. Self registration
HEMA 88 K7 35 47 38 S 137 51 27 E

361 **D'Estrees Bay Camp Ground** ☎ (08) 8553 2381
Cape Gantheaume Conservation Park
Camp Area in Cape Gantheaume Conservation Park. Permit required. Self registration. Dirt road
HEMA 88 K6 35 57 58 S 137 36 19 E

362 **Murray Lagoon Campground** ☎ (08) 8553 2381
Cape Gantheaume Conservation Park
Camp Area in Cape Gantheaume Conservation Park. Permit required. Self registration
HEMA 88 K6 35 55 26 S 137 33 40 E

363 **Vivonne Bay Campground** ☎ (08) 8553 4500
Camp Area at Vivonne Bay. Self registration. Some powered sites
HEMA 88 K6 35 59 4 S 137 10 37 E

364 **Parndana Hotel** ☎ (08) 8559 6071
Camp Area at Parndana. Cnr Wedgwood Rd & Cook St
HEMA 88 K6 35 47 27 S 137 15 51 E

365 **Rocky River Camping Area** ☎ (08) 8553 4490
Flinders Chase National Park
Camp Area at Rocky River. 300m S of Visitor Information Centre. Bookings essential
HEMA 88 K5 35 57 11 S 136 44 7 E

366 **Western River Cove** ☎ (08) 8553 4500
Camp Area at Western River Cove. Via Western River Cove Rd, 29 km W of Parndana. Dirt road. Steep in places. Small vehicles only. Self registration
HEMA 88 J5 35 40 40 S 136 58 18 E

367 **Stokes Bay** ☎ (08) 8559 2277
Camp Area at Stokes Bay. Via Stokes Bay Rd, 4 km W of Parndana. Behind café, check-in & pay at café
HEMA 88 J6 35 37 30 S 137 12 23 E

368 **Discovery Lagoon Camping Grounds** ☎ (08) 8553 5220
Camp Area 3 km S of Emu Bay or 12 W of Kingscote. 948 North Coast Rd
HEMA 88 J6 35 37 25 S 137 31 23 E
BIG RIG

369 **American River Campground** ☎ (08) 8553 4500
Camp Area at American River. Permit required. Self registration. Small vehicles only
HEMA 88 K7 35 47 15 S 137 46 14 E

Port Augusta to Birdsville

370 **Woolshed Flat Rest Area**
Rest Area16 km N of Stirling North or 18 km S of Quorn
HEMA 94 H7 32 27 45 S 137 58 7 E
B83
BIG RIG

Notes...

371 Quorn Town Park
Rest Area at Quorn. Railway Tce
HEMA 94 H7 32 20 46 S 138 2 21 E
B47

372 Warren Gorge
(08) 8648 6031
Camp Area 21 km N of Quorn, via Arden Vale Rd. Dirt road last 8 km
HEMA 94 G7 32 10 57 S 138 0 26 E

373 Argadells Bush Retreat
(08) 8648 6246
Camp Spot 25 km N of Quorn, via Arden Vale Rd. Bookings essential. Dirt road
HEMA 94 G7 32 8 20 S 138 2 25 E
BIG RIG

374 Cradock Hotel
Camp Spot at Cradock at Hotel. 27 km SE of Hawker or 43 km N of Carrieton. Free camp with a beer. Gold coin donation for showers
HEMA 95 G8 32 4 10 S 138 29 36 E
BIG RIG

375 Hawker Town Park
Rest Area at Hawker. Elder Tce
HEMA 95 G8 31 53 15 S 138 25 16 E
B47

376 Flinders Ranges Caravan Park
(08) 8648 4266
Caravan Park at Hawker. Carpenter Rd
HEMA 95 G8 31 53 4 S 138 24 51 E
BIG RIG

377 Flinders Bush Retreats - Willow Waters Gorge Bush Camping
(08) 8648 4441
Camp Area 20 km E of Hawker. Take Craddock Rd for 7.4 km then signposted road to Willow Waters. Follow road for 6 km, turn L at first house on L. Pre-booking essential
HEMA 95 G9 31 54 27 S 138 33 41 E

378 Nooltana Creek Parking Area
Parking Area 13 km N of Hawker or 76 km S of Parachilna
HEMA 95 F8 31 48 33 S 138 22 1 E
B47

379 Hookina Creek
Rest Area 18 km N of Hawker or 71 km S of Parachilna, near Wonoka Ruins
HEMA 95 F8 31 45 39 S 138 19 58 E
B47
BIG RIG

380 Moralana Creek
Rest Area 41 km N of Hawker or 48 km S of Parachilna
HEMA 95 F8 31 33 20 S 138 25 36 E
BIG RIG

381 Merna Mora Station
(08) 8648 4717
Camp Area Merna Mora Station. 47 km N of Hawker. 3 km W off the Hwy opposite the Moralana Scenic Dr
HEMA 95 F8 31 32 46 S 138 23 28 E
B83
BIG RIG

382 Brachina Creek
Rest Area 70 km N of Hawker or 19 km S of Parachilna
HEMA 95 E8 31 18 31 S 138 24 51 E
B47
BIG RIG

383 Parachilna Junction
Rest Area at Parachilna
HEMA 95 E8 31 7 54 S 138 23 51 E
B47

384 Parachilna Campground
(08) 8648 4895
Camp Area at Parachilna. Payment & keys at Prairie Hotel
HEMA 95 E8 31 7 52 S 138 23 42 E
BIG RIG

385 Beltana Station
(08) 8675 2256
Camp Area at Beltana Station. 10 km E of Beltana Roadhouse. Pets permitted only with prior authorisation. Honesty box for fees
HEMA 95 D8 30 49 18 S 138 22 17 E

386 Warraweena Conservation Park
(08) 8675 2770
Camp Area at Warraweena. 35 km E of Beltana Roadhouse. Pets permitted only with prior authorisation. Must call at homestead prior to camping. Dirt road
HEMA 95 D9 30 46 4 S 138 38 12 E

387 Aroona Dam
Picnic Area 67 km N of Parachilna. Turn W 62 km N of Parachilna or 9 km S of Leigh Creek onto Aroona Dam Rd. 5 km dirt road
HEMA 95 C8 30 35 6 S 138 21 34 E
BIG RIG

388 Leigh Creek Junction
Parking Area at Leigh Creek
HEMA 95 C8 30 35 47 S 138 24 13 E
B47

389 Leigh Creek Caravan Park
0429 012 445
Caravan Park at Leigh Creek. Acacia Dr
HEMA 95 C8 30 35 17 S 138 24 29 E
BIG RIG

390 Copley Town Park
Rest Area at Copley
HEMA 95 C8 30 33 26 S 138 25 25 E
B47

391 Iga-Warta Community Campground
☎ (08) 8648 3737

Camp Area at Iga-Warta. 62 km E of Copley. Bookings required. Dirt road

HEMA 95 C9 | 30 35 45 S | 138 56 5 E

392 Italowie Gap Campground
☎ (08) 8648 4829

Vulkathunha-Gammon Ranges National Park

Camp Area 22 km E of Nepabunna or 17 km W of the Park HQ, via the Copley - Arkaroola Rd. Self registration required

HEMA 95 C10 | 30 33 22 S | 139 10 11 E

393 Weetootla Gorge Campground
☎ (08) 8648 4829

Vulkathunha-Gammon Ranges National Park

Camp Area 110 km W of Copley. Turn N at Balcanoona into Arkaroola Rd, turn W 2.3 km N of Balcanoona. 4.5 km to campsites. Small vehicles only. Self registration required

HEMA 95 C10 | 30 29 49 S | 139 15 33 E

394 Grindells Hut Campground
☎ (08) 8648 4829

Vulkathunha-Gammon Ranges National Park

Camp Area 118 km W of Copley. Turn N 9.3 km N of Balcanoona into Arkaroola Rd, camp site is 17 km along this road. 4WD & camper trailers only

HEMA 95 C10 | 30 28 30 S | 139 12 51 E

395 Chambers Gorge

Camp Area 27 km NE of Wirrealpa. 4WD recommended

HEMA 95 D10 | 30 57 12 S | 139 12 53 E

396 Arkaroola Wilderness Sanctuary
☎ (08) 8648 4848

Camp Area at Arkaroola.130 km E of Leigh Creek. Bush camping also available

HEMA 95 C10 | 30 18 42 S | 139 20 10 E

397 Lyndhurst Hotel Motel
☎ (08) 8675 7781

B47

Camp Area at Lyndhurst

HEMA 95 C8 | 30 17 16 S | 138 21 8 E

398 Farina Station Campground
☎ (08) 8675 7790

Camp Area at Farina Station. 26 km N of Lyndhurst. Turn W 25 km N of Lyndhurst or 56 km S of Marree. Signposted

HEMA 95 B8 | 30 3 41 S | 138 16 22 E

BIG RIG

399 Oasis Town Centre Caravan Park
☎ (08) 8675 8352

1

Caravan Park at Marree. Railway Tce South

HEMA 91 K8 | 29 38 49 S | 138 3 46 E

BIG RIG

400 Marree Hotel
☎ (08) 8675 8344

Camp Spot at Marree. Fee for showers

HEMA 91 K8 | 29 38 54 S | 138 3 52 E

Birdsville to Marree

Birdsville Track

This road is seasonal and more suitable to 4WD vehicles, camper trailers and off road caravans. Road conditions phone 1300 361 033

401 Lake Harry Ruins

Camp Spot 38 km NE of Maree or 168 km SW of Mungerannie Roadhouse

HEMA 91 K8 | 29 26 3 S | 138 14 46 E

402 Clayton Station
☎ (08) 8675 8311

Camp Area at Clayton Station. 54 km NE of Marree or 152 km S of Mungerannie Roadhouse. Honesty box by toilets

HEMA 91 J8 | 29 16 32 S | 138 22 17 E

BIG RIG

403 Cooper Creek
☎ (08) 8675 9591

Camp Area 146 km NE of Marree or 60 km S of Mungerannie Roadhouse

HEMA 91 H9 | 28 37 25 S | 138 42 36 E

404 Mungerannie Hotel
☎ (08) 8675 8317

Camp Area at Mungerannie, 206 km NE of Marree or 308 km SW of Birdsville. Beside Derwent River

HEMA 91 F9 | 28 1 7 S | 138 39 47 E

405 Cowarie Station
☎ (08) 8675 8304

Camp Area at Cowarie Station. 51 km NW of Mungerannie Hotel. Bookings essential

HEMA 91 E8 | 27 42 6 S | 138 20 8 E

406 Tippipila Creek Bush Camp

Camp Spot 134 km N of Mungerannie or 181 km S of Birdsville

HEMA 91 C10 | 26 59 42 S | 139 1 1 E

Notes...

Marree to Marla

Oodnadatta Track

This road is seasonal and more suitable to 4WD vehicles, camper trailers and off road caravans. Road conditions phone 1300 361 033

407 Muloorina Station

☎ (08) 8675 8386

Camp Area at Muloorina Station. 54 km NW of Marree. Turn N off Oodnadatta Track 2 km W of Maree. Honesty box

HEMA 90 J7 29 14 20 S 137 54 23 E

408 Curdimurka Railway Siding

Parking Area 104 km W of Marree or 100 km SE of William Creek. Parking around the ruins

HEMA 90 K6 29 28 36 S 137 5 4 E

BIG RIG

409 Coward Springs Campground
☎ (08) 8675 8336

Camp Area 131 km W of Marree or 73 km SE of William Creek

HEMA 90 J5 29 24 14 S 136 48 44 E

410 Beresford Siding

Parking Area 154 km W of Marree or 50 km SE of William Creek

HEMA 90 J5 29 14 34 S 136 39 23 E

BIG RIG

411 Strangways Siding

Parking Area 167 km W of Marree or 37 km SE of William Creek

HEMA 90 J5 29 9 23 S 136 34 21 E

BIG RIG

412 Halligan Bay Campground
Kati Thanda - Lake Eyre National Park

Camp Area at Halligan Bay. Turn N 7 km SE of William Creek onto Halligan Bay access track (57 km). High clearance 4WD only. Check conditions, desert pass required

HEMA 90 H5 28 45 49 S 136 56 23 E

413 William Creek Camping Ground
☎ (08) 8670 7880

Camp Area at William Creek Hotel

HEMA 90 H4 28 54 25 S 136 20 18 E

BIG RIG

414 Warrina Siding

Parking Area 108 km NW of William Creek or 95 km S of Oodnadatta

HEMA 90 F3 28 11 38 S 135 49 42 E

415 Peake Creek Siding

Parking Area 130 km NW of William Creek or 73 km S of Oodnadatta

HEMA 90 F3 28 1 33 S 135 48 15 E

BIG RIG

416 Algebuckina Bridge, Neals Creek

Camp Spot 145 km NW of William Creek or 58 km S of Oodnadatta

HEMA 90 F3 27 54 6 S 135 48 37 E

BIG RIG

417 Mt Dutton Siding

Parking Area 160 km NW of William Creek or 43 km S of Oodnadatta

HEMA 90 E3 27 48 56 S 135 43 37 E

418 North Creek

Camp Spot 175 km NW of William Creek or 28 km S of Oodnadatta, N side of road by old railway bridge

HEMA 90 E3 27 44 15 S 135 36 15 E

BIG RIG

419 Arckaringa Station
☎ (08) 8670 7992

Camp Area at Arckaringa Station. 140 km N of Coober Pedy or 86 km SW of Oodnadatta

HEMA 90 F1 27 56 12 S 134 44 18 E

BIG RIG

420 Oodnadatta Caravan Park
☎ (08) 8670 7822

Caravan Park at Oodnadatta. Behind the roadhouse

HEMA 90 E2 27 32 56 S 135 26 53 E

421 Oodnadatta Town Camp

Camp Spot at Oodnadatta. Opposite Health Service

HEMA 90 E2 27 32 42 S 135 26 48 E

72

422 Mt Dare Hotel
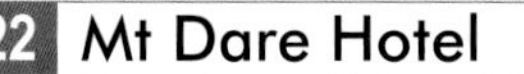
☎ (08) 8670 7835

Camp Area at Mt Dare. 75 km SE of Finke or 70 km NW of Dalhousie Springs

HEMA 90 A2 26 4 10 S 135 14 52 E

423 Dalhousie Springs Campground
☎ 1800 816 078
Witjira National Park

Camp Area at Dalhousie Springs 183 km NE of Oodnadatta or 68 km S of Mt Dare Hotel. Turn N 18 km from Oodnadatta, 91 km to Hamilton HS then turn NE 71 km to Dalhousie. Turn E 3 km. Dirt road. 4WD only

HEMA 90 B2 26 25 23 S 135 30 13 E

424 Purni Bore
☎ 1800 816 078
Witjira National Park

Camp Area 248 km NE of Oodnadatta or 65 km E of Dalhousie Springs. Campground on the Spring Creek Track. Dirt road. 4WD only. Desert Parks Pass required

HEMA 90 B4 26 17 3 S 136 5 54 E

425 3 O'Clock Creek Campground
☎ 1800 816 078

Witjira National Park

Camp Area 183 km NE of Oodnadatta or 58 km S of Mt Dare Hotel. Turn N 18 km from Oodnadatta, 91 km to Hamilton HS then turn NE 71 km to Dalhousie. Turn W 3 km. Dirt road. 4WD only

HEMA 90 B2 26 27 34 S 135 24 41 E

426 Kathleen Creek

Camp Spot 89 km NW of Oodnadatta or 129 km E of Marla. Tracks along creek

HEMA 90 D1 27 12 17 S 134 45 13 E

427 Olarinna Creek

Camp Spot 104 km NW of Oodnadatta or 114 km E of Marla. Turn N on W side of creek, follow track

HEMA 90 D1 27 9 48 S 134 37 9 E

Flinders Ranges National Park

428 Arkaba Rest Area

Rest Area 21 km NE of Hawker or 35 km S of Wilpena

HEMA 95 F8 31 43 40 S 138 31 7 E

429 Rawnsley Lookout

Parking Area 41 km N of Hawker or 15 km S of Wilpena

HEMA 95 F9 31 36 40 S 138 39 7 E

BIG RIG

430 Wilpena Pound Caravan & Campground
☎ (08) 8648 0048

Flinders Range National Park

Camp Ground at Wilpena. Bookings taken at Visitor Centre or Resort

HEMA 95 F9 31 31 37 S 138 36 23 E

BIG RIG

431 Willow Springs Station
☎ (08) 8648 0016

Camp Area at Willow Springs Station. 21 km NE of Wilpena. Some dirt road

HEMA 95 E9 31 26 56 S 138 45 32 E

432 Dingly Dell Campground
☎ (08) 8648 0049

Flinders Range National Park

Camp Area 28 km N of Wilpena, on Blinman Rd. Signposted

HEMA 95 E9 31 21 19 S 138 42 20 E

433 Youngoona Campground
☎ (08) 8648 0048

Flinders Range National Park

Camp Area 36 km N of Wilpena. Turn W 33 km N of Wilpena turnoff or 29 km S of Blinman onto Brachina Gorge Geological Trail for 3 km. Dirt road. 4 sites only

HEMA 95 E9 31 19 51 S 138 39 21 E

434 Trezona Campground
☎ (08) 8648 0048

Flinders Range National Park

Camp Area 45 km N of Wilpena. Turn W 33 km N of Wilpena onto Brachina Gorge Geological Trail for 6 km, then turn N. Dirt road

HEMA 95 E9 31 19 51 S 138 37 42 E

435 Brachina East Campground
☎ (08) 8648 0048

Flinders Range National Park

Camp Area 38 km NW of Wilpena. Turn W 5 km N of Wilpena turnoff onto Bunyeroo Valley Scenic Dr. Then turn W at T-intersection of Brachina Gorge Rd for 1 km. Dirt road

HEMA 95 E9 31 20 1 S 138 34 46 E

436 Teamsters Campground
☎ (08) 8648 0048

Flinders Range National Park

Camp Area 42 km NW of Wilpena. Turn W 5 km N of Wilpena turnoff onto Bunyeroo Valley Scenic Dr. Then turn W at T-intersection of Brachina Gorge Rd for 4.5 km. Dirt road

HEMA 95 E9 31 20 18 S 138 32 59 E

437 Koolamon Campground
☎ (08) 8648 0048

Flinders Range National Park

Camp Area 53 km N of Wilpena. Turn W 33 km N of Wilpena turnoff or 29 km S of Blinman onto Brachina Geological Trail for 10 km. Then turn N onto Aroona Rd for 4.6 km. Dirt road

HEMA 95 E9 31 17 32 S 138 35 8 E

438 Aroona Ruins Campground
☎ (08) 8648 0048

Flinders Range National Park

Camp Area 54 km N of Wilpena. Turn W 33 km N of Wilpena turnoff or 29 km S of Blinman onto Brachina Geological Trail for 10 km. Then turn N onto Aroona Rd for 6 km. Dirt road

HEMA 95 E9 31 16 45 S 138 34 45 E

439 Cambrian Campground
☎ (08) 8648 0048

Flinders Range National Park

Camp Area 33 km NW of Wilpena. Turn W 5 km N of Wilpena turnoff onto Bunyeroo Valley Scenic Dr. Dirt road

HEMA 95 E9 31 21 26 S 138 34 57 E

440 Acraman Campground
☎ (08) 8648 0048

Flinders Range National Park

Camp Area 28 km NW of Wilpena. Turn W 5 km N of Wilpena turnoff onto Bunyeroo Valley Scenic Dr. Dirt road. 4 sites only. Not suitable caravans

HEMA 95 E9 31 24 35 S 138 33 42 E

Notes...

441 Alpana Station
☎ (08) 8648 4626

Camp Area at Alpana Station. 59 km N of Wilpena Pound or 5 km S of Blinman off Wilpena Rd

HEMA 95 E9 | 31 8 25 S | 138 41 4 E

442 Blinman Hotel
☎ (08) 8648 4867

Camp Area 59 km N of Wilpena or 32 km E of Parachilna, at hotel. Dirt road from Parachilna

HEMA 95 E9 | 31 5 37 S | 138 40 40 E

443 Angorichina Station
☎ (07) 8648 4863

Camp Area at Angorichina Station. 9 km W of Blinman turn E approx 2.2 km S of Blinman. Bookings essential. Pets on request

HEMA 95 E9 | 31 5 42 S | 138 44 25 E

444 Moolooloo Station
☎ (08) 8648 4861

Camp Area at Moolooloo Station. 21 km NW of Blinman. Glass Gorge Rd. Variety of sites. Bookings essential. Dirt road

HEMA 95 D9 | 30 59 24 S | 138 34 42 E

445 Angorichina Tourist Village
☎ (08) 8648 4842

Camp Area 17 km E of Parachilna or 16 km W of Blinman

HEMA 95 E9 | 31 7 35 S | 138 33 39 E

446 Parachilna Gorge

Camp Area 10 km E of Parachilna. Various sites on riverbank

HEMA 95 E8 | 31 8 6 S | 138 31 48 E

Port Augusta to Kulgera

Stuart Highway

447 North Tent Hill Rest Area

A87

Rest Area 34 km NW of Port Augusta or 136 km SE of Pimba

HEMA 94 G6 | 32 14 30 S | 137 32 45 E

BIG RIG

448 Hesso Rest Area

A87

Rest Area 52 km NW of Port Augusta or 118 km SE of Pimba. Small vehicles only

HEMA 94 G6 | 32 7 9 S | 137 26 25 E

449 Ranges View Rest Area

A87

Rest Area 62 km NW of Port Augusta or 108 km SE of Pimba

HEMA 94 G6 | 32 2 2 S | 137 26 42 E

450 Bookaloo Rest Area

A87

Rest Area 79 km NW of Port Augusta or 91 km SE of Pimba

HEMA 94 F6 | 31 52 31 S | 137 20 52 E

BIG RIG

451 Maslin Rest Area

A87

Rest Area 94 km NW of Port Augusta or 76 km SE of Pimba

HEMA 94 F6 | 31 46 28 S | 137 17 23 E

BIG RIG

452 Monalena Lagoon Rest Area

A87

Rest Area 102 km NW of Port Augusta or 68 km SE of Pimba

HEMA 94 F6 | 31 43 6 S | 137 13 47 E

BIG RIG

453 Island Lagoon Lookout

A87

Rest Area 153 km NW of Port Augusta or 17 km SE of Pimba

HEMA 94 E5 | 31 22 45 S | 136 55 24 E

BIG RIG

454 Pimba Rest Area

A87

Rest Area at Pimba, near Hotel. Showers (cold) available for fee

HEMA 94 E5 | 31 15 23 S | 136 48 16 E

BIG RIG

455 Roxby Downs

B97

Parking Area 6 km W of Roxby Downs. Andamooka Rd

HEMA 94 C5 | 30 32 50 S | 136 56 24 E

456 Lions Park
☎ (08) 8671 2001

Parking Area at Roxby Downs, off Burgoyne St. Self Contained Vehicles only

HEMA 94 C5 | 30 33 41 S | 136 53 40 E

BIG RIG 48

457 Roxby Downs South

Parking Area 2 km S of Roxby Downs

HEMA 94 C5 | 30 34 30 S | 136 53 38 E

48

458 Andamooka Camping Ground
☎ (08) 8672 7023

Camp Area 1 km W of Andamooka. Honesty box for donation

HEMA 94 C6 | 30 27 4 S | 137 9 46 E

BIG RIG

459 Lake Hart Lookout

A87

Rest Area 42 km W of Pimba or 71 km SE of Glendambo

HEMA 94 E4 | 31 14 1 S | 136 24 17 E

BIG RIG

460 Glendambo South Rest Area

A87

Rest Area 89 km W of Pimba or 24 km SE of Glendambo

HEMA 94 D3 | 31 7 11 S | 135 55 39 E

BIG RIG

461 Glendambo Outback Resort
☎ (08) 8672 1030

Caravan Park at Glendambo. Stuart Hwy

HEMA 94 D3 | 30 58 10 S | 135 45 1 E

BIG RIG

462 Mulga Well Rest Area

A87

Rest Area 27 km N of Glendambo or 225 km S of Coober Pedy

HEMA 94 D3 | 30 48 36 S | 135 32 38 E

BIG RIG

463 Mulga Well North Rest Area
A87
Rest Area 63 km N of Glendambo or 189 km S of Coober Pedy
HEMA 94 C2 30 32 4 S 135 21 33 E
BIG RIG

464 Bon Bon Rest Area
A87
Rest Area 84 km N of Glendambo or 168 km S of Coober Pedy. Emergency phone
HEMA 94 C2 30 21 20 S 135 19 44 E
BIG RIG

465 The Twins Rest Area
A87
Rest Area 124 km N of Glendambo or 128 km S of Coober Pedy
HEMA 94 B2 30 1 41 S 135 11 43 E
BIG RIG

466 Ingomar Rest Area
A87
Rest Area 161 km N of Glendambo or 91 km S of Coober Pedy. Emergency phone
HEMA 93 K14 29 42 44 S 135 7 39 E
BIG RIG

467 Ingomar North Rest Area
A87
Rest Area 206.5 km N of Glendambo or 46.5 km S of Coober Pedy
HEMA 93 J13 29 21 0 S 134 59 12 E
BIG RIG

468 Hutchison Memorial
A87
Parking Area 240 km N of Glendambo or 12 km S of Coober Pedy. Fireplace on lower level
HEMA 93 J13 29 4 30 S 134 51 12 E
BIG RIG

469 William Creek Road
Parking Area 10 km E of Coober Pedy on William Creek Rd. Dirt road
HEMA 93 H13 29 2 3 S 134 49 20 E

470 The Clothes Barn
Parking Area at Coober Pedy. Marquardt Rd, see caretaker on arrival
HEMA 93 H13 28 59 59 S 134 45 23 E
$ BIG RIG

471 Breakaways Lookout
Parking Area 31 km N of Coober Pedy. Turn E 22 km N of Coober Pedy or 128 km S of Cadney Roadhouse. 9 km of dirt road
HEMA 93 H13 28 50 44 S 134 42 27 E
BIG RIG

472 Pootnoura Rest Area
A87
Rest Area 75 km N of Coober Pedy or 75 km S of Cadney Roadhouse. Emergency phone
HEMA 93 G12 28 33 17 S 134 15 19 E
BIG RIG

473 Evelyn Downs Rest Area
A87
Rest Area 90 km N of Coober Pedy or 60 km S of Cadney Roadhouse
HEMA 93 G12 28 25 32 S 134 11 7 E
BIG RIG

474 Mathesons Bore
A87
Parking Area 110 km N of Coober Pedy or 40 km S of Cadney Roadhouse
HEMA 93 G12 28 15 29 S 134 9 4 E
BIG RIG

475 Cadney Homestead Caravan Park
☎ (08) 8670 7994
Caravan Park at Cadney Roadhouse
HEMA 93 F12 27 54 18 S 134 3 24 E
$+

476 Marla South Rest Area
A87
Rest Area 46 km NW of Cadney Roadhouse or 35 km SE of Marla
HEMA 93 E11 27 33 21 S 133 49 13 E
BIG RIG

477 Marla Travellers Rest Caravan Park
☎ (08) 8670 7001
Caravan Park at Marla. Stuart Hwy
HEMA 93 D11 27 18 15 S 133 37 20 E
$+ BIG RIG

478 Tarcoonyinna Rest Area
A87
Rest Area 53 km N of Marla or 125 km S of Kulgera
HEMA 93 C10 26 53 47 S 133 22 51 E
BIG RIG

479 Agnes Creek Rest Area
A87
Rest Area 85 km N of Marla or 93 km S of Kulgera
HEMA 93 B10 26 38 14 S 133 16 45 E
BIG RIG

480 The Marryat Rest Area
A87
Rest Area 120 km N of Marla, 39 km S of NT Border or 58 km S of Kulgera. Emergency phone
HEMA 93 B10 26 20 29 S 133 12 4 E
BIG RIG

481 Marryat Creek North Rest Area
A87
Rest Area 128 km N of Marla or 31 km S of NT Border. 52 km S of Kulgera
HEMA 93 A10 26 16 42 S 133 11 20 E
BIG RIG

Eyre Peninsula

Lincoln and Flinders Highways

482 Half Way Rest Area
B100
Rest Area 40 km S of Port Augusta or 34 km N of Whyalla. Both sides of Hwy
HEMA 88 B6 32 43 33 S 137 30 38 E
BIG RIG

Notes...

SOUTH AUSTRALIA

483 Fitzgerald Bay
☎ (08) 8645 7900

Camp Area at Fitzgerald Bay. Turn E off B100 onto Port Bonython Rd, 65 km SW of Port Augusta or 8 km N of Whyalla, then N after 16 km to the end of bitumen. Turn L, then 2 km dirt road. Site on R. Signposted

HEMA 88 B7 | 32 55 17 S | 137 44 57 E

484 Fitzgerald Bay Bush Camp
☎ (08) 8645 7900

Camp Area at Fitzgerald Bay. Turn E off B100 onto Port Bonython Rd, 65 km SW of Port Augusta or 8 km N of Whyalla, then N after 16 km to the end of bitumen. Turn L, then 3.7 km dirt road. Track on R. Signposted. Limited space, small vehicles only

HEMA 88 B7 | 32 54 25 S | 137 45 18 E

485 Point Lowly
☎ (08) 8645 7900

Camp Area at Point Lowly, 35 km NE of Whyalla. Turn E off B100, 65 km SW of Port Augusta or 8 km N of Whyalla onto Point Lowly Rd. Adjacent to toilet block, near boat ramp. Dump Point 500m N campsite. Max stay 14 days

HEMA 88 C7 | 32 59 34 S | 137 46 51 E

BIG RIG

486 Stuart Park (Weeroona Bay Football Club)
☎ 0450 143 998

Camp Area at Whyalla. 8 km W of PO. Access off Cartledge Ave via McDouall Stuart Ave. Self Contained Vehicles only. Caretaker will collect fee

HEMA 88 C6 | 33 1 54 S | 137 30 50 E

BIG RIG

487 Hancocks Shaft Rest Area

Rest Area 49 km S of Whyalla or 57 km N of Cowell

HEMA 88 C6 | 33 15 55 S | 137 12 34 E

BIG RIG

488 Harbour View Caravan Park
☎ (08) 8629 2216

Caravan Park 3 km N of Cowell. Harbour View Dr

HEMA 88 D5 | 33 40 25 S | 136 56 20 E

BIG RIG

489 Cowell Motorhome Park

Camp Area at Cowell. Wellington Rd, S end of town. Self Contained Motorhomes only. Dump Point is at Brooks Dr

HEMA 88 D5 | 33 41 40 S | 136 55 20 E

BIG RIG

490 The Knob Beach Park Area

Parking Area 19 km S of Cowell, via Beach Rd or via Port Gibbon. Rough corrugated dirt road

HEMA 88 E5 | 33 47 55 S | 136 50 49 E

BIG RIG

491 Port Gibbon Foreshore
☎ (08) 8629 2019

Rest Area at Port Gibbon Foreshore. Access from B100 at Port Gibbon sign, through Igloo Rd. 6 km dirt road. $5 fee at Honesty box

HEMA 88 E5 | 33 48 7 S | 136 48 6 E

BIG RIG

492 Yeldulkie Weir

Picnic Area 37 km W of Cowell or 5 km E of Cleve. Donation requested

HEMA 88 D4 | 33 41 35 S | 136 32 39 E

493 Cleve Showgrounds
☎ (08) 8628 2004

Camp Area at Cleve. Rudall Rd

HEMA 88 D4 | 33 42 3 S | 136 29 26 E

BIG RIG

494 Cleve Hotel
☎ (08) 8628 2011

Parking Area at Cleve. 32 Fourth St, check in with publican. Self Contained Vehicles only

HEMA 88 D4 | 33 42 12 S | 136 29 37 E

BIG RIG 48

495 Cleve Caravan Park & Roadhouse
☎ (08) 8628 2019

Caravan Park at Cleve. 1 Cowell Rd

HEMA 88 D4 | 33 42 8 S | 136 29 59 E

BIG RIG

496 The Arno Bay Hotel
☎ (08) 8628 0001

Camp Area at Arno Bay. Tel El Kebir Tce, foreshore end. Parking at rear of hotel, check in at hotel for payment. Self Contained Vehicles only

HEMA 88 E4 | 33 54 59 S | 136 34 22 E

BIG RIG 72

497 Wharminda Soaks Picnic Area

Picnic Area 10 km W of Wharminda. Signposted at railway crossing. Dirt road. Small vehicles only, low trees

HEMA 88 E4 | 33 55 51 S | 136 9 47 E

498 Carrow Wells

Camp Spot 4 km S of Port Neill, via Coastal Rd. Alternatively turn E 25 km NE of Tumby Bay for 5 km, then NE for 10 km. Dirt road

HEMA 88 E4 | 34 8 39 S | 136 20 1 E

499 Cowleys Beach

Camp Spot 11 km S of Port Neill via Coastal Rd. Turn E into Kiandra Rd. Alternatively turn E 22 km NE of Tumby Bay along Kiandra Rd for 6 km

HEMA 88 F4 | 34 11 50 S | 136 17 56 E

BIG RIG

500 Lipson Cove
☎ (08) 8688 2101

Camp Area 13 km NE of Lipson. Turn E onto Lipson Cove Rd 52 km SW of Arno Bay or 18 km NE of Tumby Bay. 8 km dirt road. Please use Honesty box

HEMA 88 F4 | 34 15 43 S | 136 15 38 E

501 CWA Cottages & Caravan Park
☎ (08) 8688 2272

Caravan Park at Tumby Bay. 3 The Esplanade

HEMA 88 F4 | 34 22 29 S | 136 6 13 E

502 Tumby Bay Self Contained RV Park
☎ (08) 8688 2087

Parking Area 1 km N of Tumby Bay. Opposite airport turnoff & cemetery. Self Contained Vehicles only. Permits from Ritz Cafe or Tumby Takeaway

HEMA 88 F4 34 21 31 S 136 6 3 E

BIG RIG

503 Yallunda Flat Showgrounds
☎ (08) 8688 2431

Camp Area between Tumby Bay & Cummins on Bratten Way. Not available Oct long weekend. Folded note donation. Honesty box

HEMA 88 F3 34 20 51 S 135 52 49 E

504 Louth Bay

Camp Spot 27 km SW of Tumby Bay. Turn E 25 km SW of Tumby Bay or 21 km N of Port Lincoln for 2 km. First L past golf club

HEMA 88 F3 34 32 30 S 135 55 51 E

BIG RIG

505 McKechnie Springs Farmstay
☎ (08) 8684 5015

Camp Area 12 km NW of Port Lincoln. Head W on Flinders Hwy, turn N onto Wine Shanty Rd, then onto Green Patch Rd. Continue along Greenpatch Rd then turn NE onto McFarlane Rd. At Y intersection veer R. Entrance 200m from the Y jcn. 12 km dirt road. Minimum 2 night stay

HEMA 88 G3 34 35 23 S 135 46 22 E

BIG RIG

506 Axel Stenross Boat Ramp
☎ 1300 788 378

Parking Area in Port Lincoln. N end of town. Upper car park only, limited turning space. Motorhomes only, must be self contained. Permit required

HEMA 88 G3 34 42 14 S 135 51 14 E

72

507 Billy Lights Point Boat Ramp
☎ 1300 788 378

Parking Area in Port Lincoln. Via Ravendale Rd, Marina Dr & St Andrews Dr. Car park area adjacent to bush. Motorhomes only, must be self contained. Permit required

HEMA 88 G3 34 44 43 S 135 53 28 E

72

508 Horse Rock Campground
Lincoln National Park
☎ (08) 8688 3111

Camp Area 9 km NE of Park Entrance on Access Rd. Dirt road. Permit required. Small sites

HEMA 88 G3 34 48 28 S 135 51 44 E

509 Taylors Landing Campground
Lincoln National Park
☎ (08) 8688 3111

Camp Area 24 km SE of Park Entrance on Access Rd. Dirt road. Permit required

HEMA 88 G3 34 51 16 S 135 57 32 E

510 Surfleet Cove Campground
Lincoln National Park
☎ (08) 8688 3111

Camp Area 22 km NE of Park Entrance on Access Rd. Dirt road. Permit required

HEMA 88 G3 34 45 57 S 135 57 25 E

BIG RIG

511 Fishermans Point Campground
Lincoln National Park
☎ (08) 8688 3111

Camp Area 24 km NE of Park Entrance on Access Rd. Dirt road. Permit required

HEMA 88 G3 34 45 25 S 135 59 9 E

512 September Beach Campground
Lincoln National Park
☎ (08) 8688 3111

Camp Area 28 km NE of Park Entrance on Access Rd. Dirt road. Permit required

HEMA 88 G3 34 44 2 S 135 59 47 E

513 Cape Donington Campground
Lincoln National Park
☎ (08) 8688 3111

Camp Area 29 km NE of park entrance. 500m from Access Rd. Dirt road. Permit required

HEMA 88 G3 34 43 45 S 135 59 20 E

514 Engine Point Campground
Lincoln National Park
☎ (08) 8688 3111

Camp Area 25 km NE of Park Entrance on Access Rd. Dirt road. Permit required

HEMA 88 G3 34 44 21 S 135 59 20 E

515 Mikkira Station
☎ (08) 8685 6020

Camp Area at Mikkira Station. 30 km SW of Port Lincoln via Fishery Bay Rd

HEMA 88 G3 34 50 18 S 135 40 51 E

516 Whaling Station

Parking Area 31 km SW of Port Lincoln. Whaling Station Rd

HEMA 88 G3 34 54 39 S 135 41 21 E

517 Coffin Bay Lookout

Rest Area 1 km E of Coffin Bay. 250m off Hwy

HEMA 88 G2 34 37 17 S 135 29 4 E

518 Yangie Bay Campground
Coffin Bay National Park
☎ (08) 8688 3111

Camp Area 19 km W of Coffin Bay. Some dirt road. Permit required

HEMA 88 G2 34 38 24 S 135 21 38 E

BIG RIG

Notes...

SOUTH AUSTRALIA

519 Mount Dutton
☎ (08) 8685 4031

Camp Area at Mount Dutton Bay Woolshed, 5 km W of Wangary. Dirt road

HEMA 88 F2 | 34 31 53 S | 135 25 58 E

BIG RIG

520 Farm Beach Campground
☎ (08) 8676 2106

Campground 10 km NW of Wangary, via Farm Beach Rd. Dirt road

HEMA 88 F2 | 34 29 48 S | 135 23 52 E

BIG RIG

521 Coles Point

Camp Spot at Coles Point, 26 km N of Wangary. Turn W 14.6 km N of Wangary onto Coles Point Rd. 10.5 km to bush sites along coast

HEMA 88 F2 | 34 22 10 S | 135 21 14 E

522 Warrow North Rest Area

B100

Rest Area 9 km NW of Warrow or 18 km S of Mount Hope

HEMA 88 F2 | 34 15 57 S | 135 25 21 E

523 Point Drummond

Parking Area 13 km W of Mount Hope. 4 km dirt road

HEMA 88 F2 | 34 10 21 S | 135 16 4 E

524 Lake Hamilton Rest Area *(Cummings Lookout)*

B100

Rest Area 15 km N of Mount Hope or 60 km SE of Elliston

HEMA 88 E2 | 34 0 43 S | 135 16 7 E

BIG RIG

525 Sheringa South Rest Area

B100

Rest Area 25 km N of Mount Hope or 8 km S of Sheringa

HEMA 88 E2 | 33 54 40 S | 135 15 50 E

BIG RIG

526 Sheringa Beach
☎ (08) 8687 8761

Camp Area 8 km W of Sheringa. Turn W off B100, 40 km SE of Elliston or 33 km N of Mount Hope. Dirt road. Obtain permit from store

HEMA 88 E2 | 33 52 19 S | 135 10 10 E

BIG RIG

527 Dry Stone Walling Rest Area

B100

Rest Area 16 km NW of Sheringa or 24 km SE of Elliston

HEMA 88 E2 | 33 45 33 S | 135 6 5 E

BIG RIG

528 Locks Well Beach
☎ (08) 8687 8761

Parking Area 27 km NW of Sheringa or 19 km SE of Elliston. Turn W 24 km NW of Sheringa or 16 km SE of Elliston. Big rigs at top car park

HEMA 88 D1 | 33 44 32 S | 135 1 33 E

BIG RIG

529 Nationdale Bush Camping
☎ 0408 916 216

Camp Area 7 km E of Elliston via Birdseye Hwy (Elliston - Lock Rd). 5 km E of intersection. GPS at gate. 4x4 vehicle access. Follow signs & yellow markers to bush camp area

HEMA 88 D1 | 33 38 23 S | 134 57 37 E

530 Walkers Rocks Campground
☎ (08) 8687 9200

Camp Area 14 km N of Elliston. Turn W off B100, 10 km N of Elliston or 117 km SE of Streaky Bay. 5 km dirt road

HEMA 88 D1 | 33 33 34 S | 134 51 21 E

BIG RIG

531 Talia Caves

Parking Area 48 km N of Elliston. Turn W off B100, 42 km N of Elliston or 84 km SE of Streaky Bay. 6 km dirt road

HEMA 88 C1 | 33 19 0 S | 134 47 9 E

BIG RIG

532 Coodlie Park
☎ (08) 8687 0411

B100

Camping Area in Coodlie Park, 49 km N of Elliston or 16 km S of Port Kenny. Signposted turn off to W. Call at office for bush camp site directions

HEMA 88 C1 | 33 17 8 S | 134 46 50 E

BIG RIG

533 Venus Bay Wharf

Parking Area at Venus Bay. 26 km NW of Talia or 14 km SW of Port Kenny

HEMA 88 C1 | 33 13 55 S | 134 40 22 E

BIG RIG

534 Port Kenny Caravan Park
☎ (08) 8625 5076

Caravan Park at Port Kenny. Flinders Hwy

HEMA 97 K13 | 33 10 12 S | 134 41 32 E

535 Murphys Haystacks

Parking Area 10 km E of Calca. Turn W off B100, 22 km NW of Port Kenny or 39 km SE of Streaky Bay for 2 km along Benbarber Rd. Small fee to enter the "Haystacks" property

HEMA 97 J12 | 33 1 9 S | 134 29 28 E

BIG RIG 24

536 Baird Bay
☎ (08) 8626 1001

Camp Area 48 km NW of Port Kenny or 50 km S of Streaky Bay, via Calca Rd. Small vehicles only. Dirt road. Honesty system

HEMA 97 K12 | 33 8 38 S | 134 21 47 E

537 Eyres Waterhole

B100

Rest Area 59 km NW of Port Kenny or 5 km SE of Streaky Bay

HEMA 97 J12 | 32 49 5 S | 134 14 46 E

BIG RIG

538 Streaky Bay Lions Park

B100

Rest Area at Streaky Bay. N end of town

HEMA 97 J12 | 32 47 42 S | 134 13 5 E

BIG RIG

539 Speed Point ☎ (08) 8626 1001
Camp Area 16 km S of Streaky Bay. Small vehicles only. Dirt road. Honesty box
HEMA 97 J12 32 55 51 S 134 7 45 E

540 Tractor Beach ☎ (08) 8626 1001
Camp Spot 17 km SW of Streaky Bay, via Westall Way Scenic Dr. Dirt road. Honesty box
HEMA 97 J12 32 52 13 S 134 6 47 E

541 Perlubie Beach ☎ (08) 8626 1001
B100
Camp Area 21 km N of Streaky Bay or 49 km SE of Smoky Bay. Camping only allowed on beach, don't use old parking area this is private property. Beware of tide & soft sand
HEMA 97 H12 32 39 40 S 134 17 41 E
BIG RIG

542 Haslam Rest Area
B100
Rest Area 3 km S of Haslam Hwy exit, 39 km N of Streaky Bay or 31 km SE of Smoky Bay
HEMA 97 H12 32 30 45 S 134 14 25 E
BIG RIG

543 Haslam Campground
Camp Area at Haslam. Cnr Mail St & South Tce. Maximum stay 10 days. Limited sites
HEMA 97 H12 32 30 32 S 134 12 50 E
BIG RIG

544 Acraman Creek Conservation Park ☎ (08) 8625 3144
Camp Area 23 km SE of Smoky Bay. Turn W 12 km NW of Haslam turnoff or 17 km SE of Smoky Bay for 6 km of dirt road. 4WD only. Small vehicles only. Permit required
HEMA 97 H12 32 27 15 S 134 4 12 E

545 Smoky Rd Rest Area
Rest Area 2.5 km SE of the Smoky Bay turn off
HEMA 97 12H 32 23 25 S 133 59 26 E
BIG RIG

546 Smoky Bay Caravan Park ☎ (08) 8625 7030
Caravan Park at Smoky Bay. On foreshore
HEMA 97 H11 32 22 37 S 133 56 3 E

547 Laura Bay Conservation Park ☎ (08) 8625 3144
Camp Spot 19 km NW of Smoky Bay or 21 km SE of Ceduna. 3 km dirt road
HEMA 97 G11 32 14 32 S 133 49 47 E

548 Wittelbee Conservation Park ☎ (08) 8625 3144
Camp Area 10 km SE of Ceduna, via Decres Bay Rd. Signposted
HEMA 97 G11 32 12 22 S 133 44 17 E

Port Augusta to Eucla

Eyre Highway

549 Port Augusta Motorhome Park
Camp Spot behind the Port Augusta Sports & Recreation facility, Power Station Rd. 4 km E of Port Augusta. Self Contained Vehicles only. Maximum stay 14 days
HEMA 88 A7 32 30 40 S 137 47 9 E
BIG RIG

550 Lincoln/Eyre Highway Junction
A1
Rest Area 25 km SW of Port Augusta or 42 km E of Iron Knob
HEMA 88 B7 32 36 58 S 137 34 26 E
BIG RIG

551 Iron Knob Rest Area
A1
Rest Area 1 km W of Iron Knob, at Hwy A1 jcn
HEMA 88 B6 32 43 15 S 137 8 54 E
BIG RIG

552 Knobbies Camping & Caravan Area
Camp Area at Iron Knob. Dickenson St. Donation requested
HEMA 88 B6 32 43 56 S 137 9 2 E
BIG RIG

553 Mt Ive Station ☎ (08) 8648 1817
Camp Area at Mt Ive Station. 126 km W of Iron Knob via Kingoonya - Iron Knob Rd
HEMA 88 A4 32 26 18 S 136 4 5 E

554 Waltumba Camp Ground
Lake Gairdner National Park
Camp Area 30 km NW of N Mt Ive Station on Moonaree Station Rd. Access via Mt Ive Station by private access road enquires & gate key available from Mt Ive Station (08) 8648 1817. 4WD vehicle access
HEMA 94 G3 32 7 20 S 135 53 46 E

555 Iron Knob West Rest Area 1
A1
Rest Area 21 km SW of Iron Knob or 66 km NE of Kimba
HEMA 88 B5 32 51 44 S 137 0 16 E
BIG RIG

556 Iron Knob West Rest Area 2
A1
Rest Area 37 km SW of Iron Knob or 50 km NE of Kimba
HEMA 88 C5 32 57 51 S 136 53 16 E
BIG RIG

557 Kimba East Rest Area
A1
Rest Area 52 km SW of Iron Knob or 35 km E of Kimba
HEMA 88 C5 33 2 56 S 136 46 9 E
BIG RIG

Notes...

SOUTH AUSTRALIA

558 Lakes Edge Camping Area
☎ (08) 8688 3111
Lake Gillies Conservation Park

Camp Area 76 km W of Iron Knob. Turn N off Eyre Hwy 67 km W of Iron Knob or 17 km E of Kimba. 9 km track to camp area. Suitable for off road caravans & camper trailers. Signposted

HEMA 88 C5 33 2 9 S 136 35 55 E

559 Apex-Lions Park
A1

Rest Area at Kimba, Park Tce, next to swimming pool. Donation for upkeep of facilities

HEMA 88 C4 33 8 20 S 136 25 0 E

48

560 Kimba Recreation Reserve
A1

Camp Area at Kimba. Buckleboo Rd, extension of North Tce. Entry through archway Kima Pioneer Memorial. Coin shower. Donation welcome for upkeep

HEMA 88 C4 33 8 4 S 136 24 54 E

BIG RIG 24

561 Carappee Hill Campground
☎ (08) 8688 3111
Carappee Hill Conservation Park

Camp Area 8 km NE of Darke Peak or 42 km SW of Kimba. Dirt road

HEMA 88 D4 33 25 56 S 136 16 20 E

562 Koongawa East
A1

Parking Area 44 km W of Kimba or 45 km E of Kyancutta

HEMA 88 C3 33 11 49 S 135 59 57 E

BIG RIG

563 Darkes Memorial Rest Area
A1

Rest Area 55 km W of Kimba or 34 km E of Kyancutta

HEMA 88 C3 33 9 56 S 135 53 12 E

BIG RIG

564 Goyders Line Memorial Rest Area
A1

Rest Area 11 km W of Koongawa or 20 km E of Kyancutta

HEMA 88 C3 33 8 47 S 135 45 21 E

BIG RIG

565 Polkdinney Park
A1

Parking Area at Kyancutta, next to Kyancutta general store

HEMA 88 C2 33 7 59 S 135 33 9 E

566 Kopi Rest Area
B90

Rest Area 38 km S of Kyancutta or 25 km N of Lock

HEMA 88 D3 33 22 54 S 135 38 59 E

BIG RIG

567 Lock Caravan Park
☎ (08) 8689 1020
B90

Caravan Park at Lock. South Tce, near town centre. Pay at PO during week or Caretaker on weekends

HEMA 88 D3 33 34 10 S 135 45 24 E

BIG RIG

568 Peachna Rest Area
B90

Rest Area 26 km S of Lock or 55 km N of Cummins

HEMA 88 E3 33 46 54 S 135 42 47 E

BIG RIG

569 Cummins Railway Triangle

Rest Area at Cummins. Centre of town

HEMA 88 F3 34 15 56 S 135 43 33 E

BIG RIG

570 Wudinna East Rest Area
A1

Rest Area 7 km W of Kyancutta or 6 km E of Wudinna

HEMA 88 C2 33 5 5 S 135 30 4 E

BIG RIG

571 Granite Country Rest Area
A1

Rest Area at Wudinna, near Wudinna Trail turnoff

HEMA 88 C2 33 2 58 S 135 27 57 E

BIG RIG

572 Polda Rock

Parking Area 8 km NE of Wudinna, via Standley Rd. Dirt road

HEMA 88 C2 33 1 16 S 135 32 0 E

573 Mt Wudinna

Parking Area 13 km NE of Wudinna, via Standley Rd. Dirt road

HEMA 88 C2 32 59 4 S 135 32 51 E

574 Yaninee Rest Area
A1

Rest Area 3 km W of Yaninee or 13 km SE of Minnipa

HEMA 88 B2 32 55 53 S 135 14 22 E

575 Minnipa Apex Park
A1

Rest Area at Minnipa

HEMA 88 B2 32 51 16 S 135 9 3 E

BIG RIG 24

576 Tcharkuldu Rock

Camp Area E of Minnipa, via Bockelberg Rd. Dirt road. 7 day maximum stay. Donation requested

HEMA 88 B2 32 50 50 S 135 11 45 E

BIG RIG

577 Pildappa Rock

Camp Area 15 km NE of Minnipa. Dirt road. Donation requested

HEMA 88 B2 32 45 3 S 135 13 47 E

BIG RIG

578 Waganny Camping Area
☎ (08) 8688 3111
Gawler Ranges National Park

Camp Area 63 km NW of Widinna. Access via Old Paney Scenic Route. Signposted. 3 km S to campsite. Suitable for off road caravans & camper trailers

HEMA 88 B2 32 42 20 S 135 32 0 E

579 Chandada Pioneer Park
Rest Area 15 km W of Poochera or 46 km E of Streaky Bay
HEMA 88 B1 32 45 16 S 134 40 24 E

580 Poochera Rest Area
A1
Rest Area 2 km W of Poochera or 45 km SE of Wirrulla
HEMA 88 B1 32 42 39 S 134 49 22 E

581 Yantanabie South Rest Area
A1
Rest Area 25 km NW of Poochera or 22 km SE of Wirrulla
HEMA 88 A1 32 33 12 S 134 40 21 E

582 Wirrulla Caravan Park
(08) 8626 8019
A1
Caravan Park at Wirrulla. Shower key at general store or hotel
HEMA 97 H13 32 24 16 S 134 31 57 E

583 Wirrulla West Rest Area
A1
Rest Area 9 km W of Wirrulla or 84 km E of Ceduna
HEMA 97 H12 32 24 41 S 134 26 32 E

584 Old Perlubie School Site
A1
Rest Area 13 km W of Wirrulla or 80 km E of Ceduna
HEMA 97 H12 32 24 48 S 134 24 7 E

585 Puntabie East Rest Area
A1
Rest Area 48 km W of Wirrulla or 45 km E of Ceduna
HEMA 97 G12 32 12 38 S 134 7 56 E

586 Ceduna Airport Caravan Park
(08) 8625 2416
A1
Caravan Park 2 km E of Ceduna. Eyre Hwy
HEMA 97 G11 32 7 21 S 133 41 25 E

587 A1 Cabins & Caravan Park
(08) 8625 2578
A1
Caravan Park at Ceduna. 41 McKenzie St
HEMA 97 G11 32 7 25 S 133 40 49 E

588 Koonibba Rest Area
A1
Parking Area 33 km W of Ceduna or 40 km E of Penong
HEMA 97 G10 31 57 5 S 133 25 9 E

Notes...

589 Watraba Parking Area
A1
Parking Area 51 km W of Ceduna or 25 km E of Penong
HEMA 97 G10 31 56 26 S 133 16 31 E

590 Penong Caravan Park
(08) 8625 1111
A1
Caravan Park at Penong. 3 Stiggants Rd
HEMA 97 G10 31 55 31 S 133 0 32 E

591 Cactus Beach Point Sinclair
(08) 8625 1036
Camp Area 21 km S of Penong. Via Point Sinclair Rd. Dirt road
HEMA 97 G10 32 5 19 S 132 59 0 E

592 Cohen Rest Area
A1
Rest Area 16 km W of Penong or 63 km E of Nundroo
HEMA 97 F9 31 51 40 S 132 51 50 E

593 Fowlers Bay Caravan Park
(08) 8625 6143
Caravan Park at Fowlers Bay. On foreshore. Dirt road
HEMA 97 G8 31 59 20 S 132 26 12 E

594 Scotts Bay Bush Camping
(08) 8625 3144
Camp Spot 13 km W of Fowlers Bay. Via Fowlers Bay Corrabie Rd, then S onto Scotts Bay Rd for 6.6 km. W end behind dunes
HEMA 97 G8 32 0 15 S 132 23 5 E

595 Coorabie Farm
(08) 8625 6126
Camp Area at Coorabie. 15 km SE of Nundroo, turn S 5 km E of Nundroo into Fowlers Bay Rd. 10 km gravel, turn R into farm just before Coorbie
HEMA 97 G8 31 53 28 S 132 17 19 E

596 Nundroo East Rest Area
A1
Rest Area 69 km W of Penong or 10 km E of Nundroo
HEMA 97 F8 31 49 34 S 132 18 51 E

597 Nundroo Hotel Motel Caravan Park
(08) 8025 6120
A1
Caravan Park at Nundroo Roadhouse
HEMA 97 F8 31 47 33 S 132 13 29 E

598 Colona Rest Area
A1
Rest Area 27 km W of Nundroo or 25 km E of Yalata
HEMA 97 F8 31 36 19 S 132 2 9 E

599 Yalata West Rest Area
Rest Area 21 km W of Yalata or 70 km E of Nullarbor Roadhouse
A1
HEMA 96 E7 | 31 24 38 S | 131 36 53 E

600 222k Peg Rest Area
Rest Area 54 km W of Yalata or 37 km E of Nullarbor Roadhouse
A1
HEMA 96 E6 | 31 21 55 S | 131 15 58 E

601 164k Peg Rest Area
Rest Area 20 km W of Nullarbor Roadhouse or 164 km E of Border Village
A1
HEMA 96 F5 | 31 32 5 S | 130 41 32 E
BIG RIG

602 157k Peg Rest Area
Rest Area 27 km W of Nullarbor Roadhouse or 157 km E of Border Village
A1
HEMA 96 F5 | 31 33 2 S | 130 37 3 E
BIG RIG

603 Koonalda Homestead
☎ (08) 8625 3144
Camp Spot at Koonalda homestead. Turn N 94 km W Nullarbor Roadhouse or 88 km E of Border Village. 14 km to old Homestead. Fee payable at NPWSA Ceduna
A1
HEMA 96 F3 | 31 27 22 S | 129 51 28 E

604 85k Peg Rest Area
Rest Area 100 km W of Nullarbor Roadhouse or 84 km E of Border Village
A1
HEMA 96 F3 | 31 34 49 S | 129 52 27 E
BIG RIG

605 81k Peg Rest Area
Rest Area 103 km W of Nullarbor Roadhouse or 81 km E of Border Village
A1
HEMA 93 F3 | 31 35 16 S | 129 50 3 E
BIG RIG

606 Bunda Cliffs Scenic Lookout
Parking Area 109 km W of Nullarbor Roadhouse or 75 km E of Border Village. 600m S of Hwy
A1
HEMA 96 F3 | 31 36 24 S | 129 46 36 E
BIG RIG

607 52k Peg Parking Bay
Parking Area 132 km W of Nullarbor Roadhouse or 52 km E of Border Village
A1
HEMA 96 F3 | 31 37 9 S | 129 31 47 E
BIG RIG

608 38k Peg Parking Bay
Parking Area 146 km W of Nullarbor Roadhouse or 38 km E of Border Village
A1
HEMA 96 F2 | 31 38 17 S | 129 23 19 E
BIG RIG

609 25k Peg Parking Bay
Parking Area 159 km W of Nullarbor Roadhouse or 25 km E of Border Village
A1
HEMA 96 F2 | 31 38 55 S | 129 15 16 E
BIG RIG

610 17k Peg Parking Bay
Parking Area 167 km W of Nullarbor Roadhouse or 17 km E of Border Village
A1
HEMA 96 F2 | 31 39 27 S | 129 10 4 E
BIG RIG

611 Scenic Lookout (13k Peg)
Parking Area 171 km W of Nullarbor Roadhouse or 13 km E of Border Village
A1
HEMA 96 F2 | 31 39 35 S | 129 7 52 E
BIG RIG

612 10k Peg Rest Area
Rest Area 174 km W of Nullarbor Roadhouse or 10 km E of Border Village
A1
HEMA 96 F2 | 31 38 54 S | 129 5 59 E
BIG RIG

Lyndhurst to Innamincka

Strzelecki Track

This road is seasonal and more suitable to 4WD vehicles, camper trailers and off road caravans. Road conditions phone 1300 361 033

613 Freeling Rest Area
Rest Area 76 km NE of Lyndhurst or 387 km SW of Innamincka
HEMA 95 B10 | 29 59 48 S | 139 0 28 E
BIG RIG

614 Dog Fence Rest Area
Rest Area 104 km NE of Lyndhurst or 338 km SW of Innamincka
HEMA 95 A10 | 29 47 21 S | 139 5 22 E
BIG RIG

615 Murnpeowie Rest Area
Rest Area 126 km NE of Lyndhurst or 338 km SW of Innamincka. Opposite Murnpeowie Station turnoff
HEMA 91 K10 | 29 37 3 S | 139 8 56 E
BIG RIG

616 Blanchewater Ruins
Camp Spot 158 km NE of Lyndhurst or 307 km SW of Innamincka. N side of creek on the E side of road
HEMA 91 K11 | 29 33 1 S | 139 27 1 E

617 Art Barker Rest Area
Rest Area 209 km NE of Lyndhurst or 255 km SW of Innamincka
HEMA 91 K11 | 29 29 37 S | 139 55 46 E
BIG RIG

618 Montecollina Bore Rest Area
Rest Area 222 km NE of Lyndhurst or 223 km SW of Innamincka
HEMA 91 K12 | 29 24 2 S | 139 59 15 E

619 Strzelecki Creek Rest Area

Rest Area 273 km NE of Lyndhurst or 192 km SW of Innamincka. 2 km S of creek crossing

HEMA 91 J12 28 57 37 S 140 7 40 E

620 Moomba Lookout

Parking Area 174 km NE of Montecollina Bore or 105 km SW of Innaminka on New Strzelecki Track or 86 on Old Strzelecki Track

HEMA 91 F12 28 7 57 S 140 12 41 E

621 Innamincka Town Common

☎ (08) 8675 9901

Camp Area 1 km S of township on banks of Coopers Creek. Signposted, honesty box at entrance

HEMA 91 F13 27 45 5 S 140 43 58 E

622 Policemans

☎ (08) 8648 5328

Camp Area on the 15 Mile Track SW of Innamincka. At 3.5 km turn R to Policeman's Water Hole. Desert Parks Pass required, fees payable at Innamincka Store

HEMA 91 F13 27 45 31 S 140 42 12 E

623 Ski Beach

☎ (08) 8648 5328

Camp Area on the 15 Mile Track SW of Innamincka. 5.6 km turn R to Ski Beach. Desert Parks Pass required, fees payable at Innamincka Store

HEMA 91 F13 27 45 52 S 140 41 6 E

624 Kings Site

☎ (08) 8648 5328

Camp Area on the 15 Mile Track SW of Innamincka. 7 km turn R to King's Site Campground. Desert Parks Pass required, fees payable at Innamincka Store

HEMA 91 F13 27 46 40 S 140 40 29 E

625 Minkie Waterhole

☎ (08) 8648 5328

Camp Area on the 15 Mile Track SW of Innamincka. 10.8 km turn R to Minkie Waterhole. Desert Parks Pass required, fees payable at Innamincka Store

HEMA 91 F13 27 46 47 S 140 38 23 E

626 Scrubby Camp

☎ (08) 8648 5328

Camp Spot on the Coongie Lake track NW of Innamincka. 43.5 km turn L into camp site. Desert Parks Pass required, fees payable at Innamincka Store

HEMA 91 E13 27 39 38 S 140 23 3 E

627 Kudriemitchie Campground

☎ (08) 8648 5328

Camp Spot on the Coongie Lake track NW of Innamincka. 83 km turn L into camp site. Desert Parks Pass required, fees payable at Innamincka Store

HEMA 91 E12 27 21 41 S 140 12 15 E

628 Coongie Lakes Campground

☎ 1800 816 078

Malkumba-Coongie Lakes National Park

Camp Spot on the Coongie Lake track NW of Innamincka. 104 km turn L into camp site. Desert Parks Pass required, fees payable at Innamincka Store. Subject to flooding, check ahead to make sure road is open

HEMA 91 D12 27 11 27 S 140 9 12 E

629 Cullyamurra Waterhole

☎ (08) 8648 5328

Take Innamincka - Nappa Merrie Rd E from Innaminka. Turn N 14 km. Desert Parks Pass required, fees payable at Innamincka Store

HEMA 91 E14 27 42 6 S 140 50 24 E

Notes...

key map

PURNULULU NATIONAL PARK (117 G13) PHOTO: © ISTOCK.COM/SARAH WINTER

Distances are shown in kilometres and follow the most direct major sealed route where possible.

	WA-SA Border Village	Port Hedland	Perth	Newman	Mount Magnet	Kununurra	Karratha	Kalgoorlie	Geraldton	Esperance	Carnarvon	Bunbury	Broome
Albany	1400	1999	413	1546	958	3575	1892	865	799	476	1276	358	2594
Broome	3223	609	2217	1048	1654	1049	842	2314	1992	2703	1457	2592	
Bunbury	1593	1800	178	1347	723	3372	1693	770	600	669	1077		
Carnarvon	2344	862	899	1237	815	2438	634	1459	477	1600			
Esperance	924	2108	737	1655	1049	3684	2268	389	1275				
Geraldton	1867	1327	422	964	338	2983	1093	982					
Kalgoorlie	909	1719	596	1266	660	3295	1879						
Karratha	2788	238	1515	631	1219	1867							
Kununurra	4206	1590	3198	2029	2635								
Mount Magnet	1569	1059	563	606									
Newman	2175	453	1169										
Perth	1445	1622											
Port Hedland	2628												
WA-SA Border Village													

116-117
114-115
118
112-113
119
106-107
For more detail see pages 102-103 and 104-105
110-111
108-109

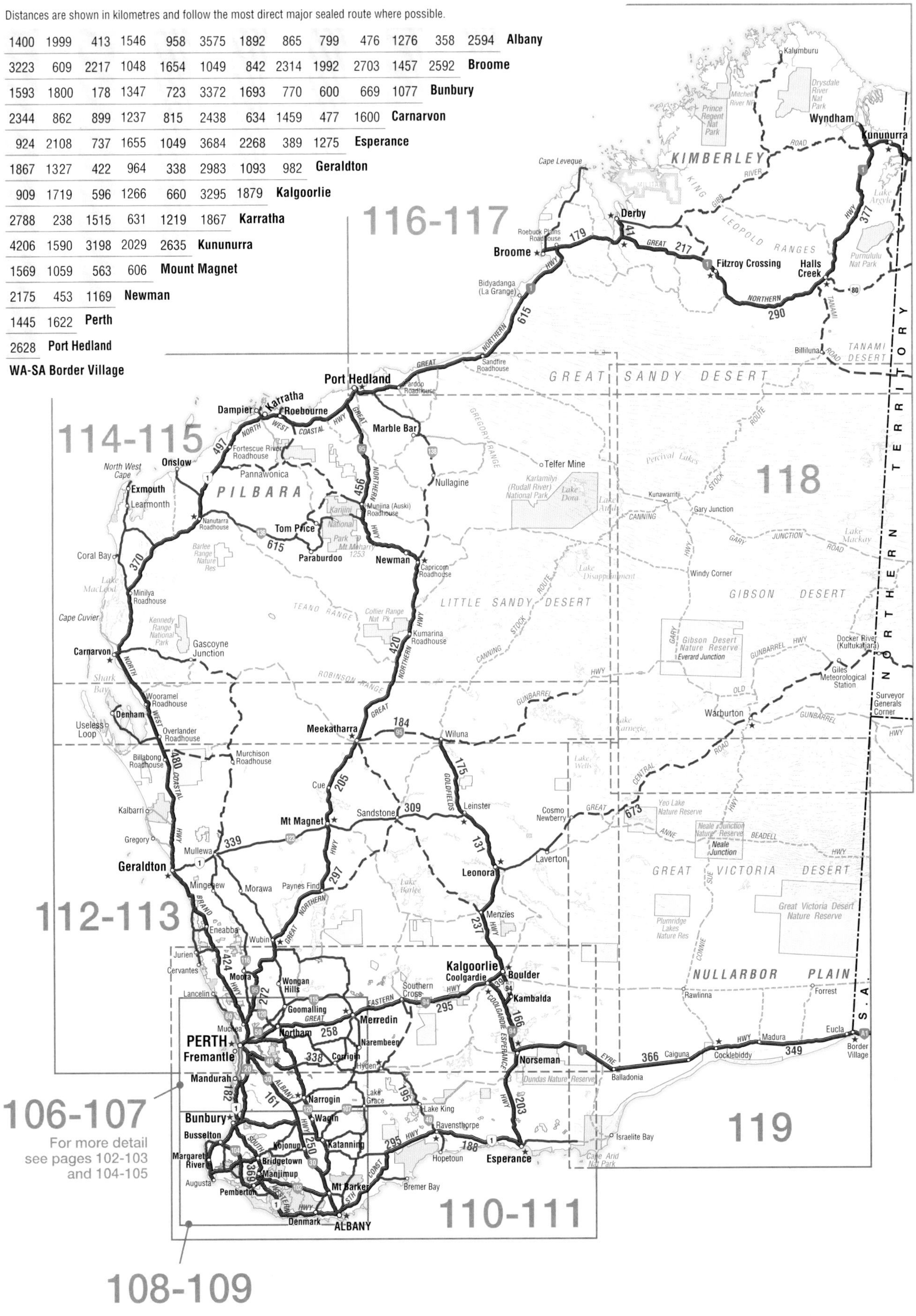

Perth CBD

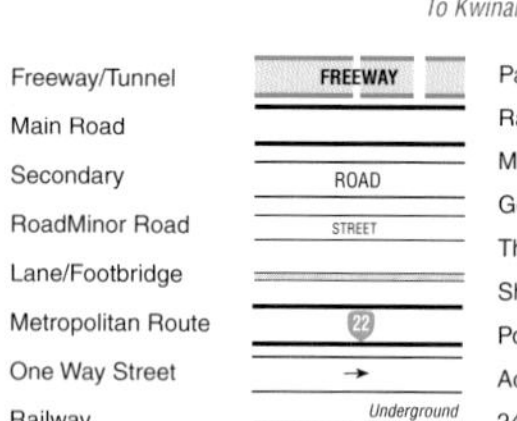

Points of Interest

1. Art Gallery of Western Australia A3
2. Barracks Archway B1
3. Cloisters, The B2
4. Deanery, The B3
5. Government House B3
6. Hay Street Mall B2
7. His Majesty's Theatre B2
8. Horseshoe Bridge B2
9. King Street Arts Centre B2
10. Kings Park B1
11. Kings Park Lookout C1
12. Langley Park C3
13. Murray Street Mall B2
14. NIB Stadium A4
15. Old Council House B3
16. Old Court House B3
17. Old Mill C1
18. Old Perth Boys School B2
19. Old Perth Observatory B1
20. Parliament House B1
21. Perth Arena A2
22. Perth Concert Hall B3
23. Perth Convention Exhibition Ctr B2
24. Perth Inst of Contemporary Arts A3
25. Perth Mint B4
26. Perth Town Hall B3
27. Perth Zoo E2
28. St George's Cathedral B3
29. St Mary's RC Cathedral B3
30. Scitech Discovery Centre A1
31. State Library of Western Aust A3
32. State War Memorial C1
33. Swan Bells C2
34. Wellington Square B4
35. Western Australian Museum A3

Accommodation

38. Aarons All Suites B3
39. Aarons Hotel Perth B3
40. Adina Apartment Hotel Perth B2
41. Citadines St Georges Terrace Perth B2
42. Comfort Hotel Perth City C4
43. Comfort Inn Wentworth Plaza Hotel Perth B2
44. Criterion Hotel B3
45. Crowne Plaza Perth C4
46. Duxton Hotel Perth, The B3
47. Four Points by Sheraton Perth A2
48. Globe Backpackers and City Oasis Resort B2
49. Goodearth Hotel C4
50. Grand Central Backpackers B3
51. Holiday Inn Perth City Centre B2
52. Hotel Ibis Perth B2
53. Hyatt Regency Perth C4
54. Ibis Styles Perth A3
55. Kings Perth Hotel B3
56. Mantra on Hay C4
57. Mantra on Murray B2
58. Marque Hotel Perth B1
59. Melbourne Hotel, The B2
60. Mercure Hotel, The B3
61. Mounts Bay Waters Apartments B1
62. New Esplanade Hotel Perth, The B2
63. Novotel Perth Hotel Langley C3
64. Parmelia Hilton Perth Hotel B2
65. Perth Ambassador Hotel C4
66. Perth City YHA B3
67. Quest West End B2
68. River View on Mount Street B1
69. Rydges Perth B2
70. Seasons of Perth B3
71. Sheraton Perth Hotel C3
72. Sullivans Hotel C1
73. Travelodge Perth Hotel B3

Travel Information

75. City West Train Station A1
76. Claisebrook Train Station A4
77. East Perth Train Station A4
78. Esplanade Station B2
79. McIver Train Station B3
80. Perth Train Station B3
81. Perth Underground Station B2
82. Perth Visitor Centre B2
83. RAC Office A1
84. Roe Street Temporary Bus Station A2

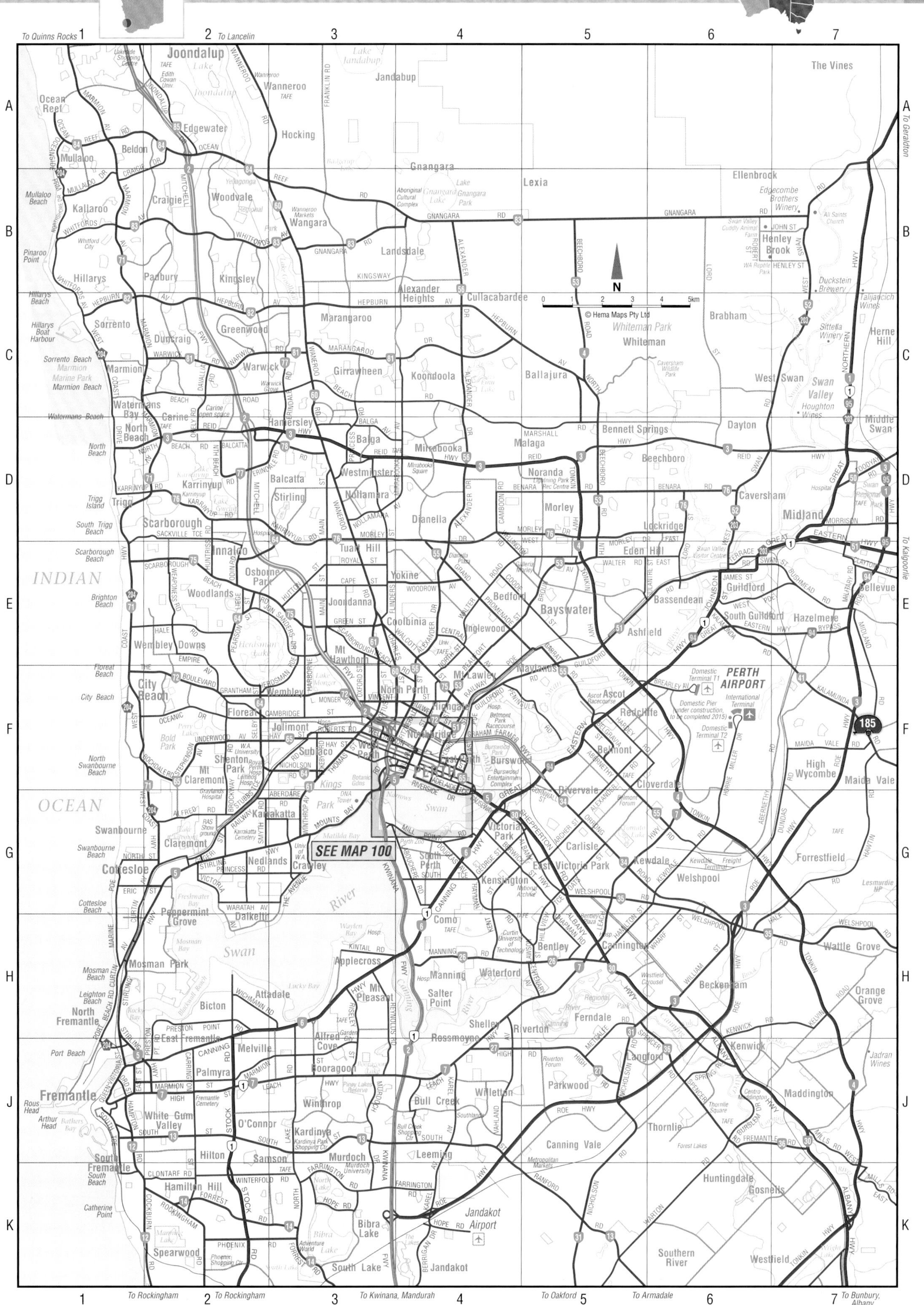
To Quinns Rocks
To Lancelin
Joondalup
Wanneroo
Jandabup
The Vines
Ocean Reef
Edgewater
Hocking
Mullaloo
Beldon
Gnangara
Lexia
Ellenbrook
Mullaloo Beach
Kallaroo
Craigie
Woodvale
Wangara
Edgecombe Brothers Winery
Whitford City
Pinaroo Point
Landsdale
Henley Brook
Hillarys
Padbury
Kingsley
Alexander Heights
Cullacabardee
Duckstein Brewery
Hillarys Beach
Taljancich Wines
Sorrento
Marangaroo
Brabham
Hillarys Boat Harbour
Duncraig
Greenwood
© Hema Maps Pty Ltd
Whiteman Park
Whiteman
Sittella Winery
Herne Hill
Sorrento Beach
Marmion
Marmion Beach
Warwick
Girrawheen
Koondoola
Ballajura
West Swan
Swan Valley
Houghton Wines
Watermans Bay
Carine
Hamersley
Balga
Mirrabooka
Malaga
Bennett Springs
Dayton
Middle Swan
Watermans Beach
North Beach
Beechboro
Westminster
Noranda
Caversham
Trigg Island
Trigg
Karrinyup
Balcatta
Stirling
Nollamara
Morley
Midland
South Trigg Beach
Scarborough
Dianella
Lockridge
Scarborough Beach
Innaloo
Tuart Hill
Eden Hill
INDIAN
Osborne Park
Yokine
Bellevue
Brighton Beach
Woodlands
Joondanna
Bedford
Bassendean
Guildford
Bayswater
South Guildford
Hazelmere
Coolbinia
Inglewood
Ashfield
Wembley Downs
Mt Hawthorn
Floreat Beach
Mt Lawley
Maylands
PERTH AIRPORT
City Beach
City Beach
Wembley
North Perth
Ascot
Highgate
Floreat
Redcliffe
Jolimont
Northbridge
High Wycombe
Bold Park
Subiaco
West Perth
East Perth
Belmont
Burswood
Maida Vale
North Swanbourne Beach
Shenton Park
Mt Claremont
PERTH
Cloverdale
Kings Park
Rivervale
OCEAN
Karrakatta
Victoria Park
Swanbourne
Claremont
SEE MAP 100
Carlisle
Swanbourne Beach
Nedlands
Crawley
South Perth
Kewdale
Forrestfield
Cottesloe
East Victoria Park
Welshpool
Kensington
Cottesloe Beach
Peppermint Grove
Dalkeith
River
Como
Bentley
Wattle Grove
Swan
Cannington
Mosman Beach
Mosman Park
Applecross
Manning
Waterford
Beckenham
Leighton Beach
Mt Pleasant
Orange Grove
North Fremantle
Attadale
Salter Point
Bicton
Ferndale
Shelley
Riverton
East Fremantle
Alfred Cove
Rossmoyne
Port Beach
Melville
Kenwick
Palmyra
Booragoon
Langford
Jadran Wines
Fremantle
Parkwood
Maddington
Willetton
Rous Head
Winthrop
Bull Creek
Arthur Head
White Gum Valley
O'Connor
Thornlie
Kardinya
Canning Vale
Leeming
Hilton
Samson
Murdoch
South Fremantle
South Beach
Huntingdale
Gosnells
Hamilton Hill
Catherine Point
Jandakot Airport
Bibra Lake
Spearwood
Southern River
Westfield
South Lake
Jandakot
To Rockingham
To Rockingham
To Kwinana, Mandurah
To Oakford
To Armadale
To Bunbury, Albany
To Geraldton
To Kalgoorlie
1
2
3
4
5
6
7
A
B
C
D
E
F
G
H
J
K

Perth Suburbs, Western Australia

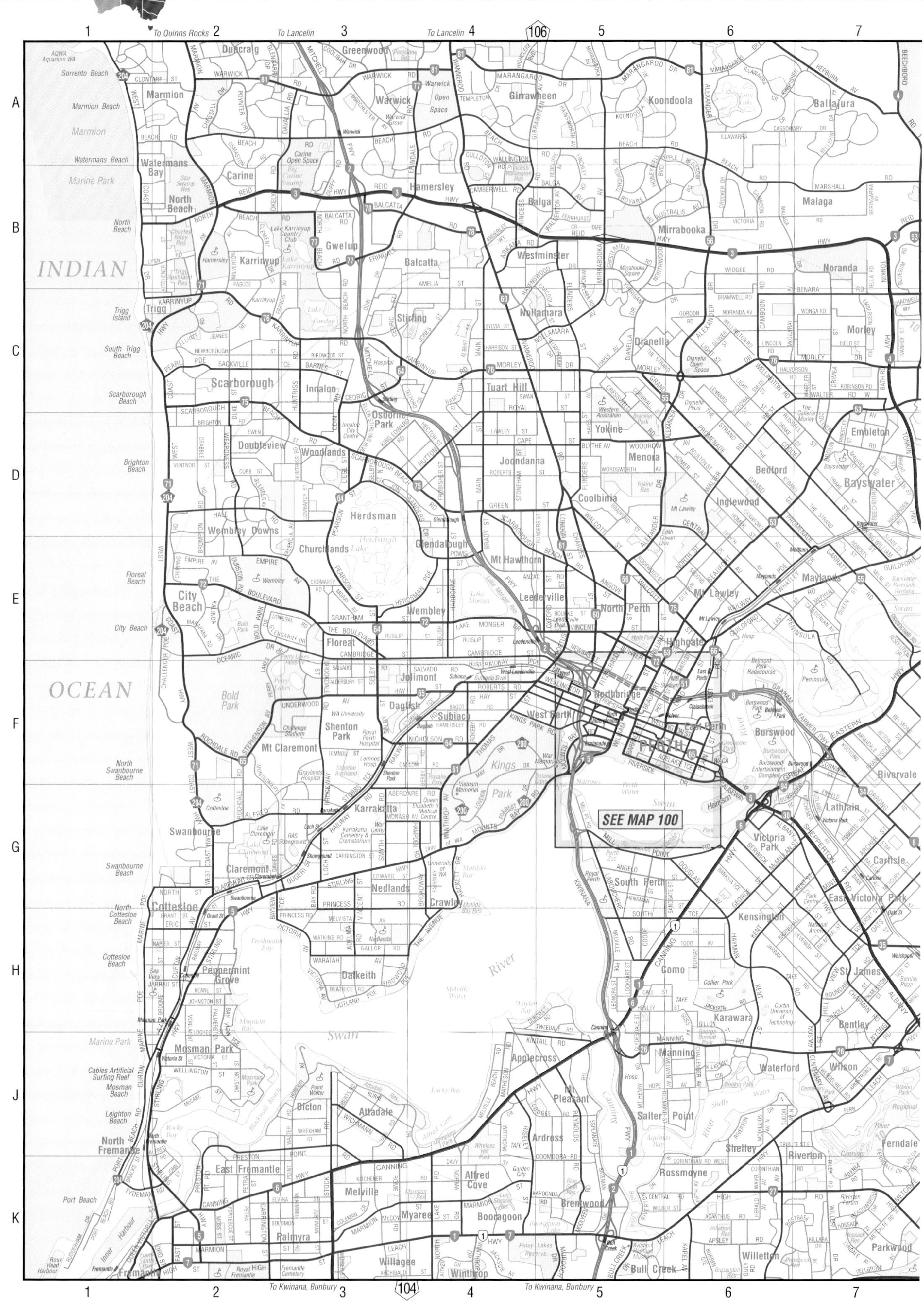

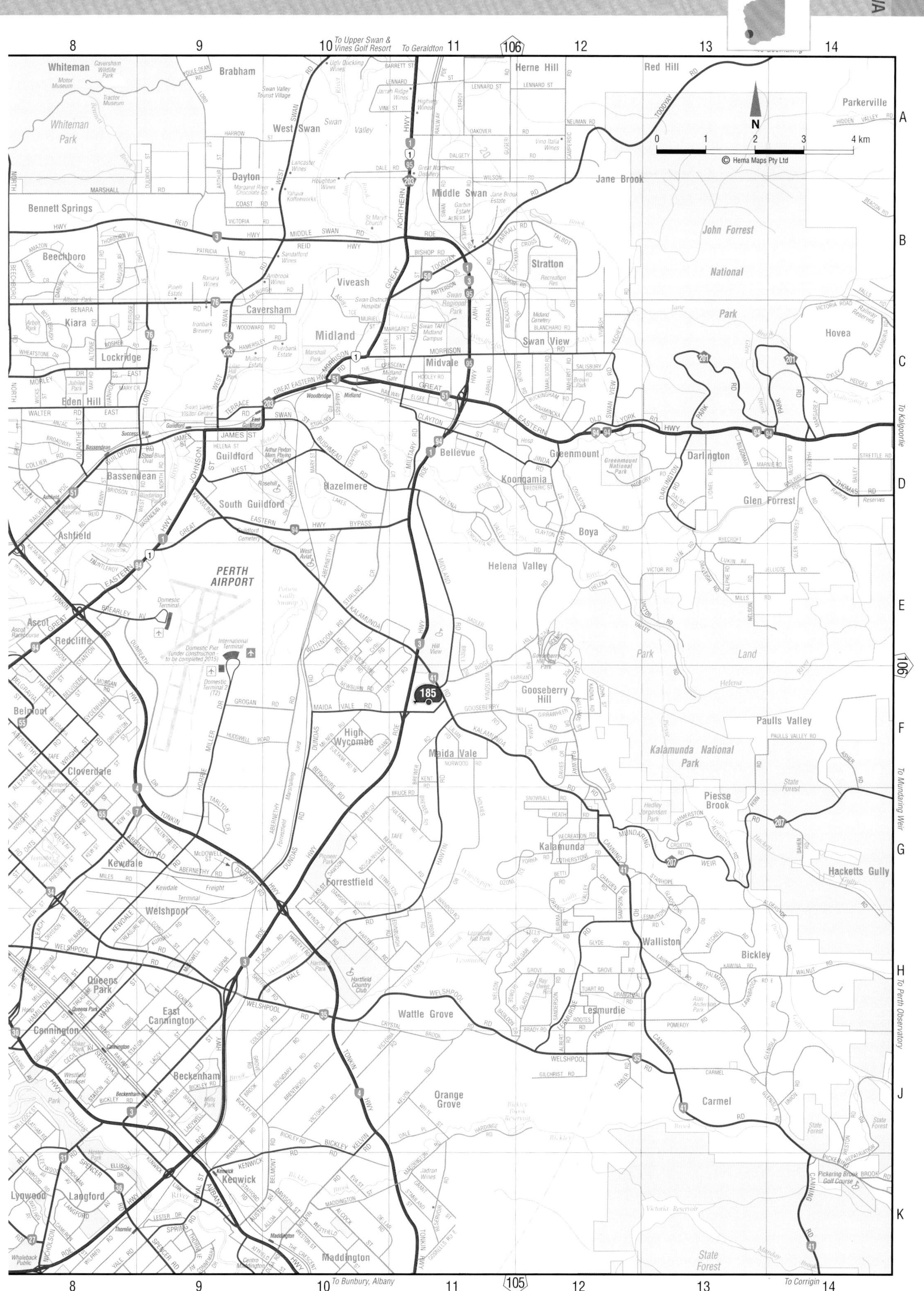
To Upper Swan & Vines Golf Resort
To Geraldton
To Bunbury, Albany
To Corrigin
To Kalgoorlie
To Mundaring Weir
To Perth Observatory
© Hema Maps Pty Ltd
0 1 2 3 4 km
N
Whiteman
Whiteman Park
Brabham
West Swan
Dayton
Bennett Springs
Beechboro
Kiara
Lockridge
Eden Hill
Caversham
Viveash
Midland
Herne Hill
Middle Swan
Red Hill
Parkerville
Jane Brook
John Forrest National Park
Stratton
Swan View
Midvale
Hovea
Bassendean
Guildford
Ashfield
South Guildford
Hazelmere
Bellevue
Greenmount
Koongamia
Darlington
Glen Forrest
Boya
Helena Valley
PERTH AIRPORT
Ascot
Redcliffe
Belmont
Cloverdale
High Wycombe
Maida Vale
Gooseberry Hill
Paulls Valley
Kalamunda National Park
Piesse Brook
Kalamunda
Hacketts Gully
Kewdale
Forrestfield
Welshpool
Walliston
Bickley
Queens Park
East Cannington
Wattle Grove
Lesmurdie
Cannington
Beckenham
Orange Grove
Carmel
Kenwick
Langford
Lynwood
Maddington
185

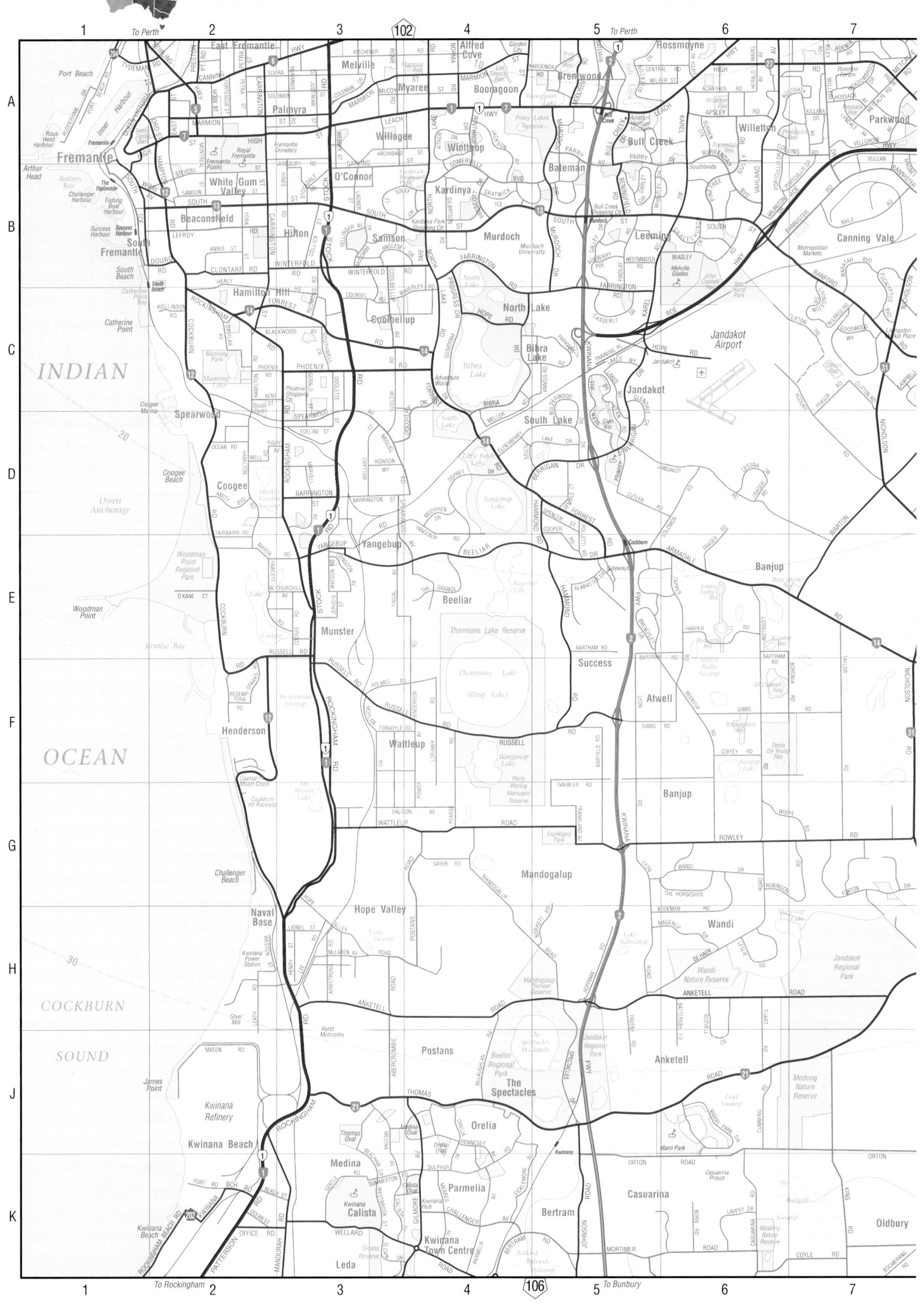
To Perth
East Fremantle
Alfred Cove
Rossmoyne
Port Beach
Melville
Myaree
Booragoon
Brentwood
Palmyra
Inner Harbour
Rous Head Harbour
Fremantle
Willagee
Winthrop
Bull Creek
Willetton
Parkwood
Arthur Head
Royal Fremantle
Fremantle Cemetery
Bateman
White Gum Valley
O'Connor
Kardinya
Canning Vale
Beaconsfield
Hilton
Samson
Murdoch
Murdoch University
Leeming
Success Harbour
South Fremantle
South Beach
Hamilton Hill
Coolbellup
North Lake
Metropolitan Markets
Catherine Point
Bibra Lake
Jandakot Airport
INDIAN
Spearwood
South Lake
Jandakot
Coogee Marina
Coogee Beach
Coogee
Owen Anchorage
Yangebup
Beeliar
Banjup
Woodman Point Regional Park
Woodman Point
Munster
Thomsons Lake Reserve
Thomsons Lake
Jervoise Bay
Success
Atwell
Henderson
Wattleup
OCEAN
Banjup
Mandogalup
Challenger Beach
Naval Base
Hope Valley
Wandi
Kwinana Power Station
COCKBURN
Wandi Nature Reserve
Jandakot Regional Park
SOUND
Postans
Anketell
The Spectacles
James Point
Kwinana Refinery
Orelia
Modong Nature Reserve
Kwinana Beach
Medina
Parmelia
Casuarina
Calista
Bertram
Kwinana Town Centre
Oldbury
Leda
To Rockingham
To Bunbury

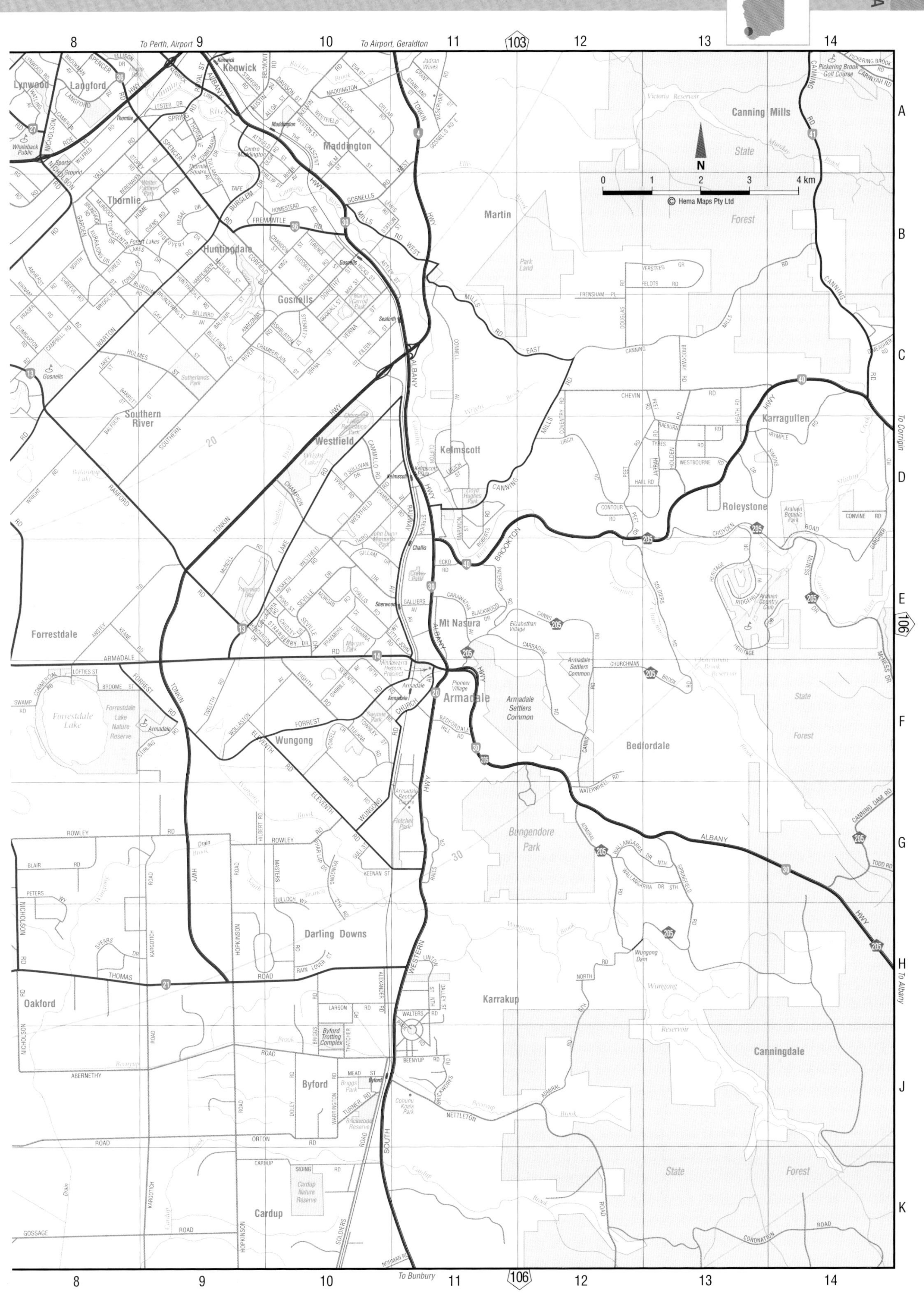
To Perth, Airport
To Airport, Geraldton
To Corrigin
To Albany
To Bunbury
0 1 2 3 4 km
© Hema Maps Pty Ltd
N
Lynwood
Langford
Kenwick
Maddington
Thornlie
Huntingdale
Gosnells
Southern River
Westfield
Kelmscott
Martin
Canning Mills
Karragullen
Roleystone
Mt Nasura
Armadale
Bedfordale
Forrestdale
Forrestdale Lake
Forrestdale Lake Nature Reserve
Wungong
Brookton Hwy
Bungendore Park
Darling Downs
Oakford
Byford
Karrakup
Canningdale
Cardup
Cardup Nature Reserve
Byford Trotting Complex
Armadale Settlers Common
Araluen Botanic Park
Araluen Country Club
Churchman Brook Reservoir
Wungong Dam
Wungong Reservoir
Victoria Reservoir
Pickering Brook Golf Course
Whaleback Public
Sutherlands Park
Champion Lakes Regatta Centre
State Forest
Albany Hwy
Tonkin Hwy
South Western Hwy
Canning Mills Rd
Armadale Rd
Thomas Road
Nicholson Rd
Rowley Rd
Abernethy Rd
Gossage Road
Coronation Road

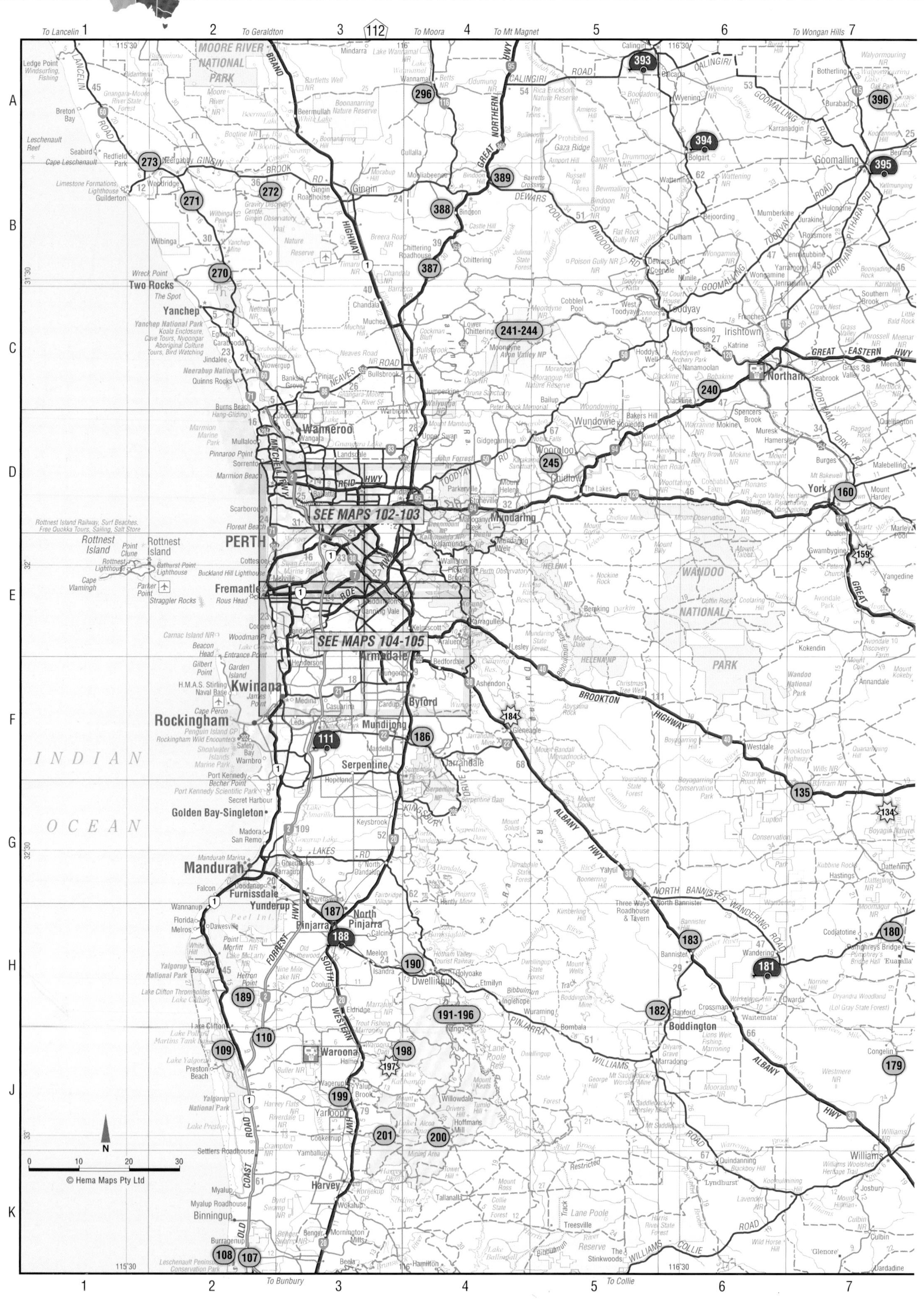
SEE MAPS 102-103
SEE MAPS 104-105
PERTH
Fremantle
Rockingham
Kwinana
Mandurah
Pinjarra
Northam
York
Toodyay
INDIAN
OCEAN
© Hema Maps Pty Ltd

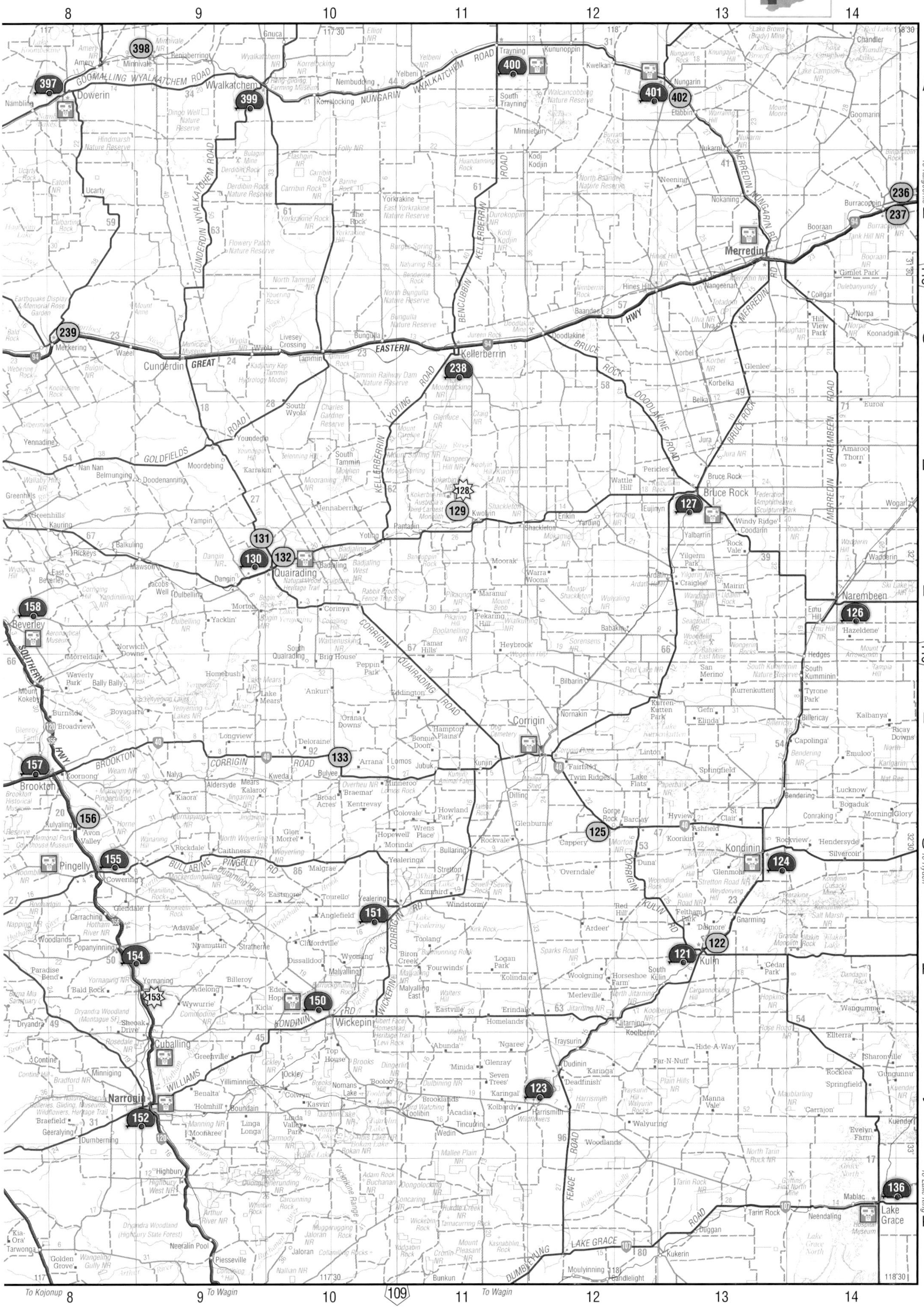
8
9
10
11
12
13
14
A
B
C
D
E
F
G
H
J
K
Dowerin
Wyalkatchem
Minnivale
Amery
Nambling
Trayning
Kununoppin
Kwelkan
Nungarin
Elabbin
South Trayning
Merredin
Burracoppin
Nokaning
Hines Hill
Nangeenan
Cunderdin
Meckering
Tammin
Kellerberrin
Doodlakine
Baandee
Bungulla
Bruce Rock
Narembeen
Quairading
Dangin
Beverley
Corrigin
Kunjin
Bullaring
Brookton
Pingelly
Kondinin
Kulin
Wickepin
Yealering
Cuballing
Narrogin
Highbury
Harrismith
Lake Grace
Mablac
Pingelly
Popanyinning
Yornaning
Jitarning
Ardath
Babakin
Gorge Rock
Goomalling Wyalkatchem Road
Nungarin Wyalkatchem Road
Merredin Nungarin Rd
Great Eastern Hwy
Goldfields Road
Bruce Rock
Doodlakine Road
Kellerberrin Yoting Road
Corrigin Quairading Road
Brookton Corrigin Road
Bullaring Pingelly Rd
Kondinin Rd
Dumbleyung Lake Grace Road
Fence Road
Narembeen Merredin Road
Williams
Southern Hwy
To Kalgoorlie
To Hyden
To Lake King
To Kojonup
To Wagin
To Wagin

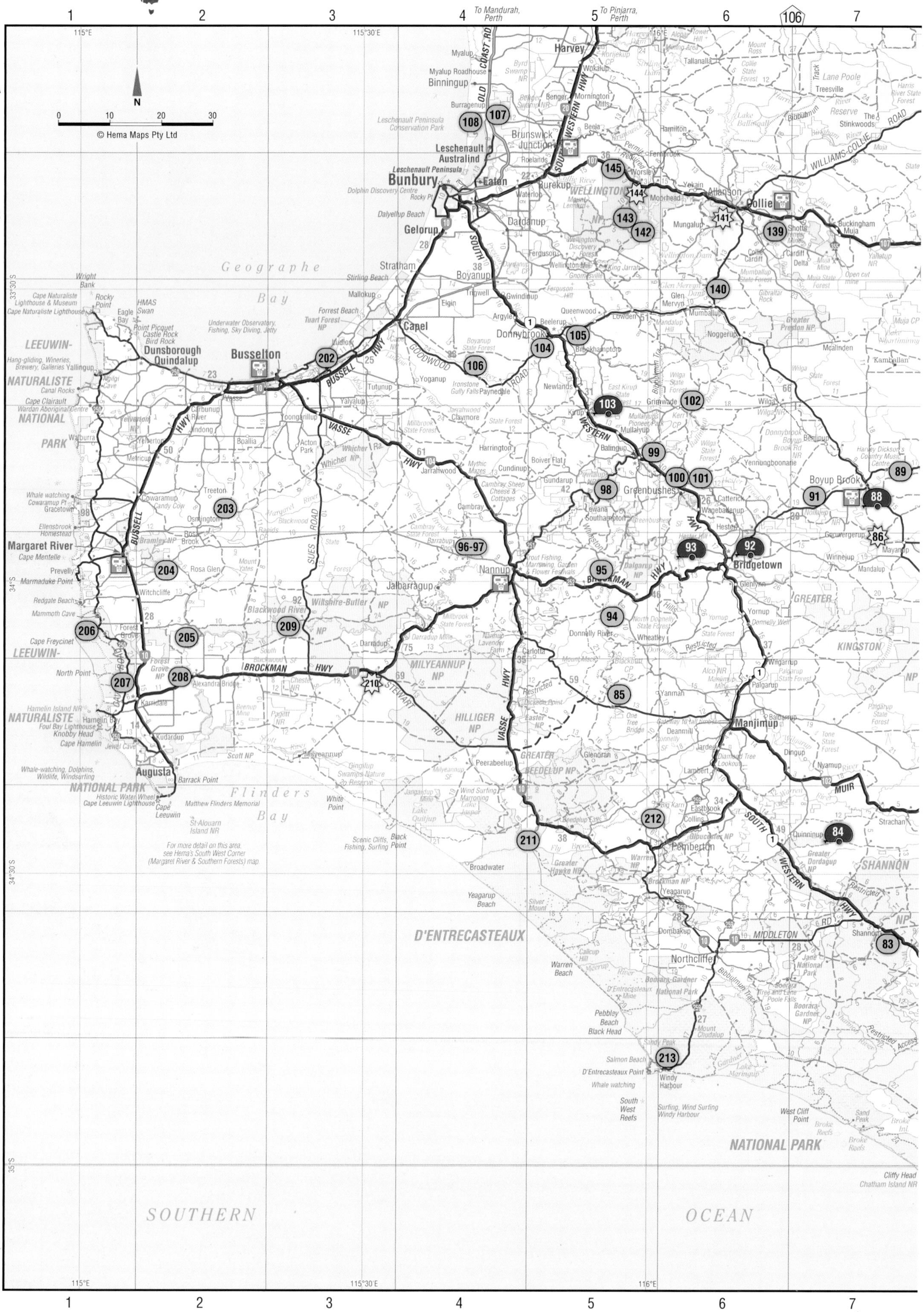

South West and South Coast, Western Australia

© Hema Maps Pty Ltd

To Mandurah, Perth
To Pinjarra, Perth

Harvey
Myalup
Binningup
Burekup
Brunswick Junction
Leschenault Australind
Bunbury
Eaton
Dardanup
Gelorup
Stratham
Boyanup
Capel
Donnybrook
Busselton
Dunsborough
Quindalup
Yallingup
Cowaramup
Gracetown
Margaret River
Prevelly
Witchcliffe
Augusta
Cape Leeuwin
Cape Naturaliste
LEEUWIN-NATURALISTE NATIONAL PARK
Geographe Bay
Flinders Bay
Nannup
Jalbarragup
Balingup
Greenbushes
Bridgetown
Boyup Brook
Manjimup
Pemberton
Northcliffe
Windy Harbour
Collie
Allanson
Shotts
Mungalup
Wellington NP
Kirup
Mullalyup
Newlands
Hester
Catterick
Wilga
Yornup
Palgarup
Deanmill
Jardee
Quinninup
Shannon
Walpole
Yeagarup
Peerabeelup
Donnelly River
Beedelup NP
Warren NP
Greater Beedelup NP
Hilliger NP
Milyeannup NP
D'ENTRECASTEAUX
NATIONAL PARK
SOUTHERN OCEAN
BROCKMAN HWY
SOUTH WESTERN HWY
VASSE HWY
BUSSELL HWY
MUIR HWY

Camp sites: 83, 84, 85, 86, 88, 89, 91, 92, 93, 94, 95, 96-97, 98, 99, 100, 101, 102, 103, 104, 105, 106, 107, 108, 139, 140, 141, 142, 143, 144, 145, 202, 203, 204, 205, 206, 207, 208, 209, 210, 211, 212, 213

For more detail on this area, see Hema's South West Corner (Margaret River & Southern Forests) map.

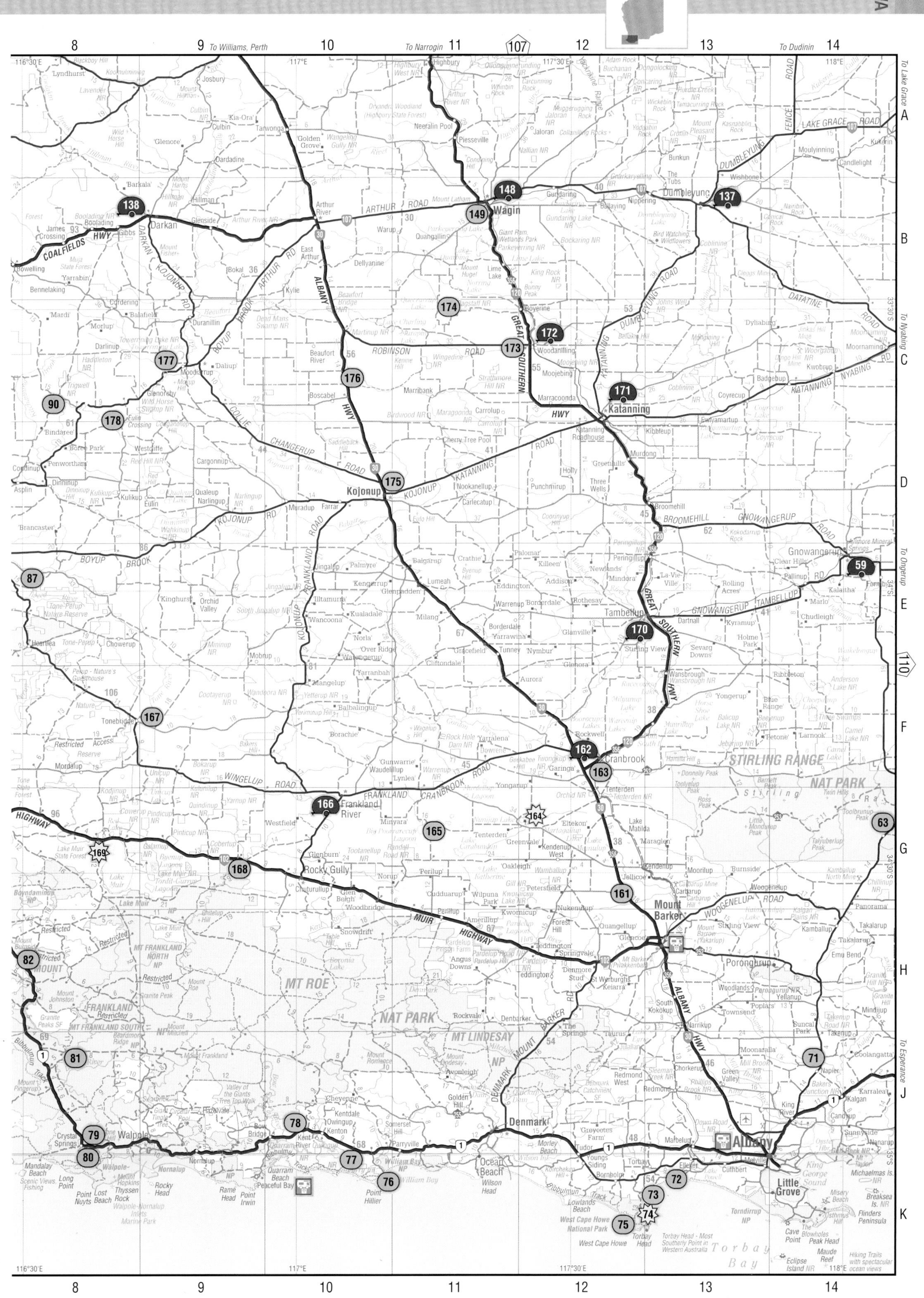

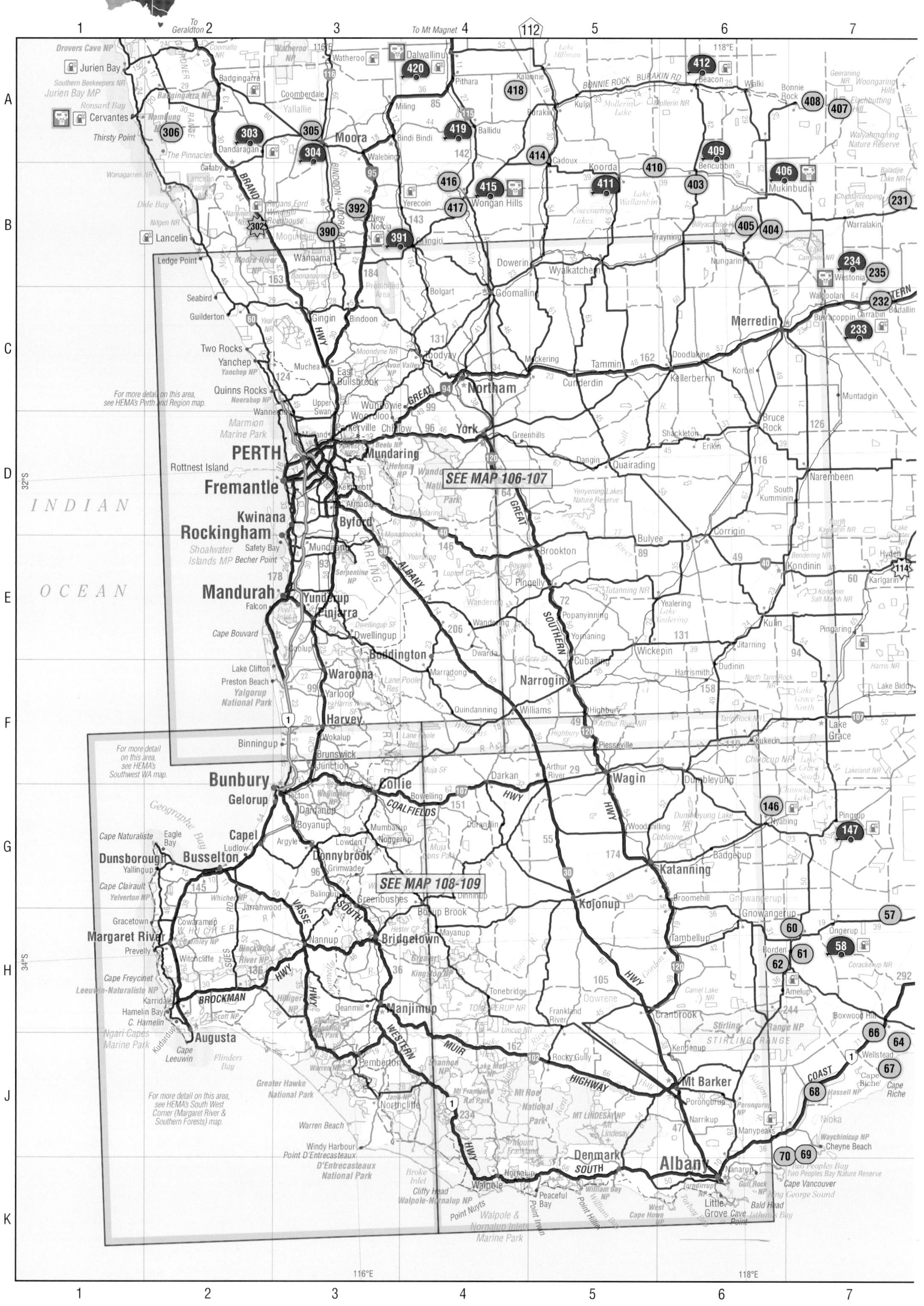
To Geraldton
To Mt Magnet
SEE MAP 106-107
SEE MAP 108-109
For more detail on this area, see HEMA's Perth and Region map.
For more detail on this area, see HEMA's Southwest WA map.
For more detail on this area, see HEMA's South West Corner (Margaret River & Southern Forests) map.
INDIAN
OCEAN
PERTH
Fremantle
Rockingham
Mandurah
Bunbury
Busselton
Albany
Northam
York
Merredin
Narrogin
Katanning
Mt Barker
Margaret River
Augusta
Dunsborough
Collie
Bridgetown
Manjimup
Wagin
Kojonup
Denmark

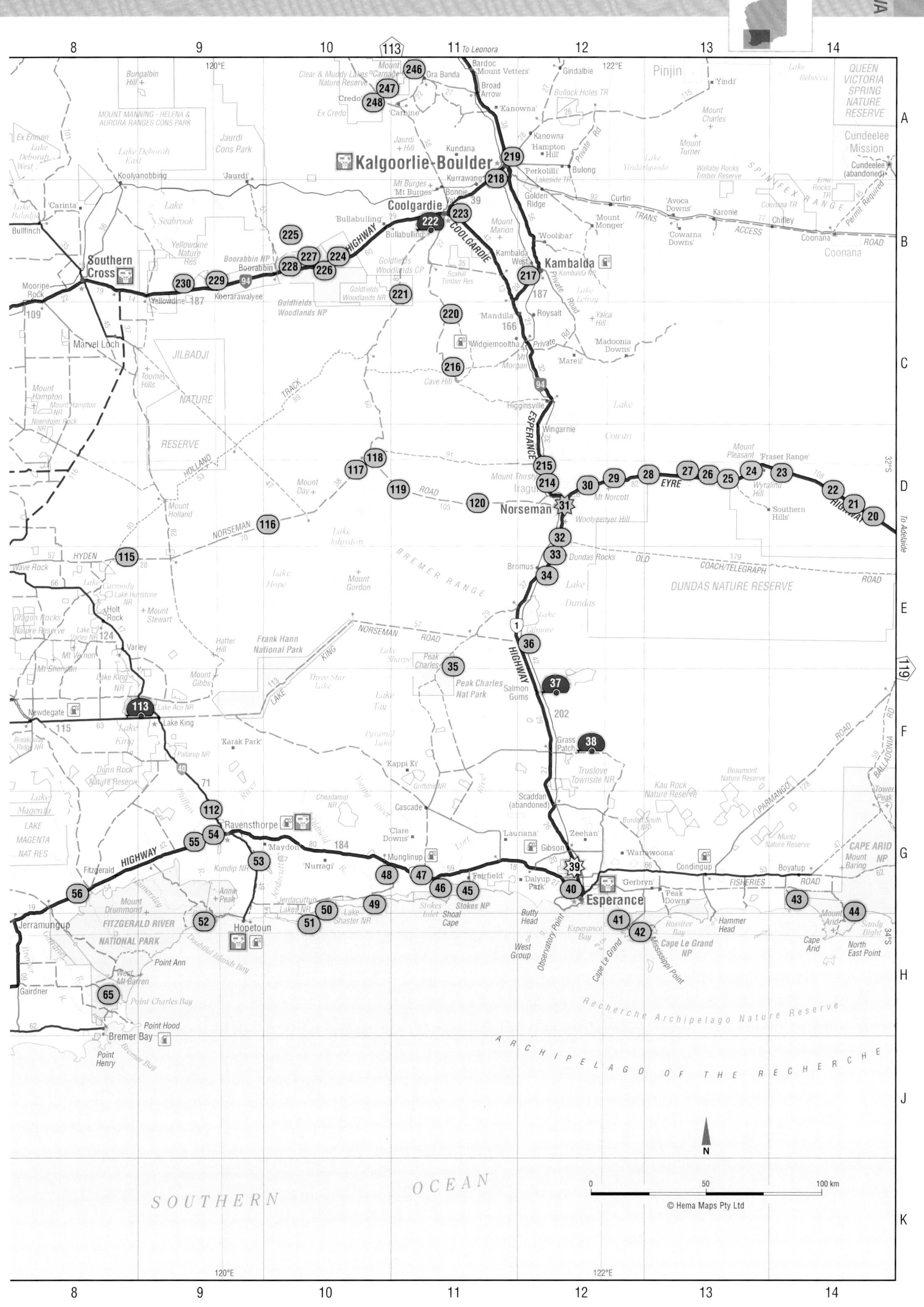

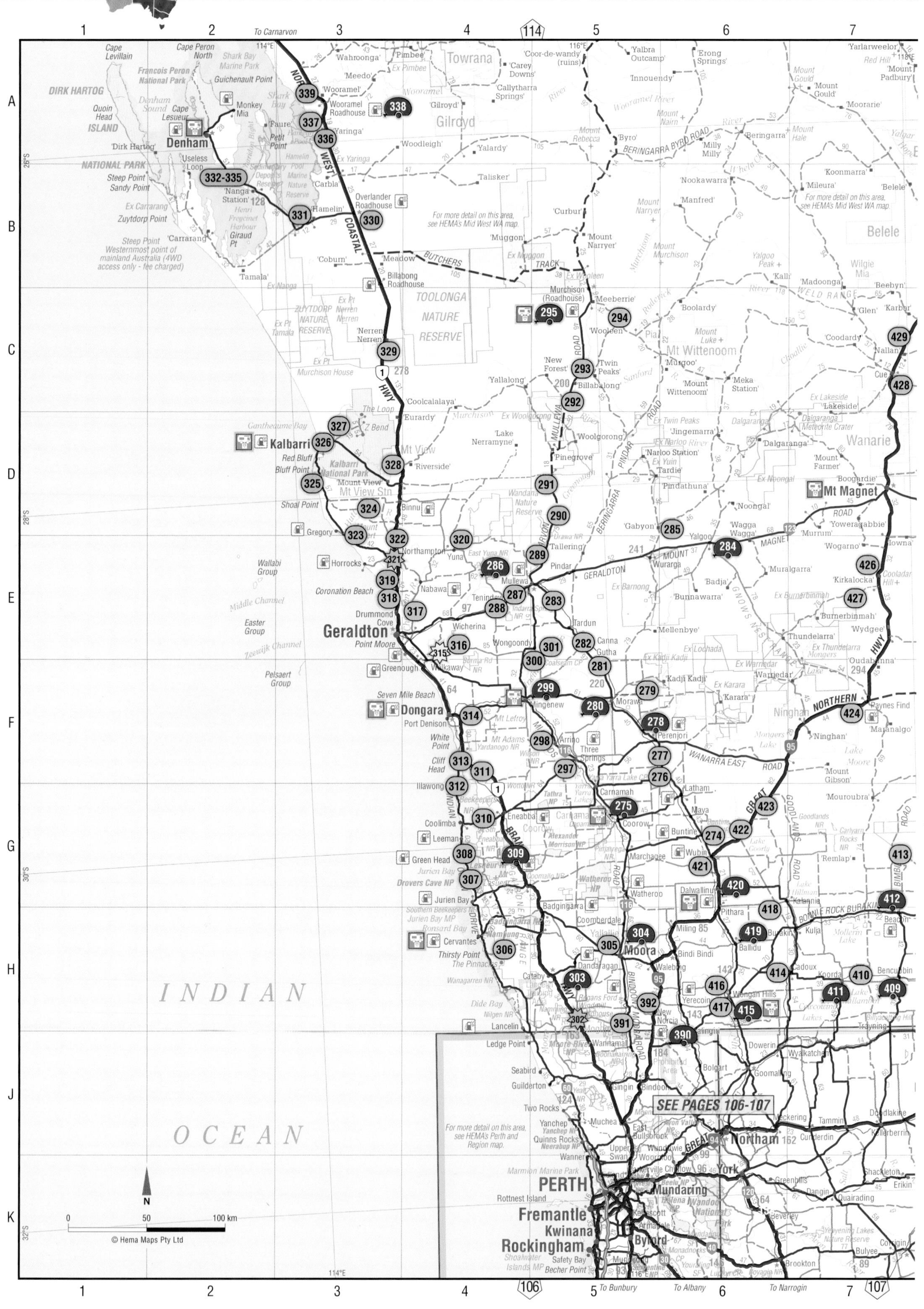
Denham
Kalbarri
Geraldton
Dongara
Mt Magnet
Moora
Northam
PERTH
Fremantle
Kwinana
Rockingham
INDIAN
OCEAN
SEE PAGES 106-107
For more detail on this area, see HEMA's Mid West WA map.
For more detail on this area, see HEMA's Perth and Region map.
© Hema Maps Pty Ltd

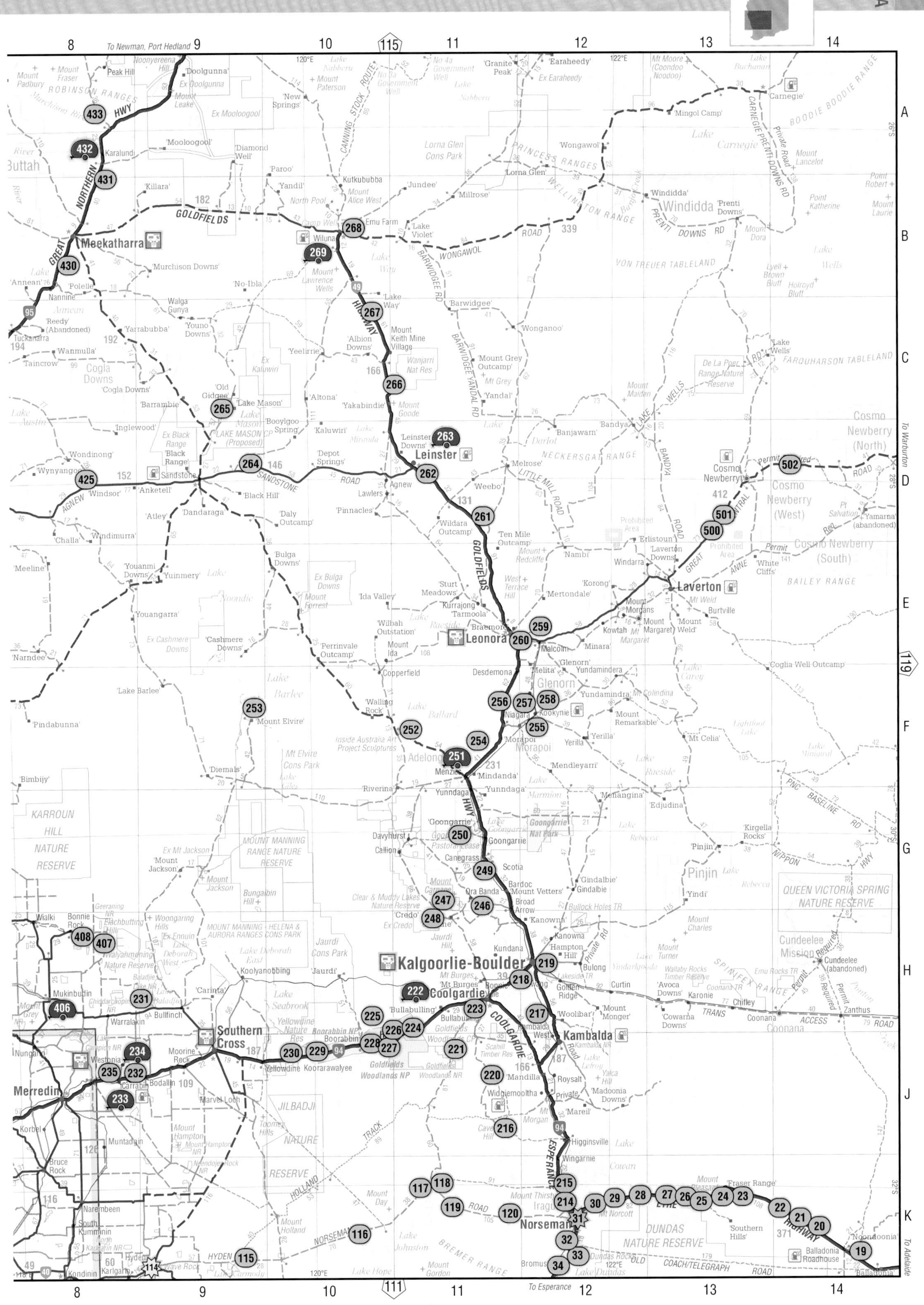

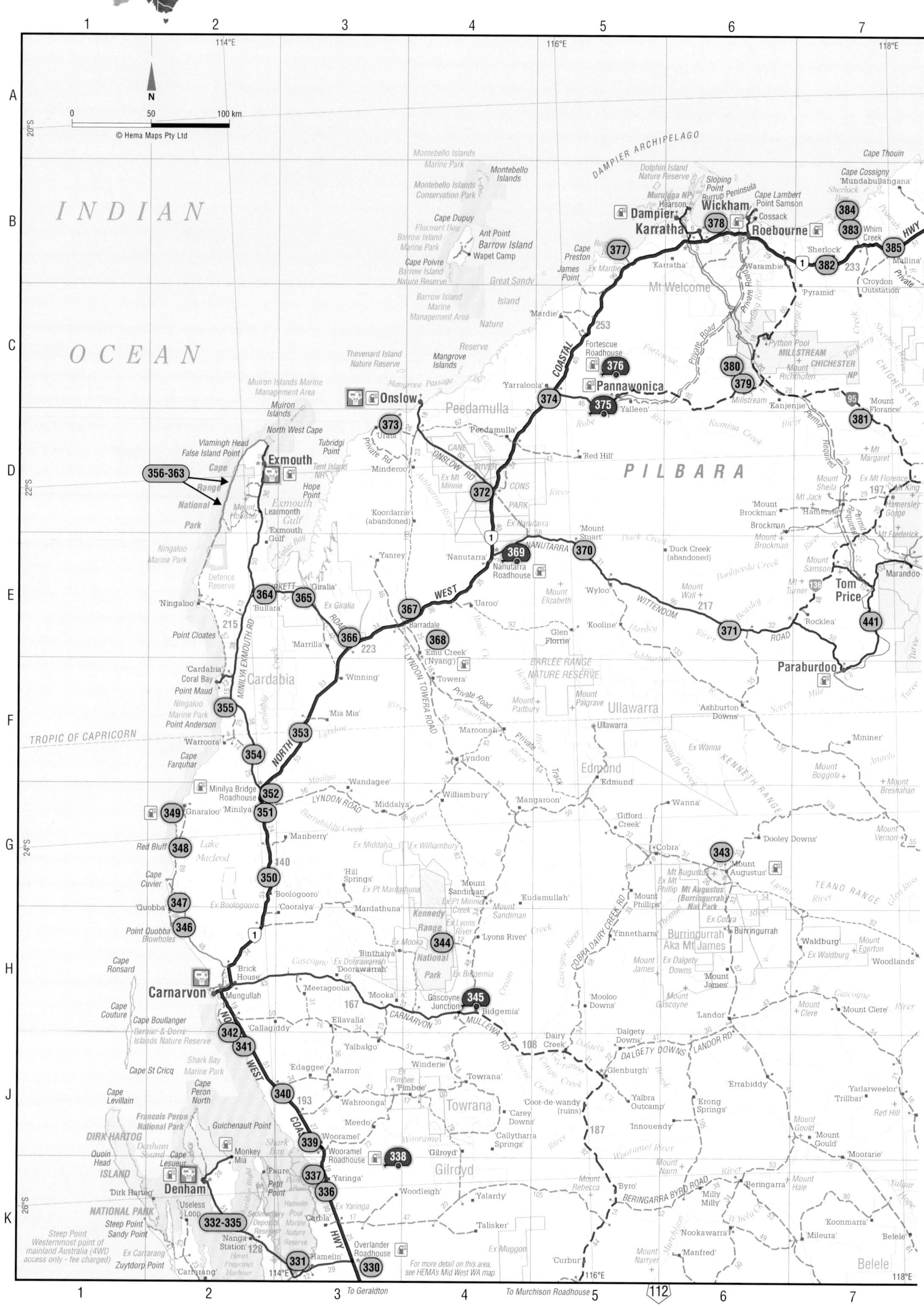
N
0 50 100 km
© Hema Maps Pty Ltd
INDIAN OCEAN
DAMPIER ARCHIPELAGO
Montebello Islands Marine Park
Montebello Islands
Montebello Islands Conservation Park
Cape Dupuy
Flacourt Bay
Barrow Island Marine Park
Ant Point
Barrow Island
Wapet Camp
Cape Poivre
Barrow Island Nature Reserve
Great Sandy Island Nature Reserve
Barrow Island Marine Management Area
Thevenard Island Nature Reserve
Mangrove Islands
Mangrove Passage
Muiron Islands Marine Management Area
Muiron Islands
North West Cape
Vlamingh Head
False Island Point
Exmouth
Tent Island NR
Hope Point
Exmouth Gulf
Learmonth
Cape Range National Park
Ningaloo Marine Park
Defence Reserve
Ningaloo
Point Cloates
Coral Bay
Point Maud
Ningaloo Marine Park
Point Anderson
TROPIC OF CAPRICORN
Cape Farquhar
Minilya Bridge Roadhouse
Gnaraloo
Red Bluff
Lake Macleod
Cape Cuvier
Point Quobba
Blowholes
Cape Ronsard
Carnarvon
Cape Couture
Cape Boullanger
Bernier & Dorre Islands Nature Reserve
Shark Bay Marine Park
Cape St Cricq
Cape Peron North
Cape Levillain
Francois Peron National Park
Guichenault Point
DIRK HARTOG ISLAND NATIONAL PARK
Quoin Head
Monkey Mia
Cape Lesueur
Denham
Dirk Hartog
Useless Loop
Steep Point
Sandy Point
Steep Point Westernmost point of mainland Australia (4WD access only - fee charged)
Zuytdorp Point
Nanga Station
Hamelin
Overlander Roadhouse
To Geraldton
For more detail on this area, see HEMA's Mid West WA map.
To Murchison Roadhouse
Dolphin Island Nature Reserve
Murujuga NP
Burrup Peninsula
Sloping Point
Hearson
Dampier
Karratha
Wickham
Cape Lambert
Point Samson
Cossack
Roebourne
Cape Preston
James Point
Mt Welcome
Cape Thouin
Cape Cossigny
Sherlock
Whim Creek
Mallina
Croydon Outstation
Pyramid
Warambie
Fortescue Roadhouse
Pannawonica
Yarraloola
Mardie
COASTAL HWY
Python Pool
MILLSTREAM CHICHESTER NP
Mount Richthofen
Millstream
Kanjenjie
Mount Florance
Onslow
Peedamulla
Minderoo
ONSLOW RD
CANE RIVER CONS PARK
Red Hill
PILBARA
Koordarrie (abandoned)
Nanutarra
Nanutarra Roadhouse
Mount Stuart
Duck Creek (abandoned)
Yanrey
Wyloo
Mount Elizabeth
Kooline
WITTENOOM ROAD
Glen Florrie
Mount Brockman
Brockman
Hamersley
Hamersley Gorge
Mt Frederick
Marandoo
Mount Samson
Mt Turner
Tom Price
Rocklea
Paraburdoo
Giralia
Bullara
MINILYA EXMOUTH RD
Cardabia
Marrilla
Barradale
Uaroo
NORTH WEST
Emu Creek (Nyang)
Towera
BARLEE RANGE NATURE RESERVE
Mount Padbury
Mount Palgrave
Ullawarra
Ashburton Downs
Winning
Mia Mia
LYNDON TOWERA ROAD
Maroonah
Lyndon
Wandagee
Williambury
Mangaroon
Edmund
Ex Wanna
KENNETH RANGE
Mininer
Mount Boggola
Mount Bresnahan
Wanna
Gifford Creek
Dooley Downs
Mount Vernon
LYNDON ROAD
Middalya
Manberry
Minilya
Cobra
Mount Augustus
Mt Augustus Nat Park
Burringurrah
TEANO RANGE
Hill Springs
Boologooro
Cooralya
Mardathuna
Mount Sandiman
Kennedy Range National Park
Eudamullah
Mount Phillips
Yinnetharra
Burringurrah Aka Mt James
Waldburg
Mount Egerton
Woodlands
Lyons River
Binthalya
Doorawarrah
Brick House
Mungullah
Meeragoolia
Mooka
Gascoyne Junction
Bidgemia
CARNARVON MULLEWA RD
COBRA DAIRY CREEK RD
Mooloo Downs
Mount Gascoyne
Mount James
Landor
Mount Clere
Ellavalla
Callagiddy
Yalbalgo
Dairy Creek
Dalgety Downs
DALGETY DOWNS
LANDOR RD
Glenburgh
Errabiddy
Winderie
Towrana
Marron
Edaggee
Pimbee
Wahroonga
Coor-de-wandy (ruins)
Carey Downs
Yalbra Outcamp
Erong Springs
Yarlarweelor
Trillbar
Red Hill
Meedo
Wooramel
Wooramel Roadhouse
Callytharra Springs
Innouendy
Mount Gould
Moorarie
Gilroyd
Yaringa
Faure
Petit Point
Woodleigh
Yalardy
Mount Rebecca
Byro
BERINGARRA BYRO ROAD
Beringarra
Milly Milly
Mount Hale
Koonmarra
Carbla
Talisker
Nookawarra
Mileura
Belele
Ex Muggon
Curbur
Mount Narryer
Manfred
Carrarang
Hamelin Pool
Henri Freycinet Harbour
114°E
116°E
118°E
20°S
22°S
24°S
26°S

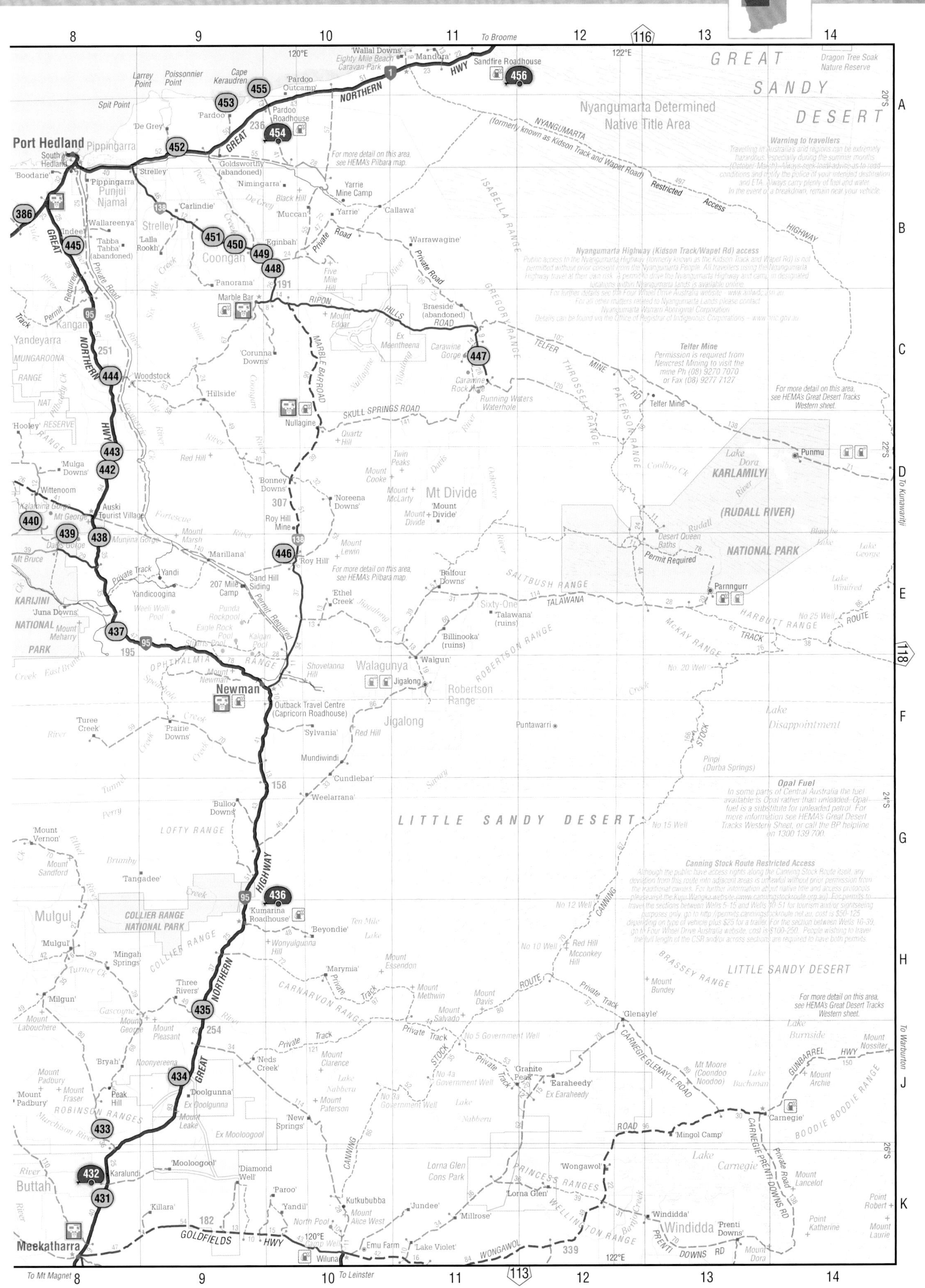
GREAT SANDY DESERT
Nyangumarta Determined Native Title Area
NYANGUMARTA (formerly known as Kidson Track and Wapet Road) Restricted Access HIGHWAY
Warning to travellers
Travelling in Australia's arid regions can be extremely hazardous, especially during the summer months (October-March). Always seek local advice as to road conditions and notify the police of your intended destination and ETA. Always carry plenty of fuel and water. In the event of a breakdown, remain near your vehicle.
Nyangumarta Highway (Kidson Track/Wapet Rd) access
Public access to the Nyangumarta Highway (formerly known as the Kidson Track and Wapet Rd) is not permitted without prior consent from the Nyangumarta People. All travellers using the Ngangumarta Highway travel at their own risk. A permit to drive the Nyangumarta Highway and camp in designated locations within Nyangumarta lands is available online.
For further details see the Four Wheel Drive Australia website - www.anfwdc.asn.au
For all other matters related to Nyangumarta Lands please contact Nyangumarta Warrarn Aboriginal Corporation.
Details can be found via the Office of Registrar of Indigenous Corporations - www.oric.gov.au
Telfer Mine
Permission is required from Newcrest Mining to visit the mine Ph (08) 9270 7070 or Fax (08) 9277 7127
For more detail on this area, see HEMA's Great Desert Tracks Western sheet.
For more detail on this area, see HEMA's Pilbara map.
Opal Fuel
In some parts of Central Australia the fuel available is Opal rather than unleaded. Opal fuel is a substitute for unleaded petrol. For more information see HEMA's Great Desert Tracks Western Sheet, or call the BP helpline on 1300 139 700.
Canning Stock Route Restricted Access
Although the public have access rights along the Canning Stock Route itself, any deviation from this route into adjacent areas is unlawful without prior permission from the traditional owners. For further information about native title and access protocols please visit the Kuju Wangka website (www.canningstockroute.org.au). For permits to travel the sections between Wells 5-15 and Wells 40-51 for tourism and/or sightseeing purposes only, go to http://permits.canningstockroute.net.au, cost is $50-125 depending on type of vehicle plus $25 for a trailer. For the section between Wells 16-39, go to Four Wheel Drive Australia website, cost is $100-250. People wishing to travel the full length of the CSR and/or across sections are required to have both permits.
Port Hedland
South Hedland
Newman
Meekatharra
Wiluna
Nullagine
Marble Bar
Sandfire Roadhouse
Pardoo Roadhouse
Kumarina Roadhouse
Outback Travel Centre (Capricorn Roadhouse)
Jigalong
Punmu
Parnngurr
Carnegie
KARLAMILYI (RUDALL RIVER) NATIONAL PARK
KARIJINI NATIONAL PARK
COLLIER RANGE NATIONAL PARK
LITTLE SANDY DESERT
Lake Disappointment
Lake Carnegie
GREAT NORTHERN HWY
GOLDFIELDS HWY
GUNBARREL HWY
CARNEGIE-GLENAYLE ROAD
CARNEGIE-PRENTI DOWNS RD
CANNING STOCK ROUTE
To Broome
To Kunawarritji
To Warburton
To Mt Magnet
To Leinster

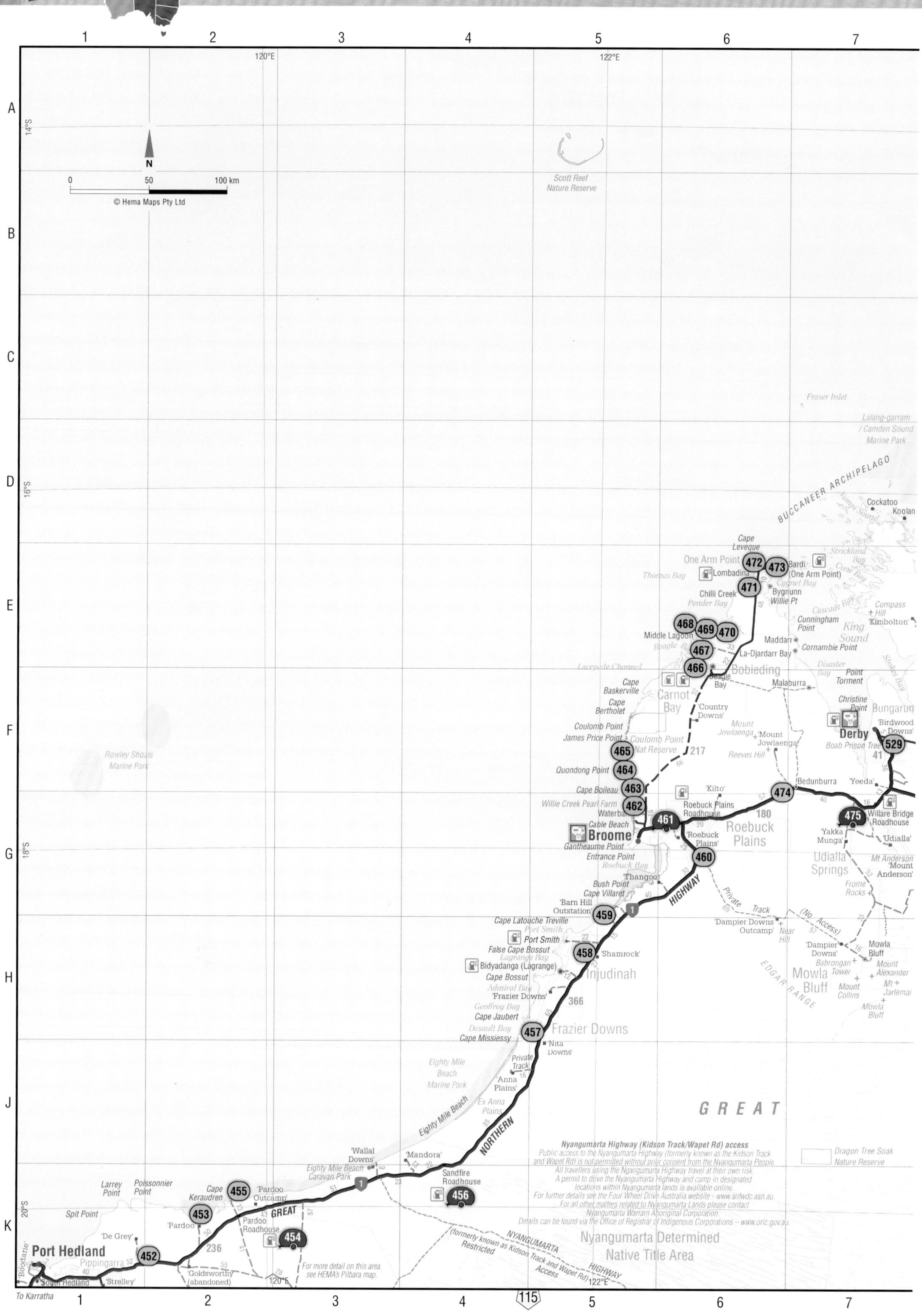

© Hema Maps Pty Ltd
Scott Reef Nature Reserve
Rowley Shoals Marine Park
BUCCANEER ARCHIPELAGO
Cape Leveque
One Arm Point
Lombadina
Bardi (One Arm Point)
Chilli Creek
Bygnunn Willie Pt
Cunningham Point
King Sound
Middle Lagoon
Maddarr
Cornambie Point
La-Djardarr Bay
Bobieding
Beagle Bay
Malaburra
Point Torment
Cape Baskerville
Carnot Bay
Cape Bertholet
'Country Downs'
Coulomb Point
James Price Point
Coulomb Point Nat Reserve
Mount Jowlaenga
Derby
Boab Prison Tree
'Birdwood Downs'
Quondong Point
Cape Boileau
Willie Creek Pearl Farm
Waterbank
Cable Beach
Broome
Gantheaume Point
Entrance Point
Roebuck Bay
'Kilto'
Roebuck Plains Roadhouse
'Roebuck Plains'
Roebuck Plains
Bedunburra
'Yeeda'
Willare Bridge Roadhouse
'Yakka Munga'
'Udialla'
Udialla Springs
Mt Anderson
'Mount Anderson'
Thangoo
Bush Point
Cape Villaret
'Barn Hill Outstation'
HIGHWAY
Private Track
'Dampier Downs' Outcamp'
(No Access)
Cape Latouche Treville
Port Smith
False Cape Bossut
Lagrange Bay
'Shamrock'
Bidyadanga (Lagrange)
Cape Bossut
Injudinah
'Dampier Downs'
Mowla Bluff
EDGAR RANGE
'Frazier Downs'
Cape Jaubert
Frazier Downs
Cape Missiessy
'Nita Downs'
Eighty Mile Beach Marine Park
'Anna Plains'
Eighty Mile Beach
NORTHERN
GREAT
'Wallal Downs'
Eighty Mile Beach Caravan Park
'Mandora'
Sandfire Roadhouse
Nyangumarta Highway (Kidson Track/Wapet Rd) access
Public access to the Nyangumarta Highway (formerly known as the Kidson Track and Wapet Rd) is not permitted without prior consent from the Nyangumarta People.
All travellers using the Ngangumarta Highway travel at their own risk.
A permit to drive the Nyangumarta Highway and camp in designated locations within Nyangumarta lands is available online.
For further details see the Four Wheel Drive Australia website - www.anfwdc.asn.au.
For all other matters related to Nyangumarta Lands please contact Nyangumarta Warrarn Aboriginal Corporation.
Details can be found via the Office of Registrar of Indigenous Corporations – www.oric.gov.au.
Nyangumarta Determined Native Title Area
Dragon Tree Soak Nature Reserve
Larrey Point
Poissonnier Point
Cape Keraudren
'Pardoo Outcamp'
Spit Point
'Pardoo'
Pardoo Roadhouse
'De Grey'
Port Hedland
Pippingarra
South Hedland
'Strelley'
'Goldsworthy' (abandoned)
For more detail on this area see HEMA's Pilbara map.
NYANGUMARTA HIGHWAY (formerly known as Kidson Track and Wapet Rd) Restricted Access
To Karratha

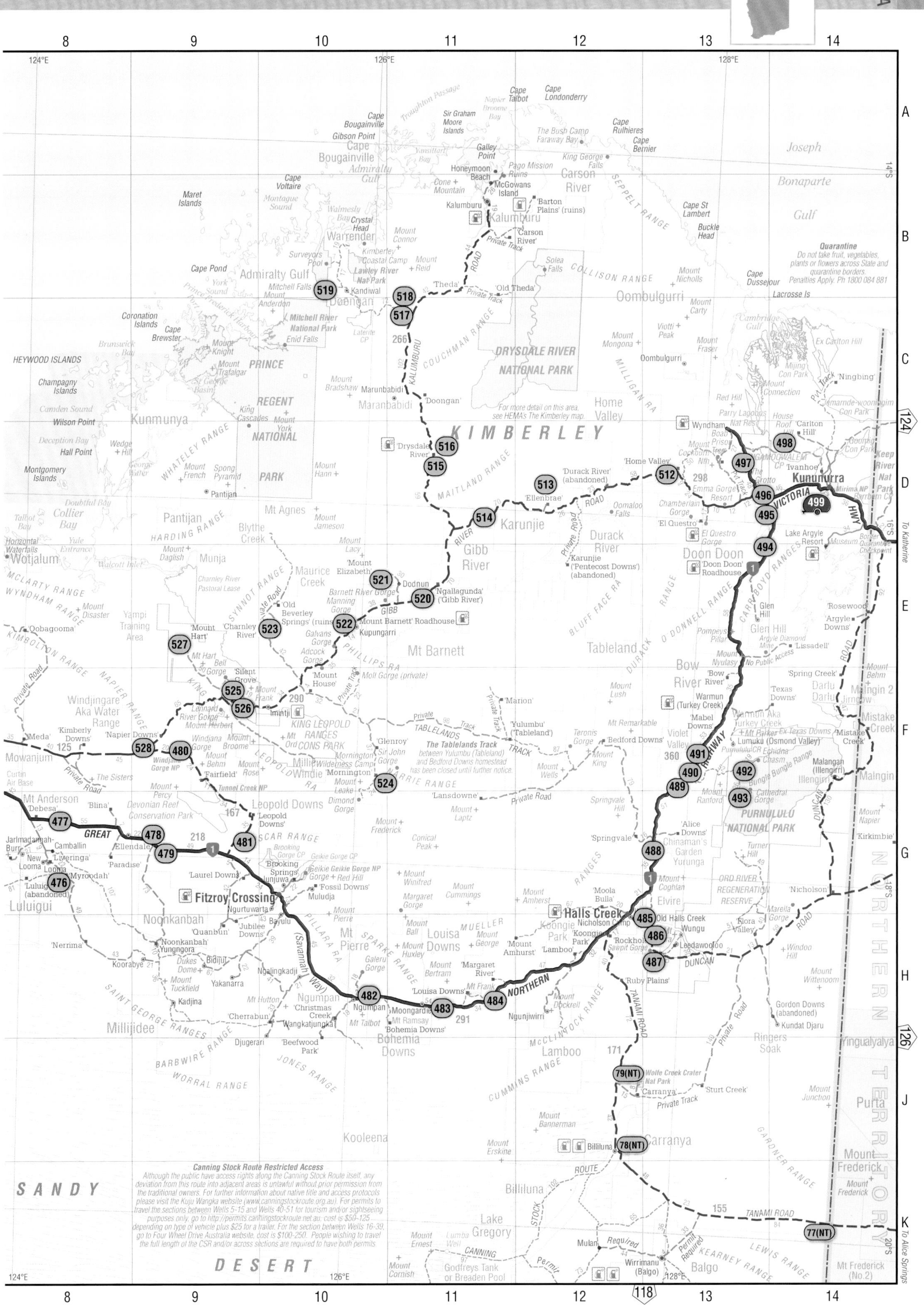
KIMBERLEY
DRYSDALE RIVER NATIONAL PARK
PRINCE REGENT NATIONAL PARK
PURNULULU NATIONAL PARK
Kununurra
Halls Creek
Fitzroy Crossing
Wyndham
Kalumburu
Quarantine
Do not take fruit, vegetables, plants or flowers across State and quarantine borders. Penalties Apply. Ph 1800 084 881
The Tablelands Track
between Yulumbu (Tableland) and Bedford Downs homestead has been closed until further notice.
For more detail on this area, see HEMA's The Kimberley map.
Canning Stock Route Restricted Access
Although the public have access rights along the Canning Stock Route itself, any deviation from this route into adjacent areas is unlawful without prior permission from the traditional owners. For further information about native title and access protocols please visit the Kuju Wangka website (www.canningstockroute.org.au). For permits to travel the sections between Wells 5-15 and Wells 40-51 for tourism and/or sightseeing purposes only, go to http://permits.canningstockroute.net.au; cost is $50-125 depending on type of vehicle plus $25 for a trailer. For the section between Wells 16-39, go to Four Wheel Drive Australia website, cost is $100-250. People wishing to travel the full length of the CSR and/or across sections are required to have both permits.
SANDY
DESERT
NORTHERN TERRITORY
To Katherine
To Alice Springs

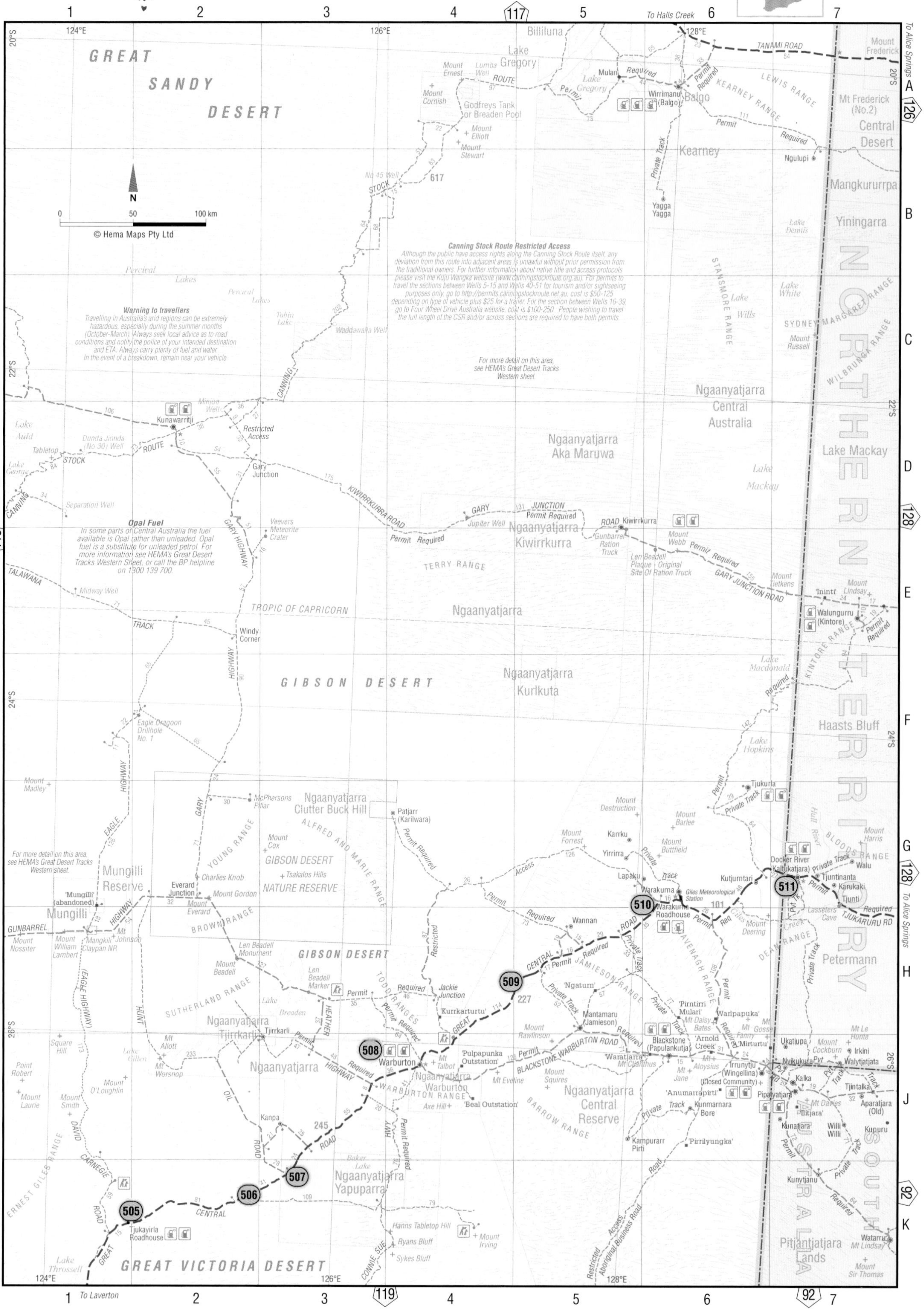

Central-East Western Australia

© Hema Maps Pty Ltd

Canning Stock Route Restricted Access

Although the public have access rights along the Canning Stock Route itself, any deviation from this route into adjacent areas is unlawful without prior permission from the traditional owners. For further information about native title and access protocols please visit the Kuju Wangka website (www.canningstockroute.org.au). For permits to travel the sections between Wells 5-15 and Wells 40-51 for tourism and/or sightseeing purposes only, go to http://permits.canningstockroute.net.au, cost is $50-125 depending on type of vehicle plus $25 for a trailer. For the section between Wells 16-39, go to Four Wheel Drive Australia website, cost is $100-250. People wishing to travel the full length of the CSR and/or across sections are required to have both permits.

For more detail on this area, see HEMA's Great Desert Tracks Western sheet.

Warning to travellers

Travelling in Australia's arid regions can be extremely hazardous, especially during the summer months (October-March). Always seek local advice as to road conditions and notify the police of your intended destination and ETA. Always carry plenty of fuel and water. In the event of a breakdown, remain near your vehicle.

Opal Fuel

In some parts of Central Australia the fuel available is Opal rather than unleaded. Opal fuel is a substitute for unleaded petrol. For more information see HEMA's Great Desert Tracks Western Sheet, or call the BP helpline on 1300 139 700.

For more detail on this area, see HEMA's Great Desert Tracks Western sheet.

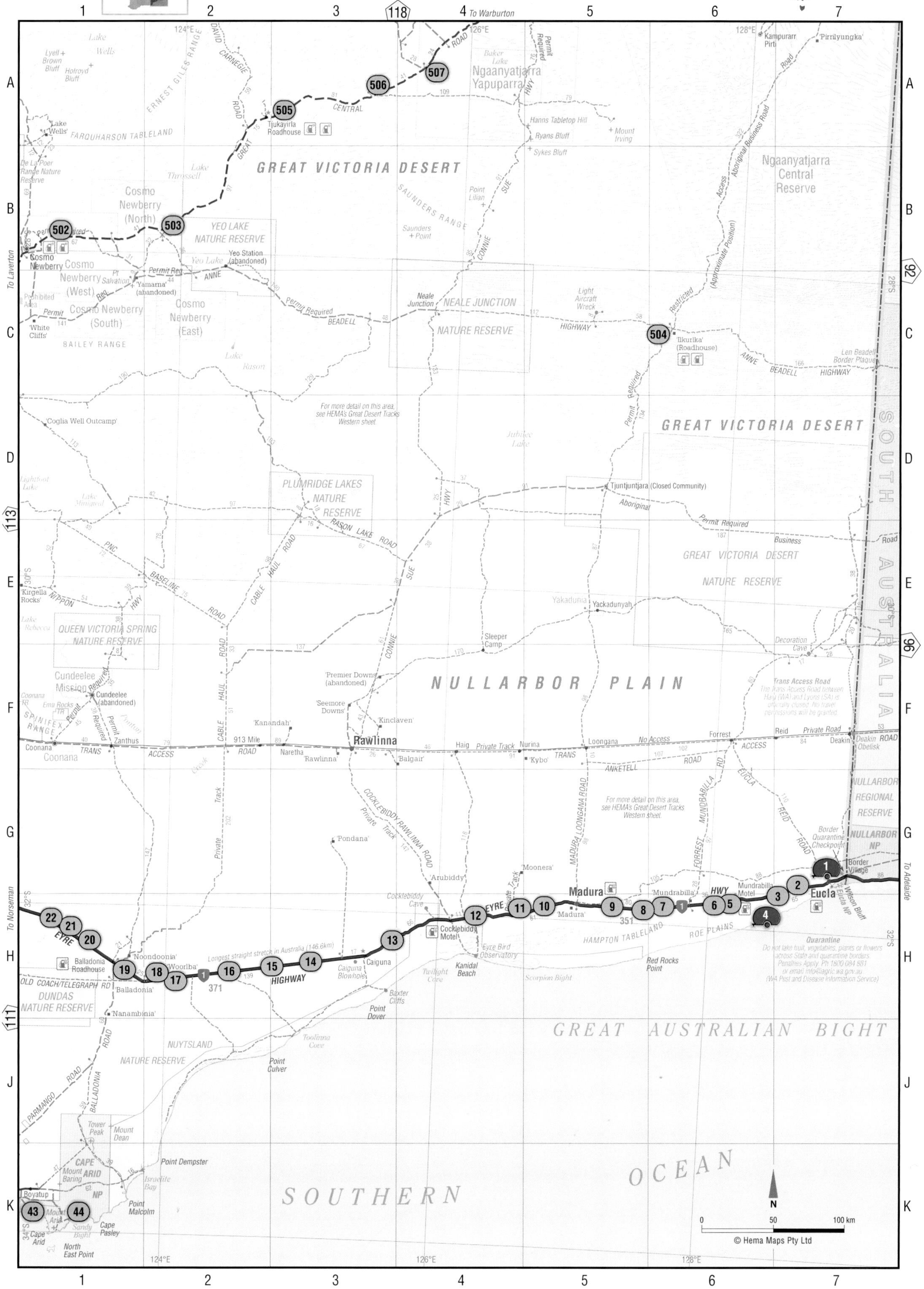

GREAT VICTORIA DESERT

Ngaanyatjarra Yapuparra

Ngaanyatjarra Central Reserve

YEO LAKE NATURE RESERVE

NEALE JUNCTION NATURE RESERVE

PLUMRIDGE LAKES NATURE RESERVE

QUEEN VICTORIA SPRING NATURE RESERVE

GREAT VICTORIA DESERT NATURE RESERVE

NULLARBOR PLAIN

NULLARBOR REGIONAL RESERVE

NULLARBOR NP

DUNDAS NATURE RESERVE

NUYTSLAND NATURE RESERVE

CAPE ARID NP

GREAT AUSTRALIAN BIGHT

SOUTHERN OCEAN

SOUTH AUSTRALIA

Cosmo Newberry (North)

Cosmo Newberry (West)

Cosmo Newberry (South)

Cosmo Newberry (East)

Tjukayirla Roadhouse

'Ilkurlka' (Roadhouse)

Tjuntjuntjara (Closed Community)

Rawlinna

Cundeelee Mission

Madura

Eucla

Border Village

Cocklebiddy Motel

Balladonia Roadhouse

Mundrabilla Motel

Caiguna

For more detail on this area, see HEMA's Great Desert Tracks Western sheet.

Trans Access Road: The Trans Access Road between Haig (WA) and Lyons (SA) is officially closed. No travel permissions will be granted.

Quarantine: Do not take fruit, vegetables, plants or flowers across State and quarantine borders. Penalties Apply. Ph 1800 084 881 or email info@agric.wa.gov.au (WA Pest and Disease Information Service)

Longest straight stretch in Australia (146.6km)

© Hema Maps Pty Ltd

Western Australia Highway Index

Western Australia Alphabetic Site Index

Eucla to Esperance

Eyre and Coolgardie-Esperance Highways

1 Eucla Ambeer Motor Hotel & Caravan Park
☎ (08) 9039 3468

Caravan Park at Eucla. Eyre Hwy

HEMA 119 G7 31 40 37 S 128 53 4 E

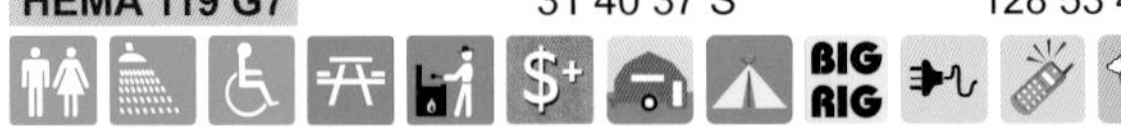

2 Najada Rockhole

Rest Area 30 km W of Eucla or 35 km E of Mundrabilla

HEMA 119 G7 31 44 46 S 128 36 1 E

BIG RIG

3 Hearder Hill

Parking Area 36 km W of Eucla or 29 km E of Mundrabilla

HEMA 119 H6 31 46 2 S 128 31 42 E

BIG RIG

4 Mundrabilla Roadhouse Caravan Park
☎ (08) 9039 3465

Caravan Park at Mundrabilla. Eyre Hwy

HEMA 119 H6 31 49 6 S 128 13 31 E

5 Kathala Pass

Rest Area 3 km W of Mundrabilla or 113 km E of Madura. 500m S of Hwy

HEMA 119 H6 31 49 53 S 128 11 43 E

BIG RIG

6 Jilah Rockhole

Rest Area 10 km W of Mundrabilla or 106 km E of Madura

HEMA 119 H6 31 50 26 S 128 7 49 E

BIG RIG

7 Boolaboola Rest Area

Rest Area 54 km W of Mundrabilla or 62 km E of Madura

HEMA 119 H6 31 53 33 S 127 39 42 E

BIG RIG

8 Carlabeencabba Rockhole

Rest Area 69 km W of Mundrabilla or 47 km E of Madura. Emergency phone

HEMA 119 H6 31 55 14 S 127 31 9 E

BIG RIG

9 Moodini Bluff

Rest Area 90 km W of Mundrabilla or 26 km E of Madura

HEMA 119 H5 31 54 35 S 127 17 15 E

BIG RIG 24

10 Olwolgin Bluff

Parking Area 24 km W of Madura or 66 km E of Cocklebiddy

HEMA 119 H5 31 55 40 S 126 46 43 E

BIG RIG

11 Moonera Tank

Rest Area 47 km W of Madura or 43 km E of Cocklebiddy. Emergency phone

HEMA 119 H4 31 59 23 S 126 32 50 E

BIG RIG

12 Observatory Turnoff

Parking Area 73 km W of Madura or 17 km E of Cocklebiddy. 1 km E of Eyre Bird Observatory turnoff

HEMA 119 H4 32 0 10 S 126 16 38 E

BIG RIG

13 Jillbunya Rockhole

Parking Area 44 km W of Cocklebiddy or 21 km E of Caiguna

HEMA 119 H3 32 10 25 S 125 40 25 E

BIG RIG

14 Domblegabby Rest Area

Rest Area 39 km W of Caiguna or 143 km E of Balladonia

HEMA 119 H3 32 19 17 S 125 4 30 E

BIG RIG

15 Baxter Rest Area

Rest Area 67 km W of Caiguna or 115 km E of Balladonia

HEMA 119 H3 32 21 26 S 124 47 14 E

BIG RIG 24

16 Woorlba East Rest Area

Rest Area 97 km W of Caiguna or 85 km E of Balladonia

HEMA 119 H2 32 23 39 S 124 28 21 E

BIG RIG

17 Woorlba Homestead Rest Area

Rest Area 132 km W of Caiguna or 50 km E of Balladonia. Emergency phone

HEMA 119 H2 32 26 12 S 124 6 17 E

BIG RIG 24

18 90 Mile Sign

Parking Area 147 km W of Caiguna or 35 km E of Balladonia

HEMA 119 H2 32 27 12 S 123 57 17 E

BIG RIG 24

19 Afghan Rock

Parking Area 177 km W of Caiguna or 5 km E of Balladonia

HEMA 119 H1 32 22 42 S 123 39 54 E

BIG RIG 24

20 Harms Lake

Rest Area 25 km W of Balladonia or 167 km E of Norseman

HEMA 119 H1 32 13 28 S 123 22 34 E

BIG RIG 24

21 Harms Lake Parking Area

Parking Area 39 km W of Balladonia or 153 E of Norseman

HEMA 119 H1 32 10 27 S 123 16 30 E

BIG RIG

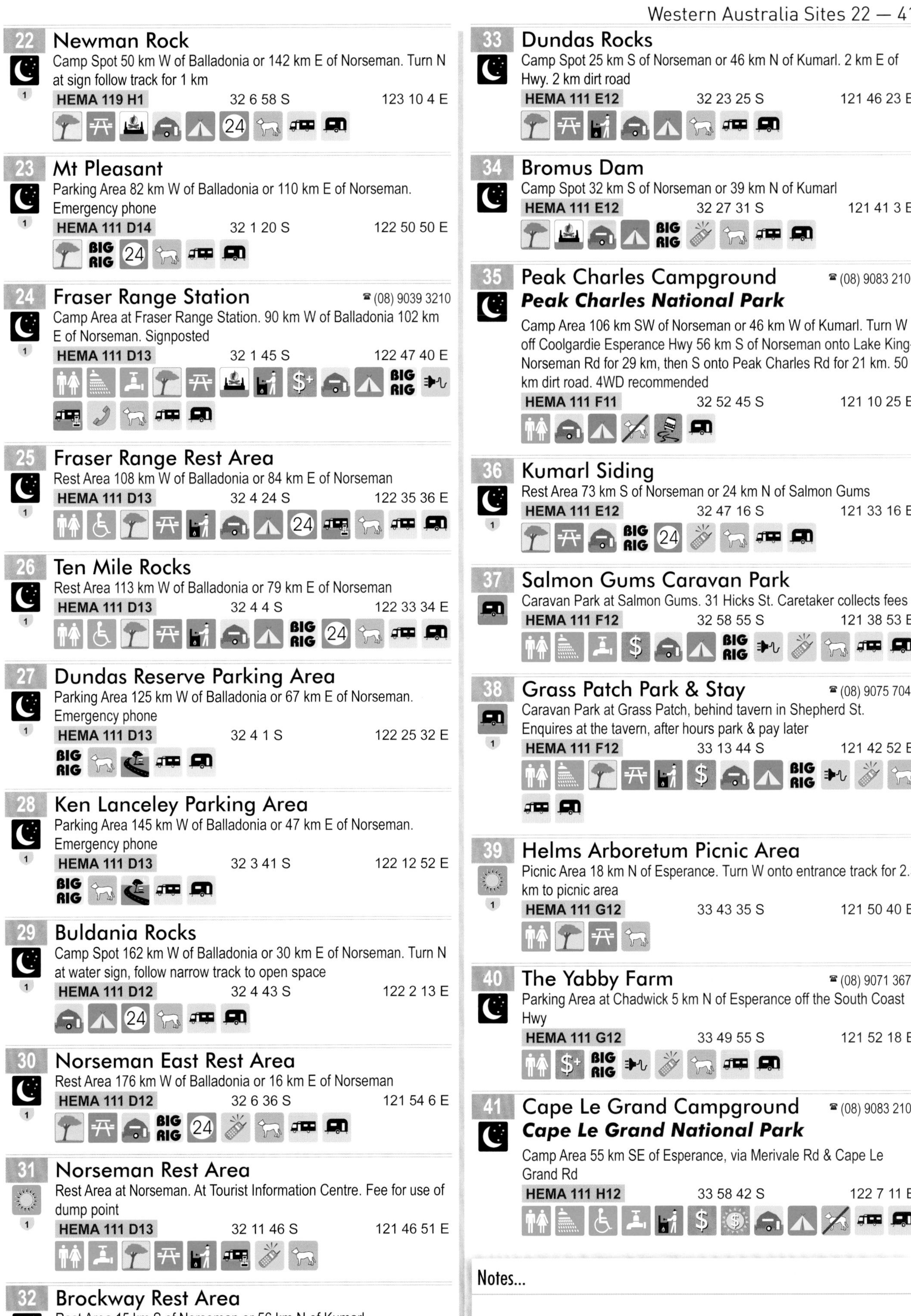

22 Newman Rock

Camp Spot 50 km W of Balladonia or 142 km E of Norseman. Turn N at sign follow track for 1 km

1 HEMA 119 H1 32 6 58 S 123 10 4 E

24

23 Mt Pleasant

Parking Area 82 km W of Balladonia or 110 km E of Norseman. Emergency phone

1 HEMA 111 D14 32 1 20 S 122 50 50 E

BIG RIG 24

24 Fraser Range Station

☎ (08) 9039 3210

Camp Area at Fraser Range Station. 90 km W of Balladonia 102 km E of Norseman. Signposted

1 HEMA 111 D13 32 1 45 S 122 47 40 E

BIG RIG

25 Fraser Range Rest Area

Rest Area 108 km W of Balladonia or 84 km E of Norseman

1 HEMA 111 D13 32 4 24 S 122 35 36 E

24

26 Ten Mile Rocks

Rest Area 113 km W of Balladonia or 79 km E of Norseman

1 HEMA 111 D13 32 4 4 S 122 33 34 E

BIG RIG 24

27 Dundas Reserve Parking Area

Parking Area 125 km W of Balladonia or 67 km E of Norseman. Emergency phone

1 HEMA 111 D13 32 4 1 S 122 25 32 E

BIG RIG

28 Ken Lanceley Parking Area

Parking Area 145 km W of Balladonia or 47 km E of Norseman. Emergency phone

1 HEMA 111 D13 32 3 41 S 122 12 52 E

BIG RIG

29 Buldania Rocks

Camp Spot 162 km W of Balladonia or 30 km E of Norseman. Turn N at water sign, follow narrow track to open space

1 HEMA 111 D12 32 4 43 S 122 2 13 E

24

30 Norseman East Rest Area

Rest Area 176 km W of Balladonia or 16 km E of Norseman

1 HEMA 111 D12 32 6 36 S 121 54 6 E

BIG RIG 24

31 Norseman Rest Area

Rest Area at Norseman. At Tourist Information Centre. Fee for use of dump point

1 HEMA 111 D13 32 11 46 S 121 46 51 E

32 Brockway Rest Area

Rest Area 15 km S of Norseman or 56 km N of Kumarl

1 HEMA 111 D12 32 19 54 S 121 45 34 E

BIG RIG

33 Dundas Rocks

Camp Spot 25 km S of Norseman or 46 km N of Kumarl. 2 km E of Hwy. 2 km dirt road

HEMA 111 E12 32 23 25 S 121 46 23 E

34 Bromus Dam

Camp Spot 32 km S of Norseman or 39 km N of Kumarl

HEMA 111 E12 32 27 31 S 121 41 3 E

BIG RIG

35 Peak Charles Campground

☎ (08) 9083 2100

Peak Charles National Park

Camp Area 106 km SW of Norseman or 46 km W of Kumarl. Turn W off Coolgardie Esperance Hwy 56 km S of Norseman onto Lake King-Norseman Rd for 29 km, then S onto Peak Charles Rd for 21 km. 50 km dirt road. 4WD recommended

HEMA 111 F11 32 52 45 S 121 10 25 E

36 Kumarl Siding

Rest Area 73 km S of Norseman or 24 km N of Salmon Gums

1 HEMA 111 E12 32 47 16 S 121 33 16 E

BIG RIG 24

37 Salmon Gums Caravan Park

Caravan Park at Salmon Gums. 31 Hicks St. Caretaker collects fees

HEMA 111 F12 32 58 55 S 121 38 53 E

BIG RIG

38 Grass Patch Park & Stay

☎ (08) 9075 7046

Caravan Park at Grass Patch, behind tavern in Shepherd St. Enquires at the tavern, after hours park & pay later

1 HEMA 111 F12 33 13 44 S 121 42 52 E

BIG RIG

39 Helms Arboretum Picnic Area

Picnic Area 18 km N of Esperance. Turn W onto entrance track for 2.3 km to picnic area

1 HEMA 111 G12 33 43 35 S 121 50 40 E

40 The Yabby Farm

☎ (08) 9071 3675

Parking Area at Chadwick 5 km N of Esperance off the South Coast Hwy

HEMA 111 G12 33 49 55 S 121 52 18 E

BIG RIG

41 Cape Le Grand Campground

☎ (08) 9083 2100

Cape Le Grand National Park

Camp Area 55 km SE of Esperance, via Merivale Rd & Cape Le Grand Rd

HEMA 111 H12 33 58 42 S 122 7 11 E

Notes...

42 Lucky Bay Campground
☎ (08) 9083 2100
Cape Le Grand National Park
Camp Area 59 km SE of Esperance, via Merivale Rd & Cape Le Grand Rd
HEMA 111 H13 | 33 59 30 S | 122 13 12 E

43 Thomas River Campground
☎ (08) 9083 2100
Cape Arid National Park
Camp Area 118 km E of Esperance, via Fisheries Rd & Tagon Rd
HEMA 111 G14 | 33 51 12 S | 123 0 58 E

44 Seal Creek Campground
☎ (08) 9083 2100
Cape Arid National Park
Camp Area 162 km E of Esperance, via Fisheries Rd & Poison Creek Rd. Small vehicles only
HEMA 111 G14 | 33 54 49 S | 123 20 1 E

Esperance to Albany
South Coast Highway

45 Quagi Beach
☎ (08) 9083 1533
Camp Area 71 km W of Esperance or 51 km E of Munglinup. Turn S off South Coast Hwy 63 km W of Esperance or 43 km E of Munglinup onto Farrells Rd for 8 km of dirt road. Honesty box for fee, caretaker on duty
HEMA 111 G11 | 33 49 45 S | 121 17 31 E

46 Benwenerup Campground
☎ (08) 9076 8541
Stokes National Park
Camp Area 83 km W of Esperance. Turn S off South Coast Hwy 78 km W of Esperance or 28 km E of Munglinup onto Stokes Inlet Rd for 5 km of dirt road
HEMA 111 G11 | 33 49 3 S | 121 8 58 E

47 Coomalbidgup Parking Area
Parking Area 88 km W of Esperance or 19 km E of Munglinup
HEMA 111 G11 | 33 45 49 S | 121 2 56 E
BIG RIG

48 Munglinup Rest Area
Rest Area at Munglinup, opposite roadhouse
HEMA 111 G10 | 33 42 17 S | 120 51 39 E
1
BIG RIG

49 Munglinup Beach
☎ (08) 9071 0666
Camp Area 31 km S of Munglinup. Turn S off South Coast Hwy 4 km E of Munglinup onto Fuss Rd for 10 km, Springdale Rd for 10 km, then Munglinup Beach Rd for 7 km. 9 km dirt road
HEMA 111 G10 | 33 53 13 S | 120 48 18 E

50 Starvation Boat Harbour
☎ 0427 264 377
Camp Area 50 km E of Hopetoun, via Springdale Rd & Starvation Boat Harbour Rd. 40 km dirt road
HEMA 111 G10 | 33 55 10 S | 120 33 19 E

51 Mason Bay
☎ 0427 264 377
Camp Area 40 km E of Hopetoun, via Springdale Rd & Mason Bay Rd. 30 km dirt road
HEMA 111 H10 | 33 57 16 S | 120 28 45 E

52 Hamersley Inlet
☎ 0427 264 377
Fitzgerald River National Park
Camp Area 26 km SW of Hopetoun. Via Southern Ocean West Rd, Hamersley Dr, Hamersley Inlet Rd
HEMA 111 H9 | 33 57 22 S | 119 55 2 E
BIG RIG

53 Kundip Rest Area
Rest Area 19 km S of Ravensthorpe or 30 km N of Hopetoun
HEMA 111 G9 | 33 41 25 S | 120 11 10 E
BIG RIG

54 Meridian Rest Area
Rest Area 4 km W of Ravensthorpe or 109 km E of Jerramungup
HEMA 111 G9 | 33 34 26 S | 120 0 8 E
1
BIG RIG

55 Phillips River Crossing
Camp Spot 15 km W of Ravensthorpe or 98 km E of Jerramungup. 1 km E of the bridge turn S onto old detour road
HEMA 111 G12 | 33 36 10 S | 119 53 6 E

56 Fitzgerald River (Jacup)
Parking Area 80 km W of Ravensthorpe or 33 km E of Jerramungup
HEMA 110 H7 | 33 49 53 S | 119 15 13 E
1
BIG RIG

57 Needilup Rest Area
Rest Area 14 km W of Jerramungup or 25 km E of Ongerup, behind hall
HEMA 110 H7 | 33 57 9 S | 118 46 19 E

58 Ongerup Caravan Park
☎ 0428 282 127
Caravan Park at Ongerup. Cnr Walker & Lamont Sts
HEMA 110 H7 | 33 58 4 S | 118 29 12 E

59 Gnowangerup Travel Stop
☎ (08) 9827 1635
Caravan Park at Gnowangerup. Richardson St. Pay at CRC or roadhouse. AH phone (08) 9827 1239
HEMA 109 E14 | 33 56 31 S | 118 0 36 E
BIG RIG

60 Louis's Lookout Rest Area - North Borden
Rest Area 4 km N of Borden at Great Southern Hwy jcn
HEMA 109 E14 34 1 31 S 118 16 22 E
BIG RIG

61 Borden Rest Area
Rest Area at Borden. Opposite General Store
HEMA 110 H7 34 4 16 S 118 15 46 E
20

62 Borden Recreation Ground
Camp Spot at Borden
HEMA 110 H6 34 4 22 S 118 15 31 E
BIG RIG

63 Moingup Springs Campground ☎(08) 9842 4500
Stirling Range National Park
Camp Area 76 km N of Albany, 65 km N of Bakers Junction or 45 km S of Borden, off Chester Pass Rd
HEMA 109 G14 34 24 3 S 118 6 8 E

64 Millers Point Reserve ☎(08) 9835 1022
Camp Area 20 km E of Boxwood Hill or 53 km W of Bremer Bay. Turn S off Borden Bremer Bay Rd 14 km E of Boxwood Hill onto Millers Point Rd. 6 km dirt road. Small vehicles only
HEMA 110 J7 34 27 14 S 118 52 42 E

65 Quaalup Homestead Wilderness Retreat ☎(08) 9837 4124
Camp Area 77 km SW of Jerramungup or 48 km N of Bremer Bay. From Jerramungup turn E after 28 km onto Devil Creek Rd. Dirt road. Limited solar power, no generators permitted, no credit cards
HEMA 111 H8 34 15 37 S 119 24 35 E

66 Pallinup River
Rest Area 67 km S of Jerramungup or 15 km NE of Wellstead. 5 km S of Bremer Bay intersection
1
HEMA 110 J7 34 24 24 S 118 43 35 E
BIG RIG

67 Cape Riche Campground ☎(08) 9847 3088
Camp Area 18 km SE of Wellstead, via Sandalwood Rd. Limited space for big rigs. Dirt road
HEMA 110 J7 34 35 52 S 118 44 56 E
BIG RIG

68 Green Range Rest Area
Rest Area 25 km SW of Wellstead or 73 km NE of Albany
1
HEMA 110 J7 34 37 41 S 118 22 51 E

Notes...

69 Normans Beach
Camp Spot 14 km S of Many Peaks. Turn SE off South Coast Hwy 3 km SW of Many Peaks or 36 km NE of Albany onto Homestead Rd for 9 km, then onto Normans Beach Rd for 2 km. 6 km dirt road
HEMA 110 J7 34 55 17 S 118 12 51 E

70 Bettys Beach
Camp Spot 17 km S of Many Peaks. Turn SE off South Coast Hwy 3 km SW of Many Peaks or 36 NE of Albany onto Homestead Rd for 9 km then onto Bettys Beach Rd for 5 km. 9 km dirt road. Limited space. Closed 15 Feb- 30 Apr for salmon season
HEMA 110 J7 34 56 12 S 118 12 30 E
48

71 Napier Creek
Parking Area 25 km N of Albany or 23 km S of Porongurup. S of Napier Bridge on L
HEMA 109 J14 34 49 51 S 117 57 36 E
24

Albany-Bunbury-Perth
South Western Highway

72 Torbay Inlet ☎(08) 9841 1088
Camp Area 28 km W of Albany or 38 km E of Denmark. Turn S off Lower Denmark Rd 24 km W of Albany or 34 E of Denmark onto Perkins Beach Rd & Torbay Inlet Rd. Dirt road for 4 km. Small area. Maximum stay 7 days
HEMA 109 K13 35 2 22 S 117 40 47 E

✓73 Cosy Corner (East)
Camp Area 30 km W of Albany or 38 km E of Denmark. Turn S off Lower Denmark Rd 25 km W of Albany or 33 km E of Denmark onto Cosy Corner Rd. Maximum stay 7 days
HEMA 109 K13 35 3 33 S 117 38 44 E

74 Cosy Corner (West)
Picnic Area 31 km W of Albany. Access as per Cosy Corner East. Low trees
HEMA 109 K13 35 3 53 S 117 38 36 E

75 Shelley Beach Camping Area ☎(08) 9844 4090
West Cape Howe National Park
Camp Area 38 km W of Albany. Access via Cosy Corner, Coombes & Shelley Bch Rds. 5.5 km dirt road, very steep descent. No caravans permitted, small vehicles only, small area
HEMA 109 K12 35 6 32 S 117 37 46 E

76 Parry Beach ☎(08) 9848 2055
Camp Area 28 km W of Denmark or 43 km E of Walpole. Turn S 22 km W of Denmark or 43 km E of Walpole onto Parry Rd for 6 km. Maximum stay 3 weeks. Maximum height limit 2.75m. Small vehicles only. Large vehicle overflow now adjacent with no facilities, fee applies time limit for overflow area is 24 hours
HEMA 109 K10 35 2 25 S 117 9 42 E

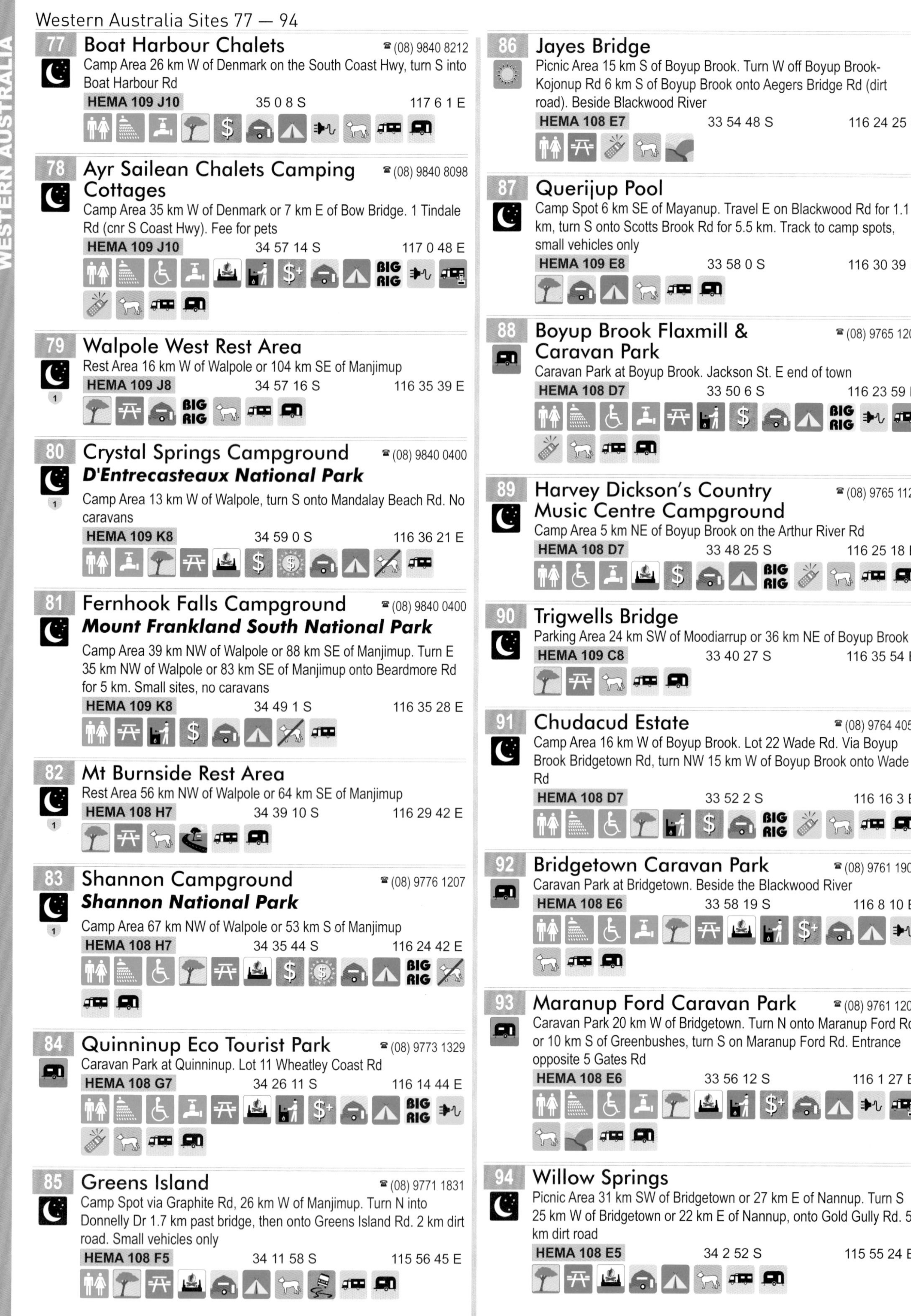

77 Boat Harbour Chalets
☎ (08) 9840 8212

Camp Area 26 km W of Denmark on the South Coast Hwy, turn S into Boat Harbour Rd

HEMA 109 J10 | 35 0 8 S | 117 6 1 E

78 Ayr Sailean Chalets Camping Cottages
☎ (08) 9840 8098

Camp Area 35 km W of Denmark or 7 km E of Bow Bridge. 1 Tindale Rd (cnr S Coast Hwy). Fee for pets

HEMA 109 J10 | 34 57 14 S | 117 0 48 E

BIG RIG

79 Walpole West Rest Area

Rest Area 16 km W of Walpole or 104 km SE of Manjimup

HEMA 109 J8 | 34 57 16 S | 116 35 39 E

BIG RIG

80 Crystal Springs Campground
☎ (08) 9840 0400

D'Entrecasteaux National Park

Camp Area 13 km W of Walpole, turn S onto Mandalay Beach Rd. No caravans

HEMA 109 K8 | 34 59 0 S | 116 36 21 E

81 Fernhook Falls Campground
☎ (08) 9840 0400

Mount Frankland South National Park

Camp Area 39 km NW of Walpole or 88 km SE of Manjimup. Turn E 35 km NW of Walpole or 83 km SE of Manjimup onto Beardmore Rd for 5 km. Small sites, no caravans

HEMA 109 K8 | 34 49 1 S | 116 35 28 E

82 Mt Burnside Rest Area

Rest Area 56 km NW of Walpole or 64 km SE of Manjimup

HEMA 108 H7 | 34 39 10 S | 116 29 42 E

83 Shannon Campground
☎ (08) 9776 1207

Shannon National Park

Camp Area 67 km NW of Walpole or 53 km S of Manjimup

HEMA 108 H7 | 34 35 44 S | 116 24 42 E

BIG RIG

84 Quinninup Eco Tourist Park
☎ (08) 9773 1329

Caravan Park at Quinninup. Lot 11 Wheatley Coast Rd

HEMA 108 G7 | 34 26 11 S | 116 14 44 E

BIG RIG

85 Greens Island
☎ (08) 9771 1831

Camp Spot via Graphite Rd, 26 km W of Manjimup. Turn N into Donnelly Dr 1.7 km past bridge, then onto Greens Island Rd. 2 km dirt road. Small vehicles only

HEMA 108 F5 | 34 11 58 S | 115 56 45 E

86 Jayes Bridge

Picnic Area 15 km S of Boyup Brook. Turn W off Boyup Brook-Kojonup Rd 6 km S of Boyup Brook onto Aegers Bridge Rd (dirt road). Beside Blackwood River

HEMA 108 E7 | 33 54 48 S | 116 24 25 E

87 Querijup Pool

Camp Spot 6 km SE of Mayanup. Travel E on Blackwood Rd for 1.1 km, turn S onto Scotts Brook Rd for 5.5 km. Track to camp spots, small vehicles only

HEMA 109 E8 | 33 58 0 S | 116 30 39 E

88 Boyup Brook Flaxmill & Caravan Park
☎ (08) 9765 1200

Caravan Park at Boyup Brook. Jackson St. E end of town

HEMA 108 D7 | 33 50 6 S | 116 23 59 E

BIG RIG

89 Harvey Dickson's Country Music Centre Campground
☎ (08) 9765 1125

Camp Area 5 km NE of Boyup Brook on the Arthur River Rd

HEMA 108 D7 | 33 48 25 S | 116 25 18 E

BIG RIG

90 Trigwells Bridge

Parking Area 24 km SW of Moodiarrup or 36 km NE of Boyup Brook

HEMA 109 C8 | 33 40 27 S | 116 35 54 E

91 Chudacud Estate
☎ (08) 9764 4053

Camp Area 16 km W of Boyup Brook. Lot 22 Wade Rd. Via Boyup Brook Bridgetown Rd, turn NW 15 km W of Boyup Brook onto Wade Rd

HEMA 108 D7 | 33 52 2 S | 116 16 3 E

BIG RIG

92 Bridgetown Caravan Park
☎ (08) 9761 1900

Caravan Park at Bridgetown. Beside the Blackwood River

HEMA 108 E6 | 33 58 19 S | 116 8 10 E

93 Maranup Ford Caravan Park
☎ (08) 9761 1200

Caravan Park 20 km W of Bridgetown. Turn N onto Maranup Ford Rd or 10 km S of Greenbushes, turn S on Maranup Ford Rd. Entrance opposite 5 Gates Rd

HEMA 108 E6 | 33 56 12 S | 116 1 27 E

94 Willow Springs

Picnic Area 31 km SW of Bridgetown or 27 km E of Nannup. Turn S 25 km W of Bridgetown or 22 km E of Nannup, onto Gold Gully Rd. 5 km dirt road

HEMA 108 E5 | 34 2 52 S | 115 55 24 E

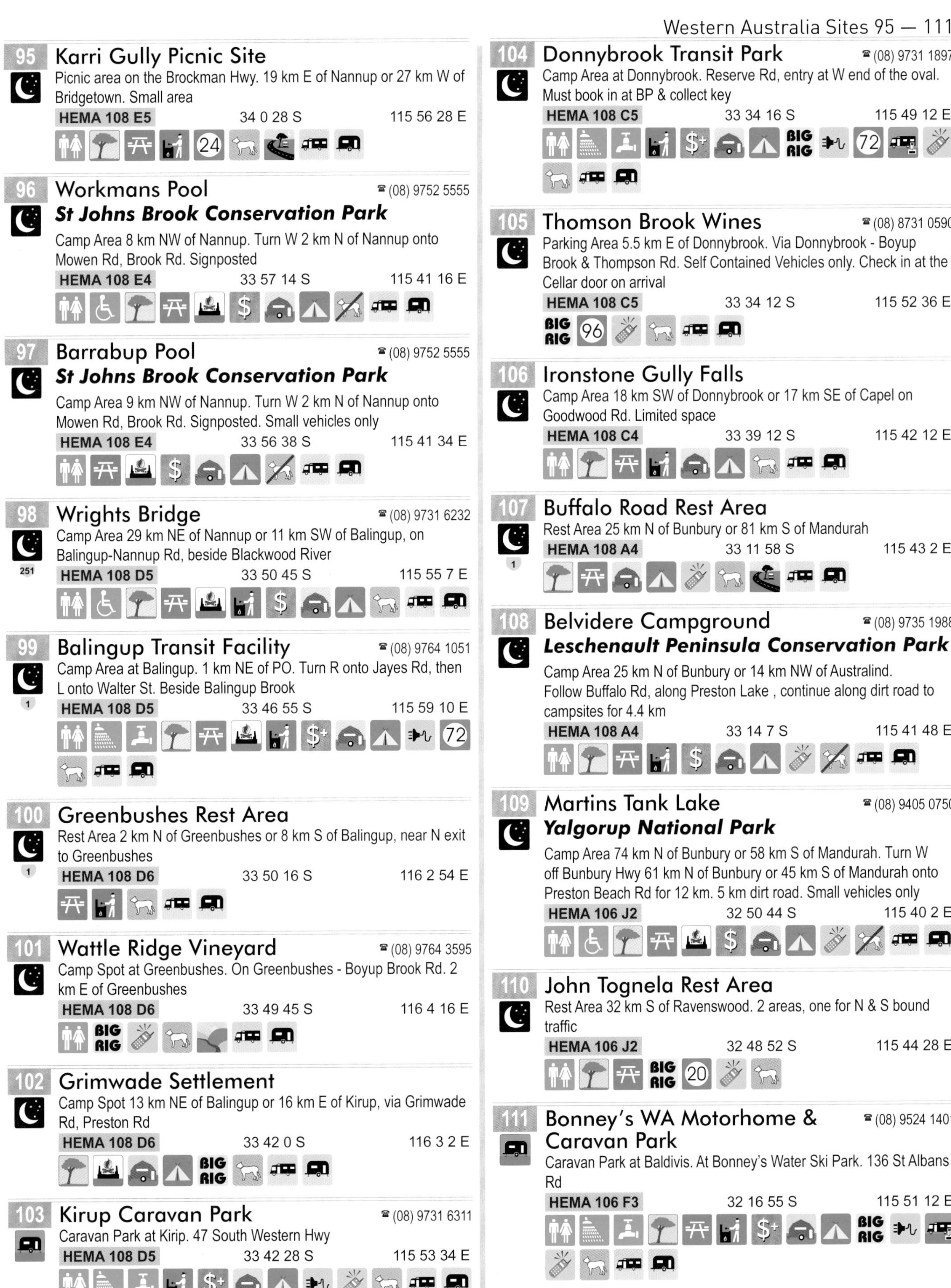

95 Karri Gully Picnic Site
Picnic area on the Brockman Hwy. 19 km E of Nannup or 27 km W of Bridgetown. Small area
HEMA 108 E5 34 0 28 S 115 56 28 E
24

96 Workmans Pool
☎ (08) 9752 5555
St Johns Brook Conservation Park
Camp Area 8 km NW of Nannup. Turn W 2 km N of Nannup onto Mowen Rd, Brook Rd. Signposted
HEMA 108 E4 33 57 14 S 115 41 16 E

97 Barrabup Pool
☎ (08) 9752 5555
St Johns Brook Conservation Park
Camp Area 9 km NW of Nannup. Turn W 2 km N of Nannup onto Mowen Rd, Brook Rd. Signposted. Small vehicles only
HEMA 108 E4 33 56 38 S 115 41 34 E

98 Wrights Bridge
☎ (08) 9731 6232
Camp Area 29 km NE of Nannup or 11 km SW of Balingup, on Balingup-Nannup Rd, beside Blackwood River
251
HEMA 108 D5 33 50 45 S 115 55 7 E

99 Balingup Transit Facility
☎ (08) 9764 1051
Camp Area at Balingup. 1 km NE of PO. Turn R onto Jayes Rd, then L onto Walter St. Beside Balingup Brook
1
HEMA 108 D5 33 46 55 S 115 59 10 E
72

100 Greenbushes Rest Area
Rest Area 2 km N of Greenbushes or 8 km S of Balingup, near N exit to Greenbushes
1
HEMA 108 D6 33 50 16 S 116 2 54 E

101 Wattle Ridge Vineyard
☎ (08) 9764 3595
Camp Spot at Greenbushes. On Greenbushes - Boyup Brook Rd. 2 km E of Greenbushes
HEMA 108 D6 33 49 45 S 116 4 16 E
BIG RIG

102 Grimwade Settlement
Camp Spot 13 km NE of Balingup or 16 km E of Kirup, via Grimwade Rd, Preston Rd
HEMA 108 D6 33 42 0 S 116 3 2 E
BIG RIG

103 Kirup Caravan Park
☎ (08) 9731 6311
Caravan Park at Kirip. 47 South Western Hwy
HEMA 108 D5 33 42 28 S 115 53 34 E

104 Donnybrook Transit Park
☎ (08) 9731 1897
Camp Area at Donnybrook. Reserve Rd, entry at W end of the oval. Must book in at BP & collect key
HEMA 108 C5 33 34 16 S 115 49 12 E
BIG RIG 72

105 Thomson Brook Wines
☎ (08) 8731 0590
Parking Area 5.5 km E of Donnybrook. Via Donnybrook - Boyup Brook & Thompson Rd. Self Contained Vehicles only. Check in at the Cellar door on arrival
HEMA 108 C5 33 34 12 S 115 52 36 E
BIG RIG 96

106 Ironstone Gully Falls
Camp Area 18 km SW of Donnybrook or 17 km SE of Capel on Goodwood Rd. Limited space
HEMA 108 C4 33 39 12 S 115 42 12 E

107 Buffalo Road Rest Area
Rest Area 25 km N of Bunbury or 81 km S of Mandurah
1
HEMA 108 A4 33 11 58 S 115 43 2 E

108 Belvidere Campground
☎ (08) 9735 1988
Leschenault Peninsula Conservation Park
Camp Area 25 km N of Bunbury or 14 km NW of Australind. Follow Buffalo Rd, along Preston Lake , continue along dirt road to campsites for 4.4 km
HEMA 108 A4 33 14 7 S 115 41 48 E

109 Martins Tank Lake
☎ (08) 9405 0750
Yalgorup National Park
Camp Area 74 km N of Bunbury or 58 km S of Mandurah. Turn W off Bunbury Hwy 61 km N of Bunbury or 45 km S of Mandurah onto Preston Beach Rd for 12 km. 5 km dirt road. Small vehicles only
HEMA 106 J2 32 50 44 S 115 40 2 E

110 John Tognela Rest Area
Rest Area 32 km S of Ravenswood. 2 areas, one for N & S bound traffic
HEMA 106 J2 32 48 52 S 115 44 28 E
BIG RIG 20

111 Bonney's WA Motorhome & Caravan Park
☎ (08) 9524 1401
Caravan Park at Baldivis. At Bonney's Water Ski Park. 136 St Albans Rd
HEMA 106 F3 32 16 55 S 115 51 12 E
BIG RIG

Notes...

Ravensthorpe-Hyden-Perth

Brookton Highway

112 Overshot Hill Nature Reserve
Rest Area 9 km N of Ravensthorpe or 61 km S of Lake King, on Ravensthorpe-Lake King Rd
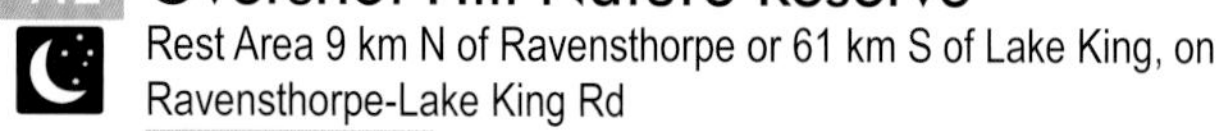
HEMA 111 G9 | 33 31 39 S | 119 59 36 E

113 Lake King Caravan Park
(08) 9874 4048
Caravan Park at Lake King, Critchley Ave. Register & pay at tavern across road
HEMA 111 F8 | 33 5 2 S | 119 41 18 E

114 Hyden Rest Area
Rest Area at Hyden. Opposite hotel
HEMA 110 E7 | 32 26 57 S | 118 51 57 E

115 The Forrestania Plots
Camp Spot 64.5 km E of Hyden on Hyden-Norseman Rd. Dirt road. Signposted
HEMA 111 E8 | 32 24 55 S | 119 32 1 E

116 The Breakaways
Camp Spot 137.4 km E of Hyden on Hyden-Norseman Rd. Dirt road
HEMA 111 D10 | 32 16 34 S | 120 15 46 E

117 McDermid Rock
Parking Area 192 km E of Hyden, or 141 km W of Norseman on Hyden-Norseman Rd. Turn N, travel 1.5 km to rock
HEMA 111 D10 | 32 1 18 S | 120 44 20 E

118 Lake Johnston
Camp Spot 200 km E of Hyden or 102 km W of Norseman on the Hyden-Norseman Rd. Access track S side of road, picnic area on edge of lake, track to campsite on R of picnic area
HEMA 111 D10 | 32 0 57 S | 120 47 7 E

119 Disappointment Rock
Camp Spot 87 km W of Norseman or 246 E of Hyden on the Hyden-Norseman Rd
HEMA 111 D11 | 32 7 48 S | 120 55 44 E

120 Woodlands
Camp Spot 48 km W of Norseman or 285 E of Hyden on the Hyden-Norseman Rd
HEMA 111 D11 | 32 11 15 S | 121 20 16 E

121 Kulin Caravan Park
(08) 9880 1053
Caravan Park at Kulin. 82 Johnson St
HEMA 107 H13 | 32 40 2 S | 118 9 31 E

122 Kulin Overnight Stop
(08) 9880 1204
Camp Spot at Kulin. Johnston St (Southside) between Kulin Resource Centre & Kulin Hostel. Self Contained Vehicles only
HEMA 107 H13 | 32 40 11 S | 118 9 20 E

123 Harrismith Caravan Park
(08) 9883 1010
Caravan Park at Harrismith. Cnr Railway Ave & Baylon St
HEMA 107 J12 | 32 56 10 S | 117 51 44 E

124 Kondinin Caravan Park
(08) 9889 1006
Caravan Park at Kondinin. Gordon St. Key & payment at Shire office or at roadhouse
HEMA 107 G14 | 32 29 43 S | 118 15 49 E

125 Gorge Rock Pool
Picnic Area 20 km SE of Corrigin or 28 km W of Kondinin
40
HEMA 107 G12 | 32 27 25 S | 117 59 45 E

126 Narembeen Caravan Park
(08) 9064 7308
Caravan Park at Narembeen. Currall St
HEMA 107 E14 | 32 3 49 S | 118 23 46 E

127 Bruce Rock Caravan Park
(08) 9061 1377
Camp Area at Bruce Rock, Dunstall St, next to swimming pool
HEMA 107 D13 | 31 52 29 S | 118 9 6 E

128 Kokerbin Rock
Picnic Area 47 km W of Bruce Rock or 43 km E of Quairading. Turn N off Bruce Rock-Quairading Rd 40 km W of Bruce Rock or 36 km E of Quairading onto Kwolyin Rd West for 7 km
HEMA 107 D11 | 31 53 12 S | 117 42 34 E

129 Kwolyin Camp
Camp Area at Kwolyin. Situated on the Old Kwolyin township site off the Bruce Rock-Quairading Rd
HEMA 107 D11 | 31 55 59 S | 117 45 46 E

130 Quairading Caravan Park
(08) 9645 1001
Caravan Park at Quairading. McLennan St
HEMA 107 E10 | 32 0 44 S | 117 24 9 E

131 Toapin Weir Rest Area
Rest Area 8 km N of Quairading. Turn W from Cunderdin-Quairading Rd 5.5 km N of Quairading. 3 km gravel road to weir. Small area
HEMA 107 E9 | 31 58 44 S | 117 21 36 E

132 Quairading Travellers Rest Area
Greater Sports Ground, McLennan St. Permit required from Shire office. Self Contained Vehicles only
HEMA 107 E10 32 0 42 S 117 24 10 E

133 Aldersyde Parking Area
Parking Area 28 km E of Brookton or 63 km W of Corrigin
HEMA 107 F10 32 19 11 S 117 16 30 E

134 Boyagin Rock
Picnic Area 36 km SW of Brookton. Turn S 19 km W of Brookton onto York Williams Rd for 10 km then E onto Boyagin Rd & Perch Rd
HEMA 107 G7 32 28 15 S 116 53 11 E

135 Brookton Highway Rest Spot
40
Parking Area 27 km W of Brookton or 87 km E of Armadale
HEMA 107 G7 32 23 57 S 116 44 14 E

Lake King to Bunbury

136 Lake Grace Caravan Park
(08) 9865 1263
Caravan Park at Lake Grace. Mather St
HEMA 107 K14 33 5 59 S 118 27 33 E

137 Dumbleyung Caravan Park
(08) 9863 4012
Caravan Park at Dumbleyung, Harvey St. Opposite Shire office
HEMA 109 B13 33 18 47 S 117 44 23 E

138 Darkan Caravan Park
(08) 9736 2222
107
Caravan Park at Darkan. Lot 274 Coalfield Rd. 1 km W of PO
HEMA 109 B9 33 20 3 S 116 43 29 E

139 Stockton Lake Recreation Area
(08) 9735 1988
Camp Area 8 km E of Collie. Turn S off Hwy 107, 53 km W of Darkan or 6 km E of Collie, onto Piavanini Rd
HEMA 108 B6 33 23 5 S 116 13 43 E

140 Glen Mervyn Dam
Camp Spot at Glen Mervyn Dam. 18 km S of Collie on the Collie - Mumballup Rd. Small vehicles only
HEMA 108 C6 33 30 18 S 116 5 50 E

141 Minningup Pool
Picnic Area 5 km SW of Collie, via Patterson St & Mungalup Rd
HEMA 108 B6 33 22 35 S 116 8 15 E

142 Potters Gorge
(08) 9735 1988
Wellington National Park
Camp Area 29 km W of Collie, via Coalfields Rd, Wellington Dam Rd & Tom Jones Dr
HEMA 108 B5 33 23 25 S 115 58 55 E

143 Honeymoon Pool (Stones Brook)
(08) 9735 1988
Wellington National Park
Camp Area 28 km W of Collie, via Coalfields Rd, Wellington Dam Rd & River Rd. Windy road small vehicles only. No caravans allowed
HEMA 108 B5 33 22 48 S 115 56 12 E

144 Wellington Dam Road Rest Area
107
Rest Area 18 km W of Collie or 18 km E of South West Hwy/ Coalfields Rd jcn, at Wellington Dam Rd. Small vehicles only
HEMA 108 B5 33 19 10 S 115 58 52 E

145 Coalfields Road Rest Area
107
Rest Area 23 km W of Collie or 13 km E of South West Hwy/ Coalfields Rd jcn
HEMA 108 B5 33 17 30 S 115 56 56 E

Cranbrook to Northam

Great Southern Highway

146 Nyabing Recreation Reserve
(08) 9829 1051
Camp Spot at Nyabing, Martin St. Key at Shire office
HEMA 110 G6 33 32 45 S 118 8 48 E

147 Pingrup Caravan Park
(08) 9820 1101
Caravan Park at Pingrup. Pingrup Lake Grace Rd, near the “Shears Shed”. See notice board for payment & keys
HEMA 110 G7 33 32 5 S 118 30 40 E

148 Wagin Caravan Park
0419 611 057
Caravan Park at Wagin. Cnr of Arthur Rd & Scadden St. 1 km W of PO
HEMA 109 B11 33 18 39 S 117 20 5 E

Notes...

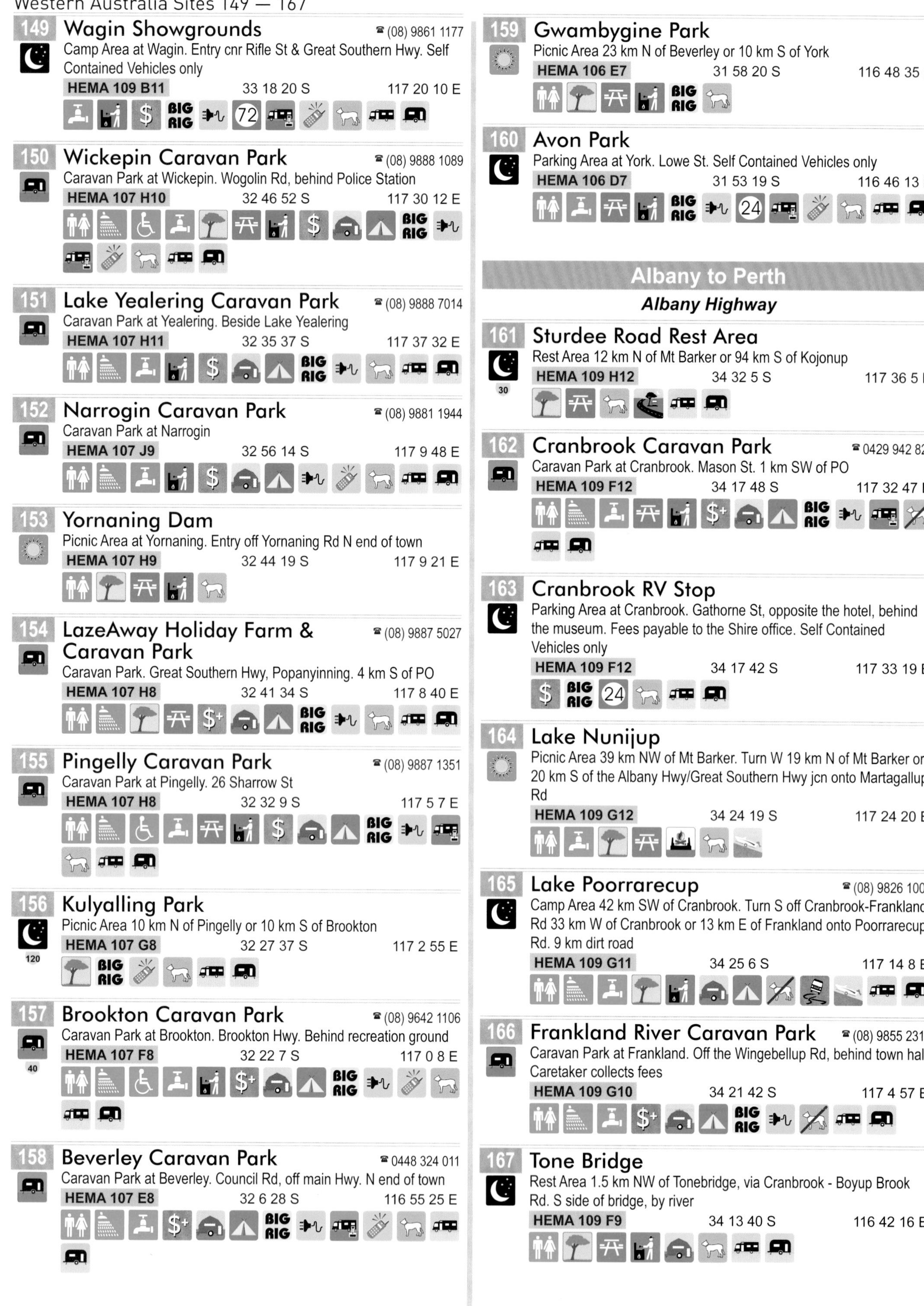

149 Wagin Showgrounds
☎ (08) 9861 1177

Camp Area at Wagin. Entry cnr Rifle St & Great Southern Hwy. Self Contained Vehicles only

HEMA 109 B11 33 18 20 S 117 20 10 E

BIG RIG 72

150 Wickepin Caravan Park
☎ (08) 9888 1089

Caravan Park at Wickepin. Wogolin Rd, behind Police Station

HEMA 107 H10 32 46 52 S 117 30 12 E

BIG RIG

151 Lake Yealering Caravan Park
☎ (08) 9888 7014

Caravan Park at Yealering. Beside Lake Yealering

HEMA 107 H11 32 35 37 S 117 37 32 E

BIG RIG

152 Narrogin Caravan Park
☎ (08) 9881 1944

Caravan Park at Narrogin

HEMA 107 J9 32 56 14 S 117 9 48 E

153 Yornaning Dam

Picnic Area at Yornaning. Entry off Yornaning Rd N end of town

HEMA 107 H9 32 44 19 S 117 9 21 E

154 LazeAway Holiday Farm & Caravan Park
☎ (08) 9887 5027

Caravan Park. Great Southern Hwy, Popanyinning. 4 km S of PO

HEMA 107 H8 32 41 34 S 117 8 40 E

BIG RIG

155 Pingelly Caravan Park
☎ (08) 9887 1351

Caravan Park at Pingelly. 26 Sharrow St

HEMA 107 H8 32 32 9 S 117 5 7 E

BIG RIG

156 Kulyalling Park

120

Picnic Area 10 km N of Pingelly or 10 km S of Brookton

HEMA 107 G8 32 27 37 S 117 2 55 E

BIG RIG

157 Brookton Caravan Park
☎ (08) 9642 1106

40

Caravan Park at Brookton. Brookton Hwy. Behind recreation ground

HEMA 107 F8 32 22 7 S 117 0 8 E

BIG RIG

158 Beverley Caravan Park
☎ 0448 324 011

Caravan Park at Beverley. Council Rd, off main Hwy. N end of town

HEMA 107 E8 32 6 28 S 116 55 25 E

BIG RIG

159 Gwambygine Park

Picnic Area 23 km N of Beverley or 10 km S of York

HEMA 106 E7 31 58 20 S 116 48 35 E

BIG RIG

160 Avon Park

Parking Area at York. Lowe St. Self Contained Vehicles only

HEMA 106 D7 31 53 19 S 116 46 13 E

BIG RIG 24

Albany to Perth

Albany Highway

161 Sturdee Road Rest Area

30

Rest Area 12 km N of Mt Barker or 94 km S of Kojonup

HEMA 109 H12 34 32 5 S 117 36 5 E

162 Cranbrook Caravan Park
☎ 0429 942 825

Caravan Park at Cranbrook. Mason St. 1 km SW of PO

HEMA 109 F12 34 17 48 S 117 32 47 E

BIG RIG

163 Cranbrook RV Stop

Parking Area at Cranbrook. Gathorne St, opposite the hotel, behind the museum. Fees payable to the Shire office. Self Contained Vehicles only

HEMA 109 F12 34 17 42 S 117 33 19 E

BIG RIG 24

164 Lake Nunijup

Picnic Area 39 km NW of Mt Barker. Turn W 19 km N of Mt Barker or 20 km S of the Albany Hwy/Great Southern Hwy jcn onto Martagallup Rd

HEMA 109 G12 34 24 19 S 117 24 20 E

165 Lake Poorrarecup
☎ (08) 9826 1008

Camp Area 42 km SW of Cranbrook. Turn S off Cranbrook-Frankland Rd 33 km W of Cranbrook or 13 km E of Frankland onto Poorrarecup Rd. 9 km dirt road

HEMA 109 G11 34 25 6 S 117 14 8 E

166 Frankland River Caravan Park
☎ (08) 9855 2310

Caravan Park at Frankland. Off the Wingebellup Rd, behind town hall. Caretaker collects fees

HEMA 109 G10 34 21 42 S 117 4 57 E

BIG RIG

167 Tone Bridge

Rest Area 1.5 km NW of Tonebridge, via Cranbrook - Boyup Brook Rd. S side of bridge, by river

HEMA 109 F9 34 13 40 S 116 42 16 E

168 Muirs Bridge

Rest Area 11 km W of Rocky Gully or 87 km E of Manjimup, beside Frankland River

102

HEMA 109 G9 34 28 38 S 116 54 7 E

169 Lake Muir Observatory

Rest Area 34 km W of Rocky Gully or 64 km E of Manjimup

102

HEMA 109 G8 34 26 25 S 116 38 58 E

170 Tambellup Caravan Park

☎ (08) 9825 3555

Caravan Park at Tambellup

HEMA 109 E13 34 2 37 S 117 38 41 E

BIG RIG

171 Katanning Caravan Park & BP Roadhouse

☎ (08) 9821 1155

Caravan Park at Katanning. 68 Cornwall St

HEMA 109 C12 33 42 4 S 117 33 36 E

172 Woodanilling Caravan Park

☎ (08) 9823 1681

Caravan Park at Woodanilling. Cnr Robinson Rd & Great Southern Hwy

HEMA 109 C12 33 33 51 S 117 25 26 E

BIG RIG

173 Woodanilling Recreation Reserve

☎ (08) 9823 1506

Parking Area in Woodanilling, Yairabin St. Self Contained Vehicles only. Limited sites. Donation required

HEMA 109 C12 33 33 36 S 117 25 59 E

BIG RIG 24

174 Queerarrup Lake

☎ (08) 9823 1506

Camp Spot 28 km NW of Woodanilling. Turn N off Robinson Rd 18 km W of Woodanilling onto Reshke Rd, follow 10 km turn L onto Douglas Rd, R onto Queerarrup Rd, veer R at T jcn, Camp Spot on L. Self Contained Vehicles only

HEMA 109 C11 33 30 55 S 117 13 27 E

175 Kojonup Rest Area

☎ (08) 9831 0500

Rest Area at Kojonup. Gordon St S end of town. Permit required from Info Centre 143 Albany Hwy. Self Contained Vehicles only

HEMA 109 D10 33 50 13 S 117 9 32 E

BIG RIG 72

176 Martup Pool

Rest Area 32 km N of Kojonup or 24 km S of Arthur River. Some low trees, follow track to riverside camping

30

HEMA 109 C10 33 32 47 S 117 5 4 E

177 Lakeside Camping (Lake Towerrinning)

☎ (08) 9863 1040

Camp Area 40 km SW of Arthur River or 64 km NE of Boyup Brook. 2 km N of Moodiarrup, via Darkan Rd S

HEMA 109 C9 33 35 2 S 116 47 32 E

BIG RIG

178 Eulin Crossing

Camp Spot 20 km SW of Moodiarrup or 49 km NE of Boyup Brook. Turn SE 16 km from Moodiarrup or 45 km from Boyup Brook onto Kulikup N Rd for 4.3 km. Turn W into Eulin Crossing Rd. Follow for 1 km, track down to camp spot. Small vehicles only

HEMA 109 C8 33 42 2 S 116 40 28 E

179 Congelin Campground

☎ (08) 9881 9200

Dryandra Woodland

Camp Area 27 km N of Williams, via York-Williams Rd. Turn N off Hwy 30, 3 km NW of Williams onto York- Williams Rd. Signposted

HEMA 107 J7 32 49 0 S 116 53 8 E

180 Pumphreys Bridge Lions Park

Camp Spot at Pumphreys Bridge. Via Wandering - Narrogin Rd, 43 km N Narrogin. NW side of the CWA building

HEMA 106 H7 32 39 45 S 116 54 17 E

BIG RIG

181 Wandering Caravan Park

☎ (08) 9884 1056

Caravan Park at Wandering. Cheetaning St. Payment at Shire office, after hours at tavern.

HEMA 106 H6 32 41 3 S 116 40 29 E

182 Boddington RV Stop

Parking Area at Boddington. In Old School Grounds off Waraming Way. Self Contained Vehicles only

HEMA 106 H6 32 47 59 S 116 28 25 E

BIG RIG 48

183 Bannister Parking Area

Parking Area 11 km N of Crossman or 4 km S of Bannister

30

HEMA 106 H6 32 42 47 S 116 32 47 E

184 Glen Eagle Rest Area

Rest Area at Glen Eagle. Some low trees at entrance

30

HEMA 106 F4 32 17 21 S 116 11 29 E

185 Advent Park Campground & Caravan Park

☎ (08) 9454 5341

Caravan Park at Maida Vale. 345 Kalamunda Rd. Bookings essential

HEMA 103 F11 31 56 42 S 116 1 8 E

BIG RIG

Notes...

Perth to Bunbury

South Western Highway

186 **Frank Lupino Memorial Park**

20

Picnic Area 16 km S of Armadale or 42 km N of Pinjarra. 2 km N of Jarrahdale turnoff

HEMA 106 F4 32 17 4 S 116 0 45 E

  BIG RIG 

187 **Pinjarra RV Parking Area**

20

Parking Area at Pinjarra. Cnr South Western Hwy & Pinjarra Williams Rd. Opposite Premier Hotel. Self Contained Vehicles only

HEMA 106 H3 32 37 41 S 115 52 43 E

 BIG RIG 24  

188 **Pinjarra Park Country Camping** (08) 9531 1604

Caravan Park at Pinjarra. 326 Pinjarra Williams Rd. 3.5 km S of PO

HEMA 106 H3 32 39 22 S 115 52 39 E

BIG RIG

189 **Herron Point**

Camp Area near Lake Clifton. Turn N off Old Bunbury Rd 16 km SW of Pinjarra or 14 km E of Old Coast Rd/Old Bunbury Rd jcn onto Herron Point Rd. Onsite caretaker for fees

HEMA 106 H2 32 44 28 S 115 42 38 E

 48

190 **Marrinup Townsite Campground** (08) 9538 1078

Camp Spot 4 km NW of Dwellingup. Turn N 2.2 km W of Dwellingup or 25 km E of Pinjarra onto Grey Rd. Travel 2.7 km, cross railway line follow signposted track up hill to open camping area

HEMA 106 H4 32 42 7 S 116 1 40 E

191 **Nanga Mill** (08) 9538 1078

Lane Pool Reserve

Camp Area 18 km S of Dwellingup, via Nanga Rd. Dirt road

HEMA 106 H4 32 48 10 S 116 6 14 E

192 **Chuditch Campground** (08) 9538 1078

Lane Pool Reserve

Camp Area 16 km S of Dwellingup. 8.5 km from entry station, via Murray Valley Rd. Small vehicles only, limited caravan sites. Bookings essential

HEMA 106 H4 32 47 18 S 116 6 43 E

193 **Baden Powell Campground** (08) 9538 1078

Lane Pool Reserve

Camp Area 9 km S of Dwellingup & 1.5 km from entry station, via Nanga Rd. Bookings essential

HEMA 106 H4 32 46 18 S 116 5 12 E

194 **Charlies Flat Campground** (08) 9538 1078

Lane Pool Reserve

Camp Area 14.5 km S of Dwellingup & 7 km from entry station on River Rd, via Nanga Rd. Dirt road. Small vehicles only, limited caravan sites. Bookings essential

HEMA 106 H4 32 48 56 S 116 6 21 E

195 **The Stringers Campground** (08) 9538 1078

Lane Pool Reserve

Camp Area 19 km S of Dwellingup, via Nanga Rd & Murray Valley Rd. Dirt road. Tents only, no caravans or camper trailers. Bookings essential

HEMA 106 H4 32 48 8 S 116 6 24 E

196 **Yarragil Campground** (08) 9538 1078

Lane Pool Reserve

Camp Area 20 km S of Dwellingup, via Nanga Rd. Dirt road. Tents only, no caravans or camper trailers. Bookings required

HEMA 106 H4 32 48 13 S 116 7 22 E

197 **Lake Navarino Spillway Picnic Area**

Picnic Area at Waroona Dam 8 km E of Waroona. Access via Nanga Brook Rd, Scarp Rd & Invarell Rd. Past Navarino Resort over dam wall, turn R at T jcn

HEMA 106 J3 32 50 58 S 115 59 0 E

198 **Navarino Lakeside Camping** (08) 9733 3000

Lakeside camping at Waroona Dam. Access via Navarino Resort. Fees payable at resort. Bookings necessary for powered site

HEMA 106 J3 32 50 29 S 115 59 52 E

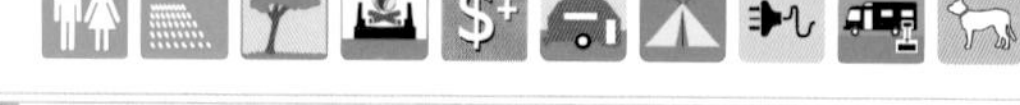

199 **Wagerup Parking Area**

20

Parking Area 6 km N of Yarloop or 6 km S of Waroona

HEMA 106 J3 32 53 36 S 115 54 30 E

BIG RIG

200 **Hoffman Mill** (08) 9735 1988

Camp Area 22 km E of Yarloop. Turn E 5 km S of Yarloop or 9 km N of Harvey, onto Logue Brook Dam Rd & Clarke Rd. 11 km dirt road. Closed between Easter & end October

HEMA 106 J4 33 0 15 S 116 4 59 E

BIG RIG

201 **Lake Brockman Bush Camping** (08) 9733 5402

Camp Areas at Lake Brockman. Turn E on to Logue Brook Dam Rd off South Western Hwy 6 km S of Yarloop, then onto Scarp Rd. Must call at Caravan Park kiosk to pay fees. Bookings preferred

HEMA 106 J3 33 0 13 S 115 58 23 E

Bunbury-Margaret River-Northcliffe

Bussell, Brockman and Vasse Highways

202 Pine Plantation Picnic Area

Picnic Area 6 km SW of Capel, on Ludlow Tuart Forest Dr. No fires

HEMA 108 C3 33 36 0 S 115 29 17 E

203 Canebrake Pool ☎ (08) 9752 5555

Rapids Conservation Park

Camp Area 25 km E of Margaret River. Turn E 4 km N of Margaret River or 7 km S of Cowaramup, onto Osmington, Canebrake & Crossing Rds. 5 km dirt road

HEMA 108 D2 33 52 55 S 115 16 52 E

204 Big Valley Campsite ☎ (08) 9757 5020

Camp Area 12 km SE of Margaret River on a sheep farm. Via Bussell Hwy 2 km, turn E onto Rosa Brook Rd 7 km & S onto Wallis Rd for 2 km

HEMA 108 E2 33 59 4 S 115 9 18 E

BIG RIG

205 Warner Glen (Chapman Pool) ☎ (08) 9752 5555

Camp Area 15 km SE of Witchcliffe or 21 km NE of Karridale. Turn E 6 km S of Witchcliffe or turn N 11 km E of Karridale onto Warner Glen Rd for 8 km

HEMA 108 E2 34 5 33 S 115 12 23 E

206 Conto Field Campground ☎ (08) 9752 5555

Leeuwin-Naturaliste National Park

Camp Area 18 km SW of Margaret River or 20 km NW of Karridale. Turn W off Caves Rd 16 km SW of Margaret River or 18 km NW of Karridale onto Conto Rd

HEMA 108 E1 34 4 55 S 115 0 55 E

207 Boranup Campground ☎ (08) 9752 5555

Leeuwin-Naturaliste National Park

Camp Area 35 km SW of Margaret River or 8 km NW of Karridale, via Caves Rd & Boranup Dr. Small vehicles only

HEMA 108 F1 34 10 41 S 115 4 4 E

208 Alexandra Bridge Camping Area ☎ (08) 9758 2244

10

Camp Area 10 km E of Karridale or 65 km SW of Nannup. Veer L into Clarke Dr, beside Blackwood River. Generators allowed

HEMA 108 F2 34 9 51 S 115 11 10 E

209 Sue's Bridge Campground ☎ (08) 9752 5555

Blackwood National Park

Camp Area 40 km NE of Karridale. Turn N 30 km E of Karridale or 46 km SW of Nannup onto Sue's Rd for 9 km

HEMA 108 E3 34 4 37 S 115 23 24 E

210 Canebreak Rest Area

10

Rest Area 42 km E of Karridale or 34 km SW of Nannup, on Nannup-Karridale Rd

HEMA 108 F3 34 9 20 S 115 31 9 E

211 Grass Tree Hollow Campground ☎ (08) 9776 1207

D'Entrecasteaux National Park

Camp Area 84 km E of Karridale or 25 km NW of Pemberton. Turn S into Boat Landing Rd. Limited tent only sites, small vehicles only. 2 km dirt road

HEMA 108 G4 34 25 33 S 115 48 20 E

212 Big Brook Arboretum ☎ (08) 9776 1207

Camp Area 10 km N of Pemberton, via Club Rd, Pump Hill Rd, Tramway Trail & Rainbow Trail. Small vehicles only

HEMA 108 G5 34 24 14 S 116 0 14 E

213 Windy Harbour Campground ☎ (08) 9776 8398

Camp Area at Windy Harbour, 28 km SW of Northcliffe. Maximum stay 3 months

HEMA 108 J8 34 50 19 S 116 1 27 E

BIG RIG

Norseman to Perth

Coolgardie-Esperance and Great Eastern Highways

214 Mt Thirsty

94

Parking Area 15 km N of Norseman or 151 km S of Coolgardie

HEMA 111 D12 32 6 3 S 121 41 40 E

BIG RIG

215 Lake Cowan

94

Parking Area 23 km N of Norseman or 143 km S of Coolgardie

HEMA 111 D12 32 2 29 S 121 40 43 E

BIG RIG 24

216 Cave Hill Nature Reserve

Camp Spot 50 km E of Widgiemooltha or 87 km SW of Coolgardie. Turn W on to Higginsville Pump Station Rd. 4WD only

HEMA 111 C11 31 39 41 S 121 13 25 E

217 Kambalda West RV Stop

Parking Area at Kambalda West. Behind Rec centre off Barnes Dr, facilites at Rec centre during opening hours

HEMA 111 B12 31 12 23 S 121 37 17 E

BIG RIG 24

Notes...

218 Lake Douglas Recreation Reserve

Camp spot 12 km SW of Kalgoorlie or 26 km NE Coolgardie. Turn S & follow signs for 3.5 km. 2 km dirt road

HEMA 111 B11 30 50 38 S 121 23 35 E

BIG RIG 72

219 Centennial Park

☎ 1800 004 653

Rest Area at Kalgoorlie. Cnr Hannan St & Patroni Rd. Self Contained Vehicles only

HEMA 111 A11 30 45 45 S 121 27 27 E

BIG RIG 24

220 Burra Rock

☎ (08) 9080 5555

Goldfields Woodlands National Park

Camp Spot 59 km S of Coolgardie, via Hunt St & Burra Rock Rd. 33 km dirt road

HEMA 111 C11 31 23 3 S 121 12 2 E

221 Victoria Rock

☎ (08) 9080 5555

Goldfields Woodlands National Park

Camp Spot 45 km SW of Coolgardie. From Coolgardie, via Jobson St & Victoria Rock Rd. Dirt road

HEMA 111 B11 31 17 35 S 120 55 32 E

222 The Haven Caravan Park

☎ (08) 9026 6123

94

Caravan Park at Coolgardie. Great Eastern Hwy. 1 km W of PO

HEMA 111 B11 30 57 18 S 121 8 43 E

$+ BIG RIG

223 Railway Museum

Parking Area at Coolgardie. Woodward St. Self Contained Vehicles only

HEMA 111 B11 30 57 22 S 121 9 47 E

BIG RIG 24

224 Yerdani Well

94

Rest Area 56 km W of Coolgardie or 129 km E of Southern Cross

HEMA 111 B10 31 8 22 S 120 37 41 E

BIG RIG

225 Wallaroo Rock

☎ (08) 9080 5555

Wallaroo Conservation Park

Camp Area 103 W of Coolgardie. Turn N off Hwy 64 km W of Coolgardie or 123 km E of Southern Cross at the Old Woolgangie Township sign. 39 km 4WD track to rock

HEMA 111 B10 31 3 29 S 120 17 53 E

226 Boondi Lookout

94

Rest Area 75 km W of Coolgardie or 109 km E of Southern Cross. S side of road, follow old road

HEMA 111 B10 31 11 21 S 120 26 43 E

BIG RIG

227 Boondi Rest Area

94

Rest Area 76 km W of Coolgardie or 108 km E of Southern Cross

HEMA 111 B10 31 11 18 S 120 25 45 E

BIG RIG

228 Boondi Rock

☎ (08) 9080 5555

Goldfields Woodlands National Park

Camp Area 83 km W of Coolgardie or 107 km E of Southern Cross. Turn N 81 km W of Coolgardie or 105 km E of Southern Cross for 2 km of dirt road. 7.5 km E of Boorabbin-Jaurdi Rd. Signposted

HEMA 111 B10 31 10 52 S 120 23 4 E

BIG RIG

229 Koorarawalyee (Boorabbin) Rest Area

94

Rest Area 114 km W of Coolgardie or 68 km E of Southern Cross

HEMA 113 J10 31 16 8 S 120 1 0 E

BIG RIG 24

230 Karalee Rock & Dam

☎ (08) 9049 1001

Camp Area 137 km W of Coolgardie or 52 km E of Southern Cross. Turn N 133 km W of Coolgardie or 48 km E of Southern Cross for 5 km of dirt road. Signposted

HEMA 113 J10 31 15 3 S 119 50 24 E

BIG RIG

231 Baladjie Rock

Camp Spot 74 km E of Mukinbudin or 21 km W of Bullfinch, via Koorda-Southern Cross Rd. 5 km dirt road N of main road

HEMA 110 B7 30 57 14 S 118 52 51 E

232 Bodallin Pioneers Park

94

Rest Area at Bodallin

HEMA 110 C7 31 22 12 S 118 51 23 E

BIG RIG

233 Carrabin Roadhouse Motel & Caravan Park

☎ (08) 9046 7162

Caravan Park at Carrabin

HEMA 110 C7 31 22 44 S 118 40 41 E

$

234 Westonia Caravan Park

☎ (08) 9046 7063

Caravan Park at Westonia. Wolfram St

HEMA 110 B7 31 18 16 S 118 41 50 E

$

235 St Lukes Church Parking Area

☎ (08) 9046 7063

Parking Area in Westonia, 69 Wolfram St. Self Contained Vehicles only

HEMA 110 B7 31 17 59 S 118 41 50 E

BIG RIG 72

236 Rabbit Proof Fence Parking Bay

94

Parking Area 6 km W of Walgoolan or 2 km E of Burracoppin

HEMA 107 B14 31 23 23 S 118 30 5 E

BIG RIG

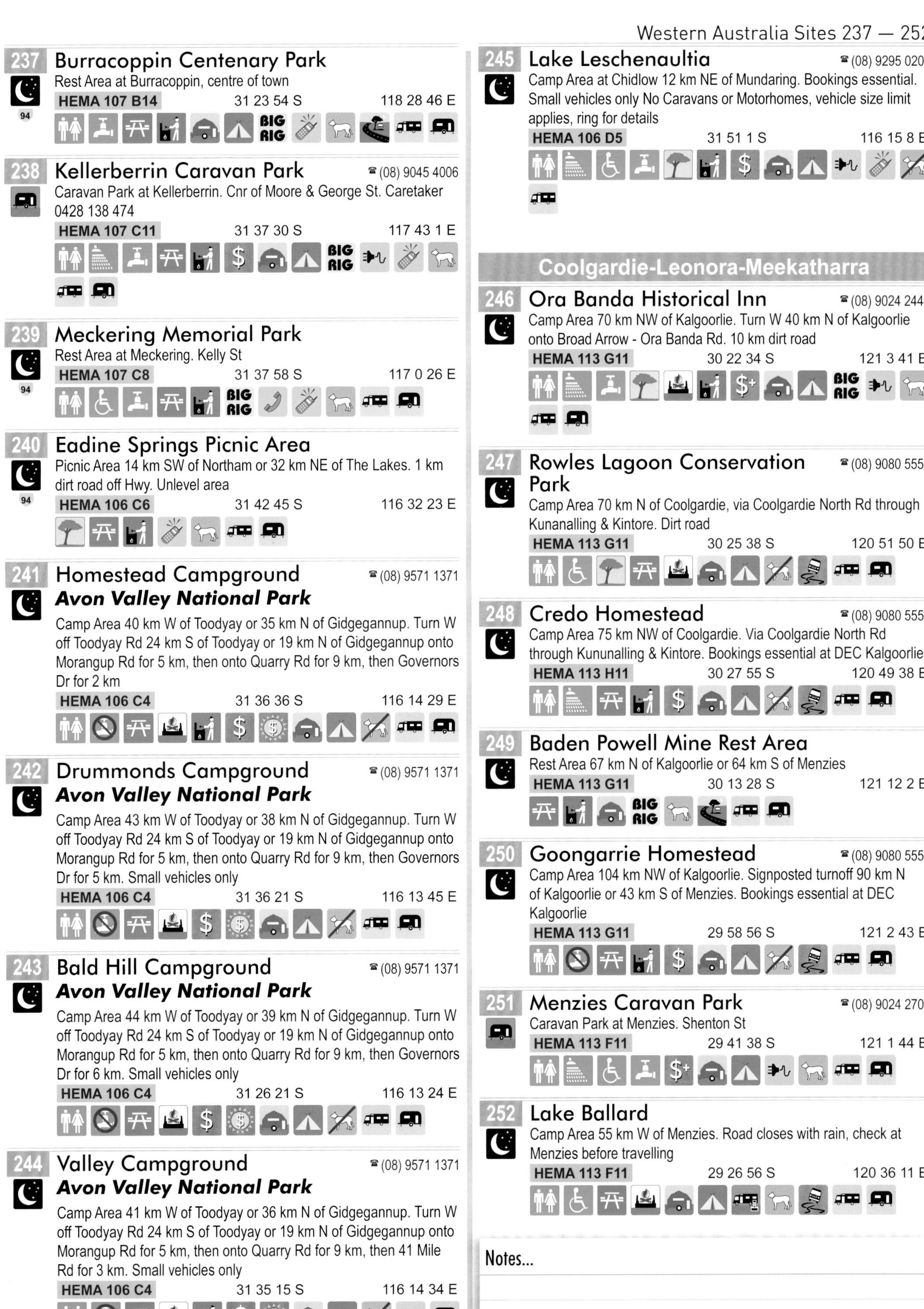

237 Burracoppin Centenary Park
Rest Area at Burracoppin, centre of town
HEMA 107 B14 31 23 54 S 118 28 46 E
94

238 Kellerberrin Caravan Park
(08) 9045 4006
Caravan Park at Kellerberrin. Cnr of Moore & George St. Caretaker 0428 138 474
HEMA 107 C11 31 37 30 S 117 43 1 E

239 Meckering Memorial Park
Rest Area at Meckering. Kelly St
HEMA 107 C8 31 37 58 S 117 0 26 E
94

240 Eadine Springs Picnic Area
Picnic Area 14 km SW of Northam or 32 km NE of The Lakes. 1 km dirt road off Hwy. Unlevel area
HEMA 106 C6 31 42 45 S 116 32 23 E
94

241 Homestead Campground
(08) 9571 1371
Avon Valley National Park
Camp Area 40 km W of Toodyay or 35 km N of Gidgegannup. Turn W off Toodyay Rd 24 km S of Toodyay or 19 km N of Gidgegannup onto Morangup Rd for 5 km, then onto Quarry Rd for 9 km, then Governors Dr for 2 km
HEMA 106 C4 31 36 36 S 116 14 29 E

242 Drummonds Campground
(08) 9571 1371
Avon Valley National Park
Camp Area 43 km W of Toodyay or 38 km N of Gidgegannup. Turn W off Toodyay Rd 24 km S of Toodyay or 19 km N of Gidgegannup onto Morangup Rd for 5 km, then onto Quarry Rd for 9 km, then Governors Dr for 5 km. Small vehicles only
HEMA 106 C4 31 36 21 S 116 13 45 E

243 Bald Hill Campground
(08) 9571 1371
Avon Valley National Park
Camp Area 44 km W of Toodyay or 39 km N of Gidgegannup. Turn W off Toodyay Rd 24 km S of Toodyay or 19 km N of Gidgegannup onto Morangup Rd for 5 km, then onto Quarry Rd for 9 km, then Governors Dr for 6 km. Small vehicles only
HEMA 106 C4 31 26 21 S 116 13 24 E

244 Valley Campground
(08) 9571 1371
Avon Valley National Park
Camp Area 41 km W of Toodyay or 36 km N of Gidgegannup. Turn W off Toodyay Rd 24 km S of Toodyay or 19 km N of Gidgegannup onto Morangup Rd for 5 km, then onto Quarry Rd for 9 km, then 41 Mile Rd for 3 km. Small vehicles only
HEMA 106 C4 31 35 15 S 116 14 34 E

245 Lake Leschenaultia
(08) 9295 0202
Camp Area at Chidlow 12 km NE of Mundaring. Bookings essential. Small vehicles only No Caravans or Motorhomes, vehicle size limit applies, ring for details
HEMA 106 D5 31 51 1 S 116 15 8 E

Coolgardie-Leonora-Meekatharra

246 Ora Banda Historical Inn
(08) 9024 2444
Camp Area 70 km NW of Kalgoorlie. Turn W 40 km N of Kalgoorlie onto Broad Arrow - Ora Banda Rd. 10 km dirt road
HEMA 113 G11 30 22 34 S 121 3 41 E

247 Rowles Lagoon Conservation Park
(08) 9080 5555
Camp Area 70 km N of Coolgardie, via Coolgardie North Rd through Kunanalling & Kintore. Dirt road
HEMA 113 G11 30 25 38 S 120 51 50 E

248 Credo Homestead
(08) 9080 5555
Camp Area 75 km NW of Coolgardie. Via Coolgardie North Rd through Kununalling & Kintore. Bookings essential at DEC Kalgoorlie
HEMA 113 H11 30 27 55 S 120 49 38 E

249 Baden Powell Mine Rest Area
Rest Area 67 km N of Kalgoorlie or 64 km S of Menzies
HEMA 113 G11 30 13 28 S 121 12 2 E

250 Goongarrie Homestead
(08) 9080 5555
Camp Area 104 km NW of Kalgoorlie. Signposted turnoff 90 km N of Kalgoorlie or 43 km S of Menzies. Bookings essential at DEC Kalgoorlie
HEMA 113 G11 29 58 56 S 121 2 43 E

251 Menzies Caravan Park
(08) 9024 2702
Caravan Park at Menzies. Shenton St
HEMA 113 F11 29 41 38 S 121 1 44 E

252 Lake Ballard
Camp Area 55 km W of Menzies. Road closes with rain, check at Menzies before travelling
HEMA 113 F11 29 26 56 S 120 36 11 E

Notes...

WESTERN AUSTRALIA

WESTERN AUSTRALIA

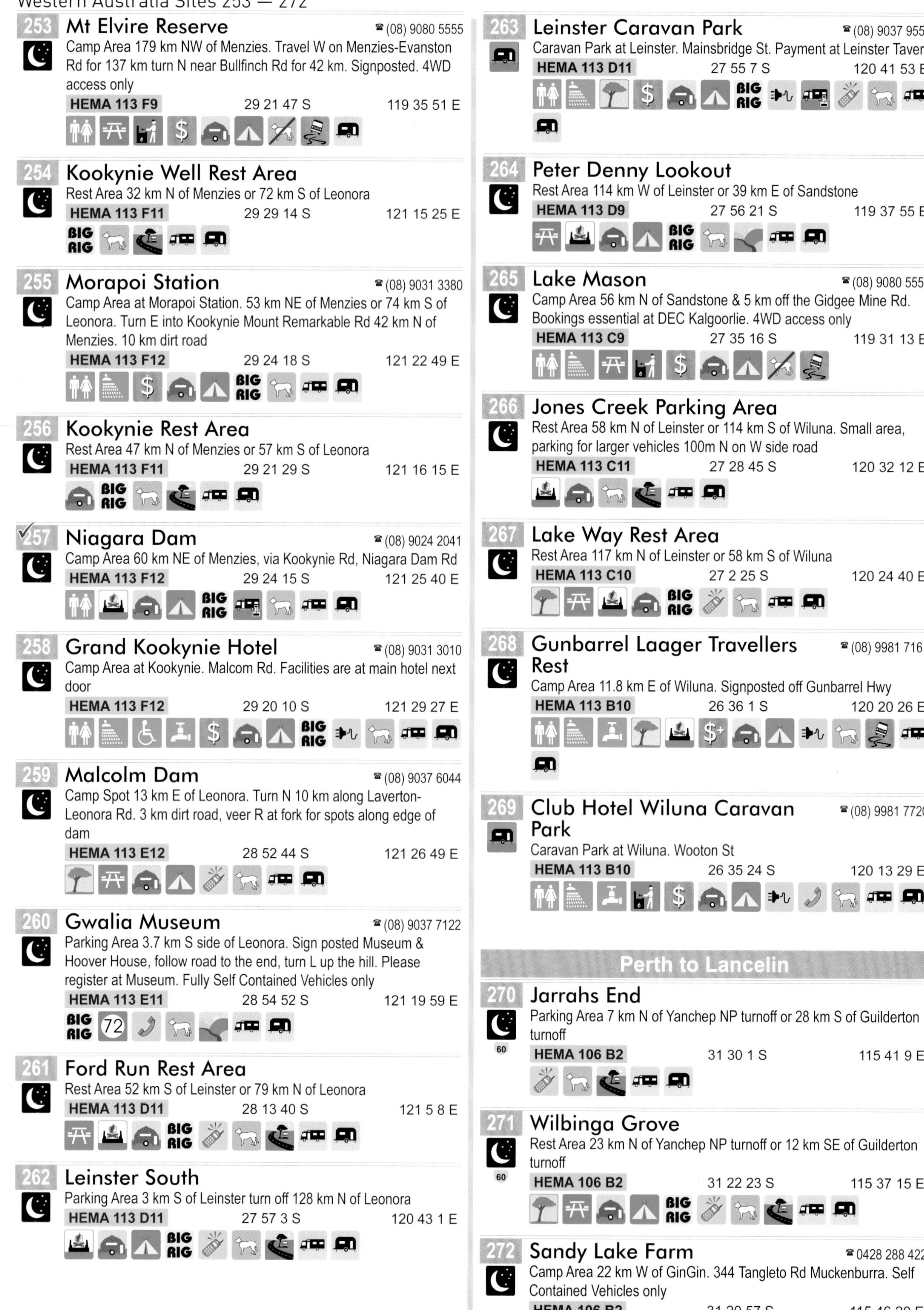

253 Mt Elvire Reserve
☎ (08) 9080 5555

Camp Area 179 km NW of Menzies. Travel W on Menzies-Evanston Rd for 137 km turn N near Bullfinch Rd for 42 km. Signposted. 4WD access only

HEMA 113 F9 29 21 47 S 119 35 51 E

254 Kookynie Well Rest Area

Rest Area 32 km N of Menzies or 72 km S of Leonora

HEMA 113 F11 29 29 14 S 121 15 25 E

BIG RIG

255 Morapoi Station
☎ (08) 9031 3380

Camp Area at Morapoi Station. 53 km NE of Menzies or 74 km S of Leonora. Turn E into Kookynie Mount Remarkable Rd 42 km N of Menzies. 10 km dirt road

HEMA 113 F12 29 24 18 S 121 22 49 E

BIG RIG

256 Kookynie Rest Area

Rest Area 47 km N of Menzies or 57 km S of Leonora

HEMA 113 F11 29 21 29 S 121 16 15 E

BIG RIG

257 Niagara Dam
☎ (08) 9024 2041

Camp Area 60 km NE of Menzies, via Kookynie Rd, Niagara Dam Rd

HEMA 113 F12 29 24 15 S 121 25 40 E

BIG RIG

258 Grand Kookynie Hotel
☎ (08) 9031 3010

Camp Area at Kookynie. Malcom Rd. Facilities are at main hotel next door

HEMA 113 F12 29 20 10 S 121 29 27 E

BIG RIG

259 Malcolm Dam
☎ (08) 9037 6044

Camp Spot 13 km E of Leonora. Turn N 10 km along Laverton-Leonora Rd. 3 km dirt road, veer R at fork for spots along edge of dam

HEMA 113 E12 28 52 44 S 121 26 49 E

260 Gwalia Museum
☎ (08) 9037 7122

Parking Area 3.7 km S side of Leonora. Sign posted Museum & Hoover House, follow road to the end, turn L up the hill. Please register at Museum. Fully Self Contained Vehicles only

HEMA 113 E11 28 54 52 S 121 19 59 E

BIG RIG 72

261 Ford Run Rest Area

Rest Area 52 km S of Leinster or 79 km N of Leonora

HEMA 113 D11 28 13 40 S 121 5 8 E

BIG RIG

262 Leinster South

Parking Area 3 km S of Leinster turn off 128 km N of Leonora

HEMA 113 D11 27 57 3 S 120 43 1 E

BIG RIG

263 Leinster Caravan Park
☎ (08) 9037 9556

Caravan Park at Leinster. Mainsbridge St. Payment at Leinster Tavern

HEMA 113 D11 27 55 7 S 120 41 53 E

BIG RIG

264 Peter Denny Lookout

Rest Area 114 km W of Leinster or 39 km E of Sandstone

HEMA 113 D9 27 56 21 S 119 37 55 E

BIG RIG

265 Lake Mason
☎ (08) 9080 5555

Camp Area 56 km N of Sandstone & 5 km off the Gidgee Mine Rd. Bookings essential at DEC Kalgoorlie. 4WD access only

HEMA 113 C9 27 35 16 S 119 31 13 E

266 Jones Creek Parking Area

Rest Area 58 km N of Leinster or 114 km S of Wiluna. Small area, parking for larger vehicles 100m N on W side road

HEMA 113 C11 27 28 45 S 120 32 12 E

267 Lake Way Rest Area

Rest Area 117 km N of Leinster or 58 km S of Wiluna

HEMA 113 C10 27 2 25 S 120 24 40 E

BIG RIG

268 Gunbarrel Laager Travellers Rest
☎ (08) 9981 7161

Camp Area 11.8 km E of Wiluna. Signposted off Gunbarrel Hwy

HEMA 113 B10 26 36 1 S 120 20 26 E

269 Club Hotel Wiluna Caravan Park
☎ (08) 9981 7720

Caravan Park at Wiluna. Wooton St

HEMA 113 B10 26 35 24 S 120 13 29 E

Perth to Lancelin

270 Jarrahs End

Parking Area 7 km N of Yanchep NP turnoff or 28 km S of Guilderton turnoff

60

HEMA 106 B2 31 30 1 S 115 41 9 E

271 Wilbinga Grove

Rest Area 23 km N of Yanchep NP turnoff or 12 km SE of Guilderton turnoff

60

HEMA 106 B2 31 22 23 S 115 37 15 E

BIG RIG

272 Sandy Lake Farm
☎ 0428 288 422

Camp Area 22 km W of GinGin. 344 Tangleto Rd Muckenburra. Self Contained Vehicles only

HEMA 106 B2 31 20 57 S 115 46 20 E

BIG RIG 72

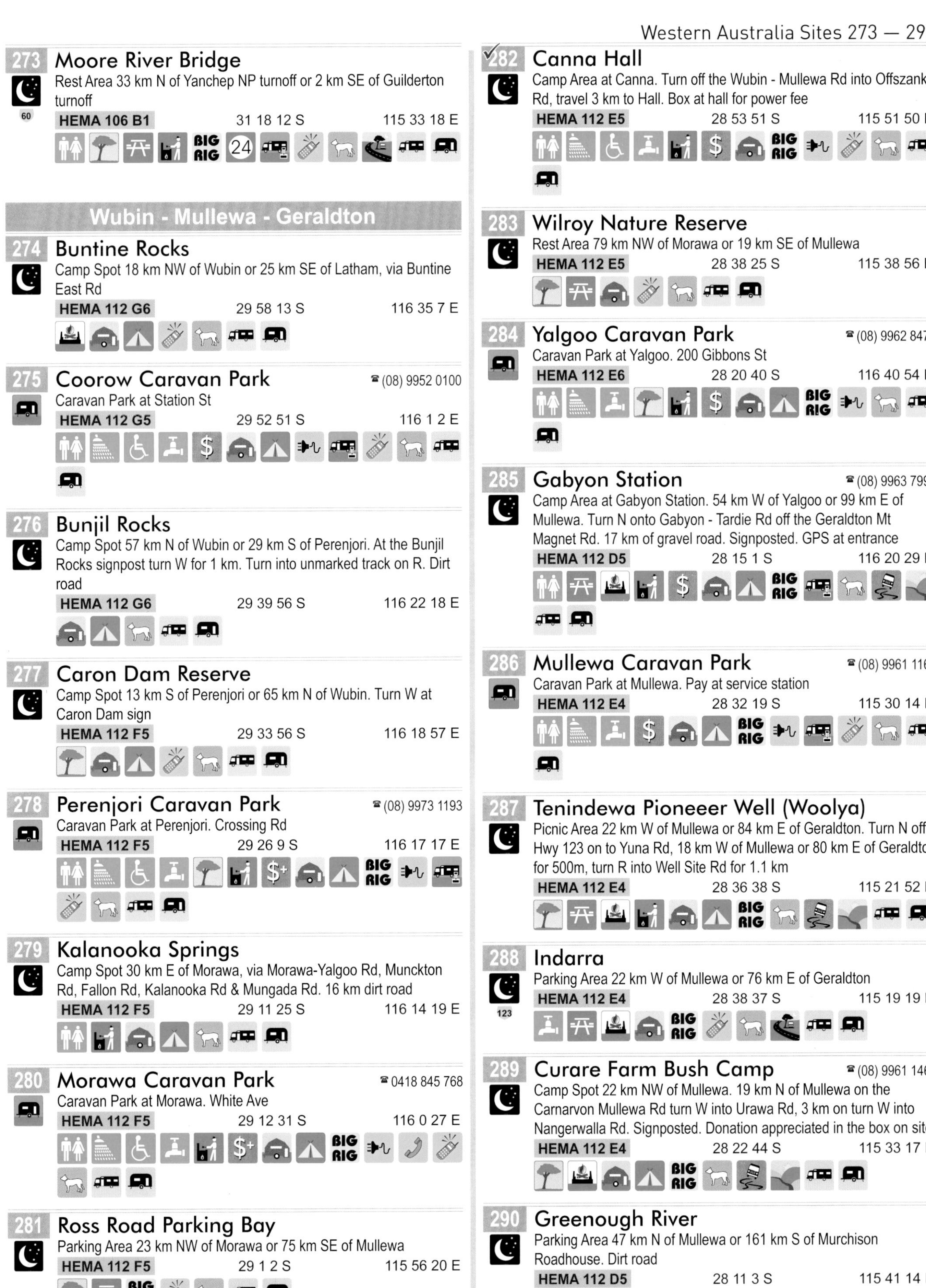

273 Moore River Bridge
Rest Area 33 km N of Yanchep NP turnoff or 2 km SE of Guilderton turnoff
60
HEMA 106 B1 31 18 12 S 115 33 18 E
BIG RIG 24

Wubin - Mullewa - Geraldton

274 Buntine Rocks
Camp Spot 18 km NW of Wubin or 25 km SE of Latham, via Buntine East Rd
HEMA 112 G6 29 58 13 S 116 35 7 E

275 Coorow Caravan Park
☎ (08) 9952 0100
Caravan Park at Station St
HEMA 112 G5 29 52 51 S 116 1 2 E

276 Bunjil Rocks
Camp Spot 57 km N of Wubin or 29 km S of Perenjori. At the Bunjil Rocks signpost turn W for 1 km. Turn into unmarked track on R. Dirt road
HEMA 112 G6 29 39 56 S 116 22 18 E

277 Caron Dam Reserve
Camp Spot 13 km S of Perenjori or 65 km N of Wubin. Turn W at Caron Dam sign
HEMA 112 F5 29 33 56 S 116 18 57 E

278 Perenjori Caravan Park
☎ (08) 9973 1193
Caravan Park at Perenjori. Crossing Rd
HEMA 112 F5 29 26 9 S 116 17 17 E
BIG RIG

279 Kalanooka Springs
Camp Spot 30 km E of Morawa, via Morawa-Yalgoo Rd, Munckton Rd, Fallon Rd, Kalanooka Rd & Mungada Rd. 16 km dirt road
HEMA 112 F5 29 11 25 S 116 14 19 E

280 Morawa Caravan Park
☎ 0418 845 768
Caravan Park at Morawa. White Ave
HEMA 112 F5 29 12 31 S 116 0 27 E
BIG RIG

281 Ross Road Parking Bay
Parking Area 23 km NW of Morawa or 75 km SE of Mullewa
HEMA 112 F5 29 1 2 S 115 56 20 E
BIG RIG

282 Canna Hall
Camp Area at Canna. Turn off the Wubin - Mullewa Rd into Offszanka Rd, travel 3 km to Hall. Box at hall for power fee
HEMA 112 E5 28 53 51 S 115 51 50 E
BIG RIG

283 Wilroy Nature Reserve
Rest Area 79 km NW of Morawa or 19 km SE of Mullewa
HEMA 112 E5 28 38 25 S 115 38 56 E

284 Yalgoo Caravan Park
☎ (08) 9962 8472
Caravan Park at Yalgoo. 200 Gibbons St
HEMA 112 E6 28 20 40 S 116 40 54 E
BIG RIG

285 Gabyon Station
☎ (08) 9963 7993
Camp Area at Gabyon Station. 54 km W of Yalgoo or 99 km E of Mullewa. Turn N onto Gabyon - Tardie Rd off the Geraldton Mt Magnet Rd. 17 km of gravel road. Signposted. GPS at entrance
HEMA 112 D5 28 15 1 S 116 20 29 E
BIG RIG

286 Mullewa Caravan Park
☎ (08) 9961 1161
Caravan Park at Mullewa. Pay at service station
HEMA 112 E4 28 32 19 S 115 30 14 E
BIG RIG

287 Tenindewa Pioneeer Well (Woolya)
Picnic Area 22 km W of Mullewa or 84 km E of Geraldton. Turn N off Hwy 123 on to Yuna Rd, 18 km W of Mullewa or 80 km E of Geraldton for 500m, turn R into Well Site Rd for 1.1 km
HEMA 112 E4 28 36 38 S 115 21 52 E
BIG RIG

288 Indarra
Parking Area 22 km W of Mullewa or 76 km E of Geraldton
123
HEMA 112 E4 28 38 37 S 115 19 19 E
BIG RIG

289 Curare Farm Bush Camp
☎ (08) 9961 1461
Camp Spot 22 km NW of Mullewa. 19 km N of Mullewa on the Carnarvon Mullewa Rd turn W into Urawa Rd, 3 km on turn W into Nangerwalla Rd. Signposted. Donation appreciated in the box on site
HEMA 112 E4 28 22 44 S 115 33 17 E
BIG RIG

290 Greenough River
Parking Area 47 km N of Mullewa or 161 km S of Murchison Roadhouse. Dirt road
HEMA 112 D5 28 11 3 S 115 41 14 E

Notes...

291 Wandina Station Stay
☎ (08) 9962 9597

Camp Area Wandina Station. 70 km N of Mullewa. Turn W onto Wandina Rd. 4 km dirt road. Limited power

HEMA 112 D5 | 27 59 10 S | 115 37 53 E

BIG RIG

292 Ballinyoo Bridge

Parking Area 132 km N of Mullewa or 76 km S of Murchison Roadhouse. Various tracks along river. Dirt road

HEMA 112 C5 | 27 31 35 S | 115 46 29 E

293 Stock Well 9

Camp Spot 53 km S of Muchison Settlement or 148 km N of Mullewa. Turn E, follow track to well

HEMA 112 C5 | 27 20 40 S | 115 53 41 E

294 Wooleen Station
☎ (08) 9963 7973

Camp Area at Wooleen Station. 50 km SE of Muchison Settlement. Sign posted on Carvarvon Mullewa Rd. Open 1st April to 31st October. Booking recommended

HEMA 112 C5 | 27 5 14 S | 116 9 36 E

BIG RIG

295 Murchison Oasis Roadhouse & Caravan Park
☎ (08) 9961 3875

Caravan Park at Murchison Settlement

HEMA 112 C5 | 26 53 46 S | 115 57 26 E

Bindoon to Dongara

Midlands Road

296 Wannamal Rest Area

116

Rest Area 26 km N of Bindoon or 59 km S of Moora

HEMA 106 A4 | 31 9 55 S | 116 3 29 E

BIG RIG

297 Three Springs Short Stay Parking
☎ (08) 9954 1001

Parking Area at Three Springs. Next to sports oval, facilities open during daylight hours

HEMA 112 F5 | 29 32 15 S | 115 45 39 E

BIG RIG 48

298 Arrino Siding

116

Rest Area at Arrino, 18 km N of Three Springs or 35 km S of Mingenew

HEMA 112 F5 | 29 26 22 S | 115 37 41 E

BIG RIG

299 Mingenew Springs Caravan Park
☎ (08) 9928 1019

Caravan Park at Mingenew. Lee Steere St. 1 km SW of PO

HEMA 112 F4 | 29 11 34 S | 115 26 17 E

BIG RIG

300 Breakaway Campground
☎ (08) 9921 5955

Coalseam Conservation Park

Camp Area 34 km N of Mingenew or 50 km S of Mullewa. Access from Mingenew is dirt road, access from Mullewa is steep in places. Maximum stay 3 nights between August - October

HEMA 112 E5 | 28 57 1 S | 115 32 23 E

BIG RIG

301 Miners Camp
☎ (08) 9921 5955

Coalseam Conservation Park

Camp Area 35 km N of Mingenew or 52 km S of Mullewa. Access from Mingenew is dirt road, access from Mullewa is steep in places. Maximum stay 3 nights between August - October

HEMA 112 E5 | 28 57 29 S | 115 33 15 E

BIG RIG

Perth to Port Hedland

Brand and North West Coastal Highways

302 Regans Ford

1

Rest Area 43 km N of Gingin or 32 km S of Cataby. Beside Moore River. Toilets only at Northern area

HEMA 110 B2 | 30 59 20 S | 115 42 17 E

BIG RIG

303 Dandaragan Transit Caravan Park
☎ (08) 9651 4071

Caravan Park at Dandaragan. Pioneer Park

HEMA 110 A2 | 30 40 13 S | 115 42 12 E

BIG RIG

304 Moora Shire Caravan Park
☎ (08) 9651 0000

Caravan Park at Moora. Dandaragan St. Next to Apex Park

HEMA 110 A3 | 30 38 17 S | 116 0 16 E

BIG RIG

305 Moora RV Short Stay
☎ (08) 9651 0000

Camp Area at Moora. Robert St . Self Contained Vehicles only

HEMA 110 A3 | 30 38 16 S | 116 0 18 E

BIG RIG 24

306 Mambung Station Stay and B&B
☎ (08) 9652 4048

Camp Area 44 km E of Cervantes via Cervantes & Munbinea Rds. GPS at gate

HEMA 112 H4 | 30 34 10 S | 115 13 44 E

307 Sandy Cape Recreational Park
☎ (08) 9652 0800

Camp Area at Sandy Cape, 12 km N of Jurien Bay or 18 km S of Green Head. 6 km dirt road

HEMA 112 G4 | 30 11 23 S | 115 0 7 E

96

308 Billy Goat Bay
☎ (08) 9952 0100

Parking Area at Billy Goat Bay. Turn W off Green Head Rd, 500m S of Indian Ocean Dr. Follow signposted track to parking area at the S end of bay. Self Contained Vehicles only

HEMA 112 G4 30 2 31 S 114 57 27 E

48

309 Halfway Mill Roadhouse Caravan Facility
☎ (08) 9952 9054

Caravan Park. Brand Hwy. 30 km S of Eneabba, entry at cnr of Coorow Rd

HEMA 112 G4 30 3 27 S 115 19 50 E

310 Lake Indoon
☎ (08) 9951 1055

Camp Spot 12 km SW of Eneabba or 16 km E of Coolimba

HEMA 112 G4 29 51 37 S 115 9 17 E

BIG RIG

311 Arrowsmith Rest Area

Rest Area 30 km N of Eneabba or 50 km S of Dongara

1

HEMA 112 F4 29 34 43 S 115 8 9 E

312 Nobby Head North

Camp Spot 35 km N of Leeman or 22 km S of Brand Hwy jcn on Indian Ocean Dr

HEMA 112 G4 29 39 14 S 114 57 56 E

72

313 Cliff Head North

Parking Area 51 km N of Leeman or 6 km S of Brand Hwy jcn on Indian Ocean Dr

HEMA 112 F4 29 30 54 S 114 59 51 E

BIG RIG

314 Dongara East Rest Area

Rest Area 70 km N of Eneabba or 7 km E of Dongara. 700m E of Brand Hwy & Midland Rd intersection

116

HEMA 112 F4 29 15 19 S 115 0 48 E

BIG RIG

315 Wind Farm Lookout Parking Area

Parking Area 10 km E of Walkaway. On Nangetty Walkaway Rd

HEMA 112 E4 28 54 9 S 114 53 33 E

316 Ellendale Pool
☎ (08) 9921 0500

Camp Area 22 km NE of Walkaway, via Walkaway-Nangetty Rd & Ellendale Rd

HEMA 112 E4 28 51 33 S 114 58 22 E

72

Notes...

317 Fig Tree Picnic & Camping Ground
☎ (08) 9920 5011

Camp Area 21 km NE of Geraldton. North West Coast Hwy, Chapman Valley Scenic Dr for 12 km

HEMA 112 E4 28 39 32 S 114 42 15 E

BIG RIG 24

318 Coronation Beach
☎ (08) 9920 5011

Camp Area 36 km N of Geraldton or 32 km S of Northampton. Turn W 28 km N of Geraldton or 24 km S of Northampton. Maximum stay 1 month

HEMA 112 E3 28 33 12 S 114 33 52 E

319 Oakabella Homestead
☎ (08) 9925 1033

Camp Area 35 km N of Geraldton or 17 km S of Northampton. Turn W onto Hatch Rd, follow signs

HEMA 112 E3 28 30 0 S 114 35 58 E

BIG RIG

320 Yuna Hall

Camp Spot at Yuna. NE of Yuna Hall, E of Tavern. Turn at school sign. Signposted

HEMA 112 E4 28 19 36 S 115 0 16 E

BIG RIG 72

321 Northampton Lions Park

Rest Area at Northampton. Access off Essex St, next to IGA

1

HEMA 112 E3 28 20 54 S 114 37 49 E

322 Northbrook Farmstay
☎ (08) 9934 1222

Camp Area 6 km N of Northampton on the NW Coastal Hwy

HEMA 112 E3 28 17 54 S 114 37 49 E

BIG RIG

323 Linga Longa Farm Stay at Lynton Station
☎ (08) 9935 1040

Camp Area at Lynton Station. 1353 Port Gregory Rd. 40 km W of Northampton or 60 km S of Kalbarri

HEMA 112 E3 28 12 40 S 114 18 18 E

BIG RIG

324 The Principality of Hutt River
☎ (08) 9936 6035

Camp Area 45 km NW of Northampton. Turn NW 8 km N of Northampton onto Chilimony Rd for 15 km, then W onto West Ogilvie Rd (dirt Rd). Alternatively, turn W onto Binnu West Rd at Binnu, then S onto Box Rd. (9 km dirt rd)

HEMA 112 D3 28 4 27 S 114 28 12 E

325 Wagoe Chalets & Camping Area
☎ (08) 9936 6060

Camp Area 84 km NW of Northampton or 20 km S of Kalbarri. Turn W off Kalbarri Coast Rd. 3 km dirt road

HEMA 112 D3 27 53 10 S 114 8 9 E

WESTERN AUSTRALIA

326 Big River Ranch
☎ (08) 9937 1214
Camp Area 4 km NE of Kalbarri on the Ajana Kalbarri Rd
HEMA 112 D3 27 41 21 S 114 11 17 E

327 Murchison House Station
☎ (08) 9937 1998
Camp Area at Murchison Station. 13 km E of Kalbarri. 4 km dirt road. Bookings essential
HEMA 112 D3 27 38 49 S 114 14 8 E

328 Galena Bridge (Murchison River)
Rest Area 13 km N of Kalbarri turnoff or 115 km S of Billabong Roadhouse
1
HEMA 112 D3 27 49 39 S 114 41 24 E
BIG RIG 24

329 Nerren Nerren Rest Area
Rest Area 82 km N of Kalbarri turnoff or 46 km S of Billabong Roadhouse
1
HEMA 112 C3 27 12 43 S 114 36 44 E
BIG RIG 24

330 Overlander Roadhouse
☎ (08) 9942 5916
Camp Area at Roadhouse. North West Coastal Hwy
HEMA 112 B3 26 24 42 S 114 27 50 E

331 Hamelin Station Stay
☎ (08) 9948 5145
Camp Area at Hamelin Station. 30 km W of Overlander Roadhouse or 100 km SE of Denham. Shark Bay Rd
HEMA 112 B3 26 26 3 S 114 12 0 E
BIG RIG

332 Goulet Bluff
☎ (08) 9948 1590
Camp Area 95 km W of Overlander Roadhouse or 38 km SE of Denham. Turnoff 93 km W of Overlander Roadhouse or 36 km SE of Denham. 2 km dirt road W of Hwy. Phone for permit or call by the Shark Bay Visitor Centre, Knight Tce Denham. Permits are booked on the day required, no advance bookings taken
HEMA 112 B2 26 12 52 S 113 41 36 E
24

333 Whalebone Bay
☎ (08) 9948 1590
Camp Area 102 km W of Overlander Roadhouse or 27 km SE of Denham. 1 km dirt road W of Hwy. Phone for permit or call by the Shark Bay Visitor Centre, Knight Tce Denham. Permits are booked on the day required, no advance bookings taken
HEMA 112 B2 26 7 46 S 113 38 27 E
24

334 Fowlers Camp
☎ (08) 9948 1590
Camp Area 109 km W of Overlander Roadhouse or 24 km SE of Denham. Turnoff 107 km W of Overlander Roadhouse or 22 km SE of Denham. 2 km dirt road W of Hwy. Phone for permit or call by the Shark Bay Visitor Centre, Knight Tce Denham. Permits are booked on the day required, no advance bookings taken
HEMA 112 B2 26 6 21 S 113 37 13 E
24

335 Eagle Bluff
☎ (08) 9948 1590
Camp Area 114 km W of Overlander Roadhouse or 23 km SE of Denham. Turnoff 110 km W of Overlander Roadhouse or 19 km SE of Denham. 4 km dirt road W of Hwy. Phone for permit or call by the Shark Bay Visitor Centre, Knight Tce Denham. Permits are booked on the day required, no advance bookings taken
HEMA 112 B2 26 4 28 S 113 34 56 E
24

336 Gladstone Scenic Lookout
Rest Area 51 km N of Overlander Roadhouse or 25 km S of Wooramel Roadhouse
1
HEMA 112 A3 25 59 9 S 114 17 55 E
BIG RIG

337 Gladstone Campground
☎ (08) 9941 0030
Camp Area 61 km N of Overlander Roadhouse or 27 km S of Wooramel Roadhouse. Turn W opposite Yaringa Homestead, 55 km N of Overlander Roadhouse or 21 km S of Wooramel Roadhouse. 6 km dirt road
HEMA 112 A3 25 57 8 S 114 14 55 E
BIG RIG

338 Wooramel Roadhouse Caravan Park
☎ (08) 9942 5910
Caravan Park at Wooramel Roadhouse. 70 km N of Overlander Roadhouse or 124 km S of Carnarvon
1
HEMA 112 A3 25 46 13 S 114 17 40 E
BIG RIG

339 Wooramel Station
☎ 0417 172 208
Camp Area at Wooramel Station. Turn E 120 km S of Carnarvon or 2.6 km N of Wooramel Roadhouse. Signposted
HEMA 114 J3 25 44 27 S 114 17 2 E

340 Edaggee Rest Area
Rest Area 43 km N of Wooramel Roadhouse or 81 km S of Carnarvon
1
HEMA 114 J3 25 27 34 S 114 3 31 E
BIG RIG 24

341 New Beach
☎ (08) 9941 0030
Camp Spot 99 km N of Wooramel Roadhouse or 41 km S of Carnarvon. Turn W 91 km N of Wooramel Roadhouse or 33 km S of Carnarvon. 8 km dirt road. Low lying, check tide charts. Must have chemi toilet
HEMA 114 J2 25 9 22 S 113 47 53 E
BIG RIG

342 **Bush Bay** ☎ (08) 9941 0030
Camp Spot 101 km N of Wooramel Roadhouse or 43 km S of Carnarvon. Turn W 91 km N of Wooramel Roadhouse or 33 km S of Carnarvon. 6 km N of New Beach. 10 km dirt road. Low lying, check tide charts
HEMA 114 J2 25 7 50 S 113 45 14 E
BIG RIG

343 **Mt Augustus Tourist Park** ☎ (08) 9943 0527
Camp Area 280 km NE of Gascoyne Junction via Dairy Creek or 360 km NW of Meekatharra
HEMA 114 G6 24 18 29 S 116 54 32 E
BIG RIG

344 **Temple Gorge Campground** ☎ (08) 9941 3754
Kennedy Range National Park
Camp Spot 59 km N of Gascoyne Junction. Turn W 47 km N of Gascoyne Junction onto Ullawarra Rd for 12 km. Mostly dirt road
HEMA 114 H4 24 39 38 S 115 10 57 E

345 **Gascoyne Junction Tourist Park** ☎ (08) 9943 0868
Caravan Park at Gascoyne Junction
HEMA 114 H4 25 3 13 S 115 12 25 E
BIG RIG

346 **Blowholes (Point Quobba)** ☎ 0408 942 945
Camp Area 72 km N of Carnarvon. Turn W off North West Coastal Hwy 24 km N of Carnarvon or 115 km S of Minilya Roadhouse. Must have chemi toilet. 30 day maximum stay
HEMA 114 H2 24 29 16 S 113 24 44 E
BIG RIG

347 **Quobba Station** ☎ (08) 9948 5098
Camp Area at Quobba Station. 82 km N of Carnarvon. Turn W off North West Coastal Hwy 24 km N of Carnarvon or 115 km S of Minilya Roadhouse. 10 km dirt road N of Blowholes
HEMA 114 H2 24 23 43 S 113 24 19 E
BIG RIG

348 **Red Bluff** ☎ (08) 9948 5098
Quobba Station
Camp Area 54 km N of Quobba Homestead via Gnaraloo Rd. Signposted turnoff 44 km N of station, 10 km sometimes rough dirt road to campsite. Suitable off road caravans
HEMA 114 G2 24 1 56 S 113 26 56 E

349 **Gnaraloo Station - 3 Mile Camp** ☎ (08) 9948 5000
Camp Area at Gnaraloo Station. 150 km N of Cararvon, via Blowholes Rd
HEMA 114 G2 23 52 29 S 113 29 48 E

350 **Lake MacLeod Rest Area**
Rest Area 49 km S of Minilya Roadhouse or 90 km N of Carnarvon
HEMA 114 G2 24 14 57 S 114 2 11 E
BIG RIG

351 **Minilya River**
Rest Area 500m S of Minilya Roadhouse S side of Minilya River Bridge or 141 km N of Carnarvon
1
HEMA 114 G2 23 49 1 S 114 0 38 E
BIG RIG

352 **Minilya Bridge Roadhouse** ☎ (08) 9942 5922
Camp Area at Roadhouse
HEMA 114 G2 23 48 53 S 114 0 34 E
BIG RIG

353 **Lyndon River**
Rest Area 48 km NE of Minilya Roadhouse or 179 km SW of Nanutarra Roadhouse
1
HEMA 114 F3 23 28 58 S 114 16 32 E
BIG RIG 24

354 **Lyndon River (West)**
Rest Area 32 km N of Minilya Roadhouse or 190 km S of Exmouth on Minilya-Exmouth Rd
HEMA 114 F2 23 32 32 S 113 57 47 E
BIG RIG

355 **Warroora Station - The 14 Mile**
Camp Area At Warroora Station. 84 km N of Minilya Roadhouse or 166 km S of Exmouth. Turn W 75 km N of Minilya Roadhouse or 155 km S of Exmouth, 5 km sandy dirt road to camp entrance, then 6 km to campsites. Report to caretaker. Must have chemical toilet. Approach from the N entrance as the S entry is sandy
HEMA 114 F2 23 17 35 S 113 50 39 E
BIG RIG

356 **Neds Campground** ☎ (08) 9949 2808
Cape Range National Park
Camp Area within National Park. Limited sites. Generators allowed. Public phone & dump point at Milyering Visitor Centre
HEMA 114 D2 22 0 1 S 113 55 58 E

357 **Mesa Campground** ☎ (08) 9949 2808
Cape Range National Park
Camp Area within National Park. Limited sites. Generators allowed. Public phone & dump point at Milyering Visitor Centre
HEMA 114 D2 22 0 24 S 113 55 38 E
BIG RIG

Notes...

358 **Tulki Beach Campground** ☎ (08) 9949 2808
Cape Range National Park
Camp Area within National Park. Limited sites. Generators allowed. Public phone & dump point at Milyering Visitor Centre
HEMA 114 D2 22 4 31 S 113 53 56 E

359 **Kurrajong Campground** ☎ (08) 9949 2808
Cape Range National Park
Camp Area within National Park. Limited sites. No generators allowed. Public phone & dump point at Milyering Visitor Centre
HEMA 114 D2 22 10 44 S 113 51 34 E

360 **North Kurrajong** ☎ (08) 9949 2808
Cape Range National Park
Camp Area 71 km SW of Exmouth. Turn W after 70 km. Limited sites. No generators allowed. Public phone & dump point at Milyering Visitor Centre
HEMA 114 D2 22 10 24 S 113 51 39 E

361 **Bungarra** ☎ (08) 9949 2808
Cape Range National Park
Camp Area within National Park. Limited sites. No generators. Public phone & dump point at Milyering Visitor Centre
HEMA 114 D2 22 14 49 S 113 50 24 E

362 **Osprey Bay Campground** ☎ (08) 9949 2808
Cape Range National Park
Camp Area within National Park. Limited sites. Generators allowed. Public phone & dump point at Milyering Visitor Centre
HEMA 114 D2 22 14 19 S 113 50 21 E
BIG RIG

363 **Yardie Creek Campground** ☎ (08) 9949 2808
Cape Range National Park
Camp Area within National Park. Limited sites. Generators allowed. Public phone & dump point at Milyering Visitor Centre
HEMA 114 D2 22 19 13 S 113 48 53 E

364 **Bullara Station** ☎ (08) 9942 5938
Camp Area At Bullara Station. 86 km S of Exmouth or 60 km N of Coral Bay. 8 km E of NW Coastal Hwy intersection. Signposted
HEMA 114 E2 22 40 39 S 114 3 15 E
BIG RIG

365 **Giralia Station** ☎ (08) 9942 5937
Camp Area at Giralia Station. 125 km S of Exmouth or 110 km N of Coral Bay. 45 km E of NW Coastal Hwy intersection. Limited power. 4 km dirt road
HEMA 114 E3 22 42 31 S 114 20 20 E
BIG RIG

366 **Burkett Road Rest Area**
1
Rest Area 116 km NE of Minilya Roadhouse or 111 km SW of Nanutarra Roadhouse. 1 km N of Exmouth turnoff
HEMA 114 E3 22 59 1 S 114 36 47 E
BIG RIG

367 **Barradale Rest Area**
Yannarie River
1
Rest Area 156 km NE of Minilya Roadhouse or 70 km SW of Nanutarra Roadhouse
HEMA 114 E3 22 51 49 S 114 57 5 E
BIG RIG 24

368 **Emu Creek Station** ☎ (08) 9943 0534
Camp Area at Emu Creek Station. Turn E onto Nyang Rd 156 km N of Minilya Roadhouse or 49 km S of Nanutarra Roadhouse. 22 km to station. Dirt road
HEMA 114 E4 23 1 54 S 115 2 31 E

369 **Nanutarra Roadhouse Caravan Park** ☎ (08) 9943 0521
1
Caravan park at Nanutarra Roadhouse
HEMA 114 E4 22 32 34 S 115 30 3 E

370 **House Creek Bridge**
136
Rest Area 62 km E of Nanutarra Roadhouse or 162 km W of Paraburdoo/Wittenoom Rd jcn
HEMA 114 E5 22 27 51 S 116 2 12 E
24

371 **Beasley River Rest Area**
218
Rest Area 171 km E of Nanutarra Roadhouse or 53 km W of Paraburdoo/Wittenoom Rd jcn
HEMA 114 E6 22 56 56 S 116 58 40 E
BIG RIG 24

372 **Onslow Turnoff**
1
Parking Area 44 km N of Nanutarra Roadhouse or 119 km S of Fortesque River Roadhouse. 1 km S of turnoff
HEMA 114 D4 22 9 3 S 115 32 28 E
BIG RIG

373 **Three Mile Pool**
Camp Spot 36 km S of Onslow or 5 km S of Old Onslow Township. Turn W 64 km NW of Hwy 1 jcn or 17 km S of Onslow, onto Twitchen Rd & Old Onslow Rd. 19 km dirt road
HEMA 114 D3 21 45 44 S 114 57 5 E

374 **Robe River**
1
Rest Area 117 km N of Nanutarra Roadhouse or 43 km S of Fortescue River Roadhouse
HEMA 114 C5 21 36 55 S 115 55 21 E
BIG RIG 24

375 **Pannawonica Transit Site** ☎ (08) 9184 1038
Caravan Park at Pannawonica. Sports Way, next to Tony Lyons Park
HEMA 114 C5 21 38 12 S 116 19 29 E

376 Fortescue River Roadhouse & Caravan Park ☎ (08) 9184 5126

1

Caravan Park at Roadhouse

HEMA 114 C5 | 21 17 42 S | 116 8 17 E

BIG RIG

377 Gnoorea Point (40-Mile) ☎ (08) 9186 8555

Camp area at Forty Mile Beach. Turn W 54 km N of Fortescue River Roadhouse or 40 km S of Karratha Roadhouse. Turn off is 200m S of Devil Creek Bridge. 12 km dirt road. Fee applies May - Sep. Maximum stay 3 months. Chemical toilet required to stay here

HEMA 114 B5 | 20 50 26 S | 116 20 51 E

BIG RIG

378 Cleaverville Beach ☎ (08) 9186 8528

Camp Area 26 km NW of Roebourne or 33 km NE of Karratha. Turn N 28 km E of Karratha Roadhouse or 14 km W of Roebourne. 13 km dirt road. Open 1May - 30Sep. Maximum stay 3 months. Chemical toilet required to stay here

HEMA 114 B6 | 20 39 40 S | 116 59 53 E

BIG RIG

379 Miliyana Campground ☎ (08) 9143 1488

Millstream Chichester National Park

Camp Area 144 km S of Roebourne. Turn S 27 km E of Roebourne or 55 km W of Whim Creek, then SE after 79 km, then SW for 18 km. Alternative access via Pannawonica, 92 km dirt road

HEMA 114 C6 | 21 35 18 S | 117 4 22 E

380 Star Gazers Campground ☎ (08) 9184 5144

Millstream Chichester National Park

Camp Area 144 km S of Roebourne. Turn S 27 km E of Roebourne or 55 km W of Whim Creek, then SE after 79 km, then SW for 18 km. Alternative access via Pannawonica, 92 km dirt road

HEMA 114 C6 | 21 35 40 S | 117 5 17 E

381 Mt Florance Station ☎ (08) 9189 8151

Camp Area at Mt Florance Station. 125 km NW Auski Roadhouse or 200 km S Roebourne. Open April - end September. Dirt road

HEMA 114 D7 | 21 47 20 S | 117 51 57 E

382 Sherlock River

1

Camp Spot 56 km E of Roebourne or 27 km W of Whim Creek. Turn N 100m W of bridge. Small area

HEMA 114 B7 | 20 56 41 S | 117 36 41 E

383 Coorinjinna Pool

Camp Spot 20 km N of Whim Creek. Turn N opposite old hotel site, travel 14 km, then R (opposite old gravel pit) onto track for 1 km. Various sites along river. 15 km dirt road

HEMA 114 B7 | 20 43 22 S | 117 48 0 E

BIG RIG

384 Balla Balla Inlet

Camp Spot 25 km N of Whim Creek. Turn N opposite old hotel site, follow Rd to end. Limited spots on higher ground, tidal

HEMA 114 B7 | 20 40 29 S | 117 46 59 E

385 Peawah River

1

Rest Area 26 km NE of Whim Creek or 92 km SW of Port Hedland

HEMA 114 B7 | 20 50 51 S | 118 4 6 E

BIG RIG 24

386 Herbert Parker (Yule River)

1

Rest Area 56 km NE of Whim Creek or 62 km SW of Port Hedland. Limited space

HEMA 115 B8 | 20 42 0 S | 118 18 0 E

Perth to Port Hedland

Great Northern Highway

387 Brockman River Parking Area

Parking Area 16 km SE of Bindoon or 28 km NE of Bullsbrook. Via Muchea East Rd, Chittering Rd. Beside Brockman River

HEMA 106 B4 | 31 29 39 S | 116 6 57 E

BIG RIG

388 Bindoon Oval ☎ (08) 9576 1020

Camp Area at Bindoon. Recreation Oval S end of town on Great Northern Hwy. Must call into PO for payment

HEMA 106 B4 | 31 23 13 S | 116 5 49 E

BIG RIG 72

389 Bindoon Hill

95

Rest Area 9 km N of Bindoon or 38 km S of New Norcia

HEMA 106 B4 | 31 19 35 S | 116 9 15 E

BIG RIG

390 Mogumber Hall

Camp Spot at Mogumber. Bindoon - Moora Rd N of town at the sports ground

HEMA 112 H5 | 31 2 4 S | 116 2 38 E

BIG RIG 24

391 New Norcia Caravan Park ☎ (08) 9654 8020

95

Caravan Park at New Norcia

HEMA 110 B3 | 30 58 25 S | 116 12 45 E

BIG RIG

392 New Norcia ☎ (08) 9654 8056

95

Parking Area at New Norcia. Great Northern Hwy near Oval S of Monastery. Self Contained Vehicles only. Pay at Visitor Centre

HEMA 110 B3 | 30 58 24 S | 116 12 48 E

BIG RIG

Notes...

393 **Calingiri Caravan Park** ☎ (08) 9628 7004
Caravan Park at Calingiri. Cavell St
HEMA 106 A5 31 5 17 S 116 26 47 E

394 **Bolgart Caravan Park** ☎ (08) 9627 5220
Caravan Park at Bolgart. George St
HEMA 106 A6 31 16 17 S 116 30 31 E

395 **Goomalling Caravan Park** ☎ (08) 9629 1183
Caravan Park at Goomalling. Throssel St. 1 km SE of PO
HEMA 106 B7 31 17 59 S 116 49 57 E
BIG RIG

396 **Oak Park & Gnamma Holes**
Picnic Area 17 km NE of Goomalling on Oak Park Rd
HEMA 106 A7 31 8 15 S 116 52 37 E
BIG RIG

397 **Dowerin Roadhouse & Caratel Park** ☎ (08) 9631 1135
Caravan Park at Dowerin. Goldfields Rd
HEMA 107 A8 31 11 43 S 117 1 55 E
BIG RIG

398 **Minnivale Rest Area**
Rest Area at Minnivale. Turn N off the Goomalling-Wyalkatchem Rd 15 km E of Dowerin or 20 km W of Wyalkatchem, along Cunderdin-Minnivale Rd for 5 km. Next to disused tennis courts. Self Contained Vehicles only
HEMA 107 A9 31 8 20 S 117 11 4 E
BIG RIG

399 **Wyalkatchem Travellers Park** ☎ 0427 814 042
Caravan Park at Wyalkatchem. Hands Dr
HEMA 107 A9 31 11 1 S 117 22 52 E

400 **Trayning Caravan Park** ☎ 0428 997 156
Caravan Park at Trayning. Enter from Bencubbin-Kellerberrin Rd, behind the swimming pool
HEMA 107 A11 31 6 38 S 117 47 37 E
BIG RIG

401 **McCorrys Old Hotel Caravan Facility** ☎ (08) 9046 5187
Caravan Park at Nungarin. Old Hotel Rd
HEMA 107 A13 31 10 35 S 118 5 58 E
24

402 **Nungarin Recreation Ground** ☎ (08) 9046 5006
Camp Area at Nungarin. Danberrin Rd. Self Contained Vehicles only
HEMA 107 A13 31 11 32 S 118 5 35 E

403 **Marshall Rock Camping**
Camp Spot 10 S of Bencubbin, via Mukinbudin Rd & Marshall Rock South Rd
HEMA 110 B6 30 50 5 S 117 54 19 E

404 **Eaglestone Rock**
Camp Spot 21 km NE of Nungarin towards Lake Brown. Via Danberrin Rd, Knungajin Rd & Lake Brown South Rd
HEMA 110 B6 31 4 0 S 118 13 49 E
BIG RIG

405 **Mangowine Homestead** ☎ (08) 9046 5149
Camp Area in Homestead grounds. 14.5 km N of Nungarin on Karomin Rd, or 24 km S of Mukinbudin
HEMA 110 B6 31 2 55 S 118 6 21 E
BIG RIG
48

406 **Mukinbudin Caravan Park** ☎ (08) 9047 1103
Caravan Park at Mukinbudin. Cruickshank St
HEMA 110 B6 30 55 8 S 118 12 21 E
BIG RIG

407 **Elachbutting Rock**
Camp Spot at Elachbutting Rock. 100 km N of Westonia. GPS at entrance, follow signposted track around rock to camping area
HEMA 113 H8 30 35 27 S 118 36 25 E

408 **Beringbooding Rock**
Camp Spot at Beringbooding Rock. Via Beringbooding Rd & Cunderdin Rd
HEMA 113 H8 30 33 30 S 118 29 32 E

409 **Bencubbin Caravan Park** ☎ (08) 9685 1202
Caravan Park at Bencubbin. Kellerberrin Rd
HEMA 110 B6 30 49 7 S 117 51 44 E
BIG RIG

410 **Gabbin**
Camp Spot at Gabbin, next to Community Heritage Hall
HEMA 112 H7 30 48 1 S 117 40 48 E
24

411 **Koorda Caravan Park** ☎ (08) 9684 1219
Caravan Park at Koorda. Scott St. 1 km N of PO
HEMA 110 B5 30 49 20 S 117 29 12 E
BIG RIG

412 **Beacon Caravan Park** ☎ 0488 025 853
Caravan Park at Beacon. Lucas St
HEMA 110 A6 30 27 3 S 117 51 56 E
BIG RIG

413 **Billiburning Rock**
Camp Spot 34 km N of Beacon, via Ingleton Rd & White Rd. 18 km dirt road
HEMA 112 G7 30 10 20 S 117 55 4 E

414 **Cadoux Camp Spot** ☎ (08) 9673 1040
Camp Spot at Cadoux. Dowerin Kalannie Rd. Payment & access key at Cadoux Trader
HEMA 110 B5 30 46 18 S 117 8 0 E

415 **Wongan Hills Caravan Park** ☎ (08) 9671 1009
Caravan Park at Wongan. 65 Wongan Rd
HEMA 110 B4 30 53 21 S 116 42 53 E

416 **The Gap**
Camp Spot 12 km W of Wongan Hills or 36 km E of Waddington on the Waddington-Wongan Hills Rd. Signposted on the L from Wongan Hills. Self Contained Vehicles only
HEMA 110 B4 30 49 49 S 116 38 2 E

417 **Lake Ninan Rest Area**
Rest Area 10 km SW of Wongan Hills on the Calingiri Wongan Hill Rd
HEMA 110 B4 30 57 7 S 116 39 31 E
20

418 **Petrudor Rock**
Camp Spot 31 km E of Pithara. Turn S off Pithara East Rd onto Petrudor Rd. 8 km dirt road
HEMA 110 A4 30 25 30 S 116 58 0 E

419 **Ballidu Caravan Facility** ☎ (08) 9674 1213
Caravan Park at Ballidu. Wallis St. Payment & caretaker info at site
HEMA 110 A4 30 35 44 S 116 46 22 E
BIG RIG

420 **Dalwallinu Caravan Park** ☎ (08) 9661 1253
Caravan Park at Dalwallinu. Dowie St
HEMA 112 G6 30 16 27 S 116 40 8 E

421 **Wubin Rocks**
Camp Spot 8 km NE of Wubin or 149 km SW of Paynes Find. Turn NW onto Manuel Rd 6.5 km W of Wubin or 147 km SE of Paynes Find. 1 km dirt road. Small vehicles only
HEMA 112 G6 30 3 51 S 116 40 31 E

422 **Jibberding Rock**
Camp Spot 22 km NE of Wubin or 131 km SW of Paynes Find. Just N of Rabbit Proof Fence Rd
95
HEMA 112 G6 30 0 9 S 116 49 29 E

423 **White Wells**
Parking Area 47 km NE of Wubin or 107 km SW of Paynes Find
95
HEMA 112 G6 29 50 10 S 116 56 45 E
BIG RIG

424 **Paynes Find Roadhouse & Tavern** ☎ (08) 9963 6111
Camp Area at Roadhouse. On Great Northern Hwy 145 km S of Mt Magnet
95
HEMA 112 F7 29 15 48 S 117 41 9 E
BIG RIG

425 **Windsor Rest Area**
Rest Area 77 km W of Sandstone or 76 km E of Mt Magnet on Mt Magnet Sandstone Rd
HEMA 113 D8 28 1 39 S 118 31 29 E
BIG RIG

426 **Kirkalocka Station** ☎ (08) 9963 5827
Camp Area at Kirkalocka Station. 60 km S of Mt Magnet or 84 km N of Paynes Find. Turn E at signpost. Limited power available
HEMA 112 E7 28 33 42 S 117 46 40 E
BIG RIG

427 **Nalbarra Station** ☎ (08) 9963 5829
Camp Area at Nalbarra Station. 80 km SW of Mt Magnet. Turn W off the Great Northern Hwy 63 km S of Mt Magnet or 70 km N of Paynes Find, then 17 km to station. Signposted, dirt road
HEMA 112 E7 28 38 55 S 117 36 29 E

428 **Garden Rock**
Camp Spot 16 km SE from Cue. Signposted from Cue on Cue to Sandstone Rd. Dirt road. 4WD when wet
HEMA 112 C7 27 29 21 S 118 1 36 E

429 **Lake Nallan Nature Reserve**
Camp Spot 20 km N of Cue or 96 km SW of Meekatharra. Only camp in the 2 designated areas
1
HEMA 112 C7 27 15 41 S 117 59 7 E
BIG RIG 48

430 **Bluebird Parking Area**
Parking Area 19 km S of Meekatharra or 106 km N of Cue
HEMA 113 B8 26 44 36 S 118 24 14 E
BIG RIG

Notes...

431 25 Mile Well

Camp Spot 41 km N of Meekatharra or 215 km S of Kumarina Roadhouse

HEMA 113 B8 26 15 54 S 118 39 31 E

BIG RIG

432 Karalundi Caravan and Camping Park

☎ (08) 9981 2000

Caravan Park 55 km N of Meekatharra on Great Northern Hwy

HEMA 113 A8 26 7 42 S 118 41 9 E

433 Bilyuin Pool

Camp Spot 88 km N of Meekatharra. Turn W 74 km N of Meekatharra or 182 km S of Kumarina Roadhouse onto Ashburton Downs Rd. On L after Murchison River, follow tracks for 1 km to sites on river. 14 km dirt road

HEMA 115 J8 25 54 15 S 118 39 47 E

434 Gascoyne River (South Branch)

Rest Area 148 km NW of Meekatharra, 276 km S of Newman or 108 km S of Kumarina Roadhouse

HEMA 115 J9 25 34 44 S 119 14 13 E

BIG RIG 24

435 Gascoyne River (Middle Branch)

Rest Area 192 km NW of Meekatharra, 230 km S of Newman or 64 km S of Kumarina Roadhouse

HEMA 115 H9 25 12 3 S 119 20 6 E

BIG RIG

436 Kumarina Roadhouse Caravan Park

☎ (08) 9981 2930

Caravan Park at Kumarina Roadhouse

HEMA 115 H9 24 42 38 S 119 36 27 E

BIG RIG

437 Mt Robinson Rest Area

Rest Area 109 km NW of Newman or 86 km SE of Auski Roadhouse. 800m E of Hwy

HEMA 115 E8 23 2 34 S 118 50 57 E

BIG RIG 24

438 Albert Tognolini Rest Area

Rest Area 179 km NW of Newman or 17 km S of Auski Roadhouse. 2 km E of Hwy. Follow tracks to the R along ridge

HEMA 115 E8 22 29 23 S 118 44 9 E

BIG RIG

439 Dales Gorge Campground

☎ (08) 9189 8157

Karijini National Park

Camp Area 8 km E of Karijini Visitors Centre. Generators allowed. Showers at Info Centre for fee

HEMA 115 E8 22 28 30 S 118 33 5 E

BIG RIG

440 Karijini Eco Resort

☎ (08) 9425 5566

Camp Area 35 km W of Karijini Visitors Centre or 79 km NE of Tom Price via Karijini Dr, Banjima Dr & Weano Gorge Rd. Dirt road

HEMA 115 D8 22 23 10 S 118 15 46 E

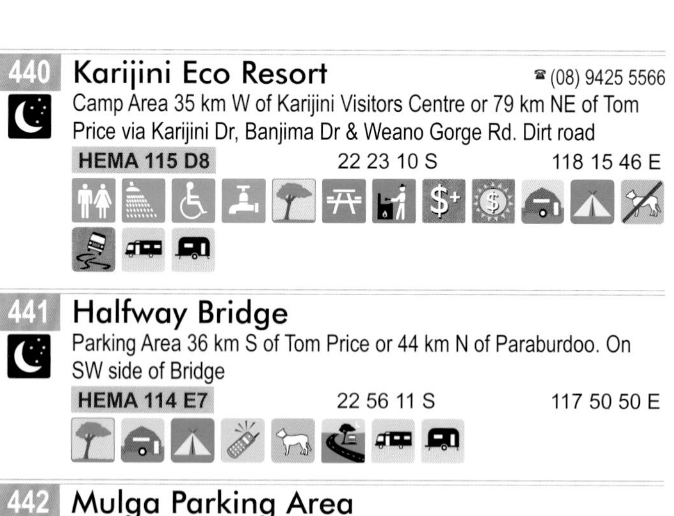

441 Halfway Bridge

Parking Area 36 km S of Tom Price or 44 km N of Paraburdoo. On SW side of Bridge

HEMA 114 E7 22 56 11 S 117 50 50 E

442 Mulga Parking Area

Parking Area 39 km N of Auski Roadhouse or 180 km S of Hwy 1 jcn

HEMA 115 D8 22 3 10 S 118 48 10 E

BIG RIG

443 Bea Bea

Rest Area 42 km N of Auski Roadhouse or 177 km S of Hwy 1 jcn

HEMA 115 D8 22 0 32 S 118 48 55 E

BIG RIG

444 Marble Bar Turn Off

Parking Area 95 km N of Auski Roadhouse or 124 km S of Hwy 1 jcn. Share with trucks

HEMA 115 C8 21 34 40 S 118 48 57 E

BIG RIG

445 Indee Station

☎ (08) 9176 4968

Camp Area at Indee Station. 185 km N of Auski Roadhouse or 25 km S of Hwy 1 jcn. Turn E onto Indee Rd for 9 km dirt road. GPS at gate, follow signs to homestead

HEMA 115 B8 20 46 41 S 118 32 23 E

BIG RIG

Newman to Port Hedland

Marble Bar Road

446 Roy Hill Rest Area

Rest Area at intersection of Roy Hill Rd & Marble Bar Rd. 93 km N Newman or 96 km S of Nullagine

HEMA 115 E10 22 40 10 S 119 57 1 E

BIG RIG

447 Carawine Gorge

Warrawagine Station

Camp Spot 162 km E of Marble Bar, via Rippon Hills Rd, Woodie Woodie Rd. Signposted to Gorge. 14 km, then veer R to sites. Dirt road. 4WD access only. No firearms permited on the Station. Watch for cattle at all times

HEMA 115 C11 21 28 55 S 121 1 43 E

448 Coongan Pool

Camp Spot 110 km SE of the Great Northern Hwy or 33 km N of the Marble Bar turn off. Turn NE opposite parking area, on Marble Bar side of river, follow tracks to Y jcn veer L. Small vehicles only, dirt track

HEMA 115 B10 20 54 18 S 119 47 25 E

449 Doolena Gorge

Camp Spot 109 km SE of the Great Northern Hwy or 34 km N of Marble Bar turn off. Turn S dirt track on Port Hedland side of river. Follow track for 1.5 km. Watch for overhanging trees

HEMA 115 B10 — 20 55 32 S — 119 47 8 E

450 Pear Creek

Camp Spot 89 km SE of the Great Northern Hwy or 55 km NW of the Marble Bar turn off. Turn NE on Marble Bar side of creek & follow track. Small vehicles only, limited space

HEMA 115 B9 — 20 50 24 S — 119 36 38 E

451 Des Streckfuss Rest Area

138

Rest Area 74 km NW of Marble Bar or 79 km SE of Hwy 1 jcn. 129 km SE of Port Hedland

HEMA 115 B9 — 20 49 33 S — 119 30 44 E

BIG RIG 24

Port Hedland to Kununurra

Great Northern Highway

452 De Grey River

1

Rest Area 82 km NE of Port Hedland or 71 km SW of Pardoo Roadhouse

HEMA 116 K2 — 20 18 28 S — 119 15 11 E

BIG RIG

453 Pardoo Station

☎ (08) 9176 4930

Camp Area at Pardoo Station. 133 km N of Port Hedland or 44 km S of Pardoo Roadhouse. Turn N onto Pardoo Station Rd 32 km S of Roadhouse or 120 km N of Port Hedland. 13 km dirt road

HEMA 116 K2 — 20 6 23 S — 119 34 46 E

BIG RIG

454 Pardoo Roadhouse Caravan Park

☎ (08) 9176 4916

Caravan Park at Pardoo Roadhouse. 153 km N of Port Hedland

HEMA 116 K2 — 20 3 14 S — 119 49 39 E

BIG RIG

455 Cape Keraudren

☎ (08) 9176 4979

Camp Area 11 km NW of Pardoo Roadhouse. Turn N off Hwy 1 at Pardoo Roadhouse. Dirt road. Maximum stay 3 months

HEMA 116 K2 — 19 57 26 S — 119 46 7 E

BIG RIG

456 Sandfire Roadhouse Caravan Park

☎ (08) 9176 5944

Caravan Park at Sandfire Roadhouse. 291 km N of Port Headland

HEMA 116 K4 — 19 46 7 S — 121 5 26 E

BIG RIG

457 Stanley Rest Area

1

Rest Area 108 km NE of Sandfire Roadhouse or 181 km SW of Roebuck Plains Roadhouse. 4 km N of Nita Downs turnoff

HEMA 116 H5 — 19 2 36 S — 121 39 56 E

BIG RIG 24

458 Nillibubica (Goldwire) Rest Area

1

Rest Area 168 km NE of Sandfire Roadhouse or 121 km SW of Roebuck Plains Roadhouse

HEMA 116 H5 — 18 36 14 S — 121 57 59 E

BIG RIG

459 Barn Hill Station

☎ (08) 9192 4975

Camp Area at Barn Hill Station. 205 km N of Sandfire Roadhouse or 95 km SW of Roebuck Plains Roadhouse. Turn W off Hwy 1, 195 km N of Sandfire Roadhouse or 95 km S of Roebuck Plains Roadhouse for 10 km of sand & dirt road. Closed Nov to April

HEMA 116 G5 — 18 22 5 S — 122 2 27 E

BIG RIG

460 Roebuck Plains Rest Area

1

Parking Area 267 km N of Sandfire Roadhouse or 22 km SW of Roebuck Plains Roadhouse

HEMA 116 G6 — 18 0 51 S — 122 35 42 E

BIG RIG

461 Broome's Gateway

☎ 0437 525 485

Caravan Park 29 km E of Broome or 5 km W of Roebuck Plains Roadhouse

HEMA 116 G6 — 17 51 22 S — 122 27 24 E

BIG RIG

462 Willie Creek

☎ (08) 9191 3456

Camp Spot 35 km N of Broome. Turn N 9 km E of Broome, along Cape Leveque Rd & Manari Rd, Willie Creek Rd. Follow red markers around lake. Camping area just past picnic shelter, veer R. Small vehicles only. Dirt road. 4WD recommended

HEMA 116 G5 — 17 45 33 S — 122 12 40 E

72

463 Barred Creek

☎ (08) 9191 3456

Camp Spot 39 km N of Broome. Turn N 9 km E of Broome, along Cape Leveque Rd & Manari Rd then turn W 9 km N of Willie Creek Rd, follow 1.5 km to various sites

HEMA 116 F5 — 17 39 42 S — 122 12 7 E

72

464 Quondong

☎ (08) 9191 3456

Camp Spot 45 km N of Broome. Turn N 9 km E of Broome, along Cape Leveque Rd & Manari Rd. Dirt road. 4WD recommended

HEMA 116 F5 — 17 35 28 S — 122 10 11 E

72

Notes...

465 Prices Point
☎ (08) 9191 3456

Camp Spot 58 km N of Broome. Turn N 9 km E of Broome, along Cape Leveque Rd & Manari Rd. Dirt road. 4WD recommended

HEMA 116 F5 | 17 29 15 S | 122 8 39 E

72

466 Banana Well Getaway
☎ (08) 9192 4040

Camp Area 135 km N of Broome. Travel along Cape Leveque Rd for approx 109 km, turn W at sign called Loongabid (Steve Arrow Rd), 7 kms to signpost, then 6 km to site

HEMA 116 E6 | 16 58 35 S | 122 35 18 E

BIG RIG

467 Gnylmarung Retreat
☎ (08) 9192 4097

Camp Area approx 150 km N of Broome. Travel along Cape Leveque Rd for 134 km, turn W onto Middle Lagoon Rd, follow signs for 28 km

HEMA 116 E6 | 16 51 40 S | 122 37 15 E

468 Nature's Hideaway at Middle Lagoon
☎ (08) 9192 4002

Camp Area 180 km N of Broome. Travel 134 km along Cape Leveque Rd, turn W onto Middle Lagoon Rd, follow signs. 40 km to site. Open 01 Apr - 31 October

HEMA 116 E6 | 16 46 26 S | 122 34 37 E

469 Whalesong Cafe & Campground
☎ (08) 9192 4000

Camp Area 175 km N of Broome. Follow the Cape Leveque Rd for 134 km, turn W onto Middle Lagoon Rd, then follow the Whalesong signs for 30 km. Reservations essential, limited sites

HEMA 116 E6 | 16 47 59 S | 122 37 22 E

470 Goombaragin Eco Retreat
☎ 0429 505 347

Camp Area 175 km N of Broome. Follow the Cape Leveque Rd for 134 km, turn W onto Middle Lagoon Rd, turn R ofter 16 km, follow signs. Reservations essential, limited sites

HEMA 116 E6 | 16 47 43 S | 122 39 58 E

471 Chile Creek
☎ (08) 9192 4141

Camp Area 190 km N of Broome, 7 km S of Lombadina Community. Turn onto Diaradgin Rd, follow signs, 6 km of sandy access track, suitable for 4WD, camper trailers & tents

HEMA 116 E6 | 16 32 6 S | 122 52 22 E

472 Kooljaman at Cape Leveque
☎ (08) 9192 4970

Camp Area at Cape Leveque, 220 km N of Broome. Small campervans only, no caravans. Minimum stay 2 nights

HEMA 116 E6 | 16 23 47 S | 122 55 38 E

473 Gambanan
☎ 0427 786 345

Camp Area 4.5 km NW of One Arm Point. Signposted, 1.5 km track

HEMA 116 E6 | 16 25 14 S | 123 1 54 E

474 Nillibubbica Rest Area
☎

Rest Area 71 km E of Roebuck Plains Roadhouse or 60 km W of Willare Bridge Roadhouse

1

HEMA 116 G6 | 17 39 21 S | 123 7 57 E

BIG RIG 24

475 Willare Bridge Roadhouse Caravan Park
☎ (08) 9191 4775

Caravan Park at Willare Bridge 14 km SW of Derby turn off or 165 km E of Broome

1

HEMA 116 G7 | 17 43 35 S | 123 39 15 E

BIG RIG

476 Myroodah Crossing

Camp Spot 38 km S of Camballin Rd & Grt Northern Hwy intersection. At 3 way intersection continue straight ahead to River Crossing. Various campspots both sides of river. Dirt road

HEMA 117 G8 | 18 4 44 S | 124 13 18 E

72

477 The Boab Rest Area

Rest Area 55 km SE of Derby turnoff or 158 km W of Fitzroy Crossing

1

HEMA 117 G8 | 17 49 26 S | 124 14 4 E

BIG RIG

478 The Lake Ellendale

Camp Spot 118 km SE of Derby turnoff or 95 km W of Fitzroy Crossing. Entry is 6.4 km W of Ellendale rest area

HEMA 117 G9 | 17 55 52 S | 124 47 0 E

BIG RIG

479 Ellendale Rest Area

Rest Area 125 km SE of Derby turnoff or 88 km W of Fitzroy Crossing

1

HEMA 117 G9 | 17 57 38 S | 124 50 10 E

BIG RIG 24

480 Windjana Gorge National Park
☎ (08) 9195 5500

Camp Area 143 km E of Derby or 151 km NW of Fitzroy Crossing. Turn S off Gibb River Rd 125 km E of Derby for 18 km or turn N 43 km W of Fitzroy Crossing onto Leopold Downs Rd for 105 km. Dirt road. Generators allowed in separate campground

HEMA 117 F9 | 17 24 42 S | 124 56 33 E

BIG RIG

481 RAAF Boab Quarry

Camp Spot 54 km NW of Fitzroy Crossing. Turn N onto Leopold Downs Rd 43 km W of Fitzroy Crossing. 11 km to Y jcn, take RH fork 700m down track to various campspots. 58 km S of Tunnel Creek turnoff. Dirt road

HEMA 117 G9 | 17 54 44 S | 125 17 48 E

482 Ngumban Cliff Lookout
Rest Area 96 km SE of Fitzroy Crossing or 192 km W of Halls Creek
HEMA 117 H10 18 44 53 S 126 6 31 E
1
BIG RIG

483 Larrawa Nature Stay & Bush Camping
(08) 9191 7025
Camp Area 143 km E of Fitzroy Crossing or 147 km W of Halls Creek. 4 km on dirt road to station. Open 01 April - 30 September. GPS at gate
HEMA 117 H11 18 47 57 S 126 32 4 E
1
$ BIG RIG

484 Mary Pool (Mary River)
Rest Area 180 km E of Fitzroy Crossing or 108 km W of Halls Creek
HEMA 117 H11 18 43 37 S 126 52 19 E
1
BIG RIG 24

485 Caroline Pool
Camp Spot 15 km SE of Halls Creek, via Duncan Rd. Turn E 13 km SE of Halls Creek. Dirt - Sandy road, small area limited turning space
HEMA 117 H13 18 13 36 S 127 45 35 E

486 Palm Springs
Picnic Spot 40 km SE of Halls Creek, via Duncan Rd. Small area close to road
HEMA 117 H13 18 25 12 S 127 50 42 E
80
24

487 Sawpit Gorge
Camp Spot 46 km SE of Halls Creek, via Duncan Rd. Last 3 km winding & corrugated. Small vehicles only. Small area
HEMA 117 H13 18 25 30 S 127 49 14 E
72

488 Little Panton River
Parking Area 46 km N of Halls Creek or 117 km S of Turkey Creek
HEMA 117 G13 17 52 32 S 127 49 54 E
1
BIG RIG

489 Leycesters Rest - Ord River
Rest Area 100 km N of Halls Creek or 63 km S of Turkey Creek
HEMA 117 F13 17 28 45 S 127 57 4 E
1
BIG RIG 24

490 Spring Creek
Rest Area 107 km NE of Halls Creek or 56 km SW of Turkey Creek. Big rigs at top car park
HEMA 117 F13 17 25 59 S 127 59 21 E
1
BIG RIG

491 Muluks Rest Area
Rest Area 121 km N of Halls Creek or 39 km S of Turkey Creek
HEMA 117 F13 17 20 19 S 128 3 8 E
BIG RIG 24

492 Kurrajong Campground
(08) 9168 4200
Purnululu National Park
Camp Area 7 km N of Visitors Centre. 4WD vehicle only, 56 km rough dirt road
HEMA 117 F13 17 23 20 S 128 19 50 E
$

493 Walardi Campground
(08) 9168 4200
Purnululu National Park
Camp Area 12 km S of Visitors Centre. 4WD vehicle only. 56 km rough dirt road
HEMA 117 G13 17 31 16 S 128 18 2 E
$

494 Dunham River
Rest Area 118 km N of Turkey Creek or 35 km S of Victoria Hwy jcn
HEMA 117 E13 16 7 54 S 128 22 52 E
1
BIG RIG 24

495 Wuggubun Aboriginal Community Campground
Camp Area 157 km N of Turkey Creek or 40 km SW of Kununurra. Turn W off Hwy. Signposted
HEMA 117 D13 15 57 13 S 128 22 45 E
1
$ BIG RIG

496 Cockburn Rest Area
Rest Area at Victoria Hwy jcn or 152 km N of Turkey Creek, 56 km S of Wyndham or 45 km W of Kununurra
HEMA 117 D13 15 52 7 S 128 22 17 E
1
BIG RIG 24

497 Maggie Creek
Rest Area 28 km N of Victoria Hwy jcn or 28 km S of Wyndham. Area not level
HEMA 117 D13 15 40 42 S 128 14 50 E

498 Mambi Island
Camp Area 54 km NW Kununurra. Turn N onto Valentine Springs Rd, travel 14.5 km to Parrys Creek Rd, turn L travel 31.5 km. Signposted access to camp. Dirt road. Steep entry
HEMA 117 D14 15 34 58 S 128 28 24 E

499 Kununurra Agricultural Showground Caravan Park
(08) 9168 2885
Caravan Park at Showgrounds. Coolibah Dr. Available to travellers with pets or big rigs only. Closed during show week
HEMA 117 D14 15 46 19 S 128 43 54 E
$+ BIG RIG

Notes...

WESTERN AUSTRALIA

Leonora to Yulara (NT)

Great Central Road

This road is seasonal and more suitable to 4WD vehicles, camper trailers and off road caravans. Road conditions phone 1800 013 314. Permits are required to travel on this road

500 Giles Breakaway

Camp Spot 50 km N of Laverton or 262 km SW of Tjukayirla Roadhouse. At Outback Way sign turn S onto track to Breakaway

HEMA 113 D13 28 16 49 S 122 42 3 E

501 Giles Breakaway Parking Area

Parking Area 56 km N of Laverton or 256 km SW of Tjukayirla Roadhouse

HEMA 113 D13 28 14 49 S 122 43 10 E

BIG RIG

502 Limestone Well Parking Area (The Pines)

Parking Area 120 km NE of Laverton or 191 km SW of Tjukayirla Roadhouse

HEMA 119 B1 27 54 55 S 123 10 41 E

BIG RIG

503 Minnie Creek Rd Parking Area

Parking Area 197 km NE of Laverton or 115 km SW of Tjukayirla Roadhouse

HEMA 119 B2 27 50 32 S 123 55 3 E

BIG RIG

504 Ilkurlka Roadhouse

☎ (08) 9037 1147

Camp Area at Ilkurlka. Facilities at roadhouse

HEMA 119 C6 28 21 1 S 127 31 5 E

505 Tjukayirla Roadhouse

☎ (08) 9037 1108

Camp Area at Tjukayirla Roadhouse

HEMA 118 K2 27 9 19 S 124 34 29 E

BIG RIG

506 Camp Paradise

Camp Spot 92 km NE of Tjukayirla Roadhouse or 163 km SW of Warburton. Turn N off road

HEMA 118 K2 26 57 55 S 125 24 43 E

BIG RIG

507 Mananytja Rockhole

Camp Spot 122 km NE of Tjukayirla Roadhouse or 133 km SE of Warburton. Turn N 100m W of rockhole follow track to breakaway

HEMA 118 K3 26 50 10 S 125 39 29 E

BIG RIG

508 Warburton Roadhouse

☎ (08) 8956 7656

Camp Area at Warburton Roadhouse

HEMA 118 J4 26 7 56 S 126 34 9 E

BIG RIG

509 Yarla Kutjarra Campground

Camp Area 95 km NE of Warburton or 136 km SE of Warakurna

HEMA 118 H5 25 36 37 S 127 13 24 E

BIG RIG 48

510 Warakurna Roadhouse

☎ (08) 8956 7344

Camp Area at Warakurna Roadhouse

HEMA 118 G6 25 2 34 S 128 18 12 E

BIG RIG

511 Kaltukatjara Campground (Docker River) NT

Camp Area at Kaltukatjara. 1 km W of town turnoff

HEMA 118 G7 24 51 48 S 129 3 41 E

BIG RIG

Gibb River Road

This road is seasonal and more suitable to 4WD vehicles, camper trailers and off road caravans. Road conditions phone 1800 013 314

512 Home Valley Station

☎ (08) 9161 4322

Camp Area at Home Valley Station. 66 km W of Wyndham-Kununurra turnoff. 1.7 km off Gibb River Rd

HEMA 117 D13 15 43 15 S 127 49 24 E

BIG RIG

513 Ellenbrae Station

☎ (08) 9161 4325

Camp Area at Ellenbrae Station. 171 km W of Wyndham-Kununurra turnoff & 180 km E of Mt Barnett Roadhouse. 5 km N of Gibb River Rd. Pay fees at homestead

HEMA 117 D12 15 57 27 S 127 3 47 E

514 Russ Creek

Camp Spot at Russ Creek 46 km W of Ellenbrae Station turnoff or 43 km E of Kalumburu Rd. On N side of road E of the creek

HEMA 117 D11 16 2 53 S 126 42 4 E

515 Drysdale River Station - Homestead Campground

☎ (08) 9161 4326

Camp Area at Drysdale River Station. 59 km N of Gibb River Rd & Kalumburu Rd intersection. Limited powered sites

HEMA 117 D11 15 42 13 S 126 22 45 E

BIG RIG

516 Drysdale River Station - Miners Pool

☎ (08) 9161 4326

Camp Area Drysdale Station. 5 km N of Drysdale River Station. Pay fees at Drysdale River Station

HEMA 117 D11 15 40 45 S 126 24 10 E

517 **King Edward River Campground No 1** ☎ (08) 9168 4200
Camp Spot 8.5 km W of Kalumburu Rd along the Mitchell Plateau/ Port Warrender Rd
HEMA 117 C11 14 53 4 S 126 12 2 E

518 **King Edward River Campground No 2** ☎ (08) 9168 4200
Camp Spot 8.2 km W of Kalumburu Rd along the Mitchell Plateau/ Port Warrender Rd
HEMA 117 C11 14 53 3 S 126 12 5 E

519 **Punamii-unpuu (Mitchell Falls) Campground** ☎ (08) 9168 4200
Mitchell River National Park
Camp Spot 16.2 km W of the Mitchell Plateau/Port Warrender Rd
HEMA 117 C10 14 49 12 S 125 43 6 E

520 **Hann River**
Camp Spot 53.8 km W of Kalumburu Rd jcn or 54.2 km E of Mount Barnett Roadhouse
HEMA 117 E11 16 30 51 S 126 21 20 E

521 **Mt Elizabeth Station** ☎ (08) 9191 4644
Camp Area at Mt Elizabeth Station. 38 km NE of Mt Barnett Roadhouse or 70 km S of the Kalumburu Rd jcn, then 30 km N to campsite
HEMA 117 E10 16 25 10 S 126 6 17 E

522 **Manning Gorge Camping Area** ☎ (08) 9191 7007
Camp Area at Manning Gorge. 7 km N of Mt Barnett Roadhouse. Permit required, fees payable at Roadhouse
HEMA 117 E10 16 39 25 S 125 55 39 E

523 **Charnley River Station** ☎ (08) 9191 4646
Camp Area at Charnley River Station. Turn N 27 km NE of Imintji Store or 47 km SW of Mount Barnett Roadhouse. Travel N for 42 km to Station
HEMA 117 E10 16 42 53 S 125 27 29 E

524 **Mornington Wilderness Camp** ☎ (08) 9191 7406
Camp Area 90 km S of Gibb River Rd. Turn S 25 km E of Imintji Store or 53 km W of Mt Barnett Roadhouse. Must report in at radio booth before entering to check availability. No generators or fires
HEMA 117 F10 17 30 29 S 126 6 45 E

525 **Silent Grove Camping Area** ☎ (08) 9192 5500
King Leopold Ranges Conservation Park
Camp Area 20 km N of Gibb River Rd on Silent Grove Rd. Turn N 8 km W of Imintji Roadhouse or 95 E of Gibb River Rd/ Leopold Downs Rd jcn
HEMA 117 F9 17 3 59 S 125 14 57 E

526 **March Fly Glen Rest Area**
Rest Area 9.7 km W of Silent Grove Rd or 220 km E of Derby. Small vehicles only
HEMA 117 F9 17 9 47 S 125 18 37 E

527 **Mt Hart Wilderness Lodge** ☎ (08) 9191 4645
Camp Area at Mt Hart Station. Turn N 65 km E of Leopold Downs Rd jcn or 38 km W of Imintji Store. 49 km to Station
HEMA 117 E9 16 49 6 S 124 55 14 E

528 **Lennard River Rest Area**
Rest Area 72 km W of Silent Grove Rd or 128 km E of Derby
HEMA 117 F9 17 23 34 S 124 45 22 E

529 **Birdwood Downs** ☎ (08) 9191 1275
Camp Area 18 km E of Derby on the Gibb River Rd. Bush camping. No generators allowed
HEMA 116 F7 17 21 28 S 123 46 6 E

Notes...

key map

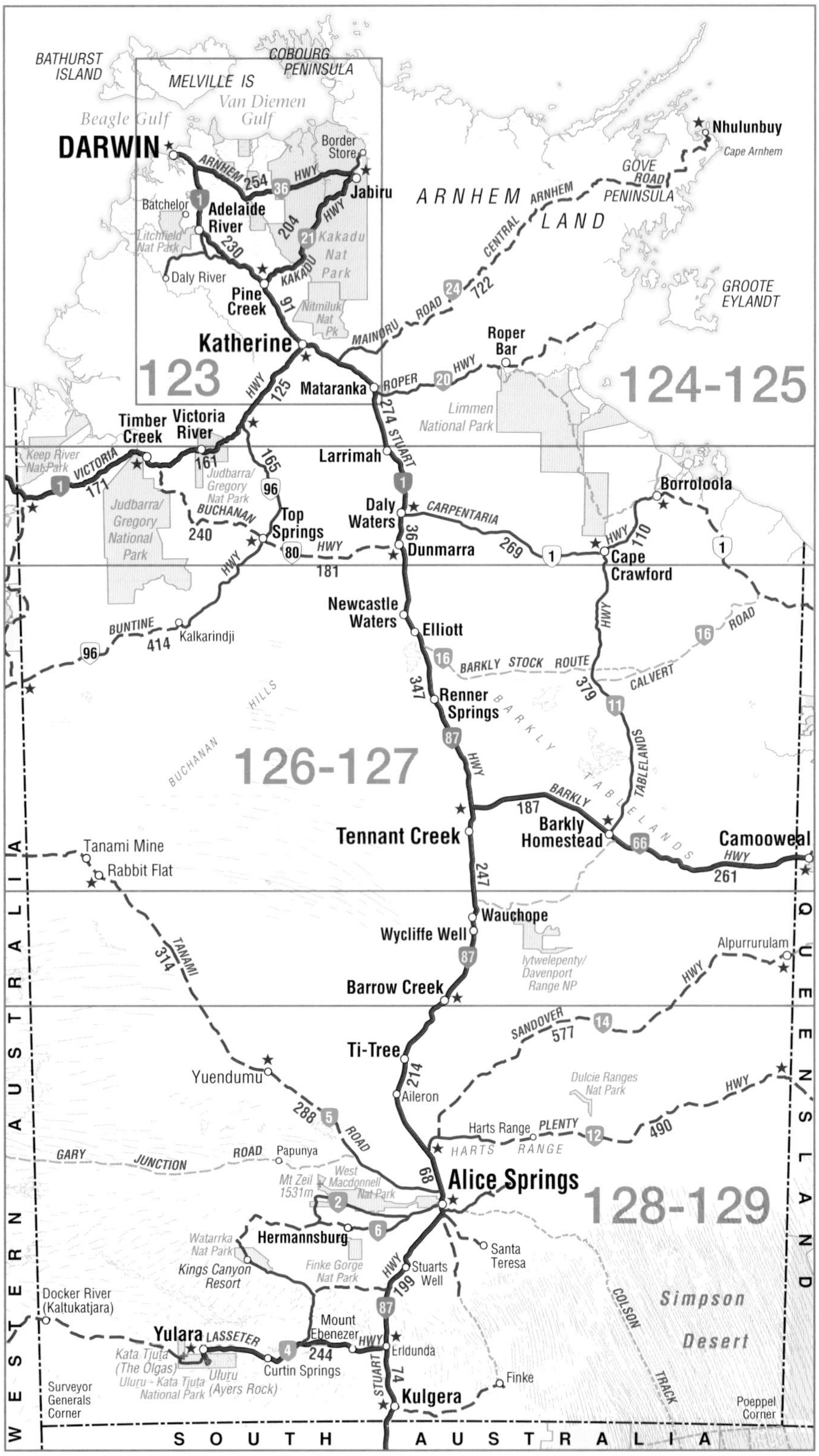

MINDIL BEACH (122 G1)

PHOTO: PETER EVE © TOURISM NT

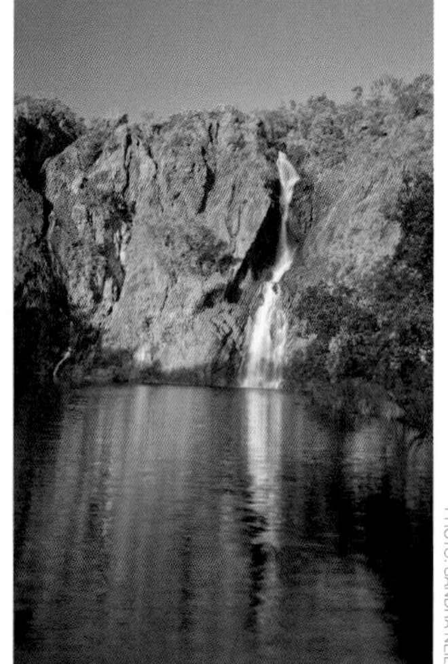

WANGI FALLS, LITCHFIELD NP (124 E3)

PHOTO: SANDRA NEILL

	Uluru (Ayers Rock)	Nhulunbuy	Mataranka	Kununurra	Kulgera	Katherine	Jabiru	Halls Creek	Darwin	Camooweal	Borroloola	Barrow Creek	Alice Springs
Barrow Creek													284
Borroloola												893	1177
Camooweal											721	694	978
Darwin										1412	940	1210	1494
Halls Creek									1187	543	1143	1310	1046
Jabiru								1169	251	1394	922	1192	1476
Katherine							299	865	317	1095	623	893	1177
Kulgera						1451	1750	1320	1768	1252	1451	558	274
Kununurra					1678	512	811	358	829	1449	1049	1247	1404
Mataranka				624	1339	112	411	977	429	983	511	781	1065
Nhulunbuy			739	1241	2078	729	1028	1594	1046	1722	1250	1520	1804
Uluru (Ayers Rock)		2267	1528	1867	337	1640	1939	1509	1957	1441	1640	747	463
Tennant Creek	970	1297	558	1024	781	670	969	1118	987	471	747	223	507

Distances are shown in kilometres and follow the most direct major sealed route where possible.

Major Road	
Minor Road	
One Way Road	→
Major Building	
Govt Building	
Theatre/Cinema	
Shopping	
Information	
Post Office	
24hr Fuel	

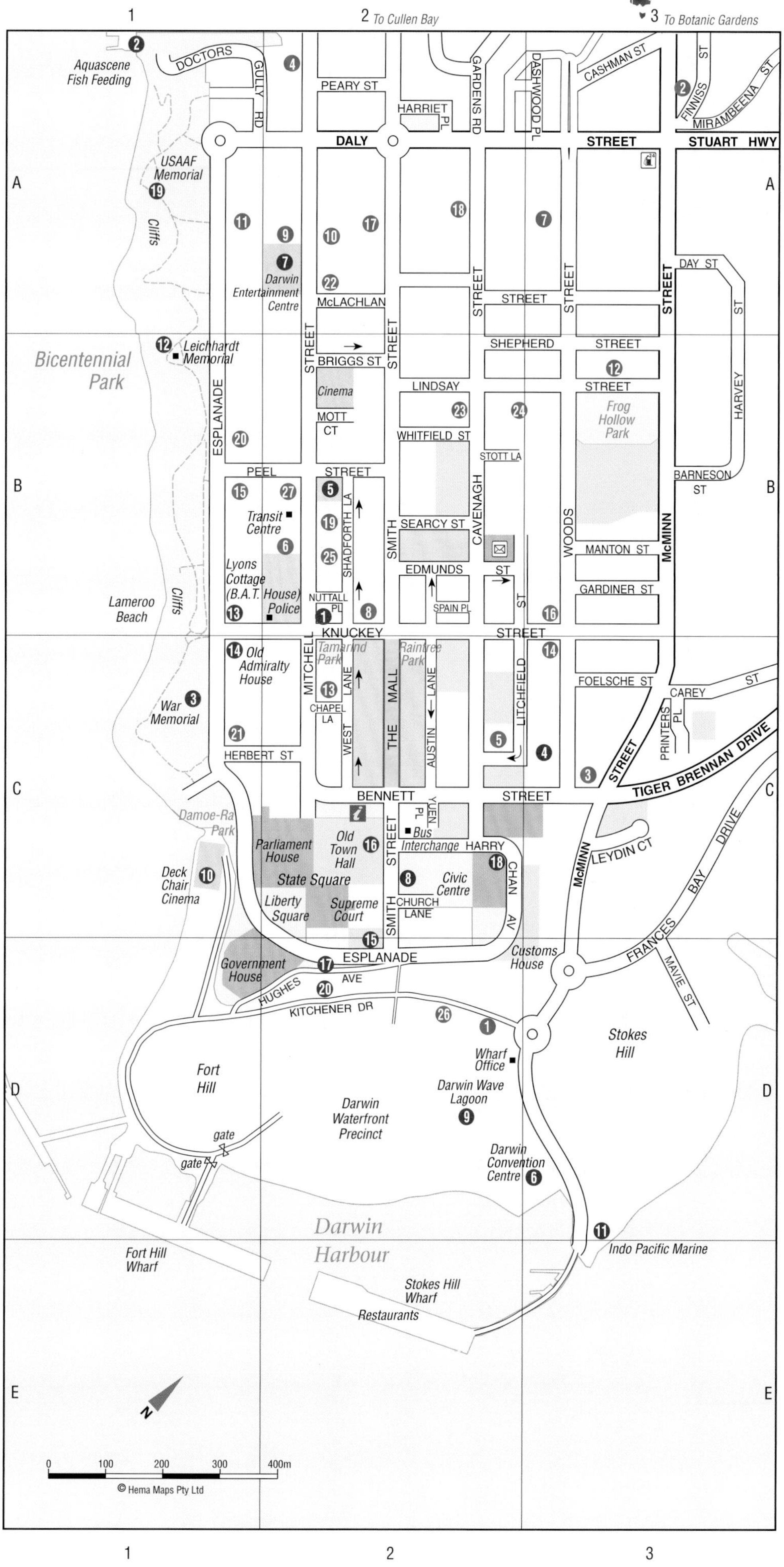

Points of Interest

1. Aboriginal Fine Arts Gallery B2
2. Aquascene Fish Feeding A1
3. Cenotaph / War Memorial, The C1
4. Chung Wah Temple and Museum C3
5. Crocosaurus Cove B2
6. Darwin Convention Centre D3
7. Darwin Entertainment Centre A2
8. Darwin Theatre Company C2
9. Darwin Wave Lagoon D2
10. Deckchair Cinema, The C1
11. Indo Pacific Marine D3
12. Leichhardt Memorial B1
13. Lyons Cottage (B.A.T. House) B1
14. Old Admiralty House C1
15. Old Court House, The C2
16. Old Town Hall, The C2
17. Survivors Lookout D2
18. Tree of Knowledge, The C2
19. USS Peary Memorial / USAAF Memorial A1
20. WWII Oil Storage Tunnels D2

Accommodation

1. Adina Apartment Hotel Darwin D2
2. Alatai Holiday Apartments A3
3. Argus Apartments C3
4. Banyan View Lodge A2
5. Cavenagh Hotel Motel, The C2
6. Chilli's Backpackers B2
7. City Gardens Apartments A3
8. Darwin Central Hotel B2
9. Darwin City YHA A2
10. Dingo Moon Lodge A2
11. DoubleTree by Hilton Hotel Darwin A1
12. Frogshollow Backpackers B3
13. Hilton Darwin C2
14. Luma Luma Holiday Apartments C3
15. Mantra on the Esplanade B1
16. Mantra Pandanas B3
17. Marrakai Apartments A2
18. Mediterranean All Suite Hotel A2
19. Melaleuca On Mitchell Backpackers B2
20. Novotel Atrium Darwin B1
21. Palms City Resort C1
22. Poinciana Inn A2
23. Quest Serviced Apartments B2
24. Travelodge Mirambeena Resort B2
25. Value Inn B2
26. Vibe Hotel Darwin Waterfront D2
27. Youth Shack, The B2

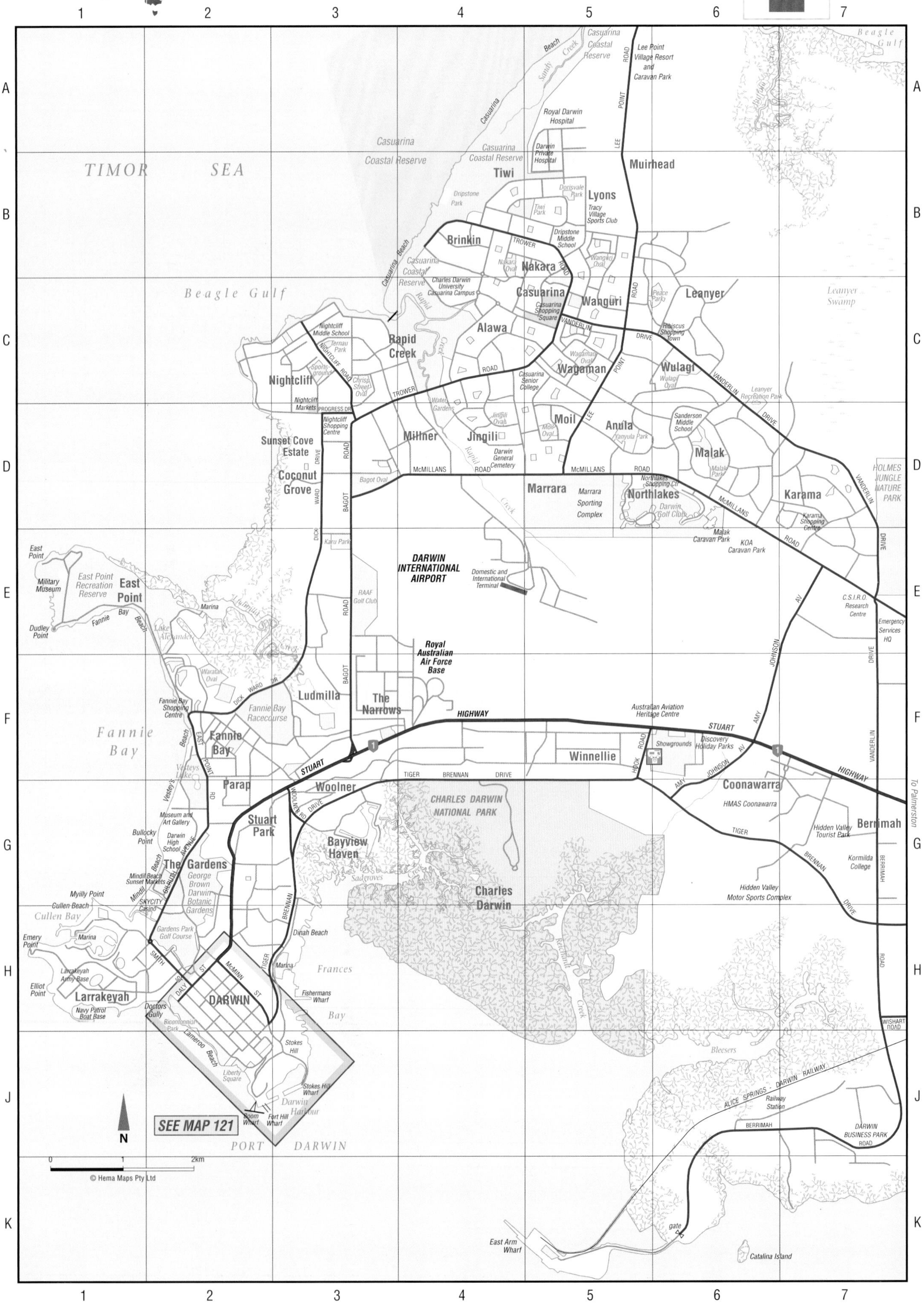

Darwin Throughroads

TIMOR SEA
Beagle Gulf
Fannie Bay
Cullen Bay
Frances Bay
PORT DARWIN
Darwin Harbour
Leanyer Swamp
Casuarina Coastal Reserve
Casuarina Beach
Lee Point Village Resort and Caravan Park
Royal Darwin Hospital
Darwin Private Hospital
Muirhead
Tiwi
Lyons
Dorisvale Park
Tiwi Park
Tracy Village Sports Club
Dripstone Park
Dripstone Middle School
Brinkin
Nakara
Nakara Oval
Casuarina
Casuarina Shopping Square
Wanguri
Wanguri Oval
Leanyer
Peace Park
Charles Darwin University Casuarina Campus
Hibiscus Shopping Town
Nightcliff Middle School
Ternau Park
Rapid Creek
Alawa
Nightcliff
Sports ground
Chrisp Street Oval
Wagaman
Wagaman Oval
Casuarina Senior College
Wulagi
Wulagi Oval
Leanyer Recreation Park
Nightcliff Markets
Nightcliff Shopping Centre
Water Gardens
Millner
Jingili
Jingili Oval
Moil
Moil Oval
Anula
Anula Park
Sanderson Middle School
Malak
Malak Park
Darwin General Cemetery
Sunset Cove Estate
Coconut Grove
Bagot Oval
Marrara
Marrara Sporting Complex
Northlakes
Northlakes Shopping Ctr
Darwin Golf Club
Karama
Karama Shopping Centre
HOLMES JUNGLE NATURE PARK
Malak Caravan Park
KOA Caravan Park
Karu Park
DARWIN INTERNATIONAL AIRPORT
Domestic and International Terminal
East Point
Military Museum
East Point Recreation Reserve
Dudley Point
Fannie Bay Beach
Lake Alexander
Marina
RAAF Golf Club
C.S.I.R.O. Research Centre
Emergency Services HQ
Royal Australian Air Force Base
Waratah Oval
Ludmilla
The Narrows
Fannie Bay Shopping Centre
Fannie Bay Racecourse
Fannie Bay
Australian Aviation Heritage Centre
Showgrounds
Discovery Holiday Parks
Winnellie
Vesteys Lake
Parap
Woolner
Coonawarra
HMAS Coonawarra
Berrimah
CHARLES DARWIN NATIONAL PARK
Stuart Park
Museum and Art Gallery
Bullocky Point
Darwin High School
Bayview Haven
Hidden Valley Tourist Park
Kormilda College
The Gardens
Mindil Beach Sunset Markets
George Brown Darwin Botanic Gardens
Sadgroves
Charles Darwin
Hidden Valley Motor Sports Complex
Myilly Point
Cullen Beach
SKYCITY Casino
Gardens Park Golf Course
Dinah Beach
Emery Point
Marina
Larrakeyah Army Base
Elliot Point
Larrakeyah
Navy Patrol Boat Base
Fishermans Wharf
DARWIN
Doctors Gully
Bicentennial Park
Lameroo Beach
Stokes Hill
Liberty Square
Stokes Hill Wharf
Boom Wharf
Fort Hill Wharf
Bleesers
Railway Station
DARWIN BUSINESS PARK
East Arm Wharf
gate
Catalina Island
To Palmerston
LEE POINT ROAD
TROWER ROAD
VANDERLIN DRIVE
NIGHTCLIFF ROAD
PROGRESS DR
McMILLANS ROAD
DICK WARD DRIVE
BAGOT ROAD
STUART HIGHWAY
AMY JOHNSON AV
HOOK ROAD
TIGER BRENNAN DRIVE
BERRIMAH ROAD
WISHART ROAD
EAST POINT RD
GILRUTH AVENUE
SMITH ST
DALY ST
McMINN ST
WOOLNER RD
ALICE SPRINGS - DARWIN RAILWAY
BERRIMAH
DARWIN BUSINESS PARK ROAD

SEE MAP 121

N
0 1 2km
© Hema Maps Pty Ltd

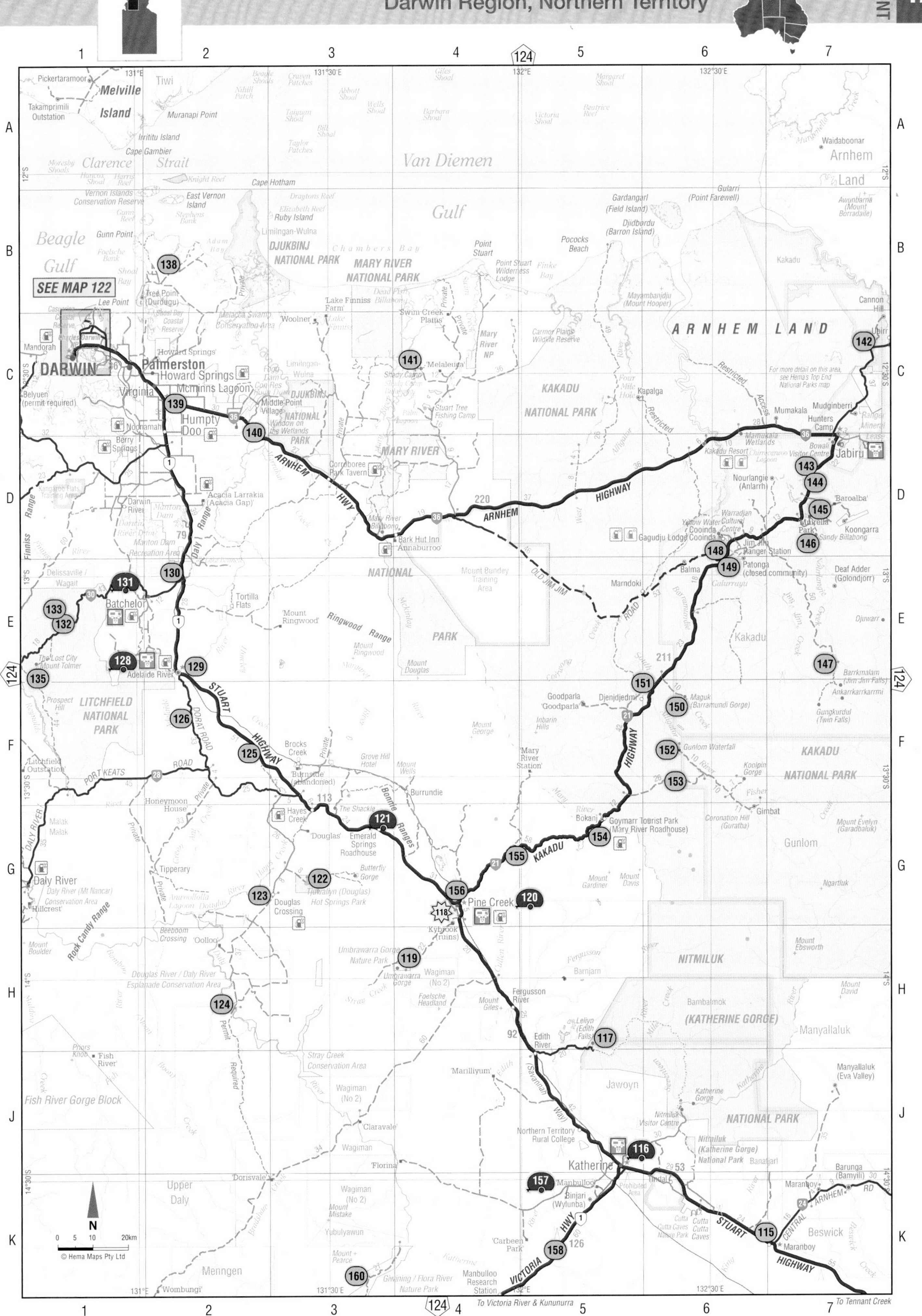
Melville Island
Tiwi
Pickertaramoor
Takamprimili Outstation
Muranapi Point
Irrititu Island
Cape Gambier
Clarence Strait
Van Diemen Gulf
Beagle Gulf
Cape Hotham
Vernon Islands Conservation Reserve
East Vernon Island
Ruby Island
Gunn Point
Limilngan-Wulna
DJUKBINJ NATIONAL PARK
MARY RIVER NATIONAL PARK
Chambers Bay
Point Stuart
Point Stuart Wilderness Lodge
Pocock Beach
Gardangarl (Field Island)
Djidbordu (Barron Island)
Gularri (Point Farewell)
Waidaboonar
Arnhem Land
Avunbarna (Mount Borradaile)
Kakadu
Cannon Hill
Ubirr
ARNHEM LAND
SEE MAP 122
Lee Point
Tree Point (Durdugu)
Casuarina Coastal Reserve
Woolner
Lake Finniss Farm
Swim Creek Plains
Mary River NP
Carmor Plains Wildlife Reserve
Mayambanjidju (Mount Hooper)
Mandorah
DARWIN
Palmerston
Howard Springs
Mcminns Lagoon
Virginia
Belyuen (permit required)
Humpty Doo
Noonamah
Berry Springs
Middle Point Village
Shady Camp
Melaleuca
Stuart Tree Fishing Camp
KAKADU NATIONAL PARK
Four Mile Hole
Kapalga
Restricted Access
For more detail on this area, see Hema's Top End National Parks map
Mumakala
Mudginberri
Hunters Camp
Jabiru
Mamukala Wetlands
Kakadu Resort
Bowali Visitor Centre
Nourlangie (Anlarrh)
Baroalba
ARNHEM HWY
Corroboree Park Tavern
MARY RIVER
Acacia Larrakia (Acacia Gap)
Darwin River
Manton Dam
Manton Dam Recreation Area
Daly Range
Finniss Range
Kangaroo Flats Training Area
Mary River Billabong
Bark Hut Inn Annaburroo
NATIONAL
ARNHEM
HIGHWAY
Gagudju Lodge Cooinda
Yellow Water Cooinda
Warradjan Cultural Centre
Muirella Park
Sandy Billabong
Koongarra
Jim Jim Ranger Station
Patonga (closed community)
Balma
Deaf Adder (Golondjorr)
Mount Bundey Training Area
OLD JIM JIM ROAD
Marrdoki
Delissaville / Wagait
Batchelor
Tortilla Flats
Mount Ringwood
Ringwood Range
PARK
Kakadu
Djuwarr
The Lost City
Mount Tolmer
Adelaide River
STUART HIGHWAY
Mount Douglas
Barrkmalam (Jim Jim Falls)
Ankarrkarrkarrmi
Gungkurdul (Twin Falls)
Goodparla
Djenjidjedmi
Inbarin Hills
Maguk (Barramundi Gorge)
Gunlom Waterfall
KAKADU NATIONAL PARK
Koolpin Gorge
Gimbat
Coronation Hill (Guratba)
Mount Evelyn (Garadbaluk)
Gunlom
Ngartluk
Prospect Hill
LITCHFIELD NATIONAL PARK
Litchfield Outstation
PORT KEATS ROAD
DORAT ROAD
Brocks Creek
Burnside (abandoned)
Grove Hill Hotel
Mount Wells
Burrundie
Bonnie Ranges
Mary River Station
Mount George
Honeymoon House
Hayes Creek
The Shackle
Emerald Springs Roadhouse
Douglas
Butterfly Gorge
Tjuwalyn (Douglas) Hot Springs Park
Douglas Crossing
Bokanj
Goymarr Tourist Park (Mary River Roadhouse)
KAKADU
Mount Gardiner
Mount Davis
Malak Malak
DALY RIVER
Daly River
Daly River (Mt Nancar) Conservation Area
Hillcrest
Tipperary
Rock Candy Range
Pine Creek
Kybrook (ruins)
Beeboom Crossing
Oolloo
Mount Boulder
Umbrawarra Gorge Nature Park
Umbrawarra Gorge
Wagiman (No 2)
Fergusson
Barnjarn
NITMILUK
Mount Ebsworth
Douglas River / Daly River Esplanade Conservation Area
Foelsche Headland
Mount Giles
Fergusson River
Bambalmok
(KATHERINE GORGE)
Mount David
Manyallaluk
Permit Required
Leliyn (Edith Falls)
Edith River
Phors Knob
Fish River
Fish River Gorge Block
Stray Creek Conservation Area
Marilliyum
Jawoyn
Manyallaluk (Eva Valley)
Katherine Gorge
NATIONAL PARK
Wagiman (No 2)
Claravale
Northern Territory Rural College
Nitmiluk Visitor Centre
Nitmiluk (Katherine Gorge) National Park
Banatjarl
Wagiman
Florina
Katherine
Tindal
Dorisvale
Manbulloo
Prohibited Area
Barunga (Bamyili)
Upper Daly
Wagiman (No 2)
Mount Mistake
Binjari (Wylunba)
Cutta Cutta Caves Nature Park
Maranboy
CENTRAL ARNHEM RD
Beswick
Yubulyawun
Carbeen Park
STUART HIGHWAY
VICTORIA HWY
Mount Pearce
Menngen
Giwining / Flora River Nature Park
Manbulloo Research Station
Wombungi
To Victoria River & Kununurra
To Tennant Creek
0 5 10 20km
© Hema Maps Pty Ltd

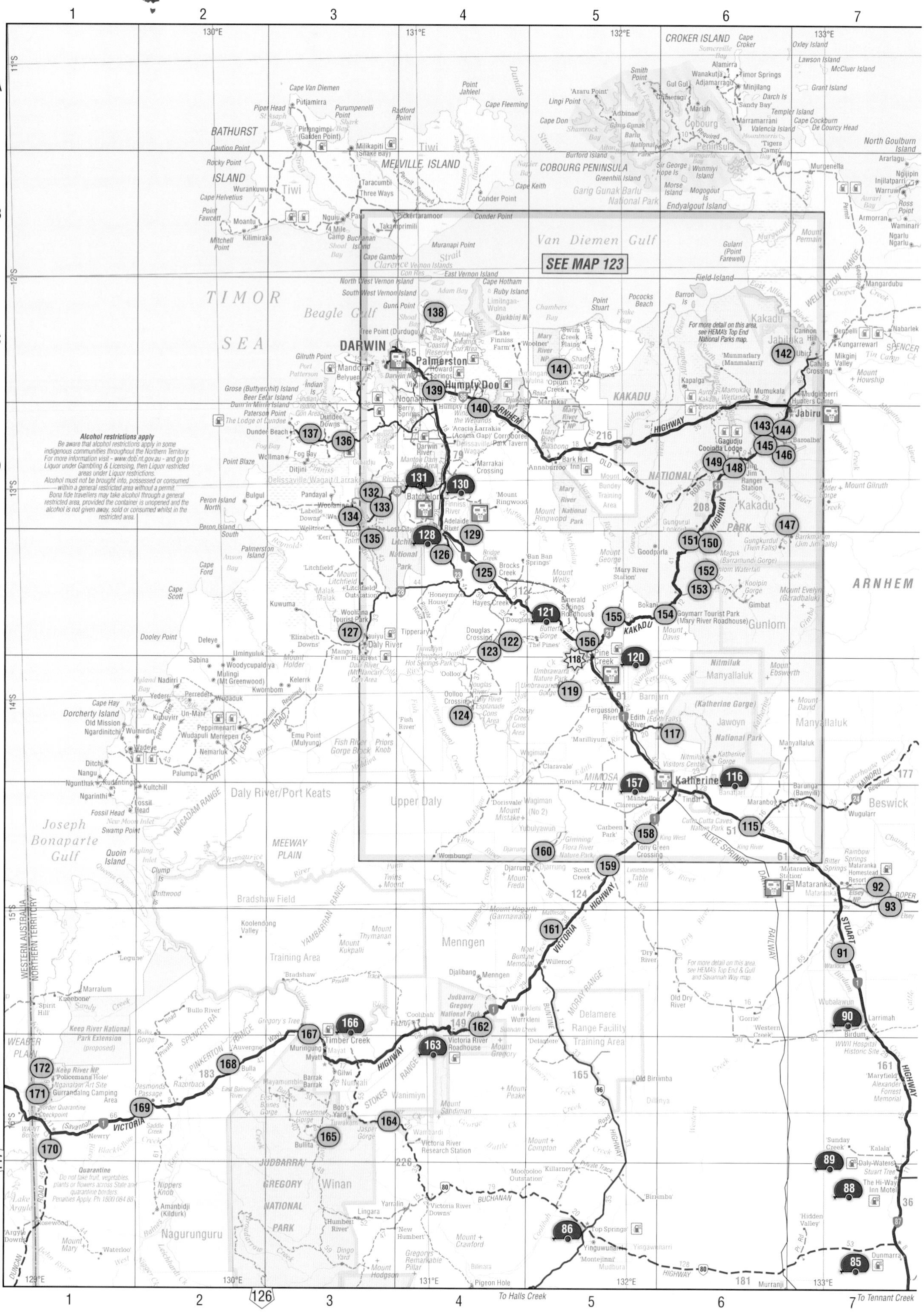

SEE MAP 123

Alcohol restrictions apply

Be aware that alcohol restrictions apply in some indigenous communities throughout the Northern Territory. For more information visit - www.dob.nt.gov.au - and go to Liquor under Gambling & Licensing, then Liquor restricted areas under Liquor restrictions.

Alcohol must not be brought into, possessed or consumed within a general restricted area without a permit.

Bona fide travellers may take alcohol through a general restricted area, provided the container is unopened and the alcohol is not given away, sold or consumed whilst in the restricted area.

For more detail on this area, see HEMA's Top End National Parks map.

For more detail on this area, see HEMA's Top End & Gulf and Savannah Way map.

Quarantine

Do not take fruit, vegetables, plants or flowers across State and quarantine borders. Penalties Apply. Ph 1800 084 881

To Kununurra

To Halls Creek

To Tennant Creek

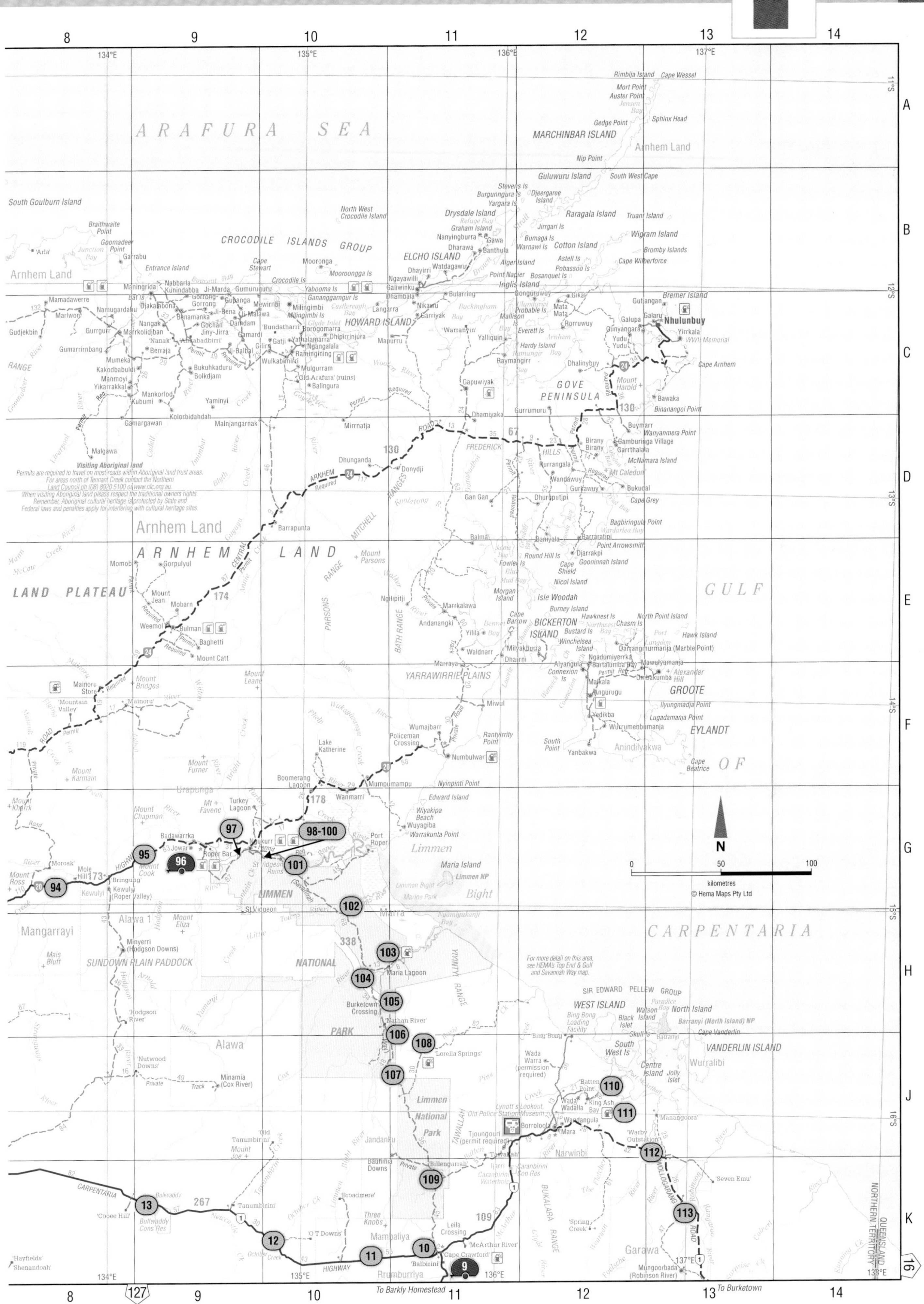
ARAFURA SEA
ARNHEM LAND
GULF OF CARPENTARIA
Arnhem Land
LAND PLATEAU
GOVE PENINSULA
GROOTE EYLANDT
LIMMEN NATIONAL PARK
Limmen National Park
SIR EDWARD PELLEW GROUP
VANDERLIN ISLAND
WEST ISLAND
CROCODILE ISLANDS GROUP
ELCHO ISLAND
HOWARD ISLAND
BICKERTON ISLAND
Nhulunbuy
Borroloola
Visiting Aboriginal land
Permits are required to travel on most roads within Aboriginal land trust areas. For areas north of Tennant Creek contact the Northern Land Council ph (08) 8920 5100 or www.nlc.org.au. When visiting Aboriginal land please respect the traditional owners rights. Remember, Aboriginal cultural heritage is protected by State and Federal laws and penalties apply for interfering with cultural heritage sites.
For more detail on this area, see HEMA's Top End & Gulf and Savannah Way map.
kilometres
© Hema Maps Pty Ltd
To Barkly Homestead
To Burketown
NORTHERN TERRITORY
QUEENSLAND

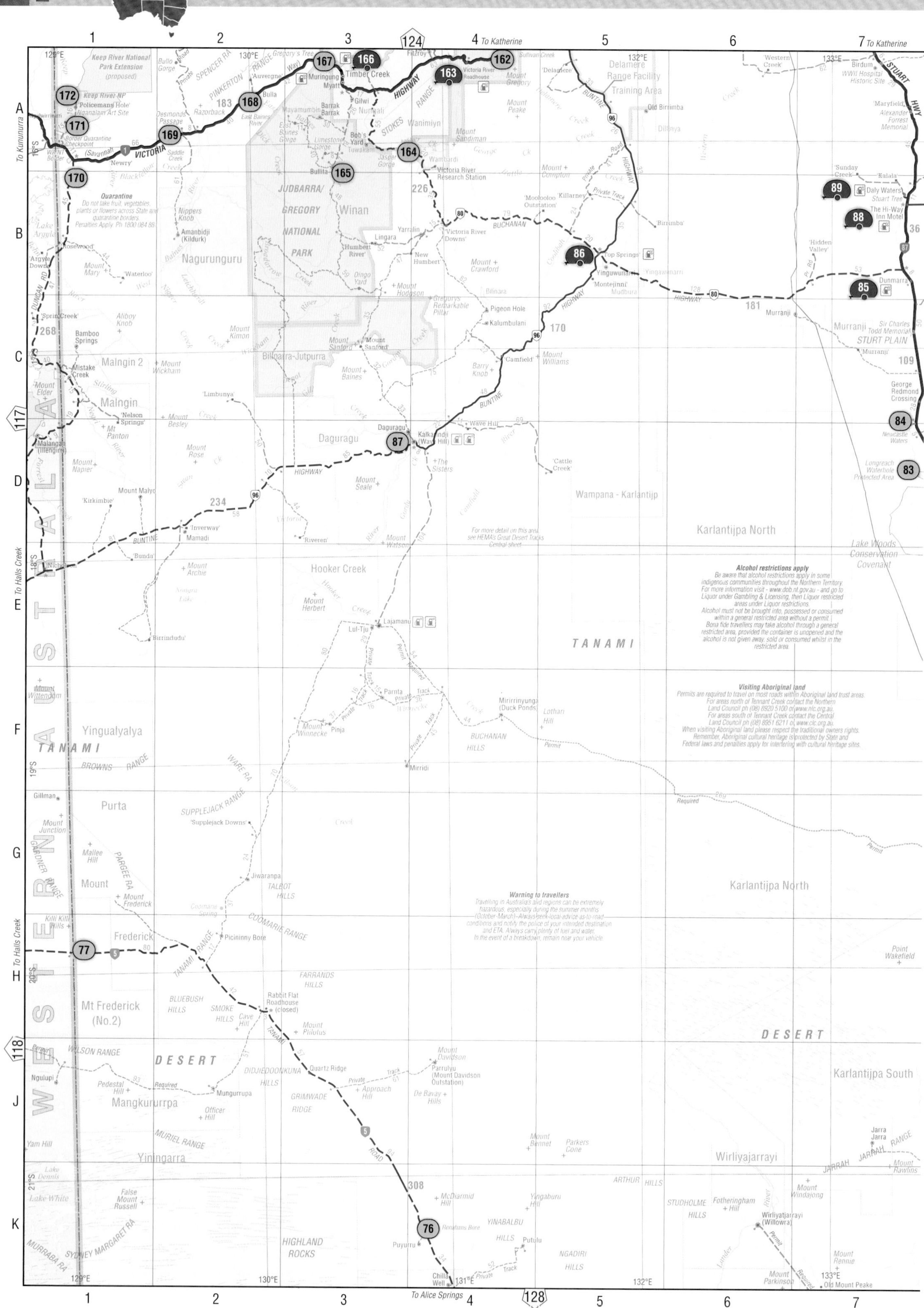

To Katherine
To Kununurra
To Halls Creek
To Alice Springs
Keep River National Park Extension (proposed)
Keep River NP
'Policemans Hole'
Nganalam Art Site
Border Quarantine Checkpoint
Quarantine
Do not take fruit, vegetables, plants or flowers across State and quarantine borders. Penalties Apply. Ph 1800 084 881
VICTORIA HIGHWAY
Timber Creek
Victoria River Roadhouse
Delamere Range Facility Training Area
JUDBARRA/ GREGORY NATIONAL PARK
Victoria River Research Station
BUNTINE HIGHWAY
BUCHANAN HIGHWAY
Top Springs
Nagurunguru
Malngin 2
Malngin
Daguragu
Kalkarindji (Wave Hill)
Winan
Bilinara-Jutpurra
Wampana - Karlantijp
Karlantijpa North
Lake Woods Conservation Covenant
Hooker Creek
Lajamanu
TANAMI
For more detail on this area see HEMA's Great Desert Tracks Central sheet.
STUART HWY
Daly Waters
The Hi-Way Inn Motel
Dunmarra
Murranji
STURT PLAIN
Newcastle Waters
Longreach Waterhole Protected Area
Alcohol restrictions apply
Be aware that alcohol restrictions apply in some indigenous communities throughout the Northern Territory. For more information visit - www.dob.nt.gov.au - and go to Liquor under Gambling & Licensing, then Liquor restricted areas under Liquor restrictions.
Alcohol must not be brought into, possessed or consumed within a general restricted area without a permit.
Bona fide travellers may take alcohol through a general restricted area, provided the container is unopened and the alcohol is not given away, sold or consumed whilst in the restricted area.
Visiting Aboriginal land
Permits are required to travel on most roads within Aboriginal land trust areas. For areas north of Tennant Creek contact the Northern Land Council ph (08) 8920 5100 or www.nlc.org.au. For areas south of Tennant Creek contact the Central Land Council ph (08) 8951 6211 or www.clc.org.au. When visiting Aboriginal land please respect the traditional owners rights. Remember, Aboriginal cultural heritage is protected by State and Federal laws and penalties apply for interfering with cultural heritage sites.
Warning to travellers
Travelling in Australia's arid regions can be extremely hazardous, especially during the summer months (October-March)–Always seek local advice as to road conditions and notify the police of your intended destination and ETA. Always carry plenty of fuel and water. In the event of a breakdown, remain near your vehicle.
Yinguaiyalya
Purta
Mount Frederick
Frederick
Mt Frederick (No.2)
Rabbit Flat Roadhouse (closed)
TANAMI ROAD
DESERT
Karlantijpa South
Mangkururrpa
Yiningarra
Wirliyajarrayi
HIGHLAND ROCKS
WESTERN AUSTRALIA

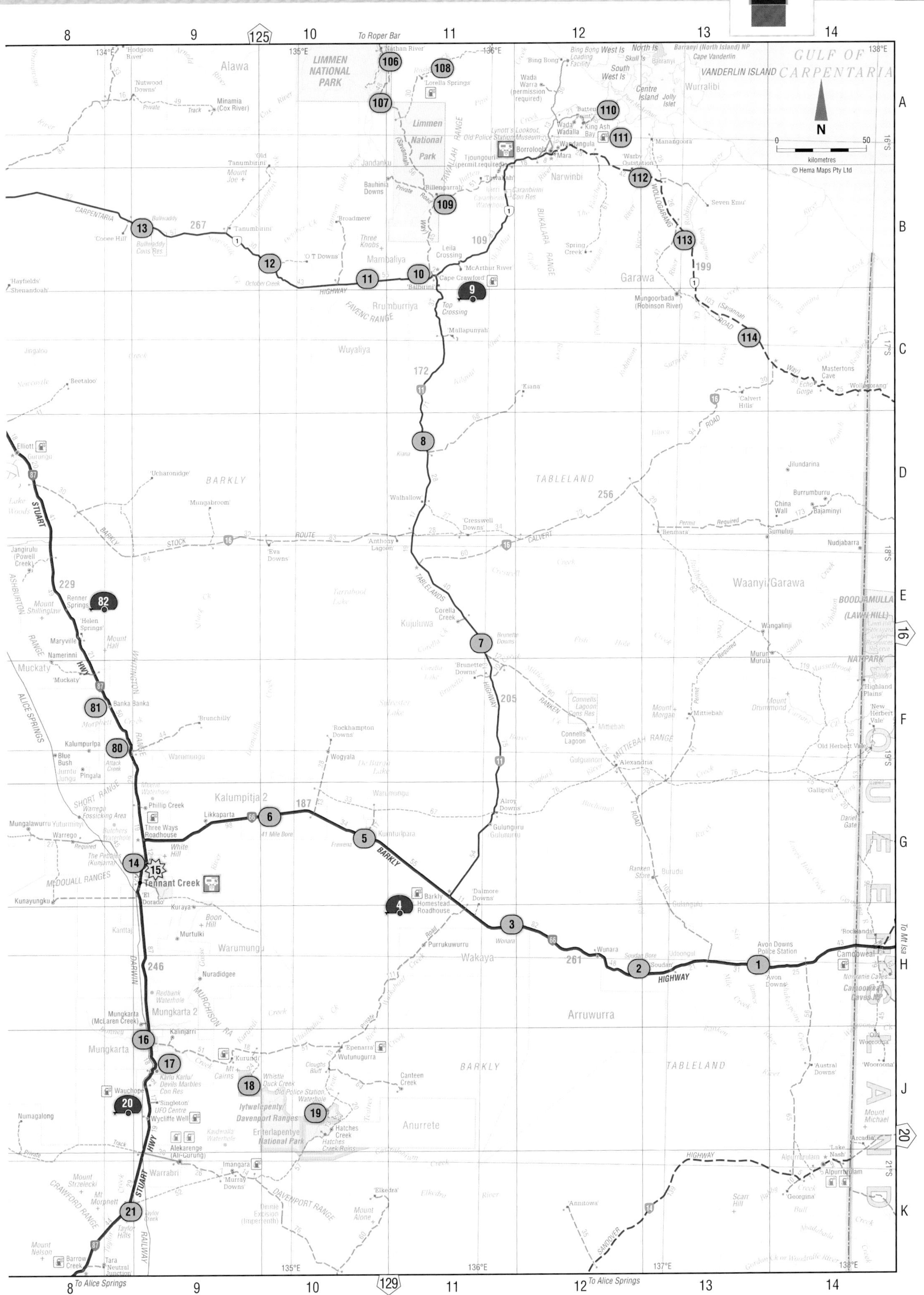
GULF OF CARPENTARIA
LIMMEN NATIONAL PARK
Limmen National Park
Alawa
Borroloola
Mambaliya
Garawa
Wuyaliya
Rrumburriya
BARKLY TABLELAND
Waanyi/Garawa
BOODJAMULLA (LAWN HILL) NAT PARK
Kujuluwa
Kalumpitja 2
Tennant Creek
Warumungu
Wakaya
Arruwurra
Mungkarta
Mungkarta 2
Anurrete
Iytwelepenty/Davenport Ranges National Park
Warrabri
Muckaty
Elliott
Renner Springs
Three Ways Roadhouse
Barkly Homestead Roadhouse
Camooweal
Avon Downs Police Station
Wauchope
Wycliffe Well
Barrow Creek
CARPENTARIA HIGHWAY
TABLELANDS HIGHWAY
BARKLY HIGHWAY
STUART HWY
SANDOVER HIGHWAY
QUEENSLAND
To Roper Bar
To Mt Isa
To Alice Springs
© Hema Maps Pty Ltd
kilometres

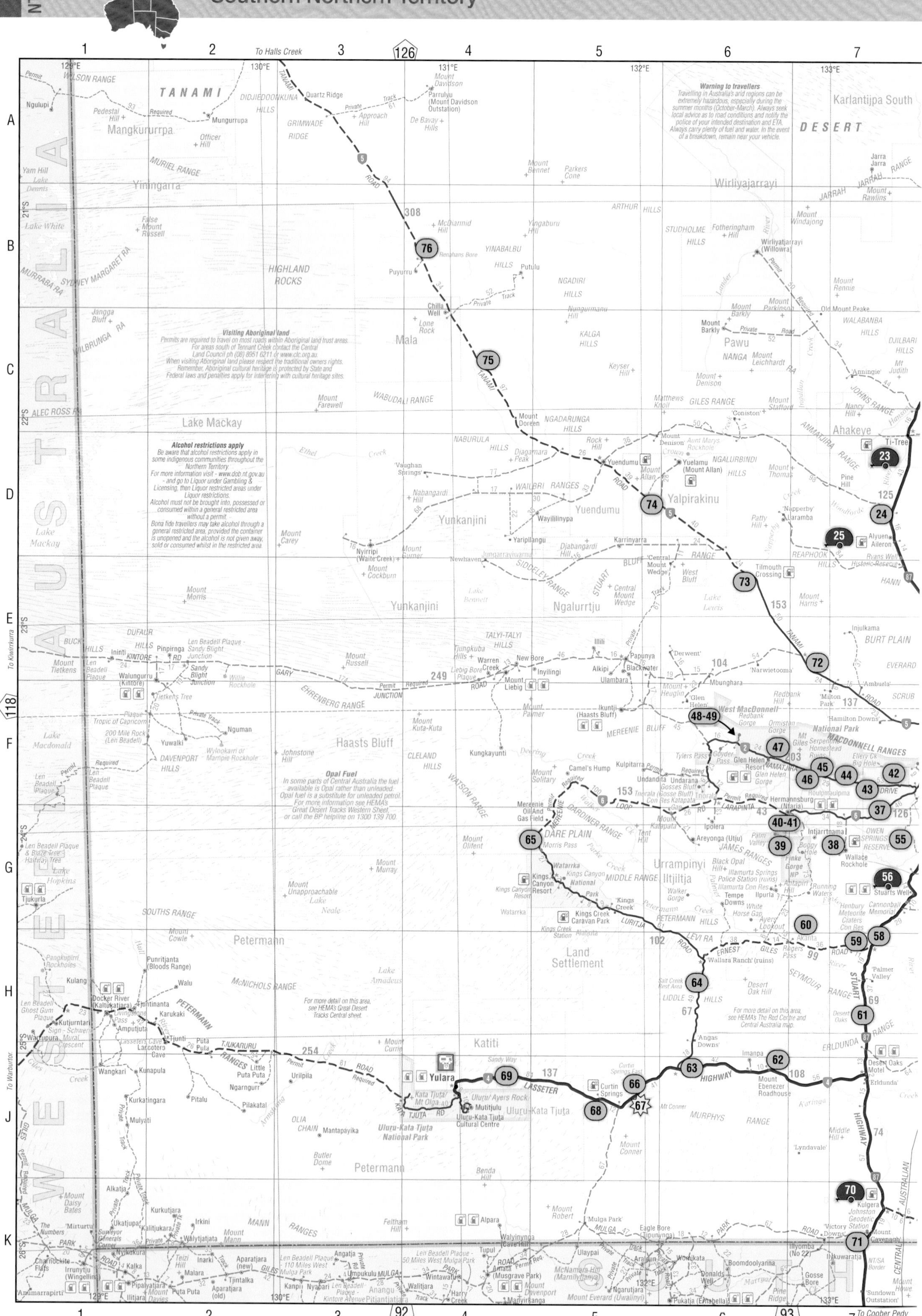
TANAMI
DESERT
Karlantijpa South
Warning to travellers
Travelling in Australia's arid regions can be extremely hazardous, especially during the summer months (October-March). Always seek local advice as to road conditions and notify the police of your intended destination and ETA. Always carry plenty of fuel and water. In the event of a breakdown, remain near your vehicle.
Visiting Aboriginal land
Permits are required to travel on most roads within Aboriginal land trust areas. For areas south of Tennant Creek contact the Central Land Council ph (08) 8951 6211 or www.clc.org.au. When visiting Aboriginal land please respect the traditional owners rights. Remember, Aboriginal land cultural heritage is protected by State and Federal laws and penalties apply for interfering with cultural heritage sites.
Alcohol restrictions apply
Be aware that alcohol restrictions apply in some indigenous communities throughout the Northern Territory. For more information visit - www.dob.nt.gov.au - and go to Liquor under Gambling & Licensing, then Liquor restricted areas under Liquor restrictions. Alcohol must not be brought into, possessed or consumed within a general restricted area without a permit. Bona fide travellers may take alcohol through a general restricted area, provided the container is unopened and the alcohol is not given away, sold or consumed whilst in the restricted area.
Opal Fuel
In some parts of Central Australia the fuel available is Opal rather than unleaded. Opal fuel is a substitute for unleaded petrol. For more information see HEMA's Great Desert Tracks Western Sheet, or call the BP helpline on 1300 139 700.
For more detail on this area, see HEMA's Great Desert Tracks Central sheet.
For more detail on this area, see HEMA's The Red Centre and Central Australia map.
Lake Mackay
Yuendumu
Haasts Bluff
Hermannsburg
West MacDonnell National Park
Kings Canyon Resort
Yulara
Uluru-Kata Tjuta National Park
Petermann
Katiti
LASSETER HIGHWAY
STUART HIGHWAY
TANAMI ROAD
To Halls Creek
To Coober Pedy
To Kiwirrkurra
To Warburton

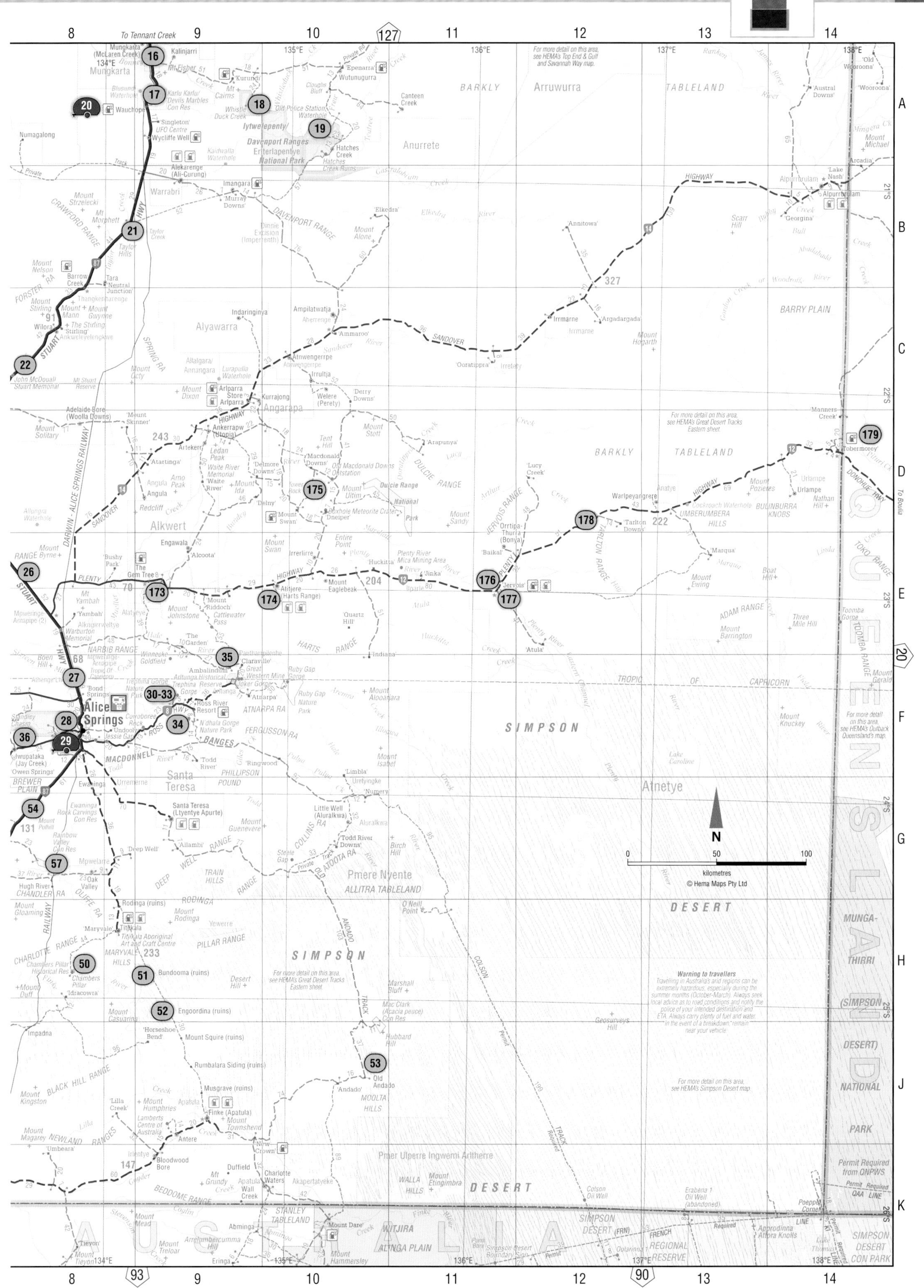
To Tennant Creek
Mungkarta (McLaren Creek)
Kalinjarri
Wauchope
Numagalong
Singleton
UFO Centre
Wycliffe Well
Alekarenge (Ali-Curung)
Warrabri
Imangara
Davenport Ranges
National Park
Old Police Station Waterhole
Hatches Creek
Canteen Creek
'Epenarra'
Wutunugurra
BARKLY
Arruwurra
TABLELAND
Anurrete
For more detail on this area, see HEMA's Top End & Gulf and Savannah Way map.
Mount Strzelecki
Mt Morphett
CRAWFORD RANGE
DAVENPORT RANGE
Dinnie Excision (Imperenth)
'Elkedra'
Mount Alone
'Annitowa'
HIGHWAY
Alpurrurulam
'Lake Nash'
'Georgina'
Scarr Hill
Mount Nelson
Barrow Creek
Taylor Hills
Tara Neutral Junction
Thangkenharenge
FORSTER RA
Mount Stirling
Mount Gwynne
The Stirling
Wilora
Anningie Mount Mann
Indaringinya
Alyawarra
Ampilatwatja
'Ammaroo'
SANDOVER
Irrmarne
'Argadargada'
Mount Hogarth
BARRY PLAIN
STUART
John McDouall Stuart Memorial
SPRING RA
Atnwengerrpe
'Ooratippra'
Irrultja
Arlparra Store
Kurrajong
Angarapa
Welere (Perety)
'Derry Downs'
'Manners Creek'
For more detail on this area, see HEMA's Great Desert Tracks Eastern sheet.
Adelaide Bore (Woolla Downs)
'Mount Skinner'
Mount Solitary
Ankerrapw (Utopia)
Artekerr
Ledan Peak
Waite River Memorial
Mount Stott
'Arapunya'
Tent Hill
'Macdonald Downs'
Old Macdonald Downs Outstation
DULCIE RANGE
Dulcie Range
National Park
BARKLY
TABLELAND
'Lucy Creek'
'Tobermorey'
DONOHUE HWY
To Boulia
Urlampe
Nathan Hill
DARWIN - ALICE SPRINGS RAILWAY
'Atartinga'
Angula
Arno Peak
'Delmore Downs'
Mount Ida
Mount Ultim
Boxhole Meteorite Crater
Dneiper
Redcliff
Alkwert
Mount Swan
JERVOIS RANGE
Orrtipa-Thurra (Bonya)
Warlpeyangrere
Anatye
Cockroach Waterhole
UMBERUMBERA HILLS
BULINBURRA KNOBS
'Tarlton Downs'
TARLTON RANGE
Engawala
'Alcoota'
Irrerlirre
Entire Point
Plenty River Mica Mining Area
'Huckitta'
'Jinka'
'Baikal'
'Marqua'
Mount Byrne
'Bushy Park'
The Gem Tree
PLENTY
Mount Eaglebeak
'Jervois'
Mount Ewing
Boat Hill
TOKO RANGE
Mt Yambah
'Yambah'
Mount Johnstone
'Mount Riddoch'
Cattlewater Pass
Atitjere (Harts Range)
'Quartz Hill'
HARTS RANGE
'Atula'
ADAM RANGE
Mount Barrington
Three Mile Hill
Toomba Gorge
TOOMBA RANGE
Mount Gerald
Mpweringe Arnapipe (2)
Warburton Memorial
NARBIB RANGE
'The Garden'
Winnecke Goldfield
Claraville
Ambalindum
Great Western Mine
Ruby Gap Gorge
'Indiana'
TROPIC OF CAPRICORN
'Bond Springs'
Alice Springs
Ross River Resort
Trephina Gorge
ATNARPA RA
Ruby Gap Nature Park
Mount Alooarrana
N'dhala Gorge Nature Park
FERGUSSON RA
SIMPSON
Mount Knuckey
For more detail on this area, see HEMA's Outback Queensland's map.
MACDONNELL RANGES
'Todd River'
Santa Teresa
PHILLIPSON POUND
'Ringwood'
Mount Isabel
Lake Caroline
Iwupataka (Jay Creek)
'Owen Springs'
BREWER PLAIN
Ewaninga
Ewaninga Rock Carvings Con Res
Santa Teresa (Ltyentye Apurte)
Mount Guenevere
'Limbla'
Urelyingke
'Numery'
Little Well (Aluralkwa)
Atnetye
N
0 50 100
kilometres
© Hema Maps Pty Ltd
Rainbow Valley Con Res
'Allambi'
Deep Well
TRAIN HILLS
COLLINS RA
'Todd River Downs'
Birch Hill
Steele Gap
ATOOTA RA
Pmere Nyente
ALLITRA TABLELAND
Hugh River
Oak Valley
CHANDLER RA
DEEP WELL
RODINGA
Mount Rodinga
O'Neill Point
DESERT
MUNGA-THIRRI (SIMPSON DESERT) NATIONAL PARK
Mount Gloaming
Rodinga (ruins)
'Maryvale'
Titjikala
Titjikala Aboriginal Art and Craft Centre
PILLAR RANGE
SIMPSON
CHARLOTTE RANGE
Chambers Pillar Historical Res
MARYVALE HILLS
Bundooma (ruins)
Desert Hill
For more detail on this area, see HEMA's Great Desert Tracks Eastern sheet
Marshall Bluff
COLSON
Warning to travellers
Travelling in Australia's arid regions can be extremely hazardous, especially during the summer months (October-March). Always seek local advice as to road conditions and notify the police of your intended destination and ETA. Always carry plenty of fuel and water. In the event of a breakdown, remain near your vehicle.
'Idracowra'
Mount Casuarina
Engoordina (ruins)
Mac Clark (Acacia peuce) Con Res
Geosurveys Hill
Impadna
'Horseshoe Bend'
Mount Squire (ruins)
Hubbard Hill
Rumbalara Siding (ruins)
Old Andado
'Andado'
MOOLTA HILLS
For more detail on this area, see HEMA's Simpson Desert map.
BLACK HILL RANGE
Mount Kingston
'Lilla Creek'
Mount Humphries
Musgrave (ruins)
Finke (Apatula)
Lamberts Centre of Australia
Mount Townshend
Antere
NEWLAND RANGES
Mount Magarey
'Umbeara'
Bloodwood Bore
New Crown
Pmer Ulperre Ingwemi Arltherre
Permit Required from QNPWS
Duffield
Mt Grundy
Charlotte Waters
Akapertayeke
Apatula Wall Creek
WALLA HILLS
Mount Etingimbra
DESERT
Colson Oil Well
Erabena 1 Oil Well (abandoned)
Poeppel Corner
BEDDOME RANGE
STANLEY TABLELAND
Mount Mead
Abminga
Mount Dare
WITJIRA
ALINGA PLAIN
SIMPSON DESERT (FRN)
FRENCH
REGIONAL RESERVE
Approdinna Attora Knolls
SIMPSON DESERT CON PARK
'Tieyon'
Mount Tieyon
Mount Treloar
Arrelumbercumma Hill
Eringa
Simpson Desert Boundary Sign
Lake Thomas
AUSTRALIA
QUEENSLAND

Northern Territory Highway Index

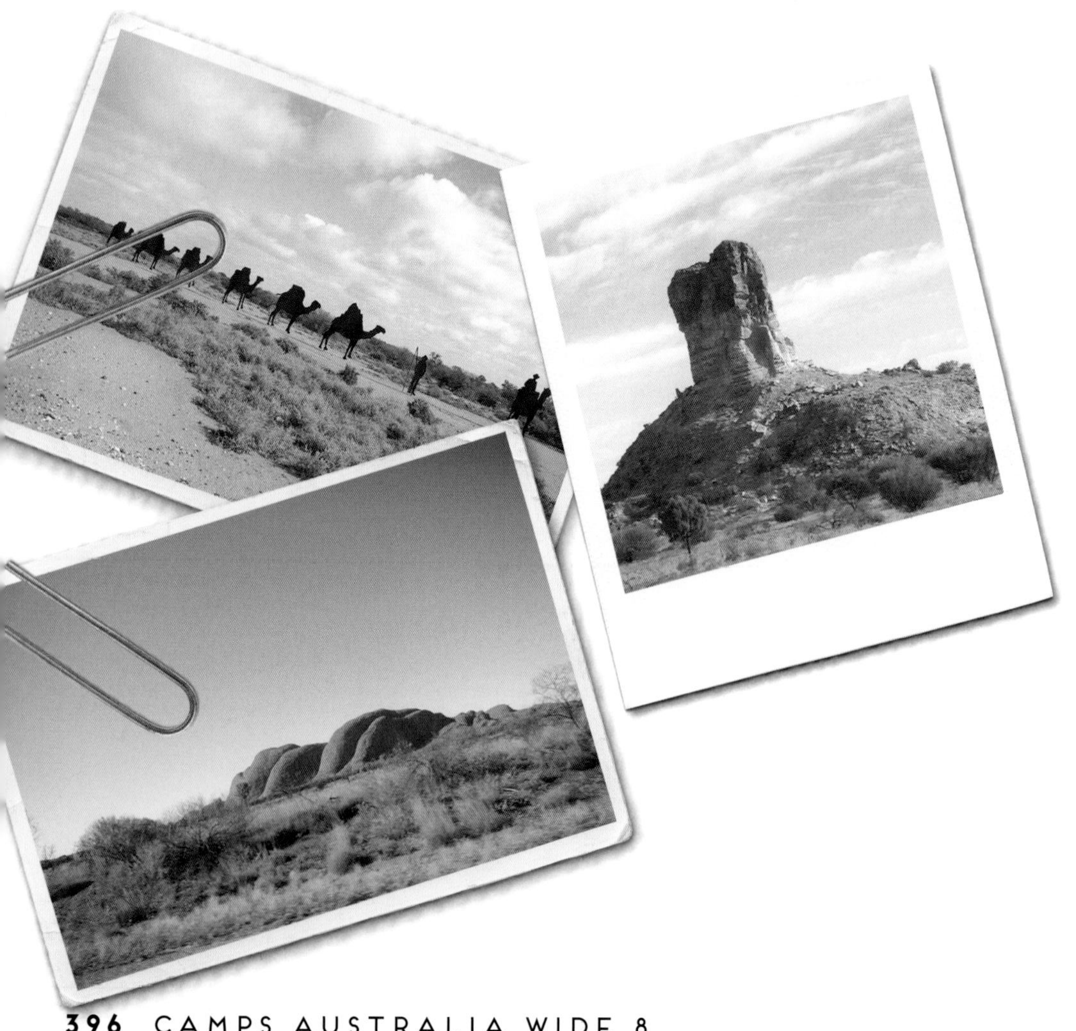

Northern Territory Alphabetic Site Index

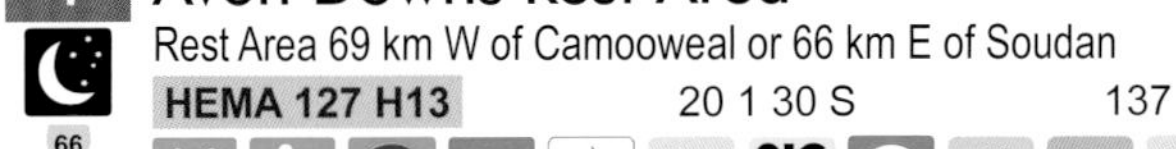

Camooweal to Three Ways

Barkly Highway

1 Avon Downs Rest Area
66

Rest Area 69 km W of Camooweal or 66 km E of Soudan

HEMA 127 H13 20 1 30 S 137 29 23 E

BIG RIG 24

2 Soudan Bore Rest Area
66

Rest Area 66 km W of Avon Downs or 32 km E of Wunara Store. 16 km W of Soudan Station

HEMA 127 H13 20 4 25 S 136 52 43 E

BIG RIG 24

3 Wonarah Bore
66

Rest Area 56 km W of Wunara Store or 43 km E of Barkly Homestead

HEMA 127 H12 19 50 33 S 136 9 23 E

BIG RIG 24

4 Barkly Homestead Wayside Inn ☎ (08) 8964 4549
66

Caravan Park 99 km W of Wunara Store or 187 km E of Three Ways

HEMA 127 G11 19 42 38 S 135 49 39 E

BIG RIG

5 Frewena Rest Area
66

Rest Area 55 km W of Barkly Homestead or 132 km E of Three Ways

HEMA 127 G10 19 25 59 S 135 24 4 E

BIG RIG 24

6 41 Mile Bore
66

Rest Area 117 km W of Barkly Homestead or 70 km E of Three Ways

HEMA 127 G10 19 19 13 S 134 51 3 E

BIG RIG 24

Barkly Homestead - Borroloola - Daly Waters

Tablelands and Carpentaria Highways

7 Brunette Downs Rest Area
11

Rest Area 145 km N of Barkly Homestead or 232 km S of Cape Crawford. At windmill

HEMA 127 E11 18 28 27 S 135 58 46 E

BIG RIG

8 Kiana Turnoff Rest Area
11

Rest Area 271 km N of Barkly Homestead or 107 km S of Cape Crawford

HEMA 127 D11 17 31 41 S 135 41 2 E

BIG RIG

9 Heartbreak Hotel Caravan Park ☎ (08) 8975 9928
1

Caravan Park at Cape Crawford. Jcn of Carpentaria Hwy & Tablelands Hwy

HEMA 127 B11 16 40 59 S 135 43 36 E

10 Little River
1

Camp Spot 10 km W of Cape Crawford or 259 km E of Daly Waters. E side of bridge, beside river

HEMA 127 B11 16 42 2 S 135 38 31 E

11 Goanna Creek Rest Area
1

Rest Area 39 km W of Cape Crawford or 230 km E of Daly Waters. 100m N of Hwy

HEMA 127 B10 16 42 16 S 135 22 3 E

12 October Creek Rest Area
1

Rest Area 99 km W of Cape Crawford or 170 km E of Daly Waters

HEMA 127 B10 16 37 54 S 134 51 31 E

13 Bullwaddy Rest Area
1

Rest Area 179 km W of Cape Crawford or 90 km E of Daly Waters

HEMA 127 B9 16 27 3 S 134 11 40 E

Three Ways to Kulgera

Stuart Highway

14 Kunjarra (The Pebbles)

Parking Area 19 km S of Three Ways or 17 km N of Tennant Creek. Turn W off Stuart Hwy 13 km S of Three Ways or 11 km N of Tennant Creek, (just N of Telegraph Station) for 4 km, then L at jcn for 2 km. 6 km dirt road. Signposted

HEMA 127 G9 19 31 57 S 134 10 49 E

BIG RIG

15 Tingkkarli (Lake Mary Ann)

Picnic Area 5 km NE of Tennant Creek. Turn E off Stuart Hwy 3 km N of Tennant Creek or 21 km S of Three Ways for 2 km

HEMA 127 G9 19 36 30 S 134 12 41 E

BIG RIG

16 Bonney Well Rest Area
87

Rest Area 87 km S of Tennant Creek or 27 km N of Wauchope

HEMA 127 J9 20 25 48 S 134 14 46 E

BIG RIG 24

17 Karlu Karlu / Devils Marbles Campground ☎ (08) 89518211
87

Camp Area 104 km S of Tennant Creek or 10 km N of Wauchope. 1 km E of Hwy

HEMA 127 J9 20 34 5 S 134 15 51 E

BIG RIG

Notes...

18 Whistleduck Creek
☎ (08) 8951 8250

Iytwellepenty / Davenport Range National Park

Camp Area 87 km S of Tennant Creek. Turn E onto Kurundi Rd for 69 km, then turn S for 25 km. Dirt road. 4WD essential

HEMA 127 J9 20 38 11 S 134 46 46 E

19 Old Police Station Waterhole
☎ (08) 8951 8250

Iytwelepenty (Davenport Ranges) National Park

Camp Area 87 km S of Tennant Creek. Turn E onto Kurundi Rd for 119 km, then turn S for 43 km. Dirt road. 4WD essential

HEMA 127 J10 20 45 15 S 135 11 12 E

20 Wauchope Hotel & Roadhouse
☎ (08) 8964 1963

87

Caravan Park at Wauchope behind Hotel

HEMA 127 J9 20 38 26 S 134 13 20 E

21 Taylor Creek

87

Rest Area 52 km S of Wycliffe Well or 40 km N of Barrow Creek. Limited space

HEMA 127 K8 21 14 52 S 134 6 53 E

BIG RIG

22 McDouall Stuart Memorial

87

Rest Area 68 km S of Barrow Creek or 21 km N of Ti-Tree

HEMA 129 C8 21 57 38 S 133 29 48 E

BIG RIG 24

23 Ti-Tree Roadhouse Caravan Park
☎ (08) 8956 9741

87

Caravan Park at Ti-Tree

HEMA 128 D7 22 7 53 S 133 25 0 E

24 Prowse Gap

87

Rest Area 45 km S of Ti-Tree or 14 km N of Aileron

HEMA 128 D7 22 31 52 S 133 19 44 E

24

25 Aileron Hotel & Roadhouse
☎ (08) 8956 9703

87

Caravan Park at Aileron

HEMA 128 D7 22 38 38 S 133 20 43 E

BIG RIG

26 Connors Well

87

Rest Area 38 km S of Aileron or 95 km N of Alice Springs

HEMA 129 E8 22 57 2 S 133 32 35 E

BIG RIG 24

27 Tropic of Capricorn Rest Area

87

Rest Area 103 km S of Aileron or 30 km N of Alice Springs

HEMA 129 F8 23 26 29 S 133 49 57 E

BIG RIG 24

28 Blatherskite Park Camping
☎ (08) 8955 5197

Camp Area in Alice Springs. Len Kittle Dr, 5 km S of city centre. Available for oversized vehicles (buses, mobile homes) & travellers with animals. Only able to take caravans if the local parks are fully booked. Prior bookings preferred

HEMA 129 F8 23 44 7 S 133 51 45 E

BIG RIG

29 Temple Bar Caravan Park
☎ (08) 8952 2533

Caravan Park at 875 Ilparpa Rd

HEMA 129 F8 23 45 37 S 133 47 13 E

BIG RIG

30 Gorge Campground
☎ (08) 8951 8250

Trephina Gorge Nature Park

Camp Area 85 km E of Alice Springs. Turn N into Trephina Gorge Nature Park 76 km E of Alice Springs for 9 km. 5 km dirt road

HEMA 129 F9 23 31 18 S 134 23 48 E

31 Panorama Campground
☎ (08) 8951 8250

Trephina Gorge Nature Park

Camp Area 85 km E of Alice Springs. Turn N onto Trephina Gorge Nature Park 76 km E of Alice Springs. 10 km to camp area. 5 km dirt road

HEMA 129 F9 23 31 20 S 134 23 49 E

32 Bluff Campground
☎ (08) 8951 8250

Trephina Gorge Nature Park

Camp Area 85 km E of Alice Springs. Turn N into Trephina Gorge Nature Park 76 km E of Alice Springs for 9 km. 5 km dirt road. No caravans or trailers, limited space

HEMA 129 F9 23 32 10 S 134 23 48 E

33 John Hayes Rockhole
☎ (08) 8951 8250

Trephina Gorge Nature Park

Camp Spot 85 km E of Alice Springs. Turn N into Trephina Gorge Nature Park 76 km E of Alice Springs. 4 km to Info Centre, turn W along rough track. High clearance 4WD only. Small area

HEMA 129 F9 23 32 24 S 134 21 18 E

34 N'Dhala Gorge Nature Park
☎ (08) 8951 8250

Camp Area 90 km E of Alice Springs. Signposted off Ross Hwy. 11 km 4WD track, 3 water crossings, first one deepest

HEMA 129 F9 23 38 19 S 134 27 47 E

35 Old Ambalindum Homestead
☎ (08) 8956 9714

Camp Area at Old Ambalindum Homestead. 135 km NE of Alice Springs on Arltunga Tourist Dr. 22 km N of Old Arltunga Hotel. Dirt road

HEMA 129 F9 23 22 53 S 134 40 48 E

36 Standley Chasm Angkerle Atwatye
☎ (08) 8956 7440

Camp Area at Standley Chasm. First night fee includes Chasm entrance, reduces for additional nights. Gates close at 1700 hrs

HEMA 129 F8 23 43 17 S 133 28 10 E

37 Mueller Creek

Rest Area 70 km SW of Alice Springs or 56 km E of Hermannsburg. 23 km SW of Namatjira Dr jcn

6

HEMA 128 G7 23 55 54 S 133 17 34 E

24

38 Wallace Rockhole Campground
☎ (08) 8956 7993

Camp Area at Wallace Rockhole

HEMA 128 G7 24 7 25 S 133 5 9 E

39 Palm Valley Campground
☎ (08) 8951 8250

Finke Gorge National Park

Camp Area 147 km W of Alice Springs via Larapinta Dr. Turn S just W of Hermannsburg. 21 km dirt road. High clearance 4WD only

HEMA 128 G6 24 3 29 S 132 44 49 E

40 Ntaria Campground
☎ (08) 8956 7480

Camp Area at Hermannsburg. Collect keys & pay at supermarket opposite

HEMA 128 G6 23 56 33 S 132 46 50 E

41 Hermannsburg Historic Precinct
☎ (08) 8956 7402

Camp Area at Hermannsburg. 800m past sports oval. Bookings & payment at precinct entrance

HEMA 128 G6 23 56 39 S 132 46 30 E

42 Hugh River Bush Camping

Camp Spots along Hugh River. Turn N off Namatjira Dr 9.4 km W of Larapinta Dr jcn, onto access track, 200m to info board & then 1 km to dispersed bush camps along river. Access track suitable for off road caravans for approx first 5 km. GPS at entrance

HEMA 128 F7 23 48 40 S 133 23 7 E

43 Point Howard Lookout

Rest Area 78 km W of Alice Springs or 53 km E of Glen Helen, on Namatjira Dr. Steep access to lookout

2

HEMA 128 F7 23 48 15 S 133 10 34 E

24

Notes...

44 Ellery Creek Big Hole
☎ (08) 8956 7799

West MacDonnell National Park

Camp Area 80 km W of Alice Springs or 43 km E of Glen Helen. 2 km N of Hwy. Small vehicles only. Dirt road. Emergency Phone

HEMA 128 F7 23 46 48 S 133 4 22 E

45 Serpentine Chalet Bush Camping
☎ (08) 8956 7799

Tjoritja - West MacDonnell National Park

Camp Area 108 km W of Alice Springs or 23 km E of Glen Helen. 600m to 2WD camping. 4WD only beyond. No caravans

HEMA 128 F7 23 45 1 S 132 54 56 E

46 Neil Hargrave Lookout

Rest Area 107 km W of Alice Springs or 24 km E of Glen Helen. 800m S off Hwy

HEMA 128 F7 23 45 2 S 132 54 19 E

BIG RIG 24

47 Ormiston Gorge
☎ (08) 8956 7799

West MacDonnell National Park

Camp Area 135 km W of Alice Springs or 12 km NE of Glen Helen. Turn N 4 km E of Glen Helen

HEMA 128 F6 23 37 57 S 132 43 29 E

48 Woodland Camping Area - Redbank Gorge
☎ (08) 8956 7799

Tjoritja - West MacDonnell National Park

Camp Area 23 km NW of Glen Helen. Turn N for 5 km off Namatjira Dr 20 km W of Glen Helen

HEMA 128 F6 23 35 25 S 132 30 46 E

49 Ridgetop Camping Area - Redbank Gorge
☎ (08) 8956 7799

Tjoritja - West MacDonnell National Park

Camp Area 24 km NW of Glen Helen. Turn N for 6 km off Namatjira Dr 20 km W of Glen Helen. Small vehicles only

HEMA 128 F6 23 34 58 S 132 30 52 E

50 Chambers Pillar Historical Reserve
☎ (08) 8951 8211

Camp Area 164 km S of Alice Springs off the Old Ghan Railway track. Turn W at Rodinga Ruins travel 57 km to site. 4WD only. Suitable for off road caravans

HEMA 129 H8 24 52 29 S 133 49 29 E

51 Bundooma Siding

Parking Area 151 km S of Alice Springs or 94 km N of Finke on the Old Ghan Railway track

HEMA 129 H9 24 53 34 S 134 15 34 E

52 Engoordina Ruins

Parking Area 173 km S of Alice Springs or 72 km N of Finke on the Old Ghan Railway track

HEMA 129 H9 25 4 10 S 134 21 51 E

53 Old Andado Homestead Camping

☎ (08) 8956 0812

Camp Area at Old Andado Station, 123 km E of Finke. 4WD only

HEMA 129 J10 25 22 49 S 135 26 30 E

54 Mt Polhill Rest Area

87

Rest Area 68 km S of Alice Springs or 132 km N of Erldunda. 32 km N of Stuarts Well. Small area, limited space

HEMA 129 G8 24 6 30 S 133 33 28 E

24

55 Redbank Waterhole

Camp Spot 64 km S Alice Springs or 25 km N of Stuarts Well. Access off Stuart Hwy, signposted Owen Springs Reserve. 5.2 km to waterhole, follow signs. GPS at entrance. Suitable off road caravans & campervans

HEMA 128 G7 24 9 9 S 133 30 40 E

56 Stuarts Well Roadhouse

☎ (08) 8956 0808

Caravan Park 97 km S of Alice Springs or 104 km N of Erldunda

HEMA 128 G7 24 20 26 S 133 27 31 E

BIG RIG

57 Rainbow Valley Conservation Reserve

☎ (08) 8951 8250

Camp Area. Turn off 75 km S of Alice Springs or 14 km N of Stuarts Well. 22 km dirt road, sandy patches. 4WD recommended

HEMA 129 G8 24 19 51 S 133 37 57 E

58 Finke River Rest Area

87

Rest Area 126 km S of Alice Springs or 75 km N of Erldunda. Beside river

HEMA 128 H7 24 33 5 S 133 14 20 E

24

59 Henbury Meteorite Craters

☎ (08) 8951 8250

Camp Area 147 km S of Alice Springs. Turn W off Stuart Hwy 131 km S of Alice Springs or 70 km N of Erldunda onto Ernest Giles Rd for 11 km, then N for 5 km. Dirt road

HEMA 128 H7 24 34 16 S 133 8 35 E

60 Akanta Bush Camping

Camp Area in Akanta settlement. Turn N off Ernest Giles Rd 48 km W of Stuart Hwy or 52 E of Luritja Rd jcn, just E of Palmer River crossing. 7.5 km to camp area, track to L 500m before homestead

HEMA 128 H7 24 31 7 S 132 48 34 E

61 Desert Oaks Rest Area

87

Rest Area 169 km S of Alice Springs or 32 km N of Erldunda

HEMA 128 H7 24 54 18 S 133 11 46 E

BIG RIG 24

62 Mt Ebenezer Roadhouse

☎ (08) 8956 2904

Camp Area at Mt Ebenezer Roadhouse

HEMA 128 J6 25 10 44 S 132 40 37 E

63 Kernot Range Rest Area

4

Rest Area 101 km W of Erldunda or 59 km E of Curtin Springs. 7 km E of Luritja Rd jcn

HEMA 128 J6 25 10 37 S 132 15 6 E

BIG RIG 24

64 Salt Creek Rest Area

3

Rest Area 48 km N of Lasseter Hwy. On Luritja Rd, 20 km S of Ernest Giles Rd jcn

HEMA 128 H6 24 46 21 S 132 18 24 E

BIG RIG 24

65 Jump Up Lookout Rest Area

Rest Area 27 km NW of Kings Canyon. Permit is required to travel on the Larapinta Dr - Meenie Loop Rd, permits available at the Servo at Kings Canyon Resort

HEMA 128 G5 24 3 38 S 131 24 31 E

24

66 Curtin Springs East Rest Area

4

Rest Area 136 km W of Erldunda or 27 km E of Curtin Springs. 25 km W of Luritja Rd jcn

HEMA 128 J5 25 15 57 S 131 58 43 E

BIG RIG 24

67 Mt Connor Lookout

4

Rest Area 142 km W of Erldunda or 21 km E of Curtin Springs. 31 km W of Luritja Rd jcn

HEMA 128 J5 25 18 21 S 131 56 23 E

BIG RIG

68 Curtin Springs Wayside Inn & Cattle Station

☎ (08) 8956 2906

4

Camp Area 163 km W of Erldunda or 84 km E of Yulara. Fee for showers

HEMA 128 J5 25 18 52 S 131 45 27 E

BIG RIG

69 Sandy Way Rest Area

4

Rest Area 56 km W of Curtin Springs or 28 km E of Yulara. Tracks over dune to camp spots

HEMA 128 J4 25 13 13 S 131 13 47 E

24

70 Kulgera Roadhouse & Caravan Park

☎ (08) 8956 0973

87

Caravan Park at Kulgera Roadhouse

HEMA 128 K7 25 50 22 S 133 18 1 E

BIG RIG

71 NT-SA Border

87

Rest Area 159 km N of Marla or 19 km S of Kulgera

HEMA 128 K7 | 25 59 54 S | 133 11 47 E

BIG RIG

Alice Springs to Halls Creek - Tanami Track

Tanami Road

This road is seasonal and more suitable to 4WD vehicles, camper trailers and off road caravans. Road conditions phone 1800 246 199 (NT) or 1800 013 314 (WA)

72 Charley Creek Rest Area

Rest Area 123 km NW of Alice Springs or 62 km SE of Tilmouth Well Roadhouse

HEMA 128 E7 | 23 16 15 S | 132 55 6 E

BIG RIG

73 Tilmouth Well Roadhouse

☎ (08) 8956 8777

Camp Area at Tilmouth Well Roadhouse. Limited powered sites

HEMA 128 E6 | 22 48 35 S | 132 35 54 E

BIG RIG

74 Yuelamu Roadside Stop

Rest Area S side of road opposite turnoff to Yuelamu Community

HEMA 128 D5 | 22 28 0 S | 132 6 9 E

BIG RIG

75 Floodout Creek

Rest Area 69 km SE of Renehans Bore or 194 km NW of Tilmouth Well Roadhouse

HEMA 128 C4 | 21 48 22 S | 131 10 38 E

BIG RIG

76 Renahans Bore Rest Area

Rest Area 152 km SE of Rabbit Flat or 263 km NW of Tilmouth Well Roadhouse

HEMA 128 B4 | 21 16 39 S | 130 50 57 E

BIG RIG

77 Border Rest Area

Rest Area on N.T. side of border N side of road

HEMA 126 H1 | 19 53 50 S | 129 1 22 E

78 Sturt Creek

Camp Spots on creek bank 46 km SE of Wolfe Creek Crater turnoff or 176 km S of Halls Creek

HEMA 117 J12 | 19 33 36 S | 127 41 37 E

Notes...

79 Wolfe Creek Camp

☎ (08) 9168 4200

Wolfe Creek Crater National Park

Camp Area. Turnoff 130 km SE of Halls Creek. 20 km to campsite from Tanami Rd

HEMA 117 J12 | 19 10 35 S | 127 47 10 E

Three Ways to Mataranka

Stuart Highway

80 Attack Creek (Stuart Monument)

87

Rest Area 47 km N of Three Ways or 87 km S of Renner Springs

HEMA 127 F8 | 19 1 24 S | 134 8 29 E

BIG RIG 24

81 Banka Banka Station

☎ (08) 8964 4511

87

Camp Area at Banka Banka Station. 74 km N of Three Ways or 60 km S of Renner Springs

HEMA 127 F8 | 18 47 32 S | 134 1 50 E

BIG RIG

82 Renner Springs Desert Inn

☎ (08) 8964 4505

87

Caravan Park at Renner Springs. At roadhouse

HEMA 127 E8 | 18 19 8 S | 133 47 43 E

BIG RIG

83 Longreach Waterhole

Camp Area 12 km W of Elliott. Turn W 20m N of first cattle grid Northern side of Elliott. 11 km of sandy track (rough patches) to camping area

HEMA 126 D7 | 17 36 58 S | 133 28 26 E

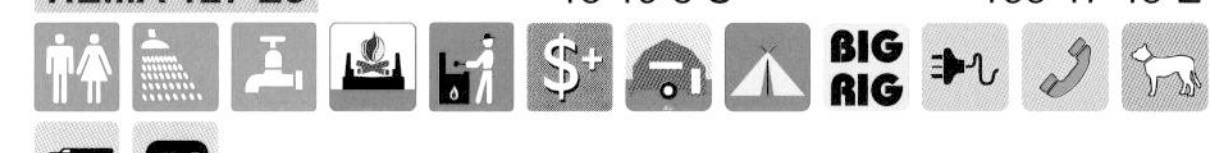

84 Newcastle Waters Rest Area

87

Rest Area 25 km N of Elliott or 77 km S of Dunmarra. Just S of Newcastle Waters turnoff. Limited space

HEMA 126 D7 | 17 22 31 S | 133 26 22 E

BIG RIG

85 Dunmarra Wayside Inn

☎ (08) 8975 9922

87

Caravan Park at Dunmarra

HEMA 126 B7 | 16 40 47 S | 133 24 45 E

BIG RIG

86 Top Springs Roadhouse Caravan Park

☎ (08) 8975 0767

Caravan Park at Top Springs. Buntine & Buchanan Hwy intersection. Limited powered sites

HEMA 126 B5 | 16 32 36 S | 131 47 49 E

BIG RIG

87 Kalkarindji (Wave Hill)

☎ (08) 8975 0788

Camp Area at Kalkarindji. Next to general store

HEMA 126 D4 | 17 26 49 S | 130 50 3 E

NORTHERN TERRITORY

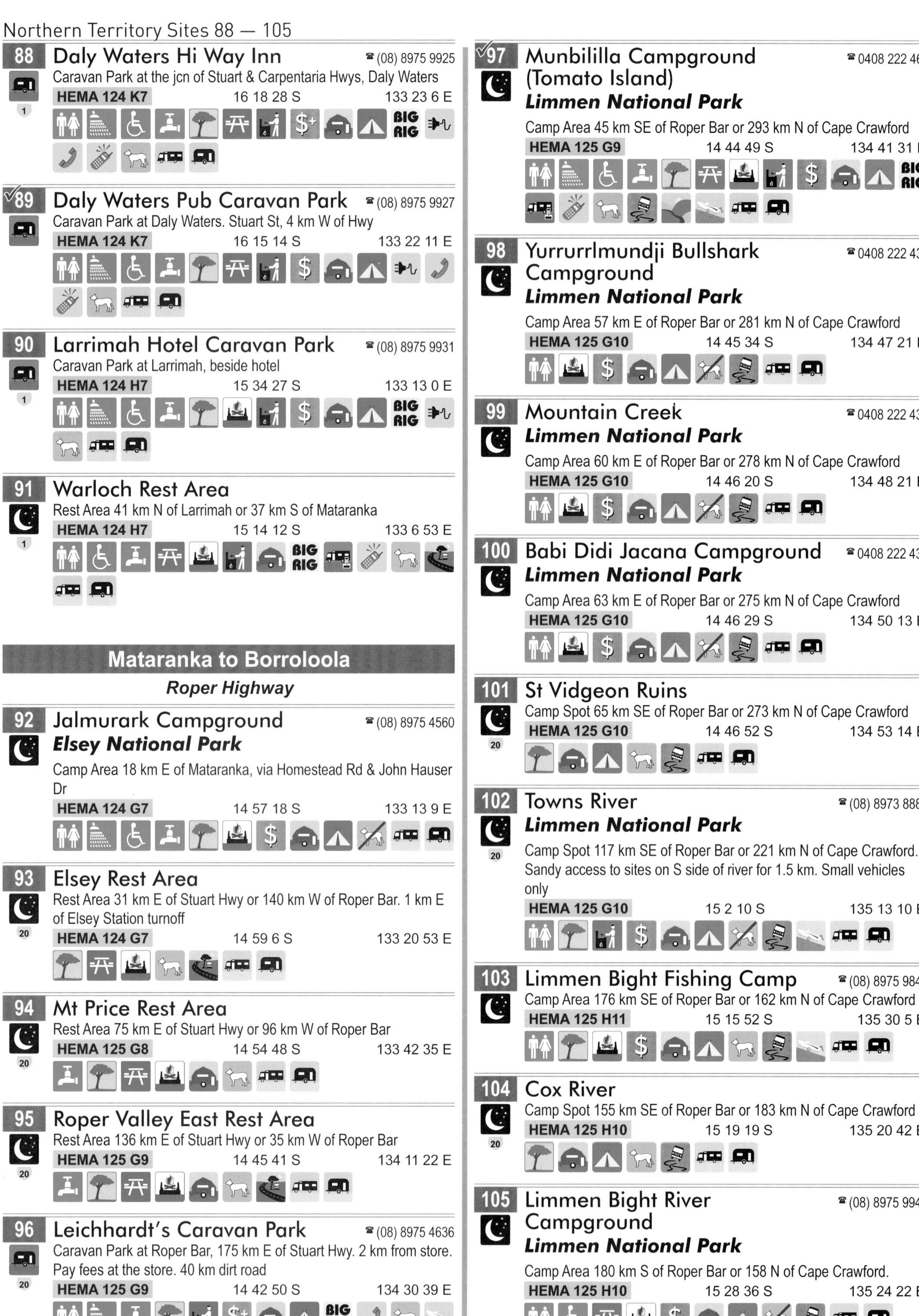

88 Daly Waters Hi Way Inn
☎ (08) 8975 9925

Caravan Park at the jcn of Stuart & Carpentaria Hwys, Daly Waters

HEMA 124 K7 16 18 28 S 133 23 6 E

1

BIG RIG

89 Daly Waters Pub Caravan Park
☎ (08) 8975 9927

Caravan Park at Daly Waters. Stuart St, 4 km W of Hwy

HEMA 124 K7 16 15 14 S 133 22 11 E

90 Larrimah Hotel Caravan Park
☎ (08) 8975 9931

Caravan Park at Larrimah, beside hotel

HEMA 124 H7 15 34 27 S 133 13 0 E

1

BIG RIG

91 Warloch Rest Area

Rest Area 41 km N of Larrimah or 37 km S of Mataranka

HEMA 124 H7 15 14 12 S 133 6 53 E

1

BIG RIG

Mataranka to Borroloola

Roper Highway

92 Jalmurark Campground
☎ (08) 8975 4560

Elsey National Park

Camp Area 18 km E of Mataranka, via Homestead Rd & John Hauser Dr

HEMA 124 G7 14 57 18 S 133 13 9 E

93 Elsey Rest Area

Rest Area 31 km E of Stuart Hwy or 140 km W of Roper Bar. 1 km E of Elsey Station turnoff

HEMA 124 G7 14 59 6 S 133 20 53 E

20

94 Mt Price Rest Area

Rest Area 75 km E of Stuart Hwy or 96 km W of Roper Bar

HEMA 125 G8 14 54 48 S 133 42 35 E

20

95 Roper Valley East Rest Area

Rest Area 136 km E of Stuart Hwy or 35 km W of Roper Bar

HEMA 125 G9 14 45 41 S 134 11 22 E

20

96 Leichhardt's Caravan Park
☎ (08) 8975 4636

Caravan Park at Roper Bar, 175 km E of Stuart Hwy. 2 km from store. Pay fees at the store. 40 km dirt road

HEMA 125 G9 14 42 50 S 134 30 39 E

20

BIG RIG

97 Munbililla Campground (Tomato Island)
☎ 0408 222 463

Limmen National Park

Camp Area 45 km SE of Roper Bar or 293 km N of Cape Crawford

HEMA 125 G9 14 44 49 S 134 41 31 E

BIG RIG

98 Yurrurrlmundji Bullshark Campground
☎ 0408 222 436

Limmen National Park

Camp Area 57 km E of Roper Bar or 281 km N of Cape Crawford

HEMA 125 G10 14 45 34 S 134 47 21 E

99 Mountain Creek
☎ 0408 222 436

Limmen National Park

Camp Area 60 km E of Roper Bar or 278 km N of Cape Crawford

HEMA 125 G10 14 46 20 S 134 48 21 E

100 Babi Didi Jacana Campground
☎ 0408 222 436

Limmen National Park

Camp Area 63 km E of Roper Bar or 275 km N of Cape Crawford

HEMA 125 G10 14 46 29 S 134 50 13 E

101 St Vidgeon Ruins

Camp Spot 65 km SE of Roper Bar or 273 km N of Cape Crawford

HEMA 125 G10 14 46 52 S 134 53 14 E

20

102 Towns River
☎ (08) 8973 8888

Limmen National Park

Camp Spot 117 km SE of Roper Bar or 221 km N of Cape Crawford. Sandy access to sites on S side of river for 1.5 km. Small vehicles only

HEMA 125 G10 15 2 10 S 135 13 10 E

20

103 Limmen Bight Fishing Camp
☎ (08) 8975 9844

Camp Area 176 km SE of Roper Bar or 162 km N of Cape Crawford

HEMA 125 H11 15 15 52 S 135 30 5 E

104 Cox River

Camp Spot 155 km SE of Roper Bar or 183 km N of Cape Crawford

HEMA 125 H10 15 19 19 S 135 20 42 E

20

105 Limmen Bight River Campground
☎ (08) 8975 9940

Limmen National Park

Camp Area 180 km S of Roper Bar or 158 N of Cape Crawford.

HEMA 125 H10 15 28 36 S 135 24 22 E

106 **Butterfly Falls** ☎ (08) 8975 9940
Limmen National Park
Camp Area 199 km S of Roper Bar or 139 km N of Cape Crawford. Turn E. Signposted Butterfly Springs, camp 2 km along dirt track. Small vehicles only
HEMA 125 J11 15 37 36 S 135 27 36 E

107 **Southern Lost City** ☎ (08) 8975 9940
Limmen National Park
20
Camp Spot 224 km S of Roper Bar or 114 km N of Cape Crawford. Turn N at sign follow track for 4 km. 4WD recommended
HEMA 125 J11 15 48 31 S 135 27 21 E

108 **Lorella Springs Wilderness Park** ☎ (08) 8975 9917
Camp Area 265 km SE of Roper Bar or 165 km NW of Borroloola. Turn E off Savannah Way 236 km SE of Roper Bar or 101 km N of Cape Crawford, 30 km to entrance
HEMA 125 J11 15 43 15 S 135 38 26 E

109 **Batten Creek**
Rest Area 289 km SE of Roper Bar or 49 km N of Cape Crawford. 4 km N of Billengarrah intersection
20
HEMA 125 K11 16 18 5 S 135 42 26 E

110 **Batten Point**
Camp Spot at Batten Point, 5 km from King Ash Bay, via Batten Rd. Pay fees to King Ash Bay caretaker
HEMA 125 J12 15 53 44 S 136 31 53 E
BIG RIG

111 **King Ash Bay Fishing Club** ☎ (08) 8975 9800
Camp Area 42 km NE of Borroloola at King Ash Bay. Turn SE off Bing Bong Rd after 21 km to Batten Point. Beside McArthur River. 28 km dirt road
HEMA 127 A12 15 56 8 S 136 28 44 E
BIG RIG

112 **Wearyan River**
Camp Spot 55 km SE of Borroloola or 223 km NW of Wollogorang. Tracks along both sides of river
HEMA 125 J13 16 10 1 S 136 45 22 E

113 **Robinson River Crossing**
Camp Spot 105 km SE of Borroloola or 149 km NW of Wollogorang. Tracks 100m on the NW side of Robinson River crossing
HEMA 125 K13 16 28 10 S 137 2 52 E

114 **Calvert Creek**
Camp Spot 177 km E of Borroloola or 85 km W of QLD border. Tracks on both sides of the river
HEMA 127 C13 16 56 1 S 137 21 29 E

Mataranka to Darwin

Stuart Highway

115 **King Rest Area**
Rest Area 59 km N of Mataranka or 46 km S of Katherine. 4 km S of King River bridge
1
HEMA 123 K6 14 38 38 S 132 37 56 E
BIG RIG 24

116 **North Bank Park** ☎ (08) 8972 1430
Caravan Park at Katherine. Lot 478 Arndt Rd
HEMA 123 J5 14 28 19 S 132 15 9 E

117 **Leliyn (Edith Falls) Campground** ☎ (08) 8975 4869
Nitmiluk National Park
Camp Area 61 km N of Katherine. Turn E 42 km N of Katherine or 49 km S of Pine Creek
HEMA 123 H5 14 10 46 S 132 11 10 E

118 **Copperfield Dam**
Picnic Area 5 km S of Pine Creek. Turn W off Stuart Hwy 3 km S of Pine Creek. 2 km dirt road
HEMA 123 G4 13 50 42 S 131 49 3 E
BIG RIG

119 **Umbrawarra Gorge** ☎ (08) 8976 0282
Camp Area 24 km SW of Pine Creek. Turn W off Stuart Hwy 3 km S of Pine Creek. 21 km dirt road
HEMA 123 H4 13 57 56 S 131 41 52 E

120 **Pine Creek Service Station Caravan Park** ☎ (08) 8976 1217
Caravan Park at Pine Creek. Moule St
1
HEMA 123 G4 13 49 29 S 131 50 6 E

121 **Emerald Springs Roadhouse Caravan Park** ☎ (08) 8976 1169
Caravan Park at Emerald Springs. 32 km N of Pine Creek or 76 km S of Adelaide River
1
HEMA 123 G3 13 37 53 S 131 37 47 E
BIG RIG

Notes...

NORTHERN TERRITORY

122 Tjuwaliyn (Douglas) Hot Springs Park
(08) 8976 0282

Camp Area 43 km SW of Hayes Creek. Turn W off Stuart Hwy 6 km NW of Hayes Creek or 62 km SE of Adelaide River onto Dorat Rd for 5 km, then SW onto Oolloo Rd for 25 km, then SE for 7 km of dirt road

HEMA 123 G3 13 45 53 S 131 26 22 E

BIG RIG

123 Douglas Daly River Esplanade Conservation Area
(08) 8978 2479

Camp Spot 2 km S of Douglas Daly Tourist Park. Various camp spots along Daly River. Must check in at Tourist Park office for site allocation. Small vehicles only. Fee includes use of toilet & shower facilities in the tourist park

HEMA 123 G3 13 47 14 S 131 21 9 E

124 Oolloo Crossing

Camp Spot 37 km S of Douglas Daly Tourist Park on Oolloo Rd. Various camp spots on Daly River bank. Small vehicles only. 28 km dirt road

HEMA 123 H2 14 4 9 S 131 15 2 E

125 Bridge Creek

Rest Area 24 km N of Hayes Creek or 33 km S of Adelaide River

HEMA 123 F2 13 26 11 S 131 18 48 E

1

BIG RIG 24

126 Robin Falls

Rest Area 59 km NW of Hayes Creek or 14 km S of Adelaide River, via Dorat Rd. 500m W of road. Dirt road. Small vehicles only, limited space

HEMA 123 F2 13 21 10 S 131 8 1 E

127 Lee & Jenny's Bushcamp
0427 030 556

Camp Area at Daly River. From Adelaide River take Dorat Rd for 32 km, turn W into Daly River Rd for 78 km, then turn W into Woolianna Rd (Cemetery Rd). 12 km to entrance

HEMA 124 E3 13 39 53 S 130 39 25 E

BIG RIG

128 Adelaide River Show Society Caravan Park
(08) 8976 7032

Caravan Park 2 km SW of Adelaide River. Dorat Rd

HEMA 123 E2 13 14 49 S 131 6 36 E

BIG RIG

129 Mount Bundy Station
(08) 8976 7009

Camp Area at Mount Bundy Station. 5.5 km NW of Adelaide River. Turn NW on to Haynes Rd 1 km S of Adelaide River

HEMA 123 E2 13 13 39 S 131 8 2 E

BIG RIG

130 Coomalie Creek RV Park
(08) 8976 0501

Camp Area at Coomalie Creek. 25 km N of Adelaide River or 88 km S of Darwin

1

HEMA 123 E2 13 1 9 S 131 7 20 E

BIG RIG

131 Pandanus on Litchfield
(08) 8976 0242

Caravan Park 9 km W of Batchelor via Rum Jungle Rd

HEMA 123 E1 13 1 35 S 130 59 17 E

BIG RIG

132 Buley Rockhole Campground
(08) 8976 0282

Litchfield National Park

Camp Area 43 km W of Batchelor. Small vehicles only, no caravans

HEMA 123 E1 13 6 46 S 130 47 10 E

133 Florence Falls Campground
(08) 8976 0282

Litchfield National Park

Camp Area 43 km W of Batchelor. Small vehicles only, no caravans

HEMA 123 E1 13 5 49 S 130 47 4 E

134 Wangi Falls Campground
(08) 8976 0282

Litchfield National Park

Camp Area 66 km SW of Batchelor

HEMA 124 D3 13 9 44 S 130 40 50 E

135 Tjaynera Falls Campground
(08) 8976 0282

Litchfield National Park

Camp Area 57 km W of Batchelor or 7 km S of Wangi Falls. 9 km dirt road. 4WD only

HEMA 123 E1 13 15 0 S 130 44 41 E

136 Sand Palms Roadhouse & Tavern
(08) 8978 2822

Camp Area at Bynoe. Via Cox Peninsular Rd, Fog Bay Rd to Bynoe Haven Rd. 1.5 km dirt road

HEMA 124 D3 12 48 29 S 130 37 1 E

137 Dundee Downs Bush Resort
(08) 8978 2900

Camp Area 90 km SW of Darwin. Lot 3040 Barramundi Dr off Fog Bay Rd. Bookings essential

HEMA 124 D3 12 46 15 S 130 29 37 E

BIG RIG

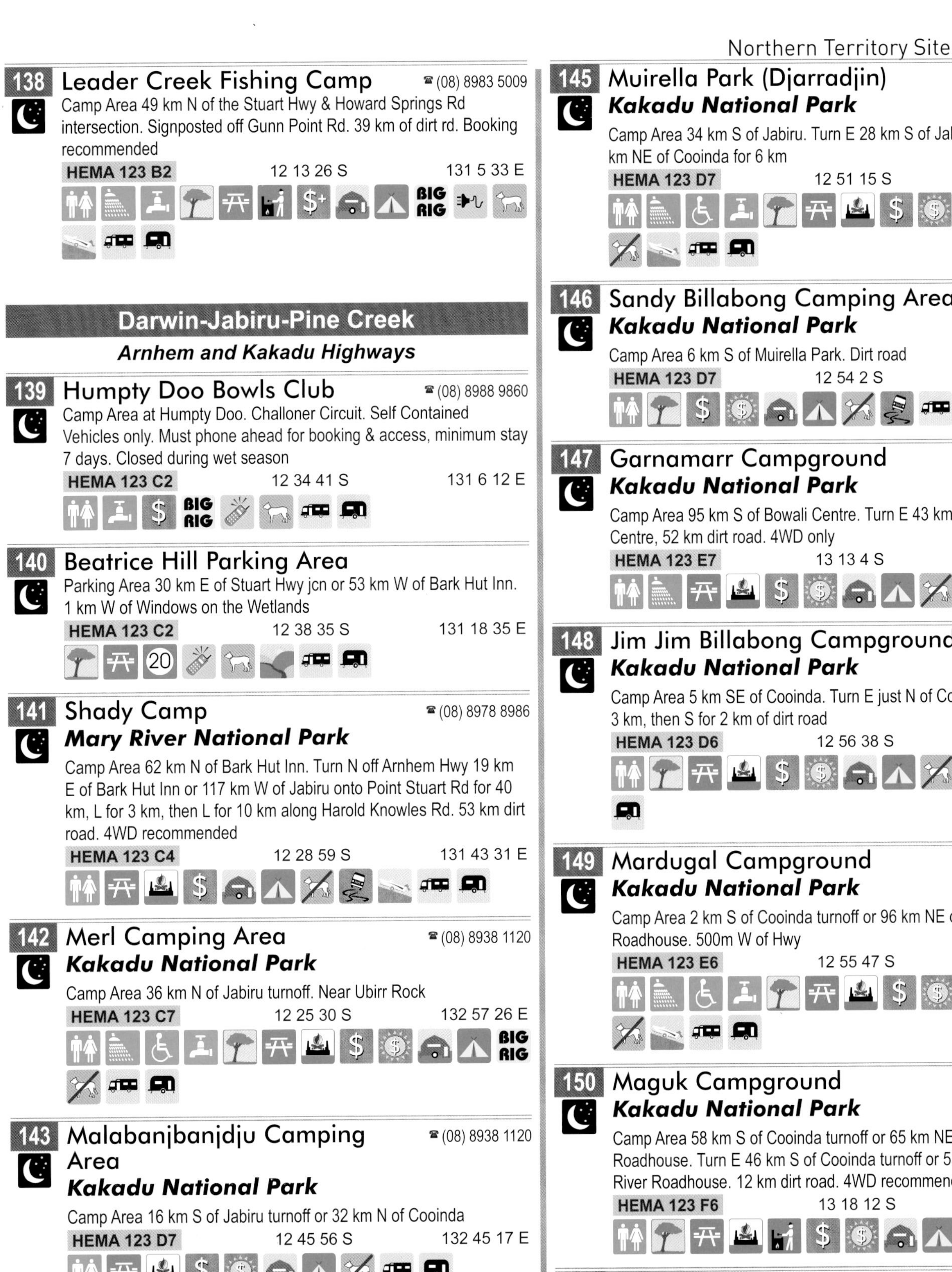

138 **Leader Creek Fishing Camp** ☎ (08) 8983 5009

Camp Area 49 km N of the Stuart Hwy & Howard Springs Rd intersection. Signposted off Gunn Point Rd. 39 km of dirt rd. Booking recommended

HEMA 123 B2 12 13 26 S 131 5 33 E

BIG RIG

Darwin-Jabiru-Pine Creek

Arnhem and Kakadu Highways

139 **Humpty Doo Bowls Club** ☎ (08) 8988 9860

Camp Area at Humpty Doo. Challoner Circuit. Self Contained Vehicles only. Must phone ahead for booking & access, minimum stay 7 days. Closed during wet season

HEMA 123 C2 12 34 41 S 131 6 12 E

BIG RIG

140 **Beatrice Hill Parking Area**

Parking Area 30 km E of Stuart Hwy jcn or 53 km W of Bark Hut Inn. 1 km W of Windows on the Wetlands

HEMA 123 C2 12 38 35 S 131 18 35 E

20

141 **Shady Camp** ☎ (08) 8978 8986

Mary River National Park

Camp Area 62 km N of Bark Hut Inn. Turn N off Arnhem Hwy 19 km E of Bark Hut Inn or 117 km W of Jabiru onto Point Stuart Rd for 40 km, L for 3 km, then L for 10 km along Harold Knowles Rd. 53 km dirt road. 4WD recommended

HEMA 123 C4 12 28 59 S 131 43 31 E

142 **Merl Camping Area** ☎ (08) 8938 1120

Kakadu National Park

Camp Area 36 km N of Jabiru turnoff. Near Ubirr Rock

HEMA 123 C7 12 25 30 S 132 57 26 E

BIG RIG

143 **Malabanjbanjdju Camping Area** ☎ (08) 8938 1120

Kakadu National Park

Camp Area 16 km S of Jabiru turnoff or 32 km N of Cooinda

HEMA 123 D7 12 45 56 S 132 45 17 E

144 **Burdulba Camping Area** ☎ (08) 8938 1120

Kakadu National Park

Camp Area 17 km S of Jabiru turnoff or 31 km N of Cooinda

HEMA 123 D7 12 46 18 S 132 44 53 E

145 **Muirella Park (Djarradjin)** ☎ (08) 8938 1120

Kakadu National Park

Camp Area 34 km S of Jabiru. Turn E 28 km S of Jabiru turnoff or 20 km NE of Cooinda for 6 km

HEMA 123 D7 12 51 15 S 132 45 18 E

BIG RIG

146 **Sandy Billabong Camping Area** ☎ (08) 8938 1120

Kakadu National Park

Camp Area 6 km S of Muirella Park. Dirt road

HEMA 123 D7 12 54 2 S 132 46 25 E

147 **Garnamarr Campground** ☎ (08) 8938 1120

Kakadu National Park

Camp Area 95 km S of Bowali Centre. Turn E 43 km S of Bowali Centre, 52 km dirt road. 4WD only

HEMA 123 E7 13 13 4 S 132 48 58 E

148 **Jim Jim Billabong Campground** ☎ (08) 8938 1120

Kakadu National Park

Camp Area 5 km SE of Cooinda. Turn E just N of Cooinda turnoff for 3 km, then S for 2 km of dirt road

HEMA 123 D6 12 56 38 S 132 33 11 E

149 **Mardugal Campground** ☎ (08) 8938 1120

Kakadu National Park

Camp Area 2 km S of Cooinda turnoff or 96 km NE of Mary River Roadhouse. 500m W of Hwy

HEMA 123 E6 12 55 47 S 132 32 16 E

BIG RIG

150 **Maguk Campground** ☎ (08) 8938 1120

Kakadu National Park

Camp Area 58 km S of Cooinda turnoff or 65 km NE of Mary River Roadhouse. Turn E 46 km S of Cooinda turnoff or 53 km NE of Mary River Roadhouse. 12 km dirt road. 4WD recommended

HEMA 123 F6 13 18 12 S 132 26 0 E

151 **Gungural Campground** ☎ (08) 8938 1120

Kakadu National Park

Camp Area 51 km S of Cooinda turnoff or 47 km NE of Mary River Roadhouse

HEMA 123 F6 13 17 25 S 132 20 8 E

Notes...

152 Gunlom

☎ (08) 8938 1120

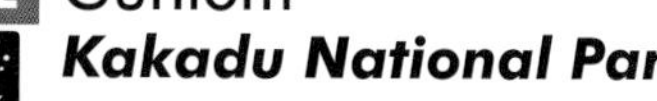

Kakadu National Park

Camp Area 124 km S of Cooinda turnoff or 48 km NE of Mary River Roadhouse. Turn E 87 km S of Cooinda turnoff or 11 km NE of Mary River Roadhouse, onto Gunlom Rd. 36 km dirt road

HEMA 123 F6 13 26 5 S 132 24 53 E

153 Kambolgie Campground

☎ (08) 8938 1120

Kakadu National Park

Camp Area 100 km S of Cooinda turnoff or 24 km NE of Mary River Roadhouse. Turn E 87 km S of Cooinda turnoff or 11 km NE of Mary River Roadhouse onto Gunlom Rd. 10 km dirt road

HEMA 123 F6 13 30 13 S 132 23 37 E

154 Goymarr (Mary River Roadhouse)

☎ (08) 8975 4564

Camp Area at Mary River Roadhouse 200m S of Kakadu National Park S entrance

HEMA 123 G5 13 36 20 S 132 13 10 E

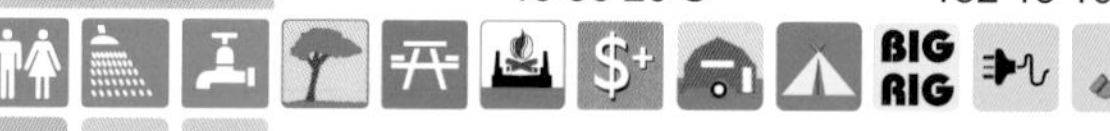

155 Harriet Creek

21

Rest Area 32 km SW of Mary River Roadhouse or 26 km NE of Pine Creek. 500m E of Hwy

HEMA 123 G5 13 40 42 S 131 59 6 E

156 Pussy Cat Flats

☎ (08) 8976 1355

21

Camp Area 56 km SW of Mary River Roadhouse or 2 km E of Pine Creek on Kakadu Rd

HEMA 123 G4 13 48 29 S 131 50 18 E

Katherine to NT/WA Border

Victoria Highway

157 Manbulloo Homestead Caravan Park

☎ (08) 8972 1559

1

Caravan Park 11 SW of Katherine. Turn N off Victoria Hwy 9 km W of Katherine onto Murnburlu Rd, follow signs

HEMA 123 K5 14 31 9 S 132 11 57 E

158 King West Rest Area

1

Rest Area 33 km SW of Katherine or 163 km NE of Victoria River

HEMA 123 K5 14 40 38 S 132 5 11 E

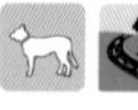

159 Vince Connolly Crossing

1

Rest Area 58 km SW of Katherine or 138 km NE of Victoria River

HEMA 124 G5 14 49 42 S 131 55 0 E

160 Djarrung Campground

☎ (08) 8973 8888

Giwining / Flora River Nature Park

Camp Area 132 km SW of Katherine. Turn NW 86 km SW of Katherine or 110 km NE of Victoria River. 36 km dirt road

HEMA 123 K3 14 45 30 S 131 35 46 E

161 Mathison Rest Area

1

Rest Area 104 km SW of Katherine or 92 km NE of Victoria River

HEMA 124 H5 15 8 23 S 131 41 1 E

162 Sullivan Campground

☎ (08) 8975 0888

1

Judbarra / Gregory National Park

Camp Area 178 km SW of Katherine or 18 km E of Victoria River. Pets allowed in campground only

HEMA 124 H4 15 35 13 S 131 16 29 E

163 Victoria River Roadhouse Caravan Park

☎ (08) 8975 0744

Caravan Park at Roadhouse. 90 km E of Timber Creek

HEMA 124 H4 15 36 57 S 131 7 38 E

164 Charlies Crossing

Camp Spot 55 km S of the Victoria Hwy & Buchanan Hwy intersection or 157 km N of Top Springs. Dirt road

HEMA 124 J3 16 1 51 S 130 48 10 E

165 Bullita Homestead Campground

☎ (08) 8975 0888

Judburra / Gregory National Park

Camp Area 60 km SE of Timber Creek. Turn S 12 km SE of Timber Creek onto Binns Track. 48 km dirt road. 4WD recommended

HEMA 124 J3 16 6 46 S 130 25 25 E

166 Circle F Caravan Park

☎ (08) 8975 0722

Caravan Park at Timber Creek. At the Creek Hotel

HEMA 124 J3 15 39 40 S 130 28 51 E

167 Big Horse Creek Campground

☎ (08) 8975 0888

1

Judbarra / Gregory National Park

Camp Area 10 km W of Timber Creek, 216 km E of Kununurra or 177 km E of NT/WA border. Pets allowed in campground only

HEMA 124 H3 15 36 44 S 130 24 9 E

168 East Baines River

Rest Area 57 km W of Timber Creek, 169 km E of Kununurra or 130 km E of NT/WA border

1

HEMA 124 J2 15 46 2 S 130 1 35 E

BIG RIG 24

169 Saddle Creek

Rest Area 117 km W of Timber Creek, 109 km E of Kununurra or 70 km E of NT/WA border

1

HEMA 124 J2 15 57 26 S 129 33 42 E

BIG RIG 24

170 Zebra Rock Mine Campground ☎0400 767 650

Camp Area at Zebra Rock Mine. Turn S onto Duncan Rd off Victoria Hwy 14 E of WA border or 170 km W of Timber Creek. Travel 5 km, turn R onto access road. 10 km dirt road. Open April - Sept. Signposted

HEMA 124 J1 16 7 23 S 129 2 53 E

$ BIG RIG

171 Gurrandalng Campground ☎(08) 9167 8827

Keep River National Park

Camp Area 202 km W of Timber Creek. Turn N 184 km W of Timber Creek or 3 km E of NT/WA border. 18 km rough, dirt road

HEMA 124 J1 15 52 31 S 129 3 5 E

$

172 Jarnem Campground ☎(08) 9167 8827

Keep River National Park

Camp Area 215 km W of Timber Creek. Turn N 184 km W of Timber Creek or 3 km E of NT/WA border. 31 km rough, dirt road

HEMA 124 J1 15 45 44 S 129 5 57 E

$

Plenty Highway

This road is seasonal and more suitable to 4WD vehicles, camper trailers and off road caravans. Road conditions phone 1800 246 199 (NT)

173 Mud Tank Zircon Field Fossicking Area

Camp Spot 17 km SE of Gemtree. Turn S off Plenty Hwy 7.5 E of Gemtree onto Alatyeye Rd, travel 9 km to access gate. Bush camp spots 500m after gate. 4WD recommended

HEMA 129 E9 23 0 45 S 134 16 13 E

BIG RIG

174 Spotted Tiger Bore Campground ☎(08) 8956 9722

Camp Area 8 km S of Harts Range Police Station. Turn S 500m W of Police Station onto Racecourse Rd. Follow for 8 km to campground

HEMA 129 E10 23 2 21 S 134 55 4 E

$

175 Mac & Rose Conservation Reserve (Tower Rock) ☎(08) 8956 9582

Camp Area 312 km NE of Alice Springs via Plenty Hwy. Turn N 20 km E of Harts Range Police Station or 335 km W of QLD border. 75 km to campground. 4WD only

HEMA 129 D10 22 28 8 S 135 5 1 E

$

176 Jervois Station ☎(08) 8956 6307

Camp Area at Jervois Station. 202 km E of Stuart Hwy or 222 km W of NT/QLD border. Dirt road

HEMA 129 E11 22 57 4 S 136 8 39 E

$

177 Marshall River Rest Area

Rest Area 202 km E of Stuart Hwy or 222 km W of NT/QLD border. Beside river. Dirt road

HEMA 129 E11 22 57 12 S 136 9 6 E

178 Arthur River

Camp Spot 62 km SE of Jervois Station or 159 km W of NT/QLD Border. Tracks beside creek. Dirt road

HEMA 129 D12 22 40 11 S 136 37 51 E

179 Tobermorey Station ☎(07) 4748 4996

Camp Area at Tobermorey Station. 218 km E of Jervois Station or 4 km W of NT/QLD border

HEMA 129 D14 22 17 2 S 137 57 53 E

$

Notes...

PUBLIC DUMP POINTS

With environmental issues becoming more of a concern to travellers, the disposal of grey and black water is of major importance. A comprehensive public dump point list has been compiled to assist you in locating the facilities for responsible disposal of your waste water.

The list is alphabetical by town within each State or Territory, with location details and contact phone numbers where available. Note that public dump points are also indicated on the maps. See "Symbols used on the maps" below for an explanation of the meaning of these map symbols.

Be aware that some situations may change and the accuracy of accessibility and type of facility cannot be guaranteed.

The use of chemicals in 'black water' is of concern, so it is advisable to use those which are biodegradable and eco-friendly rather than those containing chemicals such as formaldehyde.

Most of the dump points accessible by big rigs would require the use of a waste hose, preferably 3 metres or more in length.

Please leave the facility clean and tidy, otherwise the use may be withdrawn if abused.

Where the information is available, listings show whether the dump point is suitable for cassettes or holding tanks and whether big rigs can access it.

Please respect the courtesy extended to you if you avail yourself of this service.

Explanation of a sample Public Dump Point listing

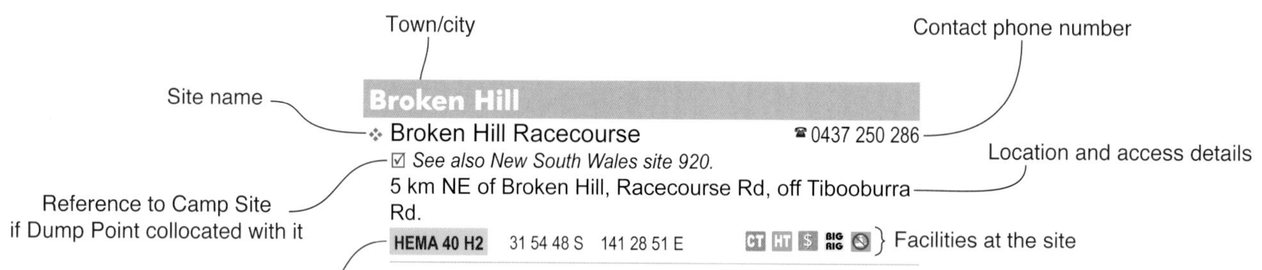

Symbols used in listing

- CT Cassette toilet use
- HT Holding tank use
- BIG RIG Access suitable for big rigs
- $ Fees applicable
- Water available

Symbols used on the maps

- 30 Day Use Site with Public Dump Point
- 115 Camping/Parking Site with Public Dump Point
- Public Dump Point not at a Listed Site

Queensland

Adels Grove
- Adels Grove Dumpoint ☎(07) 4748 5502
  Adels Grove Airfield, outside the Airport fence. GPS is approximate
  HEMA 16 G1 18 41 29 S 138 31 53 E CT HT

Agnes Water
- Council Depot
  Agnes Water - 1770 Rd. 4.2 km N of Round Hill Rd intersection. Turn L at SES HQ sign
  HEMA 15 J12 24 10 49 S 151 52 59 E CT HT BIG RIG

Allora
- Allora Apex Park
  New England Hwy, S end of town near Anglican Chruch, opposite Dalrymple Rd
  HEMA 10 G1 28 2 9 S 151 59 18 E CT HT BIG RIG

Alpha
- Alpha Dump Point
  Clermont- Alpha Rd, opposite showgrounds
  HEMA 14 H4 23 38 47 S 146 38 11 E CT HT BIG RIG

Aramac
- Aramac Shire Caravan Park ☎(07) 4652 9999
  ☑ *See also Queensland site 338.*
  Booker St. Public access
  HEMA 21 E10 22 58 2 S 145 14 20 E CT HT

Atherton
- Atherton Sewerage Works ☎(07) 4091 7937
  Grove St, off Tolga Rd, over railway. N end of town
  HEMA 18 F3 17 15 18 S 145 28 49 E CT HT BIG RIG

Augathella
- Augathella Dump Point
  Brassington Park, Bendee St - Old Charleville Ausathella St
  HEMA 21 J12 25 48 8 S 146 35 18 E CT HT

Ayr
- Shell Burdekin Travel Centre
  Cnr Bruce Hwy & Bower St
  HEMA 14 A6 19 34 59 S 147 23 56 E CT HT BIG RIG

Babinda
- Babinda Rotary Park ☎(07) 4067 1008
  ☑ *See also Queensland site 10.*
  Rest Area at Babinda. Just east of town over railway. S end of Howard Kennedy Dr
  HEMA 18 G6 17 20 54 S 145 55 35 E CT HT BIG RIG

Balgal Beach
- Balgal Beach
  ☑ *See also Queensland site 34.*
  At Rest Area 6 km E of Rollingstone. Turn E off Bruce Hwy 1 km S of Rollingstone. 5 km E of Hwy. N end of town near boat ramp
  HEMA 17 H12 19 0 37 S 146 24 18 E CT HT BIG RIG

Bang Bang
- Bang Bang Rest Area
  ☑ *See also Queensland site 251.*
  Rest Area 112 km S of Normanton or 90 km N of Burke & Wills Roadhouse
  HEMA 16 G4 18 31 36 S 140 39 11 E CT HT BIG RIG

Baralaba
- Baralaba Dump Point ☎(07) 4992 9500
  Wooroonah St, near caravan park, behind the showgrounds
  HEMA 15 J9 24 11 8 S 149 48 56 E CT HT BIG RIG

Barcaldine
- Barcaldine Showgrounds ☎(07) 4651 1211
  ☑ *See also Queensland site 336.*
  Capricorn Hwy, E end of town
  HEMA 21 F10 23 33 2 S 145 17 37 E CT HT BIG RIG
- Lloyd Jones Weir
  ☑ *See also Queensland site 337.*
  15 km SW of Barcaldine. Turn W off Landsborough Hwy 5 km S of Barcaldine for 9 km. 1 km dirt Rd
  HEMA 21 F10 23 39 0 S 145 12 57 E CT HT BIG RIG

Bedourie
- Bedourie Dump Point
  Diamantina Development Rd. 500m N of Roadhouse
  HEMA 20 G3 24 21 7 S 139 28 5 E CT HT BIG RIG

Bedourie Area
- Monkira Rest Area
  ☑ *See also Queensland site 385.*
  Rest Area on Diamantina Development Rd, 121 km E of Eyre Dev. Rd Jcn or 138 km W of Birdsville Dev. Rd Jcn
  HEMA 20 H4 24 49 11 S 140 32 28 E CT HT BIG RIG
- No 3 Bore Rest Area
  ☑ *See also Queensland site 386.*
  Rest Area on Diamantina Development Rd. 28 km E of Eyre Development Rd junction
  HEMA 20 G3 24 28 31 S 139 48 33 E CT HT BIG RIG

Betoota
- Betoota Rest Area
  ☑ *See also Queensland site 380.*
  At rest area
  HEMA 22 A3 25 41 36 S 140 44 52 E CT HT BIG RIG

Beerwah
- Gowinta Farms Caravan Park ☎(07) 5494 0365
  205 Burys Rd, Beerwah. Public access
  HEMA 9 E9 26 52 30 S 152 58 43 E CT HT BIG RIG
- Beerwah Sportsground ☎(07) 5494 0513
  Entry off Simpson St, off roundabout
  HEMA 9 E9 26 51 50 S 152 57 21 E CT HT BIG RIG

Biggenden
- Biggenden Dump Point ☎(07) 4217 1177
  Isis Hwy. 50m W of caravan park
  HEMA 13 B12 25 30 52 S 152 2 20 E CT HT BIG RIG

Biloela
- The Silo Tourist Information Centre ☎(07) 4992 2400
  Exhibition Avenue, NW end of town
  HEMA 15 J10 24 24 15 S 150 30 4 E CT HT BIG RIG

Birdsville
- Birdsville Dump Point
  South side of Rd past Airstrip
  HEMA 22 A1 25 54 14 S 139 20 41 E CT HT BIG RIG
- Birdsville East Dumpoint
  E side of Birdsville. 500m E of windmill on Eyre Development Rd
  HEMA 22 A1 25 54 28 S 139 22 39 E CT HT BIG RIG

Blackall
- Blackall Dump Point ☎(07) 4657 4637
  Paddy Behan Way (Blackall - Isisford Rd) Opposite Barcoo River Camp
  HEMA 14 J3 24 25 35 S 145 27 43 E CT HT BIG RIG
- Blackall Showgrounds
  Blackall-Jericho Rd
  HEMA 14 J3 24 25 33 S 145 28 29 E CT HT BIG RIG

Blackbutt
- Blackbutt Showgrounds ☎(07) 4163 0633
  ☑ *See also Queensland site 465.*
  Bowman Rd, by water tanks
  HEMA 8 E2 26 52 50 S 152 6 7 E CT HT BIG RIG

Blackwater
- Bedford Weir
  ☑ *See also Queensland site 320.*
  27 km N of Blackwater. Turn N 2 km W of Blackwater
  HEMA 15 H8 23 22 21 S 148 50 20 E CT
- Blackwater Dump Point
  Turpentine St, near the Showgrounds
  HEMA 15 H8 23 35 35 S 148 52 31 E CT HT BIG RIG

Bluewater
- Bluewater Park
  ☑ *See also Queensland site 36.*
  Rest Area at Bluewater, 80 km S of Ingham or 29 km N of Townsville
  HEMA 17 H12 19 10 35 S 146 33 5 E CT HT BIG RIG

Bollon
- Bollon Dump Point ☎(07) 4620 8844
  William St, behind Fire Station
  HEMA 12 H3 28 1 51 S 147 28 40 E CT BIG RIG

Boonah
- Boonah Showgrounds ☎(07) 5463 4080
  ☑ *See also Queensland site 645.*
  Entry via Melbourne St
  HEMA 10 G7 27 59 51 S 152 41 6 E CT HT BIG RIG

Boulia
- Boulia Dump Point
  West side of Diamantina Hwy, 1 km N of Boulia
  HEMA 20 E3 22 54 28 S 139 54 15 E CT HT BIG RIG

Bowen
- Bowen Showground ☎(07) 4786 5353
  Mt Nutt Rd, N side of town
  HEMA 14 B7 19 59 42 S 148 13 42 E CT HT BIG RIG

Boyne River Rest Area
- Boyne River Rest Area
  ☑ *See also Queensland site 112.*
  At Rest Area 49 km SE of Mount Larcom or 49 km N of Miriam Vale. 1 km S of Benaraby
  HEMA 15 J11 24 0 39 S 151 20 26 E CT HT BIG RIG

Bundaberg
- Hinkler Lions Park
  ☑ *See also Queensland site 127.*
  Isis Hwy, opposite airport. Key at Waste Transfer Station
  HEMA 13 A12 24 53 49 S 152 18 51 E CT HT BIG RIG

Burketown
- Burketown Dump Point
  Sloman St. Opposite caravan park
  HEMA 16 F3 17 44 31 S 139 32 48 E CT HT BIG RIG

Caboolture
- Caboolture Showgrounds ☎(07) 5495 2030
  ☑ *See also Queensland site 184.*
  4 km N of Town Centre
  HEMA 9 G9 27 4 4 S 152 56 55 E CT

Caloundra

- Caloundra Dump Point ☎(07) 5420 6240
  Behind the Information Centre, Caloundra Rd. If locked, key at Info Centre
  HEMA 9 E10 26 47 53 S 153 6 51 E CT HT

Cairns

- Cairns Southern Wastewater Depot ☎(07) 4044 8200
  Kate St, off Portsmith Rd. Business hours only. Key at Office
  HEMA 18 D4 16 57 12 S 145 45 10 E CT HT BIG RIG
- Cairns Wastewater Depot ☎(07) 4044 8200
  Macnamara St, Manunda. Business hours only
  HEMA 18 D4 16 54 46 S 145 45 0 E CT HT BIG RIG

Calliope

- Calliope Dump Point
  Cnr Taragoola Rd & Dawson Hwy. Key for lock from Calliope Store, 46 Stirrat St
  HEMA 15 J11 24 0 27 S 151 12 2 E CT HT BIG RIG

Camooweal

- Camooweal Dump Point
  East end of town, opposite the water tower
  HEMA 16 J1 19 55 18 S 138 7 27 E CT HT BIG RIG

Capella

- Bridgeman Park Showground ☎(07) 4984 9142
  Hibernia Rd, in SW corner of grounds
  HEMA 14 G6 23 5 21 S 148 0 58 E CT HT BIG RIG

Carmila Beach

- Carmila Beach
  ☑ *See also Queensland site 85.*
  6 km E of Carmila. 1 km dirt Rd. Last 300m narrow, sandy track
  HEMA 15 E9 21 54 50 S 149 27 47 E CT HT BIG RIG

Cecil Plains

- Cecil Plains Rural Retreat Caravan Park ☎0428 913 779
  ☑ *See also Queensland site 541.*
  Taylor St, in caravan park. Public access
  HEMA 13 G10 27 31 59 S 151 11 45 E CT HT BIG RIG

Charleville

- Charleville Dump Point ☎(07) 4656 8355
  Qantas Drive (Airport access Rd)
  HEMA 23 B14 26 24 59 S 146 15 7 E CT HT BIG RIG

Charters Towers

- Columbia Mine Poppet Head ☎(07) 4761 5533
  Flinders Hwy Bypass
  HEMA 14 B4 20 4 21 S 146 16 35 E CT HT BIG RIG

Charters Towers Area

- Fletcher Creek
  ☑ *See also Queensland site 278.*
  Rest Area 42 km N of Charters Towers or 157 km SE of Greenvale.
  HEMA 14 B4 19 48 57 S 146 3 14 E CT HT BIG RIG

Childers

- Childers Rest Area
  Crescent St, behind Post Office
  HEMA 13 B12 25 14 6 S 152 16 44 E CT HT BIG RIG

Chillagoe

- Chillagoe Rodeo Grounds ☎(07) 4094 7111
  ☑ *See also Queensland site 203.*
  From Queen St turn W onto Frew St, entrance 700m on R
  HEMA 17 E9 17 9 29 S 144 30 58 E CT HT BIG RIG

Chinchilla

- Chinchilla Dump Point ☎(07) 4662 7056
  Park St (Chinchilla -Wondai Rd)
  HEMA 13 E9 26 44 7 S 150 37 50 E CT HT BIG RIG
- Chinchilla Showgrounds ☎(07) 4662 7194
  ☑ *See also Queensland site 555.*
  Entrance at Cnr Zeller St & Gaske Ln
  HEMA 13 E9 26 45 2 S 150 37 5 E CT HT BIG RIG

Clairview

- Clairview Rest Area
  N end of Colonial Drive
  HEMA 15 E9 22 6 17 S 149 31 36 E CT HT BIG RIG

Clermont

- Clermont Dump Point ☎(07) 4983 1133
  Lime St, next to bowls club
  HEMA 14 G6 22 49 8 S 147 38 40 E CT HT BIG RIG

Clermont Area

- Theresa Creek Dam ☎(07) 4983 2327
  ☑ *See also Queensland site 411.*
  22 km SW of Clermont
  HEMA 14 G6 22 58 16 S 147 33 13 E CT HT BIG RIG

Cloncurry Area

- Terry Smith Lookout
  ☑ *See also Queensland site 269.*
  Rest Area 103 km S of Burke & Wills Roadhouse or 78 km N of Cloncurry
  HEMA 16 J4 20 4 49 S 140 13 39 E CT HT BIG RIG

Coen

- Coen Dump Point ☎(07) 4060 1135
  Peninsula Developmental Rd, N side of town. E side of Rd. S side of Library
  HEMA 19 G3 13 56 43 S 143 12 6 E CT HT BIG RIG

Collinsville

- Collinsville Showgrounds ☎(07) 4785 5795
  ☑ *See also Queensland site 50.*
  Entry from Railway Rd next to Showgrounds
  HEMA 14 C6 20 33 24 S 147 50 57 E CT HT BIG RIG

Cooktown

- Cooktown Dump Point ☎(07) 4069 5444
  Access from Charlotte St, opposite Sovereign Hotel
  HEMA 17 B10 15 27 58 S 145 14 57 E CT HT

Cunnamulla

- Cunnamulla Council Dump Point
  Williams St, adjacent to showground fence
  HEMA 23 F13 28 4 5 S 145 41 49 E CT HT BIG RIG

Dalby

- Dalby Dump Point
  5 Black Street
  HEMA 13 F10 27 10 34 S 151 14 41 E CT HT BIG RIG

Dalveen

- Jim Mitchell Park
  ☑ *See also Queensland site 636.*
  McCosker Drive
  HEMA 13 J11 28 29 20 S 151 58 14 E CT HT BIG RIG

Dirranbandi

- Dirranbandi Dump Point ☎(07) 4620 8844
  Theodore St, beside showground
  HEMA 12 J4 28 34 33 S 148 13 52 E CT

Duaringa

- Duaringa Rest Area
  ☑ *See also Queensland site 313.*
  Rest Area at Duaringa. E end of town
  HEMA 15 H9 23 43 18 S 149 40 20 E CT HT BIG RIG

Dululu

- Dululu Rest Area
  ☑ *See also Queensland site 419.*
  Bryant St, Dululu. Next to toilet block
  HEMA 15 H10 23 50 54 S 150 15 40 E CT HT BIG RIG

Eidsvold

- Eidsvold Dump Point ☎(07) 4166 9918
  Cnr Burnett Way & Esplanade St
  HEMA 13 B10 25 22 18 S 151 7 24 E CT HT BIG RIG

Einasleigh

- Einasleigh Dump Point
  Baroota Street
  HEMA 17 G9 18 30 55 S 144 5 36 E CT HT BIG RIG

Emerald

- Emerald Rest Area
  ☑ *See also Queensland site 323.*
  Clermont St
  HEMA 14 H7 23 31 18 S 148 9 20 E CT BIG RIG

Eumundi

- Eumundi RV Stop Over ☎(07) 5442 8762
  ☑ *See also Queensland site 177.*
  Parking Area at Eumundi, Cnr Albert St & Napier St.
  HEMA 9 B9 26 28 34 S 152 57 13 E CT HT BIG RIG

Fernvale

- Fernvale Dump Point
  Clive St
  HEMA 10 B6 27 27 14 S 152 39 1 E CT HT BIG RIG

Gayndah

- Zonhoven Park
  ☑ *See also Queensland site 441.*
  Burnett Hwy. E end of town
  HEMA 13 B11 25 37 44 S 151 37 33 E CT HT BIG RIG

Georgetown

- Georgetown Dump Point
  Normanton St, opposite toilets in Heritage Park
  HEMA 17 G8 18 17 29 S 143 32 52 E CT HT BIG RIG

Gin Gin

- Gin Gin Dump Point ☎(07) 4133 2000
  Bruce Hwy, opposite Mobil Roadhouse. N end of town
  HEMA 13 A11 24 58 55 S 151 56 58 E CT HT BIG RIG

Glenden

- Glenden Dump Point
  Gilbert Ave, at Golf Club
  HEMA 14 D7 21 21 1 S 148 7 23 E CT HT BIG RIG

Goomeri

- Goomeri Showgrounds ☎0431 520 316
  ☑ *See also Queensland site 452.*
  Cnr Burnett Hwy & Laird St. S end of town
  HEMA 13 D12 26 11 6 S 152 4 8 E CT HT BIG RIG

Goondiwindi
- Caltex Truck Stop ☎ (07) 4671 0999
  Boundary Rd, E end of town
  HEMA 13 J8 28 31 42 S 150 18 37 E CT HT BIG RIG

Goondiwindi
- Redmond Park
  Anderson St, near the driver reviver area
  HEMA 13 J8 28 33 1 S 150 19 12 E CT HT

Gregory Downs
- Council Dump Point ☎ (07) 4745 5100
  Willis Rd, next to the toilets
  HEMA 16 G2 18 38 59 S 139 15 14 E CT BIG RIG

Gympie
- Archery Park
  ☑ *See also Queensland site 152.*
  Cnr Cross St & Bruce Hwy. 4 km N of town centre
  HEMA 13 D13 26 11 19 S 152 39 13 E CT HT BIG RIG
- Six Mile Creek Rest Area
  ☑ *See also Queensland site 155.*
  Bruce Hwy, 6 km S of Gympie
  HEMA 13 D13 26 13 54 S 152 41 49 E CT HT BIG RIG

Home Hill
- Home Hill Dump Point
  Sixth St. W of railway crossing
  HEMA 14 A6 19 39 59 S 147 24 52 E CT BIG RIG

Hughenden
- Hughenden Dump Point ☎ (07) 4741 1958
  Corner of McLaren St & Swanston St. Near white tower
  HEMA 14 C1 20 51 3 S 144 11 32 E CT HT BIG RIG

Ilfracombe
- Ilfracombe Dump Point ☎ (07) 4658 2233
  Murray St, opposite caravan park
  HEMA 14 H1 23 29 27 S 144 30 37 E CT HT BIG RIG

Ingham
- Tyto Wetlands RV Stop ☎ (07) 4776 4792
  ☑ *See also Queensland site 28.*
  Cnr Bruce Hwy & Cooper St. S of town on W side of Hwy
  HEMA 17 G11 18 39 18 S 146 9 11 E CT HT BIG RIG

Inglewood
- Inglewood Rest Area
  Brook St. E end of town
  HEMA 13 J9 28 24 51 S 151 5 2 E CT HT

Injune
- Injune Truck Stop ☎ (07) 4626 1581
  Hutton St, near Roadhouse
  HEMA 12 C5 25 50 24 S 148 34 3 E CT HT BIG RIG

Innisfail
- Innisfail Dump PoInt ☎ (07) 4063 2655
  Haddrell Park, Bruce Hwy. Opposite Barrier Reef Motel. S side of town
  HEMA 18 H6 17 32 1 S 146 1 47 E CT HT BIG RIG

Ipswich
- Ipswich Showgrounds ☎ (07) 3281 1577
  ☑ *See also Queensland site 524.*
  81 Warwick Rd. Open 8.30 to 4.30 Mon to Fri
  HEMA 6 H2 27 37 38 S 152 45 33 E CT BIG RIG

Isisford
- Barcoo River Nature Park ☎ (07) 4658 8900
  ☑ *See also Queensland site 606.*
  Saint Francis St. At toilet block, SE end of town
  HEMA 21 G9 24 15 28 S 144 26 36 E CT HT

Jandowae
- Jandowae Dump Point
  Dalby St, between High & Hickey Sts. Adjacent to Lions Park, N side of town
  HEMA 13 E10 26 46 45 S 151 6 33 E CT HT BIG RIG
- Jandowae Showgrounds ☎ (07) 4668 5268
  ☑ *See also Queensland site 549.*
  Showgrounds. Warra St
  HEMA 13 E10 26 47 13 S 151 6 38 E CT HT BIG RIG

Jericho
- Jericho Showground
  ☑ *See also Queensland site 332.*
  1 km NE of Jericho
  HEMA 21 F11 23 35 42 S 146 7 54 E CT HT BIG RIG

Kalbar
- Kalbar Showground ☎ 0409 973 608
  ☑ *See also Queensland site 643.*
  N end of town
  HEMA 10 F6 27 56 15 S 152 37 32 E CT BIG RIG

Julia Creek
- Julia Creek Dump Point
  Hickman St, near Junction of Allison St
  HEMA 16 K6 20 39 10 S 141 44 30 E CT HT BIG RIG
- McIntyre Park
  In the Racecourse off Kynuna Road. Near the blue toilet block. GPS at entry
  HEMA 16 K6 20 39 50 S 141 44 32 E CT BIG RIG

Jundah
- Jundah Dump Point ☎ (07) 4658 6133
  800 m N of Jundah on Thomson Developmental Rd, near turn off to outpatient entrance
  HEMA 20 H7 24 49 23 S 143 3 43 E CT HT BIG RIG

Karumba
- Truck Stop ☎ (07) 4745 2240
  Bypass Rd, near Corner Yappar St
  HEMA 16 F4 17 29 29 S 140 50 7 E CT HT BIG RIG

Kenilworth
- Kenilworth Show & Recreation Grounds ☎ (07) 5446 0131
  ☑ *See also Queensland site 169.*
  Elizabeth St. S side of town
  HEMA 8 C7 26 35 56 S 152 43 34 E CT HT BIG RIG

Kingaroy
- Kingaroy Showgrounds Caravan Park ☎ (07) 4162 5037
  ☑ *See also Queensland site 494.*
  31 Youngman St. S side of town
  HEMA 13 E11 26 32 49 S 151 49 56 E CT HT BIG RIG
- Lions Park ☎ (07) 4162 6230
  Baron St, off Kingaroy St
  HEMA 13 E11 26 32 47 S 151 50 16 E CT

Laidley
- Laidley Dump Point
  John St, near swimming pool
  HEMA 10 C4 27 37 55 S 152 23 34 E CT

Lawnton
- Pine Rivers Showground ☎ 0459 023 346
  ☑ *See also Queensland site 189.*
  Gympie Rd
  HEMA 5 D8 27 17 7 S 152 59 13 E CT HT BIG RIG

Longreach
- Longreach Showground ☎ (07) 4658 1745
  Sandpiper St, off Eagle St. W end of town
  HEMA 21 F9 23 26 20 S 144 14 56 E CT HT BIG RIG

Lowood
- Lowood Showgrounds & Caravan Park ☎ 0455 187201
  ☑ *See also Queensland site 484.*
  Station St. Turn L at entry, between buildings
  HEMA 10 B6 27 27 45 S 152 35 1 E CT HT BIG RIG

Mackay
- Mackay Rest Area
  At the Information Centre, Bruce Hwy. Access from Nthbound only. Turn in between BP & Information Centre. Dump is on the left
  HEMA 15 D8 21 9 56 S 149 9 14 E CT BIG RIG

Mareeba
- Eales Park Dump Point ☎ (07) 4092 5674
  Doyle St, opposite Davies Park. W side of town
  HEMA 18 E3 16 59 42 S 145 24 50 E CT HT BIG RIG

Maroochydore
- Maroochy Shire Sewage Treatment Plant ☎ (07) 5475 7200
  Commercial Rd. Business hours only. For key contact Treatment plant Admin Office
  HEMA 9 C10 26 39 8 S 153 3 23 E CT HT BIG RIG

Maryborough
- Airport
  Access via Airport Drive off Saltwater Creek Rd. Follow signs around to right. 2 km from town on Rd to Hervey Bay
  HEMA 13 B13 25 31 6 S 152 42 33 E CT HT
- Maryborough Showground & Equestrian Park ☎ (07) 4123 5311
  ☑ *See also Queensland site 138.*
  Bruce Hwy. N end of town
  HEMA 13 B13 25 30 22 S 152 39 46 E CT HT BIG RIG

Meandarra
- Leo Gordon Apex Park
  Cnr Meandarra & Dillon Sts
  HEMA 12 F7 27 19 24 S 149 52 50 E CT

Miles
- Miles Council Dump Point
  Industry Lane, via Leichhardt Hwy (Sth), Waterworks Rd
  HEMA 13 E8 26 39 59 S 150 11 7 E CT HT BIG RIG

Millmerran
- Millmerran Showgrounds ☎ (07) 4695 1241
  ☑ *See also Queensland site 625.*
  Millmerran - Cecil Plains Rd
  HEMA 13 G10 27 51 37 S 151 16 40 E CT HT BIG RIG
- Walpole Park
  ☑ *See also Queensland site 624.*
  Charles St, between Walpole & Charlotte Sts. Dump Point opposite park
  HEMA 13 G10 27 52 20 S 151 16 27 E CT HT BIG RIG

Mirani

- Mirani Dump Point ☎ 1300 622 529
Victoria St, opposite Council Customer Service Centre
HEMA 15 D8 21 9 34 S 148 51 52 E CT HT BIG RIG

Mitchell

- Mitchell Showgrounds ☎ (07) 4623 8171
Alice St, near entrance
HEMA 12 D4 26 29 47 S 147 58 45 E CT BIG RIG

Monto

- Monto Showground ☎ (07) 4166 9918
Oxley St, W side of town
HEMA 13 A10 24 51 57 S 151 6 53 E CT HT BIG RIG

Morney

- Morney Rest Area
☑ *See also Queensland site 377.*
Rest Area 108 km W of Windorah or 95 km E of Betoota on the Diamantina Development Rd
HEMA 20 J6 25 22 50 S 141 37 24 E CT HT BIG RIG

Morven

- Morven Recreation Ground ☎ (07) 4654 8281
☑ *See also Queensland site 580.*
S side of town via Victoria St
HEMA 12 D2 26 25 6 S 147 6 58 E CT HT BIG RIG

Mount Isa

- Mount Isa Dump Point
Cnr George St & East St
HEMA 16 K3 20 43 16 S 139 30 10 E CT HT BIG RIG

Mount Molloy

- Rifle Creek Rest Area
☑ *See also Queensland site 195.*
Rest Area 1 km N of Mt Molloy, 33 km S of Mossman or 41 km N of Mareeba
HEMA 18 C2 16 39 58 S 145 19 42 E CT BIG RIG

Mount Perry

- Mount Perry Dump Point ☎ (07) 4156 3850
54 Heusman Street, in front of the caravan park
HEMA 13 B11 25 10 29 S 151 38 24 E CT HT BIG RIG

Mount Surprise

- Mount Surprise Dump Point ☎ (07) 4062 1233
Main Rd, outside toilet block
HEMA 17 F9 18 8 50 S 144 19 3 E CT HT BIG RIG

Moura

- Moura Dump Point
Moura Bindaree Rd, E end of town
HEMA 15 K9 24 33 54 S 149 58 27 E CT HT BIG RIG

Mundubbera

- Mundubbera Dump Point ☎ (07) 4165 5700
Bauer St, near the Lyons St intersection & the tennis courts
HEMA 13 B10 25 35 33 S 151 18 3 E CT HT BIG RIG

Murgon

- Murgon RV Stop ☎ (07) 4189 9387
☑ *See also Queensland site 486.*
3 Krebs St
HEMA 13 D11 26 14 32 S 151 56 17 E CT HT BIG RIG

Murgon Area

- Bjelke Petersen Dam.
Via Haager Dr, Yallakool Park in parking area opposite tennis courts
HEMA 13 D11 26 18 12 S 151 59 44 E CT BIG RIG

Muttaburra

- Muttaburra Caravan Park ☎ (07) 4658 7191
☑ *See also Queensland site 341.*
Caravan Park at Muttaburra. Cnr Mary & Bridge Sts
HEMA 21 D9 22 35 36 S 144 33 7 E CT HT BIG RIG

Nambour

- Nambour Dump Point
Off Bli Bli Rd. Located in the side road on the Sth side of the roundabout when taking the Western exit off Bruce Hwy. Signposted. Locked, call number on gate for combination
HEMA 9 C9 26 36 59 S 152 58 44 E CT HT BIG RIG

Nanango

- Tipperary Flat Park
☑ *See also Queensland site 456.*
Rest Area at Nanango. 1.5 km S of PO. Next to BP service station
HEMA 8 C1 26 40 48 S 151 59 47 E CT HT BIG RIG

Nebo

- Nebo Parking Bay
Peak Downs Hwy
HEMA 14 E7 21 40 58 S 148 41 34 E CT HT BIG RIG

Normanton

- Normanton Council Depot ☎ (07) 4745 2200
Old Hospital Rd. Business hours only
HEMA 16 F5 17 40 51 S 141 4 36 E CT HT BIG RIG

Oakey

- Oakey Dump Point
Cnr York St & Lorrimer St next to Works Depot
HEMA 13 G11 27 26 27 S 151 43 27 E CT HT BIG RIG

Petrie

- Wyllie Park Rest Area
☑ *See also Queensland site 187.*
Old Bruce Hwy, beside North Pine River. Gates open 8.00am - 6.00pm
HEMA 5 D9 27 16 22 S 152 58 49 E CT HT BIG RIG

Pittsworth

- Pittsworth Dump Point
Railways St, outside Showgrounds next to SWS building
HEMA 13 G11 27 42 41 S 151 38 31 E CT HT BIG RIG

Pomona

- Pomona Showgrounds ☎ (07) 5485 1477
☑ *See also Queensland site 166.*
Exhibition St
HEMA 9 A8 26 21 36 S 152 51 28 E CT HT BIG RIG

Proserpine

- Proserpine Council Caravan Park ☎ (07) 4945 1554
79 Anzac Rd. Fee for non guests
HEMA 14 C7 20 24 15 S 148 34 18 E CT $

Quilpie

- Quilpie Dump Point ☎ (07) 4995 8657
John Waugh Park. Quarrion St
HEMA 21 K9 26 36 57 S 144 15 46 E CT HT BIG RIG

Rainbow Beach

- Rainbow Beach Sewerage Works ☎ (07) 5481 0800
By sewerage pumping station.Clarkson Drive (Inskip Point Rd)
HEMA 13 C13 25 54 3 S 153 5 18 E CT HT BIG RIG

Ravenshoe

- Ravenshoe Dump Point ☎ (07) 4096 2244
Outside sewerage works, Ascham St
HEMA 18 J4 17 36 55 S 145 28 49 E CT HT BIG RIG

Redcliffe

- Redcliffe Showgrounds ☎ (07) 3283 0405
Scarborough Rd, near hospital. Daylight hours only
HEMA 5 B12 27 13 30 S 153 6 22 E CT HT BIG RIG

Richmond

- Richmond RV Parking Area
☑ *See also Queensland site 294.*
At 72 hr RV parking Area. 300m off Main Rd, via Harris St & Hillier St
HEMA 16 K7 20 43 44 S 143 8 36 E CT HT BIG RIG

Rockhampton

- Music Bowl Park
Nuttall Rd, off Yamba Rd (Bruce Hwy), N of city. Across from sports fields
HEMA 15 H10 23 19 8 S 150 30 51 E CT HT BIG RIG

Rolleston

- Beazley Park
In Rest Area, Beazley Park, Meteor St & Dawson Hwy
HEMA 14 J7 24 27 48 S 148 37 28 E CT HT BIG RIG

Rollingstone

- Bushy Parker Park
☑ *See also Queensland site 33.*
Rest Area at Rollingstone. Turn E off Bruce Hwy just N of Rollingstone, across railway line
HEMA 17 H11 19 2 46 S 146 23 37 E CT HT BIG RIG

Roma

- Roma Dump Point ☎ (07) 4622 1266
Station St, between Lewis & Major Sts. In front of council Depot
HEMA 12 D5 26 34 34 S 148 47 46 E CT HT BIG RIG

- Roma Showgrounds ☎ 0408 988 002
☑ *See also Queensland site 565.*
Northern Rd. N end of town
HEMA 12 D5 26 33 13 S 148 47 6 E CT HT BIG RIG

Sapphire

- Sapphire Reserve
☑ *See also Queensland site 326.*
Rifle Range Rd, opposite general store
HEMA 14 H6 23 27 57 S 147 43 13 E CT HT BIG RIG

Sarina

- Sarina Dump Point ☎ (07) 4956 2251
Tourist Centre, Railway Square off the Bruce Hwy
HEMA 15 D8 21 25 33 S 149 13 2 E CT HT

Shorncliffe

- Shorncliffe Boat Ramp
In boat ramp car park, off Sinbad St. Next to toilet block. Cassettes only, raised off ground
HEMA 5 F11 27 20 2 S 153 4 50 E CT

Springsure

- Springsure Dump Point ☎ (07) 4984 1166
At toilet block near museum
HEMA 14 J7 24 7 5 S 148 5 22 E CT

- Springsure Showground ☎ (07) 4984 1242
Barcoo St. S side of town
HEMA 14 J7 24 7 19 S 148 5 2 E CT HT BIG RIG

St George
- St George Showground ☎ (07) 4620 8844
  McGahan St, behind E end of showground
  HEMA 12 H5 28 1 39 S 148 35 27 E CT HT BIG RIG

St Lawrence
- St Lawrence Recreational Reserve
  ☑ See also Queensland site 91.
  1 km W of St Lawrence
  HEMA 15 F9 22 21 4 S 149 31 11 E CT HT BIG RIG

Stanthorpe
- Apex Park ☎ (07) 4681 5500
  Folkestone St, off Maryland St at toilet block
  HEMA 13 J11 28 39 29 S 151 55 55 E CT HT BIG RIG

Stonehenge Area
- Isisford Road Rest Area
  ☑ See also Queensland site 366.
  Rest Area 121 km S of Longreach or 96 km N of Jundah
  HEMA 21 G8 24 14 1 S 143 33 27 E CT HT BIG RIG

Surat
- Surat Fishing & Restocking Club Park ☎ (07) 4626 5058
  ☑ See also Queensland site 711.
  Carnarvon Hwy, 1 km N of Surat
  HEMA 12 F6 27 8 57 S 149 4 23 E CT BIG RIG

Tambo
- Tambo Lake
  ☑ See also Queensland site 597.
  Lansborough Hwy, S end of town
  HEMA 21 H11 24 52 55 S 146 15 35 E HT BIG RIG

Tara Lagoon
- Tara Lagoon
  ☑ See also Queensland site 522.
  Camp Area at Tara Lagoon
  HEMA 13 F8 27 16 21 S 150 27 36 E CT HT BIG RIG

Taroom
- Taroom Dump Point
  Woolsey St. 700m N of Post Office, outside Council Depot
  HEMA 12 B7 25 38 3 S 149 47 56 E CT HT BIG RIG

Texas
- Texas Dump Point ☎ (07) 4652 1444
  Flemming St, outside Council Depot
  HEMA 13 K10 28 51 12 S 151 10 25 E CT HT BIG RIG

Thargomindah
- Thargomindah Dump POint
  Watts St off Adventure Way. N of town, Opposite council building near cooling ponds
  HEMA 23 F9 27 59 23 S 143 49 11 E CT HT BIG RIG

Theodore
- Theodore Dump Point ☎ (07) 4992 9500
  Eastern Lane, off 7th Avenue. Next to Tennis Courts
  HEMA 13 A8 24 56 43 S 150 4 36 E CT HT BIG RIG

Thuringowa
- Ross River Dam ☎ (07) 4773 8411
  At entrance to Ross River Dam Park, Upper Ross River Rd, via Kelso
  HEMA 14 A5 19 24 27 S 146 44 0 E CT HT BIG RIG

Tin Can Bay
- Tin Can Bay Dump Point
  Snapper Creek Rd, turning point at tip
  HEMA 13 C13 25 55 24 S 152 59 27 E CT HT BIG RIG

Toogoolawah
- Toogoolawah Showgrounds ☎ (07) 5423 1336
  ☑ See also Queensland site 480.
  Ivory Creek Rd
  HEMA 8 G4 27 4 41 S 152 22 31 E CT HT BIG RIG

Toowoomba
- Toowoomba Showground ☎ (07) 4634 7400
  ☑ See also Queensland site 537.
  Glenvale Rd. 8am - 5.00pm Monday to Friday
  HEMA 10 C1 27 33 36 S 151 53 4 E CT HT $ BIG RIG

Townsville
- BP Bohle's Little Acre
  900 Ingham Rd. 'Daylight hours only'. $10.00 Key deposit, dump point at rear of service station
  HEMA 14 A5 19 15 43 S 146 42 53 E CT HT BIG RIG

Tully
- Tully Showground ☎ 07 4068 2288
  ☑ See also Queensland site 20.
  Butler St, outside Showgrounds
  HEMA 18 K5 17 56 2 S 145 55 47 E CT HT BIG RIG

Wallangarra
- Wallangarra Lions Park
  ☑ See also Queensland site 640.
  Near Cnr Margetts St & New England Hwy
  HEMA 13 K11 28 55 18 S 151 55 41 E CT BIG RIG

Wallumbilla
- Wallumbilla Showgrounds
  ☑ See also Queensland site 564.
  Main Road at the W end of town
  HEMA 12 E6 26 35 14 S 149 11 1 E CT HT BIG RIG

Wandoan
- Wandoan Water Tower ☎ (07) 4627 5148
  Jerrard St, near tower
  HEMA 13 D8 26 7 21 S 149 57 35 E CT HT BIG RIG

Warwick
- Maltilda Roadhouse ☎ (07) 4661 7450
  Cnr Cunningham Hwy & Ogilvie Rd. Nth end of town
  HEMA 10 J2 28 11 41 S 152 2 39 E CT HT BIG RIG

Windorah
- Windorah Dump Point
  Diamantina Development Rd (near water tower). E side of Town
  HEMA 20 J7 25 25 4 S 142 39 35 E CT HT BIG RIG

Winton
- Winton Dump Point
  In Riley St parking area. Cnr of Riley & Jundah Rd
  HEMA 20 D7 22 23 30 S 143 2 23 E CT HT BIG RIG
- Winton Recreation Ground ☎ (07) 4657 1188
  Vindex St, next to skate park
  HEMA 20 D7 22 23 14 S 143 1 56 E CT BIG RIG

Wondai
- Wondai RV Stop ☎ (07) 4189 9251
  Haly Street, adjacent to Old Rail Station
  HEMA 13 D11 26 19 2 S 151 52 25 E CT HT BIG RIG

WW2 Airfield
- WW2 Airfield
  ☑ See also Queensland site 307.
  Rest Area 50 km NW of Mt Isa or 139 km E of Camooweal. Near monument on Barkly Hwy
  HEMA 16 K2 20 22 23 S 139 15 50 E CT HT BIG RIG

Yeppoon
- Merv Anderson Park ☎ (07) 4939 4888
  Yeppoon Emu Park Rd, 200m E of Visitor Info Centre
  HEMA 15 G11 23 8 16 S 150 45 0 E CT HT BIG RIG

Yungaburra
- Yungaburra Dump Point
  Lot 550 Mulgrave Rd. On road outside sewerage works
  HEMA 18 G3 17 15 45 S 145 34 44 E CT HT BIG RIG

New South Wales

Aberdeen
- Taylor Park
  ☑ See also New South Wales site 195.
  New England Hwy. N end of town. At fence on N side of park
  HEMA 37 C9 32 9 39 S 150 53 17 E CT HT BIG RIG

Adelong
- Adelong Dump Point
  Travers St, off Snowy Mountain Hwy
  HEMA 43 H13 35 18 24 S 148 3 42 E CT HT BIG RIG

Albury
- Albury City Dump Point ☎ 1300 252 879
  Railway Place. Enter at Cnr Smollett & Young St to Railway Station, turn S to dump location
  HEMA 43 J11 36 5 7 S 146 55 26 E CT HT BIG RIG

Appin
- Appin Dump Point
  Appin Park
  HEMA 35 H9 34 11 53 S 150 47 19 E CT HT BIG RIG

Armidale
- Armidale Dump Point
  Galloway St. Approx 1 km S of City off Waterfall Way. Follow signs for Arboretum
  HEMA 39 G9 30 31 15 S 151 38 47 E CT

Ashford
- Ashford Caravan Park ☎ (02) 6725 4014
  ☑ See also New South Wales site 260.
  57 km N of Inverell. Bukkulla St
  HEMA 39 D8 29 19 24 S 151 5 52 E CT HT BIG RIG

Balranald
- Swimming Pool Car Park
  ☑ See also New South Wales site 760.
  Church St. In car park next to water tower
  HEMA 42 F6 34 38 7 S 143 33 43 E CT HT BIG RIG

Baradine
- Camp Cypress ☎ (02) 6843 1035
  ☑ See also New South Wales site 786.
  1 km W of PO at showground. Lachlan St
  HEMA 38 H3 30 56 49 S 149 3 21 E CT HT BIG RIG
- Baradine Dump Point
  Lions Park, cnr Wellington & Darling Sts
  HEMA 38 H3 30 56 59 S 149 4 0 E CT HT BIG RIG

Barraba

- Council Works Depot
  77 Cherry St. Outside depot
  HEMA 38 G6 30 22 49 S 150 36 46 E CT HT BIG RIG

Batehaven

- City Park
  Beach Rd, in car park opposite shops
  HEMA 44 E5 35 43 53 S 150 11 57 E CT HT

Bathurst

- Bathurst Council Depot ☎ (02) 6336 6011
  Morrisset St. Mon-Fri only 0900-1600
  HEMA 36 F6 33 24 10 S 149 34 26 E CT HT BIG RIG
- Bathurst Showground ☎ (02) 6331 1349
  ☑ *See also New South Wales site 457.*
  Kendell Ave
  HEMA 36 F6 33 25 5 S 149 35 22 E CT HT BIG RIG

Batlow

- Batlow Dump Point
  Memorial Avenue, opposite Wakehurst Ave junction
  HEMA 44 E1 35 31 12 S 148 9 0 E CT HT BIG RIG

Bellingen

- Bellingen Dump Point ☎ (02) 6655 2310
  Black St, opposite Bellingen Showground
  HEMA 39 G12 30 26 55 S 152 53 54 E CT HT BIG RIG

Bendeela

- Bendeela Reserve
  ☑ *See also New South Wales site 568.*
  In Camp Area 7 km W of Kangaroo Valley. There is a dump point near toilet block in campgrounds 1 & 2. Cassette only
  HEMA 44 C6 34 44 21 S 150 28 15 E CT

Berridale

- Berridale Dump Point
  At rear of the Southern Cross Motor Inn. Access off Middlingbank Rd
  HEMA 44 G2 36 21 35 S 148 49 52 E CT HT BIG RIG

Berrigan

- Berrigan Dump Point
  Hayes Park, Jerilderie St
  HEMA 43 J10 35 39 38 S 145 48 50 E CT HT

Berry

- Berry Showground ☎ 0427 605 200
  ☑ *See also New South Wales site 567.*
  500m S of PO. Alexandra St
  HEMA 44 C7 34 46 46 S 150 41 46 E CT HT BIG RIG

Bingara

- Bingara Showground ☎ (02) 6724 0066
  Bowen St, inside 2nd entrance gate
  HEMA 38 E6 29 52 0 S 150 33 20 E CT BIG RIG

Blayney

- Henry St Toilet Block ☎ (02) 6368 2104
  Henry St. S end, behind PO
  HEMA 36 G5 33 31 58 S 149 15 23 E CT HT

Blayney

- Blayney Showground ☎ (02) 6368 2104
  Western Hwy
  HEMA 36 G5 33 31 6 S 149 15 31 E CT BIG RIG

Boggabri

- Jubilee Park ☎ (02) 6799 6760
  Hull St in sportsground, Mon-Fri business hours only
  HEMA 38 H5 30 42 20 S 150 2 56 E CT HT BIG RIG

Bomaderry

- Bomaderry Country Winnebago ☎ (02) 4421 0122
  314 Princes Hwy. Enter at rear via Cambewarra Rd, near McDonalds. Business hours only
  HEMA 44 C6 34 50 36 S 150 35 43 E CT

Bombala

- Bombala Caravan Park ☎ (02) 6458 3817
  ☑ *See also New South Wales site 615.*
  Monaro Hwy. Public access, pay fee to office
  HEMA 44 J3 36 54 30 S 149 14 20 E CT HT $

Boorowa

- Boorowa Dump Point
  Park St, next to Caravan Park
  HEMA 36 J4 34 26 1 S 148 43 12 E CT HT $ BIG RIG

Bourke

- Back O Bourke Information Centre ☎ (08) 6872 1321
  Kidman Way
  HEMA 41 D10 30 4 51 S 145 57 0 E CT HT BIG RIG

Braidwood

- Braidwood Dump Point ☎ (02) 4842 9231
  Cnr of Kingsway & McKellar St, N side of town
  HEMA 44 E5 35 26 24 S 149 48 7 E CT HT BIG RIG

Brewarrina

- Brewarrina Dump Point
  At rear of the Information Centre on Bathurst Rd. Only accessible when info centre open. 0830-1700 weekdays
  HEMA 41 C11 29 57 35 S 146 51 28 E CT HT

Broken Hill

- Broken Hill Information Centre ☎ (08) 8088 9700
  Cnr Bromide & Blende Sts. Key at Information Centre
  HEMA 40 H2 31 57 34 S 141 27 39 E CT HT BIG RIG
- Broken Hill Racecourse ☎ 0437 250 286
  ☑ *See also New South Wales site 920.*
  5 km NE of Broken Hill, Racecourse Rd, off Tibooburra Rd.
  HEMA 40 H2 31 54 48 S 141 28 51 E CT BIG RIG $

Bulahdelah

- Bulahdelah Showgrounds ☎ (02) 4997 4981
  ☑ *See also New South Wales site 99.*
  Cnr Stuart & Prince Sts. Near Helipad
  HEMA 37 D12 32 24 18 S 152 12 16 E CT HT BIG RIG

Bungendore

- Bungendore Showground ☎ 0457 528 344
  ☑ *See also New South Wales site 633.*
  On the Bungendore - Sutton Rd. See Caretaker
  HEMA 44 D4 35 14 30 S 149 24 37 E CT HT BIG RIG

Burren Junction

- Burren Junction Dump Point ☎ (02) 6828 1399
  Hastings St. Behind toilet block at tennis courts
  HEMA 38 F3 30 6 8 S 148 57 52 E CT BIG RIG

Burrinjuck

- Burrinjuck Waters ☎ (02) 6227 8114
  ☑ *See also New South Wales site 537.*
  Burrinjuck Dam, State Park, 25 km S of Bookham
  HEMA 44 C2 34 58 46 S 148 37 11 E CT HT

Bylong

- Bylong Public Hall
  ☑ *See also New South Wales site 407.*
  Bylong Valley Way, opposite store
  HEMA 36 C7 32 24 58 S 150 6 52 E CT HT BIG RIG

Canowindra

- Canowindra Caravan Park ☎ 0428 233 769
  ☑ *See also New South Wales site 471.*
  Tilga St. Next to swimming pool. 300m S of PO. Public access
  HEMA 36 G4 33 34 8 S 148 39 50 E CT HT BIG RIG

Casino

- Casino Showground ☎ (02) 6660 0300
  Grafton Rd, S end of town
  HEMA 39 C12 28 53 2 S 153 2 48 E CT HT BIG RIG

Cessnock

- Cessnock Showground ☎ 0412 235 447
  ☑ *See also New South Wales site 213.*
  Access gates beside indoor sports centre Mount View Rd. Close Feb & early Mar for show
  HEMA 45 J4 32 49 51 S 151 20 26 E CT HT BIG RIG
- Abermain Recreation Club ☎ (02) 4930 4285
  Entry via Goulburn St, Key at reception
  HEMA 45 J4 32 48 26 S 151 25 34 E CT HT BIG RIG

Clarence Town

- Bridge Reserve ☎ (02) 4984 2680
  Durham St
  HEMA 37 D11 32 34 58 S 151 46 56 E CT HT BIG RIG

Cobar

- Cobar Visitors Centre ☎ (02) 6836 2448
  Marshall St
  HEMA 41 G9 31 29 53 S 145 50 33 E CT HT BIG RIG

Coffs Harbour

- Coffs Harbour Dump Point ☎ (02) 6648 4000
  Phil Hawthorne Dr, off Stadium Drive roundabout S of Town off Pacific Hwy
  HEMA 39 G12 30 19 26 S 153 5 47 E CT HT BIG RIG

Coleambally

- Coleambally Lions Park
  Entry from Kingfisher Ave & Kidman Way
  HEMA 43 G10 34 47 52 S 145 52 46 E CT BIG RIG

Collarenebri

- Collarenebri Primitive Campground
  ☑ *See also New South Wales site 278.*
  Gwydir Hwy, E end of town. Next to football grounds. Beside toilet block
  HEMA 38 D2 29 32 56 S 148 34 55 E CT

Conargo

- Bills Park ☎ (03) 5880 1200
  ☑ *See also New South Wales site 851.*
  Rest Area at Conargo. W end of town, near school
  HEMA 43 H8 35 18 24 S 145 10 38 E CT HT BIG RIG

Condobolin

- River View Caravan Park ☎ (02) 6895 2611
  ☑ See also New South Wales site 950.
  Diggers Avenue. S end of town. Public access
  HEMA 43 C12 33 5 40 S 147 8 50 E CT HT BIG RIG

Coonabarabran

- Neilson Park
  ☑ See also New South Wales site 793.
  Rest Area at Coonabarabran. Essex St, Eastern end of park
  HEMA 38 J3 31 16 16 S 149 16 46 E CT HT BIG RIG

Coonamble

- Riverside Caravan Park ☎ (02) 6822 1926
  Castlereagh Hwy. Inside Caravan Park, public access. Big Rigs call ahead
  HEMA 38 H1 30 57 48 S 148 23 23 E CT HT BIG RIG

Cootamundra

- Cootamundra Dump Point
  Apex Park, Hurley St off Olympic Hwy. Near toilet block
  HEMA 36 K3 34 38 40 S 148 1 30 E CT HT BIG RIG

Corowa

- Corowa Dump Point ☎ (02) 6033 1426
  Rowers Park near Ball Park CP, Bridge Rd. Deposit required, contact CP Kiosk
  HEMA 43 J10 36 0 15 S 146 23 38 E CT HT BIG RIG

Cowra

- Cowra Overnight Rest Area
  ☑ See also New South Wales site 469.
  Lachlan Valley Way
  HEMA 36 G4 33 50 8 S 148 40 55 E CT HT

Dareton

- Dareton Dump Point
  Tiltao St, next to service station
  HEMA 42 E3 34 5 44 S 142 2 29 E CT

Darlington Point

- Darlington Point Lions Park ☎ (02) 6968 4166
  Darlington St. N side of town, 200m E of caravan park
  HEMA 43 F10 34 34 0 S 146 0 29 E CT BIG RIG

Delungra

- Delungra Recreation Ground ☎ (02) 6724 8275
  ☑ See also New South Wales site 264.
  Reedy St, W end of town
  HEMA 38 E7 29 39 4 S 150 49 33 E CT HT BIG RIG

Deniliquin

- Deniliquin Rest Area
  ☑ See also New South Wales site 500.
  Cobb Hwy, N side of Town, adjacent to public toilet
  HEMA 43 H8 35 31 31 S 144 58 41 E CT HT

Dorrigo

- Dorrigo Dump Point
  Waterfall Way (Armidale Rd) S of Showground
  HEMA 39 G11 30 20 29 S 152 42 2 E CT HT BIG RIG

Dubbo

- Dubbo Showground ☎ (02) 6884 8845
  Wingewarra St. E side of town
  HEMA 36 C4 32 15 0 S 148 36 52 E CT HT BIG RIG
- Western Plains Zoo
  At Western Plains Zoo. Turn R after entering through main gate. In caravan parking area
  HEMA 36 C4 32 16 18 S 148 35 9 E CT HT BIG RIG

Dungog

- Dungog Showground ☎ (02) 4992 1810
  ☑ See also New South Wales site 331.
  Chapman St
  HEMA 37 D11 32 24 19 S 151 45 3 E CT HT BIG RIG

Eugowra

- Byrne's Park
  ☑ See also New South Wales site 476.
  Byrne's Park, Myall St, adjacent to bridge
  HEMA 36 F3 33 25 40 S 148 22 11 E CT HT BIG RIG

Euston

- Euston Dump Point ☎ (03) 5026 4244
  Nixon St, entrance between Euston Club & Motel. Key at club
  HEMA 42 F4 34 34 47 S 142 44 41 E CT HT BIG RIG

Evans Head

- Evans Head Industrial Estate ☎ (02) 6682 4392
  Memorial Airport Drive, near council depot, between Winjeel Dr & Sir Valston Hancock Dr
  HEMA 39 C13 29 6 15 S 153 25 20 E CT HT BIG RIG

Finley

- Finley Dump Point ☎ (03) 5883 5100
  Endeavour St, beside old railway station
  HEMA 43 H9 35 38 44 S 145 34 33 E CT HT BIG RIG

Forbes

- Forbes Lions Park
  ☑ See also New South Wales site 822.
  Rest Area at Forbes. Cnr of Lachlan & Junction Sts. 500m S of PO, beside lake
  HEMA 36 F3 33 23 22 S 148 0 14 E CT HT BIG RIG
- Shire Works Depot ☎ (02) 6850 1300
  Newell Hwy. Near BP Roadhouse, Fitzgeralds Bridge. 1.5 km S of PO. Business hours only
  HEMA 36 F3 33 24 7 S 147 59 5 E CT HT BIG RIG

Forster

- Forster Beach Holiday Park ☎ (02) 6554 6269
  Reserve Rd. Adjacent to amenities building. Public access
  HEMA 37 C13 32 10 46 S 152 30 42 E CT HT

Glen Innes

- Glen Innes Anzac Park
  ☑ See also New South Wales site 152.
  Cnr East Ave & Ferguson St
  HEMA 39 E9 29 44 3 S 151 44 4 E CT HT BIG RIG

Gloucester

- Gloucester Holiday Park ☎ (02) 6558 1720
  Denison St. 700m W of PO. Call at reception for payment & directions
  HEMA 37 B12 32 0 23 S 151 57 12 E CT $

Goolgowi

- Goolgowi Caravan Park ☎ (02) 6965 1900
  ☑ See also New South Wales site 491.
  Combo St. 1 km NE of PO
  HEMA 43 E9 33 58 47 S 145 42 22 E CT HT BIG RIG

Grafton

- Grafton Showground ☎ (02) 6642 2240
  ☑ See also New South Wales site 38.
  Prince & Dobie St
  HEMA 39 E12 29 41 3 S 152 56 24 E CT HT BIG RIG
- Grafton Greyhound Racing Club ☎ (02) 6642 3713
  ☑ See also New South Wales site 37.
  Cranworth St
  HEMA 39 E12 29 40 27 S 152 55 32 E CT BIG RIG

Grenfell

- Grenfell Dump Point ☎ (02) 6343 1212
  West St, near old railway station. Take 2nd driveway from cnr Camp St
  HEMA 36 H3 33 53 43 S 148 9 21 E CT HT BIG RIG

Griffith

- Willow Park ☎ (02) 6962 4145
  ☑ See also New South Wales site 959.
  Kookora St toilet block
  HEMA 43 F10 34 17 16 S 146 1 55 E CT BIG RIG

Gulgong

- Gulgong Showground ☎ (02) 6374 1255
  ☑ See also New South Wales site 403.
  Entrance on Cnr of Grevillia & Guntawang Rds
  HEMA 36 C6 32 22 15 S 149 31 41 E CT HT BIG RIG

Gulgong

- Gulgong Dump Point ☎ (02) 6374 1202
  Saleyards Lane off Station St, front of shire depot
  HEMA 36 C6 32 21 30 S 149 32 46 E CT HT BIG RIG

Gundagai

- Gundagai Dump Point
  Railway Parade
  HEMA 43 G13 35 3 55 S 148 6 45 E CT HT BIG RIG

Gunnedah

- Gunnedah Lions RV Park
  Oxley Highway (Mullaley Road)
  HEMA 38 H6 30 58 43 S 150 14 24 E CT HT BIG RIG
- Gunnedah Showground ☎ (02) 6740 2125
  South St. Located just inside entrance
  HEMA 38 H6 30 58 48 S 150 14 53 E CT HT BIG RIG

Harden

- Harden Showground
  North St
  HEMA 44 B1 34 32 46 S 148 21 27 E CT HT BIG RIG

Hay

- Hay Showground ☎ (02) 6993 1087
  ☑ See also New South Wales site 494.
  Dunera Way, N end of town. Outside emergency service building. 200m W of Showground
  HEMA 43 F8 34 29 51 S 144 50 17 E CT HT BIG RIG

Henty

- Henty Dump Point
  Henty Pleasant Hills Rd, behind the Library
  HEMA 43 H12 35 30 57 S 147 1 58 E CT HT

Hillston

- Hillston Lions Park
  Kidman Way, next to the caravan park
  HEMA 43 D9 33 28 47 S 145 32 4 E CT HT BIG RIG

Holbrook

- Holbrook Tourist Park
  Bardwell St, off Hume Hwy. Public access. Must advise park office
  HEMA 43 J12 35 43 48 S 147 18 30 E CT HT

Howlong

- Lowe Square Recreation Reserve ☎(02) 6033 8999
  Riverina Hwy, between High & Larmer sts. Near toilet block. Key from Howlong Trading Post / Shell Service Station
  HEMA 43 J11 35 58 50 S 146 38 2 E CT HT BIG RIG

Inverell

- Inverell Showground ☎(02) 6722 3435
  ☑ *See also New South Wales site 257.*
  1 km E of town, enter off Tingha Rd - in between Sporting Complex & Pioneer Village
  HEMA 39 E8 29 46 57 S 151 7 14 E CT HT BIG RIG

Jamberoo

- Jamberoo Dump Point
  Keith Irvine Oval. Church St
  HEMA 37 K9 34 38 49 S 150 46 28 E CT HT

Jerilderie

- Lakeside Parking Area ☎(03) 5886 1200
  Newell Hwy car park, 100m W of Civic Centre, beside church
  HEMA 43 H9 35 21 19 S 145 43 23 E CT HT BIG RIG

Jugiong

- Jugiong Showground
  ☑ *See also New South Wales site 539.*
  Riverside Dve. Donation requested for use
  HEMA 43 G14 34 49 24 S 148 19 34 E CT HT BIG RIG

Junee

- Willow Park ☎(02) 6924 8100
  Park Lane, 70m from entry
  HEMA 36 K2 34 51 34 S 147 34 24 E CT HT BIG RIG

Kempsey

- Kempsey Showgrounds ☎(02) 6562 5231
  ☑ *See also New South Wales site 62.*
  19 Sea St
  HEMA 39 J11 31 4 24 S 152 49 45 E CT HT BIG RIG

Kew

- iKew Information & Community Centre ☎(02) 6559 4400
  133 Nancy Bird Walton Dr
  HEMA 37 A13 31 38 7 S 152 43 20 E CT HT BIG RIG

Khancoban

- Khancoban Dump Point ☎(02) 6948 9100
  Scott St, near cnr Mitchell Ave
  HEMA 43 K13 36 13 3 S 148 7 24 E CT HT BIG RIG

Kundabung Rest Area

- Kundabung Rest Area
  ☑ *See also New South Wales site 67.*
  Rest Area 15 km S of Kempsey. Southbound only
  HEMA 39 J11 31 12 14 S 152 49 25 E CT HT BIG RIG

Kyogle

- Kyogle Showground ☎0459 537 601
  ☑ *See also New South Wales site 225.*
  N end of town. Fee if not staying at showground
  HEMA 39 B12 28 36 57 S 153 0 0 E CT HT $ BIG RIG

Lake Cargelligo

- Lake Cargelligo Shire Dump Point ☎(02) 6895 1900
  Narrandera St
  HEMA 43 C10 33 18 17 S 146 22 23 E CT

Lake George

- Anderson VC Rest Area
  ☑ *See also New South Wales site 640.*
  Anderson VC Rest Area. 7 km N of Bungendore turn off
  HEMA 44 C4 35 6 1 S 149 22 36 E CT HT BIG RIG

Leeton

- Leeton Showground ☎(02) 6953 6481
  ☑ *See also New South Wales site 731.*
  Racecourse Rd
  HEMA 43 F10 34 33 49 S 146 23 58 E CT HT BIG RIG

Lightning Ridge

- Lightning Ridge Dump Point ☎(02) 6829 1670
  Onyx St
  HEMA 41 B13 29 25 32 S 147 58 21 E CT BIG RIG

Lithgow

- Lithgow Showground ☎(02) 6353 1775
  Entry off George Coates Ave. Daylight hours
  HEMA 34 C2 33 28 51 S 150 8 42 E CT HT BIG RIG

Lockhart

- Lockhart Caravan Park ☎0458 205 303
  ☑ *See also New South Wales site 722.*
  Green St. 300m W of PO
  HEMA 43 H11 35 13 13 S 146 42 46 E CT

Maclean

- Maclean Showground
  ☑ *See also New South Wales site 30.*
  At Maclean Showground, entry off Cameron St
  HEMA 39 D13 29 27 50 S 153 11 58 E CT HT BIG RIG

Manildra

- Manildra Showground ☎0428 697 685
  ☑ *See also New South Wales site 876.*
  Orange St
  HEMA 36 F4 33 10 38 S 148 41 16 E CT HT BIG RIG

Manilla

- Manilla Park ☎(02) 6785 1304
  Charles St
  HEMA 38 H7 30 44 21 S 150 42 57 E CT HT BIG RIG

Mathoura

- Mathoura Dump Point
  Laneway behind Bowling Club. Enter off Mitchell St. Drive through
  HEMA 43 J8 35 48 30 S 144 53 56 E CT HT BIG RIG

Menindee

- Menindee Lakes Caravan Park ☎(08) 8091 4315
  ☑ *See also New South Wales site 984.*
  Menindee Lakes Shore Drive. Public access, fee at reception
  HEMA 42 B3 32 21 15 S 142 24 12 E CT HT $ BIG RIG

Merriwa

- Merriwa Dump Point ☎(02) 6548 2607
  Blaxland St, next to Caravan Park
  HEMA 37 C8 32 8 17 S 150 21 3 E CT HT BIG RIG

Milton

- Milton Showground ☎0429 934 067
  ☑ *See also New South Wales site 578.*
  Milton Showground. Croobyar Rd
  HEMA 44 D6 35 19 9 S 150 25 48 E CT HT BIG RIG

Moama

- Rich River Golf Club Resort ☎(03) 5481 333
  ☑ *See also New South Wales site 507.*
  Twenty Four Lane, via Perricoota Rd. ID required, report to reception for key
  HEMA 43 K8 36 4 35 S 144 43 35 E CT HT BIG RIG

Moree

- Moree Dump Point
  Web Ave, off Newell Hwy
  HEMA 38 D5 29 27 26 S 149 50 40 E CT HT BIG RIG

Morisset

- Morisset Showground ☎(02) 4973 2670
  ☑ *See also New South Wales site 131.*
  At showground, Ourimbah St
  HEMA 33 E12 33 6 30 S 151 28 49 E CT HT BIG RIG

Moruya

- Moruya Dump Point
  Shore St. Near sewer pump station opposite tennis courts. Via Church St off Princes Hwy
  HEMA 44 F5 35 54 27 S 150 4 35 E CT HT BIG RIG

Moulamein

- Moulamein Dump Point
  Moulamein Rd, between Tallow & Sainsberry St
  HEMA 42 G6 35 5 16 S 144 1 53 E CT HT BIG RIG

Mudgee

- Mudgee Showground ☎(02) 6372 3828
  Douro St, 200m from cnr Nicolson St. Phone first
  HEMA 36 D6 32 36 10 S 149 34 53 E CT HT BIG RIG

Mulwala

- Purtle Park
  Melbourne St. Key at Newsagent
  HEMA 43 J10 35 59 8 S 146 0 34 E CT HT BIG RIG

Murrurundi

- Wilson Memorial Park
  New England Hwy. Best entrance via Mount St through back gate
  HEMA 37 B9 31 45 51 S 150 50 11 E CT HT BIG RIG

Nambucca Heads

- Nambucca Heads Visitor Information Centre ☎(02) 6568 6954
  Cnr Pacific Hwy & Riverside Drive. Key available between 0900 - 1700
  HEMA 39 H12 30 39 9 S 152 59 25 E CT

Narrabri

- Narrabri Showground ☎(02) 6792 3913
  ☑ *See also New South Wales site 776.*
  Belar St
  HEMA 38 F5 30 20 19 S 149 45 48 E CT HT BIG RIG
- Cameron Park
  ☑ *See also New South Wales site 775.*
  Rest Area at Narrabri. 700 m S of Information Centre
  HEMA 38 F5 30 19 37 S 149 46 43 E CT

Narrandera

✧ Narrandera Showground ☎ 0407 105 846
☑ *See also New South Wales site 726.*
Elizabeth St, E side of town. Behind hall in grounds
HEMA 43 G11 34 44 57 S 146 33 52 E CT BIG RIG

Newcastle Area

✧ Australian Motorhomes, Bennetts Green Dump Point ☎ (02) 4948 0433
At rear of Australian Motorhomes, enter via, Groves Rd, Statham St, 2nd driveway on R. Mon - Fri 0900 -1700
HEMA 33 C14 32 59 50 S 151 41 25 E CT HT BIG RIG

Nowra

✧ Nowra Showground ☎ 1300 662 808
☑ *See also New South Wales site 572.*
West St
HEMA 44 C6 34 52 30 S 150 35 31 E CT HT BIG RIG

Nyngan

✧ Teamsters Rest Area
☑ *See also New South Wales site 894.*
Teamsters Rest Area, Pangee St. Approx 300m W of Information Centre
HEMA 41 G12 31 33 43 S 147 11 40 E CT HT BIG RIG

Oberon

✧ Jenolan Caravan Park ☎ (02) 6336 0344
Cunynghame St. Public access
HEMA 36 G7 33 42 6 S 149 51 28 E CT HT $

Orange

✧ Total Park ☎ (02) 6393 8000
Bathurst Rd, behind Shell Service Station. E end of town
HEMA 36 F5 33 17 27 S 149 6 34 E CT HT BIG RIG

Parkes

✧ Kelly Reserve
☑ *See also New South Wales site 817.*
Rest Area at Parkes. N end of town
HEMA 36 E3 33 7 28 S 148 10 23 E CT

Peak hill

✧ Peak Hill Dump Point
Warrah St, between Mingelo & Bogan St. W side of Hwy
HEMA 36 D3 32 43 38 S 148 11 10 E CT HT BIG RIG

Portland

✧ Kremer Park
☑ *See also New South Wales site 455.*
Kiln St
HEMA 36 F7 33 21 11 S 149 58 28 E CT HT BIG RIG

Port Macquarie

✧ Port Macquarie Dump Point
Chestnut Rd, off Lake Rd. Adjacent to sewer pumping station
HEMA 39 K12 31 27 6 S 152 53 23 E CT

Quirindi

✧ Rose Lee Park
Kamilaroi Higway
HEMA 38 K6 31 31 4 S 150 40 34 E CT HT BIG RIG

Rylstone

✧ Rylstone Caravan Park ☎ 0409 873 340
5 Carwell St. Public access. Fee applies
HEMA 36 E7 32 47 50 S 149 58 10 E CT HT $ BIG RIG

Seal Rocks

✧ Seal Rocks Dump Point
Seal Rocks Rd, opposite entry to caravan park. Near public toilets
HEMA 37 D13 32 25 57 S 152 31 28 E CT BIG RIG

Singleton

✧ Singleton Showground ☎ 0488 722 424
☑ *See also New South Wales site 204.*
Access gates in Church St, directly opposite Dight Ave
HEMA 45 E1 32 34 5 S 151 10 19 E CT HT BIG RIG

Talbingo

✧ Talbingo Dump Point ☎ (02) 6941 2555
Murray Jackson Dr, between Lampe & Bridle Sts. At entrance to water depot station
HEMA 43 H14 35 34 43 S 148 17 59 E CT

Tamworth

✧ Tamworth Rest Area ☎ (02) 6755 4555
☑ *See also New South Wales site 173.*
3 km NE of Tamworth on New England Hwy
HEMA 38 J7 31 6 30 S 150 57 16 E CT HT BIG RIG

Tamworth

✧ Tamworth Airport Rest Area
☑ *See also New South Wales site 174.*
On Hwy opposite airport
HEMA 38 J7 31 4 40 S 150 51 2 E CT HT BIG RIG

Tarcutta

✧ Tarcutta Dump Point
Sydney St. In "Changeover Bay". Beside toilets
HEMA 43 H13 35 16 33 S 147 44 17 E CT HT BIG RIG

Taree

✧ Taree Rotary Park
☑ *See also New South Wales site 87.*
Manning River Dr, via Victoria St. Just W of Information Centre
HEMA 37 B13 31 53 57 S 152 29 27 E CT HT BIG RIG

Temora

✧ Temora Showground ☎ (02) 6977 1801
☑ *See also New South Wales site 832.*
Entry via Mimosa St.
HEMA 43 F12 34 26 23 S 147 31 17 E CT HT BIG RIG

✧ Temora Dump Point ☎ (02) 6980 1100
Northern end of Airport St. Approx 200m from Hwy
HEMA 36 J2 34 25 40 S 147 31 9 E CT HT BIG RIG

Tenterfield

✧ Tenterfield Showground ☎ (02) 6736 3666
☑ *See also New South Wales site 140.*
Miles St. Entry at back gate
HEMA 39 C10 29 3 25 S 152 0 55 E CT HT BIG RIG

Tocumwal

✧ Town Beach ☎ (03) 5874 2517
☑ *See also New South Wales site 858.*
From Tocumwal - Corawa Rd turn W onto Hennessy St then S on Town Beach Rd. 700m dirt Rd
HEMA 43 J9 35 49 6 S 145 33 43 E CT HT BIG RIG

Tullamore

✧ Tullamore Showground ☎ (02) 6892 5194
☑ *See also New South Wales site 821.*
Camp Area at Tullamore. Cornet St
HEMA 36 D2 32 37 39 S 147 34 11 E CT HT BIG RIG

Tumbarumba

✧ Tumbarumba Dump Point
Cnr Cape & Bridge Sts. 100m from Visitors Centre
HEMA 43 J13 35 46 37 S 148 0 33 E CT HT BIG RIG

Tumut

✧ Tumut Dump Point ☎ (02) 6941 2555
Elm Drive
HEMA 44 D1 35 18 11 S 148 13 42 E CT HT BIG RIG

Ungarie

✧ Ungarie Showground
☑ *See also New South Wales site 953.*
Camp Area at Ungarie, Crown Camp Rd, entrance beyond school. Behind toilets, signposted
HEMA 43 D11 33 38 7 S 146 58 43 E CT HT BIG RIG

Urunga

✧ Urunga Recreation Reserve
Morgo St, S of town centre heading to Hungry Head. 250m S of intersection with South St East
HEMA 39 G12 30 30 6 S 153 1 16 E CT HT BIG RIG

Wagga Wagga

✧ Wilks Park
☑ *See also New South Wales site 705.*
Rest Area at Wagga Wagga. Turn E off Olympic Hwy at Travers St, across bridge to Hampden Ave. N side of town, E side of Murrumbidgee River
HEMA 43 G12 35 5 59 S 147 22 17 E CT HT BIG RIG

Walcha

✧ Walcha Dump Point
North St, in front of Council depot
HEMA 39 H9 30 58 40 S 151 35 18 E CT HT BIG RIG

Walgett

✧ Alex Trevallion Park
☑ *See also New South Wales site 376.*
Castlereagh Hwy. S end of town
HEMA 38 E1 30 2 4 S 148 6 55 E CT HT BIG RIG

Wallerawang

✧ Lake Wallace
☑ *See also New South Wales site 454.*
Barton Ave, beside lake. Turn N off Great Western Hwy 8 km W of Lithgow or 57 km E of Bathurst
HEMA 34 B1 33 24 56 S 150 4 24 E CT HT BIG RIG

Warialda

✧ Warialda Rest Area
☑ *See also New South Wales site 270.*
Saleyards Rest Area, Gwydir Hwy. E side of town
HEMA 38 D6 29 32 43 S 150 34 52 E CT HT BIG RIG

Warragamba

✧ Warragamba Picnic Area
Off Warradale Rd
HEMA 34 F7 33 53 37 S 150 36 6 E CT HT

Warren

✧ Warren Dump Point
Oxley Park, Coonamble Rd. Near the water tower
HEMA 36 A2 31 41 48 S 147 50 23 E CT BIG RIG

Wee Waa

✧ Dangar Park ☎ (02) 6799 6760
Cnr Cowper & George Sts, next to toilet block
HEMA 38 F4 30 13 25 S 149 26 39 E CT HT BIG RIG

Wellington

- Wellington Showground
  Bushranger Creek Rd
  HEMA 36 D5 32 33 15 S 148 56 3 E CT HT BIG RIG

Wentworth

- Fort Courage Angling & Caravan Park ☎ (03) 5027 3097
  ☑ *See also New South Wales site 996.*
  20 km W of Wentworth on Old Renmark Rd. Beside Murray River
  HEMA 42 E2 34 5 3 S 141 43 53 E CT HT BIG RIG

West Wyalong

- Ace Caravan Park ☎ (02) 6972 3061
  Cnr Newell & Mid Western Hwy's. Fee applies
  HEMA 36 H1 33 55 23 S 147 11 55 E CT $
- West Wyalong Showground ☎ 0428 518 329
  ☑ *See also New South Wales site 828.*
  At the showground. Entry by Duffs Rd only off the West Wyalong bypass Rd
  HEMA 43 F12 33 56 18 S 147 12 50 E CT HT BIG RIG

White Cliffs

- Opal Pioneer Caravan & Camping Tourist Park ☎ (08) 8091 6688
  ☑ *See also New South Wales site 914.*
  Johnstone St
  HEMA 40 E5 30 50 58 S 143 5 23 E CT HT BIG RIG

Wingham

- Wingham Showground ☎ (02) 6553 4083
  ☑ *See also New South Wales site 88.*
  Gloucester Rd. Daylight hours only
  HEMA 37 B13 31 52 25 S 152 21 43 E CT HT BIG RIG

Woodburn

- Woodburn Dump Point ☎ (02) 6660 0267
  Pacific Hwy. Beside public toilets next to Coraki turnoff
  HEMA 39 C13 29 4 25 S 153 20 20 E CT

Woodenbong

- Woodenbong Campground ☎ (02) 6635 1300
  ☑ *See also New South Wales site 217.*
  W end of town, next to swimming pool. Deposit for key at Ampol
  HEMA 39 A11 28 23 20 S 152 36 21 E CT HT BIG RIG

Wyangala Waters

- Wyangala Waters Holiday Parks ☎ (02) 6345 0877
  ☑ *See also New South Wales site 465.*
  Day fee to enter park. See reception
  HEMA 36 H5 33 57 46 S 148 57 17 E CT $ BIG RIG

Wyong

- Caltex Service Station ☎ (02) 4352 2944
  Both sides of F3 Freeway
  HEMA 33 G12 33 15 10 S 151 24 12 E CT HT BIG RIG

Yass

- Yass Dump Point
  1428 Yass Valley Way, outside council depot
  HEMA 44 C2 34 49 18 S 148 54 21 E CT HT BIG RIG

Young

- Young Showground ☎ (02) 6382 2079
  ☑ *See also New South Wales site 694.*
  In showground at Young. Entry from Whitman Ave
  HEMA 36 J3 34 18 58 S 148 18 50 E CT HT BIG RIG

Australian Capital Territory

Canberra

- Epic Exhibition Park
  Federal Hwy, Lyneham. Adjacent to camping area. Call ahead as site often closed during Dec - Jan/ Easter
  HEMA 47 C5 35 13 36 S 149 8 55 E CT HT BIG RIG

Victoria

Ararat

- Ararat
  ☑ *See also Victoria site 472.*
  Alexandra Ave
  HEMA 58 C7 37 16 50 S 142 55 59 E CT HT BIG RIG

Avoca

- Avoca Caravan Park ☎ (03) 5465 3073
  ☑ *See also Victoria site 405.*
  Liebig St. 1.2 km W of PO. Dump is outside caravan park
  HEMA 59 C9 37 5 36 S 143 28 7 E CT HT BIG RIG

Ballarat

- Eureka Stockade Caravan Park ☎ (03) 5331 2281
  104 Stawell Street South. Public access, must stop at reception
  HEMA 59 E10 37 33 49 S 143 53 9 E CT HT $ BIG RIG

Benalla

- Benalla Dump Point
  Off Samaria Rd, at old Airport Terminus Building. Signposted
  HEMA 64 C3 36 33 11 S 145 59 50 E CT HT

Bendigo

- Bendigo Showgrounds ☎ 0407 094 805
  Holmes Rd. 2 km N of PO
  HEMA 63 K10 36 44 18 S 144 16 23 E CT HT BIG RIG

Birchip

- Birchip
  At Community Leisure Centre, access from corner Morrison & Johnson Rds. Veer L to toilet block
  HEMA 62 G6 35 58 46 S 142 54 41 E CT HT BIG RIG

Bridgewater

- Bridgewater Recreation Reserve
  ☑ *See also Victoria site 368.*
  Bridgewater-Maldon Rd
  HEMA 63 K9 36 36 23 S 143 56 41 E CT HT BIG RIG

Bruthen

- Bruthen Caravan Park ☎ (03) 5157 5753
  ☑ *See also Victoria site 132.*
  Tambo Upper Rd. 600m E of PO. Pay fee at reception
  HEMA 65 H8 37 42 43 S 147 50 8 E CT HT $ BIG RIG

Cann River

- Cann River Rainforest Caravan Park ☎ (03) 5158 6369
  ☑ *See also Victoria site 5.*
  7536 Princes Hwy, just W of Cann River Bridge
  HEMA 65 G12 37 33 59 S 149 8 46 E CT

Casterton

- Island Park Caravan Park ☎ 0457 414 187
  ☑ *See also Victoria site 555.*
  Caravan Park at Casterton. M Carmichel Drive off Murray St, adjacent to swimming pool. Next to amenities block. Public access
  HEMA 58 E3 37 34 58 S 141 24 19 E CT BIG RIG

Charlton

- Charlton Travellers Rest ☎ (03) 5491 1613
  ☑ *See also Victoria site 361.*
  43-45 High Street
  HEMA 63 H8 36 16 2 S 143 21 7 E CT

Cobram

- Cobram Dump Point
  Cobram Showgrounds, entrance from Banks St into Ivy St. Follow past tennis courts to Sthn corner
  HEMA 64 A2 35 55 18 S 145 39 9 E CT HT BIG RIG

Cohuna

- Cohuna Dump Point
  Cohuna Island Rd, near caravan park
  HEMA 63 G10 35 48 17 S 144 13 33 E CT HT BIG RIG

Colac

- Central Caravan Park ☎ (03) 5231 3586
  ☑ *See also Victoria site 500.*
  Caravan Park at Colac. Bruce St. At showground. Gold coin donation for use
  HEMA 61 F9 38 20 9 S 143 36 12 E CT HT BIG RIG

Corryong

- Corryong Dump Point
  Next to toilet block at Saleyards, Donaldson St (School Lane)
  HEMA 65 B8 36 11 17 S 147 53 56 E CT BIG RIG

Daylesford

- Daylesford Victoria Caravan Park ☎ (03) 5348 3821
  Cnr Ballan Rd & Burrall St. Key at the Reception office, deposit required
  HEMA 59 D11 37 21 31 S 144 8 23 E CT BIG RIG $

Dimboola

❖ Dimboola Dump Point ☎ (03) 5391 4444
Wimmera St, near caravan park entrance
HEMA 62 J4 36 27 24 S 142 1 30 E

Dinner Plain

❖ Scrubbers End Overnight Parking ☎ 1300 734 365
☑ See also Victoria site 145.
Parking Area at Dinner Plain Alpine Village. Enter via Big Muster Dr & Scrubbers End Lane, E side of village
HEMA 64 E6 37 1 28 S 147 14 36 E CT

Donald

❖ Donald Apex Park
☑ See also Victoria site 392.
Rest Area at Donald. N end of town
HEMA 62 J7 36 22 3 S 142 58 39 E CT HT BIG RIG

Eagle Point

❖ Eagle Point Caravan Park ☎ (03) 5156 1183
☑ See also Victoria site 34.
Camp Park Rd. 12 km S of Bairnsdale. Opposite Reception
HEMA 65 H8 37 53 32 S 147 40 53 E CT HT BIG RIG

Elmore

❖ Aysons Reserve (Campaspe River)
☑ See also Victoria site 427.
At Camp Area 8 km NE of Elmore. Turn N off Midland Hwy 32 km W of Stanhope or 5 km NE of Elmore along Burnewang Rd for 3 km
HEMA 63 J11 36 27 34 S 144 40 8 E CT HT BIG RIG

Euroa

❖ Euroa Shell Service Centre
At Shell Service Centre, off M31
HEMA 64 D2 36 44 38 S 145 35 27 E CT HT BIG RIG

Foster

❖ Foster Dump Point
Cnr Main St & Nelson St, at service station
HEMA 66 H5 38 39 8 S 146 12 13 E CT HT BIG RIG

Girgaree

❖ Girgarre Town Park
☑ See also Victoria site 425.
Corner of Winter & Station St. Dump beside hall near toilets
HEMA 63 J12 36 23 53 S 144 58 48 E CT HT BIG RIG

Harcourt

❖ Harcourt Dump Point
Cnr High & Bridge Sts
HEMA 59 B12 36 59 40 S 144 15 43 E CT HT BIG RIG

Heathcote

❖ Heathcote Dump Point ☎ (03) 5433 3121
Barrack St, outside of Queen Meadow Caravan Park
HEMA 59 B13 36 55 24 S 144 42 47 E CT HT BIG RIG

Heyfield

❖ Heyfield RV Rest Stop ☎ 0418 108 691
☑ See also Victoria site 43.
700m SE of Heyfield Post Office, cnr MacFarlane & Clark Sts.
HEMA 64 J5 37 59 6 S 146 47 15 E CT HT BIG RIG

Heywood

❖ Heywood Dump Point
Hunter St East
HEMA 58 G3 38 7 51 S 141 37 57 E CT HT BIG RIG

Holland Landing

❖ Holland Landing Dump Point ☎ (03) 5142 3333
Holland Landing Rd. Near public toilets at the Jetty
HEMA 64 J7 38 3 13 S 147 27 36 E CT BIG RIG

Hopetoun

❖ Hopetoun Rest Area
☑ See also Victoria site 583.
At Rest Area 1 km NE of Hopetoun
HEMA 62 G5 35 43 21 S 142 21 53 E CT BIG RIG

Horsham

❖ Horsham Dump Point
Firebrace St, outside Caravan Park
HEMA 58 A5 36 43 21 S 142 11 58 E CT HT BIG RIG

Jeparit

❖ Jeparit Dump Point
Dimboola - Rainbow Rd, outside the shire depot
HEMA 62 H4 36 8 24 S 141 59 23 E CT HT BIG RIG

Kaniva

❖ Kaniva Caravan Park ☎ 0458 687 054
☑ See also Victoria site 495.
Caravan Park at Kaniva. Baker St. Dump is near Dungey St gates. Public access
HEMA 62 J2 36 22 54 S 141 14 25 E CT BIG RIG

Kerang

❖ Kerang Dump Point
Markets Rd
HEMA 63 G9 35 44 14 S 143 55 39 E CT HT BIG RIG

Korumburra

❖ Korumburra Showgrounds Dump Point ☎ (03) 5655 2326
Victoria St. Rear entrance gate, next to toilet block. Key must be collected from Korumburra Tourist Park in Bourke St. Deposit required for key
HEMA 57 K13 38 25 40 S 145 49 2 E CT HT BIG RIG

Kyabram

❖ Kyabram Dump Point ☎ (03) 5852 2883
Fauna Park Road, off Lake Rd. Next to toilet block. Obtain key from Fauna Park office
HEMA 63 J12 36 19 16 S 145 2 52 E CT

Kyneton

❖ Kyneton Mineral Springs Reserve
☑ See also Victoria site 380.
Parking Area 3.5 km W of Kyneton on Burton Ave
HEMA 59 C12 37 14 9 S 144 25 10 E CT HT BIG RIG

Lake Bolac

❖ Lake Bolac Dump Point
In service Rd, next to the Glenelg Hwy
HEMA 58 E7 37 42 40 S 142 50 32 E CT HT BIG RIG

Lakes Entrance

❖ Lakes Entrance-Gippsland Lakes Fishing Club
☑ See also Victoria site 32.
Opposite Information Centre. Bullock Island Rd
HEMA 65 H8 37 52 58 S 147 58 18 E CT HT BIG RIG

Lancefield

❖ Lancefield Caravan Park ☎ (03) 5429 1434
☑ See also Victoria site 381.
30 Chauncey St. Public access for a fee
HEMA 59 C13 37 16 44 S 144 43 48 E CT HT $ BIG RIG

Leitchville

❖ Leitchville Dump Point
Leitchville Recreation Reserve, Cohuna - Leitchville Rd
HEMA 63 G10 35 54 13 S 144 17 55 E CT HT BIG RIG

Leongatha

❖ Leongatha Apex Caravan Park ☎ (03) 5662 2753
14 Turner St. 800m N of PO. Fee for non guests
HEMA 57 K14 38 28 18 S 145 56 52 E CT $

Lockington

❖ Lockington Travellers Stopover ☎ 0447 787 581
☑ See also Victoria site 285.
In Camp Area at Lockington, Main St
HEMA 63 H11 36 16 15 S 144 32 8 E CT HT

Lorne

❖ Lorne Dump Point ☎ 1300 891 152
Behind Lorne Visitors Centre. Turn into Otway St, follow road towards the spit. Dump is on the RH side at 2nd toilet block
HEMA 61 G12 38 32 6 S 143 58 37 E CT BIG RIG

Macarthur

❖ Macarthur Recreation Reserve ☎ (03) 5576 1113
☑ See also Victoria site 511.
700m S of town off Port Fairy - Hamilton Rd, entry to reserve just S of river crossing. Signposted
HEMA 58 G4 38 2 15 S 142 0 27 E CT HT BIG RIG

Maffra

❖ Gippsland Vehicle Collection ☎ (03) 5147 3223
1A Sale Rd. Access by arrangement
HEMA 64 J5 37 58 24 S 146 59 5 E CT HT $ BIG RIG

Mallacoota

❖ Mallacoota Foreshore Holiday Park ☎ (03) 5158 0300
☑ See also Victoria site 3.
Allan Drive
HEMA 65 G13 37 33 26 S 149 45 32 E CT HT BIG RIG

Mansfield

❖ Mansfield Dump Point ☎ 1800 039 049
Stock Route off High St, 100 metres W of Info Centre
HEMA 64 E3 37 3 0 S 146 4 43 E CT HT BIG RIG

Maryborough

❖ Maryborough dump Point
Reservoir Rd, off the Ballarat - Maryborough Rd
HEMA 59 B10 37 3 52 S 143 43 55 E CT HT BIG RIG

Mildura

❖ Mildura Dump Point ☎ (03) 5018 8450
Benetook Avenue, between 11th & 14th Sts. Front of council depot, opposite TAFE
HEMA 62 A4 34 12 17 S 142 10 6 E CT HT BIG RIG

Mirboo North

❖ BP Service Station
Ridgway St, Mirboo North. Key from attendant, fee if no fuel purchased
HEMA 66 G4 38 24 4 S 146 9 39 E CT HT $ BIG RIG

Murrabit
- Murrabit Recreation Reserve
  ☑ *See also Victoria site 302.*
  Browning Ave, inside Rec Reserve
  HEMA 63 F9 35 31 49 S 143 57 9 E CT HT BIG RIG

Murtoa
- Murtoa Dump Point
  Lake St, near the showground & caravan park
  HEMA 58 A6 34 37 20 S 142 27 59 E CT HT BIG RIG

Nathalia
- Nathalia Dump Point
  Weir St, next to the toilets
  HEMA 63 H13 36 3 20 S 145 12 3 E CT

Neerim South
- Neerim South Recreation Reserve
  Neerim East Rd
  HEMA 66 E4 38 0 59 S 145 57 24 E CT HT BIG RIG

Nicholson
- Nicholson River Reserve
  ☑ *See also Victoria site 33.*
  Toilet block at boat ramp car park. Cassette only
  HEMA 65 H8 37 49 2 S 147 44 24 E CT

Numurkah
- Numurkah Showgrounds
  Enter via Tunnock Rd
  HEMA 64 B1 36 5 38 S 145 26 45 E CT HT BIG RIG

Nyah
- Nyah Recreation Reserve
  ☑ *See also Victoria site 308.*
  River St, adjacent to Harness Club
  HEMA 63 E8 35 10 18 S 143 22 53 E CT BIG RIG

Orbost
- Orbost Dump Point
  Forest Road behind the truck wash
  HEMA 65 H10 37 42 28 S 148 27 5 E CT HT

Paynesville
- Paynesville Progress Jetty ☎ (03) 5153 9500
  Toilet block on The Esplanade
  HEMA 65 H8 37 55 9 S 147 43 10 E CT BIG RIG

Port Albert
- Port Albert Parking Area
  ☑ *See also Victoria site 89.*
  Parking Area Wharf St, 49 Tarraville Rdnear boat ramp. Collect Key from Port Albert General Store
  HEMA 66 H6 38 40 22 S 146 41 38 E CT BIG RIG

Portland
- Portland Dump Point
  Henty Park, adjacent to amenities block, near the Cable Tram depot
  HEMA 58 H3 38 21 16 S 141 36 22 E CT

Pyramid Hill
- Pyramid Hill Caravan Park ☎ 0438 557 012
  ☑ *See also Victoria site 286.*
  Caravan Park at Pyramid Hill. 1 km E of PO. At the rear of the amenities block
  HEMA 63 H10 36 3 19 S 144 7 30 E CT HT BIG RIG

Rainbow
- Rainbow Dump Point
  Park St, off the Rainbow - Nhill Rd. Next to the bowling club.
  HEMA 62 G4 35 54 5 S 141 59 30 E CT HT BIG RIG

Robinvale
- Robinvale Dump Point
  Riverside Park, Robin Street
  HEMA 62 C6 34 34 52 S 142 46 24 E CT HT BIG RIG

Rosebud
- Capel Sound Foreshore Reserve ☎ (03) 5986 4382
  Port Nepean Rd, entry at section B just N of Elizabeth Ave. Near amentities block 3
  HEMA 56 J7 38 21 49 S 144 52 24 E CT

Rosedale
- Rosedale Bowling Club
  1 Dawson St. Near Wood St
  HEMA 64 J5 38 9 21 S 146 46 49 E CT

Sale
- Port of Sale
  Canal Rd, behind Council office. Cassettes only, access via steps behind toilet block
  HEMA 64 J6 38 6 45 S 147 3 46 E CT
- Sale Showground Caravan & Motorhome Park ☎ (03) 5144 6432
  ☑ *See also Victoria site 37.*
  Sale-Maffra Rd
  HEMA 64 J6 38 5 31 S 147 3 58 E CT HT BIG RIG
- Wellington Visitor Information Centre ☎ 1800 677 520
  8 Foster Street
  HEMA 64 J6 38 6 44 S 147 3 27 E CT BIG RIG

Sea Lake
- Sea Lake Recreation Reserve Caravan Park ☎ 0427 701 261
  ☑ *See also Victoria site 355.*
  71-91 Calder Hwy
  HEMA 62 F6 35 30 12 S 142 50 56 E CT HT BIG RIG

St Arnaud
- St Arnaud Sports Club ☎ (03) 5495 1268
  Dunstan St, off Charlton St Arnaud Rd, behind sports club
  HEMA 59 A8 36 36 32 S 143 15 34 E CT HT BIG RIG

Stawell
- Stawell Dump Point
  Scallen St, near public toilets
  HEMA 58 C7 37 3 15 S 142 46 52 E CT BIG RIG

Strathmerten
- Strathmerton Dump Point
  Murray Valley Hwy, lane behind toilet block. Opposite pub
  HEMA 63 G13 35 55 33 S 145 28 46 E CT HT BIG RIG

Sunshine
- Sunshine 7 Eleven Service Station ☎ (03) 9310 2694
  Western Ring Road, Northbound. Take truck lane, past diesel pumps. Marked as Bus Effluent point
  HEMA 52 G4 37 48 16 S 144 48 16 E CT BIG RIG
- Sunshine 7 Eleven Service Station ☎ (03) 9310 2615
  Western Ring Road, Southbound.Take truck lane, past diesel pumps. Marked as Bus Effluent point
  HEMA 52 G4 37 48 16 S 144 48 33 E CT BIG RIG

Swan Hill
- Swan Hill Showgrounds
  Entry via Stradbroke Ave. Left of the Grandstand
  HEMA 63 E8 35 20 20 S 143 22 4 E CT HT BIG RIG

Tallangatta
- Tallangatta Showgrounds ☎ (02) 6071 2621
  ☑ *See also Victoria site 112.*
  Camp Area at Tallangatta. Weramu St. Call ahead to gain entry. Gold coin donation for water
  HEMA 64 B6 36 13 10 S 147 10 5 E CT HT BIG RIG

Tatura
- Tatura Park
  Hastie St, entrance opposite Davy St
  HEMA 64 C1 36 26 44 S 145 13 58 E CT BIG RIG

Tidal River
- Tidal River ☎ 131 963
  ☑ *See also Victoria site 95.*
  At Camp Area
  HEMA 66 K5 39 1 48 S 146 19 16 E CT HT

Walwa
- Walwa Dump Point
  Ohalloran St, off River Rd. At the football oval
  HEMA 65 A8 35 57 44 S 147 44 11 E CT HT BIG RIG

Warracknabeal
- Warracknabeal Caravan Park ☎ 0400 915 125
  ☑ *See also Victoria site 600.*
  2 Lyle St. Public access
  HEMA 62 H5 36 15 11 S 142 23 15 E CT HT

Warrnambool
- Surfside Holiday Park ☎ (03) 5559 4700
  Pertobe St. Public access. Call first, fee for non guests
  HEMA 60 F2 38 23 28 S 142 28 59 E CT HT $

Wedderburn
- Wedderburn Pioneer Caravan Park ☎ (03) 5494 3301
  ☑ *See also Victoria site 364.*
  Caravan Park at Wedderburn. Hospital St. 1 km E of PO. Public Access, report to office
  HEMA 63 J8 36 24 47 S 143 36 59 E CT HT BIG RIG

Wulgulmerang
- Wulgulmerang Recreation Reserve ☎ (03) 5155 0244
  ☑ *See also Victoria site 25.*
  Snowy River Rd
  HEMA 65 E9 37 4 6 S 148 15 37 E CT HT BIG RIG

Wycheproof
- Wycheproof Dump Point
  Calder Hwy, beside Caravan Park & Sports Oval
  HEMA 62 H7 36 4 13 S 143 13 33 E CT HT BIG RIG
- Wycheproof Caravan Park ☎ (03) 5493 7278
  ☑ *See also Victoria site 358.*
  Caravan Park at Wycheproof. Calder Hwy 500m, N of PO
  HEMA 62 H7 36 4 10 S 143 13 32 E CT HT BIG RIG

Yarram
- Yarram Recreation Reserve
  Railway Ave, via Buckley St
  HEMA 66 H6 38 33 25 S 146 40 25 E CT HT BIG RIG

Victoria

Yarrawonga

- Yarrawonga Showgrounds ☎ (03) 5744 1989
  Dunlop St. Collect key from Visitor Information Centre, Irvine Pde. Deposit required. Next to cream brick amenities block
  HEMA 64 A3 | 36 1 3 S | 146 0 32 E | CT HT BIG RIG

Yea

- Yea Water Discovery Centre ☎ (03) 5797 2663
  2 Hood St
  HEMA 64 F1 | 37 12 36 S | 145 25 37 E | CT HT BIG RIG

Tasmania

Arthur River

- Arthur River Dump Point ☎ (03) 6452 4800
  S side of river, turn R to Gardiner Point. Dump point is situated at the end of the Rd at the "Edge of the World Lookout"
  HEMA 76 G3 | 41 3 27 S | 144 39 37 E | CT BIG RIG

Beaconsfield

- Beaconsfield Recreation Ground ☎ (03) 6383 6350
  ☑ *See also Tasmania site 188.*
  York St, off Grubb St. E side of town
  HEMA 74 D6 | 41 11 57 S | 146 49 19 E | CT HT BIG RIG

Bicheno

- Bicheno Beach Toilet Block ☎ (03) 6375 1333
  The Esplanade
  HEMA 75 J14 | 41 52 31 S | 148 18 36 E | CT HT BIG RIG

Bothwell

- Bothwell Dump Point ☎ (03) 6259 5503
  Market place, rear of Council CP, behind golf museum
  HEMA 73 H13 | 42 22 59 S | 147 0 31 E | CT

Burnie

- Cooee Point Reserve ☎ (03) 6431 1033
  ☑ *See also Tasmania site 168.*
  Cooee Point. 3 km W of Burnie, via Turrung St & Cooee Point Rd
  HEMA 77 F9 | 41 2 19 S | 145 52 37 E | CT HT BIG RIG
- South Burnie Dumpoint
  Esplanade, Reeve St public toilets near yacht club
  HEMA 77 G9 | 41 3 44 S | 145 54 54 E | CT BIG RIG

Cambridge

- Cambridge Memorial Oval ☎ (03) 6245 8600
  Cambridge Rd
  HEMA 69 G2 | 42 50 10 S | 147 26 41 E | CT HT BIG RIG

Campbell Town

- King Street Oval
  ☑ *See also Tasmania site 53.*
  King St, western end of oval
  HEMA 75 J10 | 41 55 47 S | 147 29 17 E | CT HT BIG RIG

Cradle Mountain

- Cradle Mountain Dump Point
  Behind the Visitor Information Centre, near the bus car park
  HEMA 72 B7 | 41 34 52 S | 145 56 16 E | CT HT BIG RIG

Cygnet

- Burtons Reserve ☎ (03) 6264 8448
  Off Charlton St, S end of town. Adjacent to toilet block
  HEMA 71 G12 | 43 9 48 S | 147 4 55 E | CT HT

Deloraine

- Deloraine East Overnight Park ☎ (03) 6393 5300
  ☑ *See also Tasmania site 138.*
  Racecourse Drive, near tennis courts
  HEMA 74 G5 | 41 31 19 S | 146 39 43 E | CT HT BIG RIG

Devonport

- Devonport South Dump Point
  Miandetta-Devonport Rd, at the sewerage facility next to bridge near Horsehead Creek
  HEMA 77 G12 | 41 11 59 S | 146 21 19 E | CT HT BIG RIG

Devonport East

- East Devonport Recreation Centre (Girdlestone Park) ☎ (03) 6424 4466
  ☑ *See also Tasmania site 148.*
  Car park at football ground in John St
  HEMA 77 G12 | 41 11 10 S | 146 22 45 E | CT HT BIG RIG

Evandale

- Morven Park
  Barclay St. W end of town. Behind clubhouse
  HEMA 75 G9 | 41 34 5 S | 147 14 49 E | CT HT BIG RIG

Fingal

- Fingal Park
  ☑ *See also Tasmania site 36.*
  Talbot St, beside public toilets
  HEMA 75 G12 | 41 38 17 S | 147 58 6 E | CT BIG RIG

Franklin

- Franklin Foreshore Reserve
  ☑ *See also Tasmania site 84.*
  Adjacent to toilet block
  HEMA 71 F11 | 43 5 34 S | 147 0 33 E | CT HT BIG RIG

George Town

- George Town Rest Area
  ☑ *See also Tasmania site 186.*
  Main Rd. S end of town, behind information centre
  HEMA 74 C6 | 41 6 33 S | 146 50 18 E | CT HT

Gordon

- Gordon Foreshore Reserve ☎ (03) 6211 8200
  ☑ *See also Tasmania site 97.*
  At Reserve, Channel Hwy
  HEMA 71 G12 | 43 15 42 S | 147 14 33 E | CT HT BIG RIG

Hamilton

- Hamilton Camping Ground ☎ (03) 6286 3202
  ☑ *See also Tasmania site 108.*
  W end of town. Beside river
  HEMA 73 J12 | 42 33 33 S | 146 49 50 E | CT HT BIG RIG

Hobart

- BP Service Station ☎ (03) 6234 3549
  200 Brooker Hwy
  HEMA 68 B2 | 42 52 12 S | 147 19 18 E | CT
- Hobart Showgrounds ☎ (03) 6272 6812
  ☑ *See also Tasmania site 75.*
  Howard Rd, Glenorchy
  HEMA 69 G1 | 42 50 2 S | 147 17 6 E | CT HT BIG RIG
- Montrose Bay Reserve
  Foreshore Rd, off Brooker Hwy
  HEMA 69 H1 | 42 49 17 S | 147 16 8 E | CT HT BIG RIG
- Rosny Sewage Treatment Plant ☎ (03) 6245 8600
  Off Rosny Esplanade, via Bastick St
  HEMA 68 B4 | 42 52 23 S | 147 21 23 E | CT HT BIG RIG

Huonville

- Huonville Foreshore ☎ (03) 6264 0326
  Channel Hwy. Next to the toilets
  HEMA 71 F11 | 43 2 5 S | 147 3 4 E | CT HT BIG RIG

Kempton

- Victoria Memorial Hall ☎ (03) 6259 3011
  Old Hunting Ground Rd, off Main St
  HEMA 73 J14 | 42 31 54 S | 147 11 59 E | CT

Kingston

- Kingston Wetlands Site ☎ (03) 6211 8242
  At entrance to Wetlands Reserve, Channel Hwy
  HEMA 69 H1 | 42 58 27 S | 147 18 50 E | CT HT BIG RIG

Latrobe

- Latrobe Motorhome Stop ☎ (03) 6421 4699
  ☑ *See also Tasmania site 153.*
  Rear of Wells Supermarket, access off Cotton St
  HEMA 77 H12 | 41 14 14 S | 146 24 37 E | CT HT BIG RIG

Launceston

- Inveresk Showgrounds (York Park Precinct) ☎ (03) 6323 3383
  Forster St, off Invermay Rd. In all day parking area near the Round House. Entry near South St
  HEMA 75 F8 | 41 25 22 S | 147 8 24 E | CT HT BIG RIG

Narawntapu National Park

- Bakers Point Campground (3) ☎ (03) 6428 6277
  ☑ *See also Tasmania site 194.*
  Camp Area 18 km N of B71/C740 junction. 6 km dirt Rd
  HEMA 74 D5 | 41 9 44 S | 146 34 5 E | CT
- Springlawn Campground ☎ (03) 6428 6277
  ☑ *See also Tasmania site 193.*
  Camp Area 13.5 km N of B71/C740 junction. 2 km dirt Rd
  HEMA 74 D5 | 41 8 52 S | 146 36 9 E | CT

New Norfolk

- New Norfolk Dump Point
  Page Ave, next to caravan park
  HEMA 71 D11 | 42 46 34 S | 147 3 57 E | CT HT BIG RIG

Nubeena

- Nubeena Dump Point ☎ (03) 6251 2400
  Nubeena Rd, opposite Police Station. N end of town
  HEMA 69 J3 | 43 5 44 S | 147 44 36 E | CT HT BIG RIG

Penguin

❖ Penguin Dump Point ☎(03) 6429 8979
Cnr of Main & Johnsons Beach Rds. If locked, key at Information Centre
HEMA 77 G10 41 6 36 S 146 4 10 E CT HT BIG RIG

Pontville

❖ Pontville Park RV Stop ☎(03) 6268 7000
☑ *See also Tasmania site 72.*
Glen Lea Rd, off the Midland Hwy
HEMA 69 F1 42 41 12 S 147 15 37 E CT HT BIG RIG

Port Huon

❖ Shipwrights Point Regatta Ground ☎(03) 6264 0300
☑ *See also Tasmania site 85.*
In Camp Area at Port Huon. Just N of wharf area, beside river. Signposted
HEMA 71 G11 43 9 31 S 146 58 47 E CT HT BIG RIG

Port Sorell

❖ Port Sorell Jetty ☎(03) 6426 2693
Darling St. N end, next to caravan park
HEMA 77 G13 41 9 50 S 146 33 23 E CT HT BIG RIG

Queenstown

❖ Queenstown Dump Point
Lyell Hwy (Batchlor St), near Mary St beside works building
HEMA 72 F5 42 4 38 S 145 33 34 E CT BIG RIG

Railton

❖ Railton Motorhome Stop
☑ *See also Tasmania site 154.*
At Camp Spot on the Esplanade. N side of Foster Street opposite Hotel
HEMA 77 J12 41 20 39 S 146 25 23 E CT HT BIG RIG

Rosebery

❖ Rosebery Dump Point
Murchison Hwy, S end of town opposite toilets
HEMA 72 D5 41 46 49 S 145 32 19 E CT HT BIG RIG

Ross

❖ Ross Dump Point
Near Caravan Park, the Esplanade, off High St
HEMA 69 A2 42 1 49 S 147 29 26 E CT HT BIG RIG

Scottsdale

❖ Northeast Park
☑ *See also Tasmania site 3.*
Ringarooma Rd. 1 km E of Post Office
HEMA 75 D10 41 9 54 S 147 31 24 E CT BIG RIG

Sheffield

❖ Sheffield Recreation Ground
☑ *See also Tasmania site 155.*
Spring St, on Rd to Recreation Grounds
HEMA 77 J12 41 22 58 S 146 20 9 E CT HT BIG RIG

Sisters Beach

❖ Sisters Beach Dump Point
Behind Fire Station, cnr Honeysuckle Ave & Cumming St
HEMA 77 F8 40 55 6 S 145 33 52 E CT

Smithton

❖ Smithton Esplanade
☑ *See also Tasmania site 177.*
West Esplanade, on W side of Duck River Bridge. RH side
HEMA 76 E5 40 50 20 S 145 7 12 E CT HT BIG RIG

Sorell

❖ Sorell RV Stop ☎(03) 6269 0000
☑ *See also Tasmania site 48.*
Montague St
HEMA 69 G3 42 47 2 S 147 33 24 E CT BIG RIG

St Helens

❖ St Helens Sporting Complex
☑ *See also Tasmania site 29.*
Tully St
HEMA 75 E14 41 19 0 S 148 14 8 E CT HT BIG RIG

St Leonards

❖ St Leonards Park Dump Point
Station Rd, off Johnston Rd. In car park. Difficult access if car park busy. Cassette only
HEMA 75 F8 41 27 45 S 147 11 35 E CT

St Mary's

❖ St Marys Sportsground & Golf Course
☑ *See also Tasmania site 37.*
22 Harefield St
HEMA 75 G13 41 35 5 S 148 11 2 E CT HT BIG RIG

Stanley

❖ Stanley Public Dump Point
Tatlow's Wharf Rd, beyond Caravan Park, next to toilet block
HEMA 76 D6 40 45 50 S 145 17 45 E CT HT BIG RIG

Strahan

❖ Council Depot
96 Harvey St (Ocean Beach Rd), outside depot
HEMA 72 G4 42 8 59 S 145 18 50 E CT HT BIG RIG

Swansea

❖ Boat Ramp Car Park ☎(03) 6257 8155
The Esplanade, near toilets & play ground
HEMA 69 B5 42 7 51 S 148 4 31 E CT HT BIG RIG

Triabunna

❖ Triabunna Dump Point ☎(03) 6257 4772
Via Boyle St, Esplanade East. Veer L over bridge
HEMA 69 E4 42 30 33 S 147 55 10 E CT HT BIG RIG

Tullah

❖ Tullah dump Point
Farrell St. GPS approximate
HEMA 72 C6 41 44 14 S 145 37 0 E CT

Ulverstone

❖ Ulverstone Dump Point ☎(03) 6429 8979
Cnr of Victoria St & Beach Rd. Key at Visitor Information Centre
HEMA 77 G11 41 9 6 S 146 10 27 E CT HT BIG RIG

Waratah

❖ Waratah Dump Point ☎(03) 6443 8342
Annie St. Opposite Council Works Depot
HEMA 72 A5 41 26 36 S 145 31 51 E CT HT BIG RIG

Westbury

❖ Andys Bakery Café ☎(03) 6393 1846
☑ *See also Tasmania site 136.*
Meander Valley Rd. E end of town, behind bakery
HEMA 74 G6 41 31 32 S 146 50 42 E CT HT BIG RIG

Wynyard

❖ Wynyard Solid Waste Transfer Station ☎(03) 6443 8342
Goldie St (W end). Business hours only
HEMA 77 F9 40 59 33 S 145 42 59 E CT HT BIG RIG

Zeehan

❖ Zeehan Dump Point
Mulchahy - Packer St, off B27 300m from Intersection on RHS
HEMA 72 E4 41 53 25 S 145 20 45 E CT HT BIG RIG

South Australia

Ardrossan

❖ Council Dump Point
Cnr Second St & West Terrace at rear of Bowling Club & Tennis Counts, enter from West Terrace
HEMA 88 F7 34 25 28 S 137 54 52 E CT HT BIG RIG

Andamooka

❖ Andamooka Camping Ground ☎(08) 8672 7023
☑ *See also South Australia site 458.*
Camp Area 1 km W of Andamooka.
HEMA 94 C6 30 27 4 S 137 9 46 E CT HT BIG RIG

Arno Bay

❖ The Arno Bay Hotel ☎(08) 8628 0001
☑ *See also South Australia site 496.*
Camp Area at Arno Bay. Tel El Kebir Terrace, foreshore end.
HEMA 88 E4 33 54 59 S 136 34 22 E CT HT BIG RIG

Balaklava

❖ Balaklava Caravan Park ☎0400 264 075
☑ *See also South Australia site 261.*
Short Tce. Next to swimming pool
HEMA 89 F8 34 8 57 S 138 25 8 E CT HT BIG RIG

Barmera

❖ Bruce Oval
☑ *See also South Australia site 136.*
Sims St
HEMA 89 F12 34 15 13 S 140 28 3 E CT HT BIG RIG

Beachport

❖ Surf Beach Dump Point
Millicent - Beachport Rd. In car park 500m W of Robe turnoff (Southern Ports Hwy)
HEMA 98 H5 37 28 26 S 140 1 52 E CT HT BIG RIG

Berri

❖ Martins Bend Campground ☎(08) 8582 2423
☑ *See also South Australia site 117.*
At Camp Area 3 km E of Berri, via Riverview Rd. Follow signs. See caretaker before using
HEMA 89 F12 34 17 24 S 140 37 49 E CT

Blanchetown

❖ Blanchetown Dump Point
South St at Lower Blanchetown Oval
HEMA 89 F10 34 21 19 S 139 36 59 E CT HT BIG RIG

Bordertown

❖ Bordertown Recreation Lake
☑ *See also South Australia site 99.*
Off Golf Rd, at Rest Area
HEMA 98 F6 36 18 21 S 140 46 31 E CT HT BIG RIG

Burra

❖ Burra Caravan & Camping Park ☎ (08) 8892 2442
☑ *See also South Australia site 226.*
12 Bridge Tce. Fee for use, see reception
HEMA 89 D9 33 40 44 S 138 56 15 E CT HT $ BIG RIG

❖ Burra Showgrounds ☎ (08) 8892 2738
☑ *See also South Australia site 227.*
Hall Terrace.
HEMA 89 D9 33 40 5 S 138 55 28 E CT HT $ BIG RIG

Bute

❖ Bute Dump Point
Railway Terrace. Near toilets
HEMA 88 E7 33 51 54 S 138 0 32 E CT BIG RIG

Cadell

❖ Cadell Recreation Ground ☎ 0497 799 284
☑ *See also South Australia site 143.*
Dalzell Rd
HEMA 89 E11 34 2 16 S 139 45 26 E CT HT BIG RIG

Callington

❖ Callington Recreation Grounds
Callington Rd
HEMA 89 H9 35 6 47 S 139 2 22 E CT HT BIG RIG

Ceduna

❖ BP Service Station ☎ (08) 8625 3407
Eyre Hwy. W end of town at Fruit Fly Checkpoint
HEMA 97 G11 32 6 48 S 133 40 21 E CT HT BIG RIG

Clayton Bay

❖ Clayton Bay Dump Point
Island View Drive, next to Boat Club entrance
HEMA 89 J9 35 29 33 S 138 55 21 E CT HT BIG RIG

Cleve

❖ Cleve Dump Point
Rudall Road. 1.8 km W of PO
HEMA 88 D4 33 41 52 S 136 28 33 E CT HT BIG RIG

Coffin Bay

❖ Coffin Bay Boat Ramp
Entry from Esplanade, near toilets
HEMA 88 G2 34 36 58 S 135 27 51 E CT HT BIG RIG

Coober Pedy

❖ Coober Pedy Waterworks
Hutchinson St, 900m N of PO
HEMA 90 H1 29 0 14 S 134 45 21 E CT HT BIG RIG

Coonalpyn

❖ Coonalpyn Soldiers Memorial Caravan Park ☎ 0427 399 089
☑ *See also South Australia site 57.*
Richards Tce
HEMA 89 K11 35 41 33 S 139 51 27 E CT HT BIG RIG

Cowell

❖ Cowell Showgrounds
Cnr Brooks Drive & North Terrace
HEMA 88 D5 33 40 48 S 136 55 32 E CT HT BIG RIG

Crystal Brook

❖ Jubilee Park
☑ *See also South Australia site 271.*
Railway Tce. Between Cunningham & Bowman Sts
HEMA 89 D8 33 21 13 S 138 12 23 E CT HT BIG RIG

Cummins

❖ Cummins Community Caravan Park
62 Bruce Tce. 2 km S of PO
HEMA 88 F3 34 16 15 S 135 43 23 E CT HT BIG RIG

Curramulka

❖ Curramulka Sports Complex
☑ *See also South Australia site 312.*
Mount Rat Rd
HEMA 88 G7 34 41 52 S 137 42 24 E CT HT BIG RIG

Dublin

❖ Dublin Lions Park
☑ *See also South Australia site 257.*
In Rest Area. Old Port Wakefield Rd. Behind toilet block
HEMA 89 F8 34 27 7 S 138 21 5 E CT HT BIG RIG

Edithburgh

❖ Edithburgh Dump Point
Blanche St, opposite caravan park. Available early 2015
HEMA 88 H7 35 5 24 S 137 44 44 E CT HT BIG RIG

Elliston

❖ Eliston Dump Point
Beach Terrace, at Info Centre
HEMA 88 D1 33 38 51 S 134 53 28 E CT HT BIG RIG

Gladstone

❖ Gladstone Dump Point
Main North Road, behind caravan park
HEMA 89 C8 33 16 6 S 138 20 59 E CT HT BIG RIG

Hamley Bridge

❖ Hamley Bridge Community & Sports Centre
☑ *See also South Australia site 165.*
Stockport Rd
HEMA 86 A3 34 21 14 S 138 40 53 E CT HT BIG RIG

Hawker

❖ Hawker Town Park
☑ *See also South Australia site 375.*
Rest Area at Hawker. Elder Terrace
HEMA 95 G8 31 53 15 S 138 25 16 E CT HT BIG RIG

Iron Knob

❖ Knobbies Camping & Caravan Area
☑ *See also South Australia site 552.*
Dickens St
HEMA 88 B6 32 43 56 S 137 9 2 E CT HT $ BIG RIG

Jamestown

❖ Jamestown Dump Point ☎ (08) 8664 0077
130 Ayr St. Outside caravan park
HEMA 89 C9 33 12 19 S 138 36 3 E CT HT BIG RIG

Kadina

❖ Kadina Dump Point ☎ (08) 8821 1600
Doswell Terrace, opposite medical centre
HEMA 88 E7 33 57 32 S 137 43 16 E CT HT BIG RIG

Kapunda

❖ Kapunda Harness Racing Club ☎ 0428 956 462
Hancock Rd
HEMA 86 A5 34 20 26 S 138 54 8 E CT HT BIG RIG

Kangaroo Island

❖ American River Dump Point
Tangara Drive, in front of toilet block
HEMA 88 K7 35 47 15 S 137 46 15 E CT HT BIG RIG

❖ Christmas Cove - Penneshaw
Christmas St, off Howard Drive. Cassette only, access is limited
HEMA 88 K7 35 43 9 S 137 56 2 E CT

❖ Kingscote
Third St. Adjacent to Nepean Bay Tourist Park
HEMA 88 J6 35 40 15 S 137 36 42 E CT HT BIG RIG

❖ Parndana Dump Point ☎ (08) 8553 4500
Jubilee Ave, adjacent to Health Centre
HEMA 88 K6 35 47 17 S 137 15 38 E CT BIG RIG

❖ Western KI Caravan Park & Wildlife Reserve ☎ (08) 8559 7201
South Coast Rd. 3 km E of Flinders Chase. Fee for non guests, must call into reception
HEMA 88 K5 35 57 39 S 136 48 28 E CT HT $ BIG RIG

Karoonda

❖ Karoonda Apex Caravan Park ☎ (08) 8578 1071
☑ *See also South Australia site 129.*
Entry off Karoonda Rd, follow track to behind Oval toilet block. Signposted
HEMA 89 H11 35 5 47 S 139 53 23 E CT HT BIG RIG

Keith

❖ Keith Caravan Park ☎ (08) 8755 1957
☑ *See also South Australia site 50.*
Naracoorte Rd. Public access
HEMA 98 F5 36 6 4 S 140 21 4 E CT HT

Kimba

❖ Kimba Recreation Reserve
☑ *See also South Australia site 560.*
Buckleboo Rd, extension of Nth Terrace. Entry through archway
HEMA 88 C4 33 8 4 S 136 24 54 E CT HT BIG RIG

Kingston SE

❖ Kingston SE Dump Point
Railway Terrace, off Cape Jaffa/ Robe Hwy, at Sale Yards
HEMA 98 G4 36 50 3 S 139 51 45 E CT HT BIG RIG

Lameroo

❖ Lake Roberts
500m E of PO
HEMA 89 J12 35 19 42 S 140 31 14 E CT HT BIG RIG

Laura

❖ Laura Dump Point
North Tce, on road outside Laura Caravan Park
HEMA 89 C8 33 10 54 S 138 18 3 E CT HT BIG RIG

Leigh Creek

❖ Leigh Creek Caravan Park ☎ 0429 012 445
☑ *See also South Australia site 389.*
Acacia Dr. Public access
HEMA 95 C8 30 35 17 S 138 24 29 E CT HT BIG RIG

Loxton

❖ Loxton Motorhome Reserve ☎ (08) 8584 8071
☑ *See also South Australia site 121.*
Coral St, outside Motorhome Reserve. Opposite Loxton Sporting Club
HEMA 89 G12 34 27 6 S 140 34 42 E CT HT BIG RIG

Maitland

❖ Maitland Showground ☎ (08) 8832 2171
☑ *See also South Australia site 345.*
Rogers Tce. Signposted, near shed on right
HEMA 88 F7 34 22 18 S 137 40 39 E CT HT BIG RIG

Mannum

- Haythorpe Reserve ☎ (08) 8569 0100
  ☑ *See also South Australia site 185.*
  In parking area 1 km NE of Mannum, on Bowhill Rd. E side of river. N of ferry crossing
  HEMA 89 H10 34 54 33 S 139 19 24 E CT
- Mannum Caravan Park ☎ (08) 8569 1402
  Purnong Rd. Public access. Fee if not a guest, must contact office
  HEMA 89 H10 34 54 30 S 139 19 3 E CT HT $ BIG RIG

Marla

- Marla Dump Point
  Cockatoo Crescent
  HEMA 93 D11 27 18 8 S 133 37 22 E CT HT BIG RIG

Melrose

- Melrose Showground ☎ 0428 662 140
  ☑ *See also South Australia site 302.*
  Main North Rd. N end of town
  HEMA 89 B8 32 48 36 S 138 11 46 E CT HT BIG RIG

Meningie

- Meningie Dump Point
  Princes Hwy, in parking bay at Southern entrance to town
  HEMA 89 J10 35 41 40 S 139 20 12 E CT HT BIG RIG

Millicent

- Millicent Information Centre ☎ (08) 8733 0904
  1 Mt Gambier St, behind Info centre. Key & hose from Info centre. Open office hours only
  HEMA 98 J5 37 35 50 S 140 21 27 E CT HT BIG RIG

Minnipa

- Minnipa Dump Point
  Minnipa Oval. Mosley Tce
  HEMA 88 B2 32 51 24 S 135 9 24 E CT HT BIG RIG

Morgan

- Morgan Dump Point
  Morgan Oval, North East Terrace
  HEMA 89 E11 34 1 46 S 139 40 8 E CT HT BIG RIG

Mount Gambier

- Mt Gambier Showgrounds ☎ 0408 492 182
  ☑ *See also South Australia site 2.*
  Pick Avenue. Key from Mobil Service Station
  HEMA 98 J6 37 50 16 S 140 47 51 E CT HT $ BIG RIG

Mount Pleasant

- Talunga Park Caravan Park (Showgrounds) ☎ (08) 8568 1934
  ☑ *See also South Australia site 192.*
  Melrose St. At showground
  HEMA 86 F7 34 46 34 S 139 2 34 E CT HT BIG RIG

Mt Barker

- Mount Barker Dump Point
  Alexandrina Road
  HEMA 85 J14 35 4 26 S 138 51 43 E CT

Mundulla

- Mundulla Showground ☎ (08) 8752 0700
  ☑ *See also South Australia site 46.*
  North Terrace
  HEMA 98 F6 36 21 30 S 140 41 25 E CT HT BIG RIG

Murray Bridge

- Murray Bridge Dump Point
  Railway Terrace. 200m NE of Post Office
  HEMA 89 H10 35 6 57 S 139 16 25 E CT HT BIG RIG

Naracoorte

- Naracoorte Showgrounds ☎ 0428 621 127
  ☑ *See also South Australia site 79.*
  Smith St
  HEMA 98 G6 36 57 16 S 140 44 48 E CT HT BIG RIG

Orroroo

- Orroroo Caravan Park ☎ (08) 8658 1444
  ☑ *See also South Australia site 244.*
  Second St. 200m W of PO. At back of the park. Call at Reception to pay fee
  HEMA 89 B9 32 43 57 S 138 36 36 E CT $ BIG RIG

Peterborough

- Peterborough Dump Point
  Don Ferguson Drive, entry beside Tourist Information Centre
  HEMA 89 C9 32 58 25 S 138 50 2 E CT HT BIG RIG

Pinnaroo

- Pinnaroo
  Cnr Mallee Hwy & Homburg Tce
  HEMA 89 J13 35 15 37 S 140 54 46 E CT HT BIG RIG

Point Lowly

- Point Lowly ☎ (08) 8645 7900
  ☑ *See also South Australia site 485.*
  Port Bonython Rd, S side past gas plant. 500m from camp spot
  HEMA 88 C7 32 59 34 S 137 46 51 E CT HT BIG RIG

Port Augusta

- Port Augusta Motorhome Park
  ☑ *See also South Australia site 549.*
  Power Station Rd
  HEMA 88 A7 32 30 40 S 137 47 9 E CT HT BIG RIG

Port Broughton

- Port Broughton Dump Point ☎ (08) 8635 2107
  Cnr Mundoora & Bute Rds, next to council depot
  HEMA 88 D7 33 36 10 S 137 56 9 E CT HT BIG RIG

Port Germein

- Port Germain Recreation Grounds
  West Terrace, adjacent to First Street
  HEMA 88 C7 33 1 9 S 137 59 39 E CT HT BIG RIG

Port Gibbon

- Port Gibbon Foreshore ☎ (08) 8629 2019
  ☑ *See also South Australia site 491.*
  Port Gibbon Foreshore Access from B100 at Port Gibbon sign, through Igloo Rd
  HEMA 88 E5 33 48 7 S 136 48 6 E CT HT BIG RIG

Port Julia

- Port Julia Oval (Reichenbach Memorial Park) ☎ (08) 8853 8115
  ☑ *See also South Australia site 311.*
  Osprey St, behind toilets
  HEMA 88 G7 34 39 46 S 137 52 38 E CT

Port Lincoln

- Port Lincoln Dump Point
  Windsor Ave, off Proper Bay Road. Next to Ravendale Sportsgrounds
  HEMA 88 G3 34 44 35 S 135 51 18 E CT HT BIG RIG

Port Pirie

- Port Pirie Dump Point
  Globe Oval, Geddes Rd
  HEMA 88 C7 33 11 9 S 138 1 25 E CT HT BIG RIG

Quorn

- Quorn Dump Point
  Silo Rd
  HEMA 88 A7 32 20 26 S 138 2 52 E CT HT BIG RIG

Riverton

- Riverton Caravan Park ☎ (08) 8847 2419
  ☑ *See also South Australia site 236.*
  Cnr Oxford Tce & Torrens Rd, at Town Oval. Fee if not a guest
  HEMA 89 F9 34 9 20 S 138 44 59 E CT HT $

Robe

- Robe Dump Point
  Corner White & Robe Sts
  HEMA 98 H4 37 10 30 S 139 45 40 E CT HT BIG RIG

Robertstown

- Robertstown Oval
  ☑ *See also South Australia site 231.*
  Parking Area at Robertstown. Entry from Church St
  HEMA 89 E9 33 59 35 S 139 4 49 E CT HT BIG RIG

Roxby Downs

- Roxby Downs Dump Point
  Near BP Service Station, Olympic Hwy. $10.00 key deposit
  HEMA 94 C5 30 33 15 S 136 53 36 E CT HT BIG RIG

Snowtown

- Snowtown Centenary Park Caravan Park ☎ (08) 8865 2252
  ☑ *See also South Australia site 264.*
  In Caravan Park at Snowtown. North Tce. Use Eastern entry for higher vehicles.
  HEMA 89 E8 33 46 42 S 138 12 59 E CT HT BIG RIG

Southend

- Southend Dump Point
  Bridges Drive, behind the public toilet at beach car park
  HEMA 98 J5 37 34 14 S 140 7 5 E CT BIG RIG

St Kilda

- St Kilda Adventure Park
  ☑ *See also South Australia site 254.*
  Parking Area at St Kilda, via Mangrove St. Dump is W end of boat ramp car park. Key at Kiosk
  HEMA 82 C3 34 44 31 S 138 32 0 E CT

Streaky Bay

- Streaky Bay Lions Park
  ☑ *See also South Australia site 538.*
  East Terrace, off Flinders Hwy
  HEMA 97 J12 32 47 42 S 134 13 5 E CT HT BIG RIG

Swan Reach

- Tenbury - Hunter Reserve ☎ (08) 8569 0100
  ☑ *See also South Australia site 169.*
  Take ferry N across to W side of river. 500m E of ferry crossing. Next to toilets
  HEMA 89 G10 34 33 43 S 139 36 1 E CT HT BIG RIG

Tailem Bend

- Tailem Bend Dump Point
  Main Rd, in parking bay at Southern end of town
  HEMA 89 H10 35 16 7 S 139 27 30 E CT HT BIG RIG

Tantanoola

- Tantanoola Rest Area
  ☑ *See also South Australia site 9.*
  Opposite hotel in rest area
  HEMA 98 J5 37 41 46 S 140 27 20 E CT HT BIG RIG

Tumby Bay
- Tumby Bay Self Contained RV Park ☎ (08) 8688 2087
  ☑ *See also South Australia site 502.*
  Northern Access Rd. N end of town
  HEMA 88 F4 34 21 31 S 136 6 3 E CT HT BIG RIG

Waikerie
- Waikerie Dump Point
  Corner of Civic Ave & Dowling St, access off Civic Ave
  HEMA 89 F11 34 10 56 S 139 59 14 E CT HT BIG RIG

Wallaroo
- Wallaroo Dump Point ☎ (08) 8823 2023
  Owen Tce. Next to Mobil Service Station
  HEMA 88 E7 33 56 4 S 137 37 53 E CT HT BIG RIG

Whyalla
- Foreshore Rest Area
  Lincoln Hwy. 350m S of Mc Douall Stuart Ave
  HEMA 88 C6 33 2 46 S 137 31 35 E CT HT BIG RIG
- Jubilee Park Dump Point (Whyalla Showgrounds)
  Jenkins Ave. Signposted at entry. Daytime only, gates locked at night
  HEMA 88 C6 33 2 20 S 137 30 31 E CT HT BIG RIG

Wilmington
- Wilmington Centenary Park
  ☑ *See also South Australia site 249.*
  Melrose Tce
  HEMA 89 B8 32 39 13 S 138 6 6 E CT HT BIG RIG

Wilpena Pound
- Wilpena Pound Dump Point
  At Wilpena Pound. At the back of the long term car park. GPS approximate
  HEMA 95 F9 31 31 40 S 138 36 29 E CT BIG RIG

Wudinna
- Gawler Ranges Motel & Caravan Park ☎ (08) 8680 2090
  Eyre Hwy. 1 km E from PO. Behind the caravan park ablution block
  HEMA 88 C2 33 3 20 S 135 28 1 E CT HT BIG RIG

Yacka
- Yackamoorundie Park ☎ (08) 8846 4077
  ☑ *See also South Australia site 291.*
  Cnr of Main Nth Rd & North Terrace
  HEMA 89 D8 33 34 6 S 138 26 43 E CT BIG RIG

Yunta
- Yunta Centennial Park ☎ (08) 8650 5009
  ☑ *See also South Australia site 218.*
  Rest Area at Yunta. Next to Telecentre on Hwy.
  HEMA 95 H10 32 34 54 S 139 33 46 E CT HT BIG RIG

Western Australia

Albany
- Brig Amity Park ☎ (08) 9841 9290
  Off Princess Royal Drive, Amity Quay
  HEMA 109 J13 35 1 44 S 117 52 45 E CT BIG RIG
- Albany Dump Point
  At Information Bay, Albany Hwy N of town. S of Drome Rd
  HEMA 109 J13 34 59 28 S 117 51 21 E CT HT BIG RIG

Balladonia Area
- Baxter Rest Area
  ☑ *See also Western Australia site 15.*
  At Rest Area 67 km W of Caiguna or 115 km E of Balladonia
  HEMA 119 H3 32 21 26 S 124 47 14 E CT HT BIG RIG

Beasley River
- Beasley River Rest Area
  ☑ *See also Western Australia site 371.*
  Rest Area 171 km E of Nanutarra Rdhouse or 53 km W of Paraburdoo/Wittenoom Rd junction
  HEMA 114 E6 22 56 56 S 116 58 40 E CT HT BIG RIG

Beverley
- Beverley Dump Point
  Council Drive. Just past & opposite the caravan park entrance
  HEMA 107 E8 32 6 27 S 116 55 26 E CT HT BIG RIG

Bindoon
- Bindoon Oval ☎ (08) 9576 1020
  ☑ *See also Western Australia site 388.*
  Next to toilets at the oval
  HEMA 106 B4 31 23 13 S 116 5 49 E CT HT BIG RIG

Boddington
- Boddington RV Stop
  ☑ *See also Western Australia site 182.*
  1 Wuraming Avenue
  HEMA 106 H6 32 47 59 S 116 28 25 E CT HT BIG RIG

Boyup Brook
- Boyup Brook & Flaxmill Caravan Park ☎ (08) 9765 1200
  Jackson St, east end of town. Public Access. Turn R at entry, white post marked "Dump"
  HEMA 108 D7 33 50 5 S 116 23 58 E CT

Broome
- Roebuck Bay Caravan Park ☎ (08) 9192 1366
  91 Walcott St. 2 km S of PO. Have to park outside, cassette only, must see reception
  HEMA 116 G5 17 58 15 S 122 14 2 E CT $

Bruce Rock
- Bruce Rock Caravan Park ☎ (08) 9061 1377
  ☑ *See also Western Australia site 127.*
  Dunstal St. Public access
  HEMA 107 D13 31 52 29 S 118 9 6 E CT HT BIG RIG

Brunswick Junction
- Brunswick Junction Showgrounds ☎ (08) 9726 1244
  At Showgrounds, Ridley St. Turn R inside grounds. Key at Eziway Supermarket, business hours
  HEMA 108 A5 33 15 11 S 115 50 14 E CT HT BIG RIG

Busselton
- Busselton Dump Point ☎ (08) 9781 0444
  Behind Churchill Park Hall, Adelaide St. Call to receive access code to unlock
  HEMA 108 C2 33 38 47 S 115 21 3 E CT HT BIG RIG

Carnarvon
- Carnarvon Dump Point ☎ (08) 9941 1146
  Hill St, off Robinson St
  HEMA 114 H2 24 52 55 S 113 39 34 E CT HT BIG RIG

Carnarvon Area
- Blowholes (Point Quobba) ☎ 0408 942 945
  ☑ *See also Western Australia site 346.*
  At Camp Area 72 km N of Carnarvon. Turn W off North West Coastal Hwy 24 km N of Carnarvon or 115 km S of Minilya Roadhouse
  HEMA 114 H2 24 29 16 S 113 24 44 E CT

Cervantes
- Waste Transfer Station ☎ (08) 9652 0806
  Seville St, entry at Estella Place. Limited opening hours
  HEMA 112 H4 30 29 52 S 115 4 48 E CT HT BIG RIG

Cleaverville Beach
- Cleaverville Beach ☎ (08) 9186 8528
  ☑ *See also Western Australia site 378.*
  At Camp Area. Turn N 28 km E of Karrratha Rdhouse or 14 km W of Roebourne. 13 km dirt Rd. Open May - Sep
  HEMA 114 B6 20 39 40 S 116 59 53 E CT

Collie
- Collie River Valley Tourist Park ☎ (08) 9734 5088
  Porter St. 2 km W of PO. Please call in at reception first
  HEMA 108 B6 33 21 44 S 116 8 44 E CT

Coolgardie
- Coolgardie RV Stop
  Woodward St, cnr of Lefroy St. Old Railway Station
  HEMA 113 H11 30 57 22 S 121 9 47 E CT HT BIG RIG

Coorow
- Coorow Caravan Park ☎ (08) 9952 0100
  ☑ *See also Western Australia site 275.*
  Station St. Public access
  HEMA 112 G5 29 52 51 S 116 1 2 E CT HT BIG RIG

Coronation Beach
- Coronation Beach ☎ (08) 9920 5011
  ☑ *See also Western Australia site 318.*
  At Camp Area. Turn W 28 km N of Geraldton or 24 km S of Northampton
  HEMA 112 E3 28 33 12 S 114 33 52 E CT

Corrigin
- Corrigin Dump Point ☎ (08) 9063 2203
  Walton St, behind toilet block
  HEMA 107 F12 32 19 51 S 117 52 23 E CT

Cuballing
- Cuballing Dump Point ☎ (08) 9883 6031
  At Old Railway Station. 301 Great Southern Hwy
  HEMA 107 J9 32 49 4 S 117 10 48 E CT HT

Dalwallinu
- Dalwallinu Caravan Park ☎ (08) 9661 1253
  ☑ *See also Western Australia site 420.*
  Dowie St. Public access
  HEMA 112 G6 30 16 27 S 116 40 8 E CT $

De Grey River
❖ De Grey River
☑ *See also Western Australia site 452.*
At rest area 82 km NE of Port Hedland or 71 km SW of Pardoo Roadhouse
HEMA 116 K2 20 18 28 S 119 15 11 E CT

Denham
❖ Denham Dump Point
Denham - Hamelin Rd, in info bay on approach to town
HEMA 114 K2 25 55 37 S 113 32 36 E CT HT BIG RIG

Denmark
❖ Cosy Corner (East)
☑ *See also Western Australia site 73.*
At Camp Area 30 km W of Albany or 38 km E of Denmark. Turn S off Lower Denmark Rd 25 km W of Albany or 33 km E of Denmark onto Cosy Corner Rd
HEMA 109 K13 35 3 33 S 117 38 44 E CT

Derby
❖ Kimberley Entrance Caravan Park ☎ (08) 9193 1055
Rowan St. See reception, donation to RFDS
HEMA 116 F7 17 18 25 S 123 37 45 E CT HT BIG RIG

Dongara
❖ Dongara Dump Point
Waldeck St, next to the Oval
HEMA 112 F4 29 14 51 S 114 55 58 E CT HT BIG RIG

Donnybrook
❖ Donnybrook Transit Park ☎ (08) 9731 1897
☑ *See also Western Australia site 104.*
Reserve St, W end of oval
HEMA 108 C5 33 34 16 S 115 49 12 E CT HT BIG RIG

Dowerin
❖ Dowerin Dump Point
Stewart St, opposite the hotel
HEMA 107 A8 31 11 43 S 117 1 50 E CT HT BIG RIG

Eighty Mile Beach Area
❖ Stanley Rest Area
☑ *See also Western Australia site 457.*
Rest Area 108 km NE of Sandfire Roadhouse or 181 km SW of Roebuck Plains Roadhouse. 5 km N of Nita Downs turnoff
HEMA 116 H5 19 2 36 S 121 39 56 E CT HT BIG RIG

Eneabba
❖ Arrowsmith Rest Area
☑ *See also Western Australia site 311.*
Rest Area 30 km N of Eneabba or 50 km S of Dongarra
HEMA 112 F4 29 34 43 S 115 8 9 E CT HT BIG RIG

Esperance
❖ Esperance Dump Point
Shelden Rd, off Norseman Rd
HEMA 111 G12 33 50 35 S 121 53 54 E CT HT BIG RIG

Exmouth
❖ Sports & Recreation Ground ☎ (08) 9949 1176
Murat Rd, in recreation reserve near visitors centre. Directions available at visitors centre
HEMA 114 D2 21 55 56 S 114 7 47 E CT HT BIG RIG

Gnoorea Point (40 Mile)
❖ Gnoorea Point (40-Mile) ☎ (08) 9186 8555
☑ *See also Western Australia site 377.*
Near Camp area at Forty Mile Beach. Turn W 54 km N of Fortescue River Roadhouse or 40 km S of Karratha Roadhouse.12 km dirt rd. Open May - Sep
HEMA 114 B5 20 50 26 S 116 20 51 E CT HT BIG RIG

Fitzroy Crossing Area
❖ Ellendale Rest Area
☑ *See also Western Australia site 479.*
Rest Area 125 km SE of Derby turnoff or 88 km W of Fitzroy Crossing
HEMA 117 G9 17 57 38 S 124 50 10 E CT BIG RIG

❖ Ngumban Cliff Lookout
☑ *See also Western Australia site 482.*
Rest Area 96 km SE of Fitzroy Crossing or 192 km W of Halls Creek
HEMA 117 H10 18 44 53 S 126 6 31 E CT HT BIG RIG

Geraldton Area
❖ Fig Tree Picnic & Camping Ground ☎ (08) 9920 5011
☑ *See also Western Australia site 317.*
Camp Area 21 km NE of Geraldton. North West Coast Hwy, Chapman Valley Scenic Drive for 12 km
HEMA 112 E4 28 39 32 S 114 42 15 E CT

Hopetoun
❖ Hopetoun Dump Point ☎ (08) 9839 0000
Cnr Hopetoun-Ravensthorpe Rd & Senna Road. 3 km N of Hopetoun
HEMA 111 H9 33 55 8 S 120 8 13 E CT HT BIG RIG

Jurien Bay
❖ Sandy Cape Recreational Park ☎ (08) 9652 0800
☑ *See also Western Australia site 307.*
2 km N of Jurien Bay or 18 km S of Green Head. 6 km dirt road
HEMA 112 G4 30 11 23 S 115 0 7 E CT

Kalbarri
❖ Kalbarri Dump Point
Porter St, 1.7 km from turn off, in industrial area
HEMA 112 D3 27 42 8 S 114 10 3 E CT HT BIG RIG

Kalgoorlie
❖ Boulder Dump Point
Hamilton St, between Piesse & Richardson St
HEMA 113 H11 30 47 0 S 121 29 29 E CT HT BIG RIG

❖ Kalgoorlie Dump Point ☎ (08) 9021 1966
Forrest St. N of Railway Station
HEMA 111 A11 30 44 38 S 121 28 12 E CT HT BIG RIG

Kambalda
❖ Kambalda West RV Stop
☑ *See also Western Australia site 217.*
Parking Area at Kambalda West. Behind Rec centre off Barnes Drive
HEMA 111 B12 31 12 23 S 121 37 17 E CT HT BIG RIG

Kojonup
❖ Kojonup Rest Area ☎ (08) 9831 0500
☑ *See also Western Australia site 175.*
Gordon St. S end of town
HEMA 109 D10 33 50 13 S 117 9 32 E CT HT BIG RIG

Kondinin
❖ Kondinin Caravan Park ☎ (08) 9889 1006
☑ *See also Western Australia site 150.*
Gordon St
HEMA 107 G14 32 29 43 S 118 15 49 E CT HT BIG RIG

Kookynie
❖ Niagara Dam ☎ (08) 9024 2041
☑ *See also Western Australia site 257.*
Downstream from Dam wall
HEMA 113 F12 29 24 15 S 121 25 40 E CT HT

Kulin
❖ Kulin Overnight Stop ☎ (08) 9880 1204
☑ *See also Western Australia site 122.*
Johnston St at the public toilets
HEMA 107 H13 32 40 11 S 118 9 20 E CT BIG RIG

Lake Grace
❖ Lake Grace Dump Point
Sport Precinct, Stubbs St
HEMA 107 K14 33 6 3 S 118 27 22 E CT HT BIG RIG

Lake Macleod
❖ Lake MacLeod Rest Area
☑ *See also Western Australia site 350.*
Rest Area 49 km S of Minilya Roadhouse or 90 km N of Carnarvon
HEMA 114 G2 24 14 57 S 114 2 11 E CT HT BIG RIG

Learmonth
❖ Burkett Road Rest Area
☑ *See also Western Australia site 366.*
16 km NE of Minilya Roadhouse or 111 km SW of Nanutarra Roadhouse. 1 km N of Exmouth turnoff
HEMA 114 E3 22 59 1 S 114 36 47 E CT HT BIG RIG

Leonora
❖ Leonora Dump Point
Goldfields Hwy, at the Information bay, S of town
HEMA 113 E11 28 53 37 S 121 19 47 E CT HT BIG RIG

Marble Bar
❖ Marble Bar Dump Point
At Rest Area in General St. Near the General Store & Service Station
HEMA 115 C9 21 10 17 S 119 44 37 E CT HT BIG RIG

Marble Bar Area
❖ Des Streckfuss Rest Area
☑ *See also Western Australia site 451.*
Rest Area 74 km NW of Marble Bar or 79 km SE of Hwy 1 junction.
HEMA 115 B9 20 49 33 S 119 30 44 E CT HT BIG RIG

Margaret River
❖ Margaret River Dump Point
Gloucester Park access Rd, off Wallcliffe Rd. Behind Youth Zone Room. Locked, key available at Civic Admin Centre or Margaret River Recreation Centre
HEMA 108 E12 33 57 14 S 115 4 12 E CT HT BIG RIG

Mary River
❖ Mary Pool (Mary River)
☑ *See also Western Australia site 404.*
Rest Area 180 km E of Fitzroy Crossing or 108 km W of Halls Creek
HEMA 117 H11 18 43 37 S 126 52 19 E CT

Meekatharra
❖ Meekatharra Dump Point ☎ (08) 9981 1002
In lane way between Savage & Porter St's behind Shire Office
HEMA 113 B8 26 35 37 S 118 29 45 E CT HT

Meekatharra Area

- Gascoyne River (South Branch)
  ☑ *See also Western Australia site 434.*
  Rest Area 148 km NW of Meekatharra, 276 km S of Newman or 108 km S of Kumarina Roadhouse
  HEMA 115 J9 25 34 44 S 119 14 13 E CT HT BIG RIG

Merredin

- Merredin Tourist Park ☎ (08) 9041 1535
  2 Oats St. Public access
  HEMA 107 B14 31 29 5 S 118 17 29 E CT HT

Mingenew

- Mingenew Dump Point
  Midlands Rd, in parking bay 100m W of Palm Roadhouse
  HEMA 112 F4 29 11 25 S 115 26 19 E CT HT BIG RIG

Minilya

- Minilya River
  ☑ *See also Western Australia site 351.*
  Rest Area 1 km S of Minilya Roadhouse or 141 km N of Carnarvon
  HEMA 114 G2 23 49 1 S 114 0 38 E CT HT BIG RIG
- Lyndon River
  ☑ *See also Western Australia site 353.*
  Rest Area 48 km NE of Minilya Roadhouse or 179 km SW of Nanutarra Roadhouse
  HEMA 114 F3 23 28 58 S 114 16 32 E CT HT BIG RIG

Minnivale

- Minnivale Rest Area
  ☑ *See also Western Australia site 398.*
  Cnr of Amery Benjaberring & Berry Rd. Next to disused tennis courts
  HEMA 107 A9 31 8 20 S 117 11 4 E CT HT BIG RIG

Moora

- Moora RV Short Stay ☎ (08) 9651 0000
  ☑ *See also Western Australia site 305.*
  Robert St at Apex Park
  HEMA 110 A3 30 38 16 S 116 0 18 E CT HT BIG RIG

Moore River

- Moore River Bridge
  ☑ *See also Western Australia site 273.*
  Rest Area 33 km N of Yanchep NP turnoff or 2 km SE of Guilderton turnoff
  HEMA 106 B1 31 18 12 S 115 33 18 E CT HT BIG RIG

Mount Magnet

- Mount Magnet Caravan Park ☎ (08) 9963 4198
  Lot 397 Hepburn St
  HEMA 112 D7 28 3 42 S 117 50 58 E CT $

Mt Barker

- Mt Barker Visitors Centre ☎ (08) 9851 1163
  Albany Highway
  HEMA 109 H13 34 37 38 S 117 39 49 E CT HT BIG RIG

Mukinbudin

- Mukinbudin Caravan Park ☎ (08) 9047 1103
  ☑ *See also Western Australia site 406.*
  Cruickshank St
  HEMA 110 B6 30 55 8 S 118 12 21 E CT HT

Munjina (Auski)

- Mulga Parking Area
  ☑ *See also Western Australia site 442.*
  Parking Area 39 km N of Auski Roadhouse or 180 km S of Hwy 1 junction
  HEMA 115 D8 22 3 10 S 118 48 10 E CT HT BIG RIG

Murchison

- Murchison Oasis Roadhouse & Caravan Park ☎ (08) 9961 3875
  ☑ *See also Western Australia site 295.*
  Murchison Settlement
  HEMA 112 C5 26 53 46 S 115 57 26 E CT HT BIG RIG

Nannup

- Nannup Dump Point
  Brockman St, next to the caravan park
  HEMA 108 E4 33 58 34 S 115 45 47 E CT HT BIG RIG

Narrogin

- Narrogin Dump Point
  Cnr Earl & Egerton St. Behind Information Centre
  HEMA 107 J9 32 56 1 S 117 10 35 E CT HT

Nerren Nerren

- Nerren Nerren Rest Area
  ☑ *See also Western Australia site 329.*
  Rest Area 82 km N of Kalbarri turnoff or 46 km S of Billabong Roadhouse
  HEMA 112 C3 27 12 43 S 114 36 44 E CT

Newman

- Newman Visitors Centre
  2 Fortescue Ave. Key required from Information centre open 8.00am - 5.00pm daily
  HEMA 115 F9 23 21 33 S 119 43 40 E CT HT BIG RIG

Newman Area

- Mt Robinson Rest Area
  ☑ *See also Western Australia site 437.*
  Rest Area 109 km NW of Newman or 86 km SE of Auski Roadhouse. 800m E of Hwy
  HEMA 115 E8 23 2 34 S 118 50 57 E CT HT BIG RIG

Norseman

- Norseman Rest Area
  ☑ *See also Western Australia site 31.*
  68 Roberts St, Key required from Tourist Information Centre. Open business hours
  HEMA 111 D13 32 11 46 S 121 46 51 E CT $

Norseman Area

- Fraser Range Rest Area
  ☑ *See also Western Australia site 25.*
  Rest Area 109 km W of Balladonia or 83 km E of Norseman
  HEMA 111 D13 32 4 24 S 122 35 36 E CT HT BIG RIG

Northam

- Northam Dump Point ☎ (08) 9622 2100
  Peel Terrace, opposite Caltex Service Station
  HEMA 106 C6 31 38 59 S 116 40 38 E CT HT BIG RIG

Northhampton

- Northampton Lions Park
  ☑ *See also Western Australia site 321.*
  Access off Essex St, near public toilets in caravan parking area, next to supermarket
  HEMA 112 E3 28 20 54 S 114 37 49 E CT HT

Northhampton Area

- Galena Bridge (Murchison River)
  ☑ *See also Western Australia site 328.*
  Rest Area 13 km N of Kalbarri turnoff or 115 km S of Billabong Roadhouse
  HEMA 112 D3 27 49 39 S 114 41 24 E CT HT BIG RIG

Nullagine

- Nullagine
  Cnr Cooke & Walter Sts, in the Rest Stop
  HEMA 115 C10 21 53 10 S 120 6 28 E CT HT BIG RIG

Nungarin

- Nungarin Dump Point
  Main St, opposite Heritage Machinery & Army Museum
  HEMA 107 A13 31 11 5 S 118 6 10 E CT HT BIG RIG

Onslow

- Onslow Dump Point ☎ (08) 9184 6644
  Cameron Avenue, adjacent to basketball court. S of Post Office
  HEMA 114 C4 21 38 28 S 115 6 47 E CT HT BIG RIG

Peaceful Bay

- Peaceful Bay Dump Point
  Peaceful Bay Rd, near public toilets
  HEMA 109 K10 35 2 30 S 116 55 40 E CT HT BIG RIG

Pingelly

- Pingelly Dump Point ☎ (08) 9887 1066
  Hall Street, behind Caravan Park
  HEMA 107 G8 32 32 5 S 117 5 6 E CT HT BIG RIG
- Pingelly Recreation Ground
  Entry off Somerset St. Near swimming pool
  HEMA 107 G8 32 31 53 S 117 5 25 E CT HT BIG RIG

Pinjarra

- Pinjarra RV Parking Area
  ☑ *See also Western Australia site 187.*
  Visitor Information Centre. Cnr SW Hwy & Pinjarra Williams Rd opposite Exchange Hotel
  HEMA 106 H3 32 37 41 S 115 52 43 E CT HT BIG RIG

Port Headland Area

- Mundabullangana
  At Rest Area, cnr Great Northern Hwy & North West Coastal Hwy 40 km S of Port Headland
  HEMA 115 B8 20 34 27 S 118 26 18 E CT HT BIG RIG

Port Smith Area

- Nillibubica (Goldwire) Rest Area
  ☑ *See also Western Australia site 458.*
  Rest Area 168 km NE of Sandfire Roadhouse or 121 km SW of Roebuck Plains Roadhouse
  HEMA 116 H5 18 36 14 S 121 57 59 E CT HT BIG RIG

Quairading

- Quairading Dump Point ☎ (08) 9645 1001
  Next to public toilets, stockyards on Quairading - York Rd. W side of town
  HEMA 107 E10 32 0 43 S 117 23 42 E CT HT BIG RIG

Ravensthorpe

- Ravensthorpe Dump Point
  South Coast Hwy, approx 400 metres SE of Hopetoun turn off.
  HEMA 111 G9 33 34 44 S 120 3 28 E CT HT BIG RIG

Regans Ford

- Regans Ford
  ☑ *See also Western Australia site 302.*
  Rest Area 43 km N of Gingin or 32 km S of Cataby
  HEMA 110 B2 30 59 20 S 115 42 17 E CT HT BIG RIG

Robe River

- Robe River
  ☑ *See also Western Australia site 374.*
  Rest Area 117 km N of Nanutarra Roadhouse or 43 km S of Fortescue River Roadhouse
  HEMA 114 C5 21 36 55 S 115 55 21 E CT HT BIG RIG

Roebuck Plains Area

- Nillibubbica Rest Area
  ☑ *See also Western Australia site 474.*
  At rest area 71 km E of Roebuck Plains Roadhouse or 60 km W of Willare Bridge Roadhouse
  HEMA 116 G6 17 39 21 S 123 7 57 E CT HT BIG RIG

Southern Cross

- Southern Cross Dump Point
  Corner of Achernar & Sirius Sts. Eastern end near old Shire yards
  HEMA 111 B8 31 13 50 S 119 19 51 E CT HT BIG RIG

Southern Cross Area

- Karalee Rock & Dam ☎ (08) 9049 1001
  ☑ *See also Western Australia site 230.*
  At Camp Area 137 km W of Coolgardie or 52 km E of Southern Cross. Turn N 133 km W of Coolgardie or 48 km E of Southern Cross. 5 km of dirt Rd
  HEMA 113 J10 31 15 3 S 119 50 24 E CT HT BIG RIG
- Koorarawalyee (Boorabbin) Rest Area
  ☑ *See also Western Australia site 229.*
  Rest Area 114 km W of Coolgardie or 68 km E of Southern Cross
  HEMA 113 J10 31 16 8 S 120 1 0 E CT HT BIG RIG

Three Springs

- Three Springs Dump Point
  Hall St, adjacent to Council building
  HEMA 112 F5 29 32 10 S 115 45 52 E CT HT BIG RIG

Trayning

- Trayning Caravan Park ☎ 0428 997 156
  ☑ *See also Western Australia site 400.*
  Caravan Park at Trayning. Entry off Bencubbin-Kellerberrin Rd, behind the swimming pool. Public Access
  HEMA 107 A11 31 6 38 S 117 47 37 E CT HT BIG RIG

Wagin

- Wagin Showgrounds ☎ (08) 9861 1177
  ☑ *See also Western Australia site 149.*
  Great Southern Hwy
  HEMA 109 B11 33 18 20 S 117 20 10 E CT HT BIG RIG

Walkaway

- Ellendale Pool ☎ (08) 9921 0500
  ☑ *See also Western Australia site 316.*
  At Camp Area 22 km NE of Walkaway, via Walkaway-Nangetty Rd & Ellendale Rd
  HEMA 112 E4 28 51 33 S 114 58 22 E CT

Waroona

- Waroona Memorial Oval ☎ (08) 9733 1506
  Enter from Millar St, off South Western Hwy. Adjacent to the Walmsley Memorial Pavilion toilets
  HEMA 106 J3 32 50 42 S 115 55 25 E CT HT BIG RIG

Westonia

- Westonia Dump Point
  Cnr Westonia - Carrabin & Boodarockin Rds
  HEMA 113 J8 31 17 48 S 118 41 21 E CT HT BIG RIG

Wickepin

- Wickepin Caravan Park ☎ (08) 9888 1089
  ☑ *See also Western Australia site 150.*
  At caravan park at Wickepin. Wogolin Rd, behind Police Station
  HEMA 107 H10 32 46 52 S 117 30 12 E CT HT

Whim creek area

- Peawah River
  ☑ *See also Western Australia site 385.*
  26 km NE of Whim Creek or 92 km SW of Port Hedland
  HEMA 114 B7 20 50 51 S 118 4 6 E CT

Wongan Hills

- Wongan Hills Dump Point ☎ (08) 9671 1973
  Wongan Hills Rd. At Information Centre
  HEMA 110 B4 30 53 35 S 116 42 59 E CT HT BIG RIG

Woodanilling

- Woodanilling Recreation Reserve ☎ (08) 9823 1506
  ☑ *See also Western Australia site 173.*
  Parking Area in Woodanilling, Yairabin St
  HEMA 109 C12 33 33 36 S 117 25 59 E CT HT BIG RIG

Wooramel Area

- Edaggee Rest Area
  ☑ *See also Western Australia site 340.*
  Rest Area 43 km N of Wooramel Roadhouse or 81 km S of Carnarvon
  HEMA 114 J3 25 27 34 S 114 3 31 E CT HT BIG RIG

Wyndham

- Cockburn Rest Area
  ☑ *See also Western Australia site 496.*
  Rest Area at Victoria Hwy junction or 152 km N of Turkey Creek, 56 km S of Wyndham or 45 km W of Kununurra
  HEMA 117 D13 15 52 7 S 128 22 17 E CT HT BIG RIG

Yannarie River

- Barradale Rest Area
  ☑ *See also Western Australia site 367.*
  Rest Area 156 km NE of Minilya Roadhouse or 70 km SW of Nanutarra Roadhouse
  HEMA 114 E3 22 51 49 S 114 57 5 E CT HT BIG RIG

York

- Avon Park
  ☑ *See also Western Australia site 160.*
  Lowe St at rear of public toilets
  HEMA 106 D7 31 53 19 S 116 46 13 E CT HT BIG RIG

Yule River

- Marble Bar Turn Off
  ☑ *See also Western Australia site 444.*
  Parking Area 95 km N of Auski Roadhouse or 124 km S of Hwy 1 junction
  HEMA 115 C8 21 34 40 S 118 48 57 E CT HT BIG RIG

Northern Territory

Adelaide River

- Adelaide River Dump Point ☎ (08) 8976 0058
  Hopwell St, adjacent to the Fire Station
  HEMA 123 E3 13 14 13 S 131 6 13 E CT HT

Alice Springs

- Alice Springs Dump Point ☎ 1800 645 199
  Commonage Rd, S of The Gap. LHS of Rd, next to Blatherskite Park
  HEMA 129 F8 23 43 57 S 133 51 37 E CT HT BIG RIG

Batchelor

- Batchelor Dump Point ☎ (08) 8976 0058
  Nurndina St, adjacent to Public Toilets
  HEMA 123 E2 13 2 49 S 131 1 43 E CT HT BIG RIG

Borroloola

- Tamarind Park ☎ 1800 245 091
  Near airport gate
  HEMA 125 J12 16 4 19 S 136 18 22 E CT

Darwin

- Winnellie Greyhound Club ☎ (08) 8936 2499
  Hook Rd, Winnellie
  HEMA 122 F5 12 25 41 S 130 53 40 E CT HT BIG RIG

Jabiru

- Jabiru Dump Point ☎ (08) 8979 2230
  Jabiru Drive, 300m past tourist information board, opposite turnoff to cemetery
  HEMA 123 D7 12 39 51 S 132 50 18 E CT HT BIG RIG

Katherine

- Katherine Dump Point
  200m from Information Centre. 300m along Lindsay St, just beyond Second St
  HEMA 123 J5 14 27 53 S 132 16 2 E CT HT BIG RIG

Katherine Area

- Vince Connolly Crossing
  ☑ *See also Northern Territory site 159.*
  Rest Area 58 km SW of Katherine or 138 km NE of Victoria River
  HEMA 124 G5 14 49 42 S 131 55 0 E CT HT BIG RIG

King River

- King Rest Area
  ☑ *See also Northern Territory site 115.*
  Rest Area 59 km N of Mataranka or 46 km S of Katherine
  HEMA 123 K6 14 38 38 S 132 37 56 E CT HT

Larrimah Area

- Warloch Rest Area
  ☑ *See also Northern Territory site 91.*
  Rest Area 41 km N of Larrimah or 37 km S of Mataranka
  HEMA 124 H7 15 14 12 S 133 6 53 E CT HT BIG RIG

Mataranka

- Mataranka Dump Point
  Cnr Stuart Hwy & Martin St, at public toilets in park
  HEMA 124 G7 14 55 21 S 133 3 59 E CT

Pine Creek

- Pine Creek Dump Point ☎ 1800 245 091
  Ward St, outside council depot
  HEMA 123 G4 13 49 28 S 131 49 55 E CT HT BIG RIG

Tennant Creek

- Tennant Creek Dump Point ☎ (08) 8962 3388
  Stuart St, near Showgrounds
  HEMA 127 G9 19 38 32 S 134 11 51 E CT HT BIG RIG

Victoria River Area

- Mathison Rest Area
  ☑ *See also Northern Territory site 161.*
  Rest Area 104 km SW of Katherine or 92 km NE of Victoria River
  HEMA 124 H5 15 8 23 S 131 41 1 E CT HT BIG RIG

Yulara

- Yulara Dump Point ☎ (08) 8956 2171
  Cnr Berry Ed & Tuit Crescent, off Giles St. Behind AAT Kings depot, on the ground under metal plate
  HEMA 128 J4 25 13 24 S 130 58 31 E CT HT BIG RIG

ACKNOWLEDGEMENTS

Special Acknowledgements

Des & Bev Fittock
Bob & Colleen Ford
Lyn Hutton
Kym Leech
T.K. Maher
Frank Norden
Grahame & Wendy Roberts
Sheng Yee

Acknowledgements

Glenoce Allman
Carole & Stephen Anderson
Colin Andrew
Colin Andrews
Rob Andrews
Phil Archer
Marie & Knox Arps
Gavin & Vanessa Atkinson
Christine Banks
Jo Barclay
Chris Barnes
Nev & Chris Barrett
Barry & Lynne
John & Dorothy Barwick
Jeff Beard
Mick & Doreen Beeston
Jacod Beinke
Margo Bellis
Erine Bennett
Dave Berry
Lindesay Blackburne-Kane
Brian Blades
Kelly & Marty Bode
Lynton Bolland
Graham Booth
Albert Borg
Graham Bower
Terry & Rhonda Boyce
Rene Braunmuller
Brian Breingan
Mayne & Aileen Brewer
Jan Bride
Denise Buckle
John Burow
Garth Camac
Noel Campbell
Rob & San Cavanagh
Kevin Cheetham
Yvonne Church
Ian & Leonie Churchill
Jo Clark
Alex Clowes
Malita Cogent
Peter & Glenys Cole
Diane Cordaire
Daryl Cossar
Mike Coward
Carol Cowling
Dave Cox
Delma Crisp
Terry Crowther
Kevin Cummins
Jayne Cunningham
Greg Dalton
Keith Dawson
Margaret Lacson de Hall
Steve Alison Denman
Brian Dillon
Debra Dillon
Blair & Mary Dixon
Steve Dixon
Ken & Tricia Docherty
Ian Donges
Graeme & Kris Downing
Beverley Driver
Rupert Duckworth
Jennifer Duncan
James Elliott
David Embury
Judy Entwisle
Shona Esson
Martin Faulkner
Wendy Fellows
Barry Flood
Ash & Wendy Frank
Geoff & Dianne Gibb
Dave Giles
Deirdre & Gordon Giles
Cheryl Gillespie
Scott Glendinning
Margaret Glover
Cliff Gmail
Ross Green
John & Hilda Greeves
John & Monica Hadlow
Ken Hall-Patch
Doug Hamilton
May Hampton
R Hanna
Len Hanrahan
Roy Hargreaves
Bob & Julie Head
Jenny Head
Les Herring
Barb Hickey
John & Hilda
Heather Hjorth
Barbara Hobson
Michael Hoffman
Lesley Hughes
Gwen Hyde
Margaret Hynoski
Ron Ireland
Peter & Julie Johnson
Helen Johnston
Carol Jones
Bill Jongsma
David Kelly
Laurie Kibblewhite
Gail Kirkpatrick
Luka Kovacevic
Leigh Labinsky
Brian Lambert
Frank Laverty
Barry Lehman
Diane Leotta
Steve Linley
Anne Lippinkhof
Tony Locandro
Sandra Mackichie
Bob Mann
Petra Maringer
Raelene Marshall
Shaun Marshall
Wayne Matthews
Bob May
Peter Mayo
David McDonald
Cheryl McGregor
Gladys Mckechnie
Ian McLaughlin
Bill McNulty
Brian McWhirter
Josephone Mihalic
Liz Miller
Philip Minotti
Jim Mitchell
Pam Montgomery
Gerald Morohett
Rohan, Fiona, Eden & Jethro Morris
Vanessa Morris
Kerri Myers
Terry & Sandra Myers
Michael Nottingham
Geoff Nowell
Mike Nowlan
Mark Odgaard
Paul & Sue O'Keeffe
Andrew Osborne
Brad Parker
Cheryl Paterson
Elaine & Eric Pearce
Maree Pennington
Anne Picker
Jenny Pickering
Max Pickworth
Karen Power
Liz Randall
Ronald & Joan Read
John Reid
Warwick & Dianne Rofe
Kate Roffey
Timothy Roper
Tom Rundle
Harley Sadler
Samantha
Ian & Jenny Scarborough
John Schipper
Norma Schreuder
Jill & Roger Sheath
Todd Simpson
Eddie Smelt
Cathy Sohler
Allan Sorohan
Paula Sporton
Stephen Spry
Bryan & Marliese Stanley
Bob & Chris Stokan
Roy Sudholz
Mark & Lauren Sulis
Margaret Surman
Bernice Tait
Cliff Taylor
Raymond Thain
Keith Thompson
Colin Toll
Barbara Tower
Diane Treoth-Telfer
Barry A Turner
Tom van Leeuwen
Denny van Maanenberg
Bob Walker
Peter Ward
Vic Ward
Rofe Warwick
Sue Wedlock
Kathy Whelan
Vicki White
Bruce & Pan Wilding
Neville Williams
John & Pauline Winchester
John Winter
Carolyn Woods
Peter Wright
Brian & Kathy Yeoman
Helen Yuille
Karl Zochan

Sample of a Site Listing

Explanation Of Symbols In Site Listings

(Aa detailed explanation is available starting at page 12)

- Toilets
- Disabled access (toilets and showers)
- Water not drinkable
- Shade
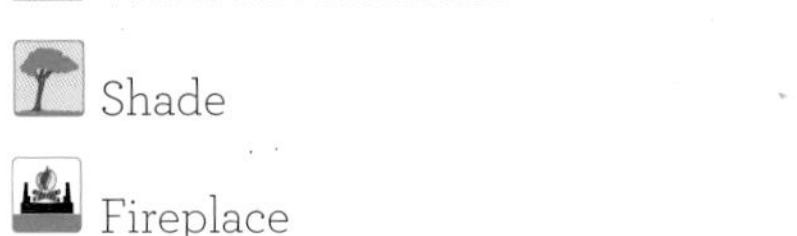
- Fireplace
- Fees applicable
- BIG RIG Site suitable for big rigs
- Power
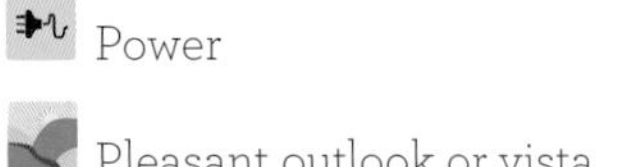
- Pleasant outlook or vista
- Suitable for motorhome

- Showers (usually hot)
- Water (drinkable)

- Suitable for camper trailer

- Picnic table

- Barbeque
- Fees above specified limit
- Day use fee applicable
- Maximum stay (hours)

- Dump point for toilet waste

- Author's Recommendation

- Boat ramp available
- Site suitable for tents
- Dry weather access only

- Site close to road
- Pets NOT allowed
- Pets allowed
- Mobile phone service
- Public phone
- Suitable for caravan

Site symbols used in listings		Equivalent site symbols used on maps
Day Use Only	=	32 or 30 if collacted with Dump Point
Overnight Camping/Parking	=	155 or 115 if collacted with Dump Point
Caravan Parks	=	121

Explanation of a sample Public Dump Point listing

Explanation of Public Dump Point Symbols

Symbols used in listing

- CT Cassette toilet use
- HT Holding tank use
- BIG RIG Access suitable for big rigs
- Fees applicable
- Water available

Symbols used on the maps

Day Use Site with Public Dump Point

Camping/Parking Site with Public Dump Point

Public Dump Point not at a Listed Site